CONSERVATION IN DEVELOPING COUNTRIES: PROBLEMS AND PROSPECTS

PROCEEDINGS OF THE CENTENARY SEMINAR OF THE BOMBAY NATURAL HISTORY SOCIETY

CONSERVATION IN DEVELOPING COUNTRIES: PROBLEMS AND PROSPECTS

PROCEEDINGS OF THE CENTENARY SEMINAR OF THE BOMBAY NATURAL HISTORY SOCIETY

edited by
J. C. DANIEL & J. S. SERRAO

BOMBAY NATURAL HISTORY SOCIETY

OXFORD UNIVERSITY PRESS
BOMBAY DELHI CALCUTTA MADRAS

Oxford University Press, Walton Street, Oxford OX2 6DP

Oxford New York Toronto
Delhi Bombay Calcutta Madras Karachi
Petaling Jaya Singapore, Hong Kong Tokyo
Nairobi Dar es Salaam
Melbourne Auckland
and associates in
Berlin Ibadan

ISBN 0 19 562652 4

PRINTED BY BRO. PAULINUS AT ST. FRANCIS INDUSTRIAL TRAINING INSTITUTE, MOUNT POINSUR, BORIVLI (WEST), BOMBAY 400 103, PUBLISHED BY THE BOMBAY NATURAL HISTORY SOCIETY AND CO-PUBLISHED BY S. K. MOOKERJEE, OXFORD UNIVERSITY PRESS, OXFORD HOUSE, APOLLO BUNDER, BOMBAY 400 039.

PREFACE

Bombay Natural History Society celebrated its Centenary on the 15th of September 1983. As a part of the Centenary programme a seminar was held on "Conservation in the developing countries — Problems and prospects" from 6th to 10th December 1983.

The 94 papers received were presented in ten sessions and covered Conservation in National Parks and Sanctuaries and National Action Plan; Ecological Diversity; Status and Conservation of Wildlife and Wildlife habitats; Conservation Education; Captive Breeding; Wildlife Trade; Resource Utilisation and Regeneration; and Ecological Planning.

Not all the papers presented are reproduced here, but only those for which manuscripts were available at the time of going to press. However, papers that have not been included are represented by abstracts submitted by the authors.

The inordinate delay in publication means that conclusions and views expressed may have changed in the intervening period. The data provided therefore refers to conditions prevailing in 1983.

A. N. D. NANAVATI
Hon. Secretary

CONTENTS

PAGE

PREFACE .. v

MONITORING LARGE-MAMMAL POPULATIONS IN NATIONAL PARKS AND NATURE RESERVES. By George A. Petrides ... 1

MARINE PARK IN THE GULF OF KACHCHH. By Sanat A. Chavan (*With two plates*) ... 7

GUIDELINES FOR THE ANALYSIS OF BIOPHYSICAL IMPACTS TO TROPICAL COASTAL MARINE RESOURCES. By Nora L. Berwick (*With five text-figures*) ... 9

THE DAJIPUR SANCTUARY AND ITS POTENTIAL AS A NATIONAL PARK. By Jay Samant (*With a map*) ... 63

POPULATION ECOLOGY AND MANAGEMENT PROBLEM OF LARGER MAMMALS IN THE PARAMBIKULAM WILDLIFE SANCTUARY, KERALA. By P.S. Easa and M. Balakrishnan (*With four plates*) ... 70

THE ECOLOGY OF THE *MALDHARI* GRAZIERS IN THE GIR FOREST, INDIA. By Marianne Berwick (*With three text-figures*) ... 81

VEGETATION TYPES OF INDIA IN RELATION TO ENVIRONMENTAL CONDITIONS. By V.M. Meher-Homji (*With two text-figures*) ... 95

STANDING BIOMASS AND NET PRIMARY PRODUCTIVITY OF TROPICAL RAIN FORESTS OF KARNATAKA. By S.N. Rai ... 111

TREE SHAPE AND LEAF ARRANGEMENT: A QUANTITATIVE COMPARISON OF MONTANE FORESTS, WITH EMPHASIS ON MALAYSIA AND SOUTH INDIA. By Egbert Giles Leigh, Jr. (*With 18 text-figures*) ... 119

ECOLOGICAL DIVERSITY. By Madhav Gadgil and V.M. Meher-Homji. (*With two text-figures*) ... 175

FISH DISTRIBUTION AS INFLUENCED BY AQUATIC HABITAT ALTERATION AND SPECIES INTRODUCTIONS. By Neil B. Armantrout ... 199

ECO-DEVELOPMENTAL STRATEGY FOR THE EASTERN GHATS. By K.S.R. Krishna Raju and C. Subba Reddi (*With a map*) ... 207

THE UNUSUAL SIGNIFICANCE OF THE GIANT SQUIRRELS (*RATUFA*). By Richard W. Thorington Jr and Richard L. Cifelli ... 212

COMMENTS ON THE RAIN FORESTS OF SOUTHWEST INDIA AND THEIR HERPETOFAUNA. By B. Groombridge ... 220

THE FAUNA OUTSIDE NATIONAL PARKS AND SANCTUARIES. By M.K. Ranjitsinh ... 233

FORESTS AND FOREST POLICY IN NORTHWEST INDIA SINCE 1800. By A.J. Gaston ... 241

PROBLEMS AND PROSPECTS FOR WILDLIFE CONSERVATION IN SRI LANKA. By R. Rudran ... 252

WILDLIFE CONSERVATION IN SRI LANKA: A BRIEF SURVEY OF THE PRESENT STATUS. By Thilo W. Hoffmann (*With a map*) ... 260

THE ENDANGERED MARINE AND TERRESTRIAL HABITATS OF MINICOY ATOLL IN LAKSHADWEEP. By C.S. Gopinadha Pillai (*With a map and two plates*) ... 267

EUTROPHICATION, A MAJOR PROBLEM IN THE CONSERVATION OF FRESHWATER RESOURCES. By H.S. Sehgal. (*With a text-figure*) ... 277

PROBLEMS IN DEVELOPING A NATIONAL WILDLIFE POLICY AND IN CREATING EFFECTIVE NATIONAL PARKS AND SANCTUARIES IN PAKISTAN. By T.J. Roberts (*With one plate*) ... 283

HERPETOLOGICAL CONSERVATION IN INDIA. By Romulus and Zai Whitaker ... 289

WILDLIFE CONSERVATION IN THAILAND: A STRATEGIC ASSESSMENT. By Warren Y. Brockelman (*With two plates*) 300

WILDLIFE CONSERVATION IN KERALA. By V.S. Vijayan ... 305

WILDLIFE CONSERVATION IN BANGLADESH. By Mohammad Ali Reza Khan ... 310

NOTES TOWARDS A DEFINITION OF CONSERVATION EDUCATION. By Man Mohan Singh ... 317

USING MUSEUM TO TEACH CONSERVATION: UNDERSTANDING LEARNER BEHAVIOUR IN THE NATIONAL MUSEUM OF NATURAL HISTORY, NEW DELHI. By. John H. Falk ... 321

SILENT VALLEY. A CASE STUDY IN ENVIRONMENTAL EDUCATION. By Dilnavaz Variava ... 326

BOMBAY NATURAL HISTORY SOCIETY'S EFFORTS UNDER NATURE EDUCATION SCHEME. By Shailaja R. Grubh ... 335

CONSERVATION EDUCATION PROGRAMME OF WORLD WILDLIFE FUND – INDIA. By Chandrakant Wakankar ... 337

PRELIMINARY OBSERVATIONS ON THE ECOLOGY AND CONSERVATION OF THE SHAMA *COPSYCHUS MALABARICUS* IN SOUTHERN INDIA. By D.N. Mathew, K. Vijayagopal, M. Sivaraman, K.J. Joseph ... 340

OBSERVATIONS ON SOME MEGAPODES OF INDONESIA AND AUSTRALIA. By T. Antony Davis (*With five plates*) ... 347

CONSERVATION OF VULTURES IN (DEVELOPING) INDIA. By Robert Grubh, Goutam Narayan & S.M. Satheesan (*With two plates*) ... 360

BIOLOGY AND CONSERVATION OF SEA TURTLES IN THE INDIAN OCEAN. By J. Frazier (*With seven text-figures*)... 364

NILGIRI TAHR, ERAVIKULAM NATIONAL PARK AND CONSERVATION. By Clifford G. Rice ... 387

BLACKBUCK CONSERVATION IN CULTIVATED AREAS OF ANDHRA PRADESH. By N.L.N.S Prasad and V.J. Ramana Rao ... 400

DILEMMA OF UNGULATE CONSERVATION IN THE RAJASTHAN DESERT. By Ishwar Prakash ... 407

THE BIOLOGY OF THE BROW-ANTLERED DEER, *CERVUS ELDI ELDI* MCCLELLAND, 1852, AT KEIBUL LAMJAO NATIONAL PARK, MANIPUR. By Kh. Shamungou Singh ... 411

LEOPARDS LIVING AT THE EDGE OF THE ROYAL CHITAWAN NATIONAL PARK NEPAL. By John Seidensticker, Melvin E. Sunquist and Charles McDougal ... 415

CONSIDERATION FOR CONSERVATION AND MANAGEMENT OF INSECTIVOROUS BATS IN THEIR NATURAL HABITATS. By K. Usman (*With a text-figure*) ... 424

CICONIIFORM BIRDS BREEDING IN BHAVNAGAR CITY, GUJARAT: A STUDY OF THEIR NESTING AND PLEA FOR CONSERVATION. By B.M. Parashyarya and R.M. Naik (*With two figures and three plates*) ... 429

AN ASSESSMENT OF THE PRESENT DISTRIBUTION AND POPULATION STATUS OF THE LESSER FLORICAN. By H.S.A. Yahya ... 446

BREEDING HABITS AND HABITAT OF THE PAINTED SNIPE AS OBSERVED IN TIRUCHIRAPALLI, TAMILNADU, SOUTH INDIA. By H.D. Wesley (*With a text-figure*) ... 456

THE ROLE OF MANAGEMENT IN THE CONSERVATION OF ENDANGERED SPECIES WITH SPECIAL REFERENCE TO INDIAN CROCODILIANS. By H.R. Bustard ... 463

ASIAN ELEPHANT MANAGEMENT IN NORTH AMERICA. By Edwin Gould (*With a text-figure*) ... 484

BREEDING THE INDIAN PYTHON (*PYTHON M. MOLURUS*) UNDER CAPTIVE CONDITIONS IN INDIA. By Shekar Dattatri .. 488

MAHSEER AN ENDANGERED SPECIES OF GAME FISH, NEEDS ARTIFICIAL PROPAGATION FOR ITS CONSERVATION. By C.V. Kulkarni. (*With a plate*) ... 496

INDIA'S FRESHWATER TURTLE RESOURCE WITH RECOMMENDATIONS FOR MANAGEMENT. By Edward O. Moll ... 501

TRENDS IN WILDLIFE TRADE FROM INDIA TO THE UNITED STATES. By Lynn Gray Schofield and Linda McMahan (*With a text-figure*) ... 516

CONTENTS

SOME ASPECTS OF THE WILDLIFE/PET TRADE IN INDIA. By Sharad R. Sane ... 523

THREATENED ENDEMIC PLANTS FROM MAHARASHTRA. By S.M. Almeida & M.R. Almeida ... 544

REGENERATION OF TREE COVER AFTER AERIAL SEEDING IN THE SAND DUNE ECOSYSTEM OF ARID REGION. By K.A. Shankarnarayan (*With four text-figures*) ... 553

DRY-ZONE AFFORESTATION AND ITS IMPACT ON BLACKBUCK POPULATION. By K. Ullas Karanth and Mewa Singh 565

UTILIZATION OF ORGANIC WASTE FOR FISH CULTIVATION. By Dhirendra Kumar, B. Venkatesh, and P.V. Dehadrai ... 571

ORCHID SANCTUARY SESSA, ARUNACHAL PRADESH — AN EFFORT TOWARDS HABITAT CONSERVATION. By Sadanand N. Hegde ... 576

ENVIRONMENTAL IMPACT OF HYDRO ELECTRIC PROJECTS. By B Vijayaraghavan ... 582

THE IMPACT OF THE LOSS OF FOREST ON THE BIRDS OF THE EASTERN GHATS OF ANDHRA PRADESH. By Trevor D. Price (*With four text-figures*) ... 594

AGASTYAMALAI PROPOSAL FOR A BIOSPHERE RESERVE IN THE WESTERN GHATS. By Rauf Ali ... 607

ECO-DEVELOPMENT AS A SOLUTION FOR INDIA'S ENVIRONMENTAL PROBLEMS. By M.A. Rashid (*With one plate*). 616

NON-GOVERNMENT ORGANISATIONS AND CONSERVATION. By E.R.C. Davidar ... 621

CONCEPTS FOR A CIVILIZATION BASED ON CONSERVATION. By R. Ashok Kumar ... 624

ABSTRACTS OF PAPERS READ, BUT NOT SUBMITTED FOR PUBLICATION

WILDLIFE AND CONSERVATION PROBLEMS IN ASHAMBU HILLS. By A.J.T. Johnsingh ... 629

ECOLOGICAL DIVERSITY OF THE VEGETATION IN THE DESERT ENVIRONMENT. By M.M. Bhandari ... 629

STOCHASTIC EXTINCTION AND RESERVE SIZE. A FOCAL SPECIES REPORT. By S. Joseph Wright ... 630

TROPICAL BEES AND ECOLOGICAL DIVERSITY: NEW PARADIGMS AND PROSPECTS. By David W. Roubik ... 631

A MULTITUDE OF FIDDLERS, AND YET THREATENED? By Rudolf Altevogt ... 631

DEER, PLANT PHENOLOGY, AND SUCCESSION IN SOUTH ASIAN MONSOONAL LOWLAND FORESTS. By Eric Dinerstein 631

CASE HISTORY OF COOPERATIVE CONSERVATION PROGRAMME. THE NEPAL TIGER PROJECT. By C. Wemmer, R. Simons and H.R. Mishra ... 632

THE NEED TO CONSERVE SPOTTED-BILLED PELICAN NESTING HABITAT IN INDIA. By G. Gene Montgomery and Ralph W. Schreiber ... 632

THE GREY PELICAN AT NELAPATTU. By V. Nagulu and J.V. Ramana Rao ... 633

HABITAT MANAGEMENT FOR THE CONSERVATION OF THE GREAT INDIAN BUSTARD *CHORIOTIS NIGRICEPS*. By Asad Rafi Rahmani ... 633

REHABILITATION OF SALTWATER CROCODILE, *CROCODYLUS POROSUS* SCHNEIDER IN ORISSA, INDIA — A CASE HISTORY. By Sudhakar Kar ... 634

BUTTERFLY FARMING AND CONSERVATION IN PAPUA NEW GUINEA, WITH CONTROLLED UTILIZATION OF RESOURCES AS A NEW VILLAGE INDUSTRY. By Angus F. Hutton ... 634

THE TRADE IN WILD FALCONS IN EGYPT. By Mostafa Abbas Saleh ... 635

IMPLICATIONS OF MUTUALISTIC SEED-DISPERSAL FOR TROPICAL RESERVE MANAGEMENT. By Henry F. Howe ... 636

DESERTIC TREES AND THEIR INFLUENCES ON COMPANION VEGETATION. By A.N. Lahiri ... 637

ENVIRONMENTAL CONSEQUENCES OF HYDRO-ELECTRIC PROJECTS IN BASTAR DISTRICT, CENTRAL INDIA. By H.R. Divekar ... 638

THE DEVELOPMENT OF BIRDLIFE IN AUROVILLE. By Pieter Centerfield ... 638

INDEX ... 641

Monitoring Large-Mammal populations in National Parks and Nature Reserves

GEORGE A. PETRIDES

Department of Fisheries and Wildlife, Michigan State University, East Lansing, Michigan. USA.

ABSTRACT

The preservation of natural landscapes with their indigenous fauna and flora is a responsibility of every nation. In many of the world's national parks and nature reserves, however, large-mammal populations have tended to increase and to destroy their vegetative habitats.

Most wild areas today exist as 'islands' surrounded by other land uses. Once destroyed, population and technological pressures will prevent their recovery. It is essential that existing wild lands be preserved through management.

Two simple but effective methods for herbivore food-preference analysis are described. These yield rapid and useful measurements of range condition and trend and enable the prevention of habitat damage. The importance of the exclosure as an index to wilderness values also is illustrated.

A fundamental objective of all governments should be the preservation of natural and unspoiled areas which contain the complete fauna and flora of the nation. Serving as living museums, these samples of wild landscape should be set aside as national parks or nature reserves. Their principal function would be to display the indigenous flora and fauna interacting with each other and the physical environment as they did before man became dominant.

In an earlier paper (Petrides 1977), I reviewed the topic of wildlife population explosions as a problem in the preservation of nature. On areas which contain populations of hoofed mammals several conditions often prevail that are natural in themselves but which often combine to threaten natural values. These are not always recognized either by the public or by scientists, yet the facts are that:

1. In many of the world's remaining national parks and wilderness areas, populations of hoofed animals tend to increase and to damage or destroy their vegetative habitats.
2. Populations of 'big game' species characteristically are not held in check by predators. Neither do such animals 'flow out' from crowded habitats, except after serious damage is done to the wilderness vegetation.
3. Beliefs that nature ever was in long-term 'balance' on local areas may not be valid. It seems much more likely (Petrides 1974) that alternating periods of habitat overuse and of range recovery have prevailed through the ages.
4. National parks and natural areas today mostly exist as 'islands' surrounded by other land uses. There, the isolated wild plant and animal species are vulnerable to over-population and other catastrophes and hence to extinction. Once destroyed, we cannot expect that present-day natural areas will be kept intact over the centuries

to await an uncertain natural recovery.

5. The problem of over-abundant ungulates in nature reserves is unlikely to vanish. Many wild areas will require control of excessive animal numbers in order to retain their wilderness character.

From my several previous visits to national parks and wildlife refuges in India, I can agree that the illegal killing of animals in nature reserves generally is a more serious problem than animal over-abundance. Damage by livestock, however, is not unusual and at the delightful Kanha National Park last year signs of incipient over-grazing by spotted deer (*Axis axis*) were evident.

Even where over-populated wildlife habitats have not yet occurred, awareness of the possible destruction of nature by natural causes should not be overlooked. There are, I believe, actions which officials responsible for nature preservation should undertake as precautions against the occurrence of herbivore over-abundance. Sometimes the precautions which I recommend will reveal that damage to wild vegetation already has occurred. Management decisions then may have to be made in order to restore the wilderness to an undisturbed condition.

What needs to be known? Wherever wild grazing animals occur, there is a natural tendency to want to count them. The public wants to know how many animals there are, and the local official wants to be able to supply answers. But to census wildlife in any except the most open grasslands is generally difficult, expensive, and inaccurate. And it is usually unnecessary from the standpoint of species management. While the number of individuals present (or even the number per unit area) is of general interest, it is absolutely critical to the preservation of both the plant and animal communities to establish that an herbivore is in balance with the foods available to it. If the animal species is below-normal in abundance, then the reason should be determined. If it is over-abundant, then the whole living community could be damaged.

Every animal species which grazes on herbaceous plant forages or which browses on shrubs or trees has its own special nutritional requirements. Not all plants are equally tasty or equally nutritious. Always some kinds are preferred over others. These preferred forages (both by species and parts eaten) are often found to be the most nutritious foods for the grazing animal involved.

The principal foods of an animal population are those which it eats in greatest quantities. These foods, however, may or may not be those which are preferred. Preferred foods are those which are proportionately more frequent in the diet than in the available environment. It is important for the nature-reserve manager to know both principle and preferred foods for each important herbivore present.

Determining food preferences. There are two good ways to determine whether a population of herbivores is in balance with its food supply. Both of these involve the determination of preference ratings for the various forage plants.

The usual method (Petrides 1975) is to determine the percentages of various forages in the diet (*d*) and then to divide these values by the percentages available of these foods in the environment (*a*). This is most easily done in the field by following randomized transect lines in areas occupied by a single herbivore species and tallying the eaten and uneaten twigs of each plant species present. (If more than one grazing species is present in an area, it may still be of value to determine food preference values for the combined animal populations. The collective results would be useful in making management decisions for the several herbivore species.

Later observations of individuals or isolated populations might enable the identification of specific foraging characteristics.)

The derived food preference values ($p = d/a$) indicate the order in which forage plants are sought out by the grazing animal. Values above 1.00 indicate which forages are preferred by the grazing animal, while values under that level indicate which available plants are neglected or avoided as foods. Plant species C in the Table, for example, is eaten 1.67 times as much as would be expected from its abundance. It is preferred four times as much by the grazing animal as species F.

Another approach to food preference analysis is by determining the percentages of various species which are eaten. The percentages removed (r) by eating are values which parallel the d/a preferred or neglected. There is no value of 1.00, however, to serve as a guide to exact status.

TABLE

CALCULATION OF FOOD PREFERENCE RATINGS AND THE DIETARY IMPORTANCE OF FORAGE SPECIES USING HYPOTHETICAL DATA (FROM PETRIDES 1975)

FORAGE 'SPECIES'[1]	QUANTITIES[2] (A) AVAILABLE	(R) REMOVED	PERCENTAGES (a) AVAILABLE	(d) DIET[3]	(r) REMOVED[4]	(P) PREFERENCE RATINGS[5]
B	1,000	900	10	30	90.0	3.00
C	1,500	750	15	25	50.0	1.67
E	2,000	600	20	20	30.0	1.00
F	2,400	300	24	10	12.5	0.42
G	2,500	210	25	7	8.4	0.28
H	400	150	4	5	37.5	1.25
I	100	90	1	3	90.0	3.00
J	100	0	1	0	0	0.00
Totals	WA = 10,000	WR = 3,000	100	100	30.0	1.00

a = A/WA d = 100R/WR r = 100R/A p = D/A

[1]Species are designated by letters which are without meaning: A and D are not used for species to avoid confusion with symbols for availability and diet.

[2]Numbers or volumes of food items available and removed (eaten).

[3]Percentage of each species removed as related to all food removed and consumed: $d = 100R/WR$.

[4]Percentage of available forage (A) which is consumed: $r = 100R/A$.

[5]Note that the relative values of percentages of foods removed (r) directly parallel the preference rating values $P = d/a$.

In the complex vegetation of the mature Malaysian rainforest, Williams and Petrides (1980) found it not to be feasible to determine the relative abundance of the many species of possible tapir (*Tapirus indicus*) forages. The most convenient (and actually the only practical) way was to determine the extent to which browse was taken from each small tree straddled by a tapir. Using this method, they found that of 46 species eaten by tapirs, 27 were browsed to a greater extent than 75 percent. These species were the most highly preferred and hence offered the greatest potential as indicators of habitat condition for tapirs. Where those plants were over-utilized, the range was probably overstocked with tapirs. If underconsumed, then some factor other than the available food supply was limiting tapir abundance.

Range condition and trend. Forage preference studies provide essential data in nature preservation. They yield information on stocking rate (herbivore density) as well as on range (habitat) condition and trend.

Both total food-intake and preference values of forage plants are important items. In the sample data of the Table, for instance, species B and I equally are the most preferred (at p = 3.00). But forage B is the most important food consumed by the test animal. Species B comprises 30% of the herbivores' diet, while species I provides only three percent of the food eaten. Obviously, it is essential that species B be watched carefully to insure that it is not over-utilized. When it begins to be heavily eaten, however, species I also can serve as an early indicator of an over-populated (over-stocked) range.

As a general rule (and in the absence of more exact knowledge), it is assumed that no more than 50% of either the vegetative or reproductive parts can be removed by foraging if a plant species is to maintain its abundance in the plant community. Where feeding is intensive, the most preferred forage species will tend to be depleted first, with the remaining species affected more or less severely according to their preference ranking. On heavily over-grazed areas, plants neglected or avoided by herbivores will tend to increase and invade new areas.

For the Table example, it would be expected under heavy grazing pressure, that preferred species A, I, C & H would decrease in that sequence. Avoided species and neglected species F and G would increase. Species E would either increase or decrease or remain neutral, depending on the degree of grazing pressure.

Regular determination of the status of preferred forage plants will indicate whether a wildlife habitat is deteriorating through overgrazing. Or the indication may be that the area is inadequately grazed and that native herbivores are either absent or prevented from increasing by some other environmental factor which should be investigated.

The preparation of a list of preferred food plants on an area yields positive results quickly. Surveys of range vegetation indicate whether preferred forages are being over-utilized and thus whether the habitat is being degraded. In such work, it is desirable but not necessary to identify the plant species accurately. Unknown plants can be called species A, B or X. Range condition and trend thus can be evaluated so long as similar plants are not confused with each other.

Calculations of the same sort can be undertaken to ascertain the prey preferences of carnivores (Petrides and Pienaar 1966; Pienaar 1969). Seldom is this a critical need in nature preservation, though, since predators rarely if ever become destructively over-abundant. Typically, their own behavioural interactions control the densities of predator populations and prevent exceptional reductions in prey abundance. Plant-eating animals, however, hold the potential for range destruction. Forage preference determinations are essential in all areas where herbivores are present.

The exclosure technique. In addition to food preference analysis, it is desirable to build exclosures in areas occupied by grazing species. These are fenced areas designed to exclude grazing animals. The objective is to keep herbivores out of a sample area of rangeland so that a comparison between the vegetation within the exclosure and outside will reveal the effects of herbivore feeding pressures.

No specific size can be recommended for an exclosure. Normally, the protection of even 0.01 hectare will yield useful results but small exclosures also may be affected by rodents or other small herbivores. If they can enter the exclosure, they may congregate where larger grazers cannot compete. Their possible effects on vegetation, therefore, must not be overlooked.

Ideally, exclosures should be large enough or numerous enough to include all vegetative species. Under the best circumstances, too, they should be partitioned so as to exclude all herbivores from a segment of the area, with another portion open only to rodents and tiny grazers. Under ideal conditions, the partitioning of exclosures permits detailed analysis of herbivore foraging effects. But usually in most wildlife areas, the effects of large herbivores on a vegetative habitat can be dramatically demonstrated by simple fenced exclosures which exclude only large mammals.

There are grounds for arguing, as a matter of interest, that exclosures should be required to monitor general land use effects. In northern Lebanon, for example, I have seen a stone fence which surrounds a Maronite churchyard of perhaps 5 hectares. Inside the fence were handsome mature Cedar-of-Lebanon trees and also seedling cedars and grasses. Outside the fence, the contryside was nearly barren of vegetation and the dry ground was covered with goat tracks.

A person travelling through Lebanon might wonder about the Biblical statement that Solomon built his ships of the cedars. Commonly it is assumed that climatic changes caused extinction of the cedar forests during the 5000 years since Solomon's time. But the Maronite churchyard, doubtless causing a merely-accidental exclusion of livestock through recent centuries, demonstrated that the climate has not changed radically. It is still suitable for tree-seedling survival. The extensive erosion evident throughout northern Lebanon, therefore, is a product of human misuse of the land. Especially it is due to the failure to prevent overgrazing.

Management to preserve nature. We all like to think that somewhere nature can be allowed to remain untouched and unaffected by human pressures. Some place, we feel (Petrides 1977), trees must be allowed to fall and decay without human intervention. Let them die naturally, we say. Let them fertilize new generations of wild forests. But, in contrast to trees, which when unharvested merely fall and enrich the site, over-abundant herbivores destroy their habitats and themselves.

The world's true wilderness areas are few and mostly isolated tracts. Just as the ancient monuments of Greece are being eroded by atmospheric pollutants, the world's wild heritage also faces dangers related to modern life. Management of natural areas and wilderness may seem like a contradiction of terms. Truly, human interference should not be undertaken unless necessary. Yet the control of animal populations often is required if wild areas are to be preserved in a natural state.

References

Petrides, George A. (1975): Principal foods versus preferred foods and their relation to stocking rates and range condition. *Biol. Cons.* 7:161-169.

____ (1977): Wildlife population explosions: A problem in wilderness management. *In* Voices of the Wilderness. Proc. First World Wilderness Cong. (Johannesburg) pp. 235-239.

____ & Pienaar, U. de V. (1966):Calculation and ecological interpretation of prey preferences for large predators in Kruger National Park, South Africa. Michigan State University, East Lansing, Michigan, mimeo, 6 pp.

Pienaar, U. de V. (1969): Predator-prey relationships amongst the larger mammals of Kruger National Park. *Koedoe* 12: 108-196.

Williams, K.D. & Petrides, G.A. (1980): Browse use, feeding behaviour, and management of the Malayan tapir. *J. Wildl. Manage.* 44:489-494.

Marine Park in the Gulf of Kachchh

(With two plates)

SANAT A. CHAVAN

INTRODUCTION

The southern coastline of the Gulf of Kachchh possesses an intricate network of islands, inlets, bays and long expanses of intertidal elevated sandstones. The intertidal zone of the Gulf is endowed with a fantastic array of marine life, topped with coral reefs and mangrove forests. The Government of Gujarat has declared this unique area (20°15′-23°35′N, 69°-70°E) as a Marine Park. An area of 162.89 sq. km is notified as a Marine National Park and 455.92 sq.km as a Marine Sanctuary.

Past records reveal that this Gulf area with its necklace of islands, had much richer marine and land fauna. Jamnagar state had a well-developed pearl fishery and the Okhamandal coast of the erstwhile Baroda state supported window-pane oyster fishery.

FAUNA

A brief survey of the animal life is given below:

Phylum PORIFERA

About 70 species of sponges (soft and calcarious types) have been recorded in the region. They occur in a fantastic array of colours, namely pink, red, brown, blue, light blue, yellow, orange etc.

Phylum COELENTERATA

Corals form the predominant types of this phylum. Examples of the commoner forms of Corals are *Favia* spp., *Porites, Siderestrea* spp. *Lytocarpus* sp., *Dendronephthya brevirama* (soft coral), *Dendronephthya dendrophyta* (soft coral), *Astromuricea stellifera* (horny coral), *Juncella juncea* (horny coral), *Lophogorgia lutkeni* (horny coral), *Virgularia rumphii* (sea pen), *Pteroïdes* sp. (sea pen).

Phylum ECHIUROIDEA

Ikedella misakiensis, Ikedosoma pirotanensis, the latter is peculiar to this area.

Phylum ANNELIDA.

Several species of marine worms occur such as *Sabella* sp. (fan worm), *Neris versicolor, Tubicolor* (Polychetes) worms, *Eurythoe complanata* etc.

Phylum CRUSTACEA

The Barnacles *Balanus complentata. Balanus* spp. are not common, and a variety of True Crabs such as *Scylla serrata, Neptunus pelagicus, Thalamita prymna, Uca* sp. *Eriphia laevimenus, Charybdis* spp., *Attergatis inermis, Pagarus* sp., and the lobsters *Panulirus polyphagus* and *Panulirus homarus*.

Phylum MOLLUSCA

This group of invertebrates is very well represented in the Gulf by snails, mussels, oysters, octopus, sea-hares, etc. More than 200 species have been recorded in the shallow, intertidal waters and also in the deeper waters.

Phylum ECHINODERMATA

The star fish and its relatives are mostly bottom-dwelling and are represented by *Lamprometra palmata, Astropecten polyacanthus, Pateria* sp., *Ophiothrix* sp. *Macrophiothrix* sp., *Salmaca bicolor, Clypeaster humilis,* sealily, feather star, starfishes, brittle star, sea urchin, sand dollar etc.

FISHES

The Gulf region supports about 200 species of fishes including about 18 types of sharks. Some of the species are peculiar to coral reefs.

REPTILES

The Green Sea Turtles (*Chelonia mydas*), are common as also varieties of sea-snakes. The Leatherback and Olive Ridley turtles are also seen. Some mangroves harbour sawscaled vipers.

BIRDS

All along the creeks in the Gulf, around Pirotan, Dera, Bugglabeli, and Shahbeli tall mangrove trees are crowded with heronries of birds like grey herons, pond herons, reef herons. Other species seen along the coast are painted storks, large and small egrets, curlew, crabplovers, darters, cormorants etc. Along with the receding tide we find hectic activity of various gulls, avocet, whimbrel, curlew, terns and the elegant crabplovers, herons, egrets, storks etc.

Migratory turnstones and sanderlings coming all the way from the Arctic region seem to follow each other in large groups. Mudflats around the creeks have fantastic collection of birds, the most elegant among them being crabplovers, sitting in close circular groups at the edge of islands at high tide.

MAMMALS

The endangered Dugong is the most noteworthy among the marine mammals seen in the Park area besides the Dolphin and the Whale.

MANGROVES

The whole coastline of the Gulf is fringed with a luxurient growth of mangroves, the unique land building, tropical plants which show remarkable ability to live in saline and tidal areas where no other trees grow. The slushy mangrove marshes with a high degree of dissolved oxygen provide a paradise for a number of marine creatures. Mangrove is the most important link in the Coastal Ecosystem.

Three species dominant in this area are *Avicennia* sp. *Rhizhophora mucronata,* and *Ceriops taqal.* In lesser concentration, *Avicennia alba* and *A. officinalis* are also present, along with *Brugeria, Salicornia* and *Salvadora* spp.

Rhizhophora and *Ceriops,* lifted above the surface of muddy marshes by prop-roots growing from their trunk and branches form excellent habitats for water and shore birds. Seeds of these two mangrove species germinate by vivipary. *Avicennia* found in the outermost zone, have gas exchanging roots, *pneumatophores,* rising out radially in mud all around the parent plant.

Mushrooming industrial activity of salt works, cement factory, cutting mangrove for fuel and grazing by camel had taken heavy toll of mangrove vegetation. Fortunately timely action by the Government of Gujarat has saved and injected new life in this precious marine ecosystem.

Above: Giant Sea Anemone in coral reef
Below: Brain Coral in coral lagoons
(*Photos*: Author)

Viviparous fruits of *Ceriops* and *Rhizophora* start germinating while still on the tree (*Photo*: Author)

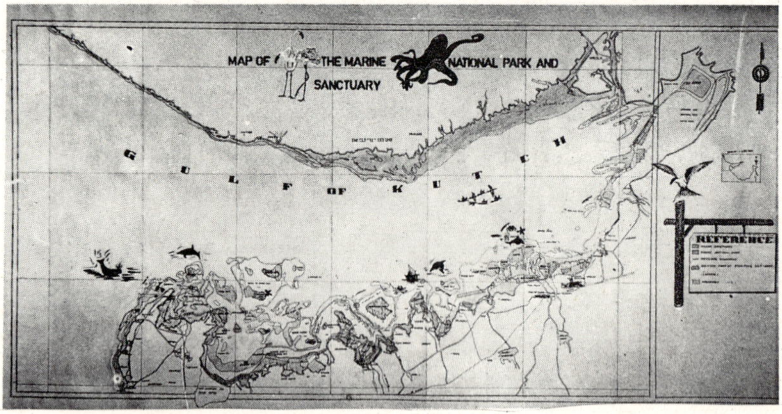

Marine Park in the Gulf of Kutch (*Photo*: Author)

Guidelines for the Analysis of Biophysical Impacts to Tropical Coastal Marine Resources

(*With five text-figures*)

NORA L. BERWICK

ACKNOWLEDGEMENTS

I would like to express special thanks to Suzi Fowler whose technical insights made the production of this paper possible.

TABLE OF CONTENTS

1.0 INTRODUCTION
2.0 ESSENTIAL ECOLOGICAL INFORMATION FOR EFFECTIVE MANAGEMENT OF TROPICAL COASTAL RESOURCES
2.1 **Mangroves**
Description
Critical Environmental Parameters for Maintenance of Ecological Processes
Major Sources of Environmental Stress
2.2 **Seagrass Meadows**
Description
Critical Environmental Parameters for Maintenance of Ecological Processs
Major Sources of Environmental Stress
2.3 **Coral Reefs**
Description
Critical Environmental Parameters for Maintenance of Ecological Processes
Major Sources of Environmental Stress
3.0 ENVIRONMENTAL ASSESSMENT
3.1 **Affected Environment**
Environmental Issues
Resources
The Region of Influence
Attributes
3.2 **Investigation and Assessment**
Determination of Baseline Conditions
Analytic Approaches & Techniques for Measuring the Physical and Chemical Parameters of the Resource
Analytic Approaches and Techniques for Measuring the Biotic Parameters of the Resource
Analytic Approaches and Techniques for Assessing the Functional Parameters of the Resource
Estimation of Future Baseline without the Development Project
Estimation of Project Effects
Determination of Impact
Determination of Significance
Determination of Appropriate Mitigation Measures
4.0 COASTAL RESOURCE MANAGEMENT RESEARCH RECOMMENDATIONS
5.0 REFERENCES

Conservation Systems, 102 Seventh St., N.E., Washington, D.C. 20002

LIST OF FIGURES

Fig. 1-1 **Hypothetical Nutrient Flow Diagram Illustrating the Complex Trophic Relationships of Tropical Coastal Ecosystems**
Fig. 1-2 **Biophysical System Processes Susceptible to Impacts**
Fig. 3-1 **Impact Analysis Procedure Flow Chart**
Fig. 3-2 **Habitat Evaluation Approach to Impact Assessment**
Fig. 3-3 **An Integrated Overview of Nearshore Catch Fisheries Sector Interactions**

LIST OF TABLES

1-1 **Comparative Productivity Values between Tropical Marine Ecosystems and Cultivated Land**
2-1 **Principal Sources and Effects of Development-Related Stress to Mangrove Ecosystems**
2-2 **Major Sources of Stress to Seagrass Ecosystems and Potential Associated Effects**
2-3 **Comparision of Primary Estimates between Coral Reefs and Vicinity Oceanic Waters**
2-4 **Major Sources of Stress to Coral Reef Ecosystems and Potential Associated Effects**
3-1 **Comparision of Component and Ecosystem Approaches to the Assessment of Tropical Coastal Marine Communities**
3-2 **Hypothetical Example of a Summary Impact Matrix Based on Data from the Segara Anakan Reclamation Project Report: Impact to Commercial Fisheries**

ABSTRACT

Tropical coastal zones with their characteristic abundance of natural resources are foci for such increasing exploitation pressures as fishing, collection of construction materials and mineral resources, development of recreation areas, transportation corridors, industrial sites, urban settlements, and waste disposal sites. Impacts of development-related activities on coastal ecosystems can not be sufficiently predicted and mitigated for without systematic data acquisition and analysis. This paper focuses on the mangrove-seagrass-coral reef complex and is intended to provide a general framework for the collection and assessment of ecological information for the management of these tropical coastal resources. Topics reviewed include: (1) interactions between the three coastal ecosystems; (2) the influences of the configuration of the land mass, coastal terrain and substratum, as well as water current patterns on these ecosystems; (3) the critical environmental parameters necessary for the maintenance of each ecosystem; (4) the major sources of environmental stress; (5) an approach to environmental assessment; (6) current methodologies for resource inventories and baseline surveys; as well as (7) recommendations for applied research related to development of realistic coastal zone management strategies. The unifying structure for such systematic evaluations is the systems analytic approach.

1.0 INTRODUCTION

Coastal zones with their characteristic abundance of natural resources are foci for such increasing exploitation pressures as fishing, collection of construction materials and mineral resources, development of recreation areas, transportation corridors, industrial sites, urban settlements, and waste disposal sites. The historical economic significance of coastal resources is perhaps best exemplified with regard to fisheries. According to Levy (1976), 90 percent of global marine fish production is caught over the continental shelf. These fishing grounds are often associated with shallow waters where highly productive coastal ecosystems such as coastal lagoons, mangrove estuaries, seagrass meadows, and coral reefs play an important role in the support systems provided the fisheries (e.g. feeding, breeding, and nursery habitat). The highly productive fisheries in the Java seas may be attributed to the increased primary productivity in oceanic waters fed by estuarine flooding from freshwater runoff into coastal waters (Maragos, *et al.* 1983). Lindall, *et al.* (1972) estimated that 98 percent of all fish caught in the Gulf of Mexico are estuarine dependent. The coral reef fishery of northwest Sabah (Indonesia), with an annual estimated value of $1.25 million, accounts for approximately 30 percent of the total landings (Langham and Mathias 1977). Fisheries of the fringing coral reef and lagoon coastline bordering much of Tanzania, Kenya and Somalia are estimated to range from 5 to 17 times that of offshore Somalian waters of equivalent area (Anon. 1974).

Coastal resources have acquired additional significance with the onset of more recent development opportunities such as petroleum and mining activities, marine-oriented tourism, the siting of ports and energy facilities, forest products exploitation, as well as the development of areas for agricultural and/or aquacultural production. The presence of such economically important resources along with their concomitant use patterns and associated infrastructure has contributed toward an estimated two-thirds of the world's population, including a majority of cities with populations exceeding one million, residing in the coastal zone (Levy 1976).

Ecologically, the coastal zone is an ecotone representing the transition from terrestrial to marine influences. It consists of the shore as well as fringing terrestrial and sublittoral regions involving several interrelated food-chains (Figure1-1) and biophysical system processes susceptible to impacts (Figure 1-2). The coastal zone does not have absolute boundaries and may include, depending on analytic requirements, upland watersheds, wetlands,

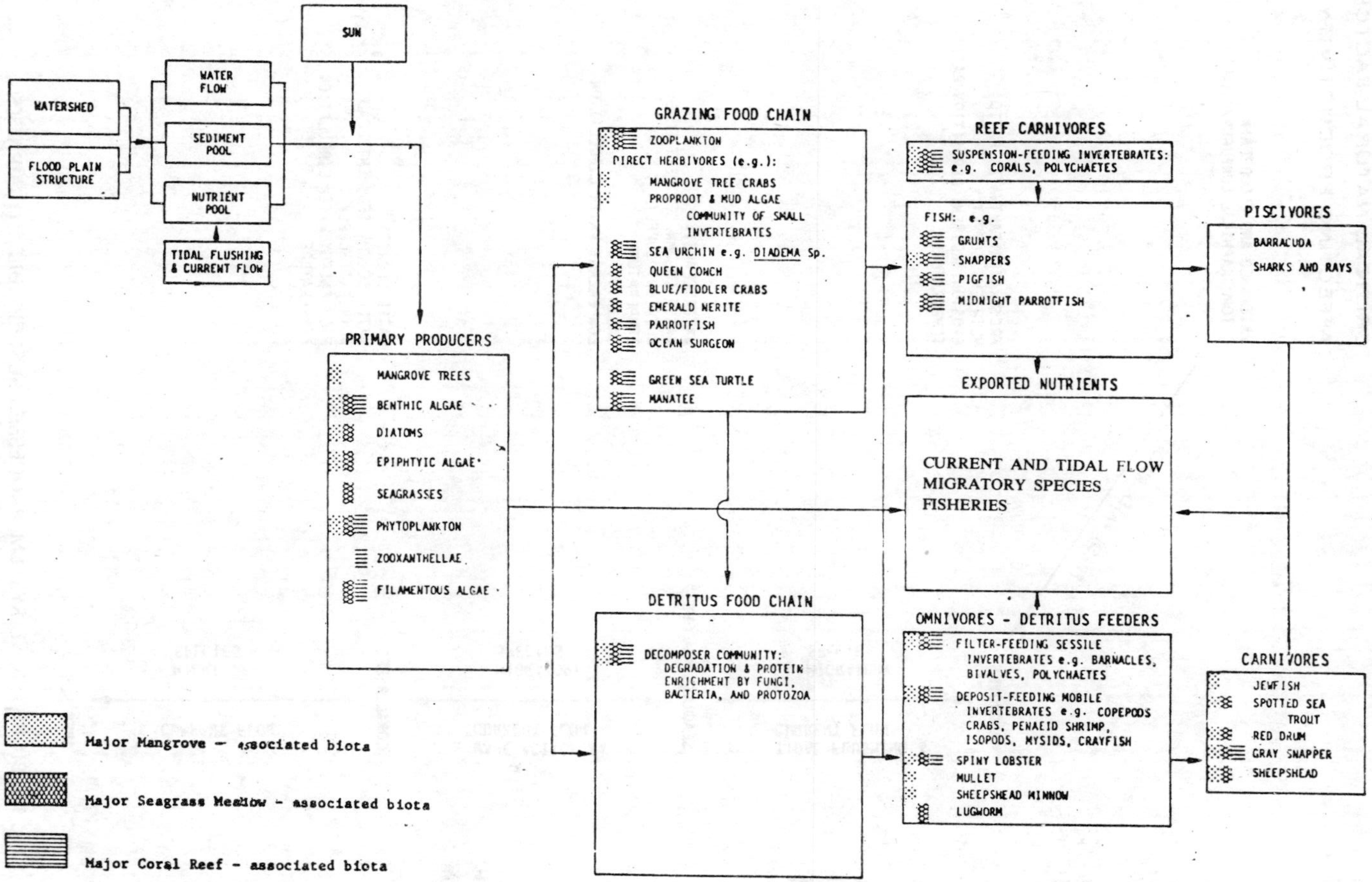

Fig. 1-1. HYPOTHETICAL NUTRIENT FLOW DIAGRAM ILLUSTRATING
THE COMPLEX TROPICAL RELATIONSHIPS OF TROPICAL COASTAL ECOSYSTEMS

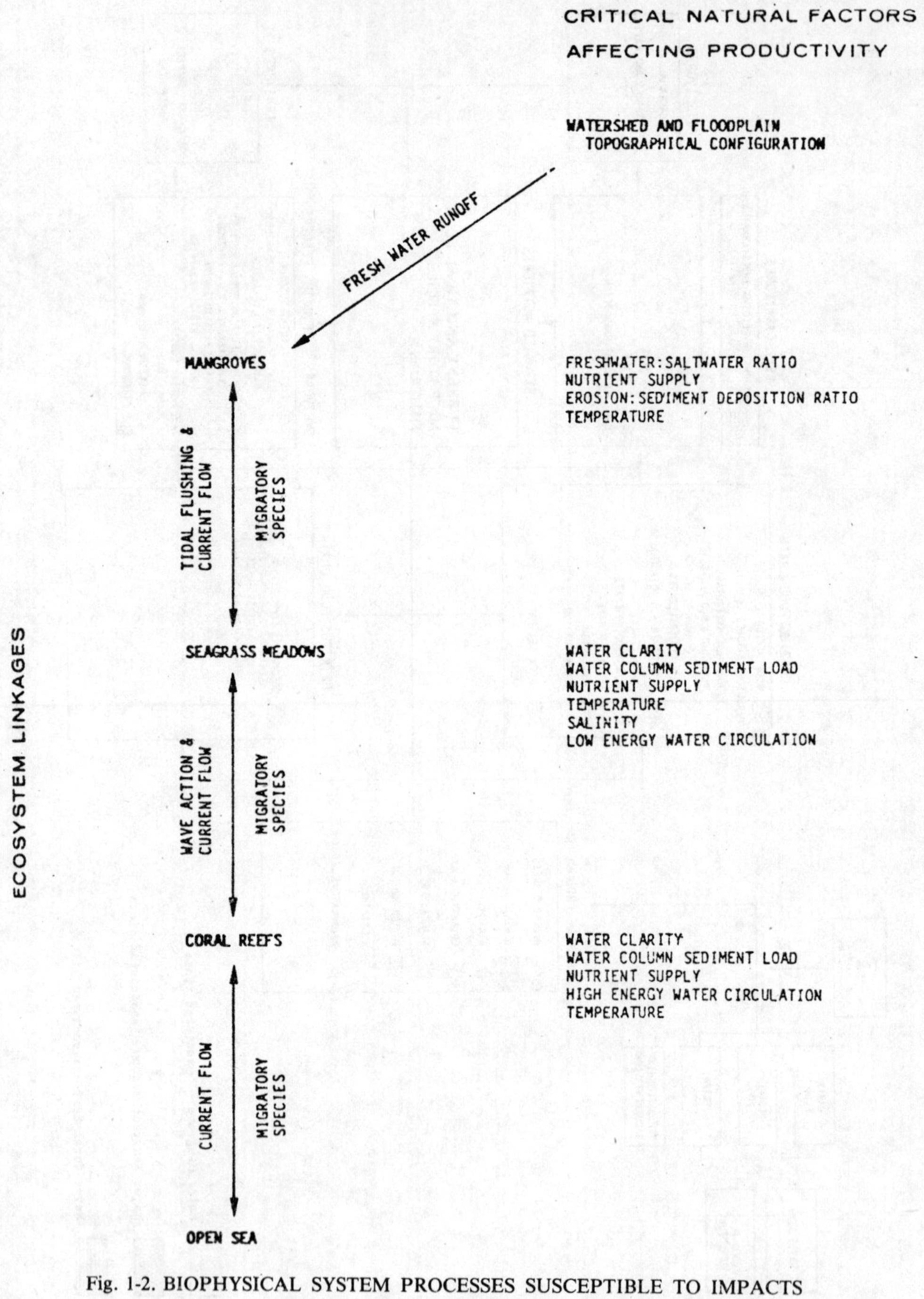

Fig. 1-2. BIOPHYSICAL SYSTEM PROCESSES SUSCEPTIBLE TO IMPACTS

estuaries, mangroves, shallow water embayments, coastal lagoons, beaches, seagrass meadows, coral reefs, and extend several hundred kilometres seaward. Sharp ecotones are not easily defined as they are determined by the gradient of physical and chemical conditions that constitute the range of tolerance for the assemblage of associated biota.

Mangroves, seagrass meadows, and coral reef ecosystems that characterize many tropical coastlines provide or influence important natural resources. An understanding of the functioning of these ecosystems is necessary for effective coastal resource management. The three ecotypes are among the most productive in the world (Table 1-1). Lewis (1977) ranks seagrass beds and coral reefs higher in gross primary productivity per m^2 per year than sugarcane fields in Java or the nutrient-rich Pervian Current. Mangrove ecosystems supplied with terrestrial nutrient input produce comparable levels of gross primary productivity (Lugo and Snedaker 1974). The presence of any one or combination of the three ecosystems in coastal areas indicates a dependence on an overall similar, yet system-specific, set of critical environmental parameters with regard to: (1) water quality, salinity and temperature regimes; (2) freshwater runoff, currents and tidal regimes; (3) sediment deposition and transport patterns; and (4) nutrient inputs.

TABLE 1-1

COMPARATIVE PRODUCTIVITY VALUES BETWEEN TROPICAL MARINE ECOSYSTEMS AND CULTIVATED LAND (FROM LEWIS, 1977; LUGO AND SNEDAKER 1974).

Ecotype	**Average Gross Primary Production gmC/m²/yr**
Mangrove Forest[1]	2300-5074
Marine Grass Beds	4650
Coral Reef	4200
Peru Current	3650
Sugar Cane Fields	3450
Field Grass, Minnesota	500

[1]Receives wet season terrestrial nutrient runoff

Characteristic of the mangrove-seagrass meadow-coral reef complex is the inextricable linkage between the ecosystem types and interrelated supporting systems by current flow and to inland areas by watershed drainage. Faunal connections are known to exist between the ecotypes (Odum, *et al.* 1982; Zieman 1982) as are energy and nutrient flux processes (Zieman 1982; Stoddart and Johannes 1978). The flow of both dissolved and particulate organic matter from mangroves is reported to enhance the primary productivity of seagrasses (Zieman 1982). Seagrass beds and mangroves enhance the secondary productivity of coral reefs and nearshore waters by providing shelter and alternative feeding sites for juvenile (and adult) forms of commercially important fin- and shellfish species. Nutrient transfer from seagrass meadows to reef ecosystems occurs as a result of the nocturnal foraging migrations of both juvenile and adult carnivorous/omnivorous fishes to the grassbeds with subsequent excretion/defecation upon return to the reef (Ogden and Zieman 1977; Meyer, *et al.* 1983). When one ecosystem functions as nursery for another, there is nutrient transport from one habitat to the other as, for example, when crustaceans and reef fishes migrate from their juvenile seagrass habitat to take up residence on reefs (Ogden and Zieman 1977). The influence of coral reef animals on reef community structure is a result of nocturnal foraging of urchins and diurnal foraging of herbivorous fishes (Ogden and Gladfelter 1982). Hay (1981) and Hay *et al.* (1983) reported that more than 90 percent of the material grazed from turtle grass beds near coral reef was due to herbivorous fishes while less than 10 percent was due to urchin grazing. Hay (1984) found this situation to be reversed in areas under intensive fishing pressure by man and conjectures that overfishing causes a reduction in the number of urchin predators (e.g. balistids).

In addition to primary production, nutrient transfer, or to interactions between their component species, interactions between coastal ecosystems may also be considered in terms of their respective modifications to the physical environment and morphological characteristics. Mangroves, seagrass beds, and coral reefs all form structures that influence water movement in such a manner that stabilizes the physical environment. All three ecosystems produce and retain sediment: mangroves and seagrass beds by depositing leaves and blades; coral reefs by producing calcareous sediments which accumulate in the back reef area. In a study performed off Bermuda, for example, it was estimated that for every acre of reef, 920 kg (1 ton) of solid coral skeleton is converted to sand annually, primarily by parrotfishes (Kaplan 1982). Encrusting coraline algae on seagrasses produce from 40 to 180 gm/m^2/year of calcium carbonate sediment off Jamaica (Land 1970) and upwards to 2800 gm/m^2/year off Barbados (Patriquin 1972).

A result of sediment production and retention is modification of water movements. Coral reefs form barriers that dissipate wave energy. By forming lagoons, coral reefs allow the existence of seagrass beds where they would otherwise not exist. Mangroves and tropical grassbeds, characteristically found in areas of reduced wave energy, also occur in the absence of coral reefs, in natural harbours or in the lee of points of land. Mangroves, by occluding and absorbing terrestrial freshwater runoff, buffer large salinity changes in coastal waters. Both mangroves and seagrasses trap and stabilize sediments thus reducing the sediment load in coastal waters (Odum, *et al.* 1982; Zieman 1982).

The role of mangroves and seagrass meadows as nurseries for many juvenile species may be more a result of the habitat structure than productivity. Primary production that goes directly into the herbivore food chain may be due to epiphytic algae which use the seagrasses and mangroves as a substrata rather than from the production of the seagrasses and mangroves themselves.

In general, interactions between mangroves, seagrass meadows, and coral reefs are not necessary for the establishment or maintenance of any one of the systems, and are of less importance to the development and productivity of these ecosystems than are the influences exerted by the coastal terrain, topography, water current patterns and rivers. Chemical nutrients, especially nitrates and phosphates, are of particular importance in influencing primary productivity in shallow tropical coastal ecosystems. The high productivity associated with mangrove ecosystems depends upon terrestrial runoff (Lugo, *et al.* 1973). Lugo and Snedaker (1974) found the topographic configuration of the coastline as well as the nature of water movements in terms of terrestrial runoff, drainage, and tidal patterns to be the determining factors in the structure and function of mangrove ecosystems. Aleem (1972) and Sutcliffe (1972, 1973) document the importance of terrestrial runoff on nearshore fisheries. Marsh (1977) and Birkeland (1982) discuss the effects of terrestrial nutrient runoff on coral reef communities.

In reviewing development activities harmful to seagrass communities in estuarine and coastal ecosystems, Thayer, *et al.* (1975) listed as particularly destructive those activities that changed water movement patterns and altered the nature of the shoreline, such as dredging and other disturbance of bottom sediments, clearing of lands for agriculture, channelling of streams thus increasing rates of erosion and inputs of sediments, stream diversions, as well as dam construction and irrigation projects.

Similarly, sedimentation resulting from poor land management practices has been reported to be the most significant pollution threat to coral reefs (Johannes 1975). The degree of coral reef sensitivity to sedimentation is demonstrated by coral die-off in the John Pennekamp Park in the Florida Keys resulting from sediment released from construction in areas more than 65 km (40 mi) away (Kaplan 1982). The rapid destruction of reef ecosystems by sedimentation is particularly prevalent in developing countries where land is cleared for agricultural development, housing and road construction or where harbour dredging activities occur.

Renewable resources of the coastal area are thus vulnerable to land-based sources of impact. Coastal zones do not function in isolation but are interrelated and interpendent not only with immediately adjacent ecosystems by coastal terrain and current flow but also with inland ecosystems by topographical configuration and patterns of watershed drainage. The quality of coastal waters and changes in water quality attributed to development exert a major influence on coastal ecosystems. The quality of the water that runs off the shoreland is determined by the sediments, nutrients and minerals, organic matter, oxygen concentration, as well as any toxic materials from land-based activities. Thus upland agricultural, grazing, and forestry practices in addition to coastal based urban or industrial development activities and marine-oriented tourism exert their influences on coastal ecosystem processes. Tables 2-1, 2-2, and 2-4 illustrate respectively the cause and effect relationships between development activities, their physical consequences, and associated ecological responses by mangrove, seagrass, and coral reef ecosystem. It is clear that effective coastal resource management must incorporate an understanding of the topographical configuration of the land mass, the coastal terrain and substratum, the terrestrial input of materials, and water movement patterns on nearshore coastal ecosystems.

Among the several factors that can influence the potential for impact of development on waste ecosystems are included: (1) the size, nature, location, and timing of the development activity; (2) the type location, and sensitivity of the ecosystems to be affected; and (3) the nature and importance of the natural functions and uses of those ecosystems. Impacts, while significant when measured in terms of specific ecological and economic costs, are difficult to detect in their early stages of manifestation for several reasons: (1) ignorance of the causes of the impacts; (2) ignorance of the associated underlying processes and linkages through which the cause-and-effect relationships manifest themselves; (3) inadequate detection and monitoring capabilities; and (4) lack of an adequate institutional framework to deal with appropriate corrective mechanisms. There is presently a paucity of data concerning the environmental consequences of existing and planned development processes on the marine resources of tropical coastlines. Impacts of development-related activities on coastal ecosystems can not be adequately predicted and mitigated or compensated for without systematic data acquisition and analysis. This paper, provides a general analytic framework for the assessment of essential ecological information necessary for effective management of tropical coastal resources.

TABLE 2-1

PRINCIPAL SOURCES OF EFFECTS OF DEVELOPMENT-RELATED STRESS TO MANGROVE ECOSYSTEMS (ADAPTED FROM SAENGER, *et al.*, 1983).

Activity	Potential Deleterious Effects	Scale of Impact* (ha)
Clearfelling	● Gradual decrease in mangrove area due to conversion to other land uses ● Changed floristic composition favour non-commercial species with the resultant decline in: - timber productivity - the mangrove's function as breeding/feeding grounds for fin- and shellfish species	100,000-500,000
Diversion of freshwater by e.g. irrigation development	● Reducing flushing and its associated increase in dry-season water/soil salinities resulting in: - shifts in species dominance to more saline tolerant species (e.g., the commercial *Heritiera fomes* in the Gangetic delta of Bangladesh) - severe alteration of the depositional character of the mangrove environment - reduced structural complexity of habitat - less favourable habitat conditions for fauna dependent on the mangrove ecosystem for freshwater and food supply (e.g., Bengal tiger) - reduced productivity and detritus export leading to unfavourable habitat conditions for mangrove-dependent fisheries ● Alteration of mangrove sediment deposition resulting in: - deprivation of inorganic nutrient input - siltation	1,000-500,000
Conversion to agriculture	● Alteration of freshwater runoff patterns and tidal exchange resulting in: - initial leaching of salts by freshwater drainage - increased salinity - development of acid sulfate soil conditions - loss of mangrove areas and their associated high productivity - habitat loss of terrestrial fauna and coastal fisheries	100-100,000
Conversion to aquaculture	● Loss of mangroves and associated biota due to major changes in: - drainage patterns - frequency of tidal inundation - nutrient availability - toxicity of runoff from impoundments and drainage channels in areas of acid sulfate soil	100-10,000
Conversion to salt ponds	● Clearfelling followed by land leveling and diking resulting in complete eradication of mangrove flora and fauna ● Alteration of soil salinity and structure that excludes future recolonization from adjacent mangrove stands	100-1,000

Activity	Potential Deleterious Effects	Scale of Impact (ha)
Conversion to urban development	● Total eradication of and reclamation of mangrove area ● Extensive peripheral effects that include - increased rainfall runoff resulting from redirected outflows and reduced penetration - increase in downstream concentrations of e.g., hig-toxicity pollutants and organic effluents - high water demand by high human density - public health management problems - vandalism and increased recreation pressure	100-1,000
Construction of harbors and channels	● Major alteration of nearshore freshwater to saltwater ratio resulting in: - chronic salinity stress - change in species dominance and composition ● Routine discharge or accidental spillages of pollutants into surrounding waters	100-1,000
Mining and mineral extraction		10-100
Activities within the ecosystem:	● Complete destruction of the system	
Activites adjacent to the ecosystem:	● Deposition of excess sediment resulting in: - blocking water, nutrient, and gas exchange within the substrate and between substrate and surrounding water - reduced productivity	
Liquid waste disposal		
Excessive concentrations of non-toxic wastes:	● Oxygen depletion ● "Toxic effects" resulting from bioaccumulation of compounds in the food chain to lethal concentrations - disruption of ecosystem equilibrium - defoliation and death of mangrove flora and fauna	1-10
Toxic wastes:	● Loss of mangroves and associated biota	
Solid waste/garbage disposal	● Loss of mangroves and associated biota ● Surface flow of material leachate and toxic substances into adjacent waterways ● Replacement of natural forms by animal scavengers ● Public health management problems	1-10
Oil and other hazardous chemical spillage	● Physical smothering effect on plant surfaces responsible for carbon dioxide and oxygen exchange ● Long-term chronic poisioning of mangroves and associated biota resulting in reduced productivity	1-10
Traditional exploitative uses	● Relatively deleterious to effects ecosystem equilibrium	1

* Indicates relative scale between activities.

TABLE 2-2
MAJOR SOURCES OF STRESS TO SEAGRASS ECOSYSTEMS AND POTENTIAL ASSOCIATED EFFECTS

Activity	Potential Deleterious Effects
Dredge and Fill Operations Waterfront real estate and industrial development, landfill for causeway construction, navigation channel dredging, and marine dumping of spoil associated with these activities, etc.	● Direct destruction by removal or burial of seagrasses at construction site ● Direct destruction of adjacent habitats by dredge spoil dumping ● Secondary effects on adjacent habitats from increased residual turbidity levels and degraded water quality including: - reduced light penetration and productivity rates - smothering effects on filter feeders - reduced dissolved oxygen levels ● Habitat loss for: - commercially valuable fisheries species and trophic intermediaries - sediment infauna ● Unsuitable sediment conditions for seagrass recolonization (Zieman, 1975b)
Clearing of Coastal and Inland Areas for Agriculture Production (Thayer, *et al.*, 1975)	● Stream channeling/diversion leading to - increased erosion rates and resulting high sediment loads - reduced light penetration and photosynthetic rates - reduced freshwater and nutrient inputs to nearshore areas - increased penetration of higher salinity waters shoreward
Sewage Discharge	● Reduced water quality resulting in: - Stimulation of excess epiphytic production reducing light, availability to leaf blades and thus productivity levels - reduced dissolved oxygen levels caused by increased microbial respiration ● Increased phytoplankton productivity leading to increased turbidity levels and reduced seagrass productivity ● Habitat loss for commercially valuable fisheries species and trophic intermediaries
Chemical Pollution Industrial discharge of organometallics and organochlorides agricultural runoff of pesticides and fertilizers, etc. etc.	● Uptake and concentration by seagrasses with the potential for toxic effects to seagrass species or higher trophic biota as a result of chemical concentrating capability (Thorhaug and Schroeder, 1980)
Industrial Discharge of Thermal Effluents	● Reduced seagrass productivity and growth within narrow tolerance limits beyond which death occurs (Thorhaug, 1981) ● Denuded seabeds and reduced abundance/diversity of associated biota in areas adjacent to heated discharge effluents (Roessler and Zieman, 1969; Thorhaug, *et al.*, 1973) ● Habitat loss for commercially valuable fisheries species and trophic intermediaries
Oil Pollution Oil spills, clean-up procedures, etc.	● Loss of associated fauna (e.g. larvel and juvenile stages of penaeid shrimp species, filter feeding amphipods and polychaetes, sea urchins, conches, holothurious, etc.) (Tatum, *et al.*, 1978; den Hartog and Jacobs, 1980; Nadeau and Berquist, 1977) ● Extensive damage to adjacent biotic interfaces of mangroves and shallow subtidal seagrass/flats (Chan, 1977) ● Direct damage to seagrass (Nadeau and Berquist, 1977) ● Minimal damage to seagrass (Chan, 1977)

TABLE 2-3

COMPARISION OF PRIMARY PRODUCTIVITY ESTIMATES BETWEEN CORAL REEFS AND VICINITY OCEANIC WATERS (FROM LEWIS, 1981)

Reef Location	Gross Production ($gmC/m^2/yr.$)	Source	Vicinity Off-Reef Waters	Gross Production ($gmC/m^2/yr.$)	Source
Hawaiian Coral Reef, Coconut Island	7300	Gordon and Kelly (1962)			
			Oceanic waters off Hawaii	21-27	Doty and Oguri (1956)
Fringing Coral Reef North Kapaa, Hawaii	2427	Kohn and Helfrich (1957)			
Eastern Reef, Rongelap Atoll, Marshall Islands	1250	Sargent and Austin (1954)	Oceanic waters off Rongelap	28	Steemann-Nielson (1954)
El Mario reefs, Puerto Richo	4450	Odum, *et al.* (1954)	North Atlantic waters off Barbados	139	Beers, *et al.* (1963)
Fringing coral reef Moorea, French Polynesia	2628	Sournia (1976)	French Polynesia: deep lagoon subject to fertilization from land	37-153	Sourina and Richard (1976)

TABLE 2-4

MAJOR SOURCES OF STRESS TO CORAL REEF ECOSYSTEMS AND POTENTIAL ASSOCIATED EFFECTS

Activity	Potential Deleterious Effects	Example
Mining, blasting, dredging and filling	• Localised reef destruction: - loss of an estimated $23 m^2$/day of reef cover or 26.8 km reef loss per year (Langham and Mathias, 1977)	Removal of an estimated 100 coral heads/day for use in road building and land reclamation in northwest Sabah, Indonesia (Langham and Mathias, 1977).
	• Increased turbidity and sedimentation in the water column - decreased productivity and growth - disruption of filter-feeding processes - decreased efficiency of respiratory activities - total loss of reef occupying over 440 hectares as a result of siltation associated with dredging at Johnston Island (Brock, *et al.*, 1966)	Removal of an estimated 25,000 tons ($60,000 m^2$) coral annually from reefs in the Gulf of Mannar and Palk Bay, India, for use in the production of calcium carbide (Mahadeven and Nayar, 1972). Removal of an estimated 25,000 tons per year of coral from the reefs off Mauritius for use in the lime industry (Walker, 1962).
	• Habitat loss for associated biota including reef-dependent fisheries	Fishing with dynamite (Ramas, 1969, Johannes, 1970; Ramas, 1969).
	• Decreased tourism and recreation attraction	Blasting of reef structure for navigation channels (Johannes, 1975). Blasting associated with dredging (Endean, 1976). Dredging activities resulting in reef destruction (Marsh and Gordon, 1974; Salm 1982).
Collection of reef biota and associated activities	• Reduction in number of large predatory fishes and molluscan "collection" specimens (e.g. giant triton) resulting in - alteration of community trophic structure - changed species dominance and composition - local extinction by selective collecting	Absence of large predatory fishes (Sharks and groupers) from reefs in the Western Indian Ocean historically documented. to harbour vast number of such fishes (Polunin and Frazier, 1974) Decrease in mollusk population at Addu Atoll, Maldives, Indian Ocean between 1936 and 1964 resulting in local species extinction (Stoddart, 1969)
	• Localized mechanical damage by direct coral removal, anchoring, and trampling (Woodland and Hopper, 1977)	Destruction of 20 percent of a staghorn coral reef in the Fort Jefferson National Monument, Florida by careless anchoring (Davis, 1977)
	• Habitat loss for associated biota including reef-dependent fisheries	
	• Decreased tourism and recreation attraction	

Activity	Potential Deleterious Effects	Example
Inland deforestation Coastal land clearance for agriculture and urban/ industrial development	• Erosion resulting in siltation of nearshore waters - destruction of reef habitat by "smothering" effects - habitat loss for associated biota including reef-dependent fisheries	Human-induced alterations in the vicinity of Kaneohe Bay, Hawaii resulting in the complete destruction of one-third the nearshore reef system with an additional third consisting of dying reefs overgrown by an alga characteristically found in polluted areas (Banner, 1974)
Overgrazing[1]	• Freshwater runoff from coastal housing developments resulting in changed salinity regimes	Heavy fish and coral die-off in Kaneohe Bay, Hawaii following heavy rains that resulted in freshwater runoff at 16 percent of the bay's volume (Bathan, 1968)
	• Decreased tourism and recreation attraction	Inadequate watershed protection in Java resulting in a six-fold increase of silt loads of the Citarum river between 1970-1972 with disruptive effects on nearshore reef systems (Ruddle, 1948)
		Sediment loss to coastal waters off the Phillipines estimated to be 60 million tons (Ruddle, 1984)
Sewage disposal		Kaneohe Bay, Hawaii (Banner 1974); U.S. Virgin Islands (Salvat, 1974)
Heated thermal effluents from coastal power facilities	• Localised loss and damage to nearshore reefs and associated biota (Johanes, 1970) • Decreased tourism and recreation attraction	Kahe Point, Oahu, Hawaii: 87 percent increase in area of dead/damaged corals in vicinity of the 1972 expansion of the coastal electric power plant (Jokiel and Coles, 1974).
Desalination effluents		St. Thomas, Virgin Islands: Total destruction of reef and associated invertebrates within 200 metres of desalination plant (Van Eepoel and Grigg, 1970)

[1]Not directly related to activity at Kaneohe Bay site indicated in the "example coloumn"

Activity	Potential Deleterious Effects	Example
Chemical pollution: (e.g. pesticides and industrial toxic substances)	● Localized "Stress" effects/loss and damage to near-shore reefs and associated biota including species-specific selective elimination resulting in alteration of community trophic structure	Indonesia: "Stress" effects produced with chlorinated hydrocarbons (DDT and endrin) with concentrations at 2 ppm (Lamberts, (1977)
	● Interference with physiological, particularly reproductive, processes and larvae development (Johannes, 1975; Loya, 1975)	Red Sea (Eliat Reserve): Destruction of one mile reef tract resulting from phosphate fertilizer runoff (Loya, 1975); prevention of reef recolonization (Loya, 1976; Mitchell and Ducklow, 1976)
	● Decreased tourism and recreation attraction	Tahit: Localized reef fish kills resulting from uncontrolled use of the insecticides dieldrin (Randall, 1972)
Oil pollution: Oil spill	● Loss and damage to reefs and associated biota when adheres to shallow water corals - smothering effect - change in texture of habitat such that area becomes unsuitable for recruitment of settlement of larva	Red Sea: Destruction of 90 percent of reef flat with subsequent recoveory of reef portion most distant from low-level chronic discharge of shore facility (Loya, 1975)
Chronic low level pollution from associated port facilities	● Localized "stress" effects such as interference with reproductive processes and aborted larvae development (Loya, 1975)	
	● Decreased tourism and recreation attraction	

2.0 Essential Ecological Information for Effective Management of Tropical Coastal Resources

2.1 **Mangroves**

DESCRIPTION. As much as 75 percent of low-lying tropical (25° N and S latitudes) coastlines characterized by reduced wave energy and freshwater drainage are dominated by the organically rich and diverse littoral mangrove swamp community (McGill 1959). The tree canopies, masses of aerial roots, muddy substrates, as well as associated creeks and embayments remaining from tidal inundation that characterize the mangrove ecosystem provide a diverse structural habitat for a complex community of invertebrates, fishes, and birds. Indirectly, mangroves play an important role as feeding and nursery grounds for commercially important fin- and shellfish species. According to Snedaker (1978) as much as 90 percent of tropical marine fish species pass at least one stage of their life cycle in mangrove estuaries. In addition to providing protective and feeding habitat, mangroves function to reduce coastal erosion and to maintain high estuarine water quality through (1) sediment entrapment from surface water runoff and (2) nutrient release in a steady-state equilibrium (Darovec 1975).

Mangrove-estuarine systems provide large nutrient inputs to adjacent waters. With productivity measurements as high as 8.23 gC/m^2/day (Golley *et al.* 1962) mangrove forests are considered among the most productive of estuarine ecosystems (Odum, *et al.* 1974). Leaf and twig litter of approximately 9 mtons/ha/yr (Heald, 1971) represents a major portion of mangrove annual productivity and forms the principal nutrient source for a detritus-based aquatic food chain in which much of the organic production is exported to surrounding waters, which in turn support highly productive nearshore fisheries. Furthermore mangrove ecosystems serve as a sink for macronutrients (e.g. nitrogen and phosphorus), trace elements, and heavy metals (Odum, *et al.* 1982). The direct commercial value of mangroves include (1) tannin using curing leather, (2) wood chip production, (3) fuelwood and charcoal, as well as (4) building materials (Chai 1974).

CRITICAL ENVIRONMENTAL PARAMETERS FOR MAINTENANCE OF ECOLOGICAL PROCESSES. The chief component controlling the presence, distribution, and stability of mangrove communities is the water regime which depends upon a number of interdependent factors. The most critical parameters are: (1) an adequate fresh water supply, (2) an adequate nutrient supply, and (3) substrate stability.

Fresh water availability and salinity concentration control the "metabolic efficiency" of the mangrove ecosystem. Water availability depends upon (1) the frquency and volume of fresh water from upland drainage systems, (2) the frequency and volume of tidal exchange, and (3) atmospheric evaporative demand. Despite the fact that mangrove species possess adaptive mechanisms that allow tolerance of salinity extremes (e.g. the salt excretion glands of the leaves and salt-excluding membrane of the proproots), the absence of freshwater inflow to the upper intertidal regions results in potential soil salt concentrations in excess of the physiological tolerances of the mangroves and associated biota. The efficiency with which an inflow of fresh water regulates soil salinity and water content depends upon soil type and drainage patterns (e.g. sandy *v.* clay soils). Changes in upland land use patterns resulting in modifications to fresh water inputs not only have the potential for critically altering the approximate salinity regime, but also for altering the necessary nutrient and sediment inputs as discussed below.

The nutrient supply of the mangrove ecosystem is regulated by several interacting processes involving the input/export of inorganic mineral ions and organic matter coupled with the internal recycling of nutrients via the detrital food web. The relative concentrations and optimal ratio of nutrients for maintenance of system productivity are determined by (1) the frequency, amount, and duration of tidal or freshwater flooding as well as by (2) the internal circulation dynamics of the detrital complex (Odum, *et al.* 1982).

Substrate stability, the ratio of erosion to sediment deposition is regulated by the current velocity of freshwater runoff and its associated sediment load, tidal flushing, and wave action. The importance of sediment deposition to mangrove species is documented by the roles played in mangrove sustainability as opposed to impact (Odum, *et al.* 1982). Positive roles of sediment deposition within critical limits include: sediment entrapment followed by substrate colonization by mangroves; nutrient, pollutant, and silt trap that retains nutrients and filters out toxic wastes.

Negative effects occur when, for example, sediment loads exceed soil drainage such that oxygen deficits and anaerobic soil conditions result. Interventions that alter existing freshwater runoff patterns or flood plain/shoreline geomorphology (e.g. impoundments, dredging activities, bulkheading, etc.) have the potential for impairment of the mangrove ecosystem structure and function.

MAJOR SOURCES OF ENVIRONMENTAL STRESS. The primary agents which degrade mangrove ecosystems may be generally characterized as (1) over-exploitative traditional use patterns, and (2) non-sustainable modern-day resource utilization patterns. Table 2-1 lists common activities, their associated effects, and impact scale.

2.2 Seagrass Meadows

DESCRIPTION. Meadows of seagrasses with their distinctive vascular structure and root/rhizome systems (as opposed to algae) generally inhabit nearshore clear shallow waters of reduced wave energy in tropical and subtropical latitudes. These highly productive, species-rich submarine meadows provide ecologically important habitats for a number of commercial fin- and shellfish species (Zieman 1982) as well as frequently provide the link between the physiochemically divergent mangrove and coral reef ecotypes (Thorhaug 1981). The migration of animals from one ecosystem to another at various life stages coupled with the flow of water transporting both organic and inorganic material from runoff and tidal flushing, bridge offshore coral reefs to nearshore seagrass beds to mangrove estuaries. The two major areas of occurrence are the Indo-West Pacific and the Caribbean (den Hartog 1970).

The primary commercial value of seagrass meadows derives from its indirect value as feeding and critical habitat for commercially valuable fisheries species as well as trophic intermediaries (Odum, *et al.* 1982; Zieman 1982). Seagrass ecosystems also play an important role in habitat stabilization. Seagrasses stabilize sediment and reduce erosion (Zieman 1982). The baffling effects of seagrasses assume additional importance in reducing turbidity and clarifying the surrounding waters, an effect beneficial not only to the seagrasses themselves and continued high photosynthetic rates, but also to filter-feeding invertebrates.

That seagrass meadows represent one of the richest of tropical marine ecosystems, rivaling mangrove forests and tropical agriculture in productivity, is well documented (Westlake 1963; Zieman and Wetzel 1980: Thorhaug 1981). According to Thorhaug (1981), seagrasses can produce as much as 2000g dry weight per m^2 per year with an additional 700-1000g/m^2/year contributed by the epiphytic algae and benthic macroalgae associated with the seagrasses. The production values of seagrasses are approximately 6 times that of plankton (100-500 g carbon per m^2 per year) which form the productivity base in contiguous offshore waters.

Photosynthetically fixed energy from seagrasses is channeled along two major trophic pathways: (1) direct herbivory by such commercially important reef fish as scarids (parrot fish) and acanthurids (surgeon fish) (Randall 1967); and (2) utilization of detritus via detrital food webs (Zieman 1981).

CRITICAL ENVIRONMENTAL PARAMETERS FOR MAINTENANCE OF ECOLOGICAL PROCESSES. The presence, distribution, and stability of seagrass ecosystems is dependent upon a number of interdependent factors. The most critical parameters are: (1) light, (2) temperature, (3) salinity, (4) substrate, and (5) current velocity.

- *Light*. The requirements of seagrasses for high light intensity to promote photosynthesis is demonstrated by the observation that their depth distribution is limited to 10 metres (Zieman and Wetzel 1980). Any activities that increase the sediment load of the water column and result in high residual turbidity (e.g. dredge and fill/dumping operations associated with real estate development, waterfront industries, intracoastal waterway construction, etc.) have the potential for limiting light penetration levels crucial to primary productivity. An example of a decreases in the distribution and abundance of seagrasses in Lindbergh Bay, St. Thomas U.S. Virgin Islands related to turbidity caused by dredging is reported by Van Eepoel and Grigg (1970). Lush growths of turtlegrass recorded at depths of up to 10 metres (33 ft) in 1968 prior to dredging activities were restricted to sparse patches occurring in waters of 2.5 metres (8 ft) in depth in 1970.
- *Temperature*. Although the wide geographical distribution of seagrass species would seem to indicate a broad range of temperature tolerance, tropical species characteristically exhibit a narrow range of tolerance, which is reflected in the seasonal range of the surrounding waters (Moore 1963). Zieman (1975a) found that turtle grass in Biscayne Bay, Florida demonstrated optimal growth in a temperature range of 28° to 30°C and that net photosynthesis declined sharply on either side of this range. According to Thorhaug (1981), studies on the effects of thermal effluents on seagrass communities in the Gulf of Mexico and the Caribbean indicate the upper lethal limit to be only a few degrees above the summer ambient temperature of 32°-34°C.
- *Salinity*. While seagrass species vary with regard to their salinity tolerances, most can tolerate large salinity fluctuations (10-40°/oo). The optimum range for growth appears to be at concentrations approaching that of oceanic water, averaging 35°/oo (Zieman 1982). According to Hammer (1968) turtle grass exhibits a linear decrease in photosynthetic activity with decreasing salinity. A 1:1 dilution of seawater with fresh water resulted in a photosynthetic rate one-third that of full-strength seawater. The damage to

seagrasses resulting from an excess of nearshore freshwater runoff is documented by Thomas, *et al.* (1961) to be more severe than the effects of high water surge. Furthermore, Zieman (1970) has noted a salinity-temperature interaction with tropical seagrasses where species, tolerant of lower than normal salinities at lower ambient temperatures are unable to survive these same salinities under increased temperature conditions.

- *Substrate.* Seagrasses occur in a wide variety of sediment types ranging from coarse mud to a bottom sediment composition of 40 percent silt and fine mud. The most important substrate requirement, however, for proper seagrass development is sufficient sediment depth (Zieman 1982). The role of substrate depth in sediment stability is two-fold: (1) an anchoring medium for the plants against water surge and currents, as well as (2) a matrix for nutrient recycling and supply. Depth requirements are species specific. Variation in sediment types is the cumulative result of (1) the source material, (2) the current flow regime, and (3) the density of seagrass leaves (Zieman 1982). The density of seagrass blades effectively increases the sedimentation rates in the beds by (1) trapping fine organic and inorganic particles on the leaf surface, (2) retaining particles (e.g., detritus) produced within the grass beds, as well as (3) binding and stabilizing the deposited sediments via the root/rhizome complex (Burrell and Schubel 1977). Thus the sedimentation process in seagrass meadow growth and development is a circular one: increased sediment depth results in increased blade length and seagrass density, which in turn result in additional sediment trapping and bonding effects.

- *Current Velocity*. Seagrass productivity appears to be influenced by current velocity. Conover (1968) who reported turtle grass and *Zostera* to exhibit maximum standing crops where current flow averaged 0.5m/sec, hypothesized that flowing waters by breaking down diffusion gradients increase CO_2 and nutrient availability. Zieman (1982) notes that seagrass samples from a mangrove-lined tidal channel demonstrate a leaf standing crop of 262g dry weight/m^2 with a total biomass of 4,570g dry weight/m^2. Comparative samples from a lagoon with minimal water movement were 185 and 1,033g dry weight/m^2, respectively.

Major Sources of Environmental Stress. The major destructive forces to seagrass meadows are human-induced and may be classified as either (1) acute single events such as an accidental oil spill, dredging and filling, etc., or (2) chronic low-level discharges involving agricultural pesticide runoff, industrial discharge of heavy metals or thermal effluents, sewage, etc. Table 2-2 summarizes common activities and their associated effects on seagrass ecosystems.

2.3 **Coral Reefs**

DESCRIPTION. Coral reefs are shallow-water, tropical marine ecosystems generally restricted to the circumglobal belt between 30° N and 30° S latitudes. Exceptions to this occur where warm currents flow out of these areas. In the

Indo-Pacific region, for example, coral assemblages extend to 35° N off Japan and to 32° S in the Tasman Sea (Sheppard 1983). Reef ecosystems, in addition to their aesthetic appeal, are the foci for a tremendous abundance and diversity of associated biota as well as high primary and secondary productivity.

Within the tropics there is no reef development in shallow coastal areas where temperature and salinity regimes as well as light penetration levels are not within the critical limits for growth and maintenance. The shores of the northern Indian Ocean, the northern Persian Gulf, and the nearshore areas around Hong Kong, for example, all have turbidity, temperature and freshwater flushing regimes that exceed the tolerance levels for reef establishment and growth. Similarly in tropical coastal areas subjected to cold currents, e.g. West Africa and most of the western coastline of both North and South America, coral reef development is absent (Sheppard 1983).

Lewis (1981) reports reef gross primary production rates to vary from 300-5000 g carbon per m^2 per year. Such figures are comparable to those produced in the most fertile of marine ecosystems (Westlake 1963) and are in marked contrast to productivity in nearby oceanic waters where gross production rates of phytoplankton are as much as 10 to 100 times lower than those measured in waters over reefs (Table 2-3). This is, of course, related trophically to extraordinary secondary productivity.

Fisheries account for the most important use associated with reef ecosystems. According to Smith (1978b), estimates of yields from coral reefs and adjacent shallow-water coastal areas range from 2.5 to 5 tons per $kilometre^2$ annually, with the potential for global reef fisheries reaching 2.7 million mtons per year. Stevenson and Marshall (1974) estimate the standing crop of reef fish populations to reach 5-15 times the crops of representative North Atlantic fishing grounds and twice the average standing crop of temperate lakes.

The major coastal tourist attractions in tropical waters are coral reefs and white sand beaches. According to Beekhus (1981), for example, within the last 50 years the Caribbean coastal based tourist industry generates tourism-related receipts ranging from 2 to 5 percent of the gross national product (GNP) in the greater Antilles to 55 percent of the GNP in the Lesser Antilles. In 1973, tourism concentrated in the coastal areas of Indonesia accounted for $90 million or 4.5 percent of the total foreign exchange and was projected to rise to 7.6 percent by 1980 (Langham and Mathias 1977). In addition to fisheries and tourism value, corals are harvested for tourist/ornamental souveniors, novel pharmacological compounds (Ciereszko and Karns 1973), and construction materials and lime production (Mahadeven and Nayar 1972).

Coral reef communities are renowned for their highly diverse structural and biotic complexity. As such, reef ecosystems represent habitat for a large assemblage of invertebrate (particularly crustaceans and molluscs) and fish species, a situation unparalleled in temperate marine regimes (Marshall 1965). Coral reefs serve a vital function by contributing to the calcareous sands of the tropical coastal beaches and by serving as natural breakwaters buffering incoming swell/storm surge and preventing coastal erosion. Fringing reefs have been described by Johannes (1975) as "self-repairing breakwaters which permit the continued existence of about 400 atolls and numerous other low tropical islands, as well as preserving thousand of miles of continental coastlines."

CRITICAL ENVIRONMENTAL PARAMETERS FOR MAINTENANCE OF ECOLOGICAL PROCESSES. The presence, distribution and stability of reef ecosystems are dependent upon a number of interdependent physical parameters, the most critical of which are (1) light, (2) temperature, (3) salinity, and (4) water turbidity, circulation and sedimentation.

- *Light.* Solar radiation plays an important role in reef formation since light penetration determines the depth to which photosynthesis can occur in the benthic algae and zooxanthellae of coral tissue. In addition to its role in primary production, light and the photosynthetic process are hypothesized to play an important role in accelerating calcification by zooxanthellae (Pearse and Muscatine 1971; Barnes and Taylor 1973; Vandermeulen and Muscatine 1974). Thus the vertical distribution of coral reefs is restricted by the effective depth of incident light with maximum reef growth occurring within 10 metres of the surface (Stoddart 1969).

  Any activities that increase the sediment load of the water column (e.g. inland/coastal deforestation resulting in erosion and sediment runoff, dredging, coral mining, fishing with explosives, etc.) have the potential for reducing effective illumination levels to the detriment of reef primary production and growth.

- *Temperature*. The geographical distribution of reef corals is influenced by temperature in that (1) no significant reef development occurs where the mean annual temperature falls below 18° C (Vaughan 1919, Mayor 1918); and (2) optimal reef development is limited to waters with temperatures ranging from 25° to 29° C (Stoddart 1969). Although Kinsman (1964) documented healthy coral reefs off the Oman coast (Arabia) in waters with a seasonal range of 16° to 40° C, the usual maximum ambient temperatures encountered by reef systems are only a few degrees below their upper lethal limit of 35-38° C depending upon the species (Mayor 1918, 1924; Edmondson 1928). According to Endean (1976), shallow water heating by solar radiation has been hypothesized to contribute to the paucity/absence of corals in the Torres Strait Queensland, Australia (Mayor 1918); Arno Atoll Marshall Islands (Wells 1951); and on the beach rock of Heron Island, Barrier Reef, Australia (Endean 1956). Thermal effluents from coastal power facilities in Biscayne Bay, Florida and Oahu, Hawaii, have caused the deaths of reef systems as far away as 1.5 km from the plants (Kaplan 1982; Jokiel and Coles 1974).

- *Salinity*. Most coral species are sensitive to higher or lower salinity regimes than those normally encountered in coastal areas (30 to 35°/oo). Although corals have survived salinity extremes from 17.5 to 70°/oo under experimental conditions for short periods of time, corals are not likely to encounter higher than normal salinity regimes, thus, increased salinity is not the usual factor causing reef devastation (Endean 1976). Rather, a decrease in salinity for example, caused by an influx of fresh water such as that described by Banner (1968) in Kaneohe Bay, Hawaii, appears to be the more likely stress factor encountered in coral destruction.

- *Water Turbidity, Sedimentation and Circulation.* The degree of turbidity affects the depth to which light penetrates and thus the production and growth rates of reefs corals as discussed above. Since normal growth rates are known to be reduced by half on cloudy days (Goreau 1961), the potential exists for increased amounts of suspended materials such as that caused from coastal erosion processes and sediment runoff, coral mining, dredging activities, etc. to have deleterious effects on reef ecosystems. Furthermore, excessive sediment loads have the potential to interfere with the suspension-feeding processes and respiratory activities of coral reef polyps. Chronic low-level sedimentation rates appear to have a greater potential for adverse effects to corals than do occasional single-event sedimentation loads with the effective impact varying according to coral species and sediment size (Endean 1976). Dodge, *et al.* (1974) found the average growth of the boulder coral (*Montastrea annularis*) in Discovery Bay, Jamaica to be significantly reduced by sedimentation rates of about 1.1 mg per cm^2 per day under normal conditions. Sediment application experiments by Rogers (1983) indicate varying effects of sediment loading with varying species and sediment particle size: The elkhorn coral *(Acropora palmata),* a species normally found in shallow areas of strong wave action, was the least resistant to calcereous sediment application and succumbed to a single dose of 20 mg per cm^2. The "palmate" or flattened morphology of the elkhorn coral and the crevices and depressions of *M. annularis* colonies make these corals more susceptible to sediment accumulation than the cylindrical branches of the staghorn coral (*A. cervicornis*) and the almost spherical structure of the brain corals (e.g. *Diploria strigosa*) (Rogers 1983).

  Finally, current flow and water circulation across the reef is critical in (1) supplying oxygenated water onto the reef, (2) the transport of nutrients and organic matter, and (3) removal of sediment (Lewis 1981). Changes in current flow as a result of interference to coastal drainage patterns have the potential for disruptive effects on reef ecosystems (Endean 1976).

Major Sources of Environmental Stress. The primary sources of coral reef destruction are characterized by (1) direct exploitation/extraction of the resource, and indirectly by (2) resource utilization patterns in linked ecosystems (e.g. sedimentation, thermal discharge, freshwater runoff, etc. from adjacent land). The fringing reef system which characteristically forms a continuous band parallelling the coastline in nearshore waters is particularly vulnerable to land-based pollution discharges and sedimentation runoff. Table 2-4 summarizes common activities and their associated effects on coral reef ecosystems.

3.0 ENVIRONMENTAL ASSESSMENT

The environmental assessment process is the mechanism by which (1) the biological, physical and socio-economic aspects of proposed development projects are identified; (2) the potential impacts are analyzed during project design prior to project implementation; and (3) these analyses are used in the decision-making processes addresses whether and how to proceed with the proposed actions (e.g. selection of alternative projects, avoidance, or mitigation of adverse consequences). The primary goal of the assessment process is to avoid or reduce significant adverse impacts of development. To accomplish this it is necessary to know (1) the physiochemical characteristics of the coastal environment and associated biota; (2) functions or processes that occur in the coastal ecosystem such as energy flows including food chains, nutrient cycling, and biotic interrelationships such as movements, succession and species interactions. Specific data requirements for assessing a particular development project depend upon the scope and phase of development and the potential for impacts.

The major steps involved in the assessment process for coastal development are illustrated in Figure 3-1 with a habitat approach to impact assessment illustrated in Figure 3-2. Modification would be required to reflect both the scale of the development project and the scope or purpose of the environmental review. Before any environmental study begins, decisions are made as to the appropriate level of detail and the specific analytic procedures to be followed. This generally reflects the judgments of environmental scientists as well as inputs from the public ("SCOPING") which are detailed in a report appended to the impact document. To facilitate understanding of the environmental assessment process, a discussion of the significant terms used throughout this paper follows.

The terms "issues", "region of influence", "resources", and "attributes", for example, have meanings that are fundamental to describing the affected environment; whereas the terms "effects", "impacts", and "significance" are important in the investigation and assessment of a project on the environment. All of these terms are used in the documentation of the assessment process.

3.1 Affected Environment

The terms "issues', "region of influence", "resources", and "attributes" are used to describe the environment. An environmental assessment or impact analysis develops from the broad general concerns or issues that result from scoping, to more specific topics called resources, to the specific, detailed and usually measurable values of attributes, resources are derived from an identification of environmental issues. Attributes (or measurable resource components) are derived from specific enivronmental resources.

Environmental Issues. Environmental issues which may be generated or exacerbated by a project are the *raison d'etre* for an environmental impact assessment that argues for project implementation, reconfiguration, mitigation, or abandonment. A recognized impact issue defines a problem or question to be investigated in the environmental process. Coastal issues, in particular, are difficult to define in that the relationships among coastal use activities are inextricably linked. For example, the issue of tourism development on a mangrove-estuary coastline with offshore coral reefs is interconnected with mangrove-dependent fisheries yields via land reclamation involving the filling of wetland areas and subsequent reduction in estuarine productivity. Although issues may be vague areas of concern, attempts should be made to define them in terms of cause and effect to render them more amenable to analysis in quantifiable terms. The following is an example of a cause and effect sequence useful in delineating the potential environmental and socio-economic impacts from a hypothetical land reclamation project involving the conversion of mangrove estuaries to agricultural use (e.g. rice fields):

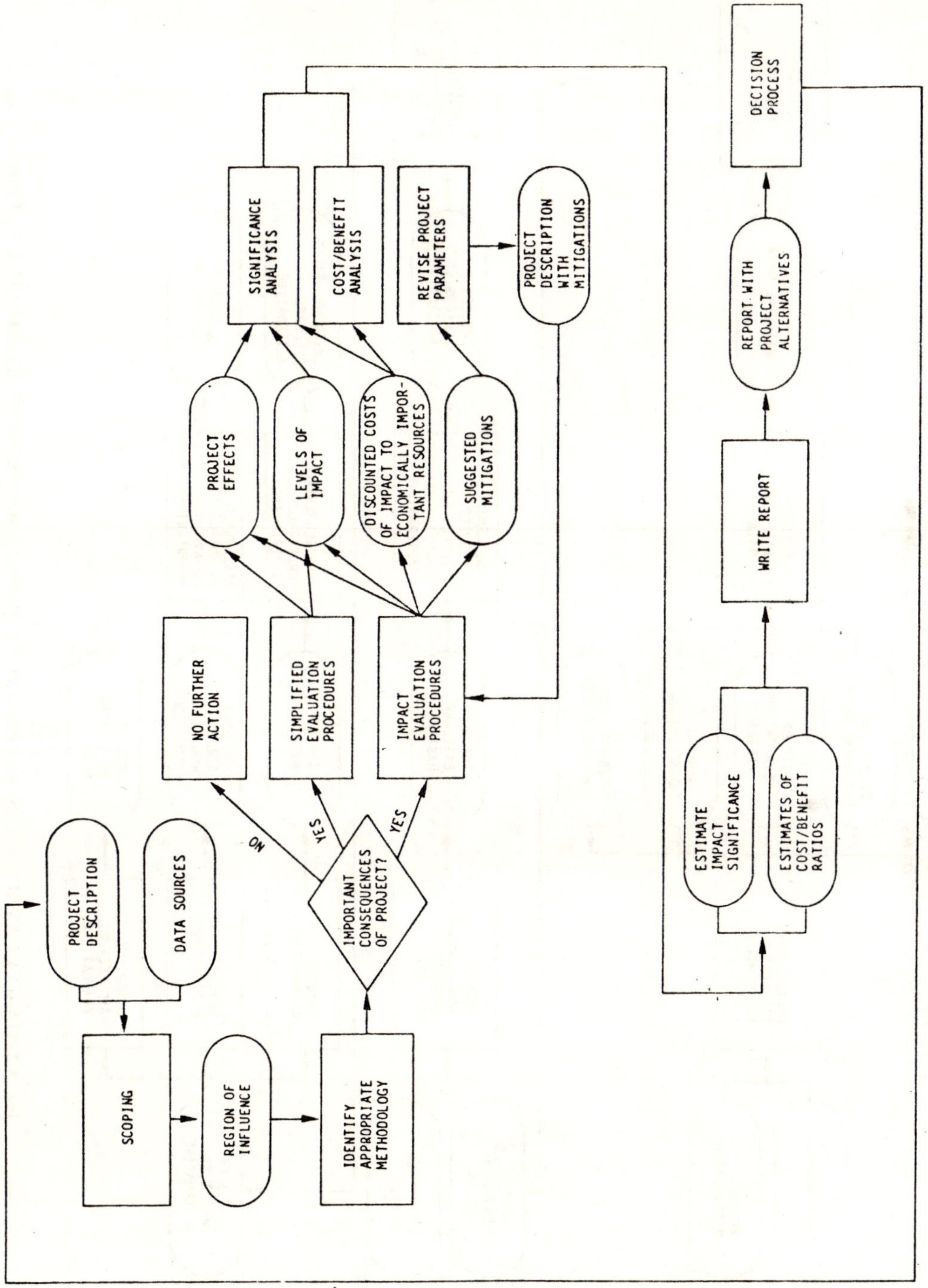

Fig. 3-1. IMPACT ANALYSIS PROCEDURE FLOW CHART

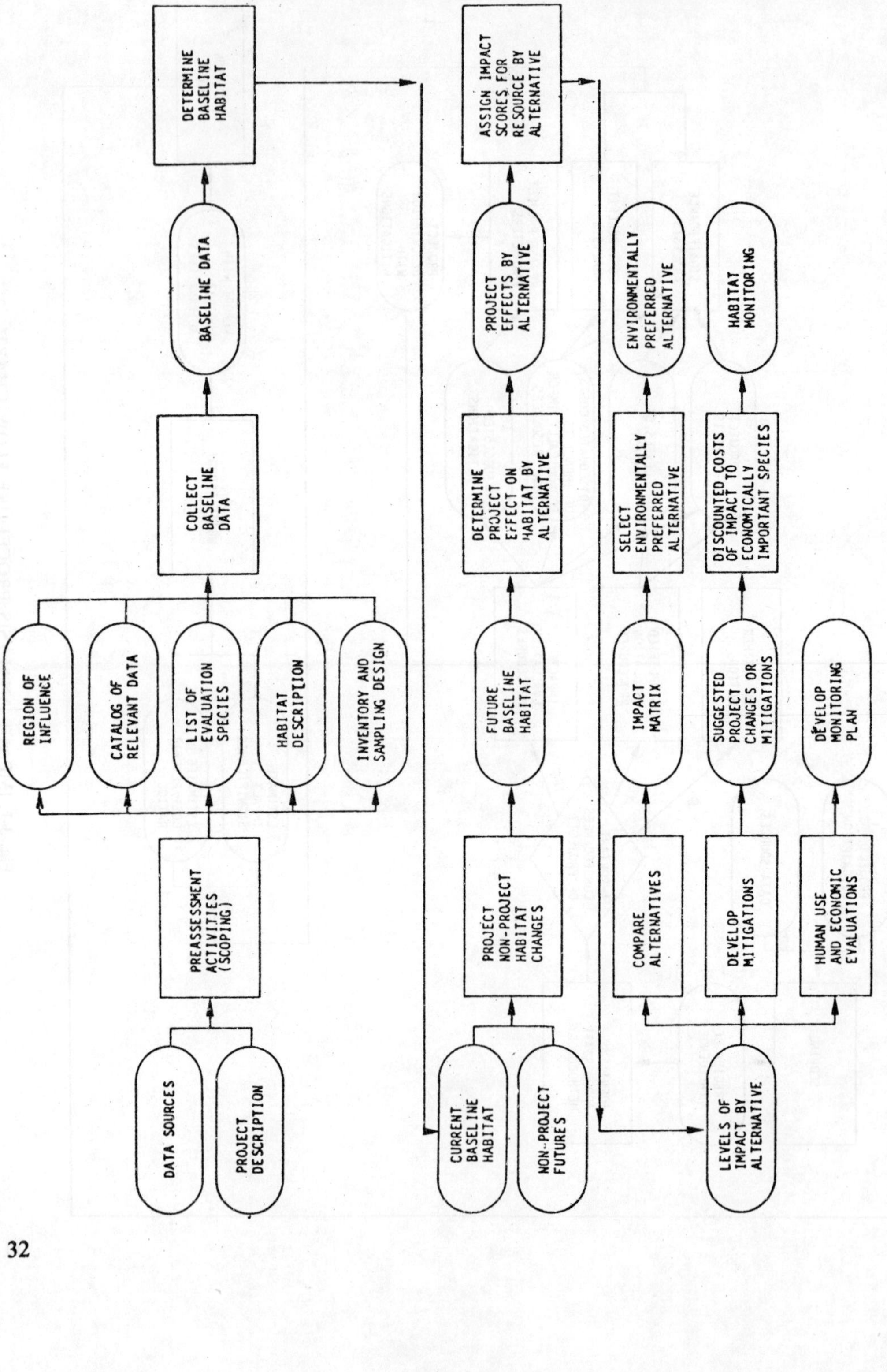

Fig. 3-2. HABITAT EVALUATION APPROACH TO IMPACT ASSESSMENT BASED ON U.S. FISH AND WILDLIFE SERVICE HABITAT EVALUATION PROCEDURES (ESM 102, 1980; ESM 103, 1980)

- **Causes.**

  - Proposed coastal use: Land reclamation and conversion of natural mangrove estuaries to rice fields.

  - Proposed activity: Alteration of freshwater runoff patterns and tidal exchange; filling in of wetland area.

- **Effects.**

  - Measurable change in environmental condition: Alteration of mangrove habitat and associated productivity levels.

  - Impact of socio-economic concern: Reduction in offshore yields of mangrove-dependent fisheries vs. increased rice production.

Multiple sequences of changes in various elements of the ecosystems may also occur prior to terminating as an impact. Increased turbidity in coastal waters, for example, results in reduced light penetration, which in turn results in reduced coral growth prior to the effect of decreased landings from coral reef fishery stocks. Both tourism and fisheries are important coastal activities and both depend upon a high level of coastal water quality. Yet, both tourism and fisheries potential are recipients of impacts such as pollution, aesthetic degradation, and loss of wildlife habitat that are generated by their very development. Impact issues associated with potential deleterious effects for the three coastal resources under discussion — mangroves, seagrass meadows, and coral reefs are delineated in Tables 2-1, 2-2 and 2-4, respectively. The level of detail required for issue identification with regard to describing cause and effect relationships will vary with the resource and potential project interaction. The effects of specific use activities, whether coastal or upland, on the environment or socio-economic value of a coastal resource must be identified.

Resources. Resources are individual or sectoral topics derived from the more general environmental issues which are concrete enough to permit analysis. For purposes of this paper, tropical coastal resources are defined as natural features/systems in the coastal area and whose value depends upon certain societal uses or perceptions. Such resources include mangroves, seagrass beds and coral reefs as well as their terrestrial and coastal supporting systems. An issue is seldom analyzed adequately in terms of a single resource; at least two resource components are usually linked to a single issue.

The Region of Influence. Impact studies are generally confined to the geographically defined area within which measurable project effects are likely to occur. The area studied is termed the project "region of influence" (ROI) and is resource-dependent. The ROI is usually influenced by several factors including (1) the project site; (2) the secondary effects based upon the type of project, e.g. increased access and illegal harvests; and (3) all key or critical areas that could be affected by project related activities such as sediment run-off and chemical/thermal discharge, as well as, for example, near- and offshore fishing grounds of known mangrove-dependent marine fisheries.

Techniques for determining the region of influence within which measurable project effects on the resource vary with the scope of the analysis from: (1) simply drawing a circle or boundary around the estimated "affected" area; (2) *manual* overlaying of selected mapped resource variables (attributes) that determine the vulnerability of the resource to project-related effects, to (3) *computer-assisted spatial analysis* for overlaying and statistical manipulation of mapped variables as described by Berwick, *et al.* (1984). Such procedures identify the geographical area where the resource is at risk. The region of influence is often species-or habitat-specific and depends upon resource attributes discussed below.

Attributes. Attributes are quantifiable characteristics of the resource with specific temporal and spatial aspects that define the resource for purposes of impact analysis. Attributes are those characteristics on which data are collected, analyses are performed, future conditions with and without the proposed development project are estimated, and mitigations are devised.

Specifically, identifying attributes that can be measured, narrows the investigations and focus of the analyses on topics crucial to the impact assessment. Tropical coastal ecosystems can be described in terms of qualitative and quantitative resource component attributes. Qualitative attributes are descriptive in nature and include habitat types, species composition and distribution, legal status, habitat requirements (e.g. migration routes, feeding and spawning areas, and cover), sensitivity to disturbance. Quantitative attributes are those by which the resource can be described numerically and include habitat morphometry, flow, water quality measurements, species abundance, some aspects of habitat requirements (e.g. depth, current velocity and direction, dissolved oxygen, salinity, temperature), productivity, measures of population dynamics, the resource monetary value, and the recreation parameters of coastal resources such as coral reefs. Effects of coastal tourism developments are determined with regard to visitor-use, crowding, and resource carrying capacity, which in turn are dependent upon resource size, location, accessibility, recreational opportunities available, and user preference. Carrying capacity is the resource sustainable use that can occur without degradation to the system (Hendee, *et. al.* 1978).

Individual resource attributes are not chosen to provide a total definition of the resource. Rather, each resource is represented by the several attributes that together represent the issue-related features of the resource. The number of attributes chosen for study and the depth of analysis are determined by the site, project and key issues identified in each specific situation.

Using the issue of tourism development as an example, the coastal resource "mangroves" might be subdivided into analysis of effects on offshore commercial fisheries. The attributes of the resource component, commercial fisheries, would be species composition, distribution and fishing grounds, habitat requirements, yield, economic value, etc. Determining the collective effects or changes in attributes, such as estimating the amount of habitat disturbed and not available to migratory commercial species, for example, would facilitate determination of the impact on the commercial fisheries resources component.

For the most part, the above list of attributes reflects the static nature of determining habitat and community composition by measuring the component items of an ecosystem. As such, these data provide little information with which to assess the interactive and integrative properties and functions that characterize an ecosystem. As noted earlier coastal ecosystems are essentially super-ecosystems consisting of the shore as well as fringing terrestrial regions and sublittoral zones involving several interrelated food chains (Figure 1-1) and biophysical system processes susceptible to impacts (Figure 1-2). System studies require additional different set of measurements. For example, species diversity is reported to be an indicator of ecosystemic health or integrity particularly in tropical coastal marine ecosystems such as coral reefs (Odum, *et al.* 1974). A diversity index such as the Shannon—Wiener index (Odum 1971; Krebs 1972) provides more information than would a list of species with regard to judging the potential impact from a development project. Resource attributes which provide ratios or indices of metabolic functions such as ecological efficiency by measurements of diurnal oxygen metabolism and subsequent determination of photosynthesis to respiration ratios would provide more information on the functional trophic state of the community than would a measurement of dissolved oxygen alone. Table 3-1 compares the component and ecosystem approaches to assessment of coastal marine communities. System properties are more difficult to measure than are the components. Definitive data on productivity process are time consuming to obtain and require more technical skill than deriving crude indices from published and unpublished data sources on densities, age, size, class distributions, food habits, and nutritive content of forage.

3.2 Investigation and Assessment

The investigation and assessment phase of the impact analysis process involves six major elements: (1) determining the pre-project "baseline" state of the resource attributes identified as subjects for analyses; (2) estimating the future baseline without the development project; (3) estimating the effects of the development project on resource attributes; (4) estimating the impacts of those effects on resources; (5) assessing the significance of the impacts; and (6) determining appropriate mitigative measures.

"Effects" refer to the empirical determination of changes to attributes that would result from a project (e.g. before-and-after changes in coastal water sediment) while the term "impacts" requires scientific and political judgment on the importance of these effects.

DETERMINATION OF BASELINE CONDITIONS

Collection of baseline information is necessary to provide a standard against which the effects of a development project are evaluated and post-project monitoring studies are conducted. Baseline data include:

- *Resource inventories* which *identify* the resource components and their characteristic attributes within the region of project influence and indicate their quantity and variety (e.g. species lists and distribution maps, habitat requirements, water quality, etc.)

- *Baseline studies* which *analyze* and *assess* the inventory information collected as well as ecosystem functional properties such as attribute linkages, productivity, trophic efficiencies, nutrient cycling, etc.

Inventory information is obtained from short-term extensive literature and reconnaissance surveys that provide little information on temporal variability. Trend analyses through incorporation of existing data from baseline studies with other predevelopment resource inventories provides a more accurate basis for project planning and design than would inventory information alone.

Baseline conditions may be determined at two levels of project resolution: regional and site specific. The data necessary for marine coastal habitat and biota baseline descriptions are defined as resource attributes. The complexities of coastal ecotypes such as seagrass beds and coral reefs coupled with logistic difficulties of systematic ground surveys dictate that baseline methods for measuring and mapping large areas of coastal marine ecotypes include remote sensing techniques as described by Kelly (1980) for seagrass meadows, as well as

TABLE 3-1

COMPARISON OF THE COMPONENT AND ECOSYSTEM APPROACHES TO THE ASSESSMENT OF TROPICAL COASTAL MARINE COMMUNITIES

Component-level Measurements	Ecosystem-level Measurements
Species inventory	Seral stage determination reflecting species composition, densities and prior knowledge of successional trajectories.
Species list, number of species and relative abundance	Species diversity indices
Fish densities, age, size, class distribution, food habitats, and nutritive content of forage	Trophic efficiency ratios of kcal consumed m^2 per year to kcal produced per m^2 per year.
Dissolved oxygen (O_2) measurements	Diurnal oxygen metabolism reflecting phytosynthesis to respiration ratios (flow respirometry)
Dissolved phosphate	Phosphate turnover rate
Phytoplankton biomass	Chlorophyll concentration (gms/m^2) as an index to primary production.
Enumeration of available prey (biomass, density, etc.)	Feeding efficiency by organic C and zooplankton measurements on e.g. landward vs. seaward sides of a reef.
Individual behaviour	Dominance hierarchies
Inventories	Integrated inventories (e.g. reconnaissance scale aerial photographs, satellite imagery/remote sensing).
	Conceptual models or processes and functional relationships.
Tide pool characterization/itemization of morphometry, water quality, species, etc.	Tide pool dynamics and modeling as reef process paradigm; impact experiments.
Measure and catalogue of direct effects of impacts on items by source of perturbation	Measure and catalogue of higher order effects (secondary effects) on system.

satellite imagery and systematic aerial photographic surveys as described by Hopley (1978) and Rützler (1978) for coral reefs. Sequential photographs and repeated mapping are useful in determining and monitoring the effects of development projects, especially those emitting thermal discharge (Conant, *et at.* 1983) or sediment or salinity changes to coastal waters (Sheppard 1983). It is essential that these repeated observation sets be formated to the same scale for geo-reference purposes. Site specific techniques for mapping of reefs and islands are described by Stoddart (1978b) and Rützler and Macintyre (1982). Choice of survey techniques is based on the survey objectives, areal extent, as well as the time, money and equipment available.

Since aquatic ecosystems are usually complex with many components not directly influencing the decision-making process, "featured" evaluation species, useful, for example, in the U.S. Fish and Wildlife Service Habitat Evaluation procedures (HEP) may be selected for analysis (ESM 102, 1980; ESM 103, 1980). These evaluation species are selected through the (1) scoping process, (2) consultation with local experts, (3) evaluation of project effects that could impact the species in question, and (4) scientific judgment. Various combinations of the above listed attributes are then measured for only these species and not all that are present.

For evaluation species, an assessment of: 1) the history of exploitation/harvest including socio-economic value of the resource/species, 2) vulnerability of the resource or species perturbations, and 3) perceptions or attitudes of the public toward the resource or species (cf. Kellert 1980) should be included in determination of baseline conditions. Information on relative abundance of the resource or species, and the vulnerability of the interrelated supporting processes characteristic of the coastal ecosystem complex dictate the magnitude and limits of a potential project.

ANALYTIC APPROACHES AND TECHNIQUES FOR MEASURING THE PHYSICAL AND CHEMICAL PROPERTIES OF THE RESOURCE. The specific techniques and level of detail required in baseline determination and subsequent monitoring studies depend upon the proposed project action and the project region of influence. Use of the previously discussed resource parameters particularly vulnerable to environmental stress for the mangrove, seagrass, and coral reef resources, coupled with information presented in Tables 2-1, 2-2, and 2-4 regarding potential stress sources and associated deleterious effects could serve, for example, as an initial basis for determining appropriate assortment of sampling methods and analyses sampling methods and analyses for baseline studies. Field techniques for sampling various physical, chemical and biotic parameters as presented below are adapted from methods presented in Conant, *et al.* (1983).

In performing field surveys, several aspects of the coastal aquatic environment must be considered. Spatial and temporal variability occur in the physical, chemical, and biological characteristics of aquatic systems. Thus, time and location are of utmost importance in designing a field survey. For example, if impacts on larval fish or migratory fish are a key issue, then the survey should be scheduled to occur when they are present. In all field surveys, detailed field notes and documented photographs are required. Data are recorded on preestablished forms, and any voucher specimens stored in a curated museum or other repository as specified in collecting permits. A description of the habitat in the field notes should include location, type, size, substrate types, amount of sub-habitats present, depths, velocity, shading/cover, and existing disturbance (e.g. water diversions). Sketch maps with an approximate scale are also useful. Photographic documentation includes recording subject and frame number. The following analytic approaches and techniques applicable to physical and chemical variables do not include all available tactics and techniques but provide a sufficiently varied cross-section of essential information for understanding the assessment process.

(1) *Surface Water* measurements that include stream flow and sediment transport are important parameters to be considered with regard to evaluating the potential "downstream effects" of land use changes in upland watersheds (e.g. grazing, clear felling for agricultural use, dam construction, etc.). Rainfall-runoff and stream-flow records provide useful baseline data. Detailed procedures for stream flow measurements and sediment transport computation are given in Chow (1974).

(2) *Tidal cycle and amplitude* influence a host of physical, geological and biological phenomena along coastlines such as currents and circulation patterns, flushing of bays and harbours, erosion and sediment transport, as well as dessication time, feeding behaviour patterns and reproductive cycles of many marine organisms. The region of influence for dredging activities also varies with regard to tidal effects. Thus tidal cycle and amplitude determination is an important baseline measurement for coastal measurements.

(3) *Current* measurements along coastlines are useful baseline determinations for many of the same reasons described above for tidal cycles. Current and circulation measurements are often difficult to obtain because of local variability in climatic conditions as well as in the temporal and spatial aspects of turbulence, mixing, and tidal effects especially in or near river-sea interfaces. Most current surveys used in coastal navigation (e.g. NOAA Current Tables) are measurements of surface currents and as such are not necessarily applicable for use in calculating flushing rates or transport volume of selected bays, estuaries, or in shore shallow waters. Volume transport calculations (amount of water flowing through a given area per unit time) depend upon current velocity estimates and involve (1) determination of the bottom profile and type of boundary layer, (2) the velocity profile away from the substrate, and (3) the stratification and movement of water layers (Conant, *et al.* 1983).

Current measuring techniques rely on two different concepts: (1) the "Eulerian Method" or velocity and direction measurements at a fixed point; and (2) the "Lagrangian" method of measurement of the movement path of a water mass over a predetermined distance. The techniques described by Pond and Pickard (1979) are all variations of these themes. For example, the use of fluorescein dye patches to trace water movement is based on the concept that neutrally buoyant matter moves with the same speed and direction as mainstream water movement

(Lagrangian). As the dye patch moves and spreads, the centre is used to estimate direction, average velocity, depth and to detect eddies. Similarly, fluids with suspended matter (e.g. pollutant discharge plumes), and freshwater or thermal effluent plumes can be used to estimate current speed and direction when coupled with successive aerial photographic documentation. An example of the Eulerian Method of particular applicability in relatively shallow water is the "drag angular deflection". A weighted object, hung by a monofilament line, for example, within 10 metres of the surface from a fixed platform such as a pier or wharf, deflects the line by an angle related to water velocity.

Two general methods used for measuring current speed and direction are (1) current meters for use at a single location, and (2) drifting objects (drogues) used to determine the direction of the drift, the time required to travel a known distance, and thus the current flow. It is important that the drogue be influenced by water currents rather than by wind (Monahan, *et al.* 1975).

(4) The chemical parameters of *water quality* influence biological productivity through interactions with the physiological processes of organisms. Parameters usually measured in conjunction with field studies include temperature, salinity, dissolved oxygen, pH, alkalinity, chloride, total ammonia nitrogen, nitrate, nitrite, sulfate, phosphate, turbidity, and conductivity. Appropriate test ranges for seawater using, for example, the Hach Chemical Company field kits such are not accurate with regard to salinity or nitrates. The accuracy and precision of field kits vary with reagent sources and interference with dissolved substances (Boyd 1977 and 1980; Cuenco and Stickney, 1980). If accuracy and precision are required, laboratory analyses that conform to those described in STANDARD METHODS FOR THE EXAMINATION OF WATER AND WASTEWATER APHA, AWWA, and WPCF, 1981) should be followed. Quality assurance checks need to be standardized.

Temperature measurements are central to most water quality baseline studies in the tropics because of the reduced thermal tolerance of tropical aquatic biota as compared to organisms from equivalent temperate waters (Moore 1963). Temperature measurements are central to subsequent sampling programmes (e.g. dissolved oxygen). Thermistor thermometers provide reliable and inexpenisve electronic field measurements (Conant, *et al.* 1983), although a series of max-min thermometers can be periodically read and reset manually.

Salinity measurements reflect another important physical-chemical parameter of coastal environments particularly with regard to estuarine biota whose existence is directly related to the magnitude of the salinity differential (Boesch 1977; Coull 1977). Salinity determination is useful in tracing freshwater or low-salinity effluent plumes in coastal waters as well as in determining boundaries between layers of stratified water bodies with freshwater input. Chlorinity and salinity measurements by silver nitrate titrations (Knudsen method) electrical conductivity measurements, or refractometry measurements (Conant, *et al.* 1983) provide important baseline/monitoring information with regard to potential projects which would alter natural salinity regimes.

Turbidity measurements are used to determine light penetration into the water, or transparency which relates light intensities at given depths to that of surface waters. Light transmission measurements are made to determine the effective "Photic" zone where photosynthesis occurs and are used in the evaluation of productivity as well as the presence of suspended or dissolved organic matter. Obtaining a representative sample is crucial because of the spatial variability in near-shore waters where land-water interface events occur, such as surface runoff or river/estuary drainage into the sea. Additional variables include the angle of incidence of sunlight, seasonal plankton blooms, and water stratification. Methods which can be used to measure turbidity or light levels include irradiance meters and transmissometers. Such instruments have the advantage of being able to measure conditions at various points in the water column. Midwater turbidity plunes are difficult to detect by surface or bottom measurements (Rogers 1982). These instruments are simple to use but expensive. For routine purposes light penetration measurements using a secchi disk are adequate. A secchi disk is a weighted white disk of predetermined diameter that is lowered into the water. The depth at which it disappears from view is recorded.

Sedimentation rate measurements both "up- and downstream" from the source of coastal development and dredging activities in addition to adequate data on "natural" sedimentation rates and coral tolerance to increased sediment loads are essential to determining impacts to reef ecosystems. Collection of sediment by "traps" followed by filtration, weighing, and "rate" calculation is the usual procedure. According to Gardner (1980 a and b) cylindrical sediment traps (e.g. PVC pipe) provide the most representative sampling device for collection of sediment at the reef surface. The ratio of diameter to height of between 2 and 3 gives an accurate measure of vertical sediment flux. Sedimentation rate is calculated from the size of the sediment trap, immersion time, and weight of collected material.

Dissolved oxygen measurements are used to estimate the metabolic activity of aquatic species. Sampling programmes should take into account the diel cycles of afternoon maximum community oxygen production/accumulation as well as the predawn minimum community oxygen production. Since oxygen solubility in water is a direct function of water temperature, with lower concentrations at warmer temperatures, seasonal variation in temperature regimes which would result in changed metabolic rates of the biota as well as changed concentration constrants should also be incorporated into sampling programmes. Dissolved oxygen measurements are useful in determining changes in metabolic activity as a result of thermal discharge into coastal waters. Either the Winkler method, or polarographic method where the oxygen concentration is measured *in situ* with an electrode on a weighted cable as described in the STANDARD METHODS FOR THE EXAMINATION OF WATER AND WASTEWATER (APHA, AWWA, and WPCF, 1981) are acceptable.

Carbon dioxide concentrations changes (free CO_2) are difficult to detect; thus measurements as indicators of metabolic activity are less sensitive than measurements of changes in dissolved oxygen content. Storage of metabolic gases present problems in determining accurate production in seagrasses, for example (Zieman and Wetzel 1980). A preferred method for carbon dioxide determination is that described in STANDARD METHODS FOR THE EXAMINATION OF WATER AND WASTEWATER (APHA, AWWA, and WPCF 1981) where calculations of the free gas are based on the known equilibrium of carbon dioxide with other forms of inorganic carbon relative to the pH and temperature of the sample. Measurements of pH, temperature, and alkalinity (bicarbonate and carbonate) usually performed as part of baseline studies are the data required to calculate free carbon dioxide. The utility of measurements of seagrass productivity by radioactive carbon uptake is discussed by Penhale (1975), Bittaker and Iverson (1976), and Capone, *et al.* (1979). Odum (1971) suggests the low Steeman-Nielson figures (1952) of C^{14} uptake in productivity measurements to be a result of the net productivity in tropical waters related to inherent high respiration rates which result in lower net productivities estimates.

- *pH* measurements are important baseline determinations since changes in water pH may not only result from direct discharge of acidic or basic substances to coastal waters but also from the indirect changes in the metabolic activity of the aquatic biota. As such, the sampling design should incorporate diel cycles as in dissolved oxygen sampling programmes. Use of pH meters such as that included in the "Hach" field kit multiple analyzer is the preferred method of pH determination.

ANALYTIC APPROACHES AND TECHNIQUES FOR MEASURING BIOTIC PARAMETERS OF THE RESOURCE. Sampling and characterization of biotic assemblages are necessary for baseline impact and subsequent monitoring studies. Species lists by habitat coupled with relative abundance may be adequate for determining changes in species numbers or shifts in species composition effected by environmental stress. Generally more information would be desirable for analyses necessary to predict effects and impacts. Low species diversity indices, relative to a control or standard norm, are indicative of stressed conditions (Odum, *et al.* 1974; Sale 1977). Population parameters such as spatial distribution, abundance determined by transect and quadrant survey data are useful in monitoring temporal changes in size-frequency distributions. Growth measurements useful as indicators of environmental quality depend upon such parameters as the physiological state of the species, habitat, crowding, food supply, etc. The following section summarizes potentially useful sampling techniques and analyses useful in baseline studies for impact assessment.

(1) *Benthic community* sampling techniques are determined by substrate categories such as a coral reef, sand channel, seagrass meadows, tree roots, and various sediment mixtures of sand, mud, and clay. Each substrate type is correlated with a unique assemblage of epi- and infaunal biota, and each requires a different sampling regime. Spatial patterns of zonation which play an important role in benthic sampling programmes should be defined and individually sampled for accurate baseline studies. Sand bottom intertidal zonation, for example, is complicated by vertical zonation within the sediment. Utilization of zonation data as indicators of impact derives from the correlation between various physical factors of the intertidal gradient and biotic distribution (Doty 1957). Furthermore, biological interactions such as grazing or predation play an important role in zonation patterns (Connell 1972; Paine 1974).

Species studied may be of commercial importance, "indicator" organisms with a known response to specific perturbations, or the numerical dominants. Soft substrates are particularly vulnerable to disturbance that renders the habitat available for new colonizing and succession of species (Simon and Dauer 1977; Woodin 1978; Sanders, *et al.* 1980). Monitoring of such changes can be accomplished by transect and/or quadrat sampling techniques. The general methods described below for benthic sampling are summarized from Conant, *et al.* (1983).

Transect sampling is based on the concept that there is a relationship between species abundances and occurrence along a randomly placed line in a two-dimensional system. Transect sampling regimes may be at even intervals or at random points (Porter 1977a and b; Poole 1974; Loya 1978; Quinn and Gallucci 1980) along the transect lines. Transect locations are best kept within a relatively homogeneous environment (stratified). For example, a single line should not cross mangroves and reefs as the variability would be excessive with a loss of both information and confidence in it. Each transect should be located within a single discrete habitat stratum. Variation with zones and transitions between zones, for example, are noted by changes in species abundances. Data on abundance, biomass, or percentage cover at each sampling site along a transect may be determined using quadrat sampling methods (Dayton 1971; Connell 1970 and 1972; Lubchenco and Menge 1978). Quadrats are better than points where measuring non-randomly distributed (e.g. clumped) organisms. The quadrat size selected depends upon the size and abundance of organisms to be sampled. Scraped samples from quadrats are useful in determining numbers and biomass (Dayton 1971). Clearance of benthic organisms from hard substrates is difficult because of the problems involved in totally excluding the organisms (Paine 1974). Photographs of organisms in permanent quadrats (Connell 1972), digitized photo-quadrats taken at specified intervals or at random along transects (Berwick and Anderson 1984), as well as time lapse photography (Paine 1974; Wilson 1974) are useful techniques for inventorying and monitoring changes in coral communities.

Coral reef epibenthic communities present several problems with regard to transect and quadrat sampling procedures because of their inherent topographical complexity and variety of microhabitats for associated biota. Visual survey techniques such as aerial photography (Laxton and Stablum 1974), free swimming observer, towed observer (Kenchington and Morton 1976), and spot check surveys (Pearson and Garrett 1976) as described by Kenchington (1978) are useful for extensive surveys of large reef areas for studies that require (1) generic descriptions of a reef area, (2) selection of representative areas for more detailed site-specific studies, and (3) monitoring of impact effects (e.g. oil spills, coral predators, etc.). With regard to site specific studies, chain transects have been used by Porter (1972 a and b) to survey coral species diversity and depth zonation. Permanent quadrats have been used by Connell (1973) to monitor long-term changes in the percentages of cover and growth/damage to individual colonies. Continuous recording linear transects as developed by Loya (1972) were used by Loya and Slobokin (1971) in coral reef studies in the Gulf of Eilat, Red Sea. General surveys and baseline studies have been performed by Birkeland, *et al.* (1976), and Amesbury, *et al.* (1975 a and b; 1976). Smith and Henderson (1978) have used photographic mapping techniques after Rützler (1978) and descriptive physiographic techniques after Pichon (1978) and Stoddart (1978 a and b). Potentially useful but theoretical and untested sampling regimes include the "plotless" and stratified random sampling regimes described by Loya (1978) and the application of plant ecology methods by Scheer (1978). The choice of appropriate methods to be used depends upon areal extent, object of survey, time and available resources.

(2) *Benthic infaunal community* characterizations are important with regard to elucidating their roles played in conjunction with the epibenthos in (1) the elaboration of reef ecosystem food chains and in (2) reef sedimentation. Quadrat sampling techniques for soft bottom epi- and endobiotic communities are defined in terms of surface homogeneity (e.g. seagrass meadows, *Halimeda* flats, sandy channels between coral ridges, mud flats adjacent to mangroves, etc.). Vertical as well as horizontal verification of apparent substrate uniformity is important since, for example, Thomassin (1969) found layered sediments in sandy channels between coral ridges to be characterized by different infaunal assemblages. Comparative studies of reef soft-bottom communities with those of seagrass meadows and fringing mangroves require that sampling methods be identical. Thomassin (1978) reviews and evaluates the utility of various grab, dredge, box core, and suction devices, as well as the trapping, trawling and net sweeping methods used in the Tulear coral reef studies. Collected specimens temporarily preserved in 10 percent formalin in seawater are identified, counted, and measured/weighed. Sediment analysis for grain size, water, and nutrient content (total carbon, nitrogen, and protein) are performed to determine the more functional aspects of endofaunal assemblages (Conant, *et al.* 1983).

(3) *Plankton* sampling methods, including mesh sizes for nets, preservation, and analysis are specific for each size category from megaplankton (2 mm) to nanoplankton (2 to 20um). General zooplankton sampling techniques (plankton traps, vertical net tows, automatic closing methods, etc.) are outlined by Conant, *et al.* (1983) after Tranter and Fraser (1968) and Steedman (1976). Sampling design should include diurnal cycles, depth and spatial distribution over the study area, seasonal changes, as well as recognition that (1) different substrate types support different assemblages of zooplankton, and (2) zooplankton distribution patterns vary in homogeneity depending upon location.

Zooplankton studies are useful in (1)

population studies for determining seasonal abundance of larval forms of specific benthic or nektonic species, (2) fisheries studies for estimating zooplankton food resources, and (3) impact studies for determining the effect of development-related environmental stress. Sampling plankton upstream and downstream of entrainment projects, such as power plant intakes and outfalls, coupled with volume transport information, are useful data in gauging the effects of thermal effluents in estuarine and shallow water littoral areas (Noth 1974). Plankton measurements can be used to demonstrate plankton depletion across reefs by coral and other predators in natural or perturbed systems (Glynn 1973). More detailed presentations of plankton sampling techniques and analyses for coral reef systems as listed by Conant, *et al.* (1983) include Emery (1968); Hobson and Chess (1978); Porter, *et al.* (1977 and 1978); Johannes (1978); and Rützler, *et al.* (1980).

(4) *Littoral vegetation* studies include survey and classification of macrophytes and macroalgae as well as determination of an index of relative abundance. Area coverage for the dominant species or types of plants may be estimated. Plants can be sampled more quantitatively by use of a square metre grid placed over the plants and those within harvested, washed, identified, dried, weighed, and pressed as herbarium reference specimens. Adequate sampling of submerged species is important in baseline studies and may require scuba equipment. Conant, *et al.* (1983) suggests aerial colour photography for mapping the distribution of emergent or floating plant beds and the use of filters to detect submerged beds by "false colour" images (Benton and Newman 1976).

(5) *Fish and fisheries* baseline data are necessary for an understanding of biological, social, and economic complexity and contributions of these elements in relation to potential development projects in coastal environments. Life history data (distribution, reproduction, food habits, etc.) of key species identified as the dominant local fisheries catch, for example, are crucial to subsequent sampling programmes and analyses. Local fisherman and fishery office personnel are sources of valuable preliminary information regarding near and offshore waters and fisheries. Such information is essential to evaluation of (1) the cultural and economic role of fishing, (2) flexibility in exploitation systems, (3) level of social and economic organization, (4) political importance, and (5) additional relevant regional factors.

The sampling design and collecting techniques required in fish surveys present an added dimension not encountered in studies of sedentary organisms — mobility and rapid response to environmental changes, including changing abundance/distribution patterns associated with habitat and food requirements. The overview and evaluation of sampling techniques provided by Conant, *et al.* (1983) are summarized below.

Habitat identification via quick reconnaissance surveys or reference to navigation charts as a prelude of in-depth field studies, serves to locate sampling design and determine equipment. With regard to sampling techniques, caution should be taken to avoid selective sampling of species and size classes (Saila and Roedel 1979; Hocutt and Stauffer 1980). Total kill methods such as rotenone poisoning avoid selective biases. Use of gill nets that have graded mesh sizes provides a more effective means of estimating abundance than would repeated trawling efforts using a single mesh-sized net. Additional factors to be considered in sampling methods and design include: water depth, bottom type, current, and presence of submarine obstructions. Furthermore, temporal and both horizontal/vertical variability in spatial distribution and movement patterns of fish dictate sampling regimes be representative of such inherent behaviour. Potentially useful shallow water sampling methods include repetitive visual surveys, traps and trap nets, purse seines, mark/recapture techniques, rotenone poisoning, and electric shocking. Common open water methods include gill nets, drag nets (trawl), and set gear where anchors and marker buoys are attached to each end of a gill net as opposed to drift net techniques which are particularly effective methods of catching scattered surface fish in darkness.

Species not readily identified in the field are preserved in 10 percent formalin (4 percent formaldehyde) neutralized with borax. The following field data are recorded: equipment used, sampling period, location and area covered, depth, time, date, and numbers of each species caught. Such "catch-per-effort" information can be used as measures of relative abundance. Standard lengths of species caught and consistently recorded throughout the study in addition to weight measurements, and collection of otoliths, spines or bones, contribute valuable information regarding the age and growth of fish. Such data are useful indicators of population condition (Bagenal 1978). A useful source of additional information with regard to length-frequency distributions and weight-length ratios of local commercial species can be obtained from fisheries harvest. Such data are required to assess the effects of fishing on the resource. For example, catch composed almost entirely of small-sized fish compared to species size in "normally" occurring populations may indicate overexploitation of the resource.

Fisheries statistics important for baseline studies include: (1) surveys of the fishery resource, (2) fishing practices, including capture methods and area covered, (3) harvest data, as well as (4) information processing, marketing, and consumption data (Saila and Roedel 1979).

Problems associated with sampling design and collecting techniques to obtain reliable quantitative data for open water fish communities are magnified when applied to reef fishes since: (1) varied reef habitats support different assemblages of fish species (Talbot and

Goldman, 1974; Hobson, 1974; Goldman and Talbot, 1976); (2) spatial distribution varies with: - bottom morphometry (Talbot, 1965; Risk, 1972); -diurnal/nocturnal changes (Collette and Talbot, 1972; Vivien, 1973); - tidal cycles (Potts, 1970; Choat and Robertson, 1975; - both intra- and interspecific interactions (Sale, 1972; Smith and Tyler 1972; Barlow, 1974 a and b; Fishelson, *et al.* 1974).

(3) Many species exhibit territorial behaviour (Myrberg 1972; Vine 1974) or maintain discrete home ranges (Sale 1971). Primarily for these reasons, Russell, *et al.* in a 1978 review of sampling and collecting procedures, advise that standard mark-recapture methods which rely on repetitive non-selective sampling techniques (Regier and Robson 1971) are not applicable to many reef species and suggests the use of a collapsible frame net technique that (1) ensures all fish are taken in a single sample, and (2) minimizes escape or predation losses, as an alternative to rotenone poisoning or explosive sampling. Underwater remote censusing techniques such as movie films provide permanent visual records of fish community structure and habitat. Such "cinetransects" have been used for fish surveys in California kelp-beds (Ebeling, *et al.* 1971) and on coral reefs (Alevizon and Brooks 1975).

ANALYTIC APPROACHES AND TECHNIQUES FOR ASSESSING THE FUNCTIONAL PARAMETERS OF THE RESOURCE. Although biotic communities may be characterized in terms of their physical habitat or major structural features (e.g. physiognomy or dominant species), functional attributes characterizing "community metabolism" and ecosystem indices provide a dynamic basis for monitoring ecosystemic "health" and detecting environmental stresses prior to irreversible structural damage. Approaches useful in (1) extrapolating from measurements regarding community composition and structure to the analyses of entire community assemblages and/or ecosystems and in (2) allowing comparisions of spatial/temporal variability in the functional roles of species include:

- Primary productivity (as opposed to photosynthetic rate determination) expressed as the ratio of photosynthesis to respiration (P/R ratios).
- Determination of total organic carbon in seawater (import, production and export of organic matter) as a measurement of energy requirements and productivity in coral reefs (Gordon 1978).
- Alkalinity depletion as a chemical measure of coral growth (Smith (1978a).
- Calcification and organic carbon metabolism in corals as indicated by CO_2 measurements (Smith and Kinsey 1978).
- Changes in the flux or flow of substances across reef platforms as an indicator of nutrient utilization, productivity, respiration, etc. Data requirements include the change in concentration of the substance(s) being measured and volume transport data (Maragos 1978).
- Nutrient flux processes as determined by the uptake and release of dissolved organic carbon, nitrogen, and phosphorus by corals (D'Elia 1978; Webb 1978; Pilson 1978).
- Coral feeding in relation to zooplankton and benthic algal detritus

flux by sampling zooplankton at upstream and downstream stations across a reef (Johannes 1978; Porter 1978).

- Secondary productivity measures:

  - numerical, biomass, or energy flow analysis as measures of food web linkages (Dayton 1975; Paine 1980), with trophic efficiency ratios or ratios between energy flow at different points along a food chain expressed as percentages of comparative ratios of Kcal consumed/per m^2 per year to Kcal produced per m^2 per year Odum 1971).

  - trapping/caging, removal and density manipulation of potential keystone species involved in predator-prey interactions to illuminate roles of community dominants and consumers for impact verification (Paine 1974 and 1977; Connell 1970; Virnstein 1977), after Conant, *et al.* (1983).

- Species diversity indices where the number of species (richness) present and the number of each species present (relative abundance or equitability) are combined in the Shannon-Wiener function to give a diversity index dependent upon the number of species and the evenness of distribution among species (Peet 1974). Diversity measurements are useful in detecting and evaluating environmental stress (Wilhm 1967; Wilhm and Dorris 1966). The diversity index obtained for each natural community under study is expressed as a ratio to the diversity of a representative community standard.

- Seral stage determination as a function of P/R ratios (Odum 1971); seral species may be used as indicators of community condition or disturbance in e.g. mangroves or seagrass meadows. Requirements include species composition and densities in comparison with an appropriate control.

- Experimental tests of stability and resilence (Conant, *et al.* 1983).

- Graphic and tubular comparisons of numbers/biomass or length-frequency and weight-length ratios involving parametric/non-parametric statistical analyses (Conant, *et al.* 1983).

- Multivariate statistical analysis of data such as clustering and ordination to determine similarities between samples or multiple regression and analysis of variance to examine source of variability. For example, normalized data for ecosystem indices of species diversity, trophic efficiency, and seral stage may be summed and placed in a similarity matrix, site by site. A cluster analysis and construction of a dendrogram would graphically display the ecological similarity of all sites one to another. The degree of divergence of any one site from controls can be assessed. An elaboration of statistical methods can be found in Gnanadesikan (1977).

- Socio-economic sampling of artisanal fishermen.

An enumeration of objectives is required to determine the sampling methods used. For example, if the study is aimed at determining community response as a function of the concentration of some element will the community under scrutiny be considered alone or in relation to the surrounding ecosystem? Is monitoring the flux of only one element sufficient to characterize the response? Furthermore, is it important that the data be integrated into diurnal/nocturnal patterns of behaviour? Sampling programmes for primary productivity, for instance, must consider the light and nutrient dependence of primary production. The measurement regimes should include sampling throughout the photic zone on an annual basis, particularly in tropical regions. Seagrasses are a major functioning element in the complex cyclical processes involved in estuarine and nearshore marine productivities (Zieman and Wetzel 1980), and therefore seagrass productivity studies must be interpreted in terms of related ecosystems.

In many instances a lack of coordination with other development sectors during the planning and design phase of coastal development projects has the potential to generate apparently unrelated adverse environmental impacts. Conversion of an estuarine-mangrove area to a freshwater lake and rice fields by removing the ecotone from tidal influence destroys the mangrove ecosystem process critical to post-larval penaeid shrimp development. Total commercial shrimp yield has been found to be directly proportional to acreage of the vegetation-water interface (Turner 1977). Turner (1975) calculated the projected removal of 22,500 hectares of mangroves in the Cilacap region on the south coast of Java (Segara Anakan Reclamation Project) to decrease Cilacap's shrimp and fish catch by 88 percent.

The basic questions to be asked in conjunction with the feasibility and design of developments involve understanding enough about the systemic interactions of the various components of a multiple resource system to plan effectively for optimal and sustainable productivity. One useful approach to integrated coastal resource planning and management involves the use of systems analysis. Systems analysis is the process of identifying the important components of the system and determining how they interact to produce a set of behaviours. Multisector coastal zone assessments employing the systems analytic approach with priority given, for example, to identifying resource use conflicts affecting coastal fisheries and related natural systems provides a means of identifying interactions with other sectors of the system in evaluating intersectoral conflicts. Figure 3-3 is a conceptual model which illustrates the typical interactions between fisheries and other sectors to create an overall system perspective. By describing sectoral resource interactions in a specific coastal development project context, a well constructed systems model acquires utility as (1) a tool for visualizing and addressing the complex of diverse disciplines and sectors as a functional unit; (2) an analytic and auditable approach for resource planners to make predictions about aggregate system behaviour to avoid potential intersectoral conflicts in coastal development; (3) a tool for rapid identification of data gaps and inconsistencies; and (4) an approach to a resource development planning with the potential for creating a climate for institutional and policy change. The conceptual model is one of a series of steps employed in the rigorous analysis of a system. One end point is a simulation model which can test the system-wide effects of various policies, interventions and project configurations. The utility lies in the fact that the human mind cannot begin to quantitatively predict the complex ripple effects of an intervention in a typical system which may contain 1000 interactions (Chamberlin, *et al.* 1984). The size of such models is effectively limited by the analyst's ability to trace unexpected behaviour through the structure (in the form of flow diagrams) of the model which represents a system. If the model is too complex, behaviours are inexplicable, if too simple, behaviours are not scientifically credible.

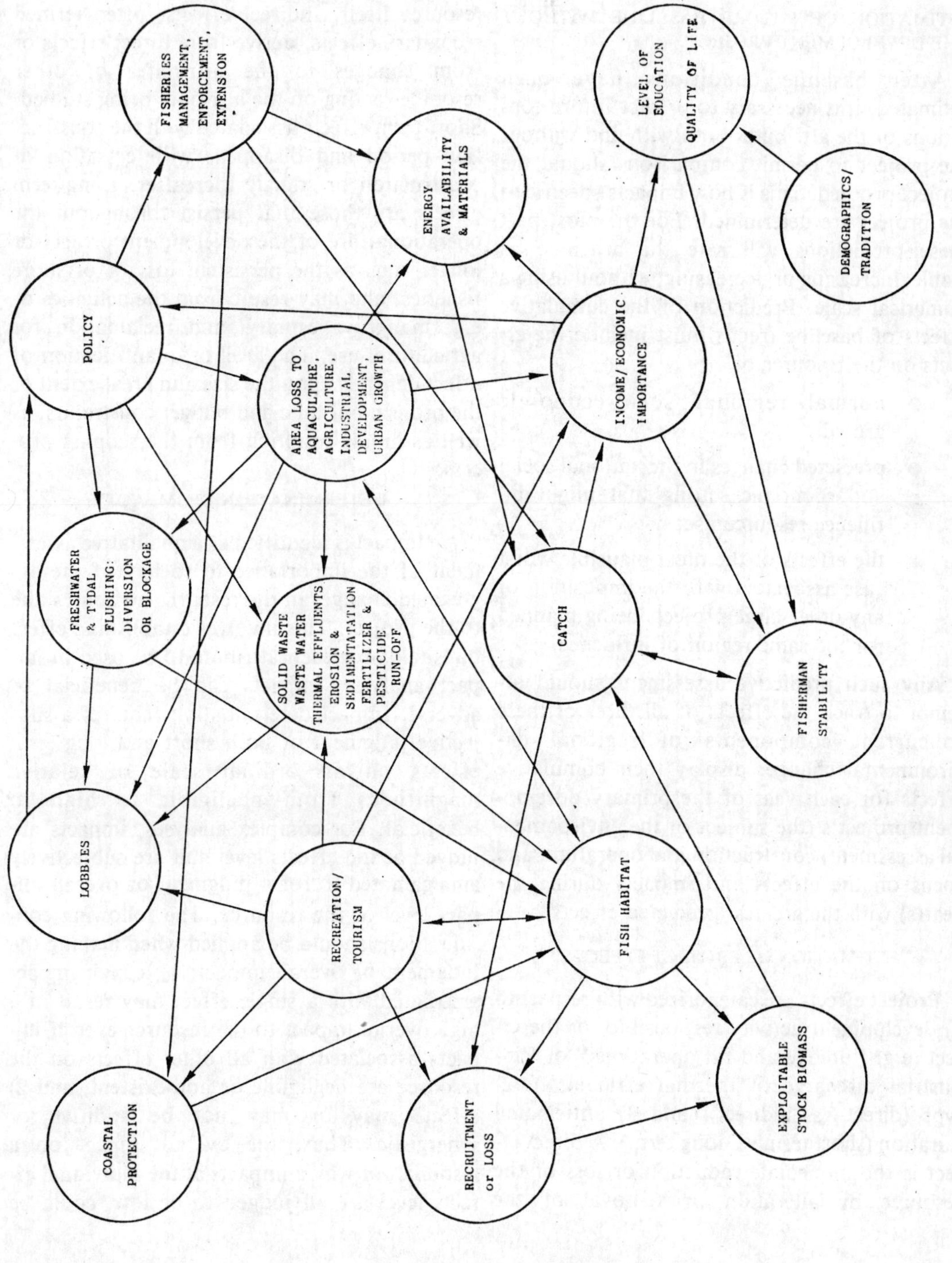

Fig. 3-3. AN INTEGRATED OVERVIEW OF NEARSHORE CATCH FISHERIES SECTOR INTERACTIONS

ESTIMATION OF FUTURE BASELINE WITHOUT THE DEVELOPMENT PROJECT.

After baseline conditions have been estimated, it is necessary to predict future conditions of the attributes both with and without the project to permit comparisons should the project proceed. This is how impacts specific to the project are determined. For the most part these predictions will rate the attribute as stable, increasing or decreasing, without using a numerical scale. Prediction of the cumulative effects of baseline trends must include the effects on the resource of

- normal regional socio-economic growth,
- predicted changes in the national social and economic setting that might influence resource use,
- the effects of the most plausible worst case associated with the imposition of any other large projects being planned for the same region of influence.

Any such predictive assessment should attempt to track the effects of all three of these concurrent components of regional environmental change; display their cumulative effects for each year of the primary development project's (the subject of the environmental assessment) construction and operation; and focus on the effects and impacts during the year(s) with the greatest predicted effects.

ESTIMATION OF PROJECT EFFECTS

Project effects are categorized with respect to 1) development activity responsible for the effect (e.g. "dredge and fill operations" or "industrial discharge of thermal effluents"); 2) type (direct vs. indirect); and 3) anticipated duration (short term vs. long term). A direct effect is the immediate reduction or loss of the resource by alteration or removal of the resource itself. Indirect effects, often termed secondary effects, derive from direct effects or from changes in the attributes of other resources acting on the attribute being studied. Short-term effects associated with the construction period and disappear with cessation of construction or shortly thereafter. Long-term effects are those that persist throughout the operational life of the development project or longer such as the persistent loss of offshore fisheries, and may result from the activities of e.g. mangrove estuary land reclamation for agricultural use. The level of quantification of effect depends upon the size and areal extent of the project and time and budget constraints, as well as inputs resulting from the scoping process.

DETERMINATION OF IMPACT

An impact is identified as a qualitative assessment of the importance to society of the aggregated changes in the resource attributes due to the project. This involves establishing effect thresholds for each attribute to be used in impact analysis. Impacts can be beneficial or adverse. Impact determination requires a subjective judgment of both short and long term effects on an ordinal scale of relative magnitudes from negligible to high to beneficial. For complex analyses, impacts are judged at the effects level and are subjectively amalgamated to form judgment of overall impact level of the resource. The following considerations should be applied when making the judgment of overall impact: 1) a high impact associated with a single effect may result in a high overall impact to the resource even if impacts associated with all other effects on the resource are negligible or non-existent, and 2) effects may or may not be additive or synergistic. Thus, the overall impact on a resource for which impacts at the individual effects level are all judged to be low, could be low, moderate, or high, depending upon the additivity or non-additivity of the individual effects.

An example of the criteria used to rate impacts in the environmental assessment of an off-shore exploratory hydrocarbon drilling operation in the Davis Strait region of the Canadian Arctic are as follows (Imperial Oil Limited, et al., 1978):

Major Impact: A *major impact* affects an entire population or species in sufficient magnitude to cause a decline in abundance and/or change in distribution beyond which natural recruitment (reproduction, immigration from unaffected areas) would *not* return that population or species, or any population or species, dependent upon it, to its former level within several generations. A major impact may also affect a subsistence or commercial resource use to the degree that the well-being of the use is affected over a long term.

Moderate Impact: A *moderate impact* affects a portion of a population and may bring about a change in abundance and/or distribution over one or more generations, but does not threaten the integrity of that population or any population dependent upon it. A short-term effect upon the well-being of resource users may also constitute a moderate impact.

Minor Impact: A *minor impact* affects a specific group of localized individuals with a population over a short time period (one generation or less), but does not affect other trophic levels or the population itself.

Project effects may be ranked in descending order of change over baseline. This allows com parision of alternatives and creates information useful in assigning impact scores. Factors to be considered in assessing and ranking effects include:

- the amount of the resource component available and the percent affected
- the resilience of the resource component, or the ability to recover from effects
- the importance of the resources to interelated supporting systems
- the effect of foreclosing future opportunities for development, use, or protection of the resource or other resources
- the legal standing and importance of the resource and the degree to which any action affecting it is foreclosed.

Each effect on a resource component is evaluated individually, with effects ranked for both short and long term as illustrated in Table 3-3.

DETERMINATION OF SIGNIFICANCE

Significance is the importance of the impact of the resource. Significance assessment in-

TABLE 3-3

HYPOTHETICAL EXAMPLE OF A SUMMARY IMPACT MATRIX BASED ON DATA FROM THE SEGARA ANAKAN RECLAMATION PROJECT REPORT: IMPACT TO COMMERCIAL FISHERIES

(adapted from Turner, 1975)

Resource Component	Project Action	Effects: Short Term	Effects: Long Term	Short Term	Long Term	Significance: L	Significance: R	Significance: N
Mangrove-dependent commercial offshore fisheries (e.g. penaeid shrimp)	Removal of 22,500 hectares of mangrove from intertidal influence	Direct habitat loss of shallow water nursery areas for post-larval penaeid shrimp development by removal of critical mangrove/water vegetative interface and resulting in reduced recruitment to adult offshore populations approximately two months later.	90% decrease in offshore shrimp landings and proportionate decrease in in fish catch even if fish are not estuarine dependent.	***	***	+	+	0
	Construction of paddy dikes and drainage canals	Alternation of freshwater discharge creating unfavorable salinity regimes and changed sedimentation rates/distribution.	New equilibrium point reached between tidal flushing, current and sedimentation resulting in less than favorable habitat conditions for developing larvae. No evidence that disruptive alteration of one portion of nursery grounds will be compensated by a greater utilization of remaining portion. Continued high loss in offshore shrimp landings.	***	***	+	+	0
	Rice field operations	Chemical and nutrient discharge with field drainage creating less than favorable habitat conditions.	Reduced shrimp catch	*	**	+	0	0
Component 2								
:	:	:	:					
Component Total				**	***	+	+	+
Overall Resource Impact				**	**	*	*	+

Impact levels: B = beneficial, - = negligible, * = low, ** = moderate, *** = high

L = Local, R = Regional, N = National, 0 = not significant, + = significant

Assumes costs of trawling to be supported by price of shrimp.

volves a subjective determination combining (1) resource attribute importance, (2) impact magnitude and duration, and (3) the anticipated level of institutional, scientific, or public concern with regard to the resource and the potential impact. Significance is a binary determination at the national, regional, and local level.

DETERMINATION OF APPROPRIATE MITIGATION MEASURES

Since the goal of the environmental assessment process is to avoid or reduce significant adverse impacts of development, impact assessment studies provide the basis to specify the appropriate mitigation measures to reduce unavoidable impacts and to identify designs, and precautions to prevent avoidable impacts. Compensation is invoked when mitigation is not possible and the resource is likely to be completely lost or altered. An example of compensation for loss of an ecosystem would be by locating a similar area nearby (usually by purchase) and designating that area for conservation. The most effective mitigative measures for the coastal zone are based on the physical separation of development activities from fragile natural systems and would include:

- selection of an alternate site for development projects not dependent on coastal productivity;
- decrease in the size of the project
- selection of a less valuable biotic/socio-economic coastal area;
- temporal concentration of activities to provide integration and localization of development activities to protect adjacent and offshore areas within the project region of influence from impact (e.g. breeding and migratory areas);
- selective routing and disposal of wastes to avoid contaminating the coastal zone;
- scheduling of the construction phase of the development phase so as to avoid disturbing fish and wildlife during its breeding and nesting seasons;
- artificial reef construction;
- protection of coastal ecosystems immediately adjacent of the development site through use of a buffer zone.

4.0 Coastal Resource Management Research Recommendations

Effective tropical coastal management schemes necessitate incorporation of applied research related to the multisectoral components involved in the synergystic impact of coastal and upland watershed development activities on, for example, fisheries. Avoidance of unnecessary ecological effects emanating from development projects require multidisciplinary studies and integrated assessments of coastal systems. The following list of priority research items, although by no means complete, are recommended for sustainable coastal resource cónservation:

- *Boundaries.* determining the boundaries of the coastal and nearshore marine areas influenced by upland watershed processes.
- *Baseline Measurements.* performing baseline studies especially within coastal zones influenced by freshwater and terrestrial sediment run-off. Such studies would include natural resource surveys, characterization of the physical environment and its underlying processes (including the effects of

the coastal terrain and water current patterns), in addition to assessments of the nature and quantity of inputs to coastal regions from inland sources.

- *Monitoring.* monitoring programmes that would include systematic surveys of terrestrial inputs influencing the coastal zone (e.g. freshwater flow, suspended sediment, contaminants, nutrients, etc.) as well as observations regarding induced changes in these processes (e.g. tidal flushing and current flow regimes) resulting from structural modification to the shore terrain.

- *System Linkages.* determining the inter-relationships of linked ecosystem processes involving upland watersheds, mangrove estuaries, seagrass beds, and coral reefs including their interrelated support systems. Additional studies, might include, for example, research on (1) the effects of coastal configuration and associated ecosystems on primary productivity and consequent secondary productivity/biomass; (2) the interactions between coastal ecosystems such as nutrient transfer by foraging animals; (3) the effects of resident nutrient levels associated with mangroves and seagrass beds or nutrient discharge "pulses" from onshore activities (e.g. agricultural runoff, sewage disposal, etc.) on secondary productivity/biomass; and (4) the influence of nearby seagrass beds and mangrove swamps on the facilitation of recruitment to the coral reef fish community.

- *Viability of Fisheries.* determining the inter-relationships and effects of land use practices on local fisheries.

- *Impact Assessment Procedures.* establishing evaluative procedures for determining the coastal implications of proposed development schemes. Both social and economic costs and benefits of current and alternative uses of coastal resources would be evaluated.

- *Impact Thresholds.* determining the threshold levels to baseline coastal processes of key terrestrial inputs and the critical environmental parameters required to maintain these processes. Additional research might include comparative studies between pristine coastal areas and those affected by nearby human activities such as reclaimed mangrove estuaries for agriculture or urban development.

- *Project Site Selection.* establishing criteria for site selection of upland/coastal development projects to minimize impacts and optimize sustainability and economic return. An example would be the use of such Geographic Information Systems as "MAP" (Berwick, *et al.* 1984).

Such studies would provide the beginnings for an integrated data base for policy analysis and coastal resource planning, management, and development. Mechanisms to link data collection, resource assessments and applied research with decision-makers are essential to the structuring of an institutional framework to integrate development activities as part and process of a coastal management plan.

References

ALEEM, A.A. (1972): Effect of river outflow management on marine life. *Mar. Biol.* **15:** 200-208.

ALEVIZON, W.S. & BROOKS, M.G. (1975). The comparative structure of two western Atlantic reef-fish assemblages. *Bull. Mar. Sci.* **25:** 482-490.

AMESBURY, S.S., TSUDA, R.T., ZOLAN W.J. & TANSY, T.L. (1975a): Limited current and underwater biological surveys of proposed sewer outfall sites in the Marshall Island District. Ebeye, Kwajalein Atoll. University of Guam Marine Laboratory Technical Report No. 22. 30 pp.

________ (1975b): Limited current and underwater biological surveys of proposed sewer outfall sites in the Marshall Island District. Darrit-Uliga-Dalap area, Majuro Atoll. Agana, Guam: University of Guam Marine Laboratory Technical report No. 23.

________ RANDALL, R.H., BIRKELAND, C. & CUSHING F. (1976): Limited current and underwater biological surveys of the Donitsch Island sewer outfall site, Yap Western Caroline Islands. Agana, Gaum: University of Guam Marine Laboratory Technical Report No. 24.

ANONYMOUS (1974): International conference on marine resources development in Eastern Africa. (A.S. Msangi and J.J. Griffin, eds.) Univ. of Dar es Salaam.

APHA, AWWA, and WPCF. (1981): Standard Methods for the Examination of Water and Wastewater, 15 ed., American Public Health Association, Washington, DC.

BAGENAL, T.. (ed.) (1978): Methods for assessment of fish production in fresh waters. Third ed. I.B.P. Handbook No. 3. Oxford: Blackwell Scientific Publ.

BANNER, A.H. (1968): Hawaii Institute of Marine Biology Technical report No. 15.

________ (1974): Kaneohe Bay, Hawaii: Urban pollution and a coral reef ecosystem. *In* A.M. Cameron, B.M. Campbell, A.B. Cribb, R. Endean, J.S. Jell, O.A. Jones, P. Mather, and F.H. Talbot (eds.), Proc. 2nd International Coral Reef Symposium, Brisbane, Queensland, Australia 2: 685-702.

____ & BAILEY, J.H. (1970): Hawaii Institute of Marine Biology, Technical Report No. 25.

BARLOW, G.W. (1974a): Contrasts in social behaviour between Central American cichlid fishes and coral reef surgeon fishes. *Am. Zool.* **14**: 9-34.

____ (1974b): Extraspecific imposition of social grouping among surgeon fishes. *J. Zool. Soc. Lond.* **174**: 333-340.

BARNES, D.J. & TAYLOR, D.L. (1973): *In situ* studies of calcification and photosynthetic carbon fixation in the coral *Montastrea annularis. Helgo. Wissen. Meeres.* **24:** 284-291.

BATHAN, K.H. (1968): A descriptive study of the physical oceanography of Kaneohe Bay, Oahu. Hawaii Inst. Mar. Bio. Technical Report No. 14.

BEEKHUS, J.V. (1981): Tourism in the Caribbean: Impacts on the economic, social and natural environments. *Ambio* **10**(6): 325-331.

BEERS, J.R., STEVEN, D.M. & LEWIS, J.B. (1963): Primary production in the Caribbean Sea off Jamaica and the tropical North Atlantic off Barbados. *Bull. Mar. Sci.* **18**: 86-104.

BENTON, A.R. & NEWMAN, R.M. (1976): Colour aerial photography for aquatic plant monitoring. *J. Aquatic Plant Management* **14**: 14-16.

BERWICK, N. & ANDERSON, M. (1984): Automated analysis of photo-quadrats as a technique for inventorying and measuring impacts to coral reefs (*in preparation*).

BERWICK, S., NISBET, R.A. & REED, K.L. (1983): Spatial analysis for determining "region of influence" when predicting impacts on wildlife and other resources. *In* R. Comer, J. Merino, J. Monarch, C. Pustmueller, M. Stalmaster, R. Soeker, J. Todd, and W. Wright (eds.), Issues and Technology in the Management of Impacted Western Wildlife. Proc. National Symposium, November 15-17, 1982, Steamboat Springs, Colorado. Technical Bulletin No. 14. Thorne Ecological Institute, Boulder, Colorado. 250 pp.

________ CHAMBERLIN, R.M. REED, K.L. FAETH, P. & BERWICK, N. 1984: A demonstration of systems analysis for development planning: A Model of Project X. Westview Press, Boulder, Co. 64 pp. (submitted).

BIRKELAND, C. (1982): Terrestrial runoff as a cause of outbreaks of *Acanthaster planci* (Echinodermata: Asteroidea). *Mar. Biol.* **69**(2): 175-185.

______ REIMER, A.A. & YOUNG, J.R.. (1976): Survey of marine communities in Panama and experiments with oil. PB 253 409/7GA. EPA Report 600/3-76/028.

BITTAKER, H.F. & IVERSON, R.L. (1976): *Thalassia testudinum* productivity: A field comparison of measurement methods. *Mar. Biol.* **37**: 39-46.

BOESCH, D.F. (1977): A new look at the zonation of benthos along an estuarine gradient. *In* B.C. Coull (ed.), Ecology of marine benthos. Columbia, SC: Univ. of S. Carolina Press, pp. 245-266.

BOYD, C.E. (1977): Evaluation of water analysis kit. *Environmental quality* **6**: 381-384.

________ (1980): Reliability of water analysis kits. *Trans. Am. Fish. Soc.* **109**: 239-243.

BROCK, V.E., VAN HEUKELEM, W. & HELFRICH, P. (1966):

An ecological reconnaissance of Johnston Island and the effects of dredging. Hawaii Institute of Marine Biology, Technical Report No. 11. 56 pp.

BURRELL, D.C. & SCHUBEL, J.R. (1977): Seagrass ecosystem oceanography. *In* C.P. McRoy and C. Helffrich (eds.), Seagrass eco-systems: a scientific perspective. Marcel Dekker, New York. pp. 195-232.

CAPONE, D.G., PENHALE, P.A., OREMLAND, R.S. & TAYLOR, (1979): Relationship between productivity and N_2 (C_2H_2) fixation in a *Thalassia testudinum* community. *Limnol. Oceanogr.* **24:** 117-125.

CHAI, P.P.K. (1974): The potential of mangrove forests in Sarawak. *The Malaysian Forester* **37**(4).

CHAN, E.I. (1977). Oil pollution and tropical littoral communities: biological effects of the 1975 Florida Keys oil spill. *In Proc. 1977 Oil Spill Conference, New Orleans, La. American Petroleum Institute, Washington, DC.* pp. 539-542.

CHOAT, J.H. & ROBERTSON, D.R. (1975): Protogynous hermaphroditism in fishes of the family Scaridae. *In* R. Reinboth (ed.), Intersexuality of the animal kingdom. Berlin, Springer-Verlag. pp. 263-283.

CHOW, V.T. (1974): Handbook of applied hydrology. New York: McGraw Hill.

CIERESZKO, L.S. & KARNES, T.K.B. (1973): Comparative biochemisty of coral reef coelenterates. *In* O.A. Jones and R. Endean (eds.), Biology and geology of coral reefs, Vol. 2, Biology 1. Academic Press, New York and London. 480 pp.

COLLETTE, B.B. & TALBOT, F.H. (1972): Activity of coral reef fishes with emphasis on nocturnal-diurnal changeover. *Bull. Nat. Hist. Mus. Los Angeles County* **14:** 125-170.

CONANT, F., ROGERS, P.P., BAUMGARDNER, M.F., MCKELLL, C.M., DASMANN, R.F. & REINING, P. (eds.) (1983): Resource inventory and baseline study methods for developing countries. AAAS, Washington, DC. 539 pp.

CONNELL, J.H., (1970): A predatory-prey system in the marine inter-tidal region. I. *Balanus glandula* and several predatory species of *Thais. Ecol. Monogr.* **40:** 49-78.

______ (1972): Community interactions on marine rocky inter-tidal shores. *Ann. Rev. Ecol. and Sys.* **3:** 169-192.

____ (1973): Population ecology of reef-building corals. *In:* O.A. Jones and R. Endean (eds.), Biology and geology of coral reefs, Vol. 2, Biology 1. Academic Press, New York and London. 490 pp.

CONOVER, J.T. (1968): Importance of natural diffusion gradients and transport of substances related to benthic marine plant metabolism. *Bot. Mar.* **11** (1-4): 1-9.

COULL, B.C. (ed.) (1977): Ecology of marine benthos. Columbia, S.C.: Univ. of S. Carolina Press.

CUENCO, M.L. & STICKNEY, R.R. (1980): Reliability of an electrode and a water analysis kit for determination of ammonia in aqua-culture systems. *Trans. Am. Fish. Soc.* **109:** 571-576.

DAROVEC, J.E. (1975): Techniques for coastal restoration and fishery enhancement in Florida. Fl. Mar. Fish. Pub. 15. Florida Dept. of Natural Resources.

DAVIS, G.E. (1977): Anchor damage to a coral reef on the east coast of Florida. *Biol. Conserv.* (11): 29-34.

DAYTON, P.K. (1971): Competition, disturbance, and community organization: the provision and subsequent utilization of space in a rocky intertidal community. *Ecol. Monogr.* **41:** 351-389.

________ (1975): Experimental evaluation of ecological dominance in a rocky intertidal algal community. **45:** 135-159.

D'ELIA, C.F. (1978): Dissolved nitrogen, phosphorous, and organic carbon. *In* D.R. Stoddart and R.E. Johannes (eds.), Coral reefs: research methods. UNESCO, Paris. pp. 485-498.

DEN HARTOG, C. (1970): The seagrasses of the world. North-Holland Publ. Co.

____ & Jacobs, R.P.W.M. (1980): Effects of the Amoco Cadiz oil spill on an eelgrass community at Roscoff (France) with special reference to the mobile benthic fauna. Helgol. Meersunters. **33:** 182-191.

DODGE, R.E., ALLER, R.C., & THOMSON, J. (1974): Coral growth related to resuspension of bottom sediments. *Nature,* London **247:** 574-577.

DOTY, M.S. (1975): Rocky intertidal surfaces. *Geol. Soc. AM. Mem.* **67:** 535-585.

______ & OGURI, M. (1956): The island mass effect. J. du Cons. *Int. pour l'Explor. de la Mer* **22:** 33-37.

EBELING, A.W., LARSON, R., ALEVIZON, W.S., & DE WITT, JR., F. (1971): Fishes of the Santa Barbara kelp fores. *Abstr. Coastal Shallow Water Res. Conf. (2): 61.*

EDMONSON, C.H. (1928): The ecology of an Hawaiian coral reef. *Bull. of the Bernice P. Bishop Museum, Honolulu, Hawaii* **45:** 64.

EMERY, A.R. (1968): Preliminary observations on coral reef plankton. *Limnol. and Oceanogr.* **13:** 293-303.

ENDEAN, R. (1956): Further records of echinodermata (excluding crinoidea) University of Queensland Papers, Dept. of Zoology **1**(5): 121-141.

________ (1976). Destruction and recovery of coral reef communities *In* O.A. Jones and R. Endean (eds.), Biology and geology of coral reefs, Vol. 3, Biology 2. Academic Press, New York and London: 435 pp.

ESM 102 (1980): Habitat evaluation procedures (HEP). Division of ecological Services, U.S. Fish and WIldlife Service, Dept. of Interior, Washington, D.C.

__________ 103 (1980): Standards for the development of

habitat suitability index models, Division of Ecological Services, U.S. Fish and Wildlife Service, Dept. of Interior, Washington, D.C.

FISHELSON, L., POPPER, D. & AVIDOR, A. (1974): Biosociology and ecology of pomacentrid fishes around the Sinai Peninsula (northern Red Sea) *J. Fish Biol* 6: 119-133.

GARDNER, W.D. (1980a): Sediment traps dynamics and calibration: a laboratory evaluation. *J. Mar. Research* **38**(2): 17-39.

_____ (1980b): Field assessment of sediment traps. ibid. **38**(2): 41-52.

GILBERT, L.E. (1980): Food web organization of neotropical diversity. *In* M. E. Soule and B. A. Wilcox (eds.), Conservation Biology. Sinauer Associates Inc. Publishers, Massachusetts. pp. 11-33.

GLYNN, P.W. (1973): Ecology of Caribbean coral reefs. The Porites reef-flat biotope. Part II. Plankton community with evidence for depletion. Mar. Biol. 22:1-24.

GNANADESIKAN, R. (1977): Methods for statistical data analysis of multivariate observations. Wiley and Sons, Inc. New York. 311 pp.

GOLDMAN, B. & TALBOT, F.H. (1976): Aspects of the ecology of coral reef fishes. *In* O.A. Jones and R. Endean (eds.), Biology and geology of coral reefs. Vol. 3. Biology 2. Academic Press, New York and London, pp. 125-54.

GOLLEY, F., ODUM, H.T. & WILSON, R.F. (1962): The structure and metabolism of a Puerto Rican red mangrove forest in May. *Ecology* **43**: 9-10.

GORDON, D.C. (1978): Total organic carbon. *In* D.R. Stoddart and R.E. Johannes (eds.), Coral reefs: research methods. UNESCO, Paris. pp. 405-408.

GORDON, M.S. & KELLY, H.M. (1962): Primary productivity of an Hawaiian coral reef: A critique of flow respirometry in turbulent water. *Ecology* **43**: 473-480.

GOREAU, T.F. (1961): Problems of growth and calcium deposition in reef corals. *Endeavour* **20**: 32.

GULLAND, J.A. (1969): Manual of methods for fish stock assessment I. Fish population analysis. FAO Manuals in Fisheries Science. No. 4. Rome: FAO.

HAMMER, L. (1968): Salzgehalt and photosynthese bei marin planzen. *Mar. Biol.* **1**(3): 185-190.

HAY, M.E. (1981): Spatial patterns of grazing intensity on a Caribbean barrier reef: herbivory and algae distribution. *Aquatic Botany* **11**: 97-109.

_______ (1984): Patterns of fish and urchin grazing on Caribbean coral: are previous results typical? *Ecology* **65**: 446-454.

_____ COLBURN, T. & DOWNING, D. (1983): Spatial and temporal patterns in herbivory on a Caribbean fringing reef: the effects of plant distribution. *Oecologia* **58**: 299-308.

HEALD, E.J. (1971): The production of organic detritus in a South Florida estuary. U. of Miami. Sea Grant Tech. Bull. No. 6.

HENDEE, J.C., STANKEY, G.H. & LUCA, R.C. (1978): Wilderness management, USDA/Forest Service, Misc. Pub. No. 1365. U.S. Govt. Printing Off., Washington, D.C. 381 pp.

HIATT, R. & STRASBURG, D.W. (1960): Ecological relationships of the fish fauna on coral reefs of the Marshall Islands. *Ecol. Monogr.* **30**: 65-127.

HOBSON, E.S. (1974): Feeding relationships of teleostean fishes on coral reefs in Kona, Hawaii. *Fish. Bull.* (72): 915-1031.

____ & CHESS, J.R. (1978): Trophic relationships among fish and plankton in the lagoon at Enewetak Atoll, Marshall Islands. *Fish. Bull.* **76**: 133-153.

HOCUTT, C.H. & STAUFFER, J.R., JR., (eds.) (1980): Biological monitoring of fish. Lexington, Mass: Lexington Books.

HOPLEY, D. (1978): Aerial photography and other remote sensing techniques. *In* D.R. Stoddart and R.E. Johannes (eds.), Coral reefs: research methods. UNESCO, Paris. pp. 23-44.

IMPERIAL OIL LIMITED, AQUITAINE CO. OF CANADA LTD., & CANADA-CITES SERVICE LTD. (1978): Summary: Environmental Impact Statement for Exploratory Drilling in Davis Strait Region.

JOHANNES, R.E. (1970): FAO technical conference on marine pollution and its effect on living resources and fishing. Rome, Italy, December 9-18, 1970. Prospectus.

_______ (1975): Pollution and degradation of coral reef communities. *In* E.J. Ferguson Wood and R.E. Johannes (eds.) Tropical Marine Pollution. Elsevier Publishing Co., Amsterdam, Oxford and New York: 192 pp.

_______ (1978): Flux of zooplankton and benthic algal detritus. *In* D.R. Stoddard and R.E. Johannes (eds.), Coral reefs: research methods, UNESCO, Paris. pp. 429-432.

JOKIEL, P.L. & COLES, S.L. (1974): Effects of heated effluents on hermatypic corals at Kahe Point, Oahu, Hawaii. *Pac. Sci.* **28**: 1-18.

KAPLAN, E.H. (1982): A field guide to the coral reefs of the Caribbean and Florida. Houghton Mifflin Co., Boston, Mass. 289 pp.

KELLERT, S. (1980): American attitudes toward and knowledge of animals: an update. *Int. J. Stud. Amer. Prob.* **1**(2): 87-119.

KELLY, M.G. (1980): Remote sensing of seagrass beds. *In* R.C. Phillips and C.P. McRay (eds.), Handbook of Seagrass Biology: An Ecosystem Perspective. Garland STPM PRess, New York and London. 353 pp.

KENCHINGTON, R.A. (1978): Visual surveys of large areas

of coral reefs. *In* D.R. Stoddart and R.E. Johannes (eds.), Coral reefs: research methods. UNESCO, Paris. pp. 149-162.

KENCHINGTON, R.A. & MORTON, B. (1976): Two surveys of the crown-of-thorns starfish over a section of the Great Barrier Reef. Canbera, Australian Government Publishing Service. 186 pp.

KINSMAN, D.J.J. (1964): Reef coral tolerance of high temperatures and salinities. *Nature* (London) **202**(4939): 1280-1281.

KOHN, A.J. & HELFRICH, P. (1957): Primary organic productivity of a Hawaiian coral reef. *Limnol. and Oceanogr.* **2:** 241-251.

KREBS, C.J. (1972): Ecology. The experimental analysis of distribution and abundance. New York. Harper and Row. 694 pp.

LAMBERTS, A.E. (1977): The effects of some pesticides on reef corals, Marine Research in Indonesia. No. 17.

LAND, L.S. (1970): Carbonate mud: production by epibenthic growth on *Thalassia testudinum. J. Sediment. Petrol.* **40:** 1361-1363.

LANGHAM, N.P.E. & MATHIAS, J.A. (1977): The problems of conservation of coral reefs of northwest Sabah. Marine Research in Indonesia. No. 17.

LAXTON, J.H. & STABLUM, W.J. (1974): Sample design for quantitative estimation of sedentary organisms on coral reefs. *Biol. J. Linn. Soc.* **6**(1): 1-18.

LEVY, J.P. (1976): Introduction and summary in inter-regional seminar on development and management of resources in coastal areas. *In* K.H. Szekielda and B. Breuer (eds.), German Foundation for International Development/UN.

LEWIS, J.B. (1977): Processes of organic production on coral reefs. *Biol. Rev.* **52:** 305-347.

_____ (1981): Coral reef ecosystems. *In* H.R. Longhurst (ed.), Analysis of marine ecosystems. Academic Press, New York and London. 741 pp.

LINDALL, W.N., HALL, J.R., SYKES, J.E. & ARNOLD, E.L, JR., (1972): Louisiana coastal zone: analysis of resources and resource development needs in connection with estuarine ecology. National Marine Fisheries Service, St. Petersburg, Florida.

LOYA, Y. (1972): Community structure and species diversity of herma-typic corals at Eilat, Red Sea. *Mar. Biol.* **13:** 100-123.

_____ (1975): Possible effects of water pollution on the community structure of Red Sea corals. *Mar. Biol.* **29.**

_____ (1976): Recolonization of Red Sea corals affected by natural catastrophe and man-made perturbations. *Ecology* **57:** 278-289.

LOYA, Y. (1978): Plotless and transect methods. *In* D.R. Stoddart and R.E. Johannes (eds.), Coral reefs: research methods. UNESCO, Paris. pp. 197-218.

____ & SLOBODKIN, L.B. (1971): The coral reefs of Eilat (Gulf of Eilat, Red Sea). *In* D.R. Stoddart and C.M. Yonge (eds.), Regional variation in Indian Ocean coral reefs. Symposium Zool. Soc. London, 28: 117-139. Academic Press: London and New York. 584 pp.

LUBCHENCO, J. & MENGE, B.A. (1978): Community development and persistence in a low rocky intertidal zone. *Ecol. Monogr.* **48:** 67-94.

LUGO, A.E. & SNEDAKER, S.C. (1974): The ecology of mangroves. *Ann. Rev. Ecol. Syst.* **5:** 39-64.

____ EVINK, G., BRINSON, M.M., BROCE, A. & SNEDAKER, S.C. (1973): Diurnal rates of photosynthesis, respiration and transpiration in mangrove forests of South Florida. *In* S.C. Snedaker and A.E. Lugo (eds.), The role of mangrove ecosystems in the maintenance of environmental quality and high productivity of desirable fisheries. Final Report submitted to the Bureau of Sport Fisheries and Wildlife. 406 pp.

MAHADEVAN, S. & NAYAR, K.N. (1972): Distribution of coral reefs in the Gulf of Mannar and Palk Bay and their exploitation and utilization. *In* G. Mukandan and C.S. Pillai (eds.), Proceedings of the symposium on corals and coral reefs. Mar. Bio. Assoc. India. Cochin, India, pp. 181-190.

MARAGOS, J.E. (1978): Measurement of water volume transport flow studies. *In* D.R. Stoddart and R.E. Johannes (eds.), Coral reefs: research methods, UNESCO, Paris. pp. 353-360.

____ SOEGIARTO, A., GOMEZ, E.D. & DOW, M.A. (1983): Development planning for tropical coastal ecosystems. *In* R.A.Carpenter (ed.), Natural Systems for Development. MacMillan Publishing Co. New York, pp. 485.

MARSH, J.A. (1977): Terrestrial inputs of nitrogen and phosphorus on firing reefs of Guam. Proceedings, Third International Coral Reef Symposium, Miami, Florida. 1. Biology: 331-336.

_______ & GORDON, G.D. (1974): Marine environmental effects of dredging and power plant construction. Univ. Guam Mar. Lab. Tech. Rep., 8: 56 pp.

MARSHALL, N.B. (1965): The life of fishes. Weidenfeld and Nicholson London.

MAYOR, A.G. (1918): Toxic effects due to high temperature. Carnegie Institution of Washington, Dept. of Marine Biology, Publ. 252, **12:** 173-178.

_______ (1924): Structure and ecology of Samoan reefs. Carnegie Institution of Washington, Dept. of Marine Biology. Publ. 340, **19:** 1-26.

McGILL, J.T. (1959): Coastal classification maps. 2nd Coastal Geography Conference. Coastal Sud. Inst., L.S.U.

MEYER, J.L., SCHULTZ, E.T. & HELFMAN, G.S. (1983): Fish schools: an asset to corals. *Science* 220: 1047-1049.

MITCHELL, R. & DUCKLOW, H. (1976): The slow death of coral reefs. *Nat. Hist.* **85**(8): 106-110.

MOORE, D.R. (1963): Distribution of the seagrass, *Thalassia,* in the United States. *Bull. Mar. Sci. Gulf Caribb.* **13**(2): 329-342.

MYRBLRG, A.A. (1972): Social dominance and territoriality in the bicolour damselfish, *Eupomacentrus partitus* (Poey) (Pisces: Pomacentridae). *Behaviour* **41**: 207-231.

NADEAU, R.J. & BERQUIST, E.T. (1977): Effects of the March 18, 1983 oil spill near Cabo Rojo, Puerto Rico on tropical marine communities. *In* Proceedings of the 1977 Oil Spill Conference, New Orleans, Louisiana. American Petroleum Inst., Washington, DC pp. 535-538.

NOAA Current Tables. Annually since 1853. U.S. Dept. of Commerce, National Oceanic and Atmospheric Admin. Washington, D.C.

NORTH, W.J. (1974): Effects of heated effluent on marine biota particularly in California. *In* J. Pearce (ed.), Modifications thermiques et equilibre biologues. Amsterdam, North Holland Pub. pp. 41-60.

ODUM, E.P. (1969): The strategy of ecosystem development. *Science* **164**: 262-270.

_____ (1971): Fundamentals of ecology. W.B. Saunders and Co., Phil. Pa., 574 pp.

ODUM, H.T., BURKHOLDER, P.R. & RIVERO, J. (1959): Measurements of productivity of turtle grass flats, reefs and the Bahia Fosforescente of southern Puerto Rico. *Publ. Inst. Mar. Sci.* **6**: 159-170.

____ COPELAND, B.J. & McMAHAN, E.A. (1974): Coastal ecological systems of the United States Vol. I. The Conservation Foundation, Washington, DC. 533 pp.

ODUM, W.E., McIVOR, C.C. & SMITH, T.J. III (1982): The ecology of mangroves of South Florida: a community profile. U.S. Fish and Wildlife Service, Office of Biological Services, Washington, DC. FS/OBS-81-24. 144 pp.

OGDEN, J.C. & ZIEMAN, J.C. (1977): Ecological aspects of coral reef-seagrass bed contacts in the Caribbean. *In* D.L. Taylor (ed.), Proceedings: Third International Coral Reef Symposium, Miami, Florida. 1. Biology. 656 pp.

_____ & GLADFELTER, E.H. (eds.), (1982): Coral reefs, seagrass beds and mangroves: their interactions in the coastal zones of the Caribbean. Report of a workshop held at the West Indies Laboratory, St. Croix, U.S. Virgin Islands, May 1982. 139 pp.

PAINE, R.T. 1974): Intertidal community structure: Experimental studies on the relationship between a dominant competitor and its principal predator. *Oecologia* **14**: 93-120.

PAINE, R.T. (1977): Controlled manipulations in the marine intertidal zone and their contributions to ecological theory. Proc. Phil. Acad. nat. Sci. Philadelphia: ANSP.

_________ (1980): Food webs: interaction strength and community infrastructure. *Anim. Ecol.* **49**: 667-685.

PATRIQUIN, D.G. (1972): Carbonate mud production by epibionts on *Thalassia:* an estimate based on leaf growth rate data. *J. Sediment. Petrol.* **42**(3): 687-689.

PEARSE, V.B. & MUSCATINE, L. (1971): Role of symbiotic algae (zoo-xanthellae) in coral calcification. *Bio. Bull.* **141**: 350-363.

PEET, R.K. (1974): The measurement of species diversity. *Ann. Rev. Ecol. Sys.* **5**: 285-307.

PENHALE, P.A. (1975): Primary production of eelgrass, *Zostera marina,* and its epiphytes in the Newport River Estuary. *In* Annual Report to the Energy Research and Development Administration, NOAA, Natl. Mar. Fish. Serv., Beaufort, N.C. pp. 184-191.

PICHON, M. (1978): Quantitative benthic ecology of Tulear reefs. *In* D.R. Soddart and R.E. Johannes (eds.), Coral reefs: research methods. UNESCO, Paris. pp. 163-174.

PILSON, M.E.Q. (1978): Determination of phosphorus. *In* D.R. Stoddart and R.E. Johannes (eds.), Coral reefs: research methods. UNESCO, Paris. pp. 163-174.

_____ & BETZER, S.B. (1973): Phosphorus flux across a coral reef. *Ecology* **54**: 581-588.

POLUNIN, N.V.C. & FRAZIER, J.G. (1974). Diving reconnaissance of twenty-seven western Indian Ocean coral reefs. Environmental Conservation 1(17: 71-72.

POOLE, R.W. (1974): An introduction to quantitative ecology. New York: McGraw-Hill.

POND, S. & PICKARD, G.L. (1979): Introductory dynamic oceanography. Pergamon Press, Oxford.

PORTER, J.W. (1972a): Ecology and species diversity of coral reefs on opposite sides of the Isthmus of Panama. *Bull. Biol. Soc. Wash.* **2**: 89-116.

____ (1972b): Patterns of species diversity in Caribbean reef corals. *Ecology* **53**: 745-748.

_______ (1978): Coral feeding on zooplankton. *In* D.R. Stoddart and R.E. Johannes (eds.), Coral reefs: research methods. UNESCO, Paris. pp. 515-522.

_________ PORTER, K.G. & BATAC-CATALAN Z. (1977): Quantitative sampling of Indo—Pacific demersal reef plankton. *In* D.L. Taylor (ed.), Proc. Third International Coral Reef Symposium. Vol. 1. Miami, Fla. Univ. of Miami Rosensteil School of Marine and Atmos. Science. pp. 105-112.

PORTER, K.G., PORTER, J.W. & OHLHORST, S.L. (1978):

Resident reef plankton. *In* D.R. Stoddart and R.E. Johannes (eds.), Coral reefs: research methods. UNESCO, Paris. pp. 499-514.

POTTS, G.W. (1970): The schooling ethology of *Lutjanus monostigma* (Pisces) in the shallow water environment of Aldabra. *J. Zool. Lond.* **161:** 223-235.

QUINN, II T.J. & GALLUCCI, V.F. (1980): Parametric models for line-transect estimations of abundance. *Ecology* **61**; 293-302.

RAMAS, C.C. (1969): *Underwater Nature* **6:** 31.

RANDALL, J.E. (1967): Food habits of reef fishes of the West Indies. *Stud. Trop. Oceanogr. Miami* **5:** 665-847.

____ (1972): Chemical pollution in the sea and the crown-of-thorns starfish (*Acanthaster planci*). Biotropica **4**(3): 132-144.

REGIER, H.A. & ROBSON, D.S. (1971): Estimating population number and mortality rates. *In* W.E. Ricker (ed.), Methods for assessment of fish production in fresh waters. Blackwell Science Publications, Oxford (IBP Handbook No. 3, 2nd edit.), pp. 131-165.

RISK, M.J. (1972): Fish diversity on a coral reef in the Virgin Islands. *Atoll. Res. Bull.* (153): 1-6.

ROESSLER, M.A. & ZIEMAN, J.C. (1969): The effects of thermal additions on the biota of southern Biscayne Bay, Florida. Proc. Gulf. Carib. Fish. Inst. 22nd Session.

ROGERS, C.S. (1982): Marine environments of Brewers Bay, Perseverance Bay, Flat Cay and Saba Island, St. Thomas, USVI with emphasis on coral reefs and seagrass beds: November 1978 through July 1981. Division of Natural Resource Management. Dept. of Conservation and Cultural Affairs. Government of the Virgin Islands.

________ (1983): Sublethal and lethal effects sediments applied to common Caribbean reef corals in the field. *Marine Pollution Buttetin* **14**(10): 378-382.

RUDDLE, K. (1984): Pollution in the marine coastal environment of ASEAN countries in Southeast Asian Seas: Frontiers for development. McGraw-Hill (*in press*).

RUSSELL, B.C., TALBOT, F.H., ANDERSON, G.R.V. & GOLDMAN, B. (1978): Collection and sampling of reef fishes. *In* D.R. Stoddart and R.E. Johannes (eds.), Coral reefs: research methods. UNESCO, Paris. pp. 329-345.

RÜTZLER, K. (1978): Photogrammetry of reef environments by helium baloon. *In* D.R. Stoddart and R.E. Johannes (eds.), Coral reefs: research methods. UNESCO, Paris. pp. 45-52.

________ & MACINTYRE, I.G. (eds.) (1982): The Atlantic barrier reef ecosystem at Carrie Bow Cay, Belize, I: Structure and Communities. Smithsonian Institution Press, Washington, DC. 539 pp.

_______ FERRARIS, J.D. & LARSON, R.J. (1980): A new plankton sampler for coral reefs. PSZN I: *Marine Ecology* **1:** 65-71.

SAENGER, P., HEGERL, E.J. & DAVIE, J.D.S. (eds.) (1983): Global status of mangrove ecosystems. IUCN Commission on Ecology. *The Environmentalist* **3**(3): 88 pp.

SAILA, S.B. & ROEDEL, P.M. (eds.) (1979): Stock assessment for tropical small-scale fisheries. Kingston, R.I.: Internat. Centre Marine Resources Development, Univ. Rhode Island.

SALE, P.F. (1971): Extremely limited home range in a coral reef fish *Dascyllus aruanus* (Pisces: Pomacentridae). *Copeia* (2): 324-327.

____ (1972): Effect of cover on agonistic behaviour of a reef fish: a possible spacing mechanism. *Ecology* **53:** 753-758.

_____ (1977): Maintenance of high diversity in coral reef fish communities. *Amer. Nat.* **111:** 337-359.

SALM, R.V. (1982): Guidelines for the establishment of coral reef reserves in Indonesia. FO/INS/78/061. Special Report, Bogor, Indonesia: 66 pp.

SALVAT, B. (1974). Degradation des ecosystems coralliens. LeCourrier de la Nature, **30:** 49-62.

SANDERS, H.L., GRASSLE, J.F., HA,MPSON, G.R., MORSE, L.S., GARNER-PRICE, S. & JONES (1980): Anatomy of an oil spill: long-term effects from the grounding of the barge Florida off West Fal-mouth, Massachusetts. *J. Mar. Res.* **38:** 256-380.

SARGENT, M.C. & AUSTIN, T.S. (1954). Biologic economy of coral reefs. United States Geological Survey Professional Papers 260-E, pp. 293-300.

SCHEER, G. (1978): Application of phytosociologic methods. *In* D.R. Stoddart and R.E. Johannes (eds.), Coral reefs: research methods. UNESCO, Paris. pp. 175-196.

SEBENS, K.P. (1984). Population dynamics and habitat suitability of the intertidal sea anemones *Anthopleura elegantissima* (Brandt) and *A. xanthogrammica* (Brandt). Ecol. Monogr.

SHEPPARD, C.R.C. (1983): A natural history of the coral reef. Blandford Press, Poole Dorset, England. 152 pp.

SIMON, J.L. & DAUER, D.M. (1977): Reestablishment of a marine community following natural defaunation. *In* B.C. Coull (ed.), Ecology of marine benthos. Columbia, S.C.: Univ. of S. Carolina Press, pp. 139-154.

SMITH, C.L. & TYLER, J.C. (1972): Space resource sharing in a coral reef fish community. *Bull. Nat. Hist. Mus. Los Angeles County* (14): 125-154.

SMITH, S.V. (1978a): Alkalinity depletion to estimate the calcification of coral reefs in flowing waters. *In* D.R. Stoddart and R.E. Johannes (eds.), Coral reefs: research methods. UNESCO, Paris. pp. 397-404.

_____ (1978b): Coral-reef area and the contribution of reefs to processes and resources of the world's oceans.

Nature Vol. 273.

SMITH, S.V. & KINSEY, D.W. (1978): Calcification and organic carbon metabolism as indicated by carbon dioxide. *In* D.R. Stoddart and R.E. Johannes (eds.), Coral, reefs: research methods. UNESCO, Paris. pp. 469-484.

_____ & HENDERSON, R.S. (eds.) (1978): Phoenix Island Repport I: An environmental survey of Canton Atoll lagoon, 1973. Atoll Res. Bull. No. 221. Washington, DC: Smithsonian Inst.

SNEDAKER, S.C. (1978): Mangroves: their value and perpetuation. *Nat. and Resources* **14:** 6-13. UNESCO, Paris.

SOURNIA, A. (1976): Oxygen metabolism of a fringing reef in French Polynesia. Helgo. Wissen. Meeres. **28:** 401-410.

SOURNIA, A. & RICHARD, M (1976): Phytoplankton and its contribution to primary productivity in two coral reef areas of French Polynesia. *J. Exp. Mar. Biol. Ecol.* **21:** 129-140.

STEEDMAN, H.F. (ed.) (1976): Zooplankton fixation and preservation. UNESCO, Paris.

STEEMANN-NIELSEN, E. (1952): The use of radioactive carbon (C^{14}) for measuring organic production in the sea. - *J. Cons. Int. Explor. Mer.* **18:** 117-140.

STEEMANN-NIELSEN, E. (1954). On organic production in the ocean. *J. du Cons. Int. pour l 'Explor. de la Mer* **39:** 309-328.

STEVENSON, D.K. & MARSHALL, N. (1974): Generalizations on the fisheries potential of coral reefs and adjacent shallow-water environments. *In* A.M. Cameron, B.M. Campbell, A.B. Cribb, R. Endean, J.S. Jell, O.A. Jones, P. Mather, and F.H. Talbot (eds.), Proc. 2nd International Coral Reef Symposium, Brisbane, Queensland, Australia. **1:** 147-156.

STODDART, D.R. (1969): Ecology and morphology of recent coral reefs. *Bio. Rev.* **44.**

_______ (1978a): Descriptive reef terminology. *In* D.R. Stoddart and R.E. Johannes (eds.), Coral reefs: research methods. UNESCO, Paris. pp. 5-16.

________ (1978b): Mapping reefs and islands. *In* D.R. Stoddart and R.E. Johannes (eds.), Coral reefs: research methods. UNESCO, Paris. pp. 17-22.

________ & JOHANNES R.E. (eds.) (1978): Coral reefs: research methods. UESCO, Paris. 581 pp.

SUTCLIFFE, W.H. (1972): Some relations of land drainage, nutrients, particulate material, and fish catch in two eastern Canadian bays. *J. Fish. Res. Bd. Canada* **29;** 357-362.

__ (1973): Correlations between seasonal river discharge and local landings of American lobster (*Homarus americanus*) and Atlantic halibut (*Hippoglossus hippoglossus*) in the Gulf of St. Lawrence **30**(6): 856-859.

TALBOT, F.H. (1965): A description of the coral structure of Tutia Reef (Tanganyika Territory, East Africa) and its fish fauna. *Proc. Zool. Soc. Lond.* **145**: 431-470.

TALBOT, F.H. & GOLDMAN. B. (1974). A preliminary report on the diversity and feeding relationships of the reef fishes at one Tree Island, Great Barrier Reef. *In* Proc. Symp. Corals and Coral Reefs, 1969, *Mar. Biol. Assoc.* India. pp. 425-44.

TATEM, H.E., COX, B.A. & ANDERSON, J.W. (1978): The toxicity of oils and petroleum hydrocarbons to estuarine crustaceans. *Estuarine Coastal Mar. Sci.* **6**: 365-373.

THAYER, G.W., WOLFE, D.A. & WILLIAMS, R.B. (1975): The impact of man on seagrass systems. *Am. Sci.* Vol. 63.

THOMAS, L.P., MOORE, D.R. & WORK, R.C. (1961): Effects of Hurricane Donna on the turtle grass beds of Biscayne Bay, Florida. *Bull. Mar. Sci. Gulf Caribb.* **11**(2): 191-197.

THOMASSIN, B.A. (1969): Les peuplements de deux biotopes de sables coralliens sur le Grand Recif de Tulear, S.W. de Madagascar. *Rec. Trav. Stn. Mar. Endoume.* Supple. **9:** 59-133.

___ (1978): Soft-bottom communities. *In* D.R. Stoddart and R.E. Johannes (eds.), Coral reefs: research methods. UNESCO, Paris. pp. 251-262.

THORHAUG, A. (1981): Biology and management of seagrass in the Caribbean *Ambio* **10**(10): 195-298.

_______ & SCHROEDER, P. (1980): Trace metal cycling in tropical-subtropical estuaries dominated by the seagrass *Thalassia testudinum. American Journal of Botany.* **67**(3): 118-129.

_____ SEGAR, D. & ROESSLER, M.A. (1973): Impact of a power plant on subtropical and estuarine environment. *Mar. Poll. Bull.* **4**(11).

TRANTER, D.T. & FRASER, J.H. (eds.) (1968): Zooplankton sampling. Genega: UNESCO.

TURNER, R.E. (1975): The Segara Anakan reclamation Project: The impact on commercial fisheries (*unpublished manuscript*).

___ (1977): Intertidal vegetation and commercial yields of Penaeid shrimp. *Trans. Am. Fish. Soc.* **106:** 411-416.

VANDERMEULEN, J.H. & MUSCATINE, L. (1974): Influence of symbiotic algae on calcification in reef corals: Critique and Progress Report, 1-19. *In* W.B. Vernberg (ed.), Symbiosis in the Sea. University of South Carolina Press. Columbia, South Carolina.

VAN EEPOEL, R.P. & GRIGG, E.I. (1970): Survey of the ecology and water quality of Lindbergh Bay, St. Thomas. Water Pollution Rep. Caribbean Res. Inst., St. Thomas, Virgin Islands.

VAUGHAN, T.W. (1919): Rep. Smithson. Inst. **17:** 189.

VINE, P.J. (1974): Effects of algal grazing and aggressive behaviour of the fishes *Pomacentrus lividus* and *Acanthurus sohal* on coral reef ecology. *Mar. Biol.* **24:** 131-136.

VIRNSTEIN, R.W. (1977): The importance of predation by crabs and fish on benthic infauna in Chesapeake Bay. *Ecology.* **58:** 1199-1217.

VIVIEN, M. (1973): Ecology of the fishes of the inner coral reef flat in Tulear (Madagascar). *J. Mar. Biol. Assoc. India.* **15:** 20-45.

VOSS, G.L. (1973): Sickness and death in Florida's coral reefs. Nat. Hist. **82**(7): 40-47.

WALKER, H.J. (1962): Coral and the lime industry of Maritius. *Geographical review* **52**(3): 325-336.

WEBB, K.L. (1978): Nitrogen determination. *In* D.R. Stoddart and R.E. Johannes (eds.), Coral reefs: research methods. UNESCO, Paris. pp. 413-420.

WELLS, J.W. (1951): The coral reefs of Arno Atoll, Marshall Islands. *Atoll Research Bull.* No. 9. 46 pp.

WESTLAKE, D.F. (1963): Comparison of plant productivity. *Biol. Review* **38:** 385-425.

WILHM, J.L. (1967): Comparison of some diversity indices applied to populations of benthic macroinvertebrates in a stream receiving organic wastes. *J. Water Poll. Cont. Fed.* **39:** 1673-1683.

_____ DORRIS, T.C. (1966): Species diversity of benthic microorganisms in a stream receiving domestic and oil refinery affluents. *Amer. Midl. Nat.* **76:** 427-449.

WILSON, D.P. (1974): *Sabellaria* colonies at Duckpool, North Cornwall. *J. Mar. Biol. Assoc. U.K.* **54:** 393-436.

WOODIN, S.A. (1978): Refuges, disturbance and community structure: a marine soft-bottom example. *Ecology* **59:** 274-284.

WOODLAND, D.J. & HOOPER, J.N.A. (1977): The effect of trampling on coral reefs. *Biol. Conserv.* **11:** 1-4.

ZIEMAN, J.C. (1970): The effects of a thermal effluent stress on the seagrasses and macroalgae in the vicinity of Turkey Point, Biscayne Bay, FL. Ph.D. thesis, U. of Miami, Coral Gables.

_____ (1975a): Seasonal variation of turtle grass, *Thalassia testudinum* (Konig), with reference to temperature and salinity effects. *Aquat. Bot.* **1:** 107-123.

_____ (1975b): Tropical seagrass ecosystems and pollution. *In:* E.J.F. Wood and R.E. Johannes (eds.), Tropical marine pollution. Elsevier Oceanography Series 12. Elsevier Publ. Co., New York.

_____ (1981): The food webs within seagrass beds and their relationships to adjacent systems. Proc. of Coastal Ecosys. Wkshp. USFWS Spec. Rep. Ser. FWS/OBS-80/59.

_____ (1982): The ecology of the seagrasses of South Florida: a community profile. U.S. Fish and Wildlife Service, Office of Biological Services, Washington, DC. FWS/OBS-82/25. 151 pp.

_____ & WETZEL, R.G. (1980): Methods and rates of productivity in seagrasses. *In* R.C. Phillips and C.P. McRoy, (eds.), Handbook of Seagrass Biology: An Ecosystem Perspective. Garland STMP Press, New York. pp. 87-116.

The Dajipur Sanctuary and its potential as a National Park

(With a map)

JAY SAMANT

Department of Zoology, Shivaji University, Kolhapur 416 004.

ABSTRACT

The Dajipur Wildlife Sanctuary is in the Western Ghats region of the Kolhapur district in the southwestern Maharashtra. The present status of the earlier game reserve has been discussed in the paper. The small sanctuary (20 sq.km) cannot support the growing wildlife in it. The adjacent areas have good forests but they are under ever increasing pressure of deforestation and poaching. The present sanctuary, the catchment areas of Radhanagari and Kalammawadi dams and adjacent forest areas have been suggested for the proposed Radhanagar National Park (200 sq.km) and the proposal is evaluated. A list of wild animals found in the area is given.

In order to conserve the wildlife and protect both the catchment areas from this region recommendations are given at the end of the paper.

INTRODUCTION

The Dajipur Bison Sanctuary (20 sq. km) is a part of the former game reserve of the late Chhatrapati Maharaja of Kolhapur. As the state of Kolhapur was situated in the Western Ghats area, much of its western province is formed by the hilly region of the Sahyadri mountain ranges. Till Independence these hill ranges of the Kolhapur state were covered by thick subtropical evergreen, semi-evergreen and moist-deciduous forests. These gave excellent protection to a variety of wildlife which was plentiful in those days.

The Maharaja had kept some of the best patches of forests reserved for game hunting by the royal family and its guests. In the days of the Kolhapur State the Dajipur forest was known for some of the peninsular hill wildlife, especially tiger, panther, sambar, gaur, etc.

After Independence the forests in Radhanagari, Bawada, Panhala, Gargoti regions have been subjected to heavy pressure for timber and fire wood. Habitat destruction is only a partial reason for the dwindling of wildlife in this area. The major reasons are legal hunting and poaching, which have led to indiscriminate killing of wildlife in this area.

LOCATION AND PHYSICAL FEATURES

The Dajipur Sanctuary (16°30′N, 73°52′E) covers an area of 19.61 sq. km. This comprises the reserved forest area of the Olvan village of Radhanagari taluka and areas from Manbet and Taliye villages of Gagan Bawada taluka of Kolhapur district. For management purposes, the sanctuary comes under Radhanagari forest range.

The sanctuary is located on the Manbet plateau where the height ranges are from 985-1010m above mean sea level. The flat crest area extends up to Manbet village and is covered with dwarf evergreen and semi-evergreen vegetation with many large barren and grassy patches in between (Plate). In the evenings this area faces strong west winds almost throughout the year.

The climate of the sanctuary is moderate. There are three seasons: summer extends from March to May, the rainy season from June to

September, and winter from October till late January. During summer the mean temperature ranges from 30°-35°C, maximum 41°C. The mean annual rainfall in the sanctuary area is 3780 mm and there are strong winds during the rainy season. The mean temperature during winter is 16°C and it drops to about 9°C in the month of December. During winter months the sanctuary sometimes gets dense fog.

An observation tower of 20 feet height has been constructed at the heart of the plateau (5 sq.km). A small and shallow tank constructed opposite the tower provides water for wildlife till the month of December. There are a number of small springs in the sanctuary which dry up during late winter and summer. The main waterholes are at Waghachepani, Margajachepani, Kasarbarichepani etc. but these cannot be considered as perennial waterholes. Recently an anicut has been constructed at Sambarkund where perennial water is found. This area has very thick vegetation.

The observation tower, in the heart of the sanctuary, is 22 km from Dajipur village, which is on the Kolhapur Sawantwadi road, an all weather state highway. It is about 62 km from Radhanagari, the nearest town and about 120 km from Kolhapur city, the nearest railway station. The nearest airport is 135 km from Dajipur at Belgaum in Karnataka.

A notification to declare the Dajipur Bison Sanctuary was issued by the Government in 1958 and the area of Manbet, Olvan and Taliye village boundaries was declared as reserved forest on 14th September 1965. Surprisingly enough the required survey of the sanctuary has not been undertaken during the last twenty-five years.

VEGETATION

The sanctuary has two distinct types of forests, sub-tropical evergreen and semi-evergreen of about 1060 ha and 901 ha respectively. In the sanctuary and adjacent areas along the crest the wooded parts are confined to the western half of the hills. The western rim and its descending slopes hold a stunted type of evergreen vegetation. The tree cover around human habitat is poor due to exploitation and shifting cultivation. The vegetation on the marginal sides on the east and the areas around the submergence of Radhanagari and Kalammawadi reservoirs are more of a degraded forest, scrub jungle and grassy wasteland.

WILDLIFE

The sanctuary and the surrounding forests hold a diversity of wildlife. The list of mammals is given in the Table below. These records are based on a study of pugmarks, droppings, trophies and on reports from local inhabitants and the Forest Department staff. There is significant wildlife population in Palsambe, and the dense forest in the Bawada range in the north, in the sanctuary area and in Patachadang, Kaladang, Surangi, Rametha and a number of ravines and valleys in the catchment areas of Radhanagari and Kalammawadi dams. However, no scientific wildlife survey of this region has been done so far.

Till recently tiger (*Panthera tigris*) was found in the Radhanagari forests including Dajipur, Patachadang, Kaladang, Rametha, Surungi, Wakighol etc. The collection of tiger trophies in Kolhapur show that this magnificent animal was not uncommon in these forests. Though there are some reports of sighting of tiger in these forests, I have not come across any authentic records of tiger pugmarks or kills.

Panther (*Panthera pardus*) is the main carnivore of the sanctuary and the adjacent areas and has been seen on a number of occasions. Pugmarks of a large female and a young one

TABLE

WILDLIFE IN THE DAJIPUR SANCTUARY AND THE PROPOSED NATIONAL PARK

SPECIES	COMMON NAME	MARATHI NAME
1) *Presbytis entellus* (Dufresne)	Common Langur	*Wanar*
2) *Panthera pardus* (Linnaeus)	Leopard	*Biblya Wagh*
3) *Felis bengalensis* Kerr	Leopard Cat	*Wagati*
4) *Felis chaus* Guldenstaedt	Jungle Cat	*Baul*
5) *Viverricula indica* (Desmarest)	Small Indian Civet	*Javadi manjar*
6) *Paradoxurus hermaphroditus* (Pallas)	Palm Civet	*Udmanjar*
7) *Herpestes edwardsi* (Geoffroy)	Common Mongoose	*Mungoos*
8) *Hyaena hyaena* (Linnaeus)	Striped Hyena	*Taras*
9) *Canis aureus* Linnaeus	Jackal	*Kolha*
10) *Cuon alpinus* (Pallas)	Wild Dog	*Kolshinda*
11) *Melursus ursinus* (Shaw)	Sloth Bear	*Aswal*
12) *Lutra perspicillata* I. Geoffroy	Smooth Indian Otter	*Panmanjar*
13) *Petaurista petaurista* (Pallas)	Giant Flying Squirrel	*Kotisar*
14) *Ratufa indica* (Erxleben)	Indian Giant Squirrel	*Shekhara*
15) *Funambulus palmarum* (Linnaeus)	Threestriped Squirrel	*Jangali khar*
16) *Hystrix indica* Kerr	Indian Porcupine	*Salindar*
17) *Lepus nigricollis* F. Cuvier	Blacknaped Hare	*Sasa*
18) *Bos gaurus* H. Smith	Gaur	*Gawa*
19) *Cervus unicolor* Kerr	Sambar	*Sambar*
20) *Muntiacus muntjak* (Zimmermann)	Barking Deer	*Bhekar*
21) *Tragulus meminna* (Erxleben)	Mouse Deer	*Pisori*
22) *Sus scrofa* Linnaeus	Wild Boar	*Randukkar*
23) *Manis crassicaudata* Gray	Indian Pangolin	*Khavalya manjar*

were recorded in May 1983, on the sanctuary road near Waghachepani. A subadult and a full grown adult male were occasionally seen near Sambarkund and near the entrance of the sanctuary in March 1983. This habitat is suitable for tiger, but perhaps presently holds only a panther population.

Wild Dog (*Cuon alpinus*) has been known to exist in the sanctuary. In March 1982, a male sambar was found attacked by a pack of wild dogs on the sanctuary road. Many times their existence was noted due to the pugmarks and they were seen near a spot called 'Margajachepani'. The deer population in the sanctuary and nearby forested area is under increasing predatory pressure of this species since poachers do not kill wild dogs.

Gaur (*Bos gaurus*). The Dajipur Wildlife sanctuary is named after this animal as 'The Dajipur Bison Sanctuary'. The name is misleading and has caused some misunderstanding. Firstly the name 'Bison' should have been corrected as 'Gaur'. Secondly this is not the only sanctuary in the country where gaur is found. Its special mention is, therefore, misleading to the local population, which thinks that 'the Dajipur Bison Sanctuary' is the only one of its kind in the country. Last but not the least is that the sanctuary has equally good fauna of other peninsular Indian species, which are almost neglected. The local forest staff gives undue importance to the gaur population, as if

DAJIPUR BISON SANCTURY AND PROPOSED RADHANAGARI NATIONAL PARK

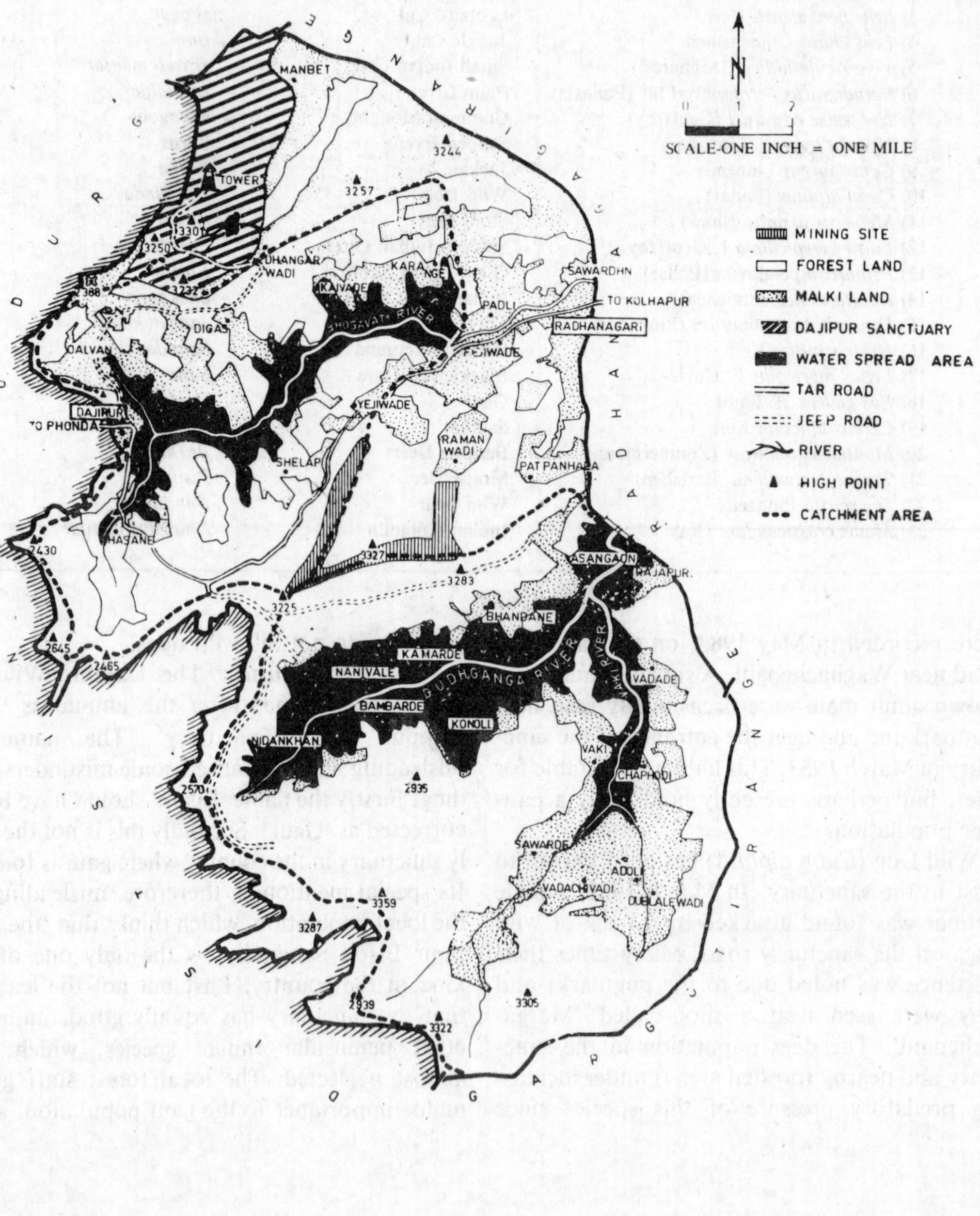

it is the only species assumed to be protected in the sanctuary.

The estimated gaur population in the sanctuary and in the neighbouring forest areas, i.e. in the south catchment areas of the Radhanagari and Kalammawadi dams, and in the north Bawada range forests, is about 200 to 300. Gaur usually gets protection because of the local religious belief that it is *Nandi,* the vehicle of Lord Shiva.

Unfortunately, the status of the gaur population is not as healthy as one would expect. Due to cattle grazing on the periphery of this small sanctuary there is always a danger of foot and mouth and rinderpest diseases spreading to the gaur population. Forest department's extraction activities and large scale illegal tree cutting (Plate) and encroachment on the neighbouring areas of the sanctuary have been destroying the gaur habitat on its local migratory routes thus restricting its movements. The hunting in May 1983 of an adult female on the outskirts of the sanctuary for trophy purpose by hunters is an example of how the so called protected gaur population still faces the danger of poaching.

To evolve suitable conservation strategies, a census of the gaur population in the sanctuary area, the Bawada range and the Kalammawadi catchment area is, therefore, urgently required.

Among herbivōres, sambar (*Cervus unicolor*), barking deer (*Muntiacus muntjak*), mouse deer (*Tragulus meminna*) have been subjected to poaching and need protection in the adjacent areas. Chital (*Axis axis*) was once recorded in considerable number in this habitat. But along with the tiger it has been wiped out from these forests because of heavy hunting pressure. The Sloth Bear (*Melursus ursinus*) has been recorded in Surangi and Kaladang forests, in the proposed national park but not in the present sanctuary.

Due to tree cutting and development of cultivation in land near degraded forests along the Radhanagari reservoir, the wild boar (*Sus scrofa*) inhabits sugarcane and other crops as its natural habitat has been destroyed. Though this causes destruction of the crop, the guns issued for crop protection are also used for poaching purposes in the neighbouring forests.

WILDLIFE MANAGEMENT

The forest staff of the sanctuary at present is one range forest officer, one forester and seven forest guards. The staff is too inadequate to look after wildlife protection and conservation activities. The main drawback is that the residential facilities for the staff are located in Dajipur village which is 22 km away by road from the heart of the sanctuary. Forest guards' quarters constructed near the entrance of the sanctuary, 4 km away from the Dajipur quarters have been vacant from the beginning.

The Sanctuary staff has no vehicle and therefore, protection cannot be done satisfactorily. The staff lack equipment and literature and are not conversant with wildlife management methods. There is also no management plan prepared for the sanctuary. No research or census work has been undertaken in the sanctuary since its beginning 25 years ago.

PROPOSED RADHANAGAR NATIONAL PARK

The Forest Department has proposed a national park in this area. The Radhanagar National Park in fact, will not merely be an extension of the existing Dajipur Wildlife Sanctuary but it will include a considerable area of mixed habitats around. These areas already have good vegetation and wildlife for conservation. This is mainly formed by the catchments of Radhanagari and Kalammawadi dams across Bhogawati and Dudhganga rivers respectively.

The total area of the proposed national park will be around 198 sq. km. The area extends from longitude 73° 50′E to 74° 03′E and latitude 16° 12′N to 16° 29′N.

The existing Dajipur Wildlife Sanctuary is about 4845 acres. This area is formed by three village boundaries, Manbet, Taliye and Olvan. An additional area of about 57,770 acres will be added from the south of the present sanctuary making the National Park area of about 62, 624 acres. This excludes the central hilly portion, separate from both the catchment areas, of about 1991 acres. This has been leased out for exploratory mining purpose. This additional area for National Park will come from 28 village boundaries but it does not include the submergence in the Radhanagari and Kalammawadi dams.

This proposal for a national park is based on the following reasons. The existing wildlife sanctuary is inadequate and cannot support the already existing wildlife population. The declaration of national park will stop the forestry activities of tree felling and fire wood extraction which destroy the different habitats of the adjacent area and which could otherwise provide excellent protection to the wildlife.

In the proposed national park there are excellent patches of evergreen forest on the crest region of the hills as also the known areas of wildlife like Surangi, Rametha, Kaladang. If the human population can be shifted out of the catchment area, there will not be any danger of grazing and illicit tree cutting in this region. If declared as a national park, the catchment area will not only help to conserve the already dwindling flora and fauna of this region but it will help to prevent silting in the reservoir. For wildlife management purpose also this will be an ideal situation.

Both the neighbouring reservoirs will form a perennial source of water to the wildlife which would be observed from boats as in the case of Periyar Wildlife Sanctuary. The submergence will cut off most of the existing roads in the Kalammawadi catchment area. This will prevent access to illegal tree cutting and poaching in the region. The forest quality also according to the Forest Department is poor in the proposed National Park area because it does not have any timber varieties and the extracted wood is normally used as fuel.

At present the 40 km Radhanagari-Dajipur tar road serves as an easy access for poachers and illegal wood traders to reach the interior of both the catchment areas on either side of the road. If the national park is created, the same road will form the only common access from the middle of the park, to both the sides. As there is no other motorable access road in the 200 sq. km area, only two checkposts at the extreme ends on the same road, i.e. one at the entrance of Phonda Ghat at Dajipur and other near the bifurcation of roads to Radhanagari and Kalammawadi dams, can easily control the entire traffic in and out of the national park.

The proposed Radhanagar National Park will have a unique place in the State of Maharashtra since this could be the only protected forest with wildlife in it in the southwest of the state in the Western Ghats region. The area has sub-tropical evergreen and semi-evergreen vegetation and forms the catchment areas of two important irrigation projects, namely Radhanagari and Kalammawadi which need to be protected even otherwise, in order to prevent erosion and silting. Another feature of the proposed National Park is that most of the area which comes under it already belongs to the State Forest Department, is mainly used for shifting cultivation.

About two-thirds area of the National Park in the south, i.e. Kalammawadi catchment area, is ideal for this purpose. It is surrounded by inaccessible hills. The population in the river valley is thin. It is proposed to shift the population out of the catchment area because of its submergence in late 1986.

RECOMMENDATIONS

1. All forest activities in the proposed National Park area, i.e. clear felling, firewood extraction etc., should be stopped immediately as it is detrimental to wildlife and leads to habitat destruction.

2. A wildlife management plan should be prepared immediately for the Dajipur Sanctuary and the entire area of the proposed National Park.

3. The crest region forest area of the western Kolhapur district should be included in the national park area in future or should at least be declared as a protected forest and ban on hunting should be enforced.

4. Wildlife management staff should be appointed and should be provided with necessary facilities.

5. The coupe working as per existing working plan should be stopped.

6. A mobile squad is necessary for the protection of the sanctuary.

7. The area forming both the catchments must be immediatley declared as closed blocks to shooting.

8. The existing hunting rights should be terminated and no big or small game licence be given in the entire protected area of the proposed national park.

9. The Dhangarwadis and other hamlets from the upper catchment areas and thick forests should be rehabilitated in the command area of the Kalammawadi and Radhanagari dams on priority basis.

10. Special rights given to the people for collection of firewood and forest products cause considerable damage to the forest wealth.

11. The National Park affected people should be given the consideration in the Government job priorities and other facilities. This man power should be mainly used in the management plan of the national park. They should be given preference in the afforestation and other conservation work in the catchment areas of both the dams.

12. The affected people should be given Forest Department and revenue wastelands from the catchment areas and neighbouring areas for social forestry purposes.

13. Tourism should not be encouraged beyond a certain extent.

14. No land should be given for mining purposes in the proposed national park.

15. The local population and specially youth should be involved in the development of the proposed national park.

16. Detailed ecological research work needs to be undertaken in this area.

ACKNOWLEDGEMENTS

I am thankful to Shri A.G. Oak, Conservator of Forest, Kolhapur Circle, for the help and guidance in this work. My thanks are also due to Shri Kinige, D.F.O., Kolhapur for providing the necessary facilities to do the field work. Without the valuable help of both these officials writing of this paper would not have been possible.

Population ecology and management problem of larger mammals in the Parambikulam Wildlife Sanctuary, Kerala

(*With 4 plates*)

P.S. EASA AND M. BALAKRISHNAN

Summary

Parambikulam Wildlife Sanctuary is situated, in Palghat District of Kerala (76°35'-76°50'E and 10°20'-10°26'N). West coast tropical wet-evergreen forests, west coast tropical semi-evergreen forests, Southern secondary moist-mixed deciduous forests, dry-deciduous forests, grasslands, swamps and teak and eucalyptus plantations form the major habitat of the sanctuary.

The whole area in the sanctuary was covered on foot and the population status of each species of larger and medium-sized mammals was recorded by direct counts. Indirect evidences such as droppings/pellets, hoof/pugmark/foot prints and calls were also taken into consideration. 25 species of larger and medium-sized mammals have been recorded from this area. They include three endangered species, the lion-tailed macaque, *Macaca silenus*; tiger, *Panthera tigris* and the Nilgiri tahr, *Hemitragus hylocrius*.

The current management problems of the sanctuary, namely cattle grazing, private plantations, taungya cultivation, forest plantations, stray dogs, bamboo extractions, forest fire and the proposed Kuriarkutty-Karappara multipurpose project have been evaluated. Effects of these human interactions on wildlife have also been discussed.

INTRODUCTION

India has a priceless legacy of wildlife, however, a large number of species are now endangered. Factors such as sustained pressure on forests and resulting habitat destruction and diverse human socio-economic problems have contributed considerably to the deteriorating status of our magnificent wildlife. Fortunately, recent trends have created a keen awareness among the general public, at least in some states of India, of the need to conserve natural habitats and forest wealth and to protect our endangered wild animals. Information on the status of the population of wildlife is however necessary for the proper management of any biosphere reserve, national park or wildlife sanctuary. Some investigations on population status of some of the wild mammals in the forests of South India have been carried out by a number of investigators (Daniel 1970; Kurup 1975; Krishnan 1976; Nair 1977; Saratchandra and Gadgil 1975; Prasad *et al.* 1980). Recently, the Asian Elephant Group has estimated the population of Asiatic Elephant, *Elephas maximus* in the subcontinent (Nair *et al.* 1980; Chaudhari 1980; Singh 1980). Further, reconnaissance survey of some of the forest reserves of South India have also been made (Vijayan and Balakrishnan 1977; Vijayan 1978; Vijayan *et al.* 1979; Nair *et al.* 1977; Nair and Gadgil 1980).

No serious attempt has so far been made to assess the abundance and the distribution of larger mammals of the Parambikulam Wildlife Sanctuary which is one of the best sanctuaries in Kerala to observe and study wildlife. The avifauna of the area was surveyed by Sálim Ali (1969). The only attempt to study the mammalian fauna of Parambikulam was that of Vijayan (1978) who made a short term survey. Sugathan (1981) made casual observations on mammals of the area while conducting a survey of Frogmouths in Parambikulam-Sholayar forests. However, none of these studies could cover all the areas of the sanctuary and hence the present study was undertaken to assess the population status of larger mammals of the sanctuary.

Study Area

Parambikulam Wildlife Sanctuary is situated in Palghat District of Kerala State, India (between 76°35′ and 76°50′ E and between 10°20′ and 10°26′ N, Fig. 1). It came into existence in 1962 when an area of 69.8 km² of the Sungam Range of Nemmara Forest Division was declared as a sanctuary. Parambikulam Range of the Division of Teak Plantation was added to this in 1973. At present the area is about 235 km² at an elevation of about 600 m above sea level. The area is bound by the south westerly flowing Karapara river in the west and the same river flowing easterly in part of the south and forest clearance running through a watershed dividing between the northerly draining stream and southerly draining streams on the south. On the eastern side the boundary is purely an administrative one with forest clearance running throughout the area. The northern boundary is defined by south westerly flowing Thekkadyar up to the central part of the area and the remaining portion by a forest clearance along the water divide between northerly and southerly flowing streamlets.

This area forms a part of Western Ghats extending from Maharashtra to Cape Comorin parallel to the West coast. The only major interruption is the Palghat Gap just north of this area. Unlike in other areas the ridges here turn eastwards due to the influence of the gap. The gap is a natural boundary and there is a total break of vegetational continuity. From the gap towards south the ridges are steep culminating in the high ridges of the Nelliampathy forests. There are only two terraces, one nearer the MSL in the gap and the second, a not so well-defined, gently undulating, plateau at a higher level. From the second plane rugged ridges stretch in different geographical directions delineating minor hydrological valleys.

Peculiar features observed throughout these mountains are the non-symmetrical and non-uniform slope characteristics spread throughout the area in different directions. The dip slope has a blanket vegetation throughout the area whereas the escarpment side with different brakes of slopes exhibits different floristic and faunistic composition. The topmost level in this slope is mostly rocks followed by areas of rich soil cover and profuse vegetation. These mountain ridges have well-defined valleys confined to lower orders of streams which permit denser vegetation along them. These lines being the shortest route to the top of hill is mostly followed by the animals. The contours even within a small lateral spread do have plenty of crenulations which are not very much persistent along the slope directions. Such a feature is indicative of differential erosions in a vertical direction.

Another important feature observed in the area is the absence of valley plains. All the ridges slope straight down to streams thus avoiding the possibility of any plain land or gently undulating land except in the Parambikulam Ar where there are human settlements. The river is in its youthful stage with sinuous course of flow in north-west, west and south-west directions.

The linear trend of the ridges and draining system make the animals travel across the ridges, thus in a defined geographical direction in a limited sector of the sanctuary. The area in general has a slope towards the west. The highest peak being Karimala Gopuram, 4721 ft. (a triangulation station of Survey of India) and the lowest 1442 ft, the bank of Chalakudi Ar.

Inside the sanctuary area. three dams (Table 1) of the Parambikulam Aliyar Project were constructed in the year 1960 for the purpose of irrigation and power generation and are still under the administrative control of the Tamil Nadu State Government.

Table 1

Name of dam	Area of water	Catchment area
	Sq. km	Sq. km
1. Parambikulam	21.22	228.34
2. Thunakadavu	4.33	43.33
3. Peruvarippallam	2.89	15.79

The temperature at Parambikulam ranges from 55°F to 90°F. The average annual precipitation is 2590 mm. The area gets both the southwest and northeast monsoons. However, southwest monsoon is the more active one in this region.

The only access to the sanctuary is by road from Pollachi which is at a distance of about 48 km from Thunakavadu, the headquarters of the sanctuary. A network of roads inside the sanctuary enables visitors to go around in motor vehicles.

METHOD OF STUDY

The whole area of the Parambikulam Wildlife Sanctuary was covered on foot by us by camping at different places. A total of 500 hours spread out in October, November and December 1981 were spent by both of us in the field for collecting data on the population status of wild animals in the sanctuary. Further, one of us (P.S.E.) has been camping at Thunakadavu, the headquarters of the Parambikulam Wildlife Sanctuary throughout 1982 and the first half of 1983 collecting additional information of the population and behaviour of some of the larger mammals with special reference to their management problems.

The following details were collected for assessing the population of the larger mammals of the area. (1) The species of animals seen, (2) Time of observation, (3) Activity of the animal/troop/herd at the time of observation, (4) Number of animals in the troop/herd/pack, (5) Indirect evidences like spoor, scats, pellets, pugmarks, calls, etc., and (6) The habitat where the animals were located. Pugmarks of tiger and leopard were drawn using pugmark tracers whenever they were sighted. Herd composition and size and individual identification marks were noted down in the case of elephants and gaurs. In the case of elephant, gaur and wildboar only direct evidences were taken into consideration. Further, night drives through various forest roads enabled sightings of some of the nocturnal animals.

OBSERVATIONS

Vegetation

Both natural and man made habitats are met with in the area. The natural habitat consists of West Coast Tropical Wet Evergreen forest, West Coast Tropical Semi-evergreen forest, Southern Secondary Moist Mixed Deciduous forest, grasslands and swamps (Fig. 2). Teak and Eucalyptus plantations form the man-made habitat. Vegetation of Parambikulam is a combination of Malabar and Deccan elements (Sebastian and Ramamurthy 1966). The former occurs in the evergreen patches and the latter in moist deciduous forests. Table 2 gives the details of vegetation types of the forests.

Table 2

Type of forest	Area in km²
West Coast Tropical Wet Evergreen Forest	55
West Coast Tropical Semi-evergreen forest	20
Southern Secondary Moist Mixed Deciduous forest	65
Grasslands and swamps	2
Plantations	93

West Coast Tropical Wet Evergreen Forest is mainly confined to Karappara, Thuthampara, Pulikkal, Orukombankutty and Kariansholai. Distribution of semi-evergreen forest is restricted to the valleys in Parambikulam. Deciduous forest has a wide range of distribution in the sanctuary. It occurs mainly on the lower slopes and the ridges.

The natural forest areas available in the sanctuary are rich in bamboo and reeds (*Bambusa* and *Ochlandra* sp.) (Fig. 3).

Plantations

Parambikulam constitutes one of the best natural teak areas in Kerala. Kannimara teak in Parambikulam is the oldest natural teak tree in the world (Fig. 4). Artificial regeneration of teak was started in 1966 following clearfelling of the original vegetation. Hybrid variety of *Eucalyptus* sp. was also raised in 1962. At present about 93 km² of the sanctuary fall under plantations.

Fauna

The sanctuary harbours a good number of almost all representatives of the larger species of peninsular Indian mammals. Three endangered species have also been recorded from this area.

Primates

All the four species of the family Cercopithecidae, so far reported from Kerala, have been observed in Parambikulam Wildlife Sanctuary.

Bonnet Macaque, *Macaca radiata* (Geoffroy)

This, the commonest of South Indian monkeys, was found in plantation fringes and moist-deciduous forests. A total of 95 individuals in 8 troops were seen during the present study.

Lion-tailed Macaque *Macaca silenus* (Linnaeus)

This endemic, endangered, arboreal macaque, occurs in evergreen forest. Four troops were seen and as they were very shy they often gave no chance for a proper count. The minimum troop size located was four (Table 3). The sanctuary harbours a minimum of 24 individuals of the species. All except the troop in Shettivara Hills were in the continuous stretch of evergreen forests in Orukomban, Muthuvarachal and Chempadipara area. The species is reported to be seen in Karimalagopuram area also.

Table 3

Locations of sightings of Lion-tailed Macaque

Locality	Troop	Numbers
Shettivara hills	1	5+
Chempadi para	1	4+
Koorankuzhi	1	9+
Muthalavayali	1	6+

Nilgiri Langur, *Presbytis johni* (Fischer)

Nilgiri Langur, *Presbytis johni* is common throughout the area. A total of 206 individuals in 44 troops were seen and 9 calls were heard during the period of the study. They were found mostly in evergreen and moist-deciduous forests (Fig. 5). However, troops were also seen in teak plantations with belts of natural forests near by.

Common Langur, *Presbytis entellus* (Dufresne)

The Common Langur, *Presbytis entellus* is rare and is restricted to the border areas of Tamil Nadu. Two troops totalling 21 animals were seen.

Cats (Felids)

Of the six species of wild cats so far recorded from Kerala, only three were seen.

Tiger *Panthera tigris* (Linnaeus)

Tracings of pugmarks of 9 different tigers were drawn from various places. In addition to these, two scats were also noted in places where no pugmarks could be located because of the peculiar nature of the terrain (Table 4).

Table 4

Locations of sightings of Tiger pugmarks and scats

Location	Pugmarks	Scats
Seechalippallam	1	1
Kannimara	1	–
Parambikulam tunnel entry	–	1
Thottiali malai	1	1
Kazhutha ketti thekku	1	–
Kuriarkutty	1	–
Muthalvayali	–	1
Parambikulam earthen dam	1	–
Kalyanakuda	1	–
Thoothampara	2	–

Leopard *Panthera pardus* (Linnaeus)

Sightings of panthers have been reported by tourists on various occasions. Two panthers with a cub were seen by the AWLPO in Padipara and one was reported to be usually seen in Parambikulam. During the survey, three pugmarks and two scats were recorded (Table 5).

Table 5

Locations of evidence of Panthers

Locations	Pugmarks	Scats
Kannimarateak road	1	–
Kariansholai	–	1
Parambikulam tunnel entry	–	1
Sungam colony	1	–
Pandaravara malai	1	–

Jungle cat, *Felis chaus* (Guldenstaedt)

Only one individual of the species was seen, sitting at night, on a tree in Muthuvarachal evergreen forest area. Indirect evidence also indicates that the species is rare in the sanctuary.

Civets

Of the four species of civets reported from Kerala, only two were seen.

Small Indian Civet *Viverricula indica* (Desmarest)

The species seems to be not common in the area. Two of them were seen at dusk and two during a night drive through the forest roads. Two droppings and two foot prints were also recorded.

Toddy Cat, *Paradoxurus hermaphroditus* (Pallas)

Occurrence of this species was recorded from indirect evidences only. A total of 14 droppings at various places in the sanctuary were recorded.

Mongooses

Of the four species occurring in Kerala, only one was seen during this study.

Ruddy Mongoose, *Herpestes smithi* (Gray)

Only three individuals of this species were seen during the study. Their number seems to be less in the reserve.

Canids

Only one of the three species recorded from Kerala was noted in the sanctuary.

Indian Wild Dog, *Cuon alpinus* (Pallas)

A pack of four Dholes was seen during the survey, feeding on a sambar doe in Thellickal area. Seven droppings and three pugmarks were also noted. Though the number of this species was said to be high in the area, they were rarely seen. Further, reports of animal kills were also rare.

Sloth Bear, *Melursus ursinus* (Shaw)

Three individuals of the species were seen near Thellickal area. A total of 87 droppings, 5 foot prints and 9 diggings were recorded.

Mustelids

The Mustelids is represented by *Lutra* sp. The lake in Thunakadavu harbours a good population of the species. Otters moving around with fishes in their mouth is a common sight here. Two packs with a total number of 13 were seen.

Larger Rodents

Giant Squirrel, *Ratufa indica* (Erxleben)

Only 20 individuals of the species were seen during the present survey. Further, 8 calls were also heard during this study period. They were noted only in the natural forests.

Indian Porcupine, *Hystrix indica* (Kerr)

Only one was seen near Kannimara teak area during a night drive. Twenty nine droppings and twenty three diggings were also recorded.

Proboscids

Indian Elephant, *Elephas maximus* (Linnaeus)

Fourteen herds with a total of 90 individuals including lone ones were seen during the survey. The largest herd seen was of eleven elephants. Herds of larger numbers after the joining of two herds were also seen occasionally. Splitting of herds was also noted during continuous observation. Table 6 shows the sex ratio of the herds seen in the sanctuary. No makhnas (male elephants without tusks) could be located during the study. Tuskers have been seen rarely with the herd (Fig. 6 and 7). Natural death of an adult cow and a baby elephant were recorded during the study period.

Table 6

Sex and age class	Number of individuals seen	Percentage
Adult tuskers	32	36
Juvenile tuskers	6	7
Adult cows	38	42
Juvenile cows	2	2
Babies	12	13
Total	90	100

Bovids

Two species of this family have been noted in the area.

Gaur, *Bos gaurus* H. Smith

The sanctuary is famous for this species as a drive through the sanctuary roads enables one to see herds of them. During this survey a total of 20 herds with a population of 157 were seen. Seven lone bulls were also recorded. It was not possible always to note down the herd composition. However, almost all herds were having calves. Two natural deaths were reported during the period.

Nilgiri Tahr, *Hemitragus hylocrius* (Ogliby)

The Vengoli Hills harbour a herd of this endemic, endangered species. The herd at present consists of seventeen heads.

Cervids

The most common deer in the sanctuary is the sambar, *Cervus unicolor* (Fig. 8). During the survey a total of 78 individuals of the species were seen of which 20 were stags, 52 does and 6 fawns. The highest number in a herd was eight. In addition to these, five calls, pellets at 48 places and hoof marks at 32 places were also recorded.

Chital, *Axis axis* (Erxleben)

Chitals were found to be confined to the areas bordering Tamil Nadu. They were seen in Padipara, Thellickal, Sungam, Anappady and Seechali areas. A total of 48 in five troops were seen which comprised of 14 stags, 28 does and 6 fawns. Call of one herd was also recorded.

Muntjak (Barking Deer), *Muntiacus muntjak* (Zimmermann)

Only three, all does. Two calls, two groups of pellets and two hoof marks were also recorded from various places. The animals sighted were solitary.

Tragulids

Only two of this small deer, the Indian Chevrotain, *Tragulus meminna* (Erxleben) were recorded from the sanctuary. Seven hoof marks and one pellet group were also recorded from different localities.

Indian Wild Boar, *Sus scrofa* (Linnaeus)

A total of 46 were seen in six sounders. Though the species is said to be very common in the sanctuary, their presence was not even noted in many places. They are however common in Anappady, Thellickal and Parambikulam areas.

Indian Pangolin, *Manis crassicaudata* (Gray)

Two burrows of this specialised mammal were located inside the sanctuary.

In addition to these large and medium sized mammals, two reptile species worth mentioning are the Mugger *Crocodylus palustris* and the Monitor lizard *Varanus*. The reservoir in Parambikulam contains a good population of crocodiles. *Varanus* was seen in plantation fringed and moist-deciduous forests (Fig. 9). A total of ten were seen during the present survey.

Management Problems of the Sanctuary

Cattle grazing

Herds of cattle have become a common sight in the sanctuary. The residents in Parambikulam Aliyar Project Colony, the settlers in Thunakadavu and the taungya cultivators along the border own most of the cattle concerned. They are often allowed to go deep inside the sanctuary and graze. Cattle were even seen grazing along with sambar, elephant and guar in Thellickal Vayal. They are also driven to the sanctuary, through Anappady, from Tamil Nadu area. The number of cattle inside the sanctuary was estimated to be around 200.

Estates

Estates and other private holdings are located mostly on the north western border of the sanctuary. In addition to this, teak plantations in vested forest areas have been given for taungya cultivation (i.e. short term cultivation of tapioca, paddy, etc., prior to raising of plantation trees). An area of about 70 hectares near Kuriarkutty was under taungya in the beginning of 1982. About 50 persons per day worked in this taungya camp for about three months. Another, 15 persons permanently lived in the area. The disturbance to wildlife from these plantations and estates was numerous. Crackers were used in taungya cultivations to scare wild animals. The estate people were also using snares and other traps for smaller mammals. Moreover, the movement of labourers through the sanctuary often disturbs the free movement of wildlife in areas such as Thekkady, in this sanctuary.

Plantations

About 42 hectares of Teak plantations near

Seechali and adjacent areas in this sanctuary have been clearfelled in 1982 (Fig. 10). The bridge connecting the two sides of the canal from Thunakadavu to Sarkarapathy falls within the clearfelled area. This area was frequently used by wild animals for crossing the deep canal. The disturbance to wildlife due to the labourers staying in Anappadi area and the work done prevents the free movement of wildlife in this area.

Stray dogs

Stray dogs are a real menace to the wildlife in Parambikulam, Thunakádavu and Sungam. They were once seen chasing a sambar deer up to the reservoir. Action is said to be taken for removing these dogs but there was no evidence of it being effective.

Bamboo extraction

Bamboo is extracted on a large scale for pulp production in the Gwalior Rayons factory, Mavoor, Calicut. About 1,25,000 pieces of bamboos (about 40,000 numbers) were transported in 1982 from Parambikulam Range of the Nemmara Forest Division as per the records of the Forest Department. The prescribed scientific methods of extraction have not been followed in the sanctuary. Moreover, the labourers staying in sheds right inside the sanctuary and plying of a number of lorries for transportation of bamboos disturb the habitat and wildlife seriously.

Forest Fire

Seasonal occurrence of forest fire is common during the months of January to April (Fig. 11). Since the area of grassland is small and the distribution patchy, fire occurs mainly in plantation. Forest edges in the evergreen forests in Muthalavayali and nearby areas have been found to be seriously affected by fire.

The Proposed Kuriarkutty – Karapara Multipurpose Project

The Kuraiarkutty-Karappara multipurpose project jointly proposed by the Kerala State Electricity Board and the Irrigation Department of Kerala contemplates the development of 95 MW of power and irrigation of about 11,736 ha of land using the tail waters from Kuriarkutty power house. This project will have three reservoirs submerging about 265 ha of reserve forests, 600 ha of vested forests and 345 ha of teak plantation (Fig. 12). Further, the approach roads from Nemmara to the power house at Kuriarkutty and dam site at Thellickal are also planned. The Project is proposed to be completed in five years.*

Discussion

Twenty four species of large and medium sized mammals have been recorded during the present survey. Vijayan (1978) has recorded *Herpstes edwardsi* also from the area. An analysis of the herd composition of elephants in the sanctuary shows a satisfactory male-female sex ratio. The distribution of animals in man-made and natural forests were similar. But this could be attributed to the belt of natural forests around plantations.

Seasonal fires have been reported to be advantageous to herbivores under some condition as they allow the sprouting of grasses with improved palatability and nutritional value. The young shoots are richer in protein and soluble carbohydrates than the dead grass (Lemon 1968). Skovlin (1972) reported that different species of grasses have different reactions to the same burning treatment. Further, he has also mentioned the possibility of

* Brief Report on Advance Action Schemes and Schemes under active investigations — Kerala State Electricity Board Publication.

geographical variation in the effect of fire on the basis of detailed experiments in parts of Kenya. Fire in forest edges prevents regeneration of tree species and kill the species which are not resistant to fire. Studies of Spinage and Guinness (1972) have shown that fire diminished the ability of an area to support large mammals owing to the selective pressure over a long period towards more fire resistant grasses which are less palatable to grazers than the vegetation that would develop in the absence of fire. However, no detailed and systematic study on this topic has so far been made in any forest in India and hence a study of this sort would be helpful for a proper management and control of fire in the Indian context. Rotational burning which establishes a mosaic of burnt and unburnt grassland during the dry season can be tried in the sanctuary.

Soil erosion is an acute problem in taungya plantations. Loss of top soil has resulted due to the lack of soil conservation measures for tuberous/rhizomatous crops. Taungya causes changes in sand, silt and clay contents, pH, organic carbon and cation exchange capacity of the soil (Alexander *et al.* 1980).

Deterioration of natural resources and allied problems arising from the unwise use of the water resources of the rivers of the Western Ghats have already been discussed in detail by Gadgil (1979). The Kuriarkutty-Karappara Project, if implemented, will affect the wildlife of this sanctuary severely. The Kuriarkutty reservoir will submerge a portion of teak plantations and moist-deciduous forests. A large portion of the existing evergreen forests of the area will be submerged by the formation of the Pulickal and Karappara reservoirs. Our studies have shown that one of the proposed dam sites, Thellickal has the highest concentration of large and medium sized mammals in this sanctuary. Moreover, Thellickal has a number of swamps where elephants, gaur and deer species are seen in large numbers. Local migration of animals from Anamalai Wildlife Sanctuary of Tamil Nadu to the Parambikulam Wildlife Sanctuary have been observed during the dry season and the route followed by them falls within the area of submergence of the proposed project. Further, the population of primates in the evergreen forests will also be affected by this project.

It is true that this project plans to bring about 11,736 ha of land under irrigation. This includes conversion of 7,236 ha from dry to wet crops, namely paddy and sugarcane, stabilisation of existing 100 ha of double crop paddy and conversion of 2,000 ha of single crop paddy fields to double crop. An increased production of about 62,200 tonnes of paddy and 2,11,300 tonnes of sugarcane has been anticipated by the implementation of this project. At the same time, there will be a loss of production of 18,100 tonnes of ground nut and 5,400 tonnes of cotton annually due to the change of land use. This will affect the 370 handloom weaving centres and the newly started cotton spinning mill in Chittur Taluk of the Palghat District.

So far, no subsurface exploration of the area to be benefitted by this project has been made. At present, about 900 ha of sugarcane fields have been irrigated by well water in the Chittur Taluk. Further, about 2,500 Mc. ft of water is made available from the Parambikulam-Aliyar Project to the area that may be benefitted by the proposed Kuriarkutty-Karappara Project as per an interstate agreement between Kerala and Tamil Nadu. It may be further advantageous for the area to tap the ground water resources rather than the proposed project, especially from the ecological and socio-economic points of view.

The motor vehicles plying through forest roads for transport of extracted bamboos and teak poles have been disturbing the free movement of the animals. Further, blowing of horns was also noticed even inside the core area during the present study. This type of noise interferes with communication of the animal and thus disturb their free life in their natural habitat (Shaw 1978).

The possibility of spread of diseases such as foot and mouth disease and rinderpest due to the cattle inside the sanctuary cannot be ruled out. Outbreak of such disease in Periyar Tiger Reserve in Kerala and Bandipur in Karnataka severely affected the gaur population during the seventies.

Though it is uneconomic to leave the plantations as a whole without extraction; this should not be permitted within the sanctuary owing to the damage that the extraction activities would cause to the wildlife. This would reduce the human interference in the sanctuary to a considerable extent and thus improve the quality of the sanctuary. Further, this will result in a better propagation of the population of various species of wildlife in this sanctuary where they can be really protected and scientifically managed for long-term benefits.

ACKNOWLEDGEMENTS

We are indebted to Dr. K. M. Alexander, Professor and Head of the Department of Zoology, University of Kerala for constant encouragement during the period of this study Dr Kenneth R. Ashby, Department of Zoology, University of Durham, U.K., and Dr P. T. Roy Chacko, Department of Geology, University of Kerala have critically read the manuscript. The suggestions of Mr J. C. Daniel, Curator, Bombay Natural History Society for improvement of the presentation of this paper are gratefully acknowledged. We are also grateful to the Chief Conservator of Forests (Wildlife), Government of Kerala, for granting permission to work in the sanctuary. Thanks are also due to the Wildlife Preservation Officer and the Assistant Wildlife Preservation Officer, Parambikulam Wildlife Sanctuary, for their timely assistance in diverse ways without which this study would not have been completed successfully. Mr. O. Jayarajan, AWLPO and a number of field staff of the sanctuary have been assisting us for field work and related activities ever since this work was initiated.

We are also thankful to the University Grants Commission, New Delhi, for financial assistance. P.S.E. was supported by a Junior Research Fellowship of the University of Kerala.

REFERENCES

ALEXANDER, T. G., SOBHANA, K., BALAGOPALAN, M. & MARY, M. V. (1980): Taungya in relation to soil properties, soil erosion and soil management. Kerala Forest Research Institute Report: *4*.

ALI, SALIM (1969): Birds of Kerala, Oxford University Press, Madras.

CHANDRASEKARAN, K. P., MOHAMMED, M. & ANANTHA SUBRAMONIAN, A. S. (1977): The first working plan for the Nemmara Forest Division (1969-70 to 1983-84), Kerala Forest Department.

CHAUDHARI, D. K. L. (1980): An interim report on the status and distribution of elephants (*Elephas maximus*) in North East India. In *The Status of Asian Elephant in the Indian Sub-Continent* IVCN/SSC Report pp. 43-58.

DANIEL, J. C. (1970): The Nilgiri Tahr, *Hemitragus hylocrius* (Ogliby) in the High Range in Kerala and the Southern hills of Western Ghats. *J. Bombay nat. Hist. Soc. 67*: 535-543.

GADGIL, M. (1979): Hills, dams and forests. Some

field observations from the Western Ghats. *Proc. Indian Acad. Sci., C2,* 291-303.

KRISHNAN, M. (1976): India's Wildlife in 1959-1970. Bombay Natural History Society, Bombay.

KURUP, G. U. (1975): Status of the Nilgiri Langur, *Presbytis johni* in the Anamalai, Cardamom and Nilgiri hills of the Western Ghats, India. *J. Bombay nat. Hist. Soc. 72*: 21-29.

LEMON, P. C. (1968): Fire and Wildlife grazing on an African Plateau. *Proc. Tall Timbers Fire Ecol. Conf. 8,* 71-88.

NAIR, S. S., NAIR, P. V. K., SHARATCHANDRA, H. C. & GADGIL, M. (1977): An Ecological reconnaissance of the proposed Jawahar National Park. *J. Bombay nat. Hist. Soc. 74*: 401-435.

NAIR, P. V. K. & GADGIL, M. (1980): The status and distribution of elephant population of Karnataka. ibid. *75*: 1000-1016.

NAIR, P. V. K., SUKUMAR, R. & GADGIL, M. (1980): The Elephant in South India — A review. In *The Status of Asian Elephant in the Indian Subcontinent* IUCN/SSC Report pp. 9-20.

NAIR, S. S. (1977): A Population survey and observations on behaviour of the blackbuck in the Point Calimere Sanctuary, Tamil Nadu, *J. Bombay, nat. Hist. Soc. 73*: 305-310.

PRASAD, S. N., NAIR, P. V. K., SHARATCHANDRA, H. C. & GADGIL, M. (1980): On factors governing the distribution of wild mammals in Karnataka. ibid. *75*: 718-743.

SHARATCHANDRA, H. C. & GADGIL, M. (1975): A Year of Bandipur. ibid. 72: 623-647.

SAHI, S. F. (1980): Report of the Asian Elephant Specialist Group, Central India Task Force. In *The Status of the Asian Elephant in the Indian subcontinent.* IUCN/SSC Report pp. 35-42.

SEBASTINE, K. M. & RAMAMURTHY, K. (1966): Studies on the flora of Parambikulam and Aliyar Submergible areas. *Bull. Bot. Sur. India, 8*: 169-182.

SHAW, E. A. G. (1978): Symposium on the effects of noise on wildlife *in* Effects of noise on wildlife. Academic Press, New York.

SINGH, V. B. (1980): Elephant in N. W. India (Uttar Pradesh). In *The Status of the Asian Elephant in the Indian subcontinent.* IUCN/SSC Report pp. 59-60.

SKOVLIN, J. M. (1972): The influence of fire on important range grasses of East Africa. *Proc. Tall Timbers. Fire Ecol. Conf. 11*: 201-217.

SPINAGE, C. A. & GUINNESS, F. E. (1972): Effects of fire in the Akagera National Park and Mutara Hunting Reserve, Rwanda. *Rev. Zool. Bot. Afr., 86*: 302-336.

SUGATHAN, R. (1981): A Survey of Ceylon Frogmouth (*Batrachostomus moniliger*) habitat in the Western Ghats of India. *J. Bombay nat. Hist. Soc. 78*: 309-315.

VIJAYAN, V. S. (1978): Parambikulam Wildlife Sanctuary and its adjacent areas. ibid. *75*: 888-900.

——————— & BALAKRISHNAN, M. (1977): Impact of hydroelectric project on Wildlife. Report of the first phase of study. Kerala Forest Research Institute, pp. I-III.

———————, BALAKRISHNAN, M. & Easa, P. S. (1979): Periyar Tiger Reserve — a reconnaissance Report. Kerala Forest Research Institute, pp. 1-171.

Above: The grasslands and swamps form the major feeding ground of most of the herbivores in the area.

Below: Bamboos near stream banks is a rare sight now in Kerala, as these have been extracted on a large scale for use as raw materials in the Mavoor Gwalior Rayons Factory, Calicut.

Above: The small patches of natural forests left in the plantation area have a major concentration of foraging animals. Here, a herd of elephants drinking and foraging in the water hole.

Below: Sambar deer, the common deer of this sanctuary, in a man-made forest.

Above: Showing clear-felling of forests in the Sanctuary which makes problems for movement of animals in the Sanctuary.

Below: Forest fire during the months of January to April is seen in all parts of forests including the forest plantations in Kerala. This eats away all the undergrowth and cover in addition to the large scale damage it has been causing to the timber species.

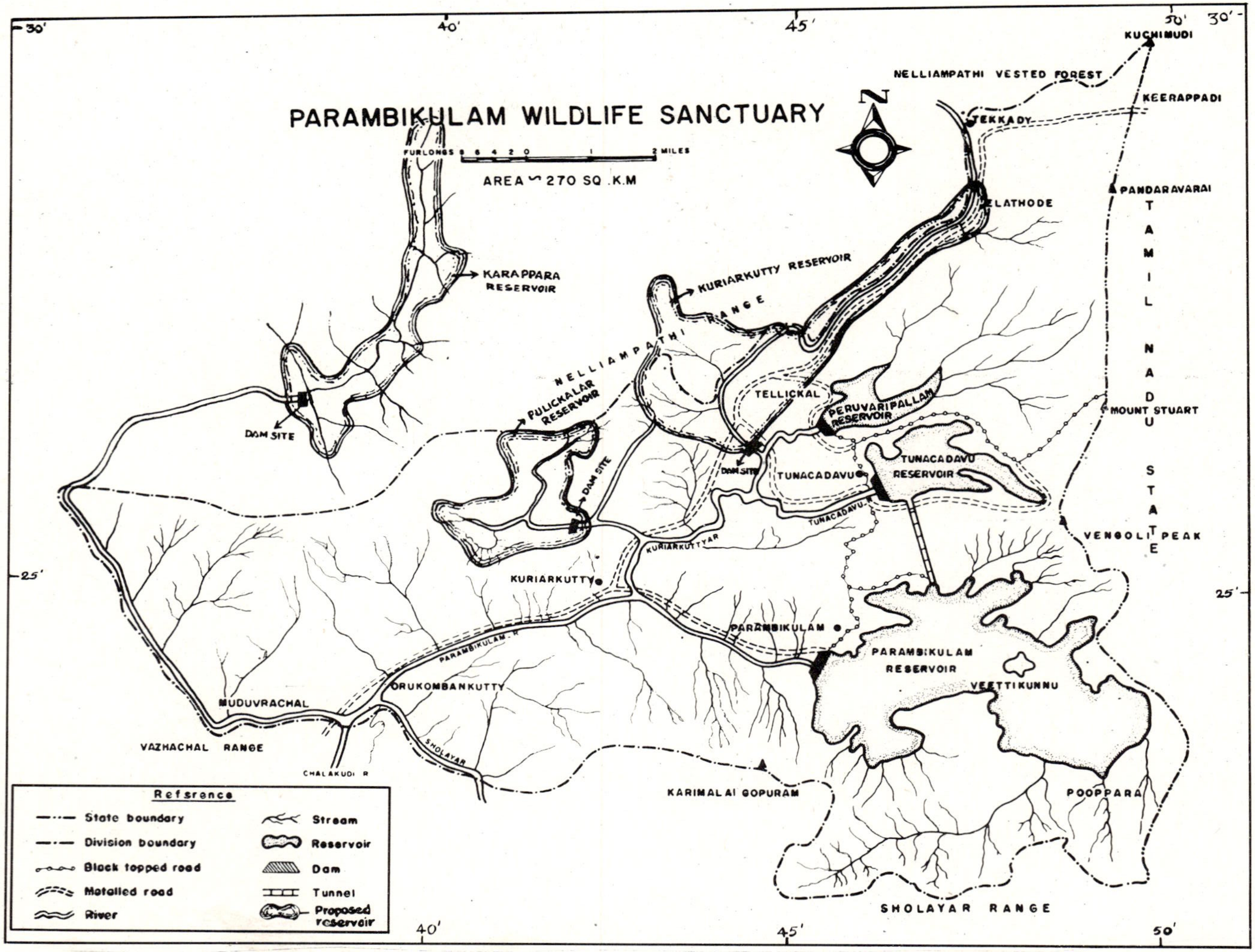

Map showing the existing and proposed reservoirs in the Parambikulam Wildlife Sanctuary.

The Ecology of the *Maldhari* Graziers in the Gir Forest, India

(*With three text-figures*)

Marianne Berwick[1]

The Gir Forest of Gujarat, India, is 1200 sq. km in area, and 200 air miles northwest of Bombay, at the tip of the Saurashtra Peninsula. It is the last remaining natural sanctuary for the Asiatic lion (*Panthera leo persica*). The cattle owners of the area known as *Maldharis* are in direct competition with the lion for territory and in indirect competition for food resources. They have been part of the Gir ecosystem for at least 125 years (Solanki 1970). It is only within the last 75 years (Santapau and Raizada 1956) that the Gir ecosystem had begun an accelerated decline — in 1900 it was about twice its present size — due to an entire complex of factors, only one of which is the *Maldharis* and their buffalo.

By 1981, at least 70 percent of the *Maldhari* population was resettled in 21 locations outside the Gir (Rashid 1981). It is the purpose of this paper to discuss the ecology of the *Maldhari* community as it functioned in 1970 in the Gir ecosystem and to extend these results to hypothesize as the current condition of the Gir Forest since the resettlement. The methods and concepts of animal ecology were applied to the general framework of this study of the ecology of the *Maldharis*. The methodology integrated well with other ecosystem studies being carried out at the Gir Forest: the behaviour and ecology of the lion, Joslin 1968-71; the impact of domestic stock on the vegetation and soil of the Gir Forest, Hodd, 1968-70; the feeding niches and limiting factors of six species of wild ungulates, Berwick 1969-71; and the ecology of the vultures, Grubh 1970-72. This approach has been incorporated into other human ecology studies (Lee 1966; Parrack 1969; Rappaport 1969; Van Arsdale 1978) and is now being applied in studies at the Wildlife Institute of India in Dehra Dun (Berwick and Saharia 1984).

Rationale

A study of the human inhabitants of the Gir Forest was seen as important in 1970 as the Government intended to start a resettlement scheme soon and little was known about the *Maldhari*'s place in the ecosystem, the extent of his direct competition with other wild species for food and territory or the indirect competition of his buffalo, cattle, and lifestyle with the wildland resources. Little reliable data were available. Of the many human groups interacting with the ecosystem — the *Maldharis*, the Forestry Department, the shikaris, the cooperative societies of forest workers, the grass cutters, the villagers on the periphery (including the Harijans), the religious pilgrims, and the three Negro villages — the *Maldharis* were chosen for study because they seemed at that time to be in most direct conflict with the lion for resources, and they seemed to be the human group most intimately part of the ecosystem.

Hypothesis

The hypothesis of our studies was that the

[1]Yale University School of Medicine, Department of Epidemiology and Public Health, 60 College Street, New Haven, CT 06510, USA

Maldharis (although participating in a market economy), like any free-living wildlife population, would show up in statistical indices as living close to the margins of survival; that they would reflect the condition of the environment in their population dynamics and in their energy utilization patterns, and that they would show the magnitude of the existing and potential human impact on the ecosystem.

STUDY OBJECTIVES

The objectives of this study were to quantify the impact of the *Maldhari* on the ecosystem and to quantify their utilization of energy within the forest ecosystem. Toward this end it was necessary to obtain basic demographic statistics, energy consumption and utilization patterns, and to identify forest use patterns. The Gir Project was formed as a joint venture of the Smithsonian Institution, the Bombay Natural History Society, and Yale University. It has also received support from the World Wildlife Fund and the National Science Foundation.

METHODS

Study design. The investigation of the *Maldharis* was divided into several phases:

(1) The collection of basic demographic data such as population size, density, sex ratio, mortality, natality, and migration. These data were necessary to get some idea of the growth rate and limiting factors of the population and to begin to quantify the extent of its effect on the forest.

(2) Utilization of the forest resources, including flora, soil, water, and territory, and

(3) Quantification of energy flow, to elucidate the *Maldharis'* place in the energy balance of the ecosystem and to assess the nutritional plane of the population.

A sample area of approximately 100 sq. km. was chosen to study as the Government planned to relocate the *Maldharis* within its perimeter; this area is now contiguous to the *sanctum sanctorum* of the National Park which is now 259 sq. km (Rashid 1981).

Data collection. Census information was collected during three separate visits to each *ness* within the sample area. (A *ness* is a small group of mud and twig huts surrounded by thorn fencing to keep predators out.) An interpreter was used to facilitate my Gujarati. The first set of visits in the winter season were introductory. During the second set of visits, prior to the monsoon, we conducted the actual first census, stopping at the house of the headman of each *ness* and enumerating each *ness* household. If information was incomplete, we then went to the household itself for clarification. The third set of visits, six months later, were conducted to gain additional information on births, deaths, migration, history, and health habits of the population. Mia Kuwa, a *ness* run by a religious group and a very significant part of the ecosystem, was not included in demographic analysis as it was composed of one family and five men who grazed 275 animals. For comparative purposes, Bhojde village, a permanent settlement village on the outskirts of the Sanctuary, was censused in the same way as the *Maldharis* in June 1971. Basic census data (sex, age, number of children, health history) were obtained. Life tables were constructed from these data to give insight into population parameters such as mean expectation of life at birth, crude birth and death rates, sex ratios, and survivorship curves. Natality data were obtained from interviews in 1970.

Utilization of Forest resources. A comprehensive list of plant uses was obtained by questionnaire (after Pinto) and observation (Table 3). Where possible, such as in soil and dung removal, measurements were made. Other data came from direct observation.

Energy flow. Detailed methods for obtaining energy flow data are described in another paper (Berwick 1984). Basically, dietary patterns were established through the 24-hour recall method. Detailed quantified data on diet were obtained by measurement of intake for three *Maldharis* of different sex and age combinations by weighing food over a 24-hour period. Activities during that period were noted and timed to the second.

RESULTS

POPULATION

Density. Table 1 indicates the number of nesses and changes in population within the 100 sq. km area from April 1970 to March 1971. Traditionally, the *Maldharis* move about the forest from ness to ness in search of better habitat for their buffalo. These data indicate that the ness is not a cohesive unit as it often fragments and does not move en masse to a new site. This pattern suggests an incohesive social structure which has implications for resettlement: that it may be easier to deal with individual Maldharis rather than the group.

The *nesses* seem to consolidate in the summer and during the monsoon, and to disperse during the winter, when the grasses and water are abundant throughout the preserve. Table 1 also shows that most *nesses* are small, the average *ness* consisting of seven houses. While *ness* size may be related to kinship, the size is necessarily small during the hot, dry season when food and water become limited. Approximately six people live in each house in a *ness*. These are extended families, consisting of the mother, father, children, and often grandparents and siblings of the mother, father, or their children.

The crude density of the *Maldharis* was 7 persons per sq. km, or one *ness* per 9 sq. km. These desnsities seem extremely low in relation to the average densities of 131 persons per sq. km in the State of Gujarat (Govt. India 1968); however, ecologic density is the limiting factor. Ecologic density is the population per sq. km of usable habitat and can be considered the "human carrying capacity" of an area. According to Berwick (1976), the Gir Sanctuary can maintain 21,816 cattle and buffalo at proper use levels (carrying capacity). In 1971 there were 25,292 cattle and buffalo using the Sanctuary, not including a nearly equal number of seasonal "outside" animals. Sinha (1967) suggested that at least 30 head of cattle and buffalo are necessary to produce the ghee and other products necessary to support a *Maldhari* household. At that rate the carrying capacity of the Sanctuary in terms of households would be 727 households, rather than the present 1105. Thus, the optimum ecologic density for *Maldharis*, with 30 head of cattle and buffalo per household, would be 4421 persons, or 3.790 persons per sq. km rather than the 7 persons per sq. km seen in 1970. Using Rashid's figures from 1981, I estimate that the *Maldhari* density was reduced to 1.12 sq. km by resettlement, well within the carrying capacity of the Sanctuary.

Age Structure. A basic demographic description can yield a great deal of information about the health of a population at one point in time. Crude mortality, fertility, and sex ratios can be inferred from life tables constructed from such data. Figure 1, an age structure pyramid of the *Maldhari* population, shows a typical young, expanding population. The noticable dips in the pyramid will modify the rate of population growth. From interviews it appears that there were major smallpox epidemics between 1945

TABLE 1
NESS SIZE AND MOVEMENT DURING 1970

Ness Name	April 1970 Present	June 1970 Tot. pop.	Hs.	November 1970 Tot. pop.	March 1971[1] Tot. pop.
1. Vakidas	x	20	3	20	not mentioned
2. Keriawala	x	20	3	20	20
3. Pichdibella	x	24	4	27	28
4. Patisla	x	25	5	29	23
5. Kankai	x	28	5	11	7
6. Kapuria	x	30	5	30	34
7. Wadrungala	x	29	5	23	19
8. Nima	x	41	7	21	10
9. Sapodela	x	42	7	24	uninhabited
10. Chodia	x	45	7	34	not mentioned
11. Kathita	x	47	6	22	4
12. Nana Gola	x	47	9	39	33
13. Junvania	x	50	7	28	42
14. Keramdadee	x	49	7	59	122
15. Kisa	x	53	10	39	60
16. Wadasli	x	60	10	49	61
17. Patriala	x	79	12	80	101
18. Panwallo Gun	x	moved to Sapodela		24	not mentioned
19. Khakrawadi (Kanta)	x	moved to Junvania and Sapodela		31	68
20. Phuvatirath	x	82	15	63	91
21. Kamleshwar	x	moved to Nannava, Sasan, Dalkania and Kathitar		0	22
22. Umervidee	x	moved to Bhuvatirath		0	uninhabited
23. Ravta	x	moved to Nana Gola and Sapodela		0	49
24. Kanta	x	moved to Kisa		11	not mentioned
25. Langagali	x	moved to Nima		0	not mentioned
26. Kodyar	x	moved to Kankai		0	uninhabited
27. Parmi	x	moved to Bhilgala		0	not mentioned
Totals: 28 nesses	25 nesses	18 nesses 771 people		684 people	794 people
Average ness size: 7 houses		Average household size:		6.08 people	

[1]Official Gujarat State Census figures for 1971.

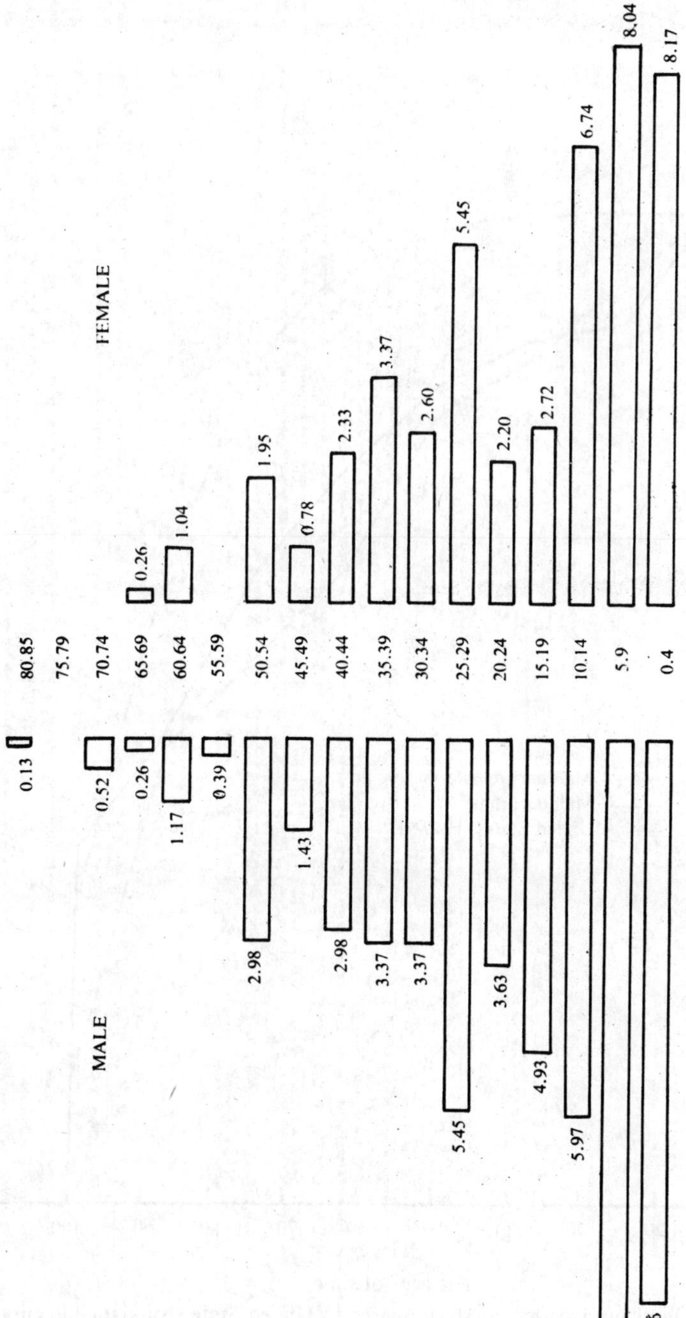

Fig. 1. The structures of the Maldhari census population, June 1970 (total 771)*
***Figures given percentage of total**

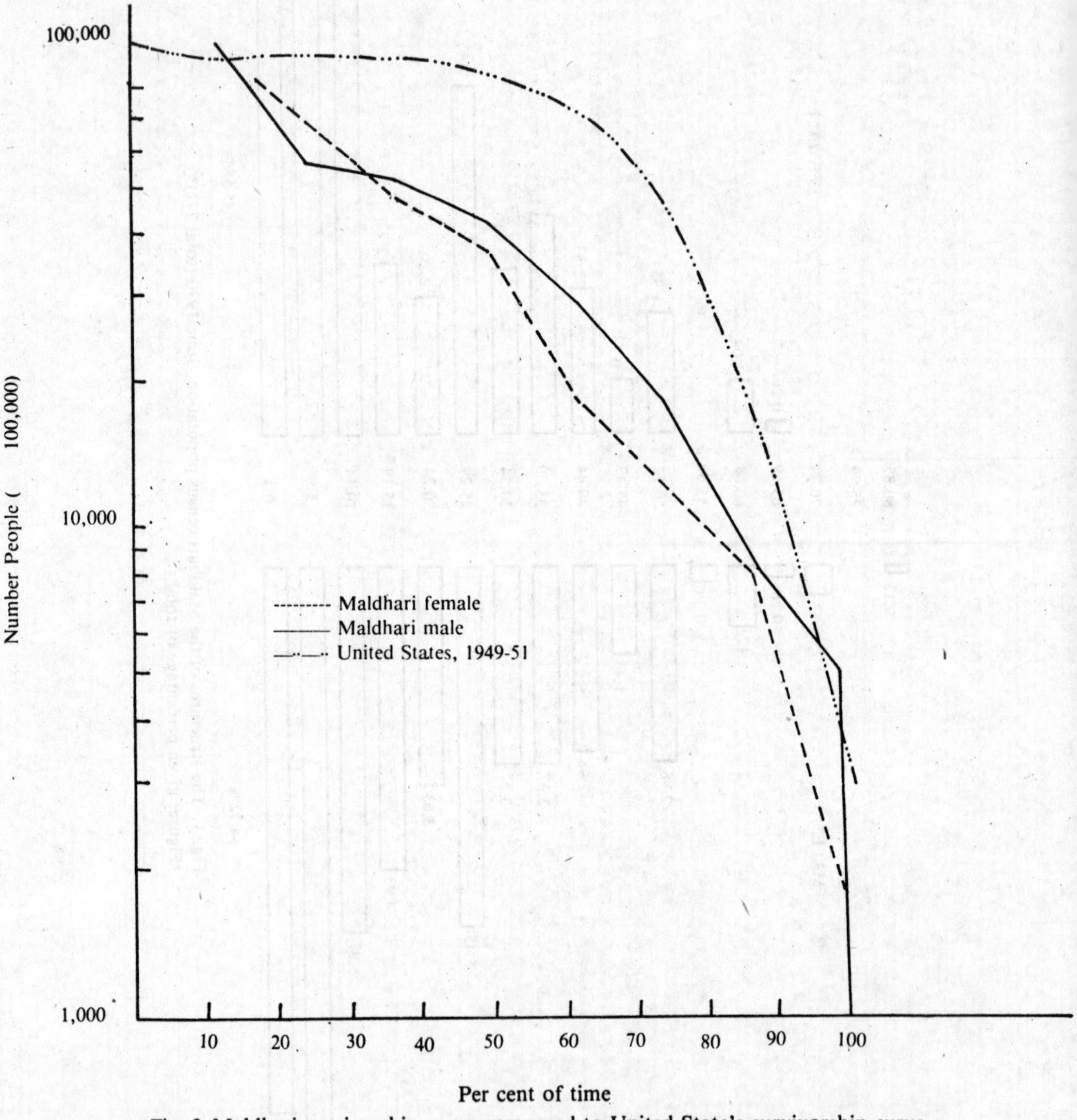

Fig. 2 Maldhari survivorship curve compared to United State's survivorship curve

and 1950 and between 1920 and 1925. In addition, there was major flooding in Gujarat in 1945 and a major drought in 1948 (Trewartha and Gosal 1957). These catastrophes might account for the low numbers of *Maldharis* in the 20-24 year and 45-49 year age classes. Life expectancy at birth for *Maldharis* was 24 years, similar to the figure for India at the turn of the century. Crude birth rate was 40 per 1000, similar to India's at that time.

Sex ratio. Table 2 compares the sex ratio at different ages for *Maldharis,* Bhojde villagers, and all-India. While a high sex ratio in India is probably due to "culturally and socially conditioned selective female mortality rates at infancy and the reproductive age groups" (Chandrasekhar 1967), that of the *Maldharis* is exceptionally high. A high sex ratio at birth was also found in the Punjab by Wyon and Gordon (1962). They suggested differential *in utero* mortality as a possible cause. Similar situations occur among wildlife populations.

TABLE 2

SEX RATIOS OF *MALDHARIS,* PHOJDE VILLAGERS, AND ALL-INDIA (MALES/100 FEMALES).[1]

Age class	Maldharis	Phojde villagers	All-India
0-14 years	96.87	105.59	105.68
15-24 years	132.5	92.06	98.97
25-40 years	108.54	85.71	107.50
40-00 years	156.52	100.41	110.49
Total	116.05	101.25	106.27

[1]All-India sex ratios derived from Table 9, India: A Reference Annual 1968, Govt. India.

Seasonality of conception. February was the peak month for conceptions resulting in live births. A distinct seasonality was noted, but with 17 births reported, the sample size is clearly too low to use with any rigour. It should be pointed out, however, that wildlife reproduction is seasonal to take advantage of optimal environmental conditions at birth.

Mortality. Figure 2 is a survivorship curve comparing the *Maldhari* population with the United States population of 1949-51. This type of curve is often calculated for wildlife populations and can indicate the type of mortality experienced by the population. Most human curves, as in the United States, are convex "in which the population mortality rate is low until near the end of the life span" (Quick 1963). Many primitive people also exhibit this type of curve in which the highest mortality is experienced in very young and old age. The *Maldharis* and the Bhojde villagers, however, exhibit survivorship curves more similar to populations such as the Tsembaga Maring (Rappaport 1968) — a stairstep type of survivorship curve which occurs when survival differs greatly in successive life history stages. In the case of the *Maldhari* female the steepest drops in survivors occur at ages 20-29 and 40-49, two important life history stages for women — childbearing and menopause. Both male populations show sharp declines during the early stages of their lives, having more stable adulthoods, more similar to other human populations, and sharp declines at the end of their lifespan. The crude death rate for *Maldharis* appeared to be 27 per 1000 while India's in 1960 was 23 per 1000. Caution must be exercised in interpreting these data as the population is not large, and wide fluctuations might not be picked up adequately in a two-year study. A major assumption of the life table analyses is that the population is stable. Planned follow-up studies will help clarify the population dynamics of the *Maldhari*. On the whole, these population parameters indicate a population living at the margin of its resources. It is likely that these parameters, if measured today, after the Government resettlement programme, would be much different. If the programme were successful, one would expect to still see a young age structure; however, there would likely be a more even distribution of the population with fewer dips indicating more resistance to environmental insult. We would also hope and expect to see a more even sex ratio, lower infant mortality, longer life expectancy at birth, and less seasonality of birth patterns.

FOREST UTILIZATION

The *Maldharis'* most obvious use of the forest was as a supply of buffalo fodder. During the hot, dry summer months the *Maldhari* buffalo grazed the dry stems of grass which contain 1-2 percent protein (Berwick 1976); while the herdsmen "lopped" green browse, such as *Acacia* and *Diospyros,* which has far more nutritive value, about 10 percent protein. During the monsoon the buffalo can subsist rather well on the green grass and probably rely on this growth, which they are inhibiting by grazing at critical growth stages until the hot, dry season. Furthermore, Hodd (1970) found that the decrement in optimal growth of certain preferred grasses fostered the growth of certain creeping annual grasses which were less palatable. A further negative impact on the forest by the *Maldharis*' buffalo is through soil compaction, which degrades the water and air-holding capacity of the soil, increasing erosion and decreasing plant production. The practice of mixing topsoil and dung (approximately one quarter soil to three-quarters dung) from an approximately a half-kilometre radius around each *ness,* to sell to cultivators outside the Sanctuary adds further to the elimination of forest nutrients and the process of erosion. The *Maldharis* used the stem of aterdi (*Hélicteres isora*) for the frames of their houses, teak for the corral, and acacia for the thorn fencing. Since they move frequently (33% of the households and 34% of the *nesses* moved in one two-month period), this use is doubled or trebled annually. The more clandestine illegal cutting and sale of teak logs also added to deforestation. Dietary analyses indicate that forest fruits and herbs are nutritionally important but a trivial contribution to biomass removal in the forest. The plants used by the *Maldhari* as food and medicine are listed in Table 3. So, in addition to the grazing by their animals, the *Maldhari* utilize all other aspects of the forest — territory, shrubs and trees, soil, and water.

ENERGY FLOW

Table 4 compares the measured caloric intake of three *Maldharis* and indicates that the adult male has a deficit of approximately 200 calories and the lactating female approximately 200 while the adolescent female shows a small surplus. The male and adolescent female are receiving nearly sufficient and complete protein while the lactating female is getting almost half her recommended needs as well as incomplete protein (Berwick 1984). On the whole it seems as if some *Maldharis* receive enough protein but not enough calories. It is important to note that the time of year during which detailed observations were made was late April, when the least amount of milk was available. *Maldharis* ingest more milk or milk products over time than Bhojde villagers; however, they lack fresh cultivated food, the green leafy vegetables, other vegetables, roots and tubers, and fruits. The vitamin most probably lacking from their diet then would be folic acid, an important item for pregnant women. Vitamin C may be supplied by the *amla* fruit (*Emblica officinalis*), frequently eaten by *Maldharis*, a single fruit equivalent in vitamin C to one or two oranges (Aykroyd 1966). Clearly, resettlement would affect this pattern by giving the *Maldharis* proximity to fresh vegetables, if not actual stores grown by themselves in their fields. It is worrisome, however, that their buffalo herds are quite likely to be reduced due to a variety of circumstances, thus decreasing their protein intake, which was barely adequate.

Weight fluctuations are often indicative of nutritional status changes (Keller, *pers.*

TABLE 3

PLANTS USED BY *MALDHARI* AS MEDICINE AND FOOD[1]

Plant Species	Common Name	Type	Use
Ipomea sp.	*Pherav*	Climber	The fruits are roasted and eaten for urinary troubles. Also the fruit hairs are given with yoghurt or buttermilk to calves for stomach germs.
Cucurbitaceae	*Ankh-fod*	Climber	The fruits are cut and applied to finger injuries.
Cissampelus pereira	*Pang*	Climber	The roots and leaves are applied on human boils.
Celastus paniculatus	*Malkangani*	Vine	The fruits are crushed and applied to body swellings.
Vitis spp.	*Gando velo*	Climber	A paste from the bark is applied to cattle injuries.
Tinospora cordifolia	*Galo*	Climber	The tender branches are boiled and drunk in a fever.
Aspargus sp.	*Nag-na-suva*	Climber	The roots are used for urinary troubles. The skinned roots are dried, powdered, and taken with sugar and milk.
Zizyphus oenoplia		Creeper	The fruits are eaten by *Maldharis* and animals.
Hemidesmus indica	*Kagdakunder*	Climber	The juice is extracted from the root pulp and is applied to affected positions of the body in eczema.
Impetians spp.			Offered to gods in prayer.
Crochorus oletorieus	*Bal*	Herb	The black seeds from the ripe fruit are eaten by *Maldhari* graziers.
Cassia punnila	*Samad*	Herb	For eye trouble the seeds, after removing the seed coat, are put into the eyes.
Corchorus triama	*Rajang*	*Herb*	*Eaten as vegetable in the young stage of the plant.*
Triumfetta rotundifolia	*Jipto*	Herb	Used for sweeping the floor as a broom in the *nesses*.
Phaseolus minima	*Popti*	Herb	Ripe fruits eaten by graziers and animals.
Barleria pratens	*Ashelio*	Herb	Juice of leaves is applied to feet infected in mud and rains.
Hibiscus spp.	*Bhindi*		Ropes are prepared from the outer layer of the stem.
Flacourtia indiaca	*Lodar*	Shrub	The portion next to the bark is boiled with water used for the bath. This relieves body itching.
Bauhinia racemosa	*Asundro*	Tree	Ripe fruits and unripe fruit seeds are eaten by *Maldharis*.
Helicteres isora	*Nardasing*, *Aterdi*	Shrub	For dysentery in children. Seeds eaten with curd. Also used in building huts.

[1]This information was obtained by S. Chavan, a fellowship student with the Gir Project on deputation from the Gujarat Forest Department. He questioned both a *Maldhari* and a permanent settlement villager in the Spring of 1971.

Acacia pinnata	*Khair-vel*	Climber	The chewed pulp of the stems is put into the eyes of cattle when infected.
Balanitis roxburghii	*Hingora*	Shrub	Fruits used as fish poison by *Kohlis*.
Randia dumetorum	*Mindhol*	Shrub	Fruits used as fish poison by *Kohlis*. Fruit tied to hand in *Maldhari* marriages.
Cassia absus	*Simedh*	Herb	Seeds applied to child's eye when infected.
Cassia tora	*Kubadio*	Herb	Seeds crushed, boiled and drunk for cough.
Celosia argentia		Herb	Seeds boiled and drunk with water for urinary troubles
Aselapiadaceae	*Karkaodo*	Climber	Paste made from bark is applied to body ache.
Grewia hirsuta	*Khaddhamni*	Shrub	Used as broom for sweeping the *ness*.
Rivea spp.	*Pang vel*	Climber	In cases of difficult delivery of calf, plant is boiled and concoction is given to buffalo. Curry is prepared from leaves.
Fluggea macrocarpa	*Shinvi*	Shrub	Fruits are eaten by children.
Aerne scandeuse	*Gorakh-Ganjaro*	Herb	Smoked in pipe.
Abutilon indica	*Khaport*	Herb	Boiled leaves are given to bullocks, in case of urine difficulty.
Tridex procumbens	*Paka-Fad, Gha-Zhadvu*	Herb	Paste of leaves applied on injuries by axes, etc.
Terminalia crenulata	*Sajad*	Tree	Harijans use bark for tanning skins.
Soymida fabrifuga	*Ron*	Tree	Paste made from bark used on injuries of cattle.
Discora hispida	*Avol-vel*	Climber	Tuber paste applied on scorpion bite.
Lepidogorthis cristata	*Kharajwoo*		Head type inflorescence is burnt and ashes applied to eczema with ghee.
Portulalia oleracea	*Jal vevri*	Herb	Eaten as vegetable.
Ficus benghalensis	*Vadlo*	Tree	Tender, columnar roots are crushed, powdered and drunk with milk and sugar for toothache.
Pongamia pinnata	*Karanj*	Tree	Oil extracted from seeds, if applied on injuries; protects from fleas.
Screbera sweiferriorrides	*Nakti, Markho*	Tree	Leaves eaten as vegetables.
Dalbergia paniculata	*Pahi*	Tree	Roots used in urinary troubles. Skinned roots are powdered and taken with milk and sugar.

TABLE 4

COMPARISON OF MEASURED CALORIC INTAKE OF THREE *MALDHARIS*, INCLUDING ENERGY UTILIZATION AND WEIGHT TREND (after Berwick 1984)

INTAKE	ENERGY FLOW	EXPENDITURE	WEIGHT
1885 calories (97% protein)*	ADULT MALE	1981 calories	lost 1.5 kg
1325 calories (58% protein)*	ADULT LACTATING FEMALE	1495 calories	lost 1.5 kg
2347 calories (121% protein)*	ADOLESCENT FEMALE	2159 calories	gained 2.25 kg

*Percent of FAO recommended protein allowance for that class.

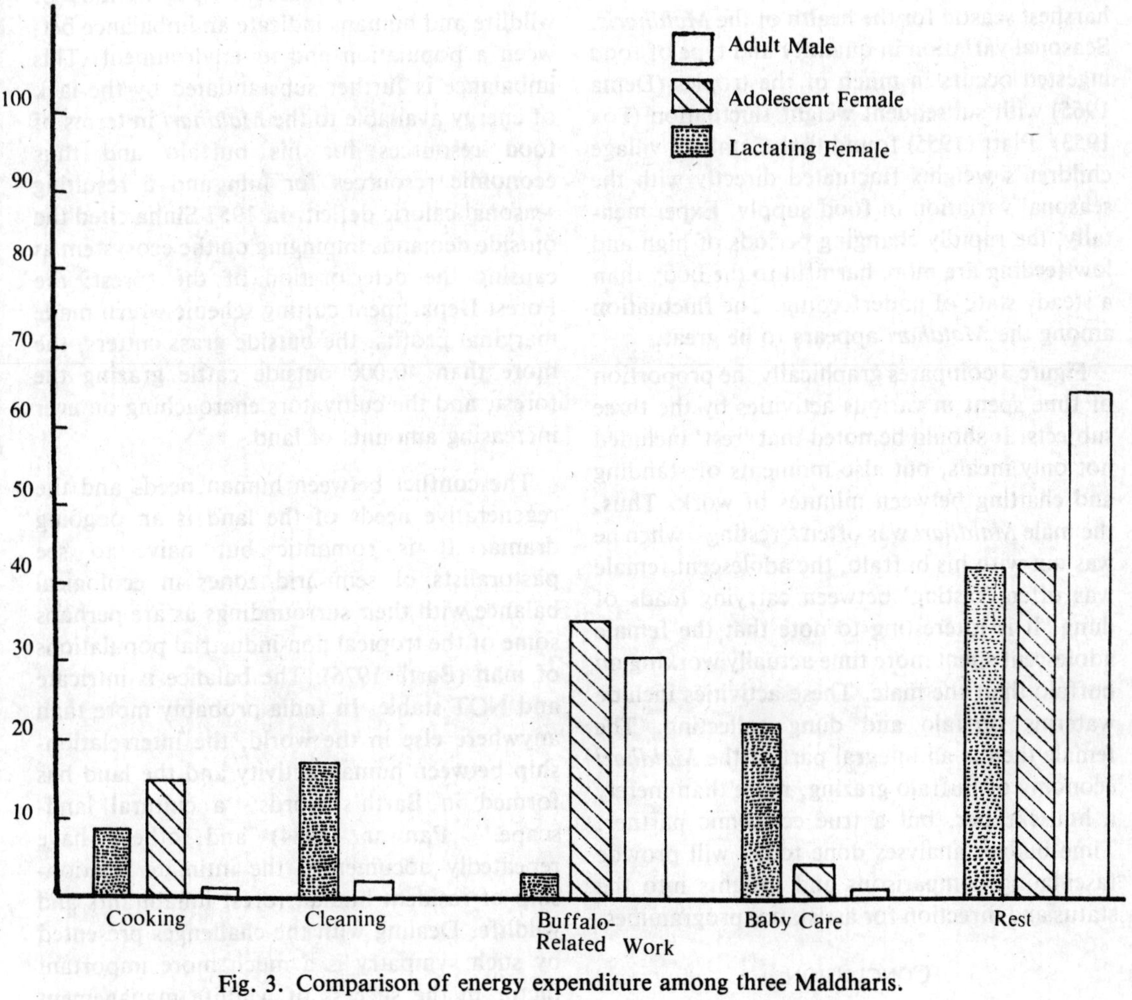

Fig. 3. Comparison of energy expenditure among three Maldharis.

comm.). Adult weight fluctuates seasonally. Analyses indicate the weight of significant numbers of *Maldharis* fluctuates seasonally, losing weight during the monsoon and gaining during the summer and winter. These data support the observation that the monsoon is the harshest season for the health of the *Maldharis*. Seasonal variation in quantity and type of food ingested occurs in much of the tropics (Dema 1965) with subsequent weight fluctuation (Fox 1953). Platt (1955) found that Gambian village children's weights fluctuated directly with the seasonal variation in food supply. Experimentally, the rapidly changing periods of high and low feeding are more harmful to the body than a steady state of underfeeding. The fluctuation among the *Maldhari* appears to be great.

Figure 3 compares graphically the proportion of time spent in various activities by the three subjects. It should be noted that 'rest' included not only meals, but also moments of standing and chatting between minutes of work. Thus, the male *Maldhari* was often "resting" when he was out with his buffalo, the adolescent female was often 'resting' between carrying loads of dung. It is interesting to note that the female adolescent spent more time actually working on buffalo than the male. These activities include watering buffalo and dung collecting. The female then is an integral part of the *Maldhari* economy of buffalo grazing, more than merely a housekeeper, but a true economic partner. Time budget analyses done today will provide fascinating comparisons and insights into the status and direction for assistance programmes.

Conclusion

Data indicate that the *Maldharis* are nutritionally and medically at risk and are living very close to their resource base with only a thin line separating them from economic disaster. Basic demographic data have revealed them to be a young population suffering high mortality, which is heavier among females. High densities, a high sex ratio, seasonality of birth, seasonal fluctuations in weight, and the stairstep shape of the survivorship curve in populations of wildlife and humans indicate an imbalance between a population and its environment. This imbalance is further substantiated by the lack of energy available to the *Maldhari* in terms of food resources for his buffalo and thus economic resources for him and a resulting seasonal calorie deficit. In 1957 Sinha cited the outside demands impinging on the ecosystem as causing the deterioration of the forest: the Forest Department cutting scheme which made marginal profits, the outside grass cutters, the more than 40,000 outside cattle grazing the forest, and the cultivators encroaching on ever increasing amounts of land.

The conflict between human needs and the regenerative needs of the land is an ongoing drama. It is romantic but naive to see pastoralists of semi-arid zones in ecological balance with their surroundings as are perhaps some of the tropical non-industrial populations of man (Barth 1976). The balance is intricate and NOT stable. In India probably more than anywhere else in the world, the interrelationship between human activity and the land has formed in Barth's words "a cultural landscape." Panwar (1984) and others have repeatedly documented the intimate relationship of resident human forest inhabitants and wildlife. Dealing with the challenges presented by such sympatry is a much more important factor in the success of wildlife management programmes in the subcontinent than in the United States with its large expanses of sparsely inhabited wildlands. While the *Maldhari* in 1970 was clearly one of many human groups degrading the Gir, it has been forcefully argued that their presence adds a vital component to a programme of conservation of the Indian lion because his buffalo provides the major supply of food to the lion, and also of tourism — because of their beauty as native forest dwellers. The data presented in this paper show that in 1970 the *Maldhari* were not doing well — that life was difficult and uncertain, in spite of the advantages to lion conservation and tourism due to their presence.

Clearly, some interventions were needed to aid the *Maldhari* and to prevent further forest degradation in spite of the above. The resettlement programme as described by Rashid (1981) appears to be a model with every possibility of success. The Government was to provide what appears to be adequate amounts of support for these buffalo herders turned agriculturalists:

(1) 3.2 HA (8 acres) of land.
(2) 610 sq. m for a house site.
(3) cultivable land ploughed and readied before relocation.
(4) Rs. 2500 grant as subsidy.
(5) Rs. 2500 loan, to be paid back in easy installments.
(6) free transportation of household effects to the new site.
(7) necessary community facilities, such as
  (a) drinking water
  (b) elementary schools
  (c) an approach road
  (d) a community centre
  (e) agricultural implements.

Rashid did not mention plans for the buffalo herds; it will be important to locate them in such a way that they do not overgraze lands in the new area. Stall feeding, grazing systems, and silage are among the successful options exercised in many places which hold some promise in mitigating such translocations. Sedentarization not infrequently leads to extreme over-stocking in settled zones, poorer diets and other forms of deterioration of the settled area, often due to concentration around water resources.

Follow-up studies should now be conducted both in the Gir and in the resettled areas to determine whether and to what extent these changes have affected the *Maldhari* population structure, nutritional status, and other health indices, as well as to quantify the effects of the reduced population pressure on the Gir ecosystem. Rashid has enthusiastically reported that "The improvement of habitat and minimizing disturbances by human beings have benefited wildlife tremendously..." and points to the May 1979 census of wildlife which shows dramatic increases in wild ungulates and a relatively steady lion population. Work needs to be done which will elucidate the relationship between the increase in biomass production which has occurred during the last 12 years at the Gir and the removal of the buffalo and other degrading forces at the Gir. The change in floral composition needs to be documented using Hodd and Berwick's range work as baseline. It will be particularly illuminating to study the *Maldharis* who remain at the Gir to see if their lot has indeed improved along with that of the wildlife, and to see if their health is better as their population size is reduced to below the carrying capacity of the forest.

ACKNOWLEDGEMENTS

I would like to thank Jino Nana Charan of Sasan, Sanat Chavan, Stephen Berwick, and Almitra Patel for their assistance with this project.

LITERATURE CITED

AYKROYD, W.R. (1966): The Nutritive Value of Indian Foods and the Planning of Satisfactory Diets. Indian Council of Medical Research, New Delhi.

BARTH, F. (1976): Socio-economic changes and social problems in pastoral lands: some concrete factors. Background paper no. 6, pp. 74-80. *In* Proc. IUCN Ecological Guidelines for the use of Natural Resources in the Middle East and South West Asia. Persepolis, Iran. 24-30 May 1975.

BERWICK, M. (1984): Energy flow among the Maldhari graziers in the Gir Forest, India. Submitted to the *J. Human Ecology*.

BERWICK, S. (1976): The Gir Forest: an endangered ecosystem. *Amer. Sci.* **64**: 28-40.

______ & SAHARIA, V.B. (1984): Wildlife Conservation in Southeast Asia. New Delhi.

CHANDRASEKHAR, S. (1967): India's population — facts, problem and policy. Mennakshi Prakashan, Delhi.

DEMA, I.S. (1965): Nutrition in relation to agricultural production. F.A.O., U.N., Rome.

FOX, R.H. (1953): A study of energy expenditure of Africans engaged in various rural activities. Thesis, University of London.

GOVERNMENT OF INDIA (1968): India 1968. Publications Division, Dir. Publ. Div., Patiala House, Ministry of Information and Broadcasting, Govt. India, New Delhi-1.

HODD, K.T.B. (1970): The ecological impact of domestic stock on the Gir Forest. IUCN 11th Tech. Meet. Vol. I. IUCN publ. N.S. No. 17, Morges, Switzerland.

LEE, R.B. (1966): Kung bushman subsistence: an input-output analysis. *In* Environment and Cultural Behaviour, Ed. A.P. Vayda, Natural History Press, Garden City, New York.

PANWAR, (1984): *In* Berwick and Saharia (Eds.). Wildlife Conservation in Southeast Asia. New Delhi.

PARRACK, D.W. (1969): An approach to the bioenergetics of rural West Bengal. *In* Environment and Cultural Behaviour. Ed. A.P. Vayda, Natural History Press, Garden City, New York.

PLATT, B.S. (1955): Cycles of good and bad feeding. *In* FAO: Human protein requirements and their fulfillment in practice. Rome, p. 94.

QUICK, R.F. (1963): Animal population analysis. *In* Wildlife Investigational Techniques. Ed. H.S. Mosby, The Wildlife Society, 1963.

RAPPAPORT, R.A. (1968): Pigs for the Ancestors, Yale Univ. Press, New Haven.

RASHID, M. (1981): The Gir Lion Sanctuary project. *In* Shaharia, V.P. (Ed.), Wildlife in India, Dept. Agriculture and Cooperation, Ministry of Agriculture, Govt. India.

SANTAPAU, H. & RAIZADA, M.B. (1956): Contribution to the Flora of the Gir Forest in Saurashtra. *Indian Forest Records* (new series), Botany—**4**:105-170.

SINHA, S.K. (1967): A draft scheme for settlement of Maldharis in the Gir Forest Division. Unpubl. report.

SOLANKI, A.S. & PATEL, T. (1970): The Rabaris of Gir, Barda, and Allech. Unpubl. Ph.D. thesis. Gujarat University, Ahmedabad.

TREWARTHA, G.T. & GOSAL, G. (1975): The regionalism of population change in India. *In* Cold Spring Harbor Symposia on Quantitative Biology 22, The Biol. Lab, Cold Spring Harbor, L.I.

VAN ARSDALE, P.W. (1978): Population dynamics among Asmut hunter-gatherers of New Guinea: Data, methods, comparisons. *Human Ecology* **6**(4): 435-467.

WYON & GORDON (1962): A long-term prospective type field study of population dynamics in the Punjab, India. *In* Kiser, Clyde V. Conf. on Research in Family Planning, New York.

Vegetation types of India in relation to environmental conditions

(*With two text-figures*)

V.M. MEHER-HOMJI[1]

INTRODUCTION

The Indian region is a well-marked geographic assemblage, limited by effective barriers like the seas, the lofty Himalayan range and the Thar desert. The variety of its climates and its geographic position at the junction of important floristic currents have permitted the penetration of the Malesian, African, Temperate, Mediterranean and Chinese floristic elements.

The inventory of the Indian flora is yet incomplete but so far over 21,000 species of higher plants have been known from the Indian region; this number represents more than one-tenth of the total species in the world (Janaki Ammal 1958). Besides the higher plants, there are more than 600 species of Pteridophytes.

Of about 11,125 species of Dicotyledons, 61.5 per cent are endemic, confined exclusively to the subcontinent, i.e. the erstwhile territory of British India, excluding Sri Lanka. However, these endemic species are not uniformly distributed throughout the subcontinent. The share of the Himalayas of the endemic dicots is 29 per cent, that of peninsular India, south of the tropic of Cancer, is 18 and of Burma 10 per cent. Five per cent of the dicotyledonous endemics are confined to the whole of the subcontinent. The figures for endemic monocotyledons are 1000 species in the Himalayas and 500 in South India (Chatterjee 1939, 1962).

[1]Institut Francais, Pondicherry

The natural barriers have helped in the development of a large number of species which are either localised in the Himalayas or in the peninsular India. The intervening area of the Indo-Gangetic plain, either because of its dry climate (in the Thar) or due to high population pressure and uniform climatic conditions (in the Gangetic valley) is poor in endemic species.

There have been several attempts to divide India into biogeographic regions according to the distribution of certain taxa, e.g. Cyperaceae by Clarke (1898), general flora by Hooker (1906) and Chatterjee (1939), migration of plants by Razi (1955) and animal distribution by Blanford.

Blasco (1979) designated the 8 divisions of Chatterjee as the ecofloristic zones enumerating the bioclimatic criteria, vegetation types and floristic peculiarities of each of these, but above all emphasising the characteristic flora (endemic species) of each zone (Table 1). However, the endemics are very often rare plants of no particular significance in constituting the vegetational landscapes.

THE BIOGEOGRAPHIC REGIONS

In the present work, we have derived the phytogeographic regions mainly from the distribution of the vegetation types which themselves show close links with the climatic and edaphic factors. Groups of allied vegetation types constitute a phytogeographic region (Fig. 1).

TABLE 1

PLANT-GEOGRAPHIC REGIONS OF CHATTERJEE (1939) WITH BIOCLIMATIC, VEGETATIONAL AND FLORISTIC CRITERIA OF BLASCO (1979)

Phytogeographic region	*Bioclimatic parameters* Annual average rainfall (mm)	Length of dry season in months	Mean temperature of the coldest month (°C)	*Forest type*	*Typical flora*	*Endemics*
Malabar	≯2000	2-6	15-25	Evergreen, semi-evergreen and moist deciduous	*Lagerstroemia lanceolata, Dalbergia latifolia, Toona ciliata, Chukrassia tabularis.*	Out of 700 dicotyledonous species at lower elevation, 400 are endemic, of which 150 are trees. In the Nilgiris: 80 endemics In Travancore: 100 endemics
Deccan	700-1500	5-8	15-25	Dry deciduous	*Tectona grandis, Anogeissus latifolia, Gmelina arborea, Pterocarpus marsupium, Terminalia* spp.	Poor in endemic flora. Bharucha and Meher-Homji (1965) enumerated 21 endemics for the southern semi-arid zone and Blasco 30 for the entire Deccan.
Indus plain or Indian Desert (Thar)	200-500	9-12	10-15	Thorny thicket	*Acacia senegal, Acacia catechu, Prosopis cineraria, Capparis decidua, Ziziphus nummularia, Calligonum polygonoides, Anogeissus pendula.*	Bharucha and Meher-Homji (1965) recorded 23 endemics for the northern semi-arid zone. Indian desert: 64 endemics (11% of the flora, Bhandari 1978).
Gangetic Plain	1200-2000	6-8	15-25	Moist deciduous sal forest, almost completely destroy in the Ganga Valley because of intensive cultivation.	Sal (*Shorea robusta*), *Terminalia* species, *Buchanania latifolia.*	
Assam	≯2000	1-6	0-15	Tropical moist deciduous, semi-evergreen, Temperate montane forest.	Sal, *Lagerstroemia, Tetrameles,* Oak (*Quercus*), Wallnut (*Juglans*), *Magnolia,* Conifers.	Rate of endemism very high
W. Himalaya, Central Himalaya, Eastern Himalayas.	Research is in progress at the University of Kashmir, Kumaun University, North-Eastern Hill University, Botanical Survey of India. For Nepal, see Dobremez (1972, 1976).					

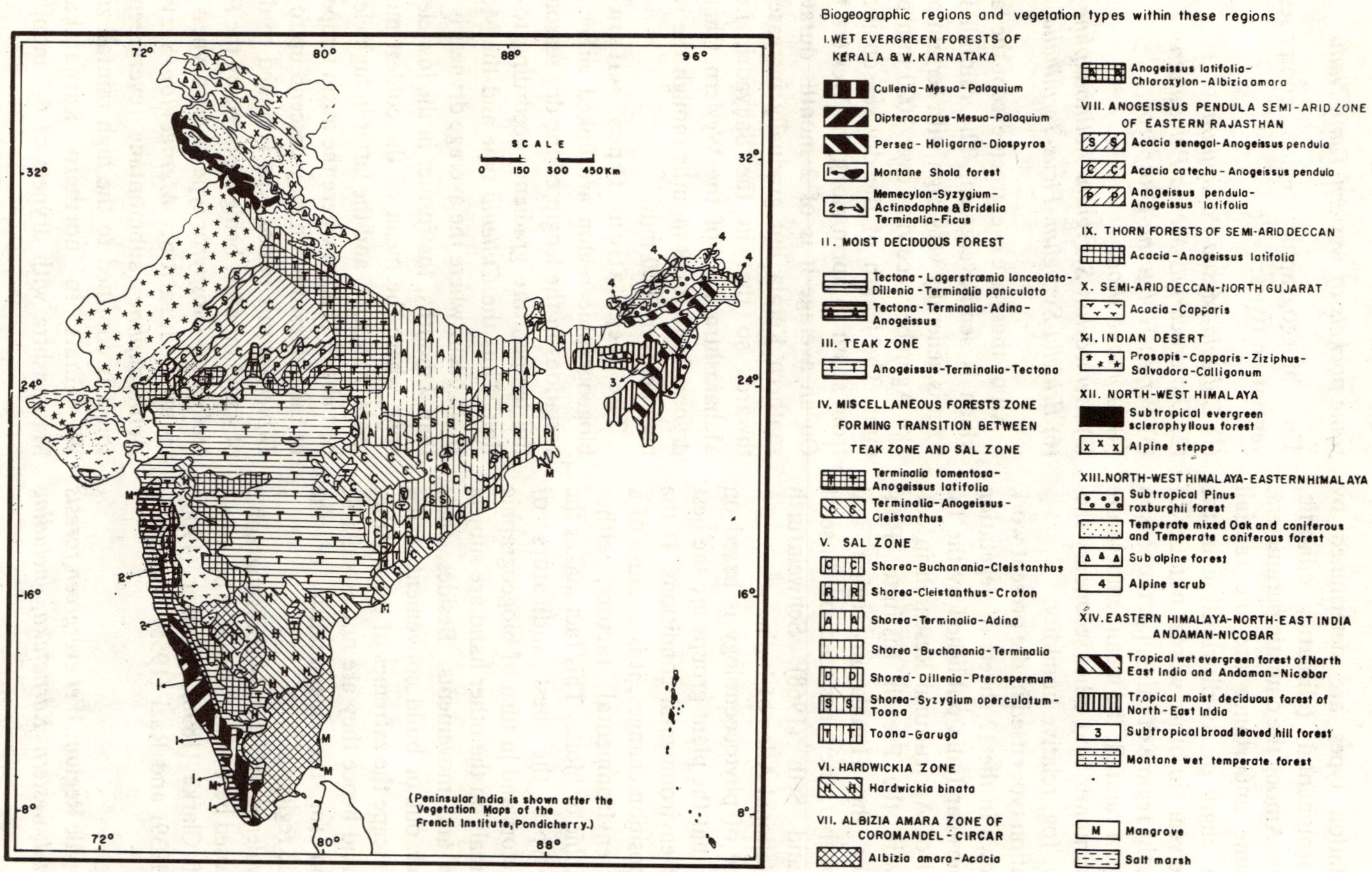

Figure. 1: Biogeographic regions and potential areas of the vegetation types

The vegetation types are determined by several environmental (climatic, edaphic, biotic) factors. Among the climatic parameters, those of prime importance are the rainfall amount, the length of its distribution in the course of the year (in other words, number of dry months), the regime of rains, i.e. the season of occurrence of rainfall, the mean temperature of the coldest month, and other secondary factors like dew, fog, relative humidity.

The vegetation types used in the present work are those shown in the 12 sheets of vegetation maps of peninsular India published by the Indian Council of Agricultural Research in collaboration with the French Institute, Pondicherry. For the Himalayan region and Andaman-Nicobar, the types used are those of Champion and Seth (1968), Schweinfurth (1957) and National Atlas of India.

The science of phytocoenology is based on the principle that the plant groups are the best indicators of environmental conditions. If the species composition changes, it is because of a change in environmental factors, either climatic, edaphic or biotic. This fact makes the vegetation types the best indicators of ecological factors and in turn of biogeographic regions. Animals on the other hand are subject to migration and movements. Besides, their ability to seek out or build convenient niches makes them escape the extremes of the weather phenomena and hence they are not as suitable as vegetation for the demarcation of the biogeographic regions.

The equivalence of the 14 biogeographic regions proposed here with the earlier botanical provinces of Clarke (1898), Hooker (1906), Chatterjee (1939) and Razi (1955) is given in Table 2.

1. **Biogeographic Region:** *Wet evergreen forests of Kerala and western Karnataka, including some pockets of western Tamil Nadu*

This biogeographic region comprises five vegetation types:

(1) *Cullenia-Mesua-Palaquium*
(2) *Dipterocarpus-Mesua-Palaquium*
(3) *Persea-Holigarna-Diospyros*
(4) *Montane shola*
(5) *Memecylon-Syzygium-Actinodaphne*
(6) *Bridelia-Syzygium-Ficus-Terminalia*

All of these are evergreen except the last one which is semi-evergreen. The rainfall in this tract is generally very high with certain patches like Agumbe, receiving over 7000 mm per annum. The length of the dry season increases from south to north along the Western Ghats. On an average it is of 2 months duration in southern Kerala but gradually increases northwards so that in the Sahyadri, i.e. the Maharashtra part of the Western Ghats, the dryness lasts for 8 months though the rainfall may be over 5000 mm.

The vegetation types within this biogeographic region are linked either to the variations in the length of the dry season or to the temperature gradients according to elevation. Thus the *Cullenia* type and the Montane shola occur where the average dryness is of less than 4 months, the former in the low elevation zone where the mean of the coldest month is more than 20°C and the latter in high elevation belt above 1500 m where the mean temperature of the coldest month may descend up to 10°C. *Dipterocarpus indica* type is linked to dryness of 4 to 5 months, being replaced by the *Persea-Holigarna-Diospyros* type where dryness is of 6 months duration. *Memecylon-Syzygium-Actinodaphne* submontane evergreen low forest is confined to the high rainfall zone of W. Ghats in northern Karnataka and Maharashtra with dryness of 6-7 months and

TABLE 2

EQUIVALENCE OF THE BIOGEOGRAPHIC REGIONS PROPOSED HERE WITH THE BOTANICAL PROVINCES OF THE EARLIER AUTHORS

Proposed Biogeographic Regions	*Correspondence with earlier Botanical Provinces of India*			
	Clarke (1898)	Hooker (1906)	Chatterjee (1939)	Razi (1955)
Wet evergreen forests of Kerala-W. Karnataka	Malabaria	Malabar	Malabar	Malabar
Moist deciduous teak forest (forming ecotone between wet evergreen forest and Teak zone)	Malabaria	Malabar	Malabar	Concan
Teak zone	Malabaria-Coromandelia	Malabar-Deccan	Deccan	Deccan-Berar-Malwa-Partly Orissa
Miscellaneous deciduous forest (forming transition between teak zone and sal zone)	Indian deserta-Gangetic plain-Coromandelia	Gangetic Plain - Indus Plain - Deccan	Gangetic Plain - Indus Plain - Deccan	Partly Bundelkhand-Upper Gangetic Plain-Malwa-Bihar
Sal zone	Coromandelia-Gangetic Plain	Deccan-Gangetic Plain	Deccan-Gangetic Plain	Bengal-Partly Upper Gagetic Plain-Bihar-Orissa
Hardwickia zone	Coromandalia-Malabaria	Deccan-Malabar	Deccan	Deccan-Khandesh
Albizia amara zone of Coromandel-Circar	Coromondelia	Deccan	Deccan	Carnatic-Mysore
Anogeissus pendula semi-arid zone of E. Rajasthan	Indian deserta	Indus Plain	Indus Plain	Rajwara-Partly Bundelkhand
Thorn forests of semi-arid Deccan	Malabaria	Malabar	Malabar-Deccan	Deccan-Khandesh
Semi-arid Deccan—North Gujarat	Malabaria-Coromandelia-Indian deserta	Deccan-Malabar-Indus Plain	Deccan-Malabar-Indus Plain	Deccan-Gujarat-Rajwara
Indian desert	Indian deserta	Indus Plain	Indus Plain	Indian desert-Punjab
North West Himalaya	West Himalaya	West Himalaya	Western Himalaya	N.W. Himalaya
Eastern Himalaya—North East India	East Himalaya-Assam	Eastern Himalaya	Central and Eastern Himalaya-Assam	Central and Eastern Himalaya-N.E. India
Andaman-Nicobar				

mean temperature of the coldest month 15 to 20°C. Finally *Bridelia-Syzygium-Ficus-Terminalia* is also a low montane type with dryness of 7 to 8 months and mean temperature of the coldest month around 20°C. Inspite of wealth of information available on soils of cultivated lands, not much work has been done on soils under forests. These have been lumped together under one category, namely "Forest Soils" in soil-classifications derived for agricultural purposes. This biogeographic region is characterised by lateritic or ferrallitic soils.

The montane shola vegetation of the south Indian hills like the Palnis, Nilgiris and Anaimalai would need a particular mention because of several peculiarities. The first one is climatic. Though the average dry season is 0 to 1 month, in over 75% years there is a real dryness of 1 to 4 months, the actual spell of drought may last 30 to 60 days at Kodaikanal and up to 80 days at Ootacamund (Legris and Blasco 1969). Mean temperature of the coldest month may reach 10°C but on winter nights, the minimum temperature may descend as low as — 9°C in the open grasslands; however, at the same time, the temperature under the forest cover remains above 0°C (Legris and Blasco l.c.). The climate of these hill-tops is often referred to as of temperate type but in view of peculiar temperature and photoperiodic regimes which differ considerably from the temperate climate, it is best to term this climate as of tropical montane type.

Plantations of tea and coffee dominate the landscape of the W. Ghats in South India from about 1000 to 1500 m and rubber below 1000 m (Dupuis 1957). *Calceolaria mexicana* is a very typical weed of tea and coffee plantations.

From vegetation point of view, the montane forests are restricted to the valleys and depressions where the moisture content is higher. Other sites carry grassy vegetation, the ligneous elements of which have their distribution range extending to the higher altitudes in the Himalayas or in the temperate regions. Whereas the winter cold proves deleterious to the regeneration of the forest species of tropical stock in the open areas, the woody species of the grasslands survive the low temperature. They are also heliophilous and some like *Rhododendron* are prophytes. This is one more reason for referring to the climate as of tropical montane type.

The prominence of *Rhododendron* and few other Himalayan plants like *Gaultheria fragrantissima, Berberis tinctoria, Mahonia, Eurya japonica* in the open landscape of the southern hills prompted some authors to emphasise, rather enthusiastically, a link between the Himalayas and these hills (See Mukherjee 1935; Biswas 1949; Razi 1955, 1955-56). Gupta (1962) went to the extent of including even the introduced species, besides the spontaneous ones and those occurring all over India and sometimes in Asia too in the list of 169 species cited as common to those two hilly areas. Blasco (1971), on the other hand, pointed out the rather strong individuality of these southern hill-tops flora, the affinity with the Himalayan species being not so marked.

Meher-Homji (1967) recognised two eco-phytogeographic groups in the ligneous montane species occurring above an elevation of 1500 m on the S. Indian hills: (1) species of extra-tropical (temperate or Himalayan) stock like *Rhododendron, Mahonia, Gaultheria* occupying open areas like shrub-savanna or margins of sholas but never occurring in the forest; (2) species of tropical stock forming the montane forest proper. These latter species as a rule belong to ancient families and are delicate. Their regeneraion is very difficult in open areas subject to winter frost, droughts and fire. Quite some species may have disappeared from the Palni, Nilgiri and Anaimalai hills. The regeneration of the montane forest, once disturbed, is practically impossible.

Amongst the genera of the montane (Shola) forests of the South Indian hills also occurring in the Himalayas, those in which the species are different in these two ranges are *Beilschmiedia, Bhesa, Cinnamomum, Euonymus, Ilex, Lasianthus, Linociera, Microtropis, Psychotria, Sideroxylon, Vaccinium*. In case of *Pygeum* even the species of the hilly regions of the eastern part of the Peninsula are different from those of the hills of S. India. None of the species of *Apodytes, Lasiosiphon, Mappia* and *Melicope* occurs in the Himalayas.

The following genera have one link species between the Himalayas and the southern hills and Sri Lanka highlands. Furthermore, the link species also occurs in the hilly regions of E. India: *Ardisia solanacea, Glochidion velutinum, Meliosma simplicifolia, Michelia champaca, Phoebe lanceolata, Photinia notoniana, Pittosporum floribundum, Schefflera venulosa, Symplocos spicata.*

In case of *Elaeocarpus ganitrus, Evodia lunu-ankenda, Glochidion heyneanum, Litsaea zeylanica, L. sebifera, Photinia notoniana* the link species does not occur in E. India.

The fact that as a rule not more than one species in a genus is common between the Himalayas and the southern hills may suggest slow rate of migration which in turn seems to favour speciation. The rate of endemism may be said to be relatively high in the South Indian montane forest flora as at the most only one species is common in the majority of the genera between these hills and the Himalayas.

The absence of the Himalayan conifers, members of Fagaceae, Betulaceae, Hamamelidaceae, etc. from the S. Indian hill-tops may be explained by the differences in the temperature and photoperiod regimes due to the latitude factor. *Quercus incana* and *Pinus roxburghii* planted in the gardens of Kodaikanal do not produce viable seeds, nor have they shown the least tendency to become naturalised. Their absence may also be explained by the dry nature of the climate during the Pleistocene glaciations which did not permit these relatively humid elements to migrate southwards as it did permit the hardy *Rhododendron, Mahonia, Gaultheria* (*Pers. Comm.* P. S. Ashton). If the climate was dry during the glaciations and not corresponding to the Pluvials, the montane forests could well have been restricted to the moister valleys and depressions as they are at present.

II. **Biogeographic region:** *Moist deciduous forests forming an ecotone between the region I, namely Wet evergreen forests and region III -Teak zone.*

It comprises two vegetation types:

(1) *Tectona-Lagerstroemia lanceolata-Dillenia pentagyna-Terminalia paniculata* type described by Champion (1936) as the "South Indian tropical moist-deciduous teak forest" occurring on the western side of the Western Ghats in Kerala, Goa, Maharashtra and on the eastern fringe of the Western Ghats in Karnataka, extending up to an elevation of 1000 m.

The range of annual rainfall is 2000 to 4000 mm with a dry season of 3 to 7 months and mean temperature of the coldest month more than 15°C. Soils are red lateritic loam.

(2) The second type is named *Tectona-Terminalia-Adina-Anogeissus* corresponding to the slightly moist teak forest of Champion and Seth (1968). Confined to the Thana, Nasik, Dangs, Nagar Haveli and Bulsar districts of coastal Maharashtra and Gujarat, it forms a transition between the above-mentioned moist-deciduous forest and the dry-deciduous teak

forest with rainfall of 1800-2500 mm, dry season of 7 to 8 months and tropical ferruginous or ferrallitic soils.

At this juncture it may be pointed out that the difference between the moist-deciduous forest and the dry-deciduous forest is mainly one of structure and architecture. Trees are taller and of larger girth in the moist-deciduous forests compared to the dry type of forests.

From floristic point of view, *Lagerstroemia lanceolata* and *Terminalia paniculata* are confined to the western half of the southern part of the Peninsula (south of 17° latitude N) and serve as an indicator of moist type, being absent in the dry type. However, in the Dharwar district of Karnataka, these species are encountered under low limit of rainfall of about 1000 mm where one would expect a dry-deciduous forest. Albeit, under drier conditions, *Lagerstroemia lanceolata* manifests xeromorphic adaptations like spines on the trunk in younger stage. In conclusion, *L. lanceolata* and *T. paniculata* are not very fidel indicators of the moist-deciduous forest, which leaves *Dillenia pentagyna* as the most characteristic tree of the moister type.

III. **Biogeographic region:** *Teak zone*

The dry-deciduous forests of India may be divided into 3 broad categories: Teak, Sal and Miscellaneous transitional zone between Teak and Sal.

The seeds of Sal (*Shorea robusta*), a Dipterocarpacea has a very short period of viability like the other members of the family. One of the main factors accounting for the occurrence of this species is the timely arrival of rains to coincide with the short period of about 10 days when the viable seeds are available. Thus the Sal is confined to the eastern part of the Peninsula receiving early monsoon and is eliminated from the regions lying further westwards where the summer rains are delayed.

Among all the biogeographic regions of India, the Teak zone occupies the second largest potential area of over 53 million ha (Gadgil and Meher-Homji 1982) extending from Kanya Kumari district in the south up to Jhansi and Guna districts in the north. Occupying a large area of the Central Deccan peninsula, it has outliers in the Gir (North Gujarat) and the Nalamalai hills (Andhra Pradesh).

The Teak zone shares many a species in common with the Sal zone and the Miscellaneous deciduous forests (Legris and Meher-Homji 1977). The dominance of the Teak in one type and of the Sal in the other type is brought about by the selective action of man. In the original forests, neither Teak nor Sal would have had the abundance that we note today as the result of preferential treatment provided by the Forest Department. These two species are favoured at the expense of many others. Dhareswar (1941) presents interesting data about the introduction of the Teak in the coastal Kanara tract of Karnataka 3 to 4 centuries ago and the dislike shown to the species then by the cultivators, a scenario reminiscent of the case of *Eucalyptus* today.

The main climatic and edaphic differences between the Teak zone and the Sal zone may be summed up as follows. The Sal withstands frost with the mean temperature of the coldest month descending to 10°C whereas the risk of frost is practically nil in the Teak zone with the mean of the coldest month above 15°C. The lower limit of rainfall in the Teak zone is 750 to 800 mm whereas it is above 1100 mm for the Sal. Besides, timely arrival of rains to coincide with the period of availability of seeds is a critical factor for Sal survival. Length of the dry season is 4 to 8 months for the Teak zone but 5 to 7 for the latter. Soils are varied under the Teak type, namely alluvial, ferruginous, black soil on trap and thin lateritic whereas these are acidic ferrallitic or ferruginous under the sal forests. Finally, Teak is a strong light demander whereas Sal is a shade bearer in early stages.

IV. **Biogeographic Region:** *Transition zone of miscellaneous deciduous forest between Teak and Sal zones*

Because of the earlier arrival of the southwest monsoon rains in the eastern half of the peninsula, the Sal zone occupies the eastern half and the Teak zone occurs further westward. Rarely does the area of Teak and Sal overlaps in what is called a "tension-belt". Sometimes the two zones occur side by side and sometimes the two dominant forest species are separated by a miscellaneous deciduous forest in which both Teak and Sal are either missing or of very rare occurrence. In the miscellaneous forest, named *Terminalia-Anogeissus latifolia-Cleistanthus* type, separating Teak and Sal zones, as a rule *Cleistanthus collinus* is a prominent species of the understorey. The rainfall in this tract of miscellaneous forest is of the order of 1000-1500 mm with 5 to 6 months dry and with the mean temperature of the coldest month above 20°C. Soils are sandy or loamy ferruginous, vertic brown or black on alluvia.

Under drier conditions (700 to 900 mm rainfall and dry season of 8 months) in parts of Gujarat, Rajasthan and Madhya Pradesh, *Cleistanthus* disappears and the forest type is termed *Terminalia-Anogeissus latifolia*. In this case, the distance separating the Teak type from the Sal type is quite considerable. Soils are either red ferruginous or brown.

V. **Biogeographic Region:** *Sal zone*

The largest potential area of over 56 million ha is under the Sal zone. Six floristic subdivisions have been recognised in the Sal zone on the basis of dominant-abundant species.

(1) *Shorea-Cleistanthus collinus-Croton oblongifolius* type occurs in the Birbhum, Chaibasa, Dhanbad, Bankura, Bardhaman, Medinipur, Puruliya, Balasore and Keonjharghar districts at elevation of 100 to 400 m.

(2) The *Shorea-Buchanania-Cleistanthus* type is distinguished by the absence of *Croton*. It occurs in the Bastar, Raipur, Kanker, Bilaspur, Raigarh, Sundergarh, Dhenkanal, Sambalpur, Bolangir, Kalahandi districts.

(3) The largest area among the Sal types (19.5 million ha) is under *Shorea-Terminalia-Adina* "series", covering a large part of the eastern peninsula and also occurring in the sub-Himalayan tract. The westernmost outlier is in the Pachmarhi hill of Madhya Pradesh, shown in Fig. 1 as *Shorea-Buchanania-Terminalia* type.

(4) *Shorea-Dillenia-Pterospermum heyneanum-Cycas circinalis* type constitutes the coastal Sal semi-evergreen forest. It is confined to the coastal belt of Orissa with rainfall of 1500 to 2000 mm, dry season of 5 to 6 months and mean temperature of the coldest month over 20°C.

(5) The moist peninsular hill Sal forest has been named *Shorea-Syzygium operculatum-Toona ciliata-Symplocos spicata* type. It is confined to elevation above 900 m over the plateaux and hills of Orissa and Bihar. Range of rainfall and dry months is the same as in the preceding coastal Sal type but the mean temperature of the coldest month is lesser: 10 to 15°C. Soils are red ferruginous or ferrallitic and lithosols in both the types.

(6) *Toona-Garuga* semi-evergreen forest of the hilly regions of Koraput, Biladila, Papikonda and Visakhapatnam hills though without Sal has been placed in the Sal zone because of the likely disappearance of Sal from this tract through over-exploitation in the historical times. In its ecological requirements (altitude,

rainfall, dry season, temperature and soil), this type closely agrees with the above-mentioned hill Sal type.

VI. **Biogeographic Region:** Hardwickia binata *zone*

This is a deciduous forest with marked dominance of *Hardwickia binata* occurring over the plateau region of Andhra Pradesh, Karnataka state and Salem district of Tamil Nadu. After a long discontinuity, it reappears in the Dhulia, Jalgaon and Nasik districts, in the Satmala and the Satpura ranges of the Deccan Trap country, and in a few parts of the Vindhya and Mahadeo ranges.

A remarkable feature of its distribution is its complete absence in the Western Ghats. It occurs on the east-west oriented Satmala, Satpura Mahadeo and Vindhya ranges but is conspicuous by its absence in the north-south oriented Sahyadris. It is found in discontinuous patches in NE-SW oriented hills of the Eastern Ghats (in Andhra Pradesh and Tamil Nadu) and near Haveri, Harihar, Chitradurga, Hiriyur and Tumkur (Karnataka) just to the east of the Western Ghats.

Rainfall range is 500 to 1200 mm spread over a period of 4 to 6 months in the areas of *Hardwickia* but the distribution of the species has not been satisfactorily correlated with climatic and soil conditions.

Because of general association of *Hardwickia* with skeletal soils, this forest type has been considered as an edaphic facies though we have observed this species on deep black soil in Andhra Pradesh.

Mall (1968) comparing the forest of Daultapur — (in Dewas division at a distance of 113 km from Bhopal) with that of Kalakund (in Mhow range about 40 km from Indore) finds that *Hardwickia* is totally absent in the former. He attributes this difference to historical factor asserting that there is no significant difference in soil characters of the two forests. Meher-Homji (1970) emphasised the role of human interference and grazing. In the open forests of the Satpura and Satmala, *Hardwickia* is generally gregarious towards the borders of the forests but not so in the interior. Because of its very hard wood it is not so easy to fell. Whereas the other species become the victim of axe at the forest margin, *Hardwickia* escapes the maltreatment. In the interior where the forests are better protected not being easily accessible, other species have a fair chance of survival and the abundance of *Hardwickia* is not so striking.

Worthy of mention is the restricted occurrence of the economic endemic Red Sanders (*Pterocarpus santalinus*) in the elevated regions of the Cuddapah, Kurnool districts and northeast portions of the Chittoor district of Andhra Pradesh (Fig. 2) where geological terrain is slate and quartzite and the rainfall regime (season of occurrence of rains) is of the transitional type between the tropical type of Kurnool (June-October rains from southwest monsoon) and the dissymetric type of Nellore (bulk of rains from the northeast monsoon in October to December) (Meher-Homji 1980).

VII. **Biogeographic Region:** Albizia amara *zone*

It is encountered along the Coromandel Coast of Tamil Nadu and Circar coast of Andhra Pradesh. The most peculiar feature of this biogeographic zone is the rainfall regime. Some light rains are experienced from the southwest monsoon during June to September but the bulk of precipitation (over 60%) is received from the so-called northeast monsoon during October to December. In fact, these are the depressions and cyclones of the autumn-winter season formed in the Bay of Bengal which provide rains because the so-called northeast monsoon is a dry wind system.

Fig. 2.. Ombrothermic diagrams & Area of the Red Sanders

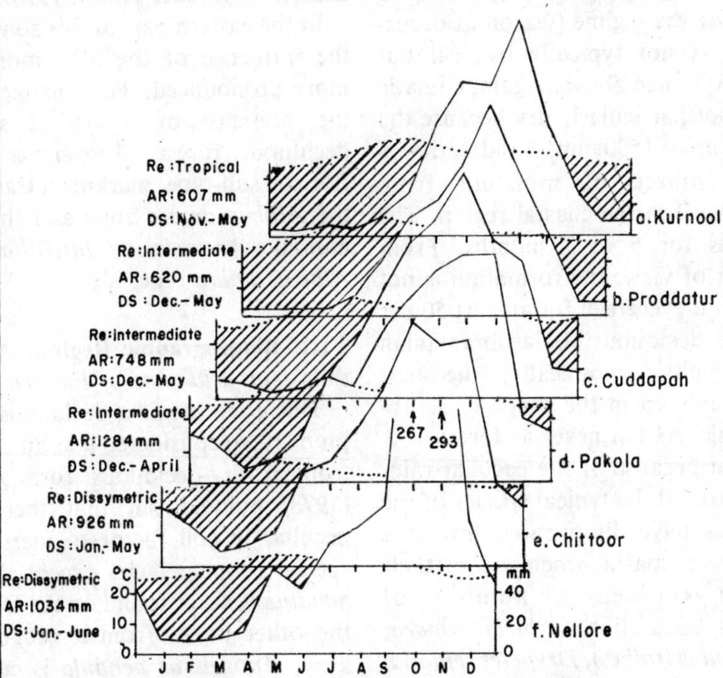

The terminology "Tropical dry evergreen forest" coined by Champion (1936) to designate this biogeographic region is a misnomer because the regime (season of occurrence of rains) is not typically tropical but dissymetric as explained above. Again, climatic conditions are not particularly dry because the rainfall range is up to 1500 mm. Besides, dew is an important source of moisture from November till April in the coastal region. The dry season lasts for 5 to 7 months. From phenology point of view, the formation is not evergreen but semi-evergreen for at least 50 per cent species are deciduous (Balasubramanian 1978). Finally, physiognomically, the best stands are encountered in the shape of scrub-woodlands or thickets but never as forest.

It appears that because of the peculiar rainfall regime, almost all the typical species of the deciduous forests have disappeared from the Coromandel-Circar coastal tract and in their absence have evolved a number of characteristic species like *Albizia amara, Pterospermum suberifolium, Drypetes sepiaria, Erythroxylon monogynum, Diospyros ferrea, Euphorbia antiquorum, Gmelina asiatica, Carmona microphylla, Hugonia mystax, Pterolobium hexapetalum* and *Cissus quadrangularis* among others.

Albizia amara avoids calcimorph soils and is therefore confined to acidic granite-gneiss rocks, avoiding the basic Deccan Trap. Soils are ferruginous or ferrallitic sandy loam. Over lateritic soil is observed *Memecylon umbellatum* which is also encountered over the lateritic caps of Mahabaleshwar and elsewhere in the Western Ghats.

In the dry coastal pocket of Ramanathapuram-Tirunelveli districts where rainfall is as low as 500 mm and dry season as long as 9 months is seen the umbrella thorn tree *Acacia planifrons*. After a long discontinuity, this species is also met with near Porbandar in Kathiawar where the climatic conditions are analogous (Meher-Homji 1970).

In the eastern part of this zone in Karnataka, the influence of the SW. monsoon becomes more pronounced. This change is heralded by the presence of a typical species of the deciduous forest, *Anogeissus latifolia*. This floristic sub-type, marking a transition between the *Albizia amara* zone and the Teak zone is named *Anogeissus latifolia-Chloroxylon-Albizia amara* type.

VIII. **Biogeographic Region:** Anogeissus pendula *semi-arid zone of Eastern Rajasthan*

This zone too is a deciduous forest. Champion (1936) considered it as an edaphic facies of tropical dry-deciduous forest. Meher-Homji (1978) pointed out that there was nothing peculiar in soil factor to merit the title of a special edaphic facies except the fact that *A. pendula* is never found on the Deccan Trap. On the other hand, from a geographic point of view, *Anogeissus pendula* is confined to subtropical latitude above 23.5°N in the Aravallis and the Bundelkhand region of Madhya Pradesh.

Three eco-floristic sub-types have been distinguished according to climatic conditions and co-dominant species:

(1) *Acacia senegal-Anogeissus pendula* type occupying the drier western part of the zone:hillocks of Jalor, Jodhpur, Barmer, Nagaur, Sirohi, Pali, Ajmer, Sikar districts, where rainfall is 400 to 700 mm, dry season is of 8.5 to 10 months duration.

(2) With moister conditions (rainfall of 550-900 mm, lesser dry season of 8 to 9 months), *Acacia senegal* is replaced by its vicariant *Acacia catechu* resulting in *A, catechu-Anogeissus pendula* type in the Aravallis.

(3) With further increase in rainfall (600-1000 mm) and lesser dry season of 8 months, *Anogeissus latifolia* associates itself with *A. pendula* in the relatively moister eastern and southeastern part of the zone in the Bundi, Kota, Shivpuri districts and in the Khichiwara, Orcha and Bundelkhand uplands of Madhya Pradesh.

Biogeographic Regions: IX *Deccan Thorn Forest;* X *(Deccan-Northern Gujarat)* and XI *(Indian desert)*

These three biogeographic regions contain one vegetation type each and have one point in common: they are deprived of forest formations, the best stands of vegetation being in the form of thorny thickets to scattered shrubs.

The *Acacia-Anogeissus latifolia* type under the biogeographic region IX occurs in the Tapti-Purna valley and in Maharashtra Deccan on alluvial or black clayey soil. Climatic conditions are not adverse (rainfall 600-800 mm with a dry season of 8 months) but the fertile soils with irrigation facilities have favoured agriculture.

The *Acacia-Capparis decidua* type of the biogeographic region X extends from Bijapur to Malegaon, covers northern Gujarat, Kathiawar and piedmont plains west of the Aravalli, under rainfall of 400-800 mm and 7 to 9 months of dryness.

Along the increasing gradient of aridity in western Rajasthan (rainfall under 400 mm, dryness of 9 to 11 months), the *Acacia-Capparis* type is replaced by the *Prosopis cineraria-Capparis-Zizyphus-Salvadora oleoides* type (of the India Desert biogeographic region) on sandy alluvial soils. The most typical plant of the sand dunes is *Calligonum polygonoides.*

This brief account presents the salient features of vegetation and environmental factors of peninsular India, with which this author has been involved for over two decades. Being less familar with the extra-peninsular area, the climatic features of the vegetation types of the Himalayas, Northeast India and Andaman-Nicobar Islands have been summarised in Table 3.

Lastly mention may be made of the mangrove vegetation occurring along the coast. Excellent reviews have been published recently by Blasco (1975) and Ananda Rao and Sastry (1972).

PAST HISTORY OF VEGETATION OF INDIA

Presently the tropical evergreen forests are confined to the Western Ghats in southern India, in Northeast India and in Andaman-Nicobar Islands. However, the plant fossils recorded from different parts of India (Cuddalore Sandstone Series in and around Pondicherry, Deccan Intertrappean Series around Chhindwara-Nagpur-Mandla, Bengal basin, Kutch, Rajasthan and the Siwaliks) point to the widespread occurrence of evergreen forests throughout the length and breadth of the country up to Miocene-Pliocene times.

Several hypotheses have been advanced for the drastic modification of the climate in the post-Miocene times resulting in conversion of the evergreen forests to deciduous forests over the major part of the Peninsula (Meher-Homji 1977).

First of all may be considered the location of the Peninsula in the late Cretaceous or early Tertiary. India occupied a more southerly position astride the equator in the Eocene (Frakes & Kemp 1972). Palaeomagnetic studies of the Traps reveal the position of Nagpur as late as in Miocene at 7°N (Deutsch *et al.* 1959; Verma & Narain). The decline in the rainfall pattern may also be attributed to the uplift of the

TABLE 3

BIOGEOGRAPHIC REGIONS, VEGETATION TYPES AND CLIMATIC FEATURES OF EXTRA-PENINSULAR AREA

Biogeographic region	Vegetation type	Altitude (m)	Annual average rainfall (mm)	Length of dry season (in months)	Mean temperature of the coldest month (°C)	Soily type
Western Himalaya	(1) Subtropical evergreen sclerophyllous forest (Subtropical dry-evergreen forest)	300-1500	500-1000 Regime bixeric with 2 dry periods and 2 rainy seasons, one in summer (maximum rains in July-August) the other in winter	5	10 (Cold winter with occasional frost)	Shallow and dry
	(2) Alpine steppe	4500	80	7	−7.5 (No. of months with frost: 3)	
Common to Western and Eastern Himalayas	(1) Subtropical *Pinus roxburghii* forest (Subtropical Pine forest)	1000-1800	1300-3000	2-6	4-10	
	(2) Temperate mixed oak and Coniferous forest (Himalayan moist temperate forest)	1800-3000	1300-2000	1-2	5	
	(3) Temperate coniferous forest (Dry temperate coniferous forest)	2000-3800	1000-1800			
	(4) Subalpine forest	2900-3500	80-650 (Snow is a regular feature)	4-7	−7 to −16 (No. of months with frost: 3 to 5)	
	(5) Alpine scrub	3500-4900	No climatic records are available (Ample snow covers the ground for 5 or more months)			
Eastern Himalaya-North-Eastern India	(1) Tropical wet evergreen forest	2000	2800-3500 (During winter there is frequently heavy dew instead of rain)	2	5-16	Alluvial over Tertiary sandstones and shales
	(2) Tropical moist-deciduous forest		2500-5000	3-4	15-18	Porous, well-drained
	(3) Subtropical broad-leaved hill forest	1000-2000	2200-11,000	2-5	10-13	Brown
	(4) Montane wet temperate forest	1750-2750	3200	2	5	Sandy loamy soil on gneissic rock
Andaman-Nicobar Islands	(1) Tropical wet-evergreen forest	upto 800	3150	2	28.7	

Himalayas in the wake of the northward drift of the Indian landmass, introducing the monsoon regime. The Himalayas were elevated in four stages, the last one being in the late Pliocene to early Pleistocene, establishing the present trend of precipitation in the Peninsula.

The subsequent northern drift, probably accompanied by a slight southern shift of the equator (Aubreville 1969), the uplift of the Himalayas and the maximum rise of the Western Ghats in the Pliocene (Krishnan 1968; Vaidyanathan 1977) contributed towards drier conditions on the Coromandel coast and a change from the wet evergreen forest to a deciduous and ultimately to a dry-evergreen type of thicket (Meher-Homji 1974). The rate of drift of India during the Tertiary has been estimated at about 6 cm per year (Meher-Homji 1976).

Whereas the major portion of the Indian subcontinent experienced a climatic change in the Tertiary, southeast Asia has retained a more or less uniformly humid climate. The pollen stratigraphy suggests that in this central part of the Indo-Malaysian region, plant evolution has continued unperturbed by any major climatic shift since the Cretaceous (Muller 1970). Aubreville (1969) proposed that the Tertiary equator was not far from the present day equator in southeast Asia and so the vegetation did not experience much change compared to Africa. Melville (1966, 1967) ascribes the climatic change in India to its rapid and exactly southnorth drift. This eliminated most of the Cretaceous gymnospers (Florin 1961) and accounted for small contribution of India to its modern flora in spite of its size, compared to southeast Asia and Africa.

REFERENCES

ANANDA RAO, T. & SASTRY, A.R.K. (1972): An ecological approach towards the classification of coastal vegetation in India— *Indian For.* **98:** 594-607.

AUBREVILLE, A. (1969): Essai sur la distribution et l'histoire des angiospermes tropicales dans le monde.—*Adansonia* 9: 189-247.

BALASUBRAMANIAN, K. (1978): Biotaxonomical studies of Marakkanam R.F., Coromandel Coast.—Ph.D. Thesis, Annamalai Univ.

BHANDARI, M.M. (1978): FLORA OF THE INDIAN DESERT. Scientific Publishers, Jodhpur.

BHARUCHA, F.R. & MEHER-HOMJI, V.M. (1965): On the floral elements of the semi-arid zones of India and their ecological significance. *New Phytol.* **64:** 330-342.

BISWAS, K. (1949): Botanical notes on the Satpura theory. *Proc. nat. Inst. Sci. India* **15:** 365-367.

BLASCO, F. (1971): Orophytes of South India and Himalayas.—*J. Indian bot. Soc.* 50: 377-381.

__ (1975): The mangroves of India. *Inst. Fr. Pondichery. Tr. Sect. Sci. Tech.* **14**(1): 1-175.

______ (1979): Les territoires biogeographiques du Sous-Continent Indien. *In Paleogeographie et Biogeographie de l'Himalaya et du Sous-Continent Indien,* pp. 25-30. Greco 12. C.R. de la Table Ronde l'Univ. Paul Sabatier, Toulouse.

CHAMPION, H.G. (1936): A preliminary survey of the forest types of India and Burma. *Indian For. Rec.* **1**:1-286.

____ & SETH, S.K. (1968): A revised survey of the forest types of India, Delhi.

CHATERJEE, D. (1939): Studies on the endemic flora of India and Burma. *J.Roy. Asiat. Soc. Bengal Sci.* **5**:1-69.

____ (1962): Floristic pattern of Indian vegetation. *Proc. Summer School of Botany, Darjeeling,* pp. 32-42.

CLARKE, C.B. (1898): On the sub-sub-areas of British India, illustrated by the detailed distribution of the Cyperaceae in that Empire. *J.Linn. Soc. (Lond.) Bot.* **34**:1-146.

DEUTSH, E.R., RADHAKRISHNAMURTHY, C & SAHASRABUDHE, P.W. (1959): Palaeomagnetism of the Deccan traps. *Ann. Geophys.* **15:** 39-59.

DHARESWAR, S.S. (1941): The denuded condition of the minor forests in Kanara coastal tract, its history and a scheme for its regeneration. *Indian For.* **67**(2): 68-81.

DOBREMEZ, J.F. (1972): Mise au point d'une methode cartographique d'etude des montagnes tropicales. Le Nepal, ecologie et phytogeographie. These-Grenoble, 373 p.

__ (1976): Le Nepal: Ecologie et Biogeographie, Cahiers Nepalais. C.N.R.S. Paris, 356 p.

DUPUIS, J. (1957): L'economie des plantations dans l'Inde du Sud.—*Inst. Fr. Pondichery. Tr. Sect. Sci. Tech.* **1**(1): 1-50.

FLORIN, R. (1961): The distribution of conifer and taxad genera in time and space. *Act. Hort. Berg.* **2**: 121-312.

FRAKES, L.A. & KEMP E.M. (1972): Influence of continental positions on early Tertiary climates. *Nature* **24**: 97-100.

GADGIL, M. & MEHER-HOMJI, V.M. (1982): Conserving India's biological diversity. *In* Indo U.S. Binational Workshop on Conservation and Management of Diversity. Dept. of Environment, New Delhi and Indian Inst. of Sci., Bangalore.

GUPTA, R.K. (1962): Some observations on the plants of the South Indian hill tops (Nilgiri and Palni plateaus) and their distribution in the Himalayas. *J. Indian bot. Soc.* **41**:1-15.

HOOKER, J.D. (1906): A sketch of the flora of British India. Oxford.

JANAKI AMMAL, E.K. (1958): Report on the humid regions of South Asia. *In* Problems of Humid Tropical Regions, pp. 43-53, UNESCO, Paris.

KRISHNAN, M.S. (1968): Physiogeographic characteristics of Peninsular ranges. In: Law, B.C. (ed.). Mountain and Rivers of India. *21st Intern. Geogr. Congr., New Delhi.*

LEGRIS, P. et BLASCO, F. (1969): Variabilite des facteurs du climat: Cas des montagnes du Sud de I'Inde et de Ceylan. Inst. Fr. Pondicery. *Tr. Sect. Sci. Tech.* **8**: 1-94.

_____ & MEHER-HOMJI, V.M. (1977): Phytogeographic outlines of the hill ranges of Peninsular India—*Trop. Ecol.* **18**(1): 10-24.

MALL, L.P. (1968): Ecology of Daultapur and Kalakund forests of Madhya Pradesh. *Proc. Symp. Recent Adv. Trop. Ecol.* **2**: 398-406. ISTE, Varanasi.

MEHER-HOMJI, V.M. (1967): Phytogeography of the South Indian hill stations.—*Bull. Torrey bot. Club* **94**: 230-242.

_________ (1970): Notes on some peculiar cases of phytogeographic distributions. *J. Bombay nat. Hist. Soc.* **67**: 81-86.

MEHER-HOMJI, V.M. (1974): On the origin of the tropical dry evergreen forest of South India. *Int. J. Ecol. Environ. Sci.* **1**(1): 19-39.

_______ (1976): On the rate of drift of India during the Tertiary. *Geobios* **3**: 23-24.

___ (1977): Tropical dry deciduous forests of Peninsular India. *Feddes Rep.* **88**(1-2): 113-134.

_____ (1978): The term subtropical in phytogeography: Facts and fallacies.—In: Sen, D.N. (ed.). Environ. Physiol. Ecol. Plants, pp. 109-115.

_____ (1980): On the ecology of the economic endemic *Pterocarpus santalinus* Linn. f. of Andhra Pradesh, India. *Int. Tree Crops J.* **1**: 143-146.

MELVILLE, R. (1966): Continental drift, Mesozoic continents and the migrations of the angiosperms. *Nature* **211**: 116-120.

____ (1967): The distribution of land around the Tethys Sea and its bearing on modern plant distribution. *In:* Adams, C.G. and D.V. Ager (eds.). Aspects of Tethyan Biogeography, pp. 291-312. Systematics Assoc. Publ. 7.

MUKHERJEE, D.B. (1935): Notes on a collection of plants from Mahendragiri. *J. Indian bot. Soc.* **14**:305-311.

MULLER, J. (1970): Palynological evidence on early differentiation of angiosperms. *Biol. Rev.* **45**:417-450.

RAZI, B.A. (1955): Some observations on plants of the South Indian hilltops and their distribution. *Proc. nat. Inst. Sci. India* **21** B: 79-89.

_______ (1955-56): The phytogeography of the Mysore hilltops. *J. Mysore Univ.* **14B**: 87-107: **15B**: 109-144.

SCHWEINFURTH, U. (1957): Die Horizontale and Vertikale Verbreitung der Vegetation in Himalaya. *Bonner Geogr. Abh.* Heft **20**, 372 p. Ferd. Dummlers Verlag, Bonn.

VAIDYANATHAN, R. (1977): Recent advances in geomorphic studies of Peninsular India: A review. *Indian J. Earth Sci.* S. Ray Vol.:13-35.

VERMA, R.K. & NARAIN, H. (   ): Palaeomagnetic studies of Indian rocks and continental drift. Proc. Upper Mantle Symp., AGU Monograph, Tokyo.

Standing Biomass and net primary productivity of Tropical Rain Forests of Karnataka

Dr S. N. Rai[1]

F. R. I. & Colleges, Dehra Dun 248 006.

Introduction

The Net Primary Production (NPP) of the biosphere is about 100.2×10^9 tonnes per year. Sixty-six percent of this is in terrestrial ecosystems (Whittaker & Likens, 1973). Primary productivity is dependent upon a number of environmental conditions, foremost among these are temperature and water. A relationship was suggested between mean annual temperature and productivity and an equation was given by Leith (1973). A computer programme was developed and that gave the expected productivity for every combination of total annual temperature and rainfall between 0 mm and — 30°C and 4500 mm and + 30°C. A world map indicating the productivity of the terrestrial ecosystem named as 'Miami Model 1971' was prepared.

There is practically very little reported data on standing biomass on Net Primary Productivity of the Tropical Rain (Wet Evergreen) forests of India. In the present study the standing biomass and Net Primary Productivity has been determined for four study areas based on regression models developed for biomass.

Review of Literature

The primary productivity of the Rain forest is considerably high, but these forests require so much autotrophic respiration for maintenance that the NPP is comparatively low. Dawkins (1967) suggested a range of potential productivity from 5 to 40 t/ha/a, for the Tropical Rain forests. Muller & Neilsen (1965) gave a dry matter production of 13.5 t/ha/a in Ivory Coast. Golley & Golley (1972) suggested a NPP of 23 to 30 t/ha/a for the Rain forest. Murphy (1977) gave a NPP of 16.2 t/ha/a for seasonal Rain forest and 24 t/ha/a for Evergreen Rain forest. He gave the range of NPP for Rain forest from 10.3 to 32.1 t/ha/a. Tanner (1980) reported a NPP of 6.5 to 7.6 for upper montane Rain forest and 16 t/ha/a for lower Rain forest from Jamaica. Whittaker and Likens (1973) gave a mean NPP of 20 t/ha/a for Tropical Rain forest and 15 t/ha/a for Tropical seasonal Rain forest.

Edwards & Grubb (1977) reported a total above ground living biomass of 505 t/ha from New Guinea. Rodin & Bazilevich (1967) suggested a relationship for the Tropical Rain forest where leaves account for 4 to 9 percent, trunk and branches 70 to 80 percent and the roots 16 to 21 percent of the biomass.

Table 1 gives the above ground biomass of the Tropical Rain forest. The average standing biomass of eleven sites is 342.66 t/ha, and its range is from 229 to 560 t/ha. Similarly table 2 gives the estimates of root biomass from nine sites with an average of 51.23 t/ha and a range of 13.7 to 132 t/ha. It is amazing to note that

[1] *Present address*: Conservator of Forests, Sandal Research Centre, Bangalore 560 003, Karnataka.

TABLE 1

ABOVE GROUND BIOMASS AND NET PRIMARY PRODUCTIVITY IN SOME TROPICAL RAIN FORESTS OF THE WORLD

Forest type	Location	Above ground biomass t/ha	NPP t/ha/a	Source
Tropical Rain	Yagambi	—	32	Bartholomew *et al.* (1953)
Tropical Rain	Khade, Ghana	265.8	—	Greenland and Kowal (1960)
Tropical Rain	Khao Chang, Thailand	324	29	Kira *et al.* (1964)
Seasonal Rain	Anguededou, Ivory Coast	—	13	Muller and Nielsen (1965)
Tropical Rain	Thailand	290.6	—	Ogawa *et al.* (1965 b)
Tropical Rain	Cambodia	348 to 415	—	Hozumi *et al.* (1969)
Lower Montane	El Verde, Puerto Rico	—	16	Odum (1970 b)
Lower Montane (60 years)	El Verde, Puerto Rico	233.4	—	Jordan (1971)
Lowland Dipterocarp	Pasoh, Malaysia	—	22	Bullock *in* Gist (1973)
Tropical Rain	New Guinea	286	—	Enright (1979)
Tropical Rain	Abidjan, Ivory Coast	560	15.5 to 17	Anonymous (1975)
Montane Rain	New Guinea	505	—	Edwards (1977)
Montane Rain	Jamaica	229 to 312	6.5 to 16	Tanner (1980)

TABLE 2

ROOT BIOMASS IN SOME TROPICAL RAIN FORESTS OF THE WORLD

Forest type	Location	Root biomass t/ha	Source
Tropical Rain	Ivory Coast	23.8	Huttel (1969)
Montane Rain	El Verde, Puerto Rico	72.3	Odum (1970 a)
Miombo	Zaire	13.7	Malaisse (1972)
Tropical Rain	Ivory Coast	49	Huttel (1975)
Tropical Rain	Central Amazonia	28.08 to 30.99	Klinge (1976)
Tropical Rain	Venezuela	132	Klinge (1978)
Tropical Rain	New Guinea	57.2	Enright (1979)
Montane Rain	Jamaica	54	Tanner (1980)

in a multistoreyed *Sequoia sempervirens* forest the estimated bole biomass itself amounted to 3461 t/ha (Fujimori, 1977). Klinge (1973a) reported a living plant biomass of 1000 t/ha from Central Amazonian forest. Ola-Adams (1974) has discussed the productivity of some natural forests and plantation in Nigeria. The highest reported values of fresh coarse root mass of 50 t/ha and fine root mass of 205 t/ha are from Central Amazonia (Klinge 1973b).

Study Area

The bulk of data collection by destructive sampling for dimension analysis of trees was done at Chakra, where clearing of a Tropical Rain forest was in progress, prior to the area going under submersion. Inventory of vegetation and monitoring of litter-cycling was done at Agumbe, Bannadpare, Kagneri and South Bhadra sites. The study sites and their floristics are briefly described below :

(a) Agumbe. The site is located around 13°31′N lat. and 75°6′E long., elevation 675 m; mean annual rainfall 7669 mm and months of June, July and August account for 82.5 percent of the annual rainfall. Months of December to April are practically dry.

(b) Bannadpare. The site is located around 12°5′N lat. and 75°42′E long., elevation 200 m; mean annual rainfall 5313 mm. Months of June to August receive 79.4 percent of annual rainfall but the months of Novembei to April are practically dry.

(c) Kagneri. The study site is located around 12°49′N. lat. and 75°36′E long., elevation 300 m; mean annual rainfall 6095 mm. Months of June, July and August receive 72.1 percent of the annual rainfall, but the months of December to April are dry.

(d) South Bhadra. The site is located around 13°15′N. lat. and 75°15′E long., elevation 800 m; average annual rainfall 6521 mm. Months of June to August receive 85.7 percent of the annual rainfall while months of December to March are practically dry.

(e) Chakra. The area is located around 13°33′N lat. and 75°6′E long., elevation 600-800 m, mean annual rainfall in the locality (a rainguage 15 km away at Vatgod) is 7034 mm. Months of June to August receive 98.4 percent of the annual rainfall, while the month of December to April are practically dry.

The mean annual temperature of Agumbe is 22.2°C (range 20.1 to 24.6); of Bannadpare 27°C (range 25.2 to 29.7) and of Kagneri 28.6°C (range 25.9 to 32.2). Mean Annual temperature of South Bhadra and Chakra can be considered to be similar to Agumbe.

Floristics of the area have been described in detail by Rai (1981). All the five sites have Wet Evergreen vegetation, which can be broadly called as Tropical Rain Forests also. They fall in the category of Southern Tropical Wet Evergreen Forests (Champion & Seth 1968). Agumbe and Chakra have dominance of *Poeciloneuron indicum — Dipterocarpus indicus* association in the overstorey and *Humboldtia brunonis* in the understorey. Bannadpare has *D. indicus-Vateria indica* association in overstorey and *Garcinias* and *Myristicas* in the understorey. Similarly, Kagneri too has *D. indicus-V. indica* dominance in overstorey and *Diospyros* and *Garcinias* in the understorey. South Bhadra is quite distinct and it has consociation of *P. indicum* in overstorey. It has *Garcinias* and other species in understorey.

All the plots have *Nothopegia, Garcinia* and *Myristica* as common constituents of understorey.

Material and Methods

Data collection for biomass was done by standard methods (Newbould, 1967). The above ground portion of a tree was sampled as Bole, Branch and current year twigs and leaves. Shrub and herb biomass was estimated by complete harvest method. In all 434 trees were sampled for bole biomass; 226 for branch biomass and 125 for current year twig and leaf biomass. The samples were dried at 85°C to a constant weight.

Litter collection was done in woven baskets, used as traps. The basket had a circular opening of 80 cm and hence had an opening area of 0.503 m². The traps were kept in the centre of a 10 × 10 m, square plot, on either side along a baseline. The baskets were kept, 30 to 40 cm above the ground level, supported on bamboo stakes. It is likely that some portion of micro-litter might have got washed down or otherwise escaped, from the woven basket, but under the circumstances the baskets were considered preferable to traps of any other kind. Such 50 baskets were kept at Agumbe, 100 at Bannadpare, 100 at Kagneri and 50 at South Bhadra for a period of 24 months.

Results and Discussion

The standing biomass of four study areas and also the root biomass is given in Table 3. The average above ground biomass is 465.6 t/ha; with a range of 410.2 to 591.2 and the average root biomass is 13.21 t/ha, with a range of 11.16 of 15.88 (Rai 1981). From the comparison of the available data it may be seen that the average above ground biomass of these forests is higher but within the reported range, however, the root biomass is lower than the reported data. It may be due to the fact that the biomass of roots, below 5 cm girth was not taken into consideration. It is expected that the root biomass would become considerably more when roots below 5 cm girth are also included.

Table 3

Total standing biomass of four study areas in tropical rain forests of W. Ghats (t/ha)

Component	Study areas: Agumbe	Bannadpare	Kagneri	South Bhadra	Average
Bole	272.834	295.050	298.835	416.130	320.712 ±64.638
Branch	120.448	121.911	126.545	169.743	134.662 ±23.531
Leaf	14.069	5.047	10.147	5.154	8.604 ± 4.351
Current year Twig	2.847	0.839	1.974	0.863	1.631 ± 0.968
Root	13.120	11.156	12.687	15.879	13.211 ± 1.968
Total	423.318	434.003	450.188	607.769	478.820 ±86.673

TABLE 4

INCREASE IN BIOMASS (kg/ha/a) OF MEAN TREES IN TROPICAL RAIN FORESTS OF KARNATAKA

DBH	Bole	Branch	Leaf & Twig	Root	Total
7.5	2.2	1.0	0.1	0.1	3.4
15	3.6	2.2	0.1	0.2	6.1
25	11.2	3.8	0.1	0.4	15.5
35	13.8	5.8	—	0.6	28.2
45	20.2	7.3	0.1	0.6	28.2
55	21.7	7.8	0	0.6	30.1
80	17.0	4.1	0	0.2	21.3

In this study leaves accounted for 1.8 percent, bole and branch for 95.44 percent and roots for 2.76 percent of the standing biomass.

ESTIMATE OF NET PRIMARY PRODUCTIVITY. There have been various estimates of standing biomass, but very few exhaustive estimates of NPP. This is primarily due to the complex nature of the uneven aged mixed forest, where an accurate estimate of rate of diameter increment (the main variable for biomass increment determination) is extremely difficult. Estimate of NPP through diameter increment of trees and allometric relationships of their components is, perhaps, the best method. The next preferable and perhaps, equally effective, method is through Basal Area increment. Another method is a multiple of the litter fall. All the three methods have been used to determine the NPP of the four study areas.

(i) ESTIMATE OF NPP THROUGH DIAMETER INCREMENT. Rai (1981) estimated general rate of diameter increment of seven tree species (five overwood and two underwood) at Agumbe in a Linear Tree Increment plot. (A portion of this plot has been used as a study area in this study.) The estimated diameter increments are given below:

DBH cm	Average mean annual increment of diameter (cm)		
	Overwood	Underwood	Weighted average
5	0.27	0.12	0.24
15	0.33	0.13	0.27
25	0.37	0.14	0.30
35	0.38	0.13	0.31
45	0.38	0.12	0.31
55	0.35	0.08	0.27
65	0.30	0.07	0.21

The diameter of the mean trees after one year will be from 7.5 to 7.75; 15 to 15.27; 25 to 25.30; 35 to 35.31; 45.31; 55 to 55.27; 65 to 65.21 and 80 to 80.1 cm.

Based on the regression equations developed for biomass estimation in these forests, and adopting them for estimating bole, branch, current year twigs, leaves and root, the increase in biomass of mean trees, for different diameters over a period of one year has been estimated and the same is given in Table 4. It may be seen that the maximal rate of diameter increment for the overwood species and the forest as a whole is in 35 to 45 cm DBH class, but the maximal rate of biomass increment is around 55 cm DBH.

Based on this analysis and considering the number of stems in various DBH classes in the plots, the NPP of four study areas has been estimated and the same is given in Table 5.

TABLE 5

NET PRIMARY PRODUCTIVITY OF VARIOUS COMPONENTS (t/ha/a) AT FOUR STUDY AREAS IN THE TROPICAL RAIN FORESTS OF KARNATAKA

	Agumbe	Bannadpare	Kagneri	South Bhadra
Bole	6.332	3.715	5.473	5.608
Branch	2.905	1.465	2.276	2.198
Leaf & Twig	0.133	0.036	0.080	0.061
Root	0.277	0.134	0.218	0.199
Total/ha	9.665	5.350	±8.048	8.067
Average	Bole	5.282 (68.30)	±1.111	
	Branch	2.211 (28.6)	±0.590	
	L & T	0.077 (1.0)	± .041	
	Root	0.207 (2.7)	± .059	
Total	7.778	±1.783	t/ha/a	

Note: Figures given in parenthesis indicate the percentage contribution of the components towards N.P.P.

(ii) ESTIMATE OF NPP THROUGH BASAL AREA INCREMENT. In another study Rai (1983) has found out the rate of basal area increment per year as the percent of the initial basal area. The average increment is 2.058 percent (the range is from 1.279 to 3.226). Considering this, the annual increase in B.A. of the study sites will be:

	B.A./ha m²	Annual Increment percent	Increase in B.A. m²
Agumbe	33.664		0.693
Bannadpare	33.934		0.698
Kagneri	35.644	2.058	0.734
South Bhadra	48.634		1.001

Presuming, an average height of 23.2 m; which is the height at 60 cm DBH; a Form Factor of 0.45 and an average dry weight of 788 kg/m³ (Rai 1981); for all the four plots, the annual increase in bole biomass would be:

Agumbe	5.701 t/ha/a
Bannadpare	5.742 t/ha/a
Kagneri	6.038 t/ha/a
South Bhadra	8.235 t/ha/a
	6.429 t/ha/a ± 1.213

Considering this to be 68.3 percent of the total NPP (Table 5) the average NPP of the study area in this case will come to 9.413 t/ha/a. It may be seen that that there is a close comparability between the two estimates of NPP, obtained by alternate methods.

(iii) ESTIMATE OF NPP THROUGH LITTER FALL. Murphy (1975), based on the data of Robin and Bazilevich (1967) concluded that the NPP is three times the litter fall. Rai (*in press*) has found a litter fall of 4.182, 4.065, 3.979 and 3.443 t/ha/a respectively in Agumbe, Bannadpare Kagneri and South Bhadra areas. Therefore the NPP of the four study areas would be: 12.546, 12.195, 11.937,

10.392 t/ha/a respectively. With an average of 11.768 ± 0.950 t/ha/a.

Based on the above three methods the average estimate of NPP for these forests is 7.778, 9.413 and 11.768 t/ha/a. The first method which is based on the rate of diameter increment may give more accurate estimate of the NPP. Table 1 has nine estimates of NPP with an average of 18.6, and the range is from 6.5 to 32 t/ha/a. The present estimate of NPP for the Tropical Rain Forest falls within this range. The NPP may be low due to the seasonality of the climate (UNESCO, 1978). Seth *et al.* (1971) have estimated the productivity of Indian forests based on a CVP Index and sample plot data, but there is no estimate for the Rain Forests of India.

Kira (1969 & 1975) has discussed the primary productivity of the Tropical Rain Forests, and gives a ceiling limit of 40 t/ha/a of NPP for the broad leaved forest. Allen (1976) reported a NPP of 27.8 t/ha/a, by leaf chamber technique from a Rain Forest near Turrialba. From the discussion of various results and the present findings it emerges, that, though the rainfall and temperature indicate a high NPP, yet the same is limited by the seasonality of rainfall. Hence any model based only on above two parameters is likely to forecast a high NPP for the forests with a marked dry season, like the one in this case.

REFERENCES

ALLEN, L. H. & LEMON, E. R., (1976): Carbon dioxide exchange and turbulence in a Costa Rican Tropical Rain forest. *In*: VEGETATION AND THE ATMOSPHERE 2, (Ed.) J. L. Montieth, Academic Press, London.

ANONYMOUS (1975): Studies on the sub-equational forest ecosystem of the lower Ivory Coast. *Terre et la Vie* 29, 169-264.

BARTHOLOMEW, W. V., MEYER, J. & LAUDELOUT, H. (1953): MINERAL NUTRIENT IMMOBILIZATION UNDER FOREST AND GRASS FALLOW IN YANGAMBI (Belgian Congo) Region, with some preliminary result on the decomposition of plant material on the forest floor. INEAC (Bruxelles). pp. 27.

CHAMPION, H. G. & SETH, S. K., (1968): THE FOREST TYPES OF INDIA. The Manager of Publications. Delhi.

DAWKINS, H. C. (1967): Wood production in Tropical Rain Forest *J. Ecol. 55*: 20-21.

EDWARDS, P. J. (1977): Studies on mineral cycling in a Montane Rain forest in New Guinea, II—The production and disappearance of litter. ibid., *65*: 971-992.

————— & GRUBB, P. J. (1977): Studies of mineral cycling in a Montane Rain forest in New Guinea, I—Distribution of Organic matter in the vegetation and soil. ibid. *65*: 1943-1969.

ENRIGHT, N. J. (1979): Litter production and nutrient partitioning in Rain forest near Bulolo, Papua New Guinea *Malay. For. 42*: 202-207.

FUJIMORI, T. (1977): Stem biomass and structure of a mature *Sequoia sempervirens* stand on the Pacific coast of northern California. *Jap. For. Socy. 59*: 535-541.

GOLLEY, F. B. (1972): (Compilers) THE TROPICAL ECOLOGY WITH EMPHASIS ON ORGANIC PRODUCTIVITY. University of Georgia Press, Athens pp. 418.

GREENLAND, D. J. & KOWAL, J. M. L. (1960): Nutrient content of the moist tropical forests of Ghana, *Pl. Science 12*: 154-174.

HOZUMI, K., YODA, K. & KIRA, T. (1969): Production ecology of Tropical Rain forest in South Western Combodia II—Photosynthetic production in an evergreen seasonal forest. *Nature & Life in South East Asia, 6*: 57-81.

HUTTEL, C. (1969): Vertical distribution of roots in a Tropical Rain forest in the southern Ivory Coast. *J. W. Afr. Sci. Ass. 14*: 65-72.

————— (1975): Root distribution and biomass in three Ivory Coast Rain forest plots. *In* Tropical Ecological systems, Springer-Verlag, Berlin.

JORDAN, C. F. (1971): Productivity of tropical forest and its relation to a world pattern of energy storage, *J. Ecol. 59*: 127-142.

KIRA, T. (1969): Primary productivity of Tropical Rain forest. *Malay For. 32*: 375-384.

KIRA, T. (1975): Primary production of forests. *In* PHOTOSYNTHESIS AND PRODUCTIVITY IN DIFFERENT ENVIRONMENTS. (Ed.) J. P. Cooper, pp. 5-40, IBP, *3*: Cambridge University Press, U.K.

———, OGAWA, H., YODA, K. & OGINO, K. (1967): Comparative ecological studies on three main types of forest vegetation in Thailand. IV—Dry matter production with special reference to the Khao Chang Rain forest. *Nature & Life In South East Asia. 5*: 149-197.

KLINGE, H. (1973a): Root mass estimation in lowland Tropical Rain forests of Central Amazonia Brazil. I. Fine root mass of a pale yellow latosol and a giant humus podzol. *Trop. Ecol. 14*: 29-38.

——— (1973b): Root mass estimation in lowland Tropical Rain forests of Central Amazonia Brazil. II. Coarse root mass of trees and palms in different height classes, *Anais Academia Basilieira de Ciencias 45*: 595-609.

——— (1976): Root mass estimation in lowland Tropical Rain forests of Central Amazonia Brazil. III. Nutrients in fine roots from giant podosols, *Trop. Ecol. 16*: 28-38.

——— (1978): Biomass studies in Amazon Cattinga forest in Southern Venezuela. I. Standing Crop of composite root mass in selected stands. ibid. *19*: 93-110.

LEITH, H. (1973): Primary production: Terrestrial ECOSYSTEM. *In*: PRIMARY PRODUCTION OF THE BIOSPHERE (Eds.) R. H. Whittaker and G. E. Likens, pp. 303-332. Plenum publishing Corporation, New York.

MALAISSE, F. (1972): The Miombo ecosystem. A preliminary study. *In*: P. M. Golley and F. B. Golley, 1972. pp. 363-405.

MULLER, D. & NIELSEN, J. (1965): Production brute, parts par respiration et production nette dans la foret ombrophile tropicale. *Det Forstlige Forssvaesen i Danmark 29*: 69-160.

MURPHY, P. G. (1975): Net primary productivity in tropical terrestrial ecosystems. *In*: PRIMARY PRODUCTIVITY OF THE BIOSPHERE (Eds.) H. Leith & R. H. Whittaker, pp. 218-231. Springer-Verlag, New York.

——— (1977): Rates of primary productivity in tropical grass lands, savannah and fores *Geo. Eco. Trop. 1*: 95-102.

NEWBOULD, P. J. (1967): METHODS FOR ESTIMAT ING THE PRIMARY PRODUCTION OF FORESTS. IBP Hand book, 3. Blackwell Publishers, Oxford, U.K., pp. 61

ODUM, H. T. (1970a): An emerging view of th ecological system at El Verde. *In* H.T. Odum and R F. Pigeon, 1970.

——— (1970b): Rain forest structure and mineral cycling homeostatis. *In* H. T. Odum and R. F. Pigeon, 1970.

OGAWA, H., YODA, K., OGINO, K. & KIRA, T. (1965): Comparative ecological studies on three main types of forest vegetation in Thailand II. Plant Biomass. *Nature & Life in South East Asia, 4*: 49-80.

OLA-ADAMS, B. A. (1974): Estimation of biomass and productivity of some natural forests and plantations in Nigeria. *Nigerian J. For. 4*: 18-23.

RAI, S. N. (1981): Productivity of Tropical Rain forests of Karnataka. Ph.D. Thesis Bombay University.

RAI, S. N. (1981): Rate of growth of some evergreen species. *Indian For. 107*: 513-518.

——— (1983): Basal Area and Volume Increment in Tropical Rain forests of India. *Indian For. 109*(4): 198-211.

RODIN, L. E. & BAZILEVICH, N. I. (1967): PRODUCTION AND MINERAL CYCLING IN TERRESTRIAL VEGETATION. Oliver and Boyd. London. pp. 288.

SETH, S. K., KAUL, O. N. & SHARMA, D. C. (1971): Potential Productivity of Indian Forests. Paper presented at International Symposium on Tropical Ecology, Emphasizing Organic Production, New Delhi.

TANNER, E. V. J. (1980): Studies on the biomass productivity in a series of montane, forest in Jamaica. *J. Ecol. 68*: 573-588.

UNESCO, (1978): Tropical Forest Ecosystems. A state of knowledge report. Prepared by UNESCO/UNEP/FAO, pp. 683.

WHITTAKER, R. H. & LIKENS, G. E. (1973): Primary production. The Biosphere and Man. *In*: THE PRIMARY PRODUCTIVITY OF THE BIOSPHERE. (Eds.) R. H. Whittaker and G. E. Likens, pp. 357-369. Plenum Publishing Corporation, New York.

Tree Shape and Leaf Arrangement: A quantitative comparison of Montane Forests, with emphasis on Malaysia and South India

(*With 18 text-figures*)

EGBERT GILES LEIGH, JR.

Smithsonian Tropical Research Institute,

Balboa, Panama

Abstract

Based on studies of forest structure, leaf size, leaf arrangement, and tree architecture in the Nilgiri Hills of South India, lowland and selected mountain-top sites in peninsular Malaysia and Puerto Rico, lowland forests in Panama and Dominica, and montane forests and scrub in Costa Rica, I find that:

1) tree density is governed by forest height, and is remarkably uniform for forests over 20 metres tall;

2) the heights of saplings or small trees of a given diameter are independent of forest height or soil fertility unless the normal height of these plants is over half that of the canopy;

3) the average area (m^2) per canopy crown is best predicted as

$$0{\cdot}1837\ (\text{forest height})^{1{\cdot}7}$$

Crowns are much larger than predicted on fertile soil and much smaller than predicted on very poor soil: climate hostile to transpiration does not mimic the effect of poor soil;

4) the average size of litter leaves is best predicted by the altitude of the forest. Leaves are larger than predicted on fertile soil, and smaller than predicted on poor soil: again, climate hostile to transpiration does not mimic the effect of poor soil. Leigh (1975) was wrong to attribute elfin forest structure to nutrient starvation induced by inability to transpire;

5) trunks, branches and twigs are unusually stout in elfin forests, and in other higher altitude forests: the smoothness of the canopy suggests that this stoutness serves to resist windsnap. Twigs and branches so stoutly built are not lightly thrown away, so trees in such forests have architecture that allow them to grow with a minimum of shedding and rebuilding.

INTRODUCTION

How alike in structure and physiognomy are the stunted montane forests in different parts of the wet tropics? To what extent do the similarities in their physiognomy reflect adaptive response to common environmental problems? What might these problems be? To answer, I will ask how altitude and climate correlate with forest structure and physiognomy within a selection of transects from forests of different stature, at different altitudes, in South India, Malaysia, Central America, and the West Indies. To be specific:

1) Why are some montane forests stunted and others not?

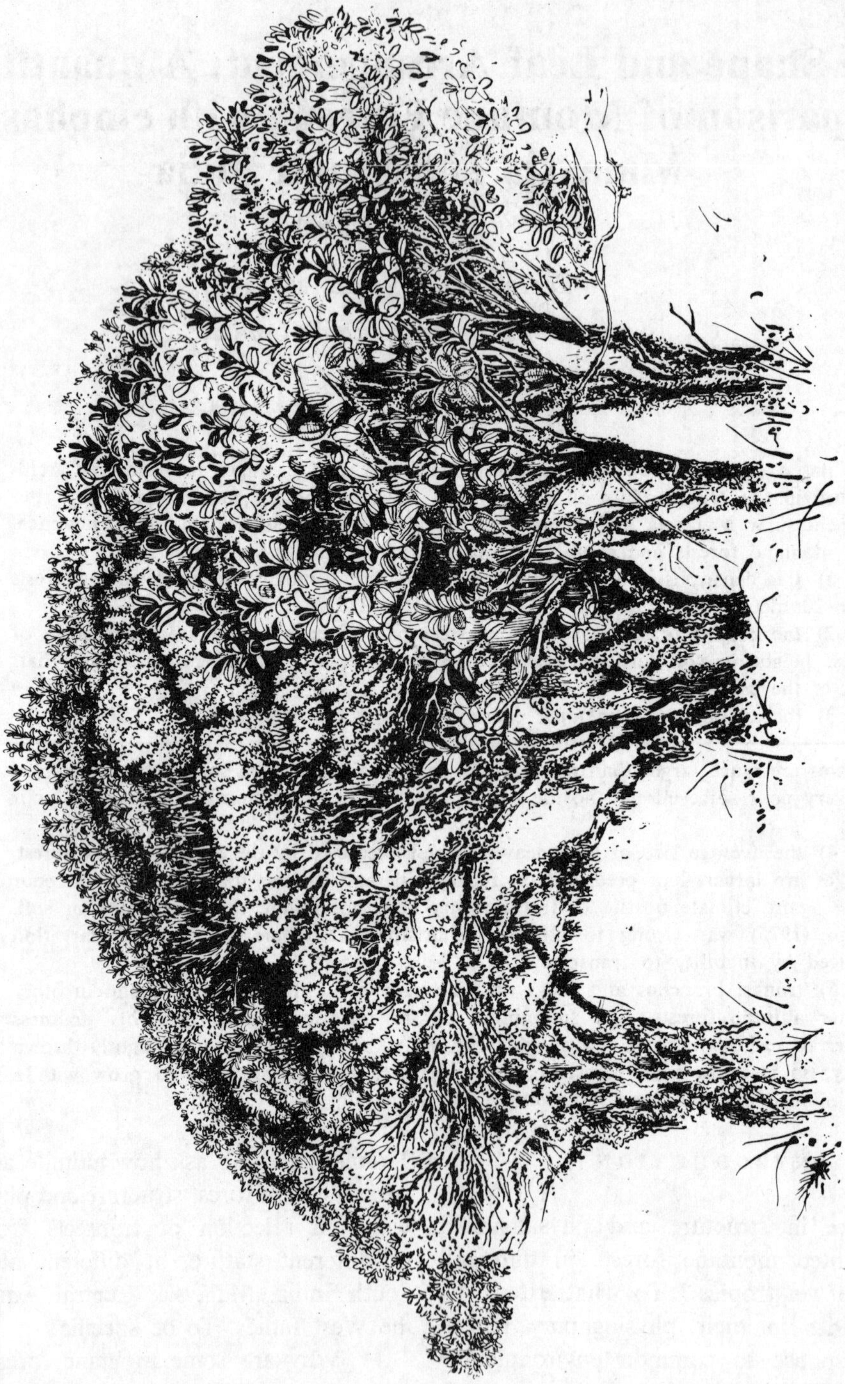

Fig. 1. Roadside patch of elfin forest shrubbery 2 m tall in paramo at 3000 m near Totoro, Colombia. Drawing by Gerardo Rivassa.

2) What aspects of forest structure and physiognomy — considering especially tree density, canopy crown size, the spectrum of tree architectures, heights of plants with different stem diameters, canopy and understory leaf size and arrangement — are simple consequences of the height of the forest, reflecting the degree to which it is stunted?

3) To what extent are these aspects of forest physiognomy independently influenced by altitude and climate?

There are many reasons why montane forest might be stunted. The soil, leached and thinned by excessive runoff, might be too poor to support taller growth (van Steenis 1972, p. 42). The acid soil might be waterlogged enough to block soil metabolism, thereby interrupting nutrient cycling and slowing plant growth. The abundant breeze and fog characteristic of many tropical mountain-tops, which occasionally persist without a break for weeks at a time, may keep leaves cool enough and the atmosphere humid enough to prevent transpiration, thus blocking nutrient uptake (Odum 1970, Leigh 1975), or rendering it more expensive (Leigh 1983). The wind may stunt the forest, blowing tall trees down (Blasco 1971), or tearing at the edges of gaps opened by previously fallen trees, and knocking trees down before they have had a chance to grow tall (Lawton and Dryer 1980, Leigh and Lawton 1981), or slowing tree growth by "forcing" trees to develop trunks stout and dense enough to resist the wind (Lawton 1982).

Effects of these processes are often hard to distinguish. Leigh (1975) proposed that where persistent breeze, fog and mist block transpiration, the forest should be organized to maximize transpiration under foggy conditions: it should have an even canopy of upright leaves, each hiding from the cooling breeze as much as possible without being shaded (Figure 1). Unfortunately, a smooth canopy is also characteristic of forests which suffer from steady winds or occasional cyclones. Moreover, I find that plants in nutrient-poor bogs and swamps tend to hold their leaves stiffly upright, whether or not fog and breeze are a problem. Leigh and Lawton (1981) and Leigh (1983) proposed that plants which have adequate light, but are short of nutrients because decomposition of litter on the forest floor is slow, should grow in a manner involving the least shedding and rebuilding. A plant which puts out horizontal sprays of foliage must shed its lower branches when later growth shades them. Therefore, when inadequate recycling restricts the nutrient supply, plants should have inclined branches and carry their leaves around twigs which point upward and outward from the crown, for such plants can grow by extending their twigs with the desired minimum of shedding and rebuilding. Unfortunately, such growth forms are also characteristic of wind-planed coastal dune scrub, suggesting that they might sometimes be a response to strong wind.

However, it may sometimes be possible to distinguish the mechanical effects of wind from the effects it might induce in wet climates by blocking transpiration. Small leaves and small crowns are thought to reflect nutrient shortage (Richards 1952, Givnish 1978). In our transects, canopy crown size is most closely correlated with forest height, and canopy leaf size with altitude. I will calculate the relevant regressions and ask whether forests in climates presumed hostile to transpiration show deviations from the regressions similar to those of forests on poor soils: if not, then we may conclude that inability to transpire does not stunt a forest by starving it of nutrient.

Methods

The Old World studies reported here are based on transects done in Malaysia in August 1970 and February 1976, and in the Nilgiri Hills in September 1970, as part of a systematic comparison of tropical forests the world around. I have revisited them since to draw and or identify the trees involved, and to classify their architectures. The studies in Costa Rica were done in October 1975 and July 1978; those in Puerto Rico, in January 1971 and April 1979; that in Dominica, in March 1972; and that in Panama, in the summer of 1977.

1. Study Areas

All transects were in areas receiving 170 cm of rain a year or more; all sites except Pasoh Reserve, Malaysia, average over 200 cm a year. Barro Colorado Island, Panama, suffers a severe dry season: in over half of the last fifty years, three consecutive months elapsed with an average of less than 3 cm of rain per month. Pasoh Reserve, Malaysia, has no predictably dry month, but it suffers a drought of a month or more every few years. Avalanchi, in the Nilgiri Hills, presumably receives little rain the first few months of the year, but the weather then is cool enough to lessen the effects of the drought. On the other hand, cyclones can spill over 200 cm of rain on Avalanchi in a single month (Blasco 1971), a figure unheard of for any of our other sites except, perhaps, Puerto Rico.

Most of our sites suffer drought only rarely, and some sites, such as the elfin forests atop the Luquillo Mountains of Puerto Rico and in the Monteverde Cloud Forest Reserve of Costa Rica, seem perpetually soggy. The air at these two sites is so moist, and the wind from the sea so constant, that the average diurnal temperature range at these two sites is 2-4°C, compared to 5-7°C at most other montane and 6-10°C at most lowland sites. The elfin forest sites in the Luquillos and at Monteverde are also uncommonly foggy: Pico del Oeste averages 260 langleys (cal/cm²/day) of solar radiation (Baynton 1968), and the Monteverde ridgetop averages 232 (Lawton 1980: both averages are based on one year of records), compared to the 400 langleys typical of lowland rain forests.

In India, one transect, "Avalanchi 2&3," was well inside, and another, "Avalanchi 4&5", was near the upper edge of the shola behind Avalanchi Rest House, at about 2100 m. The forest canopy was dominated by *Syzygium calophyllifolia* and *Syzygium arnottianum* (Myrtaceae), *Cinnamomum wightii* (Lauraceae) and *Evodia lunur-ankenda* (Rutaceae). The understory included *Lasianthus venulosa, Psychotria bisulcata* and *Psychotria elongata*: the two *Psychotria* (Rubiaceae) dominated the understory of "Avalanchi 4&5" almost to the exclusion of everything else. The upper margins of the shola were fronted by *Rhododendron arboreum* (Ericaceae) and *Rhodomyrtus tomentosa* (Myrtaceae). This forest was not heavily mossed, and although *Syzygium calophyllifolia* had the densely twigged crowns with domed subcrowns ("densely twigged cushion crowns") characteristic of mossier forest, many other species did not. A canopy story was easily distinguishable from the somewhat irregular and patchy understory, but the canopy here was no more even than that of lowland tropical forest. Trees here lacked aerial roots, and at least one tree had a spectacular woody vine 8 cm thick. Blasco (1971, pp. 194-198) has described the forest at nearby Lakkidi, and has brought together a great deal of information on the ecology of the mountains of south India.

In peninsular Malaysia, several transects were atop Gunung Ulu Kali, at about 1750

m. An "architecture walk" on level ground through the pygmy forest, about 2 m tall, was dominated by *Dacrydium comosum* (Podocarpaceae), *Leptospermum flavescens* (Myrtaceae) and *Syzygium* spp. The *Leptospermum* grew almost like krummholz plants, the trunk often rising a few centimetres or decimetres from the ground, and then turning parallel to it for a metre or more before rising to the canopy. Much of the ground, and many of the tree bases, were carpeted by sphagnum, and the forest was wreathed by the carnivorous vine *Nepenthes.* Another transect, Ulu Kali B, was in forest of *Leptospermum* and *Dacrydium* 7 m tall, whose even, seemingly wind-planed canopy often masked the unevenness of the ground. Underneath the canopy, the ground and tree trunks were largely covered by a thick carpet of sphagnum, but (in early 1976) the crowns were mossless. Saplings were abundant in patches in the understory, and *Nepenthes* were everywhere. *Leptospermum* and *Dacrydium* here grow on peaty soils with a thin iron hardpan, or on blanket peat (Whitmore and Burnham 1969): they must reflect a striking scarcity of mineral nutrient.

Ulu Kali A was in forest about 11 m high, with a canopy entirely of broad-leaved trees, abundant *Pandanus klossi* 1 to 6 m tall under the canopy, and very little *Nepenthes.* The trees there generally branched at more than half their height; their branches were mossed, often drippingly so, and often twisted. Most trunks were moderately mossed, and there were occasional tunnels formed by aerial roots. Many, but not all, the canopy trees had dense cushion crowns. This forest was far less mossy than the preceding. Ulu Kali C was on a level ridgetop, perhaps 10 m wide, with steep slopes, with forest of *Pentaphylax euryoides* (Pentaphylacaceae) and *Dacrydium comosum* 11 to 13 m tall. The canopy here was neither wind-planed nor completely closed. Most trunks and branches were moderately mossed, and aerial roots were fairly common here, forming mossy tangles. Stone (1981) describes the vegetation and flora atop Gunung Ulu Kali.

Three transects were atop Gunung Batu Brinchang in the Cameron Highlands of peninsular Malaysia, at about 2000 m. G. Brinchang N_1 was on a level ridgetop several metres wide, just the other side of the summit repeater station from the road : N_2 is a later repeat in roughly the same area. From the top, the forest canopy there looked very smooth and even, and indeed, one could easily distinguish a canopy layer 9 m tall of densely twigged monolayer cushion crowns, largely *Syzygium* sp. (very like *S. calophyllifolia* of the Nilgiris, but with larger, although similar, leaves), from the understory of woody-stemmed ground-herbs : plants of intermediate height were more sparsely, and far more patchily, distributed. Stems, trunks, and the bases of their primary branches were more thickly mossed here than at any of my other sites. The trail occasionally tunnelled under prop roots and anastomosing trunks; *Nepenthes* abounded. The productivity of this tract appeared very low : a mossy clearing 7 m wide, open to the sky, which I first saw in 1968, appeared hardly changed (and hardly disturbed) in 1970 and 1976, and had finally acquired a fair number of understory saplings by 1981 : a response twenty times slower than is usual for lowland rain forest. On the other hand, the surrounding forest apparently grew 2 or 3 m taller between 1968 and 1971.

G. Brinchang A_1 and A_2 were on a narrow ridge which leaves the road to the repeater station from the right near mile 47. The canopy over A_1 was irregular and full of openings. Each group of contiguous crowns was quite even, but separate patches of canopy were often at different levels. Story structure was evident where the canopy had matured, but not in the gaps. In places, the canopy appeared "doubled" where trees had grown up to fill gaps between canopy crowns and spread their branches just under the more compact and densely twigged crowns of the canopy. Moss and *Nepenthes* abounded, and there were extraordinary tangles of roots, as if roots and trunks anastomized at random up to 60 cm above the ground. The canopy over A_2 was more even, and among the abundant ground-herbs, numerous *Didymocarpus* sp. (Gesneriaceae), *Argostemma yappi* (Rubiaceae) and *Sonerila* sp. (Melastomaceae) were flowering in February 1976.

Fraser's Hill 1 and 2 were atop Bukit Fraser, along "Pine Tree Trail," a few hundred metres from "The Pines" bungalow, on a level place perhaps 30 m wide atop a ridge, at about 1200 m. In contrast to the other Malaysian montane transect sites, this forest was fairly tall (over 20 m), there was no sign of story structure, few crowns were unusually densely twigged, few branches were particularly gnarled, there was rather little moss, and (not the least of the contrasts) there were numerous woody vines up to 3 cm thick. *Pithecellobium* sp. (Leguminosae) and *Memecylon* sp. (Memecylaceae) were the most common canopy trees, but *Myristica*, which carries its leaves in horizontal sprays on branches radiating in layers from a central trunk, an architecture absent from the canopy atop Gunung Uli Kali or Gunung Batu Brinchang, was among the canopy trees of Pine Tree Trail. The trees of Pine Tree Trail, however, were remarkably clumped and seemed to grow from raised lumps. Moreover, in February 1976, during a great drought that afflicted all peninsular Malaysia, the ground here was soft and wet, while in lowland rain forest the ground was dry and as hard as iron. The ground cover was largely herbaceous, with many *Sonerila* (Melastomaceae), and there were a great many palms with trunks about 2 cm thick.

The lowland transects in Malaysia (Pasoh 1 and 2) were in mixed dipterocarp forest in the "IBP reserve" at Pasoh. Woody vines up to 6 cm thick were quite common here, and trunkless palms with palmate leaves made up much of the ground vegetation. The ecology of this reserve is summarized in the *Malayan Nature Journal* Volume 30, part 2 (August 1978).

In Puerto Rico my montane transects were atop the Luquillo Mountains, at about 1050 m. El Yunque 71 was done in January 1971 in forest about 5 m high on a level tract near the top of El Yunque; it was repeated in April 1979 (although overlap was not complete). This forest was dominated by *Ocotea spathulata* (Lauraceae), *Tabebuia rigida* (Bignoniaceae) and *Eugenia borinquensis* (Myrtaceae). Many tree-trunks crawled on or just above the ground before rising to the canopy. Moss was heavy, often dripping, the canopy was even, and understory shrubbery was sparse compared to the canopy. Some trees, especially *Calycogonium squamulosum* (Melastomaceae), *Tabebuia*, and canopy individuals of *Ocotea* carry monolayer crowns on dense arrays of parallel twigs. Another transect was on Pico del Este, in forest about 6 m high, dominated by *Eugenia borinquensis* and *Clusia* sp. (Guttiferae), on level ground. The canopy over the transect was quite even, but climbing a tree at its end, Robert Lawton saw the canopy downslope undulating on a scale of 3 to 5 m, with domes representing *Clusia* crowns. There was also a tree fall gap or two, and an emergent patch of canopy involving several trees. The forest was reasonably well mossed, and bromeliads were scattered from the ground to the top of the canopy. Most

Fig. 2a. *Didymopanax pittieri* (Araliaceae). Near continental divide at 1500 m in Monteverde Cloud Forest Reserve. Drawing by Alex Murawski.

Fig. 2b. *Psychotria acuminata* (Rubiaceae). Forest understory, Barro Colorado Island, Panama. Drawing by Marshall Hasbrauck.

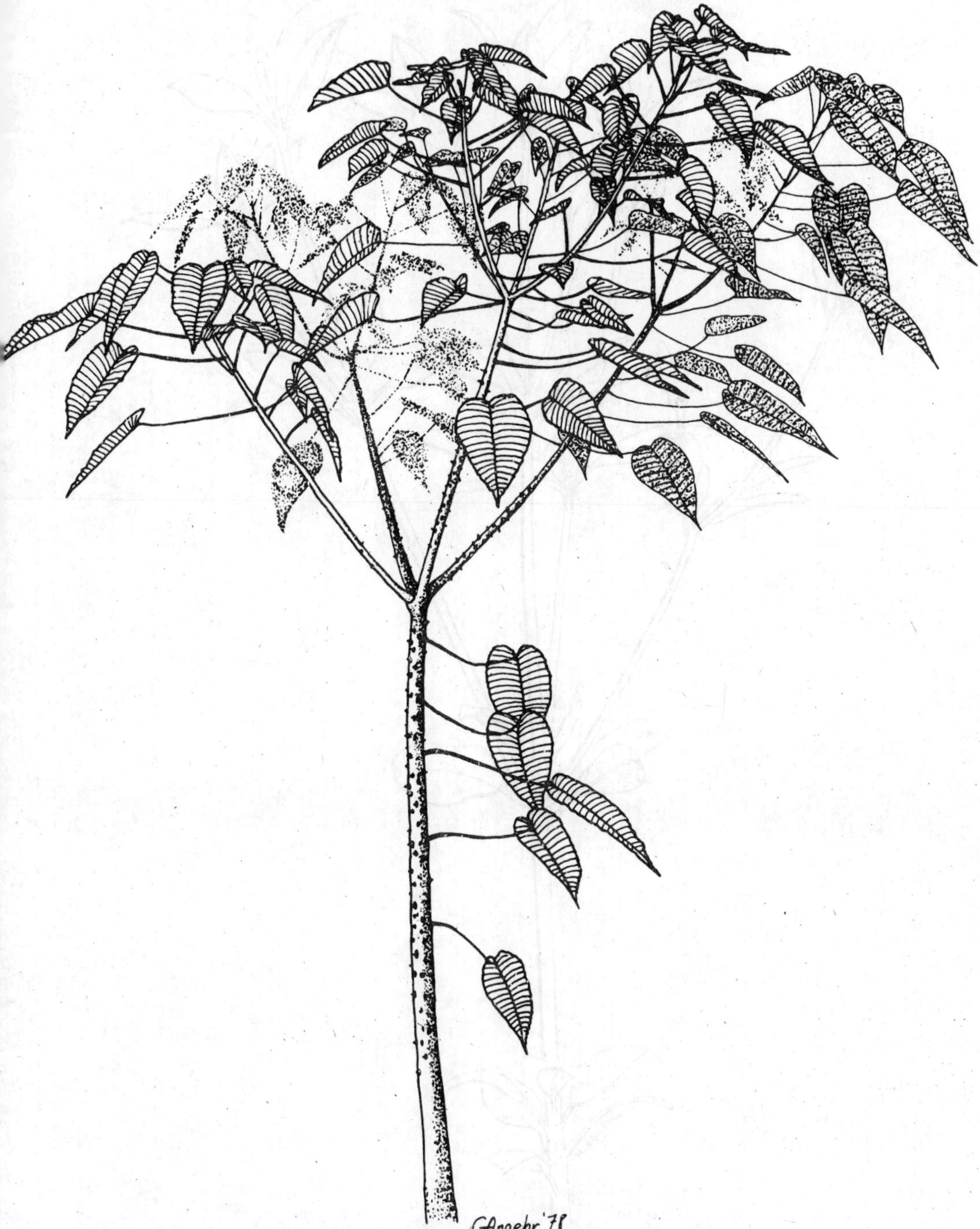

Fig. 3a. *Hura crepitans* (Euphorbiaceae), 3 m tall. Laboratory clearing, Barro Colorado Island, Panama. Drawing by George Angehr.

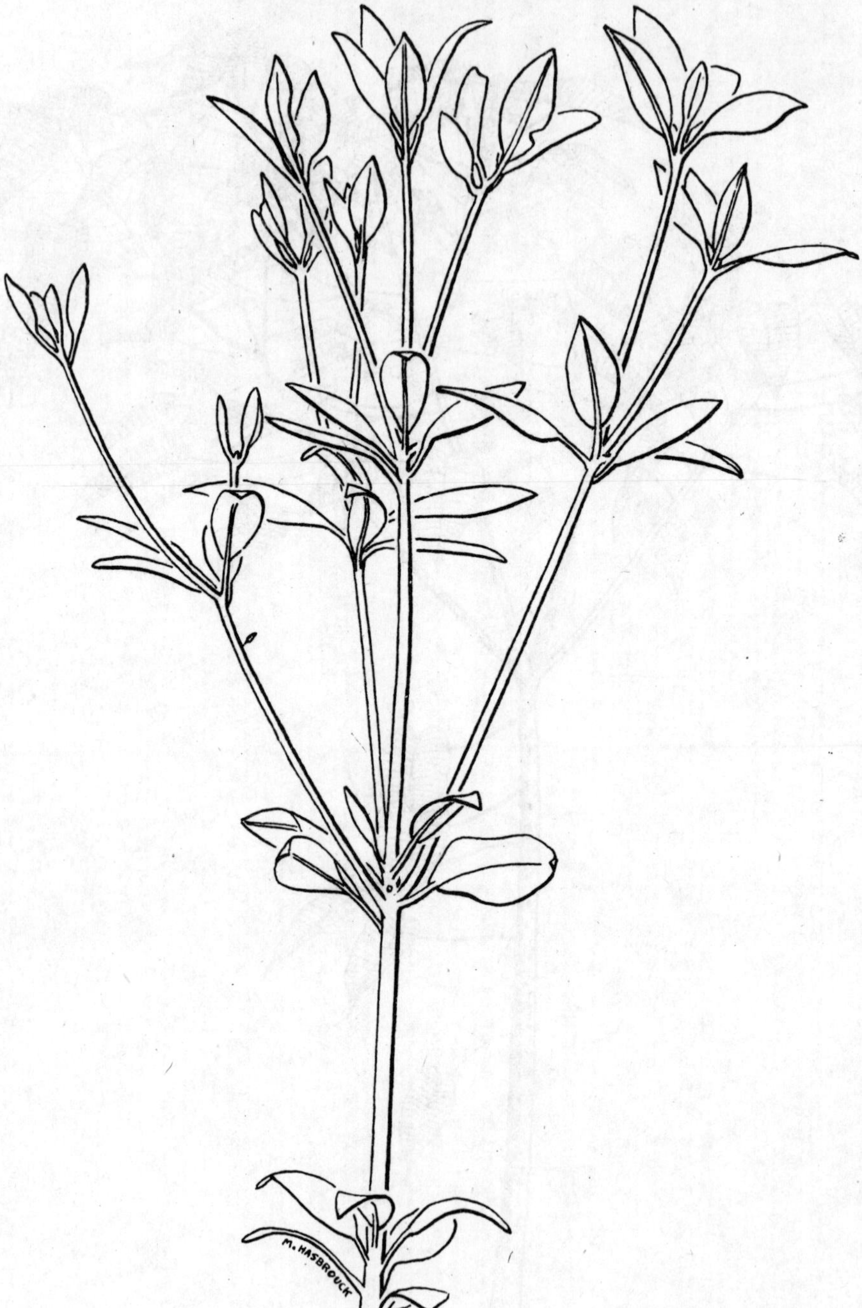

Fig. 3b. *Rhododendron malayanum* (Ericaceae). Summit heath, Gunung Ulu Kali. Drawing by Noel Holbrook, redone by Marshall Hasbrouck.

trees had aerial roots. A third transect was near the top of Mt. Britton, in a park-like stand of *Calycogonium squamulosum.* The understory here was well mossed, with some ground herbs and low *Calycogonium* seedlings, occasional ground bromeliads, and very few plants of intermediate stature. Mt. Britton was the least mossy of the Luquillo transects, and the one with the fewest bromeliads. In all the Luquillo transects, especially Mt. Britton, short squat tree ferns, *Cyathea arborea,* were common in the understory. The elfin forest of the Luquillos is remarkably unproductive : regeneration from gaps is ten times as slow as in lowland rainforest, and stump sprouts often dominate the regeneration (Byer and Weaver 1977). This forest is unusually well studied : Briscoe (1966) and Baynton (1968) described the climate, and Howard (1968) and Gleason and Cook (1927) have described the vegetation.

In Puerto Rico, the two lowland transects, Puerto Rico 1 and Puerto Rico 2&3, were in a valley at 220 m on the northern slopes of the Luquillo Mountains. The forest canopy here was rather irregular, so I also report a transect at 240 m along the top of Palmer's Ridge on the Atlantic (windward) coast of Dominica. In Dominica the lowland forest was taller and statelier, and its canopy was more nearly intact. Pinnate-leaf palms made up much of the ground vegetation in the lowland transects in Puerto Rico, and many of the small "saplings" in both Puerto Rico and Dominica.

In Costa Rica, two transects, MV Cuesta 1 and MV Cuesta 2, were in tracts of continuous canopy about 10 m tall just to the Pacific (leeward) side of the continental divide, at 1500 m in the Monteverde Cloud Forest Reserve. These sites were along the Sendero Brillante, a few hundred metres southeast of the "Ventana" (Lawton and Dryer 1980). The trees were very mossy and loaded with broad-leaved epiphytes; the canopy was often "doubled" by trees growing and spreading between crowns of the upper canopy. Crowns here were not particularly densely twigged, nor did leafy twigs necessarily point upward. Tree ferns and big-leaved plants such as marantads and heliconias made up much of the understory.

Two transects were in elfin forest. MV Elfin 1 was on a windward slope a few nundred metres east of the "Ventana". MV Elfin 2 was just southeast of the Ventana, at the top of a windward slope, in a patch of continuous wind-planed canopy 5 m high. This forest was well mossed, but the moss rarely formed the thick jackets so characteristic of Gunung Brinchang. The canopy formed an upper story of foliage about a metre thick, rarely "doubled." The understory was patchy but reasonably abundant ground herbage, with emergents a metre or more tall poking up toward the canopy. Many tree trunks were crawling on the ground, or 30 to 60 cm above it, before rising to the canopy. Fallen logs, stems and branches were well mossed up to where canopy crown foliage began. Aerial roots were everywhere, and litter accumulated on mats of such roots, masking some splendid booby-traps, and what with the anastomosing trunks around or under which one must crawl, and these "false floors", this was particularly difficult forest to move through. In general, the elfin forest at Monteverde is distinguished by the many different levels of the canopy, corresponding to the many different ages of different patches of forest. This forest is also remarkably productive and dynamic : tracts are always being eroded or blown down by the (often hurricane force) winds which assail the ridge at every season (Lawton 1980, 1982), and regeneration in the resulting gaps is remarkably rapid. The climate is very like that atop the Luquillo Mountains in Puerto Rico: the high productivity must reflect the richness of the volcanic soil at Monteverde.

Another transect, MV Ravine, was in a ravine at about 1350 m which bisects the community of Monteverde, in forest about 35 m tall. The canopy was as irregular as that of lowland tropical forest outside the hurricane belt. Many canopy trees had cushion crowns, often densely twigged, with simple leaves, held inclined, spiralled about the tips of the twigs, but some canopy trees, such as *Dussia* (Leguminosae) and *Cedrela* (Meliaceae) had compound leaves: Fraser's Hill 1 & 2, and the architecture walk at Avalanchi, were the only other montane transects where some canopy trees other than *Weinmannia* (Cunoniaceae) had compound leaves. The forest floor had large patches of the understory herb *Pavonia* (Malvaceae), and there were enough vines (some thorny) to obstruct motion through the forest.

Finally, two transects, combined as Cerro Muerte, were in oak forest about 25 m tall, with subdominant *Weinmannia,* at roughly 3000 m on Costa Rica's Cerro de la Muerte. Though the results are pooled, the transects themselves were 35 km apart. One was at the head of a ravine near the end of a logging road, 200 m from the Pan American Highway, 31.5 km west of Villa Mills and 50 km east of Cartago, and the other was in a poorly drained level area 2 km down a road which parts north from the highway 2 km east of Villa Mills. The oaks had cushion crowns, with dense sprays of twigs, each crowding inclined coriaceous leaves spiralled about its tip, and these crowns formed an even, but not fully closed, canopy. Their branches, and often their trunks, were thick with moss. In the west transect there were no lianes to speak of. The understory saplings there included a *Didymopanax pittieri,* several *Clusia,* and some leathery-leaved melastomes. Some of the sampled saplings were shoots off aerial roots: roots and fallen logs made it hard to move about this forest. At the eastern site, story structure was clear: one story formed by canopy trees and trees aspiring to the canopy, and an understory, almost exclusively melastomes, about 2 m high, with emergents. Many saplings were growing from nurse logs. The ground there was thickly mossed. The transect included two *Podocarpus,* big-leaved aroid vines were present, and *Clusia* crowns were visible in the distance. Sawyer and Lindsey (1971) describe a transect in similar forest at Villa Mills; Holdridge *et al.* (1971) supply additional information on its climate.

A transect from mature lowland forest on Barro Colorado Island, Panama, near Balboa Trail No. 10 is included for comparison. This forest is 35 to 40 m tall, and plants with compound leaves abound both in the canopy and at all levels of the understory. The soil here is basaltic (Dietrich, Windsor and Dunne 1982) and apparently quite fertile (Foster and Brokaw 1982). Croat (1978) and Leigh, Rand and Windsor (1982) describe the ecology of this forest.

2. Measurements

The transects were designed to assess

a) the density of saplings and trees of different sizes,

b) the average height of saplings and trees of different diameters, and of the canopy as a whole,

c) the average length, and the average area, of leaves carried by sampled saplings of different sizes, and of leaves sampled directly from the forest floor, and

d) the spectrum of leaf arrangements and tree architectures in different strata of the forest.

Fig. 4. *Psychotria deflexa* (Rubiaceae), 2 m high. Forest understory, Barro Colorado Island. Drawing by Karen Kraeger.

Fig. 5. *Psychotria furcata* (Rubiaceae), 1 m high. Forest understory, Barro Colorado Island. Drawing by Jane Shuttleworth.

Transects were done three ways. The pygmy forest transect at Gunung Ulu Kali and a sample of trees for architecture and leaf arrangement at Avalanchi were strip censuses, sampling trees along a trail in one case and along the edge of the shola in the other.

Some montane forest transects were plot samples: the other transects at Gunung Ulu Kali, the two transects off mile 47 of the road to the repeater station at Gunung Brinchang, the 1979 transects in Puerto Rico, and the elfin forest transects at Monteverde. In some of these transects, saplings less than 10 cm diameter at breast height (*dbh*) were sampled from a narrower strip down the centre of the plot from which trees were sampled.

Other transects followed a modified "point-quarter" sampling scheme (cf Cottam and Curtis 1956, Wadsworth 1970). The usual procedure was to lay a 100 ft or 30 m tape the floor of a suitable forest, and choose Sample Points on alternating sides of the tape, ten feet to either side, every 25 ft of the tape starting at 12.5 ft or every 8 m starting at 3 m, as appropriate. Through each sample point, I passed lines perpendicular and parallel to the tape, dividing the Sample Point's surroundings into four quadrants. In each quadrant, I chose the nearest small sapling (6-12 mm *dbh*), the nearest medium sapling (13-25 mm *dbh*), the nearest large sapling (26-100 mm *dbh*), the nearest tree (over 100 mm *dbh*) and the second nearest tree, measuring the distances of each plant from the sample point. For each plant thus encountered, I estimated the height and recorded other characteristics as described below. Usually, I also measured the distance from each sampled tree to its nearest and second nearest neighbouring trees (regardless of quadrant), adding any new ones encountered thus to the sample.

This procedure was sometimes modified. In transects MV Cuesta 1 and 2, I took only one Sample Point apiece, but in each quadrant I sampled the four nearest small and the four nearest medium saplings, the three nearest large saplings, and the four nearest trees. Fraser's Hill 1 had two Sample Points: in each quadrant I sampled the two nearest of the small, the medium, and the large saplings, the three nearest trees, and the trees nearest to each of these three.

For each small and medium sapling, I measured the length and width of a representative leaf or leaflet, and assessed the arrangement of the leaves on the twig, or, in the case of compound leaves, of leaflets on their rachis, whether they were alternate (*AHS*) or opposite (*OHS*) along the sides of horizontal twigs, forming horizontal sprays (*HS*); spiral (*F*/) or decussate (+/) around erect or inclined twigs; spiral (*F-HS*) or decussate (+–*HS*) around horizontal twigs, flattened into horizontal sprays; spiral (*F*–) or decussate (+–) around horizontal twigs, but incompletely flattened, if at all; alternate (*A*/), but not spiral, or opposite (*O*/) but not decussate, on inclined twigs; or in whorls spaced along erect or inclined stems (*wh*/).

In nearly every transect I sampled litter leaves, choosing four (sometimes more) points evenly spaced along a tape, 3 to 8 m apart (25 ft or 8 m apart along the central tape in standard point-quarter transects), and measuring the length and width of the ten leaves which were under, or whose edges were nearest, to each point (forty or more leaves per transect). In many point-quarter transects. I sampled the ground vegetation less than 1.6 m high, suspending a thread from 25 points 30 cm apart in 120 × 120 cm grids, one grid centred on each Sample Point.

In some transects I also recorded leaf orientation, whether it was held horizontally, inclined to the twig, or drooped, and whether

TABLE 1

AVERAGE HEIGHT, AND DENSITY, OF DIFFERENT SIZES OF PLANTS IN DIFFERENT FORESTS

Altitude (m)	Transect	Average height (m) of plants with dbh (mm) between: 6-12	13-25	26-50	51-101	102-203	204-406	407+	F. H.	m² per plant of size: S	M	L	T	C
1500	MV Elfin 2	1.8	2.4	2.9	3.9	4	—	—	4	9	7	3	7	3.8
	(Costa Rica)	8	11	16	12	11			19					20
1050	El Yunque 79	2.2	3.1	3.7	4.5	6	6	—	5	17	9	3	7	3.8
	(Puerto Rico)	5	9	10	18	11	1		22					22
1050	El Yunque 71	1.9	2.9	4.0	4.3	5	5	—	5	5	20	3	5	3.8
	(Puerto Rico)	9	9	8	19	29	3		32					
1050	Pico del Este	1.9	2.8	4.0	5.3	6	6	—	6	3	5	3	10	3.0
	(Puerto Rico)	12	7	3	12	3	2		16					16
1500	MV Elfin 1	1.9	3.1	3.6	4.1	5	6	—	6	5	4	3	5	9.9
	(Costa Rica)	8	6	6	6	4	2		2					3
2000	G Brinchang A_1	2.0	2.1	3.1	—	6	6	—	6	2	9	19	12	12.8
	(Malaysia)	18	4	2		13	3		14					4
2000	G Brinchang A_2	2.0	2.9	4.6	4.8	6	—	—	6	5	9	2	6	5.0
	(Malaysia)	12	6	6	25	9			11					11
2100	Avalanchi 4&5	1.9	2.6	3.4	4.0	5	6	7	6	4	5	2	5	5.0
	(India)	20	20	14	6	37	12	3	50					50
1750	Ulu Kali B	2.1	3.2	4.3	5.6	6	8	-	7	1	1	2	4	3.2
	(Malaysia)	32	-26	10	4	4	2	0	6					7
2000	G Brinchang N_1	2.1	3.3	4.6	5.9	6	6	7	6	1	3	3	6	
	(Malaysia)	18	18	12	8	33	18	4						
2000	G Brinchang N_2	2.1	2.6	4.3	8.0	9	9	10	9	2	3	2	4	4.9
	(Malaysia)	16	16	11	4	28	10	4	35					35
1500	MV Cuesta 1	2.0	2.6	3.7	3.5	5	9	10	9	4	7	9	21	32
	(Costa Rica)	16	16	1	11	3	8	5	9					10
1050	Mt Britton	—	4.1	1.7	4.2	9	9	—	9	100+	100	11	9	11
	(Puerto Rico)	0	1	2	6	10	1		9					9
2100	Avalanchi 2&3	2.0	2.6	3.5	4.0	7	7	10	—	3	4	6	10	—
	(India)	28	27	19	4	24	28	6						
1750	Ulu Kali A	2.6	4.0	6.1	6.0	10	11	—	11	3	5	3	4	6.2
	(Malaysia)	13	8	1	12	17	5		14					14
1750	Ulu Kali C	1.9	3.4	4.2	6.9	11	13	—	12	3	3	9	10	12.2
	(Malaysia)	12	9	6	6	7	4		9					9

1500	MV Cuesta 2	1.7	2.3	4.0	5.2	7	9	14	13	7	11	10	13	45
	(Costa Rica)	16	16	6	6	10	4	2	3					4½
1200	Fraser's Hill 2	2.3	3.7	5.8	8.1	11	18	21	20	2	3	2	8	27
	(Malaysia)	16	16	11	5	17	11	2	7					8½
1200	Fraser's Hill 1	2.4	3.1	4.6	6.7	11	15	23	21	4	2	4	7	26
	(Malaysia)	16	16	8	8	16	12	3	6					9
220	Puerto Rico 1	1.9	3.1	5.1	7.0	8	12	22	22	6	11	8	19	
	(Puerto Rico)	14	12	8	7	16	14	6						
220	Puerto Rico 2&3	1.8	2.4	4.8	7.3	9	13	22	23	21	16	10	15	
	(Puerto Rico)	21	16	19	5	29	18	12						
3000	Cerro Muerte	1.9	2.9	4.3	7.8	9	16	25	25	4	6	16	20	86
	(Costa Rica)	17	18	12	7	10	16	8	8					8
240	Dominica	1.8	2.7	4.3	6.8	10	14	25	29	15	26	13	16	83
		27	22	4	13	39	17	20	13					14
1350	MV Ravine	2.0	2.6	3.8	6.2	11	17	33	31	2	6	16	16	66
	(Costa Rica)	16	16	11	4	11	11	7	7					7
130	Barro Colorado	2.0	2.8	4.8	7.2	13	17	35	35	10	12	11	28	254
	(Panama)	13	16	11	5	5	6	5	5					5
100	Pasoh 2	2.2	3.2	5.7	9.2	12	18	34	38	4	6	5	18	84
	(Malaysia)	16	16	8	8	19	4	7	5					6½
100	Pasoh 1	2.0	3.5	5.0	7.2	13	20	32	43	3	5	8	13	74
	(Malaysia)	16	16	13	3	17	8	8	7					6

For each transect, the top row gives the average heights of woody plants of dbh 6-12 mm, 13-25 mm, 26-50 mm, 51-101 mm, 102-203 mm, 204-406 mm, and over 406 mm respectively; the forest height (F.H., the average height of plants fully in the canopy), and the number of square metres of ground per small sapling S 6-12 mm dbh, per medium sapling M 13-25 mm dbh, per large sapling L 26-101 mm dbh, per tree T over 101 mm dbh, and per canopy tree C, counting as ½ each tree whose crown is only half exposed. The bottom row gives the sample sizes: again, for canopy trees, each tree whose crown is only half exposed is counted as ½.

TABLE 2

AVERAGE LENGTH, L, AND SIZE, $(LW)^{1/2}$, OF LEAVES SAMPLED FROM THE FOREST FLOOR (LL), SMALL SAPLINGS (S), MEDIUM SAPLINGS (M), AND GROUND VEGETATION (GV).

Altitude	Transect		Average ± Standard Deviation (Sample Size) For LL		S		M		GV	
3000	Cerro Muerte (Costa Rica)	$(LW)^{1/2}$	36 ± 16	(59)	79 ± 23	(18)	68 ± 19	(18)		
		L	53 ± 24		123 ± 31		107 ± 26			
2100	Avalanchi 4&5 (India)	$(LW)^{1/2}$	39 ± 14	(47)	55 ± 14	(19)	69 ± 26	(20)	60 ± 20	(27)
		L	61 ± 23		85 ± 26		116 ± 52		91 ± 29	
2100	Avalanchi 2&3 (India)	$(LW)^{1/2}$	40 ± 18	(67)	63 ± 22	(28)	55 ± 18	(28)	55 ± 23	(63)
		L	60 ± 31		102 ± 41		88 ± 37		90 ± 41	
2000	G Brinchang N_2 (Malaysia)	$(LW)^{1/2}$	39 ± 26	(40)	58 ± 23	(15)	57 ± 23	(15)		
		L	51 ± 38		79 ± 37		79 ± 45			
2000	G Brinchang N_1 (Malaysia)	$(LW)^{1/2}$	30 ± 18	(52)	60 ± 28	(19)	58 ± 21	(19)	85 ± 42	(9)
		L	42 ± 29		85 ± 47		80 ± 34		127 ± 70	
2000	G Brinchang A_2 (Malaysia)	$(LW)^{1/2}$	31 ± 17	(70)	56 ± 29	(12)	37 ± 11	(6)		
		L	41 ± 25		80 ± 43		41 ± 15			
2000	G Brinchang A_1 (Malaysia)	$(LW)^{1/2}$	34 ± 13	(60)	67 ± 24	(18)	76 ± 25	(6)		
		L	45 ± 25		94 ± 40		111 ± 37			
1750	G Ulu Kali C (Malaysia)	$(LW)^{1/2}$			54 ± 37	(12)	32 ± 28	(9)		
		L			98 ± 80		41 ± 36			
1750	G Ulu Kali B (Malaysia)	$(LW)^{1/2}$	21 ± 19	(40)	60 ± 32	(32)	66 ± 25	(26)		
		L	32 ± 25		94 ± 59		101 ± 50			
1750	G Ulu Kali A (Malaysia)	$(LW)^{1/2}$	26 ± 23	(60)	87 ± 33	(12)	65 ± 30	(7)		
		L	39 ± 36		126 ± 42		94 ± 45			
1500	MV Elfin 2 (Costa Rica)	$(LW)^{1/2}$	52 ± 27	(45)	96 ± 44	(8)	94 ± 40	(11)		
		L	74 ± 35		140 ± 52		135 ± 32			
1500	MV Elfin 1 (Costa Rica)	$(LW)^{1/2}$	45 ± 22	(28)	92 ± 38	(8)	74 ± 18	(6)		
		L	72 ± 41		129 ± 52		136 ± 37			

1500	MV Cuesta 2	$(LW)^{1/2}$	38 ± 26	(41)	134 ± 73	(16)	113 ± 79	(16)		
	(Costa Rica)	L	56 ± 38		187 ± 91		163 ± 99			
1500	MV Cuesta 1	$(LW)^{1/2}$	75 ± 61	(57)	174 ± 104	(16)	240 ± 74	(16)		
	(Costa Rica)	L	99 ± 59		254 ± 135		292 ± 69			
1350	MV Ravine	$(LW)^{1/2}$	49 ± 18	(40)	88 ± 24	(16)	100 ± 70	(16)		
	(Costa Rica)	L	74 ± 29		154 ± 45		151 ± 75			
1200	Frasers Hill 2	$(LW)^{1/2}$	50 ± 16	(40)	93 ± 29	(16)	84 ± 24	(16)	75 ± 32	(33)
	(Malaysia)	L	75 ± 23		163 ± 57		368 ± 164		277 ± 157	
1200	Frasers Hill 1	$(LW)^{1/2}$	42 ± 16	(40)	91 ± 28	(16)	92 ± 22	(16)	74 ± 28	(25)
	(Malaysia)	L	62 ± 24		154 ± 45		209 ± 121		224 ± 158	
1050	Pico del Este	$(LW)^{1/2}$	63 ± 24	(50)	45 ± 32	(12)	56 ± 30	(7)		
	(Puerto Rico)	L	76 ± 29		62 ± 46		78 ± 42			
1050	El Yunque 79	$(LW)^{1/2}$	68 ± 23	(39)	46 ± 25	(5)	55 ± 30	(9)		
	(Puerto Rico)	L	91 ± 31		66 ± 39		81 ± 49			
1050	El Yunque 71	$(LW)^{1/2}$	67 ± 23	(49)	66 ± 13	(9)	60 ± 22	(9)		
	(Puerto Rico)	L	89 ± 32		104 ± 25		95 ± 41			
1050	Mt Britton	$(LW)^{1/2}$	46 ± 21	(50)						
	(Puerto Rico)	L	68 ± 27							
240	Dominica	$(LW)^{1/2}$	64 ± 22	(61)	116 ± 51	(27)	118 ± 55	(23)	106 ± 38	(27)
		L	94 ± 28		184 ± 74		208 ± 102		168 ± 58	
220	Puerto Rico 2&3	$(LW)^{1/2}$	73 ± 33	(70)	124 ± 32	(21)	148 ± 48	(15)		
	(Puerto Rico)	L	109 ± 54		227 ± 86		320 ± 206			
220	Puerto Rico 1	$(LW)^{1/2}$	67 ± 28	(39)	126 ± 70	(14)	122 ± 31	(12)		
	(Puerto Rico)	L	95 ± 40		202 ± 100		216 ± 47			
130	Barro Colorado	$(LW)^{1/2}$	88 ± 57	(37)	101 ± 48	(14)	104 ± 48	(16)		
	(Panama)	L	129 ± 72		172 ± 87		165 ± 75			
100	Pasoh 2	$(LW)^{1/2}$	59 ± 37	(40)	92 ± 21	(16)	131 ± 44	(16)		
	(Malaysia)	L	87 ± 55		176 ± 69		241 ± 90			
100	Pasoh 1	$(LW)^{1/2}$	65 ± 26	(40)	111 ± 48	(16)	111 ± 21	(16)	111 ± 61	(52)
	(Malaysia)	L	97 ± 42		206 ± 93		192 ± 42		261 ± 202	

TABLE 3

THE RELATION BETWEEN ALTITUDE AND LEAF SIZE

Average Size $(LW)^{1/2}$, in mm, of Understory and Litter Leaves, as Predicted from the Altitude, in metres, of the Forest, and as Observed.

Altitude	Transect	Average Litter Leaf Size Predicted	Average Litter Leaf Size Observed	Average Understory Leaf Size Predicted	Average Understory Leaf Size Observed
3000	Cerro Muerte	17	36	42	74
2100	Avalanchi 4&5	34	39	63	62
2100	Avalanchi 2&3	34	40	63	59
2000	G Brinchang N_2	36	39	65	58
2000	G Brinchang N_1	36	30	65	59
2000	G Brinchang A_2	36	31	65	47
2000	G Brinchang A_1	36	34	65	72
1750	G Ulu Kali C	41		71	43
1750	G Ulu Kali B	41	21	71	63
1750	G Ulu Kali A	41	26	71	76
1500	MV Elfin 2	46	52	76	95
1500	MV Elfin 1	46	45	76	83
1500	MV Cuesta 2	46	38	76	124
1500	MV Cuesta 1	46	75	76	207
1350	MV Ravine	49	49	80	94
1200	Fraser's Hill 2	51	50	83	89
1200	Fraser's Hill 1	51	42	83	92
1050	Pico del Este	54	63	87	51
1050	El Yunque 79	54	68	87	51
1050	El Yunque 71	54	67	87	63
1050	Mt Britton	54	46		
240	Dominica	70	64	105	117
220	Puerto Rico 2&3	70	73	106	136
220	Puerto Rico 1	70	67	106	124
130	Barro Colorado	72	88	109	103
100	Pasoh 2	72	59	108	112
100	Pasoh 1	72	65	108	111

TABLE 4

THE RELATION BETWEEN A FOREST'S HEIGHT AND ITS PHYSIOGNOMY

Canopy Crown Size (CCS), Understory Leaf Arrangement Index (AI: see text), Understory Leaf Arrangement Score (z) and Average Size $(LW)^{1/2}$ of Understory (S+M) and Litter (LL) Leaves, Both Observed (Obs.) and as Predicted (Pre.) from Forest Height (F.H.)

Altitude (m)	Transect	F. H. (m)	CCS (m^2)		AI		z	S+M (mm)		LL (mm)
			Pre.	Obs.	Pre.	Obs.	Obs.	Pre.	Obs.	Obs.
1500	MV Elfin 2	4	1.9	3.8	143	150	3.74	63	95	52
1050	El Yunque 79	5	2.8	3.8	140	128	3.24	65	51	68
1050	El Yunque 71	5	2.8	3.8	140	144	3.61	65	63	67
1050	Pico del Este	6	3.9	3.0	138	146	3.66	66	51	63
1500	MV Elfin 1	6	3.9	9.9	138	156	3.82	66	83	45
2000	G Brinchang A_1	6	3.9	12.8	138	119	2.96	66	72	34
2000	G Brinchang A_2	6	3.9	5.0	138	158	3.85	66	47	31
2000	G Brinchang N_1	6	3.9		138	117	2.91	66	.59	30
2100	Avalanchi 4&5	6	3.9	5.0	138	147	3.68	66	62	39
1750	G Ulu Kali B	7	5.0	3.2	136	148	3.69	68	63	21
2000	G Brinchang N_2	9	7.7	4.9	131	113	2.78	71	58	39
1500	MV Cuesta 1	9	7.7	32	131	157	3.84	71	207	75
1050	Mt Britton	9	7.7	11	131					46
2100	Avalanchi 2&3	9	7.7		131	125	3.15	71	59	40
1750	G Ulu Kali A	11	10.8	6.2	127	121	3.04	74	76	26
1750	G Ulu Kali C	12	12.5	12.2	125	97	2.24	76	43	
1500	MV Cuesta 2	13	14.3	45	123	134	3.38	77	124	38
1200	Fraser's Hill 2	20	29.9	27	107	82	1.72	88	89	50
1200	Fraser's Hill 1	21	32.5	26	105	86	1.86	90	92	42
220	Puerto Rico 1	22	35.3		103	102	2.43	91	124	67
220	Puerto Rico 2&3	23	38.2		100	92	2.07	93	136	73
3000	Cerro Muerte	25	44	86	96	138	3.49	96	74	36
240	Dominica	29	56	83	87	75	1.49	103	117	64
1350	MV Ravine	31	63	66	83	87	1.88	106	94	49
130	Barro Colorado	35	77	154	74	48	0.66	112	103	88
100	Pasoh 2	38	89	84	67	82	1.71	117	112	59
100	Pasoh 1	43	110	74	56	65	1.14	125	111	65

TABLE 5

CORRELATIONS BETWEEN FEATURES RELATED TO FOREST PHYSIOGNOMY

Matrices of Correlations and Partial Correlations between Altitude (Alt.), Forest Height (F.H.), Litter Leaf Size (LL), Understory Leaf Size (S+M) and Leaf Arrangement Index (AI)

A) All Variables

	LL	F.H.	S+M	AI
Alt.	-.82	-.60	-.65	.62
LL		.42	.52	-.36
F. H.			.67	-.83
S+M				-.54

B) Altitude Held Constant

	LL	S+M	AI
F. H.	-.15	.47	-.74
LL		-.03	.32
S+M			-.24

C) Forest Height Held Constant

	LL	S+M	AI
Alt.	-.78	-.41	.27
LL		.35	-.02
S+M			.05

D) Altitude and Forest Height Held Constant

	S+M	AI
LL	.05	.31
S+M		.18

Fig. 6. *Anacardium excelsum* (Anacardiaceae). Canopy sprig from tree 30 m high, Barro Colorado Island. Drawing by George Angehr.

Fig. 7a. *Rhizophora* sp. (Rhizophoraceae). Sprig of canopy foliage from tree 3 m tall on the Caribbean coast of Panama. Drawing by Roxane Trappe.

Fig. 7b. *Hillia* sp. (Rubiaceae). Monteverde Cloud Forest Reserve. Drawing by Marshall Hasbrouck.

Fig. 8. *Thevetia ahouvai* (Apocynaceae), 3 m tall. Forest understory, on edge of tree fall gap, Barro Colorado Island. Drawing by George Angehr.

leaves were flat, folded about their midrib, or reflexed with the base rising and the tip pointing down.

Finally, in some transects I classified sampled plants according to architecture.

3. Classifying Trees with respect to Architecture

Halle and Oldeman (1970: see also Halle, Oldeman and Tomlinson 1978) tabulated the various "models" according to which different trees grow. These models were meant to reflect different *processes*, different mechanisms of branching and growth in relation to flowering. This paper must classify the various tree *forms* found in the forest (cf Corner 1940, pp. 24-33; 1964, p. 145). As several mechanisms sometimes yield the same tree shape, I will ignore some distinctions Halle and Oldeman considered essential. Therefore I must describe my modification of Halle and Oldeman's classification: notice that though the leaf arrangement classification takes the leaflet as the basic unit, the architecture classification is based on the whole leaf, whether simple or compound.

The simplest model is the *palm*'s, where leaves are arranged spirally (or less often, decussately) around an upright, unbranched stem. Most seedlings, many saplings, most palms, and all tree ferns belong to this model. This model includes Halle and Oldeman's, Corner, Holttum, Chamberlain and Tomlinson.

The simplest modification of this model is that of the *frangipani*, whose trunk forks into two or more equal branches, which fork likewise in turn and so forth, elaborating a crown (often umbrella-like) where each terminal branch carries leaves spiralled or decussate around its tip (Figure 2). *Didymopanax pittieri* (Araliaceae, Costa Rica), frangipani (*Plumeria rubra*: Apocynaceae) and *Psychotria acuminata* (Rubiaceae, Panama) grow thus. The frangipani model includes Halle and Oldeman's Leeuwenberg and Schoute.

If, at each fork, one branch clearly dominates (as often in *Rhododendron*), we obtain Kwan-Koriba's model (Figure 3). The plants of Kwan-Koriba's model encountered in my transects nearly all elaborated monolayer crowns like those of *Didymopanax*, but this is happenstance.

Another asymmetric version of the frangipani model yields a very different form. In this version, the *deflexa* model, where a trunk or main branch forks, the more horizontal of the two forks may then branch dichotomously in a horizontal plane (Figures 4, 5), with leaves arranged along the sides of their twigs in horizontal sprays. Thus such plants carry several horizontal sprays of foliage, as do understory *Ilex myrtillus* (Aquifoliaceae, Malaysia) or *Psychotria furcata* (Panama). A plant may change from the deflexa to the frangipani model as it grows: in Malaysia I saw canopy *Ilex myrtillus* following the frangipani or Kwan-Koriba's model.

Another variant of Kwan-Koriba's model is Scarrone's. Here the trunk is (very nearly) straight, and primary branches radiate from the trunk in successive whorls or clusters. Each primary branch then forks according to Kwan-Koriba's model: together they elaborate an umbrella crown where each terminal twig carries leaves spiralled about its end (Figure 6). The mango (*Mangifera indica*: Anacardiaceae), the cashew (*Anacardium occidentale*), *Anacardium excelsum* (Panama), and *Hasseltia floribunda* (Flacourtiaceae, Panama) follow this model.

If, like the trunk in Scarrone's model, each branch bears its branches in successive discrete radiating whorls or clusters, we obtain Rauh's model. Most Rauh plants in my transects had umbrella crowns like those of *Anacardium.*

This model is perhaps best illustrated by the avocado, *Persea americana.* In practice, it is sometimes difficult to distinguish Rauh's model from Scarrone's.

Branches may also be arranged as are leaves along a branch. Primary branches may be spiralled about the trunk, secondary branches about the primary branches, and so forth, in which case I speak of a spiral Attims model. This is perfectly illustrated by the tasty-leaved weed *Chenopodium album,* and adequately illustrated by the mangrove *Lumnitzera* (Combretaceae).

If primary branches are decussately arranged about the stem, secondary branches decussate about the primary branches, and so forth, as in *Clusia* spp. (Guttiferae), the mangrove *Rhizophora,* some *Calophyllum* (Guttiferae) and many Rubiaceae, I speak of a decussate Attims (Figure 7).

In Champagnat's model, the initial stem bends over, turning up again at its tip to support a cluster of spirally arranged leaves; more branches sprout from the bend in the initial stem, leaning over in turn before turning their leafy tips upward, and so forth (Figure 8). In Panama, *Thevetia ahouvai* (Apocynaceae) illustrates this model.

Some trees in my transects supported umbrella crowns on vertical axes whose law of branching I could not distinguish (Figure 9): I lumped these under the *almendro* model.

Shrubs (or trees) of a few vertical or inclined axes, or with one or a few inclined primary stems from which issue irregularly arranged inclined or upturned twigs with spiral or decussate leaves, whose crowns are too tall, loose or irregular to be described as umbrellas, were lumped under the *psychotria* model. Notice that although many *Psychotria* find a home here, some illustrate other models.

Shrubs composed of numerous vertical or inclined axes, with leaves arranged spirally or decussately about erect or inclined twigs and branches, whose law of branching was not clear, and whose crowns were too loose or rambling to be described as *almendro,* were classified under the *coussarea* model. These last three categories are really pigeonholes, not models.

Leaves have been spiral or decussate around vertical twigs and branches in all but one of the models described thus far. In many models, however, leaves are set along the sides of horizontal twigs, forming horizontal sprays of foliage.

In Troll's model, the initial stem leans over, supporting a horizontal spray of foliage at its end; branches sprout from the bend, as in Champagnat's model, leaning over in turn to cast forth their own horizontal sprays, and so forth (Figure 10). Trees and shrubs of this model assume very different shapes, according to how strongly the part of the "main stem" below a branch stiffens and rights itself after branching. This Troll's model includes both plants like *Olmedia aspera* (Moraceae, Panama), which have wide crowns and flexible axes, and *Sorocea affinis* (Moraceae, Panama), which have stiffer axes and tall, narrow crowns. Beeches (*Fagus* spp.) are the model's best known temperate exemplars.

In Mangenot's model, an erect stem bends over 90 degrees, its distal, horizontal section carrying a horizontal spray of foliage. From the angle arises a new vertical shoot, which bends over in turn to cast forth another horizontal spray of foliage, and so forth (Figure 11). The end result is often a vertical stem with horizontal branches bearing horizontal sprays of foliage radiating out along it. Unless the topmost shoots are visible, this model can be hard to distinguish from the following *casearia* model. In Panama, Annonaceae such as the canopy tree *Guatteria dumetorum* and the understory tree *Unonopsis pittieri* are the most conspicuous exemplars of Mangenot's model.

In the casearia model, horizontal branches with leaves along the sides of the twigs emerge evenly along the main stem, spirally arranged about it, as in such Flacourtiaceae as *Zuelania guidonia* (Figure 12) and *Casearia* spp. in Panama, or decussately arranged, as in understory *Faramea occidentalis* (Rubiaceae, Panama), or *Rheedia* spp. (Guttiferae, Panama). This model includes Halle and Oldeman's Roux, Cooke and Petit (in part).

In *casearia* plants with decussate branching, secondary branches are set in opposing pairs (*OHS* or +–*HS*) on the primary branches, and so forth. In many (most?) such plants, the junctions of leaf with twig and secondary with primary branches are often a bit twisted, in a manner suggesting that naturally decussate arrangements had been flattened into horizontal sprays (+–*HS*). In plants exposed to the sun, the topmost branches may bend upward, branching and leafing according to the decussate Attims model. Thus plants of the same species may be classified as *casearia* or decussate Attims, according to whether or not they are shaded. Understory saplings of such species will be classified under the *faramea* model, after *Faramea occidentalis*, a conspicuous Panamanian exemplar, along with other Rubiaceae and Guttiferae, of this habit.

Halle and Ng (1981) describe the transformation of *Dryanobalanops aromatica* (Dipterocarpaceae, Malaysia) from an understory *casearia* sapling with horizontal branches spirally arranged about the trunk and horizontal sprays of foliage into a canopy tree with spirally arranged leaves following a spiral Attims model : it also changes from a multilayer sapling to a monolayer tree with an umbrella crown, as its leaves become progressively less tolerant of shade.

In the *virola* model horizontal branches radiate in whorls or clusters from the main stem, forming discrete layers (Figure 13). In Panama, *Quararibea asterolepis* (Bombacaceae) and *Virola* spp. (Myristicaceae) illustrate the model, as do Myristicaceae the world around. This model includes Halle and Oldeman's Massart, and Fagerlind (in part). Species differ in the rigidity with which they follow the model (Figure 14), and in canopy species, tips of the primary branches can turn upward and behave like miniature trunks, *reiterating* the model (Oldeman 1974, Halle, Oldeman and Tomlinson 1978).

Trees following the *terminalia* model have layered crowns like those of *Virola*, but each layer represents horizontal sprays of rosettes of spirally arranged leaves. At intervals, the straight trunk puts forth a whorl or cluster of initially horizontal twigs. Each such twig curves up to carry a rosette of leaves spiralled about its upturned tip, and puts out one or more horizontal branches below the rosette to repeat the process, thereby building a horizontal spray of rosettes (Figure 15). This model includes Halle and Oldeman's Aubreville, and Fagerlind (in part).

Some plants which follow this model in the shade may behave differently when they attain the canopy. In the elfin forest of Puerto Rico, understory *Ocotea spathulata* (Lauraceae) follow the *terminalia* model, but canopy individuals often support monolayer crowns on a forest of vertical axes. Unfortunately, I never drew any of these canopy individuals, so I do not know how the model was changed, but the change seemed to involve blurring the distinction between "short" and "long" shoots.

This is not a complete enumeration of the possible tree architectures, but it suffices to classify the architectures found in my transects.

4. Analyses of Data

a. PLANT DENSITY

In plot samples I found the number of square metres of ground per small (S) sapling by dividing the number of S into the area sampled for them; and similarly for medium saplings, M; large saplings, L; and trees, T.

In normal point quarter transects I estimated the number of square metres per S as $\pi/4$, or 0.7854, times the average over all quadrants of the square of the distance of each sampled S from its Sample Point. In transects where n small saplings S were sampled per quadrant, I estimated the number of square metres per S as the average over all quadrants of the mean square distance of the nth nearest S in each quadrant from its Sample Point, times $0.7854/n^2$. I estimated the densities of M, L and T in like manner. In most transects, I sampled the two nearest trees, T, in each quadrant, so I set the number of square metres per T equal to 0.3927 times the mean square distance of the second nearest trees to their Sample Points.

I estimated the canopy crown size, the number of square metres per canopy tree, C, as the number of square metres per T times n_1/n_2, where n_1 was the total number of trees sampled in the transect and n_2 was the sum of the number of trees fully in the canopy plus half the number of trees "plugging gaps in the canopy," or for which half, but not all, the crown was left unshaded by other trees.

b. FOREST HEIGHT

I estimated the height of the canopy as a whole ("forest height", or $F.\ H.$) as the average height of the trees that had fully attained the canopy, and calculated constants a and x such that $a\ (F.\ H)^x$ gave the best estimate of canopy crown size. In fitting the curve, I used only transects with five or more canopy trees (n_2 at least 5); I also excluded G Brinchang A_1 because the canopy there did not adequately cover the plot.

Other things being equal, narrow crowns seem associated with poor soils (Richards 1952). Does blocking transpiration mimic the effect of poor soil ? To answer, I check whether deviations from predicted canopy crown size are associated more with poor soil that with foggy, breezy climates (or strong wind).

c. LEAF SIZE

For each transect, I calculated the average length, and the average "size" $(LW)^{1/2}$, where L is length and W is width, for i) litter leaves, ii) leaves measured on sampled S and iii) leaves measured on sampled M, I calculated the regressions of the average size of litter leaves, the average length of litter leaves, and the midpoint $\frac{1}{2}(S+M)$ between the average leaf sizes of S and M, on altitude, as well as the regression of understory leaf size $\frac{1}{2}(S+M)$ on forest height, to try to see how best to predict leaf size.

Other things being equal, small leaves are associated with nutrient shortage (Givnish 1978, p. 102): I accordingly check deviations of actual from predicted leaf size to see whether blocking transpiration mimics the effects of poor soil.

d. LEAF ARRANGEMENT

For each transect, I represented understory leaf arrangements by an "arrangement index" AI calculated as follows :

i. Using the leaf arrangement classification of section 2, I scored each sapling whose leaf arrangement was $F/$, $+/$, or $wh/$ as 4; each sapling whose leaves were $A/$ or $0/$ as 3; each

Fig. 9a. Forest scene on Barro Colorado Island. *Dipteryx panamensis* (Leguminosae), 30 m tall, is the largest tree in the picture. Drawing by Marshall Hasbrouck.

Fig. 9b. *Leptospermum flavescens* (Myrtaceae), 2 m tall. Summit heath on Gunung Ulu Kali. Drawing by Marshall Hasbrouck.

Fig. 10. *Olmedia aspera* (Moraceae), 4 m tall. Forest understory, Barro Colorado Island. Drawing by George Angehr.

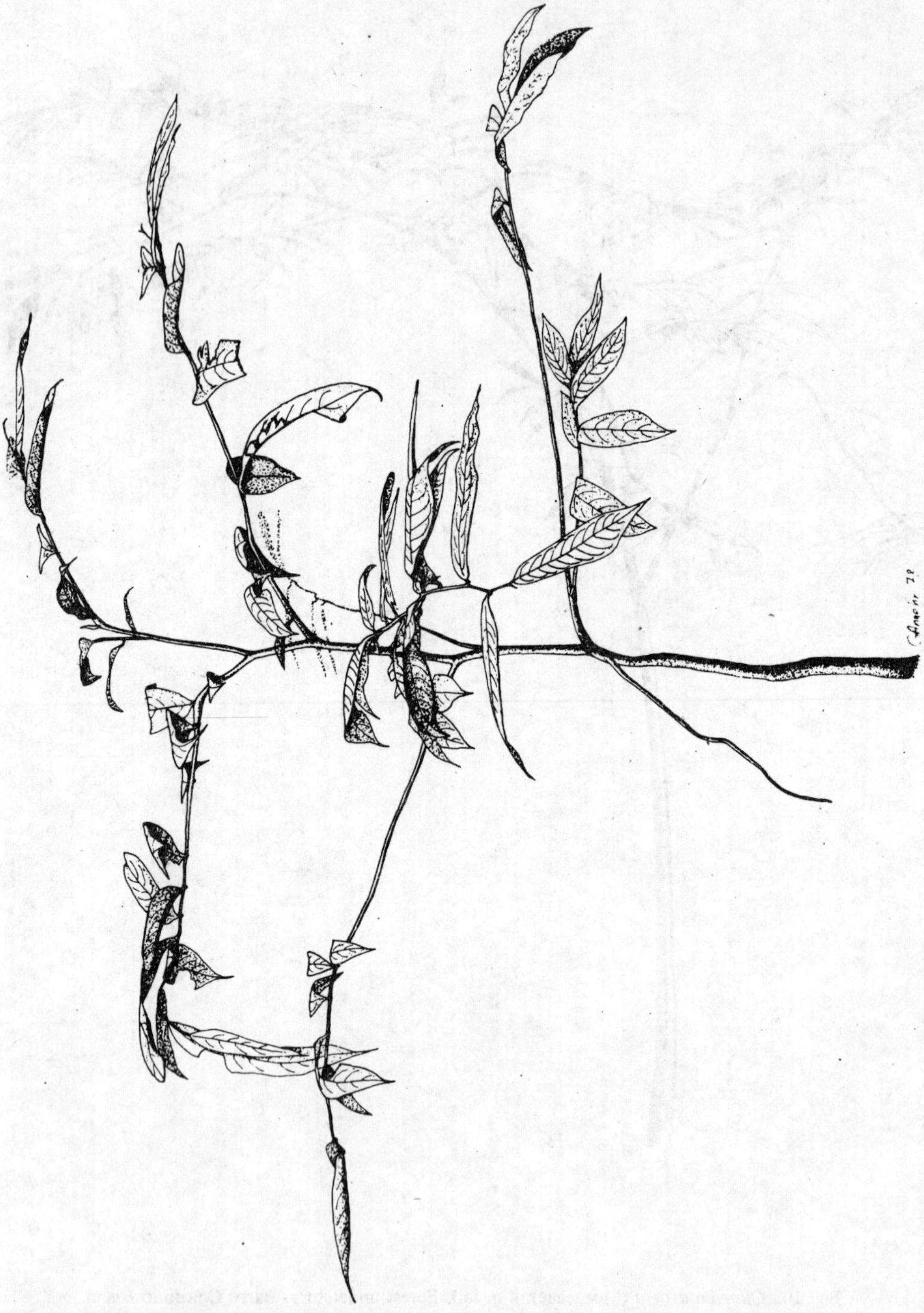

Fig. 11. *Unonopsis pittieri* (Annonaceae), 1 m tall. Forest understory, Barro Colorado Island.

sapling whose leaves were *F–* or *+–* as 2; each sapling whose leaves were *F-HS* or *+– HS* as 1; and each sapling whose leaves were *AHS* or *OHS* as 0. A sapling showing two roughly equally represented leaf arrangements was scored as the midpoint between the numbers appropriate to those arrangements.

ii. I calculated the average score for *S*, and likewise for *M*.

iii. Taking the midpoint *z* between these scores, I set the arrangement index *AI* equal to arccos $(1-z/_2)$, that is to say, the angle between 0° and 180° whose cosine is $1\text{-}z/2$. *z* itself is called the understory leaf arrangement score.

Having found the altitude; the forest height, *F. H.*; the average size $(LW)^{1/2}$ of litter leaves, *LL;* the average size of understory sapling leaves, $\frac{1}{2}(S+M)$; and the arrangement index *AI* for each transect, I calculate the matrix of the product moment correlations between these variates. To probe the nature of the correlations between these variates, and to distinguish those features representing external circumstances such as altitude from those features which are relatively direct consequences of forest height, I calculate a matrix of partial correlations with altitude removed ("held constant", as it were), and another matrix with forest height removed. The formula for the partial correlation between *x* and *z* with *y* removed is

$$(r_{xz} - r_{xy}r_{zy})/[(1 - r^2_{xy})\ (1 - r^2_{zy})]^{\frac{1}{2}}$$

where r_{xz} is the total correlation between *x* and *z*, and so on (Simpson, Roe & Lewontin 1960).

e. TREE ARCHITECTURE

I constructed an orthotropy index *OI* to represent a transect's tree architectures, in strict analogy to the leaf arrangement index *AI*. I scored plants in the Troll, Mangenot, casearia and virola models as 0; those in faramea or deflexa, or which cast their foliage in irregular horizontal sprays, as 1; those in terminalia and palm as 2; those in psychotria or coussarea as 3; and the others as 4. For a given collection of plants, I set $OI = \arccos\ (1-2p)$, where *p* was the average score for that collection of plants. I enquired how *OI* for canopy plants, and for different levels of the understory, varied with altitude and forest height.

RESULTS

1. Tree Density

The one systematic influence on plant density seems to be forest height (Table 1). Forests less than 13 metres tall nearly all have 10 or fewer square metres per tree, or over 1000 trees exceeding 10 cm *dbh* per hectare. Forests over 20 metres tall nearly all have between 13 and 28 square metres per tree, or between 360 and 770 trees per hectare. Indeed, because my transects sample such small areas, they underestimate the uniformity of tree densities in tall forests. Sapling densities vary much more from place to place than do tree densities. The rarity of small saplings in the West Indian transects, both lowland and montane, attracts attention: I have no explanation for it.

2. Plant Height

In my transects, the height of small saplings 6-12 mm *dbh* was independent of forest height. Only at MV Elfin 2, the shortest forest I studied, did medium saplings 13-25 mm *dbh* appear stunted. More generally, height appears stunted relative to diameter only when the plants would otherwise be well over half the height of the canopy.

Moreover, neither altitude, nor degree of mossiness, nor poverty of the soil, influence the height of broad-leaved plants except through their effect on forest height. In some wet places, however, such as Mt. Britton and MV Cuesta 1, angiosperm saplings may be partly replaced by tree ferns, which are much shorter for given diameter.

Canopy crown size (area per canopy crown) is best estimated by the equation

$$CCS = 0.1837\ (F.\ H.)^{1.7}.$$

The simplest derivation of the "3/2 power law" (White and Harper 1970), that mass per plant is proportional to (area per plant)$^{3/2}$, suggests that the area per canopy crown should be proportional to the square of forest height. If plants of montane forest are more likely to suffer nutrient shortage, one might expect canopy crown size to increase more rapidly than the square of forest height, so it is mildly surprising to find that the reverse is true.

Deviations of observed from predicted canopy crown size (as measured by the deviation from unity of their ratio) appear to reflect soil fertility. Excluding G. Brinchang A_1 because the canopy there covered too little of the plot, and excluding MV Elfin 1 and MV Cuesta 2 because they had too few canopy trees to give a reliable estimate of canopy crown size, observed canopy crown size exceeds the predicted most strikingly for MV Cuesta 1, Barro Colorado, Cerro Muerte, and MV Elfin 2 (Table 4), all, especially the Monteverde sites, forests on good soil. Canopy crown size falls shortest of prediction for Gunung Ulu Kali A and C, whose soils may be the worst of any on my transects. Climates hostile to transpiration do not mimic the effects of poor soil: plants in such climates, such as those at MV Elfin 2, Pico del Este, El Yunque and Mt Britton, do not have unexpectedly small crowns. Although a smaller crown presumably reduces the leverage of the wind on a canopy tree, canopy crown size is not unexpectedly small at windy sites, either those just mentioned or Avalanchi 4&5.

3. Leaf Size

In most transects, the coefficient of variation of the leaf size $(LW)^{1/2}$ is smaller than that of leaf length (Table 2), implying that longer leaves tend to be relatively narrower. In the taller forests among my transects, palm leaflets tended to be much longer than the simple dicotyledenous leaves nearby, but so narrow that the sizes $(LW)^{1/2}$ of palm leaflets and dicot leaves were quite comparable. Thus the following analyses focus on leaf size.

Litter leaf size was more predictable than understory sapling leaf size, and altitude was its best predictor. The regressions of litter leaf size $(LW)^{1/2}$ litter leaf length L, and understory sapling leaf size $\frac{1}{2}(S+M)$, in mm, on altitude (m), were, respectively.

$$(LW)^{1/2} = 74.24 - .01902\ (\text{altitude}), \quad r^2 = 0.6674;$$

$$L = 103.17 - .02478\ (\text{altitude}), \quad r^2 = 0.5575;$$

$$\tfrac{1}{2}(S+M) = 111.18 - .02293\ (\text{altitude}), \quad r^2 = 0.4182.$$

The regression for $\frac{1}{2}(S+M)$ omits MV Cuesta 2, whose understory leaf size was unaccountably huge: including it would have reduced r^2 to 0.19.

In an as yet unpublished analysis involving more transects, including ones in Peru, Venezuela, Madagascar and New Guinea, the regression of average litter leaf length L on altitude was

$$L = 114.33 - .02573\ (\text{altitude}), \quad r^2 = 0.4435.$$

Here, the average length of litter leaves correlated more closely with average temperature of the coolest month of the year (r^2 = 0.5968) than with altitude: indeed, the correlation of leaf length with altitude was simply the correlation of leaf with temperature times the correlation of temperature with altitude. Among the transects reported in this paper, the correlation of litter leaf length with altitude ($r^2 = 0.5775$) is weaker than that with temperature of the coolest month of the year ($r^2 = 0.6218$), but the correlation of litter leaf size with altitude ($r^2 = 0.6674$) is closer than that with temperature ($r^2 = 0.5837$): indeed, it is the best we have, although the differences may not be worth refining upon.

The correlation of understory leaf size with forest height is slightly better than that with altitude: the regression is

$$\tfrac{1}{2}(S+M) = 56.65 + 1.5828\ F.H., \quad r^2 = 0.4531.$$

It is quite possible that the multiple regression of understory leaf size on altitude and forest height would yield a sharper prediction than that of litter leaf size on altitude, but the latter seems a more satisfactorily direct approach, given the generality of the relation between altitude and leaf size (Grubb *et al.* 1963).

Measuring the deviation of observed from predicted litter leaf size by the difference observed minus predicted, as is appropriate for a linear regression, leaf size is most unexpectedly large at Cerro Muerte, MV Cuesta 1, and El Yunque 79, and most unexpectedly small at Ulu Kali B and C, suggesting that leaf size, like crown size, reflects the poverty of the soil. On the other hand, blocking transpiration does not mimic the effect of poor soil. At windy, foggy sites, leaf size is larger than expected at MV Elfin 1, MV Cuesta 1, El Yunque 71 and 79, and Pico del Este, while it is smaller at MV Cuesta 2, thanks to the presence of a large number of *Weinmannia* leaflets in the sample, and at Mt. Britton (Table 3). Although smaller leaves presumably offer less resistance to the wind, leaves are not unexpectedly small at windy sites: at Avalanchi, too, leaf size is a little larger than expected.

4. **Leaf Arrangement**

The leaf arrangement index *Al* correlates much more closely with forest height than with altitude: its regression on forest height is

$$Al = 151.53 - 2.2266\ F.H.,\ r^2 = 0.6969.$$

This is no surprise: understory foliage tends to be flattened into horizontal sprays on many plants which arrange their sun leaves spirally or decussately around erect or inclined twigs, and the shorter the forest, the closer the understory foliage is to the light, and the slighter the distinction between canopy species and those growing in the understory. Soil fertility seems to bear little relation to the leaf arrangement index (Table 4). Leaf arrangement is largely an expression of tree architecture, and will be considered further in the next section.

One might ask whether the inferences from my regressions are appropriate: might the deviations I ascribe to nutrient availability reflect internal relations among my variables? After all, bearing in mind that for 23 degrees of freedom a correlation of 0.40 should be just significant at the 5% level, altitude, forest height, litter leaf size, understory sapling leaf size, and understory leaf arrangement index are significantly correlated in nearly all possible ways (Table 5). Fortunately, knowledge of the partial correlations helps to clear up this confusion. Holding forest height constant, altitude correlates closely with litter leaf size and weakly with understory sapling leaf size: the other correlations are insignificant. Holding altitude constant, understory leaf arrangement index correlates closely, and understory sapling leaf size moderately, with forest height. Holding both altitude and forest height constant eliminates all significant relations between the remaining variables. Thus it seems

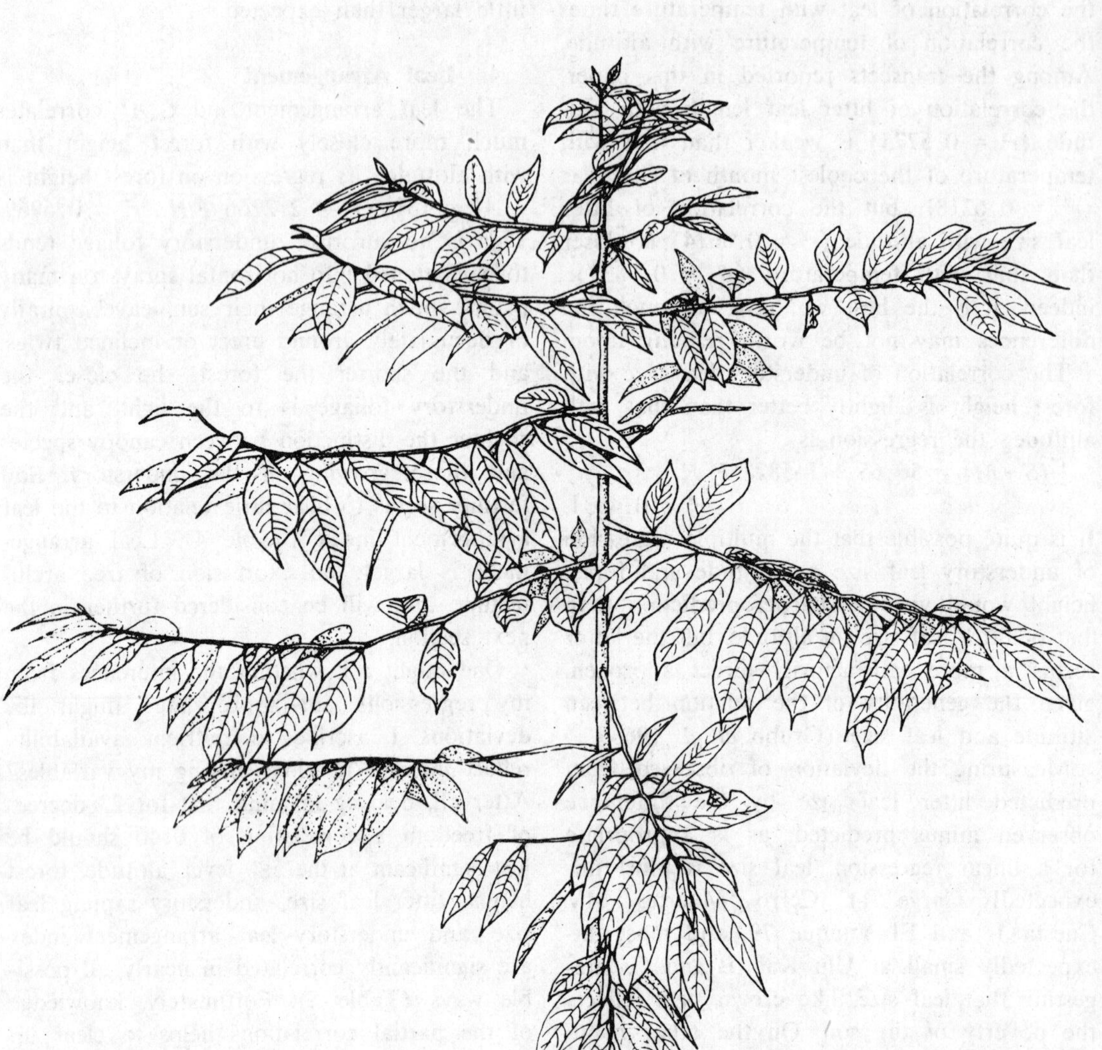

Fig 12. ***Zuelania guidonia*** **(Flacourtiaceae), 1.3 m tall. Laboratory clearing, Barro Colorado Island. Drawing by George Angehr.**

Fig. 13. *Virola sebifera* (Myristicaceae). Top of small sapling 0.8 m tall. Forest understory, Barro Colorado Island. Drawing by Alex Murawski.

Fig. 14. *Virola sebifera,* 15 m tall, on left, and *Virola surinamensis,* 30 m tall, on right; near laboratory clearing, Barro Colorado Island. Drawing by Judy Gradwohl.

Fig. 15. Spray of foliage of *Terminalia amazonica* (Combretaceae), by roadside in Parque Nacional Soberania, near Gamboa, Panama. Drawing by Alex Murawski.

TABLE 6

ARCHITECTURES OF PLANTS OF DIFFERENT HEIGHTS IN TWO TALL FORESTS

	Barro Colorado Island					Monteverde Ravine				
	Understory			canopy	Total	Understory			canopy	Total
Height (m)	0–3	3-10	10+		spp.	0–3	3-10	10+		spp.
Model										
Troll	3	6	0	1	4	2	7	1	0	5
Mangenot	2	4	2	0	5	1	1	0	0	1
casearia	1	0	2	0	2	5	3	3	0	8
virola	0	2	1	0	3	0	0	0	0	0
irregular										
horiz. sprays	1	1	5	0	6	2	2	1	1	5
faramea	1	1	0	0	2	5	1	1	0	3
deflexa	0	0	0	0	0	0	1	0	0	1
palm	6	3	3	0	9	1	0	0	0	1
psychotria	3	3	3	0	9	4	4	2	1	8
coussarea	0	1	0	0	1	1	2	0	0	3
Champagnat	3	0	0	0	3	0	0	1	0	1
Attims	0	0	0	0	0	1	1	2	1	5
Rauh	0	0	0	1	1	0	0	1	0	1
Scarrone	0	0	0	2	1	1	0	0	0	1
Kwan Koriba	0	0	0	0	0	1	1	0	0	2
almendro	0	0	2	1	3	0	0	1	4	5

Each row gives the number of plants in its model 0-3 m high. 3-10 m high. over 10 m high but still shaded, and in the canopy, and the total number of species in the transect following the model concerned.

TABLE 7

ARCHITECTURES OF PLANTS OF DIFFERENT HEIGHTS IN FOUR MONTANE FORESTS

	Gunung Ulu Kali C				Gunung Brinchang N_2				Mt Britton				Avalanchi	
	understory		canopy	Total	understory		canopy	Total	understory		canopy	Total	canopy	Total
Height (m)	0-3	3+		spp.	0-3	3+		spp.	0-3	3+		spp.		spp.
Model														
casearia	1	0	0	1	4	0	0	2	0	0	0	0	0	0
faramea	0	1	0	1	0	0	0	0	0	1	0	1	0	0
deflexa	2	4	0	1	5	2	4	2	0	0	0	0	0	0
terminalia	0	0	0	0	0	0	0	0	0	1	0	1	0	0
palm	0	2	0	1	0	0	0	0	4	0	0	1	1	1
psychotria	2	0	0	2	7	6	0	5	0	1	0	1	3	2
coussarea	0	1	0	1	5	5	0	2	0	0	0	0	0	0
spiral Attims	2	0	1	2	2	0	0	1	0	1	0	1	15	3
decussate Attims	3	4	0	2	0	1	3	1	0	0	2	1	16	2
Kwan Koriba	4	5	0	5	0	0	0	0	0	0	0	0	0	0
Rauh	0	1	0	1	1	1	1	1	0	0	0	0	6	2
Leeuwenberg	0	5	1	1	0	1	2	2	0	2	8	2	8	2
almendro	0	0	7	2	0	2	26	3	0	0	0	0	2	1

Each row gives the number of plants in its model 0-3 m high, over 3 m high but still shaded, and in the canopy, and the total number of species in the transect following the model concerned.

TABLE 8

ARCHITECTURES OF PLANTS OF DIFFERENT HEIGHTS IN DIFFERENT ELFIN FORESTS

	Monteverde Elfin 2			Pico del Este			El Yunque 79			Ulu Kali Heath	
Stature	under-story	canopy	total spp.	understory	canopy	total spp.	understory	canopy	total spp.	canopy	total spp.
Model											
Troll	2	0	2	0	0	0	0	0	0	0	0
faramea	2	0	2	0	0	0	0	0	0	0	0
terminalia	0	0	0	3	0	1	7	0	1	0	0
palm	5	0	3	1	0	1	3	0	2	0	0
psychotria	14	1	9	4	1	3	4	1	4	0	0
coussarea	0	0	0	3	0	2	3	0	1	0	0
spiral											
Attims	5	3	4	1	1	2	1	0	1	1	1
decussate											
Attims	5	7	8	0	5	1	0	0	0	3	1
Kwan											
Koriba	0	0	0	0	0	0	0	0	0	1	1
Rauh	0	0	0	1	0	1	0	0	0	0	0
Scarrone	0	0	0	0	0	0	0	0	0	2	1
Leeuwenberg	0	1	1	8	2	2	0	13	5	1	1
almendro	4	9	5	2	5	2	8	5	3	5	3

Each row gives the number of understory and of canopy plants in the model concerned, and the total number of species in the transect following that model.

TABLE 9

ORTHOTROPY INDEX (OI) AND LEAF ARRANGEMENT INDEX (AI) FOR DIFFERENT FOREST STRATA

Tall Forests					
		understory			
	height class (m)	0–3	3–10	over 10	canopy
Barro Colorado, Panama	OI	83	58	77	127
	AI	49	44	34	90
MV Ravine, Costa Rica	OI	76	68	94	136
	AI	91	71	74	102
Shorter Montane Forests					
		understory			
	height class (m)	0–3	over 3		canopy
Ulu Kali C, Malaysia	OI	125	117		180
	AI	96	—		180
G Brinchang N_2, Malaysia	OI	96	126		146
	AI	113	—		163
Mt Britton, Puerto Rico	OI	90	120		180
	AI	—	—		180
Avalanchi, India	OI	—	—		162
	AI	—	—		154
Elfin Forests					
height class		understory			canopy
MV Elfin 2, Costa Rica	OI	119			167
	AI	140			160
Pico del Este, Puerto Rico	OI	132			165
	AI	144			180
El Yunque, Puerto Rico	OI	103			167
	AI	139			180
Ulu Kali Heath, Malaysia	OI	—			180
	AI	—			180

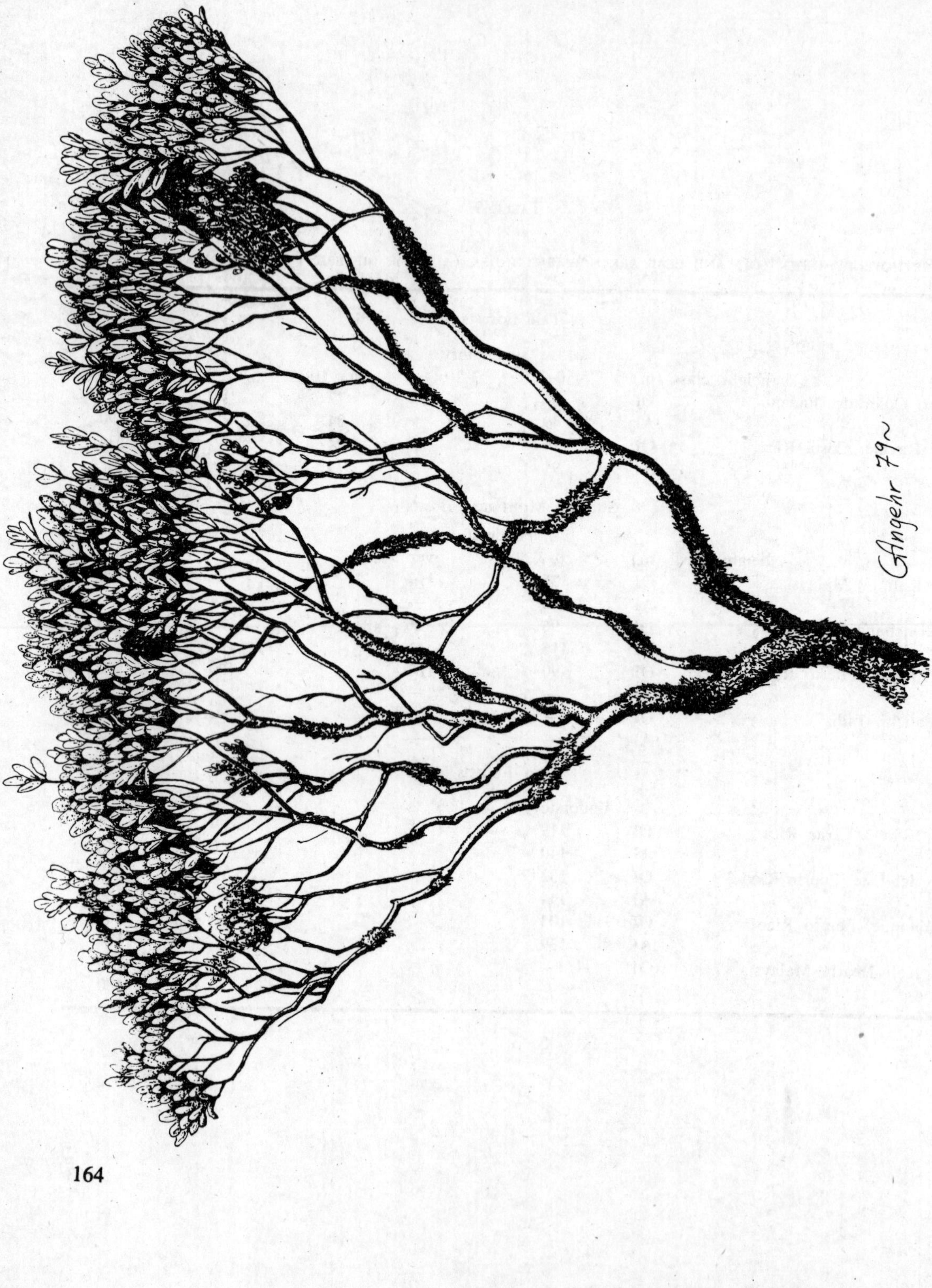

Fig. 16a. *Syzygium* sp. (Myrtaceae), sprig canopy foliage from Gunung Batu Brinchang, Malaysia. Drawn by George Angehr from photograph by Elizabeth Leigh.

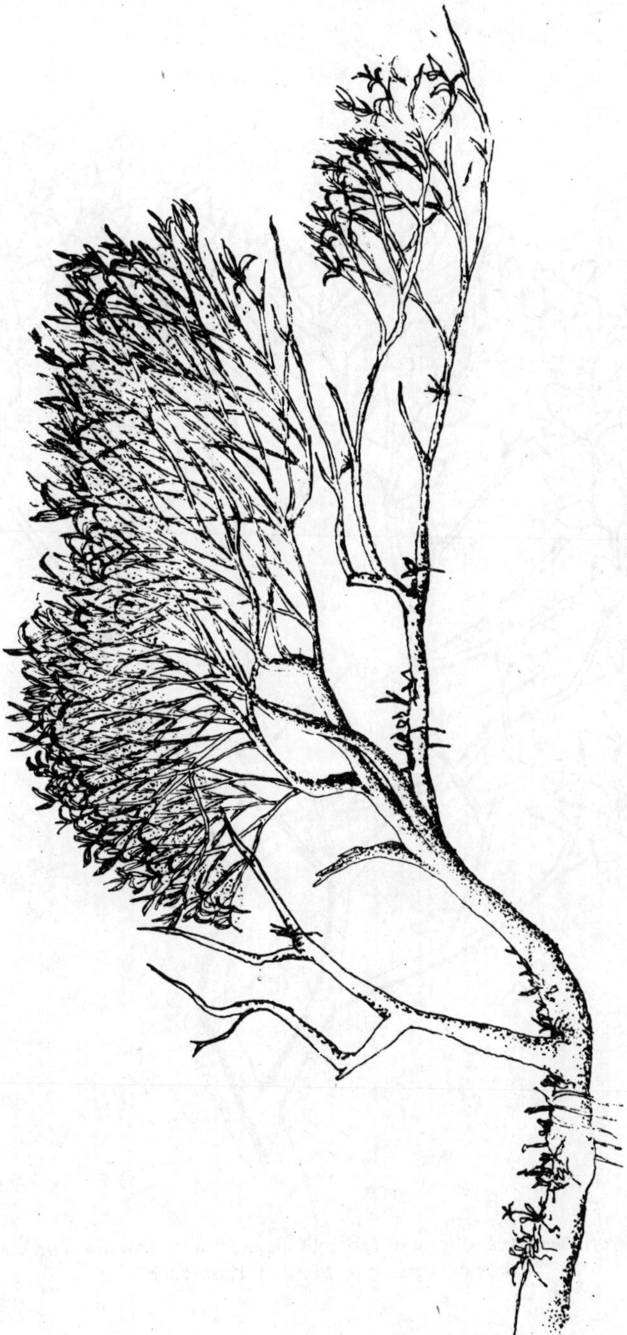

Fig. 16b. Canopy foliage of unidentified shrub, elfin forest, Monteverde Cloud Forest Reserve. Drawing by Noel Holbrook.

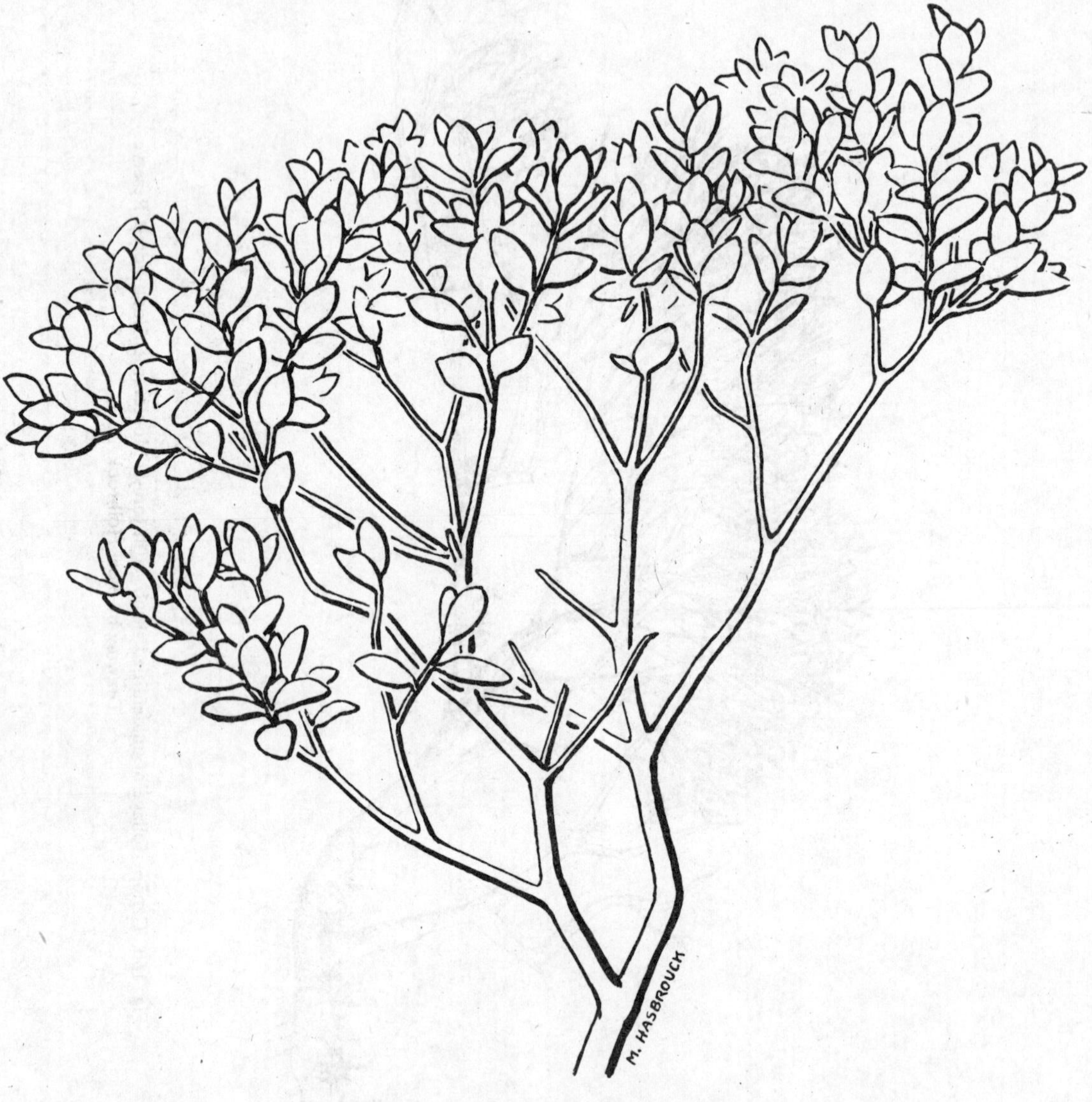

Fig. 17a. *Syzygium wrayi* (Myrtaceae), sprig of canopy foliage from summit heath on Gunung Ulu Kali, Malaysia. Drawing by Marshall Hasbrouck.

Fig. 17b. *Wikstroemia* sp. (Ternstroemiaceae), shrub 2 m high growing under large gap in canopy at Gunung Batu Brinchang, Malaysia. Drawing by Marshall Hasbrouck.

just for me to suppose that, of my five quantitative variables, altitude and forest height are the "decisive" factors, and to accept the regressions of litter leaf size on altitude, and of understory leaf arrangement index on forest height, as normative.

5. **Tree Architecture**

Although, given the crudity and vagueness inherent in my architectural classification, it may be dangerous to depend too precisely on it, the number of models per transect drops in passing from tall montane forest, which averages 14 models apiece (Table 6), to shorter montane forest, which averages 9 (Table 7), or elfin forest, which averages 8 (Table 8). To some extent this may reflect the lower number of species in transects through shorter forest: the tall forests of Barro Colorado and MV Ravine were the only architectural transect sites which could not be described in terms of dominant tree species. This process is countered somewhat by the greater likelihood of an elfin forest species having individuals classified in more than one model.

There is a pattern in which models drop out. I rarely found individuals of Troll's or the casearia model, and never found individuals of the virola or Mangenot's model, in architectural transects through shorter montane forest. In other words, models with an orthotropy score of 0 (see Methods, Analyses, section e) are most likely to drop out as forest height decreases.

The "orthotropy index," which represents the prevalence of models with erect or inclined branches and twigs, is relatively insensitive to the vagaries of my architectural classification. This index is higher in the canopy than in the understory (Table 9): orthotropy is particularly characteristic of canopy plants. The shorter the forest, the higher the orthotropy index for its understory. Perhaps this is because shorter forests have fewer species, and far fewer tree species restricted to the understory. If so, most species of tree or shrub in stunted montane forest have some prospect of reaching the canopy, and must have architectures suitable for the purpose: models whose foliage is invariably cast in horizontal sprays might thus be too rare to be sampled by my transects.

The orthotropy index is also higher for canopy plants in short montane forest than for those in tall mid-montane or lowland forest. Most canopy trees on Barro Colorado Island are orthotropic, but the canopy there contains the occasional tree of Troll's model, such as *Platypodium elegans* (Leguminosae) or *Luehea seemannii* (Tiliaceae); Mangenot's model (*Guatteria dumetorum*), the casearia model (*Zuelania guidonia*), or the virola model (*Quararibea asterolepis* or *Virola surinamensis*). Moreover, some of these species are among the most common in the canopy. Trees of such models, however, are utterly absent from the canopy of elfin forest. *Ocotea spathulata* normally casts its foliage terminalia-fashion in successive layers of rosettes, but when it reaches the canopy of wind-planed elfin forest it adjusts its growth form so as to support a monolayer crown on a plethora of erect axes, rather after the fashion of Scarrone's model. Similarly, holly (*Ilex*) in the eastern United States, which normally grows *Virola*-fashion, with many flat layers of foliage, elaborates a monolayer crown on erect axes when it attains the canopy of wind-planed dune scrub on the barrier beaches of North Carolina.

The leaf arrangement index behaves rather similarly to the orthotropy index (Table 9). In tall forests it is lower than the orthotropy index because many of the orthotropic trees of mid-montane and lowland tall forest have compound leaves: these trees form "throw-away twigs" (Givnish 1978b), but their more important branches are built to last, with a minimum of shedding and rebuilding, making an orthotropic model appropriate. In stunted montane forest, the orthotropy and leaf arrangement indices of canopy trees are very similar. The trees there make leathery leaves, built to last (cf Janzen 1974); they make simple leaves, so as to avoid discarding the twigs with the leaves they support (Givnish 1978b), and when the trees attain the canopy, their trunks and twigs thicken (Lawton 1982). Perhaps because such stout limbs are more valuable, we sometimes find plants elaborating dense arrays of parallel twigs rather than undergoing the shedding and rebuilding needed for a more efficient twig arrangement (Figure 16). Lawton (1982) is probably just to ascribe the tough construction of leaf, branch and trunk in elfin forest to the need to resist the wind, whether the wind is steady, seasonal, or episodic. The resemblance of the smooth elfin forest canopy to that of wind-planed dune scrub is suggestive, and Odum (1970) has commented on the smoothness of forest canopy in the hurricane belt. The toughness of the construction in turn demands a certain conservatism of the mode of growth, favouring models with a minimum of shedding and rebuilding.

In most forests, understory leaves are held horizontally, and are flat, as if to concentrate the maximum amount of light per unit leaf surface. Canopy leaves, on the other hand, are held at an angle to spread the strong sunlight over a wider surface. In lowland forests canopy leaves may be stiffly drooped, reflexed, with the base rising and the tip drooping, and folded about the midrib, or inclined to the twig. In forests at very high altitude, and in montane moss forests, both elfin forests and tall forests such as the oak forest atop Cerro de la Muerte and the *Nothofagus* forest atop the 2300 m Mt Kaindi in New Guinea, leaves are much more likely to be inclined to the twig and set in tufts at its end (Figure 17), although exceptions exist (Figure 18), particularly at Monteverde. In such forests, inclining the leaves may enable them to warm up more quickly when the sun comes out, and may be the botanical counterpart of the darkened wings on butterflies of moss forests and alpine meadows. In lowland shrubbery of very poor soils, such as peat bogs, leaves are usually inclined to the twig, but they are not necessarily arranged in a tuft about its tip.

Concluding Remarks

This analysis is distinctly preliminary. To begin with, I have no appropriate data from a sufficient variety of forests: the geographical net, wide as it is, should be spread wider. Only thus can I avert the reproach that the features which I ascribe to soil quality reflect only the taxonomic peculiarities of the regions where the poor soils happened to be. Moreover, my methods of analysis are rather antiquated: for my part, I find them serviceable and simple enough to understand, but others might know better ways of analyzing the data. With these caveats, I would summarize my conclusions, and their implications, as follows:

1) Tree density is governed by forest height. For mature forests over 20 metres high, tree densities are remarkably uniform.

2) The relation between height and diameter of understory plants seems related only to forest height. Moreover, plants are stunted relative to their diameter only after they have attained half the height of the canopy. This result is a bit surprising. Where soils are poor, plants build coriaceous leaves that are meant

to last (Janzen 1974). One might argue by analogy that on poor soils stems, too, would be built to last, and would be thicker relative to height on poorer soils. However, understory saplings are not stouter on poor soils. Lawton (1982) is probably just to attribute the stoutness of his elfin forest trees to the need to resist snapping in strong winds. It would clearly be inappropriate to associate this stoutness with nutrient shortage.

3) Canopy crown size decreases in a regular fashion with decrease in forest height. Canopy crowns are unusually small relative to forest height where the soil is poor, but a climate hostile to transpiration does not mimic the effect of poor soil.

4) Litter leaf size decreases with increased altitude, and bears no independent relation to forest height. Litter leaves are unusually small for their altitude where the soil is poor, but a climate hostile to transpiration does not mimic the effect of poor soil.

I was thus wrong to ascribe the form of elfin forest to nutrient starvation induced by inability to transpire (Leigh 1975). It likewise seems implausible to ascribe the low stature of elfin forest (over and above that due to the delay from diverting resources to the construction of wind-resistant trunks and branches) to low transpiration.

5) Most elfin forests appear to be stunted either by strong wind, or by very poor soil.

6) Canopy trees are more likely than understory plants to be constructed orthotropically, that is to say, of erect or inclined axes, and to arrange their leaves spirally or decussately around erect or inclined twigs. Moreover, canopy trees of stunted forest, or of tall moss forest, are more likely to be constructed orthotropically than canopy trees of lowland forest, or of mossless mid-montane forest. Elfin forest canopies are seemingly windplaned, and the canopies of tall moss forests are also rather smooth, as if trees in the cloud belt are subject at least at times to strong winds. Trees of elfin forest are apparently built stoutly to resist the wind. Such stout construction presumably makes it desirable to minimize the shedding and rebuilding of branches as a tree grows, and orthotropic architectures may prevail in elfin forest canopies because they facilitate growth with the minimum of rebuilding.

ACKNOWLEDGEMENTS

A paper by G. E. Hutchinson (1941) deducing the recycling of phosphorus in stratified lakes, struck a chord in me long ago, of which this paper is but a faint echo. Much of Hutchinson's analysis hinged on the study of deviations from "expectation" Martin Moynihan, then director of the Smithsonian Tropical Research Institute, enabled me to realize my interest in evolutionary convergence by arranging for me to travel around the world in 1968 and 1970, comparing the physiognomy of tropical rain forests, lowland and montane. He also showed how to relate art and science: again, this paper is but a faint echo of his example. It would be even fainter but for the many artists — Alex Murawski, Gerardo Rivassa, Judy Gradwohl, George Angehr, Roxane Trappe, Noel Holbrook, Karen Kraeger and Marshall Hasbrouck — who through the years have drawn plants for me, and who more than once have revealed to me through their art the order inherent in a plant's growth.

A large company have helped me along my way. Elizabeth Leigh interested me in plants, and played an integral role in all my field work before 1978, and in much since. Members of the Institut Francais de Pondichery introduced me to a suitable research site in the Nilgiris. B. C. Stone and F. E.

Fig. 18a. Unidentified sapling of a fairly common canopy tree, Gunung Batu Brinchang, Malaysia. Drawing by Marshall Hasbrouck.

Fig. 18b. Crown of *Didymopanax pittieri* (Araliaceae). Monteverde Cloud Forest Reserve: note leaflets held flat. Drawing by Noel Holbrook.

Putz guided me to many study sites in Malaysia, helped me to identify many plants, and recommended other study sites to me; John Terborgh took me on a student field trip to Puerto Rico in 1971; P. L. Weaver arranged my second field trip to Puerto Rico in 1979; James McClammer, the only one of my company who felt at home driving in a Puerto Rican rush hour, helped me on this second trip; and Robin Andrews and Ch. Maximae helped me in Dominica. Robert Lawton guided me about Monteverde, choosing suitable transect sites and identifying many plants; he helped me with transects in Puerto Rico and on Barro Colorado Island; and, finally, I benefitted greatly from his views on elfin forest structure which, despite my initial disbelief, have proved far more nearly correct than my own. It is a pleasure to remember their help.

Finally, I am most grateful to the Smithsonian Tropical Research Institute for consistent support and encouragement, not only for travel but also for artists' fees, and to the Smithsonian Institution's Office of International Activities, which paid my airplane fares in 1970, and its Fluid Research Fund, which contributed toward subsequent trips.

REFERENCES

BAYNTON, H. W. (1968): The ecology of an elfin forest in Puerto Rico. 2. The microclimate of Pico del Oeste. *Journal of the Arnold Arboretum 49*: 419-430.

BLASCO, F. (1971): *Montagnes du Sud de l'Inde. Forests. Savanes, Ecologie*. Institut Francais de Pondichery, Pondichery, India.

BRISCOE, C. B. (1966): Weather in the Luquillo Mountains of Puerto Rico. Forest Service Research Paper ITF-3, Institute of Tropical Forestry, Rio Piedras, Puerto Rico.

BYER, M. D. & WEAVER, P. L. (1977): Early secondary succession in the Luquillo Mountains of Puerto Rico. *Biotropica 9*: 35-47.

CORNER, E. J. H. (1940): Wayside Trees of Malaya. Government Printer, Singapore.

——— (1964): The Life of Plants. World Publishing Co., Cleveland, OH.

COTTAM, G., & CURTIS, J. T. (1956): The use of distance measures in phytosociological sampling. *Ecology 37*: 451-460.

CROAT, T. B. (1978): Flora of Barro Colorado Island. Stanford University Press, Stanford, CA.

DIETRICH, W. E., WINDSOR, D. M. & DUNNE, T. (1982): Geology, climate and hydrology of Barro Colorado Island. pp. 21-46 *in* E. G. Leigh, Jr., A. S. Rand and D. M. Windsor, eds. The Ecology of a Tropical Forest. Smithsonian Institution Press, Washington, D. C.

FOSTER, R. B., & BROKAW, N. V. L. (1982): Structure and history of the vegetation of Barro Colorado Island. pp. 67-81 *in* E. G. Leigh, Jr., A. S. Rand and D. M. Windsor, eds. The Ecology of a Tropical Forest. Smithsonian Institution Press, Washington, D. C.

GIVNISH, T. J. (1978): Ecological aspects of plant morphology: leaf form in relation to environment. *Acta Biotheoretica 27*: 83-142.

——— (1978b): On the adaptive significance of compound leaves, with particular reference to tropical trees. pp. 351-380 *in* P. B. Tomlinson and M. H. Zimmermann, eds. Tropical Trees as Living Systems. Cambridge University Press, Cambridge, England.

GLEASON, H. A. & COOK, M. T. (1927): Plant Ecology of Porto Rico, Parts 1 & 2. Scientific Survey of Porto Rico and the Virgin Islands 7: 1-173.

GRUBB, P. J. (1977): Control of forest growth and distribution on wet tropical mountains, with special reference to mineral nutrition. *Annual Review of Ecology and Systematics 8*: 83-105.

———, LLOYD, J. R., PENNINGTON, T. D. & WHITMORE, T. C. (1963): A comparison of montane and lowland forest in Ecuador. I. The forest structure, physiognomy and floristics. *Journal of Ecology 51*: 567-601.

HALLE, F. & NG, F. S. P. (1981): Crown construction in mature dipterocarp trees. *Malaysian Forester 44*: 222-233.

HALLE, F. & OLDEMAN, R. A. A. (1970): Essai sur l'architecture et la dynamique de croissance des arbres tropicaux. Masson et Cie, Paris.

________________, & TOMLINSON, P. B. (1978): Tropical Trees and Forests: an Architectural Analysis. Springer-Verlag, Berlin, Western Germany.

HOLDRIDGE, L. R., GRENKE, W. C., HATHEWAY, W. H., LIANG, T. & TOSI, J. A., JR. (1971): Forest Environments in Tropical Life Zones. Pergamon Press, New York.

HOWARD, R. A. (1968): The ecology of an elfin forest in Puerto Rico. 1. Introduction and composition studies. *Journal of the Arnold Arboretum 49*: 381-418.

HUTCHINSON, G. E. (1941): Limnological studies in Connecticut. IV. The mechanism of intermediary metabolism in stratified lakes. *Ecological Monographs 11*: 21-60.

JANZEN, D. H. (1974): Tropical blackwater rivers, animals, and mass fruiting by the Dipterocarpaceae. *Biotropica 6*: 69-103.

LAWTON, R. O. (1980): Wind and the Ontogeny of Elfin Structure in a Costa Rican Lower Montane Rain Forest. Ph.D. Thesis. University of Chicago, Chicago, IL.

__________ (1982): Wind stress and elfin structure in a montane rain forest tree: an adaptive explanation. *American Journal of Botany 69*: 1224-1230.

__________ & DRYER, V. (1981): The vegetation of the Monteverde Cloud Forest Reserve. *Brenesia 18*: 101-116.

LEIGH JR., E. G. (1975): Structure and climate in tropical rain forest. *Annual Review of Ecology and Systematics 6*: 67-86.

__________ (1983): Tree shapes in elfin forest. To appear in the Silver Jubilee Symposium of the International Society for Tropical Ecology.

__________ & LAWTON, R. O. (1981): Why are elfin forests stunted? pp. 20-31 *in* B. C. Stone, The Summit Flora of Gunung Ulu Kali (Pahang, Malaysia) Federation Museums Journal. vol 26 (Part 1), New Series, 1-157.

LEIGH JR., E. G., RAND, A. S. & WINDSOR, D. M. eds. (1982): The Ecology of a Tropical Forest. Smithsonian Institution Press, Washington, D. C.

ODUM, H. T. (1970): Rain forest structure and mineral cycling homeostasis. pp. H3-H52 *in* H.T. Odum and R. Pigeon, eds. A Tropical Rain Forest. Division of Technical Information, United States Atomic Energy Commission, Washington, D.C.

OLDEMAN, R. A. A. (1974): L'architecture de la foret guyanaise. Memoires ORSTOM, vol. 73.

RICHARDS, P. W. (1952): The Tropical Rain Forest. Cambridge University Press, Cambridge, England.

SAWYER, J. O. & LINDSEY, A. A. (1971): Vegetation of the Life Zones in Costa Rica. Indiana Academy of Sciences, Indianapolis, IN.

SIMPSON, G. G., ROE, A. & LEWONTIN, R. C. (1960): Quantitative Zoology. Harcourt, Brace and World, New York.

STONE, B. C. (1981): The Summit Flora of Gunung Ulu Kali (Pahang, Malaysia). *Federation Museums Journal* vol. 26 (Part 1), New Series, 1-157.

VAN STEENIS, C.G.G.J. (1972): The Mountain Flora of Java. E. J. Brill. Leiden.

WADSWORTH, R. K. (1970): Point-quarter sampling of forest type-site relations at El Verde. pp. B97-B104 *in* H. T. Odum and R. Pigeon, eds. A Tropical Rain Forest. Division of Technical Information, United States Atomic Energy Commission, Washington, D. C.

WHITE, J. & HARPER, J. L. (1970): Correlated changes in plant size and number in plant populations. *Journal of Ecology 58*: 467-485.

WHITMORE, T. C. & BURNHAM, C. P. (1969): The altitudinal sequence of forest and soils on granite near Kuala Lumpur. *Malayan Nature Journal 22*: 99-118.

Ecological Diversity

(With two text-figures)

Madhav Gadgil[1] and V.M. Meher-Homji[2]

Contribution No. 7 from Centre for Ecological Sciences, Indian Institute of Science

Abstract

With its great variety of ecological conditions, and its position at the confluence of three biogeographic realms, the Indian subcontinent has a tremendous diversity of plant and animal species. About 80,000 species of animals and 15,000 species of flowering plants have so far been described from India, and another 25 to 50 thousand remain to be described. The distribution patterns of these organisms permit us to divide the country into 16 biogeographic zones and 42 vegetation types. The present paper reviews the status of the natural plant and animal life in each of these zones and vegetation types based on a detailed analysis of all the available vegetation maps and other sources of information. These estimates are however clearly overestimates due to certain intrinsic biases in our data base. Furthermore, while certain vegetation types, such as the evergreen forest types of the Western Ghats are reasonably well preserved, others such as the *Acacia-Anogeissus latifolia* thorn forests of semi-arid Deccan are almost entirely wiped out. This destruction of our natural vegetation has rendered nearly two-thirds of our land not under cultivation or human settlement totally unproductive. Nevertheless, little is being done to revegetate this land; instead more and more natural vegetation is being destroyed to raise forest plantations which often fail or to support marginal cultivation which cannot be sustained. We now need to devise programmes of rehabilitating these wastelands to generate rural employment on a massive scale and to reduce the pressure on our few remaining pockets of natural vegetation. This should be coupled to a conservation programme which would stress the conservation of the country's overall biological diversity. We identify key localities representing all the vegetation types of the country to ensure this overall preservation of biological diversity. In addition, certain communities which have been totally destroyed will have to be artificially reconstructed.

Introduction

Much of the fascination of living creatures resides in their incredible variety. The smallest of these, the viruses, could be packed in millions on the head of a pin; while the largest animals exceed a hundred feet, and the largest trees a hundred metres in height. They occur everywhere, from the lightless depths of oceans and caves to the heights of mountain ranges, and from the icy expanses of Antarctica to the sweltering heat of Amazonia. At the latest count a million and half different kinds of living creatures have been named by scientists, while another two to ten million species remain to be described. And that is not the end to the variety of life, for in most living species each individual is different from every other member of the species.

So far as we know, this fantastic variety of life has risen from a single origin in the primaeval oceans of three billion years ago. That is why all living creatures are made up of the same chemical building blocks, and run the business of life using the same biochemical machinery. The riddle of how and why life

[1]Indian Institute of Science, Bangalore 560 012

[2]French Institute, Pondichery 605 001

diversified so much from these beginnings has been intriguing biologists for quite some time.

The solution appears to lie in the variety of environmental challenges. For living organisms are finely tuned to their environment, the struggle for survival ensuring that the ill-adapted are weeded out. Hence, each kind of organism survives well in some specific combination of environmental factors, which constitute its ecological niche. Thus a polar bear survives well in cold latitudes and a sloth bear in warm. But the living environment of an organism is even more important to it than the non-living one, and determines where it will live. A woodpecker feeds on certain kinds of insects which live under barks of trees. Cleaner fishes need cavities in corals to live in, and ectoparsites of other species of coral fishes to feed on; and so on. Thus the coming into being of one kind of organism makes possible the existence of another in an apparently ever expanding circle. Notably enough, organisms arising from different lineages develop similar solutions in response to similar environmental pressures. For instance, in Tasmania there was a marsupial wolf remarkably similar to placental wolves elsewhere, and on the Galapagos islands a woodpecker finch has learnt to use a cactus thorn to pry out insect prey in the absence of a strong beak.

This diversity of life is not evenly distributed on the surface of the earth, so that some regions are much richer than others. The warmer latitudes by and large have much greater variety of life than the colder ones. Hill tracts with their greater range of environments also harbour higher levels of diversity than an equal area of plains at similar latitudes. Finally regions colonized by organisms from different evolutionary lineages have greater diversity than those colonized by a single or fewer lineages.

INDIA'S BIOLOGICAL WEALTH

The Indian subcontinent is exceedingly fortunate on all these three counts. It is essentially a tropical country with the Himalayas keeping out the cold air masses even from our northern latitudes. It therefore has in common with other tropical regions a greater wealth of living organisms. The country supports a tremendous variety of environmental regimes from the warm, humid tracts of Kerala to cold, dry heights of the Ladakh plateau, and the hot desert of Rajasthan to the swamps of Sundarbans. It is also a country situated at the trijunction of African, European and Southeast Asian realms and derives characteristic elements from each of them. To these are added elements that developed independently in peninsular India from its history as a part of a southern Gondvana land (Mani 1974).

This renders India one of the biologically richest tracts in the world. The full diversity of the country's plant and animal life is only imperfectly known. Some groups, such as birds have been well studied, and very few new species are likely to be added to the 1200 or so already described. On the other hand, groups such as insects have been only partially investigated and another 20 to 50 thousand species may easily be added to the 67 thousand species already described from India. As of today, the number of animal species so far described from India, apart from the 67,000 insects includes 4,000 molluscs, 6,500 other invertebrates, 1400 fishes, 140 amphibians, 420 reptiles, 1200 birds and 340 mammals. Thus about 80,000 species of animals have been described from India, compared to the world total of 1.5 million (Zoological Survey of India 1980). Out of the 240,000 species of higher plants known from the world, some 15,000 have been described from India (Mani 1974).

Thus around 5 to 6% of the known species of living organisms of the world occur in India with a land surface of only 2.2%. If India's biota was to be fully described the total number of species will climb at least to 1.25 to 1.5 lakhs, although the overall share may drop if an even greater number of new species is discovered in the American tropics taking the world total to 5 million or more that it is expected to reach (Myers 1979).

ECOLOGICAL DIVERSITY

Individuals of these more than a lakh of plant and animal species, along with a whole variety of micro-organisms about which we know very little, are not uniformly distributed over the surface of the Indian subcontinent. They maintain viable populations only where their own specific set of requirements are fulfilled in terms of the physical environment, as well as the complex of populations of other species of living creatures. Generally, a set of species, dependent on each other and on a specific configuration of physical conditions for their existence tend to be distributed together. Thus, the banks of fast flowing Himalayan rivers or the intertidal zone or rocky shores of the east coast of India, or the exposed hills at high elevations of the Western Ghats each harbour their own assemblages of living organisms. Such ecosystems are natural units that go to constitute the total biosphere. Some of these ecosystems may be very restricted in occurrence, as for instance the spray zones at the base of major waterfalls, while others such as the flat arid plains of Rajasthan desert may be very widely distributed. In order to make sense of this complex pattern, we classify similar ecosystems into broad biome types such as tropical rain forests or hill streams. Biomes such as tropical rain forests are zonal, i.e. coincide with broad climatic zones; while others like the hill stream are azonal. For reasons of convenience, broad ecological classifications emphasize zonally distributed biomes. Further, such biomes are identified with the major plant species, rather than with the more mobile and less obvious animals and micro-organisms. Ecological diversity of a region is therefore summarised in the form of zonally defined biomes identified with their dominant vegetation type.

BIOGEOGRAPHIC PROVINCES

Particular assemblages of living organisms differ not only because they may be subject to different environmental regimes, but also because of their different evolutionary histories. Thus the African grasslands and forests have a variety of antelope species, while species of deer play a similar ecological role in many Asian grasslands and forests. The alpine grasslands in the Himalayas support a different species of mountain goat, *Hemitragus jemlahicus* from grasslands of the Western Ghats which harbour *H.hylocrius*. Biologists classify the world in different biogeographic realms and provinces to account for this variation in composition of their biota due to historical factors. Each such biogeographic realm and its provinces tend to possess their own characteristic, though not necessarily completely unique set of plant and animal species.

The terrestrial world has been divided into 8 biogeographic realms, and as mentioned above, the Indian subcontinent comes under the influence of three of these; Palaearctic, Afrotropical and Indomalayan. Physically, parts of our Thar desert and northwestern Himalayas are included in the Palaearctic realm, while the rest of the country is included under the Indomalayan realm. However, the desert as well as some other adjoining semi-arid tracts show a significant incursion of Afrotropical elements.

The distribution of plant and animal species is therefore best summarised through a joint consideration of the distribution in terms of ecological regimes via biomes and biogeographic provinces. Dasmann (1973, 1974) and more recently Udvardy (1982) have attempted to do so for the terrestrial environments of the world as a whole. In their latest classification the world is divided into 8 biogeographical realms and 14 terrestrial biome types. Employing these they derive a total of 227 biogeographic provinces. In this classification the Indian subcontinent is divided into 2 biogeographic provinces of the Palaearctic realm and 6 biogeographic provinces of the Indomalayan realm. These divisions are, however, not entirely satisfactory. Thus the province Deccan teak forest (4.15.4) ranges all the way from the moist-deciduous teak through dry deciduous teak to *Acacia-Capparis* scrub of semi-arid Deccan; while the sal zone is split into Ganges monsoon forest, Andhra Pradesh, which is not a very happy term, to parts of so-called Bengalian rain forest.

VEGETATION TYPES OF INDIA

Given that the divisions proposed in Udvardy's (1982) global classification are inadequate, one naturally turns to the classical work on forest types of India by Champion (1936) and Champion and Seth (1968). Unfortunately, this classification is based not on mapping the vegetation of the entire country, but on a few selected stands. Puri *et al.* (1983) bring out a number of other deficiencies in this classification including a confusion between biotic and climatic influences, an improper demarcation into northern and southern types (although in India latitude does not differentiate vegetation the way it does in Europe), and poor use of terms such as subtropical and semi-evergreen.

The best vegetation classification available to us is that developed by Gaussen (1959) and the French Institute school based as it is on a detailed careful mapping of the vegetation of the entire country except the Himalayas. This classification of vegetation introduces the notion of series of vegetation. A series includes the various physiognomic stages ranging from the forest to scattered scrub created through degradative biotic influences (Fig. 1). The final stage of the series, expected to be reached if successional processes were permitted to proceed without human interference, is termed as plesioclimax, the potential vegetation of a place. A series is named after three or more species of its plesioclimax stage. These species are selected because of their dominance, abundance, fidelity or economic value. A fuller exposition of this system is provided by Puri *et al.* (1983). For the Himalayas the best available work again based on fairly extensive vegetation mapping is that of Schweinfurth (1957). We have therefore decided to base our own treatment on 16 biogeographic provinces and 42 vegetation types derived from a combination of these two bodies of work (Fig. 2). These 42 vegetation types are then taken to represent the basic units of ecological and biological diversity of the Indian subcontinent. Table 1 gives details of these types and their equivalences with other standard classifications.

INFORMATION BASE

The French Institute has published a series of twelve vegetation maps covering the entire peninsular India (Gaussen *et al.* 1961a,b, 1963a,b, 1965a,b, 1968a,b, 1971, 1973, 1978). The main map of vegetation at 1:1 million scale

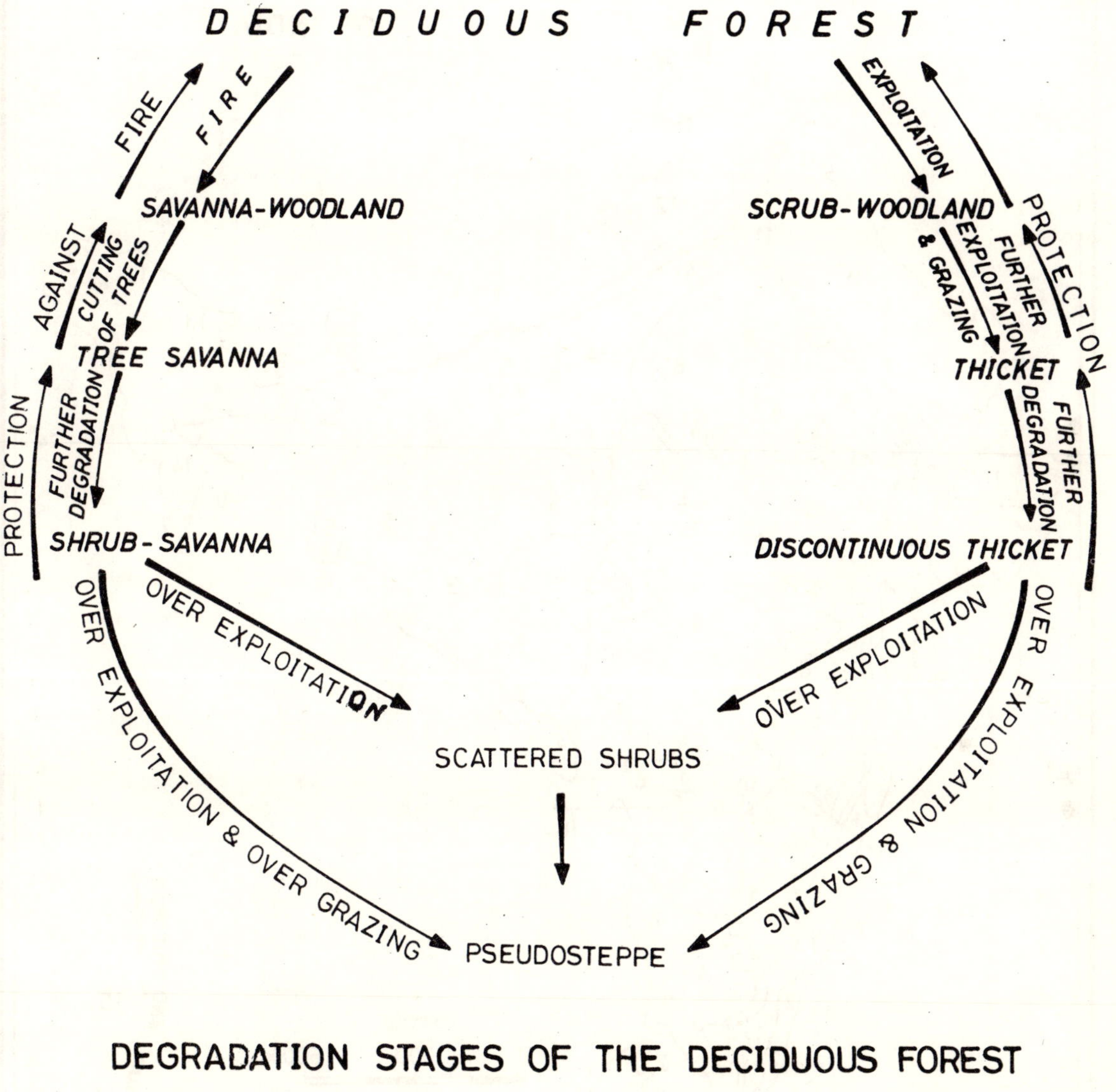

Fig. 1. Various degradation stages of a dry deciduous forest constituting the series for this vegetation type.

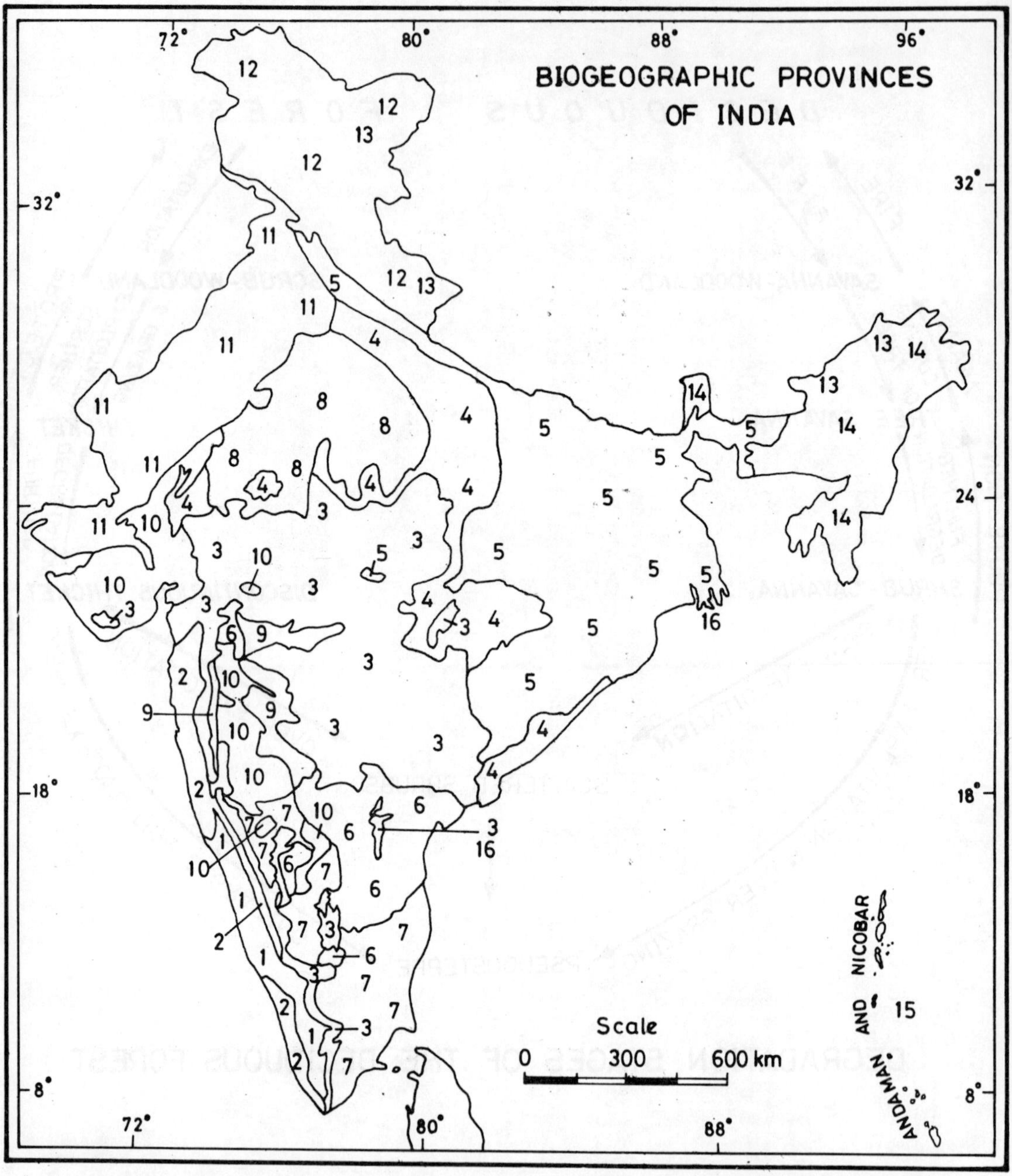

Fig. 2. Biogeographic provinces of the Indian subcontinent. (1) Wet evergreen forest of west coast — Western Ghats. (2) Transition zone between wet evergreen forests and teak forests. (3) Teak zone. (4) Transitional zone between teak and sal. (5) Sal zone. (6) *Hardwickia* zone. (7) *Albizia amara* zone. (8) *Anogeissus pendula* zone. (9) Deccan thorn forest. (10) *Acacia-Capparis* scrub. (11) Indian desert. (12) Western Himalayas. (13) Himalayas. (14) Eastern Himalayas-Northeastern India. (15) Andaman-Nicobar. (16) Mangroves.

TABLE 1
VEGETATION TYPES OF INDIA

Biogeographic Province	Potential maximum (Climax) Vegetation type	Equivalence with Champion (1936) or Champion and Seth's (1968) type	Equivalence with UNESCO International classification (1973)
I. Wet evergreen forests of West Coast and Western Ghats	(1) *Cullenia-Mesua-Palaquium*	Western tropical wet evergreen forest (West Coast tropical evergreen forest)	Tropical ombrophilous lowland/sub-montane forest (Tropical or subtropical evergreen seasonal lowland/sub-montane forest)
	(2) *Dipterocarpus-Mesua-Palaquium*	Western tropical evergreen forest (West Coast tropical semi-evergreen forest)	Tropical ombrophilous lowland forest (Tropical or subtropical evergreen seasonal lowland forest)
	(3) *Persea-Holigarna-Diosphyros*	Western tropical evergreen forest (West Coast tropical semi-evergreen forest)	Tropical ombrophilous lowland forest
	(4) Montane shola	Southern wet temperate forest, Southern montane wet temperate forest	Tropical ombrophilous montane forest
	(5) *Memecylon-Syzygium-Actinodaphne*	Bombay subtropical evergreen forest. Western subtropical hill forest	Tropical or subtropical evergreen. seasonal sub-montane forest
	(6) *Bridelia-Syzygium-Terminalia-Ficus*	Bombay subtropical evergreen forest. Central Indian subtropical hill forest	-do-
II. Transitional zone between wet evergreen forests and teak forests	(1) *Tectona-Lagerstroemia paniculata-Dillenia-Terminalia paniculata*	South Indian tropical moist deciduous (Teak) forest	Tropical or subtropical semi-deciduous lowland forest
	(2) *Tectona-Terminalia-Adina-Anogeissus*	Slightly moist teak forest	-do-
III. Teak zone	(1) *Anogeissus-Terminalia-Tectona*	Southern tropical dry or very dry deciduous teak bearing forest	Drought-deciduous broad-leaved lowland and sub-montane forest
	(2) *Tectona-Terminalia*	Intermediate between dry slightly moist deciduous teak forests	-do-
IV. Transitional zone between teak and sal	(1) *Terminalia-Anogeissus latifolia*	Northern dry mixed deciduous forest.	-do-
	(2) *Terminalia-Anogeissus-Cleistanthus*	Northern tropical dry mixed deciduous forest	-do-
V. Sal zone	(1) *Shorea-Buchanania-Cleistanthus* (2) *Shorea-Cleistanthus-Croton*	Transition between dry deciduous sal forest and moist peninsular sal forest	Drought deciduous broad-leaved lowland and submontane forest. Tropical or subtropical semi-deciduous lowland forest

Biogeographic Province	Potential maximum (Climax) Vegetation type	Equivalence with Champion (1936) or Champion and Seth's (1968) type	Equivalence with UNESCO International classification (1973)
	(3) *Shorea-Buchanania-Terminalia*	Dry peninsular sal type	Drought decuiduous broad-leaved lowland and submontane forest
	(4) *Shorea-Terminalia-Adina*	Moist peninsular sal type (Locally, dry type of northern tropical, deciduous forest)	Tropical or subtropical semi-deciduous lowland forest
	(5) *Shorea-Dillenia-Pterospermum*	Moist tropical primary seral type: Coastal sal	Tropical or subtropical semi-deciduous lowland forest
	(6) *Shorea-Syzygium-operculatum-Toona*	Moist peninsular sal forest of the northern tropical moist deciduous forest	Tropical or subtropical semi-deciduous lowland forest
	(7) *Toona-Garuga*	Tropical semi-evergreen forest	Tropical or subtropical evergreen seasonal sub-montane forest
VI. *Hardwickia* zone	(1) *Hardwickia binata-Albizia amara*	South Indian dry deciduous forest: - Hardwickia forest - Red Sanders forest	Drought deciduous broad-lowland and sub-montane forest/woodland
VII. *Albizia amara* zone	(1) *Albizia amara-Acacia*	Tropical dry evergreen forest	Tropical or subtropical evergreen seasonal lowland forest. Evergreen broad-leaved sclerophyllous shrubland or thicket
	(2) *Anogeissus latifolia-Chloroxylon-Albizia amara*	South Indian dry mixed deciduous forest	Drought deciduous broad-leaved lowland and sub-montane forest
	(3) *Manilkara-Chloroxylon*	Tropical dry evergreen forest	Tropical or subtropical evergreen seasonal lowland forest. Evergreen broad-leaved sclerophyllous shrubland or thicket
VIII. *Anogeissus pendula* zone	(1) *Acacia senegal-Anogeissus pendula*	Edaphic climax type of dry tropical forests: *Anogeissus pendula* forest (with *Acacia senegal*)	Drought deciduous broad-leaved lowland and sub-montane forest
	(2) *Acacia catechu-Anogeissus pendula* forest	Edaphic climax type of dry tropical forests: *Anogeissus pendula* forest (with *Acacia catechu*)	Drought deciduous broad-leaved lowland and sub-montane forest
	(3) *Anogeissus pendula-Anogeissus latifolia*	-do- (with *Anogeissus latifolia*)	-do-
IX. Deccan thorn forest	(1) *Acacia-Anogeissus latifolia*	Dry savannah forest, Dry deciduous scrub	Drought deciduous shrub, Woody synusia broad-leaved deciduous
X. *Acacia capparis* scrub	(1) *Acacia-Capparis*	Northern thorn scrub, Desert thorn forest, Southern Cutch thorn forest, Southern thorn forest	Purely deciduous thorn forest

Biogeographic Province	Potential maximum (Climax) Vegetation type	Equivalence with Champion (1936) or Champion and Seth's (1968) type	Equivalence with UNESCO International classification (1973)
XI. Indian desert	(1) *Prosopis-Capparis-Ziziphus-Salvadora-Calligonum*	Northern desert thorn forest, tropical Euphorbia scrub (degradation stage)	Purely deciduous thorn forest. Deciduous shrubland (with or without succulents like *Euphorbia*)
XII. Western Himalaya	(1) Subtropical evergreen sclerophyllous forest (2) Alpine steppe	Subtropical dry evergreen forest	Tropical or subtropical evergreen lowland forest. Temperate deciduous thickets. Evergreen broad-leaved sclerophyllous shrubland or thicket. Alpine and sub-alpine medows.
XIII. Himalayas	(1) Subtropical *Pinus roxburghii* forest	Subtropical Pine forest	Tropical or subtropical montane and subalpine evergreen needle-leaved forest
	(2) Temperate mixed oak and coniferous forest	Himalayan moist temperate forest	Temperate evergreen seasonal montane forest
	(3) Temperate coniferous forest	Dry temperate coniferous forset	Temperate and subpolar evergreen needle-leaved forest. Evergreen needle-leaved woodland
	(4) Subalpine forest	Subalpine forest	Evergreen needle-leaved forest with conical crowns.
	(5) Alpine scrub	Alpine scrub	Subalpine or subpolar thickets. Evergreen dwarf broad-leaved shrubland.
XIV. Eastern Himalayas-North-Eastern India	(1) Tropical wet evergreen forest	Tropical wet evergreen forest	Tropical ombrophilous submontane forest
	(2) Tropical moist deciduous forest	Tropical moist deciduous forest	Tropical or subtropical semi-deciduous lowland forest
	(3) Subtropical broad-leaved hill forest	Subtropical broad-leaved hill forest	Tropical or subtropical evergreen seasonal sub-montane forest
	(4) Montane wet temperate forest	Montane wet temperate forest	Temperate evergreen seasonal broad-leaved forest
XV. Andaman-Nicobar	Tropical wet evergreen forest	Tropical wet evergreen forest	Tropical ombrophilous lowland forest
XVI. Mangrove	Mangrove	Mangrove scrub and forest	Mangrove forest

is accompanied by six inset maps showing potential vegetation types and environmental features and agricultural regions on 1:5 million scale. On these maps the cultivated areas are left in white with symbols for cultivated crops, while the natural vegetation is depicted in a colour code. In the natural vegetation are recognized various physiognomic stages like forest, open forest, scrub-woodland, thicket, savanna-woodland, tree-savanna, shrub-savanna and scattered shrubs. These represent stages of progressive degradation under human interference. We have employed these maps to estimate the total area under plesioclimax, the proportion that remains under other degraded physiognomies, and the number of major patches of vegetation. For the Himalayas we have attempted to derive similar information from Schweinfurth's (1957) maps and the Forest Atlas of India of the National Atlas Organization (1976). The information available from these sources is however much less complete and somewhat unreliable. By and large, all these maps are rather outdated and consequently our estimates are on the high side compared to the actual state of affairs today.

This has been supplemented by a more recent important source, namely the document assessing the forests retaining primary characters by the Forest Survey of India (1982). This information, although much more up to date, is also defficient in that it is not based on fresh field work, but on circulation of a questionnaire to the State Forest Departments. The meaning of forests retaining primary characters was apparently not well defined in this exercise, and many states have simply listed wildlife sanctuaries and national parks under this head. The original biological communities are often much disturbed or replaced by monocultures in such nature reserves. In addition to these, many states have also listed other undisturbed areas outside of nature reserves. By and large, this compilation is also a considerable overestimate of vegetation retaining primary character. To these sources we have added other available literature on India's wildlife sanctuaries and national parks (Mukherji 1982). A number of knowledgeable people have supplemented this information of the state of our vegetation with personal observations kindly communicated to us. Basing on all these sources, we shall now proceed to consider the status of India's terrestrial ecological diversity in terms of the 42 vegetation types defined by us. We must warn that this assessment, although qualitatively reasonably accurate, is likely to be rather over optimistic quantitatively. Nevertheless, we do quote the quantitative estimates with this warning to provide a beginning of a proper assessment (see Tables 2 and 3).

STATUS OF TERRESTRIAL BIOTA

(I) Wet Evergreen Forests of West Coast-Western Ghats

The West Coast and the western face of the Western Ghats enjoy high levels of precipitation ranging from 2000 to 8000 mm a year. The rainfall is better distributed over the year towards the south, with the number of dry months increasing from 3 to 8 per year as one passes northwards. The belt of evergreen vegetation therefore attenuates as one passes northward, becoming confined to the crestline in southern Maharashtra.

This tract is second only to the Himalayas in its biological wealth. It harbours some 1500 species of flowering plants that are endemic to the Western Ghats and is notable for its limbless frogs (caecilians) and burrowing snakes (uropeltids). Its endemic mammals include Nilgiri langur, liontailed macaque, Nilgiri

TABLE 2

STATE OF CONSERVATION OF VEGETATION TYPE: POTENTIAL AREA UNDER EACH TYPE AND ACTUAL AREA UNDER VARIOUS PHYSIOGNOMIES

Biogeographic Region	Vegetation type	Potential area (Thousand ha)	Area under plesioclimax (Thousand ha)	Area under other physionomic stages (thousand ha): Open forest	Scrub woodland, Sav. woodland or clump. Savanna	Tree savanna	Thicket	Shifting cultivation	Area under physiognomies as percentage of potential area	Floristic diversity (maximum number of plant species with references)
I. Wet evergreen forests of West Coast and Western Ghats	1. *Cullenia-Mesua-Palaquium*	2,150 2,250	390-Evergreen 155-Semi -do- = 545 = 25% (11) +		90 (1)		10 (2).		30	2000 (Vajravelu and Joseph, 1971; Fischer, 1921)
	2. *Dipterocarpus-Mesua-Palaquium*	2,250	215-Evergreen 286-Semi -do- and deciduous = 501 = 22% (5)				665 (2)		52	1700 (Saldanha and Nicholson, 1976)
	3. *Persea-Holigarna-Diosphyros*	1,075	310-Semi-evergreen 335-deciduous = 645 - 60% (3)						60	
	4. Montane shola	356	28 - 8% (5)			Grass-land (85) (2)	10 (1)		35	850 (Shetty and Vivekanathan, 1971; Blasco, 1971; Mathew, 1969; Fyson, 1915-32)
	5. *Memecylon-Syzygium-Actinodaphne*	675	80 - 12% (6)		Clump 85(3) Savanna 5(1)		10		25	400 (Puri and Mahajan, 1960)
	6. *Bridelia-Syzygium-Terminalia-Ficus*	275	113-Open forest 41% (7)		Clump 70(3) Savanna 29(5)				77	1000 (Bhandari and Mehta, 1978; Jain, 1967; Rao and Kanodia, 1962-63)
Wet evergreen forest-Teak forest ecotone (transitional zone)	1. *Tectona-Lagerstroemia lanceolata-Dillenia-Terminalia paniculata*	4,975	870-18% (28)	Open forest 128 (7)	114 (5)		128 (3)		25	1500 (Santapau, 1960; Vartak)
	2. *Tectona-Terminalia-*	1,625	432 - 27% (22)	83 (10)	83 (4)				37	450 (Jain, 1963; Inamdar, 1968)
III. Teak zone	1. *Anogeissus-Terminalia-Tectona*	36,090	1728-5% (41)	3015 (90)	936 (42) 936 (42)	511 (19)	463 (12)		18	800 (Sharma *et al.*, 1978; Subba Rao and Kumari, 1967; Kapoor and Kapoor, 1973; Shah *et al.*, 1971; Shah, 1967. Malhotra and Moorthy, 1971)

1	2	3	4	5	6	7	8	9	10	11
	2. *Tectona-Terminalia*	17,250	2651-15% (33)	4015 (39)			1088 (14)		45	**400 (Joseph and Vajravelu, 1967; Joseph, 1963)**
IV. Teak-Sal Transition zone	1. *Terminalia-Anogeissus latifolia*	11,975	664 - 6% (15)	1,109 (16)		95 (12)	47 (3)		16	
	2. *Terminalia-Anogeissus Cleistanthus*	10,375	839 - 9% (29)		1919 (19)		137 (10)		28	
V. Sal zone	'1. *Shorea-Buchanania-Cleistanthus*	8,375	1129 - 14% (29)		1582 (28)		511 (9)		39	550 (Subrahmanyam and Henry, 1966; Saxena, 1973)
	2. ***Shorea-Cleistanthus-Croton***	10,750	726 - 7% (12)	625 (7)			145 (3)		14	400 (Malick, 1966)
	3. *Shorea-Buchanania-Terminalia*	100	15 - 15% (1)	75 (1)					90	700 (Rao and Narayanaswamy, 1960; Saxena, 1971; Kapoor and Yadav, 1962)
	4. *Shorea-Terminalia Adina*	19,510	7240 - 37% (95)	1,503 (20)			425 (6)	10 (1)	47	700 (Sen Gupta and Ram Lal, 1973; Saxena, 1970)
	5. *Shorea-Dillenia-Pterospermum*	1,875	110 - 6% (3)		20 (1)		40 (1)		9	160 (Rao and Banerjee, 1970)
	6. *Shorea-Syzygium operculatum-Toona*	4,950	1214 - 25% (16)		1395 (12)		220 (7)	455 (2)	66	850 (Panigrahi *et al.*, 1964)
	7. *Toona-Garuga*	1,000	172 - 12% (18)						17	200 (Arora, 1968; Saxena, 1973; Raju, 1964)
VI. Hardwickia zone	1. *Hardwickia binata-Anogeissus latifolia*	12,125	1425 - 12% (46)	Open forest			89 (8)		13	475 (Vajravelu and Rathakrishnan, 1967)
VII. *Albizia amara* zone	1. *Albizia amara--Acacia*	15,350	746 - 5% (34)	Scrub wood-land		20 (3)	92 (5)		6 (Marakanam under destruction as an e.g.)	400 (Mathew, 1970; 1975; Sebastine and Henry, 1960)

1	2	3	4	5	6	7	8	9	10	11
	2. *Anogeissus latifolia-Chloroxylon-Albizia amara*	2,725	10 0.5% (1)	Scrub wood-land			7 (1)		0.6	
	3. *Manilkara-Chloroxylon*	2,750	6 - 0.2.% (1)	Scrub wood-land			125 (5)		5	300 (Balasubra-manyam, 1975)
VIII. *Anogeissus pendula* Semi-Arid zone of East Rajasthan	1. *Acacia senegal-Anogeissus pendula*	3,460	42 - 1% (8)	Low forest	11 (2)		96 (21)		4	600 (Sharma, 1978)
	2. ***Acacia catechu-Anogeissus pendula***	15,805	1226 - 8% (28)	-do-	245 (6)		200 (22)		11	700 (Majumdar, 1971; Maheshwari, 1963)
	3. *Anogeissus pendula-A. latifolia*	5,000	121 - 2% (9)	103 (11)			31 (4)		5	400 (Kaushik, 1969)
IX. Deccan Thorn Forest	1. *Acacia-Anogeissus latifolia*	9,780	Nil				27 (3)		0.3	
X. Deccan—Indian Desert	1. *Acacia-Capparis*	17,250	Nill						Existing vegetation is only in the shape of discontinuous thicket or scattered shrubs	500 (Santapu and Raizada, 1955; Vaidya, 1967)
XI. Indian desert	1. *Prosopis-Capparis Zizyphys-Salvadora-Calligonum*	30,875	Nil							550 (Blatter and Hallberg, 1918; Blatter, 1908; Jain and Deshpande, 1960; Kapadia, 1945)
XII. North-west Himalaya	1. Subtropical evergreen sclerophyllous forest	1,340							312-23% (17)	
	2. Alpine steppe	5,600			232 (5)	(Steppe)				
XIII. North-West Himalaya-E. Himalaya	1. Subtropical *Pinus roxburghii* forest	4,900							940-19% (31)	

1	2	3	4	5	6	7	8	9	10	11
	2. Temperate mixed Oak and Coniferous forest	2,360							1288-55% (21)	
	3. Temperate coniferous forest	912							124-14% (7)	
	4. Subalpine forest	5,076							192-4% (21)	
	5. Alpine scrub	512					48-9% (4)			
XIV Eastern Himalaya-N.E. India	1. Tropical wet evergreen forest	5,860							860-15% (14)	
	2. Tropical moist deciduous forest	5,472							1784-33% (45)	
	3. Subtropical broad-leaved hill forest	300							148-49% (5)	
	4. Montane wet temperate forest	2,828							180-6% (3)	
XV. Andaman-Nicobar	Tropical wet evergreen forest	684	488-70% (14)						90	1000 (Thothathari, 1960, 1962)
XVI. Mangrove		681								58 (Blasco, 1977)

+ Number of patches under each physiognomy are given in brackets.

TABLE 3

AREA UNDER PLESIOCLIMAX, AND UNDER OTHER DEGRADED PHYSIOGNOMIES OF VEGETATION AND AREA PROTECTED THROUGH WILDLIFE SANCTUARIES, NATIONAL PARKS, TIGER RESERVES OR DUE TO INACCESSIBILITY AS A PERCENTAGE OF THE POTENTIAL AREA OF VEGETATION TYPE. THE VEGETATION TYPES HAVE BEEN ORDERED IN DECREASING ORDER OF PERCENTAGE AREA UNDER ALL PHYSIOGNOMIES

Sl. No.	Vegetation type	% under Plesioclimax	% under all Physiognomies	% under sanctuaries etc.
1.	Tropical wet evergreen forest of Andaman-Nicobar	70	90	1
2.	*Shorea-Buchanania-Terminalia*	15	90	65
3.	*Bridelia-Syzygium-Terminalia-Ficus*	41	77	5
4.	*Shorea-Syzygium operculatum-Toona*	25	66	1.3
5.	*Persea-Holigarna-Diospyros*	60	60	2.6
6.	Mangrove	30	60	50
7.	Temperate mixed oak and coniferous forest of Himalayas	—	55	7
8.	*Dipterocarpus-Mesua-Palaquium*	22	52	8
9.	Subtropical broad-leaved forest of Eastern Himalayas	—	49	0
10.	*Shorea-Terminalia-Adina*	37	47	6
11.	*Tectona-Terminalia*	15	45	9
12.	*Shorea-Buchanania-Cleistanthus*	14	39	0.5
13.	Montane Shola	8	35	4
14.	Tropical moist deciduous forest of NE India	—	33	7
15.	*Tectona-Terminalia-Adina-Anogeissus*	27	33	5
16.	*Cullenia-Mesua-Palaquium*	18	30	11
17.	*Terminalia-Anogeissus-Cleistanthus*	9	28	1
18.	***Tectona-Lagerstroemia-Dillenia-T. paniculata***	18	25	15
19.	*Memecylon-Syzygium-Actinodaphne*	12	25	0.8
20.	Subtropical evergreen sclerophyllous forest of NW Himalaya	—	23	0.8
21.	Subtropical *Pinus roxburghii* forest of Himalayas	—	19	3
22.	*Anogeissus-Terminalia-Tectona*	5	18	2.7
23.	*Toona-Garuga*	17	17	4
24.	*Terminalia-Anogeissus latifolia*	6	16	0.8
25.	Tropical evergreen forest of NE India	—	15	4
26.	Temperate coniferous forest of Himalayas	—	14	8
27.	*Shorea-Cleistanthus-Croton*	7	14	0.4
28.	*Hardwickia binata-Anogeissus latifolia*	12	13	3
29.	*Acacia catechu-Anogeissus pendula*	8	11	1.5
30.	Alpine scrub of Himalayas	—	9	0
31.	*Shorea-Dillenia-Pterospermum*	6	9	1.3
32.	Montane wet temperate forest of eastern Himalayas	—	6	1.5
33.	*Albizia amara-Acacia*	5	6	0.1
34.	*Anogeissus pendula-Anogeissus latifolia*	2	5	2
35.	*Manilkara-Chloroxylon*	0.2	5	2
36.	Alpine steppe of NW Himalayas	—	4	4
37.	Subalpine forest of Himalayas	—	4	3.6
38.	*Acacia senegal-Anogeissus pendula*	1	4	0.01
39.	*Acacia-Anogeissus latifolia*	0	0.3	0
40.	*Acacia-Capparis*	0	0	0.04
41.	*Prosopis-Capparis-Ziziphus-Salvadora*	0	0	1
42.	*Anogeissus latifolia-Chloroxylon-Albizia amara*	0.5	—	—

tahr and Malabar civet. The tract possesses a number of wild relatives of cultivated plants, including pepper, cardamom, mango and jakfruit.

The coastal strip is thickly populated and the natural vegetation has been entirely replaced by paddy, tapioca and coconut plantations. The only remnants of natural forests found on most parts of coast are groves protected on religious grounds. The steep hill slopes, particularly in Karnataka and Kerala retain much better the cover of natural vegetation. This is why vegetation types of this biogeographical province are amongst the best preserved anywhere in the country. Even then tea, coffee, rubber, cardamom, and eucalyptus plantations and heavy, thoughtless exploitation for plywood, matchwood and railway sleepers have resulted in extensive disturbance to these forests. In fact there are now only a few patches of genuinely virgin forests left; even the core area of Periyar Tiger Reserve being subject to regular fires, collection of minor forest produce and poaching.

Kalakkadu, Eravikulam, Periyar, Wynad, Mukambika, Someshwar, Karnala and Mount Abu (which is included here for convenience) constitute the important nature reserves of this province. It has been suggested that Periyar and Silent Valley (*Cullenia-Mesua-Palaquium* type), Govardhangiri, Pushpagiri and Narasimhaparvat (*Dipterocarpus-Mesua-Palaquium* type), Eravikulam, Ebanadu and Kanbatti (Montane shola), Kankumbi (*Memecylon-Syzigum-Actinodaphne* type) and Mt. Abu (*Bridelia-Syzygium-Terminalia-Ficus* type) should be formed into well-protected biosphere reserves on a priority basis to save the biological diversity of this rich tract.

(II) Wet Evergreen Forest-Teak Zone Ecotone

This province abuts on the previous province at lower levels of precipitation around 2000 mm a year. At its climax it supports a moist-deciduous forest characterized by *Lagerstroemia, Adina, Terminalia* and *Tectona*. Such forests are rich in wildlife dominated by Indo-Malaysian elements like elephant, sambar and gaur. The coastal tracts of this province have been brought under paddy and coconut, and the hill forests extensively converted to teak plantations, as witness the famous teak plantations of Nilambur, Kanara, Thana and Dangs. Two major wildlife sanctuaries of this province have recently been written off; Dandeli because of the giant Kali hydel project and Dangs because of the temptation to convert all natural forest to teak. Still it has left a few good nature reserves such as Parambikulam, Anaimalai, Nagarhole and Borivali. There are, however, rather extensive teak plantations in all of these. It is now necessary to declare at least Anaimalai, Nagarhole, Anashi ghat and Purna as biosphere reserves on a priority basis to protect the overall ecological diversity of this province.

(III) Teak Zone

This, the largest of India's biogeographic provinces covers much of the southern and central peninsula with an average annual precipitation of 800 to 1800 mm a year. To its east and north, sal replaces teak in a somewhat moister regime. There is good grass growth on the floor of these deciduous forests which consequently supported good populations of ungulates and their predators. The tract is also notable for supporting the slender loris.

Much of this type of vegetation of the Deccan plateau has been cleared for cultivation, but better forested tracts still persist in the central Indian region. Notable nature reserves of this vegetation type include Bandipur, Mudumalai, Gir, Taroba and Kutru, the last being one of the very last strongholds of wild buffalo in peninsular India. Unfortunately Kutru is being drastically affected by proposed river valley projects. To preserve the biological diversity of this vegetation type on a long term basis, we should set up a network of biosphere reserves including Mudumalai, Bandipur and the southern and eastern slopes of Nilgiris, Talamalai, Madeswarmalai, Kutru, Indravati, Taroba, Ganjan and Panna on a priority basis.

(IV) TEAK-SAL Transition Zone

This zone lies to the north and east of the teak zone and south and west of the sal zone, with a moderate rainfall of 700-1500 mm a year. It also supported good populations of ungulates. It has now been largely replaced by cultivation, although there are some good pockets of forest in the Bhandara district and on parts of the Eastern Ghats. Its major wildlife sanctuaries are Nagjhira and Nawegaon which should be set aside as biosphere reserves on a priority basis.

(V) Sal Zone

Covering much of central India and the eastern Gangetic plains with rainfall in the range of 1000 to 2000 mm a year, the sal zone is the second largest biogeographic province of India. The climax forest in this zone is of the moist-deciduous type with a high frequency of sal whose incidence depends on the availability of moisture when its short-lived seed is produced in the month of March. The tract has many mammalian species with Indo-Malayan affinities such as the elephant, gaur and sambar. The region also harbours populations of the threatened swamp deer or barasinga. Interestingly enough, the giant squirrel occurs here as on the Western Ghats. A number of bird genera are distributed over the sal zone, the Western Ghats and the Himalayas. This suggests that there was once a continuous distribution of many forest forms from the Himalayas to the Western Ghats and that they were probably exterminated from intervening areas by the clearance of forest.

Substantial fragments of natural vegetation of the sal zone still remain in the Central Indian tribal belt of Madhya Pradesh, Bihar, Orissa and West Bengal, although wiped out over areas such as Koraput through shifting cultivation and many other places by forest monocultures. The sal forests of the Gangetic and Brahmaputra plains in Uttar Pradesh, Bihar, West Bengal and Assam have been replaced by intensive cultivation, although fragments still remain near the foothills of the Himalayas.

This moist-deciduous forest is an excellent habitat for the larger mammals and a number of good wildlife areas in this tract are preserved as nature reserves. These include Dalma, Manas, Palamau, Kanha, Corbett, Dudhwa and Simlipal. Most of these are however under one threat or other from river valley projects or stepped up forest exploitation. It is therefore urgently needed to convert all these into an effective network of biosphere reserves.

(VI) *Hardwickia* Zone

The plateau region of Karnataka and Andhra Pradesh and part of Salem region of Tamilnadu with a relatively low annual rainfall in the region of 500 to 1200 mm is covered with a dry-deciduous forest dominated by *Hardwickia binata* and *Anogeissus latifolia* with the characteristic occurrence of *Pterocarpus santalinus*. Along with other dry tracts this region harbours the truly characteristic endemic mammals such as nilgai, blackbuck and sloth bear. Most of the natural plant and animal life of this province has been wiped out. The only significant nature reserve of this zone is Nagarjunsagar which should be made a biosphere reserve on a high priority.

(VII) *Albizia amara* Zone

The dry east coastal plains of Tamilnadu and Andhra Pradesh and parts of the Deccan plateau which have a low annual rainfall in the range of 500 and 1500 mm support vegetation characterized by the occurrence of *Albizia amara*. This tract once supported the characteristic peninsular Indian wildlife with blackbuck and wolves. However, as with other dry tracts almost all of this natural biota has been wiped out. The natural vegetation is replaced by *Eucalyptus* monoculture even in wildlife sanctuaries such as Ranebennur. The fast vanishing biota of this tract must be immediately protected by declaring its two worthwhile sanctuaries, Tungabhadra and Point Calimere as biosphere reserves.

(VIII) *Anogeissus pendula* zone of Eastern Rajasthan

Hills of the Aravalli range in eastern Rajasthan and the adjoining parts of Madhya Pradesh have a characteristic vegetation distinguished by the presence of *Anogeissus pendula*. In the drier tract (annual rainfall 400-700 mm), it is usually associated with *Acacia senegal,* but in the more humid parts of eastern Rajasthan (550-900 mm annual rainfall), the associated species is *Acacia catechu*. Further east in Rajasthan, Shivapuri plateau of Madhya Pradesh and Bundelkhand *Anogeissus latifolia* comes in. This deciduous forest tract was rich in ungulates, showing a mingling of the Afrotropical chinkara, the autochthonous nilgai and blackbuck, and the Indomalayan sambar. Much of its natural vegetation and animal life been wiped out, to be replaced by an almost barren landscape with only a few low bushes of *Euphorbia caducifolia* and *Zizyphus nummularia*.

There are three important nature reserves in this province, all former hunting preserves of Maharajas, Ranthambhor, Sariska and Shivapuri. They should be forthwith constituted into biosphere reserves to protect the biological diversity of this tract.

(IX) Thorn Forest of Semi-Arid Deccan

Parts of the Deccan plateau and Purna-Tapti valley with an annual precipitation of 600-800 mm possess a natural vegetation dominated by *Anogeissus latifolia* with *Acacia nilotica*. It must once have possessed large herds of blackbuck and other animals of semi-arid tracts. All of this is now completely gone so that there is nothing left to protect. Rather we should systematically attempt to restore the ecological regimes characteristic of the province in a few well-protected tracts.

(X) *Acacia - Capparis* Scrub

The driest regions of the Deccan plateau of Andhra Pradesh, Karnataka, Maharashtra, Saurashtra and the plains west of the Aravalli hills receive rainfall in the range of 400-850 mm a year. The natural vegetation is dominated by species of *Acacia* and characterized by *Capparis decidua*. The region once harboured large populations of blackbuck, chinkara, wolf, and the Great Indian Bustard. Essentially all of this natural vegetation and animal life has been eliminated. The only nature reserve of this province is the tiny Velavadar national park of *c.* 34 km^2 in Bhavnagar district of Gujarat harbouring blackbuck, fourhorned antelope, wolf and the Great Indian Bustard. This should be made a biosphere reserve, and further areas should be brought under a programme of ecological restoration of the characteristic biota of this province.

(XI) Indian Desert

The true Indian desert of Western Rajasthan and Cutch with an annual precipitation below

450 mm a year has a natural vegetation of *Prosopis, Capparis, Salvadora* and *Zizyphus* which grades into a vegetation dominated by *Calligonum* in the very driest parts of sand dunes. This province is really a part of the Palaearctic realm. The fauna is rather poor, but has some notable species such as the wild ass with Palaearctic affinities, and others like the hyaena and chinkara with Afro-tropical affinities. It also harbours the Great Indian Bustard.

The natural biota of the desert has been nearly wiped out, except where the religious feelings and traditions of the local population have given it protection as in Orans or village groves, and around Bishnoi villages of Rajasthan. Very recently a desert national park has been set up west of Jaisalmer to protect this biota; it also receives some protection in the wild ass sanctuary of the Little Rann of Cutch. We should extend the latter to cover the Great Rann as well and incorporate the Jaisalmer desert national park and the Ranns of Cutch in our network of biosphere reserves.

(XII) North-West Himalayas

The Himalayas, along with the contiguous hills of northeastern states represent the biological treasure trove of the Indian subcontinent. This whole region has been divided into three provinces; northwest Himalayas to include the alpine steppes and subtropical evergreen sclerophyllous forest restricted to this region; Himalayas to include the coniferous, mixed coniferous and alpine scrub forest extending all across from northwest to eastern Himalayas and northeast India to include the broad-leaved forests restricted to the east.

The northwestern Himalayas are basically a part of the Palaearctic realm and are notable for wild goats and sheep of the genera *Capra* and *Ovis,* the Tibetan wild ass, Tibetan antelope, and the musk deer. The natural vegetation of this tract is very much disturbed and there are no large nature reserves protecting this biota. Three alpine reserves in Jammu and Kashmir, Shang Gaui Reserve, Hemis High Altitude National Park and the Overa-Aru reserve need to be urgently constituted as biosphere reserves with full protection.

(XIII) Himalayas

The Himalayan slopes above 1000 m possess a rich biota reaching all the way from Hazra and Kashmir to Mishmi hills. The rainfall ranges from 750 to 3500 mm gradually increasing to the east. The eastern Himalayas are better clad with forest cover and more tropical in nature. The biota is predominantly Indo-malayan with Palaearctic elements such as the hangul restricted to the west. Red panda (*Ailurus*) is the only mammalian genus almost totally confined to the Himalayas. Other notable forms include snow leopard and clouded leopard, both threatened with extinction, the spotted linsang, the giant flying squirrel, the Himalayan tahr and the goat-antelopes — serow, goral and takin. It also harbours many notable species of pheasants.

The Himalayan biota has been very much disturbed, particularly in the western and central portions, but is a little better preserved in the east. Larger nature reserves of this tract include Govind Pashu Vihar of Uttar Pradesh and Kistwar and Dachigam national parks in Jammu and Kashmir. This biologically rich area is evidently in need of urgent protection, and the following biosphere reserves should be constituted to this end: Kaibul Lambjo in Manipur (subtropical *Pinus roxburghii* forest), Kistwar in Jammu and Kashmir (temperate mixed oak and coniferous forest), Dachigam and Gulmarg in Jammu and Kashmir and Sainj-Tirthan valley in Himachal Pradesh

(Temperate coniferous forest), and the Valley of Flowers — Rudranath tract, and Nandadevi in Uttar Pradesh (subalpine forest).

(XIV) Eastern Himalayas — Northeastern India

This province embraces the broad-leaved forests of the eastern Himalayas — northeast below the altitude of 2500 m. This is a humid tract with an annual rainfall ranging from 2500 to 11000 mm and the climax vegetation ranging from moist-deciduous and wet-temperate to wet-evergreen forest. It is an exceedingly rich region from the view point of biological diversity, and its notable mammalian fauna includes hoolock gibbon, slow loris, golden langur, ferret badger, onehorned rhinoceros, wild buffalo, swamp deer, thamin, the takin, the pygmy hog, the clouded leopard and the marbled cat.

This rich biota has suffered tremendous assaults in recent years from both the stepped up pace of shifting cultivation by the tribals and the rapacious behaviour of forest-based industry. Strong measures are obviously called for to protect it urgently,and it is suggested that the following be immediately constituted as biosphere reserves: Kaziranga National Park in Assam (tropical moist-deciduous forest), Intanki wildlife sanctuary in Nagaland (tropical wet-evergreen forest), and Namdapha wildlife sanctuary in Arunachal Pradesh (montane wet temperate and subalpine forest).

(XV) Andaman and Nicobar Islands

The Andaman and Nicobars are a group of over 300 islands, islets and reefs in the Bay of Bengal extending from 6°N to 14°N latitude. These tropical islands receive an annual rainfall of over 3000 mm. Their steeply undulating topography with hills as high as 700 m, and an extensive system of sheltered creeks and shallow bays, coral reefs and mud-and-sandbanks have generated in this archipelago a rich variety of habitats. Added to this is the fact that because of their location they have received biotic elements from Polynesian, Indo-malayan as well as Assam-Burmese provinces. All of this, coupled with the barriers to migration created by the sea between the islands has led to the establishment of an exceedingly rich biota with a number of endemic species of this group of islands. This has been so little studied that in fact most species of living organisms from this archipelago are yet to be described. Notable endemic forms amongst the better studied groups such as birds are the Nicobar megapode, Nicobar pigeon, Andaman teal and the Narcondam hornbill. The islands also harbour 220 endemic species of plants found nowhere else, and another 1300 species found here and in other parts of the world, but not on the Indian mainland. The islands also support large populations of estuarine crocodile and provide nesting grounds for four marine turtles.

Relatively little touched till 30 years ago, this biota has been increasingly disturbed in recent years through massive, unrecorded encroachment by cultivators and escalating demands of forest based industry. Although a few small islands have so far been constituted into wildlife sanctuaries, little serious thought has been given to long term conservation of this rich biological heritage. We should therefore think of setting up a viable network of biosphere reserves including the following elements: Saddle Peak in North Andaman island, Mount Harriet National Park with appropriate additions along the entire isthmus in South Andaman island, Tarmugli group of coral reef islands, North, Middle, and South Button islands, Interview Island, the Jarawa Reserve along the west coast of South and Middle Andaman islands, Little Andaman Island, Great Nicobar, Little Nicobar and Tillanchong islands.

(XVI) **Mangrove**

India has a long coastline and its creeks and estuaries offer extensive mangrove habitat. This vegetation has however been largely eliminated from the west coast and persists today only in the Sundarbans and on the Andaman and Nicobar islands. To protect this biota we should constitute a biosphere reserve in an appropriate location on Saurashtra coast, accord biosphere status to the Sundarabans, as also create the above mentioned biosphere reserves in the Andaman-Nicobar Islands.

AQUATIC ECOSYSTEMS

The Indian subcontinent possesses a rich variety of aquatic habitats ranging from glaciers and streams in the high Himalayas and great estuaries on the sea coast, high altitude lakes like Mansarovar, jheels like Bharatpur and brackish lakes like Chilka to the extensive continental shelf off the west coast of India and coral reef islands of Lakshadweep. Our notable aquatic animals include the Gangetic dolphin and the gharial. This biota has received even less attention from the view point of conservation than the terrestrial life; and is quite seriously threatened from river valley projects, siltation and chemical pollution. There are of course a few aquatic nature reserves, the best known of them being the jheel at Bharatpur, a great centre of congregation of migratory waterfowl. Three sanctuaries, covering several hundred square kilometres of the length of Chambal, Ken and Son rivers have been created to protect the Gharial habitat. Finally, there are proposals to create two marine biosphere reserves, one off Saurashtra and the other in the Gulf of Manaar to protect coral reef areas. Careful analysis and conservation action relating to the aquatic ecosystems is evidently needed, although we are not in a position to offer concrete suggestions.

DISCUSSION AND CONCLUSIONS

With its tropical climate, its great range of environmental regimes and its position near the junction of three biogeographical realms, nature has endowed the Indian subcontinent with a great potential for biological wealth. While the physical conditions set the context within which the variety of life can develop, its realization depends on the interactions amongst living creatures themselves. Thus, the substratum of life on land, the soil is itself a product of the activity of plants, earthworms, soil micro-organisms and other creatures. Trees also provide many special habitats for organisms ranging from epiphytic orchids, tree-hole breeding birds and mosquitoes, symbiotic nitrogen fixing micro-organisms to parasitic mistletoes, fungi, bacteria and viruses, and so on. Left to itself, nature favours specialization of living organisms to a fairly narrow set of environmental conditions. This is especially so in the tropics where the living world develops into a fantastically variegated mosaic of ecosystems. The richness of this mosaic is generated by and can be maintained only through the interactions of diversity of the living creatures which constitute its fabric.

Man, with his command over tools and fire, acts as a great homogenising influence on the biosphere. In nature fires occur, but at restricted times and places; many ecosystems such as the rain forest are never subject to it. Man has however uniformly spread fire over much of the surface of the earth since he first began to employ it 3.5 lakh of years ago. Later, when he began to till the land, some 10,000 years ago, he deliberately converted vast tracts of forests into grasslands. His herds of domestic animals, developed around the same time, exerted far greater and more uniform grazing pressure over vast areas.

The hunter-gatherers with their fire and efficient hunting were responsible for substantial habitat change and many species extinctions. On the Indian subcontinent, we have evidence of the occurrence of baboons and hippos in the Narmada beds of 10,000 years ago. Primitive hunter-gatherers were undoubtedly responsible for their extinction, as of wild cattle some time later. The agricultural civilization had even more drastic effects as it eliminated the thick forests over much of the fertile Gangetic and west coast plains. However, these civilizations retained respect for ecological diversity and protected it through a variety of religious and cultural practices (Gadgil 1984, Gadgil and Malhotra 1983). We owe the survival of coastal evergreen forests in Kerala and continuing survival of many creatures like the monkeys solely to these traditions.

This respect for ecological diversity was totally abandoned by the aggressive industrial civilization of Europe which established its sway over India in the second half of the eighteenth century. With this India entered the "pre-bulldozerozoic" era, to use Michael Soule's terminology. Initially they unleashed a spree of destruction of India's forests and wildlife, which lasted till 1860's when it was brought under some check. The pace picked up again as we entered the "bulldozerozoic" era in 1945. In this era, which may be dated from 1945-1965 there were massive projects of colonization of natural habitats for agriculture, as in the Terai, Dandakaranya and Wynad, a spurt of river valley projects, and extensive over-exploitation of forests to meet the needs of industry. The era left in its wake only fragments of natural habitats scattered here and there.

With natural habitats totally fragmented, we may be said to have entered the insulozoic era beginning in 1965. In this era we have brought vast tracts of the land of our country under a single homogeneous set of environmental conditions: regular summer fires, high levels of human exploitation of woody plant material for fuel and industry, and high levels of grazing by cattle and goats. This combination of factors has converted about 88 million hectares (out of a total of 305 million hectares) or over two-thirds of the country's potentially productive land not under cultivation or human settlements into barren wastelands (Vohra 1980). These wastelands are increasingly being covered either by a few species of spiny, non-palatable grasses such as *Heteropogon contortus* or noxious weeds, *Parthenium* in the drier and *Eupatorium* (= *Chromalaena*) in the more humid tracts. At the same time our polluted water bodies are being covered by a uniform carpet of water hyacinth (*Eichornea*).

While the country is being converted into large, homogeneous expanses of *Parthenium* or *Eupatorium* interrupted by monocultures of teak, *Eucalyptus,* paddy or wheat, the natural diverse ecosystems are being fragmented into smaller and smaller bits. Our analysis of the vegetation maps of peninsular India by the French Institute suggests that the median size of the largest remaining patch of each of the vegetation types is now 1100 km^2; while the median for potential area of each vegetation type was as much as 49000 km^2. Even this 1100 km^2 is an overestimate. But using this as an index, a crude calculation of species-area relationships suggests that we are already committed to a loss of 70% of our biological diversity in the longer run (Soule and Wilcox 1980). We are thus bound to eventually lose more than a lakh of our estimated 1.5 lakh species of plants and animals, even if we stop all further erosion of our natural ecosystems.

We have clearly already entered Soule's last geological era: catastrophozoic. A huge portion of our land mass, which could be making a significant contribution to national economy and provide much needed employment to our rural population is lying unproductive and barren. We have totally lost all traces of many of our natural ecosystems, especially of the drier tracts. We have hardly a couple of percent or less of genuinely well-preserved natural ecosystems left to us. Even these are nowhere truly undisturbed with fire and other human interferences creeping into every nook and corner of our land.

In spite of this, rapacious vested interests are waging a war against our few remaining natural ecosystems. They will not rest content till they have cut down the last tree in the Andamans or Silent Valley to be converted into plywood or matchsticks; nor till every stream of water is dammed or polluted. This is done in the name of development for eliminating poverty, when in fact this pattern of development is pushing more and more of our people below the poverty line.

It is obviously time for us to take stock of the situation, and initiate some rational action. This will have to rely on two major planks: rendering productive our vast tracts of barren land to bring employment for our rural poor; and protecting the remaining few patches of our country's natural ecosystems through a well thought out programme of biosphere reserves. All conservationists must now dedicate themselves to these two supremely important, but equally difficult tasks.

ACKNOWLEDGEMENTS

We greatly appreciate the help of P. Legris, J.P. Pascal, Members of the Man and Biosphere Committee of the Department of Environment, Government of India and a large number of colleagues who kindly responded to our enquiries. Timely assistance of Kessavane, Krishnaswamy, Anandam and Petrus is also acknowledged.

REFERENCES

CHAMPION, H.G. (1936): A preliminary survey of forest types of India and Burma. *Indian For. Res. N.S.* 1.

________ & SETH, S.K. (1968): A revised survey of forest types of India. Govt. of India, Delhi.

DASMANN, R.F. (1973): A system for defining and classifying natural regions for purposes of conservation. IUCN occ. pap. 7.

__________ (1974): Biotic provinces of the world. IUCN. Occ. pap. 9.

FOREST SURVEY OF INDIA (1982): Assessment and delineation of forests retaining primary characters. (Mimeo). Dehra Dun.

GADGIL, M. (1984): Social restraints on resource utilization: the Indian experience in J. McNedy and D. Pitt (ed.) Culture and Conservation (*Dublin*).

__________ & MALHOTRA, K.C. (1983): Adaptive significance of the Indian caste system: an ecological perspective. *Ann. Hum. Biol.* (*10:465-78*).

GAUSSEN, H. (1959): The vegetation maps. Inst. Fr. Pondichery. *Trav. Sect. Sci. Tech.* 1: 155-79.

GAUSSEN, H., LEGRIS, P. & VIART, M. (1961a). Sheet Cape Camorin. Int. Map of Vegetation, ICAR, New Delhi.

________________________(1961b): Sheet Madras, ibid.

____________, MARLANGE, M. & MEHER-HOMJI, (1963a): Sheet Godvari. ibid.

______________________ (1963b): Sheet Jagamath. ibid.

GAUSSEN, H., LEGRIS, P., VIART, M., MEHER-HOMJI, V.M. & LABROUE, L. (1965a): Sheet Mysore. ibid.

______________________ (1965b): Sheet Bombay. ibid.

__________, BLASCO, F., MEHER-HOMJI, V.M., & TROY, J.P. (1968a): Sheet Kathiwar. ibid.

_________________________(1968b): Sheet Satpura. ibid.

GAUSSEN, H., MEHER-HOMJI, V.M., LEGRIS, P., BASCO, F., GUPTA, R.K. & TROY, J.P., (1971): Sheet Rajasthan, ibid.

________FONTANEL, J., LEGRIS P., & TROY, J.P., (1973): Sheet Orissa. ibid.

_______, PASCAL, J.P., (1978): Sheet. Allahabad. ibid.

MANI, M.S. (ed.) (1974): Ecology and Biogeography in India. W. Junk. The Hague.

MUKHERJI, A.K. (1982): Endangered Animals of India. Zoological Survey of India, Calcutta.

MYERS, N. (1979): The Sinking Ark. Pergamon Press, Oxford.

NATIONAL ATALS ORGANIZATION (1976): Forest Atlas of India, Calcutta.

PURI, G.S., MEHER-HOMJI, V.M., GUPTA, R.K. & PURI, S. (1983): Forest Ecology, Vol. I, Phytogeography and Forest Conservation. Oxford and IBH, New Delhi.

SCHWEINFURTH, V. (1957): Die Horizontale und Verticale Verbeitung de Vegetation im Himalaya. Bonn.

SOULE, M.E. & WILCOX, B.A., (ed.) (1980): Conservation Biology. Sinauer. Sunderland, Mass.

UDVARDY, M.D.F. (1982): Biogeographical classification system for terrestrial environments. Proc. World Natl. Park Congress, Bali. (Mimeo).

VOHRA, B.B. (1980): A policy for land and water. Dept. of Environment. New Delhi.

ZOOLOGICAL SURVEY OF INDIA (1980): State of Art Report: Zoology. Calcutta.

Fish distribution as influenced by aquatic habitat alteration and species introductions

NEIL B. ARMANTROUT

INTRODUCTION

Worldwide there has been a growing concern for natural resources. A growing number of books and articles discuss the decline in natural systems and the potential impacts of such a loss. There has also been a growing concern for preserving some natural systems through creation of national parks and wildlife preserves. Yet, for most developmental efforts, natural resources and natural ecological systems are not considered in developmental planning. Nowhere is this more apparent than with the aquatic systems. Most often when preservation occurs, or where developmental plan modifications are made, they are for terrestrial plants and animals. Yet the aquatic systems, which include streams and lakes and wetlands and their associated flora and fauna, are among the most altered of natural systems. As a result of rapid development and the growing world population, few natural aquatic systems remain. Most have been altered or essentially lost. Unfortunately, little is being done to study or preserve the remaining natural aquatic systems. This paper will discuss in more detail some of the activities impinging on aquatic resources, with examples primarily from the U.S. and Iran. A further discussion on the situation in Iran is contained in Armantrout (1981).

BACKGROUND

Streams are basically transport networks, while lakes are storage units. Streams are formed by runoff of water, while lakes form in low spots where water can accumulate. The aquatic system is shaped by the interaction through time of water, soil, geomorphology and vegetation. The basic geomorphology and climatic patterns guide the overall evolution of the system. While there is considerable variability among aquatic systems — compare, for example, the Amazon and Ganges systems — the same basic processes are found in all systems. Water enters the system as rainfall or groundwater discharge, then follows the path of least resistance, continuing to flow until it reaches a depression, where it can accumulate, or flowing into the sea. The smaller headwater streams, while often short, are the most numerous, making up on an average 70-80 percent of the actual stream length in a basin. The flow patterns and water quality in the undisturbed system reflect the basic climatic and geomorphic patterns. Vegetation has a major influence, since it to a large extent controls runoff rates and erosion.

The fish that inhabit aquatic systems in their natural condition evolved adaptations to the particular conditions of the aquatic system. Those habitat conditions were determined by the flow patterns, water quality, vegetation and physical form of the stream channel. Major groups of fish show differential distribution patterns, a result of evolution and opportunities for transference from one area to another. Within regional groupings, the fishes often show similar adaptations to similar conditions. Morphology, food habits and breeding strategies reflect the conditions under which the fish evolved. In an unaltered state, each aquatic system or closely related systems contain a relatively unique faunal assemblage. In India, this can be dramatically demonstrated by the differences between the southern Deccan fishes and the much more recent and diverse Gangetic fauna.

With development, the natural aquatic systems are altered. Flow patterns, channel characteristics and streamside vegetation are all subject to alteration. Because a stream is really the result of all upstream influences, changes in one part of the system influence conditions downstream. Unlike actions on terrestrial resources, alteration of aquatic systems can have major impacts at some distance from the site of the impacts. With an alteration of the aquatic system comes an alteration in the suitability of the aquatic system for the indigenous flora and fauna. There is often a major change in the fish fauna, with a shift in assemblage from fish adapted to specific conditions to the more tolerant forms that can survive alterations. Changes in the aquatic system can lead to reduced flows and water quality, a reduction in food supplies, loss of spawning and rearing capabilities, and loss of protection and refuge areas. Quite commonly, when aquatic systems are altered, introduction of exotic species occurs. As a result of the alterations of habitat and introduction of exotics, the numbers and species of fish are changed. In many cases, the changes are unintentional, and often unnecessary, a result of lack of information or concern for natural systems during development. Following are some of the major actions which alter natural aquatic systems and some recommendations.

Actions affecting aquatic habitat

1. **Loss of Vegetation.** The loss of vegetation is the single most important element in the decline of aquatic systems worldwide. Upslope vegetation acts as a major retardant to runoff. The slowed runoff has a greater chance to enter groundwater reservoirs, to be released slowly. When vegetation is lost, the rate of runoff increases, resulting in increased flooding. At the same time, a more rapid runoff reduces groundwater recharge, so that less water is available during low flow periods. The increased rate of runoff increases the erosive capabilities of the water. Without vegetation to hold the soil, it is more rapidly washed away. As the soil enters the stream system, water quality declines, and the channel is altered. Soil deposits downstream, filling streambeds, covering rocks and gravel, raising the bottom of channels. Filled streambeds contribute to even more severe flooding.

Riparian vegetation, or vegetation closely associated with wet areas, is important in protecting stream channels and lake margins. It prevents the banks from eroding during high flow. In addition, it shades the water, provides food through insects and other organic matter entering the water, and contributes to fish habitat. Removal of the riparian vegetation exposes the channel to degradation, and reduces the potential fish habitat, particularly in smaller streams.

For fish, the loss of habitat can be complete. The feeding, reproduction and life cycles are evolved to a particular set of conditions. The changes following major alteration in vegetation in the basin can cause loss of food production, loss of spawning and rearing areas, and loss of cover and refuge areas. Many fish have reproductive cycles clued to natural flow and temperature patterns. Changes in these patterns can cause a decline or loss of reproduction.

Many activities can contribute to the decline of vegetation, but grazing and timber harvesting are probably the most important. The two often go together, with grazing following felling of timber. Clearing for agriculture, construction and urbanization, and other activities contribute to the removal of vegetation. There is often a loss of cover and diversity, with replacement by less desirable species. Because of the role of vegetation in influencing flow patterns and water quality, major changes in upslope and riparian vegetation can totally alter the suitability of aquatic systems for native species.

2. **Impoundments.** Impoundments have a major impact on aquatic resources. The impacts can be positive, negative or neutral. At the project site, a major shift from a riverine to a lacustrine situation occurs. Since native populations in a river are adapted for life in flowing water, the conversion to still water usually results in loss of some species and proliferation of others. Frequently new species, migrating in or introduced, contribute to a new fish fauna.

Impoundments can greatly increase the available habitat, resulting in a potential for increased fish production. The larger, more desirable food species are often the ones most adapted to lakes and resorvoirs. The increase in production of food fish often exceeds any losses of native fishes at the reservoir site.

The impacts can often be felt downstream, and these impacts are usually negative. The alteration of natural flow cycles changes spawning cues and can lead to a decline in larger riverine fishes. The natural transport capabilities are reduced with reduced flows, and silt and nutrients from upstream are no longer carried downstream. In cases where the high flows help to transport deposits, the decline in flows leads to accumulation of silts; pools are filled and gravels covered.

Upstream migrants of important species can be blocked. For example, in Iran, when the Menjil Dam was built on the Sefid Rud, downstream beaches were littered for several years with salmon and sturgeon that could not reach upstream spawning beds. A similar loss occurred in the U.S. with Grand Coulee Dam that blocked the whole upriver area to salmon. Successful spawners must also move downstream. If unprotected power generators are used, fish are lost as they pass through the turbines. More importantly, where water is used for irrigation, unscreened diversions attract fish that are then lost in the maze of canals.

3. **Dewatering.** Dewatering has a very direct impact on fish: no water, no fish. Rather than totally dewatering a stream, withdrawals usually reduce the flow but leave some water in the channel. Severely reduced flows reduce habitat. They also contribute to a decline in water quality, since temperatures usually become extreme, and oxygen levels a problem in warmer weather. Reduced flows are often associated with discharges from irrigation systems or industrial plants; these discharges retain a greater toxicity due to reduced dilution capability.

Dewatering can also result from changes in vegetation and erosion in a basin. When runoff increases and groundwater recharge decreases, the result can be greater flooding during high flows, but decreased flows during low water periods. Downcutting in alluvial areas, deposition leading to increased subsurface flows, and other changes in the flow patterns can lead to reduced flows or even loss of flows at some periods.

Problems are most acute in arid countries, where essentially all useable water is eventually diverted. In smaller, isolated springs, seeps or stream sections, habitat can be totally lost. More often, dewatering occurs only during periods of peak use, but these periods can be sufficient to wipe out aquatic populations. In Iran, this periodic dewatering has had a major impact along the Caspian, where the onset of irrigation in the spring often coincides with the downstream movement of the young of anadromous species. Unable to reach the Caspian Sea as a result of the dewatering, the young fish perish, reducing potential future runs.

4. **Channel alterations.** This is a general category of actions that includes physical alteration of stream channels by actions such as diking, channelization and dredging. The actions are usually to facilitate transport of water past a given area, to facilitate construction in the floodplain, or to halt periodic flooding of riparian and floodplain areas. In more mountainous areas, travel routes most often follow stream channels, and roads and railroads constructed close to waterways. Canals and bypasses may be constructed to divert or speed the movement of runoff. In arid areas in particular, springs and seeps are developed, with pipes and rocks to capture and direct flows. Other types of actions could be mentioned, all with the purpose of developing or controlling flows through alteration of channels.

These actions have several impacts, direct and indirect. A direct impact is alteration of natural flow patterns, and associated transport functions of the streams. Changes in the natural channels greatly reduce fish habitat. The associated riparian and floodplain vegetation are reduced or eliminated, removing another component of habitat. In addition to fish habitat, many other plants and animals that utilize riparian and floodplain areas are impacted.

5. **Decreased water quality.** A decrease in water quality is a problem that has already been identified in all countries. Water pollution comes from many different sources. Some are called point sources, and include the direct discharge pipes, drainage ditches, etc. Other sources are diffuse sources, such as from overland flow or seepage from contaminated groundwater.

Many of the impacts of reduced water quality are well documented. Because of the need for water for domestic, industrial and agricultural uses, humans can be directly impacted by the reduced water quality.

Aquatic flora and fauna are also affected. The impacts may be the result of toxic materials in the water, increased disease organisms, or an increase in temperature and reduction in oxygen that make it impossible for plants and animals to live. A decline in water quality may not eliminate plant and animal communities, but may eliminate the less resistant forms leaving a reduced population of only the most tolerant forms.

INTRODUCTIONS OF EXOTIC SPECIES

The introduction of exotic species is a worldwide phenomenon. At least three fish, the carp (*Cyprinus carpio* L.), rainbow trout (*Salmo gairdneri* Richardson) and mosquito fish [*Gambusia affinis* (Baird and Girard)] are now practically worldwide in distribution.

Several other fish, such as *Tilapia* and the grass carp [*Ctenopharyngodon idella* (Val.)], have been introduced in many areas. Many of the introductions have altruistic purposes, but are made without proper consideration of native species or local conditions. Many other introductions are inadvertent or accidental.

Three illustrations from Iran demonstrate the problem. During the 1960s, Iran undertook a massive programme of malaria control. Among other steps, *Gambusia* were introduced in many streams, lakes and springs throughout the country. The aggressive *Gambusia* successfully colonized many of these areas, and aggressively replaced the native fish species. Iran had native mosquito fish which could have been used instead, but, since no work had been done on the native mosquito fish, malaria control workers instead imported the *Gambusia,* which had been studied extensively, from the U.S. Also in the 1960s, in an effort to improve sport fishing opportunities, rainbow trout were imported, mostly from sources in Denmark. These were widely introduced into major stream systems. However, in many of the streams in the north and west, native trout were already present. In a situation very analogous to what happened in the western U.S. with cut-throat trout, the native species interbred with the introduced fish. The native fish, which were better adapted to local conditions, were eventually replaced by the more aggressive exotics. Among the trout plants were apparently some eggs or young of the fathead minnow (*Pimephales promelas* Rafinesque) which were thus accidently introduced into Iranian waters.

Exotics selected for introduction are usually fish which have been well studied, introduced into other areas, and which can be bred in captivity. Unfortunately, there are often native species which can achieve the same purpose. However, since it is rare that any work has been done on the native species, their suitability is unknown. The exotics often are highly adaptive forms, species which are able to successfully compete with, and often replace, native populations. This is particularly true in situations where harsher natural conditions have been modified, such as by construction of a dam, to create more favourable conditions in which the exotics are much more competitive.

Introductions of exotics can play a useful role in resource management. The basic problem is often lack of sufficient knowledge of native species to know what impacts the introductions will have on native flora and fauna, and even whether native species are already present that are suitable for the purposes for which the exotics are introduced. The native fishes may have values which are unknown as a result of the lack of study. Every effort should be made to become familiar with native fishes, learn their habitat needs, and to plan for their protection during resource development.

Discussion

Soil and water are basic elements of life. Without them, no food would be produced and life as we know it would be impossible. The key to maintaining soil and water resources is sound vegetation management. The three elements, soil, water and vegetation, are inseparably intertwined in resource management. The protection and sound management of water, soil and vegetation is necessary to ensure long-term productivity. To state that sound management is too expensive is simply to state that the manager is willing to sacrifice the future uses of the resources for a small short-term advantage. When these vital resources are lost, they either cannot be replaced, or can be replaced or substituted for only at a much greater cost.

The aquatic system is an indicator of the condition of basic resources. A stream system at any one point is a summation of conditions upstream. Studies of water quality, flow and aquatic organisms can show the overall condition of a basin. Some changes are direct and obvious, such as channelization or point source pollution discharge. Other changes are more indirect and gradual, as with loss of vegetation from grazing. With monitoring or studies, the observer can see these changes reflected in condition of the habitat and fish community. Changes may be localized, as with channelization, or may be evident for many miles downstream, as with pollution.

Most of the changes that occur in a basin are neither sudden nor dramatic. An exception would be a major alteration such as a large dam and reservoir. Instead, changes in a basin are gradual. It is ongoing activities such as wood cutting, extended grazing, or spreading urbanization that produce the gradual changes. Impacts are cumulative. Usually no real changes are seen in the aquatic system in the initial phases of an activity. The aquatic system has a built-in resiliency that permits some deterioration to be absorbed without a noticeable decline in quality. Once a threshold level has been passed, the system declines, sometimes rather precipitously. Some of the results, such as changes in fish communities are obvious only with monitoring. Others may be obvious, such as increased flooding in monsoon areas or declining flows in arid areas. Sediment loads increase. Water quality deteriorates. Fish habitat declines. Tolerant fish species become more dominant in the fish community and overall diversity and biomass decline.

With good baseline studies of aquatic systems, it is possible to see changes developing. Patterns of change reflect upstream and localized activities. Monitoring can give an early warning, not only of changes in the aquatic systems, but of problems with the other basic resources in the basin. It is the decline of the other resources that usually produces changes in the aquatic system. Major change in the aquatic system is a cause for concern, since it may indicate serious deterioration of the soil and vegetation resources in the basin.

A problem is the lack of baseline information on aquatic resources. Except for specific development projects, such as a hydroelectric project or irrigation diversion, little effort has been made to study aquatic systems of their associated biota. Even with these projects, any studies relate directly to the project and not to the impacts on the associated aquatic systems. In areas, such as southern Asia, where human settlement began thousands of years ago, there are few unaltered systems left. But even in areas with long-term inhabitation, there have been changes, some rapid, in the aquatic systems in recent years. Unfortunately, these changes are poorly documented, and are reported mostly because of impacts on humans.

With few exceptions, the life history and potential value of native fish species are only poorly known. There is an overall lack of knowledge. Basically, few trained people are available in aquatic sciences, and those that exist are usually product-oriented. As a result, there is the problem of a resource whose value is only poorly understood, but a resource which is seldom studied because so few people are sufficiently trained to recognize the values. This is especially unfortunate given the value of aquatic resources as one of the most basic natural resources.

Recommendations

I would make several recommendations. None are new, but all bear reiteration. They do not include a recommendation for cessation of development efforts; the need for development is recognized as imperative. However, there are many options on development, from siting of projects to planning and implementation which can provide for reasonable environmental safeguards. With proper consideration development efforts can proceed while preserving the basic resources for future uses. Additional short-term costs may be encountered, but the long-term benefits far outweigh any short-term cost increases.

1. Use long-term planning to identify important and critical resources and provide for their retention for continued benefits. This type of planning is especially necessary to protect the basic soil, water and vegetation resources where large areas need to be considered in planning.

2. Incorporate environmental considerations into project planning. As an example, in building a dam on a river, passage can be provided for upstream and downstream movement of fish. Water release cycles can be developed to approximate normal cycles to preserve downstream flora and fauna. Diversions can be screened to prevent the loss of young and adults. Species management can consider native fishes and desirable compatible introductions. Spawning and rearing areas and hatcheries can be developed. While other design elements could be suggested, this gives an idea of the types of things that can be considered in project planning.

3. Recognize the interrelationship of resources. Major changes in one resource can often cause major changes in other resources. This is most pronounced with vegetation, where abuses, such as indiscriminant wood cutting or excessive grazing, leads to the deterioration in the soils and aquatic system. Planning for development should not concentrate only on a single resource, but should consider the interrelatedness of all resources.

4. Develop a programme for the study and monitoring of aquatic systems to establish baseline conditions and as a total for monitoring conditions in basins.

5. Where undisturbed aquatic systems remain, or where there are systems with unusual biological or other values, establish a system to protect these systems. Most countries have a system of parks, refuges or sanctuaries. Almost always, these are for birds or other terrestrial species. Aquatic systems and fish are seldom considered, usually because knowledge of aquatic systems is lacking.

6. Develop a policy to control unrestrained transfers and introductions of exotic species. Introductions of exotics should occur only when no suitable native species are available for the proposed purpose, and when introductions would not have unacceptable negative impacts on native aquatic systems.

7. In order to effectively manage and use

native species knowledge of life histories and habitat requirements is needed. A regular programme of studies should be implemented to obtain such knowledge in order to assist planners and managers in making sound biological decisions.

SUMMARY

Water, together with soil and vegetation are basic resources on which life depends. They are interrelated, and the deterioration in one resource can lead to deterioration in the other resources. The condition of the aquatic system is a good indication of the condition of other resources. It is imperative that better consideration be given to the aquatic resources in development and resource utilization, and that a programme of study and protection be implemented. The long-term, continued use of resources should guide development, with monitoring as an indicator of resource condition.

BIBLIOGRAPHY

ARMANTROUT, N. B. (1981): The freshwater fishes of Iran. Ph.D. thesis, Oregon State University. Corvallis, Oregon. 472 pp.

Eco-Developmental strategy for the Eastern Ghats

(*With a map*)

K.S.R. Krishna Raju[1] and C. Subba Reddi[2]

The Eastern Ghats of India is one of the rich and least explored biotic regions of the country. However, large-scale and indiscriminate harvest (both legal and illegal) of mixed natural forests, extensive pernicious *Podu* or *Jhum* (slash and burn) cultivation, inadequate and half-hearted soil conservation efforts, unchecked habitat destruction and poaching, encroachment by migrant tribals and consequent creation of new settlements in the midst of virgin forests, laying of extensive roads for mining purposes and creation of large tracts of so called commercial monoculture plantations have all contributed greatly to the rapid deterioration of the Eastern Ghats region.

To assess the present status we undertook an ecological reconnaisance of some select areas under the financial sponsorship of the WWF-India during October 1981 and March 1982 (Krishna Raju 1982) and on behalf of the Andhra Pradesh Natural History Society. The results are briefly reported here.

General Perspective

"Unlike the Western Ghats, the Eastern Ghats are not by any means a range of mountains or escarpment, but represent the much broken and weathered relicts of the peninsular plateau, marked by a series of isolated hills".

Geographers consider the Khondmal hills in the Phulbani district of Orissa as the northern extremity of the Eastern Ghats, while we generally consider the hills south of the River Mahanandi as the northernmost part (see Map). Running southwards in the Koraput and Kalahandi districts, with an average elevation of 1000 metres, the Ghats culminate at a point near Mahendragiri in the Ganjam district of Orissa. South of Orissa, they run through Srikakulam, Vizianagaram, Visakhapatnam, East Godavari etc., to the banks of River Godavari.

Vegetation

The predominant vegetation in the Ghats is dry-deciduous with patches of moist-deciduous and semi-evergreen forests in some localities with higher rainfall. *Shola*-like patches and bald hill tops are common features at higher elevations in Orissa and northern Andhra.

Sal is the prominent economic timber species, replaced in the south by teak, the limit of which almost runs parallel to the River Sabari near Sunki and Konta in Madhya Pradesh. The Bastar plateau is considered the transition zone where *Sal* and Teak occur together in some parts.

The slash and burn cultivation significantly affected vegetation in several parts of the

[1]K.S.R. Krishna Raju, Honorary Secretary, A.P. Natural History Society, 11-2-6 Dasapalla Hills, Visakhapatnam-3.

[2]Dr. C. Subba Reddi, Department of, Environmental Sciences, Andhra University, Waltair 530 003.

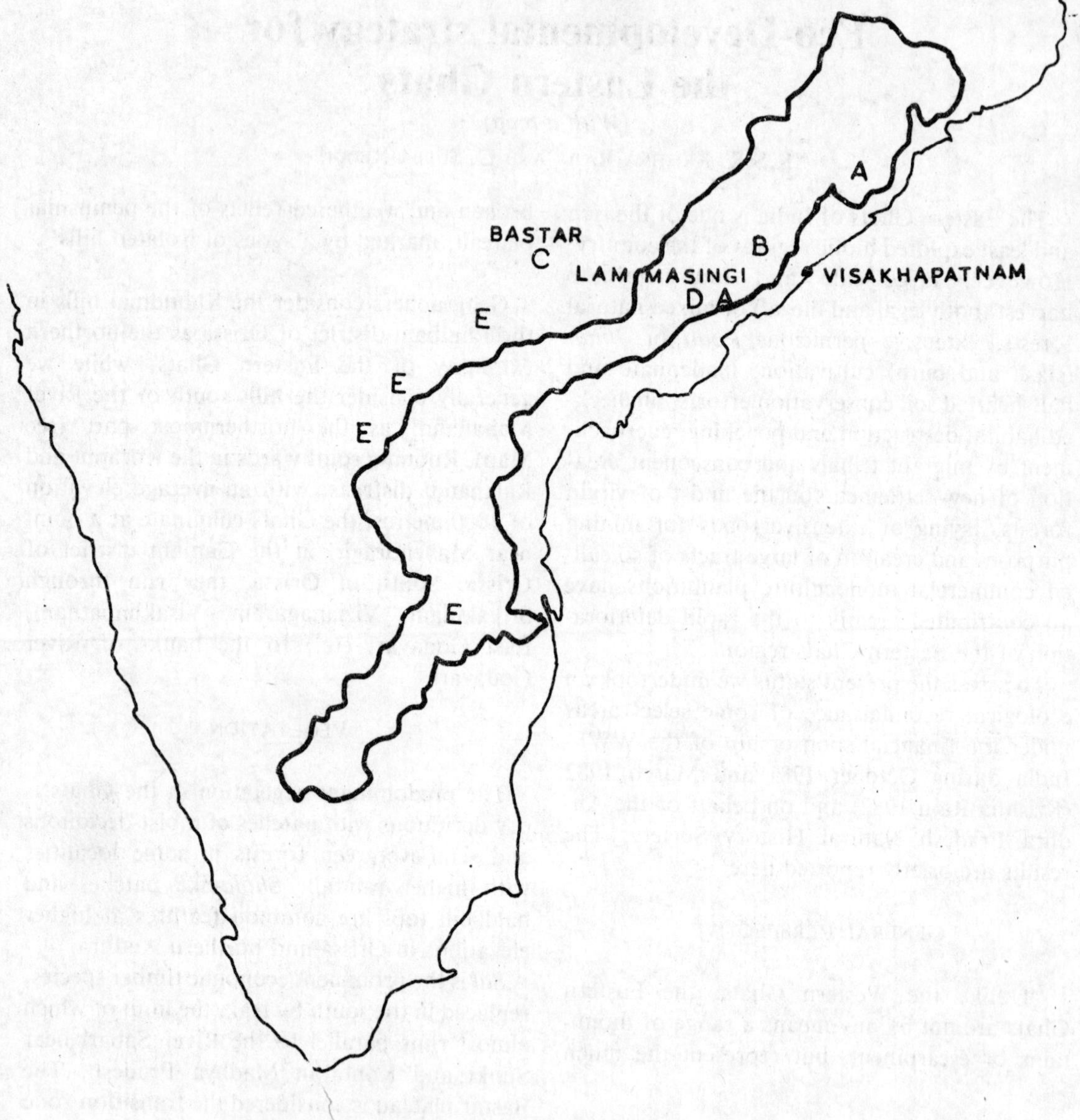

A — Known localities of Abbott's Babbler and the Little Spiderhunter
B — Known locality of the Tree Sparrow
C — Wild Buffalo localities
D — Probable localities of *Eurostopodus macrotis* and *Anthreptes singalensis*

Ghats, where natural vegetation gave way to secondary shrub and weedy pests like *Eupatorium, Lantana* and *Parthenium*.

MINERAL RESOURCES OF THE GHATS

The Ghats are rich in several minerals like Hematite, Manganese, Bauxite etc. Bailadila Iron Ore mines are just outside the western limits of the Ghats in Madhya Pradesh. Next to Iron ore, the recently discovered Bauxite deposits in Orissa and Andhra Pradesh near Damanjodi (Orissa) and Gudem (A.P.) are on a large scale. Bauxite is likely to be exploited by strip mining and transported long distances by road and probably a ropeway through some of the excellent patches of moist-deciduous forests.

TRIBALS

About 30 lakhs tribals live in the Ghats; both in Andhra Pradesh and in Orissa, most of them practising slash and burn cultivation. Though exact figures of the extent of land under this mode of cultivation are not available, huge areas are reportedly under use in Orissa and in Andhra Pradesh and year after year such areas are growing at an alarming rate.

WILDLIFE RESOURCES

The Eastern Ghats are rich in wildlife (Whistler & Kinnear 1930-37). A survey of this resource, particularly of birds and mammals, was undertaken in the years 1929-30 by the Bombay Natural History Society. Subsequently investigations on specific problems were made by Abdulali (1945, 1953), Daniel & Grubh (1966), Krishna Raju & Selvin (1971), Krishna Raju & Price (1973), Price (1978, 1980) and Ripley (1979) that resulted in the publication of several miscellaneous, status and ecological notes. However, the data available are far from complete and almost every scientific survey 'discovers' several new records to the Ghats.

Most of the common mammals of the Indian subcontinent are known to occur in the Eastern Ghats. About 300 species of birds, 55 reptiles and 15 amphibians (Pillai & Murthy 1983) are also recorded from the area while no published records are available for smaller forms like rodents and insects such as butterflies.

Leopard and tiger were not uncommon in these forests till as late as 1875 and rewards were given to hunters for killing as many as 85 tigers, 365 leopards and 75 sloth bears in Vizag district alone in the year 1864.

Indian gaur, sloth bear, leopard, sambar, spotted deer, barking deer, tiger, wild boar, porcupine are some of the common mammals of the Ghats while elephant and dhole are restricted to some areas like Lekhari. Several among these large mammals occur in good numbers in and around Jyothimamidi, Sapparla, Gudem, Marripakala, Bhadrachalam, Gumsoor, Udaigiri, Parlakhemidi, Rayagada area. Rhesus monkey is seen only in select areas around Darakonda and Sapparla etc. Common Langur is now restricted to interior forest areas and is being hunted in large numbers by tribals as a delicacy. Poaching, though contained to a large extent, is still going on and organised skin trade occurs through Vizag, Jeypore and Kakinada.

The last known records for two bird species (Jerdon's courser at Bhadrachalam and Blewitt's owl in Western Orissa) which are now considered as possibly extinct are from the Eastern Ghat regions. Some very interesting records of bird species like Tree sparrow and the Little spiderhunter from the Vizag Ghats are the first records of these Indomalayan forms in this part of the country and are of considerable significance from the zoo-geographic point of view.

Many bird and animal species are facing serious threat from habitat destruction and the resultant damage to the general environment is considerably serious. The Balimela Hydel Dam resulted in the complete disappearance of wild buffalo in Orissa, while the Sileru project area opened up vast stretches of virgin forests and destruction of wildlife. The moist-evergreen biotope that supports such scientifically interesting birds like the spiderhunter is fast disappearing. The increasing instances of sloth bear attacks on man around Seethampeta in Srikakulam district are possibly the result of habitat destruction and drying up of water resources in the forests. Ripley (1979) noted changes in bird species diversity in artificial plantations, while we collected evidence to attribute the decline of species abundance and diversity to the interference of man in several areas like monoculture teak plantations, hydel reservoirs and other man altered habitats.

General observations

The Eastern Ghats are of great scientific interest as far as zoo-geography is concerned. There are many 'relict' populations of Himalayan forms of fauna and flora, that show the possible routes and extent of migration of Indomalayan elements into peninsular India.

From economic point of view, the industrial catchment areas like Nallamalais and Godavari Valley sustain several forest-based industries. The Sileru river yields about 1500 MW of hydel power at four major hydel power stations. Millions of tons of several valuable mineral deposits are available. Therefore, sufficient safeguards have to be taken through proper planning to ensure sustained yields with least possible damage to the resource base in particular and the ecosystem in general.

The forest resources of Orissa are not yet fully evaluated though there are indications that the forest-based industries like paper mills are certain of not getting adequate raw material beyond the next few years. Any additional licensing capacity for those forest-based industries should therefore be stopped immediately, pending an evaluation of the present resources and a review of the success of the ongoing plans to generate more resources like pulp wood etc.

The signs of environmental damage are clear at Bailadila, particularly in the Malinger Valley and the nearby streams, as a result of Iron ore shale. Efforts need to be made not only to correct this damage but also to prevent recurrence of such damages at other mining areas in the Ghats.

Eco-developmental efforts and recommendations

The Department of Environment, Government of India, had sponsored a National Seminar at Visakhapatnam on the Resources, Development and Environment of the Eastern Ghats in March 1982, which was conducted jointly by the Andhra University and the Andhra Pradesh Natural History Society. Based on the recommendations of the Seminar the Government of India is reportedly contemplating constituting a high level committee to oversee eco-development and research needs in the Eastern Ghats. We feel that immediate implementation of the following suggestions is essential:

The first and foremost requirement is to adopt a suitable regional conservation strategy, which should be open for discussions and alterations. Such a regional strategy should encompass wildlife resources, forest resources, hydel resources, mineral resources, tribals etc.

We suggest that serious consideration be given to stoppage of additional licensed capacity for forest-based industries; total ban on clear felling of miscellaneous natural/mixed forests; complete protection to the already identified critical habitats like Lekhari and Jyotimamidi and for protection of threatened species such as the Tree sparrow, wild buffalo etc.

Since no measure of conservation action will be successful unless its economic benefits are demonstrated, we suggest that all possible steps be taken to start wildlife farming in respect of at least such species as wild boar.

ACKNOWLEDGEMENT

KSR is grateful to Dr Salim Ali and Mr. J.C. Daniel of Bombay Natural History Society for having him initiated in the study of Natural History during his college days. He is also thankful to Dr S. Dillon Ripley, Secretary, Smithsonian Institution, Washington for his interest in the rich avifaunal resources and their conservation in the Eastern Ghats, and for initiating several ongoing conservation oriented researches in the Ghats. The authors' thanks are due to World Wildlife Fund—India for the financial support and the Forest Department of Andhra Pradesh and Orissa for the facilities provided.

REFERENCES

ABDULALI, H. (1945): Birds of the Vizagapatam District. *J. Bombay nat. Hist. Soc.* **45**: 333-347.

_________ (1953): More about Vizagapatam birds. ibid. **51**: 674-747.

DANIEL, J.C. & GRUBH, B.R. (1966): The Indian wild buffalo *Bubalus bubalis* (Linn.) in peninsular India: A preliminary survey. ibid. **63**: 32-53.

KRISHNA RAJU, R.S.R. (1982): A preliminary Ecological Survey of the Eastern Ghats. Report submitted to WWF-India.

_________ & SELVIN, J.P. (1971): Little spiderhunter *Arachnothera longirostris* (Latham) in the Eastern Ghats. *J. Bombay nat. Hist. Soc.* **68**: 454.

_________ & PRICE, T.D. (1973): Tree sparrow, *Passer montanus* (L.) in the Eastern Ghats. ibid. **70**: 557.

PILLAI, R.S. & MURTHY, T.S.N. (1983): The Herpetofauna of the Eastern Ghats. pp. 81-84. *In* Proc. National Seminar on Resources, Development and Environment on Eastern Ghats, Andhra University, Waltair.

PRICE, T.D. (1978): Some observations on the warblers of the upland perennial wetlands in the Eastern Ghats. *J. Bombay nat. Hist. Soc.* **75**: 488-490.

_________ (1980): The seasonality and occurrence of birds in the Eastern Ghats of Andhra Pradesh. ibid. **76**:379-422.

RIPLEY, S.D. (1978): Changes in the bird fauna of a forest area; Simlipal Hills, Mayurbhanj District, and Dhenkanal District, Orissa. ibid. **75**: 570-574.

WHISTLER, H. & KINNEAR, N.B. (1930-37): The Vernay scientific survey of the Eastern Ghats. Ornithological section. ibid. 16 parts, Vol. 34-39.

The unusual significance of the Giant Squirrels (*Ratufa*)

RICHARD W. THORINGTON, JR AND
RICHARD L. CIFELLI

INTRODUCTION

The giant tree squirrels (*Ratufa*) are a distinctive element of the fauna of southern Asia. Four species are presently recognized (Ellerman and Morrison-Scott 1951; Moore and Tate 1965; Lekagul and McNeely 1977; Honacki *et al.* 1982): *Ratufa affinis, R. bicolor, R. indica,* and *R. macroura*. Of these, three species occur in India: *Ratufa bicolor gigantea* in the northeast, *R. indica* throughout much of peninsular India, with six subspecies recognized by Abdulali and Daniel (1952), five by Ellerman (1961), and four by Moore and Tate (1965); and *R. macroura dandolena* in a few places in the very south. *R. indica* and *R. macroura* are reported to be sympatric in the Palni Hills, although occurring at different elevations (Moore and Tate 1965; Agrawal and Chakraborty 1979a). The genus includes the largest tree squirrels in the world, with some individuals exceeding 2 kg in mass. It is the objective of this paper to review several aspects of the biology of *Ratufa* and to emphasize unusual and significant features, with particular emphasis on its ecology and potential importance as a biological indicator of habitat quality.

ECOLOGY

Ratufa occurs in evergreen forests in many parts of southern Asia. In the lowland forest of the Krau Game Reserve in Malaya, Payne (1980) estimated that *R. bicolor* occurred at a density of 11 animals per 100 ha (a biomass of 15.9 kg/100 ha) and *R. affinis* at a density of 26 animals per 100 ha (a biomass fo 28 kg/100 ha). *R. affinis* is probably more stringent in its ecological requirements, for it occurs only in Malaya, Sumatra, Borneo, and some of the small nearby islands. In contrast, *R. bicolor* has an extensive mainland distribution, occurring from Singapore to southern China and northeastern India in a variety of tropical and subtropical forests, as well as on Sumatra and Java (distribution maps may be found in Moore and Tate 1965; Payne 1980). *R. indica* occurs in a variety of forests in peninsular India, but it is not clear how deciduous a forest can be and still provide adequate habitat for this species. Hutton (1949) noted that it occurred only in evergreen forests in the High Wavy Mountains, but Krishnan (1972) reported *R. indica* in deciduous and semi-evergreen forests throughout the Peninsula, although not in open, dry forest. Abdulali and Daniel (1952) indicated that *R. i. dealbata* occurs in moist-deciduous forest and *R. i. centralis* inhabits "moist and dry deciduous jungle". In southern India, *R. macroura* seems to occur in drier forests than *R. indica* (Moore and Tate 1965) although Khajuria (1955) listed both as members of the "humid element" of the Deccan mammalian fauna. In Sri Lanka, *R. macroura* occurs in a wide variety of forest

Department of Vertebrate Zoology, Smithsonian Institution

types, from very humid to quite dry (Phillips 1935).

Several detailed studies of the ecology of *Ratufa* have recently been published, mostly based on studies in Malaya (MacKinnon 1978; Payne 1979a, 1979b, 1980). In the Krau Game Reserve, where these studies were conducted, there are seven species of diurnal squirrels. Both MacKinnon and Payne documented significant differences in the levels of the forest at which the various squirrel species are most commonly seen. The two species of *Ratufa* occur commonly in the canopy. MacKinnon gives an average height of 86.7 feet for *R. bicolor* and 73.9 feet for *R. affinis*. Payne observed *R. bicolor* at heights in excess of 120 feet more than 20% of the time. Only *Callosciurus prevostii* among the squirrels shares the canopy with these two species of *Ratufa*. *Callosciurus notatus* lives at lower levels in the forest (MacKinnon reported it at an average of 44.5 feet). In Vietnam, *Ratufa bicolor* has also been reported to live in the highest stratum of the forest, with both *Callosciurus erythraeus* and *C. pygerythrus* occurring at lower levels (Tien 1972). In peninsular India *Callosciurus* does not occur and there are not as many species of squirrels as in southeast Asia. If ecological competition influences the vertical distribution of squirrels, *Ratufa indica* and *R. macroura* might be expected to occur more commonly at lower levels than in Malaya. In apparent agreement with this hypothesis, Hutton (1949) reported that *R. indica* frequently foraged on the ground, but Crump (in Wroughton 1915b) reported that he never observed them below 12 feet. But it is more probable that vertical distribution of the squirrels is influenced more by the distributions of their resources, which may differ from forest to forest, than by the presence or absence of other species of squirrels. Unfortunately, quantitative data bearing on this point are not available.

The foods consumed by *Ratufa affinis* and *R. bicolor* in Malaya are listed by MacKinnon (1978) and Payne (1980). Both species feed extensively on seeds and nuts, but include fruit pulp, leaves, flowers, and bark in their diets in lesser amounts. Payne (1980) emphasized the differences in the diets between *Ratufa* and the primates sharing the same habitats — the primates feed much more extensively on leaves and the squirrels feed heavily on hard nuts and seeds which are not utilized by the primates. Krishnan (1972) provided notes on the foods of *R. indica*, including leaf-buds, leaves, twigs,

TABLE

OBSERVATIONS OF *Ratufa indica* AT MUDUMALAI WILDLIFE SANCTUARY, TAMIL NADU, INDIA, 25-29 NOVEMBER 1983. TOTAL OBSERVATION TIME WAS 2086 MIN.

Food	Feeding Bouts	Total Time	Average Time/Bout
Seeds:			
Tectona grandis	8	445 min.	55.6 min.
Terminalia tomentosa	5	310	62.0
Total	13	755	58.1
Bark:			
Anogeissus latifolia	10	189 min.	18.9 min.
Grewia tilaefolia	3	55	18.9 min.
Melia? (twigs)	2	37	18.5
Oegenia dahlbergioides	1	13	13.0
Tectona grandis	3	28	9.3
Terminalia tomentosa	1	15	15.0
Total	20	337	16.9
Leaves:			
Tectona grandis	1	6 min.	6.0 min.
Terminalia tomentosa	6	59	10.0
Total	7	65	9.3
Flowers:			
Dendrophthoe falcata (Loranthaceal)	14	148 min.	10.6 min.
Insects:			
Termites	1	5 min.	5.0 min.
Grand Total	55	1310 min.	

and hard fruits, but did not provide quantitative data permitting comparison with the diets of *Ratufa* in Malaya. Of particular interest are his notes on insect feeding by *R. indica,* because insects are conspicuously lacking from the diets of *Ratufa* in Malaya, although *R. bicolor* has been noted to eat insects and bird eggs in other areas (Blanford 1888). Our data on foods eaten by *Ratufa indica* (Table), collected during a five-day visit to Mudumalai Wildlife Sanctuary, corroborate Krishnan's observations, but the most interesting differences from the Malayan observations are the high percentages of bark and flowers in the diet. The squirrels spent more than 25% of their feeding time eating bark. They stripped the bark and ate the cambial layer of five species of trees; they completely devoured twigs of a sixth species. More than 11% of the time they fed on flowers of a single species. The *Ratufa indica* at Mudumalai did not feed at all on fruit pulp, in contrast to Payne's (1980) observations that *R. bicolor* feeds on fruit pulp 20% of the time and *R. affinis* 14%. However, until other data become available, we cannot be sure whether these data for *R. indica* indicate only a seasonal specialization or represent a real dietary difference between the species of *Ratufa.*

Very little is known about the home range and territorial behaviour of any species of *Ratufa,* because most observations have been conducted on unmarked individuals. Crump (*in* Wroughton 1916) noted *R. bicolor* in Sikkim was usually found in pairs, but that *R. indica* in Bihar seemed quite gregarious (Wroughton 1915b). Hutton (1949) stated that *R. indica* in the High Wavy mountains was not at all territorial. Krishnan (1972) observed an incident of aggressive chasing in Tamil Nadu, which he suggested was territorial behaviour. We also observed chases at Mudumalai. One of these was a long chase and seemed to bear no relationship to a territorial boundary. Another case, involving two adult males, was a back-and-forth chase in which dominance changed depending on the location of the squirrels. Therefore we interpreted it to be territorial defence. Payne (1980) carried out observations on the same individuals of *R. bicolor* and *R. affinis* for two-week periods, during which time they ranged over an area of 9 ha. At Mudumalai, our observations of *Ratufa indica* were made on six different squirrels in a total area of 10 ha, suggesting that their home range was significantly smaller than this. Within the home range, giant squirrels build large nests or dreys, in which they sleep (Lindsay 1927; Webb-Peploe 1946; Hutton 1949). Hutton suggested that they use the same nests for several years. Krishnan (1972) concluded that one squirrel would build several nests within its home range.

Although the ecology of *Ratufa* is not well known, especially that of the Indian species, it is obvious that the giant squirrels could be used very effectively as indicator species. Because they feed extensively on hard seeds and nuts, their ecological requirements are different from those of primates and birds. Thus they are indicators of different environmental parameters than most of the other diurnal vertebrates. Because they are large and conspicuous, have distinctive and easily recognized vocalizations, and because they also build nests, it should be relatively easy to assess their abundance in forests. These factors all suggest that the presence or absence of giant squirrels should be very useful to ecologists assessing the quality of habitats.

Systematics and Anatomy

The giant tree squirrels (*Ratufa*) are clearly members of the subfamily Sciurinae, but their tribal relationships within the subfamily have been variously debated. They were originally included in the genus *Sciurus,* together with the Holarctic tree squirrels (Blanford 1897), but their distinctiveness was soon acknowledged (e.g. Wroughton 1910); Gray had described the genus in 1867 but its general recognition did not come until the turn of the century). Since then, three different classifications, representing distinct phylogenetic hypotheses, have been presented. 1. Pocock (1923) allocated *Ratufa* to the tribe Funambulini, together with the south Asian genus *Funambulus* and all the genera of African tree squirrels, based primarily on the morphology of the baculum. 2. Moore (1959) and Moore and Tate (1965) allocated *Ratufa* to its own tribe, Ratufini, and noted seven cranial characters in which it differed from the Funambulini. In these respects, *Ratufa* is most similar to *Rubrisciurus,* which Moore placed in the Hyosciurina, a subtribe of the Callosciurini. Many of these similarities are lacking in the other hyosciurines (*Hyosciurus, Exilisciurus*), however, and it is likely that several of them are merely primitive features rather than shared, derived characters indicative of special relationship. Moore (1961) also argued that similarities in the number of mammae corroborated a special (albeit distant) relationship between the Ratufini and Callosciurini, but the phylogenetic significance of this characteristic is likewise uncertain. 3 Callahan and Davis (1982) suggested that *Sciurotamias,* the Chinese rock squirrel (variously allocated to the Tamiasciurini by Moore 1959, or to the Callosciurini by Allen 1940, and Black 1963), should be included in the Ratufini, because of the similarities of the reproductive tracts. They suggested that the cranial differences result from the allometry of gigantism in *Ratufa.* Long and Captain (1974) also had noted similarities between *Sciurotamias* and *Ratufa,* in the morphology of the pollex. These three classifications remain unsubstantiated, however, because no one has addressed the issue of character polarity in the Sciurinae, with the exception of several cursory observations made by Emry and Thorington (1982).

These three different hypotheses have drastically different zoogeographic implications. Pocock's arrangement suggests that *Ratufa* is derived from African tree squirrels; Callahan and Davis's classification suggests an Asiatic origin and perhaps the evolution of arboreality in *Ratufa* independent from that of other tree squirrels; Moore's classification suggests that the *Ratufa* lineage, although distantly related to the Callosciurini, has evolved independent of that of other tree squirrels for a very long time. The resolution of this systematic conundrum is therefore of particular evolutionary interest.

The earliest known fossil squirrel, *Protosciurus,* from the Oligocene, 35 million years ago, is very similar to modern tree squirrels in body proportions and postcranial anatomy (Emry and Thorington 1982). One of the few ways in which it differs, especially from the Holarctic tree squirrels, Sciurini, is in the morphology of the tarsus. The ankle in modern tree squirrels is highly modified for reversing the hindfeet when the animal comes down a tree head first. This is accomplished by strong plantar flexion at the crurotarsal joint coupled with extreme inversion at the midankle joint. *Ratufa* is very similar to *Protosciurus* in ankle morphology and hence is even a better analogue of the Oligocene fossil than other tree squirrels, which Emry and Thorington (*in press*) have called "living fossils". One of the intriguing aspects of this analogy is that *Ratufa* is able to reverse its hindfeet when hanging by them or descending a tree head first (illustrated in Nowack and Paradiso 1983: p. 495), although it is not clear at what joints this rotation is accomplished. In body proportions, however, *Ratufa* is dissimilar to *Protosciurus* and most other living tree squirrels (Thorington and Heaney 1981). The African giant tree squirrel, *Protoxerus,* is similar to *Ratufa* in some proportions, but not in others. In the shoulder girdle, *Ratufa* exhibits a number of characteristics which we interpret as derived. For example, the cranial border of the scapula is expanded, providing a more cranial origin of the subscapularis and supraspinatus muscles than is normal in squirrels. Also, the subclavius muscle, which is normally restricted to the clavicle in its insertion, extends onto the scapula in *Ratufa.* Both these specializations may be associated with the large body size of *Ratufa.* The increased size of the scapular "rotator cuff" muscles, which help fix the humerus in the glenoid joint, could be important for giant squirrels landing after a long jump, when the forelimbs accomplish the abrupt deceleration of the animal. (Giant squirrels are arboreal leapers of some accomplishment; Wroughton 1915b; Krishnan 1972; Nowak and Paradiso 1983.) In other mammals, like the large platyrrhine primates, the extension of the subclavius muscle onto the scapula appears to be associated with vertical climbing (Konstant *et al.* 1982). Thus the specializations of the shoulder girdle may all be associated with arboreal gigantism. The systematic significance of these data are not clear, for various features could be interpreted to support the systematic arrangements of Pocock, Moore and Tate, or Callahan and Davis. Further comparative studies of the anatomy of squirrels are needed to test these hypotheses and to resolve the systematic problems of the giant tree squirrels.

The specific and subspecific taxonomy of *Ratufa* also poses some interesting zoogeographic puzzles. As pointed out by Moore (1960), the occurrence of two species of *Ratufa* in peninsular India and the other two species east of the Garo-Rajmahal gap poses an interesting question, because the gap has proved to be a barrier to other squirrels, being the eastern limit of the Funambulini and the western limit of the Callosciurini, some of which are true tree squirrels and others of which are quite at home on the ground. At least two interpretations of these distributions are possible: that the *Ratufa* distribution is more ancient than that of the other two tribes or that there are some unknown ecological characteristics of *Ratufa* which enabled it, but not *Funambulus* or *Callosciurus,* to cross the gap. The former seems more probable, an interpretation which would be in agreement with Moore and Tate's systematic conclusions about the genus.

Within India, the occurrence of *Ratufa macroura* in the southern part of the peninsula is one of many demonstrations of the close link between the faunas of southern India and Sri Lanka (Wroughton 1915a; Thomas and Wroughton 1915). Since the work of Wroughton (1920), it has been accepted that the form found on the mainland is not even distinguishable as a subspecies from the form found in the lowlands of Sri Lanka, though Agrawal and Chakraborty (1979b) have noted morphological differences. The subspecies of *Ratufa indica* have been variously argued, with major contributions from Blanford (1888, 1897), Wroughton (1910), Ryley (1913), Abdulali and Daniel (1952), Ellerman (1961) and Moore and Tate (1965). Most of the remaining problems and differences of opinion involve questions about the nature of the observed geographic variation: whether some of the distinguishable forms are independent local populations, merely colour variants, or whether they represent zones of intergradation between other recognized subspecies (Abdulali and Daniel 1952, 1953; Moore and Tate 1965; Agrawal 1973; Agrawal and Chakraborty 1979a). The resolution of these arguments are of particular interest, because they will lead to a clarification of the nature of the geographic variation of *R. indica* and suggest to what extent it shows gradual clinal variation suggestive of long-term contiguity of populations or to what extent the distribution has been fragmented in the past and presently demonstrates areas of secondary intergradation. Distinction of *R. indica* subspecies has been based essentially on differences in their elegant pelage; unfortunately the variation among the subspecies and circumscriptions of their geographic ranges are not altogether clear (see, e.g. Abdulali and Daniel 1953; Ellerman 1961). Coat colour variation gives only one kind of clue, however, so it is important that geographic variation in other characters be documented as well. This exercise is important not only for interpreting the past of this species, but also as a basis for conservation efforts. There should be strong concern for the conservation of any populations of *R. indica* which can be demonstrated to be morphologically and genetically distinct. Other species of arboreal mammals may have similar patterns of geographic variation but exhibit them more subtly, in which case the giant squirrels would again be useful as an indicator species, but in this respect of interest to conservationists as well as ecologists.

CONCLUSIONS

The giant tree squirrels (*Ratufa*) are biologically interesting and significant animals in a number of respects. Ecologically, they exhibit a number of characteristics which make them of considerable interest and potential use as indicator species. Morphologically, they exhibit a combination of primitive and derived characters which make them intriguing subjects for studies of evolution and functional anatomy. Zoogeographically, they present conundrums for historical interpretation and distributions which may prove to be important for strategies of conservation.

ACKNOWLEDGEMENTS

This report was supported by grants from the Scholarly studies Programme and the PL 480 Programme of the Smithsonian Institution. The field work of RWT at Mudumalai Wildlife Sanctuary was arranged through the courtesy of the Tamil Nadu Forest Department. We are especially grateful for the assistance of Mr. J. Mangalaraj Johnson, Wildlife Warden of Mudumalai.

REFERENCES CITED

ABDULALI, H. & DANIEL, J.C. (1952): Races of the Indian giant squirrel (*Ratufa indica*). *J. Bombay nat. Hist. Soc.* **50:** 469-474.

________ (1953): A colour variation and albinism in the giant squirrel *Ratufa indica*. ibid. **51:** 731.

AGRAWAL, V.C. (1973): Notes on a collection of mammals from Goa. *Rec. zool. Surv. India* **67:** 261-280.

______ CHAKRABORTY, S. (1979): Catalogue of mammals in the Zoological Survey of India. Rodentia Part I. Sciuridae. ibid. **74:** 333-481.

______ (1979b): Taxonomic notes on some Oriental squirrels. *Mammalia* **43:** 161-172.

ALLEN, G.M. (1940): The mammals of China and Mongolia. Natural History of Central Asia, *Amer. Mus. Nat. Hist., New York* **9:** 621-1350.

BLACK, C.C. (1963): A review of the North American Tertiary Sciuridae. *Bull. Mus. Comp. Zool.* **130:** 113-248.

BLANFORD, W.T. (1888): The Fauna of British India, including Ceylon and Burma. Mammalia. London, xx + 617 pp.

______ (1897): The large Indian squirrel (*Sciurus indicus*) and its local races or subspecies. *J. Bombay nat. Hist. Soc.* **11:** 298-305.

CALLAHAN, J.R. & DAVIS, R. (1982): Reproductive tract and evolutionary relationships of the Chinese rock squirrel, *Sciurotamias davidianus*. *J. Mamm.* **63**: 42-47.

ELLERMAN, J.R. (1961): Rodentia. *In.* The Fauna of India, M.L. Roonwal, ed. Zoological Survey of India, Calcutta, vol. 3, xxx + 883 pp.

MORRISON-SCOTT, T.S.C. (1951): Checklist of Palaearctic and Indian mammals, 1758 to 1946. British Museum (Natural History), London, vi + 810 pp.

EMRY, R.J. & THORINGTON, R.W. (1982): Descriptive and comparative osteology of the oldest fossil squirrel, *Protosciurus* (Rodentia: Sciuridae). *Smithsonian Contributions to Paleobiology* **47**: 1-35.

_______ (In press): The tree squirrel *Sciurus* (Sciuridae, Rodentia) as a living fossil. *In* Casebook on living Fossils (Eldredge, N., ed.), Plenum Press, New York.

HILL, W.C.O. (1940): On the penis of *Ratufa macroura melanochra*. *Ceylon Jour. Sci.*, sec. B, Zool. Geol. **22**: 131-134.

HONACKI, J.H., KINMAN, K.E. & KOEPPL, J.W. (1982): Mammal Species of the World. Allen Press, Lawrence, Kansas.

HUTTON, A.F. (1949): Notes on the snakes and mammals of the High Wavy Mountains, Madura District, South India. Pt. 2 — Mammals. *J. Bombay nat. Hist. Soc.* **48**: 681-694.

KHAJURIA, H. (1955): Mammalian fauna of the semi-arid tracts of the Deccan and its bearing on the appearance of aridity in the region. *Sci. and Culture* **21**: 293-295.

KONSTANT, W., STERN, J.T., FLEAGLE, J.F. & JUNGERS, W.L., (1982): Function of the subclavius muscle in a non-human primate, the spider monkey. *Ateles. Folia primatologica* **38**: 170-182.

KRISHNAN, M. (1972): An ecological survey of the larger mammals of peninsular India. *J. Bombay nat. Hist. Soc.* **69**: 26-54.

LEKAGUL, B., MCNEELY, J.A. (1977): Mammals of Thailand. Kurusapha Ladprao Press, Bangkok.

LINDSAY, H.M. (1927): Mammal survey of India, Burma and Ceylon. Report No. 43. *J. Bombay nat. Hist. Soc.* **32**: 591-597.

LONG, C.A. & CAPTIAN, J. (1974): Investigations of the sciurid manus. I. Some new taxonomic characters and their importance in the classification of squirrels. *Z. f. Saugetierk.* **39**: 98-102.

MACKINNON, K.S. (1978): Stratification and feeding differences among Malayan squirrels. *Malay. Nat. J.* **30**: 593-608.

MOORE, J.C. (1959): Relationships among the living squirrels of the Sciurinae. *Bull. Amer. Mus. Nat. Hist.* **118**: 153-206.

MOORE, J.C. (1960): Squirrel geography of the Indian Subregion. *Systematic Zoology* **9**: 1-7.

_______ (1961): Geographic variation in some reproductive characteristics of diurnal squirrels. *Bull. Amer. Mus. Nat. Hist.* 122: 1-32.

_______ TATE, G.H.H. (1965): A study of the diurnal squirrels, Sciurinae, of the Indian and Indo-Chinese subregion. *Fieldiana*, Zool. **48**: 1-351.

____ (1965): A study of the diurnal squirrels, Sciurinae, of the Indian and Indo-Chinese subregion. *Fieldiana*, Zool. **48**: 1-351.

NOWAK, R.M. & PARADISO, J.L. (1983): Walker's Mammals of the world (4th ed.). Johns Hopkins University Press, Baltimore, pp. 1-1362.

PAYNE, J.B. (1979a): Abundance of diurnal squirrels at the Kuala Lompat Post of the Krau Game Reserve, Peninsular Malaysia. pp. 37-51 *in* The Abundance of Animals in Malaysian Rain Forests, A.G. Marshall (ed.). Department of Geopgraphy, University of Hull.

_______ (1979b): Synecology of Malayan tree squirrels, with particular reference to the genus *Ratufa*. Unpublished Thesis, University of Cambridge.

_______ (1980): Competitors. pp. 261-277 *in* Malayan Forest Primates, D.J. Chivers (ed.), Plenum Press, New York and London.

PHILLIPS, W.W.A. (1935): Manual of the mammals of Ceylon. Dulau and Co., London. xxviii + 373 pp.

POCOCK, R.I. (1923): The classification of the Sciuridae. *Proc. Zool. Soc. London* **1923**: 209-246.

RYLEY, K.V. (1913): Scientific results from the mammals survey. *J. Bombay nat. Hist. Soc.* **22**: 434-443.

THOMAS, O. & WROUGHTON, R.C. (1915): Scientific results from the mammal survey. B. The giant squirrels of Ceylon. ibid. **24**: 34-37.

THORINGTON JR., R.W., & HEANEY, L.R. (1981): Body proportions and gliding adaptations of flying squirrels (Petauristinae). *Journal of Mammalogy* **62**: 101-114.

TIEN, D. VAN, (1972): Donnees ecologiques sur 1 ecureuil geant de McClelland (*Ratufa bicolor gigantea*) (Rodentia, Sciuridae) au Vietnam. *Zoologische Gart. Lptz.* **41**: 240-243.

WEBB-PEPLOE, C.G. (1946): Field notes of the mammals of S. Tinnevelly, S. India. *J. Bombay nat. Hist. Soc.* **46**: 629-644.

WROUGHTON, R.C. (1910): Some notes on the giant squirrels of India, Burma, and Ceylon. ibid. **19**: 880-896.

_______ (1915a). Bombay Natural History Society's mammal survey of India, Burma and Ceylon. No. 18. ibid. **24**: 79.

_______ (1915b): Bombay Natural History Society's mammals survey of India, Burma, and Ceylon. Report No. 19: Bengal, Bihar and Orissa. ibid. **24**: 96-110.

WROUGHTON, R.C. (1916): Bombay Natural History Society's mammal survey of India, Burma and Ceylon. Report No. 23. Sikkim and Bengal Terai. ibid. **24:** 468-493.

_______ (1920): The mainland representative of *Ratufa macroura dondolena*. ibid. **27:** 249-250.

WROUGHTON, R.C. & RILEY, K.V. (1913). Bombay Natural History Society's mammal survey of India, Burma and Ceylon. Report No. 7. ibid. **22:** 45-58.

Comments on the Rain Forests of Southwest India and their Herpetofauna

B. GROOMBRIDGE

SYNOPSIS

Tropical Moist Forests (TMF) occur in mainland India only in parts of the northeast, and on the southerly portions of the Western Ghats. There is very high endemism among plant and animal groups of the southwest forests, notably among the amphibians and reptiles. The diversity, highest among frogs, caecilians and snakes, does not appear to be surpassed by any other region of Indo-Malaysia of comparable size. The southwest TMF also still supports sparse populations of hunter-gatherer tribal societies. The uniqueness and importance of this TMF area is not sufficiently appreciated, certainly not internationally. Despite recent work the biota of the southwest forests in general remains poorly known; many amphibian and reptile taxa are known by a handful of specimens, often collected in the nineteenth century and not recorded since. In contrast, modification and destruction of TMF has continued throughout the twentieth century. Few patches of relatively undisturbed rain forest persist. While the option to design an effective conservation strategy still exists, further field and systematic work on the biota is urgently required. The needs of the persisting tribal groups must be taken into account, and a balance evolved between maintenance of intact rain forest and loss of forest to development projects.

INTRODUCTION

The purpose of this paper is to briefly characterise the rain forests of southwest India, their importance as refuges for plant and animal species and for hunter-gatherer tribal societies, and to note in particular the rich and distinctive herpetofauna of the area. It will be stressed that more work on taxonomy, distribution and ecology is urgently needed, within the framework of an overall conservation strategy for the Western Ghat forests.

Conservation Monitoring Centre, 219(c) Huntingdon Road, Cambridge CB3 ODL, U.K.

TROPICAL MOIST FORESTS IN SOUTHWEST INDIA

The Western Ghats, and parts of the Assam region in the northeast, are the only areas of mainland India to receive an annual rainfall of over 250 cm (Ramdas 1974). These two zones are also the only parts of mainland India to support evergreen tropical rain forest (also found in the Andaman and Nicobar islands) (Mani 1974a; Puri 1960). The Southwest Indian forests, together with the remnant forest in southwest Sri Lanka, constitute the isolated westernmost outliers of the Indo-Malaysian Formation (Richards 1952) of Tropical Moist Forest (TMF), represented in its most typical form by the lowland dipterocarp forests of Malaysia and western Indonesia.

The peaks, hills and plateaus associated with the western escarpment of the Indian peninsula, collectively termed the Western Ghats, extend along much of the west coast, 50-100 km inland, but are particularly well defined in the south. Here a string of more or less discrete hill ranges occur from southwest Karnataka southward along the state border of Kerala and Tamil Nadu.

Although there are appreciable variations due to local topography, the windward portions of the Western Ghats, especially in the south, receive abundant orographic rainfall in most months of the year; however, there is typically a short but well-marked dry season. This is considerably intensified during the southwest monsoon, and while the Western Ghats zone as a whole typically receives over 250 cm annual rainfall (Ramdas 1974), this may rise to between 500 and 800 cm in the higher southern hills, including parts of the Anaimalais.

Whilst a modified type of evergreen forest is found on central parts of the Western Ghats in Maharashtra State, more typical semi-evergreen and evergreen rain forest is not found until further south in parts of Goa and Karnataka, and reaches full development in a relatively narrow belt, between about 450 and 1500 m altitude, along the windward slopes of the Nilgiris, Anaimalais, and ranges to the south (Puri 1960; Subramanyam & Nayar 1974).

Correlated with local climatic and topographic variations, evergreen forest grades, with decreasing rainfall, into semi-evergreen and seasonal (deciduous) monsoon forest. Such gradations can occur over relatively short distances. At higher elevations in these ranges the lofty rain forest trees give way to much smaller temperate evergreen types, and ultimately to *shola* forest in the valleys of the dissected and undulating upland plateaus, surrounded by scrub and grassland, probably largely a result of centuries of clearance and burning by man (Mani 1974a; Puri 1960; Subramanyam & Nayar 1974).

These southwest rain forests are biologically the richest area of the peninsula (Mani 1974c), second only to the Himalayan region in the subcontinent as a whole. Many of the approximately 1500 plant species endemic to the Western Ghats occur in these forests. The overall floristic relationships are with forests in Sri Lanka on one hand, and in Assam, Burma and Southeast Asia on the other (Mani 1974a; Puri 1960). Characteristic woody plant families include the Dipterocarpaceae, represented here by *Dipterocarpus indicus* and species of *Hopea, Shorea, Valeria, Vateria* and others; also the Guttifereae, with giant trees such as *Mesua ferrea* and *Calophyllum* species; and the Myristaceae (Mani 1974a; Puri 1960; Subramanyam & Nayar 1974).

Similarly there is high endemicity among the animals of the southwest forests, notably among the amphibians and reptiles, but also among fishes, birds (chiefly at the subspecies level), and certain invertebrate groups; in parallel with the plants, the overall faunal relationships are with Sri Lanka and Assam-Burma-Southeast Asia (Ali 1969; Jayaram 1974; Mani 1974b, c).

Most importantly the southwest forests have sheltered sparse populations of semi-nomadic hunter-gatherer peoples, such as the Kadar of the Anaimalais, the Pandaram of the Pandalam Hills, and several others (Thurston & Rangachari 1909; Morris 1982). Early anthropologists regarded some of these tribal groups as among the last vestiges of a pre-Dravidian ethnic stratum, related to the Australian aboriginals and the Veddas of Sri Lanka (Thurston 1913); this, however, is difficult to substantiate. Although the relative isolation of the tribes in the Ghat forests has enabled them to remain free of the caste hierarchy and the feudalistic labour system pervading the surrounding agricultural lowlands, it is likely that there have long been significant trading contacts between the two communities (Morris 1982).

UTILIZATION OF FOREST RESOURCES

In terms of resources, the moist forests of Southwest India are important for:

(i) so-called 'minor forest products' such as bamboo, cane, rattan, honey, spices, oil-seeds, resins, etc.,

(ii) hard and softwoods for the timber trade,

(iii) wild relatives of tropical crops (e.g. Pepper *Piper nigrum,* Cardamom *Elettaria car-*

damomum, Jakfruit *Artocarpus heterophyllus*),

(iv) wild plants of potential medicinal significance, including those utilized by tribal groups. It appears that relatively little research has been done on medicinal usage of plants by tribal peoples in the Western Ghats, this is required as a matter of some urgency as their traditional lifestyle is becoming increasingly modified.

The Malabar coast has been renowned since Roman times as the source of spices, sandalwood, precious oils, ivory, and other produce originating from the forests of the Western Ghats. Then, as now, it was doubtless certain of the forest tribes who initially collected this produce.

The 'minor forest products' are of fundamental importance both in local utilization and in trade as raw materials and manufactured goods. Today those forest tribes that retain a semi-nomadic lifestyle live jointly by the collection and sale or barter of such produce, and by direct consumption of other forest resources of plant and animal origin.

Forest products are deemed to be national resources and as such their exploitation is under the control of the State Forest Department. The right to market minor forest produce from a given range is leased out to contractors whose agents handle the local purchase or barter of produce collected by the tribals. It has been stressed (Morris 1982) that this relationship is essentially exploitative; trade in minor forest products results in significant income to the State and to the merchants, who can make large profits at the expense of the tribals. On the other hand, for the Hill Pandaram at least, the dietary staples such as rice and tapioca obtained through trade appear to supplement wild-collected food sources, rather than the reverse (Morris 1982).

Forest animals, including certain mammals, birds and reptiles, provide a crucial protein source for tribal groups (although no quantitative data are yet available). Wild yams provide much of the carbohydrate intake. The reptiles utilized by tribes such as the Kadar and the Hill Pandaram comprise Indian Monitor lizard *Varanus bengalensis*, the Travancore Tortoise *Geochelone travancorica*, and the Cane Turtle *Heosemys silvatica* (apparently absent from the range of the Hill Pandaram).

Although both the chelonian species are considered to be under some threat, and are listed in the IUCN Red Data Book (Groombridge 1982), no attempt should be made to discourage the forest tribes from utilizing them as a food source. Instead, efforts should be made to ensure that sufficient areas of undisturbed forest are left to allow the chelonians and other target species to maintain a population level that can withstand exploitation. This is especially important in the case of the chelonians, since they (*H. silvatica* in particular) appear to be collected and eaten most regularly by children, and must make a very significant contribution to the nutrition of this vulnerable age group. Although the tribals forage very widely and can be extremely efficient collectors, they themselves exist at low population densities. A realistic estimate is required of the minimum area of forest able to support the necessary biomass of prey species, and the total area of forest necessary to support the tribal way of life.

Despite the enduring importance of wildlife resources and minor forest products, it appears that during the nineteenth and twentieth centuries, initially as a result of British commercial exploitation, the forests have been valued primarily as sources of hardwood for a variety of constructional and decorative purposes, and more recently for plywood timbers also.

The forests of the former state of Cochin (now incorporated into Kerala), on the Nelliampathi Hills and the western Anaimalais, in many ways typify the overall pattern of exploitation throughout the Western Ghats. These forests were recognized as one of the state's most valuable assets soon after colonial penetration of the area, but reckless over-exploitation of this resource was already acknowledged around the turn of the last century (Anon 1908). In the early nineteenth century great quantities of timber had been taken from the Cochin forests (and other parts of the Anaimalais) for use in the shipyards of Bombay, and timber was also in much demand for railway sleepers and pit-props. Because of inefficient cutting techniques the major part of the potentially useful timber in any given tree was often completely wasted (Peet 1887). The moist-deciduous forests present in areas of more seasonal or lesser rainfall, containing teak and other hardwoods, were most valued for their timber resources (Fischer 1921; Peet 1887). However, prized hardwoods, including *Dipterocarpus, Calophyllum* and *Mesua,* also occurred abundantly in the evergreen forests (Fischer 1921).

The semi-evergreen and evergreen forests were also extensively cleared for plantation crops (Fischer 1921). Coffee planting started in the mid-nineteenth century on the northern slopes of the Anaimalais, other areas in the west, including the catchments of the Periyar and Sholayar rivers, were opened up in 1896. Overall, several thousand acres of evergreen forest were cleared for plantations of tea, coffee, rubber, and to a lesser extent, cardamom and cinchona (Fischer 1921).

Although an improved system of forest administration was inaugurated in Cochin State around 1898, in which the Forest Department came under the control of a Conservator, the fact that a few tracts of partially undisturbed forest still exist today in certain areas (in the vicinity of Parambikolam and Kavalai for example) appears to be due as much to local topography, which rendered timber extraction difficult and costly, as to good management.

Plantations of tea, rubber, teak and exotic timber species (notably Eucalyptus), also logging and hydroelectric projects are at present further reducing the area under TMF. There are few relatively undisturbed tracts of TMF remaining, and particularly few patches of evergreen rain forest (Mani 1974; Saharia 1981; Fischer 1921). In the region of the headwaters of the Chalakudi river for example (the Parambikolam and Sholayar rivers), construction of dams has not only resulted in submergence of large areas of virgin forest (Sebastine & Ramamurthy 1966), but the increased usage of the area concomitant with construction and operation of the dams must have adverse effects on the integrity of habitats and on populations of certain animal species (Vijayan 1978). There are already four dams built in the area and more are planned. Lower down the Chalakudi the hill forest has been largely cleared for rubber and teak plantations, or otherwise modified. Hydroelectric power and irrigation water are vital commodities in southern India, but it is equally vital to ensure that only truly essential projects are undertaken and that their impact on the environment is minimised.

The natural hill forests also play a vital, but as yet poorly quantified, role in watershed protection and in local climatic cycles; it is widely asserted that loss of forest cover has led to decrease or irregularity in annual rainfall in some areas (Mani 1978).

THE HERPETOFAUNA OF THE WESTERN GHATS

It is not the intention here to attempt a

zoogeographic discussion of the Indian herpetofauna (one reason for this is the inadequacy of current systematic knowledge). The suggestion (Ali 1969; Mani 1974b,c) may be noted that the southwest hill forests in part constitute refugia for the numerous plant and animal species occurring there; these taxa appear to represent components of a moist-tropical forest community formerly widespread over the Indian peninsula, including both autochthonous elements and intrusive elements having dispersed westward from southeast Asia through the Assam region. Both climatic and anthropogenic factors are implicated in the withdrawal of this community from most of the Peninsula. The hypothesis that the species assemblage now restricted to southwest India was formerly more widespread is based largely on the occurrence of a few species of this group as relict populations on hills of the Eastern Ghats and other isolated sites in the east and northeast (for example, two *Uropeltis* species in the Shevaroy Hills and two *Ichthyophis* species in northeast Tamil Nadu), and on the occurrence of taxa related at the specific or generic level in the Assam region and southeast Asia. However, the high number of local endemics suggests that much *in situ* speciation has also occurred.

While modification and destruction of these forests have continued steadily throughout the present century, our scientific knowledge of the biota of these areas — with the partial exception of certain birds and larger mammals such as the Nilgiri Tahr *Hemitragus hylocrius* (Rice 1983) and Liontailed Macaque *Macaca silenus* (Green & Minkowski 1977) — has remained virtually at a standstill until very recently. The situation has improved somewhat in the past few years following work by the Zoological and Botanical Surveys of India, and the Madras Snake Park. However, many species are still known from a very few specimens, often with imprecise locality data, and very frequently have not been recorded since collection of the type material several decades ago. The present extent of clearance and disturbance of TMF means that many plant and animal species must be actually or potentially threatened by habitat loss.

Despite the sparsity of present data on the systematics and distribution of the amphibians and reptiles of the southwest rain forests, it is clear that the herpetofauna of the region is extremely rich. There are approximately 150 described endemic species and 12 endemic genera (see Appendix). Very many additional species are present that range into Sri Lanka, or other parts of southern India, or are more widespread in the Peninsula.

This high species-richness is rarely equalled by any other area of Indo-Malaysia of comparable size, and may be greatly surpassed only in parts of Central and South America. The mountain rain forests of eastern Tanzania, including the Usambaras and Ulugurus, widely ragarded as major centres of high diversity and endemism, have 17 endemic frogs (Schiotz 1981) whereas the Ghat forests of southwest India have 54 named species and probably at least 40 true species (however, the latter forests do cover a somewhat larger area). Borneo, the third largest island in the world and a well-known centre of diversity, has a similar number of endemic amphibians (Inger 1966), or fewer if all the named species of southwest India are valid. West Malaysia has about 10 endemic snakes (Tweedie 1953), southwest India has about 55.

Perhaps most notable among the amphibians are the Black Microhylid *Melanobatrachus indicus,* an endemic monotypic genus (Beddome 1878) known only from a handful of specimens collected in the Anaimalais in the 1870s, and possibly most closely related to two relict genera in the mountains of east Tanzania

(Parker 1934); the Malabar Tree Toad *Pedostibes tuberculosa,* the only species of this bufonid genus in peninsular India (other species range from extreme northeast India through parts of southeast Asia); the endemic ranid genera *Nannobatrachus* and *Nyctibatrachus;* and a significant radiation of caecilians, including an endemic subfamily for the genus *Uraeotyphlus* (Nussbaum 1979). Among the reptiles may be noted the two near-endemic arboreal agamid genera *Otocryptis* and *Salea;* an important radiation of the gekkonid genus *Cnemaspis* (Smith 1935); the rare endemic genus of burrowing snakes *Xylophis* (Smith 1943); and the major radiation of primitive but specialised burrowing snakes of the family Uropeltidae, known only from peninsular India and Sri Lanka (Gans 1966, 1973; Murthy 1981). Because most scientific collecting and descriptive work on these groups was carried out around the turn of the century, it should be recognized that we have only a first approximation of the actual number of biological species and their true distribution areas.

In order to design an effective strategy for conservation and utilization of TMF in southwest India it is clearly essential to know more about the taxonomy, distribution and ecology of the fauna and flora. It is quite possible that a significant number of the local or rare species may in fact be more widespread than known at present. The urgent need for more fieldwork is clear: not only has recent fieldwork resulted in new data on the status of rare plant and animal species not previously reported for many decades, but new species are still being discovered. Dr Pillai of the Zoological Survey of India has described five new anurans from the Western Ghats in the last five years (Pillai 1978, 1979, 1981; Pillai & Pattabiraman 1981), and he reports (*in litt.* 1982) that two new caecilian amphibians await description. The urgency of the situation has been stressed by Rom Whitaker of the Madras Snake Park, he reports (Whitaker 1982) that although the moist forest of one particular *shola* in the Palni Hills has been largely degraded, a recent survey in the remaining forest revealed one specimen of an undescribed species of Kukri Snake *Oligodon* sp. The implication is that continuing habitat loss could so easily have led to the species' extinction before its discovery.

Prominent among rediscovered taxa is the terrestrial emydid turtle *Heosemys silvatica* (Henderson 1912). Until 1982 this species was known to science by only two reported museum specimens, both collected in 1911 in hill forest around Kavalai, at about 450 m, in the former 'Cochin State Forests' (we now know that one and perhaps two later specimens have found their way, unreported, into museum collections). Two colleagues and I were able to visit the type area in late 1982 and, with the essential aid of Kadar tribals, were very gratified to locate a healthy wild population (Groombridge, Moll & Vijaya 1983). Work in late 1983 has further demonstrated the great importance of the *Heosemys* site. In addition to the two threatened chelonian species we have found groups of two threatened primate species (Liontailed Macaques and Nilgiri Langurs) and other notable fauna such as Indian Python and Great Pied Hornbill. In this instance *H. silvatica* served as an indicator species for a relatively intact, but apparently unreported, moist forest fauna.

The fact that new species are still being discovered, even if already threatened, coupled with recent rediscoveries of rare plant and animal taxa, illustrates that work in the field can still provide the data on which strategic conservation policies should be based.

RECOMMENDATIONS

The southwest tropical-moist forests must on

no account be dismissed as simply an isolated and relatively unimportant patch of the Indo-Malayan Formation, that requires little specific concern. On the contrary, while many plant and animal species of the rich biota of northeast India extend into China, Burma and other parts of Southeast Asia, a high proportion of the southwest flora and fauna are taxa found nowhere else. For this reason, and because the biota to some extent represents the vestiges of a community once (even into historical times) more widespread over the Indian peninsula, the southwest forests require much greater taxonomic and conservation attention than they have hitherto received. The over-riding need is for *an overall strategy for conservation and utilisation of TMF resources in India*—covering both the southwest peninsular forests and those of the northeast frontier zones.

It is necessary that all relevant groups of fauna and flora, and especially the needs of the few remaining forest tribal groups, are taken into account. Among the prerequisites for effective legislation we need to know: (i) what actual type and coverage of forest remains, and where, (ii) more about the biota of these forests, (iii) which are the priority sites for conservation, (iv) what forms and levels of utilization are feasible, (v) what further forms of disturbance are justifiable. A complete and accurate appraisal, based on ground, air and perhaps satellite surveys, of the present distribution of Tropical-Moist Forest types and the degree to which they are intact or degraded, is an important preliminary to future conservation action. Many of the requisite data should now be supplied by the variety of programmes initiated by the relatively new (1980) Department of Environment, within the overall framework of a National Conservation Strategy; for example, the Forest Survey of India was established in 1981 with the task of assessing and monitoring the country's forest resources.

For the amphibians and reptiles the urgent needs are for:

(i) adequate new field and systematic work on the many characteristic and endemic species, especially the many species at present known by only a few specimens or not recorded for several decades,

(ii) surveys in existing protected areas to determine which taxa are covered in the present network,

(iii) investigation of the role of amphibians and reptiles in the ecology of TMF communities in southwest India, preferably within the framework of a broader study of the ecology and dynamics of Indian TMF systems,

(iv) input relevant to the herpetofauna into discussion on location of future protected areas (e.g. Biosphere reserves).

ACKNOWLEDGEMENTS

My fieldwork in Kerala could not have been performed without the generous cooperation of officials of the Kerala Forest Department, notably Mr G. Mukundan (Additional Chief Conservator of Forests), Mr R. Nair (Conservator of Forests, Trichur District) and Mr Joseph (Divisional Forest Officer, Chalakudi Division of Trichur District). I am also extremely grateful to the People's Trust for Endangered Species and the Fauna and Flora Preservation Society for providing the vital financial support (in 1982 and 1983 respectively), to Ms. J Vijaya and the Madras Crocodile Bank for essential assistance in the field, and to the IUCN Conservation Monitoring Centre for granting leave of absence.

Appendix. Preliminary informal list of nominal

amphibian and reptile taxa endemic to southwest India. Not all these taxa are moist-forest forms, but the great majority are. Many additional taxa not listed here occur in the area but extend also to southeast India and/or to Sri Lanka, or are more widespread in the Peninsula. A few taxa that occur in the northern extremities of the Western Ghats, or just extend to one or two localities in the Eastern Ghats, are also listed (enclosed in brackets).

It should be stressed that (a) more species almost certainly remain to be discovered, and (b) many of the taxa listed (e.g. among the rhacophorids) may well be synonymized when specimens are subjected to critical scrutiny. The total number of valid endemic species may be similar to the present total of named species (approximately 150).

AMPHIBIA

ANURA (frogs and toads)

Bufonidae

Ansonia Torrent Toads
A. ornata (Günther, 1875); Brahmagiri Hills (Coorg; Karnataka)
A. rubigena Pillai & Pattabiraman, 1981; Silent Valley (Kerala)

Bufo

B. beddomii Günther, 1875; 'Travancore Hills'
B. hololius Günther, 1875; 'Malabar'
B. parietalis Boulenger, 1882; 'Malabar' and 'Travancore'
B. silentvalleyensis Pillai, 1981; Silent Valley (Kerala)
Pedostibes tuberculosa (Günther, 1875) Malabar Tree Toad; 'Malabar', recently recorded in Silent Valley. The only species of the genus in peninsular India, otherwise known from northeast India and Southeast Asia.

Microhylidae

Melanobatrachus indicus Beddome, 1878; Anaimalais and other hill ranges in Kerala. Endemic genus. This species is usually assigned to a distinct subfamily, Melanobatrachinae. The species does not appear to have been collected since the original series, described in 1878.
Ramanella triangularis (Günther, 1875); 'Malabar', Nilgiri Hills.

Ranidae

Micrixalus
M. fuscus Boulenger, 1882; N. Kanara to Tinnevelly
M. herrei Myers, 1942; 'Travaneore'
M. nudis Pillai, 1978; Wynaad (Kerala)
M. opistorhodos (Günther, 1868); 'Malabar', Nilgiri Hills
M. saxicola (Jerdon, 1853); 'Malabar', Wynaad (Kerala)
M. silvaticus Boulenger, 1882; 'Malabar'
M. thampii Pillai, 1981; Silent Valley (Kerala)

Nannobatrachus, endemic genus.
N. anamallaiensis Myers, 1942; Anaimalai Hills (Kerala)
N. beddomii Boulenger, 1882; 'Malabar', Tinnevelley
N. kempholeyensis Rao, 1937; Kempholey Ghat, Hassan (Karnataka)

Nyctibatrachus, endemic genus
N. major Boulenger, 1882; Wynaad (Kerala), Kerala
N. humayuni Bhaduri & Kripalani, 1955; N. Kanara, Mahabaleshwar, Khandala
N. pygmaeus (Günther, 1875); Anaimalai Hills
N. sanctipalustris Rao, 1920; Brahmagiris, Shimoga (Karnataka)
N. sylvaticus Rao, 1937; Hassan (Karnataka)

Rana

R. aurantica Boulenger, 1904; 'Travancore'
R. beddomii Günther, 1875; 'Malabar', 'Travancore'
R. bhagmandlensis Rao, 1922; Bhagmandla (Karnataka)
R. brevipalmata Peters, 1871; 'Malabar', Wynaad (Kerala)
R. curtipes Jerdon, 1853; Kanara to 'Travancore'
R. diplosticta (Günther, 1875); 'Malabar', Anaimalai Hills
R. dobsoni Boulenger, 1890; 'Malabar'
(*R. leithii* Boulenger, 1888; S. India west only?)
R. leptodactyla (Günther, 1875); 'Malabar', 'Travancore'
R. murthii Pillai, 1979; Gudallur (Tamil Nadu)
R. phrynoderma Boulenger, 1882; 'Malabar', Anaimalai Hills
R. rufescens (Jerdon, 1854); Salsette Id (Maharashtra), 'Malabar'
R. sauriceps Rao, 1937; Coorg (Karnataka)
R. semipalmata Boulenger, 1882; 'Malabar'
R. verrucosa Günther, 1875; 'Malabar' 'Travancore'

Rhacophoridae

Philautus
P. beddomii (Boulenger, 1882); SW. India
[*P. bombayensis* (Annandale, 1919); Bombay]
P. charius Rao, 1937; Kadur (Karnataka)
P. elegans Rao, 1937; Hassan (Karnataka)
P. glandulosus (Jerdon, 1853)
P. kottigeharensis Rao, 1937; Kadur (Karnataka)
P. longicrus Rao, 1937; Hassan (Karnataka)
P. melanesis Rao, 1937; Hassan (Karnataka)
P. montanus Rao, 1937; Hassan (Karnataka)
P. narainensis Rao, 1937; Kadur (Karnataka)
P. pulcherrimus Ahl, 1927; Wynaad (Kerala)
P. swamianus Rao, 1937; Kadur (Karnataka)
P. travancoricus Boulenger, 1882;

Rhacophorus
R. calcadensis Ahl, 1927; Anaimalais, 'Travancore'
R. malabaricus Jerdon, 1870; 'Malabar'
R. noblei Ahl, 1927; 'Malabar'
R. parkeri Ahl, 1927; 'Malabar'

GYMNOPHIONA (caecilians)

Caeciliidae

Gegeneophis (the third species of the genus is known by the type only, from Manipur, northeast India)
G. carnosus (Beddome, 1870); Wynaad, Kotegehar (Karnataka)
G. ramaswamii Taylor, 1964; Tenmalai, Trivandrum (Kerala)
(*Indotyphlus battersbyi* Taylor, 1960; Pune District, Maharashtra)

Ichthyophiidae

Ichthyophis

(*I. beddomei* Peters, 1879; Nilgiris, Wynaad, and extends to a locality near Madras)
I. bombayensis Taylor, 1965; near Bombay (Mararashtra)
I. malabarensis Taylor, 1960; Maduvangard ('Travancore')
(*I. peninsularis* Taylor, 1960; 'Malabar', 'Travancore', also extends to Chingleput District, Tamil Nadu)
I. subterrestris Taylor, 1960; Kerala
I. tricolor Annandale, 1909; Kerala, Nilgiri Hills

Uraeotyphlus, endemic genus

U. malabaricus (Beddome, 1870); 'Malabar', Nilgiri Hills
U. menoni Annandale, 1913; Kerala
U. narayani Sesachar, 1939; Kerala
U. oxyurus (Dumeril & Bibron, 1841); Kerala

REPTILIA

SAURIA (lizards)

Agamidae

Calotes
C. ellioti Günther, 1864; 'Malabar', Sivagiris, etc.
C. grandisquamis Günther, 1871 Anaimalais, Brahmagiris, etc.
C. nemoricola Jerdon, 1853; Nilgiris
(*C. rouxi* Dumeril & Bibron, 1837; 'Travancore', 'Bombay Presidency')
Draco dussumieri Dumeril & Bibron, 1837; W. Ghats from Goa southward
Otocryptis beddomii Boulenger 1885; Sivagiris, Cardamom Hills (a near endemic genus, second species in Sri Lanka).
Salea (near endemic genus, third species in northeast)
S. anamallayana (Beddome, 1878); Anaimalais, Palnis, 'Travancore'
S. horsfieldii Gray, 1845; Nilgiris, Palnis

Gekkonidae

Cnemaspis (12 of the 22 spp. occur in south India and Sri Lanka).
C. beddomei (Theobald, 1870); Tinnevelly, Wynaad, 'Travancore'
C. goaensis Sharma, 1976; Canacona (Goa)
C. indica (Gray, 1946); Nilgiris, 'Travancore'
C. littoralis (Jerdon, 1853); Nilgiris
C. ornata (Beddome, 1870); Anaimalais, Tinnevelly, etc.
C. sisparensis (Theobald, 1870); Sispara Ghat (Nilgiris)
C. wynadensis (Beddome, 1870); Wynaad

Cyrtodactylus albofasciatus (Boulenger, 1885); Kanara
Dravidogecko anamallensis (Günther, 1875); Anaimalais, Palnis, Tinnevelly

Lacertidae

Ophiops beddomei (Jerdon, 1870); Satara District, Kanara, Wynaad (a high altitude grassland form).

Scincidae

[*Chalcides pentadactylus* (Beddome, 1870); near Beypore (Kerala coast) (single specimen known)]
Dasia subcaerulea (Boulenger, 1891); Bodinaikkanur, High Wavy Mtns (only two specimens known)
Scincella (formerly *Leiolopisma*)
S. beddomei (Boulenger, 1887); Nilgiris, 'Travancore'
S. bilineatum (Gray, 1846); Nilgiris
S. laterimaculatum (Boulenger, 1887); Nilgiris, Tinnevelly, 'Travancore'
S. palnicum (Boettger, 1892); Palni Hills, Coimbatore
S. travancoricum (Beddome, 1870); 'Travancore', Anaimalais, Palnis
Riopa goaensis Sharma, 1976; Molem (Goa)
Ristella, endemic genus
R. beddomei Boulenger, 1887; W. Ghats from Kanara southward
R. guentheri Boulenger, 1887; Anaimalais, Tenmalai, Madura
R. rurkii Gray, 1839; Anaimalais, Palnis, 'Travancore'
R. travancorica (Beddome, 1870); Tinnevelly

SERPENTES (snakes)

'Colubridae'

Ahaetulla

A. perroteti (Dumeril & Bibron, 1854); Kanara to Nilgiris
A. dispar (Günther, 1864); W. Ghats from Nilgiris southward

Amphiesma

A. beddomei (Beddome, 1863); W. Ghats south of Mahableshwar
A. monticola (Jerdon, 1853); W. Ghats from Goa to 'Travancore'
Boiga dightoni (Boulenger, 1894); Pirmed (Travancore) (only 3 specimens).

Dendrelaphis grandoculis (Boulenger, 1890); W. Ghats from Wynaad southward
Oligodon Kukri Snakes
O. affinis Günther, 1862; W. Ghats from Wynaad southward
O. brevicauda Günther, 1862; W. Ghats from Nilgiris southward
O. travancoricus Beddome, 1877; W. Ghats from Anaimalais southward
O. venustus (Jerdon, 1853); W. Ghats from Wynaad southward
Rhabdops olivaceus Beddome, 1863); Wynaad (near endemic genus, the second species from Assam-Yunnan).
Xylophis, endemic genus
X. perroteti (Dumeril & Bibron, 1854); W. Ghats from Wynaad southward
X. stenorhynchus (Günther, 1875); W. Ghats from Anaimalais southward

Elapidae

Calliophis Coral Snakes
C. beddomei Shevaroy Hills, Koppa (Karnataka)
C. bibroni (Jan, 1858); W. Ghats from Coorg southward
C. nigrescens Günther, 1862; W. Ghats

Typhlopidae

Typhlops Worm Snakes
[*T. beddomei* Boulenger, 1890; W. Ghats, (also Vizagapatam ?)]
T. thurstoni Boettger, 1890; Nilgiris, Trichur
T. tindalli Smith, 1943; Nilgiris

Uropeltidae (Shield-tail snakes, a family endemic to India and Sri Lanka).

Brachyophidium rhodogaster Wall, 1921; Palni Hills, Tenmalai (Kerala) (endemic genus)
Melanophidium, endemic genus
M. bilineatum Beddome, 1870; Wynaad (known by the three types only)
M. punctatum Beddome, 1871; Anaimalais, 'Travancore', Telewady (Karnataka), Atapadi (Tamil Nadu)
M. wynaudense Beddome, 1863; Manantoddy, Coorg
Platyplectrurus, (possibly an endemic genus, the single Sri Lanka record is in doubt).
P. madurensis Beddome, 1877; Palnis, Munnar, 'Travancore'
P. trilineatus (Beddome, 1867); Palnis, Anaimalais
Plectrurus, endemic genus
P. aureus Beddome, 1880; Chambra Hill (Wynaad)
P. canaricus (Beddome, 1870); Kudremukh (Karnataka)
P. guentheri Beddome, 1863; Nilgiris
P. perroteti Dumeril & Bibron, 1854; Karnataka

Rhinophis

R. fergusonianus Boulenger, 1896; Cardamon Hills (Kerala) (type only)
R. sanguineus Beddome, 1863; Koppa, Kelsa (Karnataka), Wynad, Nilgiris, 'Travancore', Tirunelveli
R. travancoricus Boulenger, 1893; Trivandrum, New Ambadi (TN), 'Travancore'
Teretrurus sanguineus (Beddome, 1867); (endemic genus) Tirunelveli Hills, Munnar, Wynaad

Uropeltis

U. arcticeps (Günther, 1875) W. Ghats south of Palghat
U. beddomii (Günther, 1862) Anaimalais
U. broughami (Beddome, 1878) Nilgiris, Palnis, Sirumalais (Madurai Dist.)
U. ceylanicus Cocteau, 1833 W. Ghats from Castle Rock to Travancore, also Shevaroy Hills (E. Ghats)
U. dindigalensis (Beddome, 1877) Sirumalai

Hills (Madurai Dist.)
U. ellioti (Gray, 1858) W. Ghats south of the Goa gap, also Shevaroy Hills, Nadur, Javadi and Ganjam Hills (Orissa) (E. Ghats)
U. liura (Günther, 1875) Madurai, Tirunelveli Hills
U. macrolepis (Peters, 1862) Bombay Hills, Mahableshwar (Maharashtra)
U. macrorhynchus (Beddome, 1877) Anaimalais (inc. Upper Aliyar)
U. maculatus (Beddome, 1878) Anaimalais and hills to south
U. myhendrae (Beddome, 1886) W. Ghats south of Goa gap
U. nitidus (Beddome, 1878) Anaimalais (Kerala side)
U. ocellatus (Beddome, 1863) Agumbe, N. Kanara (Karnataka), Wynaad, Nilgiris, Anaimalais (inc. Kavalai)
U. petersi (Beddome, 1868) Anaimalais
U. phillipsi (Nicholls, 1929)
U. pulneyensis (Beddome, 1863) Palnis, Alagar Hills, High Wavy Mtns., Madurai, Munnar
U. rubrolineatus (Günther, 1875) Bhimshankar, Pune (Maharashtra), Pachiparai, Palali (TN), Anaimalais, 'Travancore'
U. rubromaculatus (Beddome, 1867) Nilgiris, Anaimalais, Munnar
U. smithi Gans, 1966 Anaimalais
U. woodmasoni (Theobald, 1876) Palnis, Anaimalais, Tirunelveli, Nilgiris, 'Travancore'

Viperidae

Trimeresurus Arboreal Pit-vipers
T. huttoni Smith, 1949; High Wavy Mtns (Madura Dist.)
T. macrolepis Beddome, 1862; W. Ghats from Nilgiris southward
T. malabaricus Jerdon, 1854; W. Ghats
T. strigatus Gray, 1842; W. Ghats from Nilgiris southward

TESTUDINES (turtles, tortoises)

Emydidae

Heosemys silvatica (Henderson, 1912), Cane Turtle; western Anaimalais (also Calicut Hills ?)

Testudinidae

Geochelone travancorica (Boulenger, 1907), Travancore Tortoise; W. Ghats from Coorg southward

REFERENCES

ALI, S. (1969): Birds of Kerala. Bombay. Oxford University Press.

ANON. (1908): Imperial Gazetteer of India, Provincial Series, Madras (Vol. II, The Southern and West Coast District, Native States, and French Possessions). Calcutta: Superintendent of Government Printing.

BEDDOME, R.H. (1878): Description of a new Batrachian from southern India, belonging to the family Phryniscidae (*Melanobatrachus indicus,* gen. et. sp. nov.). *Proceedings of the Zoological Society of London,* 1878:722-723.

FISCHER, C.E.C. (1921): A survey of the flora of the Anaimalai Hills in the Coimbatore District, Madras Presidency. *Rec. bot. Surv. India* 9:1-218.

GANS, C. (1966): Uropeltidae. *Das Tierreich,* 84:1-29.

____ (1973): Uropeltid snakes — survivors in a changing world. *Endeavour* 32:60-65.

GREEN, S. & MINKOWSKI, K. (1977): The liontailed monkey and its South Indian rain forest habitat. Pp. 289-337, *in* Bourne, G.H. & H.S.H. Rainier (Eds), Primate Conservation. Academic Press.

GROOMBRIDGE, B. (1982); The IUCN Amphibia-Reptilia Red Data Book. Part 1. Testudines, Crocodylia, Rhynchocephalia. Gland (Switzerland): IUCN.

______, MOLL, E.O. & VIJAYA, J. (1983): Rediscovery of rare Indian turtle *Heosemys silvatica* (Reptilia: Emydidae). *Oryx* 17(2):130-134.

HENDERSON, J.R. (1912): Preliminary note on a new tortoise from South India. *Rec. Ind. Mus.* 7: 217-218.

INGER, R.F. (1966): The systematics and zoogeography of the Amphibia of Borneo. *Fieldiana:* Zool., 52.

JAYARAM, K.C. (1974): Ecology and distribution of freshwater fishes, amphibia and reptiles. Chapter XVII, pp. 517-584. *In* Mani, M.S. (Ed.) 1974.

MANI, A. (1978): How Man modifies climate. *J. Bombay nat. Hist. Soc.* 75(3): 580-588.

MANI, M.S., (Ed.) (1974). Ecology and biogeography in India. Monographiae Biologicae, No. 23. The Hague. W. Junk.

________ (1974a): The flora. Chapter VI, pp. 157-177, *in* Mani, M.S. (Ed.) 1974.

__ (1974b): Biogeographical evolution in India. Chapter XXIV, pp. 698-724. *In* Mani, M.S. (Ed.) 1974.

______ (1974c): Biogeography of the Peninsula. Chapter XIX, pp. 614-647. *In* Mani, M.S. (Ed.) 1974.

MORRIS, B. (1982): Forest Traders: A Socio-economic study of the Hill Pandaram. London School of Economics Monographs on Social Anthropology, No. 35. Athlone Press, New Jersey.

MURTHY, T.S.N. (1981); Checklist and key to the uropeltid snakes of India. *The Snake* **13**: 142-150.

NUSSBAUM, R.A. (1979): The taxonomic status of the caecilian genus *Uraeotyphlus* Peters. *Occ. Pap. Mus. Zool. Univ. Mich.*, No. 687.

PARKER, H.W. (1934): A monograph of the frogs of the family Microhylidae. London: British Museum (Natural History).

PEET, A.W. (1887): The forests of Coimbatore. Chapter XIV, pp. 398-413. *In* Nicholson, F.A. 1887. Manual of the Coimbatore District in the Presidency of Madras. Madras. Govt. Printer.

PILLAI, R.S. (1978): A new frog of the genus *Micrixalus* Boul. from Wynad, S. India. *Proc. Indian Acad. Sci.* (Anim. Sci.-2), 87B(6): 173-177.

________ (1979): A new species of *Rana* (family Ranidae) from Western Ghats, S. India. *Bull. zool. Surv. India* **2**(1): 39-42.

_______ (1981): Two new species of Amphibia from Silent Valley, S. India. ibid. **3**(3): 153-158.

___________ (1982): *In litt.*, 25 February.

________ & PATTABIRAMAN, R. (1981): A new species of Torrent Toad (Genus: *Ansonia*) from Silent Valley, S. India. *Proc. Indian Acad. Sci.* (Anim. Sci.) **90**(2): 203-208.

PURI, G.S. (1960): Indian Forest Ecology. 2 vols. New Delhi: Oxford Book and Stationary Co.

RAMDAS, L.A. (1974): Weather and Climatic patterns. Chapter IV, pp. 99-134, *in* Mani, M.S. (Ed.) 1974.

RICE, C.G. (1983): Nilgiri Tahr, Eravikulam National Park and Conservation. Paper presented at Centenary Seminar of the Bombay Natural History Society, 6-10 December.

RICHARDS, P.W. (1952): The Tropical Rain Forest. Cambridge: Cambridge University Press.

SAHARIA, V.B. (1981): Wildlife in India. Ministry of Agriculture, Government of India.

SCHIOTZ, A. (1981): The Amphibia in the forested basement hills of Tanzania: a biogeographical indicator group. *Afr. J. Ecol.* **19**:205-207.

SEBASTINE, K.M. & RAMAMURTHY, K. (1966): Studies on the flora of Parambikolam and Aliyar submergible areas. *Bull. Bot. Surv. India,* **8**:169-182.

SMITH, M.A. (1935): Reptilia and Amphibia, Vol. II, Sauria, *in* series, The Fauna of British India, Ceylon and Burma. London: Taylor and Francis.

____ (1943): Reptilia and Amphibia, Vol. III, Serpentes, *in* series, The Fauna of British India, Ceylon and Burma. London: Taylor and Francis. Reprinted 1957, Calcutta: Govt. of India.

SUBRAMANYAM, K. & NAYAR, M.P. (1974): Vegetation and phytogeography of the Western Ghats. Chapter VII, pp. 178-196, *in* Mani, M.S. (Ed.) 1974.

THURSTON, E. (1913): The Madras Presidency with Mysore, Coorg and the Associated States. In series, Provincial Geographies of India. Cambridge: University Press.

________ & RANGACHARI, K. (1909): Castes and Tribes of Southern India. Vol. VII. Madras: Govt. Printer.

TWEEDIE, M.F.W. (1953): The Snakes of Malaya. Singapore: Govt. Printing Office.

VIJAYAN, V.S. (1978): Parambikulam Wildlife Sanctuary and its adjacent areas. *J. Bombay nat. Hist. Soc.* **75**(3):888-900.

WHITAKER, R. (1982): Introduction; aims and objectives of the Snake Specialist Group. Proceedings of the IUCN/SSC Snake Specialist Group, First Meeting, 8-12 November 1982, pp. 1-4.

The Fauna outside National Parks and Sanctuaries

M. K. RANJITSINH

Till as late as the 19th century human settlements were but islands amongst areas that were in a state of nature. In the first half of the present century with the inexorable rise in population and the conversion of ecosystem people into biosphere people (Dasmann 1975) — from those who derived sustenance from individual ecosystems to those who depended upon the resources of the globe — there was almost a *volte face*. The nature areas, especially the forests, became islands in a sea of humanity. In the second half of the 20th century, these islands shrunk and are shrinking, to the effectively protected national parks and sanctuaries. In south Asia these islands predictably, are miniscule, Yet if present trends continue — and there seems to be no significant signs of change — let alone wild animals and birds but nature itself would perhaps only survive in these parks and sanctuaries.

The population of Asia excluding the USSR, has risen from approximately 1887 million in 1950 to about 4000 million by 1975, and is expected to reach 6350 million in 2000 A.D. The major increase, of course, is in south Asia, where the population is rising at the ratio of 2:1 in relation to economic growth, and the majority of the rural people are even today living below the subsistence level. India has over 180 million cattle and 60 million buffaloes, more than any country in the world. Can nations, in the face of such circumstances restrict, excessive exploitative practices and set aside more areas of arable land, man's most precious possession, for effective conservation? What future is there then for the fauna outside the national parks and sanctuaries? Can even these 'island' areas survive and save on a long term basis the majority of the species of plant and animal life that they purport to protect?

Today, in this region, only Bhutan has over 10 per cent of its land under national parks and sanctuaries. In most cases including Indonesia, Burma, Pakistan and Afghanistan, this is less than 2 per cent. Sri Lanka has about 9.3 per cent of her area under the protected areas system — but not all are national parks and sanctuaries. The average size of 41 of a total of 54 such protected areas is less than 50 sq. km and many are just one sq. km. Can they fulfill the purpose for which they were created?

The status and distribution of the tiger in India provides an interesting example, and a portent of future trends. Of the 1827 tigers enumerated in 1972, the 9 Tiger Reserves set up initially contained 268 tigers. By 1977 the number of tigers in these 9 had more than doubled to 612, while the total population in the country was estimated to have increased to 2484. Hence, while the increase in the 9 reserves was 344, that in the rest of the country was 313, which also was almost entirely in the other national parks and sanctuaries including the 2 Tiger Reserves subsequently created. By 1979 the tiger population in these 9 Reserves was reaching or had crossed the optimum holding capacity, and had risen to 658. In the meanwhile the count for the whole country had increased to 3015. This increase has very largely been in the national parks and sanctuaries other than the Reserves mentioned and which altogether, still comprise less than 15% of the total 'forest area' of the country. The remaining were mainly those tigers which had moved out of the parks and sanctuaries with the filling up of the niches and territories therein. What are their prospects? With the increased enforcement of the Wildlife (Protection) Act, 1972, and the cost of motor oil being what it is, 'White Collar' poaching has certainly reduced very considerably. So has poisoning of carnivores, with the cash compensations being paid for livestock killed. But habitat destruction is still going apace, the incidence of grazing has increased, and the wild ungulate populations are not increasing in most parts outside the parks and sanctuaries. So what are the options before a subadult tiger, especially a male, seeking his own home range. Either he remains within his natal area in an already crowded park or sanctuary and runs the risk of intraspecific aggression, the increased incidence of which is already coming to notice, or throw his lot with the area outside and subsist on livestock. It takes but one 'successful' poison consumption to do the trick for a troublesome tiger.

The case of the elephant is but a variation of this 'cat in the manger' syndrome. Large ranges are a prerequisite for their survival. Not only are these being increasingly denied, but edible crops are being grown at their doorstep, resulting in man-animal confrontation which does good neither to the elephant nor to the conservation movement. Their numbers in Uttar Pradesh increased from 350 in 1967 to 500 in 1976, but their habitat decreased from 2,55,000 ha to 1,74,000 ha during the same period (V.B. Singh 1978). Instances of poisoning of elephants and poaching for ivory are on the increase in the country. Studies in south India have shown how habitat fragmentation is decimating the elephants (Nair & Gadgil 1980). The large majority of the elephant population on the mainland of the Indian subcontinent, estimated at between 11 and 13 thousand by the Asian Elephant Specialist Group of the IUCN (1978), is outside of parks and sanctuaries, especially in the northeast. Those that are within these protected areas, need to move out periodically. Of all the wild mammalian species in south Asia the elephant is the most adversely affected by the insularization of protected areas.

Hangul (*Cervus elaphus hanglu*) is another animal which seasonally moves out of protected areas and whose predicament is far graver. From their winter quarters in the Dachigam Sanctuary they move to the neighbouring Sindh and Liddar valleys in spring, some going as far as Wardhwan and upper Kishtwar, which also are said to have a resident population. Their number in all likelihood is less than 200, and there is hardly an animal which has hovered on the brink of extinction so long, mainly because it is unsafe outside the sanctuaries. Their main summer abodes need the protection of newly established sanctuaries as it may not be feasible to extend the existing ones to cover the annual range of the animal. Before that, studies need to be made to determine the extent of the summer ranges. The long awaited montane national park in upper Kishtwar would be a great asset. Special protective staff need to be stationed at strategic points to cover the migration route in September, when the stags return to Dachigam for the autumn rut, giving away their presence by their unmistakable roars.

The mammals of the Himalaya and trans-Himalaya have suffered a greater decline than the peninsular fauna in the last 3 decades. This is primarily because of the lack of adequate number of viable and effectively protected parks and sanctuaries. Indeed, this has been the single greatest failure of the conservation movement in India in the way of establishment of protected areas. The remoteness, the lack of staff, the presence of graziers who depend upon the pasture, the harsh climate and the feeling, often not expressed but latent, that there is nothing really to protect there, have all contributed towards this predicament. The result is that of all the endangered mammals listed under Schedule I of the Indian Wildlife (Protection) Act whose main populations today are outside parks and sanctuaries, the montane ones are the most threatened.

Notable amongst them, are the Shapu (*Ovis vignei*), Tibetan antelope (*Pantholops hodgsoni*), Wild Yak (*Bos grunniens*), Tibetan gazelle (*Procapra picticaudata*), Mishmi Takin (*Budorcas taxicolor*), Pallas's cat (*Felis manul*). lynx (*Felis lynx isabellina*), snow leopard (*Panthera uncia*), Nayan, or Great Tibetan Sheep (*Ovis ammon hodgsoni*), musk deer (*Moschus moschiferus*), markhor (*Capra falconeri*) and the Red Panda (*Ailurus fulgens*). With the exception of the snow leopard, lynx, musk deer and the red panda, the other species are not protected in a single effective park or sanctuary.

The difference between what I saw in 1958 and those met with in 1970 in Ladakh, was startling. I barely saw any bharal (*Pseudois nayaur*) on the second trip; in 1958 they were almost ubiquitous. The Shapu, the yak, the Nayan, gazelle and the takin are on the verge of extinction in India, the others under serious threat.

Nepal has done better with the establishment of Sagarmatha and Langtang National Parks and the Shey and Lake Rara Sanctuaries. Pakistan has created the Khujerab National Park to protect with the other mountain fauna, the incomparable Marco Polo Sheep (*Ovis poli*). The greatest hope for Himalayan fauna, however, is in Bhutan, where the Jigme Dorji, Laya and Ghasa sanctuaries cover the entire northern portion of the country.

Consider the other larger mammals whose major populations are outside parks and sanctuaries. The number is the most from the north-east of the Indian subcontinent. The golden langur (*Presbytis geei*), the Pygmy hog (*Sus salvanius*) and the Hispid hare (*Caprolagus hispidus*) are found in only one safe area each — Manas and the contiguous Bhutan Manas. With the rapid sub-montane reduction of the high grasslands, and the regular burnings of the remnant ones, the hare and the hog may easily fade into oblivion. It is doubtful whether Manas alone can save them. Almost nothing is known of the present status and distribution of the golden cat (*Felis temmincki*) and that arboreal phantom of the forest, the clouded leopard (*Neofelis nebulosa*). They may occur in Chitwan and one or more sanctuaries in India, or they may not. Both are gravely endangered. With protection now being accorded viable remnant populations of the golden langur and of the lion-tailed macaque (*Macaca silenus*) exist in some sanctuaries. The hoolock gibbon (*Hylobates hoolock*) which is not so fortunate is perhaps the most threatened primate in India now. Again, little is known of their status.

In South India though the major populations of the Nilgiri tahr (*Hemitragus hylocrius*) are in parks and sanctuaries, sizeable populations exist outside, notably in the Anamalais and the High Wavy Mountains where the tahr, having been completely closed to hunting now, have lost their greatest guardians, the sport-loving tea and coffee planters. Nothing is known of the Malabar civet (*Viverra megaspila*). It is not reported from any park or sanctuary.

Of the Caracal (*Felis caracal*) also almost next to nothing is known. The surviving populations would be in areas outside parks and sanctuaries — Kutch, western Madhya Pradesh and eastern and southern Rajasthan.

With the destruction of habitat the problem is common to the other smaller cats — the marbled cat (*Felis marmorata*), the rusty spotted cat (*Felis rubiginosa*). Very little is known of their numbers and distribution and the major surviving population lives outside of parks and sanctuaries.

The same also held true till very recently with the three crocodilians found in the Indian subcontinent, and the gharial then was amongst the most endangered animals in this part of the world. With captive breeding and the creation of a number of reserves, the position is happily very greatly improved. However, as in the case of carnivores, the crocodiles moving out of sanctuaries and those released from captivity, will come in conflict with man with intensive fishing with nylon nets and destruction of nests. Their numbers outside crocodile sanctuaries can only increase substantially with regular captive breeding, which has had a very good beginning in India. The status of the other great reptile, the python (*Python molurus*), is causing concern. With habitat destruction, reduction of its natural prey, exploitation for the sake of skins and with no godfather to clamour for their interests, its position outside the protected areas is not secure.

One of the largest rookeries of marine turtles in the subcontinent has now been given the protection of a sanctuary on the Orissa coast. Elsewhere their nesting grounds are not secure, but the status of marine turtles in the Indian Ocean is far better than that of the freshwater turtles, terrapins and of the tortoises. The once common star-shelled tortoise, exploited for the pet trade and harmed perhaps by pesticide spraying and certainly by habitat destruction, is now rare. The Travancore tortoise (*Geochelone travancorica*), endemic to eastern Kerala and Coorg (The IUCN, 1982) is now declining in numbers. The even more restricted Kavalai forest turtle (*Heosemys silvatica*), the last specimen of which had been collected in 1911 in the Cochin forests of Kerala, has been rediscovered in the same locality. Extremely circumscribed in distribution, it urgently needs protection, its habitat not being in a park or sanctuary.

The position of some of the larger mammals whose populations are mainly outside the protected areas, is safer. Of the 22,500 to 24,500 blackbuck (*Antilope cervicapra*) estimated to survive in India at present, approximately 12,000 live inside the parks and sanctuaries and the rest without (Ranjitsinh 1982). They have survived because of the religious zeal and sentiments of the local people, the Bishnois, the Wala Kathis, the Vala Roppiats and others, and their main concentrations — Velavadar, Doli, and Tal chapar — were protected by these people long before they became sanctuaries. Even now sizeable populations live by the courtesy of religious sentiment — Sathin, Khejarli, Lohawat and Guda Bishnoia in Jodhpur district, Vetnoi and Purshottampur in Orissa, Botad in Saurashtra. The Chinkara (*Gazella bennetti*) severely reduced and threatened, also lives mainly outside of parks and sanctuaries and due almost entirely to religious sentiment and the remoteness of their remaining habitats. The largest concentration that survives today, which I estimated at over 2000 in 1974, is in the area around Jamobji, the main shrine of the Bishnois in western Rajasthan. The plains wolf (*Canis lupus pallipes*) too is found almost entirely outside parks and sanctuaries. Severely reduced, this resourceful animal, now very largely dependent upon livestock for its survival, is making a slow comeback in a number of areas, and reappearing in areas where it had disappeared in the recent past.

With the exception of Rannebenur in Karnataka, Karera and Ghatigaon in Madhya

Pradesh and the newly created Desert National Park in Rajasthan, the large majority of the world population of the great Indian bustard (*Choriotis nigriceps*) numbering 650 to 830 birds (Rahmani, *et al.* 1983), lives outside of parks and sanctuaries. The largest single concentration in a small area that is known of, Shakaliya in Ajmer district, is not a sanctuary, but is presently safe with favourable opinion and support of the local people. Elsewhere it has survived because of the remoteness of its habitat and the non-hunting habit of the local people, the numbers seem to have stablized at a low level. The bird, however, continues to be threatened by hunting, habitat destruction and disturbance, and the difficulties that its seasonal movements create towards the setting up of effective protected areas.

Equally endangered, by habitat destruction is the Bengal florican (*Eupodotis bengalensis*). Though its range in the subcontinent extends from the Uttar Pradesh Terai to eastern Assam, it is now being largely confined to the few scattered parks and sanctuaries in these alluvial grasslands. Unless short grass areas large enough to meet with their needs, and adequate protection to safeguard this very localised bird are provided, it will vanish outside the protected areas, a situation which seems most likely under the present circumstances. But perhaps the most threatened of the 21 species of the endangered bustard family of the world, and also its smallest member, is the exquisitely handsome lesser florican (*Sypheotides indica*). Endemic to the drier parts of western India, its habitats other than for the monsoon breeding period are unknown. This bird too occurs entirely outside parks and sanctuaries, other than the four sanctuaries in Madhya Pradesh, two of them just recently created. Shot and plagued by habitat modification, the bird is appearing in its breeding grounds in decreasing numbers, even in their former strongholds in Kutch and Saurashtra. In Wankaner in Saurashtra, despite the excellent rains this year, four were found in areas which traditionally should have harboured at least 20. It is possible that adverse factors are affecting their other non-monsoon grounds.

Habitat destruction has also affected the resident white-winged wood duck (*Cairina scutulata*) in India, Bangladesh as well as in Southeast Asia. They frequent perennial streams lined with large shady trees, flowing for some length in disturbance-free forest areas, a tall order these days. There are no existing parks or sanctuaries in their habitat and the bird is still left to the mercy of the local people.

The most endangered member of that other threatened group, the tragopan pheasants, is Blyth's (*Tragopan blythi*) with its variation *T.b. molesworthi*. Endemic to Nagaland, Manipur and the adjacent areas of Burma, there is no safe haven for them in those lands of inveterate hunters and shifting cultivation. In the western Himalayas, the status of the endangered cheer pheasant (*Catreus wallichi*) and of the Western tragopan (*Tragopan melanocephalus*) is not precisely known, but the populations do not appear to be increasing.

The oceanic islands present a different dilemma. The remoteness, the relative lack of demographic pressures in some, the impression of idylic unspoilt paradises, inculcate a feeling of lethargic security. In 1973 after an extensive tour I had submitted a report recommending protected areas. Till now almost none has been set up. The Narcondam hornbill (*Rhyticeros narcondami*), endemic only to this volcanic island, is safe today because of the terrain and its remoteness. But that is no reason why no sanctuary should be established. Will not lumber felling commence someday otherwise?

Two birds which may soon become the most

threatened with extinction in this part of the world, are the Andaman teal (*Anas andamanensis*) and the Nicobar megapode (*Megapodius freycinet*), the only member of the family west of the Wallace line. The Andaman teal inhabits freshwater lakes, which are both few and the first to receive human settlements on their shores, in the Andaman Archipelago. I only saw one flock in a small lake on the Little Andaman Island in 1973. Some of these lakes like this and the one on Neil Island need to have sanctuaries established. Unlike the white-winged wood duck, the Andaman teal has not bred in captivity in the Slimbridge Wildfowl Trust. The megapode, which builds its conspicuous, large mounds in the lowland areas of the main Nicobar Islands, would have to deal with human settlements in their habitats, and it is doubtful whether man or his dogs will spare the nests.

A sanctuary needs also to be established in the Great Rann of Kutch, where the largest breeding colony of the greater and lesser flamingos (Phoenicopteridae) in Asia occurs. Pelicans also breed there. The same argument which has till now prevented the establishment of a protected area there — the place is already safe; who goes there — was also trotted out when I was trying to persuade the Gujarat Government to set up a sanctuary in the Little Rann for the wild ass (*Equus hemionus khur*). If conservation does not go to the area, something else will someday. Besides, with the finding of substantial numbers of the wild ass in the Great Rann for the first time during the ennumeration this year, and the lesson from the anti-locust pesticide spraying which washes down into the salt pans and must destroy the crustaceous and other food chain of the flamingos, should be incentives now to the setting up a sanctuary in the Great Rann.

With the failure on the mountain front, the second non-performance of the conservation effort in India is in the way of marine protected areas. Protective efforts have been made in the coral-rich Pirotan Island off the Jamnagar coast in Saurashtra. But nowhere has a marine park come up, not even to protect the magnificent coral bed of Krusadai and Shingle islands off Rameshwaram coast. The corals, the fish fauna and the dugong (*Dugong dugon*) continue to be exploited all along the Indian coast and around the Laccadives.

Lest all the above should give the impression of failure on the part of the decision makers in India and read like a catalogue of candidates for extinction, it must be stated in all fairness that conservation has made a greater headway in this country than any other in southern Asia. The obstacles that have to be surmounted in implementing appropriate conservation policies and programmes, are unparalleled for their magnitude. In some cases the state governments concerned have already brought the entire or major portions of the habitats of remnant populations of endangered fauna under parks and sanctuaries, and it is very difficult to obtain others. In the state of Madhya Pradesh over 12% of its forest area and 5% of the total area is covered under these two categories of protected areas.

There is, however, in some quarters a sense of euphoria, of having settled issues for all time to come when in reality only time has been bought. There is often a reluctance to set up new sanctuaries and parks when experience is proving over and yet over again that fauna and its habitat have a long-term assured future, with but a few exceptions, in these areas alone. There is even a feeling that the areas already notified are enough. I think it should be evident to all that nature reserves that are created in the current decade may well be the last to be created in India.

The approach, however, must be different. The play in the past has been to get areas for the animals; the strategy henceforth should be to get the areas with the animals, ecosystems and watersheds for the sake of man.

Studies in island biogeography and colonization, extinction and survival of species therein, have revealed some very dramatic evidence. With the nature reserves increasingly becoming insular islands with modification of the surrounding areas, these data could well be of relevance. If the majority of the habitat is destroyed and a fraction of the area is saved as a reserve, the reserve will initially contain more species than it can hold at equilibrium. The excess will gradually become extinct. If only 10% of the area occupied as a habitat is saved for a reserve in a contiguous and composite form, approximately half the number of species found in the preserved habitat may survive in it. The smaller and more isolated the reserve, the higher the rates of extinction (Diamond 1975). The highest extinction percentage will be of species whose initial populations were of fewer individuals either because the species is a carnivore, or because it has a specialized habitat requirement, or because it is a large animal (Brown 1971).

The above statements are of relevance to those reserves which still have a 'buffer'. It would be wise to add wherever possible to the existing buffers which surround notified sanctuaries and national parks. A 'buffer' has no legal relevance anyway.

But there must always remain large habitat areas outside of parks and sanctuaries. What must be the approach there? Game farming is a suggestion often put forth. It has not been a form of land use that has had an auspicious beginning on this subcontinent, for reasons obvious to all. But that does not imply that it has no potential whatsoever. Even if African prototype may be difficult to establish in this region, there are other approaches. To cite but some examples, the harvesting of marine turtle eggs, if scientifically implemented, would be certainly feasible and could become a very valuable protein diet resource. The fur export of Kashimir alone is valued at some 60 million rupees annually (Mir Inayat Ullah, *pers. comm.*).

In the Reserve and Protected forests a more appropriate land-use practice would have to be adopted if these forests and rangelands are to remain productive and be able to contribute to the national economy. Over-grazing and over-exploitation would have to be stopped ultimately. The managers of these lands must also alter the priorities and attitudes. The pride and job satisfaction must enumerate what they have been able to save and to raise in the way of forest wealth, not what they have been able to raise at the annual auctions. If the land-use is improved, the fauna will survive and perhaps even thrive. If not, then we shall have barren hills and a sterile land and far more fauna lost.

As would be evident, the so-called 'buffer' zones and habitats around the parks and sanctuaries would now constitute as a class the most important conservation units outside of the protected areas. It would be into these areas that the excess carnivores and even herbivores would move into. These areas, if adequately safeguarded, would prevent the biological and ecological isolation of the parks and sanctuaries, and in case this does happen, provide at least 'land bridges' to other habitats. Here the involvement and support of the local people would play a most crucial part. These are the major areas of 'conflict' with the people, and they highlight most of all the third world problems and the greatest failure of the conservation effort in India—the failure to obtain popular support to conservation, especially of the rural people most affected.

Albeit, it is very difficult. But has a serious attempt been made on a wide scale? The approach of the park managers is often of "us" *versus* "they" — the insiders *versus* the outsiders. There are reasons for such an approach, some of them valid. But will such a policy pay lasting dividends? As Norman Myers (1982) says, all forms of land use, especially their administrators, need to maintain cordial relations with their neighbours: if neighbours are treated as enemies they may start to behave as enemies. The park manager may find it worthwhile to spend more time in dealing with the lands and peoples outside his boundary, than in 'developing' his charge. In the words of Aldo Leopold "Development is a job not of building roads into lovely country, but of building receptivity, into the still unlovely human mind".

SELECT BIBLIOGRAPHY

DASMANN, R, (1975): National parks, nature conservation, and "future primitive". *Ecologist* **6**(5): 164-167.

DIAMOND, J.M., (1975): The island dilemma: lessons of modern biogeographic studies for the design of natural reserves. *Biol. Conserv.* (7): 129-146.

BROWN, J.H., (1971): Mammals on mountaintops: nonequilibrium insular biogeography. *Am. Nat.* **105**: 467-478

IUCN, The 1982. The Amphibia — Reptilia Red Data Book. Part I, Gland, Switz.

MYERS, N. (1982): Eternal values of the parks movement and the Monday morning world. Paper for Session VII C, World National Parks Congress, Bali.

NAIR, P.V., GADGIL, M. (1980): The status and distribution of elephant populations of Karnataka. *J. Bombay nat. Hist. Soc. vol.* **75** supplement.

RANJITSINH, M.K. (1978): Wildlife conservation and development. *Cheetal,* Vol. **19** (4): 7-16.

________(1979): Forest destruction in Asia and the South Pacific. *Ambio,* Vol. VIII (5): 192-201.

________(1980): The tiger in the twenty-first century. *Tigerpaper,* FAO, Vol. VII (1) 1-3.

________(1982): Ecology and behaviour of the Indian blackbuck (*Antilope cervicapra* Linn.): With special reference to the Velavadar national park, Saurashtra, India, Ph.D. dissertation. 290.

SINGH, V.B. (1978): The elephant in Uttar Pradesh, (India)—re-survey of their status after 10 years. *J. Bombay nat. Hist. Soc.* **75**(1): 71-82.

Forests and Forest Policy in Northwest India since 1800

A.J. GASTON
Canadian Wildlife Service, Ottawa KIA OE7, Canada

ABSTRACT

Recent interest in the state of forests in India has given the impression of a precipitous decline in forest cover over the whole country during the past few decades. Examination of the writings of British forest officials during the second half of the nineteenth century does not support this conclusion as far as the Western Himalayas are concerned. Instead it seems likely that in this area the extent of forests has changed only moderately over the past 150 years, despite periods of rapid forest destruction associated with the laying down of the Indian railways and with incendiarism protesting British rule in India.

Awareness of the environmental impact of forest destruction seems to have been high among forest officers in the last century, but political constraints probably prevented this awareness from being translated into adequate forest protection and re-afforestation. Insufficient notice seems to have been taken of factors retarding forest regeneration so that plans consistently over-estimated the amount of forest being replaced. A combination of these factors probably led to a gradual deterioration of forest cover during the period of British rule, despite better motives on the part of forest officials than are frequently ascribed to them.

If there has been no recent abrupt change in forest cover, how can we account for recent accelerations in siltation rates and flooding along Himalayan rivers? These may be caused by destruction of shrubs and ground vegetation in the forest as a result of over-grazing by domestic animals. In seeking to reduce soil erosion and flooding we must ensure protection for all vegetation layers. Simply maintaining tree cover may not, in itself, be sufficient.

INTRODUCTION

A great deal has been written in recent years on the state of India's forests (Roy 1978, Eckholm 1979, Gupta and Bandhu 1979, Baig 1980, Gribbin 1982, Manohar 1982). The general concensus is that forest cover in India has been diminishing rapidly at least since Indian independence and probably earlier. Particular concern has been expressed over deforestation of the Himalayas because of drastic consequences for the adjacent plains (Gupta and Bandhu 1979, Moddie 1981).

Responsibility for the diminution of forests is generally placed on State forest departments, which have the job of managing the nation's forest wealth. Forest officials are frequently accused of being solely interested in producing revenue, rather than considering the whole environment (Kayastha and Juyal 1979, Baig 1980). This attitude is believed to have originated with the former British administration (Raina 1979, Patel 1980, Centre for Science and Environment 1982).

Deforestation of the Himalayas is believed to be a primary cause of increased soil erosion and consequent rapid siltation of reservoirs in the Himalayan foothills (Kayastha and Juyal 1979, Moddie 1981, Centre for Science and Environment 1982). Other undesirable consequences attributed to deforestation are an increased incidence of flooding in the adjacent plains and reduced flow of rivers during the dry season (Bhasin *et al.* 1979, Rieger 1981, Centre for Science and Environment 1982).

The current outburst of interest in India's forests and their associated problems gives the impression that deforestation and its results are a fairly recent phenomenon in India. By examining evidence of former forest distribution,

P-16

records of felling, statements of forest policy, and comments of early British forest officials in India I have tried to assemble evidence on the progress of forest management and trends in forest cover over the past 150 years, particularly in the Western Himalayas.

PROGRESS OF DEFORESTATION

For the period prior to 1870 I have relied heavily on Stebbing's (1922) historical survey of the Indian forests. During this period two important forest surveys were carried out in the Western Himalayas; by Longden in 1851-53 and by Cleghorn (1864) in 1862-63. During the past ten years I have been able to visit practically all parts of the Indian Himalayas visited by Cleghorn and have therefore been able to compare my own impressions with his written account. For the period from 1870-1900 I have examined Forest Department reports and the Indian Forester. For later periods most of my information came from Forest Department working plans. I have not attempted to deal with the period subsequent to Indian independence.

Social, economic and political aspects of forest policy and its effects in the Western Himalayas have been dealt with by Tucker (1983). I shall concentrate here on the environmental lessons that can be learnt from the history of West Himalayan forests and the implications for future management of the problems associated with deforestation.

Forest cover in prehistoric times

Prior to the initiation of agriculture in India, perhaps 5-6000 years B.P., forests probably covered most of the land area (Puri 1965, Whyte 1968). Exceptions possibly occurred in low-lying seasonally flooded or frost-prone areas where grasslands may have constituted a climax vegetation (Whyte 1968). It is clear from the descriptions of the epics (Mahabarata, Ramayana) that even at the period when these accounts were being formalized (*c.* 800 B.C., Van Buitenen 1973) forest cover was very extensive in lowland India. However, the attitude towards forests at that period is exemplified by the story in the Mahabarata (Book 1.19, Van Buitenen 1973) of the burning of the Khandava forest, which surely reflects similar deliberate forest destruction taking place in many areas at that time to make way for agriculture. In the Indo-Gangetic plain settlements, agriculture and hence presumably forest clearance, were widespread by 4000 B.P. (Allchin and Chakrabarti 1979). Evidence for settlements in the temperate zone of the Western Himalayas goes back at least 1500 years (Goetz 1969) and we can probably assume that early encroachments in this area began at least 2000 years B.P.

The establishment of a forest policy in India

With the development of British power in India during the 18th and 19th centuries the management and exploitation of India's timber resources became a concern of the colonial administration. By the mid-19th century the State of India's timber resources was giving rise to concern, as the development of infrastructure in the form of railways, bridges, buildings and wood-burning industries began to make inroads on the forests. As early as 1842 a reafforestation programme was initiated at Nilambur in Kerala to redress losses of teak *Tectona grandis* (Anon. 1920), one of the most popular Indian timbers for building and furniture-making.

Early attempts to map India's forest resources show that by the mid-19th century the distribution of commercially exploitable timber was essentially the same as is seen today. The main forest blocks occurred along the crest of the Western Ghats and through the hilly areas of the northern Deccan, in Madhya Pradesh, western Orissa and southern Bihar; in a belt along the Himalayan foothills and extending into the mountains to the limit of tree growth;. and in the northeast, where the largest single block of virgin forests were found in Assam and adjacent States and Burma (Baden-Powell 1874).

By the middle of 19th century there was a general appreciation within the British administration that something was seriously wrong with India's forests. This led to the announcement, in 1855, of a forest policy for British India, followed by the setting up of a forest department, and the appointment, in 1863, of an Inspector General of forests.

Three trees were regarded initially as being the most important for commercial exploitation:— the teak of the southern and central Deccan; the Sal (*Shorea robusta*) of the Himalayan foothills and eastern Deccan; and the Deodhar Cedar (*Cedrus deodara*) of the West Himalayan temperate zone. British policy in its early stages was directed principally at maintaining sufficient stocks of these three species (Baden-Powell 1874). At the same time, particularly before the advent of large-scale coal mining in India, maintenance of sufficient stocks of fuel-wood for the steam locomotives of the railways, was also given a high priority. In the 1860's extensive fuel-wood plantations of native leguminous trees (*Acacia* spp.) were initiated at Changa-Manga (now in Pakistan) to replace losses from the forests of Lahore, Gujranwala and Jhilam (Jhelum) districts used to supply the Calcutta-Lahore railway (Pearson 1872a).

Demarcation of forests and definition of local grazing and timber rights was carried out as an important part of the land settlements that continued throughout the 19th century in British India. Forests were classed either as 'reserved', with all activities controlled (in theory) by the forest department, 'protected', in which local rights were enshrined, and unprotected, where no control was exercised by the forest department (Anon. 1920). In the Himalayas protection forests maintained to preserve soil and water were designated as reserved, and most other commercially useful forest was classed as protected. However, local rights were often extensive and included the right to fell timber for building.

Right from the start of forest management in India there was friction between the forest service and the local forest contractors who actually felled and supplied the timber at the government's behest. Methods employed in the Western Himalayas were condemned by practically all the British officials who witnessed them. Lord William Hay, writing in 1860 (quoted by Cleghorn 1864) gives a graphic description of timber operations in temperate coniferous forests around Simla:

> "The woodcutter enters, fells many trees and damages many others by the tree falling down a steep slope, the branches not having been cut off. A heap of chips and debris remains which takes fire, by accident or otherwise; the villagers send their cattle for pasturage and in a very few years some scattered pines are all that remain of a once flourishing forest"

Even where felling was carried out economically there was a tremendous wastage in transport. Baden-Powell (1874) estimated that only 1 in 10 of the logs cut in the Himalayas actually reached the potential users in the plains, the rest being rotted, splintered or pilfered in transit. This applied particularly to areas outside British control (Kashmir, Chamba), where the contractors generally carried out their work without any supervision. The general distrust of private forest contractors has persisted to the present and culminated recently in the formation, in many States, of State Forest Corporations; public monopolies to run all aspects of the forest industry.

Development of awareness of the environmental role of forests

By the second half of the 19th century the philosophy of Indian Forest Service had noticeably shifted from commercial exploitation towards conservation. Baden-Powell (1877a) notes that protection of soil and water resources should be the primary aim of forest demarcation in the Himalayas, recommending that all headwater areas, as well as feeder streams, and all slopes of more than 50° should be exempt from felling. He also recommended a system of local management with forest revenues going to local people which appears remarkably prescient in the light of recent calls for 'social forestry'. This recommendation was never implemented. However, the designation of large areas in major river catchments as reserved forest illustrates the importance attached to protection at the time of original forest demarcations, which took place in the Western Himalayas mainly between 1860-1900 (Barnes 1862, Trevor 1921, Walters 1922, Glover 1927).

Soil erosion and ravine formation were recognized as major problem in the silt-covered plains of Uttar Pradesh by Brandis (1885) who recommended the re-afforestation of 100,000 acres of wasteland and ravines in Etawah District. Courthope (1915) calculated that ravines had been encroaching in Etawah District at a rate of 2.5% of total land area per century for the past 400 years. Benskin (1922) chronicled the success of the reclamation works which recovered about 100,000 acres of ravines over forty years. Despite this success, however, he noted that "there is scarcely a tree (in U.P.) between the Himalayan terai and the Satpuras".

This was in an area which, at the time of Akbar (16th century), was a well-forested hunting ground. Benskin also noted that evidence from past settlement patterns suggested a considerable lowering of the mean water level in the River Jumna over the previous 400 years, which he attributed to deforestation in the headwaters, although by this time extensive canal irrigation upstream may also have affected matters. In any case, the lowering of the river level was a powerful cause of ravine erosion which continues to expand (Baig 1980).

The role of forests in mitigating downstream floods was well known by the mid-19th century as a result of work in Europe. Warth (1880) stated: "...damage done by floods may be diminished by creating and improving forests on hitherto more or less barren hill tracts".

He also drew attention to the fact that, although most people agreed with his statement, such policies were rarely implemented because it was not of any direct value to anyone to do so. This theme crops up also in relation to other forest problems.

Interest in the environmental consequences of forest policies extended to the influence of forest cover on local climates. The Government of India instituted an inquiry into this subject in 1906 which tried to relate records of rainfall and flooding to changes in forest cover. No relationship was found between climate and forest cover, but evidence was acquired to show that loss of forest cover led to increased run-off and consequent downstream flooding. The report also testifies that a considerable contraction in forest area had taken place over the previous 50 years (Hills 1916). Over the whole of British territories at that time (including Pakistan, Bangladesh and Burma) the proportion of land supporting forest was estimated as 15%. This is not very different from various recent estimates for India which range from 11% (Patel 1980, Manohar 1982, Centre for Science and Environment 1982) to the 'official' figure of 23% (Chopra 1975).

Events with a major impact on forests in Northwest India

During the British period the need for timber increased dramatically; particularly for railway sleepers. Deodar was considered the best timber for sleepers, lasting an average of 20 years; about twice the life of Pine or Sal ('A.S.' 1896). This tree is common in the Western Himalayas but not dominant (Champion and Seth 1968). Pure stands suitable for commercial exploitation are local, being found particularly in the upper valleys of the major rivers; Sutlej, Jumna, Beas, Ravi and Chenab (Cleghorn 1864). Very large numbers of these trees were exported during the period of rapid expansion of the railways in northern India during 1850-1870.

Some sample statistics given by Cleghorn (1864) show the impact of the railways' requirements. In 1861, 14,000 and in 1862, 18,000 logs were floated down the Ravi, probably about half of the deodars of suitable size then standing. In Bashahr, on the Sutlej, 6000 deodar trees were cut in 1861 (reported by R.J. Strong), while between 1853-1863, 74,000 first class (more than 2 ft. D.B.H.) trees were felled in Pangi (upper Chenab, in Chamba State) and Cleghorn notes: "It is obvious that no forest in the world can bear such excessive cutting".

By 1874 Baden-Powell (1874) was writing that the forests of the Ravi were exhausted and even in 1896 McDonell (1896) reports an absence of commercial timber in that area.

Timber for the Lahore-Peshawar segment of the northern railway came mainly from the Ravi, Chenab and Jhelum valleys, the latter in the independent state of Kashmir. Pearson (1877a) was so distressed at the damage caused by the felling techniques of local contractors in Kashmir that he urged opening up reserved forests in British India instead to mitigate the damage that increased run-off from the catchment areas would have in the Punjab plains (part of British India).

For the Rajputana railway deodar sleepers came mainly from the area around the headwaters of the Ganges, in U.P. About 10,000 trees providing 270,000 sleepers were felled around Gangotri, while another 45,000 Sal sleepers came from Kumaon and Garhwal (Pearson 1872b). Much of the timber used on railway lines in Uttar Pradesh at this period came from the Gogra, Gandak and Kosi valleys in Nepal (Pearson 1872a). By 1872 Baden-Powell was recommending the use of creosoted Chil Pine (*Pinus roxburghii*) instead of deodar for sleepers, apparently because of a dearth of deodar.

Following the great assault on West Himalayan forests caused by the initial expansion of the Indian railways there seems to have been a period of retrenchment. Some pressure on timber resources was alleviated by the decline of the indigenous iron smelting industry which flourished in the 18th and early 19th centuries at Kotkhai, Hatkoti, Mandi, Shil and other centres in the Tons, Giri and Sutlej valleys. Charcoal for smelting is estimated to have required 2800 trees annually at Bir alone (Stebbing 1922).

In the Himalayan front ranges at altitudes from 1500-2500 more forest was cleared for temperate agriculture; particularly potatoes and fruit orchards. On the Mahasu ridge, near

Simla, large areas of oaks (*Quercus dilata* and *Q. incana*) were felled in the 1860's to make room for potatoes, but by 1881 the soil was exhausted and a programme of re-afforestation was undertaken jointly by the British and Patiala authorities which provided most of the, mainly coniferous forest that now adorns the area. Other clearances at the same period, which were later abandoned, may not have regenerated since.

Oaks also fared badly in the hills of Uttar Pradesh where they were reported much diminished by 1916 due to 'impecuniosity of the zamindars and improvidence of the raiyots' (Hills 1916). In other words, everyone wished to exploit the forests, and no one gained from protecting them. The tendency for oaks and deodars to be replaced after clear felling by Blue Pine (*Pinus excelsa*) was noted by D'Arcy (1887) and Gorrie (1936). Although oaks probably form the climatic climax vegetation over most of the temperate zone in the Western Himalayas there are at present only small areas of pure oak forest remaining (Gaston *et al.* 1983).

Some more positive events were occurring at the same period. Cleghorn (1864) noted that, during his visit in 1862, the only pure stands of deodars in the Upper Beas valley were along the right bank of the river above Manali. This forest has entirely disappeared and the area now supports only rough pasture. However, during the 1880's Duff, the local conservator, established large plantations of deodars nearby, which form the magnificent forest stands which surround the modern Manali bazaar. A comparison of modern forest maps of the Kulu Valley with one provided by Cleghorn (1864) suggests that there has been little change in the area covered by forest in the interim, although the distribution has changed in some cases. Similarly, comparison of the present distribution of forest in Brahmaur district, on the upper Ravi, with maps prepared by D'Arcy (1887) suggests that the extent of forests has not altered much in that area either.

In 1921 forests in the Western Himalayas suffered another important setback. According to Wright (1917, quoted in Gorrie 1936), a rumour circulated throughout the hills that the Congress Party, led at that time by Mahatma Gandhi, had suggested the burning of State forests as part of a civil disobedience campaign. Apparently, the rumour was untrue, but before it was countermanded a huge outbreak of incendiarism had occurred which, coming at a period of prolonged drought, caused enormous damage. In Mandi District 37,000 acres of demarcated forests, about 30% of the total, were burnt (Gorrie 1936). Kulu lost 65,000 acres, more than three-fourths of all the fire damage during the period 1905-1930 (Samler 1935), while a third of the forests in Kotkai and Kotgarh ranges were also burnt (Glover 1927). The incendiarism also extended to Kangra, Chopal and Nahan and the hill districts of Uttar Pradesh (Tucker 1983). Setting fire to public forests seems to have been a traditional form of protest. Stewart (quoted by Henniker-Gotley 1932) claims that the forests of the Kagan valley (in Pakistan) in the late 19th century still bore the scars of fires set at the onset of the British administration in that area (1849). In Uttar Pradesh large-scale incendiarism occurred early this century in response to the demarcation of reserved forest (Joshi 1979).

The Second World War created a sharp increase in demand for timber in India and felling within government forests was accelerated to meet it (Kayastha and Juyal 1979). Much of the timber was Sal from the foothills zone of the Himalayas. Further destruction of these forests occurred during the resettlement of refugees after the partition of India and Pakistan in

1947. The *terai* of sub-Himalayan foothills had been sparsely populated throughout historic times because of endemic malaria and still supported large areas of Sal forest. In India many refugees were allowed to take over land in this area and considerable areas of forest were cleared and settled, a process abetted by the introduction of measures to control malaria (Das 1979).

Chronic problems affecting Indian forests

By and large the chronic problems affecting forests in India have been well described by others (Ekholm 1979, Gupta and Bandhu 1979, Baig 1980, Centre for Science and Environment 1982). I would like merely to confirm that these are long-standing problems that have been recognized for many years. One of these is the problem of deliberate burning practised in many areas to provide the growth of fresh grass. A conference held at Simla in 1875 was almost entirely devoted to the problem of preventing forest fires. Brandis, in his opening address, claimed that "a very large proportion of the reserves (forest) are not better than ... vast extents of blanks with here and there groups of scrub and trees. The main cause of this ... are the jungle fires of the hot season. For the improvement of these forests there is no measure which equals fire conservancy in importance" (Brandis and Smythies 1876).

More recently, fire as a hazard to lowland forest has probably diminished somewhat because, with the general fuel-wood crisis in India, people range everywhere to collect the slightest scrap of combustible material and undergrowth fires are therefore less fierce, feeding only on small amounts of dry leaves and grasses.

The problem of grazing by domestic animals also has a long history. The control of grazing in reserved forests was a major issue in land settlements. Grazing rights were established over certain forest areas and totally excluded from certain classes of reserved forest. It is clear, however, that though the policy was sound, the practice was faulty. In 1921 Trevor (1921) writing of the forests in Kulu reported: "During the past fifty years no regeneration of any sort has become established in many of the fir forests of Upper Kulu ... it is only a question of years before their destruction is complete. Such management makes the closure to grazing of all areas under concentrated regeneration a matter of compulsion. Without such closure nothing can be done ... should this fail the whole structure of the (forest working) plan falls to pieces".

Trevor identified the major weakness of forest plans in India. Estimates of forest yield made by forest officers have often assumed automatic regeneration of felled forests. In practice this has rarely occurred. The reason is almost certainly the huge density of domestic animals; about 350 million all told, including 230 million cows and buffaloes. This population has been increasing more or less at the same rate as the human population, with a 33% increase between 1945 and 1966 (Chopra 1975). The animals browse the young tree seedlings before they can become established. Most trees cannot withstand even moderate grazing before they are at least five years old (Baden-Powell 1877, Samler 1935).

Recent examination of forests in Kulu District shows a similar picture to that painted by Trevor. Large areas of mature or over-age forest show no sign at all of natural regeneration (Gaston *et al.* 1983). The current plans of the forest department rely almost entirely on replanting to grow new trees. Not only is there no sign of forest regeneration. In many areas the shrub and ground layer, even in well-preserved, demarcated forests, is very sparse, leaving large areas of bare soil. Like the lack of tree seedlings, this seems to be the result of heavy grazing by domestic animals, which penetrate everywhere in the forest.

Fagan (1885) notes that over large areas of the Deccan closure to grazing was prevented in order to obtain the revenue paid by graziers. He condemns this short-sighted policy and shows that the value of timber which would grow if grazing was excluded would much exceed the revenue obtained from grazing. From a social perspective, his argument was flawed because it considered only the profit to the State, not taking into account the welfare of the graziers themselves. His point was valid, however, insofar as it indicated the difficulty of establishing true economic criteria for forest management.

DISCUSSION

Changes in forest cover in the Western Himalayas

A review of the evidence from early British forest officials does not support the contention that there has been a recent rapid decline in the extent of forest cover in the Northwest Himalayas. On the contrary, it appears that the extent of forest cover at least in the temperate zone of the Western Himalayas, has changed only moderately in the last 100 years, after the onslaught of felling for railway construction in the mid-19th century. The importance of this period, too, must be seen in perspective. Practically all the timber removed was deodar, which probably never covered more than 20% of the temperate zone and some was subsequently replaced by replanting. In areas such as the Kulu Valley there is as much or more deodar now than there was in Cleghorn's time.

Some very fragmentary information on the state of forests in the Western Himalayas before the arrival of the British can be obtained from paintings published by Frazer (1820) who accompanied an expedition of Sikh troops on a campaign in the hill areas of Uttar Pradesh and Himachal Pradesh against the Gurkhas. Although the majority of areas depicted cannot be identified, those that can show scenery remarkably similar to that found today. Through the kindness of Penelope Chetwode I was able to examine two of the plates (of Sarahan and Manan in the Sutlej Valley) beside photographs that she had taken from the identical view point. If anything, the recent pictures actually show more forest cover than Frazer's. Taken as a whole, the collection of 20 plates suggests that the Himalayan front ranges at that date supported very little forest and were typically covered in grass.

If the temperate zone of the Western Himalayas had suffered extensive deforestation by the early 19th century then the same probably applied to lowland India. Rather than a recent and catastrophic denudation of the landscape it seems more realistic to assume that the current state of forests in India is the result of processes that have been continuous for many centuries.

Implications for the role of vegetation in soil conservation and flood control

If there has been no recent rapid decline in forest cover in the Western Himalayas, what has caused the recent acceleration of siltation in the foothill reservoirs and the increased incidence of floods on the Himalayan rivers? Two answers to the question are possible. The first is that changes in siltation and flooding have been less severe than is popularly supposed. The second is that the lower layers of the forest vegetation have been reduced by heavy grazing, leading to increased soil erosion and run-off, despite the maintenance of fairly constant tree cover. If this is true, then we should treat over-grazing within the forest on a par with deforestation in causing environmental damage. The simple idea that clothing the mountains in trees will alleviate floods and erosion should be tempered with the realization that other vegetation layers may be equally important. Policies for flood and erosion control should try to preserve as much vegetation cover as possible, whether it be trees, shrubs or grass. This can only be done through strict control of grazing.

Political constraints on forest conservation

A second conclusion that is inescapable from the writings of early Indian foresters is that the recognition of a problem by people within the forest service was not sufficient to lead to a solution. Presumably this failure was the result of political realities. The feeling that the political wing of the British administration viewed the needs of forest conservancy with some distaste is clearly indicated by the foreword to the "Working Plan of the Chamba leased forests" in which the responsible Secretary to the Government of the Punjab notes: "(Forest regulations) produce at times a very formidable feeling of discontent and irritation among the people ... Every effort should be made to avoid imposing any restriction which is not really necessary for some definite purpose" (Tupper *in* D'Arcy 1887).

It is easy to imagine that opinions on what constituted a "really necessary" measure might have differed between foresters and their political bosses. Baden-Powell (1877b) made this clear when he accused the government of weakness towards enforcing forest regulations. Such differences may well be at the root of the continued deterioration in Indian forests that took place during the British period.

To further illustrate the lag between the appreciation of forest problems and the application of solutions I should quote Sir M. Visvesvaraya who made the following prescient statement in his presidential address to the 10th Indian Science Congress in 1924: "The world supplies of coal and oil which represent the conservation of solar energy of former ages are diminishing; the use of solar energy by means of sun engines is not yet commercially feasible and the best known way of utilizing solar energy for further use is by the cultivation of trees of rapid growth" (Parker 1925).

Notwithstanding this well-informed suggestion it has taken nearly 60 years for the idea to be put into practice in India on a large scale.

Trevor's (1921) complaint that assumptions about regeneration were unjustified stems from the same root cause. Regeneration did not occur because grazing was not controlled as the regulations demanded. This was either because civil authorities were reluctant to proceed with prosecutions, or because insufficient funds were allotted for wardening. In either case the decisions were political; the situation remains the same today.

Finally, Worth's (1880) statement that sensible policies such as reafforestation to prevent downstream flooding were not pursued because no one person stood to profit from them rings very true today. The forest contractors damaged the forest beause it belonged to the government. The forest services were judged on the timber that was standing, and gained nothing from replanting slopes that could not be harvested in their life-time. The graziers ignored restrictions because they gained nothing from forest regeneration. None of this appears to have changed (Eckholm 1979, Baig 1980, Rieger 1981). If reafforestation is to be achieved on a large scale in India the attitudes of all those involved; forest officials, guards, contractors and local people, and their motivation towards preserving the forest, will be the crucial ingredients for success.

ACKNOWLEDGEMENTS

I would like to thank P. Garson, P. Phillimore, M. Ridley, and R. Tucker for helpful comments on this manuscript. I am very grateful to Lady P. Betjeman for showing me Frazer's book and for many stimulating discussions on the Western Himalayas.

REFERENCES

ALLCHIN, F.R. & CHAKRABARTI, D.K. (1979): A source book of Indian archaeology, Vol. 1. New Delhi, Munshiram Manoharlal.

ANON. (1920): The work of the Forest Department in India. London, H.M. Stationary Office.

A.S. (1896): Durability of railway sleepers. *Indian Forester* **22**(6):232-233.

BADEN-POWELL, B.H. (1872): Annual report on the Punjab forest administration for 1871-72. Appendix D (56 + xv pp.). *In* Report on the administration of the Forest Department in the several provinces under the Government of India, 1871-72, ed. by G.F. Pearson, Appendix D. Calcutta, Government of India.

______ (1874): Report of the administration of the Forest Department, 1872-73, Vol. 1. Calcutta, Government of India.

____ (1877a): Note on the demarcation of the forest area in districts containing hill or mountain ranges. *Indian Forester* **2**(3):239-265.

____ (1877b): The political value of forest conservancy. ibid.**2**(3):281-287.

BAIG, M.A. (1980): Plundering the forests. *India Today*. March-April.

BARNES, G.C. (1862): Report on the settlement in the District of Kangra. Lahore, Hope Press.

BENSKIN, E. (1922): Afforestation in the United Provinces, India. Allahabad, U.P. Government Press.

BHASIN, V., BHASIN, M.K. & SINGH, I.P. (1979): People and forests of Bharmaur Tehsil, Chamba, Himachal Pradesh. *In* Ecology and Development, ed. by D. Bandhu and V. Bhardwaj, 247-254. New Delhi, Indian Environmental Society.

BRANDIS, D. (1885): Mr. Brandis' work in the N.W. provinces and Oudh. *Indian Forester* **11**(4):147-158.

____ & SMYTHIES, A. (1876): Report of the proceedings of the forest conference held at Simla, October 1875. Calcutta, Government of India.

CENTRE FOR SCIENCE AND ENVIRONMENT (1982): State of India's Environment — 1982; Citizen's Report. New Delhi, Centre for Science and Environment.

CHAMPION, H.G. & SETH, S.K. (1968): A Revised Survey of the Forest Types of India. New Delhi, Government of India.

CHOPRA, P.N. (1975): The Gazetteer of India: Indian Union, Vol. 3. New Delhi, Government of India.

CLEGHORN, H. (1864): Report upon the forests of the Punjab and the Western Himalayas. Roorkee.

COURTHOPE, E.A. (1915): A report on the ravines of Bhadawar estate (1915), Agra District. *In* Afforestation in the United Provinces, India, ed. by E. Benskin. U.P., Allahabad, Government Press.

D'ARCY, W.E. (1887): Working plans of the Chamba leased forests and of the Dalhousie forests, Chamba Division, Punjab. Calcutta, Government of India.

DAS, B.N. (1979): Management trends in forestry. *In* Man and forest, ed. by K.M. Gupta and D. Bandhu, 100-106. New Delhi, Today and Tomorrow's Printers and Publishers.

ECKHOLM, E. (1979): Forest renewal in India. *Nat. Hist. (New York)* **88**:12-27.

FAGAN, R.A. (1885): Forest pastures in the Deccan. *Indian Forester* **114**:158-172.

FRAZER, J.B. (1820): Views in the Himalaya Mountains. London, Rodwell and Martin.

GASTON, A.J., HUNTER, M.L. & GARSON, P.J. (1983): The status of wildlife in Himachal Pradesh, Western Himalayas. *Biol. Cons.* **27**:291-314.

GLOVER, H.M. (1927): Revised working plan for the Kotkai and Kotgarh forests. Lahore, Government of India.

GOETZ, H. (1969): Studies in the History and Art of Kashmir and the Indian Himalaya. Wiesbaden.

GORRIE, R.M. (1936): Forest working plan for Mandi State Forests, Sambat 1994-2113 (1937-1956). Lahore, Civil Military Gazette Press.

GRIBBIN, J. (1982): The other face of development. *New Sci.* **25**, Nov. 489-495.

GUPTA, K.M. & BANDHU, D. (1979): Man and Forest. New Delhi, Today and tomorrow's Printers and Publishers.

HENNIKER-GOTLEY, G.R. (1932): Revised working plan of the Hazara Forest, Hazara, N.W.F.P., 1931-32 to 1960-61. Peshawar, Government of India.

HILLS, M. (1916): Note on an enquiry by the Government of India into the relationship between forests and atmospheric and soil moisture in India. *Indian Forests Bull.* **33**:41 pp.

JOSHI, D.P. (1979): Evaluation of forest conservancy and panchyat forest system and their contribution to forest development in U.P. *In* Man and Forest, ed. by K.M. Gupta and D. Bandhu, 88-99. New Delhi, Today and Tomorrow's Printers and Publishers.

KAYASTHA, S.L. & JUYAL, G.N. (1979): Forests, environment and development. *In* Man and Forest, ed. by K.M. Gupta and D. Bandhu, 28-43. New Delhi, Today and Tomorrow's Printers and Publishers.

MANOHAR, R.M. (1982): India setting new forest bill and policy. *World Environment Report,* Oct. 30.

MODDIE, A.D. (1981): Himalayan environment. *In* The Himalaya: Aspects of Change, ed. by J.S. Lall, 341-350. New Delhi, Oxford University Press.

PARKER, R.N. (1925): Eucalyptus in the plains of northwest India. *Indian Forest Bull.* **61**. 34pp.

PATEL, H.M. (1980): National Forest Policy: an Ecological Expediency. *In* Studies in Himalayan Ecology and Development Strategies, ed. by T. Singh and J. Kaur, 81-88. New Delhi, The English Book Store.

PATHAK, S.L. (1896): Reafforestation of the Mahasu-Fagu ridge, Punjab. *Indian Forester* **22**:44-49.

PEARSON, G.F. (1972a): Report of the Administration of the Forest Department, 1870-71. Calcutta, Government of India.

_________ (1872b): Report on the administration of the Forest Department in the several provinces under the Government of India, 1871-72. Calcutta, Government of India.

PURI, G.J. (1865): Indian Forest Ecology. Vol. I and II. New Delhi, Government of India.

RAINA, V. (1979): Forest and soil conservation in Himachal Pradesh: fifth five-year plan and its progress. *In* Man and Forest, ed. by K.M. Gupta and D. Bandhu, 256-262. New Delhi, Today and Tomorrow's Printers and Publishers.

RIEGER, H.C. (1981): Man versus mountains. *In* The Himalaya: Aspects of Change, ed. by J. Lall, 351-376. New Delhi, Oxford University Press.

ROY, S.K. (1978): Forests and wildlife for the people. *World Wildlife Fund-India. Newsletter* **26**:1-3.

SAMLER, W.H.G. (1935): Revised working plan for the Kulu forests, 1934-35 to 1973-74. Lahore, Supt. of Govt. Printing.

STEBBING, F.B. (1922-26): The Forests of India, 3 vols. London, The Bodley Head.

TREVOR, C.G. (1921): Revised working plan for the Kulu forests. Lahore, Government of India.

TUCKER, R.P. (1983): The British colonial system and the forests of the Western Himalayas, 1815-1914. *In* Global Deforestation and the Nineteenth Century World Economy, ed. by R.P. Tucker and J.F. Richards. Durham, N. Carolina, Duke University Press.

VAN BUITENEN, J.A.B. (1973): The Mahabharata, I. The Beginning. Chicago, University of Chicago Press.

WALTERS, O.H. (1922): A revised working plan for the Kangra and Hoshiarpur Divisions. Lahore, Government of India.

WARTH, H. (1980): Fire protection and floods in the Siwaliks. *Indian Forester* **6**:95-97.

WHYTE, R.O. (1968): Grasslands of the Monsoon. London, Faber and Faber.

Problems and Prospects for Wildlife Conservation in Sri Lanka

R. RUDRAN

Department of Zoological Research, National Zoological Park, Washington, D.C. 20008

ABSTRACT

Rapid human population increases have caused some of the most serious problems to wildlife conservation in Sri Lanka. They have led to the implementation of large agricultural development projects, and increased slash and burn agriculture, poaching and other marginal forms of human livelihood. These in turn have resulted in the destruction of several habitat types and the reduction of many wildlife populations. Declining populations of wildlife include representatives of the island's megafauna endemic species and plants of medicinal value. Another major problem to wildlife conservation in Sri Lanka is the lack of environmental awareness among the people. This has resulted in a scarcity of personnel trained in wildlife management and a lack of public and administrative support for environmental agencies.

The prospects for wildlife conservation which remained bleak until recently have improved due to the Government's concern for environmental conservation. During the last few years the Government adopted an integrated approach to development, and approved the establishment of several new national parks. Other important measures were also taken to protect the environment. This augurs well for wildlife conservation, but given a past filled with unhappy environmental experiences the future full of promise should be viewed with cautious optimism.

In most, if not all, developing countries human population increases produce some of the most serious problems to wildlife conservation. Sri Lanka is no exception to this general rule (Table 1). In the 1950s when Sri Lanka's population consisted of about eight million people, nearly 45% of the total land was under forest cover (Andrews 1961). However, by the 1970s when the human population reached nearly 13 million, forest cover had been rapidly reduced to 24% of the total land area (Economic Review 1978). Thus, within a matter of about two decades, 46% of the existing forest cover was destroyed as the human population increased between four and five million. Similar numerical increases in the human population of Sri Lanka also occurred during the 1900-1950 period. Evidently, this increase had very little effect on the extent of forest cover, and only a 0.8% reduction was recorded during the first 50 years of this century. This suggests that the human population's numerical increase *per se* was not the reason for the rapid decline of forested areas.

The reasons for the rapid disappearance of Sri Lanka's forests are varied, but they are usually rooted in the attitudes of the human population in an ever changing natural, social, and economic environment. Employment opportunities in Sri Lanka have always lagged far behind the human population increases in this island. Thus, with time a progressively larger proportion of the country's population was

TABLE I

HUMAN POPULATION INCREASES AND THE DECLINE OF FOREST COVER OF SRI LANKA

Year	Human Population Size ($\times 10^6$)	Forest Cover ($\times 10^6$ ha)	% of total land area
1901	3.6	-	-
1902	-	2.92	45.9
1953	8.1	-	-
1956	-	2.87	45.1
1971	12.7	-	-
1978	-	1.55	23.6
1984	15.0	1.34	21.0

Source. Department of Census and Statistics (1982), Economic Review (1978), Andrews (1961)

TABLE 2

ENDANGERED AND THREATENED SPECIES FOUND IN SRI LANKA AND THEIR WORLD DISTRIBUTION

Species	Known Distribution	Portion of range where Endangered or Threatened
	ENDANGERED	
Elephant	India, Burma, Laos, Thailand, Cambodia, Malaysia, Sri Lanka, Vietnam	Entire
Leopard	Africa, Asia	Entire
Redfaced malkoha	Sri Lanka	Entire
Swamp Crocodile	Sri Lanka, India	Entire
Estuarine Crocodile	Sri Lanka, Malay Peninsula, Philippines, New Guinea, Australia, Fiji	Entire except New Guinea
Bengal Monitor	Iran, India, Burma, Afghanistan, Sri Lanka, Vietnam, Thailand, Malaysia	Entire
Python	Sri Lanka, India	Entire
	THREATENED	
Purplefaced langur	Sri Lanka	Entire
Toque Macaque	Sri Lanka	Entire

Source. U.S. Federal Register (January 1978 and December 1979)

forced into marginal forms of existence of which the traditional slash and burn agriculture was the most common. This form of agriculture when practised by an ever increasing number of people affected forests in two ways. Firstly, the total area under slash and burn increased, and secondly, the cycle of slash and burn in a particular area was progressively shortened. These two effects of slash and burn agriculture combined with the relatively slow rate of regeneration of tropical forests (Richards 1952, Struhsaker 1978) were the most important bases for the rapid decline of forest cover. Recent land use studies indicated that slash and burn agriculture was the primary reason for the reduction of forest cover in several vegetation zones of Sri Lanka (TAMS 1980).

Another factor which exacted a toll on forest cover was the implementation of government sponsored agricultural development schemes. The major objectives of these schemes have been to provide employment opportunities to the growing population, and to increase the agricultural productivity of the country. Unfortunately, these objectives have invariably led to extensive deforestation for the establishment of new agricultural lands, although increasing the productivity of existing agricultural lands has always been an alternative option. A case in point is the Accelerated Mahaweli Development Programme which was inaugurated by the present government in 1977. By 1984, this development scheme and other on-going agricultural projects are expected to reduce the island's forest cover from 24% to 21% of the total land area (Economic Review 1978). This reduction will further depress the extent of forest cover below the minimum required for climatic and hydrological stability of the country (Hoffmann 1979).

Although forests have shown the greatest decline, other wildlife habitats of Sri Lanka have also undergone substantial reduction during recent decades. In particular, natural grasslands, marshes and mangroves have been severely impacted by human interference (Cramer 1979). As would be expected, this general decline of wildlife habitats has led to population depletion in numerous species. The most conspicuous of these reductions are found in relatively wide ranging large mammal species such as elephant (*Elephas m. maximus*) and leopard (*Panthera pardus fusca*). Both species have declined mainly due to repeated habitat fragmentation resulting from unplanned human activities. Habitat fragmentation has virtually eliminated elephants from the Wet Zone of Sri Lanka. At present only 9% of this zone is forested (Perera 1979) and it consists of numerous little forest patches which cannot maintain viable elephant populations. The largest of these forest patches is the Sinharajah, with an area of about 9,000 ha (Gunatilleka 1978). In the dry zone as well, the Accelerated Mahaweli Development Programme will divide the elephant's range into unconnected north-west and south-east sectors. Even within these sectors elephant habitats are so fragmented that only a few areas could support elephants in the future.

Habitat fragmentation has also magnified the edge effect problems of elephants and leopards by increasing the frequency of their disastrous contacts with man. In the 1950s agricultural crop protection accounted for 50% of the known elephant deaths, whereas in 1979, this figure has risen to 70% (Sessional Paper 1959, De Alwis *pers. comm.*). Leopards, on the other hand, are killed when they prey on cattle and poultry, and both species are poached for either tusks or skins. Animal populations are more vulnerable to habitat manipulation than to manipulation of their numbers (Caughley 1977). In Sri Lanka the elephant and leopard have experienced both types of manipulations, and have declined by as much as 75% during this century (McKay 1973, Santiapillai *et al.* 1982).

In addition to elephant and leopard, Philips (1957) listed the following as declining mammalian populations: bear (*Melursus ursinus*), Sambar (*Cervus unicolor*), spotted deer (*Axis axis*), grey langur (*Presbytis entellus*), purple-faced langur (*Presbytis senex*), toque monkey (*Macaca sinica*), giant squirrel (*Ratufa macroura*) and both species of flying squirrels (*Petaurista petaurista* and *Petinomys fuscocapillus*). Among birds, the comb duck (*Sarkidiornis melanotos*) and the glossy ibis (*Plegadis f. falcinellus*) have become extinct as breeding residents, and several birds of prey and water birds have also shown substantial population reductions (Phillips 1957). Decreasing populations of reptiles included both species of monitor lizards (*Varanus salvator* and *V. bengalensis*) and the swamp crocodile (*Crocodylus palustris*). All of these vertebrates have declined primarily through habitat destruction, although some of them have been reduced by hunting for meat and skins as well. At present four mammalian species, one bird and four reptiles are listed as endangered or threatened in Sri Lanka (Table 2).

The status of wildlife species which are unique to Sri Lanka, the endemics, also presents a disturbing picture. Recent faunal surveys indicated that the Accelerated Mahaweli Development Programme will probably have detrimental effects on 42 species of endemic vertebrates (TAMS 1980). This includes 8 species of fish, 2 amphibians, 18 reptiles, 8 birds, and 3 endemic mammals (Table 3). The majority of these species were found to prefer riverine forest habitats which will be substantially reduced during development. The development area also includes 3 endemic plant genera, and at least 53 endemic plant species of which 17 are considered rare (Cramer 1977, Kostermanns *pers. comm.*). These endemic plants as well as 31 other species with confirmed medicinal value are expected to decline within the development area as a result of habitat alteration.

TABLE 3

ENDEMIC VERTEBRATES FOUND WITHIN THE MAHAWELI ACCELERATED DEVELOPMENT PROJECT AREA

FISH

Barbus titteya
Barbus bimaculatus
Barbus srilankensis
Barbus cummingi
Garra lamta
Belontia signata
Labeo fisheri
Channa orientalis

AMPHIBIANS

Bufo atukoralei
Rana (Hylarana) gracilis
Polypedetes cruciger
Ichthyophis sp. (at least one species)

REPTILES

Calatodactylus sp.
Gymnodactylus frenatus Günther
Geckoella yakhuna Deraniyagala
Hemidactylus depressus Gray
Cnemaspis podihuna Deraniyagala
Dasia haliana (Haly et Nevill)
Anguinicephalus deraniyagalei
Anguinicephalus hickanala
Calotes liocephalus
Calotes ceylonesis (Muller)
Otocryptis weigmanni Wagler
Cylindrophis maculatus
Bungarus ceylonicus
Pseudotyphlops philippinus
Rhinophis oxyrhynchus (Schneider)

Chrysipelea taprobanica Smith
Trimeresurus trigonocephalus (Sonnini et Latrelle)
Sphenomorphus fallax

BIRDS

Galloperdix bicalcarata (J.B. Forster)
Gallus lafayetti Lesson
Psittacula calthropae (Blyth)
Loriculus beryllinus (J.B. Forster)
Megalaima flavifrons (Cuvier)
Pellorneum fuscocapillum
Phaenicophaeus pyrrhocephalus (Pennant)
Zoothera spiloptera (Blyth)

MAMMALS

Macaca sinica
Presbytis senex
Paradoxurus ceylonensis

Thus, the effects of Sri Lanka's human population increases such as habitat destruction, hunting and poaching pose serious survival problems to the ecologically important megafauna, the biologically significant endemics, and plants of medicinal value.

Another major problem to wildlife conservation in Sri Lanka is the general lack of awareness of the intimate relationship between man and his natural environment. The problem has its roots in the country's educational system which has largely ignored the teaching of environment related subjects in schools and universities. Thus, the problem of environmental ignorance pervades the entire fabric of Sri Lankan society, and has many ramifications. For instance, the general public has remained unaware of the long-term benefits of environmental conservation, or the urgent need for it in the light of a rapidly increasing population. Consequently, the people have responded to increased population pressure and scarcity of jobs by indiscriminately exploiting the environment for short-term gains. In fact the destruction of wildlife and natural habitats through slash and burn agriculture, charcoal manufacture, hunting, coral dynamiting and gem mining is partly the result of the lack of environmental awareness among the general public.

There has also been a lack of environmental awareness among the country's decision makers which is reflected by the implementation of numerous development programmes with poor environmental planning (see Hoffman 1977, 1978, Perera 1978). The frequent disregard for environmental concerns also suggests that decision makers have viewed conservation as being incompatible with human progress or development. As a result there has been a dearth of high level support for the agencies which are involved in environmental conservation. These agencies tend to be small, poorly manned outfits which are financially ill-equipped to effectively deal with environmental problems.

The effectiveness of these agencies is also undermined by the lack of personnel trained in wildlife management. This problem is again an outcome of the educational system, but is compounded by financial considerations which compel the few trained scientists to take on jobs which involve an excess of teaching and administrative duties. Consequently, field research is neglected, and without a scientific data base convincing arguments or suitable plans for wildlife management cannot be developed. Also in the absence of scientific research, wildlife management becomes reduced to law enforcement, anti-poaching and other protectionist activities which bring wildlife personnel into conflict with an unenlightened public. This conflict makes wildlife conservation unpopular among the local people who in their ignorance view conservation as an antisocial pastime of a privileged few. The question that is frequently posed even by the educated elite is whether wildlife is more important than human lives.

Thus the lack of environmental awareness and the effects of human population increases are the bases of a variety of conservation problems in Sri Lanka. These problems have escalated through several decades, and hence cannot be resolved immediately. However, recent government decisions provide some hope that Sri Lanka's natural environment will enjoy greater protection in the future. In 1979, the government initiated Sri Lanka's first environmental assessment project to study the impact of the Accelerated Mahaweli Programme. This project was implemented after forest clearing and some other development activities had commenced, but it served to focus international attention on Sri Lanka's environmental issues and led to a series of recommendations to resolve these problems (TAMS 1980). With regard to wildlife, the most important recommendations were the plans for establishing several new national parks and improving the institutional capacity of conservation agencies. Both recommendations were later incorporated into an environmental action plan for the Accelerated Mahaweli area (TAMS 1981). In 1982 the wildlife component of this plan received 6.9 million dollars from the Sri Lanka government and the U.S., and work is now in progress to upgrade the status of wildlife conservation.

The environmental impact study of the Mahaweli project also served other useful purposes. Partly as a result of it, the government decreed that all future development projects should be preceded by assessments of their impacts on the environment. Environmental agencies of the government were also authorized to become involved in all phases of agricultural development. These measures were designed to ensure an integrated approach to development in the future. Steps were also taken to remedy some environmental problems of the past. A reforestation project was implemented to rehabilitate the catchment area of the Mahaweli river. An agricultural project which degraded the natural grasslands of Horton Plains, and a logging project which threatened the lowland rainforest of Sinharajah were also terminated.

In order to improve the institutional capacity of environmental agencies the government allocated funds for an increase in personnel and technical training. Consequently, the Department of Wildlife Conservation is expected to increase its staff (of 432) by nearly 55% in the next few years (de Alwis *pers. comm.*). Financial support also enabled wildlife management personnel to regularly participate in training programmes conducted locally and abroad. The Smithsonian Institution's Wildlife Conservation and Management Training Programme has been involved in this training effort, and since 1982, it has provided training to 13 Sri Lankans through field courses conducted in the U.S. and Sri Lanka. Since Sri Lanka does not possess adequate training facilities at the moment, the government has also proposed the establishment of a fully equipped wildlife management institute (TAMS 1981). In addition to personnel training this institute would be involved in dealing with current wildlife problems, particularly with regard to elephants. In order to avoid these problems in the future, the government is in the process of drafting stricter wildlife laws and an environmental conservation strategy for the entire island.

The government's concern for the environment was a source of encouragement for private organizations interested in environmental conservation. Consequently, these private organizations initiated a conservation awareness programme (March for Conservation) which was designed to capture the interest of a wide cross section of people. Thus the programme emphasized Sri Lanka's traditional respect for wildlife based on the teachings of

Gautama Buddha. It also highlighted the benefits of environmental conservation through an annual programme of lectures, poster parades, wildlife exhibitions, scientific seminars, and field research. Since the inception of this programme four years ago, average attendance at environmental lectures has increased twenty fold. The 1983 poster parade which included a seventy two mile route march to commemorate World Environment Day, involved much larger numbers than previous years. Public participation in other environmental activities has also increased. These suggest that there is a growing awareness of environmental conservation among the public of Sri Lanka.

Private organizations and the government of Sri Lanka must be lauded for their recent efforts to promote environmental conservation. These efforts have produced very favourable conditions for the growth of environmental conservation. Thus the current prospects for environmental conservation in Sri Lanka seem rather bright. However, the prevailing conditions must be sustained over several more years before the growing conservation ethic becomes firmly rooted in the country. Whether this would happen will depend largely on the attitudes of the people and the Government. Given a past filled with unhappy environmental experiences, the future full of promise should be viewed with cautious optimism.

ACKNOWLEDGEMENTS

I thank the Bombay Natural History Society for inviting me to present this paper at its Centenary Scientific Seminar held in Bombay in December 1983. Financial support to attend the seminar was provided by the Smithsonian Institution's foreign currency programme. This paper is partly an outcome of my numerous discussions with several Sri Lankan conservationists. I thank all of them and also Mr Naren Chitty, Sri Lanka Embassy, Washington D.C. for directing me to some of the human population statistics of Sri Lanka.

BIBLIOGRAPHY

ANDREWS, J.R.T. (1961): A Forestry Inventory of Ceylon. A Canada-Colombo Plan Project, Government Press, Ceylon 116 p.

CAUGHLEY, G. (1977): Analysis of Vertebrate populations. John Wiley, London.

CRAMER, L.H. (1977): The significance of the indigenous flora in the area of the Mahaweli complex. *Sri Lanka Forester* **13**:9-18.

__________ (1979). The Natural Environmental. *Vidurava* **4**:15-21. National Science Council of Sri Lanka, Colombo.

Department of Census and Statistics of Sri Lanka (1982): Statistical pocket book of Sri Lanka. Department of Government Publications, Colombo, Sri Lanka.

Economic Review (1978): Forests—Their Role in Human Welfare and Value. *Economic Review* **3**:3-15.

GUNATILLEKA, C.V.S. (1978): Sinharajah Today. *The Sri Lanka Forester* **13**:57-64.

HOFFMANN, TH. W. (1977): Major Threat to Oldest Wildlife Reserve. *Loris* **14**:133-137.

__________ (1978): The Mahaweli Diversion Project — Its effects on wildlife and environment. ibid. **14**:282-284.

__________ (1979): The forest of the lion king. *Animal Kingdom* **82**(5):23-30

MCKAY, G. (1973): Behaviour and Ecology of the Asiatic elephant in Southeastern Ceylon. *Smithsonian Contributions to Zoology* **125**:1-113.

PERERA, W.R.H. (1978): Thotapolakanda — An Environmental Disaster? *The Sri Lanka Forester* **13**:53-56.

__________ (1979): Catchment areas and the protection of the environment. ibid. **13**:49-52.

RICHARDS, P.W. (1952): The Tropical Rainforest: An Ecological Study. Cambridge University Press, Cambridge.

SANTIAPILLAI, C., CHAMBERS, M.R., ISHWARAN, N., (1982): The leopard in the Ruhuna National Park, Sri Lanka, and observations relevant to its conservation *Biol. Conserv.* **13**:5-14.

SESSIONAL PAPER (1959): Report on the committee on preservation of wildlife. Government Press, Colombo.

STRUHSAKER, T.T. (1978): Bioeconomic Reasons for Conserving tropical rainforests. Pages 87-94 *in* Recent Advances in Primatology, Vol. 2 (D.J. Chivers and W. Lane-Pttter eds.). Academic Press, London.

TAMS (1980): Environmental Assessment — Accelerated Mahaweli Development Programme, Vol. 2, Terrestrial Environment. Mahaweli Authority of Sri Lanka, Colombo.

_______________ (1981): Environmental Plan of Action —Accelerated Mahaweli Development Programme. Mahaweli Authority of Sri Lanka, Colombo. 101 p.

U.S. FEDERAL REGISTER (1978). List of endangered and threatened wildlife and plants 43:58029-58048.

Wildlife Conservation in Sri Lanka: A brief survey of the present status

(*With a map*)

THILO W. HOFFMANN

ABSTRACT

During the last three decades the face of Sri Lanka has changed greatly. Large tracts of land have been cleared of jungles to make room for the growing population. The forest cover has dwindled from over 50% to around 20%. Wildlife and species of wild animals have had to retreat before this onslaught and are now, or will soon be mostly confined to national parks and similar reserves. Not all national ecosystems are protected and it is essential that adequate samples of these (including marine) are urgently defined and effectively conserved. A survey of changes in the status of some wild forms of animals is given. On the whole numbers and ranges are greatly depleted; nevertheless there is hope that the loss of species can be prevented if plans for ecosystem conservation (National Conservation strategy) and good intentions can be put into effective practice.

The paramount importance of sufficiently large and coordinated wildlife and forest reserves for the survival of practically all forms of Sri Lanka's splendid wildlife is demonstrated.

INTRODUCTION

During the first half of this century Sri Lanka, of all the countries in Asia, probably had the most and the best wildlife conservation areas, both relatively and absolutely. Sanctuaries and other reserves (initially to protect prime shooting grounds) were established, and in the mid-'30s the two main national park complexes (both now over 500 sq. miles in extent) were established by law. Habitat conservation went hand in hand with legal protection (the Fauna and Flora Protection Ordinance, regularly revised and updated), shooting as well as trade in and export of wildlife (except fish) being carefully controlled and eventually banned altogether. In common with most developing countries, Sri Lanka has experienced unprecedented changes during the last three decades. An explosive population growth (3.5 million in 1900, 7.5 million in 1950 and 15 million in 1980) brought about equally explosive economic development. This has meant above all the clearing of forests and jungles and turning them into arable land. Unfortunately this process was not an orderly one. Large tracts of jungle land were opened without an overall land use policy, without coordination and consultation between various branches of Government and the administration. In addition there has been illicit land clearing, illicit gemming and felling.

As a result the environment in general, ecosystems and wildlife in particular, have suffered grievously. Since the 2nd World War the forest cover in Sri Lanka has been reduced in this manner from over 50% to 20%, and it will fall further in the course of the completion of the last major development projects now in progress (Mahaweli and South-Eastern River Basins), as forest planting and replanting lag far behind. Following the control of malaria in the early '50's, almost all of this development took place in the Dry Zone which covers very roughly two-thirds of Sri Lanka. During this period valiant efforts were made by the Wildlife and Nature Protection Society of Sri Lanka to stem the tide. Successes have been few but now and again there were achievements as when in 1973 the main national parks were consolidated and extended; 2 new national parks were created — Gal Oya in 1954 and Uda Walawe in 1972. In 1980 the small but important Lahugala National Park was added. A triumph was the saving from mechanical logging of the Sinharaja forest, the last Sri Lankan rain forest of some size in the southern portion of the island (now an MAB Reserve).

During the last five years there has been a gradual change in official thinking and popular feeling. It is now accepted and appreciated that no proper development can take place without environmental assessments, without an overall enforceable policy and discipline in land use. More and more attention is being paid to all aspects of conservation, and at the time of writing there is at work a Task Force appointed by H.E. the President of Sri Lanka to prepare a National Conservation Strategy; this will be ready by October 1983. It is hoped that this strategy will bring order into chaos and mismanagement which prevailed earlier.

CLIMATIC CONDITIONS

Traditionally Sri Lanka, 65,000 sq. km in extent, has been sub-divided into three main climatic zones (1): The Low-country Dry Zone comprising the northern half and the east of the island (one Monsoon, 600-1900 mm rainfall), the Low-country Wet Zone in the south-west (two Monsoons, 1900-over 5100 mm), and the Montane or Hill Zone in the centre of the southern half (one or two Monsoons, 2000-5100 mm). Sub-divisions and refinements include 2 Arid Zones in the north-west and the south-east, an Intermediate Zone between the Dry and the Wet Zones, as well as elevational subdivisions in the Hill Zone. More recently, Vegetational Zones have been established which by and large conform with the earlier divisions and sub-divisions based on rainfall.

The total extent of relatively effective wildlife reserves and sanctuaries covers less than 10% of the land surface of Sri Lanka. All the national parks and many other sanctuaries are situated in the Low-country Dry Zone. The imbalance in favour of this zone is mostly historical; tracts of land set aside for hunting and as sanctuaries, the forerunners of national parks, had to be rich in wildlfie, suitable for hunting and practically unpopulated. These conditions could only be found in the Dry Zone. New proposed national parks under the Mahaweli Project are also situated in the Dry Zone because the other zones are mostly developed. Some corrections have been made when recently the country's highest plateau, the Horton Plains (2300 m elevation) was made into a Nature Reserve, and the Wet Zone Sinharaja forest into an MAB Reserve. There is also the Peak Wilderness Sanctuary, the largest tract of hill forest in Sri Lanka, but unfortunately it is not well protected (4).

The forest cover in the Wet and Hill Zones is no more than 8% of the extent of these 2 zones and it is urged that all the few remaining natural forests in these zones be strictly conserved to serve as climatic, protective and genetic reserves. These forests contain the relict fauna and flora of Sri Lanka with a great concentration of endemic forms.

There are plans to establish substantial new wildlife reserves in the region of the Mahaweli Development Project north-east of the central mountain massif, including the forests over 4000 ft in the Knuckles range of mountains with unique, mostly unexplored, ecosystems (2).

Wildlife conservation areas now tend to become isolated and efforts are being made to link them up with each other through Forest Reserves and corridors.

Areas which have received little or no attention are the wetlands (3), marine, estuarine and

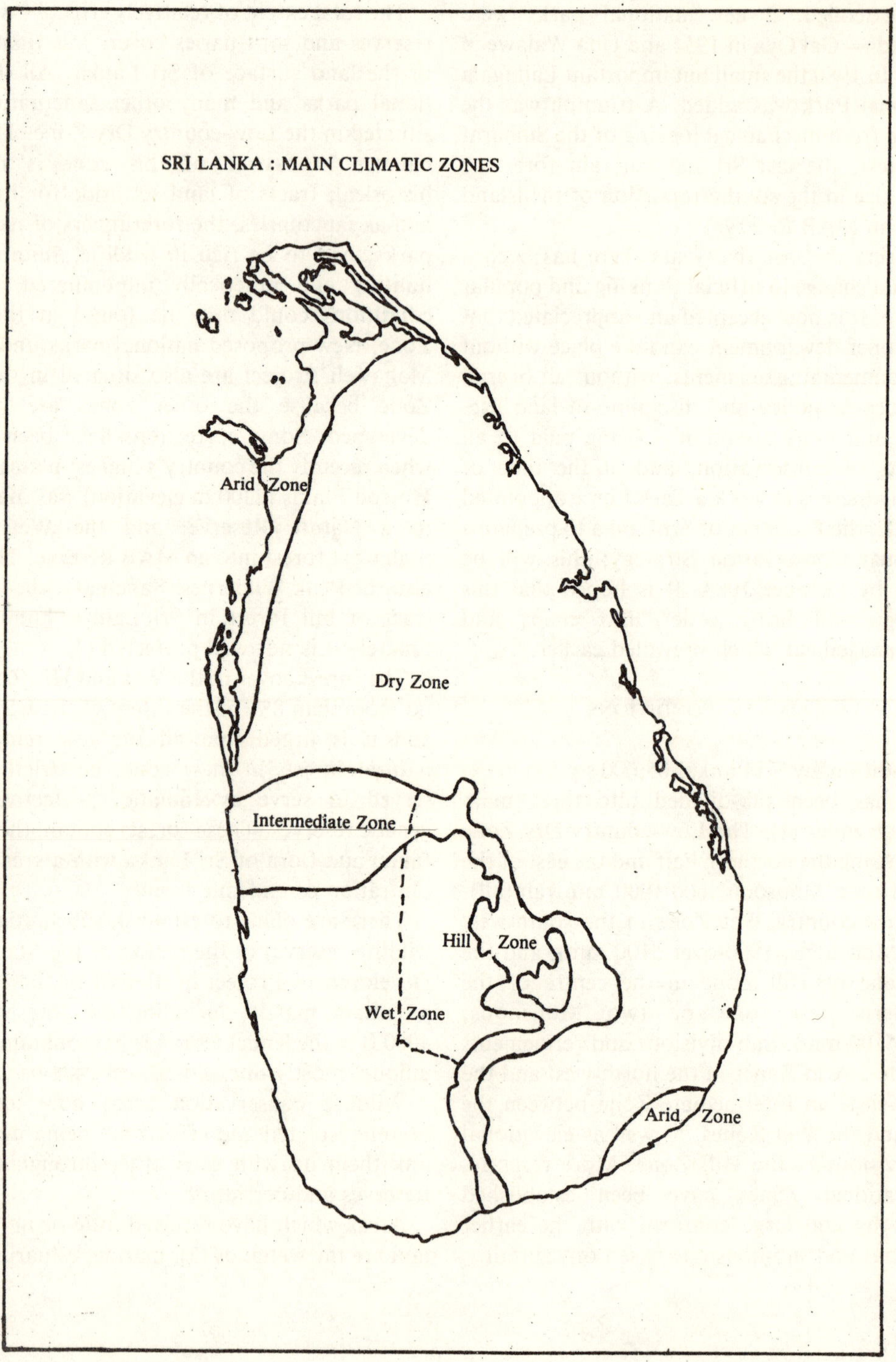
SRI LANKA : MAIN CLIMATIC ZONES
Arid Zone
Dry Zone
Intermediate Zone
Hill Zone
Wet Zone
Arid Zone

coral ecosystems and mangrove swamps which remain unprotected (except any which by chance lie in a national park). The few sanctuaries covering water surfaces are insufficiently or not protected (e.g. Chundikkulam).

WILDLIFE

As can be seen from the foregoing, wildlife in Sri Lanka has lost large extents of vital habitats during the last 3 decades and in many cases critically low levels have been reached. There have been major changes in the status of many species as a result of these developments.

MAMMALS

The most spectacular species of Sri Lankan wildlife is the elephant (*Elephas maximus*). A century ago it was found in all zones throughout the country from the north (Elephant Pass) to the extreme south and in the highest hills. Habitat loss (tea, rubber and coconut plantations) has banished the herds to the Dry Zone (with the exception of a few small isolated populations holding out in the Wet Zone). Now the elephant is about to lose even most of its remaining Dry Zone habitats and will only be able to survive in the reserves. This is the main reason why these reserves must be large and linked with each other as well as with other suitable habitats (e.g. natural forests and forest reserves). Present plans envisage such coordinated contiguous conservation areas, but every day diminishes the extents available. There are 3000 (current official estimate) to 5000 (author's estimate) wild elephants left in Sri Lanka and not all of these can be accommodated in existing and proposed reserves. It will, therefore, be necessary to capture for domestication a large number of surplus animals. Driving has generally not proved successful in Sri Lanka, and 'enrichment' of parks to the extent of satisfying the needs of hundreds of elephants is in any case not a practical proposition.

The primates have managed to survive as they are more adaptable than most other forms of wildlife. All 3 main forms of Monkeys (Grey Langur, *Presbytis entellus;* Leaf-monkey, ***Presbytis senex vetulus;*** Macaque, *Macaca sinica*) can be found in close proximity to human habitations. In parks and reserves they thrive. Rodents too are generally adaptable, but the Giant Squirrel (*Ratufa macroura*) and the 2 Flying Squirrels (*Petaurista petaurista* and *Petinomys fuscocapillus*) have been reduced in numbers by hunting for food and due to habitat loss. The status of the smaller and nocturnal forms of mammals such as mice, rats, shrews, bats, etc. is difficult to assess in the absence of scientific studies. All have experienced habitat losses and have been reduced in numbers like all other wildlife. Some forms may just barely survive, especially in the Wet and Hill Zones.

The Leopard (*Panthera pardus*), arguably Sri Lanka's most attractive species of wildlife, formerly ubiquitous like the elephant, has no chance of survival anywhere outside the reserves. It has been persecuted for its skin by shooting, trapping and poisoning with singular ruthlessness. The Sloth Bear (*Melursus ursinus*) has lost practically all its habitats outside national parks and reserves (it is one of the few species of larger wildlife naturally confined to the Low-country Dry Zone). The same is basically true of the Jackal (*Canis aureus*) though it will survive in pockets outside reserves. The small wild cats survive in reserves and small patches of jungle and uncultivated land. They are not in danger, with the exception perhaps of the Fishing Cat (*Felis viverrina*).

Ungulates too have suffered massive habitat losses, but are able to survive in existing reserves, with the exception of the Hog Deer (*Axis porcinus*) which does not have a secure habitat. Wild Buffalo (*Bubalus bubalis*), Sambar (*Cervus unicolor*) and Spotted Deer (*Axis axis*) will only survive in wildlife and some forest reserves, but the smaller and nocturnal forms such as the Muntjak (*Muntiacus muntjak*) and the Mouse Deer (*Tragulus meminna*) are yet found in many small patches of forest and scrub and stream reservations, especially in the hills. The ungulates have also suffered great losses due to uncontrolled hunting in the past; large tracts of former habitats are now empty of the larger forms.

Despite legal protection the Dugong (*Dugong dugon*) has been so decimated that today it can be regarded as extinct in Sri Lanka territorial waters. Only extreme protective measures along the Puttalam-Mannar coast, might achieve re-establishment of the species from neighbouring Indian waters.

The Cetacea in the seas around Sri Lanka have recently attracted attention, and some foreign researchers have found that the deep sea east of Trincomalee is a practically undisturbed haven for Whales of different kinds. Ten species of Whales and 8 species of Porpoises, Dolphins and Killer-Whales have been recorded earlier (1). Unfortunately foreign researchers and promotors of wildlife conservation often adopt patronizing attitudes, suggesting that only the bait of material benefit would make countries such as Sri Lanka adopt effective conservation measures. They are unaware of Sri Lanka's enviable record of wildlife and habitat conservation, and that it has the will and the capability as well as the collective conscience to conserve for conservation's sake and to protect what is in need of protection without outside prodding. Nothing could be more destructive in the long run and alien to the traditions and culture of Sri Lanka, than the promotion of uncontrolled touristic Whale watching or similar commercial activities in the national parks and sanctuaries.

Birds

Consequent to the opening up of vast tracts of land in the Dry Zone and loss of habitats in the hills (e.g. shade trees in tea), there have been many changes in the status and distribution of birds since about 1950. Some species have been greatly reduced in numbers, some are now practically confined to national parks and reserves, e.g. the Peacock (*Pavo cristatus*) more and more also Sri Lanka's national bird, the Junglefowl (*Gallus lafayetti*). The Painted Partridge *Francolinus pictus watsoni* (an endemic subspecies) which requires a special habitat (dry patna) has been reduced to a critical remnant population in the Gal Oya National Park and west of it.

During this century 3 resident forms have been lost (the Comb Duck *Sarkidiornis melanotos*), the Fairy Blue Bird (*Irena puella*), the Glossy Ibis (*Plegadis falcinellus*). Some other forms have reached critically low numbers, such as the Broadbilled Roller (*Eurystomus orientalis*), the Blue-eared Kingfisher (*Alcedo meminting phillipsi*), the Whiteheaded Starling (*Sturnus senex*), the Greenbilled Coucal (*Centropus chlororhynchus*), etc. Almost all of the 21 endemics of Sri Lanka are latently endangered because of the contraction of their special habitats (4). The Fruit Pigeons and the Malabar Pied Hornbill (*Anthracoceros coronatus*) will only survive in the parks and forest reserves. The same may be true of the Grey Pelican (*Pelecanus philippensis*), but Storks, Herons and Egrets have maintained their status or even increased in numbers (vast extents of new rice fields favour certain forms) despite continuing illicit shooting.

Shooting has become a sport of the rich as cartridges are very expensive and it has, therefore, on the whole rather diminished. As a result some forms have increased in numbers, e.g. the Grey Partridge (*Francolinus pondicerianus*) in the coastal belt from Kalpitiya to Mannar and Jaffna. In the North guns had to be surrendered as an anti-terrorist measure which has benefited the avifauna of the area, especially hundred thousands of wintering migrants, chiefly Ducks and Waders.

Raptors surprisingly seem to hold out so far, with the exception of the Rufousbellied Hawk-Eagle (*Lophotriorchis kienerii*) which is endangered. Low numbers exist in respect of the Shahin Falcon (*Falco peregrinus peregrinator*), Legge's Baza (*Aviceda jerdoni*) (loss of habitat), the Mountain Hawk-Eagle (*Spizaetus nipalensis*) and several owls.

Some of the more adaptable and robust species have, on the other hand, increased in numbers and are extending their ranges, e.g. both the House and the Black Crow (*Corvus splendens* and *C. macrorhynchos*), the Common Myna (*Acridotheres tristis melanosternus*), the Roseringed Parakeet (*Psittacula krameri*), and also the Spotted Dove (*Streptopelia chinensis ceylonensis*). There is a tendency for some species to extend their ranges to higher elevations in the hills (e.g. Yellowfronted Pied Woodpecker (*Dendrocopus mahrattensis*). An interesting case is that of the Common Coot (*Fulica atra*) which used to be known only from a few specimens at Giant's Tank near Mannar. It has spread in recent years to tanks in the Anuradhapura region, where it is now found in some numbers, to Villus in Wilpattu National Park, and has recently even been noted in the south (5).

REPTILES

The Estuarine Crocodile (*Crocodylus porosus*) has become all but extinct in the populated parts of the island and survives only in suitable habitats within national parks (Yala) and in some remote areas. The Swamp Crocodile (*Crocodylus palustris*) too has been decimated in numbers, but is not endangered.

The Terrapins (*Melanochelys trijuga* and *Lissemys punctata*) have almost disappeared from areas outside reserves as they are taken for food. The Star Tortoise (*Testudo elegans*) too is much reduced in numbers, as is the Land Monitor (*Varanus bengalensis*) outside national parks. Of the Snakes, especially the relict forms in the hills and the Wet Zone, many are reduced through continuing loss of habitats and may be endangered, e.g. the 3 species of *Ceratophora*. Other vulnerable species are *Haplocerus ceylonensis* and *Ceraspis carinatus* (6),

FISHES

Endemic forms of sweet water fishes have suffered greatly from collection as aquarium fish for export; it is claimed that as a result some species have become nearly extinct.

The situation is no better or even worse in respect of coral fish where totally uncontrolled exploitative collection for export has in recent years impoverished all the coastal reefs to an unbelievable extent. There are no laws or regulations to check this damaging activity and trade. Coral reefs are also exploited for lime, causing great changes in and loss of habitats. In addition, coral fish and coastal forms continue to decline as a result of dynamiting and other illicit forms of fishing. Control over these abusive practices is utterly inadequate, mostly non-existent.

PROTECTION LAWS

The main instrument for the conservation of wildlife in Sri Lanka is the Fauna and Flora

Protection Ordinance, which is revised and updated from time to time. It regulates the establishment and administration of national parks and other reserves (sanctuaries and nature reserves, strict nature reserves, buffer zones). It also regulates hunting today, with the exception of the Wild Boar (*Sus scrofa*), the Hare (*Lepus nigricollis singhala*) and a small list of game birds, no wildlife can be legally hunted in Sri Lanka. The Ordinance gives special protection to the Elephant (*Elephas maximus*). In the latest revision (prepared more than 3 years ago, but held up by bureaucratic obstacles), the reverse listing method has been employed throughout to indicate the few forms of fauna which in Sri Lanka are not protected (e.g. Wild Boar, Crow, Sparrow, etc.). Penalties which currently are grossly inadequate, are to be much enhanced with mandatory fines and jail sentences for serious offences. The protection of the flora in Sri Lanka is inadequate, but for wildlife the Fauna and Flora Protection Ordinance is a good instrument. The problem is proper enforcement, Political interference is commonplace, and the Department of Wildlife Conservation is understaffed and under-funded. The situation is similar in respect of forests. Unfortunately available resources are not utilized on first priorities; for instance the active protection of declared conservation areas is greatly insufficient or even totally absent in a number of important cases, e.g. the Peak Wilderness and some wetlands which are Sanctuaries. There is no systematic patrolling of boundaries in any of the national parks. The result is considerable, in some cases critical, loss in the quality of these reserves.

The recent introduction in the administration of Sri Lanka of high powered environmental agencies of various types has so far had little practical impact on wildlife conservation.

References

1. Phillips, W.W.A. (1980): Manual of the Mammals of Sri Lanka, 2nd revised edition, Pts. I and II, Colombo, Pt. III (*in preparation*).

2. Environmental Plan of Action (1981): Accelerated Mahaweli Development Programme, Colombo.

3. Hoffmann, Thilo W. (1982): A Provisional Inventory of Wetlands in Sri Lanka, *Loris* 16(2).

4. ______ (1983): A List of endangered and rare species of birds in Sri Lanka. Colombo. (*in preparation*).

5. Ceylon Bird Club Notes, (monthly) Colombo.

6. De Silva Anslem: *Pers. comm.*

The Endangered Marine and Terrestrial Habitats of Minicoy Atoll in Lakshadweep[1]

C.S. GOPINADHA PILLAI[1]

(*With a map and two plates*)

Central Marine Fisheries Research Institute, Cochin-18[2]

ABSTRACT

Continuous observations on the terrestrial and lagoon habitats in the Minicoy Atoll (8°17′N, 73°′E) in Lakashadweep over a period of 15 years, have indicated noteworthy changes in the environment and the resources. On the terrestrial side, various construction works have defaced the natural surface morphology of the atoll while intensive clearing has resulted in the depletion of the only existing atoll natural vegetation in our country. Expansion of agriculture and introduction of exotic plants, goats and cattle that exerted much grazing pressure have also affected the ground vegetation. The rats and insects are causing significant damage to coconuts.

On the marine side, blasting of the reef flat and lagoon shoals and dredging of the lagoon bottom have resulted in a high degree of sediment transport into the lagoon as well as shifting of the bottom sand due to water current thus killing most of the corals in the lagoon. The mass mortality to corals has effected a chain of ecological changes in the marine communities. The most significant among them is the depletion of the coral associated fishes in the lagoon, many of which are of value as live-baits for tuna. The marine habitat is modified, there is depletion of all living organisms. The traditional tuna fishery by pole and line is threatened due to paucity of live-baits. The various links in the ecosystem changes are traced and a few measures of conservation are suggested.

INTRODUCTION

Since dawn of this century, coral reefs and coral islands, throughout the tropics have become places of intense human activities, as areas of settlement, testing grounds for atomic weapons, sites of military operations, tourist spots, agricultural areas and centres of biological and geological researches. Oceanic atolls are known to be centres of faunal diversity. Due to lack of large buffer zones around them the environmental changes are very conspicuously manifested in the atoll ecosystems and they undergo ecological stress very easily. The corals and coral reefs form the most dominant tropical sedentary marine benthic community at present. But sadly today, as Campbell (1976) puts it "these fascinating and complex communities of plants and animals are being increasingly at risk from the pressure of man's expanding activities". Their depletion is also accelerated at several places by natural calamities. A world-wide recession of reef building and reef dwelling organisms have been recently reported by many workers (Gardiner 1936; Stoddart 1969; Pillai 1971a, 1971b,

[1]First read in December, 1983. Revised in December, 1984.

[2]*Present address:* Research Centre of CMFRI., Vizhinjam P.O., Via Trivandrum, Kerala.

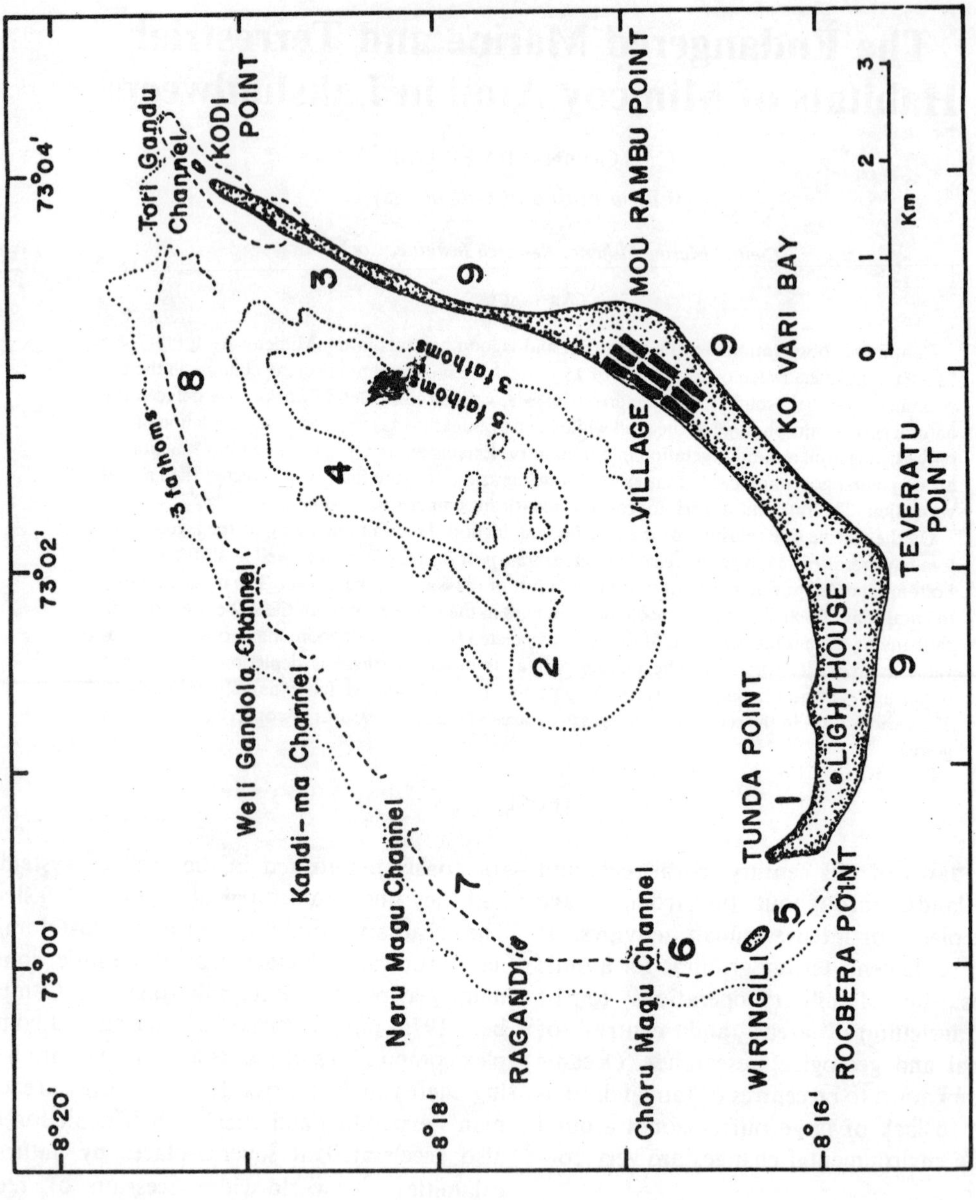

Minicoy, lagoon and reef zones described (1-9)
(After Pillai 1971a)

1971c, 1975, 1977; Banner 1974; Endean 1976; Nishihira and Yamazato 1974; Margos and Chave 1973; Wiens 1971). In our waters, mass mortality to corals due to various reasons and the resultant ecological changes have been earlier reported from Palk Bay and Gulf of Mannar (Pillai 1975) and Gulf of Kutch (Pillai *et al.* 1979). In the present paper an attempt is made to document some of the major changes observed in the various habitats of Minicoy during the last 15 years and their possible interactions and implications, both on the terrestrial and marine sides, with stress on fishery resources.

THE ATOLL OF MINICOY

Minicoy is an oval-shaped atoll with a crescent-shaped island. The island has a maximum length of 9.5 km and a maximum width of 650 m. The total land area is 4.4. sq. km. The maximum height from MSL is 1.8 m. Both the southwest and northeast monsoons contribute to the total annual rainfall, which on the average is 1600 mm. The island is located in the cyclonic belt and it often experiences heavy to very heavy wind, especially during the monsoons. The atmospheric temperature fluctuates between 29 to 31° Celsius with an average daily variation of 3°C Mannadiar (ED.) 1977 . According to the 1981 census, the total population is 6658. A steady upward trend in the demographic growth is registered since 1951 and is mainly due to better medical facilities and living conditions made available during the post independent days. The people of Minicoy are believed to have settled from Maldives and still speak Mahal. They practised the best system of unimposed socialism from time immemorial by collective farming and fishing, enjoying the produce on a percapita division basis.

THE CHANGING FACE OF MINICOY

My work on the corals and coral reefs of Minicoy was started as early as 1968 and during the last 15 years especially during the three years from 1981 to 84 with my continuous stay in the island, I have gained some intimate knowledge of the changing environments. This enables me to record here some of the ecological changes and their impact on the living resources.

The Terrestrial Environment

Vegetation. Mangroves are not developed. The natural vegetation is dominated by coconut palms with an undercover of tall trees like, *Calophyllum inophyllum, Erythrina variegata, Barringtonia* sp., *Prunus amygdalis, Ficus* sp., *Thespesia populnea, Azadiracta indica* and at settlement areas with *Artocarpus altilis, Caryca papaya, Morinda* sp., and *Casuarina equisetifolia.* A middle strata of *Pandanus odaratissimus* flourished at the southern part of the atoll till recently. *Pemphis acidula* forms isolated thickets both on the windward and leeward sides. A still lower strata of *Ricinus communis, Clerodendron* spp. and many creepers are also seen. The ground cover of vegetation is composed of many species of graminae, *Aerva lanata, Phyllanthus niruri, Vinca rosea, Boerhavia diffusa* and many others. (No attempt is made here to provide a complete list of plants.) In general, the natural vegetation is more or less in agreement with any other tropical atoll in the Indian Ocean (Wiens 1971).

The fauna. No indigenous mammal is reported, Cattle and goats are introduced in the last 25 years. Only rats among the rodents, *Mus rattus* and *M. rufescens* are very common and form a serious pest on coconuts. The avifauna is rich with sea gulls. Crows are in plenty, though they were not present in the atoll till the dawn of this century (Gardiner 1900). Many of them can be seen flocking on the exposed reef flats, probably feeding on the reef flat organisms at low tides. The land reptiles include a species of *Gecko* and *Mabuya carinata*, both of them probably introduced by chance. Land snakes are not hitherto recorded, however, a non-poisonous snake collected is present among the collections of the Minicoy Research Centre of CMFRI. Probably this is a recent introduction from mainland brought along with construction materials.

Interference on Terrestrial Habitats.

Changes on surface morphology. Human settlement is believed to have started in Minicoy much earlier than in the rest of Lakshadweep (Mannadier 1977). Early settlers had removed a lot of surface soil to make some parts of the land cultivable and the soil thus removed has been piled into hillocks, many of which are still seen in the central part of the island. A large number of small and large ponds have been made either as a source of potable water or for use as retting sites for coconut husks. All along the windward side coral boulders have been removed not only from the surface but by deep mining for construction work or for the preparation of lime. These activities have changed the natural appearance of the atoll as is the case with most of the habitated atolls.

Damage to natural vegetation. The fast deteriorating state of the natural vegetation of Minicoy should serve as a classic example to illustrate the effect of human interference on atoll vegetation. The natural vegetation at the southern part of the island, largely remained undisturbed till three years ago, except for cutting a tree or some *Pandanus* for construction or use as fire wood. However, the distribution of land three or four years ago on percapita basis (till that time the land remained a collective property resulted in individual ownership of small plots. The owners, keen on improving the land, have mostly cleared the vegetation both by clear felling and setting on fire (Plate 1, Fig. 2). The ecological implication of this loss of vegetation remains to be watched. Only in Minicoy we had some good natural atoll vegetation to boast of, but now unfortunately that is almost lost.

Grazing pressure. While the human activities are threatening the undercover vegetation, the recent increase in the number of cattle and goats to boost the "white revolution" has exerted much grazing pressure on the ground vegetation. The goats seem to do the maximum damage. No stall-fed quadruped exist in Minicoy. The sustaining number of cattle and goat in Minicoy as on 31-iv-83 is 106 and 850 respectively (data from veterinary surgeon). The clearing of the *southpandaram* land for agricultural operations has restricted the pastureland and in the long run the island is going to face fodder problem, if the population of the cattle and goats is steadily increasing at the present level.

Introduction of exotic plants. Minicoy is no exception to other habitated atolls where man has introduced exotic garden plants at the cost of natural vegetation. At several sites, the natural vegetation has slowly and steadily given way to exotic garden plants. The agricultural area has increased, though, the island has not attained self sufficiency in vegetables, and may never make it.

Pests and diseases. Rats among the coconut pests loom large in the economy of the island, causing destruction to roughly 25% of the annual nut production. Another pest that attack the coconut trees is the rhinoceros beetle, *Oryctes rhinoceros.* Fortunately, the deadly rootwilt and leafrot diseases have not taken toll of the coconut palms here.

THE MARINE HABITAT

The shores of the island and the lagoon habitats are under severe environmental stress. Sea erosion, sediments, predators and over-exploitation, especially that of the lagoon fishes are the major factors that exert pressure in the marine environment of Minicoy.

Interference

Sedimentation. The rate of sediment deposit and sediment transport in the lagoon have significantly increased in the last few years. The major reason for this is undoubtedly the blasting of the reef flats and the lagoon shoals and dredging of the lagoon bottom to deepen the channel to permit entry of ships. The main channel *Tori Gandu* (Map. 1) at the northern tip of the atoll was dredged between 1968 and 1977 by the harbour department. A good part of the soil thus dredged was deposited at zone 3 (see Map 1 for zones mentioned). A lot of accretion has resulted there and new plants have taken root. The dredging also caused stirring up of the bottom sand and its transport towards the south along with the water current. Today, there is at least 0.5 m thick of additional deposit of soil at the central and southern parts of the atoll (zones 2 and 5) when compared to early seventies (vide *infra*).

Sea erosion. The "hungry ocean gaining advantage of the kingdom of the shores "has become very rampant in the last few years. Land, several metres wide along with rows of coconut palms are being lost. The erosion is very serious at the central and southern parts of the island along the lagoon, though accretion is taking place near the Wiringili island. The recent dredging and deepening of the channel should have increased the rate of sea erosion by permitting a greater influx of water into the lagoon at high tides (Plate 1, Fig. 1).

Predation of coral polyps. The "Thorn-of-spines", the starfish *Acanthaster planci,* is a major predator of coral polyps and its infestations have been recorded from various parts of the Indo-Pacific, from Red Sea eastward to Tuamoto Archipelago. A recent review of the magnitude of the damage and its ecological implications are found in Endean (1976). This starfish was also recorded from Minicoy in 1979 (Murty *et al.* 1979) in fair numbers and death of corals due to their predation was observed at zones 2 and 3. However, by 1981 they were not found in the lagoon though careful search was made for a long time. The exact reasons for the sudden infestation of this species on reefs and its disappearance are not fully understood.

Exploitation of resources. Both the corals and the coral associated living resources of all types are exploited from this area. But at no time live corals were quarried in large quantities for industrial purposes as was done in the Gulf of Mannar and Palk Bay along the southeast coast of India (Pillai 1975, 1977). However, significant direct damage was done to several coral shoals when the lagoon was dredged. The dead boulders from the shore and reef flat are generally collected for construction work in appreciable quantity.

Among the reef associated fishes, many resident and migratory species are exploited by the local fishermen as live baits for the traditional tuna fishing. The commonly used species include, *Spratelloides delicatulus, S. japonicus, Archamia* spp. *Apogon* spp. *Diplerygonatus leucogrammicus, Lepidozygus tapeinosoma, Caesio* spp. and *Chromis caeruleus.* For a detailed account of the live baits of Minicoy, reference may be made to Jones (1964).

Effect of Environmental stress in Lagoon Habitats

Mass mortality of corals. Many natural and artificial (man-made) factors have been identified in the past as causative agents for the mass mortality of corals observed throughout the tropics (Stoddart 1969; Şalvat 1981; Pillai 1976). The major natural factors are excessive rains, influx of fresh water, prolonged exposure due to tidal fluctuations, mechanical force of cyclones, post hurricane changes in the environment, tectonic upheavals and possibly the natural senescence of corals itself. Predation by *Acanthaster* and siltation are also major disturbing factors on reef environs. Artificial factors are mostly man-made and include, thermal and oil pollution, dredging and over-exploitation.

Among all the factors mentioned above, excessive siltation and predation of polyps by *Acanthaster planci,* in that order, seem to have brought about large scale killing of corals in Minicoy in the recent past. Dredging of the area and the resulting siltation was reported by many workers as major deleterious agent to corals from several parts of the world (Banner 1974; Nishihira and Yamazato 1974; Margos and Chave 1973). My studies during 1968 from Minicoy (Pillai 1971a) showed a luxuriant growth of corals of both massive and ramose types, with a rich and varied fauna of reef-associated invertebrates and fishes throughout the lagoon shoals. No significant death of corals was observed. In 1979 there was death of corals at many pockets especially at zones 1 and 3. Further there was sign of accumulation of sand at the central and southern parts of the lagoon where ramose corals were very profuse. A few colonies of *Acropora* were found killed by *Acanthaster planci.* However, the icthyofauna associated with the corals did not reveal any stress or deterioration. In early 1982, the situation changed markedly. Both massive and ramose corals met with large scale death and majority of the shoals in the lagoon harbourred comparatively very few living coral colonies. The *Acropora* thickets were all dead (Plate 2, Figs. 3 and 4). I have measured many colonies of *Acropora palifera* at the south tip of the lagoon in 1968 which were more or less 1 m in greater spread and stood 0.75 to 1 m above the level of the sandy bottom. *Acropora corymbosa, A. aspera, A. teres* and *Pocillopora* spp. were also very rich. However, in 1982 only the distal branches of these colonies were observed above from the sand. This means that the colonies were buried *insitu* by deposition of sand. It appears that, at least there was an additional deposit of sand to the tune of 0.5 m thick during 1968 and 1981. At zones 5,6 and 7 also there was large scale death to massive poritids and faviids as well as *Heliopora.* Many of them are partly buried and the top is dead due to silting. The living zones are confined to the sides and undersides. At zone 3 where most of the dredging was done, there existed a shoal near the shore to a width of 50 m and about 100 m in length with a profuse growth of huge colonies of *Goniastrea retiformis, Diploastrea heliopora* and *Lobophyllia* spp. along with colonies of *Porites* (Nair and Pillai 1972).

At present there is little sign of any live corals there and the shoal is mostly buried under the soil dredged and deposited over it. In essence the excessive siltation due to the direct effect of dredging and subsequent sea erosion has killed almost all the corals in the lagoon. The damage is about 75%.

Effect of mass mortality of corals

Ecosystem modification. Soon the corals are dead, they get coated by algae and many smaller organisms mostly cryptobionts vanish from the coral colonies. Tabular coral colonies may remain *insitu* for two or three years but the more fragile ramose species will breakdown soon and fall to the bottom. Algal incrustation and disintegration of corals prevent the overgrowth of live skeleton on dead ones (Endean 1979). This leads to a fresh succession of communities based on marine algae and seaweeds. A few of the reef associated fishes may remain for some time on freshly killed corals but in long run they totally disappear. *Chromis caeruleus,* the most dominant resident species at Minicoy was observed to dwindle from dead corals while its co-existing species *Dascyllus aruanus* could adapt a little to dead corals.

Re-colonisation of corals by the settlement of planulae will largely depend on the physiographic conditions. Planulae can settle only on hard substrata, and even in such cases restoration will take a minimum of 15 to 20 years with regard to fast growing genera like *Acropora* and *Montipora*. However, the restoration of a well-consolidated reef ecosystem may take several hundred of years, even if the conditions are suitable. It seems that at Minicoy the chances of recolonisation of corals at many places where mortality is significant is very remote since the bottom is covered by moving sand that will prevent the settlement of fresh planulae.

Impact on fishery. The traditional tuna fishery of Lakshadweep largely depends on the availability of live baits. Of recent, there is a general complaint from the fishermen at Minicoy that the live baits are not meeting their demands. This situation merits consideration from at least three angles as follows: (1) environmental deterioration; (2) fluctuation of recruitment, and (3) over-exploitation of the resources. It has already been stated that the deterioration of the lagoon habitats has affected the live bait fishery. It is the resident forms such as *Chromis caeruleus, Archamia* spp., *Apogon* spp. and *Spratelloides japonicus* on ramose corals that are quickly vanishing from the lagoon due to the large scale death of corals. Generally it is these species that form a steady supply of bait.

A second category of live baits is constituted by migratory pelagic species that enter into the lagoon at intervals. They include *Dipterygonotus leucogrammicus, Caesio* sp. and *Lepidozygus tapeinosoma,* the last mentioned being the most useful live bait. They mostly enter the lagoon at the post-larval stage, after completion of the pelagic phase, during the post-monsoon period. The recruitment of these species is subjected to annual fluctuation It is already known that the recruitment of post-larvae of reef fishes with an early pelagic life, is mostly controlled by the prevailing oceanographic conditions, especially the direction of the surface current and it involves an element of chance (Sale 1979; Pillai *et al.* 1983). In the last few years there was a significant fall in the rate of recruitment of these species in Minicoy, and *Lepidozygus,* has not turned up. This failure of recruitment of migratory forms has exerted additional pressure on the resident species. Even if the resident forms that live among the live coral, get recruited, they will not remain in the lagoon for long, since their specific habitats, namely ramose corals are mostly dead. It was observed that several coral shoals that harboured live corals and resident fishes such as *Apogon, Archamia* etc. in the past are at present devoid of both live corals and fishes.

There is no published data on the annual catch and utilisation of live baits from Minicoy or Lakshadweep as a whole. Hence it is not possible to show figurewise the catch trend against the concept of a diminishing bait fishery as claimed by the local expert fishermen. It may be pointed out that the introduction of mechanised vessels in tuna fishery after setting up the tuna canning factory has considerably increased the fishing efforts. It has resulted in some sort of over-exploitation, particularly of the resident species, especially due to failure of recruitment of pelagic migratory species in the last few years. *Chromis caeruleus,* a strictly resident species and the one which is available in all seasons is subjected to severe fishing pressure. Larger adults are scarcely seen. Yet another species that will soon be under fishing pressure is *Spratelloides delicatulus.* This species lives on sandy beds and is planktophagous. Scarcity of coral associated and pelagic species have caused intense fishing of this species at present. The cumulative effect of all these is the dwindling of live baits in Minicoy. Needless to say that a shortage of live baits will effect the tuna fishery by pole and line. If this state of diminishing rate of recruitment of pelagic forms continues and resident forms which are under pressure from environmental crisis, already dwindling, are over-exploited, a serious situation may arise where the demand for live baits will exceed the available resources.

THE PROBLEM AND PROSPECTS FOR CONSERVATION

Conservation is the need of the hour. Both the terrestrial and lagoon habitats are fast undergoing changes and the ecosystem is not only modified but is on the way to transformation. The IUCN-WWF-UNEP has already identified, Lakshadweep as one of the western Indian Ocean areas needing highest priority for the protection of representative samples of ecosystem as a centre of high diversity (Anon, 1978). The lagoon habitats of all the islands in Lakshadweep need immediate attention since the live bait resource is vital for the tuna fishery.

The problem of conservation. The oceanic atolls face special problems with regard to conservation since they lack buffer zones with large biological communities, unlike in continents. Hence they are more at risk from environmental impacts (Anon. 1981). According to Ray (1976) all problems of conservation of endangered critical habitats should centre around an "ecological planning" and the strategy should envisage a practical approach involving survey, selection, description, suggestions for management, implementation and fruitful research for refinement.

The pioneering works of Gardiner *et al.* (1900-6); Jones (1964) and Jones and Kumaran (1981) along with my own work provide some basic information on the ecology and fauna of Minicoy. From the observations presented on the ecological stress and ecosystem linkage above, it seems that the following habitats are under environmental stress from natural and artificial factors that need our attention from a conservation point of view. On the terrestrial side destruction to vegetation by human activity and grazing particularly by goats and pests on agricultural crops especially on coconut palms. These need control. Use of pesticides in large quantities have to be regulated. On the marine side blasting of the reef and dredging of the lagoon and over-exploitation of the resources should be banned.

Some guidelines for conservation. Planting of trees suited to atoll soil to offset the imbalance created by destruction to natural vegetation.

CONTROL OF SEA EROSION. Already actions are on the way, but the problem still continues. All efforts should be made to control sea erosion.

Effective implementation of schemes for the control of pests and predators on coconuts has to be taken up.

Some pockets of coral shoals still with living corals and fishes may be left as reserve areas without any interference. This is especially important as far as strictly resident species like *Chromis caeruleus* is concerned, so that a breeding stock will be available. At present fishes of all ages are exploited even before they attain first sexual maturity.

Introduction of closed season for lagoon fishery has not much significance, and in effect it is being indirectly implemented since there is no fishery during monsoon when most of the reef fishes spawn.

Research needed. Information on sedimentological aspects, particularly with reference to rate of sediment deposit at various parts of the lagoon, influence of bottom current on sediment transport and zones of least interference should be of help in transplanting corals to restore the environment, if required.

Practically no serious study has been carried out on the biology of reef associated fishes, especially of live baits. Information on the food, feeding, fecundity, spawning and larval development and recruitment of these species all over Lakshadweep will aid in their management.

Monitoring of the rate of recruitment and available resources of live baits from year to year will help in the judicious exploitation. Culture of live baits in Lakshadweep may not meet with the anticipated results at present due to lack of facilities. Among all the species perhaps *Spratelloides delicatulus* may be the easiest to maintain in the laboratory since it lives on sandy areas.

Tilapia (*Sarotherodon mosambicus*) which was introduced into the islands as an alternative to local live baits has not received the approval of fishermen. There are many small and large ponds in Lakshadweep that could serve as rearing sites, if an alternative, small, brackish or freshwater species of fish could be acclimatised. This will control the mosquito and thus the malaria in the islands.

ACKNOWLEDGEMENTS

I thank the Director, Central Marine Fisheries Research Institute, Cochin for granting permission to present this paper. The author wishes to acknowledge his gratefulness to Shri Chacko Mathew, Scientist, C.P.C.R. Institute, Minicoy for going through the manuscript at the initial stage of its preparation and to Shri C. Mukundan and Shri K. Prabhakaran Nair, Scientists at CMFR Institute for all the constructive suggestions and help rendered during the final revision of the text. I am indebted to Shri Madan Mohan, my colleague at Minicoy for some information on live-baits and constant company during field work. I wish to place on record my appreciation and heartfelt thanks to my colleagues, Shri K. Kunki Koya, D. Kojan Koya, C. Mohammed Koya, O. Ismail and N. Pookoya without whose help in the field the present work would not have been possible. I am also indebted to many experienced fishermen of Minicoy (whose names are not mentioned herein) for divulging their life long experience on the habit and habitat of many live-baits which helped me to have a better understanding on the problem.

REFERENCES

ANONYMOUS, (1978): Second Draft of World Conservation Strategy. *IUCN. UNEP-WWF. General Assembly Paper.* pp. XXXI 94. Morges.

———— (1981); Conservation of Islands. *IUCN Bull.* **12**(5-6): 29.

BANNER, H. ALBERT (1974): Kaneohe Bay, Hawaii: Urban pollution and a coral reef Ecosystem. *Proc. IInd. Inter-*

nat. Symp. Vol. 2: 685-702. Great Barrier Reef Committee. Australia.

CAMPBELL, C.A. (1976): *The Coral Seas.* Orbis Publishing Lond. 1-128.

ENDEAN, R. (1976): Destruction and recovery of coral reef communities. In: *Biology and Geology of Coral Reefs* (Ed. Jones and Endean), Vol. 3 (Biol.2): 215-255. Academic Press.

GARDINER, J.S. (1900): The Atoll of Minicoy. *Proc. phil. Soc. (biol.)* 2(1): 22-26.

_______ (ED.) (1903-6): *The fauna and Geography of the Maldives and Laccadives.* Vol. 1 and 2: 1-1057. Cambridge Univ. Press.

_______ (1936): The reefs of the Western Indian Ocean. *Trans. Linn. Soc. Lond., (zool.)* 19:393-465.

JONES, S. (1964): A preliminary survey of the common Tuna bait fishes of Minicoy and their distribution in the Laccadive Archipelago. *Proc. Symp. Scombroid Fishes,* Part II: 643-680. Mar. biol. Ass. India.

_____ & KUMARAN, M. (1980): *Fishes of the Laccadive Archipelago.* The nature conservation and aquatic Science, Trivandrum: 1-760.

MANNADIER, N.S. (ED.) (1977): *Gazetteer of India. Lakshadweep Administration:* 1-374.

MARAGOS, J.E. & CHAVE, K.E. (1973): Stress and interference of Man in Bay. In: *Atlas of Kaneohe Bay* (Ed. Smith *et al.*): 119-123.

MURTY, A.V.S. *et al.* (1979): On the occurrence of *Acanthaster planci* (The Crown of Thorns) at Minicoy Atoll. *Mar. Fish. Infor. Serv. T & E ser.*, No. 13: 10-12. CMF Institute, Cochin.

NAIR, P.V.R. & PILLAI, C.S.G. (1972): Primary productivity of some Coral Reefs in the Indian Ocean. *Proc. Symp. Corals and Coral Reefs.* Mar. Biol. Ass. India: 33-42.

NISHIHIRA, M. & YAMAZATO, K. (1974): Human interference with coral reef community and *Acanthaster* infestation at Okinawa. *Proc. IInd. Internat. Coral Symp.* Vol. 1 577-590. Great Barrier Reef Committee-Australia.

PILLAI, C.S.G. (1971a): Distribution of shallow water stony corals at Minicoy Atoll in the Indian Ocean. *Atoll. Res. Bull. Wash.* 141: 1-12.

_______ (1971b): The distribution of corals on a reef at Mandapam Palk Bay. *J. mar. biol. Ass. India* 11 (1&2): 62-72.

PILLAI, C.S.G. (1971c): Composition of the coral fauna of the Southeastern coast of India and the Laccadives. *In* Regional Variation in Indian Ocean Coral reefs. *Symp. Zool. Soc. Lond.* 28: 301-327. Acadamic press.

____ (1972): Stony corals of the seas around India. *Proc. Symp. Corals and Coral Reefs.* Mar. biol. Ass. India: 191-216.

__ (1973): Coral resources of India with special reference to Palk Bay and Gulf of Mannar. *Proc. Symp. Living Resources of the seas around India*: 700-705. CMFRI. India.

____ (1975): An assessment of the effects of environment and human interference on the coral reefs of Palk Bay and Gulf of Mannar, along the Indian coast. *Seafood Export J.* 7(12):1-13.

__ (1977): The structure, formation and species diversity of South Indian Reefs. *Proc. IIIrd. Internat. Symp. Corals. Miami:* 47-53.

________ RAJAGOPAL M.S. & VARGEHEES, M.A. (1979): Preliminary report on the reconnaissance survey of the major coastal and marine ecosytems in Gulf of Kutch. *Mar. Fish. Infor. Serv. T&E ser.*, No. 14:16-20. CMFRI. Cochin.

_______ MADAN MOHAN & KUNHIKOYA, K. (1983): On an unusual massive recruitment of the reef fish *Ctenochaetes strigosus* (Bennet) (Perciformes, Acanthuridae) to Minicoy Atoll and its significance. *Indian J. Fish.* 30:(2): 261-268.

RAY, G. CARLETON (1976): Critical Marine habitats. *An international conference on Marine Parks and Reserves.* IUCN Pub (New Ser.) *37:* 15-63. Tokyo.

SALE, F. PETER (1979): Recruitment and co-existence in a Guild of territorial coral reef fishes. *Oecologica* (Berl.) 42: 159-177.

__________ (1980): The ecology of fishes in coral reefs. *Oceanogr. Mar. Biol. Ann. Rev.* 18: 367-421.

SALVAT, B. (ED.) (1981): Human activities that cause damage to Coral Reefs. *Coral Reef News Letter* No. 3-20-21. IUCN Survival Service Commission. Paris.

STODDART, D.R. (1969): Ecology and Morphology of Recent Coral Reefs. *Biol. Review* 44: 433-498.

WIENS, J. HEROLD (1971): *Atoll Environment and Ecology.* Yale Univ. press Newhaven pp. 532.

Above: Recently dead coral shoals in the lagoon at lowtide owing to silting.
Below: Dead and disintegrated branches of *Acropora* lying at the lagoon bottom.

Above: Eroded shore of Minicoy, result of sea-erosion.
Below: Natural forest of *Pandanus* being set on fire for new settlement.

Eutrophication, a major problem in the conservation of freshwater resources

(*With a text-figure*)

H.S. SEHGAL

Fisheries Research Complex, Department of Zoology, Punjab Agricultural University, Ludhiana

INTRODUCTION

Eutrophication has been defined differently. But in the words of Schindler (1974), a major contributor to the subject, "eutrophication" is the rapid growth of algae and aquatic weeds in natural waters. This is one of the most serious and pressing of the contemporary problems in the conservation of natural resources. Rapid eutrophication leads to a quick extinction of not only the desired species of aquatic organisms but the aquatic system as a whole. Principally, there are two kinds of eutrophication: (i) The natural eutrophication and (ii) the cultural eutrophication. Natural eutrophication is brought about by the reduction in the water volume through natural sedimentation and the filling up of the basin. It may take thousands of years for a lake to transform ultimately into a ground by natural eutrophication. The cultural eutrophication is due to the allochthonous supply of nutrients through sewage, industrial effluents and agricultural by-products thrown into the water bodies.

The deleterious effects of hyper-eutrophication are mainly through the oxygen depletion and other vital changes in the chemistry of the water. There are numerous examples of this kind including that of Budha nala, a tributary of River Satluj in Punjab. This stream one of the best fish spawning and catching grounds just 20 years ago, has been reduced to small strips with water densely black in colour. The water chemistry is altogether changed. Out of 56 species of fish existing in 1964 only 4 are left at present. This has occurred mainly through the release of industrial effluents and the untreated sewage into it (Sehgal 1984).

Different from eutrophic, there are oligotrophic water bodies which are poor in nutrients and productivity as a whole. The characterization of a water body whether eutrophic or oligotrophic and even the degree of eutrophication (important in formulating policies to conserve a particular aquatic habitat) has been based on its physical, chemical and biological parameters. The few available data on the indices of eutrophy are contradictory and unconvincing. This has urged a comparison of the available limnological data and the trophic status of some global lakes including a few studied by me in the North-western part of India. By this, an attempt has been made to review various factors used as indices of eutrophy and the consistency among them. Ways and means of controlling eutrophication and thus conserving freshwater ecosystems have been suggested.

MORPHOMETRY

Mean depth (z) of lakes, the ratio of volume (m^3) to surface area (m^2) has been considered as an index of lake productivity; low values usually indicating the eutrophic nature. A perusal of table shows that lakes classified as eutrophic usually have low *z* values, while those with higher *z* values are classified as oligotrophic or non-productive.

TABLE

MEAN DEPTH (Z) AND TROPHIC STATUS OF SOME GLOBAL LAKES

S. No.	z (range)	Trophic status	No. of lakes
1.	14.8-154 m	Oligotrophic	14
2.	3.1-14.5 m	Eutrophic	16

PHYSICO-CHEMICAL FEATURES

Transparency. A range of Secchi disc transparency drawn out from a few reported works (Mendis 1956; McColl 1972; Mathew 1975; Sehgal 1980) is 0.58 to 2.06 m for eutrophic, 7.89 m for mesotrophic (moderately eutrophic) and 11.0 to 11.9 m for the oligotrophic lakes.

Chemical stratification. Prevalence of a clinograde dissolved oxygen curve (see figure) during the period of thermal stratification has been considered an important feature of eutrophy by Sreenivasan (1969), Timms (1970) and McColl (1972). Similarly but inversely, a well defined vertical gradient showing an increase in carbon dioxide, bicarbonates and total alkalinity from surface to bottom and an absence of carbonates in bottom layers have also been used as indices of eutrophy.

Vertical differences in pH have also been used as an index of eutrophy in lakes. Sreenivasan (1969) compared Lake Ooty, with a pH difference of 2.5 units from surface to bottom, with a highly productive water body (Sylvan lake) described by Wetzel (1966).

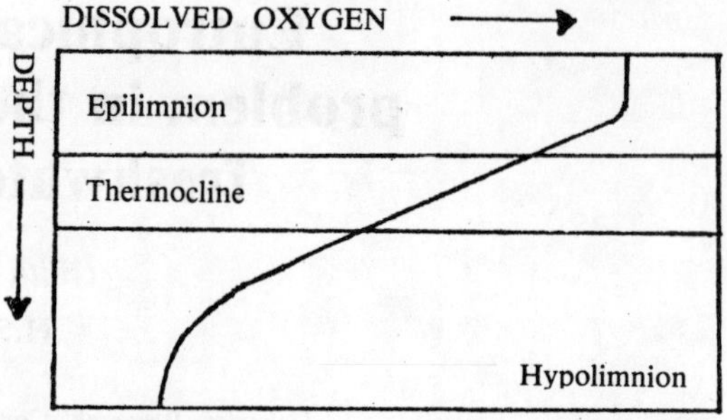

Fig. A typical clinograde dissolved oxygen curve.

Phosphorus and Nitrogen. Phosphorus and nitrogen, which are highly concentrated in most organic wastes and fertilizers, are responsible for nearly all of the world's eutrophication problems (Schindler 1974). Lakes fertilized both with nitrogen and phosphorus have much higher chlorophyll concentrations and productivities than the unfertilized ones and those treated with either of these nutrients individually show weaker responses (Fee 1979). According to Moyle (1964) and Banerjea (1967) lakes with less than 0.20 ppm of phosphate-phosphorus are oligotrophic while those with 0.20 to 0.85 ppm are eutrophic. However, Hutchinson (1957) has defined the eutrophic system as one in which total potential concentration of nutrients is high no matter even if there was an extremely low concentration of these in a water body at any time. Recently, Recknow and Simpson (1980) have used the phosphorus concentration prediction to assess the trophic status of lakes. Similar studies have been made by Wahby & El-Moneim (1979).

Calcium. Ohle, as back as 1934, classified lakes for their productivity on the basis of calcium concentrations, the index which was later on used by many workers like Welch (1952), Hutchison (1957) and Sreenivasan (1967). Lakes with 10 mg/1 of calcium are considered as poor (oligotrophic), with 10-25 mg/1 as medium (mesotrophic) and with 25 mg/1 as rich (productive or eutrophic).

BIOLOGICAL FEATURES

Species lists. It is well known that many plant and animal species act as biological indicators of either a specific feature of a habitat (Jyoti and Sehgal 1979) or the overall trophic status of a water body. Hooper (1969), Hergenrader (1980) and Ringleberg (1980) consider succession of biological communities as one of the most useful indices of eutrophication. Davydova and Trifonova (1979) have correlated the diatom flora of two different types of lakes with the state of their eutrophication. Many phytoplanktonic species like *Fragilaria corotonesis*, *Microcystis aeruginosa* and *Aphanizomenon flosaque* are recorded as the indicators of eutrophy in some New Zealand lakes (Cassie and Freeman 1980). *Filinia oplienssis, Hexarthra mira, Keratella tropica, Brachionus angularis* and *Polyarthra vulgaris* among rotifers and *Chydorus sphaericus, Alona guttata* and *Simocephalus vetulus* among Cladocera are the species of eutrophic waters (Forsyth and McColl 1975; Sehgal 1980).

Species diversity. Use of species diversity index has been preferred over the species lists to determine the maturity levels or the trophic status of water bodies. From the studies carried out on some water bodies in North-western India (Sehgal, unpublished data), it has been revealed that water bodies with almost same levels of maturity are quite different in the percentage of commonness of species and vice-versa. Species diversity is a better and reliable tool to assess the maturity level of water bodies.

Primary productivity. The rate of primary production per unit volume of the trophogenic zone is an index of the degree of eutrophication (Ruttner 1964). Wetzel (1975) used this index to compare potential productivity of water bodies in many diverse habitats. The mean rates of primary production vary from 300 to 1000 mg^C/m^2/day and from 1500 to 6090 mg^C/m^2/ day in naturally eutrophic and culturally eutrophic lakes respectively. (Edmondson 1969; Rhode 1969; Fee 1979; Hickman 1979, Khan 1979) though Wetzel (1975) reported a range of 89.0 to 996.0 mg^C/m^2/day for a mesotrophic lake, Olin in Indiana.

In polluted or culturally eutrophic waters the contribution of nannoplankton quite often becomes greater than any other form of life (Ryther 1956). Khan (1979) reported a contribution of 50-92% of nannoplankton to the total phytoplankton production in a eutrophic lake, Manasbal.

Biomass. Biomass has also been correlated with the trophic status of lakes. Phytoplankton biomass in eutrophic water bodies is over 8 mg/1, sometimes reaching as high as 30 mg/1 (Spodnieweski 1979).

Production/biomass ratio. Mature ecosystems are assumed to be characterised by a low productivity (P)/biomass (B) ratio (Margalef/1968; Odum 1969). These ecosystems are more efficient, i.e. they can maintain a greater biomass per unit of primary productivity.

COMPATIBILITY OF THE INDICES OF EUTROPHY

After comparing various indices, the entire concept of eutrophy, as it has been applied to lake ecosystems, becomes questionable. If the indices measure the condition (maturity/eutrophy) of the same ecosystem, there should exist an agreeable relationship between them (the indices). But this is not true. Lake Michigan though productive and considered eutrophic, has exceptionally high mean depth (84 m) (Wells and Mclain 1973). Similarly, lakes Leake and Tooms in Tasmania, on the basis of almost all other indices are oligotrophic despite very low values (2.2 and 3.7 m respectively Croome and Tyler 1972). Thus, the inverse relationship between and productivity of lakes seems to be of little value. It seems to be an empirical relation which is rather a result of a more fundamental casual relation.

A clinograde dissolved oxygen curve albeit used as suggestive of eutrophic condition does not hold true universally. In lake Itasca, higher summer values of dissolved oxygen at bottom falsely suggested it to be an oligotorophic water body despite its proposed eutrophic characteristics like shallowness, greater transparency and greater trophogenic zone (extending up to hypolimnion) which are responsible for higher oxygen production at the bottom (Cole 1975). Another observation, contrary to above but supporting the view, is of Green *et al.* (1973) who recorded marked stratification and deoxygenated hypolimnion in a deep oligotrophic lake, Barombi Mbo in West Cameroon. Similarly, Sreenivasan (1977) found a considerable oxygen deficiency at the bottom of a tropical Indian reservoir (Sholiar) which otherwise showed many characters of oligotrophy (e.g. low electrical conductivity, low total alkalinity, negligible phosphorus content etc.).

Winner (1972) ranked the lakes of his study on the basis of three functional (P/B ratios, assimilation numbers and net productivity) and three structural (pigment ratios, phytoplankton diversity and zooplankton diversity) indices. He concluded that there is no agreement between the structural indices, between any one of the structural and any one of the functional indices or between any one of the structural indices and the degree of eutrophication. He, however, observed an agreement between three functional indices in ranking of the lakes of his study.

Conclusions and Suggestions

Despite the extensive studies carried out in various parts of the world it cannot be definitely concluded as which particular characteristic can be assigned as the single or the fundamental index of eutrophy and the degree of eutrophication. In the light of the knowledge accumulated so far, it can only be said that lake trophic state is a multi-dimensional hybrid concept which may find its deposition from a number of morphometric, physical, chemical and biological indices. However, there is hardly any doubt that nutrients like phosphorus and nitrogen are basically the cause of eutrophication and their total may reflect its state. Thus, it is indispensable to use the net primary productivity (P), biomass (B), P/B ratios (all dependent upon the inflow of nutrients) at least for some decades to come as the indices of eutrophy and the degree of eutrophication in lakes.

It is suggested, therefore, that the diversion or release of water rich in nutrients like phosphorus and nitrogen at desirable rates in lakes and other water bodies can considerably control the process of cultural eutrophication in them and thus can help in their conservation.

Literature

Banerjea, S.M. (1967): Water quality and soil conditions of fish ponds in some states of India in relation to fish production. *Indian J. Fish.* **14**(1 & 2): 115-114.

Cassie, V. & Freeman, P.T. (1980): Observations on some chemical parameters and the phytoplankton of fine west coast dune lakes in Northland, New Zealand, *N.Z. J. Bot.* **18**(2): 299-320.

Cole, Gerald A. (1975): Text Book of Limnology. The G.V. Mosby Company, Saint Louis. 283 pp.

Croome, R.L. & Tyler, P.A. (1972): Physical and chemical limnology of lake Leake and Tooms lake, Tasmania Arch. *Hydrobiol.* **70**(3): 341-354.

DAVYDOVA, N.V. & TRIFONOVA, I.S. (1979): Diatoms of plank and bed sediments and chlorophyll concentration in sediments of two different types of lakes the Karelian Isthemus as indicators of the eutrophication process. *Bot. Zh.* **64**(8):11.

EDMONDSON, W.T., (1969): Eutrophication in North America, in Eutrophication: Causes, consequences, correctives. *Nat. Acad. Sci. Washington:* 124-149.

FEE, EVERETT J. (1979): A relation between lake morphometry and primary productivity and its use in interpreting whole-lake eutrophication experiments. *Limnol. Oceanogr.* **24**(3): 401-416.

FORSYTH, D.J. & MCCOLL, R.H.S. (1975): Limnology of lake Nagahewa, north Island, New Zealand. *N.Z. Jour. Mar. Freshwat. Res.* **9**(3): 311-332.

GREEN, J., CORBETT, S.A. & BETNEY, E. (1973): Ecological studies on crater lakes in West Cameroon. The blood of endemic fishes of Barombi Mbo in relation to stratification and their feeding habits. *J. Zool.* **170**(3):299-308.

HERGENRADER, G.L. (1980): Eutrophication of the Salt Valley reservoirs, 1968-73.1. The effects of eutrophication on standing crop and composition of phytoplankton. *Hydrobiologia* **71**(1-2): 61-82.

HICKMAN, M. (1979): Phytoplankton production in small eutrophic lake in central Alberts, Canada. *Int. Rev. Gesamten Hydrobiol.* **64** (5): 643-659.

HOOPER, R.F. (1969): Eutrophication indices and their relation to other indices of ecosystem change. In Eutrophication. Causes, consequences, correctives. *Nat. Acad. Sci. Washington:* 225-235.

HUTCHINSON, G.E. (1957): A treatise on Limnology vol. 1., Geography Physics, and Chemistry. John Wiley & Sons. New York: 1015 p.

JYOTI, M.K. & SEHGAL, H. (1979): Ecology of rotifers of Surinsar, a subtrophical freshwater lake in Jammu (J&K), India. *Hydrobiol.* **65**(1):23-32.

KHAN, M.A. (1979): Some observations on the trophic evolution of monomictic flood-plain lake, *Indian J. Ecol.* **6** (2) 27-30.

MARGALEF (1968): Perspectives in ecological theory. Univ. Chicago Press: 111 pp.

MATHEW, P.M. (1975): Limnology and productivity of Govindgarh lake, Rewa, Madhya Pradesh. *J. Inland Fish. Soc. India* **7**:16-24.

MCCOLL, R.H.S. (1972): Chemistry and tropic status of seven New Zealand lakes. *N.Z. Jour. Mar. Freshwat. Res.* **6**(4): 399-447.

MENDIS, A.S. (1956): A limnological comparison of four lakes in Saskatchewan. Fisheries Report No. 2 of Fisheries branch Department of Natural resources, Province of Saskatchewan: 5-23.

MOYLE, J.B., (1949): Some indices of lake productivity. Trans. Am. Fish Soc., **76**:322-334.

ODUM, E.P. (1969): The strategy of ecosystem development. *Sci.* **164**:252-270.

OHLE, W. (1934): Chemische und. Physikalische unkssuchungen norddentscher seen. *Arch. Hydrobiol.* **26**:386-464.

RECKHOW, K.H. & SIMPSON, J.T. (1980): A procedure using modelling and error analysis for the prediction of lake phosphorus concentration from land use information. *J. Fish. Aquat. Sci.* **37**(9): 1439-1448.

RHODE, W. (1969): Crystalization of eutrophication concepts in northern Europe. *In* Eutrophication. Causes, consequences, correctives. *Nat. Acad. Sci. Washington*: 50-64.

RINGLEBERG, J. (1980): Eutrophication: Introduction to the process and some ecological implications. *Hydrobiol. Bull.* **14** (1-2): 30-35.

RUTTNER, FRANZ (1964): Fundamentals of Limnology. Translated by D.G. Frey and F.E.J. Frey. Univ. Toronto Press: 295 pp.

RYTHER, J.H. (1956): Photosynthesis in the Ocean as a function of light intensity. *Limnol. Oceanogr.* **1**:61-70.

SCHINDLER, D.W. (1974): Eutrophication: from: the Allocative Conflicts in Water-Resources Management. Aquassiz Center for Water Studies. Univ. Manitoba. F.W.I. reprint no. **342**:255-267.

SEHGAL, H.S. (1980): Limnology of lake Surinsar, Jammu, with reference to zooplankton and fishery prospects. Ph.D. Thesis, Univ. of Jammu, India: 367 p.

________ (1984): Status of Natural Aquatic Resources in Punjab. Proc. Symp., "Status of Wildlife in Punjab." Nov. 1 & 2, 1983: 95-106.

SPONDNUEWSKI, I. (1979): Phytoplankton as the indicator of lake eutrophication. 2. Summer situation in 25 Masurian lakes in 1976: *Ecol. Pol.* **27**(3): 481-496.

SREENIVASAN, A. (1967): Application of limnological and primary production studies in fish culture. FAO Fish. Rep. No. 3 **44**:104-113.

____ (1969): Eutrophication trends in a chain of artificial lakes in Madras (India). *Indian J. Environ. Hlth.* **11**:392-401.

____ (1977): Oxygen depletion and thermal stratification in two newly formed tropical impoundments. *J. Inland Fish. Soc. India* **9**:67-71.

TIMMS, B.S. (1970): Chemical and zooplankton studies on lentic habitats in North-eastern New South Wales. *Aust. J. Mar. Freshwat. Res.* **21**:11-33.

WAHBY, S.D. & EL-MONELM, M.A.A. (1979): The problem of phosphorus in the eutrophic lake Maryat. *Estuar. Coast. Mar. Sci.* **9**(5):615-22.

WELCH, P.S. (1952): Limnology. McGraw Hill Book Company, New York. Toronto, London: 538pp.

WELLS, LARUE & ALBERTON, L. McLain (1973): Lake Michigan. Man's effects on native fish stocks and other biota. Great lakes Fishery Commission. Technical Report No. 22: 1-55.

WETZEL, R.G. (1966): Variations in productivity of Goose and hypertrophic Sylvan Lakes. Indiana. Invest. Indiana lakes Stream 7:147-184.

__________ (1975): Limnology W.B. Saunders Co. Philadelphia, 743 p.

WINNER, R.W. (1972): An evaluation of certain indices of eutrophy and maturity in lakes. *Hydrobiol.* 40(2):223-240.

Problems in developing a National Wildlife Policy and in creating effective national parks and sanctuaries in Pakistan

(*With one plate*)

T.J. Roberts

Introduction

Pakistan today has three extensive national parks, totalling 570,369 hectares or 2200 square miles, which have been recognised by the International Union for Conservation of Nature and Natural Resources as conforming to the guidelines and principles applicable to a national park. One is a high Himalayan, one a desert park and one an arid foothill park. In addition there are nearly a dozen smaller-area wildlife sanctuaries including one for Markhor in Chitral, Punjab Urial in Mianwali District, tropical dry deciduous forest in Margalla Hills, plus three wetland sanctuaries in lower Sind, and Government supported projects for protecting the Indus Dolphin, Green Turtle nesting beaches, Cheer Pheasant re-introduction and so forth.

All this really has its origins since 1967 when the Pakistan Tourist Development Corporation invited an international team of World Wildlife Fund experts to survey the wildlife resources of the country under the leadership of Guy Mountfort, an International Trustee of WWF. Following from the two WWF expeditions led by Mountfort in 1967 and 1968, a national Wildlife Inquiry Committee was set up, which in 1970 made recommendations for the immediate establishment of various national parks and wildlife sanctuaries and the setting up of a National Council for Wildlife Preservation under the Chairmanship of the Federal Minister for Agriculture, Food and Cooperatives. This heralded a new era in which the focus was no longer on game preservation for sports hunters but upon the need to protect all wildlife and to preserve unspoiled, at least some unique wilderness areas.

Development of Administrative Agencies

The overall body in Pakistan is the National Council for Wildlife Preservation, which falls within the responsibility of the Ministry of Agriculture and has a wide official and non-official membership. This has an administrative headquarters, which is headed by a Cabinet Secretary in Islamabad. At the provincial level in Punjab and Sind, special Wildlife Advisory Boards have been set up with independant wildlife officers. In the less affluent provinces of Baluchistan and the North West Frontier Province financial restraints have dictated that wildlife responsibility remain a branch of the Forestry Service but here also officials make a career within this department and are not expected to be transferred to other duties. The National Parks are administered within provincial budgets and the Wildlife Boards under the chairmanship of provincial governors, have wide powers in appointing officials, amending or proposing new protective legislation and so forth.

One innovative idea introduced first in Sind in the early 1970's and since adopted in Punjab, was the appointment of local residents of high repute or social standing such as tribal Sirdars

[1]In Pakistan it is an autonomous corporate body titled Water and Power Development Authority.

and heads of land-owning families, as Honorary Game Wardens with considerable legal powers, in each district. These men have done more to control poaching and to protect the sanctity of the National Parks and Wildlife Preserves than was possible before with enforcement only by low paid Game or Wildlife Department staff. Efforts have also been made now in Punjab and Sind to provide game watchers with motorcycles and Provincial Wildlife Department heads with four-wheel drive vehicles. There is however, still a problem in developing a professional cadre of properly trained wildlife officials.

To meet this need, wildlife management courses were introduced into the College of Forestry located at Peshawar, and collaboration of Food & Agriculture Organisation was sought to set up such training courses. Since this has still not met the need, scholarships for overseas post-graduate training have been specially awarded to officials in the Provincial Wildlife Service or at National Council Headquarters. At this particular moment three senior officers, one each from the Pakistan Forest Institute, the National Council and the Provincial Wildlife Service of Punjab, are on secondment for such training and are taking MSc. courses overseas. Until we can develop an adequate body of professionally trained specialists there will still be a tendency to rely upon Forestry Department secondment and for a wide cross section of officials to assume that they can become experts in this special field without possessing the necessary special scientific background.

HUMAN PROBLEMS

Sport hunting has been one of the first things to be well controlled even since the late 1960's, perhaps because Pakistan was a nation of sport-hunting lovers and the decision makers were quick to appreciate the need for some self regulation if game stocks were not to be depleted beyond the point of national recovery. A system of totally closed hunting areas by rotation, and a limited number of fixed days in each month when shooting was permitted was successfully introduced. Checkpoints were set up, manned by Wildlife Department staff on road barriers outside the main cities to inspect incoming vehicles especially on weekends when hunting was allowed. This has proved to be very successful. A much more intractable problem has been that of the high placed official with ideas of entrenched privilege, who openly flaunts the game laws. There have been instances of both prominent political leaders and defence service personnel particularly in frontier regions where some of our rarer wildlife still precariously survives, indulging in poaching. Fortunately the present government has recently taken stringent action against one or two high-ranking offenders and set a salutary example. There is another problem stemming from the trapping or catching of migratory cranes by tribesmen in the frontier, and the North West Frontier Province government has started a village to village educational campaign, besides increasing licencing fees for keeping live cranes etc. so that this can be gradually controlled and limited. The hunting of the Houbara Bustard by visiting Arab dignitaries has also posed a similar delicate problem which has constantly thwarted efforts by conservationists to ban hunting. From the winter of 1984 all hunting of the Houbara will be banned, as a result of recommendations made in October 1983 by conservationists from 12 countries who attended a symposium on bustards hosted by Pakistan in Peshawar. This hunting, in view of the country's oil-import problems and wishes to attract foreign investors, has been a sensitive political and economic issue for the past fifteen years; so, this decision is a milestone in marking Pakistan's commitment to wildlife preservation.

HUMAN DISTURBANCE IN WILDLIFE SANCTUARIES

This is still a major problem but not from excessive disturbance by visitors as is the case in many American and European national parks, where there has been serious erosion of footpaths, and accidents arising from over-confident visitors and potentially dangerous wild animals. The problem, shared with India, is rather that of illegal domestic grazing stock and their potential for transmitting disease and an even more intractable problem is related to the 'pre-park' traditional right of local villagers for gathering fuel wood and fodder. This is especially acute in semi-arid zones where fodder is always scarce. This problem has been largely overcome in the Margalla National Park, by re-settlement of some farming families. A very costly operation only made possible because of the availability of special additional funds and the proximity of the new capital of Islamabad. However it has not been solved elsewhere.

In wetland sanctuaries we have had problems from reed cutting for roof thatch and commercial fishing. It had come to be expected that the Irrigation and Water and Power Development Authorities[1] could supplement their budgets because reservoirs and irrigation barrage head-ponds could provide income by auctioning of fishing rights to commercial fishermen. This has now been banned on two important lakes which are game sanctuaries, namely Lal Sohanran and Haleji, but still does not go far enough. The Wildlife Council is seized of this problem and continues to press the Provincial services involved to forego the revenue from their barrage headponds and reservoirs.

ON-GOING CONSERVATION PROJECTS

Captive breeding of Green Turtles (*Chelonia mydas*)

There are eleven known nesting beaches in the world for this species. One is Karachi coastline. In Pakistan, fortunately local sentiment or prejudice save the eggs from consumption, though in other Muslim countries such as along the Omani seacoast, and west Malaysia seacoast, this doesn't prevent them from being dug up and consumed. But Karachi is now a city of 8 million and recreational use of the nesting beaches, located so close to the city, is heavy and this constantly disturbs the nesting turtles. Since, patrolling of the beaches to protect the Turtles was not feasible, instead clutches of newly laid eggs are dug up and reared in protected enclosures, and the Turtle hatchlings are subsequently taken after dark and released in the sea. Of course this does not stop all natural predators but it does eliminate predators such as pie-dogs and gulls. So far over 45,000 hatchlings have been released. It has been noted already that in years of a strong monsoon with higher tides and higher humidity, hatching success seems to be greater. Adult breeding females are being tagged, and various aspects of their biology studied by a team of scientists, but so far no successful method has been devised for tagging or marking the hatchlings.

Indus river Dolphin (*Platanista indi*)

Construction of irrigation barrages has split up the dolphin population into isolated pockets. Regrettably, no one thought of the necessity for suitable fish ladders when these barrages were constructed. Drawing off of river water for irrigation also has drastically reduced available habitat for the Dolphin in winter. The best surviving viable population lies between the Guddu and Sukkur barrages on the main Indus river. Here in the late 1970's about 180 *Platinista indi* Blind Dolphins were thought to survive. A Dolphin sanctuary covering a 23 mile stretch of the river was created and a warden-cum-research officer of the rank of Divisional Forest Officer was appointed. The first major problem was commercial catching of dolphins by professional tribes of fishermen, living on the river and specialising in this art. Oil extracted from Dolphins was reported to have medicinal properties. Eventually after repeated warnings and petty finings, they were brought to court and heavily penalised and compulsorily re-located further upstream. Jobs were arranged for some of the men with commercial river fishing outfits as an incentive to them to agree to the relocations. This was a classic example of the use of the "carrot and the stick", which seems to have worked. A detailed survey by an IUCN foreign expert in the summer of 1977 showed very successful breeding ratios of this Dolphin and the present day population inside the Sanctuary is estimated to have increased to nearly 300 individuals.

Re-introduction of the Cheer Pheasant (*Catreus wallichii*)

This is a project which has been on-going over the past nine years with very little success so far, though a good many valuable lessons have been learned. It was initiated by World Wildlife Fund—Pakistan in association with pheasant enthusiasts in Britain. Young men were selected for training in the U.K. in pheasant rearing techniques. The following year they were put in charge of incubating aviary bred eggs especially flown out (and donated) by the World Pheasant Association, from the U.K. Artificial incubation, as well as hatching under broody hens has been employed with varying success. Over the years, no less than four different sites have been chosen for the introductions, with specially constructed rearing and pre-release pens. The main problems have been low hatchability due to red-tapism in clearing eggs and occasionally holding them too long in order to make bulk shipments. An equally serious problem has been posed by predators which repeatedly broke into enclosures and the pen design had to be repeatedly changed, even including employment of electric fences and heavy-duty expanded metal mesh. The young poults could and did injure themselves on the sharp edged expanded metal, which was overcome by an inner fence of softer chicken mesh-wire netting. Jackals, Yellow-throated Martens and Himalayan Palm Civets all proved problems even with night-long watchmen or guards being posted. Poults were radio-tagged and released, but unfortunately most appear to have succumbed after release to natural predators. More birds have been reared again this summer with much improved dietary and rearing techniques and it remains to be seen if there is more success in subsequent location or sighting of liberated birds. They are being introduced into two different foothill zones where the Cheer was actually hunted within living memory. It is probably extinct now in Pakistan, but only since the 1960's.

Re-introduction of Blackbuck (*Antilope cervicapra*) into Lal Sohanran Desert Park

This project started in 1971 when the newly established branch of WWF—Pakistan received an offer of collaboration from WWF—U.S.A., and WWF—Holland. The latter country donated fencing for a pre-release enclosure and raised funds to cover air freight shipment of a donation of ten animals from a Texas ranch, 8 were females and 2 were males. Due to the highly congested and noisy environment available at Karachi Zoo where the animals were received and partly due to an unfortunate accident, one female was fatally injured during trans-shipment and off-loading. The remaining seven females and 2 males reached the desert park successfully but having received a donation of chain-link fencing, we had not anticipated the very high local cost of providing termite-proof fence posts for a captive enclosure and the animals had to be held for two years in a relatively small, though skillfully sited, natural enclosure until adequate funds could be obtained to make fence posts. Here due to the excessively aggressive behaviour of the two bucks another doe was fatally injured and breeding success continued to be low. Within 4 or 5 years we had a serious imbalance in the sex ratio with more males and fewer females. Lack of experience and skills prevented the local staff from being able to successfully capture and remove surplus males, even though the Punjab Wildlife Department imported a special 'capchur' gun with darts, from Australia.

Finally we have achieved some success by a combination of: (a) Receiving a second import of Blackbuck does from Copenhagen Zoo, and (b) rans-locating several males by construction of a very skillfully designed netting capture tunnel and shute, lined with stout cord netting. There are now over 65 Blackbuck in this captive herd and it is hoped soon to be able to release some of them into the desert park.

Captive breeding of Western Horned Tragopan (*Tragopan melanocephalus*)

Perhaps the rarest of the five known species of Tragopan in the world today, only the Western Horned is not held in any aviary and both the Pheasant Trust of Norfolk and subsequently the World Pheasant Association have been under very considerable pressure to initiate a captive breeding project in collaboration with the Government of the North West Frontier Province. This has continued since about 1968 when the first adult bird, a female, was captured in the Pakistan hills near the so-called Cease fire line and flown to the Pheasant Trust. Unfortunately a male as mate could not be secured before this female four years later died. Subsequently two males were captured but both of these died, one in captivity in Abbotabad and the second just after arrival in the U.K. In one case the bird was only kept alive by force feeding and in both instances they appeared to suffer some trauma from the experience of being held captive. In the past three or four years two more males have been captured but to date a healthy breeding pair has not reached Belgium where an expert with the most experience in breeding Tragopans remains ready to receive them.

Recent surveys indicate a barely viable population of this Tragopan survives in two areas of Pakistan but it is a serious moral question that we should ask ourselves when considering such captive breeding schemes, whether the risk of losses by encouraging capture by local hunters/trappers, as has been done in this case, of the remaining birds are not too high a price to pay for the still remote possibility of establishing a viable captive population. The controversy which has raged around the proposals to rescue the Californian Condor from extinction, through captive breeding, do indeed have parallels and this is a complex question which I will only refer to in passing.

PROBLEMS OF INTRODUCING EXOTIC SPECIES

Sports Associations and particularly the USA Fish and Wildlife Department have in the past 20 years obtained donations from Pakistan of Black Partridges (*Francolinus francolinus*) and

Chukor (*Alectoris chukor*). In exchange local wildlife authorities requested and received shipments of such birds as Ring-necked Pheasants (*Phasianus colchicus*) and Mountain Quail (*Oreortyx pictus*) and attempts have recently been made in all four provinces to release pheasants and quail into the wild. Fortunately the Quail did not survive and there is no evidence so far of the Ringnecked Pheasants successfully breeding in the wild. In areas where our own native highly adapted endemic partridges are already dwindling, the introduction of exotic game birds as competitors for the last remnant of natural cover and food resources, is only to be deplored.

SUMMARY

Pakistan in common with all neighbouring Asian countries has, as its major problem, the rapidly expanding human population which lessens, if not actually cancels out, improvements in living standards and the quality of human life resulting from better utilization of natural resources. This poses the greatest dilemna today for wildlife conservationists. The increasing pressure to exploit natural resources to a greater extent often leads to national park encroachments. Sometimes such encroachments are directly the activity of government sponsored projects, more frequently they are by tacit acceptance of illicit use. Foreign aid agencies often have to share part of the responsibility or blame for such encroachments. In Pakistan in the recent past it would not be unfair to state that a number of Himalayan located forestry projects have been accepted with a wholly exploitative bias at the expense of projects emphasising erosion control, catchment improvement and re-afforestation techniques, none of which can yield short-term dividends so eagerly sought by the planners. Fortunately the emphasis is now changing rapidly and major efforts at re-afforestation are under way in several key areas such as lower Kaghan Valley and the vale of Swat.

The only hope for striking a sensible balance and saving an adequate cross section of our wilderness area and their original wildlife resources, lies in trying to change people's attitudes through a long-term educational programme. This may sound trite or obvious, but it is a challenge in which all of us must be engaged. The most urgent need now is for conservationists to promote a better understanding amongst the less well-educated and more inaccessible human populations wherein our retreating wildlife is now most likely to be found, and where it is most likely to be most seriously threatened. People's attitudes will always be more potent than any imposed legislation. As wilderness areas shrink or disappear, and wildlife dwindles, the remnant wildlife retreats into more remote areas. Often for valid logistic reasons, the human populace of such areas is neglected and struggling daily with the problems of sheer survival. It is not surprising therefore that people in such areas are not only poorly educated, but that they regard wildlife as an unlimited resource, if not a hostile force, either way to be exploited. The need of the hour is not so much to make the decision-makers in government aware of the problems associated with development projects, as to make people in so-called backward areas, aware of modern attitudes towards wildlife and the benefits which can accrue in the long run from utilization at a level which will allow continued replenishment and enjoyment of wildlife resources for future generations.

Above: Kirthar National Park. Cliffs in background are inhabited by Wild Ibex (*Capra hircus*).
Below: Hawk's Bay, Karachi. Green turtle hatchlings emerging inside protected enclosure at night time.
(*Photos:* T.J. Roberts)

Herpetological Conservation in India

ROMULUS AND ZAI WHITAKER

During the last fifty years, there has been an excessive and largely unmeasured exploitation of Indian reptiles for the skin, live animal and curio industries in that order of importance. As early as 1935 Malcolm Smith, the author of the FAUNA OF BRITISH INDIA — Reptilia volumes, was concerned about the slaughter of reptiles for trade purposes and expressed the view that "Unless measures are taken to control it, certain species are in great danger of being exterminated". Sadly, the same commentary applies today, the only difference being that certain species seem already to have succumbed to the heavy commercial pressure. The Government of India has banned the export of snake skins since 1976 and some snake, turtle and lizard species are listed in the 1972 Wildlife Protection Act. But as with other animal groups, even when there is firm protection on paper, the heavy stakes involved and the more or less skeletal law enforcement branches of the Wildlife Departments encourage the poacher, dealer and exporter to try their luck. For instance the periodical seizures of snake skins in Madras, each involving 20 to 30 thousand skins, represent only the tip of a gigantic iceberg and at this moment there are reported to be several million skins awaiting shipment. And this is just one centre in one state. The ecological implications of this deadly harvest have never been examined. This paper will deal with current development of conservation projects in India, and where applicable in the subcontinent.

AMPHIBIANS

No one seems to know how rare the Himalayan newt (*Tylotriton verrucossus*) is. When the biological supply dealers found out they could make money selling specimens to colleges eager to have this species in their collection, it was heavily collected around Darjeeling and elsewhere. It is also likely to be suffering from ill effects of the rampant deforestation and resultant erosion of its hilly habitat.

In 1981 the frogleg industry in India killed at least 70 million frogs (20% of the frog's weight is exported, the rest dicarded) for export largely to the USA. (which, ironically has supplied some of the nastiest pesticides to India). The ecological effects of removing these great numbers of insect predators from the environment may be profound although there is little data. The Indian bullfrog (*Rana tigerina*) and the green frog (*Rana hexadactyla*) are the two main species killed. The harvest was worth Rs. 12 crores in 1981 and at least a portion of that went to the catchers, mainly Scheduled Tribes like the Irulas.

The past few years have seen a dramatic surge of interest in protecting unique biotopes. No example in India has been given more notoriety than Kerala's Silent Valley in the Kundah Hill Range. About 57 (64%) of India's approximately 89 species of frogs are found in the Western Ghats. It is not surprising that the Zoological Survey of India recently described 4 new species of frogs from Silent Valley, considering that it is one of the last relatively untouched rainforests in Kerala. It seems ludicrous to have to use four endemic amphibians to plead for the survival of a unique biotope. Particularly when the odds lined up against them include political, contractor and electricity board interests.

Conservation measures and studies needed include:

1. Studies on the frogleg industry, starting with the biology of the main species exploited, notably breeding biology and feeding habits.

2. Studies on sustained yield use, ranching and/or farming of frogs.

3. Status and biology studies on the lesser known amphibians, including the legless caecilians and the Himalayan newt. Propose areas suitable for protected areas for the latter.

4. Extensive survey and collection, particularly in northeast and southwest India to determine taxonomy, distribution and status of Indian amphibians.

SNAKES

Currently only 2 species, the Indian python (*Python molurus*) and the egg eating snake (*Elachistodon westermanii*) are protected under Schedule I of the Indian Wildlife (Protection) Act of 1972. The former suffers heavily from over-exploitation for the illegal skin industry and steady loss of even its small scrub jungle habitats. There were a few attempts at breeding this hardy and adaptable species. Up to now only 3 institutions in India have been successful; the Nandankanan Zoological Park, Orissa (Acharjyo and Misra 1976), the Jaipur Zoological Gardens (Yadav 1969) and the Madras Snake Park Trust (Dattatri 1983). Madras Snake Park Trust now has a regular planned breeding programme with 4 years of success. At present hatchlings are reared for 2 years to be released in protected habitats such as sanctuaries and national parks. In 1982 Madras Snake Park Trust and the Tamil Nadu Forest Department released four 2 metre long captive bred pythons in the Mudumalai Wildlife Sanctuary in Tamil Nadu (Dattatri 1983).

Very little information is available regarding *Elachistodon westermanni;* there are only a few preserved specimens in museum collections. Live captive specimens or breeding groups in captivity are non-existent. Though its range is fairly extensive, if it can be determined that it is as rare as it seems, this is an excellent candidate for a captive breeding programme.

No quantitative survey of either species has been carried out so far but are envisaged in the near future (Whitaker 1983). In contrast to the egg eating snake the Indian python is very widely distributed and though extirpated from most of its former range it remains common in certain locations in Andhra Pradesh, Uttar Pradesh, Rajasthan and perhaps elsewhere. The regal python (*P. reticulatus*) is known to be in the Nicobar Islands in unknown numbers. So far its occurrence in northeast India is only a conjecture, though it is known from Chittagong Hill Tracts in Bangladesh. In the Nicobars (where it has been recorded from Car Nicobar, Teressa, Trinkat, Nancowry, Great Nicobar and Little Nicobar) its occasional fondness for domestic fowl often gets it into trouble. A status survey would help bolster arguments for protecting the forests of the Nicobars (where avaricious attention is being directed as the end of the easily reachable Andaman timber is in sight).

The other 233 known snake species are protected under Schedule IV of the Indian Wildlife (Protection) Act of 1972. It was estimated that in 1932 reptile skin export figures were up to about 12,000,000 reptile skins per year (Smith 1935). The modern snake skin industry peaked in 1966-67 when an estimated 10,000,000 snake skins alone were exported (Whitaker 1978). Although it is now illegal to trap snakes without a licence and all trade in skins is banned, the underground trade is still noticeable though hard to estimate. The species under heavy pressure around the country are (in order of magnitude):

1. *Naja naja* (both the spectacled and the northeastern subspecies, *kaouthia*) Common cobra.
2. *Ptyas mucosus* Rat snake (called "Whipsnake" in the skin trade)
3. *Python molurus* Indian python

Loss of Habitat

Loss of habitat constitutes one of the major threats to secretive and non-exploited species. Particularly vulnerbale are the specialised inhabitants of fast disappearing biotopes such as evergreen and semi-evergreen forests, particularly in the Western Ghats of Tamil Nadu, Kerala and in northeast India. Although there is no statistical data, we can assert empirically that species such as the king cobra (*Ophiophagus hannah*) and the burrowing snakes (the unique uropeltids) many of them, face the very real threat of extinction. The uropeltids are endemic to South India and Sri Lanka; deforestation and the conversion of their prime habitats into plantations may have caused local extinction of populations in many parts of their range. No amount of paper protection can help these species. Large tracts of habitat must be preserved if these unique and little-studied animals are to survive.

Smuggling

In spite of the Wildlife Act and the skin export ban, India continues to be one of the leading "exporters" of snake skins. The Economist (April 11th, 1981) states that an estimated US$60 million worth of snake skins are smuggled out of the country each year. During May 1983, 130,000 snake skins were confiscated by customs officials at Madras harbour. The cargo, bound for Singapore was declared to contain handloom materials. The value of the shipment was estimated to be Rs.3 million (*c.* US$300,000). Where such high stakes are involved, control of the illegal trade is a difficult job. And as the Chief Wildlife Warden, Tamil Nadu points out, the tanning of snake skins has become a clandestine cottage industry. Detecting a few of these small tanneries makes little dent on the overall trade.

Loopholes

The recent Government decision to let Bharat Leather Corporation (a Government of India undertaking) buy up and use the over a million "old stock" remaining with skin dealers was unfortunate. It is to be hoped that they take note of where the fresh, wet salted "old stock" originates for future reference.

Alternatives

The problem of alternative employment for the thousands of tribals who have lived from snake hunting for five generations has been a severe limiting factor to the success of the crackdown on the snake skin industry. As long as the only profitable employment for these subsistence hunters is selling snake skin they will do it to buy their rice. Recently the Irula Snake Catchers' Cooperative started marketing venom produced from snakes caught in licensed numbers. The snakes are released back to the wild after four weekly extractions. 52 Irula tribal families are enrolled in the scheme at its beginning. It is hoped to expand the Irula Cooperative in several directions, utilizing their expert talents for rodent control, termite control and scientific research.

Important studies and conservation measures include:

1. Stricter implementation of the now comprehensive laws on snake capture, trade and export of the skins.
2. Examination of value of snakes in rodent control.
3. Examination of possibility of sustained yield cropping of wild snakes.
4. Provision of alternate employment for tribal snake catchers (mainly in Tamil Nadu, Andhra Pradesh and West Bengal).

SEA TURTLES

The Olive Ridley (*Lepidochelys olivacea*), the Green (*Chelonia mydas*), the Hawksbill (*Eretmochelys imbricata*), the Leatherback (*Dermochelys coriacea*) and the Loggerhead (*Caretta caretta*), in that order of abundance, feed close offshore along our coasts (Valliappan 1974) and nesting beaches have been found of all but the Loggerhead, on the mainland and the Lakshadweep and Andaman-Nicobar island groups (Bhaskar 1979).

Until 1976, millions of Olive Ridley eggs were harvested by Calcutta based agents from the unique "arribada" (mass nesting) area of Gahirmatha, Orissa, first reported by J.C. Daniel. This is possibly the largest turtle rookery in the world with up to 300,000 females landing to nest each February. The Orissa Forest Department is to be commended for having organized beach patrols to protect nesting females and including Gahirmatha in the recently established Bhitar Kanika Crocodile Sanctuary. The poaching of mating pairs close offshore is a lucrative business during the breeding season (January-February) and thousands are still brought to the beach-head at Digha, West Bengal, destined for sale in Calcutta markets. Following the publication in *India Today* of a report by J. Vijaya (Research Associate, Madras Crocodile Bank Trust), the trade went underground and this year, groups of poachers were arrested by the combined forces of the Navy, Coast Guard and Forest Department. At Chandbali, Orissa in February 1983, poachers were caught with 500 Ridleys, flippers wired together ready for shipment.

The Olive Ridley is the most heavily pressurized species because of its wide distribution and mainland nesting habits. Greens and Hawksbills are also eaten although Hawksbill meat is sometimes toxic and causes fatalities (Whitaker 1978). Markets such as the one in Tuticorin (also underground now), trade in the blood (drunk as an elixir), eggs and meat of turtles (Valliappan 1974). Vizagapatnam is the centre of an extensive trade in Hawksbill shell from Lakshadweep (via Cochin and Mangalore) and from the Andamans and Nicobar Islands (via Madras and Calcutta), though large-scale export at least has stopped.

A greater threat to sea turtles is the coral mining on offshore islands where they feed. The coral islands in the Gulf of Mannar, the prime and perhaps only feeding grounds of the Green in South India, are being destroyed and Bhaskar (1978) reports that lime companies in Gujarat are mining coral and beach sand in Kutch. Recently a Marine National Park was gazetted in the Gulf of Kutch and Sanat Chavan, Warden, informed us that coral and sand removal has been stopped.

During the last ten years there have been efforts at both collection of eggs as well as captive incubation and hatching. The Madras Snake Park Trust (MSPT) established the first hatchery in India on the Tamil Nadu coast releasing some 15,000 Ridley hatchlings into the Bay of Bengal between 1973 and 1976. This has now been continued by the Wildlife Department which this year (1983) hatched and released 76,000 young from coastal hatcheries. In addition, the Central Marine Fisheries Research Institute is undertaking growth and feeding studies on the Ridleys and the Madras Crocodile Bank Trust (MCBT) has published captive rearing data for the Ridley, Green and Hawksbill (Whitaker 1979).

Since 1976, Satish Bhaskar has been surveying and reporting on sea turtle nesting beaches on the mainland and offshore islands, sponsored by the Madras Snake Park Trust and World Wildlife Fund. His work has given an impetus to sea turtle conservation by discovering an important rookery of the Leatherback in Little Andaman (Bhaskar 1979), studying the monsoon nesting of the green turtle on Suheli island (unpublished), and reporting on the large scale sand excavation and coral mining in several states.

All sea turtles are protected under Schedule I of the Wildlife (Protection) Act. We now have enough information on nesting and feeding grounds, mainly through Bhaskar's surveys, to implement at least some necessary safeguards. The Gulf of Mannar, Lakshadweep and important beaches in the Andaman and Nicobar groups must acquire national park status along the lines of Pirotan in Gujarat. Low population areas where there has been heavy egg and turtle collection require hatcheries. It may be possible to re-introduce the Leatherback in Kerala (where it no longer nests) using eggs laid in the Andaman Islands.

Egg collecting, hatching and release is obviously one of the answers to the problem of heavy predation on turtle eggs by man and animals such as jackals, wild pigs and domestic dogs. But project personnel must be well informed. For example it is found that incubation temperatures determine sex ratios of the hatchlings (Mrosovsky 1982). Inexperienced management could result in dangerously biased sex ratios!

The new Department of Environment now has a standing sea turtle advisory group which is an optimistic improvement. To implement effective conservation action we need academic/technical inputs as well. The major areas where this is needed are: temperature and sex determination, migration, captive rearing and ranching, and sea turtle mortality from trawlers.

FRESHWATER TURTLES AND LAND TORTOISES

India's thirty freshwater turtles and land tortoises have received scant attention since M.A. Smith's FAUNA OF BRITISH INDIA, Volume 1 in 1931. In fact most information on the breeding habits of Indian species comes from collectors and herpetologists in Europe and the United States! Turtles are very popular for eating however, and appear mainly in north Indian markets, with Bengal consuming the majority. The commonest species found in markets are the large trionychids (soft-shells), like *Trionyx gangeticus, T. hurum* and the rarer *Chitra indica,* with the small but ubiquitous flapshell *Lissemys punctata* accounting for the largest numbers. However, the smaller hard-shell species are eaten as well: *Melanochelys,* for instance, and even the rare south Indian Cane Turtle (*Heosemys silvatica*) and the Travancore tortoise (*Geochelone travancorica*) are heavily hunted for the pot in Kerala (Vijaya 1982). Star tortoises (*Geochelone elegans*) are killed for

TABLE 1

PROTECTED INDIAN REPTILES

Reptiles under Schedule I of the Indian Wildlife (Protection) Act.	Common name	CITES Appendix	Red Data Book IUCN	Present status of the Indian populations
CROCODYLIDAE				
Crocodylus palustris	Mugger	I	Endangered	Vulnerable
Crocodylus porosus	Saltwater crocodile	I	Vulnerable	Endangered
GAVIALIDAE				
Gavialis gangeticus	Gharial	I	Endangered	Endangered
VARANIDAE				
Varanus griseus	Desert monitor	I	-	Indeterminate
Varanus bengalensis	Bengal monitor	I	-	Common
Varanus salvator	Water monitor	-	-	Vulnerable
Varanus flavescens	Yellow monitor	I	-	Vulnerable
CHELONIDAE				
Chelonia mydas	Green turtle	I	Endangered	Vulnerable
Eretmochelys imbricata	Hawksbill	I	Endangered	Vulnerable
Lepidochelys olivacea	Ridleys	I	Endangered	Vulnerable
Caretta caretta	Loggerhead	I	Vulnerable	Endangered
Dermochelidae				
Dermochelys coriacea	Leatherback	I	Endangered	Endangered
Trionychidae				
Lissemys punctata	Flapshell	I	-	Common
Trionyx gangeticus	Ganges softshell	I	-	Common
Trionyx hurum	Peacock softshell	I	-	Common
EMYDIDAE				
Kachuga tecta	Roofed turtle	I	-	Common
OPHIDIA				
DASYPELTIDAE				
Elachistodon westermanii	Indian egg-eater	II	-	Indeterminate
BOIDAE				
Python m. molurus	Indian python	I	Vulnerable	Vulnerable
Python reticulatus	Regal python	I	-	Indeterminate

TABLE 2

REPTILES ON SCHEDULE II OF THE WILDLIFE ACT. CAPTURE AND TRADE RESTRICTED AND CONTROLLED BY LICENSE.

SQUAMATA (Lizards)				
Suborder LACERTILIA				
CHAEMELEONIDAE				
Chamaeleon zeylanicus	Chameleon	II		Common
Uromastix hardwickii	Spiny-tailed lizard	II		Vulnerable
OPHIDIA (Snakes)				
All snakes not listed in previous Schedules				

TABLE 3

OTHER INDIAN REPTILES NOT IN THE WILDLIFE ACT SCHEDULES BUT RECEIVING INTERNATIONAL PROTECTION

SNAKES				
Eryx conicus	Common sand boa	II	-	Common
Eryx johnii	Red sand boa	II	-	Common
TURTLES				
EMYDIDAE				
Melanochelys trijuga	Black pond turtle	II	-	Common
Melanochelys tricarinata	Ridged pond turtle	I	-	Indeterminate
Heosemys silvatica	Cane turtle	I	Indeterminate	Endangered
Batagur baska	Batagur turtle	I	Endangered	Endangered
TRIONYCHIDAE				
Trionyx nigricans	Black softshell	I	Rare	Indeterminate (not known in India)
TESTUDINIDAE				
Geochelone elegans	Star tortoise	II	-	Vulnerable
Geochelone travancorica	Travancore tortoise	II	Indeterminate	Vulnerable
Geochelone elongata	Elongated tortoise	II	-	Indeterminate

AMPHIBIANS PROTECTED UNDER THE WILDLIFE ACT

Common Name	*Schedule*	*CITES*	*Red Data Book*	*Our opinion*
Himalayan newt	I *Tylototriton verrucosus*			Vulnerable
Freshwater frogs	*Rana* ssp. IV			Common
Viviparous toads	*Nectophrynoides* sp.			Vulnerable

their ornamental shells and are simultaneously losing their scrub habitat to the charcoal manufacturers in areas like Pudukottai (Whitaker 1977).

Several turtle species are protected under the Wildlife Act but due to an unfortunately confused association between exploitation and rarity, the most common are listed in Schedule I and afforded full paper protection while the rarest receive the minimum protection under Schedule IV (see Table). These listings need to be urgently changed. E.O. Moll (1983) has reorganized the listing based on field survey work and submitted it to the Government for consideration.

The Madras Crocodile Bank Trust began a comprehensive turtle and tortoise study and breeding programme in 1982. Over 130 turtles of 21 species and subspecies are maintained by the project. Table 2 records the rearing and breeding of turtles there.

Extensive surveys are required to determine main turtle and tortoise populations and their ranges. In the short time that the Crocodile Bank has been involved in chelonian work much interesting data have materialized, mainly due to the surveys of E.O. Moll who did the field work during 1982 and 1983 with J. Vijaya and Satish Bhaskar in nine Indian states. In 1982, the senior author confirmed the existence of a substantial (100-200 adults caught per year) population of *Batagur baska* in Bangladesh, near the mouth of the Sibsah river in the Sunderbans Forest Reserve (Whitaker 1982). This may be the last population in the Reserve and one of the last populations in the subcontinent. The once common *Batagur* is threatened by hunters and egg collectors. In this case it may be possible for the West Bengal and Bangladesh Forest departments to co-operate in protecting *Batagur*. Vijaya (*in* Moll 1983) found that *Batagur* still survives in the Indian Sunderbans as well. In March/April, 1983 Dr Moll advised the Madhya Pradesh Forest Department in setting up India's first freshwater turtle hatchery for rehabilitating *K. kachuga* and *K. dhongoka* and any other species determined to be rare and/or under pressure.

Though all the freshwater turtles are listed in the schedules of the Wildlife Act, enforcement has been sporadic and the Calcutta markets are still full of protected species each morning. The Uttar Pradesh Forest Department has taken a somewhat more enlightened approach by allowing licensed commercial dealing in *Lissemys,* which though the most common turtle in India, enjoys Schedule I protection. Methods of storage, transport and butchering turtles are among the most inhumane in the world and emphasize the need for management if the industry is to be permitted.

Apart from reorganising and implementing its protective legislation, the government must in the interests of highly exploited or rare species, set up hatcheries. University level and private studies on turtle and tortoise biology should be encouraged. Ultimately, sustained yield usage, commercial farming and ranching of turtles should be investigated and undertaken in place of the unregulated slaughter and egg collection that nearly exterminated one species (*Batagur baska*) as long ago as the turn of the century.

CROCODILIANS

The Government's efforts to save crocodilians came in the form of a successful, FAO/UNDP advised and aided rehabilitation project. It started in 1975 and among other things, halted the almost certain extinction of the gharial (*Gavialis gangeticus*). The various state projects are the subject of another paper, so this section will outline non-government work on crocodile conservation, mainly that of Madras Snake Park Trust and Madras Crocodile Bank Trust. In 1970 and 1971 following Zoological Survey of India (ZSI) and Bombay Natural History Society (BNHS) reports on the rarity of crocodilians, MSPT started two activities: crocodile survey work and collection of mugger (*Crocodylus palustris*) eggs from the wild in Tamil Nadu for captive hatching and rearing (Whitaker 1974). In 1973 a 5000 km survey of gharial habitat was undertaken (Whitaker 1974). Other crocodile surveys included the Andamans, Nepal and Sri Lanka.

The MSPT survey reports supported the ZSI and BNHS findings and demonstrated the existence of less than 200 gharial (*Gavialis gangeticus*) in the wild (Whitaker *et al.* 1974). Mugger (*Crocodylus palustris*) still existed in scattered remnants totalling perhaps 2000 throughout the subcontinent. The saltwater crocodile (*C. porosus*) was (and is) hanging tenuously on in the Sunderbans Tiger Reserve of Bengal, Bhitar Kanika Sanctuary in Orissa and in some parts of the Andamans and Nicobars (Whitaker and Daniel 1979).

In 1975 the MCBT was set up with MSPT, WWF-US and Tamil Nadu Tourism Department help, with 12 adult mugger and 50 juveniles. Now the Bank has over 1500 mugger and has supplied 500 captive bred offspring to State rehabilitation projects in India (Table 3). The Bank receives nearly ½ million visitors per year who learn about the value of crocodiles in nature. Besides the 1500 mugger, visitors can see American alligators, breeding groups of South American caiman, gharial and saltwater crocodiles (*C. porosus*). The main ongoing objective of the MCBT is to build up safe breeding groups of all the world's 26 species of crododilians, eventually (where necessary), to restock protected habitat in the countries of origin.

While rehabilitation schemes for crocodilians are doing well in some states, notable exceptions include Karnataka and Gujarat where much could be done to salvage the few pockets where mugger survive. Possibly the most tragic resource waste is happening in the Andamans (and gradually the Nicobars as settlers move in) where the saltwater crocodile is being quite literally pressured out of existence by legal and illegal settlement. The high price of the fat and gall bladder for purported medicinal purposes is just as fatal to crocodilians here now as the skin trade once was (Whitaker 1979). Its only hope (and indeed for many plant and animal species in this unique archipelago) is the rapid appraisal and formation of strictly protected reserves. Even if viewed merely as a commercial resource, millions of rupees could be earned annually by carefully managing the Andamans and Nicobars crocodile populations for commerce.

Some vitally needed conservation steps for Indian crocodilians include:

1. Studies on the relationships of crocodiles and commercial fisheries (productivity, nuisance value etc.)
2. Dam construction and other drastic habitat alteration has never taken crocodile survival into account. In the light of recent findings on the value of crocodiles both ecologically and economically it must now be considered.
3. Experimental commercial farming and ranching of mugger.
4. Surveys to ascertain optimum restocking areas and follow-up to measure success.
5. Positive publicity for crocodiles.
6. Continued implementation of existing protective laws on a strict basis.

LIZARDS

Lizard conservation in India has so far been limited to the passage of the Wildlife Act, affording legislative protection to the four monitors (varanids), the spinytailed lizard (*Uromastix hardwickii*) and the chameleon (*Chamaeleon zeylanicus*). The water monitor (*Varanus salvator*) has been bred in captivity at Ahmedabad Zoo and MSPT where the common monitor (*Varanus bengalensis*) has also bred but no systematic attempt has been yet made to breed Indian lizards in captivity.

There is no field guide to the Indian lizards which puts them out of reach for anyone but academic herpetologists few of whom contribute directly to Indian reptile conservation. As already pointed out, habitat loss is threatening the existence of many rain forest species, but all are small agamids, skinks, geckos and rare burrowers like *Dibamus* and *Typhloscincus*. It is a sad axiom that obscure, "non-game" wild species are always very late in receiving protective attention; and how much more so cryptic reptiles! It seems that protection of the habitats of these species as vital watersheds and biosphere reserves is their only hope.

The Andamans administration has in recent years had a strict policy against collecting wildlife there, though unpoliced. While it is heartening that there seems to be some sensitivity towards protecting these fragile islands with their wealth of reptile and amphibian life, it is equally discouraging to see the mammoth destruction of virgin rain forest there to serve the timber and plywood interests of private companies as well as the Forest Corporation. The Andamans and Nicobars contain 8 unique, endemic lizards, endemic snakes and endemic frogs all dependent on forest cover. One of the most interesting is *Phelsuma andamanense,* the Andaman day gecko or green gecko, a living key to evolution and the theory of continental drift.

The monitor lizards are of course the only heavily exploited lizards (other than *Uromastix*) in India. Trade in their skins is now banned but the water monitor remains in a critical position on the mainland in the only two protected areas they have: the Sunderbans Tiger Reserve (West Bengal) and Bhitar Kanika Crocodile Sanctuary (Orissa). Populations in the areas of the Andamans presently under intensive clearance and settlement are rapidly disappearing. Though still under heavy pressure in many states (where the meat and fat are often considered medicinal), the other three monitors appear to be holding their own. The cessation of the legal skin trade must be helping them somewhat, though no quantitative data exist.

Monitor lizards all over the country have been destroyed for skins and meat. One reference, 50 years old, tells of 600,000 skins, mainly monitor lizard, being exported from Calcutta in the month of September, 1932 (Smith, 1935). The desert monitor (*Varanus griseus*) is restricted in range and vulnerable to heavy hunting pressure. The water monitor is particularly susceptible to habitat loss and is now found only in those areas where the saltwater crocodile still occurs (Whitaker and Whitaker 1980). The common or Bengal monitor (*Varanus bengalensis*) still makes up the largest percentage of the annual illegal monitor kill but it is by far the most common and widely distributed of the four in this country.

The spinytailed lizard, an agamid, (*Uromastix hardwickii*) is the only other lizard under direct pressure. It is mainly caught for its fat and meat which is sold by itinerant "medicine men", who catch most of them in Rajasthan and Uttar Pradesh.

As far as the "lesser" species are concerned, there are many small forest skinks and geckos we may never even learn about as they are likely disappearing with the rapidly vanishing forests.

IMPORTANT CONSERVATION MEASURES INCLUDE

1. Accurate status surveys of lizards known or suspected to be rare and or under pressure. Identifying optimum habitat, particularly for the forest species, can help determine which areas should be protected to include as many important species as possible.
2. Positive publicity about the crop-pest destroying potential of lizards in the wild. It is worth mentioning that most people believe one or the other Indian lizard is venomous which is, of course, false. The spinytailed lizard is, without any scientific basis, considered to have medicinal properties; publicising the truth about these locust-eating lizards might help save many thousands from being killed.
3. Studies to quantify the rodent destroying value of monitors.
4. Studies on the potential for ranching and farming of monitor lizards for skin and meat should be made.
5. A policy decision should be examined to include on the higher schedules (I & II) of the Wildlife Act any lizards (and indeed, other reptiles and amphibians) which are known from the available data (eventually to be substantiated by survey work) to be endemic, very restricted in range, or known by only a few specimens.

ACKNOWLEDGEMENTS

Our thanks to the Madras Crocodile Bank Trust for facilities and support. Shekar Dattatri and J. Vijaya assisted with data collection; Brenda Bhaskar typed the several drafts; to these people, many thanks.

REFERENCES

BHASKAR, SATISH (1978): Notes from the Gulf of Kutch *Hamadryad* 3(3).

______ (1979): Sea turtles in the South Andamn Islands ibid. 4(1).

DATTATRI, S. (1983): Breeding the Indian Python (*Python m. molurus*) under captive conditions in India. Bombay nat. Hist. Centenary Seminar.

KAR, C.S. & BHASKAR, S. (1981): The status of sea turtles in the Eastern Indian Ocean — Smithsonian Institution in cooperation with WWF, Inc. pp. 365-372.

MOLL, EDWARD O. (1983): A status survey of freshwater turtle resources in India. Sept. June '82-'83.

MROSOVSKY, NICHOLAS (1982): Sex ratio bias in hatchling sea turtles from artificially incubated eggs. *Biological Conservation* 23: 309-314.

VALLIAPPAN, S. & WHITAKER, ROMULUS, (1974): Olive Ridleys on the Coromandel coast — Report of the Madras Snake Park Trust.

__________ & SOLOMON, PUSHPARAJ (1973): Sea turtles in Indian waters. *Cheetal* 16(1): 26-30.

VIJAYA, J. (1982): Rediscovery of the cane turtle (*Heosemys silvatica*) of Kerala. *Hamadryad* 7(3).

WHITAKER, ROMULUS (1978): Common Indian Snakes — a field guide — Macmillans, Rep. 1982.

________ (1979): Captive rearing of marine turtles — *J. Bombay nat. Hist. Soc.* 76(1): 163-166.

____ (1982): *Batagur baska,* alive and well. *Hamadryad,* 7(3).

______ (1982): Introduction, Aims and objectives of the Snake Specialist Group. *Proc. of IUCN-SSC Snake Group.*

__________ & DANIEL, J.C. (1978): The status of Asian Crocodilians. *Tiger Paper* 5(4).

______ *et al.* (1974): Gharial survey report — Report of the Madras Snake Park Trust.

_________ & WHITAKER, ZAHIDA, (1978): A preliminary survey of the saltwater crocodile (*Crocodylus porosus*) in the Andaman Islands. *J. Bombay nat. Hist. Soc.* 75(1).

______ (1978). Turtle meat poisoning. *Hamadryad* 3(1).

_________ (*In press*): Herpetological survey in Pudukottai Gazetteer. *In press.*

___________ (1980): Distribution and status of *Varanus salvator* in India and Sri Lanka. *Herpetological Review* 11(3).

SMITH, M.A. (1935): Fauna of British India. Snakes.

YADAV, (1969): Python breeding in captivity. International Zoo Year Book.

Wildlife Conservation in Thailand: A Strategic Assessment

(With two plates)

WARREN Y. BROCKELMAN

Environmental Biology Programme, Faculty of Graduate Studies, Mahidol University, Rama VI Road, Bangkok 10400, Thailand

SYNOPSIS

Thailand has developed a fine system of national parks and wildlife sanctuaries, but local villagers in most areas do not respect protected area regulations and continue to poach animals and plants and encroach on boundaries. Bloody clashes with enforcement personnel occur often, and enforcement of regulations through the use of armed force alone does not seem feasible. The basic difficulty stems from the uncritical application of Western-style protectionist management policies in a developing tropical country where conservation strategy sorely needs to be integrated with social and economic development. The needed remedies are (1) drastic changes in the missions, organization and budgets of wildlife and park management agencies, and (2) a management strategy which analyzes the problem of generating conservation action in motivational terms and attempts to create direct socio-economic rewards for desirable behaviour.

INTRODUCTION

Thailand has an extensive system of national parks and wildlife sanctuaries totalling about 43,000 km^2 in area (about 7.4 percent of the kingdom), and plans to increase this total further. Administrative and protective staff have been placed in nearly all protected areas, and management of the areas is improving. The parks and sanctuaries serve more than a million visitors each year.

In the forest, however, hunters and tree poachers roam almost unimpeded. Hunters sometimes shoot game for meat to sell to restaurants, but most appear only to hunt for food while collecting minor forest products such as resins, incense woods, rattans, etc. Sometimes people cut down large trees to obtain ripe fruit. "Protected areas" may be 90 percent unprotected, and patrolling the forest is hazardous. Park and sanctuary guards are not college-educated "rangers" as in many Western countries; they receive only labourers' wages with few fringe benefits. Many Forest Department personnel nevertheless risk their lives to protect the areas; there is no comparable conservation duty in the more affluent Western countries. A few encounters with poachers have been reported in the press during the last few years.

CONSERVATION *versus* PEOPLE

Huai Kha Khaeng is perhaps the finest of the large wildlife sanctuaries in Thailand, containing populations of many endangered species. "One official was killed while five others were injured when they were fired on with such high-powered weapons as RPG rockets, M-16 and other automatic rifles" reported the *Bangkok Sunday Nation Review* on May 13, 1979.

"Police had earlier suspected illegal hunters to be responsible for the bloody ambush but they later found evidence to believe that the ambushers were local insurgents.

"This is not an isolated incident, many murder attempts were made on the lives of many forestry officials before.

The chief of the sanctuary always carries a .357 Magnum pistol on his hip, but that "does not always make him feel safe enough." He must be constantly on the move.

Khao Yai, the best known of Thai national parks here and abroad, is also facing severe difficulties. The headquarters and expanding tourist facilities are located in a safe enclave in the centre, where all residents are in some way employed. The extensive outside border of the park is surrounded by villagers whose only benefits from the park come from breaking the laws. These 'enemies' of the park roam at will over nearly the entire area hunting and searching for valuable woods. When they come too close to the park headquarters area, they sometimes clash with park guards.

One shooting incident in 1979 was reported by a villager to the press as a "massacre" in which five villagers poaching a special type of wood were "executed" by forestry guards in the forest (Anonymous 1979). Forestry officials deny that it was an "execution". If the violators are captured and brought to justice, they invariably get off with light sentences or fines and simply go back into the forest. There is no way that the borders of the park can be protected or guarded, due to difficult terrain and vegetation and small number of access roads. The park cannot be fenced.

A few summers ago about 40 reputed insurgents attacked a guard station near the edge of the park where a training session was in progress. Four National Park Division personnel were killed and five wounded. Local villagers complained bitterly to the press about mistreatment by park guards, but the accounts seemed exaggerated. After this, patrolling by park guards virtually ceased. Insurgents were said to be in control of certain areas, but evidence of any real political insurgents in the park appears to be lacking. Poachers, however, gained more freedom to hunt almost anywhere in the park, and trees have been felled for incense wood and traps set for animals within 500 metres of headquarters and other guard posts.

The few dozen officials and guards who man headquarters and guard posts in most parks and sanctuaries are not nearly enough to protect the areas under their jurisdiction. A sanctuary chief must perform a difficult balancing act between better enforcement, and better security and survival prospects for his men. A few more guards or guns will not improve the situation, as the guards are usually outnumbered by exploiters at least 10 to 1. Greatly increasing enforcement powers would in effect be resorting to police state tactics which are not condoned in Thailand. The government generally backs down from coercive methods when popular protest becomes too strong.

Thailand over the last two decades has developed a Western style approach to parks and wildlife management which, in retrospect, is not working properly. The Western approach is based partly on the conservation ethic, and partly on the belief that we will benefit or save ourselves by saving the natural world. This belief contains a large measure of faith, even though it may turn out to be true. The West has nothing at stake, so it can afford such beliefs but when poor villagers do not share these beliefs the problem is considered to be one of "education".

The villagers are generally well aware of the value of forests and wildlife to their lives; it is the conservationists who often need the education. Villagers know that living things may be of no value to them unless they shoot and eat them, or chop them down before someone else gets to them. Hypothetical or long term benefits are of little utility; they feel only short term survival needs. Therefore care should be taken that our environmental wisdom does not turn into self-serving nonsense or oppression in the villagers' minds.

A RENEWED MANDATE

If continued progress is to be made in conservation in Thailand and in other Asian countries, emphasis will have to be shifted from mere administration and protection to "conservation for development". By "development" is meant the satisfaction of human material and spiritual needs without having to depend on destructive use of more forests and wildlife. Conservation must be designed to benefit local people just as irrigation or public health projects; otherwise, it will become increasingly difficult to justify and implement. Environmentalists have been taking better cognizance of and have been more articulate about the costs of development programmes and the benefits to mankind therefrom. If programmes are to sell and work, they must have immediate and local benefits. Even if everyone agreed that conservation measures were necesary and desirable, they could not necessarily be implemented if they required the poor people to make all the personal sacrifices.

The recommendations of the recent World National Parks Congress (IUCN 1982) emphasize "the role of protected areas in sustainable development". It is urged that "tangible benefits should accrue to local people from living near protected areas". For this to be achieved, however, there need to be fundamental changes in management goals and organization of agencies responsible for managing protected areas. This also includes agencies responsible for tourism, which is usually promoted to increase revenue and benefit the more affluent economic sectors rather than poor local residents. At present, there are few or no officials responsible for implementing such recommendations.

Other writers have also cited the need for integrating local human communities into the ecosystem (e.g. Lusigi 1980; Edsvik, 1980; Halffter 1981). In African countries the importance of wildlife-based tourism in providing revenues to governments and employment for local people is well established, although it is also appreciated that such short term benefits alone should not provide the sole rationale for conserving wildlife (e.g. Afolayan 1980; Sayer 1981). In the Royal Chitwan Park, Nepal, local residents' needs are also considered in park management. Here the development of an elaborate and specialized tourism has not been able to produce enough revenue to support maintenance costs or fully compensate local residents (Mishra 1982). But tourism here, as in other places, was not initially designed to maximize benefits to locals.

Although "rural development" is increasingly recognized as an important concern of conservation, it still needs to be made conceptually and operationally a part of wildlife and parks management. The first imperative, therefore, is that wildlife and park agencies incorporate as a central objective the fulfillment of local human needs in and around ecosystems to be protected. Protected areas obviously cannot be sealed off; the boundaries of management areas thus need to be expanded to include neighbouring human communities.

The second imperative concerns more directly the implementation of conservation objectives. Most of the utilitarian arguments used to justify conservation concern collective benefits to humans on a regional or global scale. It is naive to believe, however, that individuals (other than the relatively affluent) can be educated or persuaded to behave in ways which add to the collective welfare but not to personal welfare (Hardin 1968). A reasonable assumption in understanding the economic behaviour of people is that they will behave in ways which serve their own self-interests. Thus, once conservation goals are established, the problem of implementation must be analyzed from the standpoint of *motivation:* How are relevant parties to be motivated to behave in a manner which serves conservation objectives?

Initially, the parties whose actions (or inactions) are limiting conservation progress must be identified. A whole hierarchy of such parties exists, and their activities and needs must be carefully evaluated. For example, in one area, poor peasants may be the limiting factor; in another, wealthy businessmen, and in a third, a governmental policy.

Second, once the critical parties have been identified, ways must be found by which benefits can be provided to motivate positive actions by those parties. The necessary education must of course be carried out, as sometimes a lack of awareness does stand in the way of action (especially among government officials whose responsibilities cover extremely broad areas). More often, however, it is a lack of ways by which peoples' self-interests can be advanced. These must be designed and incorporated into the system: new policies, community projects, markets for products, etc. Below is a hierarchical list of parties and examples of possible relevant benefits.

(1) The individual and his or her family. Benefits may be a job, market for products, meat from game harvesting, etc.

(2) Local village community. Team employment, profits from cooperative economic projects, schools, improved transportation, water supply.

(3) Provincial or regional government. Benefits on a regional scale which may fall within the sphere of responsibility of this level. May be relatively weak in some countries but strong in others.

(4) The nation. Revenue from tourism, increased agricultural production and stability, national employment level, per capita income, national security, economic growth, public health indices, etc.

(5) Local business interest. Profits, future growth, availability of consumers, favourable image and publicity, etc.

(6) Multinational corporations. Profits, public image, investment opportunities, markets. This may be a difficult level to provide significant benefits for. An alternative is to appeal to governments to regulate the multinationals—also difficult.

(7) International foundations and agencies. Success in achieving their stated objectives (e.g. population control, environmental education, species conservation, etc.), ability to attract and please donors, opportunities for consultation, etc.

We may envision a grand hierarchy of motivational feedback loops. This feed-back must be designed into the conservation strategy in some way to motivate the relevant parties. The creation of appropriate loops will not necessarily be easy or possible in all cases. It will also not eliminate the need for law enforcement for the protection of common interests; my hope is that it will increase the mandate for enforcement in the public's eye and perhaps make conservation possible.

ACKNOWLEDGEMENTS

I thank the following persons for their useful comments on the manuscript or for encouragement during its preparation: Rauf Ali, Gordon

Congdon, Ardith Eudey, Madhav Gadgil, Alfred Gardner, F. Wayne King, Pong Leng-EE, Joe Marshall, Norman Myers, Jeff McNeely, J.D. Ovington, Jeremy Raemaekers, Jeffrey Sayer, Tem Smitinand, Kasem Snidvongs and Chew Wee-Lek. The opinions expressed are my sole responsiblity.

REFERENCES

AFOLAYAN, T.A. (1980): A synopsis of wildlife conservation in Nigeria. *Environ. Cons.* **7**: 207-212.

ANONYMOUS (1979): 5 persons 'executed' in Khao Yai—villagers. *The Nation Review, Bangkok*, July 22, p. 1.

BANDHARANGSHI, T. (1979): Constant fear of the forestry officials. ibid; May 13, p. 6.

EIDSVIK, H. (1980): National parks and other protected areas: some reflections on the past and prescriptions for the future. *Environ. Cons.* **7**: 185-190.

HALFFTER, G. (1981): The Mapimi Biosphere Reserve: Local participation in conservation and development. *Ambio* **10**: 93-96.

IUCN (1982): World National Parks Congress, Bali, Indonesia, 11-22 October, 1982; Recommendations. IUCN, Gland, Switzerland.

LUSIGI, W.J. (1981): New approaches to wildlife conservation in Kenya. *Ambio* **10** (2-3): 87-92.

MISHRA, H.R. (1982): Balancing human needs and conservation in Nepal's Royal Chitwan Park. ibid. **11**(5): 246-251.

POOMPRADIT, P. (1977): Efforts to protect wildlife just a saga of frustrations. *The Nation Review, Bangkok*, Feb. 11.

SAYER, J.A. (1981): Tourism or conservation in the national parks of Benin. *Parks* **5**(4): 13-15.

WESTERN, D. & HENRY, W. (1979): Economics and conservation in Third World national parks. *BioScience* **29**(7): 414-418.

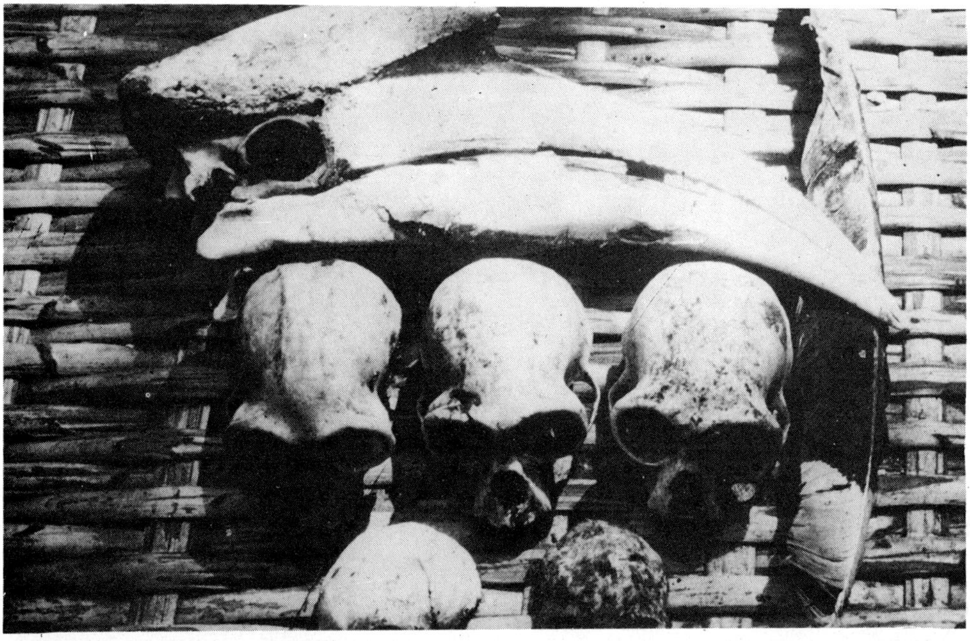

Above: Skulls of great hornbill, pileated gibbons, and monkeys found at the camp of a villager who raises cardamom spice in Khao Soi Dao Wildlife Sanctuary, Southeast Thailand.

Below: Large tree (*Aquilaria crassna*) felled in Khao Yai National Park by villagers searching for decayed wood in the core which is sold to merchants for making incense and food flavouring.

(*Photos*: W.Y. Brockelman)

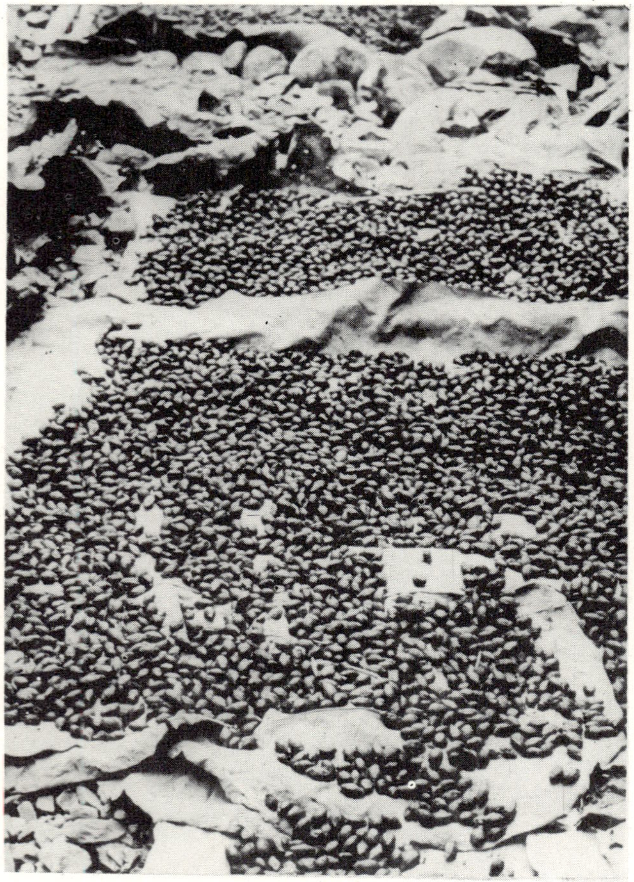

Left: "Samlong" fruit which was collected by felling a large tree of *Scaphium lichnophorum* in Khao Soi Dao Wildlife Sanctuary.

Right: Local villager arrested for choping down a *Parkia streptocarpa* tree to collect edible beans in Khao Chainao National Park, Southeast Thailand.

(*Photos*: W.Y. Brockelman)

Wildlife Conservation in Kerala

V.S. VIJAYAN[1]

INTRODUCTION

Kerala, the southernmost state of India, has a land area of 38,870 sq. km of which 8220 sq. km (21%) is forest. Inspite of the heavy demand for land for agriculture and settlement, the state could so far preserve 1851 sq. km area as sanctuaries and national parks.

The forest is composed mainly of Southern tropical wet-evergreen, Southern tropical semi-evergreen and Southern tropical moist-deciduous types of vegetation. The composition of vegetation is given in table I, following Chandrasekharan (1973).

TABLE 1

FOREST TYPES OF KERALA

Type of forest	Total area in sq. km	Percent of total area
Evergreen and semi-evergreen	4,750	57.78
Moist-deciduous	3,140	38.78
Dry-deciduous	170	2.06
Montane sub-tropical and temperate	160	1.94
	8,220	

Note. Forest plantation not included; *c.* 1,180 sq. km.

[1]Bombay Natural History Society, Ecological Research Centre, Bharatpur 321 001. India.

Since Chandrasekharan's assessment, the forest area has been reduced considerably and, according to the landsat data of 1980-1982 the total forest area is only 7376 sq. km, i.e. about 19% of the total geographical area of the state (Anon. 1983). Of the total forests, 22.5% has been brought under sanctuaries and national parks. Almost all the sanctuaries are on the Western Ghats, lying contiguous to the forest of the neighbouring states.

FORMATION OF SANCTUARIES

Of the nine sanctuaries (Table 2), none was formed with the long-term objective of conservation. Five of them are the catchment areas of hydro-electric dams, namely Neyyar, Periyar, Idukki, Parambikulam, and Peechi-Vashani. When dams were constructed in these areas it was found necessary to protect the catchment areas for preventing silt formation in the reservoirs. This might have led to the declaration of these areas as sanctuaries.

TABLE 2

WILDLIFE SANCTUARIES OF KERALA

Sanctuary/Park	Area in sq. km
Periyar Wildlife Sanctuary (Tiger Reserve)	777
Wynad Wildlife Sanctuary	344
Parambikulam Wildlife Sanctuary	285
Neyyar Wildlife Sanctuary	128
Peechi-Vazhani Wildlife Sanctuary	125
Eravikulam National Park	97
Idukki Wildlife Sanctuary	70
Thattakad Bird Sanctuary	25
Silent Valley National Park	85

Area and extent of all the sanctuaries were decided arbitrarily without giving any consideration to the criteria laid out for the formation of nature reserve, namely disease potential (Soule & Wilcox 1980, Frankel & Soule 1981); island biogeography (MacArthur & Wilson

1967, Frankel & Soule 1981); community ecology (Foster 1980, Gilbert 1980, Frankel & Soule 1981) and genetic diversity (Frankel 1970, 1974, Franklin 1980, Soule 1980, Senner 1980, Frankel & Soule 1981, Gadgil & Meher-Homji 1982).

Obviously, these criteria have developed only very recently. Based on these criteria it is now necessary to have a fresh look at these sanctuaries. While selection of the area was motivated either by the construction of dams or by some political reasons, the boundary limitation was mainly based on convenience of administration. Most of the sanctuaries lie on the Western Ghats and their boundaries are common to Tamil Nadu and Kerala. Either state borders or borders of forest divisions form the boundary of sanctuaries. Even if a more ecologically viable community existed in the contiguous forests, these forests were not included in the sanctuary. Hence, these areas become more vulnerable to the wood and animal poachers; exploitation of forest resources is also legally permitted in these areas, leading to a total disturbance of wildlife. At times such anthropogenic activities lead to the splitting of populations. Typical examples of this are:

1. *Parambikulam — Sholayar area:* There is a large tract of evergreen forest on the western border of Parambikulam wildlife sanctuary which is contiguous to the adjacent Sholayar Reserve Forest. Both the areas have populations of liontailed macaque, *Macaca silenus* (Vijayan 1978). While Parambikulam was declared a sanctuary, the contiguous forest of Sholayar Reserve was left out and intensive tree felling was allowed (Sugathan 1980). Destruction of forest in the Sholayar Reserve not only affects the liontailed macaques in that area but also the viability of the whole population of liontailed macaques in this region.

2. The evergreen forests on the southern and south-western border of Periyar Tiger Reserve are contiguous to similar types of forest in Ranni and Konni forest divisions. Faunistically also they are similar (Vijayan *et al.* 1980). Yet, they are not included in the Tiger Reserve. Felling of trees is allowed in these two forests which actually are part of the home range of many of the larger mammals.

3. On the eastern aspects of the Periyar Tiger Reserve dry-deciduous forest dominates but this is not part of the Reserve, presumably because it lies in the neighbouring state. Had these forests been constituted into a reserve by the Tamil Nadu government, the two together would have covered more diverse wildlife habitats and become ecologically more viable. Such a step at present looks formidable, but the concerned state Government can be persuaded to declare the area as a sanctuary.

So is the case with all other sanctuaries. The last declared sanctuary at Thattakkad in 1983 is only about 25 sq. km in area. Apparently no scientific considerations have been given to the size of the sanctuary. Existing reserve borders have been chosen, probably for administrative convenience.

It is, therefore, essential to review the entire design of wildlife reserves in the light of the recent thinking on the subject.

MANAGEMENT

None of the existing sanctuaries has a sound management programme. Baseline information such as the flora and fauna, population of each species of wildlife, their breeding season, breeding success, food and feeding habitat, and the major ecological requirements of the species are totally lacking for any of the sanctuaries. Sanctuaries are left to the vagaries of nature. This is a matter of serious concern. As the area of these reserves are too small, the largest one is only 777 sq. km (Table 2), maintenance of viable population of larger carnivores will be a problem. Intensive management based on scientific knowledge of the species and the ecosystem in general is the only possible solution to the above problem. Genetic management (Frankel & Soule 1981) of several of the dwindling species is desirable.

ADMINISTRATION

The State has a Wildlife Advisory Board which discusses the wildlife problems and programmes periodically. The Board is headed by the Forest Minister of the State. The Chief Wildlife Warden of the rank of Chief Conservator of Forest is the administrative head of sanctuaries and national parks. He is required to translate into action the policy recommendations of the Board, duly accepted by the State Government. A Deputy Chief Wildlife Warden is in-charge of each wildlife reserve, under whom there are many rangers, guards and watchmen. This is probably the typical pattern of staff we have been following for the last several decades, with one notable exception that till recently there was no separate Chief Conservator of Forest for Wildlife which was under the Chief Conservator of Forests whose main concern was forestry operations. Wildlife management is still a part of activities of the Forest Department, whose main objective, it appears, is exploiting the forest for short-term economic gains. It is high time that an independent Wildlife Department is formed and trained people employed as managers of wildlife reserves.

Most of the staff are trained only for conventional forestry operations and hence, we do not have qualified wildlife managers. In fact, our country has no such system for those interested to obtain degrees in Wildlife Management. Faculty for wildlife studies has yet to be developed in most of the Universities. A person trained in forestry cannot be expected to manage wildlife. A wildlife manager must be well-versed in the principles and practices of wildlife management and should have a good knowledge of other related biological subjects. He should also be aware of the latest findings in conservation biology. Only such trained managers can manage a wildlife preserve effectively.

PEOPLES' PARTICIPATION IN ADMINISTRATION OF PARK/SANCTUARY

Often, people living around the wildlife reserves make various complaints. Chief among them are:

1. Declaration of an area as park/sanctuary and the subsequent strengthening of protective measures have deprived them of the benefits they have been drawing traditionally from the forest, namely firewood, minor forest produce and grazing facility.

2. Declaration of an area as park/sanctuary attracts more tourists, which subsequently results in soaring of prices in the market. Middle class people are the worst affected.

3. They get no benefit from the newly declared sanctuary.

These complaints are very valid and deserve sympathetic consideration if one has to succeed in conserving the wildlife reserves. It is also to be noted that these problems are not specific to Kerala alone, they are for the whole country.

The only effective way of getting the cooperation of the villagers is to make them feel that they are one of the most important parts of the conservation movement and that they would be ultimately benefited by such movements. A discussion on the various ways of achieving this is beyond the scope of this paper. Only some of the most important practical steps are given here.

Participation of the representatives of people in the management of wildlife reserves and creation of an awareness among the people of the economic gains from the reserve are the two prerequisites for ensuring the co-operation of the villagers in the conservation movement. To achieve this I recommend the following:

1. Each park/sanctuary should have a Managing Committee consisting of: the chief wildlife warden, deputy chief wildlife warden, representative of research organizations, police chief of the area, district collector, representatives of the villagers and the local M.L.A.

All programmes should be discussed in this Committee and each measure which may directly or indirectly affect the villagers should have the approval of the Committee. It is very essential to take the representatives of the villagers into confidence before taking any action which may affect their interest. Absence of such a step may lead to unfortunate tragedies as had happened at Bharatpur in 1982.

2. The revenue earned by the park/sanctuary each year should be made known to the Committee, so that representatives of the villagers know the material benefit from the park/sanctuary.

3. A portion of the annual revenue of the park/sanctuary may be earmarked for some developmental programmes for the villages.

4. No management action should be taken without obtaining a scientific opinion.

SUMMARY

Kerala has five wildlife sanctuaries, two national parks, one bird sanctuary and one tiger reserve. While forming these sanctuaries and parks no consideration was given to the size, genetic viability and ecological diversity of the area. Administrative convenience appeared to have influenced the decision. Qualified wildlife managers are rarely available. The villagers around the park are non-cooperative to conservation movements largely because of their non-involvement.

It is suggested that an independent Wildlife Department may be formed. A thorough review of the present sanctuaries and parks may be made in the light of the advanced knowledge on the criteria for reserve design. Wildlife courses may be started in Universities and people possessing degrees in wildlife may only be appointed in the Wildlife Department. Each sanctuary and park should have a management committe in which representation for villagers who live around the reserve may be given. A portion of annual revenue of the park/sanctuary may be spent for the developmental programmes around the park/sanctuary.

REFERENCES

ANON. (1983): Nation wide mapping of forest and non-forest areas using landsat false colour composites for the periods 1972-1975 and 1980-82. Project Report, Vol. 1. National Remote Sensing Agency Department of Space, Hyderabad.

CHANDRASEKHARAN, C. (1973): Forest Resources of Kerala — A Quantitative Assessment, Kerala Forest Department, Trivandrum.

FOSTER, B. ROBIN (1980): Heterogeneity and disturbance in tropical vegetation. In Conservation Biology: An Evolutionary and Ecological Perspective: ed. M.E. Soule and B.A. Wilcox, Sinauer Associates, Inc. Sunderland, Massachusetts.

FRANKEL, O.H. (1970): Variation, the essence of life—Sir Williams Macleary Memorial Lecture. *Proc. Linn. Soc. NSW* 95: 158-69.

__________(1974): Genetic Conservation: Our Evolutionary Responsibility — *Genetics* 78: 53-65.

__________ & SOULE, M.E. (1981): Conservation and Evolution. Cambridge University Press.

FRANKLIN, ROBERT IAN (1980): Evolutionary Change in Small populations. *In* Conservation biology: An Evolutionary and Ecological Perspective: ed. M. Soule & B.A. Wilcox. Sinauer Associates, Inc. Massachusetts.

GADGIL, M & MEHER-HOMJI, U.M. (1982): Conserving India's Biological Diversity. Indo-U.S. Binational Workshop on Conservation and Management of Biological Diversity. Indian Institute of Science, Bangalore.

GILBERT, E. LAWRENCE (1980): Food Web Organization and Conservation of Neo-tropical diversity. *In* Conservation Biology: An Evolutionary and Ecological Perspective. ed. M.E. Soule & B.A. Wilcox. Sinauer Associates Inc. publishers, Massachusetts.

MACARTHUR, H. ROBERT & WILSON, O. EDWARD (1967): The Theory of Island Biogeography. Princeton University, Princeton, New Jersy.

SENNER, W. JOHN, (1980): Inbreeding depression and the Survival of Zoo Populations: *In* Conservation Biology — An Evolutionary and Ecological Perspective. ed. M.E. Soule & B.A. Wilcox. Sinauer Associates Inc. Publishers, Massachusetts.

SOULE, M.E. (1980): The Thresholds for survival: Maintaining fitness and Evolutionary Potential. ibid.

SOULE, M.E. & WILCOX, B.A. (1980): Conservation Biology: An Evolutionary and Ecological Perspective. Sinauer Associates Inc. Publishers, Massachusetts.

SUGATHAN, R. (1981): A Survey of the Ceylon Frogmouth (*Batrachostomus moniliger*) habitat in the Western Ghats of India. *J. Bombay nat. Hist. Soc.* 78(2): 309-315.

VIJAYAN, V.S. (1978): Parambikulam Wildlife Sanctuary and its adjacent areas. ibid. 75(3): 888-900.

___________ BALAKRISHNANA, M. & EASA, P.S. (1980): Periyar Tiger Reserve — An Ecological Reconnaissance. Kerala Forest Research Institute, Peechi — Report 5.

WHITEMORE, T.C. (1980): The Conservation of Tropical Rain Forest. In Conservation Biology: An Evolutionary and Ecological Perspective. ed. M.E. Soule & B.A. Wilcox, Sinauer Associates Inc. Publishers, Massachusetts.

Widlife Conservation in Bangladesh

MOHAMMAD ALI REZA KHAN[1]

Department of Zoology, University of Dhaka, Dhaka 2, Bangladesh[1].
Present address: Curator, ALAIN 2002 Aquarium, P.O. Box 1204, Alain, Abudhabi, U.A.E.

INTRODUCTION

Because of its zoogeographical location Bangladesh, though a small country, is one of the richest wildlife holding areas of the Indian subcontinent. Husain (1977) has aptly described Bangladesh as a transitional zone between the Indian and Malayan subregions of the Oriental Region. The country is sandwiched between the foothills of the Himalayas and the Bay of Bengal. Because of this eco-zoogeographical feature, Bangladesh has received some faunal elements from the Indian and Malayan subregions, as for example serow, banteng, Malayan sun bear, crabeating macaque, crabeating mongoose, stumptailed macaque, Phayre's leaf monkey, Burmese and Indian peafowls and common batagur. Bangladesh represents the eastern boundary for the common langur, nilgai, Indian peafowl, common house lizard (*Hemidactylus flaviviridis*), etc. It also serves as the westernmost limit for the capped langur, hoolock gibbon, Burmese peafowl, Burmese brown tortoise, Malayan box turtle, etc.

The number of species of wildlife, excluding invertebrates and fishes, is around 875. Of these, amphibians are represented by about 20 species, turtle — tortoises 25 spp., lizards, skinks and monitor lizards 20 spp., snakes 80 spp., 2 spp. of crocodiles and a gharial; about 400 spp. of resident birds, 200 spp. of migratory birds and 125 spp. of mammals (Khan 1982a, 1985).

The peculiarity of Bangladesh fauna is that it is literally devoid of any endemic species. Only exception is the Bostami turtle (*Trionyx nigricans*) living semi-captive life in a pond at Chittagong district. Bangladesh would have remained a good wildlife country if the human population could have been controlled long back in ninteen thirties or so. When India was partitioned in 1947, Bangladesh, former East Pakistan, had a population of about 30 million. During the last 35 years it has shot up to 90 million which is likely to go further up by 1990 to scale 100 million. This tremendous population pressure is causing serious threat to the survival of wildlife, especially the mammals. The situation is further aggravated by the unethical export of wild animals and the erroneous government policy of clearfelling operations in the reserved forest areas. These together have resulted in the extinction of many species which survive well in the neighbouring countries. The present status and distribution of the endangered species are to be considered in the above context.

WILDLIFE HABITAT

In addition to village groves in over 68,000 villages of the country, Bangladesh has moist- and dry-deciduous sal forest, mangrove, semi-evergreen and evergreen forests within its

1,44,054 km^2 area. The forested area is said to cover some 15% of the total area of the country, including 8 to 9% as reserved forest. The sal forest is found in the Dhaka, Tangail, Mymensingh, Jamalpur and Dinajpur districts; mangrove forest in the Sunderban area of Khulna; semi-evergreen and evergreen forests in Chittagong, Bandarban, Chittagong Hill Tracts and Sylhet districts (Map 1). Both man-made and natural mangrove formations occur patchily along the coastal belt and on the islands of the international river Naaf, bordering Burma.

EXTINCT WILDLIFE

According to the district gazetteer reports of the 19th century, reports of the government forest department and its working plans, Mitra (1957), Husain (1974) and Khan (1982 a,b,c,d, 1984, 1985) Bangladesh has lost marsh crocodile; pinkheaded duck, king vulture and Indian peafowl; wild buffalo, gaur, banteng, hog deer, swamp deer, grey wolf, Malayan mouse-deer, blackbuck and nilgai. The occurrence of the last two species and cheetah in Bangladesh has been doubted by many. But their presence in the drier Dinajpur district of Bangladesh, close to the Purnea district of Bihar, India, cannot be ruled out altogether. It is feared that Bangladesh has also lost grey partridge, black partridge, greater adjutant stork, scavenger vulture, Burmese peafowl and sarus crane.

The crocodile occurred in almost all the major rivers of the country even during the fifties. The killing of the adults, destruction of eggs and nests and siltation of the major rivers, and the loss of habitat have caused the extinction of the crocodile. The bird species have disappeared mainly due to the loss of habitat, non-availability of nesting and roosting sites, and the removal of the eggs and chicks by the nomads and tribals. Game birds have been hunted mercilessly. The bird species now extinct were all seen during the last decade except the pinkheaded duck, which vanished about half a century ago. Some Burmese peafowl may still be present in the Rangkheong and Sangu-Matamuhuri valley reserves of the Chittagong Hill Tracts (CHT) district.

The mammalian species, other than the wild buffalo, were lost due to over-hunting, and loss of habitat in the ninteen hundred sixties and seventies. All rhinoceros species were exterminated in the 19th century. The buffalo has been shot, captured and put to domestic use, and some migrated to the forests of the neighbouring countries. The wild stock failed in competition with the domesticated cattle. Moreover most pasture land and low-lying areas were transformed into either human habitations or arable lands, or both.

ENDANGERED WILDLIFE

The list of the wild animals threatened with extinction is too long to be incorporated here. Major species are listed under the different groups.

Amphibians. Of some 20 species *Kaloula pulchra, Uperodon globulosum* and *Rana hexadactyla* are represented by small and non-viable populations in restricted areas. *Kaloula* occurs in the northern and eastern forests, *Uperodon* in the sal forest of Tangail and Mymensingh and *R. hexadactyla* in the coastal areas. If the present rate of exploitation of the frog-legs of *R. tigerina* continues it is going to become badly affected. Already it has disappeared from many areas. Amphibians do not enjoy protection under the Bangladesh Wildlife Preservation Act 1973.

Reptiles. Burmese brown tortoise (*Geochelone emys*), common batagur (*Batagur baska*), Sylhet roofed turtle (*Kachuga sylheten-*

sis), bostami turtle (*Trionyx nigricans*), water monitor (*Varanus salvator*), rock and reticulated pythons (*Python molurus* and *P. reticulatus*), ratsnake (*Ptyas mucosus*), king cobra (*Ophiophagus hannah*), estuarine crocodile (*Crocodylus porosus*) and gharial (*Gavialis gangeticus*) are endangered.

Burmese brown tortoise is occasionally found in the evergreen and semi-evergreen forests of Chittagong and Chittagong Hill Tracts district; Sylhet roofed turtle is recorded from an area of Sylhet district bordering Khasia and Jaintia hill ranges of India. The record is based on the collection of a single shell in 1982. Common batagur is found only in the estuarine rivers of the Sunderbans mostly in the Sarankhola and Chandpai ranges. Bostami turtle, numbering 250 to 300 as the world population, is restricted to a pond at Chittagong. A few specimens have been seen outside the bostami pond. The distribution of water monitor is limited to the coastal river of the Bay of Bengal. A viable population still survives in the Sunderbans mangrove ecosystem. Estuarine crocodile numbering some 200 is present in the Sunderbans only. The number of gharial has come down between 20 and 30, occurring in two isolated populations — one in the Padma 'Ganges' and other Jamuna 'Brahmaputra' river systems.

The Indian and reticulated pythons, and king cobra have been wiped out from the countryside and the sal forest, but are present in small numbers in the mangrove vegetation of the Sunderbans. They are occasionally sighted in the evergreen forests of Chittagong, Chittagong Hill Tracts and in Sylhet. Reticulated python is rarer than the rock python, and the king cobra is the rarest. The ratsnake is disappearing at an alarming rate, export and smuggling of the skins depleting the natural populations of the snakes from Bangladesh.

Birds. I have earlier listed over 60 species of non-passerine birds of Bangladesh as endangered or vulnerable (Khan 1981). Some of these are the Indian shag, all species of storks other than the lesser adjutant and openbill, pelicans, black and glossy ibises, whitebellied and goliath herons, nakta or comb duck, whitewinged wood duck, Jerdon's baza, rufousbellied hawk-eagle, black eagle, Pallas's fishing eagle, whitebellied sea eagle, all species of vultures, resident falcons, swamp partridge, kalij, and peacock-pheasants, masked finfoot, Bengal florican, great pied hornbill, etc. Among these only the Pallas's fishing and whitebellied sea eagles may have a viable population in the Sunderbans mangrove forest.

Mammals. The mammals as a class are more threatened than other classes. There are ten species of prosimians, monkeys, langurs and gibbon in Bangladesh. Among these, the slow loris, stumptailed macaque, longtailed or crab-eating macaque, Phayre's leaf monkey, common langur and hoolock gibbon may not even have viable populations. Seven out of the eight species of both big and small cats of Bangladesh may be considered as endangered. Only the jungle cat has still the widest distribution as it is found both in the jungles and around villages. Clouded leopard, leopard-cat and golden cat are very rare and are restricted to the forests of eastern part of Bangladesh. The fishing cat may have a viable population in the Sunderbans. It is occasionally met outside the forest too. So far there has been no report of the marbled cat in Bangladesh. The tiger has disappeared from Bangladesh excepting the Sunderbans where the population is said to be between 300 and 400 according to a forest department report of 1984. The leopard has been exterminated in Bangladesh except a small nomadic population in the evergreen and semi-evergreen forests which may pay occasional visits to the forests of India and Burma. The pangolins, hog-badgers, binturong, crabeating mongoose, serow, hispid hare, common and Hodgson's flying squirrels and Ganges dolphin come under endangered list too. The terrestrial, arboreal and flying mammals mentioned here occur only in the evergreen and semi-evergreen forest of Chittagong, Chittagong Hill Tracts and Sylhet. The Ganges dolphin now occurs in the major river systems only (Khan 1985).

The Red Data Book of the International Union for Conservation of Nature and Natural Resources rated 14 species as endangered and one as vulnerable whereas the Convention on International Trade in Endangered Species of wild fauna and flora (CITES) included 18 species in its appendix I and 15 in appendix II (See Table). All the 34 species have been designated in this paper as endangered.

TABLE

WILDLIFE LISTED IN RDB AND APPENDICES I AND II TO CITES

Species	Status in RDB *endangered*	CITIES *vulnerable*	Appendix *I*	Appendix *II*
Batagur baska	x		x	
Geochelone emys				x
Trionyx nigricans	x		x	
Lepıdochelys olivacea	x		x	
Varanus salvator				x
Python molurus	x		x	
Crocodylus porosus		x		x
Gavialis gangeticus	x		x	
Sarkidiornis melanotos			x	
Cairina scutulata	x		x	
Polyplectron bicalcaratum				x
Pavo muticus	x		x	
Eupodotis bengalensis			x	
Nycticebus coucang				x
Macaca arctoides				x
Macaca mulatta				x
Presbytis entellus				x
Presbytis phayri				x
Presbytis pileatus				x
Manis crassicaudata				x
Cuon alpinus	x			x
Selenarctos thibetanus			x	
Melursus ursinus	x			
Leo tigris	x		x	
Leo pardus	x		x	
Neofelis nebulosa	x		x	
Felis temmincki	x		x	
Felis bengalensis			x	
Felis viverrina				x
Felis chaus				x
Elephas maximus	x		x	
Capricornis sumatraensis			x	
Caprolagus hispidus	x		x	
Platanista gangetica			x	

The table does not include migratory birds.

CAUSES OF VULNERABILITY AND ENDANGERED STATUS

There are a few causes which are general for the extinction and threatened status of various species of wildlife of Bangladesh, and several other causes are species specific.

1. *Habitat destruction.* Forests of north-west, north and eastern regions of the country are continuously destroyed by the regular, systematic clearfelling or selected logging operations by the authorised persons and timber poachers. Their major causes are destruction of forests for jhooming (slash-and-burn) operations by the tribals and the local people, accidental forest fire, construction of roads through the reserved forest areas, etc.

2. Conversion of forested areas into human habitations either legally or illegally. The situation is further worsened by the destruction of mangrove vegetation and introduction of shrimp culture in the same area.

3. Forest peripheries, close to existing villages and new settlements are gradually encroached by the local people.

4. Introduction of agriculture in the forested areas and conversion of forested lands and wetlands into arable areas.

5. Establishment of new human settlements in the reserved forest areas. Typical example being the settlements at Durgapur range of Mymensingh forest division and in some ranges of the Chittagong Hill Tracts forest divisions back in the sixties and in the recent past respectively.

6. Unchecked increase of human population demands more and more land for housing and for agriculture which are usually met from the pasture, fallow lands and by clearing the backyard jungles of the countryside.

7. Rapid urbanisation and industrialisation without paying proper attention to environmental planning eats up vast tracts of the countryside and forests.

8. Indiscriminate use of pesticides, insecticides, chemical fertilizers and aerial spray of malathion upsets the aquatic and terrestrial ecosystems.

9. Egg collection and destruction of nests seriously endangers natural populations of several species of wildlife.

Among the specific causes hunting and poaching animals for their skin, meat, antlers, horns with head have exterminated the felines, cervids and bovids. Conversion of natural forests into tea gardens, rubber plantations, pineapple orchards, oil palm and other forms of monoculture are possibly the root cause for the patchy distribution of several species. These create artificial barriers which prevent genetic exchange between neighbouring populations of the same species. Construction of dams and barrages, both at home and in the neighbouring countries seriously affects the wildlife of either countries.

CONSERVATION MEASURES ADOPTED

As Gittins (1981) pointed out conservation of wildlife is achieved through two main approaches; endangered species should be protected by law from being disturbed or killed, and representative areas of each habitat should be set aside as sanctuaries where wildlife can continue to exist in a natural state.

Most of the wildlife of Bangladesh is fully protected from disturbance, hunting, killing and export under the Bangladesh Wildlife Preservation Act, 1973, except wild boar, rufoustailed hare, Indian fox, cattle egret, little egret, pond heron, some ducks and geese, sandpipers and plovers, which may be hunted on a game licence. The Act also protected some forest areas as wildlife sanctuaries, national parks and game reserves. Bangladesh is a signatory to the Convention on Trade in Endangered Species of wild fauna and flora, which has been ratified in 1982. Unfortunately there is no organisation to implement the Act and manage the protected areas, except a conservator of forest who is also to look after the administration of the forest department.

Suggested Conservation Measures

The measures suggested are not much different from those I have already mentioned elsewhere (Khan 1984).

1. Clearfelling operations suggested under the existing forest working and management plan must be stopped in the moist-deciduous, evergreen and semi-evergreen forests immediately. Instead selective felling be practised.

2. Areas which have already been clearfelled must not be planted with a single commercially important species. Rather a group of species be planted and the undergrowth, which provide cover for the wild animals, be encouraged. In case of some monoculture, such as tea and rubber plantations, efforts must be made to leave some forested areas as corridors connecting the fragmented forests. This will ensure free movement of the animals through the corridors.

3. No forestry operations be allowed in the reserved areas. All such activities must be restricted to the unclassified state forest, protected, acquired and vested forests and on the newly accreted islands along the coastal belt.

4. All jhooming operations be stopped and in its place terrace gardening be introduced through cooperative farming.

5. The villagers should be encouraged to keep some vegetation behind their houses, the way their forefathers did. Roadside shrubberies be encouraged and cities and industries be planted with trees and shrubs.

6. Insecticides and pesticides with residual effects must be banned and aerial spray of chemicals be declared illegal. Industrial effluents must be treated before these are released into waterbodies.

7. The Bangladesh Wildlife Preservation Act 1973 needs vigorous publicity through radio and television, and news media. Every now and then its clauses which ban shooting and procurement of skins of wild animals should be publicised.

8. The Wildlife Act needs certain amendments to give protection to the habitat of the wildlife, in addition to the existing provisions for the protection of the animals.

9. All trade dealings in furs or skins of wild animals be declared illegal.

10. As Bangladesh is now a party to the CITES, export of wild animals belonging to the appendixes I and II of the CITES and those rated as endangered in the Red Data Book of IUCN must be banned.

11. Areas that have been so far declared as game reserves, wildlife sanctuaries, bird sanctuaries and national parks be properly managed by employing sufficient number of trained personnel. All human activities in these areas be stopped.

12. All cities to be supplied with natural gas for domestic usage thereby reducing dependency on fuel wood.

Farming of exportable wildlife, such as frogs, turtles, snakes, monitor lizards, crocodiles and primates should be encouraged both in the private and public sectors.

References

Gittins, S.P. (1981): A survey of the primates of Bangladesh. Report submitted to Fauna Preservation Society of London and Conder Conservation Society Trust, England. p. 64.

Husain, K.Z. (1974): An introduction to the wildlife of Bangladesh. F. Ahamed, Dacca. p. 81.

HUSAIN, K.Z. (1977): Wildlife, recreation and environment. *Proc. 1st Bangladesh nat. conf. forestry. Dacca.* pp. 375-380.

KHAN, M.A.R. (1981): The endangered birds of Bangladesh. *Newsletter for birdwatchers* 21(12):4-7.

_________ (1982a): Wildlife of Bangladesh - a checklist. Dhaka Univ., Dacca. p. 173.

_________ (1982b): Chelonians of Bangladesh and their conservation. *J. Bombay nat. Hist. Soc.* 79(1): 110-116.

______(1982c): On the endangered snakes of Bangladesh. *Proc. 1st meeting of the IUCN/SSC snake specialist group* pp. 57-60.

KHAN, M.A.R. (1982d): Present status and distribution of the crocodiles and gharials of Bangladesh. *Proc. 5th meeting Croc. sp. group IUCN/SSC Florida, 1980*, pp. 229-236.

_________ (1984): Endangered mammals of Bangladesh. *Oryx* 18(3): 152-156.

_______ (1985): *Mammals of Bangladesh — a field guide.* Nazma Roza, House 25, Dhanmandi, Dhaka p. 92.

MITRA, S.N. (1957): Banglar Shikar Prani (Bengali). West Bengal Govt. Press, India. p. 136.

Notes towards a definition of Conservation Education

MAN MOHAN SINGH

Joint Secretary & Financial Adviser Ministry of Education and Culture, Government of India, New Delhi

The basic question in Conservation Education is one of the kind of world we are shaping or for that matter misshaping into being in terms of future perspectives.

In a sense, we are living in a state of void or perhaps a schism of beliefs. The most crucial imperative of our times is the decline and in some cases, complete disintegration of traditional beliefs in conservation and the failure of science and contemporary education to fill that void. Conservation which was once upon a time a question of an integral faith has now perhaps become set of words and jargon.

Today we talk of inducting elements of Conservation Education into even the non-formal system of education. Yet there was a time when Conservation Education in a non-formal sense was transmitted from one generation to other. The scenario then was different from the contemporary situation.

The traditional pattern of living was based on a subtle and silent relationship of complete integration with nature. The only conservation instruction or education set of fables and folklore, the myths and superstitions. As against this we have today armed ourselves with words and vocabulary of conservation and in the process have upset the linkages though perhaps soothed ourselves with an air of pretended concern. We have taken debate on conservation to an alien setting where it does not really matter. Conservation should begin where it hurts people's livelihood. The Third World in its understandably relentless pursuit of progress can think of conservation while it moves ahead in the process of development. We in the Third World are very unfortunately placed as we can neither pay the price of upsetting the balance of nature, nor the price of post-surgery conservation therapy.

While I strongly believe that Conservation Education must reckon with traditional beliefs, I do not, however, minimise in any way the fact that in the last two decades concrete attempts have been made in India to frame curriculum and strategies in the introduction of environmental education. A special Unesco Regional Office Report from Bangkok represents the best account so far of environmental education in Asia and the Pacific. We have undoubtedly come to a point where environmental education at the primary, middle, secondary, university and non-formal education levels has come to acquire a meaning, a pattern and the articulation of a system. My purpose in this paper is not to delineate the programmes concerning teacher education and the preparation of special teaching materials. I am more concerned with our limitations and yet with the immense possibilities even in the context of financial, structural, administrative and institutional constraints. My long experience in educational administration has led me as if inexorably to the unshakable belief that very often what we need more desperately in educational planning is not the liquidity of finance but the solidity of imagination.

To examine possibilities of conservation education one has to look at the sheer gigantic statistical scenario of education in India. We have today half a million primary schools, 1.20 lakh middle schools, 53,000 secondary schools. These cater to about 12 crore students. As against this the total budgetary allocation in monetary terms accounts for barely 2.5% of the total Central and States budgets and education in this context for reason of other higher priorities tends to have a low priority. We had in 1980 undertaken a survey of efforts in Environmental Education in which one national institution (NCERT) very gallantly attempted pilot and trial workshops, regional workshops and a few hundreds of field centres. We have had also sporadic attempts at organising nature exhibitions, conservation drawing competitions and at places such technological innovations as tape and slide sequences designed specifically for the use of training of teachers. We also have NCERT films on learning science through environment dealing with fauna and flora as also of rocks and soils.

The question is whom are we trying to reach? It is not so much a student in a public school in an urban setting. As it is, he or she would tend to carry the message of Conservation Education from the urban setting into the drawing room. This is not to minimise in any way the significance of urban section of population being conservation oriented. We have to think of a wayside school in rural setting, far away from even the reach of a road. How do you ever teach the children in such an environment the significance of conservation? Perhaps his father and his grandfather who had not gone to school were in tune with the trees, birds and animals. Now that scheme of values has been undermined. While returning home he probably has to pass through a cluster of trees, cut a few branches or even a sapling for his evening meal's cooking. He should be the focus of our Conservation efforts.

The basic questions are: Is our Conservation Education currently and predominantly urban oriented? If conservation be a question of saving our natural heritage of the fauna and flora the proper canvas for operation is the rural scene. No models, least of all the western, can help us though that may look extremely attractive and well designed. In this context I was very impressed when I viewed the other day an album showing Environment Education Teaching Resources Problem by the Fish and Wildlife Service of the United States Department of the Interior. In one of its model lessons concerning an endangered species, a part of the exercise relates to the measurement of temperatures of the habitats, sunlight and water pollution in terms of life requirements. A visual is to be enacted through slide projections and eventually the data to be compiled in terms of a computer and the solution to be founded on the blackboard through yet another projector. The basic question in the Indian context is that let alone our teachers being trained, we have often even a semblence of a blackboard missing from the school scenario. According to a conservative estimate of the coverage of Conservation Education, if we were to reach all the school children in all the rural primary schools, it may take us yet another decade or may be the end of this century. But can we wait and will not much of what we treasure end by the end of this century?

The situation is not as depressing as it may sound. In life as in any planning one cannot escape from stark and brutal realities. My faith in our capacity to face the challenge still centres around our traditional value system. In my survey of the contemporary efforts at Conservation Education I found that there has been a distinct departure from conservation as a part of poetry in favour of prose lessons in language books. I am not suggesting that we should not build up Conservation Education as a system of scientific exhibition's population education courses or lessons on biology and on other life sciences. The basis of conservation has to be eventually a kind of a faith verging on the holiness of beliefs. A great part of one's respect for values of conservation in the rural context sprung from traditional beliefs and text-book poems or fables. I am not again implying that we should use Keat's Nightingale and Shelley's Skylark as conservation poems. There is nevertheless need to build into our textual structures readable and suitable illustrated material, which imparts lessons in a subtle manner on trees and birds and animals and reptiles. More often in the rural areas one acquired a solid core of conservation faith from early primary school exposures to poems on a sparrow or for that matter from a very moving and pathetic description of separation of a Koonj (in fact a Sarus Crane) from her mate. My basic point is that till we are able to invest more in Conservation Education in technological and in financial terms, we have to rely heavily on building up beliefs and faith.

I could not have again remotely implied that we return to the middle ages and to bird images in our folk poetry or in our religious books. The Indian scenario in Environmental Education presents a picture of the void referred to above. While attempts have been made to build up the three strands in terms of education for, about and through environment a mass and pervasive application of these has not yet been achieved. The attempts made within institutional framework are faint and very often inarticulate. The attempt so far has been to publish journals, hold exhibitions include component of population education in courses, and achieve it to some measure in terms of new teaching aids in some selected areas on a pilot basis.

I am not even for a moment suggesting that we should accept mythical beliefs in the origin of life and there are any number of stories concerning how pigeons, parakeets and peacocks originate or why hoopoe has a crest on its head. In a sense most of these superstitions and beliefs had unmistakable basis in conservation and respect for all living things. Only the message was reached through a myth or fable.

Back again to the Western conservation theology, I used the word theology as many western orations on ecology have lately tended to be pontifical. In a recent issue of *Natural History* there is a centre spread on human wants and misuse of lands with reference to the need to combine development with ecological protection in the Third World. Here are two very pungent paragraphs:

> The rural landless have their counterparts in the slums and shantytowns of Third World cities. Because the urban poor are much more visible and politically threatening, they tend to receive disproportionate attention from the media and politicans in comparison with the more numerous, and usually worse off, rural poor. Nonetheless, hundreds of millions of city dwellers live in abysmal environments.

In this rather incisively treated theme, there are some very profound observations:

> Culturally rural people fare little better. Where physical extinction no longer threatens, cultural extinction remains a constant possibility. Insensitive educators, along with modern technologies and communications, can destroy the traditional culture without providing a workable new spiritual basis of existence.

Even more valuable than their intricate knowledge of particular species may be the understanding of the dynamics of ecological systems that some tribal peoples have. Modern man has not had great success in finding sustainable ways to use the rain forests and the desert fringes. Many of the native dwellers of these zones have, by necessity, developed a sensitive understanding of the ecological interdependencies and seasonal variations, and know how to exploit the land without destroying it. But the ecological knowledge of tribal (and rural) cultures, most of which lack written languages, is seldom recorded on paper. It is passed by word of mouth. As the culture disintegrates, the accumulated knowledge of centuries is lost to humanity forever.

That was precisely the point I have been trying to make. There yet remains a vast and pervasive area of darkness. In a conservation sense, the situation is one of a world being dead and the other being powerless to be born. The battle lines are drawn in starkly brutal and realistic terms between means of livelihood aspirations for economic development and the effort to achieve these economic objectives in harmony with nature and ecological balances. I still feel that we need to evolve an integral faith concerning the whole domain of human consciousness and the answer to this is an integral conservation ethics. In myths and fables, folklore and legends, a whole web of morality is perceived in wildlife and is preached in terms of human virtues.

The aim of conservation education should therefore, be inbuilt in a subtle manner in the process of assimilation of information and knowledge. The United Nations Declaration of the Rights of the Child should be so interpreted as to prepare a child to inherit a world free from pollution and degradation of physical and natural landscape. This inevitably implies duty of the present generation to so shape the system of education as to make the child aware of his role in the world in which he would be required to play a dynamic role. In a sense the right of the child to inherit a peaceful world should not be interpreted as merely a question of a condition of absence of war or hostilities. The world that we owe to him is a world free from ecological disturbances and tensions which we can overcome by conscious efforts. We owe it right now to children in terms of Malta Declaration of the Child's Right to Play, a sense of priority to play-fields in the planning of human settlements.

The tasks that lie before us have certain crucial imperatives:

(a) We have to evolve subtle and inexpensive teaching aids,
(b) Over a period of time a curriculum has to be framed on Conservation Education as a faith and code of conduct, relying wherever it can on traditional beliefs,
(c) The thrust of Conservation Education should take care of the participative aspect in the student so as to arouse his concern for the world he is growing into in terms of his personal stakes in it.
(d) We have to work out a long term plan which envisages a comprehensive approach for meeting these objectives in the context of the existing and future financial administrative and institutional limitations and implications.

Conservation was once upon a time the Word itself. All our efforts at instruction and teaching must discover that Word which we have lost in words.

Using Museums to teach Conservation: Understanding Learner Behaviour in the National Museum of Natural History, New Delhi

JOHN H. FALK, PH. D.

Director Office of Educational Research, Smithsonian Institution, Washington, DC, USA

Worldwide, informal institutions of learning, such as museums, zoos, aquaria, and nature centres, have grown in popularity. At the same time, they are being increasingly viewed as important adjuncts to the formal, school-based educational system. This trend is particularly evident in environmental science, where museums of science and natural history have assumed a leadership role in promoting general public environmental literacy, particularly in developing countries, where access to scientific ideas and concerns are often extremely limited (c.f. Glaser, 1982; Falk, 1982). The National Museum of Natural History (Department of Environment) is an excellent example of such an effort. As more and more people look to informal institutions as places where environmental education occurs, increased attention has been focused upon understanding how learning occurs in these settings.

Although a number of studies have shown that learning can and does occur in museums (c.f. Koran & Baker, 1979; Falk, 1983), the unique nature of these free choice learning settings demands a more thorough investigation of what influences learning positively and negatively. My colleagues and I have conducted a series of studies designed to specially understand setting effects on learning (Falk, Martin, and Balling, 1978; Martin, Falk, and Balling, 1981; Falk and Balling, 1983; Balling, Falk, and Aronson, *in review*). In particular, we have focused upon the role of setting novelty. We have discovered that children will learn about the setting in which the trip occurred, but only those in a moderately novel environment will learn much about the information the museum intended for them to learn. In settings where novelty is either extremely great or extremely small, imposed learning will be inhibited. The study I will discuss today is an amplification of this research. Specifically, the investigation sought to determine if novelty effects change visitor behaviours/learning over the course of a museum visit.

METHODOLOGY

The study was conducted at the National Museum of Natural History (NMNH), New Delhi, India. The subjects were 320 (a subsample of over 2500) Municipal Corporation Delhi fourth and fifth form schoolchildren (8-10 years old) visiting the museum during winter 1982. All the children were low socio-economic status residents of New Delhi. The lesson was taught by docents in Hindi, the native language of the children. The majority of the children had not previously visited the NMNH; 22% of the subsampled children were second-time visitors.

The children arrived by bus, approximately 50 at a time. They were divided into roughly equal groups and led through the gallery by a docent. The gallery consisted of a series of natural history displays including dioramas, aquaria, and prepared specimens in cases. Half of the children started from the left side of the gallery, and half from the right side. All children were given the same lecture/discussion by a docent while seated in front of predetermined exhibits. Thus, for the experimental exhibits, the only thing that differed between the two groups was the order, and hence the time from the beginning of the tour, in which the exhibits were experienced. For example, all children saw and heard about Indian small mammals, but half within the first ten minutes of their tour, and half forty-five minutes into the tour. If the exhibition was the major determinant of behaviour (learning), there should have been no difference between the behaviour of children in front of any specific exhibit, regardless of when in the tour they encountered it, but there should have been differences across exhibits. If the docent was the major determinant of behaviour, behaviour should have remained constant across all exhibits, but might have differed across docents. If, however, other factors, namely novelty, were important, differences would have been expected to occur as a function of the elapsed time into the tour when they saw a particular exhibit.

My previous research (c.f. Falk, 1974; Falk and Balling, 1982) showed a consistently high correlation between certain observable, non-verbal behaviours and cognitive learning. Following up on this work, I conducted a study at the British Museum (Natural History) which demonstrated the feasibility of using observable, non-verbal behaviours as reliable predictors of learning (Falk, 1983). I therefote chose to use a simplified version of my British Museum scale as the dependent variable. A total of six items, all describing locus of attention, plus "Can't Tell," were utilized. They were, attending to: "Self"; "Docent/Exhibit", "Teacher"; "Peers"; "Other Visitors/Exhibits"; and "Observer".

Upon arrival of a class of schoolchildren, and after they were split into two tour groups, she would randomly select one of the two groups, and from this group randomly select 10 students. She would then follow the selected group as they were directed through the museum. Thus from each class of 50, only 10 would be sampled. As the group sat down in front of one of the exhibits picked for inclusion in this study, she would begin making observations, one every five seconds (cued by a micro-cassette tape recorder concealed on her person). She would begin with subject 1, make two observations, then two observations of subject 2, etc. until all ten subjects had been observed. She would continue cycling through the subjects, observing during the total duration of the docent's lecture/discussion at that exhibit. In this way, a profile of the task-relevant behaviour could be ascertained at each exhibit.

For the purpose of the analysis discussed here, scores were based on a dichotomous scale, attending to docent/exhibit was considered "on task", all other loci of attention were considered "off-task". The data were summarized by dividing the total number of observed "off-task" behaviours by the total number of observations and expressing it as "percent off-task behaviours". Based upon my previous work, if the off-task behaviour was less than 25%, there would generally be significant learning. An off-task percentage of greater than 35% would strongly suggest non-significant learning. The 25-35% off-task behaviour range is a grey area — learning may or may not be occurring (Falk & Balling, 1982).

The sampling protocol was as follows. A Hindi speaking Indian woman, from the education staff NMNH was used as an observer.

Instruction was handled by six different docents (4 women, 2 men). For each subject observed, the following information was recorded: 1) Sex; 2) docent leading the tour; 3) morning class or afternoon class; 4) whether there was a change in the docent leader mid-way through tour; 5) at which end of the exhibition hall they began their tour; and 6) first or second visit (determined after tour completed).

RESULTS

A summary of the percent of off-task behaviours for first-time visit and second-time visit children is presented in the Table. Subjects were divided into exhibit 1 "starters" and exhibit 5 "starters". In general, it can be seen that there was a trend for the percent of off-task behaviours to decline from early in the field trip towards late in the trip. First-time and second-time visitors showed similar patterns of declining off-task behaviours, but second-timers exhibited generally lower incidences. Statistical analysis of the data, using frequencies of off-task behaviours adjusted by total observations to compensate for unequal N's, revealed the following results. The exhibits seen by all subjects first (whether mammals or biome dioramas), had significantly higher incidences of off-task behaviours than exhibits seen last ($X^2(1) = 11.82$, p 0.001). Pooling the first two exhibits seen by the children and the last two exhibits seen by the children yields similar results — exhibits seen early had higher incidences of off-task behaviour displayed than the same exhibits seen late in the visit ($X^2(2) = 7.69$, p 0.01). No difference existed between the percent off-task behaviour of children seeing the biome dioramas first and those children seeing the mammals exhibit first ($X^2(1) = 0.15$). Likewise, the last seen exhibits by the children was also not significantly different ($X^2(1) = 0.44$). A comparison of the off-task behaviours of the two groups of subjects when viewing the insects exhibit (located half-way through the trip for both groups), yielded no significant difference ($X^2(1) = 2.30$).

TABLE

The percent of off-task behaviours (off task/(on-task + off-task) × 100 exhibited at each exhibit

	EXHIBIT				
	1	2	3	4	5
Start Exhibit 1					
First Visit	33	26	27	24	27
Second Visit	30	21	24	13	20
TOTAL	32	25	27	21	26
Start Exhibit 5					
First Visit	23	29	32	33	34
Second Visit	31	10	32	22	33
TOTAL	24	27	32	31	34

Despite similar overall patterns of behaviour, there was a significantly lower rate of off-task behaviour among second-time visitors compared with first-time visitors ($X^2(1) = 7.59$, p 0.01).

No differences were found between sexes, docents, time of day, or groups with switched versus non-switched docents.

DISCUSSION AND CONCLUSIONS

The data appear to convincingly suggest that Indian children visiting the NMNH, New Delhi exhibit patterns of behavour very similar to those of their counterparts visiting museums in the United States — behaviours which we have previously referred to as the novel field trip phenomenon. On the average, 28% of all the children's exhibited behaviour was directed away from either the docent presenting the tour or the exhibit in question. The children were thus distracted — by other visitors, exhibits, the observer, their peers, etc. — a significant percentage of the time. If the model John Balling and I developed based on American children (Falk & Balling, 1982) is at all applicable, we would predict that a large percentage of the children in these groups were not learning a great deal about the contents of the exhibits, though, of course, many of the children were. An average, though, conceals a large part of what was really happening. The detail provided by this study allows us to see how locus of attention changes across a museum visit.

To begin with, there was strong evidence that the greatest influence on the children's behaviour was the length of time they spent in the museum. Specifically, children seemed more attentive to an exhibit if it was presented to them after they had been in the museum 40-50 minutes, than if it was presented within the first 10 minutes of the visit. Clearly, the content of the exhibit had not changed. What caused this shift in attention? One possible explanation is that it took time for the children to adjust to the docent. Hence, initial inattention was docent-related. However, in serveral cases, the docents switched groups half-way through the tour or worked in shifts. No effect of this docent switching could be discerned in the data. Consequently, I am left with the conclusion that the change, as predicted, was due to some time-dependent shift in the psychological state of the children themselves — namely a growing familiarity with the museum setting, and resultant reduction in anxiety or environmental curiosity. This dampening of anxieties or environmental curiosity allowed the children to allocate a greater amount of attention to the docent and the exhibits towards the end of the tour. This finding was reinforced by the lack of significant difference between the two groups in attention to the insect exhibit. The insect exhibit was located mid-way through the tour, thus each group encountered it at roughly the same time relative to the beginning of the tour. The major finding of the study then was, early in the tour, the children were exhibiting high levels of off-task behaviours, which correlates well with low levels of task learning. By the end of the tour, they were strongly attending to the docent and the exhibit and thus were probably learning quite a bit. Content of exhibit, quality of docent, and consistency of instructor all had no significant effect on this outcome.

Another finding that emerges from this study, also reinforcing findings from our earlier studies, is the importance of repeat visits. Despite the same general pattern of behaviour among second-time visitors as first-time visitors (i.e. increased attention to task over time), second-time visitors showed a significantly lower percentage of off-task behaviours across the entire visit (inferentially, then, they learned significantly more than first-time visitors). This is the exact finding we have obtained time and time again, particularly with lower socio-economic populations. Repeat visits may be the only way to insure significant on-task museum field trip learning for certain groups.

In conclusion, this study reinforced the importance of understanding setting effects upon learning. It once again suggested that consideration of the visitor's need for acclimation to a new environment, either through pre-visit materials (c.f. Balling *et al.*, in review) or through an on-site orientation, may lead to dramatic increases in museum field trip learning. Despite the importance of exhibit design and docent training, nothing can replace the importance of being sensitive to the needs and agendas of the museum visitor. The visitors will always meet their own needs and agendas *first*. Museums are excellent places for teaching about environmental and conservation issues, but they are only effective if we understand the needs and capabilities of the people who visit them.

ACKNOWLEDGEMENTS

Thanks to Dr S.M. Nair and his staff for facilitating this study, particularly Miss P. Gupta, E. Jacob and R. Saha, Mrs. S. Varghese, and Shri S. Gupta and D.P. Singh. I am especially indebted to Miss K. Usha, who collected all the data and provided initial summaries. Also J. Balling for consultation on data analysis and comments on the manuscript, and K. Severson for typing assistance. Partial support for this research was provided by the Indo-U.S. Sub-Commission on Education and Culture, the National Museum of Natural History, New Delhi, and the Smithsonian Institution.

REFERENCES

BALLING, J.D & FALK, J.H. (1981): A Perspective on field trips: Environmental effects on learning. *Curator 23:* 229-240.

BALLING, J.D, FALK, J.H. & ARONSON, R. (   ): In review. Pre-trip programs: An exploration of their effects on learning from a single-visit field trip to a zoological park. *American Educational Research Journal.*

FALK, J.H. (1976): Outdoor education: A technique for assessing student behaviours. *School Science and Mathematics 75:* 226-230.

_____ (1983): Time and behaviour as predictors of learning. *Science Education 67*(2): 267-276.

____ BALLING J.D., (1982): The Field Trip Milieu: Learning and Behaviour as a Function of Contextual Events. *Journal of Educational Research 76(1):* 22-28.

_________ MARTIN, W.W. & BALLING, J.D. (1978): The novel field trip phenomenon: Adjustment to novel settings interferes with task learning. *Journal of Research in Science Teaching 15:* 127-134.

GLASER, J. (ED.) (1982): PROCEEDINGS OF THE "CHILDREN IN MUSEUMS" INTERNATIONAL SYMPOSIUM, Smithsonian Institution, Washington, DC.

KORAN, J.J. JR. & BAKER, S.D. (1979): Evaluating the effectiveness of field trip experiences. *In:* M.B. Rowe (ed.), WHAT RESEARCH SAYS TO THE THE SCIENCE TEACHER. Vol. II. Washington, D.C.: National Teacher's Association.

MARTIN, W.W., FALK, J.H. & BALLING, J.D., (1981): Environmental effects on learning: The outdoor field trip. *Science Education 65:* 301-309.

Silent Valley : A case study in Environmental Education

MS. DILNAVAZ VARIAVA : *Member, Save Silent Valley Committee, Bombay; BNHS/IUCN Education Commission*

At a height of approximately 1100 metres in the Palghat District of Kerala lie the 8950 ha of the rich and almost unfrequented forests of the Silent Valley. These form part of a contiguous forest block of approximately 40,000 ha, the largest such block in the rapidly deforested State of Kerala. These forests contain one of the only two viable populations of the Lion-tailed macaque — apart from the Nilgiri Tahr, the tiger, the Nilgiri Langur and the Giant Squirrel. Wild relatives of agricultural and commercial crops have been found in the Silent Valley, apart from medicinal plants. Although an attempt to start a coffee plantation was initiated in the Silent Valley in the 19th century, it was soon abandoned, and only the sporadic and selective felling of large girth trees for railway sleepers — not more than 3 or 4 per acre — disturbed this area from time to time. Unlike most of the forests of India, the Silent Valley has been free of any village settlements or tribal populations and in fact the forests appear to have evolved with minimal human intervention over millenia. It was in 1929 that the British first identified the Silent Valley as an ideal site for a hydro-electric project because of its steep and narrow gorge, which could be easily dammed, and the techno-economic advantages of the excellent head provided by the steep drop of its River Kunthi to the plains of Mannerghat below.

It was almost 30 years later, in 1958, that technical investigations were carried out by the Kerala State Electricity Board (KSEB) and it was only in 1973 that the Silent Valley hydro-electric project was finally sanctioned for implementation by the Planning Commission of the Central Government. Preliminary work started in 1973-74, but halted soon after because of paucity of funds. In 1976-1977, when the project was to be resumed, the Task Force of the National Committee for Environmental Planning, headed by Zafar Futehally, submitted its report on the Western Ghats which categorically recommended, *inter alia,* that the Silent Valley project be abandoned, but added that if this was not possible, certain safeguards should be implemented when undertaking the project. The release of this report provided the starting point for a 6-year battle over the fate of this once-Silent Valley. In an incredible display of unity for a State which is renowned for political factionalism, the Kerala State legislature passed a unanimous resolution asking that the Silent Valley hydel project be implemented. An all-party delegation obtained clearance from Prime Minister Morarji Desai for implementation of the project on the basis that the State Government would implement all the safeguards recommended by the Task force through suitable legislation. An Act to Protect the Ecological Balance of the Silent Valley Protected Area was unanimously passed by the State legislature. The Silent Valley hydro project was not, in fact, a project which the political party in Kerala could afford to oppose, for the following reasons :

1. The Malabar Region of Kerala, where the project was to be located, had a long-standing and well-justified grievance that it had not received its fair share of economic development. If per capita consumption of energy is a criterion of development, Malabar's consumption is only one fourth of the average of Kerala State, which itself was low. The local people had therefore been agitating for the Silent Valley project for over 20 years.
2. Kerala State was itself economically backward compared to the rest of India and had been generating revenue by export of electricity to neighbouring States. By 1984-85, however, Kerala was expected to be deficient in power, unless Silent Valley project was implemented.
3. Since Kerala has neither coal fields, nor nuclear plants, but is abundantly blessed with rivers, the need to develop hydro-power was considered almost sacrosanct. It was repeatedly emphasised that hydro-power is the least polluting and cheapest energy source and utilizes water which would otherwise flow uselessly to the sea.
4. The Silent Valley project with an installed capacity of 120 Mega Watt was expected to generate 500 million units of energy, which was projected as essential for the Malabar area for averting the impending energy crisis for the State.
5. The project was estimated to irrigate 10,000 hectares of land.
6. The project would reduce unemployment by generating 3000 to 4000 jobs during the construction phase.
7. Inspite of these many pressing reasons for implementation, strong social and political pressures for its implementation and multiple clearances by the Central Government, the project has now been officially dropped on ecological grounds. Essentially the Silent Valley campaign provides a case study on environmental education in the widest sense and it is therefore useful to assess whether any aspects of this campaign are replicable and whether any conclusions or pointers can be drawn for future campaigns of this type.

Although the earliest reference to the Silent Valley project that I can recall was an article by Romulus Whitaker in the *World Wildlife Fund-India* (*WWF*) *Newsletter* in 1974 there was very little follow up on this article. On publication of the subsequent Task Force report letters were written by WWF-India, the Bombay Natural History Society and others to the Government of India, resolutions for the abandonment of the project were passed at the 7th Congress of the International Primatological Society, at the Symposium on Floristic Studies organised by the Botanical Survey of India and in the meeting of the Indian Science Congress and by various other bodies. Mr. J.C. Daniel of the BNHS moved a resolution which was adopted by the IUCN General Assembly for abandonning the project. WWF-International, the IUCN and other conservation organisations wrote to the Prime Minister and Chief Minister of Kerala etc. While the Central Government was responsive to such representations, the Kerala Government and all political parties in Kerala rejected such appeals. They asked why an impoverished State like Kerala should abandon a project which would bring vital benefits to its most economically deprived region for the ecological luxury of preserving a few monkies and for the intangible potential benefits to the world at large through potential and hypothetical future discoveries.

The publication of the Task Force report had also sparked off a series of articles in the Kerala language dailies, perhaps largely at the initiative of the Kerala State Electricity Board who wished to create public pressure on the Central Government for implementation of the project. A few naturalists in Kerala visited this controversial area and started writing in the newspapers calling for the abandonment of the project. One of these Prof. M.K. Prasad of the Government College Calicut, was a member of the Executive Committee of the Kerala Shastra Sahitya Parishad (KSSP) — a science-for-the-people movement which had, in the 20 years since its inception, moved from merely propagating science among laymen to becoming actively involved in people's issues with the goal of making Science a tool for Social revolution. Its membership of approximately 7000 includes a wide spectrum of people : teachers, doctors, lawyers, engineers, scientists, trade union workers, agriculturists, and the educated unemployed. The KSSP first became involved with environmental issues when it actively campaigned against the pollution of the Chaliar river by the Birla Pulp factory in Movoor. Prasad wanted the KSSP to similarly take up the fight to save the Silent Valley. His first task was to convince the 60 member Executive Committee of the KSSP to share his concern. The pros and cons of the project were argued within the KSSP Executive Committee, who appointed a 5 member multi-disciplinary Task Force consisting of M.K. Prasad (Biologist), M.P. Parmeswaran (Neuclear Engineer), V.K. Damodaran (Electrical Engineer), K.N. Syamasundaram Nair (Agricultural Scientist-cum-Economist) and K.P. Kannan (Economist). Their booklet on the techno-economic and socio-political assessment of the hydel project gave the KSSP Executive Committee and all those concerned with the Silent Valley issue, a basic document that took a holistic approach to the Silent Valley project not merely in ecological terms, but in the context of Kerala's total power situation. The report, while highlighting the need for increasing energy supply to the Malabar area also highlighted that the energy contribution of the Silent Valley Project was (a) marginal in the context of Kerala's total power needs; (b) that irrigation could be more effectively provided by tapping ground water; and that (c) employment generation could be more effectively done by expanding small and medium scale industries rather than implementing one large project whose employment potential would end once the project was complete. It questioned the traditional policy of the KSEB to export power from Kerala for quick and easy revenue instead of more effectively distributing it in Kerala State where it could be the trigger for increased economic development. The report showed that the Malabar Region itself could be supplied more quickly through improved transmission facilities and urged the Central Government to effect a change in Kerala's total dependence on hydel power by commissioning a thermal plant in the area.

On the ecological side it highlighted the important role of forests in conserving soil and water and emphasised the importance of the Silent Valley as a gene pool. Unfortunately, the data base on the environmental side was initially thinner than on the energy side. Statements that the Silent Valley was unique, that it contained "India's last substantial stretch of tropical evergreen forest" and that it contained about half of the known world population of Lion-tailed macaques were amply exploited by the KSEB in an attempt to discredit the report.

It was probably the KSEB who financed an intensive public campaign by local professors to write books denigrating the importance of the Silent Valley. Their objective was to show that scientific opinion on the ecological importance of Silent Valley was divided. The KSSP's single booklet, written mainly for intellectuals — was countered by not less than 6 publications denigrating the importance of the Silent Valley. The debate was projected as an issue of man versus monkey, economic necessity *versus* ecological emotionalism, of neo imperialism by developed countries *versus* the needs of developing countries and even of the Central Government *versus* the State Government. The press was taken by busloads to the dam site, already devastated by the KSEB, to show how ecologically poor the Silent Valley forests were compared to the forests of Kerala and to emphasise how ideal the site was for a hydro-electric project. The KSEB campaign had a strong motivation since it affected the promotion prospects of approximately 20 engineers thereby gaining the support of all Trade Unions. Personal and non-official/pecuniary benefits are also a valued by-product for many of the officials connected with any large project. Kerala officials contacted Keralites in key positions in the Central Government with their publications. Feelings were whipped up among the local population of the district, that their economic deprivation would be perpetuated by the abandoning of the project — to the extent that anyone advocating the dropping of the project was received with hostility.

The campaign was really intensified after 1979 when the KSSP, after its 1½ years of internal debate and study, unanimously committed to calling for a halt to the project. The KSSP activists who had earlier been working in their individual capacities, now officially gave talks and lectures, participated in seminars and debates, organised exhibitions and slide-shows throughout Kerala. A general campaign to save Kerala's forests was also propagated through the KSSP's unique *Shastra Kala Jàtha* — an annual 37 days march, covering 6000 km from one end of Kerala to the other, visiting 300 to 400 villages where folk music, drama, dance, poetry and other cultural forms were used to create a scientific approach to socio-economic problems.

Other individuals and groups in Kerala had also been active ever since the public debate started. Dr Satischandra Nair, a biologist and founder Secretary of the Kerala Natural History Society, who had studied the area, fought for the Silent Valley with missionary zeal. Dr V. S. Vijayan formerly with the Kerala Forest Research Institute (KFRI) risked his job by cabling the Central Government when his report on the Silent Valley was suppressed by the Kerala Government, who controlled the KFRI. Leading poets, writers and intellectuals — people like Sugatha Kumari and K.P.S. Menon who were admired throughout Kerala, pleaded for saving Silent Valley. M.P. Parmeswarana, P. Govinda Pillai and others in the forefront of the Marxist party risked the hostility of their colleagues by propagating the undesirability of the project, especially among students. S. Sharma did the same within the Communist Party (India) Prof. John C. Jacob of the Society for Environmental Education in Kerala who organises one of the WWF's Nature Club movements, activated children to lobby against the project. Joseph John of the Friends of the Trees (FOT) campaigned in public fora. The FOT and the Society for Protection of Silent Valley filed a case in the Kerala High Court which though ultimately lost, bought precious time for the public education campaign. The scientific community in India responded magnificently to the cause of saving Silent Valley. Salim Ali, Madhav Gadgil, Dr Ganguly, Dr Meher Homji, and other well-known scientists were ever ready to make a public statement whenever the KSEB intensified its campaign to show that the Silent Valley was not ecologically valuable. Zafer Futehally, as Chairman of the Task Force and all non-governmental members of the Task Force sent letters for publication, regretting that the inclusion of safeguards in their report had obscured their substantive recommendation to drop the project. The French Institute Pondichery provided study data on the area and the Government run organisations like the Geological Survey of India (who sent a multidisciplinary team to the area), the Botanical Survey of India and the Zoological Survey of India did valuable studies. Dr M. S. Swaminathan, the then Secretary Agriculture, wrote a balanced report ending with a plea to postpone the project till the area could be studied. The report which emphasised the gene pool-concept and the alternatives for economic development of Malabar was printed and made available for distribution.

Silent Valley Committees were formed by 1978-79 in various parts of the country, the most active of which was the Save Silent Valley Committee in Bombay. Mr S. P. Godrej, a keen Conservationist and a Trustee of WWF-India, Vice President of Friends of the Trees, Bombay, called together a few environmentalists to discuss the problem and the Save Silent Valley Committee was formed as an informal activist group. Virtually all of us were office bearers of other conservation organisations. WWF-India (Western Region), the BNHS, the Friends of the Trees (Bombay), Save Bombay Committee all of whom had wanted to act on the Silent Valley issue but could not do so because the structure and functions of these organisations were not conducive to the type of action contemplated. One of the members of the Committee, Mr David Fernandes, came back from a visit to the Silent Valley with information that alternative projects existed, with information about the KSSP and with the names of other activists in Kerala with whom we established contacts. The SSVC (Bombay's) self appointed task was to help our colleagues in Kerala in whatever way was necessary. Specifically:

a) To feed the national press — especially the English language dailies which had extensive readership in Kerala with information since many of the Malayalam language dailies were strongly influenced by the KSEB. Similar activity by individuals or groups in Madras and Delhi resulted in national dailies from these locations also strongly supporting the move to save the Valley.

b) To enhance channels of communication between the information sources in Kerala and those who could influence decisions in the Central Government. Another service that could be provided in this way was to keep Dr Salim Ali authentically informed of developments and, through him, the Prime Minister.

At a stage when it appeared that the Central Government and the State Government were seriously attempting to find a solution which would permit the Silent Valley Project to be dropped, these channels of communication with members in the Central Government resulted in de-escalating the public controversy so that there was a more appropriate climate for dialogue. The most memorable of such discussions was with the Chairman of the Central Water Commission — a Keralite, who strongly resented the last minute controversy over a project which had been worked on for years and the fact that environmentalists in the National Committee for Environmental Planning, of which he was also a member, provided no convincing arguments about the ecological value of the area. The 4 hour dialogue which commenced with a series of aggressive questions on his part ended with a shared commitment on both sides to help in de-escalating the public conflict so that the right atmosphere could be created for the Central and State Governments to work on viable solutions.

c) To provide informal channels of communication between the IUCN and WWF headquarters on appropriate and inappropriate interventions. International bodies are regarded with considerable suspicion in Kerala — which has a strong Communist tradition. It was considered equally important that a non-Kerala based organisation like the Save Silent Valley Committe, Bombay, should keep as low a public profile as possible since its role was primarily to support efforts of conservationists within Kerala itself.

d) To raise funds — primarily for travel and for re-doing the sound track of a film on Silent Valley prepared by some sympathetic but poorly informed young film makers whose original commentary — but butterflies or energy, birds or employment — would only have hastened the demise of the Valley. No funds were sought by, or provided to the KSSP.

As part of the effort to find a politically and socially acceptable solution, the Central and State Government agreed on appointment of an 8 member committee consisting of 4 representatives of the Central Government and 4 of the State Government and with Prof. M.G.K. Menon, formerly Secretary of the Government of India's Department of Science and Technology and now a member of the Planning Commission. Himself a Keralite, Prof. Menon managed to have a unanimous report prepared and the Central and State Governments officially declared, in November '83, that the hydro-electric project had been shelved. A National Park was to be opened in the area.

An unprecedented drought in 1983 has made the effects of deforestation a living reality and not a theoretical possibility for the people of Kerala. The KSSP activists including Prasad and Achutan, a hydraulic engineer who is Dean of Calicut University, conducted a special 12 days Jatha during April/May '83 covering all districts in Kerala which have forests, addressing 350 meetings and talking to 10,000 people. They learnt from village elders that in past droughts the streams and wells had never dried up as they had this year — and collected 200,000 signatures asking the Government of Kerala to stop all clear felling, to stop felling on steep slopes and to have a moratorium on all development projects in forested areas. In the Palghat district of the Malabar region, where once those who asked for dropping the Silent Valley project were likely to be hounded, the people suggested to the KSSP that a felicitation be held for the Prime Minister for dropping of the Silent Valley project. There has been no public outcry in Kerala about the dropping of the project, but the Electricity Minister continues to state that he is 'unconvinced' about the ecological worth of the area. The KSSP task is not yet over. Movements for the effective protection of the Silent Valley and the adjacent forests with which it forms an integral part, are going to be continued, and so also the task of seeking ecologically acceptable development plans for the area.

This expanded approach to conservation issues and to environmental education, encompassing the entire gamut from top decision makers to the people affected provides the direction in which the environmental movement in developing countries must proceed if it is to be effective. In the short period that has elapsed between the need for action and the need for reflection, it has not been possible to exhaustively reassess a campaign that stretched over 6 years, nor to do justice to all the people who were actively involved in the efforts to conserve the Silent Valley and to the various facets of what was largely an environmental education effort. Many aspects, especially in the realm of human motivations at all levels, still remain as "grey" areas and conjectures. Each campaign must necessarily be tailor-made to suit specific situations, and replication is therefore impossible. Certain elements of the Silent Valley campaign could perhaps provide useful pointers to others engaged in a similar task and the following is therefore an attempt to share some tentative conclusions from the Silent Valley experience.

1. The traditional focus on endangered species, e.g. the lion-tailed macaque — while useful in obtaining resolutions of support from international conservation bodies was counter productive when used at the local level. The environmental education focus must therefore start with an understanding of the needs and problems of the local people and effectively project how the proposed conservation movement is directly beneficial to them.
2. In fact a major requirement in such a campaign is a constant sensitivity to what is the most appropriate environmental education message, to whom should it be addressed and by whom. The decision not to have public propaganda and the efforts to restrain it when necessary so that official positions do not harden, can be as important as the effort to create public opinion.
3. The general level of public education and awareness on environmental imperatives is so low that the burden of proving, in tangible concrete terms, why the project should be dropped was repeatedly placed on environmentalists by almost all levels of the decision making process, rather than on the Electricity Board who were insisting on implementing the Silent Valley project. This attitude could be somewhat shifted only after the KSSP study, which caried the battle into the Electricity Board's court by questioning the project on the grounds of power generation, irrigation and employment. The KSSP was fortunate in having eminent persons in various fields within its own ranks, but in other situations too environmentalists could benefit by developing specific multi-disciplinary task groups when taking up a specific programme. This requires good homework, much effort and persuasiveness on the part of environmentalists, but it is useful to recall that with the KSSP itself those biologists who pleaded for abandonning the project had to do the same kind of work to convince their colleagues in other disciplines of the need to re-examine the project.
4. For most development projects in ecologically sensitive areas alternatives do exist. In the case of the Silent Valley the thrust of the KSSP position, and that of Dr Swaminathan's report, was that alternatives in ecologically less valuable areas should be taken up first, and the Silent Valley hydro-electric project should be considered at a much later stage if still required, after the floristic and faunistic wealth of the area had been explored. It is more acceptable to ask for the postponement of a project than for its total abandonment.
5. Though the Prime Minister's own concern for environmental protection was a key factor in the reception that the plea to drop the Silent Valley received from her, the decisive factor was the fact that the Left Front government changed to one led by the Congress (1). In a democratic country — where politicians must face their electorate — the Prime Minister's interest does not provide a simplistic solution to such a politically sensitive problems. There is a need for public education to create a

climate which makes the choice a politically acceptable one. A science-for-the-people movement as effective as the KSSP, does not yet exist in other parts of the country where literacy and social awareness are lower, but a tremendous step forward could be secured by environmentalists if they convinced other organisations working in the field of rural uplift of the validity of their case, and thereby harnessed such grass root workers to the cause in hand. The combination of a grass roots movement supported by access to the national media and to nationally or internationally influential personalities enhances the chances of success.

The need to respond speedily to changing situations and to interact freely with all those concerned with the issue are of paramount importance. In this context, the existing national conservation bodies, with rigid and well-defined organisation structures, appeared to be less effective in responding to the demands of situation. An ad-hoc group like the Save Silent Valley Committee Bombay, strongly focuses on a single environmental issue, with no heirarchical decision making structure and no requirement to perpetuate itself once the problem is resolved, could draw together interested members from various organisations and thereby pool the expertise and contacts that each member had acquired, and focus them on a shared task. The Committee never got itself registered, formulated no by-laws etc. Donations were routed through the BNHS for tax exemption and accounting functions for which the BNHS got a small administration fee — and the SSVC can now either dissolve itself or take on a new name and a new task if the need arises.

7. Government officials who do not have a direct personal interest — in terms of income or prestige — in a project, can indeed be most helpful if they are convinced of the position. There are considerable advantages to be reaped through an open and co-operative dialogue with them. Among the government officials there are some who are ardent conservationists, and in a position to supply useful data. There are others who have an open mind and who should not be blamed if the pro-project lobby does a better job of communicating with them than environmentalists do.
8. Since the poverty and lack of public awareness amongst the population directly affected by a project is so great, it is difficult for them to directly sympathise with an environmentalists position of long-term benefits, sustainable development etc., when it involves sacrificing even small tangible short-term benefits. A more effective approach may be to lead the people to question the supposed benefits to themselves of projects in their area. This approach has also been followed in other areas where dams are coming up, e.g. in Bedthi.

The Silent Valley environmental education campaign was largely one of responding rapidly and effectively to the demands of an ever changing situation. The very late stage of intervention by environmentalists in a project that had been initiated many years ago and the inedequate data base with which the campaign was started made the task a longer one, an unnecessarily bitter one and costlier to the nation as a whole than it need have been. The search now should be for ways in which such movements for ecologically sound development are based on planned and timely interventions through collaborative efforts between governmental agencies and non-governmental bodies and between non-governmental agencies working in the same or different fields. An approach of this type would be an appropriate expression of the holistic approach which is part of the conservationists own philosophy.

BNHS Centenary Seminar
8th December, 1983.

Bombay Natural History Society's efforts under Nature Education Scheme

Mrs Shailaja R Grubh

Nature appreciation through nature education in schools has been an important activity of the Bombay Natural History Society for the past 36 years. The aim is to train school children so that, as they grow they would provide leadership for nature conservation. The Project since its inception has been financed by the Government of Maharashtra.

Nature Education is imparted through field trips to areas of natural beauty, through the exhibits at the natural history section of the Museum, Aquarium, through nature orientation courses for biology teachers, through exhibitions, drawing and essay competitions on wildlife, film shows, articles on wildlife in newspapers, radio programmes and publication of low priced booklets on nature.

The Nature rambles are usually conducted at the Sanjay Gandhi Park at Borivli, a suburb of Bombay and occasionally to Karnala Bird Sanctuary and other nearby natural areas. The field trips are mainly arranged for young students studying in standards, 8th to 10th. Usually a group of about 25 to 30 children is taken out to the field. In a complete academic year about 40 such field trips are conducted and 1200 to 1500 students take advantage of this activity every year. The study of Environment forms a certain portion in the biology syllabus but is inadequate. During the field trips children are exposed to various facets of nature and are taught to recognise common birds, common trees, seasonal flora, insect life and to understand the general natural environment as a whole. A group discussion is held at the end of each field trip.

At times overnight camps are held for under privileged school students.

These field trips have shown us that the lack of interest shown by our people is largely due to lack of exposure to Nature and its significance in our lives.

Nature Orientation Courses have been arranged for Biology Teachers as well as teacher trainees with considerable success. Such an investment, we believe, will go a long way towards realising our objectives of spreading nature education.

The courses for teachers include organisation of field projects. A freshwater pond life cum-Aquarium Project was taken up two years before for biology teachers. Physical factors and animal life cycles as well as seasonal changes of life in freshwater ponds and streams were described. This was followed by demonstration of aquatic invertebrates collected from Bombay area and also slides of *Daphnia, Cyclops, Paramecium, Spirogyra,* etc. Information on food chain and energy pyramid, was provided and practical demonstration on setting up a freshwater aquarium, namely the type of sand to be used, quality of water and plants and other material was described. This was followed by a question and answer session and a general discussion on using the aquarium as a classroom tool for studying various natural phenomena such as respiration and phototropism. The project was very well received and we were successful in inculcating a love of nature in teachers which would help spread the message of nature appreciation faster and more intimately by the teachers in the hearts of impressionable children.

Nature Education through exhibits includes visits to the aquarium as well as to the Natural History Section of the Prince of Wales Museum and the Zoo. This method was used largely for education of small children from the 5th to 8th std. The students were able to learn details of the physical characteristics of wildlife which otherwise cannot be approached closely. Lessons on visits to the zoo included understanding animal life as well as getting to know common trees and flowering plants maintained at the Bombay Zoo.

Every year approximately 12 visits to the Prince of Wales Museum, about 15 visits to Victoria Garden, and about 15 visits to Taraporewala aquarium are conducted and about 2000 children take advantage of this programme.

Wildlife exhibitions for school children are arranged during Wildlife Week each year. The theme varies; in 1982 it was "conservation of wildlife". The exhibitions have proved very useful as thousands of students view them including even physically handicapped school children. Experience in organising these exhibitions has enabled us to give guidance to colleges and schools in programming nature exhibitions.

Wildlife essay and painting competitions we find are useful tools to create interest in nature among children as competitions make children and parents take greater interest in nature and environment, particularly when prizes are involved. Educational aids in the form of low priced publications on Nature including attractively illustrated and printed booklets on birds, mammals and plants in English as well as in Indian languages is a continuing nature education programme.

The success of radio talks and articles in newspapers have greatly assured us on our education programme. Feedback received indicates that people who otherwise may not have become committed to the cause of nature conservation became so after reading our newspaper articles and hearing the radio talks.

The feedback on participation in field trips, Museum and Aquarium visits show that some schools feel that they could have used more days for such activity as only one class could participate at a time. Approximately 10,000 students take advantage of our different activities throughout the year.

What we have done so far under the Nature Education Scheme is a fraction of what requires to be done.

Our expansion plans include reaching out to more school children and teachers and the general public through expanding and intensifying the existing activities as well as incorporating additional ones such as setting up permanent and mobile nature exhibits, publishing informative charts on birds and mammals, and a nature magazine for children. We also plan to provide a natural history syllabus for schools and training colleges as this is a very necessary and important need at the moment.

Conservation Education Programme of World Wildlife Fund — India

CHANDRAKANT WAKANKAR, WWF - INDIA

ABSTRACT

Nature Clubs of India was launched by the WWF-INDIA as a youth movement under its Conservation Education Programme in 1975. Literature (quarterly newsletter, topical features and projects), audio-visuals, and field activities (camps, nature trails and conservation activities) are the principal media through which the programme is administered. The programme, which had initial concentration in the Western Region, has expanded to a total of about 400 Nature Clubs in 20 of the States and Union Territories of India. Originally conceived for school students, Nature Club Movement has spread among university students as well.

With the experience acquired so far WWF-INDIA plans to develop the programmes further in scope and size so as to reach specifically targetted audiences among youth and adult groups.

A nationwide conservation education programme with continuing and lasting impact down to the grassroot levels can be achieved if the Government and non-Government Organisations (NGOs) coordinate their efforts and pool their resources and experience. WWF-INDIA's experience indicates that such a task is complex but desirable, essential and feasible.

Note: Difference between the title of this paper and that in the catalogue of the abstracts is due to the fact that the author was asked to change the topic later.

HISTORY AND PRESENT STATUS

Nature Clubs of India

The programme envisages Nature Clubs of students under the guidance of a Nature Club Advisor as the appropriate channel to administer the programme to give it the form of a movement which is not possible through individual enrollment. However, nominal rolls of the clubs give the students a feeling of individual identity as against the anonymity of a club. Membership is limited at present to students between 10 and 25 years of age.

Nature Club as a concept has been found popular and effective at school and university level. Number of Nature Clubs has remained approximately at 400 over last three years. Limitations of the number of staff and trained volunteers available impose a restriction on servicing the Nature Clubs, especially those in remoter areas.

Nature Clubs are registered with WWF-INDIA by submitting the registration form, nominal roll with the ages of the members and annual subscription at Rs 5/- per member and one time Club registration fee of Rs 10/-. Annual subscription is charged at Rs 2/- per member for economically backward clubs. No concerted publicity drive is undertaken to propagate the movement.

Of late, demand for Nature Clubs for adults has also come to the fore and we are considering the ways to meet it.

Literature

Quarterly newsletter, features on conservation topics and show-and-do projects have been produced in English and sent to the Nature Clubs, the number of copies depending upon the Club strength. Marathi and Gujarati (mimeographed) translations are sent to those clubs asking for them. Widening of age group to 10-25 years has posed problems on the level of contents due to differences in the degree of maturity. Steep increase in the cost of paper and printing is, of course, another limiting factor, especially for bringing out vernacular editions. Efforts are under way to overcome these restrictions.

It needs to be stressed here that there is a great need for literature on basic natural history in Indian context for differnt age groups and categories of amateur naturalists.

Field Activities

(a) Concepts and rationals of nature conservation can be communicated in an effective manner if field activities are made an integral part of the education programme since direct sensory experience alone can motivate an individual for action.

(b) *Camps.* WWF-INDIA conducts the following categories of camps of varying duration. The camps are held in some kind of nature reserve. Programme consists of nature trails and interpretation, talks, discussions, games, audio-visuals and voluntary work. Camps are organised by education staff, volunteers or sister NGOs under aegis/sponsorship of WWF-INDIA. Camps are subsidised, especially for economically deserving students. Camps are organised at National/Regional/State/Local/Institutional level.

i) Nature Orientation Camps: For beginners (Duration 3-15 days)

ii) Nature Leadership Camps: For teachers/senior students/volunteers/Club Advisers (Duration 7 days)

iii) Environmental Education Workshops: For mature Nature Club Advisers and volunteers (Duration 7 days)

(c) It should be mentioned here that Hingolgad Conservation Education Programme conducts camp programme with maximum participation and receives sponsorship from WWF-INDIA and Gujarat State Government. The Society for Environmental Education in Kerala also conducts camp programme with sponsorship from WWF-INDIA.

(d) Nature trails are encouraged at institutional level and also at local level where experienced volunteers are available to lead them.

(e) Conservation activities are undertaken at some of the centres where dedicated volunteers are active. Some examples are as follows:

i) Kerala: Exhibitions, peace marches, demonstrations by Nature Club members under coordination by the Society for Envioronmental Education in Kerala.

ii) Tamil Nadu: Turtle egg collection and hatcheries, help in apprehending poachers.

iii) Maharashtra/Gujarat: Tree planting, tree saving, local representations, fund-raising.

iv) New Delhi:Peace marches and representations.

v) West Bengal:Peace marches and representations, survey projects.

Audio Visuals

WWF-INDIA has 14 Audio-Visuals, majority of which have been created by us. They are made available to Nature Clubs at a price which is one hundred rupees less than what is charged to the others. Visual appeal makes this medium very effective. Non-availability of equipment at institutions and small number of volunteers to take AVs around are the major limiting factors in using the medium on a larger scale. Financial resources of individual charitable NGOs are insufficient at present to create and distribute/display quality audio-visuals though expertise is available.

Future Plans

An organised, intensive outreach of the Nature Club Movement to specifically targetted audiences among important categories of students, decision makers and rural population is being planned.

Literature programme is being restricted to cater to a wider age group and provide guidelines for suitable activities.

Coordinated efforts at National level

Financial support for camp programme received from the Central and Gujarat State Governments, and cooperation with the Society for Environmental Education in Kerala and Hingolgad Conservation Education Programme are indicators that a nationwide effort in coordination of resources and experiences between the Government and Non-Governmental Organisations (NGOs) can take conservation education to grassroot level and make deep impact on strategically important audiences. Such a task would be complex but far more rewarding than the sum of fragmented efforts. It may be stressed that such coordination does not envisage faceless centralisation but rather augmenting individual efforts by pooling the resources and expertise without wasteful duplication of efforts.

Preliminary observations on the ecology and conservation of the Shama *Copsychus malabaricus* in Southern India

D.N. MATHEW, K. VIJAYAGOPAL, M. SIVARAMAN, K.J. JOSEPH

During the last four years (1980-83) we had observed the behaviour and ecology of the Shama (*Copsychus malabaricus*) in different localities in the course of an extensive University Grants Commission assisted survey project for studying the vocalisation of birds in four Southern Indian States. We believe that the Shama and some of the other species of song birds coexisting with it are in danger of local extinction in some localities.

AREA, MATERIALS AND METHODS

Our main study area was Nedungayam near Nilambur (*c.*11°12′N, 76°8′E) Malappuram district. We observed the Malabar Shama (*Copsychus malabaricus malabaricus*) at Nedungayam for 2-3 days, twice a month, July 1981 to December 1982, and less regularly for many of the months in 1983. Some observations were made near Sultan's Battery (Wynaad District), Pilachikkara reserve forest (Cannanore District) and on the Indian Shama *C.m indicus* at Amirdhi near Vellore (North Arcot) and at Lamasingi, Visakhapatnam District, Andhra Pradesh.

STATUS AND DISTRIBUTION OF THE MALABAR SHAMA

The Malabar Shama (*C.m. malabaricus*) is a resident, and locally distributed bird of the Western Indian peninsula from Gujarat, south along the Western Ghats complex to southern Kerala and Tamil Nadu, south of the River Cauvery, occurring both in the plains and up to elevation of 700 m (Ali and Ripley 1973).

At Nedungayam we observed the feeding and nesting habits of the shama. Notes were kept about the pattern of flowering and fruiting of some of the characteristic plants of the bird's home range in Nedungayam and about the quantitative changes of invertebrates which could form the prey of the shama. The number of birds met within the course of a transect walk of about 2 km within two hours was regularly recorded.

Nedungayam a tiny hamlet situated in the centre of an extensive teak plantation in the Karulai range of Nilambur Forest Division, lies at the foot of a series of hills which lead to the Nilgiri mountains in the north. Our study area was in a small and narrow strip of about 5 ha of nearly original evergreen forest bordering a hillstream, Karimpuzha. Annual floods of the stream bring considerable quantities of alluvial sediment to enrich the small strip of ecotonal riverine forest which forms the habitat of the shama. This rich soil supports a luxurient growth of vegetation which is now disappearing fast as firewood for the people of the Karulai range. Rapid deforestation is destroying the habitat of several other species of song birds as well.

Table 1 lists some of the characteristic plants of the home range of the shama.

The shama lived in the shaded areas of the gallery forests. It sang almost throughout the day and during all parts of the year, perched on the low branches or vines. Only rarely was it seen in bright sunlight. Bathing was carried out both in the water stagnating in the hollow stumps of dead trees and in the stream.

The data collected on the insect population (Fig. 2) suggested that the insects and other invertebrates increased progressively from May and stayed high till September. The schedule of nesting of the shama at Nedumgayam appeared to be timed so as to let the newly fledged young exploit the abundance of insects in the second half of the year.

TABLE 1

CHARACTERISTIC PLANTS OF THE MALABAR SHAM'S HABITAT AT NEDUNGAYAM

Species	Description	Flowering	Fruiting
Dalbergia latifolia	Large tree	Janu.-Mar.	Nov.-Jan.
Lagerstroemia lanceolata	”	Mar.-May	June-Aug.
Tectona grandis	”	June-April	Nov.-Jan.
Terminalia paniculata	”	Aug.-Dec.	Nov.-Feb.
Xylia xylocarpa	Tree of medium height	Mar.-April	Nov.-Dec.
Hydnocarpus laurifolia	Large evergreen tree	Feb.-April	Oct.-Dec.
Sapindus emarginatus	Medium sized tree	Nov.-Dec.	Jan.-Mar.
Cassia fistula	”	Mar.-April	April
Ficus hispida	Small weak tree	Throughout the	year
Clerodendrum viscosum	Soft wooded tree	Throughout the	year.
Strychnos nux-vomica	Large tree	Feb.-April	Nov.-Jan.
Lantana camara	Aromatic straggling shrub weed	Throughout the	year.
Calycopteris floribunda	Large straggling shrub	March-July	
Eupatorium odoratum	Shurb, weed	Dec.-May	

In between sessions of song the shama foraged on the ground (40% of the observations) and among the leaves and herbs (50%) tree trunks and in the air. The food of shamas formed spiders, grasshoppers, termites, adult and larval lepidoptera, flies, ants, centipedes and snails. The most frequent items of food were ants, termites and lepidoptera. Once a shama was observed swallowing a small frog.

The plant phenology in the shama's home range is contained in Table 1.

BREEDING ECOLOGY

During the year 1981-82 the shama nested at Nedungayam from April to July. As we found a pair of adult shamas in the same area and following the same foraging route month after month throughout our study, we suspect that pair bond of this bird is of long duration. The home range of this pair was about 2 ha in area. During March and April the shamas sang very frequently moving from one end to the other of their long home range. Nests were built in holes in trees 1-20 m from the ground. We have not observed any nest building activity by the male shama. The female carried twigs and leaves of *Xylia xylocarpa* in her bill and formed a saucer-shaped nest. The male accompanied the female to the nest but merely perched on a branch close to the nest and called softly. The frequency, duration and loudness of calling were reduced as the nest progressed. The eggs were bluish green with brownish spots. The clutch size was three. The female incubated silently while the male watched around the nesting site. Three out of the four shama nests studied by us were built on *Xylia xylocarpa* and the only successful nest on *Hydnocarpus laurifolia*. Out of the three nests built on *Xylia* trees in 1981 (Table 2) only two resulted in clutches, three eggs each. The first nest was deserted in the course of incubation. Magpie robins which were always present in the area were seen entering a nest and were most probably responsible for the loss of the eggs. The second clutch of shama's eggs was destroyed by the entry of rainwater in the nest; the 3rd nest was given up before egg-laying. There were two pairs of adult shama in our area of observation from April to June 1981. There was only one pair after June 1981.

Out of the only clutch of 3 eggs (observed in April) in a hollow tree trunk 1 m above ground in the breeding season in 1982, two airborne young were produced. Both sexes restricted their vocalisation during the period after egg-laying. The female incubated silently and occasionally produced a soft and unmusical guttural alarm call. Both parents cared for the nestlings. The female brooded the young in the early nestling period. The male brought caterpillars to the nest and passed them to the female or directly fed the young.

Both parents fed the fledglings which followed one or both of the parents in the closed canopy gallery forests. Their chief food was caterpillars. The nesting activities we had noted at Nedungayam are summarised in table 2.

The nesting success was thus poor, the breeding season short and the possible number

TABLE 2

SUMMARY OF THE NESTING ACTIVITIES OF THE SHAMA AT NEDUNGAYAM

Year	No. of nesting pairs	Nesting tree location and height of the nest from ground	Number of clutches	Number of eggs	Nestlings	Fledglings	Possible cause of failure
1981-82	2	*Xylia xylocarpa* Holes. 15-20 m from ground	2	6	Nil	Nil	Interference by Magpie-Robin in the nest, wood cutting, entry of rain water in the nesting hole
1982-83	1	*Hydnocarpus laurifolia* Hallow 1 m	1	3	2	2	

of brood a pair could raise per season limited. When we began our nesting studies at Nedungayam in 1981 there were 2 pairs of adult birds in the study area. Careful observations did not reveal any other adult shama in about 10 ha of the area including the spot of intensive study. One pair disappeared in the first year, the female first and then the male too. In December 1983 we could see only two adult and one juvenile bird. With many unfavourable factors like the continuous removal of trees and shrubs by men and wild elephants, interference in nesting by Magpie robins and the likelihood of rains washing out nests from holes, the prospects of the shama increasing in number at Nedungayam are none too good.

PRELIMINARY OBSERVATIONS ON THE POPULATIONS OF SHAMA IN OTHER PLACES

In order to see whether the status of shama was better in other forests we kept a record of the number of adult shamas we could see while walking a transect of about 2 km within two hours, between 6-8 hours in the morning at other localities we visited for our survey work. Table 3 gives the number of shamas seen at our Nedungayam study area and table 4, those in the other areas. As we had to cover these areas several times for the purpose of recording bird vocalisation there was little chance of our missing the shama if it were present.

TABLE 3
NUMBER OF SHAMAS SEEN AT NEDUNGAYAM

Year	Approximate hour of observations	Number of Shamas seen within 2 hours
1980	864	2 adults
1981	900	2 pairs of adults
1982	600	one pair of adult; 2 fledglings
1983	150	One pair of adult; 1 juvenile

The shama and several other species of song birds of these localities are definitely living in highly stressed environments, which are disturbed by the following factors.

TABLE 4
NUMBER OF SHAMAS OBSERVED AT OTHER LOCALITIES

Year	Month	Locality	Aproximate duration (hrs) of field work	Number of adult shamas seen within 2 hours
1980	April	Pilachikkara Reserve Forest Cannanore Dt. Kerala	12	1 adult
1980	September	Chethalayam, Sultan's Battery, Kerala	12	2 adults
1981	September	” ”	12	2 adults
1982	August	Pilachikkara	12	Nil
1982	December	Chethalayam, Sultan's Battery, Kerala	6	2 adults
1982	December	Muthanga, ” ”	8	4 adults

1981	August	Thekkumthottam, Palni Foot hills, Tamil Nadu	18	2 adults
1982	June	,, ,,	6	2 adults
1982	October	,, ,,	12	Nil
1983	January	,, ,,	12	Nil
1981	December	Lamasingi, Vizakhapatnam, Andhra Pradesh	12	4 adults
1982	January	Amirdhi reserve forest, Near Vellore, North Arcot District	36	2 adults
1983	December	Chethalayam, Sultan's Battery, Kerala	6	1 adult
1983		Muthanga, ,,	4	1 adult

Tribal and other collectors of firewood and hill-produce remove vegetation without any restriction. Two places at Sultan's Battery (Chethalayam and Muthanga) were the only spots where we did not see any firewood collection. In all the reserve forests cattle were allowed to graze freely. The habitats of shama in the Palni Hills and Lamasingi forests were camps of illicit distillers. Both firewood and illicit alcoholic drinks were sold on the roadside in the reserve forest between Narasipatnam and Lamasingi, within the home range of the Indian shama.

In table 5 the factors disturbing the shama are listed. The worst of all and the most universal one threatening all song birds was the rapid destruction of reserve forests for timber and fuel.

TABLE 5

LIST OF THE FACTORS DISTURBING SHAMA AT VARIOUS PLACES

No.	Factors disturbing	Places disturbed					
		Nedumgayam	Muthanga	Palni Hills	Amirdhi forest	Lamasingi	Pilachikkara
1.	Firewood collection by removal of living trees	+		+	+	+	+
2.	Wild elephants which break branches, destroy ground vegetation	+		+			

3.	Grazing cattle and goats	+	+	+			+
4.	Illicit distillation			+		+	
5.	Disturbances by monkeys and Magpie Robins	+					
6.	Encroachment into Reserve forest						+

STEPS SUGGESTED FOR PROTECTING SHAMA AND OTHER SONG BIRDS

1. Ban the unsupervised collection of firewood from all reserve forests. Social Forestry units must be started near all villages and the rural poor who now live by selling firewood should be engaged to grow more trees, to erect terraces and bunds to prevent erosion and to exploit the rainwater more productively. The Government could open depots in villages to supply firewood cheaply and without destroying the forests.

2. Restore and diversify the habitat of shama and other song birds by growing more of the local plants.

The following species of song birds were present in all localities where we had observed the shama and shared its home range.

1. The Racket-tailed Drongo; 2. The Fairy Blue Bird; 3. The Rubythroated Bulbul; 4. The Yellowbrowed Bulbul; 5. The Spotted Babbler; 6. The Scimitar Babbler.

3. Ban illicit distillation and grazing of cattle in reserve forests, supervise hill-produce harvest properly.

4. In view of the potential of the shama for destroying insects (figure 1) particularly caterpillars, flies and termites from forests it will be worthwhile from the point of view of forest economy to conduct systematic survey on the population of this species. With its melodious song the Shama could enhance the attractiveness of the wildlife sanctuaries and parks to tourists. Restoring the quality of the shama's habitat will have beneficial effect on many other song bird species which share its habitat.

From among the areas surveyed by us we recommend that the shama be reintroduced to areas suitable for the species in the following localities.

1. Thekkinthottam, Palni Foot hills.
2. Silver Cascade, Kodaikkanal.
3. Curtallam Forest Rest House and old Courtallam.
4. Karian shola in Topslip and parts of Parambikulam.
5. Mundanthurai Forest Rest House of Mundanthurai wildlife sanctuary.

It is possible that shama is present in very small number in some of these places but almost everywhere we had seen them we felt that their population was too small to ensure successful reproduction and continued survival.

ACKNOWLEDGEMENTS

We are grateful to the University Grants Commission for the grants which supported the research and to Shri. J.C. Daniel, Curator of the Bombay Natural History Society for his interest and encouragement.

We are grateful to Chief Conservators Shri Puspakumar IFS and Shri A. Hassankutty IFS of the Andhrapradesh and Kerala Forests respectively and to Shri Chandpasha, Conservator of North Kerala Forests for their help and cooperation. We thank the Chief Wild Life Wardens of Tamil Nadu and Karnataka State for permission to work in Sanctuaries and forests of their states.

REFERENCES

ALI, S. & RIPLEY, S.D. (1973): Handbook of the birds of Indian and Pakistan, Vol. 8: 244.

Observations on some Megapodes of Indonesia and Australia

(*With five plates*)

T. Antony Davis

Introduction

A unique, small group of birds of the family Megapodiidae (Aves: Galliformes) which display certain primitive reptilian habits, are known popularly as Megapodes or Incubator Birds. The members of the family (7 or 6 genera and 12 species) are distributed mainly in and around Papua New Guinea and Australia, some of the species, however, going as far as Java or even to Nicobar Is., in the west, the Philippines and Marianas Is., in the north, and upto the Samoa Group in the east. South Australia forms the southern limit. Though the megapodes (birds with big powerful legs) vary in colour, size and form, they share the common character of not brooding their eggs the way other birds do. Instead, they exploit nature's heat to hatch the eggs. They select convenient locations in slopes of volcanic hills for laying their eggs where the temperature is just adequate to enable them to incubate and hatch out. They also make use of the heat from hot water springs as well as the sun's heat for hatching the eggs. There is one more elaborate system of incubation followed by some members of megapodes, the prominent ones being the mallee-fowl of Australia and the brush-turkeys. Some genera of Papua New Guinea are also mound-builders. They build huge mounds (sometimes over 10 m diameter and 4 m high) with a mixture of soil, leaves and other vegetable matter that ferments and raises the temperature within the mound as the monsoon sets in. Eggs are laid in holes in the fermenting heap and covered with organic matter, which is topped with a layer of soil. In most species, the birds have no further responsibility over the eggs or the chicks that hatch out of them. The only exception is the mallee-fowl which continues to guard the nest mounds in order to prevent sudden fluctuations in temperature that would affect the viability of the incubating eggs. Because of the longer incubating period, the chicks are very precocious at hatching. They burrow themselves up out of the thick layer of sand, stone chips or vegetable matter. Within hours of their emergence, they take to wing and reach the forest where their parents dwell, sometimes many kilometres away. It is not yet understood how the young reach such forests though they have never seen their parents. The megapodes, thus, are a very fascinating group of birds, some of which are being threatened by intense poaching of eggs at breeding sites by man. There are also a few other animal predators for megapode eggs.

J.B.S. Haldane Research Centre, Nagercoil 2, Tamilnadu, India

Discovery of Incubator Birds

Antonio Pigafetta was attributed to be the first person who made a good description of the incubator bird of the Philippines, locally known as 'tabon'. Pigafetta, a member of the Magellan's Expedition of 1519-1521, while returning from the Philippines reported to the European audience on the strange habits of a bird native to the Philippines. The bird was as large as a domestic fowl, but it laid eggs as big as a duck's and buried them in holes in sand for getting hatched by the heat of the sun. Frith (1962) quotes another recording on the above Filippino bird, this time by a Dominican monk named Navarrete who was returning from his mission duty in China via the Philippines. According to him, the bird known as 'tabon' was no bigger than an ordinary chicken, though long-legged, but it laid an egg larger than a goose's. In order to lay its eggs, it digs in the sand above a yard in depth. After laying, it fills up the hole and makes it even with the rest. The eggs hatch with the heat of the sun and sand. Another report was one by Gemelli Careri in 1699, some of whose descriptions were rather imaginatory. He alleged that when the eggs of 'tabon' are about to be hatched, the female ran around the nest calling out with all her might so that the chicks, excited by the sound, struggled out vigorously and escaped. However, many people did not believe in such strange habits of the Philippine bird. Especially the 18th century French naturalist, Buffon, dismissed the tales of incubator birds as pure fabrication. But in 1821, that is, three hundred years after the first reporting of Pigafetta, John Latham described the brush-turkey from Australia, although he regarded the bird as a vulture. Nevertheless, the group of birds became well known during 1835-1840 when John Gould, a great British ornithologist, gave a real description of the megapodes. Thereafter, many investigators watched and reported on the brush-turkey, the mallee-fowl, the maleo and some other species of Megapodiidae from Australia, New Guinea, the Philippines and Sulawesi (Indonesia). The most well-known and intensively studied member of the family is the mallee-fowl of Australia. The brush-turkeys are also fairly well known compared to the common shrub-fowl (*Freycinet* sp.) distributed throughout the South-East Asian countries and in some regions of the Pacific.

Distribution and Classification of Megapodes

Of the seven (according to some ornithologists, only six) genera of Megapodiidae, two are confined exclusively to the continent of Australia, and the rest are distributed in islands commencing from Nicobar Is. in the west to Samoa in the east, and as far north as the Philippines and beyond, and to southern Australia in the south, with the centre of distribution in Papua New Guinea. On the basis of their appearance and size, the megapodes can be divided into three distinct groups. *Megapodius* (shrub-fowl) is one of the main groups whose members are found throughout the islands of the Philippines, Pacific Is., Papua New Guinea, Indonesia, East Malaysia and Nicobar Is. as well as in Northern Australia. The other members of this group are *Macrocephalon* (maleo) and *Eulipoa* (painted megapode) which strictly confine respectively to Sulawesi and Maluku islands of Indonesia. Practically all the birds of this group of megapodes are smaller than the domestic fowl, dark or dark-brown-coloured and long-legged. Ripley (1960; 1964) includes the genus *Eulipoa* as a species under *Megapodius.*

The second group comprises the brush-turkeys, of which there are three. One of them, endemic to the eastern coast of Australia is *Alectura.* The other two, *Talegalla* and *Aepypodius* are native to Papua New Guinea. Brush-turkeys are larger than the shrub-fowl, have large tail, but they fly less frequently.

The third group of megapodes, represented by *Leipoa* (mallee-fowl), is white and black but resembles the brush-turkeys in shape. Its coloration is in harmony with the red-brown soil of the mallee. While all the other species of megapodes live in tropical or sub-tropical regions with heavy rainfall and lush vegetation, the home of the mallee-fowl is in the arid scrubs of inland Australia.

Thanks to the arduous explorations and pioneering investigations made by Wallace (1860; 1883), Lister (1911), Ashby (1922), Frith (1956b), Ripley (1960; 1964) and Clark Jr. (1960; 1964a; 1964b), the various members of megapodiidae are clearly defined. At an early stage, however, even eminent naturalists like John Latham and William Swainson did not consider the brush-turkey to be a megapode (Frith 1956). Misled by the turkey's barren red skin on the head and neck as well as the yellow fleshy collar, and because of its hooked upper bill, they regarded it as a bird of prey and named it the New Holland vulture. While systematists generally agree to the family comprising 7 genera, Clark Jr. also suggests to merge the genus *Eulipoa* with *Megapodius*. There is difference of opinion on the number of species while Rand and Gilliard (1970) mention 18 species. Flieg (1970) mentions only ten species for the family. Further, the genus *Megapodius*, the largest member with widest distribution, was regarded comprising 9 species and 28 subspecies. Careful examination of the birds of these groups made it possible to reduce them to just 3 species and 15 or 16 subspecies. Presumably more intensive surveys of the thousands of islands of South-East Asia and the Pacific region (Indonesia alone has over 13,000 islands, most of which are yet to be inhabited by man) are likely to reveal more species and perhaps new genera of this unique group of incubator birds. The fact that some populations occur very much isolated also suggests that more species are likely to be added on to the present list. For instance, the *Megapodius freycinet* population in Nicobar is about 1,600 km away from its nearest fellow-species in Kalimantan or Java. Similarly, *M.pritchardii* in the islands of Niuafou is separated by about 1,300 km. from the nearest population of megapodes in the west. Table 1 lists the various species of the 7 genera of Megapodiidae. This list is incomplete so far as the subspecies are concerned. The Polynesian species of *Megapodius* (*M. laperouse* and *M. pritchardii*) demonstrate wide variation among the members, some of them deserving to be separated into subspecies.

Visits to Megapode Breeding Sites

My duty station at Manado, the capital town of North Sulawesi Province (Indonesia) is close to Ternate of north Maluku (one hour flight by small Twin-Otter air plane). One could reach Galela a small village town in the famous bird island, Halmahera, in 30 minutes by air from Ternate. I was in Galela on August 27, 1977 searching in vain for a stall to get some fruits or drinks. The local people, being Moslem, observe the fasting season seriously and so, closed all the food shops during the daytime. A girl carrying some large eggs in loosely woven baskets made of coconut leaflets for sale came across. My excitement over seeing those megapode eggs for the first time was so great that I immediately made arrangement for a boat trip and reached a calm open beach covered with dark volcanic ash some 10 km away. This was a preferred egg-laying site for the species (*Eulipoa wallacei*) bearing the name of the famous naturalist, A.R. Wallace. This breeding site stretching along the coast to a distance of about 5 km, was marked with bamboo poles at close intervals of 150 m each. Crossing the sandy beach, which was covered with a kind of thorny bush here and there, we reached the thatched hut of a local inhabitant, Haler, where he and his son were seen packing the 98 eggs they had in possession, in coconut leaf bags.

TABLE 1

MEMBERS OF THE FAMILY MEGAPODIIDAE

Genera	Species/sub-species and their distribution
I. *Megapodius*	
	1. *Megapodius freycinet* : Common shrub-fowl or jungle fowl.
	s.s. *M. f.* *nicobariensis* : North Nicobar Ie., Bay of Bengal,
	M. f. *abbotti* (*M.f. nicobariensis abbotti*): South Nicobar Ie.
	M f. *cummingi:* Is. north and east of Borneo, Palawan, Balabac, Banquay, Lebuan and others (the Philippines)
	M. f, *sanghirensis:* Sangihe Talaud Is., North Sulawesi
	M. f. *gilbertii:* Sulawesi
	M. f. *bersteinii:* Sula Island,
	M. f. *tenimberensis:* Tenimbar — ?
	M. f. *reinwardt:* Kangean, Solombo Besar, Arena etc. (Java Sea), Kisui, Tiur, Kur, Banda, Kai, (South Maluku)
	M. f. *buruensis:* Buru,
	M. f. *forstenii:* Seram, Ambon, Haruku, Goram (South Maluku)
	M. f. *freycinet:* Obi, Bacan, Halmahera, Ternate, Tidore, Kajoa, Mareh, Morotai, Rau, Tifore, West Papuan Is., Waigeu, Batanta, Gebe, Gagi, Boni, Salawati, Misool, Kofiau and small islands off North-West New Guinea, Sorong, Pulu Hum
	M. f. *aruensis:* Aru
	M. f. *duperryii:* Western and Southern New Guinea
	M. f. *macgillivrayii:* D'Entraecaux and Louisiade Archipelago and Trobiand Group, Woodlark Group, Bouvouloir Group
	M. f. *affinis:* North New Guinea from head of Geelvink Bay to Mambere River, Southern slopes of Nassau Mountain in South New Guinea to upper Utakwa River, Yapen, Manam, Tarawai and other smaller islands
	M. f. *geelvinkianus:* Biak, Numfor, Manim, Meos Mum, Meos Korwar and possibly small islands off the coast of Yapen
	2. *Megapodius laperouse:* Marianus shrub-hen, Polynesia
	3. *Megapodius pritchardii:* Polynesian shrub-hen, Polynesia
II. *Macrocephalon:* Celebes Maleo,	
	4. *Macrocephalon maleo:* North Sulawesi, Central Sulawesi, South-East Sulawesi
III. *Eulipoa:* (some authors regard this genus as *Megapodius*)	
	5. *Eulipoa wallacei:* Moluccan shrub-hen, Bacan, Halmahera, Ternate, Buru, Seram, Ambon, Haruku
IV. *Alectura:*	
	6. *Alectura lathami:* Brush-turkey, North! Eastern coastal strip of Australia
V. *Talegalla:*	
	7. *Talegalla cuvieri:* Red-billed Talegalla or Brush-turkey, Misool, Salawati, North-West New Guinea, eastward to Warbusi (Geelvink Bay) and on south coast to Mimika and Utakwa Rivers
	8. *Talegalla fuscirostris:* Blackbilled Talegalla or Brush-turkey
	T. f. *occidentalis:* Aru Ie. and Southern New Guinea from the head of Geelvink Bay and Mimika River eastward to Oriomo River
	T. f. *fuscirostris:* South coast of South-East New Guinea from Hall Sound (Yule Ie.) to Port Moresby district (Rigo)
	9. *Talegalla jobiensis:* Brown-collared Talegalla or Brush-turkey
	T. j. *longicauda:* South-East New Guinea, westward in the north to Sepik River, in the south to Aroa River.
	T. j. *jobiensis:* Yapen Ie. and Northern New Guinea from Mamberamo River to Humboldt Bay
VI. *Aepypodius:*	
	10. *Aeypypodius arfakianus:* Misool Ie., New Guinea
	11. *Aepypodius bruijni:* Waigen Ie., New Guinea
VII. *Leipoa:* The mallee-fowl.	
	12. *Leipoa ocellata:* Southern Australia.

Haler took us to his collection territory and unearthed an egg to our astonishment, as the egg was buried at a depth of about 70 cm and well above the high-tide mark. When asked whether they were not destroying a fascinating and useful bird by removing thousands of eggs every week, Haler told us that this had been their way of living for a very long period, and still the birds came to his area for laying eggs year after year. According to him, several eggs inspite of diligent search by the collectors, are left-over and these eggs hatch out and maintain the population of the species. It is easy for one to dig out all the eggs the birds lay immediately after a rain, as he (or she) only needs to follow the fresh diggings. But when the top ash is dry, it is difficult to distinguish new diggings as the bird closes the hole and makes it almost even with soil surface before it returns to the forest a few kilometres away from the sea coast. The egg pits of the maleo are only partially filled in to cover the eggs. The local people, according to Haler, neither trap the adult birds nor catch the chicks of *mamua* (local name for *Eulipoa*) because many of them owe their living to this bird which provides them with eggs. Eating *mamua* meat is almost taboo. The birds visit the breeding sites only during nights (very few visiting during full moon nights, as reported by local people), and they fly back to the nearby forest before dawn. But most other megapodes especially maleo, mallee-fowl and brush-turkey are diurnal by habit. We bought some eggs from Haler at Rp 150 per egg for trying to hatch them in the laboratory. These eggs are much cheaper than maleo eggs, each costing between Rp 600 and Rp 1,000. My first visit to a megapode breeding site where solar heat is utilized for hatching the eggs, prompted me to visit during the following six years to a variety of breeding sites, near volcanoes, near hot springs, in mallee dry country and in lush and dense rain forests. Some details on the locations visited are given in Table 2.

Reptilian Traits in Megapodes

Certain breeding habits displayed by the megapodes would push this group of birds back to the reptilian era in the scale of evolution. Much unlike the way the common birds brood over and hatch the eggs with their body warmth, the eggs of the megapodes are incubated underground in pits, or in the interior of huge mounds. Such methods of incubation may be correlated with the large size of eggs and the staggering of laying spread over a long period with long interval between layings. The incubation period is considerably longer than that for birds of similar size (about 80 days for maleo, 75 days for brush-turkey, 50-90 days for mallee-fowl, etc.). The slow early development increases the size of the young at hatching and also enables it to be highly precocious which is necessary for its survival. The slow development of embryo is due to the relatively slow incubation temperature. But a low temperature requirement is much safer especially for the nests/egg-pits unattended by parent birds. The ratio by weight of yolk to whole egg is higher in incubator birds compared to eggs of other birds which is an advantage for the over-development of the chick within the shell. The young, like the reptiles, start an independent life as soon as they emerge from the egg. Practically in all the species of megapodes, the young hatches out of the eggs with practically developed feathers, and unaided they wriggle out of the thick layer of soil/compost. Total absence of parental care and gradual hatching of eggs are conducive to precocity. Long gaps in laying each egg is inevitable as the ratio of egg to body weight of hen is very high in megapodes. Laying of eggs at intervals leads to hatching at intervals which

TABLE 2
BREEDING SITES OF MEGAPODES IN INDONESIA & AUSTRALIA VISITED BY DAVIS

Month/Year	Site	Region/country	Species of magapodes	Observations made/materials collected/remarks
August 1977	Galela, Halmahera	Maluku, Indonesia	*Eulipoa wallacei*	Saw numerous nests on volcanic ash sea coast. Inspected hundreds of eggs from 'poachers'.
February 1978 & in 1979	Tangkoko Batuangus forests	North Sulawesi, wesi, Indonesia	*Macrocephalon maleo* & *Megapodius freycinet*	Two adult maleos, numerous nests of both the species.
November 1978	Sanghe Talaud	North Sulawesi	*Megapodius freycinet*	Two adult birds and several nest-holes observed.
August 1979	CSIRO Wildlife Research	Lineham, A.C.T., Australia	Preserved specimens and skins of many spp.	Recorded their measurements and photographed them.
September 1979	Dumoga area: Molabang	North Sulawesi	*Macrocephalon maleo*	4 adult birds, about 250 nest-holes and many eggs.
May 1980	Dumoga area: Bone	North Sulawesi	*Macrocephalon maleo*	saw 12 adult birds & hundreds of nest-holes in two areas.
August 1981	Tempy, mallee area	Victoria, Australia	*Leipoa ocellata*	2 adults and 14 huge nest mounds. Photographed them.
September 1981	Mackenzie Fauna Park	Victoria, Australia	*Alectura lathami*	2 adults, one nest-mound of fresh eucalyptus leaves.
April 1983	Dumoga Park, Kosigolan Dulududio	North Sulawesi, Indonesia	*Macrocephalon maleo*	8 adults, about 1000 nest-holes within one km diameter area.
April 1983	Dumoga Park, Kosigolan	North Sulawesi	*Macrocephalon maleo*	2 adults and about 500 nest-holes near hot spring.
June 1983	Banggai	Central Sulawesi	*Macrocephalon maleo*	Heavy rains, no bird seen, saw about 100 eggs, purchased some.
August 1983	Little Desert Park	Victoria, Australia	*Leipoa, ocellata*	2 reactivated nests photographed. Fresh leaf material added.
August 1983	Dorrigo Park	N.S.W., Australia	*Alectura lathami*	6 nest-mounds, 2 adult birds. Some nests old and abandoned.
September 1983	Dorrigo Park	N.S.W., Australia	*Alectura lathami*	20 huge nest-mounds, saw 15 adult male and female brush-turkeys.
September 1983	New England National Park	N.S.W., Australia	*Leipoa ocellata*	2 old nests, saw no bird.
September 1983	Zoological Park	Toronga, Australia	*Leipoa ocellata*	2 adults, one nest-mound.
October 1983	Galela Halmahera	Maluku, Indonesia	*Eulipoa wallacei* (*Megapodius freycinet*)	

Above: Maleo (*Macrocephalon maleo*) of Indonesia. Solid crest used as thermometer.
Below: Mallee-fowl (*Leipoa ocellata*) of southern Australia.
(*Photos*: Author)

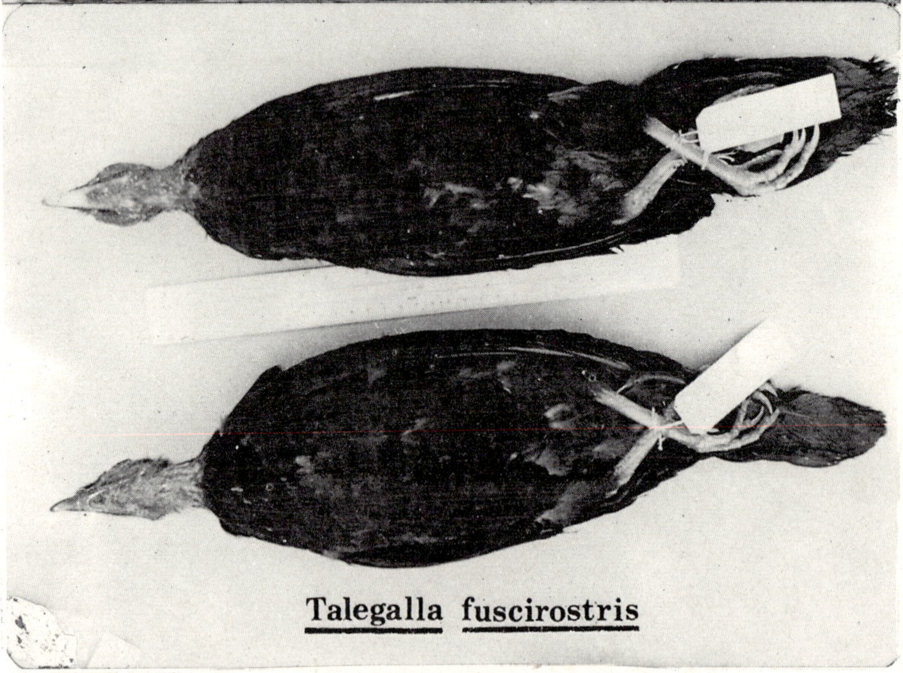

Above: Brush-turkey (*Alectura lathami*) of northeastern Australia.
Below: *Talegalla puscirostris* of Papua New Guinea
(*Photos*: Author)

Above: Giant mound-nest of Mallee-fowl of Australia measuring up to 10 m along diameter.
Below: Nests of Maleo of Indonesia are simple pits dug out in forests near hot water springs.
(*Photos*: Author)

Above: Smallest two eggs are of domestic chicken; largest four are of Maleo; intermediate sized are of *Eulipoa wallesi,* the Painted Megapode of Alukku, Indonesia.

Below: Maleo eggs packed in palm leaves to facilitate safe transport.

(*Photos*: Author)

Above: Brush-turkey chick emerging from a huge nest-mound.

Below: The first ever hybrid produced by Mr Roy Small of Brisbane, Australia, between domestic chicken hen (Phasianidae) and Brush-turkey cock (Megapodiidae).

(*Photos*: Author)

is an advantage for the young to escape from predators. Large size of egg and the long period of development brings out the chick as a miniature adult. According to Clark Jr., temperature detection by the mouth region of male and/or female bird is correlated with the methods of incubation. The megapode chicks have no egg-tooth (again in common with reptiles) since the use of such a tooth is not practicable because of the large size of the chicks at hatching. The chicks kick out of their shells instead of the normal hatching in other birds.

THE DIFFERENT KINDS OF NESTS/INCUBATORS OF MEGAPODES

The simplest method of incubation is employed by maleo and the painted megapodes, both of which do nothing more than bury their eggs in the ground. During the breeding season, these birds which usually live in forests far away from the coast, move nearer to the sea or to areas within forests with open sandy pockets. Many choose beaches which are fully exposed to the sun. The breeding site of the painted megapode near Galela is a typical example. The fully exposed volcanic ash gets heated up during the day and the temperature remains constant throughout the night for depths below 2 feet up to the tide mark. Even immediately after an hour's pouring rain, when I visited the beach and tried to retrieve an egg from a deep pit dug out by Haler, my fingers could feel the warmth of the pit. I was told of the presence of another smaller nesting area of *mamua* about 15 km away located on the slope of a hill where earlier volcanic lava flowed through. Thus, open areas with volcanic ash is a much favoured niche for the painted megapode to lay eggs. But in the several nesting sites of maleo that I examined in North and Central Sulawesi, there was not even a single case where volcanic ash seems to have been preferred for burying eggs. Patches of white sand fully exposed to sun, even within forests or areas around sources of volcanic heat, are used by the maleo. Where volcanic heat is available (hot springs) maleo cares little for open areas. They even dig pits close to stem of forest trees or under a thick canopy of low bush and brambles as it is the case in many sites in North Sulawesi.

The greatest diversity in the method of incubation displayed by *Megapodius* (shrub-fowl) would suggest that the members of this first group of megapodes are rather haphazard and inefficient in the way they deposit their eggs. However, they are diligent in selecting suitable sites. they don't lay eggs unless the hot ash, fissure in a rock face or exposed sand patch maintains constant temperature and adequate humidity for a fairly long time.

Where suitable niches for burying the eggs are not available, even the shrub-fowl builds an incubator with ground litter. Members of the second group build mounds for incubating eggs. But the size of the mound is not very large. As for example, the mound of brush-turkey is just over one metre in height and 3-5 metres in diameter. Different quantities of soil are used in the mound. The brush-turkey is reported to follow some pattern while building the incubator. This consists of raking on to the mound successive layers of different materials. *Talegalla* and *Aepypodius* also construct similar mounds, but they are more cone-shaped compared with those of the brush-turkey.

The mounds of the mallee-fowl are the most sophisticated among incubator birds. It is clear that the male and female mallee-fowl come together only during the breeding season even though the male may be engaged in working on the mound up to 8 months of the year.

THE EGG OF MEGAPODES

1. **The process of egg-laying.** I have not watched in detail the way the megapode hen lays her eggs. But some ornithologists who studied closely the nesting behaviour of megapodes have described vividly the laying processes in some species. Frith (1962b) recorded lucidly this aspect in the mallee-fowl. Mackinnon (1978) described the egg-laying in the maleo. The description by David Fleay (1936) on the process of egg-laying in the Australian brush-turkey is more vivid. According to him, 'The hen excavated a V-shaped hole 19 inches in depth, one limb of which, nearest the central axis on the mound, was vertical. Into this hole she pushed and rammed her head several times until reassured that the temperature was suitable. Then sitting across the hole with wings spread on either side and tail slightly elevated, she laid her large white egg, narrow end down, vertically in the hole. The actual laying process occupied three minutes. Then rising, she proceeded hastily to scratch material in from the side of the hole and to stamp it down, turning slowly around as she did so. More and more material was added and stamped with alternate feet, in a rapid prancing fashion, and finally material was thrown and scratched across the top before the hen departed.' In the case of the mallee-fowl, however, the female's role is over just when she drops the egg in the hole which was already prepared by the hard-working male. As soon as the female lays her egg, being exhausted, she rests for a couple of minutes at the egg hole itself and slowly moves away from the mound and relaxes in the shade of a nearby eucalyptus tree. Then the male, who has been motionlessly watching her laying ordeal, takes over the rest of the job. Initially, he fills sand around the vertically placed egg and when the egg is fully covered, more sand/soil is pulled over the egg vigorously. For about three hours, the male continues to work on the mound to see that the egg is sufficiently covered and assured for its successful hatching. During this period, the female continues to rest outside or makes occasional visits to the nest as if to encourage her hard-working mate.

2. **Size of Eggs.** In relation to body weight, the weight and size of megapode eggs are the largest among birds. Through a study of graphs prepared on the weights of eggs and body size of hen mallee-fowl, this species having an average body weight of 1,800 g should lay eggs of only 80 g each. The mean weight of mallee-fowl egg is 190 g, or one egg weighs roughly just over 10% of body weight. During a year of good laying, the females produce more than thrice their body weight in eggs. Other birds hardly produce eggs weighing half their body weight in one year. Domesticated birds like the chicken, duck, goose and quail are exceptions. As mentioned, the ratio of the yolk to weight of egg is very high for megapode eggs compared to eggs of other birds.

As the body size of different species of megapodes differ, their eggs also vary in weight considerably. Also for a given species, birds of one locality lay larger/smaller-sized eggs compared to those of another locality. This is clear from the data presented on the eggs of maleo from different localities of North and Central Sulawesi.

In Table 3, data on the weight and measurements of the painted megapode (*Eulipoa wallacei*) from North Maluku are given. These eggs were purchased from Haler of Galela.

On an average, one egg of *Megapodius* weighs twice that of a standard domestic hen egg. But the maximum thickness of both the kinds of eggs is almost the same. This is because while

TABLE 3

PAINTED MEGAPODE: WEIGHTS AND MEASUREMENTS OF EGGS FROM NORTH MALUKU

No.	Wt. egg (g)	Length (cm)	Maximum thickness (cm)	Maximum girth (cm)
1.	104.5	8.0	4.6	15.3
2.	108.0	7.6	5.1	18.3
3.	97.8	7.8	4.7	15.1
4.	103.4	7.8	4.8	15.7
5.	107.5	8.0	5.0	15.8
6.	110.4	7.8	4.9	18.1
7.	107.1	8.0	4.8	15.6
8.	94.6	7.7	4.7	15.0
9.	103.9	7.9	4.7	15.5
10.	98.0	7.5	4.9	15.5
11.	105.7	7.6	4.9	15.8
Total	1140.9	85.7	53.1	175.7
Mean	103.72	7.79	4.82	16.0
Eggs of domestic hen				
1.	51.8	5.7	3.9	12.6
2.	55.1	5.7	4.0	12.9
3.	49.2	5.2	4.0	12.9
4.	55.0	5.3	4.2	13.5
Total	211.1	21.9	12.1	51.9
Mean	52.78	5.48	4.03	12.98

the egg of domestic hen is broader at one end, both the ends of megapodius eggs are uniformly thick.

Data on eggs of maleo are given in Tables 4 and 5. The 12 eggs shown in Table 4 were purchased from a restaurant in Manado. I was told that a supplier from Dumoga area about 270 km south of Manado delivered the eggs. Each egg cost me Rp. 700. Six of them were kept inside an incubator in the laboratory for hatching trial. Table 5 shows data from 2 centres of Central Sulawesi (Banggai Ie. and from Moilong village).

It is obvious that the weights of eggs from the three centres vary considerably. Those from Moilong area are the heaviest and longest, while those of Banggai are the smallest. Eggs from North Sulawesi are intermediates. The differences in the size of eggs between localities may be due to the quality of the food available in the regions as well as to the genetic variation between birds of different ecological environments. It is desirable to obtain the weights of adult birds of these localities to verify whether the ratio of weights of egg and body weight is the same for the different groups of birds or not.

TABLE 4

Macrocephalon maleo: WEIGHTS AND MEASUREMENTS OF EGGS FROM NORTH SULAWESI

Eggs	Wt. of egg (g)	Length (cm)	Maximum thickness (cm)	Maximum girth (cm)
1.	230.6	10.50	6.20	19.45
2.	237.1	10.50	6.30	19.90
3.	244.8	10.55	6.25	19.93
4.	227.3	10.60	6.05	19.20
5.	Broken	10.50	5.80	18.80
6.	221.0	10.01	6.40	20.00
7.	221.3	10.59	6.29	19.55
8.	210.4	10.60	6.12	19.50
9.	199.5	9.71	6.21	19.50
10.	193.1	9.80	6.10	19.10
11.	208.9	10.40	6.25	19.50
12.	210.9	10.80	6.05	18.77
Total	2404.9	124.56	74.02	232.85
Mean	218.63	10.38	6.17	19.40

TABLE 5

Macrocephalon maleo: WEIGHTS AND MEASUREMENTS OF EGGS FROM CENTRAL SULAWESI

No.	Wt. of egg (g)	Length (cm)	Max. Diameter (cm)	Girth lengthwise	Girth Widthwise	Volume (cc)
From Banggai						
1.	151.0	9.4	5.4	24.7	18.9	200
2.	190.0	9.9	5.9	26.2	19.1	202
3.	173.0	9.5	5.7	25.0	18.8	200
4.	170.0	9.5	5.7	25.3	19.0	200
5.	162.0	9.7	5.7	26.8	19.4	202
Mean	169.2	9.6	5.68	25.6	19.04	200.8
From Moilong village						
5.	220.0	10.4	5.9	27.2	19.5	227
7.	231.0	10.5	5.8	27.3	19.8	245
8.	221.0	10.6	6.1	27.6	20.4	250
9.	250.0	10.8	5.9	27.6	19.5	237
Mean	230.5	10.58	5.95	27.43	19.80	239.8

3. **Destruction to Eggs.** The major predator for the mallee-fowl in Victoria is reported to be dingo, the wild dog. I was shown some deep holes close to active mounds of mallee-fowl where the dingo lived and destroyed many eggs at Tempy area of Victoria. The eggs of brush-turkey in N.S.W. are being actively destroyed by the ant-eater (ekidna) which is reportedly increasing in population. *Megapodius freycinet* eggs in Komodo Is. of Indonesia, according to Lincoln (1974) are dug out and eaten by the Komodo dragon (*Varanus komodoensis*). Other species of *Varanus* should be serious predators of megapode eggs in other parts of Indonesia as well as in the Philippines, Papua New Guinea and nearby countries.

Man is by far the greatest destroyer of megapodes. Even during the off-season, Haler collected a little less than one hundred eggs in one week from a 150-metre wide strip of the coast in North Maluku where the painted megapode nest. Like Haler there are many others who gather eggs from the same breeding territory 'legally'. The District Collector, Sub-District Officer or even the Forest Officer gives licence to local people to collect eggs from strips of 150-metre beach area by receiving Rp. 4,600 as annual tax. Thus, every year several thousands of eggs are removed from this breeding site. If this system is not put an end to very soon, undoubtedly, this beach will not be visited by any megapode for laying eggs after a couple of decades. The local government officers make use of the money thus collected by leasing out megapode breeding sites for developmental activities such as building a hospital, a school or to construct roads. More striking instances of destroying breeding centres on Maleo in Sulawesi have been reported by Mackinnon (1980) while discussing methods for the conservation of maleo birds.

Megapode eggs are considered not only wholesome, rich food, but they are also attributed having invigorating and aphrodisiac properties. The Chinese in particular have a special fancy for maleo/mamua eggs, and they buy from the poachers who lift them 'legally' or illegally from breeding sites. Three people who travelled with us in the same flight from Galela to Ternate carried with them bags of mamua eggs for their personal use. After several requests made to a Manado restaurant owner and making himself convinced that I am a harmless person, I could purchase some maleo eggs. They failed to hatch when I placed them in our laboratory incubator. A colleague at the Industrial Crops Research Institute at Manado received as recently as March 1983 a dozen eggs from Kothamobagu purchased through poachers at the Dumoga area. Even though collecting and consuming eggs of both maleo and mamua are forbidden by law, there seems to be a flourishing trade on these eggs in some parts of Sulawesi. Mackinnon (1978) laments over the alarming rate of destruction of eggs by man which is bound to wipe out the species which are already in the list of endangered birds.

4. **Ceremony of 'Bringing Home of Maleo Eggs'.** One of the traditional ceremonies unique to the district of Banggai in Central Sulawesi is 'Bringing Home of Maleo Eggs' in vogue during the past over seventy years. According to local history, a few maleos were brought originally by two sons of a king, which were the gift from their father who lived in Java. Because of the uncongenial conditions in Banggai for the survival and breeding of maleos, the birds were brought to the Sub-District Batui where the grandmother of the two princes lived. Batui is ideal for the multiplication of maleos. While handing over the birds to their grandmother, the princes made one important wish, that is, during every breeding season, the first

set of eggs the birds lay should be brought to Banggai. A specified number of eggs were required to be brought to Banggai every year as an evidence that the maleos continue to thrive there. This traditional custom is rigidly followed because the people believe that if they do not carry out the orders given by the ancestors, some misfortune might overtake them. To fulfil the ceremony, hundreds of eggs are dug out of a rich breeding site, wrapped beautifully in leaves of palms such as the coconut, nipa or a wild palm (*Livistona rotundifolia*) and carried ceremoniously to the District Officer at Banggai where many people enjoy eating them. After the ceremony, digging out of eggs continues unabated. With the rapid increase of the local inhabitants, poaching is also on the increase. It looks certain that unless the breeding site is protectd, the people's promise cannot be kept for long. Latest reports about this rich breeding site is very alarming. Due to the volcanic eruption in nearby Una Una Island, the inflicted people were accommodated in a refugee camp provided not far from the breeding site of the maleo. Within a year of the establishment of the camp, the inmates have almost wiped out the excellent breeding territory.

LITERATURE CITED

ALI, S. & RIPLEY, S.D. (1969): Handbook of the birds of India and Pakistan, Family Megapodiidae, **2**: 1-3.

ASHBY, E. (1922): Notes on the mound-building birds of Australia with particulars peculiar to the mallee-fowl, *Leipoa ocellata,* and a suggestion as to their origin. *Ibis* (11), **4**: 702-709.

BANFIELD, E.J. (1913): Megapode mounds and pits. The *Emu* **12**: 281-283.

BELLCHAMBERS, T.P. (1916-1918): Notes on the mallee fowl, *Leipoa ocellata rosinae. South Austr. Ornithol.* **2**: 134-140; **3**: 78-81.

BENNET, K.H. (1884): On the habits of the mallee hen, *Leipoa ocellata. Proc. Linn. Soc., N.S.W.* **8**: 193-197.

BESTE, H. (1978): Incubator birds. *Wildlife 20*(5): 204-209.

BRICKHILL, J. (1980): Endangered animals of New South Wales. Mallee-fowl. *Parks and Wildlife J., N.S.W.*: 49-55.

CLARK JR., G.A. (1960): Notes on the embryology and evolution of the megapodes (Aves: Galliformes). *Yale Peabody Mus. Postilla* No. 45: 1-7.

_____ (1964a): Life histories and the evolution of megapodes. *Living Bird,* 1964: 149-167.

_____ (1964b): Ontogeny and evolution in the megapodes (Aves: Galliformes). *Yale Peabody Mus. Postilla* No. *78:* 1-37.

FLEAY, D.H. (1936): Nesting habits of the brush-turkey. *The Emu* **36**: 153-163.

FLIEG, G. (1970): Breeding the yellow-wattled brush turkey in North America. *British Aviculturists' Club.*

FRITH, H.J. (1955): Incubation in the mallee fowl, *Leipoa ocellata* (megapodiidae). Acta XI Congressus Internationalis Ornithologici, pp. 570-574.

_____ (1956a): Temperature regulation in the nesting mounds of the mallee fowl, *Leipoa ocellata* Gould. *C.S.I.R.O. Wildl. Res.* **1**: 79-95.

_____ (1956b): Breeding habits in the family megapodiidae. *Ibis* **98**: 620-640.

_____ (1957): Experiments on the control of temperature in the mound of the mallee fowl, *Leipoa ocellata* Gould (Megapodiidae). *C.S.I.R.O Wildl. Res.* **2**: 101-110.

_____ (1959): Breeding of the mallee fowl, *Leipoa ocellata* Gould (Megapodiidae). ibid. **4**: 31-60.

_____ (1962a): Conservation of the mallee fowl, *Leipoa ocellata* Gould (Megapodiidae). ibid. **7: (1): 33-49.**

_____ (1962b): The mallee fowl, the bird that builds an incubator. Angus and Robertson, Sydney.

GOUD, J. & RUTGERS, R, (1970). Birds of New Guinea. London.

LE SOUEF, D. (1899): On the habits of the mound-building birds of Australia. *Ibis* **9**: 19.

LEWIS, F. (1940): Notes on the breeding habits of the mallee fowl. *The Emu* **40**: 97-110.

LINCOLN, G.A. (1974): Predation of incubator birds (*Megapodius freycinet*) by Komodo dragons (*Varanus komodoensis*). *J. Zool., London* **174**: 419-428.

LINT, K.C. (1967): The maleo, a mound builder from the Celebes. *Zoonooz* 40 (10): 4-8.

LISTER, J.J. (1911): The distribution of the avian genus *Megapodius* in the Pacific Islands. *Proc. zool. Soc. London* **52**: 749-759.

MACKINNON, J.R. (1978): Sulawesi megapodes. *World Pheasant Assn. J.* **3**: 96-103.

________ (1980): Methods for the conservation of maleo birds (*Macrocephalon maleo*).

MATTINGLEY, A.H.E. (1909): Thermometer-bird or malee-fowl. *The Emu* **8**: 53-61.

MEES, G.F. (1965): The avifauna of Misool. *New Guinea Zoology* **31**: 151-153.

RAND, A.L. & GILLIARD, E.T. (1970): Handbook of New Guinea birds.

RIPLEY, S.D. (1960): Distribution and niche differentiation in species of megapodes in the Moluccas and Western Papuan area. *Proc. XII Internat. Ornith. Cong., Helsinki,* 1958, pp. 631-640.

________ (1964): A Systematic and ecological study of birds of New Guinea. *Yale Peabody Mus. Bull.* **19**: 1-87.

SERVENTY, V. (1967). The mallee fowl's year. *Animal Behaviour:* 483-87.

STATER, P. (1970): A Field guide to Australian birds. Non-passerines. Rigby Ltd., Sydney.

UNO, A., HEINRICH, G. & MENDON, J.J. (1949): Het natuurmonument panoea (N. Celebes) en het maleohoen (*Macrocephalon maleo* Sal. Muller) in het bujzonder. *Tectona* **39**: 151-165.

WALLACE, A.R. (1860). The Ornithology of northern Celebes. *Ibis* **2**: 140-147.

________ (1883): The Malay Archipelago. London.

LINT, K.C. (1967): The maleo, a mound builder from the Celebes. *Zoonooz* **40** (10):4-8.

Conservation of Vultures in (Developing) India

(*With two plates*)

ROBERT GRUBH, GOUTAM NARAYAN & S. M. SATHEESAN

Vulture is the popular name for a few species of birds that are basically carrion feeders and have bare head and neck as an essential adaptation for feeding on tough carcasses. In fact the name vulture or condor is a functional one to denote two different groups of birds from two different geographical areas but having the same ecological role to play, which is, to feed on the flesh of large mammal carcasses. Vultures come under two remote taxonomic categories, namely Cathartidae, comprising New World vultures, and Accipitridae (subfamily Aegypiinae) comprising the Old World vultures. In this group are also included not ecologically but taxonomically, a few other species which do not chiefly feed on carrion and hence do not have bare necks, and often have only a portion of the head bare.

Here we discuss the conservation prospects of the Indian, particularly the meat eating, vultures in the present period (when India is still at the status of a Developing Country), and in comparison with the status and conservation of vultures in other parts of the world.

THE GLOBAL SITUATION

Before we get into the details of the global situation of predominently meat-eating vultures it is necessary to list the species coming under this functional group.

Basically we have three genera and nine species of birds under this ecological category and these have a global distribution. These are California Condor *Gymnogyps californianus* and the Andean Condor *Vultur gryphus* of the Americas and seven species of griffon vultures of the genus *Gyps* extending from Africa to Asia,with four species for the Indian subcontinent.

THE ANDEAN CONDOR AND THE CALIFORNIA CONDOR

The Andean condor which is the largest present day vulture has a distribution covering the entire Andes and the foothills in South America. This majestic vulture was a very common bird throughout its range of distribution until half a century ago. The Andean condor is still common at certain localities but sparse or totally absent in the rest of its original range of distribution. The decline of this species in many areas has been attributed to several factors, chiefly, wanton shooting of this easy target.

The California condor which was once numerous in California and the surroundings is now limited to a small area and the number reduced to around 20 in 1982. The gradual reduction of the California condor has been attributed to various causes, the major ones being reduction of habitat and natural food sources and killing by ignorant ranchers who own a sizeable area of this vulture's home range and feeding grounds. Accumulation of pesticide content in the body tissues, lead poisoning through gun-shot carcasses, and poisoning through baited rodent pests have been put forward as some of the major causes of their death and decline (Snyder 1982).

Whitebacked Vultures feeding on slaughter house wastes in Delhi
(*Photo*: Goutam Narayan)

Vultures soaring on thermals near Delhi
(*Photo*: Goutam Narayan)

There has been a national alert to save this bird from extinction and the measures adapted include (1) legal protection of the species and part of its home range, (2) ecological study of the species, (3) research on increasing the number through double clutching and hand rearing of the hatchlings from retrieved eggs, (4) indirect protection through public education and awareness (California Condor Conference 1982).

THE GRIFFON VULTURES

Of the total seven species, four occur on the African Continent, which are the Fulvous griffon *Gyps fulvus,* Ruppell's Griffon *G. ruppellii,* African Whitebacked Vulture *G. africanus* and Cape Vulture *G. coprothers.* Among these species the Cape vulture alone appears to have an uncertain future whereas the remaining three appear to be safe as of now.

According to the latest studies the Cape vulture is losing ground to the changing times through calcium deficiency. The Griffon vultures usually take care of their calcium requirements through swallowing pieces of weather worn bones (Grubh 1973). When the foraging grounds of the Cape vulture was still very much a wilderness it managed its calcium requirements from dried bone chips left over by hyenas. But the hyenas have receded with the advance of human exploitation of the land and the Cape vultures which still get a reasonable supply of carcasses, do not get dried bone chips, with the result that many young suffer from malformed bones and do not fledge (Mundy & Ledger 1976).

Whereas it is next to impossible to restore the hyenas to the Cape, the Vulture Study Group in South Africa has started vulture "restaurants" as a bid to save this species from further decline (Friedman and Mundy 1979). Old bone chips are provided at selected sites at these "restaurants" where the Cape vulture could drop in without disturbance. This conservation measure appears to have a favourable impact on the well-being of this species.

Griffon vultures seem to be holding ground along most of their range further east through central Asia; or rather, we do not have definite reports of their status from these areas.

THE INDIAN SITUATION

As for India the griffon vultures seem to be thriving when seen from the surface. In fact there isn't any decline in the population of griffon vultures in totality and they are thriving to the extent that a certain species (Indian Whitebacked *Gyps bengalensis*) has phenomenally proliferated in many areas. But the very nature of proliferation of this species gives a foreboding of the future status of griffon vultures in India. This forms the subject matter of further discussion, below:

Griffon vultures of India, their distribution and relative abundance

The Fulvous Griffon *Gyps fulvus fulvescence*

This is a winter visitor to western India, coming in small numbers down to Kathiawar Peninsula. The proportion of this species in the Gir hills was from 5 to 10% of the other griffons. Only individuals having immature plumage were noted at Gir and it appears that most adults have stayed behind at their breeding grounds elsewhere. The fulvus griffon is dominant over the other two griffons, namely the Indian whitebacked and the Longbilled vultures.

The Himalayan Griffon *Gyps himalayensis*

The species is restricted to the Himalayas and the foothills and their status appears to be fairly stable and safe as far as the reported information suggests.

The Longbilled Vulture ***Gyps indicus***

According to the existing literature this species has a wide range of distribution and is quite common and at some places even in equal numbers with the Whitebacked vulture. But this may not be exact because the immature Whitebacked vulture often are mistaken for Longbilled vulture by many ornithologists.

The Whitebacked Vulture ***Gyps bengalensis***

This is the commonest and most abundant vulture in India; distributed throughout the Peninsula. Although smaller than the other Indian griffons and easily chased away by others at carcasses, the Indian whitebacked vulture thrives and manages to obtain food by its sheer numbers (Grubh 1978). Besides, the Whitebacked is essentially a species of the plains thereby having an advantage over the others.

STATUS AND CONSERVATION PROSPECTS

As mentioned earlier, the Indian griffons seem to be thriving when looked at superficially. Wherever we see vultures at carcasses, they appear to hold ground and do not in any way appear to be threatened. However, underneath this apparent prosperity there are some serious problems, a calamity yet to surface but likely to strike if the prevailing situation is permitted to drift and take its own course. We see two major problems threatening the Indian griffons: one is diminishing of natural habitat and natural food sources and the other is the unnatural proliferation of this griffon around large towns and cities.

Diminishing of natural habitat and natural food sources

The griffons have a valuable role to play in Indian forests where they are the most effective scavengers of carrion and left overs of animal kills. As such, these vultures thrive at all natural forests in India where food supply from large mammals is assured. However, with the fast deterioration of our natural forests and depletion of large wild ungulates vultures are gradually disappearing from such areas. This is particularly applicable in southern India where food supply from domestic livestock carcasses is meagre and hence not dependable as a regular supplementary or alternate food supply. What is necessary here therefore is to restore the natural forests and the wild population of large mammals.

UNNATURAL PROLIFERATION OF THE VULTURES

We have a different picture in the upper parts of India where cattle cannot be slaughtered owing to religious sentiments. Here the vultures have a superabundance of meat supply, particularly at dairies around towns and cities. Besides cattle meat the griffon vultures also get plenty of slaughter house wastes (such as offal and intestines) from buffaloes which are allowed for slaughter (Plate I).

The griffons have proliferated so much, and have come to depend on towns and cities to such an extent, that the size of a town or a city can be roughly guessed by the amount of vultures soaring over these. And this is where the problem is. These vultures have lately become the major hazard for aircraft in India owing to their phenomenal proliferation around towns and cities. Before and after meal the vultures, especially the Whitebacked, soar on thermals in gigantic spirals and come in the way of aircraft at low altitudes (Plate 2).

This problem is gradually driving the aviation authorities towards decisions favouring mass killing of the vultures using chemicals.

The Indian Agricultural Research Institute already has an ongoing[1] project to do such research and work out the details of this mass killing of vultures.

But mass killing methods if efficiently employed can result in extermination of most of the vulture species in India that come to the carrion. It will then be an immense loss to the world and can also cause havoc with the ecology, environment, and human health: Natural forests and countrysides would lose the only efficient scavangers which can "incinerate" even putrified meat and carcasses of diseased animals. And the towns and cities will be exposed to serious health problems as an outcome of rotting offal of livestock carcasses.

So we have suggested an alternate method, based on sound ecological principles, to solve vulture problem to aircract, without adverse effects on the vulture species and the human environment (Ali and Grubh 1983).

Our recommendations include: 1. setting up of modern slaughter houses which use up all animal wastes including intestines and hence not provide sustenance for vultures and 2. setting up of carcass processing centres which would turn soft tissues of dead livestock into valuable chicken feed and tallow. If these two recommendations are effectively carried out there will be very few vultures trespassing the airspace of aircraft and the country will save valuable lives and property otherwise lost every year through vulture strikes. In addition to this the country will also benefit considerably from the enormous quantities of chicken feed and tallow which is now wasted on vultures.

[1]Presently discontinued.

After all this, the vultures will still continue to thrive in natural forests and in the country side in the northern states, in optimum numbers. That is the role for which the vultures are equipped. The ecological control of vultures recommended above would only help in removing the excess population of vultures, which are an unhealthy byproduct of unplanned development of towns and cities in India.

References

ALI, SALIM & GRUBH ROBERT, (1983): Ecological Study of Bird Hazards at Indian Aerodromes Phase-2 Final Report. Bombay Natural History Society — Bombay.

CALIFORNIA CONDOR CONFERENCE (1982): Recommendations and Santa Barbara Museum of Natural History, Santa Barbara, California.

FRIEDMAN, RUSSEL & MUNDY, PETER (1979): Vulture restaurants in Southern Africa. International Symposium on the Vultures. Santa Barbara Museum of Natural History, Santa Barbara, California.

GRUBH, ROBERT (1978): Competition and Coexistence in Griffon Vultures. *J. Bombay nat. Hist. Soc.* **75** (3): 810-814.

__________ (1973): Calcium intake in Vultures of the Genus *Gyps*. ibid. **70**(1): 199-200.

MUNDY, P.J. & LEDGER, J.A. (1976): Griffon Vultures, Carnivores and Bones. *South African Journal of Science* **72**: 106-110.

SNYDER, NOEL (1982): Oral presentation on the status and management of California Condor. California Condor Conference, Santa Barbara Museum of Natural History. Santa Barbara, California.

Biology and Conservation of Sea Turtles in the Indian Ocean

(With seven text-figures)

J. Frazier[1]

Introduction

The Indian Ocean, with its contiguous seas and gulfs, is mankind's oldest ocean; and has been intimately related with his history and development. Ancient civilizations arose along its shores and traded across its waters. Yet, this great ocean, one-seventh of the earth's surface (Figure 1), has been forgotten in the last Century, and despite man's long attendance, the Indian Ocean is one of the most poorly known of the great seas. This lack of knowledge extends throughout the general realm of marine biology, including marine turtles.

That some of the world's largest nesting populations have been found in the Indian Ocean in the last decade is evidence of our ignorance: *Chelonia mydas* nests in the thousands on Europa Island, Comores, Southern Yemen, Oman and Pakistan (Hughes 1971; Servan 1976; Frazier 1972, 1975a; FAO 1968, 1973; Ross *pers. comm.* 1979; Zaidi and Ghalib in Salm 1975a). *Eretmochelys imbricata* may have some of its most concentrated nesting areas in the world in the Suakin Archipelago and Persian Gulf (Moore and Balzarotti 1977; Walczak and Kinunen 1971). The largest known rookery of *Caretta caretta* is on Masirah Island (FAO 1973; Anon. 1978). Tens or hundreds of thousands of *Lepidochelys olivacea* evidently nest in Paikstan and east India (Singh *in lit.* 20 July 1976; Davis 1976; Davis and Bedi 1978).

[1] Department of Zoological Research, National Zoological Park, Smithsonian Institution, Washington, D.C. 20008, USA.

Despite this great lack of knowledge, two of the earliest studies of marine turtles, which still stand as invaluable benchmarks, were conducted in the Indian Ocean: Hornell (1927) in Seychelles and Deraniyagala (1939) in Sri Lanka. After the studies of Hornell and Deraniyagala, no *detailed* studies were made in the region until 1963 (McAllister *et al.* 1965) when research in Natal was begun; this continues (Hughes 1977a, 1982), and the programme expanded to encompass the southwest Indian Ocean (Hughes 1971, 1973a, 1973b, 1974a, 1974b, 1982).

Other short term projects, funded by FAO (1968, 1973) made valuable contributions in southern Arabia. Studies in Seychelles, BIOT, Comores and East Africa extended from 1968 to 1976 (Frazier 1971, 1972, 1975a, 1977, *in press;* Gibson 1979). During this time attempts were made to collate information on the western Indian Ocean Region and to stimulate preliminary studies, distributing questionaires and preliminary synopses to hundreds of addresses (Frazier 1974, 1975b). Subsequently, studies have been conducted in Sudan (Moore and Balzarotti 1977); Siani (Sella *in lit.* Jan. 1976, 1982); Yemen Arab Republic (Walczak 1975, 1979); and India (Bhaskar 1978a-f, 1979a-d; Kar and Bhaskar 1982), and a long-term study continues on Cousin Island, Seychelles (Diamond 1976; Garnett 1979; Frazier *in press*). A joint IUCN/Oman Government study has been initiated on Masirah Island and Oman (Annon. 1978; Ross and Barwani 1982), and preliminary marine park surveys were done in Sri Lanka, India and Pakistan (Salm 1975a, 1975b, 1976b).

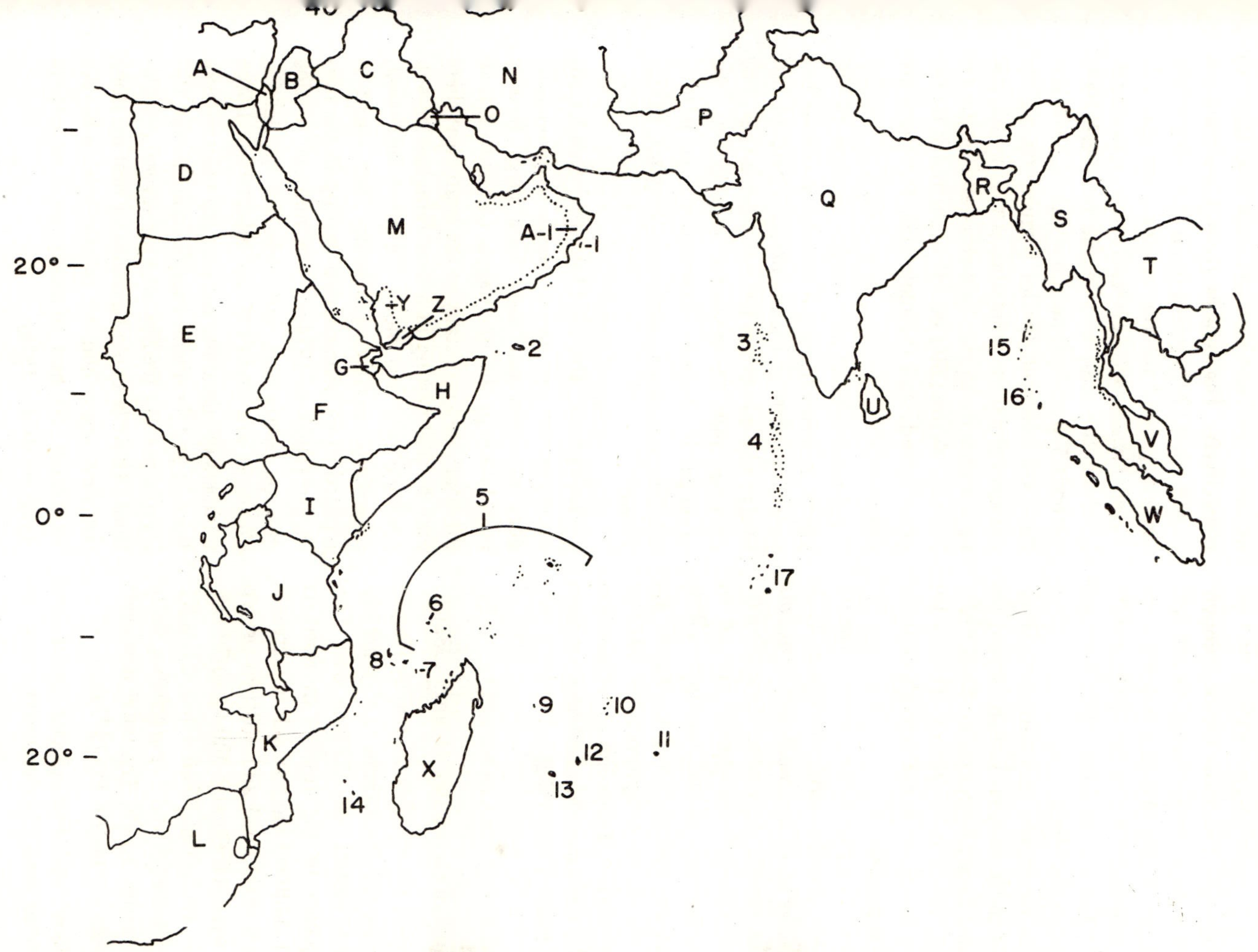

Figure 1

The Indian Ocean. Mainland Countries: A = Israel, B = Jordan, C = Iraq, D = Egypt, E = Sudan, F = Ethiopia, G = Djbouti, H = Somalia, I = Kenya, J = Tanzania, K = Mozambique, L = South Africa, M = Saudi Arabia, N = Iran, O = Kuwait, P = Pakistan, Q = India, R = Bangladesh, S = Burma, T = Thailand, V = Malaya, W = Indonesia, X = Madagascar, Y = Yemen Arab Republic, Z = People's Democratic Republic of Yemen, A-1 = Oman.

Islands: 1 = Masirah (Oman), 2 = Socotra (PDRY), 3 = Laccadives (India), 4 = Maldives, 5 = Seychelles, 6 = Aldabra (Seychelles), 7 = Mayotte (France), 8 = Comores, 9 = Tromelin (Reunion, France), 10 = St. Brandon (Mauritius), 11 = Rodriguez (Mauritius), 12 = Mauritius, 13 = Reunion (France), 14 = Europa (Reunion, France), 15 = Andamans, 16 = Nicobars, 17 = BIOT (Chagos).

Much remains to be surveyed, but of the 31 territories in the western Indian Ocean, 19 have had recent surveys. The most recent compendium of information on the Indian Ocean is in the proceedings of the World Conference on Sea Turtles, held in 1979 (Frazier 1982a, 1982b; Hughes 1982; Kar and Bhaskar 1982; Ross and Barwani 1982; Sella 1982).

The present paper will summarise the situation over the entire western Indian Ocean; the eastern Indian Ocean, from the east coast of India eastward, will not be treated. Details for each territory are given in the references at the end of each summary.

Five species of marine turtles occur in the Indian Ocean: *Dermochelys coriacea* (L.); *Chelonia mydas* (L.); *Eretmochelys imbricata* (L.); *Caretta caretta* (L.); and *Lepidochelys olivacea* (Eschscholtz). Subspecies for all of these turtles have been named, but there is little evidence that any subspecific populations are identifiable except on geographic grounds (see Fraizer *in press* a). A discussion of exploitation in each of the territories dicussed here has been presented (Frazier 1980, 1982).

Account by Countries

Southwest Indian Ocean (see Hughes 1982):

South Africa. Thoroughly studied by Hughes and colleagues, the programme is 15 years old. Concentrated nesting of *Caretta* and *Dermochelys* occurs in the reserve in northern Natal. Their numbers have evidently increased in response to continued and efficient protection. Now, over 400 *Caretta* and some 70 *Dermochelys* nest each year. *Chelonia,* and less frequently *Eretmochelys* and *Lepidochelys,* occur as vagrants farther south. The latter nests very rarely (Hughes 1974a, 1974b, 1977a).

Mozambique. All five species occur and breed. *Caretta* and *Dermochelys* nest on mainland beaches in the southern half; annual numbers are perhaps 300 and less than 50 respectively. Tag returns from Tongaland indicate that Mozambique is an important feeding ground for the nesting population in Natal. *Lepidochelys* evidently nests sporadically along the mainland in the northern half. Perhaps 500 to 1000 nest in a year. *Chelonia* is the most common species frequenting marine pastures along the mainland. An estimated 200 nest annually on the Primeiras and Segundas Islands. Nesting also occurs in the north on the other islands and the mainland, but there are few.

Eretmochelys is also more common in the north. It seems nesting is mainly on islands but may also occur on the mainland. There are not likely to be more than 100 nesting in a year. The *Caretta* and *Dermochelys* populations are doomed if intense exploitation on nesting females and nests continues (Hughes 1973a, 1976).

Madagascar. There are fair-sized populations of all turtles but *Dermochelys, Lepidochelys* does not nest but there is a large feeding population in the northwest. *Caretta* nests in the south and especially in the southeast; there may be 300 nesting in a year (Hughes 1974a). *Eretmochelys* nest along the north and west, apparently preferring islands, but there is reputed to be concentrated nesting in the northeast (Hughes 1974b). The number nesting may be substantial, but there are no details. *Chelonia* are common on all coasts. Large numbers of subadults and also tag returns from Europa and Tromelin Islands indicate that this is an important feeding area for several populations. There is a small amount of nesting along the west coast and on offshore islands. An estimated 300 nest annually on Chesterfield (Hughes 1974a, 1976).

Reunion. The main island has no significant turtle populations, although any but *Lepidochelys* might occur on occasion. The four tropical islands that are dependencies have important populations. Glorieuse has an estimated 250 *Chelonia* and 50 *Eretmochelys* nesting annually (Frazier 1975a). Tromelin has a large *Chelonia* rookery, estimated to have 2000 nesting yearly (Hughes 1976) although it was previously estimated to have only 200 to 400 (Hughes 1974a) see Hughes 1982 for other recent estimates. Europa's population is one of the largest in the western Indian Ocean region. It was first estimated to have 5000 to 9000 annual nesters (Hughes 1974a), but the estimate has since been reduced to 2000 (Servan 1976), and then increased substantially (see Hughes 1982). Iles Barren or Bassas da India, were estimated to have 200 nesting in a year (Hughes 1976).

Mauritius. Turtle populations at the large islands of Mauritius and Rodriguez are insignificant, but *Chelonia* and *Eretmochelys* may occur. Subadult *Caretta* evidently occur in transit during their pelagic phase, and *Dermochelys* are rare. The low-lying St Brandon Islands have a nesting population of *Chelonia,* from which about 300 are cropped annually (Hughes 1975). The total number nesting is evidently less than 1000; it may be only 300 (Hughes 1976). *Eretmochelys* probably nest in small numbers. *Eretmochelys* and *Chelonia* may nest in small numbers on Agalega Island.

Central and Western Indian Ocean: (see Frazier 1982a)

British Indian Ocean Territory (BIOT). This territory consists of the Chagos Archipelago, which was formerly a dependency of Mauritius. Before independence of Seychelles in 1976, BIOT, included also Aldabra, Farquhar and Desroches Atolls. The 65 islands in the Archipelago offer large areas of feeding and nesting habitat to both *Chelonia* and *Eretmochelys.* However, the only nesting known involves small numbers, although little of the Archipelago has been surveyed. Chagos is not known for turtles, although there is some indication that the islands may have once supplied large amounts of tortoise-shell to Mauritius, they seem to have been of little importance generally. Only 300 *Chelonia* are estimated to nest in a year, and the peak nesting season is during the southeast trades, from June to September. The maximum estimate for the number of *Eretmochelys* nesting annually is 300, and peak nesting is evidently during the northwest monsoon. Perhaps a few hundred of each species were captured annually. The lagoons may serve as important nursery grounds for *Chelonia* and there are many uninhabited islands and beaches (Frazier 1977).

Seychelles. This island republic covers hundreds of thousands of square km of the western Indian Ocean, including half a dozen major island groups and over 50 major islands. There are extensive reefs and many remote beaches. All but *Lepidochelys* have been documented. *Dermochelys* and *Caretta* are rarely reported. *Eretmochelys* feeds and nests throughout the territory, but seems most abundant in the Granitic Islands, and at some of the coraline islands with large lagoons (e.g. Cosmoledo and Providence). Nesting has been recorded in all months but June, and the peak is from October to January. The most concentrated nesting occurs on Cousin, where 30 to 40 nest a year. There are evidently less than 600 nesting annually in the whole territory. *Chelonia* also feeds and nests throughout the territory, but most nesting occurs in the Aldabra group of islands. Throughout the whole territory an estimated 2500 nest in a year. Nesting is year-round with a peak during the southeast trades, from about May to September. The Seychelles are world famous for both *Chelonia* and *Eretmochelys,* but *Chelonia* populations have declined after heavy exploitation and *Eretmochelys* are under heavy pressure (Frazier 1971, 1975a, 1979, *in press* a; Gibson 1979).

Mayotte. Geographically part of the Comoro Archipelago, but politically a department of France, the island offers rich reef and lagoon habitats. Only *Chelonia* and *Eretmochelys* are recorded, and numbers seem to be smaller than the habitat could support. Estimates were 500 *Chelonia* and 25 *Eretmochelys* nesting annually. The most important rookery for *Chelonia* is on Pamanzi Island in the northeast. Nesting is probably year-round, peaking about June-July. The island supplies small amounts of tortoise-shell and *Chelonia* meat, but has never been known as an important turtle area (Frazier 1972, 1975a, *in press* b).

Comores. Only *Chelonia* and *Eretmochelys* are recorded, although *Dermochelys* may also occur. The two larger islands of the Republic have few beaches and small neritic habitats. Neither Ngazidia (Grand Comore) nor Anjouan has nesting of significance; possibly a few dozen *Chelonia* nest on both islands. There may be small nursery areas, such as in the northwest of Ngazidia; and Anjouan may have rich reefs, but the areas are small and turtle populations probably number only a few hundred. Moheli, on the other hand, has many beaches and considerable shallow water with offshore islands and rich reefs. Of 89 beaches, 6 had large nesting populations of *Chelonia* and the total estimate for Moheli was 1850 nesting annually. The total estimate for the Republic was 1900. Possibly 50 *Eretmochelys* nest annually at Moheli.

The Comores are not noted for their turtles, and the presence of such a large nesting population of *Chelonia* was not expected. Dense human populations and lack of sufficient food leave the two larger islands of little value to turtles, but disturbance on Moheli seems low enough to be sustainable (Frazier 1972, 1975a, 1977, *in press* b).

Tanzania. Rich reefs and marine pastures are abundant, but much of the coast is unsuitable for nesting. Off-lying islands near Mafia and Zanzibar do offer excellent, but restricted, nesting habitat. All five turtles occur. *Dermochelys* and *Lepidochelys* are rarely reported, but may be more common than is often assumed. The latter nests, but in small numbers. *Caretta* are seen uncommonly, but females tagged in Natal have been recaptured as far north as Zanzibar, and southern Tanzania seems to be part of the feeding range for animals that nest in Natal. *Eretmochelys* nests throughout the Republic. On Maziwi, the best rookery, 20 might nest annually, and perhaps a total of 50 nest yearly in the entire country. There is nesting year-round but from February to March it peaks. *Chelonia* nests on Maziwi round the year, but mostly from June to October. Less than 200 nest annually. Shungu-Mbili Island also has considerable nesting, and there is some nesting on the mainland south of Dar es Salaam. Yet, the grand total nesting in a year is estimated at less than 300. Zanzibar was once a major clearing house in tortoise-shell importing and exporting from and to all parts of the world, however, Tanzania itself was not a major producer. Turtle populations are probably reduced from previous levels from persistent predation on reproducing animals and human habitations on nesting beaches (Frazier 1975b, 1975c).

Kenya. Much of the coast is unsuitable for nesting, but there are large marine pastures and some rich reef areas. All five turtles probably occur, but *Caretta* has not been documented. Only *Eretmochelys* and *Chelonia* are recorded nesting, although *Lepidochelys* probably also nests, but in smaller numbers. *Eretmochelys* and *Chelonia* nest along much of the coast, but most nesting is in the north, especially on islands. The most *Chelonia* nesting occurs on the mainland around Ras Tenewi, after August. However, nest predation here is great and recruitment is probably insignificant. Probably less than 50 *Eretmochelys* and less than 200 *Chelonia* nest in a year (Frazier 1975d).

Somalia. Thousands of kilometres of sandy beach and rich upwelling currents characterize this coast. All five species of turtle are known to Bajun fishermen in the south (Grotanelli 1955), but only *Chelonia* seems to be common. It occurs along the entire eastern coast (Ninni 1937). At least *Chelonia* nest (Cozzolino 1938) and there are accounts of large nesting grounds and rich turtle areas (Travis 1967; Travis *in* Goodwin 1971), but little is documented. There might be a few thousand nesting annually on several stretches of the eastern coast. Rich marine pastures support dugongs and also *Chelonia* (Travis 1967). South Arabian turtles evidently migrate to Somalia for feeding (FAO 1968, 1973). *Eretmochelys* are exploited, but the numbers taken indicate a small population (Frazier, this volume). This is to be expected, given the cold upwelling waters off the Somali coast. Evidently other species are uncommon or rare.

Gulf of Aden and Red Sea (see Frazier *in press* c; Frazier and Salas *in press*; Ross and Barwani 1982; Sella 1982).

Djbouti. Nothing seems to be recorded, but *Eretmochelys* and *Chelonia* are likely to occur, at least in small numbers.

Ethiopia (*Eretria*). Off the arid coastline is the Dhalak Archipelago, and this seems to be the only important turtle area. It provides rich reef areas and numerous beaches. Last century *Lepidochelys* and *Eretmochelys* were collected (Ruppel 1835; Steindachner 1900), and *Chelonia* and *Eretmochelys* were collected in this century (Hoofien and Yaron 1965). *Chelonia* has been reported nesting (Urban 1970; Minot *n.d.*), and *Eretmochelys* also suspected to nest. The numbers of the latter may be, or have been, substantial, but there are no records. The *Chelonia* population is probably small, but there may be large pastures along the mainland coast. The nesting population on the Dhalak Islands may have been heavily exploited (Minot *n.d.*).

Sudan. Numerous islands, including the Suakin Archipelago, lie off the arid coast. *Eretmochelys* is recorded from the north (Steindanchner 1900) and the Suakin Islands where they nest (Moore and Balzarotti 1977). *Chelonia* have been seen along the mainland coast and a specimen of *Lepidochelys* was seen in a market. *Chelonia* may nest in large numbers on the islands. Over 300 *Eretmochelys* are estimated to nest annually in just the Suakin Archipelago (Moore and Balzarotti 1977), but there are a great many more islands that may also have nesting. This represents the greatest known concentration of nesting *Eretmochelys*. Present-day exploitation is little, although it may have been intense in the past.

Egypt. Islands lie off the desert coast and from them *Chelonia* and *Eretmochelys* have been recorded (Steindachner 1900); *Eretmochelys* has also been recorded from the southern mainland (Marx 1968). Both these turtles are likely to breed, but little else is recorded.

Siani (see Sella, 1982). All five species are recorded; in order of increasing abundance: *Caretta, Lepidochelys, Dermochelys, Eretmochelys* and *Chelonia*. Only *Chelonia* is frequently seen, and only it is known to nest. An estimated 80 per year nest at Abu-Rodes, but there is some nesting also at Ras Muhammad and on Tiran and Sanafir Islands. Exploitation is mainly incidental or accidental, through underwater bombings or catches in nets (Sella *in lit.*, January 1976; 1 March 1976; 20 August 1976).

Israel. There are only about 12 km of coast, in the Gulf of Eilat, and although an active marine station is at the town of Eilat, there seems to be absolutely no . information available on marine turtles.

Jordan. There is only a short stretch of coast, about 12 km long in the Gulf of Eliat, and nothing seems to be recorded. Pollution by crude oil is evidently bad (Fitter *in lit.* 2 October 1975).

Saudi Arabia (Red Sea coast). A long coast with large numbers of islands, including the Farasan Archipelago, must harbour many nesting and feeding habitats for turtles. The only documented information seems to be a specimen of *Eretmochelys* taken in Jedda in the last century (Steindachner 1900). There are reports of commerical exploitation, probably of *Chelonia* (Walczak *in lit.* 1974).

Yemen Arab Republic. Despite a relatively short coastline, there are numerous offshore islands, and evidently rich areas of reef and marine pasture. *Eretmochelys* were collected in islands in the last century (Steindachner 1900), and it and three other species have been reported in a recent survey: *Dermochelys, Chelonia* and *Lepidochelys*. *Chelonia* is most common, but *Eretmochelys* are often encountered. Nesting occurs on coral islands, and possibly also on larger volcanic islands and the mainland. Probably both *Chelonia* and *Eretmochelys* nest, but neither has been confirmed. Human predation on eggs may be substantial in some areas (Walczak 1975, 1979).

People's Democratic Republic of Southern Yemen. Three species are recorded from both the mainland and Socotra Island: *Chelonia, Eretmochelys* and *Dermochelys*. The latter is rare. *Eretmochelys* nest on Perim and Jabal Aziz Islands. Over a ten-day period on Jabal Aziz, 46 turtles laid eggs, and it seems that the annual nesting population is in the hundreds. Far fewer nest at Perim. The major pastures for *Chelonia* are in the west of Khor Umaria. Nesting occurs all along the mainland, but especially in Quaiti State. At Sharma, the major beach, there are evidently several thousand nesting annually, with a similar quantity at Ithmurn beach. With year-round nesting there may be 10,000 Chelonia nesting in a year, mainly on these beaches in the east of the country. Females tagged on Sharma beach have turned up east of Aden and along the coast of Somalia from Hordio to Chismaio (Hinds 1964-5; FAO 1968, 1973; Hirth and Carr 1970).

Arabian Sea, Gulf of Oman and Persian Gulf (see Ross and Barwani 1982):

Oman. Masirah Island and Oman's mainland have been well studied since 1977. All five species are recorded from the Island, and all but *Dermochelys* nest. An estimated 30,000 *Caretta* and several hundred *Chelonia* nest annually on the Island. This is the largest known nesting population of *Caretta*. On the mainland, some thousands of *Chelonia* a year may nest, mainly at Ras Al Hadd. Perhaps 100 *Eretmochelys* and a similar number of *Lepidochelys* nest yearly on the island. Turtles are protected on nesting beaches and there is restricted fishing in nesting areas. The Government is committed to a management programme (FAO 1973; Anon. 1978; Ross *pers. comm. 1979)*.

United Arab Emirates. Little is documented.

Qatar. *Chelonia mydas* were said to have

nested on the mainland, but not to nest now. *Eretmochelys* nest on islands, and *Dermochelys* has been reported. *Caretta* and *Chelonia depressa* have also been reported, but these records are not confirmed (Hunnam *in* Ross and Barwani 1982).

Baharin. *Chelonia mydas* may feed around the island (Gallagher 1971).

Saudi Arabia. *Chelonia mydas* and *Eretmochelys* are reputed to nest especially on Karan Island, but also on Jana, Kurayn and Jurayd Islands, *Dermochelys* are uncommon (Basson *et al.* 1977).

Kuwait. *Chelonia mydas* occur (Ross and Barwani 1982).

Iraq. *Dermochelys* and *Eretmochelys* are listed (Khalaf 1959; Mahdi and Georg 1969).

Iran. The long, arid remote coast line has hardly been surveyed, but some islands in the Persian Gulf have been studied (Bullock and Kinunen 1971; Kinunen and Walczak 1970, 1971; Walczak and Kinunen 1971). Four species are recorded: *Dermochelys, Lepidochelys, Chelonia* and *Eretmochelys;* the last two are common around islands, where there are marine pastures. There are fair numbers of turtles off the rocky eastern coast (Nehring *in lit.* 25 Feb. 1975). A small fishery for *Dermochelys* on Larak Island may take 10 to 15 a year, and render them to oil for boat maintenance. *Lepidochelys* were seen at Lavan Island.

Turtles (*Eretmochelys* ?) nest on Larak and Lavan Islands in April and June (Bullock, Kinunen, Walczak *op. cit.*); and *Eretmochelys* nests in April and June at Nakhilu (Anderson *in lit.*, 13 April 1977), Hormus and Qeshm Islands, but the most nesting by this species is on Shitvar Island where there may be 100 a year. Nesting on the mainland is uncommon; it has been seen in October, in the east near the border with Pakistan, and in April inside the mouth of the Persian Gulf. These may have been *Chelonia,* but there may be only a few hundred nesting annually (Bullock, Kinunen, Walczak *op. cit.*).

Indian Subcontinent: (see Kar and Bhaskar, 1982)

Pakistan. The coast is highly variable, with cliffs over 100 m high in the west to the vast low-lying mangrove forests in the south at the mouth of the Indus. All five turtles are listed (Minton 1962; Mohiuddin 1975; Salm 1975a, 1975b), but there is some question as to whether *Eretmochelys* or *Caretta* occur (Mertens 1969). *Dermochelys* is rare (Minton 1966; Mertens 1969). *Chelonia* nests at Hawks Bay, evidently in the thousands, and also at Sandspit, Buleji and Paradise Point (Sind) and Ormara, Somniani and Ras Jiunri (Baluchistan). Nesting is year-round with a peak from about August to October. *Lepidochelys* also nests at Hawks Bay and Sandspit during the same season, but in fewer numbers (Murray 1884; Burton 1918; Shockley 1949; Hatt 1957; Minton 1966; Mertens 1969; Minton and Minton 1973; Mohiuddin 1975; Salm 1975a, 1975b, 1976a, 1976b). A large scale exporting business, dealing in turtle skins from Baluchistan, slaughters thousands of nesting animals; these have been reported to be *Chelonia,* but may in fact be *Lepidochelys;* details are not available (Salm 1975a, 1975b, 1976a, 1976b; Telford *in lit.,* to H. Campbell 1976).

India (See Kar and Bhaskar 1982). The western and southern coasts, while providing thousands of kilometres of sandy beach, are densely inhabited in general. All five species occur, possibly all nest. Nesting is evidently dispersed along most of the western coast but may be concentrated on uninhabited islands in the Gulf of Mannar.

The four chelonids are listed from the Gulf of Mannar (Gravely 1929; Kuriyan 1950). *Dermochelys* reputedly nested in small numbers in southern Kerala at the end of the last century, and was occasionally caught in the earlier part of this century (Cameron 1923). There may also have been sporadic nesting farther north, e.g. at Goa (Deraniyagala 1939; Salm 1976a). It is occasionally seen in the Gulf of Kutch (Bhaskar 1978d, 1978e). *Eretmochelys* may occur, or nest, on islands in the Gulf of Kutch (Abdulali 1963). It is reputed to nest also along the Gulf of Mannar, especially on offshore islands (Mudaliar *in* Salm 1975a). *Chelonia* occurs in numbers in the gulf of Mannar where it grazes marine pastures, and there is a fishery (Sundara Raj 1930) but nesting is rarely recorded. There is one published record from the Bombay area (Mawson 1921), and evidently there was frequent nesting in this area in the 1930's (Abdulali *in lit.*, 6 Sept. 1976). They may still nest in small numbers from February to April (Salm 1976a). They nest on islands in the Gulf of Kutch and may nest sporadically along the west coast (Bhaskar 1978d, 1978e). *Lepidochelys* evidently nests along much of the coast; it is recorded from the Gulf of Kutch (Bhaskar 1978d, 1978e), Bombay area (Greaves 1935), near Goa (Salm 1976a), as well as Krusadai Island in the Gulf of Mannar (Chacko 1942; Luther 1959). It evidently nests along much of peninsular India, both east and west (Whitaker 1977), but nowhere in the concentrated numbers recorded in Orissa (cf. Bustard *in lit.*, 7 July 1976; Singh, *in lit.*, 20 July 1976; Davis 1977).

Turtles are common in the Lakshadweep (Laccadives) where four species nest: *Chelonia, Eretmochelys, Lepidochelys* commonly and *Dermochelys* rarely (Alcock 1902; Hornell 1908; Ayyangar 1922; Deraniyagala 1939; Bhaskar 1978a, 1978b, 1978c, 1978f). The same species are also recorded from the Andamans and Nicobars (Bhaskar 1979a, 1979c, 1979d). (Andamans and east coast of India are in the eastern Indian Ocean and are mentioned here only to complete the national picture.)

Maldives. This nation of hundreds of atolls and thousands of islands offers large areas of habitat to nesting and feeding turtles. *Eretmochelys* were said to be plentiful at the turn of the century (Boulenger 1890; Laidlaw 1902) and tortoise-shell has been an important export item for centuries. *Chelonia* is also common and both these turtles nest, evidently in fair numbers. *Dermochelys* has been recorded but it is rare (Gardiner 1906). *Caretta* was suspected to nest, but this was on the basis of egg sizes in a nest (Deraniyagala 1956) and may be invalid. *Lepidochelys* seems to be common although it may not nest (Frazier and Didi *in prep.*). Maldives are probably one of the most important areas for *Eretmochelys* in the region, and the population probably once numbered tens or hundreds of thousands. *Chelonia* were evidently less numerous and other species, uncommon. Heavy exploitation is probably reducing feeding and nesting populations considerably, but no figures are available.

Sri Lanka (see Bhaskar 1982). Marine turtles were extensively studied by Deraniyagala (1939). All five species have been collected. *Dermochelys* nests especially from May to June and notably in the southeast, on the Yala coast; probably less than 100 nest annually. *Lepidochelys* is the most abundant species, evidently nesting throughout much of the year and around most of the island, although it is concentrated from September to January in the Southwest. Several thousands may nest yearly. *Chelonia,* reported by Deraniyagala, nests infrequently and is recorded from July and November, from the south and from the northwest. However, Salm (1975a) reported year-round nesting. They are frequently caught in the Gulf of Mannar, and were once common all round the island (Kelaart 1852), particularly Trincomalie Harbour. *Caretta* may nest around the Gulf of Mannar from June to August. In the 1930's, it was 1/20th as common as *Lepidochelys*. *Eretmochelys* may have two distinct nesting seasons: from November, or December to February and from April to June; these correspond to two general localities: the north and southwest (Deraniyagala 1939). It was once "abundant", particularly in the south (Kelaart 1852), or "plentiful" (Boulenger 1980) —but no longer.

Summary and Conclusions

Distributions of nesting areas are shown in Figures 2, 3, 4, 5, and 6, and a tabular summary is given in the Table. It must be emphasized that many of these estimates are preliminary and should be taken as indications only.

Dermochelys has the fewest rookeries and the smallest nesting population, with a total of less than 300 breeding in only four countries. *Caretta* also has very few rookeries, nesting in four or five countries, but the Masirah population, with some 30,000 nesting yearly, gives a total estimate of over 40,000 turtles nesting in a year. *Lepidochelys* may have many rookeries, involving at least eight countries; however, none of these appears to be large and the total number nesting may be little more than 4000. Of course, the rookery in Orissa, eastern India, would swell this figure by hundreds of thousands. *Eretmochelys* has scores of nesting beaches and is known to nest in most countries. Yet none of these rookeries are large and the total number nesting annually in the entire region may be in the order of 4000. *Chelonia* is by far the most common turtle in the western Indian Ocean, with rookeries in nearly every country, and 10 rookeries each with more than 1000 nesting annually. The total number estimated to nest yearly in the region is nearly 40,000.

The status of the five different species in the western Indian Ocean is related to the sizes of their nesting populations. *Dermochelys* is in a precarious state, with less than 300 annual nesters and only two rookeries in reserves, i.e., Tongaland, Natal and Yala, Sri Lanka. This is ample reason to establish nesting reserves wherever *Dermochelys* nests regularly, i.e. southern Mozambique and perhaps also the Laccadives. In populated areas where nesting is irregular, e.g. west and south coasts of India, the situation is more urgent, for these populations are smallest and under heavy pressure.

Caretta is numerically superior, and this is due especially to one rookery, Masirah. Yet, only two rookeries are in protected or managed areas: Tongaland and Masirah. The nesting turtles in Mozambique and Madagascar, while protected by law, are under heavy pressure. It is essential that the protected areas be maintained, for the future of the other populations is bleak.

Lepidochelys, with rookeries spread over the region, is generally more common than *Caretta*. However, the only major rookeries are likely to be in Pakistan and Sri Lanka, not including the east coast of India or other rookeries in the Bay of Bengal and eastern Indian Ocean. Nesting elsewhere is at a low level, and very few turtles seem to nest within protected areas, other than in Sind, Pakistan, and perhaps Sri Lanka. Protection for the major nesting populations in Baluchistan, Pakistan and Sri Lanka, as well as the smaller populations elsewhere, is needed—in the case of Baluchistan, it is needed urgently.

TABLE

ESTIMATED NUMBER OF TURTLES NESTING ANNUALLY FOR DIFFERNT SPECIES IN DIFFERENT COUNTRIES. ? INDICATES THAT THE NUMBER GIVEN IS AN "EDUCATED GUESS." IN FACT, MOST OF THE NUMBERS IN THIS ARE PRELIMINARY ESTIMATES AND SHOULD BE TREATED AS SUCH. (EASTERN INDIA AND THE ANDAMANS ARE NOT INCLUDED).

Country	*Dermochelys*	*Chelonia*	*Eretmochelys*	*Caretta*	*Lepidochelys*
South Africa	70	0	0	400	0
Mozambique	50	300	100	300	?1,000
Madagascar	0	400	?300	300	?0
Reunion	0	5,200	50	0	0
Mauritius	0	300	25	0	0
BIOT	0	300	300	0	0
Seychelles	0	2,500	600	0	0
Mayotte	0	500	25	0	0
Comores	0	1,900	50	0	0
Tanzania	0	300	50	0	25
Kenya	0	200	50	0	25
Somalia	0	?2,000	?	0	0
Ethiopia	0	?100	?100	0	0
Sudan	0	?100	?500	0	0
Egypt	0	?50	?25	0	0
Sinai	0	100	0	0	0
Israel	0	0	0	0	0
Jordan	0	0	0	0	0
Saudi Arabia	0	?100	?500	0	0
Yemen A. Rep.	0	?100	?50	0	0
P. Dem. Rep. Yemen	0	?10,000	?300	0	0
Oman	0	7,000	100	30,000	150
UAE	0	?	?	?	?
Qatar	0	?	100	0	0
Bahrain	0	?	?	?	?
Saudi Arabia	0	500	100	0	0
Kuwait	0	?	?	?	?
Iran	0	200	200	0	?0
Pakistan	0	5,000	0	0	1,000
India	25	200	150	0	500
Maldives	0	?2,000	500	0	?
Sri Lanka	100	100	50	?	2,000
TOTAL	245	39,450	4,225	40,000	4,700

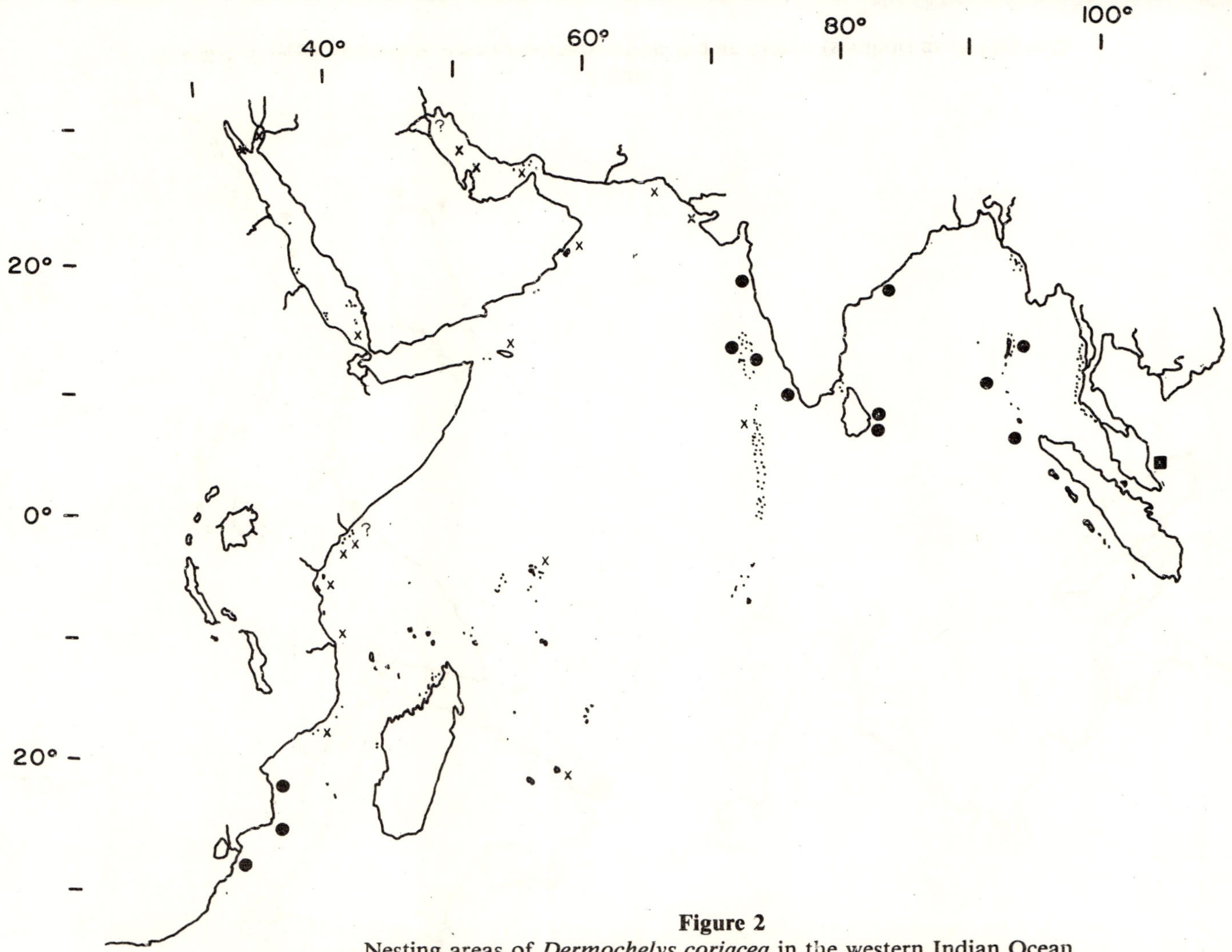

Figure 2

Nesting areas of *Dermochelys coriacea* in the western Indian Ocean.

Symbols: ? = Questionable record, or suspected to occur; × = Occurs; ⋇ = Occurs in large numbers; ○ = Suspected to nest; ● = Less than 100 nest annually; ▲ = 100 to 1,000 estimated to nest annually; ■ = 1,000 to 10,000 estimated to nest annually; ★ = Over 10,000 estimated to nest annually.

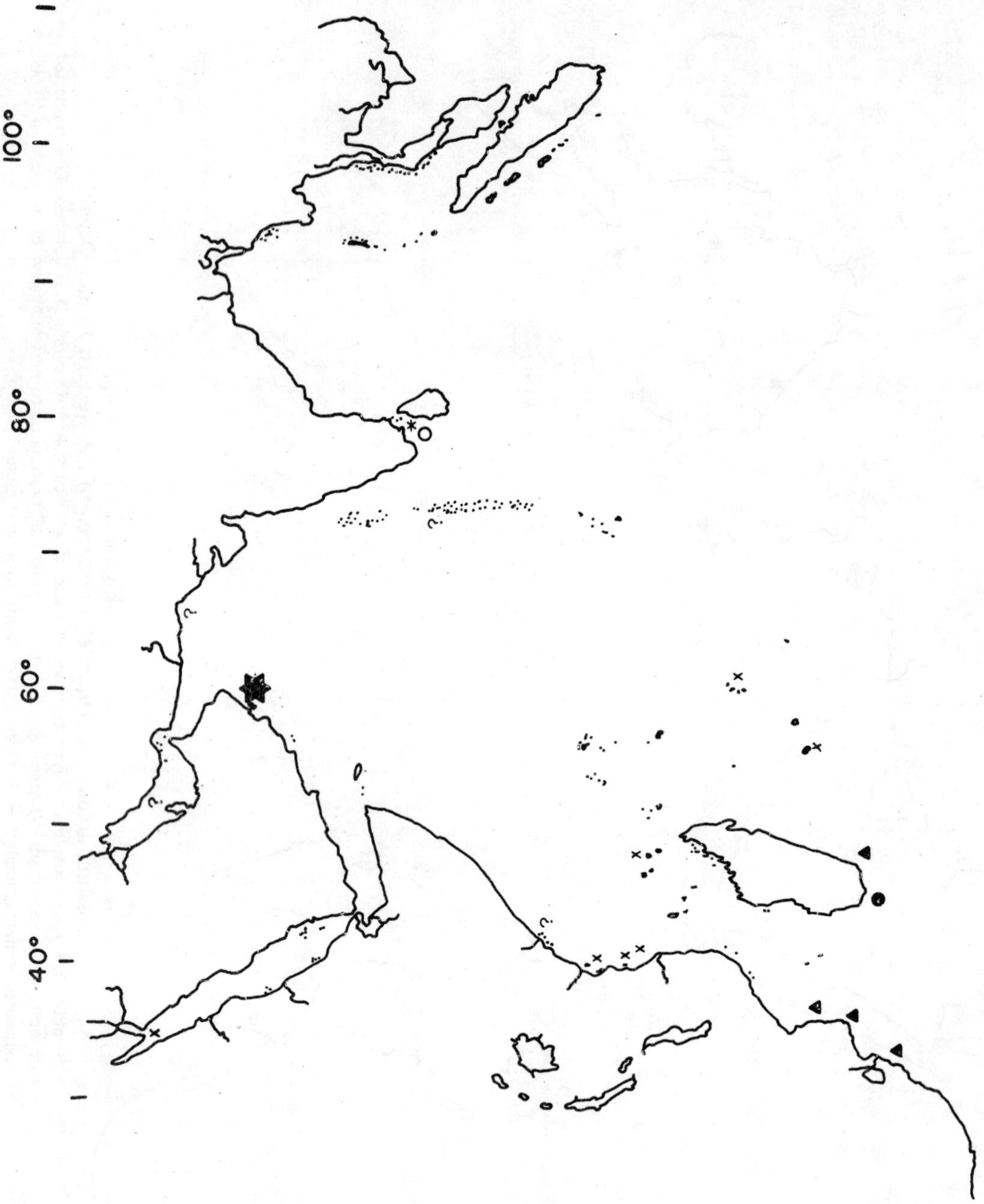

Figure 3
Nesting areas of *Caretta caretta* in the western Indian Ocean (symbols as in Figure 2).

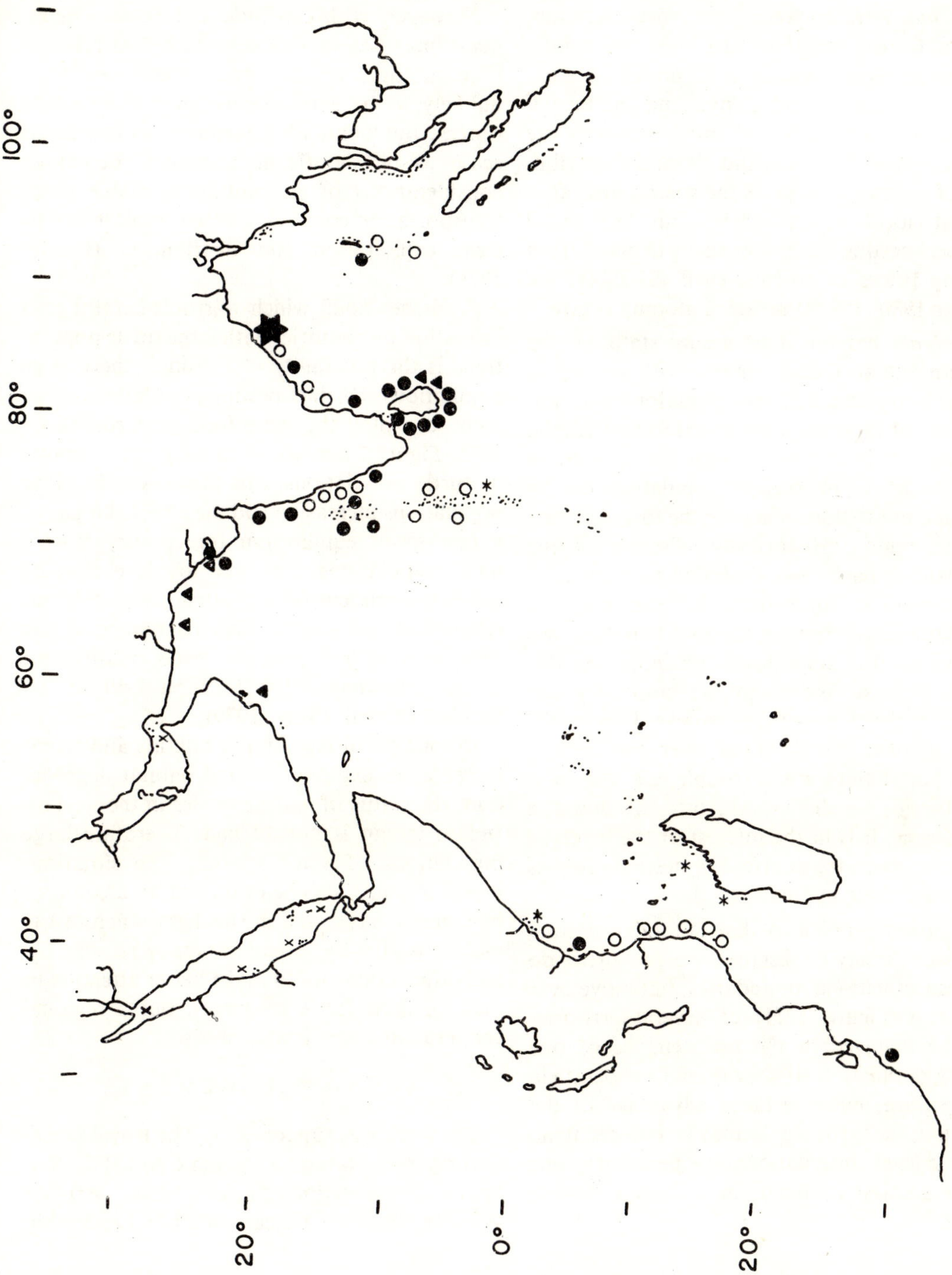

Figure 4
Nesting areas of *Lepidochelys olivacea* in the western Indian Ocean (symbols as in Figure 2).

Eretmochelys rookeries are very common, although the turtles are not especially numerous. Some nesting is in protected areas (e.g. in Tanzania and Kenya and on several islands in Seychelles), but most rookeries are not protected. The wide and abundant distribution of nesting areas gives the species insurance against local catastrophies, but the small numbers nesting under increasing demand from soaring prices of tortoise-shell ($100/kg, see Frazier 1980, 1982b) makes a gloomy future.

Chelonia has the most secure status in the western Indian Ocean region, with nesting in almost every country, several major rookeries, and tens of thousands estimated to nest yearly. However, it is imperative with this species, as with the others, to consider populations one by one, and not to think solely of the total estimate for the region. Historically, discrete nesting populations have been exploited by individual countries. The Seychellois, for example, can take little consolation in the fact that there are major rookeries in Pakistan and Oman, for this makes little difference in the crop they can realize or the status of their stocks. Despite the large number of *Chelonia* over the region, many populations are in trouble, e.g. Assumption Island; Seychelles; Mayotte; St Brandon and Kenya. It is in the interest of the involved countries to establish effective nesting reserves to protect these populations.

A further problem is that, although nesting populations may be discrete, marine turtles do not respect national boundaries, but move over vast areas (Figure 7). Hence, several territories may be involved in the maintenance of one nesting population. If they do not cooperate in this venture, but one takes advantage of the situation, the turtle stocks may be reduced to an inviable level. International cooperation is one of the greatest problems in managing marine turtles.

However, with *Chelonia* and *Eretmochelys,* questions of extinction seem to be less relevant than questions of economics. These species are unlikely to be exterminated over their whole ranges, but populations reduced to low levels cease to be significant resources. Economic considerations of the minimum viable crop, transportation costs, etc., often result in inefficient exploitation and distribution (Frazier 1979).

A further point which warrants careful consideration by countries with large turtle populations is the possibility of "losing" these large populations. Distinct nesting populations often seem to exploit the same food resources (Carr 1975; Figure 7 herein). If country "A" reduces its turtle populations, this may result in other populations increasing and the establishment of a new lower equilibrium for country "A"'s turtle populations. This new low level may be quite independent of any attempts by "A" to rehabilitate its stocks. This phenomenon has been seen with population levels of different species of whales that feed on krill in the Southern Ocean (May, 1979).

Despite centuries of turtle hunting and recent increases in exploitation and habitat degradation, the status of marine turtles in the western Indian Ocean is not all bad. There are large populations of some species. The situation, however, must also be examined on a country-by-country basis, and in this light much of the picture is gloomy. There are many reasons for individual countries to make better attempts to manage their turtle resources, but a regional cooperative effort is also needed.

ACKNOWLEDGEMENTS

The work was supported by The Royal Society (London); Natural Research Council (U.K.); Fauna Preservation Society; East African Wildlife Society; African Wildlife Leadership

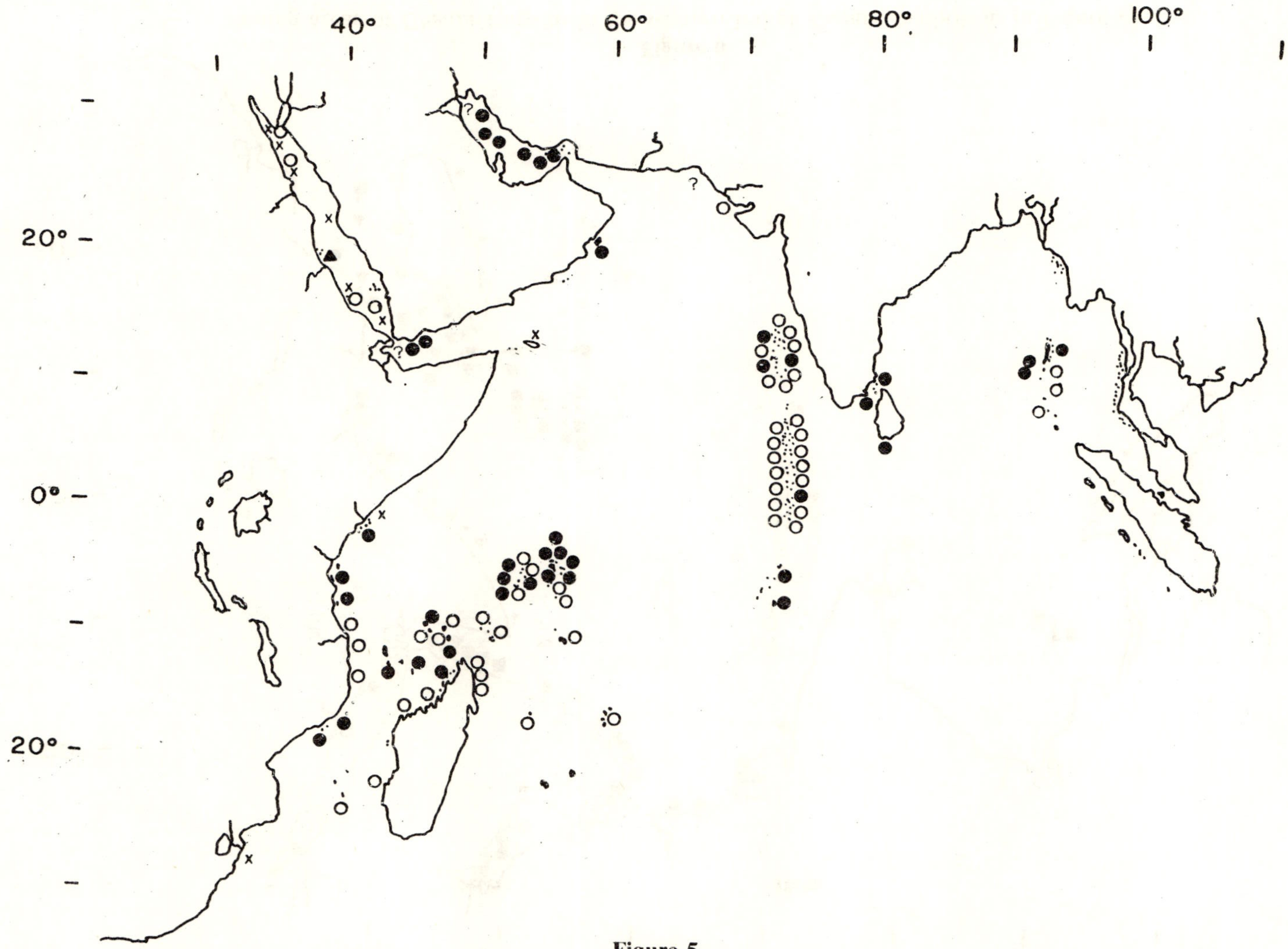

Figure 5
Nesting areas of *Eretmochelys imbricata* in the western Indian Ocean (symbols as in Figure 2).

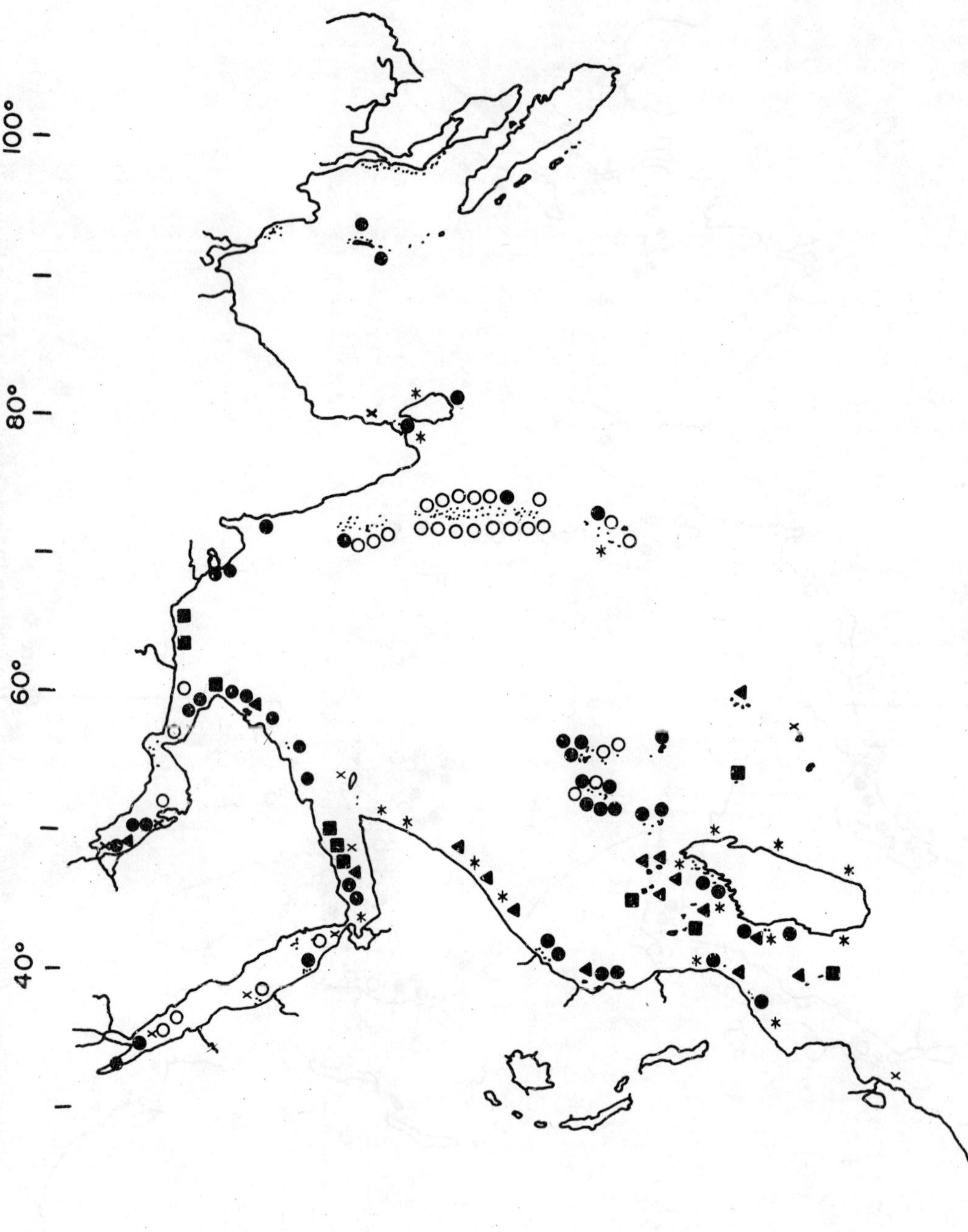

Figure 6
Nesting areas of *Chelonia mydas* in the western Indian Ocean (symbols as in Figure 2).

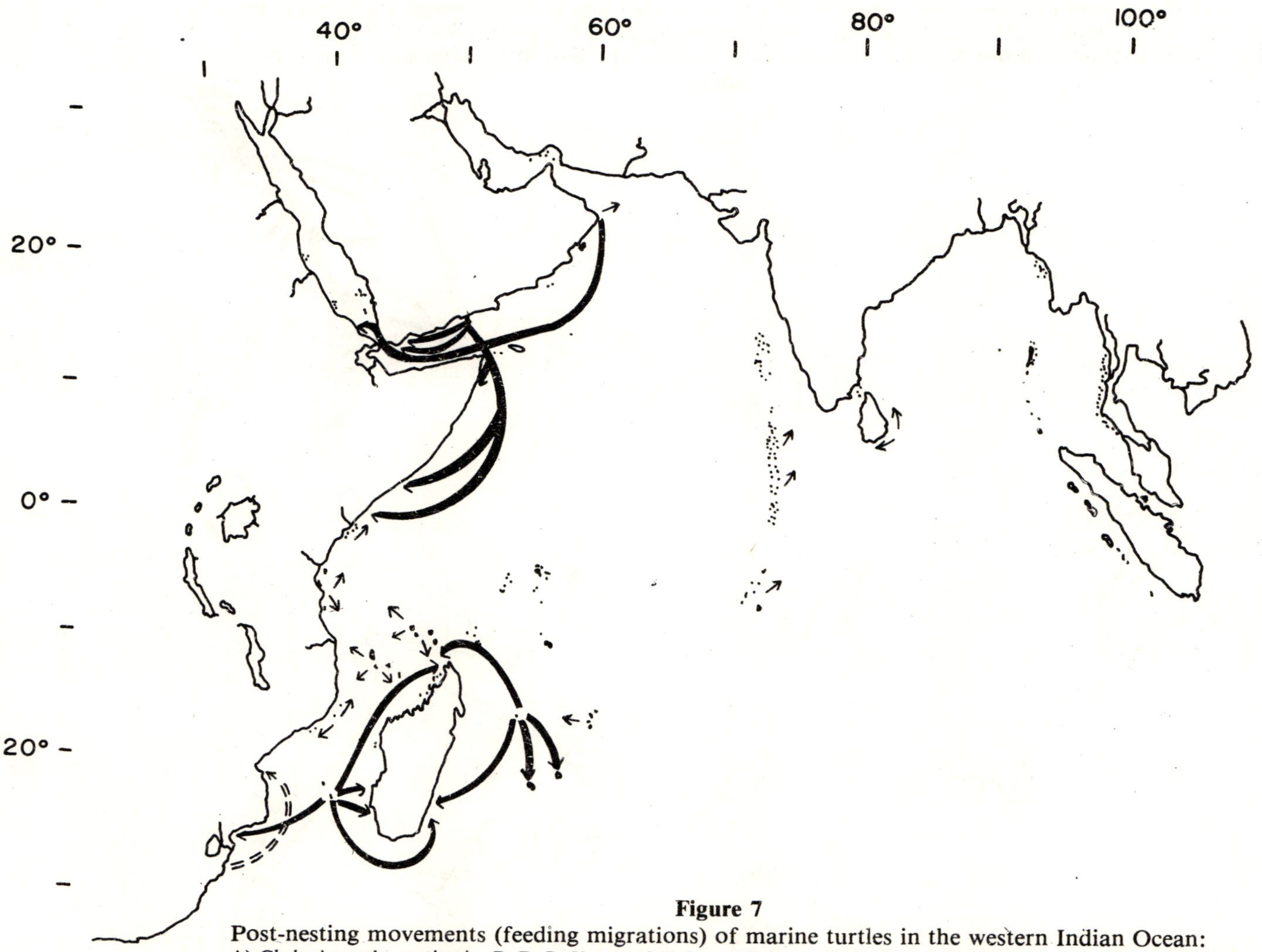

Figure 7

Post-nesting movements (feeding migrations) of marine turtles in the western Indian Ocean: A) *Chelonia mydas* nesting in: P. D. R. Yemen (data from Hirth and Carr, 1970; FAO, 1973); Tromelin Island and Europa Island (data from Hughes, 1974b, 1977b) and Ras Al Hadd, Oman (data from Ross and Barwani, 1982); and *Dermochelys coriacea* nesting in Natal (dashed line) (data from Hughes 1974b).

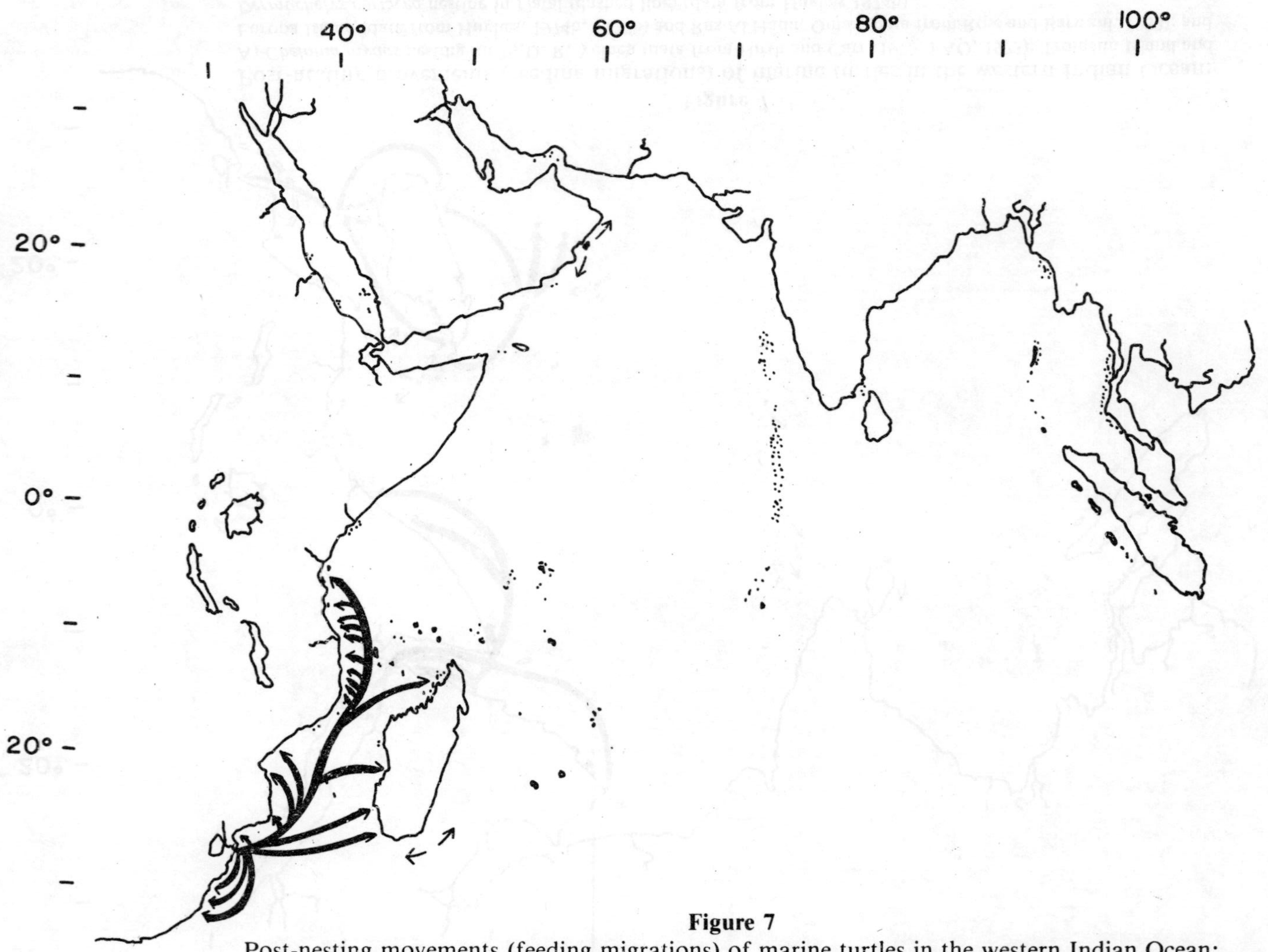

Figure 7

Post-nesting movements (feeding migrations) of marine turtles in the western Indian Ocean:
B) *Caretta caretta* nesting in Natal (data from Hughes 1974b, 1975b, 1977a, 1977b, 1982).

Short arrows show possible dispersions from other major nesting areas of these species. Arrows show only locations of tagging and releasing and locations of recapture—not routes taken by dispersing turtles.

Foundation; Department of Agriculture, Government of Seychelles; Government of BIOT; Game and Fisheries Departments of the Governments of Kenya and Tanzania; the Department of Zoological Research, National Zoological Park and the Division of Reptiles and Amphibians, Smithsonian Institution; and a grant from the Smithsonian Scholarly Studies Programme to Dr J.F. Eisenberg. Many colleagues in many countries provided information. The expert assistance of Mrs Wy Holden and Ms Virginia Garber in typing and Ms Sigrid James in illustrating was invaluable.

LITERATURE CITED

ABDULALI, H. (1963): Ornithological notes of a second trip to the Gulf of Kutch. *J. Bombay nat. Hist. Soc.* **60**(3): 703-708.

ALCOCK, A. (1902): A NATURALIST IN INDIAN SEAS. E.P. Dutton & Co., New York. 328 pp.

ANON. (1978): Oman goes for good management. *IUCN Bulletin*, New Series 9(1/2): 11.

AYYANGAR, S.R. (1922): Notes on the fauna and fishing industries of the Laccadive Islands. *Madras Fisheries Bulletin* **15**(2): 45-69.

BASSON, P.W., BURCHARD, J.E., HARDY, J.T. & PRICE, A.R.G. (1977): Biotopes of the Western Arabian Gulf. Arabian American Oil Co. Dahran, Saudi Arabia, 284 p. (Cited by Ross and Barwani, this volume).

BHASKAR, S. (1978a): Marine Turtles in India's Lakshadweep Islands. *Marine Turtle Newsletter*. Mimeogrphed. (Madras Snake Park).

_________ (1978b): Sea Turtles and other Marine Life in Lakshadweep. *Hornbill* (April-June): 21-26.

_________ (1978c *in press*?): Sea Turtles in the Arabian Sea Islands of Lakshadweep. *Tigerpaper*. (F.A.O., Bankok).

_________ (1978d): Preliminary Report on Sea Turtles in the Gulf of Kutch. *Marine Turtle Newsetter*. Mimeographed (Madras Snake Park).

_________ (1978e): Notes from the Gulf of Kutch. *Hamadryad* 3(3): 9-11.

_________ (1978f): Sea Turtles in the Lakshadweep Islands (India). *Marine Turtle Newsletter*. Mimeographed (Madras Snake Park), pp. 85-115.

_________ (1979a): Sea Turtles in the South Andaman Islands. *Hamadryad* **4**(1): 3-5.

BHASKAR, S. (1979b): Notes from Lakshadweep (Laccadive Islands). Ibid. **4**(1): 7-8.

_________ (1979c): Sea Turtle Survey in the Andaman and Nocobars. Ibid. **4**(3): 2-23, 1 fig., 2 maps.

_________ (1979d): Report on Sea Turtles and other miscellaneous notes from the Andaman and Nicobar Islands. Typescript. (Madras Snake Park), 61 pp + Appendix.

BOULENGER, G.A. (1890): REPTILIA AND BATRACHIA (The Fauna of British India, including Ceylon and Burma). Taylor and Francis, London. 541 pp.

BULLOCK, S. & KINUNEN, W. (1971): Lavan Island Aquatic Survey. Mimeographed (Division of Research and Development, Iran Game and fish Department). 9 pp + 2 maps.

BURTON, R.W. (1918): Habits of the green turtle (*Chelone mydas*). *J. Bombay nat. Hist. Soc.* **25**(3): 508.

CAMERON, T.H. (1923): Notes on turtles. Ibid. **29**(1-2): 299-300.

CARR, A. (1975): The Ascension Island green turtle colony. *Copeia* 1975(3): 547-555.

CHACKO, P.I. (1942): A note on the nesting habits of the olive loggerhead turtle, *Lepidochelys olivacea* (Eschscholtz) at Krusadai Island. *Current Science* **12**(2): 60-61.

COZZOLINO, A. (1938): Osservazioni Etologiche Sulla *Chelone mydas* Delle Coste Della Somalia Italiana. *Revista di Biologia Coloniale* **1**(4): 241-248.

DAVIS, T.A. (1977): Tragedy strikes sea turtles. *Hindustan Times*, Magazine Section, 24 April 1977 (New Delhi, India).

_________ & BEDI, R. (1978): *Hamadryad* (Newsletter of the Madras Snake Park Trust) 3, No. 3, September 1978, p.8. (Reprinted in Mrosovsky, N. (ed.), Marine Turtle Newsletter (1979) No. 12, IUCN/SSC).

DERANIYAGALA, P.E.P. (1939): TETRAPOD REPTILES OF CEYLON. Dulau & Co., Ltd., London, xxxii + 412 pp + 24 pls.

_________ (1956): Zoological collecting at the Maldives in 1932. *Spolia Zeylan* **28**(1): 7-15.

DIAMOND, A.W. (1976): Breeding biology and conservation of hawksbill turtles, *Eretmochelys imbricata* L., on Cousin Island, Seychelles. *Biological Conservation* **9**(3): 199-215.

FAO (1968): Report to the Governments of the People's Republic of Southern Yemen, and the Seychelles Islands on the green turtle resource of South Arabia, and the status of the green turtle in the Seychelles Islands. Based on the work of Dr. H. Hirth, FAO/TA Marine Turtle Biologist. *Rep. FAO/UNDP(TA)*, (2467): 59 pp.

FAO (1973): Report to the Government of the People's Democratic Republic of Yemen on Marine turtle management, based on the work of H.F. Hirth and S.L. Hollingworth, Marine Turtle Biologists. *Rep. FAO/UNDP(TA)*, (3178): 51 pp.

FRAZIER, J. (1971): Observations on sea turtles at Aldabra Atoll. *Philosophical Transactions of the Royal Society London*, B., **260**: 373-410.

_________ (1972): Marine turtles in the Archipel des Comores. Typescript (Fauna Preservation Society). 7 + 12 + 2 + 3 pp + 2 figs. + 2 tables.

_________ (1974): The status of knowledge on marine turtles in the Western Indian Ocean. Mimeographed (East African Wildlife Society, Nairobi), 12 pp.

_________ (1975a): Marine turtles of the Western Indian Ocean. *Oryx* **13**(2): 164-175.

_________ (1975b): The status of knowledge on marine turtles in the western Indian Ocean (revised). Mimeographed (East African Wildlife Society, Nairobi), 16 pp.

_________ (1975c): Maziwi Island—Interim Report, June 1975. Mimeographed (East African Wildlife Society), 2 pp.

_________ (1975d): Marine turtle survey. Mimeographed (East African Wildlife Society), 2 pp.

_________ (1977): Marine turtles in the western Indian Ocean: British Indian Ocean Territory, Comores. Typescript (Fauna Preservation Society, London). ii-33, vi-114.

_________ (1979): Marine turtle management in Seychelles: A Case-Study. *Environmental Conservation* **6**(3): 225-230.

_________ (*in press a*): Marine turtles in the Seychelles and adjacent territories. *In*: Stoddart, D.R. (ed.), 'The Biogeography and Ecology of the Seychelles Islands'. Junk, The Hague.

_________ & DIDI, N.T.H. (*in prep.*): Marine turtles of the Republic of Maldives, with a new locality record for *Lepidochelys olivacea.*

GALLAGHER, M.D. (1971): The Amphibians and Reptiles of Bahrain. Private printing, Bahrain. 40 pp. (Cited by Ross and Barwani, this volume.)

GARDINER, J.S. (1906): THE FAUNA AND GEOGRAPHY OF THE MALDIVE AND LACCADIVE ARCHIPELAGO, 2 Vols. Cambridge University Press.

GARNETT, M.C. (1979): The breeding biology of hawksbill turtles (*Eretmochelys imbricata*) on Cousin Island, Seychelles. Typescript (International council for Bird Preservation, London). 17 pp + 32 tables.

GIBSON, T.S.H. (1979): Green turtle (*Chelonia mydas* (L.)) nesting activity at Aldabra Atoll. *Philosophical Transactions of the Royal Society, London, B.*, 286: 255-263.

GOODWIN, M.M. (1971): Some aspects and problems of the use and exploitation of marine turtles. In: *Marine Turtles, IUCN Publ.* New Series, Supplementary Paper No. 31: 98-101.

GRAVELY, F.H. (1929): Administration Report, 1927-28. *Madras Fisheries Bulletin* **23**(1): 1-86.

GREAVES, J.B. (1935): Note on the Loggerhead turtle (*Caretta c. olivacea* (Eschscholtz)) depositing its eggs. *J. Bombay nat. Hist. Soc.* **(37)**(1-2): 494-495.

GROTTANELLI, V.L. (1955): PESCATORI DELL'OCEANO INDIANO. Cremonese, Rome. 409 pp.

HATT, R.T. (1957): Turtling at Hawks Bay, a beach on the Arabian Sea. *Newsletter Cranbrook Institute of Science* **26**(5): 53-58.

HINDS, V.T. (1964-5): The green turtle in South Arabia. *Port Aden Annual*: 54-57.

HIRTH, H. & CARR, A. (1970): The green turtle in the Gulf of Aden and the Seychelles Islands. *Verhandelingen der Koninklijke Nederlandse Akademie van Wetenschappen, Afd. Natuurkunde, Tweede Reeks* **58**(5): 1-44, vii pls.

HOOFIEN, J.H. & YARSON, Z. (1965): A collection of reptiles from the Dahlak Archipelago (Red Sea). *Bulletin Sea Fisheries Research Station, Haifa* **35**: 35-40.

HORNELL, J. (1908): Report on the results of a cruse along the Malabar coast and to the Laccadive islands in 1908. *Bulletin Madras Fisheries Bureau* **4**(iv): 71-126.

_________ (1927): THE TURTLE FISHERIES OF THE SEYCHELLES ISLANDS. HMSO, London. 55 pp.

HUGHES, G.R. (1971): Sea turtle research conservaton in South East Africa. A Status Report. Mimeographed (Oceanographic Research Institute, Durban). 11 pp.

_________ (1973a): The sea turtles of Mozambique. Mimeographed (Oceanographic Research Institute, Durban). 1-17 Fig + map.

_________ (1973b): The survival situation of the hawksbill sea-turtle (*Eretmochelys imbricata*) in Madagascar. *Biological Conservation* **5**(2): 114-118.

_________ (1974a): The sea turtles of South-East Africa. I. Status, morphology and distributions. Investigational Report Oceanographic Research Insititute (Durban). No. 35, 144 pp.

_________ (1974b): The sea turtles of South-East Africa. II. The biology of the Tongaland loggerhead turtle *Caretta caretta* L. with comments on the leatherback turtle *Dermochelys coriacea* L. and the green turtle *Chelonia mydas* L. in the study region. *Investigational Report Oceanographic Research Institute (Durban)*, No. 35: 96 pp.

_________ (1975) The St Brandon turtle fishery. *Proceedings of the Royal Society of Arts and Sciences of Mauritius* **3**, pt. 2: 165-189, 3 pls.

_________ (1976): Sea turtles in South East Africa. *In*:

Proceedings of the Symposium "Endangered Wildlife in Southern Africa". University of Pretoria, 22-23 July 1976. Endangered Wildlife Trust, pp. 81-87.

HUGHES, G.R. (1977a): Report for the period January 1977-June 1977. Mimeographed (Natal Parks Board) 2 pp.

_________ (1977b): SEA TURTLES. Natal Parks Board, 24 pp.

KELAART, E.F. (1852): PRODROMUS FAUNAE ZEYLANICAE (with appendices) (Vol.1), II, pt. 1, 1 vol. & 1 pt. in 1 vol. Colombo, for the author.

KHALAF, K.T. (1959): REPTILES OF IRAQ WITH SOME NOTES ON THE AMPHIBIANS. Ministry of Education, Baghdad. 96 pp.

KINUNEN, W. & WALCZAK, P. (1970): Green sea turtles at Chah Bahar, Baluchistan. Mimeographed (Division of Research and Development, Iran Game and Fish Department) (cited by Walczak and Kinunen, 1971).

_________ (1971): Persian Gulf sea turtle nesting surveys. Mimeographed (Division of Research and Development, Iran Game and Fish Department). 12 pp + 4 maps.

KURIYAN, G.K. (1950): Turtle fishing in the sea around Krusadai Island. *J. Bombay nat. Hist. Soc.* **49**(3): 509-512.

LAIDLAW, F.F. (1902): *In:* Gardiner, J.S. 1906, Vol. I, pp. 119-122.

LUTHER, G. (1959): On an abnormal egg of the turtle, *Lepidochelys olivacea olivacea* (Eschscholtz) with observations on hatching of the eggs. *J. Marine Biol. Ass. India* **1**(2): 261.

MAHDI, N. & GEORG, P.V. (1969): A systematic list of vertebrates of Iraq. *Iraq Natural History Museum, University of Baghdad,* Publication No. 26: iv + 104 pp.

MARX, H. (1968): CHECKLIST OF THE REPTILES AND AMPHIBIANS OF EGYPT. Special Publication, United States Naval Medical Research Unit, No. Three., Cairo, Egypt, U.A.R. 91 pp, 37 maps.

MAWSON, N. (1921): Breeding habits of the green turtle (*Chelonia mydas*). *J. Bombay nat. Hist. Soc.* **27**(4): 956-957.

MAY, R.M. (1979): Ecological interactions in the Southern Ocean. *Nature* **277**:86-89.

MCALLISTER, H.J., BASS, A.J. & VAN SCHOOR, H.J. (1965): Marine turtles on the cost of Tongaland, Natal. *Lammergeyer* **111**(2): 10-40.

MERTENS, R. (1969): Die Amphibien und Reptilien West-Pakistans. Stuttgarten Beiträge zur Naturkunde aus dem Staatlichen Museum für Naturkunde in Stuttgart, 197: 1 *et seq.*

MINOT, F. (ED.). (NO DATE): RED SEA AND ISLAND RESOURCES OF ETHIOPIA. African Wildlife Leadership Foundation, Nairobi. 26 pp.

MINTON, S.A. (1962): An annotated key to the amphibians and reptiles of Sind and Las Bela, West Pakistan. *Novitiates* 2081: 60 pp + 72 figs.

_________ (1966): A contribution to the herpetology of West Pakistan. *Bull. Amer. Mus. nat. Hist.* **134**: 27-184.

_________ & MINTON, M.R. (1973): GIANT REPTILES. Charles Scribner's Sons, New York. xiii + 346 pp.

MOHIUDDIN, S.Q. (1975): Pakistan National Report for the Regional Meeting on Marine Parks and Reserves. In: Regional Meeting on Marine Parks and Reserves, Tehran, Iran, 6-10 March 1975. 5 pp + map.

MOORE, R.J. & BALZAROOTTI, M.A. (1977): Report of 1976 Expedition to Suakin Archipelago (Sudanese Red Sea). Results of marine turtle survey and notes of marine and bird life. Mimeographed, iv + 27 pp.

MURRAY, J.A. (1884): THE VERTEBRATE ZOOLOGY OF SIND. Richardson & Co., London. xvi + 424 pp., pls.

NINNI, E. (1937): La pesca indigena. *In:* Corni, G., SOMALIA ITALIANA, Vol. 1. Azte e Stozia, Milano. pp. 411-467.

RÜPPELL, E. (1835): NEUE WIRBELTHIERE ZU DER FAUNA VON ABYSSINIEN GEHÖIG, AMPHIBIEN. Frankfurt am Main. 18 pp.

SALM, R.V. (1975a): Preliminary report of existing and potential marine park and reserve sites in Sri Lanka, India and Pakistan. Mimeographed.

_________ (1975b): Summary report on existing and potential marine parks and reserves around Sri Lanka, Southeast and Western India and Pakistan. *In:* Regional Meeting on Marine Parks and Reserves, Tehran, Iran, 6-10 March 1975. 7 pp.

_________ (1976a): Critical marine habitats of the northern Indian Ocean including Sri Lanka, India and Pakistan. Typescript (IUCN, Morges).

_________ (1976b): Marine turtle management in Seychelles and Pakistan. *Environmental Conservation* **3**(4): 267-268.

SERVAN, J. (1976): Ecologie de la tortue vert a l'ile Europa (Canal de Mozambique). *Tierre Vie* **30**(3): 421-464.

SHOCKELY, C.H. (1949): Herpetological notes for Ras Jiunri, Baluchistan. *Herpetologica* **5**(6): 121-123.

SUNDARA RAJ, B. (1930): Administration Report for the year 1928-29. *Madras Fisheries Bulletin* **24**(1): 1-104.

STEINDACHNER, F. (1900): Expedition S.M. Schiff "Pola" in das Rothe Meer, nördliche und süliche hälfle. 1895/96 und 1897/98. Zoologische Ergebnissen. XVII. Bericht über die herpetologischen aufasammlungen. *Denkschr. Akad. Wiss., Wien 69*: 325-335 + pls 2.

TRAVIS, W. (1967): VOICE OF THE TURTLE. George Allen and Unwin, London.

URBAN, E.K. (1970): Nesting of the green turtle (*Chelonia*

mydas) in the Dahlak Archipelago, Ethiopia. *Copeia* 1970(2): 393-394.

WALCZAK, P.S. (1975): The status of Marine turtles in the waters of the Yemen Arab Republic. UNDP/FAO Fisheries Development Project. Yem 74/003. *Fisheries Investigations Report* No. 59. 4 pp.

________ (1979): The Status of Marine Turtles in the Waters of the Yemen Arab Republic. *British Journal of Herpetology* 5(12): 851-853).

WALCZAK, P. & KINUNEN, W. (1971): Gulf of Oman turtle nesting survey. Mimeographed (Division of Research and Development, Iran Game and Fish Department). 4 pp + 2 figs.

WHITAKER, R. (1977): A Note on Sea Turtles of Madras. *Indian Forester*.

ADDITIONAL REFERENCES

FRAZIER, J. (1980): Exploitation of Marine Turtles in the Indian Ocean. *Human Ecology* 8(4): 329-370.

________ (1982a): Status of Sea Turtles in the Central Western Indian Ocean. *In:* Bjorndal, K. (ed.) BIOLOGY AND CONSERVATION OF SEA TURTLES. Smithsonian Institution Press, Washington, D.C. pp. 385-389.

________ (1982b): Subistence Hunting in the Indian Ocean. *In:* Bjorndal, K. (ed.) BIOLOGY AND CONSERVATION OF SEA TURTLES. Smithsonian Institution Press, Washington, D.C. pp. 391-396.

FRAZIER, J. (*in press b*): Marine Turtles in the Comoro Archipelago. *Proc. Kon. Ned. Akad. Wet.*, Amsterdam.

________ (*in press c*): Marine Turtles in the Red Sea. *In:* Edwards, A. and S. Head (eds.) The Red Sea (Key Environment Series), Pergamon Press.

________ & SALAS, S. (*in press*): The Status of Marine Turtles in the Egyptian Red Sea. *Biological Conservation.*

HUGHES, G.R. (1982): *Conservation of Sea Turtles in the Southern African Region. In:* Bjorndal, K. (ed.) BIOLOGY AND CONSERVATION OF SEA TURTLES. Smithsonian Institution Press, Washington, D.C. pp. 397-404.

KAR, C.S. & BHASKAR, S. (1982): Status of Sea Turtles in the eastern Indian Ocean. *In:* Bjorndal, K. (ed.) BIOLOGY AND CONSERVATION OF SEA TURTLES. Smithsonian Institution Press, Washington, D.C. pp. 365-372.

ROSS, J.P. & BARWANI, M.A. (1982): Review of Sea Turtles in the Arabian Area. *In:* Bjorndal, K. (ed.) BIOLOGY AND CONSERVATION OF SEA TURTLES. Smithsonian Institution Press, Washington, D.C. pp. 373-383.

SELLA, I. (1982): Sea Turtles in the Eastern Mediterranean and Northern Red Sea. *In:* Bjorndal, K. (ed.) BIOLOGY AND CONSERVATION OF SEA TURTLES. Smithsonian Institution Press, Washington, D.C. pp. 417-423.

Nilgiri tahr, Eravikulam National Park and Conservation

CLIFFORD G. RICE

Department of Wildlife & Fisheries Sciences, Texas A & M University College Station, TX 77843, U.S.A.

INTRODUCTION

The Nilgiri tahr (*Hemitragus hylocrius* Ogilby, 1838) is restricted in distribution to the hills of South India. It is congeneric with the Himalayan tahr (*Hemitragus jemlahicus*) found from Kashmir to Bhutan (Schaller 1973), and the Arabian tahr (*Hemitragus jayakari*) which is confined to the mountains in Oman (Munton 1979). In contrast to the thick long pelage of the Himalayan and Arabian tahrs, the Nilgiri tahr has a short grey-brown or dark brown coat. The facial markings, which are particularly distinct in mature males, consist of a dark brown muzzle separated from a dark cheek by a white stripe running down from the base of the horns. The horns are more circular in cross section than those of Himalayan and Arabian tahr, with a flattened inner margin. The frontal keel projects towards the centre, and the horn tips flare much less than those of the other two species of tahr.

Due to its restricted distribution and limited numbers, the Nilgiri tahr is included in the Red Data Book as a vulnerable species (Goodwin and Holloway 1972), and has been barred from sport hunting under Schedule I of the Indian Wildlife Act (1972).

This paper is on a study conducted at Eravikulam National Park, Kerala. Since this area has the largest population of Nilgiri tahr, and is perhaps ideal habitat for the species, the patterns described here may vary somewhat for other areas, particularly those with smaller, more isolated, and more disturbed populations. Some topics considered here will be given complete coverage in later publications.

The study was conducted from 8 July 1979 to 27 September 1981. The Park, which covers an area of just over 100 sq. km lies on the boundary between Tamil Nadu and Kerala along the crest of the Western Ghats. Anai Mudi, at 2697 m, is the highest point south of the Himalayas and falls in the southern portion of the park. Figure 1 shows the approximate boundary of Eravikulam National Park in relation to local landmarks.

The primary study method was by direct observation of animals in the wild, with intensive study of the tahr ranging between Vaguvarrai Estate and the Eravikulam Hut. These animals were habituated to the close presence of an observer, which allowed observations to continue throughout the poor weather of the monsoon which coincides with the rutting season. In addition, about 60 animals, mostly adult females, were marked with colour-coded collars to aid in individual identification. For censusing, the park was divided into a number of sections. The boundaries of these sections were along natural divisions of the habitat and the tahr population. All the tahr in each section were then counted on consecutive days. Because of the tahr's tendency to live in open country, it was possible to count and classify virtually all animals within the park with the aid of binoculars and a spotting scope.

Visits were also made to the Grass Hills of the Anamalais adjoining to the north, and to the Mukerti area of the Nilgiri plateau to gather comparative information.

As is recounted by Baig and Henderson (1978), modern settlement of the High Range began with the establishment of the North Travancore Land Planting and Agricultural Society in 1879. Estates were developed in the ensuing years, which yielded such crops as tea, coffee, and cinchona. Over the years, tea became the predominant crop and commercial control was vested in the Kanan Devan Hills Produce Corporation.

The early plantation managers were from the United Kingdom and they maintained an active interest in outdoor sports including hunting and fishing. Game taken included Nilgiri tahr, sambar, barking deer, gaur, wild boar, leopard, and tiger, while angling focused on the introduced brown and rainbow trout. To improve and regulate these activities, the High Range Wildlife Preservation Association, and the High Range Angling Association were formed in 1928 and 1933, respectively. The high country, including the plateau of what is now Eravikulam National Park were too high and too cold, and had soils unsuitable for plantation crops. Such lands under the Associations' purview were maintained in a wild state for use in outdoor sport. The harvest levels of fish and game, monitored by the Associations, were very low, and the land was kept in its original condition. Mudhuvan tribals were employed as game watchers, and the managers of nearby estates were appointed as wardens for the various areas.

In 1971 the Kanan Devan Hills (Resumption of Lands) Act ruled that all land not actually under cultivation be vested with the government as part of a land reform programme. This caused some concern that the unspoiled land of the Eravikulam Plateau would be converted to agricultural uses. However, thanks to the representations on behalf of preserving the area by J.C. Gouldsbury, then chairman of the High Range Wildlife Preservation Association, and the foresight of the Kerala state government, the area was declared a wildlife sanctuary in 1975, and then, in 1978, upgraded to a national park.

The planting community in the Nilgiri Hills filled a similar role. Formed in 1877, the Nilgiri Wildlife Association gave support and advice on the regulation of sportsman's activities in the area. However, with the current total ban on sport hunting, its influence has diminished.

Although the Western Ghats span three states, similar ecological economic and social conditions are found along their length. For this reason, conservation issues pertinent to one area in the Western Ghats are often relevant to the range as a whole. With increasing human activity and development in the area, there is a need to integrate ecological and conservation concerns into the planning and execution of these activities.

NILGIRI TAHR

Distribution and Population size. Nilgiri tahr are found only along the Western Ghats in South India, and even within this small area they are confined to the crest of the range, usually at altitudes of over 1200 m. It is thought that tahr once ranged through most of the Western Ghats (Davidar 1978), but current populations are distributed between the Nilgiri Hills in the north, and the Tiruvannamalai Peaks in the south. We owe our knowledge of the distribution of Nilgiri tahr populations to the dedicated survey work of E.R.C. Davidar and others (see Davidar 1978). The results of these surveys, updated for Eravikulam National Park and the Grass Hills of the Anamalais, are shown in Figure 2. It should be noted that these locations do not necessarily represent distinct population units. For instance, some are distributed over ecologically continuous habitats, such as the Nilgiri Hills and Silent Valley populations, or the Eravikulam National Park and the Grass Hills of the Anamalais populations. On the other hand, some locations represent a number of scattered populations, such as those from the Topslip and Parambikulam area, or the Amaravati slopes. Due to the ruggedness and inaccessibility of the terrain, the shyness of the animals, and constraints of time, not all populations were actually censused. Many of the populations were estimated based upon sign and accounts given by local informants. Probably no populations have been overlooked and therefore, the best estimate of the current wild Nilgiri tahr populations is the resulting total of 2235.

In addition, there are four captive groups of Nilgiri tahr. Of these one is located in India at the Trivandrum Zoo, Kerala. The other 3 groups are in the United States, at the Memphis Zoo and Aquarium in Tennessee, the Minnesota Zoological Garden (near Minneapolis), and the San Diego Zoo in California. The group at the Trivandrum Zoo consisted in 1981 of 1 adult male, 2 adult females, and 2 offspring born that year. In 1983 the Memphis Zoo group was of 10 adult males, 13 adult females, and 1 young born that year; the Minnesota group was of 6 adult males, 5 adult females, and 4 young; and the San Diego Zoo group was of 2 adult males and 2 adult females. All of the animals in captive groups were originally from what is now Eravikulam National Park, and all of those in the United States are descendants from an original group of 1 male and 2 females.

Habitat. Tahr typically inhabit the fringes of the rolling grassy plateaus of the Western Ghats and the adjacent cliffs and steep rock slabs (Figure 3). This grassland is composed of perennial grasses, and at Eravikulam National Park, cover values usually exceeded 90%. The common grasses, *Eulalia phaeothrix, Ischaemum indicum, Arundinella fuscata, Tripogon bromoides, Tripogon ananthaswamianus* (a species discovered during the study), *Andropogon lividis,* and *Sehima nervosum* accounted for most of the cover. In the upland grassland, sedges were about 1% of the cover, with forbs between 1% and 3%. Some areas were thickly covered with the shurb *Strobilanthes kunthianus.* Valleys and hollows contained patches of evergreen forest known as sholas, which varied in breadth from a few metres along streams to extensive forests in the lower valleys. Steep gneiss outcroppings and cliffs often form the edge of the plateau, and while rarely vertical, these areas serve as excellent cover for escape and parturition. Often slopes along the base of the cliffs are covered with taller shrubs and grasses, including *Chrysopogon zelanica, Strobilanthes kunthianus,* and *Eupatorium glandulosum.*

Group size and composition. In social grouping, Nilgiri tahr show a pattern similar to that of most other Caprini (Schaller 1978, Geist 1971, and Nievergelt 1974). The basic units of the mixed groups were associations of adult females and their subadult offspring. Adult males joined these groups during the rut and departed during the rest of the year. The proportion of time spent away from the mixed groups was positively correlated with the age or maturity of the males. Females and subadults occurred in groups of all sizes ranging from 2 to a maximum observed of 150 (that included a dozen adult males). These groups were open, and the animals forming them split and reunited often. Females were rarely seen alone, and such sightings were usually in the context of isolation associated with parturition. By contrast, male groups reached a maximum size of 21, and single males were common. Like the mixed groups, male groups split and reformed freely.

Movements. Nilgiri tahr did not distribute themselves evenly throughout their range. Rather, they frequented the plateau areas adjacent to the steep cliffs and slabs. The grassland of the plateau offered the best grazing, but only those areas near cliffs were visited. Figure 4 shows the area of Eravikulam National Park and environs used by Nilgiri tahr. This area used by tahr was further subsivided into about 7 areas termed common home ranges. These common home ranges were shared by a subpopulation of females and subadults. They were discrete and usually did not border on one another. The females and subadults, whether they were in one large group or several smaller ones, remained within each area, and generally had no contact with animals from adjacent ranges. Adult males, on the other hand, moved frequently between adjacent ranges, and also spent large portions of their time in areas outside the mixed group common home range. Such wanderings took them toward the centre of the plateau, onto areas of the plateau margin extending past the usual movements of the mixed groups, and onto the slopes below the steep cliffs and slabs. Mixed groups did not venture as far onto the plateau and they did not use the slopes below the cliffs and slabs as much as the adult males. This pattern of movement contrasts markedly with that shown by Himalayan tahr in Langtang National Park, Nepal, where the males separate from the mixed groups and move to higher elevations (Green 1978). This is impossible for Nilgiri tahr males, since the mixed group common home range areas include the tops of the highest peaks.

The annual reproductive cycle. Nilgiri tahr gave birth to single young, most of them between about 10 January and 15 February (in 1981). During this time of year, the nights were clear and cold, and the days clear and sunny. Since the best grazing occurs with the fresh regrowth after the grassland fires in February and March, this would seem to indicate that weather conditions, rather than forage production, are the major determinant of the birth season. In addition, the few females which lost their young soon after birth conceived again almost immediately, and gave birth again in the middle of the monsoon.

With a gestation period of about six months (Caughley 1971), a rut in mid summer corresponds to the mid winter birth season. This places the rut in the middle of the monsoon. Weather during the rut also played an important role in determining the timing of conceptions, and consequently that of the births. Although the reproductive cycle of the females seems to be geared for oestrus during the summer (possibly by photo period or weather cues), stimulation from courting by the males apparently plays an important role in bringing about the oestrous period (as it is for domestic sheep, Shelton 1960). During the violent storms of the monsoon, almost any activity, including courtship, is inhibited. Thus it appears that females receive the courting stimulation required only during the breaks in bad weather. Oestrus, and the subsequent conception are therefore confined to definite periods within the monsoon.

The rut. Males joined the mixed groups just before the rut and courting began. Male competition was focused on the "right" to court a particular female. When a female came into oestrus, the dominant male stayed with her, courting her occasionally. By his presence and threats he prevented subordinate males from courting or copulating with her, a practice referred to as tending. Since it was not possible for a single male to keep control of the courtship directed to two independently moving females, when a second female came into oestrus she was tended by the second highest male in the hierarchy. Males which were tending made no attempt to influence the movement or activity of "their" female.

Occasionally a male which was tending was challenged, either by a previously subordinate male, or by a newly arrived male. Rather than deferring to the dominance or threat displays of the dominant male, they reciprocated, and such interactions rapidly escalated into violent fights. These fights usually started with side clashing, the animals standing at an acute angle, clashing the outside of each horn against the opponent's, but generally changed to reverse parallel fighting. In reverse parallel fighting the tahr stood roughly shoulder to shoulder facing opposite directions. Each male attempted to deliver blows with the horns towards the belly or flank of the opponent, while at the same time, pivoting with his hindlegs to avoid his opponent's blows. These fights continued until one male gained a decisive advantage, or until one of the contestants gave up and took flight. The winner then proceeded to chase the loser, usually out of the group.

Population dynamics. All accounts attest to the satisfactory reproductive performance of Nilgiri tahr populations. That is, however, not to say that there is not considerable variation. The estimated number of young per 100 adult females in various populations ranges between a low of 32 (Eravikulam in June 1978, Rice 1979) to a high of 89 (Eravikulam in October 1969, Schaller 1971), with a mean (of values obtained at various times of the year), of about 60 young per hundred females. The reproductive rate probably varies with minor fluctuations in populations levels and the availability of food resources to the tahr.

However, despite a healthy production of young, the sizes of populations for which we have information have remained almost constant. Since there are no indications of significant emigration, on the average the mortality rates of these populations must equal the birth rates. This means that in Eravikulam National Park, for instance, about 125 tahr die each year. Although it is not possible to state the exact extent the various factors are responsible for these deaths, the major causes of mortality can be identified. During the study these were predation by leopard, by Asiatic wild dog, and by man in the form of poaching. There was no indication that tahr died directly from disease, but parasitic infection may play a role in determining which animals fall prey to predators. For example, one female showed remarkable lethargy in her response to being attacked by Asiatic wild dogs, and examination of her intestines revealed a heavy tapeworm infestation.

Food habits. Tahr are primarily grazers, most of their diet being grasses, and to a lesser extent grassland forbs, and the forbs and shrubs which grow on the steep slopes near cliffs and slabs. They also grazed along the fringes of the sholas, and (apparently) when grazing was at its worst, they penetrated a maximum of about 10 m into the sholas.

OTHER SPECIES

In addition to Nilgiri tahr, a number of other species of conservation interest occur within Eravikulam National Park.

Plants. Although the vegetation of Eravikulam National Park closely resembles that of the Nilgiri Plateau, the region is unique in some ways, particularly in the diversity of the species in the family Balmaceae (Shetty and Vivekananthan 1971). This family is well represented in the park. Shetty and Vivekananthan list 7 plant species endemic to Eravikulam National Park and an additional 16 species which are endemic to High Range.

Gaur (*Bos gaurus*). Although they are primarily forest animals, gaur come onto the open plateau to graze, and inhabit the forests of the peripheral areas of the park. Wildlife Preservation Officer, Mohan Alambuth and I agreed on a population estimate of approximately 70 gaur in the area.

Tigers (*Panthera tigris*). Tigers are present, but not in great numbers. In fact, all sightings during the course of my study in which I was close enough to note the facial markings were of the same adult female. Occasionally pugmarks of an adult male were seen, and M. Alambuth (*pers. comm.*) saw a subadult and pugmarks of its mother and siblings, indicating that reproductive potential has not been lost. Their primary prey were sambar (*Cervus unicolor*) and gaur to a lesser extent.

Leopard (*Panthera pardus*). Leopards are present in Eravikulam National Park in both spotted and black phases. Their numbers were difficult to estimate, but there were probably several present. They preyed on sambar, tahr, and barking deer (*Muntiacus muntjak*) in that order of frequency. On the other hand, judging from the examination of leopard droppings, Nilgiri tahr are the main prey of leopard in the Mukerti area of the Nilgiri Plateau.

Asiatic Wild Dog (*Cuon alpinus*). Asiatic wild dogs were seen only occasionally either alone or in pairs during most of the study. However, a pack of 9 (including 2 pups) were active in the area during the last 9 months (January to September 1981). During that time they made numerous kills, mostly of sambar fawns, and of a few young and adult tahr. In 1981, the High Range Wildlife Preservation Association wildlife guide, R. Mudhuvan, told me that for the previous 5 years, these wild dogs had followed cyclical vertical migration in the Western Ghats. They were said to operate in packs of 20 to 25 animals in the jungles to the northeast (around Chinnar), and move up onto the highlands and break up into smaller groups about every 6 months. They then remained in the high country for 6 to 8 weeks before returning to lower elevations. He also maintained that their numbers were increasing.

Asiatic Elephant (*Elephas maximus*). Although there were no elephants resident within the national park, small groups did pass through occasionally. They spent little time on the plateau and they usually crossed it in the course of a night. On the other hand, droppings and trails indicate that their use is more extensive in some of the forested areas in the park (e.g. the northern extension of Turner's Valley), and those on the fringes of the park (e.g. the upper portions of Inaccessible Valley), or the area around Erumal Patti.

Nilgiri Marten (*Martes gwatkinsi*). Little is known about the Nilgiri marten and even its distribution and status remain unclear. Although they are a forest animal, Nilgiri marten were seen crossing grassland on three occasions during the study: one pair, and 2 solitary animals. R. Mudhuvan (*pers. comm.*) reports that they may be readily located in the nearby lowland jungle to the northeast (between Marayoor and Chinnar).

CONSERVATION AND MANAGEMENT AT ERAVIKULAM NATIONAL PARK

Burning. Current policy is that some grassland should be burned every spring using a rotational system, so that any given area is burned every 2 or 3 years. Areas near Vaguvarrai and Eravikulam are burned intentionally as part of a management scheme, while more remote areas are often set ablaze by trespassers. Given adequate moisture, the perennial grasses quickly sprout succulent green shoots, which are favoured by the tahr. So favoured in fact, that about 60 tahr deserted their common home range in 1981 to graze on these shoots. In addition, observations on play in young suggest that burning is beneficial to the tahr. In January 1980, recently born young were commonly observed running, playing and fighting, but such activities were seldom seen during February and March. However, with the improved foraging conditions following burning, these activities resumed and increased in frequency. For these reasons, it is suggested that the practice of burning be maintained.

However, certain aspects of the burning programme could be improved. In 1980 for instance, burning in the Vaguvarrai and Eravikulam areas was carried out over a period of 3 days, with the result that the entire home range of some animals was burned. Although this did not seem to cause any hardship, a staggered burning programme would probably be more beneficial. Burning during the fair weather in October might also be possible, and this would make fresh vegetative regrowth available to females late in gestation and early lactation. A more detailed burning plan could easily be devised, but its execution would require a greater amount of manpower and supervision than has been allotted to the task.

National Park boundaries. As is shown in Figure 4, there is a considerable area used by Nilgiri tahr which is situated outside the National Park. Much of this area is used primarily by a few adult males. These peripheral portions of the male ranges are often at lower altitudes, and are therefore much more accessible to poachers. The finger of tahr range projecting into Inaccessible Valley (which is, in actuality, quite accessible) is a case in point. I once watched 3 armed men with the aid of dogs pursue an adult male in that area. In other instances, substantial parts of common home ranges for females and subadults lie outside the National Park, particularly on the north side of Anai Mudi, at the head of Inaccessible Valley and on the gently west sloping side of Erumal Patti. It should be pointed out that tahr are completely protected, both inside and outside the National Park. However, forest officers in charge of area bordering the Park have numerous other responsibilities, and strict protection of wildlife in the most distant portions of their areas of jurisdiction cannot be reasonably expected. Therefore, it is recommended that areas which tahr utilize that do not receive adequate protection at present be included within the park. Since wildlife protection is a high priority within the park, this would place the entire Eravikulam tahr population under this protection.

In addition, forested areas immediately adjacent to Eravikulam National Park are essential to many of the other large mammal species found there. Since the National Park boundary often follows the edge of the plateau, most of the terrain included is grassland. Although tiger, gaur, elephant, leopard, and other forest species do visit the grassland, they primarily inhabit the forests. Therefore, the effectiveness of the Park in preserving a wide variety of species would be greatly enhanced by including additional forested areas within the park.

Consequently, in addition to the minor boundary adjustments needed to include all the terrain used by the tahr, the 2 larger additions listed below would be very advantageous in conserving these other species. Considering the convenience and improved effectiveness of making park boundaries coincident with geographical features or political boundaries, these additions are recommended along the following lines :

1) The upper reaches of Inaccessible Valley. It is my understanding that an addition to the park has been suggested previously in this area. It had as its boundary, two tributaries of the Nadalkal Ar (the river which drains Inaccessible Valley); one originating on the plateau just east of Samba Malai, and the other dropping from the northeast slopes of Raja Malai. It is recommended that the northern half of this addition be extended further to the west. This would be an excellent addition, as it would include the area Nilgiri tahr use on the north side of Anai Mudi, and all the area tahr use at the head of Inaccessible Valley, besides offering additional protection to forest species.

2) Besides being a frequently used part of a tahr common home range, the grassy west facing slopes of Erumal Patti are probably the best place in the area to see gaur, as they frequently move out of the adjacent forest and onto the meadows to graze. There is ample evidence that elephant move through the area as well. However, this area falls outside the park and it is therefore recommended that the northern boundary of the park be made to coincide with the state line between Kerala and Tamil Nadu in this area, to encompass all the area used by tahr and some of the forest below.

Boundary demarcation. At present, the boundary of the National Park, as described by the Kerala Government notification, is clearly marked only where it coincides with the state boundary, or the old Kanan Devan Hills Produce Corporation boundary. In other areas, the distinction between National Park, Reserve Forest and tea company land is not clear. Such is the case, for instance, with the ridge that extends west from the Rajamallay salt lick, between Rajamallay and Kadalaar Estates, or the region between Perumal Malai and Chattamunnar Estate along the eastern boundary. Both the enforcement officers and leading conservationists in the area were not completely clear on the extent of the park in these areas and, to my knowledge, no adequate map of the National Park exists. Therefore, it seems advisable that a survey of the boundary be completed, and an authoritative map produced (including extensions and additions).

Reducing disturbances. People enter the Eravikulam National Park illegally to obtain both animal and plant products. Sambar and gaur are often pursued with firearms, and Nilgiri tahr are also often hunted with the aid of domestic dogs. Wire snares are also used, particularly in areas near settlements where they can be easily checked. It can be extremely difficult to reduce this type of disturbance since it requires constant vigilance on the part of the enforcement staff, and a willingness to patrol portions of the park not accessible without considerable effort. Also, since the violators are armed, pursuit and capture by enforcement personnel is impossible if they are not armed as well. In addition, effective reduction in this type of activity can only be accomplished if those apprehended are punished accordingly which requires the cooperation of the local judiciary.

There are two plants which are harvested from Eravikulam National Park. Cane grows in the lower forested valleys, is used for handicrafts such as furniture. The second is a small insectivorous plant, *Drosera peltata.* This is gathered from the grassland in October, a time when it is widely distributed throughout the park (and presumably other grassland areas). This plant is desired for its medicinal properties. Curtailment of these activities has been hampered in the past by the practice of local forest offices in issuing permits for their collection within the park, despite their lack of authority to do so. Thus, the cooperation of Forest Department Officials and their superiors is needed in order to halt these activities.

Management and Development. Given the near pristine conditions prevailing within Eravikulam National Park and its small size, and the fact that the major object of the park is the protection and preservation of the natural system, an extremely conservative attitude towards management and development is suggested. Special consideration should be given to maintaining the ecological and scenic integrity of the area. The healthy and stable population of Nilgiri tahr is an indication of the health and stability of the park as a whole. Consequently, there is no evidence that any remedial management is needed. Rather, the major focus should be upon removing, or at least minimizing, disturbances.

Although the presence of Nilgiri tahr may have been the primary reason for creating the National Park, this does not mean that maximizing the tahr population should be the primary management objective, especially considering the large population. Rather, the objective should be to maintain the tahr and the entire ecosystem in which they have evolved. In this context provisioning and pasture development are inappropriate. Also, despite indications of a fairly high incidence of parasites in tahr, there is no indication that this is threatening the population. It is more likely that the parasites, in conjunction with varying levels of forage, the density of the tahr, and the predators in the park, act as an important natural mechanism maintaining the tahr population at ecologically sound levels. Therefore, it is recommended that no therapeutic or prophylactic measures be undertaken in this regard.

Public use should also be considered in light of the uniqueness and majesty of the area. Every year more and more grassland in the Western Ghats is lost to plantations of wattle and eucalyptus (Davidar 1976, 1978), and before long Eravikulam National Park may remain as a last vestige of the original plateau grassland habitat. It therefore seems appropriate that this remnant should be kept in its original condition as much as possible. This will benefit, not only the plant and animal species now found within the National Park, but visitors to the park as well. Just as every year more and more Indians are discovering the value of their natural wildlife heritage, so are they discovering the value of the little undisturbed wilderness that India has left. Those who wish to see the park and Nilgiri tahr without leaving their cars may do so at the Rajamallay checkpost. With roads penetrating every other corner of the high country, it would seem fitting to leave Eravikulam National Park as a last remnant of wilderness in South India, where people can come to appreciate their natural heritage without the help of internal combustion engines.

Future investigations. Continued monitoring and study of the ecology of Eravikulam National Park is needed, both to better understand the functioning of the ecosystem, and to assess the status of conservation issues. Consequently the following investigations are suggested:

1) *Annual census and estimate of reproduction of Nilgiri tahr.* Eight to 12 days are required to completely census all areas of the park. If personnel or time are limiting, all com-

mon home range areas need not be counted every year. If the personnel have adequate experience, then all animals should be classified by sex and age, which would give an estimate of reproduction for the year, provided the counts are done after most of the births, i.e. in March.

2) *Faunal and floral species inventory.* The only systematic plant collections done to date have been those by Shetty and Vivekananthan (1971) in the area of Anai Mudi, and my own collections from grassland areas. A more comprehensive floral collection and survey should be undertaken or encouraged to identify key floral elements and endangered and rare species. At present only incidental observations are available for vertebrates other than large mammals. The park's assets in these areas should be inventoried.

3) *Continued research on the ecology of Nilgiri tahr and other species.* The Nilgiri tahr population at Eravikulam National Park should be studied further. Such information will be highly useful for future conservation efforts, both within the park, and elsewhere. In addition, the park's capability to support sustainable populations of other mammals, particularly the large predators, needs to be investigated.

4) *The effects of fire on grassland.* Burning should be continued because it is a practice of long standing, and is beneficial to the tahr. However, the long-term effects of burning on the grassland in terms of species composition, vegetative cover, productivity, nutrition and soils need to be assessed.

Captive Propagation

With only about 2200 Nilgiri tahr in the wild, the success of captive breeding is reassuring. However, such efforts may flounder due to the results of inbreeding depression if the entire captive stock continues to be developed entirely from the original small group (Frankel and Soule 1981). Proposals to augment the genetic material in the captive populations has met with approval from the Indian authorities on the state and national levels. However, current regulations governing the importation of both wild animals and semen into the United States have blocked all efforts in this direction. Continued efforts to find ways of increasing the genetic diversity in captive groups without endangering the health of domestic and native American stock are essential if captive breeding programmes of this and other species are to be successful in the long run.

Regional Strategies for Conservation

Sport Hunting. In view of the historical significance played by sport hunters and their organizations in conserving the two largest populations of Nilgiri tahr, the possibility of reopening tahr to sport hunting should not be dismissed. Although it may seem strange to hunt an animal of which only a couple of thousand survive, such a policy might be the most effective method of perpetuating some populations. This is simply because it is in the vested interest of these organizations to maintain a healthy standing crop of animals from which to select a small number of trophies. Since sport hunting is for trophies, the mortality from hunting would be confined to adult males. Thus, as Davidar (1976) has pointed out, hunters who maintain a population of tahr for hunting purposes, give absolute protection to over 90% of the population (the females and subadults)

Without any prospect of pursuing their traditional interest in sport hunting, many members of the High Range Wildlife Preservation Association and the Nilgiri Wildlife Association have lost much of their previous interest in wildlife and conservation in their respective regions. As a consequence the cause of conservation in those areas has lost a valuable ally. By removing Nilgiri tahr from Schedule I of the Wildlife Act, and reopening hunting at one or two selected sites, the involvement, participation and support of these and other similar organizations could be re-established. For such a system to work as well as it has in the past, these organizations should be afforded a large role, if not the primary role, in the protection, management, administration and costs of maintaining the hunting activities in such areas.

Any plan for hunting would require close management and supervision. This would be required to guard against overharvest and excessive stress being incurred as a result of the social disruption associated with harvesting trophy males only (Stringham and Bubenik 1975).

Reintroductions. Davidar (1978) has made an assessment of the status and condition of all areas where he located Nilgiri tahr, or where they have existed in the recent past. While reintroductions can in no way compensate for effective enforcement and protection, and will never be successful without these measures, Nilgiri tahr are likely candidates for reintroductions into parts of their range once the agents responsible for their extirpation have been eliminated. Although they do show affinities for particular ranges, their fidelity to these areas is not absolute, and Nilgiri tahr are probably able colonizers of new range, as their close relatives the Himalayan tahr have proved to be in New Zealand (Caughley 1970).

Such reintroductions might require some experimentation, but would probably best be done with groups of animals. Because males leave their original birth ranges, and travel more widely than do females, the initial group might best be a group of males. They would presumably be more accustomed to new terrain, and also less essential to the maintenance of the parent population. The male group could then be followed by a group of females if it manages to survive the initial few months of adjustment. On the other hand, if the males desert the reintroduction site immediately, a group of the more sedentary females might prove more successful. For mountain sheep (*Ovis canadensis*), Geist (1975) proposed that lambs imprinted to humans be led over the new range, and after a year wild yearlings be released with them. Such an involved scheme would probably not be necessary with tahr, but the possibility of using it should be kept in mind, should the initial efforts fail.

Reintroduction might be coupled to a proposal for sport hunting to great advantage. A club or organization could take on the responsibilities for the protection of the new area and assist in the logistics of the transfer. In return they would have the right to hunt the tahr once the population reached a level at which it could support a sustained yield.

Other large mammals. Because of the small size of many parks and sanctuaries in this region, large mammals, particularly elephants and the large carnivores, cannot be effectively conserved within their boundaries. For these species, populations of adequate size can only be maintained through cooperative management policies in adjoining areas of forest, with greater emphasis placed upon conservation and the maintenance of ecological stability in these areas. This implies a reassessment of current policies which are directly focused on the generation of revenue, a change needed in the formulation of policy on forestry operations as well (Gadgil *et al.*).

Conclusions

Thanks to the efforts of the individuals, organizations and governments involved, the survival of Nilgiri tahr seems assured in the near future. While there is ample cause for a feeling of satisfaction at having arrived at that state, the potential exists for improvement and development in the maintenance and study of these populations. Current recommendations include the need to continue to monitor the status of existing populations, and integrate management of wildlife areas in the region in a more coordinated manner. As conditions improve, the opportunity to renew sport hunting activities may be considered as an effective conservation strategy for Nilgiri tahr.

Acknowledgements

I am grateful to the American Institute of Indian Studies, the Caesar Kleberg Programme in Wildlife Ecology at Texas A&M Universtiy and the New York Zoological Society for providing funds for the study. In addition I thank the Government of India and the Kerala State Government for their cooperation and their permission to carry out the field work. For their assistance with many logistical aspects of the field work, I am very grateful to the High Range Wildlife Preservation Association, particularly M.P. Lappin, S. Singh, and I.P. Prem. I also thank P.R. Chandran, J. Lewis, C. Penny and C. Wilson for sharing information concerning their captive groups of Nilgiri tahr, P.V. Shreekumar for identifying plant specimens, and colleagues at Texas A&M for their reviews and criticisms of the manuscript.

Literature Cited

Baig, A. & Henderson, W. (1978) : A Centenary of Planting in the Kanan Devan Hills Concession, 1879-1978. Tata Finlay Ltd.

Caughley, G. (1970) : Liberation, Dispersal and Distribution of Himalayan Tahr (*Hemitragus jemlahicus*) in New Zealand. *New Zealand J. Sci.* 13 : 22-39.

__________(1971) : The Season of Births for Northern-hemisphere Ungulates in New Zealand. *Mammalia* 25 : 204-219.

Davidar, E.R.C. (1976) : Census of the Nilgiri Tahr in the Nilgiris, Tamil Nadu. *J. Bombay nat. Hist. Soc.* 73 : 142-148.

______(1978) : Distribution and Status of the Nilgiri Tahr (*Hemitragus hylocrius*) —1975-78. ibid. 75(3) : 815-844.

Frankel, O.H. & Soule, M.E. (1981) : Conservation and Evolution. Cambridge.

Gadgil, M., Prasad, S.N. & Ali, R. (1983) : An Alternative Forest Policy. *WWF-India Newsletter,* No. 44. 4(1) : 2-4 & 10.

Geist, V. (1971) : Mountain Sheep. Chicago.

________(1975) : On the Management of Mountain Sheep : Theoretical Considerations. pp. 77-100. *In :* J.B. Trefethen (ed). The Wild Sheep in Modern North America. New York.

Goodwin, H.A. & Holloway, C.W. (1972) : Red Data Book. Vol. 1, Mammalia. Morges.

Green, M.J.B. (1978) : The Ecology and Feeding Behaviour of the Himalayan Tahr (*Hemitragus jemlahicus*) in the Langtang Valley, Nepal. Unpublished M.Sc. Thesis. Univ. of Durham, England.

Munton, P. (1979) : The Conservation of the Arabian Tahr *Hemitragus jayakari*. Project 1290 IUCN/WWF Joint Operations (unpublished manuscript).

Nievergelt, B. (1974) : A Comparison of Rutting Behaviour and Grouping in the Ethiopian and Alpine Ibex. pp. 324-340. *In* : Geist, V. and F. Walther (eds). The Behaviour of Ungulates and Its relation to Management. IUCN New Series No. 24. Morges.

Rice, C.C. (1979) : Further Observations on Nilgiri tahr (*Hemitragus hylocrius*) in Eravikulam National

Park, Kerala, India. Unpublished Report to the New York Zoological Society.

SCHALLER, G.B. (1971) : Observations on Nilgiri Tahr (*Hemitragus hylocrius* Ogilby 1838). *J. Bombay nat. Hist. Soc.* **67** : 365-389.

(1973) : Observations on Himalayan tahr. ibid. **70** (1) : 1-24.

SCHALLER, G.B. (1978) : Mountain Monarches. Chicago.

SHELTON, M. (1960) : Influence of the Presence of Male Goat on the Initiation of Estrous Cycling and Ovulation of Angora Does. *J. Anim. Sci.* **19** : 368-375.

SHETTY, B.V. & VIVEKANANTHAN, K. (1971) : Studies on the Vascular Flora of Anaimudi and the Surrounding Regions, Kottayam, Kerala. *Bull. Bot. Surv. India.* **13**(1&2) : 16-42.

STRINGHAM, S.S. & BUBENIK, A.B. (1975) : Condition Physique et Taux de Survie du Chamois, *Rupicapra rupicapra* L. en Fonction des Classes d'age et de Sexe de la Population. *Bulletin de 1 office National de la Chasse. Etudes Scientifiques et Techniques.* Special No. 3 : 199-224.

Blackbuck conservation in cultivated areas of Andhra Pradesh

N.L.N.S. PRASAD[1] AND J.V. RAMANA RAO

Department of Zoology, Osmania University, Hyderabad 500 007

ABSTRACT

The habitat types in which the present day populations of blackbuck are distributed in India show tremendous variation. Despite reduction in their natural habitat due to interference of man for cultivation, they have quite well adjusted. This is an encouraging sign for the species' survival. Studies on blackbuck populations at Mudmal and other areas in Andhra Pradesh reveal that careful habitat manipulation in these areas can profit both blackbuck and the locals. Reclamation of blackbuck habitat wherever possible, payment of compensation to cultivators for crop damage, employment to trained local people as enforcement-staff, careful management of habitat to reduce blackbuck dependency on crops, minimisation of competition by cattle, sheep, and goat for resources, development of certain areas of blackbuck concentration as tourism centres are among the conservation measures suggested.

INTRODUCTION

Consequent to the demands of man available land for various economic development, enormous changes were brought about in the natural habitat of several species of wildlife. In many habitats this was a predicament for the inhabiting wildlife and either caused heavy damage to their populations or placed their very existence in jeopardy. Blackbuck, the Indian antelope, is one among the endangered species.

Blackbuck once occurred throughout India (Wallace 1876, Lydekker 1907, and Schaller 1967). Loss of its preferred habitat — the grassy plains and open scrub, and large scale poaching decimated the populations in most areas. In certain pockets, however, they are thriving well primarily because of the protection measures taken by the Government as well as by local people due to their religious sentiments. The distribution of present day populations totally estimated to be over 10,000 (Ramana Rao and Prasad 1982) reveal blackbuck occupying different habitat types. These habitats range from the sandy scrub vegetation in the desert area of Rajasthan and open river bed of the Godavari in Andhra Pradesh to marshy coastal plains of Point Calimere in Tamilnadu and areas with deciduous forest type. These areas show a variations in altitude and vegetational structures as well as environmental factors. Any attempt towards blackbuck conservation would complement its high adaptability to different habitats and changes in the habitat to facilitate survival of the species. The paper identifies the stress under which blackbuck exist in different parts of Andhra Pradesh and the possible conservation measures in these areas.

[1]Caesar Kleberg Wildlife Research Institute, Campus Box 218, Texas A&I University, Kingsville, Texas 78363.
Present address: D-62, Labs Quarters, Kanchanbagh Colony, Hyderabad 500 250.

TABLE 1
DETAILS OF HABITAT STRUCTURE OF BLACKBUCK IN DIFFERENT AREAS OF STUDY IN ANDHRA PRADESH

S.No.	Place	Geographical location	Area (approx.)	Habitat Description
1.	Mudmal	*c.* 16°24′N and 77°27′E	80 km^2	Situated 0.25 km from River Krishna. Area with rocks and boulders and a few tanks. Mainly cultivated fields interspersed with grasslands. *Acacia* sp. on grasslands and *Phoenix* sp. in water-logged areas. Main crops: paddy, jowar and other millets.
2.	Mogallur	*c.* 15°20′N and 79°25′E	25 km^2	Cultivated fields flanked by reserve forests with grasslands on the edge. *Acacia* sp. sparsely distributed on grasslands. Forest areas dominated by *Diospyros montana, Xeromphis* sp. Main crops: jowar and tobacco.
3.	Seetarampuram	*c.* 15°24′N and 79°29′E	20 km^2	
4.	Gattumala	*c.* 17°40′N and 80°40′E	10 km^2	Situated about 10 km from the River Kinnerasani with reserve forest of 3 km. Cultivation on the edges of forest. Crops include jowar, tobacco and pulses Forest area with trees such as *Terminalia tomentosa, T. bellerica.*
5.	Bayyaram	*c.* 18°05′N and 80°40′E	20 km^2	Plains area situated on the banks of River Godavari. 5-7 km off the banks — reserve forest. Few tanks here and there. All the area under cultivation mainly for tobacco, chilly, and a variety of pulses.
6.	Ravulapalem	*c.* 16°41′N and 81°47′E	25 km^2	Godavari river bed and the islands exposed form habitat during summer. River banks with cultivated fields and scrub. The latter dominated by *Inga dulce* and *Cassia* sp. and serve permanent abode. Main crops: tobacco, chilly, pulses and groundnut. Also plantain crops about 2 km off the river banks.
7.	Kedarlanka and Madanapalle	*c.* 16°42′N and 81°49′E	30 km^2	

TABLE 2

BLACKBUCK POPULATION STRUCTURE IN DIFFERENT AREAS OF STUDY IN ANDHRA PRADESH

S.No.	Place	No. of herds	Details of populations									
			T. Male	Ad. Male	S.Ad. Male	Adl. Male	Ad. Female		S.Ad. Female	Fawn	Unsexed	Total
1.	Mudmal	5	5	9	5	10	49		9	8	-	95
2.	Bayyaram	3	3	2	2	5	8		-	-	5	25
3.	Gattumala	2	2	-	-	-	5		-	1	-	8
4.	Seetaram-puram	4	2	7	5	6		34		8	-	62
5.	Mogallur	4	3	7	3	1		38		9	-	61
6.	Ravulapalem	5	8	3	2	5	22		7	9	-	56
7.	Kederlanka & Madana-palle	12	8	11	3	3	33		6	2	-	66

Mean herd size : 11.13 (SD 11.97)

T. : Territorial, Ad. : Adult, S.Ad. : Subadult, Adol. : Adolescent

STUDY AREAS AND METHODS

The main study was centred around Mudmal and adjoining villages (*c.* 16° 24′ N and 77° 27′ E), conducted from 1978 through 1980. Other areas covered included Seetarampuram, Mogallur villages in Prakasam District, Bayyaram and Gattumala villages in Khammam District and Ravulapalem and Kedarlanka villages in West Godavari District of Andhra Pradesh. The population structure, habitat variations and other factors including stresses due to man were critically examined.

OBSERVATIONS

1. HABITAT. Fig. 1 shows the different habitat types occupied by blackbuck in Andhra Pradesh. Majority of these study sites were situated along river banks. Mudmal, which was the principal area of study, was primarily a habitat of cultivated fields. There were a few grasslands distributed in small patches here and there. Other details of the habitat were described by Prasad and Ramana Rao (1984). The habitat structure of blackbuck in other areas of study are briefed in table 1. Most of the areas were under cultivation. Paddy, jowar, chilly, and a variety of pulses were common crops in these areas. There were a few tanks which became dry during summer and attracted blackbuck due to fresh grass and other palatable plants growing there. In Ravulapalem area the river bed of Godavari and the exposed islands in it formed its habitat during summer. Except for a few narrow watercourses, the river in this area became dry in summer. Blackbuck rested for prolonged periods during hot hours in these cooler areas. They fed on the *Cyperus* sp. growing on the river bed. The islands harbour *Sacchrum* sp., a tall reed which is used as a material for roof construction as well as fodder for cattle by the locals. Blackbuck also seemed to graze on the fresh leaves of this plant.

2. POPULATION STRUCTURE. The details of blackbuck in the areas of study are given in table 2. The maximum herd size was 61 (Seetarampuram) while the minimum was 2 (in other areas). Lone individuals constituted only 6%, mostly territorial males. Herds of 7 individuals or below it were more frequent (40%). Herds of 25 or more individuals were not uncommon. The mean herd size was 11.13 (SD 11.97). This was more or less similar to the mean herd size of 11.05 (SD 6.22) observed at Mudmal for two years (Prasad 1982).

3. HABITAT MANIPULATION. A major portion of the habitat occupied by blackbuck in the areas is formed of cultivated fields. Hence the pattern of cultivation and the phenological events that follow form an important source blackbuck's response to various changes. A detailed account of the phenological events of crops recorded in Mudmal area during 1978-80 is listed in table 3. Just before the onset of the Southwest monsoon, i.e. by late May, people start ploughing the land. The soil is prepared well by ploughing two or three times since the previous harvest. After the monsoon has set, the seeds are sown, which usually begins during the middle of June and continues till the first week of July. In this first crop season, usually known as *kharif*, millets, groundnut, and pulses are raised on slopes. Some crops such as horsegram, cowpea are practised as intercrops with groundnut and pigeonpea. These dry crops require water only at initial stages. These crops come to harvest at different times of the year although sown simultaneously. The harvest starts as early as in the 4th week of September (groundnut) and continues till the end of

TABLE 3
PHENOLOGICAL EVENTS OF CROPS AT MUDMAL DURING 1978-'80

Botanical name	English name	Time of sowing	Seedling emergence	Flowering starts	Earhead appearance	Milk stage	Maturation stage	Harvest	Parts eaten by blackbuck
Kharif crops									
1. *Paspalum scrobiculactum*	Kodo-millet	III and IV weeks of June	8-10 days after sowing	of Oct.	1 week of Oct.	11 and III weeks	11 week of Nov.	IV week of Nov.	Fresh leaves as well as fruits
2. *Pennisetun typhoideum*	Bulsrush millet	III and IV weeks June	I week of July	III and	II IV weeks of Oct.	III and	week of Nov.	IV weeks of Nov.	Fresh leaves and all stages of earhead
3. *Setaria italica*	Italian millet	IV week of June	I week of July		II week of Sep.	III and IV weeks of Oct.	II week of Nov.	III week of Nov.	Fresh leaves and fruits
4. *Arachis hypogea*	Groundnut	IV week of June	I and II weeks of July	III and IV weeks of Aug.			of Nov.	IV week of Sep. to I week	All stages are eaten including groundnuts
5. *Cajanus indicus*	Pigeonpea	III and IV weeks	I week of July of June	I week of Nov.	Fruiting .week of	starts IV		II week of Dec.	Mostly fruits
6. *Vigna catjung*	Cow pea	III and IV weeks June	I week of July	II week of Sep.	Fruiting week of	starts Sep.	I V	IVweek of Nov. to II Week of Dec.	Leaves and fruits
7. *Sesamum indicum*	Samame	IV week of June	I week of July of Aug.	II and III weeks	Fruiting week of	starts Aug.	IV	III week of Sep. being eaten	Not seen any part
8. *Phaseolus aureus*	Green gram	II week of June	III week of June	1 week of Aug.	Fruiting	starts week of	I I I	III week of Sep.	Fruits and leaves
Rabi crops									
9. *Phaseolus aconitifoleus*	Horse gram	II week of Sep.	III week of Sep.	I week of Nov.	Fruiting week of	starts Dec.	1	IV week of Dec.	Fruits are highly preferred
10. *Andropogon sorghum*	Great millet	III week of Oct.	I week of Nov. of Dec.	II and III weeks of Dec.	Earhead IV week III week of Dec.	Earhead milk stage		II week of Feb.	All stages of crop are highly preferred

FIGURE LEGEND

Fig. 1. Distribution of study areas with major habitat type in Andhra Pradesh.

December during which most of the pulses are harvested.

Paddy, the main crop, is cultivated in the low-lying areas and areas with an access to water supply, for it requires huge quantities of water. Paddy nurseries are raised in small areas which get water supply from wells. When the tanks in the area get filled up during monsoon, water is supplied to the fields through small canals. Paddy transplantation starts in late June. The crop comes to harvest by the end of September.

The second crop, known as *rabi,* starts in September. Jowar, horsegram are the main crops during this period. In a given area only one crop is cultivated per year in general. However, in areas of paddy cultivation, since the harvest is complete in September, either paddy or jowar is raised as a second crop, the former if sufficient water supply is available.

All the crops are harvested by the end of February and the fields remain vacant till the start of the rains once again. Even during summer, cultivation of groundnut and vegetables such as tomato, brinjal, onion, and chilly can be seen in small areas near wells. This, however, is an exception.

In other areas, the cultivation pattern being more or less the same, the type of crop, the commencement and harvest of crop, and the related activities slightly differ. This mainly depends on the availability of water supply in these areas.

4. HABITAT UTILIZATION BY BLACKBUCK. Observations at Mudmal reveal that blackbuck movements are greatly influenced by the quality of food material available in the area from time to time. To start with, blackbuck are attracted by the lush vegetation on the slopes during monsoon. Their concentration in the cultivated fields follows this. The reason: grasses and other plants growing as weeds in the fields are tender and more palatable compared to those on the grasslands. Their visit to these fields continue till the completion of the harvest. In the *kharif* season, grains of kodo-millet and paddy, pods of pulses constitute the supplementary diet. Blackbuck even scrape the loose soil or pull out the whole plant at times to get the groundnuts. An increased concentration of the animals in the fields results during December when the jowar crop is with ear-heads. Apart from the benefit as a forage material, the jowar crop also forms a cover for the fawns to hide. At the end of *rabi* crop harvest in February, blackbuck are practically left with dry grasses on grasslands and the sproutings of the harvested crops. They survive this pinch period by shifting on to the pods of *Acacia nilotica* and fruits of *Phoenix sylvestrix* as well as *Tridax procumbens* which grow abundantly everywhere. Their choice is also open to the summer crops near the wells, mostly the groundnut (all parts) and vegetables. With the onset of monsoon, the whole cycle is repeated.

5. RESPONSES OF BLACKBUCK TO HUMAN INTERFERENCE. When we focus our attention on the other side of the aspect, namely how blackbuck get along with cultivators?, — their position is not happy. Blackbuck face a certain amount of stress throughout. Activities of cultivators, shepherds, cattle, trained dogs, and movement of jeeps are the main sources of disturbance. This forces blackbuck to be always on the vigil. When they are at rest, it is rather difficult to locate them. More often they will leave the place for some secluded place. If blackbuck are located by cultivators, they are driven away from their fields. At times trained dogs are used for this purpose which forces blackbuck to move as far as 7 km away from the place occupied by them. After a few hours

blackbuck return to their area.

The observations made in other areas, although of short duration, reveal that blackbuck conveniently adjust to all changes, chiefly created by man, in their native habitat. To cite an example, in Gattumala and Mogallur areas, where the plains area was converted into cultivated fields, blackbuck move to grasslands flanked by forests. They go into the cultivated fields at dusk and have a bite at the crops and other plants growing on the bunds.

B. Conservation Measures proposed

Observations at Mudmal revealed that grassland habitat is the most preferred (Prasad and Ramana Rao 1984). The first and foremost of the conservation measures of blackbuck hence should be to protect its remaining natural habitat — the grasslands. The government lands which were not distributed to the local people as yet, be left for blackbuck. Other wastelands and areas under grasslands which were yet to be brought under cultivation by locals be recovered, for these areas form the focal points and useful for full expression of different activities by blackbuck.

In most of the areas, the damage to crops in general is not severe. The poor farmers with few *bighas,* however, are greatly affected by crop raiding by the animals. By tightening the protective measures, blackbuck populations in these areas increase further. This is bound to increase pressures on the cultivated fields. Hence, provision should be made to pay compensation for damage to crops in the areas concerned. This would encourage the locals to participate in the conservation of the species and help blackbuck free from any disturbance.

In areas such as Mogallur, Seetarampuram and Ravulapalem where protection measures are not satisfactory, local people be employed as enforcement-staff for blackbuck protection and to check poaching. The staff in other areas should be continued as poaching may recur once again as the populations here are on the increase. A better land-use planning be adopted in these areas. By creating continuous water supply in some part of the grassland area, fresh plants would be available and this reduces pressure on the adjacent fields. For such activities the trained watchman can be utilized.

Grazing activities by cattle and sheep in the areas be controlled such that the competition with blackbuck will be the minimum.

Where more concentrations of blackbuck occur, the places may be developed as tourist resorts. This would accrue economic benefits to the locals at the same time promote safety to blackbuck.

Acknowledgements

We express our gratitude to the Andhra Pradesh Forest Department and the local people for extending help during our field work in different areas. One of us (N.L.N.S.P.) received a Junior Research Fellowship from the President FRI & Colleges, Dehra Dun for the present work which is gratefully acknowledged.

References

LYDEKKER, R. (1907) : Game animals of India, Vol. II. Fredrik Warue and Co. Ltd. London, 400 p.

PRASAD, N.L.N.S. (1983) : Seasonal changes in the herd structure of blackbuck. *J. Bombay nat. Hist. Soc.* **80** (3) : 549-54.

______________& RAMANA RAO, J.V. (1984 : Evaluation of habitat structure of blackbuck (*Antilope cervicapra*) in Andhra Pradesh with special reference to Mudmal and its relevance to behaviour. *Geobios* **11** (1) : 17-21.

RAMANA RAO, J.V. & PRASAD, N.L.N.S. (1982) : Management and Husbandry of blackbuck. F.A.O. Regular Programme. No. RAPA 53. Bangkok. 75 p.

SCHALLER, G.B. (1967) : The Deer and the Tiger. The Univ. of Chicago Press, Chicago. 370 p.

WALLACE, A.R. (1876) : The Geographical distribution of Animals. Vol. II. Macmillan and Co. London, 607 p.

Dilemma of Ungulate Conservation in the Rajasthan Desert

ISHWAR PRAKASH

INTRODUCTION

The Rajasthan desert was till 1950 governed by princes. The Maharajas created Game Reserves of their own shooting blocks and maintained them by regularly restocking. The sagacity of the former maharajas of Bikaner with regard to wildlife management — for game purposes of course — speaks for itself in the form of the beautiful Gajner sanctuary, the winter resort of the Imperial Sandgrouse and the favourite playground of the chinkara, the blackbuck and the bluebull (Prakash and Ghosh 1978). The Jodhpur maharaja's hunting region was the Sardasamand-Kharda Reserve, well stocked with wild boar, blackbuck and the Indian gazelle, besides a variety of other animals and birds. The princes usually carried out logical and seasonal harvesting of wildlife and followed some rules. Besides themselves only a few nobles and British officers were allowed to hunt the wildlife. Poachers and defaulting commoners were severely punished for any violation of the rules. Along with attaining Independence in 1947, people also got the freedom to annihilate the wildlife (Prakash 1958). However, three strong factors came into the way of thoughtless, merciless and ruthless killing by the trigger-happy in the desert: a) a group of people called the Bishnoi, b) the difficulty to negotiate desert terrain, and c) availability of fast-growing natural grasslands. Despite these, we have lost the wild boar from the desert scene, but the blackbuck, the Indian gazelle, and the nilgai are plentiful in this arid zone — a situation unparalleled in the country.

Professor of Eminence, Central Arid Zone Research Institute, Jodhpur 342 003, INDIA.

FACTORS AMELIORATING UNGULATE SURVIVAL

A desert community called the Bishnoi occupies a distinctive position in this arrangement. These people possess an aversion for killing of the blackbuck. To a Bishnoi the blackbuck (*Antilope cervicapra*) represents one of his ancestors and as such it is an object of veneration. It will be no exaggeration to say that but for the aggressive protection afforded by the Bishnois to this beautiful antelope species, it would have vanished from the desert scene, as have vanished (or almost vanished) the panther and the wild boar. We have witnessed what results people's active involvement in wildlife preservation can achieve. In the Dhawa-Doli blackbuck 'sanctuary' situated about 40 km west of Jodhpur and managed by the Rajasthan Forest Department, there are now about 300 blackbuck of all age groups. The area is fortunately surrounded by Bishnoi villages and is thus not the least dependent upon vigilence of government guards for the blackbuck's protection. The populace even provides foodgrain and water to the animals during droughts and engage people to look after the needs of the animals in the remoter areas — an act worthy of emulation all over the world.

The undulating desert terrain interspersed with shifting *barchan* sand dunes is not easily negotiable even by four-wheel driven vehicles. The gazelles, in particular have learnt about this shortcoming of the poachers and taken shelter beyond the sand dunes (Prakash (1975).

The gazelles are, therefore, commonly found near the *barchan* dunes which are bereft of any vegetation and one is left to wonder as to what they feed upon? I have observed herds of gazelles browsing the green or even dry undershrub, *Crotalaria burhia,* a plant avoided by other animals!

Vast natural grasslands are still available to the roaming ungulates in the desert region. In western parts of the Bikaner and Barmer districts and whole of Jailsalmer district, the nutritious perennial grass, *Lasiurus sindicus* holds the ground, more or less singularly. In these parts of the desert the presence of the omnipresent livestock is lower than in other parts of the desert and grazing pressure is lower than the regeneration capability of *Lasiurus.* As a consequence, for example, around Sam, herds of 40-50 chinkara remain hidden in the tall grass. Besides providing food to them, the grasslands provide shelter to chinkara. The large size clumps of *L. sindicus* make the terrain impossible to be negotiated by a jeep.

Present status of Ungulates

Wild Boar. The Indian wild boar, *Sus scrofa* was once widely distributed in the Indian desert in as much as that pig-sticking was a famous sport. Even around Jodhpur city, their population was so dense that after sunset people had to keep a watch against their attack. Since the forties, however, the pig has almost vanished from the desert (Prakash 1981). A few herds have been recently reported in the dry bed of the Ghaggar river in the northern desert and around the Gajner Sanctuary, near Bikaner.

Bluebull or Nilgai. The Bluebull, *Boselaphus tragocamelus* is found near irrigated croplands. Herds of 20-30 are not uncommon. They are not molested by people as they are considered as *gai* (= cow).

Blackbuck or the Indian antelope. The Blackbuck, *Antilope cervicapra* is found in the vicinity of Bishnoi villages which are scattered throughout the desert. They are, however, abundant along the Aravallis and along the ephemeral Luni river (Prakash 1978). In this region, a number of *nadis* (rainwater ponds) occur and these animals restrict their activites around them. In some clusters of Bishoni villages, their congregaton has risen beyond the carrying capacity of the land which is severely degraded by livestock grazing and owing to stress from human activities (Prakash 1982).

Chowsingha or the Fourhorned antelope. *Tetracerus quadricornis* is not a very common animal and is found over low hills along the Aravallis in Pali and Sirohi districts (Prakash 1974).

Pest status of the Ungulates

The bluebull has an insatiable appetite. Its herds freely enter crop fields (millet, sorghum, sesame, wheat, barley, mustard etc.) and cause serious damage to the crops. In the northeastern part of the Rajasthan desert where larger herds of bluebull occur they ravage vegetable crops like carrot, cauliflower, cabbage etc. (Prakash 1960, 1964). Blackbuck is essentially a grazing animal and mostly thrives on roughage with high fibre content. It mostly feeds on *Cynodon dactylon* but when the large herds enter crop fields they cause colossal damage. The Indian gazelle is a browser, concentrate-feeder and prefers to feed on *Crotalaria burhia, Zyzyphus nummularia* and *Mayteanus emarginatus* and other shrubs and herbs (Gosh *et al.* 1983). However, like other ungulates its herds also extensively ravage standing crops. No quantified data is, however, available on loss owing to these ungulates.

THREATS TO UNGULATE CONSERVATION

As a result of the severe damage inflicted to crop by ungulates a number of Bishnoi villagers are thinking to minimise them. Fences do not yield fruitful results as they are able to jump over them. Driving the herds out of crop fields during the day works, but at night they enter the crop fields to browse. As a result it is felt that the determination among he Bishnois to protect them is fast declining. This is further aggravated by the price hike, a kilogramme of wheat lost means over Rs 2.00 nowadays, whereas earlier it was not so. The growing population of blackbuck is becoming a drain to the economy of Bishnoi villages. The dilemma is, on one side the blackbuck is in Schedule I of the Wildlife (Protection) Act and must be protected, on the other it has attained a pest status, and has to be controlled.

Another threat to ungulate survival is the Rajasthan Canal. About 12 per cent of the Rajasthan desert will come under its command. The vast grassland in Bikaner and Jaisalmer districts has been and will be transformed into croplands, the gazelles living away from humans will be in danger — either they would perish or should be driven away owing to changes in their habitat (Prakash 1975a).

COMBATING THE THREATS

We are facing a dilemma: the ungulate numbers have increased around Bishoni villages to an extent that they are destroying the crops and disturbing the economy of the people, as a consequence of which the religious sentiment of Bishnois to protect them is fast dwindling. *A. cervicapra* cannot be ranched or culled as they enjoy total protection under the law.

The best solution to the problem the author has been suggesting, is to capture adequate numbers and to re-introduce them in areas where they were commonly found in the near past (Prakash 1975). For example in Pali, Sirohi and Jalore districts blackbuck occurred in great numbers (Adams 1899). They have now almost vanished from this region. It would be worthwhile to re-introduce them in these districts and lessen the pressure in the over-populated habitats. Prior to materialising and implementing this idea, however, it will be essential to evaluate the

—food and shelter resource of the new habitat
—carrying capacity of land vis-a-vis grazing pressure of livestock
—predator population
—Standardisation of capturing/tranquilising techniques
—mode of transport.

The process of re-introducing should be implemented at a slow pace. Only a few herds be released and their ability to adjust to the new environment should be carefully watched and studied. If this pilot experiment succeeds and the animals start breeding in the area of their current introduction, more animals should be introduced. Full time researchers and forest officers should join together to make this venture a success. To start with, following is suggested.

Species	To be captured from	Re-introduced in
Wild boar	Gajner/Ghaggar bed	Sardarsamand — Khadra area
Blackbuck	Dhawa Doli Ghuda Bishoni	Jalore, Pali districts
Chinkara	Phalodi-Bap	Around hillocks in Pali, Jodhpur and Nagaur districts

ACKNOWLEDGEMENT

Gratitude is expressed to Dr. K.A. Shankarnarayan, Director, Central Arid Zone Research Institute, Jodhpur for his support.

REFERENCES

ADAMS, A. (1899): The Western Rajputana States. Taylor and Francis, London.

GHOSH, P.K., GOYAL, S.P. & BOHRA, H.C. (1983): Habtat utilization by wild and domestic ungulates — A case study in a desert biome. *J. Arid Environment* (In press).

PRAKASH, I. (1958): Extinct and vanishing mammals from the desert of Rajasthan and the problem of their preservation. *Indian For.* 184: 642-645.

___________, (1960): Shikar in Rajasthan. *Cheetal* 2(2): 68-72.

PRAKASH, I. (1964): Some vertebrate pests in the Rajasthan desert. *Indian For.* 90: 106-112.

___________, (1974): The ecology of vertebrates of the Indian desert. In: Biogeography and ecology in India (Ed. M.S. Mani). Dr. Junk b.v. Verlag, The Hague, pp. 369-420.

___________, (1975): Wildlife ecology and conservation. In: Environmental analysis of the Thar desert. (Eds. R.K. Gupta and I. Prakash). English Book Depot, Dehradun pp. 468-480.

___________,(1975a): The Amazing Life in the Indian Desert. Illustrated Weekly of India Annual: 96-121.

___________, (1978): Wildlife resources and management. CAZRI Souvenir: 61-65.

___________, (1981): Wildlife Conservation in the Thar. *Arid Lands Newsletter* No. 14, pp. 2-8.

___________, (1982): The Living Thar Desert. *Sanctuary.* III (2): 130-137.

___________, & GHOSH, P.K. (1978): Human animal interactions in the Rajasthan desert. *J. Bombay nat. Hist. Soc.* 75: 1259-1261.

The Biology of the Brow-antlered Deer, *Cervus eldi eldi* McClelland, 1852, at Keibul Lamjao National Park, Manipur

KH. SHAMUNGOU SINGH[1]

INTRODUCTION

The Brow-antlered Deer, *Cervus eldi eldi* McClelland (locally called *Sangai*) is the rarest and the most endangered deer, and is found only in the Keibul Lamjao National Park, Manipur (93.50°E., and 24.29°N., and 2250-2600 ft above MSL). Keibul Lamjao is a small park, the total area of which is only 40.0 sq. km, but its importance arises from the fact that it is the only habitat holding *Sangai* (*Sa* = animal, *ngai* = in waiting) which is in danger of extinction. The unique ecosystem of Keibul Lamjao holds other animals like Hog deer (*Axis porcinus*), wild boar (*Sus scorfa*), Civet cat (*Viveria zibetha*), Jungle cat (*Felis chaus*) and many other smaller mammals, birds and reptiles.

The need for protection of the *Sangai* has been felt even earlier. It was Capt. Harvey (1931), the then president of the erstwhile Manipur State Darbar who promulgated the first game rule of Manipur, in which the deer was fully protected. Even then the animal was recklessly hunted by the local inhabitants and the army personnel, and as a result *Sangai* was considered to be extinct in Manipur. But about 1950 a remnant population of the deer was discovered in Keibul Lamjao area and that led to the creation of a sanctuary covering an area of 50 sq. km. This sanctuary was officially gazetted in 1966 and on 28th March 1977, Keibul Lamjao National Park was erected with an area of 40.0 sq. km under the Wildlife (Protection) Act 1972.

The present paper includes a preliminary study on the complex ecosystem of Keibul Lamjao and the biology of *Sangai* in its natural habitat as well as in captivity at Iroisenba Zoological Garden.

MATERIALS AND METHODS

The technical equipments used in the field observation consist of 10 × 50 binocular, 35 mm camera with telescopic lens and other accessories. I visited the park regularly and observed the animals from the towers (6 to 9 a.m., and from 4 p.m. to dusk). At Iroisenba Zoo the best time for observation is in the morning during the feeding time. Studies on the growth of antlers were from captive animals.

The antlers dropped from the captive and wild deer were collected and measurements taken. Female skull (2.5 years old) at the State Museum, Imphal, was studied to find out a probable mean for determining age in the *Sangai*. The nature of dentition, tooth eruption and replacement were studied according to the method employed by Giles (1981). Relative density for certain leading food plants of the animals was measured according to the method described by Misra (1973).

[1] Dept of Life Sciences, Manipur University, Canchipur 795 003

Results and Discussion

ANTLERS. A feature of *Sangai* is the development of the antlers on a bony pedicel about 1-1.5 inches, and from this the antler extends horizontally with the brow-tine sweeping forward and the main beam backward in one continuous, graceful arc. Unlike in other deer the brow-tines are exceptionally well developed and show no distinguishable angular junction from the main beams.

The antler growth starts from the second year. These are curved and directed backward with a thin and light coloured velvet covering. In the third year, the antler can be distinguished into antler-tine and main beam. Later the length of the antler increases with the appearance of branch-tines from the main beam. An outgrowth of finger-like process from the anterior-tine near to the junction with the main beam indicates old age.

Usually stags shed their antlers by mid August and are out of velvet by the end of December, when the horns are at their best. This finding is in accordance with that described by Prater (1980). In captive *sangai* two out of four dropped their antlers at the end of February and the remaining one dropped its antlers in the beginning of July and the record of the fourth is not available as it died on 1.ii.1983 before shedding its antlers. Before dropping, the stags rub their antlers against trees, shrubs or sometimes on hard ground and accordingly colour changes slightly.

It is found that total length from the tip of the anterior tine up to the tip of the posterior beam varies from 95.0 cm to 124.5 cm. Gee (1961) stated that the usual length is 107 cm and the record is 113 cm. The horns are cylindrical and a rare spatula type is also found. Ususally the main beam is provided with a single branch-tine, but the main beam with two branches is also noticed.

SKULL and DENTITION. The skull is long, narrow with fairly straightline from the forehead to the nose. The length is more than double of its width. The eye socket is large (*c.* 40 × 30 mm).

$$i\,\frac{0\text{-}0}{3\text{-}3},\quad c\,\frac{0\text{-}0}{1\text{-}1},\quad pm\,\frac{3\text{-}3}{3\text{-}3},\quad m\,\frac{3\text{-}3}{3\text{-}3} = 32$$

In a 2.5 year old female, all incisors, canines and molars were permanent teeth whereas the pre-molars were still in deciduous condition. This nature of tooth eruption and succession may be used as a means of determining the age of *sangai* as has been done in *Axis* by Graf, *et al.* (1966), in whitetailed deer by Severinghus (1949) and Cohen (1977).

Habitat utilization

Grassland structure. The entire National Park can be divided into three zones — the eastern zone, beyond the Khordak river, the northern and the southern zones to the north and south of Thangbiral-Yangbi respectively. There are three hillocks, the Padot and the Chingjao in the northern zone and the Toya in the southern zone. These hillocks serve as important observation points and constitute a significant factor in the ecosystem of Keibul Lamjao as they, along with Thangbiral-Yangbi are the only hard ground in the entire park on which animals can take shelter during floods. The rest of the park area is made of organic debris, called *Phumdi.*

The distribution pattern of certain important vegetative types and their relative density are calculated by recording the occurrence of grass species from six different spots, each consisting of 10 quadrats. From spot No. 7, relative density is not calculated as the area is 100% occupied by *Leersia hexandra* species only. The percentage composition of certain species, especially that of *Zizania latifolia, Phragmitis karka,* and

Saccharum munja shows remarkable changes from the vegetative type as has been shown by Ranjit (1975). *Saccharum procenus* which he claimed as 2% occurrence in the park is totally absent presently. However, he did not specifically mention the methodology of the percentage calculations.

Seasonal food habit. A favourite food of *sangai* is *Zizania latifolia.* Its luxuriant growth is favoured by the floating nature of the *phumdi* base. About onethird of the erstwhile park comprises of *phumdi;* the rest remains submerged under water for nearly six months in a year except the Thangbiral-Yangbi area and the hillocks. The thickness of the *phumdi,* varying from 1 to 5 feet or more, remains afloat above water the level of which varies with seasons. In the cool and dry season (Jan.-April), certain *phumdi* area especially along the edge of the park rests on the hard ground below. The entire park is situated at a central location of a chain of wetlands, namely Loktat lake, Pumlen-pat (*pat* = lake), Soibu-pat, Kharung-pat, Ikop-pat etc. Therefore, in most of the park area, especially near rivulets and shady parts green sprouts of many grasses are continuously produced even in the driest month of March. During the cool-dry period *sangai* eats even dry but sweet stalks of *Z. latifolia, S. munja* etc.

Burning of the dry grassland of the park is a regular practice during the dry season. This with the onset of monsoon may stimulate the growth of new sprouts of certain grass species. With this, preferences for certain grass species as seen during the cool-dry season becomes less conspicuous. During the flowering season (Sept.-Oct.), *Setaria* sp., *Carax* sp., *Narenga porphyrochroma,* various species of *Polygonum* etc. offer further forage to the animal.

Group size and daily movement. The best season for observation of *sangai* is from January-March, when the tall grass dries up and is burnt to ashes. During this period, herds consisting of 2 or 3 (sometimes 4 to 5) animals (irrespective of sex or age, but mostly stags with hinds) are seen together grazing on the sprouts. They were seen mostly in the early morning and in the evening until dusk. During the rutting season they were seen in the open meadow sometimes up to late night. They rest during the heat of the day in the shade of unburnt tall grasses of the *phumdi* or on trees on the hillocks. In the cool winter months the deer could be seen active until mid morning, while in the hotter weather activity ceases earlier and again starts later in the afternoon. This seems probable that as in the case of *Axis axis* the deer is more influenced by heat rather than daylight or darkness. Also during this period the deer are seen more in the northern and southern zones, mostly in between the Pabot and Toya hillocks, where human activity is less. On rainy days they remain under cover instead of coming out in the open for feeding.

POPULATION STRUCTURE

Census result. The population census of the *sangai* under cover of dense and tall grass over the *phumdi* at Keibul Lamjao may not be accurate to the last individual. The population structures were taken from the records of the Wildlife Conservator, Manipur. In all the cases, census were conducted from a low-flying helicopter in the month of February-March when the grass cover was low.

IMPACT OF LOKTAK HYDRO PROJECT

A significant new aspect which has a very important ecological ramification in the Keibul Lamjao is the Loktak Hydro-electric Project. During the monsoon period, Loktak lake has a water spread area of 495 sq. km. The water of the lake is being and will be used for a major lift irrigation project. A coffer dam has been constructed on the Imphal river at Ethai, which may permanently raise the water level of Keibul Lamjao at 769.12 m (2527 ft) above MSL. This would certainly seriously inhibit the rich cycling of the nutrients because it will prevent the *phumdi* from settling down and coming in contact with the soil below, which normally occurs during the dry month. Also, the burning of *phumdi* and grassland is practised with the hope that it may accelerate the growth of sprouts of certain food plants of the animal which would no longer be possible in case of maintaining high water level permanently. This would lead to disturbance of the entire Loktak ecosystem endangering the survival prospects of the *sangai*. However, Panwar (1979) has disclaimed of this idea.

The present preliminary investigation indicates that some grass species which were used as an important food item for the animal are deteriorating. A marked change in the percentage composition of certain grass species is noticed. *S. procerum* and *N. porphyrochroma* which were abundantly found in the entire *phumdi* base are now discarded from this area except that they occur in the hillocks as small patches. Similarly the percentage of *P. karka* and *S. munja* are also in decline and *L. hexandra* and *Z. latifolia* are in luxurient growth. We do not know in definite terms as to whether these are the impacts of the Ethai dam or illegal cutting or burning of the grass species in the off season or both.

Leopards living at the edge of the Royal Chitwan National Park Nepal

JOHN SEIDENSTICKER[1], MELVIN E. SUNQUIST[2]
AND CHARLES MCDOUGAL[3]

ABSTRACT

The leopard (*Panthera pardus*) is known for its use of habitat edges and its ability to live in close proximity to people; it shows remarkable plasticity in changing behaviour as conditions change. In this paper the numerical and behavioural responses of leopards to the edge of Nepal's Royal Chitwan National Park are presented. Based on sightings and radiotracking, home range and food habits are examined in relation to the composition and distribution of prey at the edge of the Park near Sauraha. Home range size for an adult female leopard residing in the park was 7 km^2, and 6 and 13 km^2 for 2 females residing outside the Park. The composition of leopard prey killed inside the Park was predominately non-refuging species below 50 kg in size. Domestic stock below 50 kg made up the bulk of the diet of leopards living outside the Park. Interbirth intervals at Sauraha and Tiger Tops were 20 and 21 months. Mean litter size estimated by sightings of young about 1/3 adult size and young 1/2-2/3 adult size was 2.3 and 1.3, respectively. Only one of 3 dispersing young we radiotracked lived to 23 months of age, the age at first reproduction. Assuming an equal sex ratio for dispersing young, it took a female on average 46 months to produce one female to replace herself. The average duration of females at the two study sites was 37 months. Mortality of adult leopards is high and we suggest that the population is not replacing itself; this conclusion is corroborated by the observation that suitable habitat areas are not used by leopards for extended periods of time. Results are discussed in terms of leopard research and conservation needs.

INTRODUCTION

Wildlife reserves and national parks in South Asia are becoming increasingly insular in character and many boundaries of these protected areas are wll-defined habitat edges where "natural" forest and grasslands interface with plantation forests, forest scrub, and/or cultivation. A positive numerical and behavioural response to these edges, particularly by large mammals, can result in substantial losses of agricultural and forest products and undermine support from local residents for these protected sites. This "boundary problem" demands resolution and a first step is to understand species-specific responses to different classes of these habitat edges.

In this report we outline the landscape pattern (environmental template), how this influenced the composition and distribution of leopard (*Panthera pardus*) prey, and how leopards responded to this, behaviourally and numerically. We watched leopards near Sauraha and the Tiger Tops Lodge in and at the

[1] National Zoological Park, Smithsonian Institution, Washington, D. C. (U.S.A.).

[2] Florida State Museum, University of Florida, Gainesville, FL (U.S.A.).

[3] Tiger Tops Lodge, Box 242, Kathmandu, Nepal.

edge of the Royal Chitwan National Park in Nepal's *terai.*

STUDY AREA

Detailed descriptions of the natural systems and land-use changes in Chitwan Valley are available in Bolton (1975), Seidensticker (1976a), McDougal (1977), Milton and Binney (1980), Sunquist (1981), Laurie (1982), and Mishra (1982). The Chitwan is a *dun* valley. The north side is the Mahabharat Lekh (2800 m); the south side is the Churia and Someswar hills (650 m). Most of Chitwan Valley lowlands (elevation = 150 m) north of the Rapti river were cleared during a large-scale agricultural development programme in the mid-1950's. There was a resettlement programme and most of the people living south of the Rapti (the Padampur Panchayat is an important exception) were moved to the north bank and to other areas. A 544 km² area south of the Rapti extending over the Churia and Someswar hills to the boundary with India was gazetted as the Royal Chitwan National Park in 1973; the Park area was increased to 932 km² in 1977.

Drainage, a monsoon climatic system, floods, and fires determine the natural vegetational mosaic in the valley. It is a pulse-stable system (Odum 1971) resulting from flooding during the monsoon and from fires from late Jan.-April. There are 4 major physiognomic classes of vegetation of concern to this report: 1) Open farm land which now includes most of Chitwan Valley. Maize, wheat, mustard, and paddy are grown depending on season and drainage. 2) Patches of scrub and riverine forest along the north bank of the Rapti composed of *Bombax, Trewia, Lantana, Clerodendrum, Callicarpa, Colebrokea, Artemisia,* and *Pogostemom.* 3) Riverine forest and tall grass areas which now are found only inside the Park. There are 2 distinct types of riverine forest: one on new alluvium with *Dalbergia* and *Acacia* and the other on old farm sites dominated by *Bombax* and *Trewia* with understory shrubs of *Callicarpa* and *Phyllanthus.* Tall grasses can reach 6 m in height and include species of *Saccharum, Phragmites,* and *Arundo.* 4) Sal (*Shorea robusta*) forest dominates over the hills and on well-drained sites in the valley. The Tiger Tops Lodge area differs from Sauraha in that rather than being situated near the centre of the Valley, it is situated at the interface of the tall grass/riverine forest habitat and the sal forest-clad Someswar Hills.

METHODS

J. S. and M. E. S. observed leopards in the vicinity of our base camp near the village of Sauraha situated on the north bank of the Rapti at the northeast corner of the Royal Chitwan National Park; C. M. watched leopards in the vicinity of Tiger Tops Lodge, a tourist facility located 1.9 km inside the western boundary of the Park on the south bank of the Reu river. Records of leopards living near Sauraha were obtained between November 1973, when the Nepal-Smithsonian-World Wildlife Fund Tiger Ecology Project was initiated, until observations were terminated in February 1981. Observations at Tiger Tops were made between November 1972, and June 1981. We have previously published our data on leopard-tiger (*Panthera tigris*) interactions (Seidensticker 1976a), early maternal behaviour in the leopard (Seidensticker 1977) and leopard dispersal (Sunquist 1983).

Seven leopards were captured and eartagged near Sauraha between 1973 and 1977; radio collars were attached to 6 of these. Methods of capture were described in Seidensticker *et al.* (1974), and methods for radio tracking in Sunquist (1981). Leopards at the Tiger Tops Lodge were individually recognizable based on spot patterns and behaviour. Systematic observation at baiting sites provided a continuous record of the temporal occurrence of leopards in the vicinity of the Lodge. These were supplemented by tracking.

Wild ungulate densities were estimated using line transect techniques; domestic ungulates were counted by blocks using a team of observers (Seidensticker 1976b).

RESULTS

Refuging by ungulates at the Park boundary. Milton and Binney (1980) and Mishra (1982) have investigated the tourist/farmer/wildlife interface in the Sauraha area. The damage done to farmers' crops by greater Indian onehorned rhinoceros (*Rhinoceros unicornis*), axis deer (*Axis axis*) and wild swine (*Sus scrofa*) was extensive. In 1977 there was an average annual loss of 48% for 9 villages in the Padampur Panchayat located south of the Rapti, adjacent to the Park. Milton and Binney (1980) showed there was a direct positive correlation between distance from the Park boundary and the degree and rate of increase in loss of crops from the proceeding year. Crop losses were 100-50% in the first 2 km from the boundary and 50-25% in the next 4 km.

Each evening, groups of axis deer and wild pigs and single rhinos or females with their calves moved from the Park to feed in the agricultural areas. This rhythmical dispersal

TABLE 1

ESTIMATES OF NUMERICAL AND BIOMASS DENSITY OF UNGULATES IN THE SAURAHA AREA, CHITWAN VALLEY, NEPAL, JAN-APRIL, 1974. DATA ARE FROM SEIDENSTICKER (1976b)

	WITHIN THE NATIONAL PARK				OUTSIDE THE NATIONAL PARK			
	Riverine forest/ tall grass		Sal forest		Riverine forest/ Scrub forest		Sal forest	
	N/km²	kg/km²	N/km²	kg/km²	N/km²	kg/km²	N/km²	kg/km²
Wild ungulates								
Rhinoceros	11.2	15792			4.7	6627		
Cervus	2	308	2.9	447	3.9	600	11.5	1771
Sus	5.8	360			4.7	291		
Axis axis	17.3	951	15.4	847	1.6	88	19.2	1056
A. porcinus	35	1085			10.9	368		
Muntiacus	6.7	94			4.7	65		
Total N-kg/km²	78.0	18590	18.3	1294	30.5	8029	30.7	2827

	SOUTH OF THE RAPTI (OUTSIDE THE PARK)		NORTH OF THE RAPTI (TANDI BAZAAR)	
Domestic Ungulates	N/km²	kg/km²	N/km²	kg/km²
Cattle	131	30392	72	16704
Buffalo	37	10804	37	10804
Sheep	26	295	7	80
Goats	24	273	27	307
Total N-kg/km²	218	41764	143	27895

from a refuge to feed in an arena is called refuging (Hamilton and Watt 1970). Elephants (*Elephas maximus*), wild water buffalo (*Bubalus bubalis*), and swamp deer (*Cervus duvauceli*) are potential refuging species in the Indian subcontinent fauna, but they are no longer in the wild ungulate assemblage in the Valley. Three species which do not refuge to any great extent in this system are hog deer (*Axis porcinus*), barking deer (*Muntiacus muntjak*) and sambar (*Cervus unicolor*). In the terminology of Hamilton and Watt (1970), the Park and the forest corridors along the Rapti are the core; the first 2 km from the boundary is the trampling and biodeterioration zone; and 2-4 km is the feeding arena. We estimated the ecological density of wild and domestic ungulates in the core and in the arena (Table 1).

Food of leopards inside and outside the Park. Sequential kills made by an adult female leopard with a home range adjacent to cultivated areas 201 were: axis deer (yearling female), barking deer, axis deer (yearling female), axis deer (fawn), hog deer, hog deer, sambar (fawn), sambar (fawn). In this sample of 8 kills, 3 were of potentially refuging species. The majority of the food came from those ungulates that obtained their resources within the Park.

All the leopard kills collected by J. S. and M. E. S. in the Sauraha area are listed in Table 2. Potentially refuging species comprised 43% of the leopard's diet within the Park; this is consistent with the sequential sample we obtained. Wild ungulates comprised only about 1/4 of the leopard kills found outside the Park. Outside the Park, leopards switched to domestic prey in the same size-classes as they took inside the Park. Our estimates of

TABLE 2

PREY OF LEOPARDS INSIDE AND OUTSIDE THE ROYAL CHITWAN NATIONAL PARK NEAR SAURAHA

	Size classes (kg)				
	<25	25-50	50-100	100-200	Total
Inside the Park					
Cervus		1		1	2
Sus	1				1
A. axis	3	4	2		9
A. porcinus		5	2		7
Muntiacus	3	1			4
					23
Outside the Park.					
Goat	5	2			7
Sheep		2			2
Cow		1	1	2	4
Dog	2				2
Vulture	1				1
Sus	1				1
A. axis		1			1
Cervus		1	1		2
					21
Total	16	18	7	3	44
%	36	41	16	7	

ungulate densities show the great preponderance of domestic stock at the boundary. The pattern of switching in leopard predation reported on a macroscale for Asia (Seidensticker 1983) is confirmed here for leopards living side-by-side.

Leopard home ranges and refuging prey. We attached radio collars to 6 leopards in the vicinity of Sauraha (Table 3): 3 adult females (201, 202, 206) and 3 males of dispersing age that were offspring of these females. We established home ranges for the adult females by determining their locations during our systematic radio-tracking coverage of the Park and surrounding areas. We could identify leopards long after the batteries in transmitters were exhausted by their colour-coded radio collars. The home ranges, with

TABLE 3

SUMMARY OF OBSERVATIONS ON RADIOTAGGED LEOPARDS IN THE SAURAHA AREA AT THE NORTH-EASTERN CORNER OF THE ROYAL CHITWAN NATIONAL PARK

ID Nos.	Observation period	Offspring fate
Adult females		
201	Nov., 1973—Oct., 1975: Radiotracked for 5 months; 22 observation months	2 cubs born Jan., 1974; cub dispersal in April and May, 1975 (203, 204); Oct., 1975, disappeared, presumed dead.
202	Nov., 1972—April, 1975: Radio-tagged twice; tracked over 3 months; 16 observation months	Dead, presumed poisoned when transmitter was found in a village house in April, 1975; pregnant when captured in April, 1974, 1 young observed in 1975, too young to survive
206	April, 1974—Feb., 1981: First captured Dec., 1975, radio-tracked over next 6 months; 83 observation months	Living when observations were terminated; litters: —Nov., 1974, 205 survived and dispersed in May, 1976 —Mid-1976, 207 marked, 1 young lived to April, 1977 —Dec., 1978, 3 young first observed in March, 1979 —Mid-1980, 1 young seen in Feb., 1981
Dispersing young males.		
203	Born, Jan., 1974; dispersed from natal area in May, 1975; last located in Dec., 1975	Last located 10 km east of natal area; transmitter failed
204	Born, Jan., 1974; dispersed from natal area in April, 1975	Found dead in July, 1975, 9 km west of the natal area
205	Est. birth, Oct., 1974; dispersed from natal area in May 1976	Found dead in July, 1975 10 km west of natal area.

Adult female leopard observation months = 121;
Litters observed = 6

the habitat composition, of these females and sizes of their ranges calculated by connecting the outermost locations (except along the bend in the Rapti river which they did not cross) were 7, 6, and 13 km³ for 201, 202, and 206, respectively.

The Rapti river formed a distinct boundary between the home ranges of 201 and 202 and 206. The river was not a clear boundary for resident tigers in the area (Sunquist 1981). There is a small degree of overlap between the home ranges of 202 and 206. There is a temporal gap between the times these ranges were established by telemetry but tracks showed the area was used by the two females before radio-tracking commenced for 206.

We rarely encountered sign or tracks of adult male leopards in the Sauraha area and we never captured one. Male leopards occurred at bait sites in the Tiger Tops area more irregularly than did females. Our impression was that males occurred at low density. This suggests that the land tenure system is one in which a male home range enclosed the home ranges of a number of females. Alternate land-tenure systems that have been reported for solitary-living felids include the ranges of a number of males overlaping the distinct territories of a number of females (bobcats, *Lynx rufus*, Bailey 1974) and areas being used almost exclusively by a single male and single female reported by Muckenhirn and Eisenberg (1973) for leopards in Sri Lanka's Wilpattu National Park.

The home ranges of these female leopards included the core areas of a large biomass of refuging prey, but this did not comprise the bulk of their diet. The same was true outside; the leopard's primary food source in the forest and scrub was the biomass input provided by domestic ungulates. Only the removal of this energy input to leopard habitats on the north bank at the edge of the Park would tell us if leopards could continue to exist there. If this subsidy were reduced, we predict that the size of home ranges that leopard used would increase significantly, and thus, leopard density at the edge would be reduced.

Note that leopards are not using sal forest habitats to any great extent in the Sauraha area. Seidensticker (1976a) discussed the relations between tigers and leopards. Tigers through social-dominance restrict the activities of leopards; leopards and tigers coexist where habitat structure restricts the opportunity of tigers to interact with leopards and when there is an abundant prey biomass in the smaller size classes. These conditions are not met in the sal forest and sal forests cover about 70% of the Park.

Leopard reproduction and survival at the edge of the Park. What happens to leopards at the edge of the Park? Our observations on the temporal distribution of leopards in the vicinity of Sauraha and Tiger Tops Lodge allow us to estimate the numerical response of leopards to this environmental setting. At Sauraha, our total adult female leopard observation months (LOM) were 121 (Table 3); at Tiger Tops Lodge, 63 (Table 4). Mean duration of the period of observation for a female leopard was 40 and 32 months respectively. Combining observations for both areas LOM = 184; mean duration of observation = 37 months. We think the duration of observation approximates survivorship because 1 of the 5 females was killed and the other 2 that disappeared were presumed to be dead. One other adult female leopard with 3 fetuses was poisoned just outside of our study area in 1981.

We observed 6 litters at Sauraha and 3 at Tiger Tops; the mean inter-birth intervals were 20 and 21 months for leopards in the Sauraha and Tiger Tops areas respectively. Mean size for litters sighted at up to 1/3 the size of adults was 2.3 (N=3); for young of 1/2-2/3 of adult-size it was 1.3 (N=6). Only

TABLE 4

LEOPARDS OBSERVED IN THE TIGER TOPS LODGE AREA, ROYAL CHITWAN NATIONAL PARK, OBSERVATIONS WERE MADE FROM NOVEMBER 1972 TO JUNE 1981

Nov. 1972	Observations initiated	
Jan. 1974	First leopards observed Female A+2 cubs; 2/3 size of adult; one cub killed by a tiger	Male B
Jan. 1976	Female A + 1 cub, 1/2 adult size	
June 1977	Female A last seen	Male B last seen
	June 1977—Oct. 1979 No sightings except for one male, Nov., 1978	
Oct. 1979	Female C first observed	Male D first observed
Oct. 1980	Female C + 2 very small cubs	
June 1981	Observations terminated Female C present	Male D present

Leopard observation months for females = 63
Leopard observation months for males = 63
Litters observed = 3

1 of 3 dispersing young males we radiotracked lived to be 23 months of age which can approximate age-at-first-reproduction for leopards (Sunquist 1983). Assuming the sex ratio of young leopards at dispersal is parity, it would take a female leopard on average about 4 years (46 months) to produce a single female offspring to replace herself. This is markedly short of the mean duration females remained in the population at our study sites.

These data suggest that this leopard population is having trouble replacing itself. This conclusion was corroborated from our observations on the behavioural response to habitats where female leopards had lived and reared young. Both at Tiger Tops and at Sauraha there were no obvious immediate attempts by new females to establish residence after the disappearance of adult females and these suitable habitats remained open for extended periods of time.

DISCUSSION

If you are a villager and a leopard kills your goat, clearly there are too many leopards. If, on the other hand, the villager did not take his goats into leopard habitat to graze, our data suggest there would be fewer leopards. It also appears that the technology to kill leopards (pesticides and cable snares) is in the hands of local people and this is having a very significant negative impact on the numbers of leopards which inhabit the edge of this national park.

We do not think the data warrant a call for alarm or any specific action on the part of wildlife management authorities at this time. The leopard is already listed as a threatened species and our findings confirm that. But this data set, and it is the only such data for Asia, should serve to make managers aware that you cannot assume that leopards will automatically disperse from parks and reserves at a rate sufficient to replace those killed at the edge. The leopard is certainly not a locally "over abundant" threatened species as Cobb (1981) indicates is the case in many areas of Africa. Cobb, however, did not provide long-term data to support this contention.

It seems trite to suggest that what is needed is more study. However, it took us nearly a decade to come to the conclusions presented here for the edge of the Royal Chitwan National Park, and the results were counter to our intuition. Leopard populations need to be monitored in a low-key way at many other sites and under different habitat conditions for us to know if the Chitwan situation is the general trend or not. The data simply are not there to make that judgement.

ACKNOWLEDGEMENTS

We thank the Departments of National Parks of His Majesty's Government of Nepal for allowing us to watch leopards in Chitwan. Financial support was provided by the World Wildlife Fund — U.S., Smithsonian Institution, and Tiger Tops Lodge. Drs C. Wemmer, J. F. Eisenberg, D. G. Kleiman, and E. Gould have provided continual counsel and support for the National Zoo's wildlife conservation programme. Drs Wemmer, H. Mishra, and D. Smith provided some of the leopard observations from Sauraha. Over the years our research has greatly benefitted from the advice and efforts of our *shikaris* and we especially thank P. B. Rai, *Subedar* of *Shikaris*, for his many contributions. Dr S. Lumpkin edited the manuscript. Travel to the Bombay Natural History Society's Centenary Seminar was provided by Smithsonian Special Foreign Currency Programme.

REFERENCES

BAILEY, T. N. (1974): Social organization in a bobcat population. *J. Wildl. Manage.* 35: 847-849.

BOLTON, M. (1975): Royal Chitawan National Park Management Plan. United Nations Development Programme and Food and Agricultural Organization, Kathmandu. 105 pp.

COBB, S. (1981): The leopard — problems of an overabundant, threatened, terrestrial carnivore. Pages 181-191 *in* P. A. JEWELL, S. HOLT, and D. HART, eds. Problems in Management of Locally Abundant Wild Mammals. Academic Press, New York. N.Y.

HAMILTON, W. J. & WATT, K. E. F. (1970): Refuging. *Ann. Rev. Ecol. Syst. 1*: 263-286.

LAURIE, A. (1982): Behavioural ecology of the greater one-horned rhinoceros (*Rhinoceros unicornis*). *J. Zool., Lond. 196*: 307-341.

MCDOUGAL, C. (1977): *The Face of the Tiger.* Rivington Books and Andre Deutsch, London. 182 pp.

MILTON, J. P. & BINNEY, G. A. (1980): Ecological planning in the Nepalese Terai. Threshold. International Center for Environmental Renewal, Washington, D. C. 35 pp.

MISHRA, H. R. (1982): Balancing human needs and conservation in Nepal's Royal Chitwan National Park. *Ambio 11*: 274-251.

MUCKENHIRN, N. A. & EISENBERG, J. F. (1973): Home ranges and predation of Ceylon leopards. Pages 142-175 *in* R. L. EATON, ed. *The World's Cats. 1 — Ecology and Conservation.* World Wildlife Safari, Winston, OR.

ODUM, E. P. (1971): *Fundamentals of Ecology, Third Edition.* W. B. Sanders Co., Philadelphia, Penn. 574 pp.

SEIDENSTICKER, J. (1976a): On the ecological separation between tigers and leopards. *Biotropica 8*: 225-234.

————— (1976b): Ungulate populations in Chitawan Valley, Nepal. *Biol. Conser. 10*: 183-210.

————— (1977): Notes on early maternal behavior of the leopard. *Mammalia 41*: 111-113.

SEIDENSTICKER, J. (1983): Predation by *Panthera* cats and measures of human influence in habitats of south Asian monkeys. *Inter. J. Primat. 4*: 323-326.

———, TAMANG, K. A., & GRAY, C. W. (1974): The use of CI-744 to immobilize free-ranging tigers and leopards. *J. Zoo Animal Med.* 5:(4): 22-25.

SUNQUIST, M. E. (1981): The Social Organization of Tigers (*Panthera tigris*) in Royal Chitawan National Park, Nepal. *Smithsonian Contrib. Zool.* 336: 1-98.

——— (1983): Dispersal of three radiotagged leopards. *J. Mamm. 64*: 337-341.

Consideration for Conservation and Management of Insectivorous Bats in their natural habitats

(*With a text-figure*)

K. Usman
Dr. Zakir Husain College, Ilayangudi, 623702, Tamil Nadu

Relatively little is being done for the development of conservation programmes through the effective management of insectivorous bats as a useful and renewable resource. The procedures and technology for wildlife management, especially for certain game species, have been developed to a high level of efficacy; but very little has been done in this regard for microchiroptera. In order to encourage the conservation and ecological management of insectivorous bats, it is necessary to assess the status of wild populations and design programmes that will provide both the protection and the support necessary for their stability and permanance. A field study of insectivorous bats was carried out between 1978 and 1981. The status of the native bat population was observed intermittently in their natural habitats during 1982 and 1983. There seems to be a continuing depletion in many native areas. There seems to be no awareness that these flying mammals are a valuable natural resource. Man contributes considerably to the reduction in the number of bat species. His ruthless hunting of bats for food is a direct attack. The pesticide residues entering during foraging, also seem to contribute to this depletion phenomenon. This presentation discusses the potentials and priorities for programmed conservation of microchiroptera.

Introduction

The term Conservation in true sense is relatively recent. It is essentially a social attitude as well as a social movement. It advocates practices that will perpetuate the resources of the earth on which man depends. One cannot deny that biologists and conservationists have realized the value of conservation and much is said and done on, and for the conservation of fauna and flora of very many categories; but pitiably very little attention has been focused on the conservation of insect-eating bats. As a matter of fact bats are one of the neglected species.

Nevertheless bats are unique among mammals: because they can fly, are secretive, nocturnal and surrounded by mystery. They display a wide range of habits and they are part of our living environment. Some are economic liability to man — damaging crops, injuring livestock (Greenhall and Paradiso 1968), and being a nuisance in houses. Many, though, are valuable as destroyers of noxious insects, and the guano produced by bat species is valuable as fertilizers and they are renewable resources.

There are a number of important studies detailing aspects of population ecology and behaviour of *Myotis grisescens* (Tuttle 1976); *M. velifer* (Kunz 1971) and aspects of the mortality of the bat *Eptesicus fuscus* (Kunz 1974). Most efforts to document accumulation of pesticide residues in insectivorous bats (Kunz *et al.* 1977, Humphrey and Cope 1977; Clark *et al.* 1978, Gelusa *et al.* 1976) arose out of concern for declining bat populations (Mohr 1972). Apart from Sarkar *et al.* (1980) there are no systematic field studies on population strategies for bats of South India. I have attempted here to evaluate some of the data pertaining to microchiropteran bat, *Rhinopoma hardwickei*.

Materials and Methods

Field studies were conducted in the Nagamalai ridge areas of Madurai (9°58′N; 78°10′E) during 1978 through 1980. The status of the native bat population was observed intermittently in their natural habitats till 1983. The ridge is characterized by small escarpments. In some places the ridges are eroded leaving solid rocks jutting out here and there. Elevation throughout the areas is variable from west to east (from 200 m to 100 m). Heavy rains cause dendritic drainage patterns and run off is relatively rapid. The natural vegetation in the cave area contains components of scrub jungle plants. Extensive local cultivation, mostly to the north of the ridge includes paddy, sugar cane, mango, coconut etc. The general climatic conditions of this area are typical of tropical plains. The summers are long, hot and dry. Precipitation is in the form of rain and occurs primarily in September through December.

A number of natural caves, caverns, crevices are located in the study area. The cave that is known to be occupied by resident population of *R. hardwickei* was intensively studied. The Nagamalai structure has been occupied by transient (e.g. *Tadarida aegyptiaca*) and resident populations of *R. hardwickei, Hipposideros speoris, H. bicolor, Taphozous melanopogon, T. kachenensis, Megaderma lyra* and *Pipistrellus* sp. Lower disturbance level makes these habitats attractive for occupation by bat populations. Accumulation of bat droppings and stained roosting areas indirectly indicate the perennial presence of bats.

Aluminium bands with numbers engraved weighing *c.* 200 mg. were used for banding the bats as suggested by Bonaccorso *et al.* (1975). Since these bands were flanged as per the specification of Stebbings (1978), the bats were not injured. One thousand bats of the species, *R. hardwickei* were marked and released for the study of population ecology.

Population analyses were studied following 'single marking and multiple recaptures' method (Roff 1973a, 1973b, Bailey 1951). Changes occur in the ratio of marked animals and I have considered this change at a relatively constant rate. So the rate of change was measured and was used to project backward. The value of the ratio at the instant the marked animals were released into population size was obtained for the study period. The recapture values were corrected to the number of marked recaptures per 100 animals marked and per 100 in the capture sample. A weighted ratio showing the rate of decrease of the recapture values was calculated. With this weighted ratio, the theoretical number of recaptures that would have been obtained at the time of release were calculated. With the theoretical recapture value for the time of release of the marked animals, estimation of population size was obtained by substituting this value (for further details please see Roff 1973a, 1973b, Bailey 1951).

The foraging grids of my study subjects were identified by using chemiluminescent (Cyalume) substance and bat detectors (Unit of animal behaviour, Madurai Kamaraj University). This facilitated me to have periodic insect collection in the foraging areas with the aid of sticky and light traps as recommended by McNutt (1976). The difference between prefeeding and postfeeding weights yielded the insects harvested by one bat per night (Kunz 1971).

Bats were recaptured on the first week of every month. The degree of recaptures in relation to the period after banding decreased after a lapse of time. In the first month after banding recaptures were relatively high. Frequency of recaptures for the second and the third times were more during the first few months. My efforts to locate the bats during this period at other alternate roosting sites were not successful. This is not caused by bats leaving the cave after being first handled and banded but to come back in greater numbers the following year. *Rhinopoma* seem to be relatively a stable population.

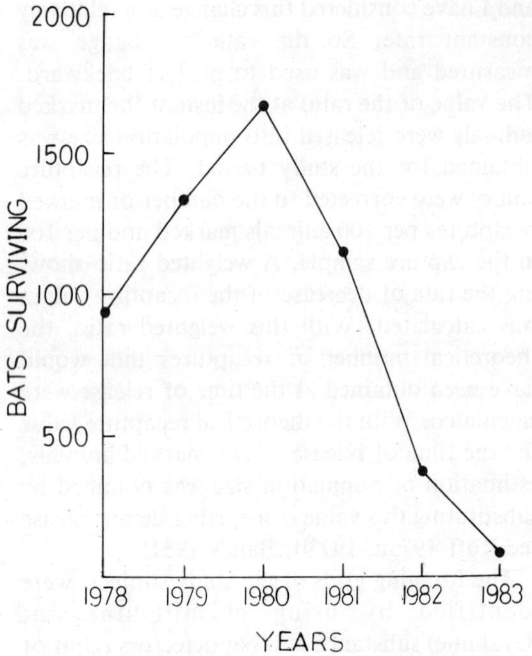

Pattern of fluctuation in the population of the bat species, *Rhinopoma hardwickei* during the years 1978 through 1984. The first half represents the "protected period" and the second half represents the "unprotected period" of research. Please see the text for other details.

Population analysis of *R. hardwickei* by single marking and multiple recaptures for the years 1978 through 1983 is presented in the accompanying figure. It illustrates an increase in the population during my intensive study period whereas the population has markedly started declining since 1981 till date.

DISCUSSION

At the onset of discussion of the observed data of *R. hardwickei* population, I feel it is of critical importance to mention that there is a point of distinction in these species between the 'protected' and the 'unprotected' years of research. It is apparent from the figure that the population of bat species steadily grows in the first three years whereas a chaotic fall begins to wean their number in the second half of the study period. This does not mean that the roosting site has become inhospitable to the bats owing to a sudden change in its environmental parameters. It is agreeable that habitat selection of appropriate roosting sites by bat species eliminate several requirements for successful and continuous living (Studier and O'Farrell 1972). The roosting sites of Nagamalai ridge furnish all the immediate environmental demands of the microchiropteran bats such as relative constancy of temperature and humidity, darkness, inaccessibility to predators, insect abundance etc. (Usman 1981). It seems therefore that there is no correlation between environmental stress and reduction in population of bats.

Natural disasters have been reported as important in bat mortality by Gillette and Kunbrough (1970). Dead bats have been seldom found under the roost in bat caves. Further meteorological data of the Unit of animal behaviour, Madurai Kamaraj University confirms that the cave and its core area afford satisfactory and conducive climate for the normal living of microchiropteran bats. They suffered neither a flood nor a freezing cold.

Banding produced no observable mortality. The bands weighed just 200 mg each, which do not hamper the aerodynamic manoeuvrability of bats. The bands were all flanged as per the specification of Stebbings (1978). Occurrence of band injury or slit of wing membrane was critically at low ebb that had no statistical significance. Multiple recaptures and recaptures after sevei al years confirm the statement.

Probable predators in the region studied have been snakes, redheaded merlins, owls and owlets. I could observe merlins and owls often chasing the emerging bats, however, most of them were unsuccessful attempts for the predators. The actual roosting sites are inaccessible to snakes, but they could prey upon fallen animals. The chances of predation for merlin disappear with the vanishing sunlight. Predatory awareness of the bats has been earmarked by their ability to forage under the canopies during moonlight hours of the nights (Morrison 1978, Usman *et al.* 1980). So predation pressure for the decline in population may be ruled out.

It is a general phenomenon that the availability of food has a great impact over the population density. The data on the availability of insect food and the number of insect-eating bats in my study grid revealed that the available biomass of insects (Usman, *unpublished*) was too large to be harvested by bat species alone. It is inferred that food was not a limiting factor for the observed depletion in bats.

Bats generally do not modify their surroundings to make a better roost (Greenhall and Paradiso 1968). Loyalty to particular summer or winter roosting sites appear to be a rather general phenomenon (Tuttle 1976). My study subject demonstrated a similar philopatry by showing continuous occupation of the roost. My attempt to find a banded animal elsewhere proved negative. This is in full agreement with the general opinion of roost fidelity. Brosset (1962) studied these animals and observed in them a similar non-migratory attitude. Hence the concept of migration does not come into picture for the cause of decline.

It has been found that pesticide residues reach the brain and cause symptoms of poisoning after fat mobilization. These chemical body burdens were obtained naturally under free living conditions (Gelusa *et al.* 1976). Major foraging areas of my study subjects cover a wide array of land under cultivation. The farmers periodically apply all types of organic poisons to protect their crops. It could not be the only cause but, no doubt, contributed sharply.

In addition to the pesticides, land clearing has caused considerable damage. The areas of caves, caverns and other roosting sites are often shelled as a part of quarry operation. These disrupt their long used dwelling places.

Protein hungry local people harvest as and when they like a good number of insectivorous bats too for the pot. This periodical devastating operation sweeps away a large number of bats.

As a matter of fact bats are a highly productive and renewable resource. They have virtually insatiable appetite, their exceptional need for food is due to the nature of the skin. Incidentally one can say that 500 bats, each weighing 15 g, will harvest one metric ton of insects per year (Gelusa *et al.* 1976; Usman 1981). This involves a major quota of noxious insects such as mosquitoes, other vectors and pests. It has been calculated that 1500 bats will yield one tone of guano annually which can be used as fine manure. The usefulness of bats as insect feeders and the value of their guano led to several attempts to encourage colonial species to occupy artificial bat towers built from Texas to Florida where malaria mosquitoes were prevalent (Greenhall and Paradiso 1968). Proper conservation and management of these 'birds of the night' will give us a helping hand to promote economy by way of manure and to down partially, if not fully, the annoying insects.

It is a pity that a number of bat species are dwindling on account of the actions of man. Several countries, including Britain, realising the crucial role that bats play in maintaining an ecological balance, have placed bats on their list of protected species (Kumar 1984). So it is high time that we undertook a long term programme to study the population status of these creatures surrounded by mystery. The delicate balance of ecosystem and man's influence on the ecosystem should be given priorities to prepare for the Red Data Book. Emphasis should be given to involve the people of the region so as to make them understand the value of conservation. Adequate knowledge of roosting sites is an essential prerequisite for any conservation measure. Intensive study in unexplored area has to be undertaken. Insects infest every part of the world and a diverse community of bats are to be studied and fostered with proper monitoring. Delaying will surely affect the population of the bewitching bat species.

ACKNOWLEDGEMENTS

This work, as a part of the Indo-German project on animal behaviour, was supported by the UGC (India), a Government of India Scholarship, and by the Alexander von Humboldt-Stiftung, DFG, DAAD (West Germany).

I thank Prof. Dr. M.K. Chandrashekaran, Madurai, and Prof. Dr. G. Neuweiler, Munchen, for their assistance. I thank Prof. Dr. S. Liakath Alikhan for help in writing this paper.

REFERENCES

BAILEY, N.T.J. (1951): On estimating the size of mobile populations from recapture data. *Biometrica* **38**:293-306.

BONACCORSO, F.J., SMYTHE, N. & HUMPHREY, S.R. (1976): Improved techniques for marking bats. *J. Mamm.* **47**:383-396.

BROSSET, A. (1962): The bats of central and western India: pt., I. *J. Bombay nat. Hist. Soc.* **59**:1-57.

CLARK, D.R. JR., KUNZ, T.H. & KAISER, T.E. (1978): Insecticides applied to a nursery colony of little brown bat (*Myotis lucifugus*): lethal concentrations in brain tissues. *J. Mamm.* **59**:84-91.

GELUSA, K.N., ALTENBACH, J.S. & WILSON, D.E. (1976): Bat mortality; pesticide poisoning and migratory stress. *Science* **194**:184-186.

GILLETTE, D.D. & KIMBROUGH, J.D. (1970): Chiropteran mortality. Southern Methodist Univ. Press, Dallas. pp. 262-283.

GREENHALL, A.M. & PARADISO, J.L. (1968): Bats and bat banding. Bureau of sport fisheries and wildlife resource publication. Washington. **72**:1-46.

HUMPHREY, S.R. & COPE, J.B. (1977): Survival rates of the endangered Indiana bat, *Myotis sodalis, J. Mamm.* **58**:32-36.

KUMAR, P. (1984): Bats. *Sanctuary* **1**:26-35.

KUNZ, T.H. (1971): Ecology of the cave bat, *Myotis velifer* in south central Kansas and north western Okalahoma. Ph.D. dissertation, Univ. Kansas.

______ (1974): Reproduction, growth and mortality of the vespertilionid bat, *Eptesicus fuscus* in Kansas. *J. Mamm.* **55**:1-13.

KUNZ, T.H., ANTHONY, E.L.P. & RUMAGE III, W.T. (1977): Mortality of little brown bats following multiple pesticide applications. *J. Wildl. Manage.* **41**:476-483.

MCNUTT, D.N. (1976): Insect collection in tropics.

MOHR, C.E. (1972): The status of threatened species of cave dwelling bats. *Bull. Nat. Spel. Soc.* **34**:33-47.

MORRISON, D.W. (1978): Luna phobia in a Neotropical fruit bat, *Artibeus jamaicensis* (Chiroptera: Phyllostomidae). *Anim. Behav.* **26**:852-855.

ROFF, D.A. (1973a): On the accuracy of some mark-recapture estimators. *Oecologia* **12**:15-34.

______ (1973b): An examination of some statistical test used in the analysis of mark-recapture data. ibid. **12**:35-54.

SARKAR, H.B.D., RAO, B.S.B., SUVARNALATHA, M. & THYAGARAJA, B.S. (1980): Banding bats for the study of population ecology. *J. Bombay nat. Hist. Soc.* **75**:989-999.

STEBBINGS, R.E. (1978): Marking bats. Proc. R.S.P.C.A. Symposium, London. *In* 'Marking animals' (ed. B.Stonehouse): 81-94.

STUDIER, E.H. & O'FARRELL, M.J. (1972): Biology of *Myotis thysanodes* and *M. lucifugus* (Chiroptera: Vespertilionidae) I. Thermoregulation. *Comp. Biochem. Physiol.* **41**:567-595.

TUTTLE, M.D. (1976): Population ecology of the gray bat (*Myotis grisescens*): Philopatry, timing and pattern of movement, weight loss during migration and seasonal adaptive strategies. *Occ. Papers., Mus. Nat. Hist. Univ. Kansas.* **54**:1-38.

USMAN, K., HABERSETZER, J., SUBBARAJ, R., GOPALAKRISHNASWAMY, G., & PARAMANANDAM, K. (1980): Behaviour of bats during a lunar eclipse. *Behav. Ecol Sociobiol.* **7**:79-81.

USMAN, K. (1981): Ecological and Ethological studies on the insectivorous bat, *Rhinopoma hardwickei hardwickei* Gray, 1831. Ph.D., dissertation, Madurai Kamaraj Univ. Madurai.

Ciconiiform birds breeding in Bhavnagar City, Gujarat: A study of their nesting and plea for conservation

(*With 2 figures and 3 plates*)

B.M. PARASHARYA & R.M. NAIK[1]

SUMMARY

Nesting histories of *Ardea alba, Ardeola grayii, Babulcus ibis, Egretta gularis, Nycticorax nycticorax, Mycteria leucocephala, Threskiornis aethiopica* and *Platalea leucorodia* in an urban setting at Bhavnagar (21°46'N, 72°11'E), Gujarat, are described. Three distinct areas of the city are distinguished and nest distribution in these areas is explained. The availability of food as well as the safety of nesting sites are discussed. A number of adjustments in the breeding biology of the birds brought about by the urban habitat are listed. The recreational, educational and scientific values of the nesting colony are discussed and a need for the management of colony is stressed.

INTRODUCTION

The herons, egrets and ibises in the Saurashtra region of Gujarat breed commonly in the heronries located in urban areas (Naik and Parasharya 1984a). The most spectacular among heronries of Saurashtra is the one located in Bhavnagar City. This heronry has been existing for a long time, though it has not been described or publicized.

We became interested in this heronry during our study of the Indian Reef Heron (Naik and Parashraya, 1984b) on the coast of Gujarat, realised its potential use for recreation, education and scientific study and paid a special attention to it for a few years.

The present paper deals with the nesting of eight species of Ciconiiform birds, namely the Large Egret (*Ardea alba*), Pond Heron (*Ardeola grayii*), Cattle Egret (*Bubulcus ibis*), Indian Reef Heron (*Egretta gularis*), Night Heron (*Nycticorax nycticorax*), Painted Stork (*Mycteria leucocephala*), White Ibis (*Threskiornis aethiopica*) and Spoonbill (*Platalea leucorodia*), in the Bhavnagar heronry and the conservation measures necessary for conserving this heronry which is now being increasingly threatened by urban development.

MATERIALS AND METHODS

The study was conducted in Bhavnagar (21°46'N, 72°11'E), a city in the Saurashtra region of Gujarat State located on the western coast of Gulf of Khambhat (Cambay).

Prior to 1977, one of us (B.M.P.) lived in Bhavnagar, watched the waterbirds nesting there and recorded some of the nesting events. We started a systematic study of the colony from 1979. A thorough survey of the nesting birds was first made in the second half of 1979 and was followed up by a survey at intervals of 10 to 20 days throughout the nesting seasons in 1980 and 1981 and at irregular intervals in 1982. During the survey, each nesting tree was located, numbered and plotted on a scaled map. Number of nests of each species per tree were counted while standing under the tree. The nesting stage for each nest was determined by closely observing the nest through field glasses. Three stages of nesting cycles were distinguished: (1) nest-building was indicated when the actual process of nest-building was in progress, or

[1]Departmet of Biosciences, Saurashtra University, Rajkot-360 005, India.

an incomplete nest was being guarded by a bird, (2) incubation period is inferred when the eggs were seen through the nest, or when a bird was tightly sitting in an incubating posture on a nest, and (3) nestling period was inferred when a chick was observed, and/or heard, in or near the nest. Any nest in any one of the above stages, was considered to be an active nest. Number of nesting pairs at any time were estimated to be the number of active nests at that particular time.

The starting and termination of nesting season of a species had to be estimated from our data in most cases; the starting was estimated from the condition of the earliest nest during the first checking and the termination from the age of the last chicks at the time of last checking of the season. People living in, or visiting, the bird-nesting areas were also watched, some of them were interviewed and their attitudes towards the birds were recorded.

The feeding areas of the nesting species were visited from time to time during the nesting season, and the feeding habitat preference of each species was noted.

Two other nesting colonies, one at the New Port and the other at Gogha, were also under our observations from 1979 onwards. While full report of our studies there, will be published elsewhere (Naik and Parasharya 1984b), we have drawn in some of the observatons to interpret the history of Bhavnagar Colony.

In this paper, the Reef Heron includes the Little Egret (*Egretta garzetta*). The white morph of the Reef Heron cannot be distinguished always from the Little Egret around the Gulf of Khambhat (Parasharya and Naik 1983). This is attributed to the fact that these two species of *Egretta* interbreed in Bhavnagar and some other locations across the Gulf (Naik and Parasharya 1984c).

RESULTS

Nesting areas

There were three distinct areas in Bhavnagar where the birds nested (Fig. 1). These areas were (1) Old City, (2) Peile Garden and its immediate vicinity, and (3) the suburban areas of Krishnanagar and Takhteshwar.

(1) **Old City.** This is the oldest part of the city, which grew out of a small settlement established around a village in 1723 A.D. by a local chieftain. The area that was urbanised around this nucleus settlement, and was at one time surrounded by a fortified wall, is designated as Old City. This area is like many other old towns in India having narrow winding streets, lanes and by-lanes. One main road traversing the city from south to north and extending up to the old port, is flanked by shopping areas with various bazaar-streets branching off from different points. Most of the city blocks are completely built-up, the adjoining buildings sharing a common wall and a building rarely having its own free space either in front or back. In such a congested area, there should not be any room for trees, but, the Peepul (*Ficus religiosa*) has managed to find some space for itself. Many of these trees grow on the sides of narrow streets and hinder the smooth flow of traffic; it also grows in the tiny courtyards of temples, and occasionally one may even see a tree emerging through the roof of a house. Some of these trees (particularly those around the railway station) are planted, but, most others have managed to grow on their on. This remarkable situation, where the Peepuls thrive under apparently impossible conditions, comes about in several urban areas of Gujarat and Rajasthan and is attributed to the fact that the uprooting or cutting a Peepul is a religious taboo for the Hindus, who form a dominant

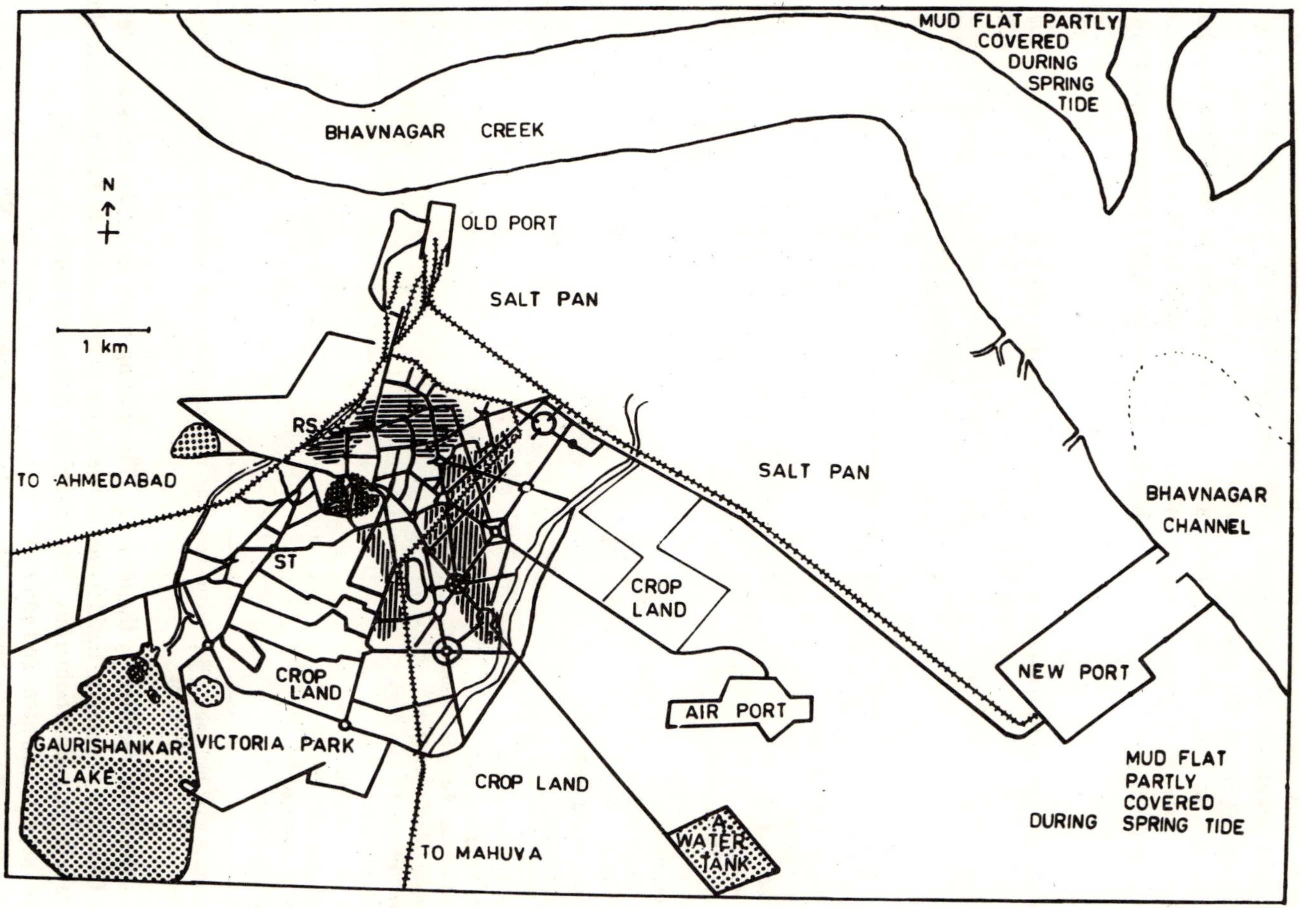

Map of Bhavnagar and its surroundings showing the nesting and feeding areas of Ciconiiform birds. The nesting area in Old City is hatched by horizontal lines, that in the suburban areas by vertical lines and that in the Peile Garden and its immediate vicinity by crossing lines. The freshwater reservoirs are stippled. In the city, the main roads are shown by single thick lines, railway tracks by single lines hatched with short lines and two creeks draining the rain water by thin double lines. R.S. — Railway Station; B.S. — Bus Station; A. WATER TANK — Akawada Water Tank.

religious group in these parts of the country. Once a Peepul seed germinates and takes root, it is fully protected by the taboo and there is nothing any one can do about it; any future house construction or road alignment has to make an allowance for it.

and Large Egret in Bhavnagar, had nested in this area (Table 2). A majority of the Night Heron, a small proportion of the Cattle Egret and a variable number of the White Ibis had also nested here. Only the Pond Heron, Spoonbill and Painted Stork did not nest here (Table 2). The nesting birds and their nests were left alone by the people and no one ever dared to do them any deliberate harm.

TABLE 1

NUMBER OF DIFFERENT TREE SPECIES USED FOR NESTING BY THE BIRDS IN THE OLD CITY(C), PEILE GARDEN(P) AND SUBURBAN(S) AREAS OF BHAVNAGAR

Species[1]	Number of trees			
	C	P	S	Total
Aegle marmelos, Bael	—	—	2	2
Albizia lebbek, **Siris or Lebbek-tree**	—	—	1	1
Azadirachta indica, Neem	—	6	3	9
Cocos nucifera, Coconut	—	—	2	2
Cordia gharaf, Gundi*	—	—	1	1
Drypetes roxburghii, Putranjiva*	—	3	—	3
Ficus amplissima, Peeper*	1	3	—	4
Ficus benghalensis, Banyan	1	1	—	2
Ficus racemosa, Cluster Fig	—	1	—	1
Ficus religiosa, Peepul	30	11	4	45
Limonia acidissimia, Wood apple	2	—	—	2
Mangifera indica, Mango	—	1	68	69
Millingtonia hortensis, Indian Cork tree	—	—	2	2
Mimusops elengi, Spanish-cherry	—	2	1	3
Moringa oleifera, Drumstick tree	—	—	1	1
Peltophorum pterocarpus, Rusty Shield-bearer	—	13	1	14
Pithecolobium dulce, Manila tamarind	—	1	2	3
Prosopis cineraria, Khijedo*	—	1	—	1
Sapindus laurifolius, Soapnut	—	1	1	2
Sterculia foetida, Wild almond	—	5	1	6
Syzygium cumini, Jambolana	1	1	43	45
Tamarindus indica, Tamarind	3	4	1	8
Zizyphus mauritiana, **Jujube**	2	1	1	4

[1]The scientific names as given by Shah (1978); the common names marked with asterisk are local names and the rest are as given by Maheshwari and Singh (1965).

The Peepul is the main tree used by the birds for nesting in Old City (Table 1). Besides the Peepul which is relatively most numerous, only a few other trees grow in this area, and some of them were also used by the nesting birds (Table 1). Almost all the pairs of Indian Reef Heron

(2) **The suburban areas.** When the Old City started expanding eastward and southward, the

Heronry in Old City

(a) Location of a Peepul tree used by the Large Egret and Indian Reef Heron for nesting. (b) Location of a Banyan tree used by the Large Egret. (c) Location of a Tamarind tree used by the White Ibis. (d) A pair of the Indian Reef Heron on a Peepul branch.

Suburban areas and their nesting birds.

(e) A general view of Bhavnagar with Takhteshwar in the foreground and Old City in the background. (f) A Spoonbill on its nest in Krishnanagar. (g) The White Ibis nestlings and their nest.

The nesting birds and trees in the Peile Garden area

h) The Painted Stork nestlings and an adult on a Tamarind. (i) A Wild Almond tree used for nesting by the Painted Stork in the garden. (j) Chicks of the Night Heron on a Mango tree.

progressive adminstrators of the princely state of Bhavnagar laid out two suburban housing projects known as Krishnanagar and Takhteshwar. In Fig. 1 Krishnanagar is on the east and Takhteshwar is on the west of the railway tract which is generally running from north to south and leading towards Mahuva (a nearby coastal town). The main roads of these suburbs some of which are aligned with the roads emerging from the Old City, are about 21 m (metres) wide (12 m for vehicular traffic and 4.5 m on either side for the footpath) and the internal roads are about 10 m wide. Each residential building is usually placed in a large plot of land, so that all around the building there is considerable space in which large decorative and fruit trees grow. There is also considerable open space; Krishnanagar has a spacious playground and both the suburbs have small unbuilt plots, which were the favourite places of the Cattle Egret for the collection of nest-building materials, particularly the thorny twigs of *Prosopis juliflora*.

The birds had a relatively wide choice of nesting trees of varying height and crown structure in these areas (Table 1). All the pairs of Spoonbill and Pond Heron, the majority of Cattle Egrets and some Night Herons had nested in these areas (Table 2). Here too, no one did any physical harm to the nesting birds

TABLE 2

NESTING DISTRIBUTION OF THE CICONIIFORM BIRDS IN THE THREE LOCALITIES OF BHAVNAGAR DURING THE PEAK NESTING SEASON OF 1980 AND 1981

Species	Year	Total No.* of pairs	No. of pairs%		
			Old City	Peile Garden	Suburbs
Indian Reef Heron	1980	109	94	6	0
	1981	100	100	0	0
Night Heron	1980	176	56	27	17
	1981	159	66	6	28
Large Egret	1980	67	100	0	0
	1981	70	100	0	0
Cattle Egret	1980	2041	9	14	77
	1981	1187	4	7	89
Pond Heron	1980	6	0	0	100
White Ibis	1980	74	26	70	4
	1981	48	100	0	0
Spoonbill	1980	123	0	0	100
	1981	99	0	0	100
Painted Stork	1980	96	0	100	0
	1981	70	0	100	0
All species combined	1980	2692	36	27	37
	1981	1733	53	16	31

*Estimated from the maximum number of active nests observed at one time.

or their broods. However, some house owners resented the birds nesting on their property close to their residence; they disliked the smell of excreta and regurgitated food of the nesting birds and chicks and considered the thorny twigs and branches falling off the nest on the ground a nuisance. These people severely pruned their trees, outside the nesting season, so that birds would be forced to go elsewhere to nest. They also fired crackers to scare away the nesting birds. Besides such activities of some people the pressure on land is increasing and nesting habitat is shrinking. With a phenomenal increase in the price of land in these areas during the present decade, the large housing plots are being subdivided and the trees being cut off to make way for new buildings. If the present trend continues, the birds would lose their important nesting habitat in Bhavnagar in the near future.

(3) **Peile Garden area.** Wedged between the Old City and the newer Takhteshwar is Peile Garden, established in the time of princely state. The Peile Garden area includes Peile Garden, the Town Hall area, a school campus and Panwadi area extending southwest up to the Bus Station (Fig. 1). Some of the tallest exotic as well as indigenous trees of Bhavnagar were located in Peile Garden and its vicinity until a cyclone up-rooted many of them in November 1982. A small pond next to the northern boundary of Peile Garden is now filled up and used as a play-cum-exhibition ground.

All Painted Storks in Bhavnagar had nested in the tall trees of Wild Almond and Tamarind. A small proportion of the other birds, except the Spoonbill, had also been nesting in this area (Table 2). Peile Garden being a public park and much of the property around the garden owned by the public bodies, the Painted Stork and its brood enjoyed full protection. It was not uncommon to see the stork chicks that have survived the fall from the tree, being tended and looked after till fledging by the regular visitors to the garden.

The storks nesting here had to pass through two difficult periods, the Diwali and Kite-flying festivals. The fireworks at night during a week long Diwali festival in October-November scared the birds. During the kite-flying festival which occurs around mid-January, the stork chicks were learning to fly. When they took short flight they often got injured by the strings of the flying kites.

Victoria Park — a potential nesting area

Victoria Park (area of about 2 km^2) is a fenced up area controlled by the Gujarat State Forest Department. A small part of the park is planted into a garden, whereas the rest is thorny deciduous forest. A small pond (Krishnakunj) located within the park is dependent on the Gaurishankar lake for its water (Fig. 1). When Gaurishankar fills up (as it happened in 1979) or overflows (as in 1976), the pond in the park retains water almost up to the next monsoon. Within the pond, there is a small island on which there is a luxuriant growth of thorny bushes and trees. In addition, there are also some thorny trees growing from the bed of the pond.

During the years when the water in the pond remained until the next summer, a number of birds nested on the partially submerged trees and those growing on the pond island; the birds reported to have bred are: Indian Reef Heron, Night Heron, Cattle Egret, Pond Heron, White Ibis, Spoonbill and Little Cormorant, *Phalacrocorax niger* (Dharmakumarsinhji 1977; Shukla 1978). In recent years, however, Gaurishankar rarely fills up during the monsoon, the pond in the park dries up by about the beginning of summer and the birds have not been nesting at this site.

Other heronries near Bhavnagar

The number of ibis and stork pairs nesting in the Bhavnaar colony has fluctuated from year to year. It is now recognised that the Ciconiiform birds are prone to change their nesting place, presumably in response to their shifting food supply (Ogden 1978), and that a short term study of the population fluctuations in a local colony is hard to interpret, unless other colonies in the neighbourhood are also kept under simultaneous observations. While a survey of the heronries in the Saurashtra region is being carried out, we know at present only two other colonies within the radius of at least 20 km from Bhavnagar; one of them is at New Port, Bhavnagar (Naik and Parasharya 1983), and the other at Gogha (Naik *et al.* 1981).

The port area in which the New Port colony is located (Fig. 1), is fully enclosed, the entry of people in it is severely restricted and the birds nesting there are fully protected by the port employees. Here, the Indian Reef Herons have been nesting in the short stunted trees on the roadsides, and the White Ibis has been nesting mainly on the big trees with compact crowns (*Ficus amplissima* and *Tamarindus indicus*) growing near the port office building. Occasionally, a few pairs of the Pond Heron have nested in association with the Reef Heron.

Gogha is a small coastal town 19 km southeast of Bhavnagar. The core nesting area of the Gogha colony is a quadrangle of the office of Mamlatdar (an administrative officer of the smallest administrative unit in India). Here, a grove of small young trees is favoured by the Reef Heron and an old tamarind tree just inside the boundary wall of the quadrangle, is favoured by the Painted Stork. The Painted Stork here, unlike that in Bhavnagar, enjoys only a partial protection. A substantial proportion of the Gogha population (about 7000 people) belongs to the fishing and seafaring communities and their boys occasionally sneak in to stone and kill the young and adult Painted Stork for food, despite the deterring influence of the Mamlatdar's staff. A small number of the Pond Heron, Night Heron and Spoonbill have also nested in Gogha; in 1983, even some White Ibises too nested here.

Feeding Areas

Long distance feeding flights are common in Ciconiiformes (Dusi *et al.* 1971; Custer and Osborn 1978), and it is probable that the birds nesting in Bhavnagar covered very wide area. All the same, the resources of the feeding sites adjacent to the colony were quite important to the birds. The principal feeding areas adjacent to the Bhavnagar colony were (as shown in Fig. 1) the coastal mudflats and Bhavnagar creek north and northeast of the city, the saltpans northeast and east of the city, and the freshwater reservoirs, namely Gaurishankar and the Akawada tank south and southwest of the city. A reservoir (not shown in Fig. 1), about 20 km southwest of the city, was also frequently used by the Painted Stork.

The Indian Reef Heron had been observed feeding mainly on the mudflats and shallow waters of the creek, but, sometimes also on the saltpans and occasionally in shallow waters of the freshwater reservoirs. The Night Heron fed largely at the coastal mudflats, to a certain extent also at the freshwater reservoirs and occasionally at the saltpans. Preference of the White Ibis for feeding from the coast was obvious, but, it fed also at saltpans, freshwater reservoirs, and very rarely on land. The Large Egret fed often in the coastal water and sometimes at the saltpans and in the freshwater reservoirs. The Spoonbills and Painted Storks were seen feeding relatively more often in the freshwater reservoirs, but, they fed sometimes on the saltpans and sea-coast as well (Table 3).

TABLE 3

FEEDING HABITATS OF THE CICONIIFORMES NESTING IN BHAVNAGAR AND FREQUENCY WITH WHICH THEY ARE USED

Species	Frequency of feeding habitat use %*			
	Sea coast	Salt pans	Fresh water reservoirs	Land
Indian Reef Heron	60	30	10	
Night Heron	60	10	30	
White Ibis	50	25	25	
Large Egret	50	25	25	
Cattle Egret			10	90
Spoonbill	25	25	50	
Painted Stork	25	25	50	

* 50 to 90% = Usually or mainly used
30 to 25% = Used sometimes
10% = Used occasionally

The Cattle Egret, which is primarily a terrestrial feeder (Table 3) was seen feeding on the playfields and other open areas within the city and also in and around the croplands southeast of the city (Fig. 1). It fed occasionally on the edge of the freshwater reservoirs also.

Nesting histories

Indian Reef Heron. Nesting of the Reef Heron in Gogha and Bhavnagar was reported by Naik *et al.* (1981). While a comprehensive paper on the breeding of reef heron in Gujarat will be published elsewhere, a brief account of nesting events of this bird in Bhavnagar is given here.

The reef heron was the first bird to start nesting in the Bhavnagar colony; the nesting occurred from March to October (Fig. 2). It built a shallow platform-type nest in which the thorny twigs and branches were often incorporated. The House Crow was the main predator of eggs and chicks. The White Ibis while robbing the nest-material occasionally destroyed the nests. A heavy wind took a toll of eggs and chicks which fell out of the nests.

The reef herons nested mainly on the Peepul in Old City during both the years 1980 and 1981; only a small number nested in the Peile Garden area and a few others during a later part of the season in Krishnanagar.

Night Heron. While the reef heron was the first to start nesting in Bhavnagar, the Night heron was the next to start and the last among the herons and egrets to terminate nesting. The bird nested from March-April to October-November (Fig. 2). It usually selected for its nesting the trees on which some reef herons were already nesting, whereas during the later part of the season it also selected the trees in which the Cattle Egrets were nesting. The bird's tendency to nest in a mixed heronry was most obvious in Krishnanagar, where despite a wide selection of trees available for nesting, the bird nested mainly on the trees that were being used by the Cattle egret. In a mixed nesting, the Night Heron preferred to nest on the topmost parts of the tree. The bird occasionally had agonistic encounters with the reef heron and cattle egret, while stealing nest materials from their nests.

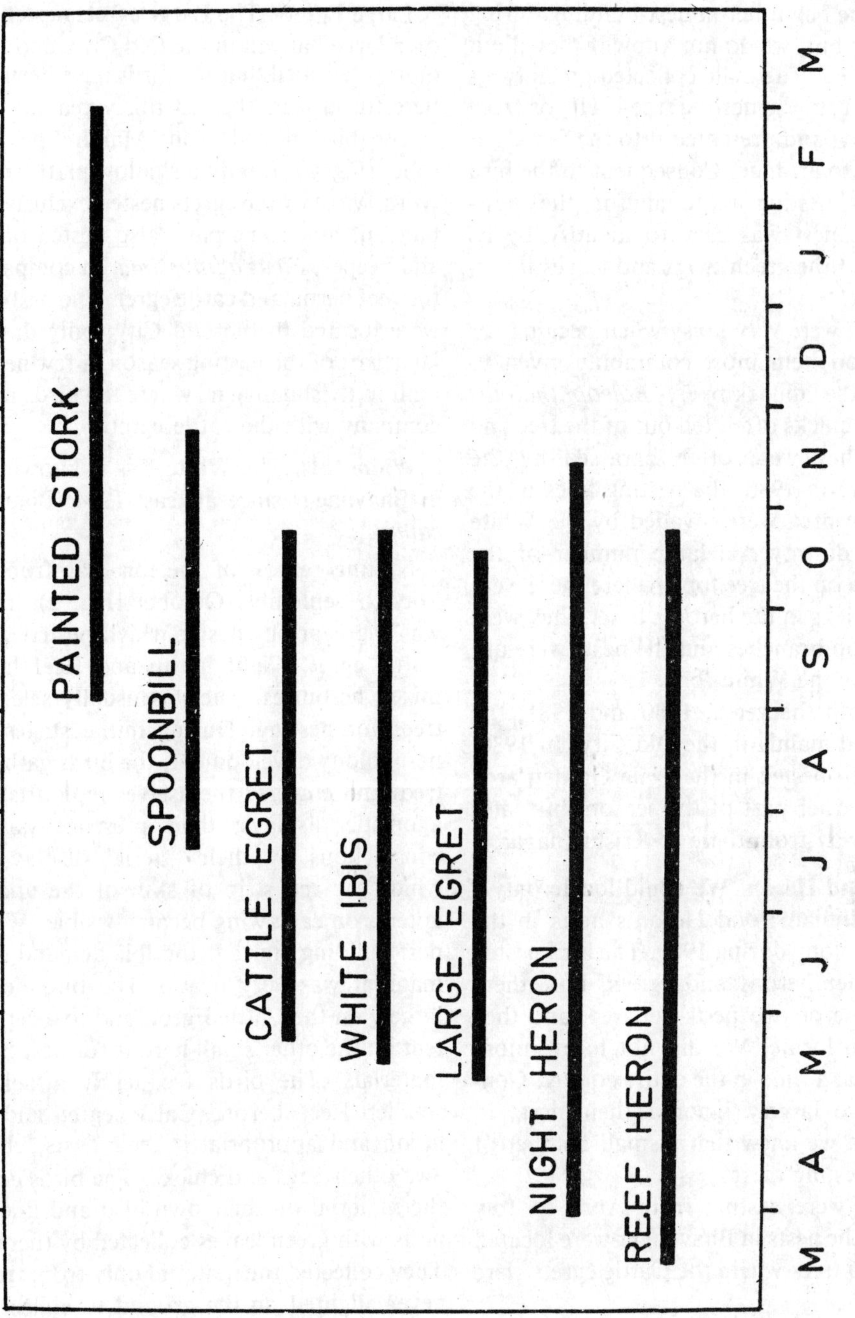

A summary of the nesting schedules of birds in the Bhavnagar Colony. The span of nesting season for each species is shown by a horizontal bar.

We saw the Night heron nest-building during the daytime, but, we do not know if they did it at night as well. The male collected green twigs with leaves from the nesting tree itself, or from a tree near by, and presented it to the female at the nest-site to arrange. Consequent to the bird using green nesting material for the nest-building, its nest was easy to identify by its bulkiness and the green twigs and leaves incorporated in it.

The chicks were very noisy when begging for food. A food item most commonly given to them was the mudskipper, *Boleophthalmus* species. The chicks often fell out of the tree and died, and they were often harassed by the House Crow. In 1980, the nesting trees in the Peile Garden area were invaded by the White Ibis, which destroyed a large number of the heron's nests on the tree tops; where there were grown up chicks in the heron's nests, they were pushed out on branches and the nests were appropriated by the White Ibis.

During both the years, 1980 and 1981, the herons nested mainly in the Old City. In 1980, some of them nested in the Peile Garden area during the earlier part of the season, but later on moved away from there to Krishnanagar.

Indian Pond Heron. We could locate only a few of the Indian Pond Heron's nests in the Bhavnagar colony during 1980. The bird nested with the other herons and egrets, but, there were only one or two nests per tree, and they were hard to locate. We did not locate more than 6 nests at a time in the entire colony. Consequently, we largely ignored their nests in 1981, though we knew that a small number of them were nesting there.

The birds were nesting from April to July (Fig. 2). All the nests in Bhavnagar were located in the mango trees where the Cattle egrets were also nesting.

Large Egrets. The Large egrets nested mainly on a large banyan in the Old City, and local inquiries revealed that the birds have been nesting here for at least the last thirty years.

The bird nested from March-April to October (Fig. 2). It built a shallow platform of dry twigs. Most of the egrets nested exclusively on a banyan, but, some pairs also nested on peepul and peeper, *Ficus amplissima,* in company with the reef heron and cattle egret. The nesting trees were located in the Old City; only during the later part of the nesting season, a few nests were built in Krishnanagar, where the birds nested in company with the cattle egret.

White Ibis. The White Ibis is known to nest in Bhavnagar since at least 1974 (Bhatt, *pers. comm.*).

Nesting season of the ibis was from April-May to September-October (Fig. 2). The bird was a gregarious nester which nested with the Cattle egret, Night heron and Reef heron in mixed heronries. The ibis usually selected big trees for nesting. During initial stages of the nest colony development, the birds gathered on trees and engaged themselves in courtship and agonistic displays; their presence was made conspicuous by their aerial display during which the red strip of skin of the underwing apteria on each wing became visible. When the nest-building started, the ibis demand of nest-material was very heavy. The bird depended largely on the Cattle Egret, and to a certain extent on the other small herons for nest-building materials. The birds frequently attacked the smaller Reef heron, Cattle egret and Night heron and appropriated their nests, chucking away their eggs and chicks. The birds collected the material on their own also and lined their nests with green leaves collected by themselves. They collected the material only from trees and never alighted on the ground to collect it. As the nests came up crowded together on a tree top, their rims almost touched.

The ibis was notorious for changing its nesting sites. One reason for a change of sites was apparently the bird's dependence on the Cattle egret for nesting material. It often had to shift its nesting sites to wherever the Cattle egrets were nesting in Bhavnagar. In 1980, the birds settled down where the Cattle egrets were nesting in the Peile Garden area. However, the Cattle egrets had just started their nests there, so that there was very little nesting material that the ibis could appropriate. Perhaps because of this, some of the ibises deserted their nesting sites and went over to the Old City area where the Cattle egret's nesting was well advanced. In 1981, when only a few pairs of the Cattle egrets nested in the Peile Garden area, all the ibises nested with the Cattle Egrets in the Old City (where only some ibises had nested in the previous year). If the change of nesting sites in 1980 and 1981 was related to the dependence of the ibis on the Cattle egret for nesting material, we have no explanation for the fact that during these years there were hardly any ibis nesting in the suburban areas, which were patronised by the majority of the Cattle egrets. In 1982, almost the whole population of ibis (except for a pair nesting in Peile Garden) shifted out of Bhavnagar all together; the reason for this exodus was not clear. In 1983, the birds arrived late in early July and nested in Takhteshwar and other areas wherever there were large concentrations of the nesting Cattle egret.

Annual variations in the number of White ibis nesting in the Bhavnagar colony as well as in the New Port colony were considerable. It appears that about 126 to 136 pairs nesting in this part of the country get distributed mainly between the Bhavnagar and New Port colonies in different proportion in different years.

Cattle egret. The Cattle egret has been nesting mainly in Krishnanagar, but some pairs have nested in the Peile Garden and the Old City areas. The nesting in Krishnanagar has been observed by the local residents since 1962, though they report that the nesting has often shifted from one group of trees to the other in different years. One of us (B.M.P.) has seen the Cattle egret nesting in a school compound in the Peile Garden area since 1970 and the local inquiries revealed that the egret has been existing there since at least 20 years. We do not know the history of the egret nesting in the Old City.

The nesting season was from May to October (Fig. 2). The bird had a tendency to segregate from the other species for nesting. The mango trees were most commonly used for nesting in Krishnanagar. The birds collected dry or green twigs, thorny branches and even metal wires for nest-building; these materials, were collected from trees as well as from the ground. The birds also stole the material from the unguarded nests of conspecific nesters and in doing this they occasionally ejected the nest contents. The Cattle egret's habit of stealing nest-material has been recorded by other workers as well (see, Siegfried 1971, for a review). Most of the other species stole or robbed nest-materials from the egret's nests, and in doing this they too sometimes ejected the egret's eggs or chicks. In th Peile Garden area as well as in the Old City, the White ibis occupied some of the egret's nests and demolished several others while robbing the nest-material.

Spoonbill. The Spoonbill is a common resident in the Saurashtra and Kachchh regions of Gujarat. However, there are only two published records of its nesting here (Ali 1954; Shukla 1978). One of us (B.M.P.) has seen the Spoonbill nesting in Bhavnagar since 1974.

The bird was a late nester and started nesting in mid-July when the monsoon had properly set in. The nesting terminated in November (Fig. 2). It nested only in Krishnanagar, mainly on the Jambolana tree. A nest-building bird simply bent the pliable terminal branches of the tree to make a base for its nest and piled over it the Jambolana branches and twigs, which snap easily under gentle pressure. The birds usually collected nesting material directly from the nesting tree and sometimes thorny branches from the deserted Cattle egret's nests in the nearby trees. It also used materials, such as, dry twigs, metal wires and iron scrap from the deserted nests of the House Crow and had a tendency to collect nest-material from the unguarded nests of conspecific neighbours. The nest-building once started, proceeded at a fast pace. During the initial stages of the colony formation, the Spoonbills visited from time to time, the trees selected for nesting, but did not stay there; however, when the nest-building started the birds were on or around the nesting trees throughout the day (they probably went out for feeding at night). Mortality of the eggs and chicks was primarily because of their falling out of the nests. During a cyclone in November of 1982, some of the nestling fell out and were lost.

The number of nesting pairs were 123 in 1980, 99 in 1981, 48 in 1982 and 146 in 1983. Except a few pairs observed nesting in Gogha, we know of no other colony of the Spoonbill outside Bhavnagar, and therefore we have no indication of where a large number of spoonbills missing from the Bhavnagar colony in 1981 and 1982, might have gone.

Painted Stork. The Painted Stork is the only stork common in the arid and semi-arid regions of Saurashtra, but its breeding colonies have not been documented. The stork colony in Bhavnagar has been there for the last twenty years, and that in Gogha for the last 50 to 60 years (Desai, *pers. comm.*).

The storks usually arrived at their nesting sites in the Peile Garden area during late August or early September when the monsoon started withdrawing. Some birds occupied the old nest-platforms, whereas the others looked for suitable sites. The nesting season lasted from September to March (Fig. 2). The birds broke green twigs and branches from the nearby trees and brought them to their nests. They also brought in thorny branches of *Acacia* from a long distance. The nests were always built at a height of 40-50 feet off the ground on top of tall trees. There were no other birds nesting with the storks on their nesting trees, except that a few White ibis might still be attending their nestlings in advance stages, when the storks arrived to breed there. The Flying Foxes (*Pteropus giganteus*) had been roosting in the nesting trees of the storks throughout the year. The stork nestlings (in early stages) occasionally fell out of the nests. Falling from a great height they usually died of injury, but, if they survived they were looked after by the regular visitors to Peile Garden, aided by the gardeners.

The number of nesting pairs varied in the Bhavnagar colony in different years, but these variations were more or less parallel with those in the Gogha colony suggesting thereby that the variations were influenced by the casual factors common to both the colonies.

The only time that we know of, when the storks did not breed was in 1974 and 1982; Gaurishankar was nearly dry in late August of these years.

Other birds

Black Ibis. This bird had nested in Krishnanagar during our study period. As it nested solitarily, or in a loose colony, we paid attention to its nesting only when we happened to come across its nest during our routine check of its colonial relatives' nests. We saw three pairs nesting in 1980 and one each in 1981 and

1982. The nests were on the peepul or coconut trees. the consolidated data indicated that the bird nested in Bhavnagar from February-March to October. It did not associate with the other colonial nesters.

Little Cormorant. This bird had nested in Bhavnagar only occasionally but if the right conditions are provided they may nest here regularly. A number of pairs were reported to be breeding in Victoria Park in March 1977 (Shukla 1978). During 1979, there were four nests of the cormorant in the Peile Garden area in August. In 1980, there were about 400 cormorants in the same area but none of them nested anywhere in the city.

DISCUSSION

While the Ciconiiform birds commonly nest in several cities and villages of Gujarat, none of these colonies surpasses the Bhavnagar colony in the diversity of its nesting birds. The geographical location (direct rail-link with Ahmedabad and a connection with Bombay by an air-route) increases potential of the colony as a tourist attraction. The Bhavnagar colony is also ideal for imparting education about wildlife to our children and for providing recreational facilities to those urbanites who would not forgo the comforts of urban living for wildlife-watching. Moreover, an urban nest-colony is of special scientific interest, since it represents the birds' adjustment to the loss of their natural nesting habitats.

Primary nesting requirements of the tree-nesting colonial Ciconiiformes are the availability of adequate food for themselves and their chicks and safe sites for nesting. These requirements are met with to a large extent, and therefore the nesting colony is flourishing in Bhavnagar since long.

Many of the Ciconiiform birds seem to feed on a wide variety of prey species. However, since each species has its distinctive physical and behavioural traits it can efficiently forage only in certain types of habitats. The location of a species' nesting colony would, therefore, be largely dependent upon the availability of a particular habitat type. A wide variety of habitats, namely marine, freshwater and terrestrial, available close to the colony is one of the reasons for a great diversity and number of birds breeding in Bhavnagar. The reef and night herons which foraged exclusively, or mainly, in marine habitats throughout the year, roosted in Bhavnagar during the non-nesting season as well; their numbers apparently swelled in the nesting season as the birds from the surrounding areas converged to Bhavnagar for nesting. The Large egret did not roost in Bhavnagar outside the nesting season, but, it heavily depended on marine food when it was nesting there. These three species of herons, because of their abilities to exploit the marine habitat for food, were nearly unaffected by the yearly fluctuations in the food supply from the freshwater habitat and had more or less stable nesting populations in Bhavnagar. On the other hand, the numbers of Painted Stork and Spoonbill were heavily dependent on the supply of freshwater food, and consequently the number of their nesting pairs was related to the water level in the freshwater reservoir at the start of the nesting season (Parasharya and Naik 1984). The White Ibis seemed to shift between Bhavnagar, Gogha and New Port colonies for the reasons which were not clear. The Cattle Egret is a terrestrial feeder; the availability of its insect food, and consequently the number of nesting pairs would vary with the annual rainfall pattern.

The colonial nesting being conspicuous, the prime requirement for such a nesting is a nesting place inaccessible to the predators. The tree-nesting colonial water birds usually nest on trees standing in a marsh, where they are relatively safe from the interference and predation by land animals. Such a nesting habitat does not exist any more in most parts of Saurashtra so that the birds have taken to nesting in cities and villages where they are usually not molested. In Bhavnagar, the birds are well protected. The cultural environment of a dominant religious group among the residents of the city does not permit deliberate harassment, persecution or killing of birds and cutting of the peepuls, which are almost the only trees in the fully built-up areas.

The switch over from the marshy to urban habitat has induced the birds to make adjustment in their breeding biology. One of the main problems of urban nesting is the scarcity of nesting material; while smaller species meet their requirement by collecting nesting material dropped on the ground, the larger species extensively rob or steal materials from the nests of small species (Naik and Parasharya 1984a). Another adjustment is changes in their breeding timing. While nesting in marshy habitats, the birds start nesting after the monsoon breaks and the ground around nesting trees gets flooded to make the trees safe from the approach of ground predators. In the urban habitat, the safe nesting sites are available all the time so that as soon as the availability of food is assured the birds start nesting; several species of Ciconiiformes in Bhavnagar nest earlier than those in marshy habitat (Naik and Parasharya 1984a; Parasharya and Naik 1984). Birds also seem to have adjusted to newer predators; they face now the urban crows and domestic cats instead of traditional marshland predators, such as, the snakes, birds-of-prey and tree-climbing mammals. Further on available to the birds as nesting substrate a greater diversity of plant species, differing widely in crown and branching structure, in the suburban gardens (Table 1) than in a marshland.

Having established recreational, educational and scientific values of the Bhavnagar colony, we submit that a management programme for conserving this colony should be drawn up and executed. In drawing up such a management programme, the following conservation measures suggested on the basis of the facts brought out by the present study may be considered.

No conservation programme can be carried out without the full cooperation from the Bhavnagar citizens. Though proportion of the populace knowledgeable about the birdlife is higher in Bhavnagar than elsewhere in Gujarat, a large number of them are still not aware of the birds nesting in their town. An extensive publicity programme should be immediately undertaken to make the general public and city-fathers aware of the nesting birds and a need for conserving their nesting colony.

The mudflats and estuaries on the Bhavnagar coast, where the nesting birds feed, have been relatively free from pollution so far, and they should be left undisturbed in the future. The mangroves on these mudflats, because of indiscriminate exploitation, are in extremely poor condition. If the mangroves are protected and allowed to regenerate, they may provide yet another important habitat (which is marginal at present) for the birds to forage. The pressure of urban development on the freshwater reservoirs needs to be eased up. Gaurishankar is almost totally neglected by the urban development authorities, despite the fact that this lake is a source of water supply to the Bhavnagar city. Instead of looking for an alternative source of water for the city, a development plan for a multipurpose use of the lake should be undertaken so that the water level can be maintained in the lake for the advantage of the people and birds throughout the year.

Among the nesting areas, there is not much that could be done to improve the situation in the old city, but, a better condition for the nesting birds can be created in the suburban and Peile Garden areas. Further divisions of the housing plots and cutting of trees in Krishnanagar and Takhteshwar should be severely restricted. Peile Garden should be extensively planted with selected tall trees even at the expense of the flower-beds and lawns. Besides, possibilities of creating new nesting areas should be explored. Victoria Park would turn into a permanent nesting area if the Krishnakunj pond within the Park fills up every year and the water level is regulated during the dry season. Krishnakunj would retain water round the year, only if the water level in Gaurishankar is regulated as suggested herein before.

It is necessary to constitute an authority for an overall management of the colony. This task can be accomplished by the Bhavnagar Municipal Corporation, in collaboration with the wildlife wing of the State Forest Department which is already looking after Victoria Park at present. The minimum routine work to be carried out by the proposed colony management authority would be to keep the ground below the nesting trees free from the thorny twigs and food items falling from the nests, the stocking of nest-building materials off the ground at suitable places in the city so that the materials are readily available to the birds for their use, and maintaining a record of the number of nesting birds and their breeding performance in different areas.

The value of Bhavnagar colony would only enhance if some conservation measures are carried out simultaneously in the New Port and Gogha colonies. The New Port area is out of bounds for the general public and visiting tourists, but, it is an important reserve from which the Bhavnagar colony draws it nesting birds from time to time. The dock workers in New Port have been doing commendable job of giving total protection to the nesting birds in their work area. However, there is an acute shortage of tall trees for the birds to nest and this can be easily remedied by the port authority. The quadrangle of the Mamlatdar's office in Gogha is extensively planted with trees, every one of which is used by the nesting birds. Most of the birds nesting there are protected, but, the chicks of Painted Stork do not enjoy full protection; this situation can be remedied by the Mamlatdar's staff residing on the spot.

ACKNOWLEDGEMENTS

One of us (B.M P.) is grateful to the Council of Scientific and Industrial Research, New Delhi, for providing the Junior Research Fellowship. We are thankful to the people of Bhavnagar for permitting us to work on their private property and their kind cooperation during the study period. Deep interest taken by the Saurashtra Branch of World Wildlife Fund —India in this work was a source of encouragement to us, and it gives us pleasure to acknowledge it. We are grateful to Messrs P.K. Desai, H.V. Shukla and K.H. Bhatt for permitting us to use their unpublished observations and Mr N.K. Pandya, Deputy Town Planner, Bhavnagar Area Development Authority, for patiently answering our numerous queries and providing us with the maps of the city.

REFERENCES

ALI, S. (1954): The Birds of Gujarat I. *J. Bombay nat. Hist. Soc.* **52**(2 & 3): 374-458.

CUSTER, T.W. & OSBORN, R.G. (1978): Feeding habitat use by colonially-breeding herons, egrets, and ibises in North Carolina. *Auk* **95**: 733-743.

DHARMAKUMARSINHJI, K.S. (1977): Nesting of Night Heron (*Nycticorax nycticorax* Linnaeus). *Pavo* **15**: 165-166.

DUSI, J.L., DUSI, R.T., BATEMAN, D.L., MCDONALD, C.A., STUART, J.J. & DISMAKES, J.F. (1971): Ecological impacts of wading birds on the aquatic environment. *Water Resour. Res. Inst. Bull.* No. 5.

MAHESHWARI, P. & SINGH, U. (1965): Dictionary of Economic Plants of India. Indian Council of Agricultural Research, New Delhi.

MORSE, D.H. (1974): Niche breadth as a function of social dominance. *Amer. Nat.* **108**: 818-830.

NAIK, R.M. & PARASHARYA, B.M. (1984a): Problems of urban nesting. Communicated for publication.

__________ (1984b): Impact of the food availability, natural habitat destruction and regional cultural variations of human settlements on the nesting distribution of a coastal bird *Egretta gularis*, in western India. Communicated for publication in *J. Bombay nat. Hist. Soc.*

__________ (1984c): Breeding season of the Indian Reef Heron. Communicated for publication.

__________, PATEL, B.H. & MANSURY, A.P. (1981): The timing of breeding season and interbreeding between the phases in the Indian Reef Heron, *Egretta gularis* (Bosc). *J. Bombay nat. Hist. Soc.* **78**: 494-497.

OGDEN, J.C. (1978): Recent population trends of colonial wading birds on the Atlantic and Gulf coastal plains. *In*: Wading Birds. Res. Rep. No. 7 of Natl. Aud. Soc. pp. 137-154.

PARASHARYA, B.M. & NAIK, R.M. (1983): The juvenile plumage of the Little Egret compared with that of the whitephase Indian Reef Heron. *J. Bombay nat. Hist. Soc.* **81**(3): 693-5.

__________ (1984): Breeding seasons of Ciconiiform birds in the coastal areas of western India. Communicated for publication.

RIPLEY, S.D. (1982): A Synopsis of the Birds of India and Pakistan. Bombay Natural History Society, Bombay.

SHAH, G.L. (1978): Flora of Gujarat, Part I & II. Sardar Patel University, Vallabh Vidyanagar.

SHUKLA, R.H. (1978): Early breeding in Bhavnagar. *Newsletter for Birdwatchers* **18**(2): 7-9.

SIEGFRIED, W.R. (1971): The nest of the Cattle Egret. *Ostrich* **42**: 193-197.

__________ (1972): Breeding success and reproductive output of the Cattle Egret. *Ostrich* **43**: 43-55.

APPENDIX

The Executive Committee of the Saurashtra Branch of World Wildlife Fund—India met at Bhavnagar on 27 November 1983 to consider the study report of the Bhavnagar heronry by Parasharya and Naik. The Committee accepted the report and adopted following resolutions for further action:

1. RECOGNISES the recreational, educational and scientific value of the urban heronries of Saurashtra, and notes that the heronry at Bhavnagar, where on the average about 2000 pairs of the Large Egret, Indian Pond Heron, Cattle Egret, Indian Reef Heron, Night Heron, Painted Stork, White Ibis, Black Ibis and Spoonbill have been regularly nesting since years, is the most spectacular among the urban heronries.
2. PUTS it on record that the successful nesting of birds in the Bhavnagar heronry owes it to a large extent to public interest in the wildlife, generated by K.S. Dharmakumarsinhji, M.K.S. Shivbhadrasinhji and the Wildlife Conservation Society of Bhavnagar.
3. URGES the people of Bhavnagar to bear with the nesting birds of their heronry and continue to give them the protection which they have been giving for all these years.
4. PROPOSES that the Government of Gujarat acknowledges the wildlife conservation practised silently by the people of Bhavnagar by protecting the Bhavnagar heronry even at their personal inconvenience.
5. REQUESTS the Department of Tourism to record the Bhavnagar heronry as an important tourist spot of Gujarat and to give it due publicity.
6. REQUESTS the Bhavnagar Municipal Corporation to set up a Committee in association with the Wildlife Conservation Society of Bhavnagar, to prepare a working plan for the development and management of the Bhavnagar heronry immediately.
7. RECORDS that the New Port area of Bhavnagar supports the single biggest nesting colony of more than a thousand pairs of the In-

dian Reef Heron, in India, and

RECOGNISES with due humility that in protecting the New Port heronry, the Port Officer, his staff and dock workers are doing a better job of wildlife conservation than many agencies directly concerned with the Wildlife,

and

on considering the number of nesting trees to be the only factor limiting the size of the New port heronry, URGES the Port Officer to get more of some appropriate trees planted at suitable places in the Port area.

8. PUTS it on record that the Gogha heronry continues to exist only because the Mamlatdar of Gogha and his staff have been actively protecting the core area of heronry located within the quadrangle of their office premises.

9. REQUESTS the Wildlife Conservation Society and Department of Forests, Government of Gujarat, to extend their Nature Education Programme to Gogha so as to create a public awareness of the importance of birds nesting in that town.

SHIVRAJKUMAR KHACHAR
Chairman
SAURASHTRA BRANCH
WORLD WILDLIFE FUND – INDIA.

An assessment of the present Distribution and Population Status of the Lesser Florican

H.S.A. YAHYA

ABSTRACT

The Lesser Florican, or the 'leekh' as it is commonly known is the smallest of the four species of Bustards (Otididae: Gruiformes) found in the Indian Subcontinent. Recent reports on the status of this species, endemic to India, have been quite alarming and therefore the Bombay Natural History Society decided to investigate the status and ecology of the species under the aegis of the Society's Endangered Species Project. As a first step a survey of florican habitat in the states in which the species occurred was undertaken. This report records the findings of the survey undertaken in Madhya Pradesh, Gujarat, Maharashtra and Bihar between June 1982 and January 1983. Altogether 90 birds were seen in their breeding ground in Madhya Pradesh and Gujarat. Hunting by local shikaris and tribals still persists in the areas where the Floricans occur. A long-term study on the ecology and biology of this endangered species is urgently needed to plan for its affective management.

HABITAT

All birds seen were in "grass birs" (grassy fields) interspersed with *Butea, Acacia, Tectona, Lantana* and *Zizyphus* bushes. Most of the birs were bounded by Soyabean, Cotton, Millet and Groundnut cultivations. This type of "Grass bir" are owned by medium to big cultivators for the lush fodder grass. The Maharaja of Sailana owned the largest bir of about 1000 hectares of Sailana in which we observed the maximum number of Floricans at a time (Table 2). Ungrazed grasslands with a few bushes, had the largest number of birds. The best soil for luxuriant growth of a good grass bir is Black Cotton Soil. Birds were not found in grass birs which were over-grazed or grew on other than black cotton soil. Incidentally as is obvious from the map, Lesser Floricans breed only in the area the soil is of the black cotton type — there is no report of their breeding beyond this limit. Floricans are shy birds and do not normally occur in the smaller grass birs (less than 1 hectare or so in size) and near human habitation. However, at Guman Pura (Table 2) it was reported that two females were living permanently near wells and were quite bold and could be seen throughout the year. This was not found true on my three successive visits.

STATUS AND DISTRIBUTION

According to Ali & Ripley (1980) the Lesser Florican which was once very common in the greater part of the Peninsula is presently rare or absent over much of its former range. The distribution is now much restricted and the numbers are dwindling due to human population pressure—encroachment on its habitat by cultivation plus direct persecution. Though the birds had been reported to occur in parts of Punjab, Gujarat, Karnataka, Tamil Nadu, Kerala, Uttar Pradesh, Terai region of Nepal, Bihar, Orissa, West Bengal and in Bhutan Duras, the present authentic report of its occurrence is known only from some parts of Madhya Pradesh, Gujarat and Maharashtra. Since the bird is an irregularly local migrant their non-breeding habitat is not known. Inspite of widespread advertisement through newspapers, handbills, and questionaires, no report has been obtained on their non-breeding habitat. However, it is certain that their breeding and non-breeding habitats do not coincide (Dharakumarsinhji 1950). According to Isakov (1976) the Great Bustard *Otis tarda* also has different breeding and non-breeding habitats. The monthwise occurrence of the lesser florican in different localities is not clear from the existing literature (Table 1). There is no report of their whereabouts during the months December to March, except a few stray sightings, based on very old reports. Since then there have been considerable changes in the habitats and large areas of grassy fields no longer exist. Even in Madhya Pradesh and Gujarat where intensive survey was made and floricans breed today, it was understood that within 10 years more than 50% of the grasslands have been converted into agricultural fields and rest are also being converted on a large scale. As stated above, the best habitats we found during the survey are at Sailana. Sailana is 17 km north-east of Ratlam. The Sailana grass bir is a continuous stretch of about 100 hectares of good undulating grass land. However, several grass birs around Jaora, Sardarpur and Dhar are also very suitable habitats. Table 2 gives the breakdown of the birds seen at different locations in Madhya Pradesh.

Fortunately the Madhya Pradesh Government has declared Sailana grass bir as a florican sanctuary. Around Sardarpur also Charavatkibir, Gomanpura, Tarkheri and Halatari Bir are very suitable places where the Lesser Florican breed every year. Although the tribals kill incubating females and eat the eggs (see observations) Sardarpur and Sailana, at a distance of about 160 km each other can be two ideal places for establishing research stations for the intensive study of the Lesser Florican in Madhya Pradesh.

Besides many cultivated areas, altogether 40 grass birs were visited in Bhavnagar, Amreli, Gir (East and West) Junagarh, Rajkot, Jamnagar, Panchnagar, Ahmedabad and Saberkantha districts of Gujarat. Among the areas visited Bhavnagar had the best rain last year and 6 Lesser Floricans were seen. In Jamnagar and Rajkot the Lesser Florican has been reported in good number (Table 3) but as at the time of my visit grass had grown tall, the display activities of the bird were reduced, and we could see only 18 birds. However, we obtained some interesting information.

At Rajkot I met a group of 4 persons who exclusively shoot the Lesser Floricans; each year, each of them bag about 20 birds. This they have been doing for 20 years. According to one of them (who kindly showed me ten very good grass birs around Rajkot) the other factors such as spraying of pesticides by helicopter, inadequate management by the forest department, over-grazing in reserved areas etc. were more adverse in their effect than the shooting of the birds. However, I was able to convince him that shooting of the birds was an equally severe factor for the decline of the Florican population. The conservator of forests, Junagarh, reported having seen many lesser floricans in their non-breeding plumage in Banni tract of Kutch during Jan.-Feb. 1969. This requires confirmation. Bhavnagar, Jamnagar and Junagarh areas have excellent potential as the Lesser Florican breeding habitats, but their number is declining in these localities as well as in the other areas and hence Baker (1921) had opined long back that the lesser florican might be extinct in another half-a-century. However, the floricans still exist in some numbers in central and western India.

Although lesser floricans have been reported to occur in some numbers in some parts of Maharashtra in recent years, I could not see any during my visit to Sholapur, Karnala, Karzat, Mirajgaon, Hiradgaon, Davelgaon, Araygaon areas. This could be due to the drought in the localities at the time of visit. Around Nagpur and Umrer area where adequate rain had been recorded, no lesser florican was seen during a five days visit. Chittampali, (*pers. comm.*) who had undertaken a survey of Lesser Florican status in 8 districts (Nagpur, Akola, Vardha, Bhandara, Yeotmal, Amravati, Buldhana and Chandrapur) of Vidharba region of Maharashtra did not see any lesser florican in these areas. According to him at Umrer a Pardhi (a tribe of nomad shikari) killed a female florican in 1981 and thus the occurrence of the Florican in some number could not be ruled out in this area.

TABLE 1

MONTHWISE OCCURRENCE OF LESSER FLORICAN IN DIFFERENT AREAS

Areas	J	F	M	A	M	J	J	A	S	O	N	D	Source
Various breeding grounds in Central India, Gujarat, Maharashtra (Deccan), Rajasthan							×	×	×	×	×		Hume & Marshall 1879
Trichinopoly (South India)								×	×	×	×		-do-
Meerut (U.P.)												×	-do-
Bihar				×	×								C.M. Inglis in Baker 1921
Maldah (West Bengal)				×	×	×							Baker 1921 GAME BIRDS OF INDIA
Ratnagiri		×											-do-
Kathiawar, Deccan etc.							×	×	×	×			Baker 1935
Kathiawar						×	×	×	×		×?	×?	Dharmakumarsinhji 1950
Punjab, Rajasthan, M.P., Gujarat, (Saurashtra)							×	×	×	×			Ali & Ripley 1980
Peninsular India	(During non breeding season?)												-do-
Bhavnagar						×	×	×	×	×	×		Personal enquiry from various people and Shivbhadrakumarsinhji
Madhya Pradesh (Sardarpur, Dhar areas)							×	×	×	×	×		Personal observations and enquiry

TABLE 2

BREAKDOWN OF THE LESSER FLORICANS IN DIFFERENT AREAS BETWEEN 3rd and 13th AUGUST AND OCTOBER 2nd to 16th, 1982 in MADHYA PRADESH

Locality	App. area	Birds seen			Local information on occurrence	Local contact	Remarks
		seen	*heard	total			
Gumanpura Bir (Private) 19 km from Sardarpur	50 acrs	1	1	1	2	Bharat Singh/Bheru Singh, Vill. P.O. Gumanpura, Via Bagh, Dist. Dhar	Visited again after 9 days. A male perhaps the same was seen on both occasions.
Holataris Bir 19 km from Sardapur	10 acrs				2	-do-	
Gumanpura plantation 24 km from Sardapur	70 acrs (adjacent to plantation)				2	-do-	
Tarkheri 35 km from Sardapur	8 to 10 acrs	5	1	5	1	Sajjan Singh Vill., & P.O. Tarkhari Dist. Jhabua	One female was reported nesting last year. Sajjan Singh had once taken 8 eggs which hatched after 22 days incubation under domestic hen. The florican chick survived for 14 days and then all were killed by a cat?
Semlia grass vid/ panpura grass vid (Govt. grass vid) 25 km from Sardarpur							Visited twice but did not see bird. The grassland is over-grazed.
Sindurka (Govt.) vid. 15 km from Jaora (By the side of the road)	—	—	—	—			Appears to be good area for florican.
Kharwa 20 km from Jaora	—	—	—	—			-do-
Bal Kheri. Vakil Sahib ki vid. 8 km from Agra	—	—	—	—	2	Omkarlal Jai, teacher, Umerca village dist. Shajapur	Not investigated thoroughly.
Buchilipather (Govt. vid)	700 acres	—	—	—	—	The D.F.O., Ujjain	Proposed Florican Sanctuary. Dry at the time of visit. No bird reported to be seen in this area. A pack of 12 wolves reported living permanently 6 km from this place.

Locality	App. area	Birds seen: seen	*heard	total	Local information on occurrence	Local contact	Remarks
Bhalwa	—	—	—	—	3♂♂, 2♀♀	Bharat Singh MLA Jaora	Seen by Dr. Salim Ali and party last year.
Bharat Singh's grass vid near polytechnic 3 km from Jaora	—	—	—	—	1 1	-do-	One was shot by a tribal 15 days before our visit.
Nagdiv	—	—	—	—	—	-do-	Looks to be a good area out near to the village.
Ratimali (Charavat. Kabir) (Pvy) 16 km from Sardarpur	7-8 acres three patches of the same size	9	1	9	3	Bhupendra Singh vill. & P.O. Ratimali, via Sardarpur dist. Dhar.	Maximum number in a particular area. Very easy to locate and study reported to be nesting there. Bhupendra, Singh used to shoot 8-10 birds each year. Has left shooting since last year. He says his father must have shot 500 birds.
Bola Shaitan, Kiwid 6 km from Sardarpur	5 acres	1	1	1	—	Mr. M.P. Lad Conservator of forests	He had seen a Bird (o) at the same place last year also.
Sailana 2 km from Sailana	1000 acres	9	2	9	4	Mr. Vikram Singh Rajkumar Sailana	The biggest grass vid seen so far. Earlier shooting preserve of the Ex Maharaja, most ideal place for the floricans; can be taken up as intensive study area.
Puniya Kheri Bamboo Plantation Camp No. 2	—	—	—	—	—	Chowkidar Puniya Kheri	Undulating grass land, Hillocks interspersed with teak plantations. Bamboo was planted in 1981-82 season.
Sherpur vid (govt.) 10 km from Sailana	150 acres	1		1	—	Udai Singh Sherpur village P.O. Sailana dist. Ratlam	Proposed florican sanctuary. One tribal was caught with a muzzle loading gun on 5.8.82. Good area.
Kalalia near Ringnoda (Pvy.) 14 km from Jaora	5 acres	2	—	2	—	Bharat Singhiji MLA, Jaora	Seen last year also. Very good grass bir. Birds appear to be bold; can be seen any time. Area be taken up for intensive study.

*not included in total

TABLE 3

DETAILS OF GRASS BIRS VISITED IN GUJARAT AND NUMBER OF LESSER FLORICANS SEEN

Name of grass bir	Nature	Area (acres)	Condition for occurrence of L. florican		Birds seen/Recent report & remarks
Bhavnagar dist.					
Velavadar National Park	R	1000+	P	—	Visited earlier also
Thala (Sihor)	R	913	G	—	Grazing stopped recently.
Piparla, Govt.	R	1460	P	—	Nearby private birs better
Piparla, Private		—	G	3	Ideal habitat surrounded by G. nut fields.
Sajensar (Jorsingh Garh)	R	825	G	—	Visited earlier also
10 km on Ghagh Rd., from Bhavnagar	C	—	G	2	Males seen by Shivbhadra K. Sinhji
Victoria Garden	R	—	P	—	Earlier, Excellent shooting place: S.K. Sinhji
27th km from Bhavnagar	Private	—	Vg	—	Report of occurrence in most years.
Dolthi (*Gir east*)	Private	—	Vg	2	Seen by Walimond Rathod (local panch)
Sarasia	R	1000+	Vg	—	Visited by **Ridley *et al.* also.
Karamdhari	R	—	Vg	—	
Vakaria	R	—	G	—	Visited by Ridely *et al.* also.
Romia *Gir West:*	R	2350	G	—	,, ,,
Jhinjhura	R	738	E	17	Ridley saw 11
Natalya	R	138	G	—	Visited by Ridley also
Khoria	R	90	G	—	4 grass birs are adjoining each other, excellent area for florican sanctuary.
Juthergaon	G	—	G	—	
Manpura	Private	—	Vg	2	Seen recently
Darbar Ki Bir	Private	—	Vg	—	Report in most years
Rajkot					
Lapari Lake area	Private	—	G	—	Adoining to lake good grass patches
Shapur Bir	Private	—	Vg.	—	Frequently visited
Khamba I	,,	150	Vg.	—	By Shikaris
Khamba II	,,	200+	Vg.	—	,, ,,
Rib	,,	150+	Vg.	—	,, ,,
Piparia	,,	1000+	E	—	7 shot recently
Narayenka	,,	500+	Vg	—	Visited by Shikaris
Bhadva	,,	750	Vg	—	,, ,,

Name of grass bir	Nature	Area (acres)	Condition for occurrence of L. florican		Birds seen/Recent report & remarks
Pal	,,	—	Vg	4	4 shot recently
Anadpara	R	480	G	—	
Jamnagar					
Niatra	Non R	100	P	—	Visited by Ridley also
Sapda	R	—	Vg	—	,, ,,
Pasaya	R	—	G	—	Near to Sapda
Rajsingh Bir	Private	—	G	—	Very near to Sapda
Morpur	R	388	G	—	Visited by Ridley *et al.* also.
Harshedpur	Private	90	E	11	Seen by Ridley *et al.* after grazing is allowed birds move off
Kengarpura	R	805	E	10	Seen by Ridley *et al.*
Pipartoda Non	R	750	G	1	,, ,,
Panchmahal					
Bannanbora	R	—	G	—	
Dahod					
Bannapura todder					
Farm	R	113	Vg	6	Near Dahod again, can be monitored from Sardarpur
Rampura grass Bir	R	1000+	Vg	—	,, ,,

*Key: R — Recerve, C — Cultivation, P — Poor, G — Good, Vg — Very good, E — Excellent.

**Ridley *et äl:* A group of birdwatchers from Paul Goriup Camp visited the area in August 1982.

No report of the occurrence of Lesser Florican has been received in recent years from Rajasthan except, from the Udaipur district (Tehsin, *pers. comm.*) where lesser floricans are said to occur in good number. This needs further verification. During the 2 months survey in different parts of Bihar I could not see any lesser florican nor could I obtain reliable information on their occurrence. However, it was gathered that the Bengal Florican *Eupodotis bengalensis* breed in some number in Singhia and Champanagar forests of Purnea district and in Bulbul area of East Champaran. Unfortunately I visited these areas in the non-breeding season. The habitat nevertheless is ideal.

OBSERVATIONS

Although during the survey I had little time for persistent observations, some first hand data recorded in the field are worth mentioning. Among the 90 birds seen 77 were males; 13 females. Only the males in the breeding plumage of the black and white are quite distinctly seen from afar. Further their repeated calls in the early morning and late afternoon is an additional point for detecting their presence. With each call they jump and thus make themselves visible above the grass. Otherwise they are very difficult to locate unless flushed out. The black plumes on the head, are clearly seen when the bird is alarmed or excited during the jumping display. The female which are slightly bigger than males (+ domestic hen) and brown all over, streaked with dark-tipped feathers are usually inconspicuous.

The males call while jumping. The call which sounds like a frog's croak is repeated at each jump after every 25 seconds or so. I once heard the call while the bird was flying near by. The call can be syllabilised as *terrr. terrr,* and appears to be uttered while the bird is at the peak of its jump: but this is yet to be verified. There is a belief that the sound is mechanical and is produced by wing beats but this does not seem to be correct because the sound is much louder and 'harder' (castanet-like) and is audible from quite a long distance—400 m or so.

Jumping: During the early morning and late afternoon, if the bird is present in an area, it is bound to jump and call. On overcast, drizziling days it jumps and calls at any time of the day. The jumps are planned and not abrupt, that is, the bird selects a bushy spot in grassland, stretches up and looks around, coils its neck in a 'S' and jumps vertically a metre or two. The height jumped depends on the height of the bush or grass—the higher the vegetation the higher the jumps. On each jump the wings are fluttered. After completing each jump the bird looks around as if expecting a response. During the jump the white patches are very prominent. Once we played back a tape recorded call at a male which was at some distance. As soon as it heard the call, it looked around and called and jumped. Then it moved towards the bush where the tape recorder was hidden but stopped some distance away, looked around, and jumped and called. Then it probably noted the difference in the mechanical call and moved away. Obviously the bird showed concern at the taped calls, and if the recording is of finer quality, this method may be quite useful for locating and counting the birds.

On two occasions two males were seen at a distance of about 250 m from each other and it was noted that whenever one called the other responded almost with the same intensity.

On two occasions one male was seen chasing another. In both cases the intruder flew away while the dominant bird remained feeding, running and moving around.

On one occasion, a male was seen crouching for about 25 minutes when disturbed by us. At first I did not see the bird but when I heard the call about 75 m away I saw a male but it also saw me and ducked among the grass—I could see only its black head. It remained in that position for about 18 minutes then looked around and moved into taller grass and again crouched. I waited for 5 minutes but as the bird did not come out, I moved forward. When I was at a distance of about 25 m the bird flew away and settled in a groundnut-maize field about 150 m away. The bird keeps alert all the time. If it sees an observer, it runs, very fast with the neck and head held horizontally and tries to hide among the vegetation.

Altogether 7 nests were located around Sardarpur area but only one female could successfully hatch: we observed the broken egg shells. The local watchman employed by the Forest Department reported incubation period as 20+ days; there were 4 eggs. Four females were killed by the local tribals while incubating. The half decomposed body of one of these females, was collected by us and weighed 350 gm. Decomposed parts of soft green leaf and small pieces of stones were recorded from the stomach. Another nest with three eggs was located at Gomanpura plantation. Out of curiosity, a local Range Officer took away one egg. We watched the nest for the next 4 days but the remaining eggs were left unattended. The feamle was either killed or disturbed and abandoned the nest. When there was no activity on the 5th day, I collected the eggs for measurement. Two unequal sized eggs measured as below:

48.3 × 39.9 mm Weight 32.70 g
47.8 × 38.2 mm Weight 28.25 g

Eggs round, ends not distinct. Colour olive-green, spotted. A pair of floricans lived in a grass bir at Gomanpura. Two young hatched, but on the third day of hatching both chicks were taken away by two different tribals on the instruction of the owner of the bir for raising in captivity: Both the chicks died the very next day.

This was the 6th clutch we know of being lost during this season around Sardarpur area. There might have been more casualities of females on incubation.

Problems and Prospects

It is obvious from this study that the main causes of decline of the Florican population is the loss of its habitat. Each year large areas of grasslands are being converted into agricultural fields. Owing to the spiralling increase in the human population, this is but natural. The second reason is the lack of education, especially about wildlife among the people in general and among the tribals in particular. The tribals are greatly destructive to the lesser florican by their killing of the female while incubating. Since they roam in the grass birs, most of the time and know the whereabouts of the nests, they collect eggs or kill the females in considerable numbers. The local shikaris, who do know that the number of the lesser florican is fast declining in their area still shoot some each year; and are a great threat to this endangered, and for that matter to many other species. Spraying of pesticides and insecticides in Gujarat by helicopter, specially in areas where the lesser floricans and peafowl, *Pavo cristatus*, congregate will have far reaching effect on the fauna of the area. Although the data collected so far are not enough to give a complete management plan, the following recommendations are made to prevent further decline of the florican.

1. *Declare as many florican sanctuaries as possible in the areas mentioned above—mainly in Gujarat and Madhya Pradesh States.* This will not be heavy financial burden to the authorities if the existing grass birs are declared "closed" and strict vigilance maintained. As the florican requires a very specialized type of habitat their population density and survival are directly dependant on the availability of suitable grassland and savana forests. It is evident from the foregoing account that floricans were quite abundant before the larger chunk of grasslands were converted into agricultural fields.

2. *Stop grazing earlier than normal.* In some *bir*, private or public, we found that the grazing stopped at a certain time. If this is done 20-30 days earlier than normal, the grass would be tall enough to provide cover to the birds when they arrive and are more vulnerable to shooters.

3. *Delay the grass cutting.* If the grass cutting is delayed for about 25 days longer than usual, it may help the young floricans to fledge successfully. On an experimental basis some patches of grass may be left as such to see whether the floricans stay there after the breeding season is over. In fact almost entire area, whether grassland or cultivated fields where the florican breed, become exposed after November and that may compel the birds to migrate.

4. *Restrict aerial spraying of insecticides and pesticides* to the minimum especially in areas where floricans, peafowl and painted partridge breed.

5. *Education of local people.* People must be educated about the importance of wildlife and made to understand the magnitude of problems and have to be taken into confidence to protect this already endangered species. While surveying I found these people quite amenable to the need for conservation when persuaded properly.

6. *The watch and ward staff of the forest department* of the known florican areas should be trained and strict vigilance and protection maintained specially while the females incubate and males display and make themselves more vulnerable.

7. *A long-term intensive study* on the ecology and biology of the lesser florican should commence without further delay to develop a complete conservation programme.

ACKNOWLEDGEMENTS

The survey was funded by the Bombay Natural History Society's Endangered Species Project financed by the U.S. Fish and Wildlife Service through the Dept. of Environment, Government of India. I am grateful to the officials and field staff members of the forest department—Governments of Bihar, Maharashtra, and Madhya Pradesh who were very cooperative and helpful during the survey. Dr Salim Ali showed keen interest in the study and kindly visited the study area. I am grateful to Mr J.C. Daniel, Curator, Bombay Natural History Society for giving me an opportunity to work on this interesting species.

REFERENCES

ALI, S & RIPLEY, S.D. (1980): *Handbook of the Birds of India and Pakistan* Vol. 2, IInd Edn. Delhi. Oxford University Press.

BAKER, E.C.S. (1921): The Game birds of India, Burma & Ceylon. Vol. 2.

——— (1935): Nidification of Birds of Indian Empire Vol. 4: 334-336

DHRAMAKUMARSINHJI, K.S. (1950): The Lesser Florican its courtship, display, behaviour and habit, *J. Bombay nat. Hist. Soc.* **49**: 201-216

HUME, A.O. & MARSHALL (1879): Game birds of India, Burma & Ceylon 33-40

ISAKOV, A.Y. (1976): Present distribution and Population Status of the Great Bustard *Otis tarda* Linnaeus: *J. Bombay nat. Hist. Soc.* **71(3)**: 433-444.

Breeding habits and habitat of the Painted Snipe as observed in Tiruchirapalli, Tamilnadu, South India

(*With a text-figure*)

H.D. WESLEY

Bishop Heber College, Tiruchirapalli 620017.

INTRODUCTION

Rostratula benghalensis is the Old World Painted Snipe being found throughout non-Saharan Africa, the Middle East, including Turkey (but not Europe), India, China, most of South-East Asia and Australia (Gooders 1975). It is said to occur throughout the Indian Union upto 5000 ft in the Himalayas, Bangladesh, Ceylon and Burma (Ali, Salim & Ripley, S.D. 1969; Ali, Salim 1979; Ripley, S.D. 1982).

Wherever it occurs, the bird affects reedy marshes (Austin 1962); flooded samphire (Lowe 1963); roadside reedy water pans and near irrigation canals (Beste 1970); rush-covered low-lying grazing land (Lowe 1970); marshes interspersed with deep pools, soft muddy patches and thick shrubby vegetation (Ali, Salim & Ripley, S.D. 1969); and swamps (Muller 1974).

STUDY AREA

I have been observing painted snipes in Tiruchirapalli for about eighteen months now. Tiruchirapalli, lying between 78°N and 10° and 11°E, is in Tamilnadu, India. The birds were observed for their breeding behaviour: courtship, nest building and incubation. This paper presents some of the activities observed of the birds that are of immediate relation to the title. Polyandry is not discussed as it has not been observed thoroughly; it remains a conjecture and its study a desideratum. Figure gives the lie of the land under study. The entire housing colony is lying wedged between two northerly flowing irrigation canals. Between the northernmost row of house-plots and the vast stretch of paddyfield beyond is a strip of fallow land (FL) about 673 feet long and about 96 feet broad. Plot No.4 was the observation post. There were no houses on plots Nos. 5,6,9,10,13,15 and 16; houses were under construction in plots Nos. 7 and 8; plots Nos. 11, 12 and 14 had occupied houses. The land intended for a park (hereinafter also referred to as 'park') is on the east of the observation post and has an area of 26,595 sq.ft. On the south of it were three plots: Nos. 2 and 3 vacant, and No. 1 had an occupied house. The total area of the 'Park' and the two vacant plots together was 34, 115 sq. feet. The plants growing therein were mostly *Cyperus* sp. and some bushes of *Prosopis juliflora,* besides some trailing grass and *Acanthus* sp. In the back fallowland the dominant ones were horse-tail in the western sector, *Cyperus* sp, *Oldenlandia* sp. and *Acanthus* sp. in the eastern.

Between the plots Nos. 2 and 3 and the 'park', and between the 'park' and the fallowland were raised bunds. The fallow land behind was in three pieces with two bunds and was in direct communication with the eastern canal at one or two places in its bank. Water

A BREEDING TERRITORY OF PAINTED SNIPE AT TIRUCHIRAPALLI, TAMIL NADU.

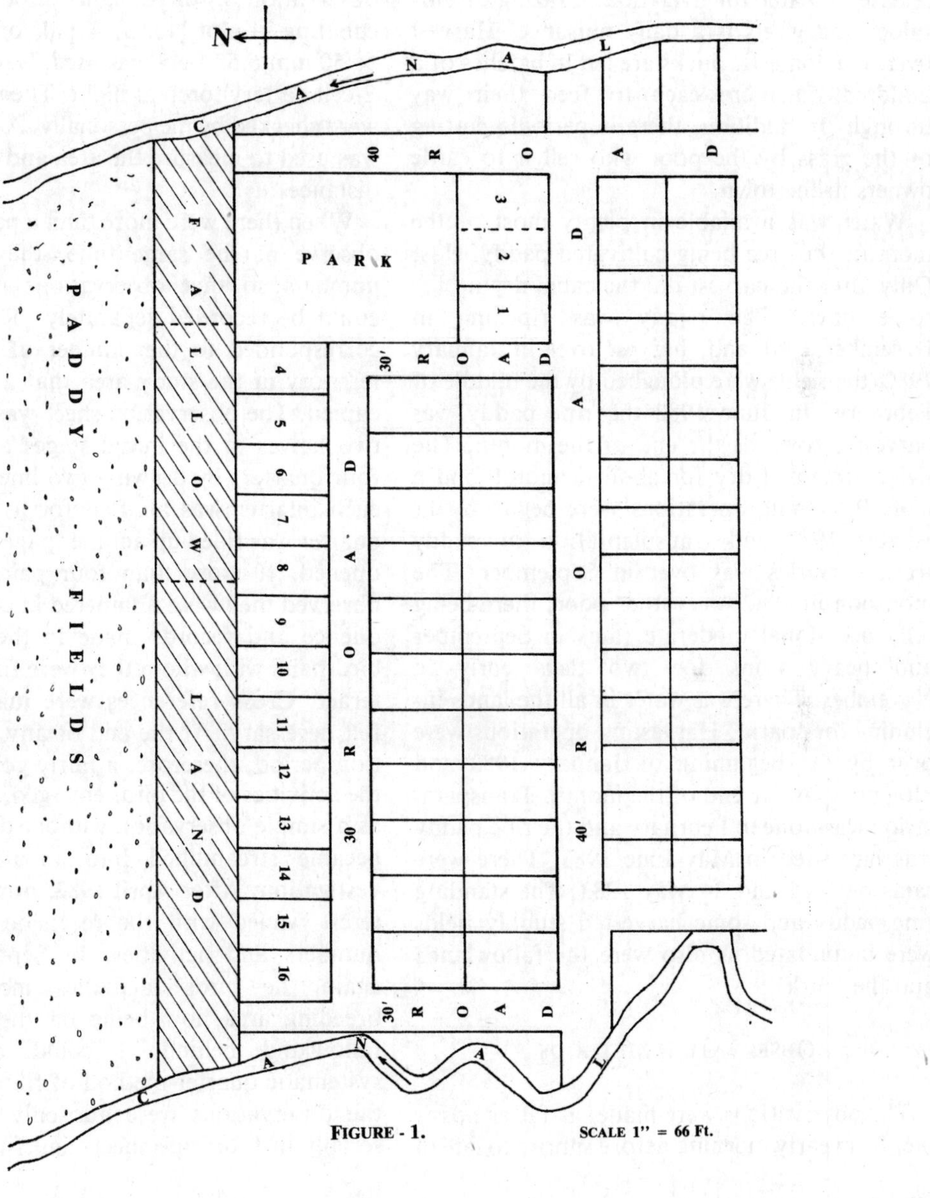

FIGURE - 1.   SCALE 1" = 66 Ft.

from the canal would not come into the 'park' because of the road between them. The vacant plots in the row of the observation post received water from the fallowland as and when the canal overflowed due to rain or excessive release of water for irrigation. Grazing of buffaloes and goats is a daily nuisance. Harvest over, the domestic ducks are led in batches of a hundred on more each to feed their way through. In addition, there is periodic cutting of the grass by the poor who sell it to cattle owners in the town.

Water was available in plenty most of the months, the area being cultivated paddyfields. Only after the harvest did the canal dry up for some days. The paddy was ripening in December 1981 and, harvest over in January 1982, the fields were ploughed by the middle of February. In June 1982 the ripe paddy was harvested towards the end of the month. The fields remained dry for about a month and a half. Ploughing operations were begun by 11 August 1982 and transplantation of paddy from nurseries was over in September. The monsoon in 1982 was rather poor, there being only occasional moderate rains in September and heavy rains for two days early in November. There was water in all the lands including the 'park'. Harvesting operations were over by the beginning of January 1983 and ploughing by the end of the month. Transplantation was done in February and the ripe paddy was harvested in May-June 1983. There were rains on 9,15 and 24 May 1983. The standing ripe paddy and some harvested stubbly fields were innundated as also were the fallowlands and the 'park'.

Observation Methods

The observations were made, as far as possible, from early morning before sunrise to late in the evening, even after sunset. They were concentrated more on the courtship activities when a pair would be together. During the waking hours in the nights the bird's calling times were recorded. Once in April 1982 I made a night observation on three nights on a male bird incubating in plot No. 5. A pair of binoculars 8 × 50 mm 6.5° field was used. Besides, I used a 2-cell battery torch at night. The nests and eggs were checked by me personally. A 100-foot tape was used to measure the area and the inter-nest distances.

When there were more than a pair of birds to observe at the same time, they were given numbers so that observations on each pair could be recorded separately. These numbers corresponded to the number of the breeding territory in the study area that a pair had occupied. The observation sheet was divided into two halves in the initial stages and later into four quarters by drawing two lines across, and each quarter was allotted for a bird. As one quarter was filled up another page was similarly opened. If more than four pairs were being observed they were numbered in continuous sequence and records made in the quarters of bird-pairs with whom they were first seen to interact. Cross references were made whenever felt necessary. At the end of any one observation period, therefore, a fairly good picture of the activities of the birds emerged. What started as a simple observation without direction soon became streamlined into an interesting investigation. After April 1982, however, the interest waned with the recession in the bird numbers and activities. In September 1982, again the birds' activities increased. The breeding area now being on the west in the fallowland behind, I could not keep a systematic quarter-method of filing the details; the observations were hurriedly jotted down serially in foolscape sheets and filed.

Observation on the bird's activities were made from the house in plot No. 4. The 'park' area could be seen in a sweep from a window of a room, from the front grill ventilation on the portico upstairs and the back terrace. The fallowland behind could be viewed from the terrace or even from windows when occasion demanded. Often I had to crouch on the terrace and look over the parapet wall. Plot No. 5 could be conveniently observed from another room upstairs and from the terrace. During the periods of observation I was constantly on the alert shifting positions quickly from one place to another to check the birds and to verify if there was no mixing up in the identity of the birds. One very useful means of being sure of the identity of a bird was its territory which does not change, once fixed; the place of rest, copulation path and spot remained unaltered. I checked to my satisfaction the various spots for the presence or absence of any of them in the territories at any given time of observation, particularly when a new arrival was suspected. Any intruding pair or bird was resented and chased off by the owners of the territory. A new arrival would thus be known.

OBSERVATION

Breeding season and abundance. A total of 55 birds, an unequal sex ratio of 30 males to 25 females, were observed in their breeding activities in two concentrations between December 1981 and November 1982. There were 18 females and 21 males between December 1981 and May 1982; and 7 females and 9 males between September 1982 and November 1982.

Among the first set of birds, five pairs established territories and nests of eggs in the breeding area of 34,115 sq.ft east of the observation post. A total of 16 eggs were laid by the five females. The least and the greatest distance between the nests were about 45 ft and 125 ft respectively. In the fallowland behind, two pairs had a total of 7 eggs in their two nests established in February 1982. The last of the first set of nests was lodged in plot No. 5 close to the observation post; it had 4 eggs in it.

Two of the 9 females of the second set of birds established their nests with 3 and 4 eggs in September and November 1982 respectively. Altogether 34 eggs were laid by ten females.

In May-June 1982 when there was water only in small pockets of the fallowland, the general condition being dry, the standing crops ripening and ready for harvest in June 1982, the breeding calls were still heard around them. No nests were found however. Now, May 1983, at the time of the writing of this paper there are a few pairs in their breeding activities, water being present in the already harvested fields and grass growing liberally there.

Breeding behaviour. A very secretive bird, the painted snipe did its courting in the grass, the pair trekking through the grass, one leading the other, occasionally lying down in and inspecting a grass growth as though for its nestworthiness. A part of the courtship involved both the birds bathing simultaneously within a few metres of each other, dabbling water over the head and the body with the vigorous dipping movements of the head, the hind part and the fluttering wings. The wide open eyes with the little spectacle gave a comical appearance indeed. Most other times they lay quietly preening or stood motionless on one leg in the shade of a herb or a bush.

Eleven copulations were observed. The male closely followed the female who waved her hind quarter up and down as she went along a track barren of grass. After what appeared to be a tediously long time of meandering, the male mounted her fowl-fashion and slipped down. Both remained for some seconds motionless before moving back to the favourite spot.

Nest and nesting material. The bird selected for its nest-bed a mud surface free of grass with standing grass around; a ground with creeping vegetation was never preferred. The female pressed the moist mud into a depression with her breast, the body thrust forward with the legs anchored behind she rotated, as she did so the legs changing positions.

Only decaying grass blades and grass stems were collected and formed the nesting material. They were collected from under the water around the nest-site itself. Very little of nest bed material was used by the pair that nested in April 1982 in plot No. 5. None of the birds under observation ever used over material such as sticks and green leaves. As a result the nest-bed matched the rest of the muddy surface. The nest being in the middle of a bunch of standing grass on the ground raised above the prevailing water level, the standing stems formed the 'wall'. The blade-tips were worked into an arching dome of canopy both by the female and the male whenever they were in. However, the sun shone through interstices in the wall and canopy. A 'hole' was always left in the wall for entering and leaving the nest that was formed more by constant movement in and out than by any deliberate effort.

While most of the nests observed were in the open fields, at least two (February 1982, April 1982) were located under horizontal branches of an *Oldenlandia* sp. of herb and a *Prosopis juliflora*. In another instance (November 1982) the pair established their nest in the midst of four paddy saplings on a clod in the badly ploughed field behind; this field was fallowland for a year. *Cyperus* sp. grew around the nest but the canopy was of slantingly growing paddy, the former being still short. In all the cases cited there was *Cyperus* sp. growing around the nest-site. The nest in the first case was open, the shade plant being a herb; that of the second was perfectly covered although the side was exposed occasionally by the grass wall being eaten away by the buffaloes, making it easy of observation from 25 feet away. The third nest, like the first one was inadequately covered so that the bird could be viewed from a distance of about 100 feet.

The eggs were a perfect camouflage in the breeding ground, the black and yellow markings merging with the black muddy nest-bed and the alternate light and shade cast over them by the sun.

During incubation, particularly as the grass dried up, the canopy sagged which the male kept overhead by pulling the blades over him, holding it in the beak and slipping the latter to the leaf tip, sitting within the nest. The male birds in the 'park' did not desert the nests when the area dried up. The plumage now perfectly merged with the grass around.

Reproduction and mortality. Of the total number of 34 eggs recorded only one was known for certain to have hatched successfully. The others were lost to predators(?), the buffaloes in the 'park' area, and sudden rise in the water level in the fallowland. The buffaloes kicked the eggs out of the nests as they sauntered along. Only on one occasion did I observe a rat snake being successfully frightened off (the 'snake stood gazing for quite some time, tongue flicking in and out before crawling away) by the beautiful wing display of the incubating male snipe. On two occasions the male snipes battled in vain against the rising water by trying to add more bed-material to their nests. About 11.7% of the eggs laid were infertile and would not hatch. The percentage of mortality was as high as 97.06%, the hatching success being 2.94%.

DISCUSSION

Breeding season. In the present study actual breeding was observed in January, February, April, September, November and December. The birds were seen in March and heard in the months of May and June, although no nests were recorded. It is likely that the painted snipe in Tiruchirapalli is a round-the-year breeder, the birds of a population or different populations coming into breeding mood, as it were, in different months. Judging from the periods of breeding in the present study the bird's sexual cycle seems to be conditioned by the availability of water. Baker (1934) believes that the "controlling factor is water supply and the attendant increase in food".

Breeding behaviour. Courtship is a long drawn-out process and it is done in the grass and water pools in the territory. The birds preen, lying in the grass or under short shade-plants. Bathing is also an important element in courtship. While they are resting, the birds remain under cover of bushy plants. Grass cover and water in the habitat are the primary requirements for the bird to occur there.

The nest is placed on raised ground in shallow water with high grass cover (Schmidt 1961; Lowe 1963; Thomas, 1975). This habit is also exhibited by the bird in Tiruchirapalli. Here the bird has always required stand of grass around and the nest is built on wet ground. The grass preferred is *Cyperus* sp. However, grass alone is inadequate and even useless if the ground is not raised above the water level in the area at the time of setting the nest.

Decaying leaf blades and stems of the grass required for the nest-bed are pulled up easily where there is water. At the time of nest building, therefore, water is desirable.

Courtship culminates in mating. The copulation drill requires to be performed in a relatively grass-free and dry area in the territory. As such, habitat with uniform grass cover has not been preferred.

The high mortality observed was due to natural and man-made causes. Infertility of the eggs is a natural cause. It is not known as to whether there is disturbance from grazing cattle and goats, and from innundation in other breeding territories. The birds here have not been able to raise the nest level to avoid the rising waters. This breeding territory seems to have been a kind of experimental area. While the two kinds of disturbances could be prevented, infertility is beyond prevention by man. Round-the-year breeding and polyandry may perhaps be compensatory alternatives for the high mortality that seems obvious.

CONCLUSION

Rostratula benghalensis, occurring in Tiruchirapalli, Tamil Nadu, requires special ecological conditions for breeding.

These are optimum water level always below that of the nest-site during nesting season, a grass covered terrain with relatively dry and barren mating-spot. Birds in other areas may or may not be similar in their requirements.

Inundation and grazing of cattle lead to desertion and high mortality, particularly when several nests with eggs are established in one small area. The harvesting of the standing grass removes the cover necessary for courtship and incubation. Conversion of marshlands and paddyfields into residential and industrial complexes poses a grave danger to this bird.

A marsh-loving bird, *R. benghalensis,* it is suggested could be attracted to planned grassy habitats with controlled optimum conditions of water, throughout the year with relatively dry and grass-free mating spots and hummocks for nests.

REFERENCES

ALI, SALIM (1979): The Book of Indian Birds. Bombay Natural History Society Bombay, Eleventh Ed.

ALI, SALIM & S. DILLON RIPLEY, (1969): Handbook of the Birds of India and Pakistan. vol.2. Oxford University Press. Bombay. London. New York.

AUSTIN, OLIVER L.JR. (1962): Birds of the World. Hamlyn, London. New York. Sydney. Toronto.

BAKER, E.C. STUART, (1934): The Nidification of birds of the Indian Empire. Taylor and Francis, London.

BESTE, H. (1970): The sighting of the painted snipe. *Aust. Bird Watcher.* **3**, No.7: 220-21.

GOODERS, JOHN (1975): The Great Book of Birds. Dial Press, New York. pp. 137.

LOWE, V.T. (1963): Observations on the painted snipe. *Emu* **62**.

____ (1970): Notes on the Behaviour of the painted snipe. *Aust. Bird Watcher* **3** No.7: 218-19.

MULLER, K.A. (1974): Observations on the Old World painted snipe, *Rostratula benghalensis* at the Taronga Zoo. *Avicult. Mag.* **80**(1):1-3.

RIPLEY, S.D.(1982): A Synopsis of the Birds of India & Pakistan. Second Edn. Bombay Natural History Society. Bombay.

SSHMIDT, R.K. (1961): Incubation period of the painted snipe, *Rostratula benghalensis. The Ostrich* **32**:183-4.

THOMAS, E (1975): Painted snipe breeding at Barham, New South Wales. *Aust. Bird Watcher* **6**(4):133.

The role of Management in the Conservation of Endangered Species with special reference to Indian Crocodilians

H.R. BUSTARD

Airlie Brae, Alyth, Perthshire, Scotland

Following some general remarks on aspects of management critical to conservation of endangered species, the paper describes the role of these same aspects of management in the achievements of the all-India Project, Crocodile Breeding and Management.

INTRODUCTION

This paper, in as far as it relates to crocodilians, discusses one aspect — one extreme — of management, here described as 'active management', where there is deliberate, well-planned, interference in the life-history of the species under management. The management used is of the most 'active' type, in that individuals of the species are reared in captivity, under as natural conditions as possible, in order to provide maximum boost to the size of the populations in the shortest possible time. This management regime is illustrated throughout with reference to the crocodilians, since this is the author's specialist field, but more importantly, because there has been a large-scale project on crocodilians in India extending over many years, which many of you will know about, and this Project provides a yard-stick against which the achievements of active management of this type can be measured. This is most important, as in suggesting active management as an invaluable tool in the case of extremely rare and greatly endangered species, it is vital that the likely results of this approach can be quantified.

MANAGEMENT

The Scope of Management

Management can be extremely 'light' — it could involve merely keeping visitors out of a part of a sanctuary at a particular time of year — when ground nesting birds are nesting for instance — or delaying the cutting of grass by several weeks to allow part of the life cycle of some small animal, ground-nesting bird, or insect, to be completed. On the other hand it could involve — as in the case of crocodilians in India — the 'production' of large numbers of release-sized animals to repopulate whole areas of the natural habitat. Management may involve captive breeding of an endangered species, and rearing of the resultant young in captivity for release back into the wild, management of the natural area etc.

Since wildlife needs space in which to live wildlife management is about land and the use of this land. Often man need not be excluded from the land if his activities are compatible with the particular forms of wildlife being managed.

Since even relatively undisturbed areas of the natural habitat are now becoming rare, in many/most parts of the World, management involves the preservation of certain tracts of land in as near to natural conditions as possible. Such tracts of land, which may constitute only a small fraction of the total land area being managed, are an integral part of management programmes but such (drastic) action will not be needed in most instances. What will be necessary is to prevent poaching and to ensure that activities which are permitted are compatible with the type of wildlife being managed. Elephants, for instance, will survive well in natural forest tracts being worked on a well-planned, sustained yield utilisation basis by the Forestry departments, provided these departments are able to ensure the long-term survival of their reserved and Protected Forests. Elephants provide an excellent example of the need to manage large areas of land for certain species. They do not need exclusive access to the land but the land must be maintained under natural, mixed, forest bamboo cover. Furthermore, many of the problems facing elephants in India today are problems that are equally acute for the Forest Service. It is the alienation of large tracts of land within the Reserved forests which has provided a major problem for the future of India's elephant populations. Due to man invading the forests, and clearing and settling large areas of forest for agricultural settlement, he is increasingly coming into conflict with elephants.

It is not to downgrade the deleterious effects of large-scale 'economically-oriented' poaching, to state that land is the first and foremost need in wildlife management. An endangered species may have become endangered while the habitat remained abundant, and in good/ecological shape, as a result of poaching, but increasingly today, pressure is on the land, and there is no possibility of using modern techniques to build up the populations of endangered species unless land is available for their use. The ultimate need will always be for habitat — land.

Hence the first role of management has to be to retain — or where this has already been lost — to build up — a 'land bank' for the concerned species.

Major Management Activities

We now come down from generalisations to the specific, and the above ideas are expanded and illustrated using, not theory, but the *practical* results of many years of hard work by dedicated Indians, with whom I have had the very great pleasure to work, in many parts of your enormous country, from Gujarat to West Bengal, and from northern Uttar Pradesh to Tamil Nadu.

Although the large-scale Government of India/FAO/UNDP Project Crocodile Breeding and Management which I recommended be initiated in my 1974/FAO Report to the Government of India, and for which I was Chief Technical Adviser for many years (1975-1981), covered all three species of Indian crocodilians — the gharial (*Gavialis gangeticus*), the saltwater or estuarine crocodile (*Crocodylus porosus*) and the mugger or marsh crocodile (*C. palustris*) we will here concentrate mainly on the gharial as its conservation is already well known, and the saltwater crocodile, as it illustrates the land management problem ideally, in a fascinating, but little-known, and very fragile, ecosystem.

We faced the extremely difficult problem initially that the animal which we were charged with conserving — the gharial — itself as elusive throughout most of the year as the tiger — was very little known. Even its nesting season was incorrectly stated by Malcolm Smith (1931), an error never corrected in the literature until the present Project started publishing its results. Accordingly we had to study its biology from scratch as we went along — we could not afford ourselves the luxury of doing this first before initiating the Project as the gharial would have been extinct before we had learned very much.

With many other species being managed, or proposed for management, the biology may be much better known so this aspect can be downgraded.

There are four (sequential) aspects in setting up a conservation project of this type, although in the present instance, due to the endangered status of the gharial as a species, and of the saltwater crocodile as a member of the Indian fauna (this latter species has a wide extra-Indian distribution also) these four separate, but inter-related, tasks had to commence simultaneously.

These steps are:

1. land management
2. protection
3. getting to know the animal — in the Konard Lorenz sense that to adequately study the behaviour of a dog one must first become a dog — leading to research projects as where necessary
4. active management of the endangered species

These four topics are discussed separately below, first in general terms, and then illustrated using examples from the crocodilian project. Although the examples are, therefore, all Indian, the same type of problems occur everywhere — it is the matter of degree that differs from country to country. Incidentally, in many countries known to the author the problems are very much greater than in India.

1. *Land*. The first considerations are: (*a*) if not already known, to locate key areas of land for the species concerned and; (*b*) to decide what degree of management control must be exercised over these in order to provide adequate long-term protection to the species.

Phase (*a*) may entail extensive surveys in the first instance in order to delineate key areas of the natural habitat in which all the species' requirements are met at all seasons of the year. If this is not possible — in a migratory species for instance — land corridors may have to be incorporated in the land plan at this stage linking two or more areas of land in order to achieve this objective.

In phase (*b*), it is important to fully appreciate that land, as the most basic commodity in the lives of most people, is intensely political. While the sincere conservationist will have to fight for the land that it required he/she should not ask for more control (or more land) than is absolutely necessary for the Project to achieve its objectives. We are hopefully passing out of the phase in which eager conservationists state that 'all' that needs to be done in order to save species X is to build a wall around land area Y, keep people out, and stop every kind of activity within. This approach — even if it were feasible — is likely to be counter-productive, and is at the opposite extreme from active management here proposed, which appreciates the 'political realities' of life, and tries to actively manage in the interests of the species in order to ameliorate other considerations *which cannot be changed*.

Wherever possible multi-land use should be encouraged, but this should not be an excuse for land alienation and/or poaching (the subject of the next section). There is no question but that multi-land use, good as the idea is, requires the 'manager' to be constantly on his toes and 'manage' in order to detect and deflect intrusions of all kinds. It can be likened to a guerilla war.

In concluding this very brief discussion on land I would point out that it will not be possible to fulfill considerations (*a*) and (*b*) set out at the start of this section without good biological information on the species under management. This will involve *good basic research,* if the work has not been adequately carried out already, and I must state that such 'good basic research' is, unfortunately, not the norm in a great many conservation projects. It is essential to have one's facts right. Enthusiasm, important as it is, is not an adequate substitute for 'hard data' when it becomes a matter of bargaining over land. Nor should it be.

2. *Protection.* It is a straightforward matter to formulate protection requirements or to *write* suitable protective legislation. The problems are *practical,* at the implementative stage. Many sanctuaries may have superb management plans but if the actual staff on the ground have never seen the management plan then it is of little use.

A preliminary observation, relating to India, based on my eight years' practical experience in many areas of the country, is that even a low and extremely simple level of protection can have an amazing effect. This sometimes reflects virtual absence of any form of protection in the area previously, but quite clearly reflects the deeply ingrained attitude of the ordinary people of India — Indian villagers are basically respectful and law-abiding. The problems lie elsewhere.

There are several basic factors to get right at the start in formulating any protective programme. These include:

1) *The status of the land.* Penalties are automatically doubled for poaching offences committed in sanctuaries or National Parks. Hence it may be useful, for this reason alone (but also for others set out below), to have key management areas gazetted as sanctuaries and where appropriate later upgraded to National Park status.

2) *Appointment of protection staff.* Staff must be appointed solely for protection duties. It is no use putting people already engaged on other work onto part-time protection work also. If the existing staff (let us assume the protection area is already a State Forest) are not sufficiently motivated then *new recruits* should be used. As far as India is concerned, there is frequently in my experience, an unfortunate lack of liaison with lower staff — those who actually have to do the work. Furthermore, staff should not be diverted from their duties to other activities.

3) *Supporting the staff.* I have found a major problem in protection short-comings is that the staff are not sufficiently motivated which invariably means that their superior officer(s) are not wholehearted in their task. There is a great willingness to please superiors in India and if catching poachers is not likely to please their superiors the field staff will divert their energies elsewhere. So there must be no doubt about the commitment of the senior officers, including the O-I-C. This commitment must be *demonstrated* regularly if protection is to succeed. It should be self-obvious that all these staff (seniormost as well as field guards) must live in or on the edge of the area they are protecting. This point requires heavy *emphasis* as it is apparently not obvious here in India, where officers-in-charge of National Parks, often live at a remote distance from their jurisdiction where contact with them is difficult at best, and extremely time-consuming.

The above three factors are prerequisites without which there is no point in drawing up a protection operating plan.

It is not possible to generalise here about how

protection should be carried out. Even within India there are markedly different regional attitudes to such matters as, for instance, the arming of protection staff. While this is the norm in certain northern States it is virtually unknown in many other areas of the country. My own feeling is that it is unfair to expect unarmed and often ill-equipped guards, to overcome gangs of armed poachers. Of course, even today the British police are unarmed, but there are key differences. The British police do not operate in remote areas against people (in this case poachers) who are always armed. Wildlife guards have, by the very manner of their duties, to operate in remote areas where they can be shot and the murderer is unlikely ever to be apprehended. To expect unarmed men under such circumstances to be thoroughly dedicated in their work may be expecting too much. This is a topic which I frequently pointed out during my many years in conservation work in Australia. I can think of many areas of the World where such a situation exists. In a sense the status (which includes arms and training in their proper use) of the wildlife guards, reflects the importance the country or state places on the proper protection of its wildlife resources.

However, it can be stated as a general rule, that wildlife guards must patrol constantly by day and night, on an irregular schedule. It will be ideal if they are trained to carry out basic research duties as has been the case in the crocodile project (see below) as this gives them a reason to be actively moving around the sanctuary/National Park in the course of collecting data. The senior staff should join patrols as frequently as possible.

Poachers know whether guards are active or not. Patrolling as an end in itself can become extremely boring, especially as the more successful the patrols, the fewer people will risk poaching, so encounters become greatly reduced. We have found in the crocodile project that the presence of an active research group, working on the animals in the wild, backed up by a skeleton protection staff, has worked wonders for protection.

Guards to protect everything. It must be made clear at the outset that the guards are not employed merely to protect tiger, or gharial, or rhinoceros. Their job is to prevent any unlawful activity within the boundaries of the protection area whether it be illegal cutting of grass or felling of trees, as opposed to game poaching. The former activities, of course, may in the long term, be as deleterious to the survival of the species being protected as direct killing by poachers, which is why such activities are banned under such circumstances. They will not be obvious to the protection staff, however, and the reasons should be carefully *explained* to them.

3. *Getting to know the animal.* This need not, and should not, be restricted to the research staff. The more familiar the protection staff are with the habits of the animal(s) on which protection is concentrated the better. Furthermore, in India, as in many parts of the World, the right sort of protection staff (see below) may know much more about the animals than the newly-appointed research staff — at a practical level at least. This is a tremendous advantage. Protection staff should always be local people. Quite apart from the advantage of their local wildlife and geographical knowledge, they will have invaluable contacts among the local people. Government policy is usually the reverse — to take people away from their local areas, where it is thought they may use their contacts for improper purposes. Furthermore, transfers are frequent — often absurdly so — the stated reason being to prevent their building up local contacts which can be used improperly. To my

mind this is a defeatist attitude. Furthermore, in wildlife work frequent transfers of staff cannot be tolerated.

One does not require rigorous scientific training to be able to collect research data *under supervision*. Illiterate or semi-literate field guards can collect extremely valuable data as will be shown below by selected examples from the crocodile project. The scientific skills lie in experimental design and in interpretation of the data, data collection in itself being largely a routine affair requiring honesty and reliability, traits which I have found to be readily available in the Indian countryside.

4. *Active management.* Before moving on to what, in the context of this paper, is active management, we should briefly list various degrees of active management, arranged loosely in *ascending order* of management involvement:

1. *Fire prevention activities* as carried out by the State Forest Departments are an interference with the natural habitat designed to reduce incidence of forest fires. Such activities benefit most of the wildlife.

2. *Seasonal burning of grass* provides an extension of: 1) above in that it may prevent more serious fires by deliberately starting man-made, controlled, cool grass fires. This also serves to maintain open grazing areas and perhaps to provide a crop of young grass shoots (e.g. rhino). Where these have been carried on since time immemorial they have become part of the ecology (one must remember that man has influenced the ecology since the early days of 'man the hunter-food gatherer'). Not to burn would be to have the forest encroach on such open areas, so essential to many grazing animals, and in time they would become completely forested.

3. *Provision of better nesting areas* provides another example. For instance, in the case of sea turtles, which nest extremely densely on restricted areas of beach, it has been shown (Bustard, 1972) that the configuration of vegetation on the beach results in uneven nesting, some areas being several times overutilised (in the sense that putting down a nest there results in a high probability of destroying an existing nest). In the simplest case removal of large tree trunks, especially those lying parallel to the beach, opens up areas previously barred to nesting activities (as sea turtles cannot surmount such obstacles), and greatly reduces 'funnelling' effects into areas in between. No one, I would think, would object to such activities in the interests of conserving an endangered sea turtle species. This is, however, active management, although of a comparatively low order.

4. *Manipulation of the food supply* can vary from a low to a medium-high level of active management, and is a widespread management tool. It may only take place in times of duress (such as drought),. but by preventing large-scale deaths at such times its effect on the population being managed may be dramatic. Quite apart from supplementary feeding under conditions described in 2) above, and fire which can greatly affect food supply (such as in 1) and 2) above) a more common activity today is manipulation of the predator-prey relationship. It may be necessary to improve the predator's food supply before the numbers of the predator species can be built up. The main prey species may have been lost due to illegal hunting activities (as in the case of ungulates for instance) or from over or uncontrolled fishing in the case of the gharial's food supply.

5. *Translocation of endangered species* may help to enhace the populations of many species,

using carefully controlled introductions of animals from another area. Introductions may even be into areas where the species has become completely extinct. In the latter case, a strong incentive for carrying out what is a complicated and essentially long-term task, may be to better ensure the survival of an endangered species by distributing it more widely. Many endangered species have become restricted to a few or even a single area at least within the boundaries of one country. Here in India the Indian lion and the Great Indian Rhinoceros are important examples.

6. *Captive breeding/rearing of endangered species* provides a virtual gradation from 5) into this, the highest category of management, as translocated individuals, must, of course, be taken into captivity before translocation, and may have to be held for some time in the new area and then slowly allowed their freedom. Other activities, set out above, such as supplementary feeding, may be involved in this gradual release process.

Under the head 'captive breeding/rearing of endangered species' we include collection of wild-laid eggs for captive hatching and rearing of young for subsequent release back into the wild as has been so very extensively carried out by the crocodile project here in India, and which, since it is described below, will not be further mentioned here. As I have pointed out to our President, Dr Salim Ali, this is a technique applicable to many species of birds, especially those where only one or two eggs laid, or otherwise less than the full egg complement will be reared under normal conditions, the 'surplus' can be collected and placed in an incubator. The technique can also be used in the case of birds which will continue to lay if eggs are removed while the normal egg complement is being built up (Lack, 1954). Such species offer tremendous scope.

Although this is an outstanding technique, of wide applicability, it should, I believe, be operated according to a set of very definite rules where animals are to be released back into the wild. Even in the case of crocodilians, the idea is to rear them to release size as quickly as possible, under as natural conditions as possible, and using natural food throughout. We set out, therefore, not to produce pet animals, and animals conditioned to unnatural conditions in captivity, as these may not readily adapt to life back in nature following release. Proof of the efficacy of our methodology comes from the very pleasing sight of released crocodilians catching fish in the wild within minutes/hours of release and in the longer term in the very high survival rates achieved by released animals.

Although it is a very controversial subject I do not believe the technique is suitable for master predators which quickly lose their respect/fear of man and which when released may then attack humans. I consider tiger and other large cats to be a prime example of this problem. A problem which, I might add, we have never encountered with crocodilians.

Animals which are captive-bred — provided they are of a suitable species for release, can be released just as captive hatched/reared young. Zoological gardens have the opportunity to provide such material for release from a wide range of species, and a first step in this direction is to become self-sufficient so that more need not be captured, often extremely wastefully (e.g. apes) from the wild.

Finally we come to captive breeding groups which may be retained in captivity indefinitely to ensure the gene-pool of species which have poor prognosis for continued survival in the wild, the hope being that at some stage some safe natural areas can be made available for releases. In all such cases stud books should be kept and sufficient out-breeding organised (by exchanges of stock) to ensure the continued genetic diversity of the stock.

MANAGEMENT IN THE CROCODILE PROJECT

Turning to the practical achievements of the Crocodile Project we will review the topics briefly set out above in the light of the Project's practical experience on the ground in many parts of India. Further details of the Project are given by Jayal (1980) and Bustard (1981).

1. *Land*. As stated above, in the case of the Crocodile Project, all four areas of work had to commence simultaneously. However, in the preliminary report to Government (Bustard 1974) the emphasis was on status and the need for sanctuary areas offering good protection.

In the 1974 report, which formed the basis of the Project initiated the following year, three areas were recommended for creation as sanctuaries. These were Ranapratapsagar on the Chambal river in Rajasthan, Satkoshia Gorge on the Mahanadi river in Orissa—both for the gharial — and Bhitarkanika in Orissa for the saltwater crocodile. The last mentioned had already been highlighted and recommended as a sanctuary by our Curator, Mr. J.C. Daniel (Daniel and Hussain 1973). In all these areas, together with many more — the Project was responsible for the creation of no less than eleven new sanctuaries — the Project assited in the development of protection/management regimes, including the preparation of several management plans, quite apart from becoming involved in strengthening the management in a number of existing sanctuaries/National Parks. A list of the sanctuaries which were created as a result of the Project is given in the Table.

This substantial achievement requires elaboration. At the start of the Project in April 1975 India was under-represented as far as sanctuaries were concerned, and, as is so often the case, those very areas where sanctuaries were most needed, were often where progress was slowest. The Project tried to provide momentum in key areas of crocodilian need. These areas, were often of national importance, quite apart from crocodilians and, their management has benefited all other species as well.

TABLE

SANCTUARIES DECLARED THROUGH THE PROJECT'S ACTIVITIES

Name	*State*	*Area (Sq. km.)*
Ranapratapsagar	Rajasthan	-
Bhitarkanika	Orissa	250
Satkoshia Gorge	Orisa	796
Katerniaghat	U.P.	400 approx.
Coringa	A.P.	236
Lanja Modugu	A.P.	20
Papikonda	A.P.	591
Hadgarh	Orissa	191
Krishna (Nagarjunasagar/Srisailam)	A.P.	3,588
Manjira	A.P.	20
Chambal National Gharial Sanct.	U.P./M.P./ Rajasthan	12,568

It may be profitable to consider this topic on a State-by-State basis:

1. *Orissa*. Since this was the first State to join the Project, from April 1975 I lived in Orissa on the banks of the Mahanadi river in the heart of the area which I had recommended for Satkoshia Gorge Sanctuary. The first sanctuary declared in Orissa was Bhitarkanika which covers an area of about 250 sq. km. Its creation was a major achievement for the State Forest Department as it lies in a very rich alluvial deltaic area of mangrove forests fronting onto the Bay of Bengal. The mangrove vegetation can be cleared, and the ground prepared for cultivation (the technique practised for centuries), and the land outside the sanctuary is already all under rice cultivation. A brief aerial

inspection graphically illustrates (*a*) the need for the sanctuary, and (*b*) its vulnerability. Anyone doubtful of the need for sanctuaries should see this from the air, as it illustrates a situation which will become increasingly the norm in the not too distant future. Such a sanctuary, of course faces enormous management difficulties even in (just) maintaining its integrity (see below).

Satkoshia Gorge sanctuary takes in a 22 km stretch of the Mahanadi river in an area where the river passes between high hills, and although not a gorge in the properly accepted sense, forms deep pools greatly favoured by gharial. The sanctuary boundaries were selected to take in much of the surrounding catchment and includes rich forest cover with (amongst others) good tiger and gaur populations in its 790 sq. km. There were delays in getting this sanctuary gazetted, meanwhile the Oriyan race of the gharial (the most southerly surviving, and also the most isolated, so potentially the most distinctive) was brought to the verge of extinction. The final, extremely swift, gazettement of this beautiful sanctuary was brought about by the personal interest of the Prime Minister, Smt. Indira Gandhi. We are extremely fortunate in India to have this deep-rooted interest in wildlife at the highest level. We are also fortunate that in the Indian Administrative Service there are a number of dedicated individuals with keen interest in wildlife matters. This combination should augur very well for wildlife. Unfortunately it does not appear to have achieved its potential.

The third sanctuary sponsored by the Project in Orissa is Hadgarh, also a most scenic area, and selected for a mugger rehabilitation programme. It comprises 191 sq.km, and the large lake is surrounded by densely wooded areas. Full details of the Orissa programme, including a rich presentation of background material, is provided in a Report which is a model of its kind, by Kanungo (1976).

2. *Uttar Pradesh.* In U.P. we have been extremely fortunate to have Mr V.B. Singh as Chief Wildlife Warden from the inception of the Project (but not in 1974 when I was surveying). Mr Singh, whose achievement in the conservation of the gharial in north India is unique, has provided a detailed account of the status and rehabilitation of the gharial in U.P. (Singh 1978). In U.P. in addition to the creation of Katerniaghat sanctuary on Girwa river, for what is the most dense remaining gharial population in the country, Mr Singh has worked endlessly to bring about the country's largest sanctuary. This has been gazetted for the gharial and takes in some 350 km. of the Chambal river in an approximately east-west direction. The Chambal sanctuary is a tri-State sanctuary in the States of U.P. Madhya Pradesh and Rajasthan and 12,568 sq.km. in size.

In the creation of this enormous sanctuary I would also like to acknowledge the debt that we owe to the interest and perseverance of Mr Seth, Inspector General of Forests at the time that this sanctuary was at the proposal stage. Mr Seth well appreciated the need for large sanctuaries — a point I have constantly stressed — and that we should develop several *National* homes for the gharial. The Chambal National Gharial Sanctuary — to give it its proper name — is an area of outstanding potential, and when management finally reaches the desired level, can be a truly national home for the gharial assisted by a number of well-run State sanctuaries/National Parks. I will not feel that we have achieved our target, however, until the Chambal is raised to National Park status.

3. *Andhra Pradesh.* With the growth of the Project I had to move to a more central point with telephone facilities etc. I was relocated in

Hyderabad. The Project has assisted in the creation of five sanctuaries in A.P. These are the Krishna Sanctuary (still given the unappealing and lengthy name Nagarjunasagar (Srisailam sanctuary by the State Forest Department). This was the country's largest sanctuary at the time of its creation at 3,588 sq. km. Properly managed it can provide one of the National homes for the mugger as well as protecting some of the State's best tiger areas and a wide range of other wildlife.

Few people know that gharial, until very recently, occurred in South India. Our own reference to this (Bustard and Choudhury 1983) is the first in the literature. In A.P. we have selected an outstanding area of the Godaveri river for the State's re-introduction of the gharial. Reminiscent in many ways of Satkoshia Gorge in Orissa, this 591 sq.km. sanctuary can be an important asset to A.P.

The saltwater crocodile is extinct in South India, the last recorded individuals having been shot more than forty years ago. Bustard and Choudhury (1980a) recorded a recent capture in the Godaveri estuary which we think was a stray individual, probably from the Andamans. However, a suitable area of Godaveri delta has been created a sanctuary (Coringa sanctuary, 236 sq. km.) specifically for re-introduction of the species and the first few individuals have been released there.

The two remaining sanctuaries are both small areas, and despite what has been stated above, there is a place for special areas of small size provided that they are additional to, and do not replace, larger, more viable areas. Both of these small areas are for mugger, one is Janju Modugu on the trans-Godaveri (20 sq.km), an ideal and beautiful area of mugger habitat where several mugger nest each year (a very rare phenomeon in Andhra Pradesh nowadays), and the other is Manjira sanctuary on the river of the same name. This latter sanctuary is conveniently located for a visit from Hyderabad (about one hour's drive from the city) and offers good viewing of several very large mugger which are not frightened of people. In both of these latter areas there are no problems with local people (who seldom prove a problem) and at Manjira small boys wash their family's buffaloes or swim in the water in close vicinity to the large mugger. This provides an excellent illustration for city dwellers — who consider all crocodiles to be extremely dangerous man-eaters — of the way in which people and animals can co-exist where protection is nowadays given to the crocodiles.

Creation of sanctuaries requires very hard and unremitting work. Of the eleven sanctuaries described above, all of which were initiated by the Project, eight were created in the two States where I was resident over many years fulfilling a major aspect of the United Nations involvement which is meant to help to move things along. Unfortunately through the system under which the Project worked, I was the sole crocodile expert throughout, and obviously greatly over-extended in a country the size of India where twelve States were co-operating with the Project and many more wished to become involved. It was a case of doing the best one could.

The United Nations policy of short-term appointments only, makes it impossible for most people to take up appointments, thus greatly hampering the calibre of person who can be recruited, other than on short-term consultancies. Except for specific, well-circumscribed roles, short-term consultancies in my view, at least in the wildlife field, are less likely to be of lasting benefit, than people who will come, stay and see a Project through.

In concluding this section I would say: (*a*) that many ideal sanctuary areas remain to be gazetted, often due to lack of someone to 'push' for them, many examples being known to me, and (*b*) what is needed above all is a *National Review* of the 'state of the art' as far as sanctuaries/National Parks are concerned in India. Sanctuaries tend to come up haphazardly and what we need is an indepth review, published in book form, of all existing wildlife areas, their flora, fauna and protection status. The author(s) would need to personally visit each area to ensure consistency of editorial approach. This would then provide a blue-print for further gazettements in areas — both geographical and flora/faunistically — un-or under-represented at the present time.

In concluding this section I would not like to suggest that the sanctuary programme has not faced any difficulties. It has; however, these have been containable. The worst has been serious encroachment of the Bhitarkanika sanctuary in Cuttack district of Orissa. The continued integrity of this sanctuary in the face of people of Bangaladesh origin who wish to cut down the mangrove forests and cultivate the area will depend on continued strong support from the Government of India.

2. *Protection*. Protective duties have been of maximum importance in the crocodile project. Animals may become endangered for a number of reasons, including loss of habitat. In the crocodile project the gharial had been driven to the brink of extinction before the project was initiated, yet much of its natual habitat remained in a more or less virgin state. Hunting for its skin (Bustard 1974) had been responsible for the large-scale catastrophic drop in numbers. Only an effectively-enforced, cessation of all hunting activities, could save it. Furthermore, with numbers reduced to an estimated 60-70 adult or subadult gharial throughout its extensive Indian range, any further losses would quickly become irreversible, as it would no longer be possible for the few remaining, and mostly scattered individuals, to find mates. In Orissa for instance by 1975 the population was reduced to four adults, two of each sex, all living within the Satkoshia Gorge proposed sanctuary area. Natural breeding in the wild, however, stopped. The last successful hatch was reported to me by local staff to have taken place in 1974. I personally collected a nest of eggs in 1975 but the eggs were infertile. The same was the case in 1976, and thereafter no further nests were recorded. Without protection, and without the Project to focus attention on its critical status and concurrently to tackle the problem, the gharial would have slipped away like the cheetah.

Protection by itself might not have been enough, at least for many population remnants, which is why an active management programme was initiated (see 3 below).

The Orissa gharial project provides a good illustration of protection in practice. This is briefly described below.

Protection antedated the declaration of Satkoshia gorge sanctuary by about a year. Protection staff were minimal at the outset comprising four river-borne staff and four land-based forest guards. The river staff were specially-recruited, local fisherman-caste villagers with an intimate knowledge of the river, since they were normally on it each day in the course of their fishing activities. The river staff moved two to a boat. The boats were their own canoes, ideal for moving on the river in monsoon torrents or summer drought. Two were from Tikerpada village near the top of the 'gorge' and two from a village near the southern river limits of the sanctuary. They patrolled daily. The time of greatest threat to the gharial is always during winter when they lie out to bask for much of the day. The threat is greatest following failure of the monsoon due to the abnormally reduced water levels which then result. This then had to be the season of maximum alertness.

None of the first three instances of poaching detected by these guards concerned gharial. I had made it very clear from the outset, that any illegal act within the proposed sanctuary boundaries was to be stopped. I had sat with the guards on the banks of the Mahanadi and pointed out the high sandbanks which the gharial use for nesting and explained how their maintenance was helped by the massive trees of the riverine forest.

The first three poaching incidents involved one case of teak log poaching and two of illegal bamboo cutting and attempted removal. We also had dramatic incidents involving attempted poaching of gharial, but first I would like to discuss other activities within the river portion of the sanctuary and how these were modified in the interests of the gharial without adversely affecting the legitimate interests of the local people.

Although it is correct to say that the catastrophic drop in gharial numbers was brought about by commercially-oriented hunting for their skins, the introduciton of the use of nylon gill nets (set nets) further decimated those individuals which had survived the poachers. Crocodiles learn fast — there are even scientifically documented instances of single instance learning in crocodilians (Bustard 1968) — and lage individuals — the breeding stock — are very wary of man where they are actively hunted, and normally cannot be caught by conventional means. Chinks in their armour — which make them extremely vulnerable — are basking, in those species where seasonally in the winter this is essential on climatic grounds (as in gharial), and nest guarding, where this trait is well developed (e.g. the saltwater crocodile).

Nylon gill nets are set across rivers — sometimes right across the river — and the normal behaviour of a captured crocodile is to twist round, which results in it becoming more and more entangled in the net. The nets are put out in the evening and taken in the next morning so are in place during the crocodiles time of major activity. Very large individuals seem to become wary of nets (presumably following a previous encounter and successful escape) but smaller individuals are caught, like fish, before they can learn to avoid them. Even in areas where the local people do not hunt crocodiles, individuals caught in nets will still be killed in order to save the extremely valuable net from damage. In the mid-seventies in Satkoshia Gorge a net was worth the equivalent of the average annual cash income of a fisherman, so that the investment, offered as a loan from the fishing contractor, is enormous.

Fishing contractors (the auctioning of lengths of rivers or lakes is widespread), and set nets, are political. Let it suffice to say that the policy of the crocodile project has been: 1) to ban the use of set nets for the above reasons, and 2) to get rid of the contractor system, 3) to advise the local villagers that the nets are not in their long-term best interests in river systems since they are over-efficient and catch all the fish. (As the larger fish become scarce they catch the recruiting individuals, on which replenishment of the breeding stock depends, by reducing the mesh spacing. 4) to allow fishing to continue using traditional methods — baited lines, small throw nets, fishing scoops etc. 5) to restrict fishing to those people living within the area and enjoying traditional rights, 6) to help the local people to set up fishing co-operatives to enable them to obtain the best price for their fish.

The people of Tikerpada within Satkoshia Gorge sanctuary will tell the enquiring visitor that the set nets destroyed their fishery resource and that following banning of the use of set nets the resource is recovering under local fishing, using traditional means, and without the very large number of outside people which the revenue staff had licensed.

One of the most significant things for the conservationist to realise is that conservation is always in the interests of the local people. When their area is ruined — the forest resource gone, the fish all caught — they cannot go away — it is their home. hence a long-term policy of sustained yield utilisation, properly explained, provided it is implemented early enough in the destructive process, will always have their approval. The contractor system, on the other hand, be it for fish or timber, is quite the reverse. The contractor is given a short-term contract. He wants to extract the maximum pecuniary advantage from this contract in the shortest possible time. He has no vested interest in the long-term ecological health of the contract area. When it is finished he will go off and start again elsewhere.

We like to think that much can be learned from the 'set net' saga. But it was not — and is not — easy, and there are many conflicting vested interests at stake. Conservation is an intensely political activity. I often tell my students that conservation is 90% politics and 10% conservation science. By politics I do not mean *talking* to politicians. Any sensible conservationist will retain the traditional civil servants' apolitical stance as far as any particular party is concerned, but the questions of land use form the very basis of political doctrine in most countries.

As our conservation staff in Satkoshia Gorge sanctuary grew, and we were able to patrol over a longer stretch of the river, we continued our policy of appointing local riverine staff for river patrols. We have deliberately, in some cases, selected former pachers' assistants. In the early seventies, in this area, one individual was reportedly responsible for the loss of most of the small number of remaining gharial. He arrived with two vehicles each winter from another State complete with a Forest Department permit to shoot sambar. He contacted local villagers and offered them a reward if they would take him to a spot where a gharial basked. He would then try to shoot it. I have talked personally to several people who claim to have helped him. The reward they obtained for showing the gharial was Rs 125. Since gharial were already scarce, there was little money to be made from this activity. Such people were very willing to work for the Forest Department as protection staff on a regular monthly salary, which I explained would continue as long as they were able to show the gharial to me or sanctuary officers on patrol that they were appointed to protect.

The above may all sound very simple. Anyone who knows India will know it is not. This is not the way the Forest Departments recruit their staff. They go to the labour exchange, and since villagers from remote areas are not registered, get towns people who know nothing about interior areas, hate them, and spend their time manipulating a transfer back to the town. I could fill a whole book about this in a single sanctuary in Orissa — Bhitarkanika. But we should think, and try to act, positively, while yet being aware of all the pitfalls.

I would like now to briefly mention two attempted poaching cases foiled by our protection staff. I have heard much criticism of the staff during my many years in India. I have nothing but admiration for many of them — particularly where they have been given proper guidance by their senior officers — as these two instances will demonstrate.

The first instance concerns a winter poaching

attempt by three armed men on our largest gharial male, which at 21 ft 6 in. is equal to the World record for the species (Pitman 1924). This was foiled by two of our villagers, fisherman-caste guards who spotted the people just as they were creeping up to take aim at the gharial, and unarmed, managed to persuade them not to shoot it. We were extremely fortunate both in the timing of their appearance, and the quality of our protection staff. The plan, of course, is to try to apprehend poachers before they reach the river area.

The second instance concerns a rich city-dweller who wanted to shoot a trophy gharial, and who came, perfectly legally, and took up residence in one of our Forest Rest Houses within the Sanctuary. I had long advocated complete searches of the boots of all vehicles entering or passing through the sanctuary. The facility existed as we had forest gates manned on a twentyfour hour basis. It seemed ludicrous to me that a signature was required to pass through, but searches were not carried out. So our trophy hunters arrived armed. When his intention became known to the local project forester, he visited him and explained the position. The man remained extremely keen, and offered extensive bribes, eventually totalling Rs 25,000 so I am advised. The forester remained adamant, and the life of a large gharial was again saved. Without the Project the importance of gharial conservation would not have been known to more than a handful of dedicated forest officers, and the gharial would have gone the way of the cheetah.

I do not have time to go deeper into protection. The type of approach that I have in mind is perfectly obvious from the above examples.

3. Getting to know the animal — research projects as required.

It is important to get a 'feel' for the animal being studied. This is exactly what Konrad Lorenz meant in the example cited above. Extensive field work by the right sort of person will provide this. This 'feel', incidently, is present in many country folk, and well developed in all the better poachers or hunters. Many senior Indian Forest Officers — S.P. Shahi is an outstanding example — will tell you how they moved from shikar to conservation with the decrease of India's wildlife. It will not be sufficient, however, to merely develop this trait. On some aspects, at least rigorous research will be needed.

Research, particularly where supported by outside conservation society funds, should be *relevant* to the conservation programme. As a research scientist, I have seen the scientific community done great disservice — and also the supply of such grants jeopardised in the future — by individuals who have used conservation funds for work of doubtful if any relevance to the particular project. This does not mean that the research should be weak. It should be of the highest quality so that its results cannot be set aside.

At the start of the gharial project we had to decide on the size of the riverine portion of Satkoshia Gorge sanctuary. Nothing was known about gharial movements. Dr L.A.K. Singh, then one of my Ph.D. students, and I commenced a study in August 1975 which showed that gharial move considerable distances in the river and may do so quite quickly (Bustard and Singh 1983). Both the large male and large female moved maximum distances of 44 km between August 1975 and January 1976 and a smaller male and female 28.8. and 22.8 km in the same time span. This showed the need for long river stretches within sanctuaries to afford adequate protection. Of great interest were distances of 12 km. over 2 hours and also in one day, and 3.6 km in 30 minutes, all three being up river. The contribution of the field protection staff in collecting the data for this paper was paramount. Without their help the paper could not have been written.

We also developed a method of estimating gharial size without seeing the individual from measurement of certain scutes at the base of the tail which leave a good impression on slightly moist sand (Bustard and Singh 1977). This technique is excellent in that even an illiterate guard can collect the data in the field. We measure three scutes and average the measurement and the guard brings back three sticks or one larger stick notched with the scute lengths. Singh and Bustard (1977) also developed individual identification using a technique called 'tail printing' — using the natural colour bandings on the tail — which has very wide applicability.

In order to collect extensive data on gharial and crocodilian biology in various geographic regions I undertook the supervision, through their Ph.D.'s, of seven Indian M.Sc's in Zoology acting in each case with an internal University guide also. This has proved an outstanding method of data collection as well as training future potential managers for India. One of these students has worked on the Pacific Ridley sea turtle in Orissa, sea turtles being my other specialist interest.

Since we were extensively involved in the handling and incubation of crocodilian eggs, on a very large-scale, much of our research was centred on eggs, and naturally, extensive data collected on such topics as clutch size, nesting behaviour, nesting season and related topics.

In the case of the saltwater crocodile, which is assumed to be a 'Vicious maneater', Dr. S.K. Kar (another former student) and I carried out research in the Bhitarkanika wildlife sanctuary of Orissa extending over 10 years (Bustard and Kar 1982) and showed that man-eating was a very rare event. On the basis of this careful scientific study we were forced to conclude that saltwater crocodiles, like many other animals, avoid man. Before the control of fishing in the sanctuary, local people daily waded into the muddy creeks to fish. Crocodiles could have attacked them unseen yet these attacks hardly ever took place. We documented only four instances of human attack over a ten year period yet this sanctuary contains some of the largest surviving crocodiles of this species in the World — the very individuals which one would expect to be responsible for such attacks.

The gharial is considered harmless to man and Dr Singh and I, therefore, documented surprising attack on a man on the Mahanadi (Bustard and Singh 1981).

Following on from the studies on human attacks by the saltwater crocodile we published a study of attacks on domestic livestock (also extremely rare in a situation where countless opportunities occur daily) (Bustard and Kar 1981a), and the obverse situation, of local people stealing the crocodile's kills (Bustard and Kar 1981b). Such publications often have immediate management implications. For instance concerning the occasional losses of cattle to saltwater crocodiles we wrote.

'The attacks all occurred at (four) locations where the natural mangrove cover had been destroyed. Unless this is the case domestic livestock cannot come to the river bank. Cattle attacks increase the unpopularity of the saltwater crocodile and increase the forces working against its conservation. Ideally crocodiles and cattle should be separated — there should be no grazing in sanctuaries. This idea, however, is difficult to achieve in much of the developing world inhabited by crocodiles. The solution lies in maintaining a strip of undisturbed mangrove forest, at least 50 m wide, along all creeks adjacent to cultivated land.

Since this fringing forest cover is important for the crocodiles themselves this should form a key aspect of management.'

In the paper dealing with crocodile kills taken as human food we concluded. 'The implication of kill stealing for the management of crocodile (and tiger) sanctuaries is clear. There is a need to separate crocodiles from local people. The *sanctum sanctorum* or core area of such sanctuaries must be free from human habitation or intrusions. In sanctuaries the animals must have 'right of way' at all times, otherwise the sanctuaries will ultimately prove of little value in the conservation of their endangered species.'

Bustard (1980) and Bustard and Choudhury (1981a) pointed out the crucial situation facing the saltwater crocodile in India and the steps that need to be followed if it is to survive. Bustard and Choudhury (1980a) in a paper on parental care in the saltwater crocodile pointed out the management implications of this trait. Due to incomplete nest guarding, vulnerability to human attack while at the nest, and the difficulty of guarding such a large brood of siblings, which also disperse too early for female protection to be effective, the authors feel that collection of eggs for hatchery incubation and captive rearing of the resultant young provides a much greater survival rate than the mother is able to achieve.

Extensive work has been carried out on the post-release monitoring of released 1.20 m long crocodilians of all three (Indian) species. Since this work clearly could not commence until we had raised large numbers of crocodilians to this size and released them back into the wild few of these studies have as yet appeared. An outstanding account, showing very little movement and excellent survival — probably 100% after several years back in the wild — has recently appeared for the Indian mugger (Choudhury and Bustard 1983). These mugger are the first captive-reared and released crocodilians to have bred following their return to the wild (Choudhury and Bustard *in press*). Much of this basic data was collected by the protection staff and their contribution is clearly set out in the paper's tables.

Kar and Bustard (*in press*) document 80% survival of a small group of fifteen saltwater crocodiles rehabilitated into Bhitarkanika after two years back in the wild. Survival figures are always minimal ones, as failure to record an animal does not mean that it has died, it may reflect human error, or the crocodile in question may have moved outside the census area.

In order to carry out subsequent monitoring, all released crocodiles must be marked. They should be marked in a way which is cheap, easy to carry out in remote areas, and which, most importantly, *can be seen without having to catch the crocodile*. This last aspect is crucial as crocodiles learn very fast (Bustard 1968), so censusing based on physical handling will result in markedly decreased recapture success, and animals which are maintaining themselves well in the population, but evading recapture, will appear to have disappeared. There are two further considerations. A tag physically applied to the crocodile may become detached, and the marking method should be one requiring minimum literacy (if any). We published our methodology in the *Indian Forester* (Bustard and Choudhury 1981b). This includes scute-clipping of the single row of scutes on the tail. Regeneration does not take place. The clip can be seen easily when the animal is basking (the clipping includes a sex code), literacy is not required to record presence of the clip. Crocodiles often swim or float with the tip of the tail above water and an experienced observer can record the clip at such times. Both Dr Kat and I have had no difficulty in recording it using a spotlight at night in Bhitarkanika, when recruiting-sized individuals come into shallow water at the edge of mudbanks and elevate the tail clear of the muddy water. Using this methodology it is possible to individually mark crocodiles also, as detailed in the paper. For general use, however, we recommend only the use of a single recognition clip, the scute clipped changing each year, so that at a glance one can see if the animal is a released individual, and at the same time the year of release. Since we release approximately 2.5 females per male, deliberately we do not clip the more abundant females for sex, but clip males. So all the above information is incorporated in a single clipped scute for females and two in the case of males.

The above few examples should serve to indicate the type of research that is needed. We in the Project have published some one hundred research papers, many in the Society's *Hornbill*. Although we publish internationally, we have always made a point of publishing papers of major conservation importance here in India. Further details of these publications together with an annotated bibliography of Indian crocodilians was published by the Project (Bustard and Singh 1982) and is available free on request. A further useful publication on crocodile conservation and research in India is that of Singh and Choudhury (1982).

4. *Active management*. In my 1974 report I recommended that an active management approach be undertaken of the gharial and other Indian crocodilians in order to boost numbers quickly. In crocodilians and other animals which produce large numbers of eggs, wastage is very large. Management, by vastly reducing this wastage at various levels of the life-history has the capacity to rapidly raise population size with the result that it is possible to re-establish whole populations *rapidly*. This is not the place to go into an evaluation of the techniques involved (Bustard 1975), nor the necessary safeguards (Bustard *in press*), of which perhaps the most important is to maintain genetic diversity in the population. It would clearly be most unwise to repopulate an entire river system with the successive progeny of one pair of crocodilians on genetic grounds, although due to their fecundity, this was a practical proposition in terms of numbers of young required, over a ten year re-introduction time scale.

The main reason for my recommending an active management programme was that otherwise recovery, in the case of the gharial, would have been patchy at best, with possible recovery limited to one or two areas in the country at best, and with the remnant populations elsewhere failing to maintain themselves and being lost. This clearly would have been unsatisfactory. In the case of the saltwater crocodile, without the active management programme I felt — and still feel — this species would have been lost from the Indian fauna over a period of time.

It may be worthwile to point out that mugger numbers were so low in many areas of the country that only active management has maintained the *geographical spread* of the mugger, although the species itself was not endangered, only seriously depleted.

There were other good reasons to adopt this approach:

1) The proposals which were contained in my 1974 FAO/Report to the Governmet of India included the creation of many new sanctuaries in the country, many of substantial areas (see 1 above). It would have been extremely difficult to justify their creation for only a handful of animals.

2) In a conservation programme of this size

there is tremendous scope for conservation education. Although saving the animal must take precedence over everything else, conservation education would provide a most valuable spin-off. If people interested in learning about the Project cannot even see the animal that is being conserved when they travel to an interior sanctuary, it is difficult, if not impossible, to generate this.

3) The active management programme focussed attention on the sanctuaries themselves, as the captive rearing stations were located as far as possible within the sanctuaries themselves. The success of this approach was obvious — the rearing stations quickly became tourist attractions in their own right, in a number of States, notably in U.P., Orissa and West Bengal. Furthermore, by focussing attention on the rearing centres people were 'streamed' away from the river itself, where large-scale tourism, such as the rearing centres encountered, would have been a serious disturbance, to the wild gharial.

4) The captive rearing stations were a tangible demonstration of what was being done to conserve the species.

5) The population parameters of the crocodilian species lent themselves superbly to this approach.

The core of the active management programme focussed on the species itself — as opposed to the parallel, extremely active programme of sanctuary selection, gazettement and protection — consisted of protection of eggs during their lengthy (approximately two and a half month) incubation period, together with protection of hatchlings until they were large enough to look after themselves.

The only way to effectively protect eggs on a large-scale, in widely separated nesting areas, spread over numerous remote areas in the country, was to collect them, preferably as soon as laid, bring them to a series of central points, and incubate them in predator-proof hatcheries. That was carried out in association with the Project in the states of Orissa, Uttar Pradesh, Andhra Pradesh, Tamil Nadu, West Bengal, Kerala, Rajasthan, and Gujarat shows the size and geographical spread of the undertaking.

Collection of wild-laid eggs for captive incubation saves the eggs from a wide range of natural predators including man. It is not always appreciated that in many areas of India, tribal man, may be the most serious — and effective — predator. For instance in Nepal, and adjacent Bihar when gharial were still present in the latter area, all eggs were collected. In extensive surveys of the Narayani river of Nepal in the mid-1970's I found no recruiting individuals implying that egg collection had been 100% over many years. In the Andamans in 1978 my student, Mr B.C. Choudhury, in a nest study on no less than 30 nests of the saltwater crocodile found that *only one nest* or 3.3% of those studied hatched. Human predation accounted for 84.6% of nest losses (Choudhury and Bustard 1980). Add to this level of predation, nests lost through flooding during incubation, and the arguments for nest collection become overwhelming.

Juvenile crocodiles are very small, averaging around 30 cm (slightly more in the case of the gharial), soft and delicate, and form easy prey for a wide range of predators, including fish, aquatic birds, mammals and other reptiles. Hence the greatly enhanced numbers which can be hatched in captivity can be further multiplied by keeping the young in specially designed pools in captivity until they are through this critical phase. Taking into account varying conditions in different areas — as is essential in a National Project — it was decided that 1.0-1.20 m (3-4 feet) was an ideal release size. The plan calls for rapid growth under semi-natural conditions, using natural food throughout in order to attain this size as quickly as possible. Under ideal husbandry conditions, in climatically favoured areas experiencing reduced winter effects, it is possible to attain this size within 18-20 months of hatching and thus operate a two year cycle in the hatchling and yearling pools (Bustard 1975). This fits in well with release times which should be set to enable the released animals to become familiar with their new habitat before onset of the monsoon. The Project recommended release in February in the warmer southern areas, with this delayed until March in the extreme north.

This activity, comprising collection of eggs and rearing of young for subsequent release into protected sanctuary areas in ideal natural habitat, has been called the 'rear release' technique. It is, of course, essential that the 'protected sanctuary areas' are created simultaneously with the rearing programme, but the 'production' of very large numbers of an endangered species provides tremendous impetus for pushing ahead with the sanctuary creation/management goals. The efficacy of this approach can be seen in the results — sanctuaries declared (See Table) and animals released upto 1982. These figures (Singh and Choudhury 1982) are:

Gharial — 855 (approximately *twelve times* the estimated 60-70 adult/subadult individuals surviving in the entire country when the project was initiated.

Saltwater crocodile — 278 (approximately *ten times,* the probable wild population of adults and sub-adults in 1974), and *mugger* — 490.

In addition substantially larger numbers of each species than these, were currently being reared for future release.

Concluding Remarks

I would briefly sum up by saying that in the crocodilian project the role of management was paramount — without the active management programme there would be no gharial today, and the saltwater crocodile would be on the verge of extinction in India.

Management entails always putting the legitimate interests of the species first. One has got to argue very strenuously for one's beliefs in the World today. One can argue more effectively if it is obvious to all parties that you have no vested interest other than the best interests of the animal itself.

Addressing myself to the younger members of the audience I would say that conservation — or science itself for that matter — is not an easy career. One must be dedicated. Conservation is a world-wide war. Furthermore, it is a war that can never be won. One can win encounters, skirmishes or minor engagements' (which if you lose will have a catastrophic effect on your animal or ecosystem), but you can never win the ultimate battle, as even when your 'animal' (for want of a better word) is numerous, and in what you believe is a secure National Park, even in the most-developed countries, such places have not proven to be sacrosanct.

In concluding this paper I would like to point out that the approach set out in this paper is one that can be adopted, with only minor variations in the conservation of a wide range of endangered animals both here in India and overseas.

Acknowledgements

The Crocodile Project is indebted to a very large number of people all of whom obviously cannot be mentioned here, but I am listing a few of those whose contributions were outstanding. They are mentioned in chronological order as they assisted the Project in time: Mr M.K. Rajitsinh, then Deputy Secretary, GOI, who helped to bring the Project into existence, Mr K.L. Lahiri, then Inspector General of Forests who told me to travel throughout India to get a 'birds eye view' of the problem, the late Mr S.R. Choudhury who ensured Orissa was the first State to take up the Project and whom I was proud to have as a friend and counsellor, Mr S.P. Shahi, then Chief Conservator of Forests, Bihar, who assisted me greatly with his knowledge of the gharial both in discussion and in the field, Mr V.B. Singh, Chief Wild Life Warden, Uttar Pradesh whose contribution to the conservation of the gharial was outstanding, Mr N.D. Jayal, Joint Secretary, GOI, who guided the Project tirelessly throughout most of its life and was an inspiration to us all, Mr Seth, then Inspector General of Forests, Mr B.P. Srivastava, then Inspector General of Forests, whose active interest and support we had even when he was C.C.F., U.P., and Mr Samar Singh, Joint Secretary, GOI who guided the Project in its final period. Lastly I owe a special debt to the enthusiasm and hard work of my Ph.D. students, particualrly Dr L.A.K. Singh on gharial, Dr S.K. Kar on saltwater crocodiles and Mr B.C. Choudhury on the mugger.

References

BUSTARD, H.R. (1968): Rapid learning in wild crocodiles (*Crocodylus porosus*). *Herpetologica* 24(2):173-175.

_____ (1972): Sea Turtles: Natural History and Conservation. Collins, Sondon & Sydney.

________ (1974) India: A preliminary survey of the prospects for Crocodile Farming. FAO Rome (FO:IND/71/033) Oct. 1974.

________ (1975): India: Gharial and Crocodile Conservation Management in Orissa. FAO Rome (FO:IND/71/033) Dec. 1975.

______ (1980): India's most endangered crocodile — will the saltwater crocodile survive? *Makara* 2(1):2-3.

BUSTARD, H.R. (1981): Crocodile Breeding Project. *In Wildlife in India*, V.B. Saharia (ed.) Government of India, New Delhi, pps. 147-164.

_____ (in press); Captive breeding of the gharial. *Proc. 1981 Intnl. Oxford Herpetological Congr.*

________ CHOUDHURY, B.C. (1980a): Parental care in the saltwater crocodile (*Crocodylus porosus* Schneider) and management implications. *J. Bombay nat. Hist. Soc.* 77(1):64-69.

________ (1980b): Long distance movement of a saltwater crocodile (*Crocodylus porosus* Schneider). *Brit. J. Herpetol.* 6(3):87.

________ (1981a): Conservation future of the saltwater crocodile (*Crocodylus porosus* Schneider) in India. *J. Bombay nat. Hist. Soc.* 77(2):201-214.

________ (1981b): Marking crocodiles for release back into the wild for subsequent indentification. *Indian Forester* 102 (8): 477-485.

________ (1983): The distribution of the gharial. *J. Bombay nat. Hist. Soc.* 79(2): 427-429.

________ & KAR, S.K. (1981a): Attacks on domestic livestock by the saltwater crocodile (*Crocodylus porosus*) in Orissa, India. *Brit. J. Herpetol.* 6:135-136.

________ (1981b): Crocodile kills taken as human food. ibid. 6(4):137.

________ (1982) Crocodile predation on man. ibid. 6:222-223.

________ & SINGH, L.A.K. (1977): Studies on the Indian gharial *Gavialis gangeticus* (Gmelin) (Reptila, Crocodilia) — I. Estimation of body length from scute length. *Indian Forester* 103(2):140-149.

________ (1981): Gharial attacks on man. *J. Bombay nat. Hist. Soc.* 78(3):610-611.

________ (1982): An annotated bibliography on Indian Crocodilians. India: Crocodile Breeding & Management Project, Field Document No. 9 (FO:IND/74/046). FAO, Rome, Dec. 1982.

________ (1983): Movement of wild gharial, *Gavialis gangeticus* (Gmelin) in the River Mahanadi, Orissa (India). 6(8): 287-291.

CHOUDHURY, B.C. & BUSTARD, H.R. (1980): Predation on natural nests of the saltwater crocodile (*Crocodylus porosus* Schneider) on north Andaman Island with notes on the crocodile population. *J. Bombay nat. Hist. Soc.* 76(2):311-323.

DANIEL, J.C. & HUSSAIN, S.A. (1973): The record (?) saltwater crocodile (*Crocodylus porosus*). ibid. 71(2):309-312.

JAYAL, N.D. (1980): Crocodile conservation in India. *Tigerpaper* 7(4): 1-3.

KANUNGO, B.C. (1976): An intergrated scheme for conservation of crocodiles in Orissa with management plans for Satkoshia Gorge and Bhitarkanika sanctuaries. *State Forest department*, Cuttack, Orissa. pps. 1-128.

LACK, D. (1954): The natural regulation of animal numbers. O.U.P.

PITMAN, C.R.S. (1924): The length attained by and the habits of the gharial (*Gavialis gangeticus*). *J. Bombay nat. Hist. Soc.* **30**:703.

SINGH, L.A.K. & BUSTARD, H.R. (1977): A method to identify individual young gharial (*Gavialis gangeticus*). *Brit. J. Herpetol.* **5**:669-671.

__________ & CHOUDHURY, B.C. (Eds.) (1982): Indian crocodiles — conservation and research. Proc. First Indian Croc. Res. Symp. Katerniaghat, U.P. 21-25 January 1979.

SINGH, V.B. (1978): Status of the gharial in Uttar Pradesh and its rehabilitation. *J. Bombay nat. Hist. Soc.* 75(3):668-683.

Asian Elephant Management in North America

(*With a text-figure*)

EDWIN GOULD

The first elephant came to the United States from India in 1796; eight years later a second arrived. By 1973 well over 400 elephants had arrived in North America. The two major consumers, zoos and circuses, have exchanged elephants over the years.

The name of an elephant often changed when ownership changed hands. The pattern makes accurate demographic estimates very difficult, particularly for the non-zoo animals. Most major zoos in the United States report their animal holdings to a computer centre at the International Species Inventory System (ISIS) in Minnesota. Circuses have no systematic record keeping device; however, a few hobbyist historians exist (Sabu, W. Woodcock, L. Bagget).

POPULATION SIZE

The earliest published account of Asian elephant populations listed a total of 299, including 80 in zoos and 130 in travelling circuses; an additional 60 African elephants were listed in zoos only (Knecht 1933).

In 1976, Kawata and Bennett reported 9.94 or a total of 103 Asian elephants in ISIS reporting institutions. Kawata and Bennett estimated another 50 Asian elephants went unreported.

Lash (1982) reported that in 1982:

275 (14.132) elephants were held by ISIS reporting institutions

277 elephants were held by circuses, some of which were Africans

9 elephants were held privately in Canada

561 total

Currently, 1983, nine male and 86 female Asian elephants are held by ISIS reporting institutions. Increased reporting, more inclusive reporting and, less likely, an increase in the actual number of elephants probably accounts for the marked differences in population estimates.

According to circus historian Sabu (1983), there are currently 24 bulls held by 16 different private individuals and circuses. An additional nine bulls are held by zoos, for a total of 33. The above figures include holdings of 1.12 *E. maximus maximus*. One bull at Calgary in Canada is the sole source of breeding bull if purity of subspecies is valued.

Geographic distribution of bulls is relatively widespread, but shipping distances, management practices, and inadequate facilities have played a part in limiting breeding programmes.

AGE STRUCTURE

More than half (49/86 or 57%) are more than 20 years of age (Figure). The largest age cohort less than 20 years old is the 12-13 year old group. The great majority of captive elements were imported into the United States. The preponderance of elephants in the more than 20, the 12-13 and the 17-19 years age classes probably represents three or more major importations in the history of animal acqusition.

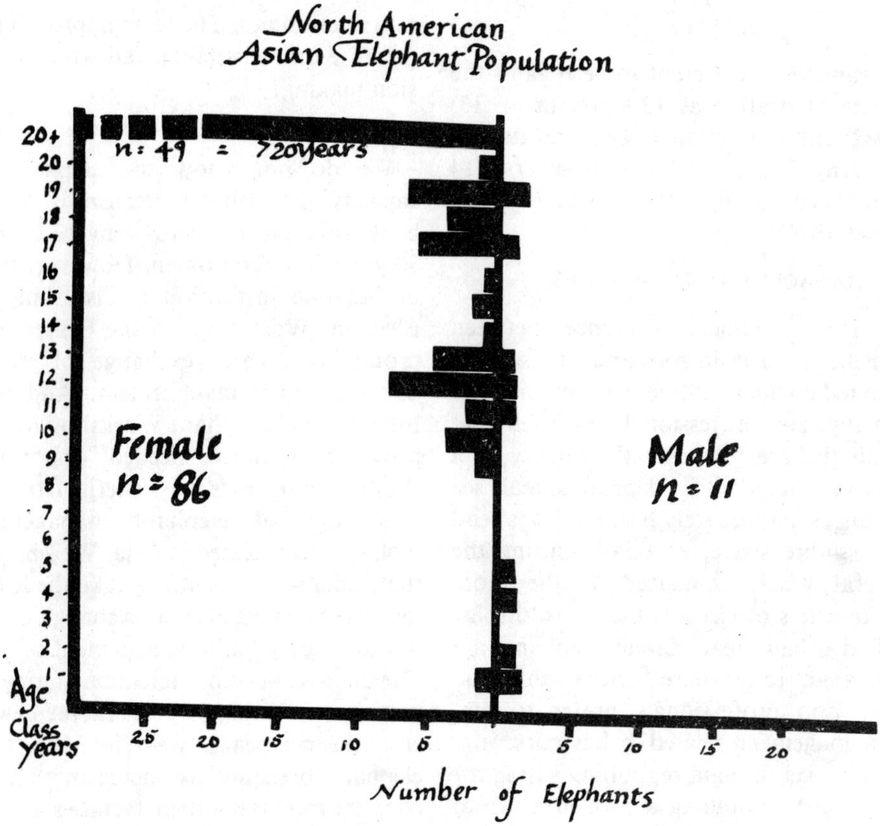

Age class composition of Asian elephant population in North American zoos in 1983.

BIRTHS

According to Keele (1983), of 37 calves born in the United States 12 (32%) lived less than one year, 18 (49%) lived longer than one year, 12 of which are still alive. Five (14%) are alive today but under one year of age. Of 18 calves which survived longer than one year, three (8%) have matured to breed. Ten bulls sired the 35 captive bred calves born to 15 cows (Keele 1983). Cows in the Portland herd account for 21 (60%) of the births. Twenty-one (60%) of the calves were male and 14 (40%) were females. Since 1977, five facilities and one private owner produced calves (Keele 1983). The first International Elephant Breeding Symposium occurred in September, 1983, at the Washington Park Zoo in Portland, Oregon. Discussions about artificial insemination, bull mangement and reproductive physiology highlighted the discussions. There were no provocative statements that revealed any particular formula for breeding success other than the "gestalt" display of the entire Portland complex of breeding facility and its management. Portland's accomplishment is remarkable.

Deaths

In two samples of different zoo elephants the median age at death was 18 years (n = 13) (Lash 1982) and 14 years (n = 12) (Kawata and Bennett 1976). Causes of death are diverse: 14 deaths included 11 different causes (Kawata and Bennet 1976).

Management Techniques

There is a distinct difference between management practices in zoos and circuses and rather limited communication between the two. Traditionally, zoo professionals have felt that circus activities are "beneath the dignity of a wild, captive animal". Circus professionals see zoo animals as inadequately trained. Zoos tend to provide more space, especially during the past several years, compared to the more cramped quarters of circuses that must display in modified urban areas. Circus elephants are generally taught to do more "tricks" than zoo elephants. Zoo professionals prefer to emphasize management related behaviours, e.g. carrying a bucket of manure, pulling a drag for levelling a yard or holding a foot in a tub to facilitate medication when the veterinarian prescribes it . Because zoo keepers usually care for other animals in the collection, they tend to spend much less time with the elephants than circus trainers. However, there seems to be general agreement that actively trained elephants are mentally and physically healthier than untrained elephants in the relatively confined facilities of any captive setting.

There has been a strong shift in zoos away from a single "bull man" handling the elephants toward a team or committee approach. The latter has been spearheaded by Don Meyers. Both systems have management problems in the zoo setting. The single person develops problems at vacation, sick leave and retirement times. The team approach may compromise on consistency and struggle with decision making.

The Future

We do not know the elephant carrying capacity of North American zoos. We can probably say that the increase by 12 over the past 30 years is a good omen. However, the success of but one institution is disturbing. Annual Elephant Workshops in the United States are promoting greater exchange of information about elephant management. And the recent International Elephant Workshop held in India provided a much needed opportunity for Western biologists to benefit from the rich knowledge of elephant management and biology accumulated in Asia. We sincerely hope that India will continue to take the lead in promoting the international exchange of information on biology and management of elephants. The increase in communication among elephant managers in the zoo world and the new spurt of enthusiasm speaks well for the future of elephant breeding as increasing numbers of zoos are modifying their facilities and developing techniques to handle bulls.

Elephants are among the most popular animals for the visiting public. Exhibiting the interaction between animal and human is a particularly captivating spectacle to the zoo visitor. At the National zoo 25 volunteers from the Friends of the National Zoo describe to the public why we train elephants to do what they do; as a part of an elephant demonstration they emphasize elephant management. The docents explain why the hook (*ankus*) is used, why the animals are trained and why the public's concern is vital to the preservation of natural habitats and the survival of elephants.

Shoshani (*pers. comm.*) has emphasized the importance of saving the elephant; because of

its size and function in the ecosystem, if you save it, you save the entire array of associated biota.

LITERATURE CITED

KAWATA, KEN & BENNETT. J. (1979): Elephants in U.S. Zoos mid-1976. AAZPA Regional workshop proceedings. pp. 164-180.

KNECHT, KAE K. (1933): Three hundred elephants. The White Tops, July-August, pp.10-11. Publisher: Circus Fans Association, Evansville, Indiana.

KEELE, MICHAEL N. (1983): Breeding Asian elephants in the United States. Manuscript: Elephant Breeding symposium, Washington Park Zoo, Portland, Oregon.

LASH, SANDRA S. (1982): Captive elephant population of North America: 1982 update. Elephant 2(1): 147-150.

Edwin Gould, Curator of Mammals, National Zoological Park, Smithsonian Institution, Washington, D.C. 20008.

Gloria C. Fenney, Museum Studies Programme, George Washington University, Washington, D.C. 20006.

Breeding the Indian Python (*Python m. molurus*) under captive conditions in India

SHEKAR DATTATRI
Research Associate, Madras Snake Park Trust,
Madras-600 022, India

ABSTRACT

This short paper attempts at providing a guide for breeding the Indian Python (*Python m. molurus*), an endangered species, under captive conditions in India. Dealt with herein are aspects of housing, general care and breeding biology, with special emphasis on problems commonly encountered with captive breeding, strategies employed in inducing breeding, artificial incubation of eggs and care of hatchlings.

INTRODUCTION

Despite its popularity in zoos, adaptability, wide distribution *and* endangered status, breeding the Indian python (*Python m. molurus*) in captivity in India still remains a novelty. Although almost every zoo in the country maintains a few individuals of this species, breeding success is seldom achieved due to lack of initiative or know-how on part of the keepers. This short paper attempts at providing a guide for breeding Indian pythons under Indian conditions and is based primarily on observations made at the Madras Snake Park Trust (MSPT) where this species has been bred for the past few years.

HOUSING

Space and habitat. Many workers maintain that, for best results, breeding populations should be housed in enclosures undisturbed by visitors. While this is probably true, it is seldom practical in a zoo where hundreds of other animals have to be taken care of. The solution therefore, is to design the enclosure in such a way as to satisfy both the public and the snakes. The python enclosure at MSPT consists of interconnected indoor and outdoor units and appears to provide an ideal environment for breeding. The inner enclosure is box-like, 6 feet × 4 feet, with a wire mesh screen in front for viewing and to allow free circulation of air. It is dimly lit and several degrees cooler than outside. At one corner in the posterior end is a small opening which leads into the 7 feet × 5 feet outside enclosure which is covered on the top and sides with weld mesh. A small concrete-lined pond and a stone basking ledge are contained within this enclosure. There are two such enclosures with 3 snakes (1 male and 2 females) in each. The open outdoor enclosures are used extensively for basking and swimming and the inner, when conditions outside get unfavourable. This simple setup ensures maximum visibility to the public while at the same time providing comfort and security to the snakes. To facilitate observations, feeding and maintenance, the inner enclosures are furnished only very sparsely. The outdoor enclosures on the other hand are contoured and landscaped to resemble the natural environment. The landscaping is fairly important as people like to see not only the snakes but also the type of habitat they live in.

FOOD

MSPT pythons are fed once a week on live fowl or rodents such as mole rats (*Bandicota benghalensis*) or bandicoots (*Bandicota indica*). Feeding is normally done late in the evening after the public has left. Live prey are introduced into the inner enclosure and left overnight, the advantage of this being that, if they are not eaten one night, they can be offered the next, thereby eliminating wastage. It is advisable to separate the snakes during feeding to avoid the risk of accidental cannibalism resulting from two snakes catching the same prey animal. Although this has never occurred at the Snake Park with adult pythons, it is a wise precaution nevertheless.

IDENTIFICATION

Maximum success with rearing or breeding can only be achieved if individual attention is paid to each snake in the group. Even with regard to food, some individuals may take only a particular type of prey; ignorance of this fact can cause the snake to waste away, or retard its growth. The need for a good identification system is therefore necessary. We employ the following two methods and have found them both effective.

Scale clipping. Brown and Parker (1976) give a simple, yet practical and effective clipping system wherein the left half of the ventrals represents tens, hundreds and thousands while the right half represents the units 1-9. The clipping can be done with a small pair of scissors and the scars left by them are easy to distinguish even after two or three years. Several thousand snakes can be marked using this system.

Body patterns. A simpler and, perhaps, more practical means of identification is to make use of body patterns. A particularly conspicuous, unique or distinct marking on each snake is photographed and the details of identificaton and marking number noted in a register. Immediate identification is possible with just a little practice if a right marking is chosen. This method has tremendous advantages over the preceding, both in captivity and in the wild, as it makes possible identification even at a distance or without having to disturb the snake.

SEXING

Sexing snakes is easy with a little practice. In pythons probing is much easier than hemipenis eversion. A thin, lubricated soft metal rod is inserted into the tail posteriorly. If the snake is a male, the rod will go in several inches (5-6) without hindrance while in the case of females it stops short due to blockage.

SEX RATIO

Most python workers are of the opinion that several males should be used for each female whenever available. The hypothesis behind this being that grouping several males with a female elicits competitive behaviour which consequently stimulates courtship and mating. However, when there is a shortage of either sex, a single male can be rotated among several females or *vice versa.*

MATING

Mating in Indian pythons appears to be a seasonal event. Acharjyo and Misra (1976) report that a pair of pythons at the Nandankanan Zoological Park in Orissa mated on the 4th and 5th February 1974 for one hour duration. At MSPT matings commence in early February and continue till early April.

TABLE 1

RECORDED MATINGS AT MSPT

Date	Time	Duration	Temperature	Remarks
4.2.81	16.15	—	25.5 C	
28.2.82	20.00	—	—	—
9.3.83	04-9.00	5 hours	28.5	Big male and female No. 5
10.3.83	10-11.00	1 hour	29.0	Same pair
10.3.83	14.50 on	over 3 hours	31.0	Small male and female No. 4
12.3.83	7.15-8.30	1 hour 15 min.	27.0	Big male and female No. 3
15.3.83	04-9.50	5 hours 50 min.	29.0	Big male and female No.3
22.3.83	12.40 on	—	32.0	Same pair
29.3.83	08.55 on	—	—	Same pair
1.4.83	6.15-9.35	3 hours 20 min.	—	Same pair
7.4.83	09.20 on	—	—	Big male and female No. 1

The big male (223 cm) was introduced with two females at a time and was thus rotated among the four females.

GESTATION

TABLE 2

GESTATION PERIOD

Institution	Location	Mating	Oviposition	Gestation Period
Nandankanan Zoological Park	Orissa	4 and 5 Feb. 1974	28. Apr. 1974	82-83 days
MSPT	Madras	28 Feb. 1982	14 May 1982	75 days
MSPT	Madras	First: 15th Mar. 1983 Last: 1st April 1983	1st June 1983	61-77 days 77 days after 1st mating 61 days after last mating

Egg laying and Hatching

Eggs are normally deposited at night and take between 55-60 days to hatch under optimum conditions.

Strategies and Techniques employed in captive breeding

Huff (1980) and Dattatri (1982) have given detailed accounts of strategies and techniques employed in captive breeding. Since this paper deals with breeding pythons under Indian conditions I will restrict myself to those which are applicable here.

Temperature and photoperiod. Photoperiod, (i.e. the length of time during which an animal is exposed to the sunlight) is considered by many workers as more important than previously suspected. Jones (1978) recognises it as "an important factor which may increase reproductive potential in captive reptiles" and states that "the effects of exposure can be negligible or severe depending upon the wavelength (colour), intensity, changes in either of these, length of exposure time ....". Citing Aronson, he further states that "one of these effects can be an increase in gonadal size and hormonal activity". Artificial lighting and heating are unnecessary when a species is raised in its native environment and housed in an enclosure such as the one described earlier.

Artificial stimulation to induce mating

Sometimes an apparently healthy pair of snakes may fail to mate even if housed together for several years, becoming lethargic and losing all interest in sexual activity. Huff (1980) has termed this condition "captive stagnancy" and states that "snakes exhibiting such a condition will seldom breed unless a change is effected in the routine". Change in feeding schedule, type or quality of food offered and other interuptions and alterations in the maintenance of the reptiles are recommended for breaking captive stagnancy.

The release of musk, brought about by aggression between males in a breeding group is known to play an important role in bringing the sexes together initially and subsequently stimulating courtship and mating. The release of musk may be brought about by manual prodding, slapping or poking (Huff 1980). Subjecting the pair to an unnatural situation or moving them to new quarters may also work. A pair of pythons at MSPT started to copulate after being transported together in a cloth bag by jeep. However, artificial stimulation is unnecessary in most cases and should be attempted only with animals exhibiting captive stagnancy.

Separation of sexes

It is an established belief among captive breeders that separation of sexes prior to the mating season and reintroducing at the right time greatly enhance the chances of fertile matings. The reintroduction presumably renews tactile and olfactory stimuli leading to courtship and mating. At MSPT males are removed from the breeding group in early December and shifted to separate air cooled quarters. Many workers feel that cooling of the males is an essential prerequisite to mating and that it is vital for inducing mating and/or enhancing fertility. Smith (1953) states that mating in north India takes place during hibernation (i.e. the coolest part of the year). Reintroduction of MSPT males into the breeding enclosure containing the females is done in early February, the start of the mating season. Male pythons in our park usually go off food during and prior to the mating season and also exhibit a marked restlessness.

After each female in the breeding group has

mated two to three times, the males are once again removed to separate quarters, for the reason that they actively use their spurs on the females during courtship and, if left for too long with unreceptive females, can inflict severe injuries on them. Concurrent matings are not absolutely necessary but certainly improve the chances of fertile mating.

SIGNS OF GRAVIDITY

It is often difficult to determine whether a female is gravid or not based on external appearance. Behaviour, however, can give important and, often, unmistakeable clues. Gravid females usually go off food about 2 weeks prior to egg laying. Some gravid females bask with the posterior portion of their body turned ventral side up, perhaps the amount of warmth reaching the ovidual eggs. Body twitching during the cooler hours of the day to raise the body temperature is also occasionally and is usually a sure sign that egg laying is imminent.

INCUBATION OF EGGS

Maternal Incubation. Female pythons coil around their eggs and actually regulate the temperature. Maternal incubation is preferable to artificial incubation and there is a preponderance of higher hatch rates associated with it. Given a suitable environment the female will successfully incubate her eggs. If conditions are unsuitable the female may suddenly terminate incubation, placing the eggs in jeopardy. At MSPT 'L' shaped plywood structures measuring 2 feet × 2 feet are propped up at the corners of the inner enclosure when egg laying is imminent to provide a dark and undisturbed environment for the females to lay. Since eggs are laid during the hottest part of the year when temperatures often shoot upwards of 44°C, the temperature of the inner enclosure is brought down to 32°C by covering the roof with tiles, wet gunny bags and palm thatches. Relative humidity inside the enclosure, more specifically, inside the 'L' structure, is maintained at a constant 80% by placing a large bowl of water (which incidentally, also provides drinking water to the snake) close to the incubating snake and with the help of wet gunny sacks. The female herself gives a clue as to the optimum temperature for the eggs. When too hot, she coils loosely around the eggs and when the temperature drops below optimum, coils tightly around the eggs and twitches her body periodically to raise the temperature. Thus, conditions can be manipulated to achieve optimum temperature merely by watching the mother snake.

Artificial incubation. Artificial incubation of eggs poses several problems, and if the utmost care is not taken, failure will definitely result. The success or failure of a captive breeding programme employing artificial incubation is hinged upon three critical factors: temperature, humidity and handling of eggs. The following points are noteworthy:

1. Eggs should be removed for artificial incubation only if the female fails to incubate them.
2. If the eggs are removed soon after they are laid, they may be separated from each other to facilitate artificial incubation.
3. Force should never be applied while separating agglutinated eggs as it may cause rupture of the egg shell.
4. Optimum temperature for incubation of python eggs is 32°C ± 1.
5. Optimum humidity is in the range of 80-100%.

At MSPT, eggs for artificial incubation are placed in closed plastic containers which are then placed in a wooden box with a mesh top.

We have found cottonwool to be an excellent substrate as it readily absorbs and retains moisture. Temperature is constantly monitored using a thermometer inserted through a hole in the lid. To raise temperature to the required 32°C a special wooden holder with two 40 watt light bulbs is placed over the mesh top. Under hot conditions an air cooler in the room where the eggs are kept is switched on. Humidity is maintained by moistening the cottonwool under the eggs as and when required. The humidity is measured using a dial hygrometer. All artificially incubated eggs are pencil marked on top to ensure that their original position remains unchanged. It should be stressed here that eggs not be moved about or handled unnecessarily, and then, only with the utmost care.

The importance of a constant temperature and high relative humidity cannot be over emphasized. Unnatural or drastic fluctuations in temperature can kill the developing embryos. Eggs incubated below 30°C and above 35°C may altogether fail to hatch. Temperatures above 35°C have been shown to have a teratogenic effect on the embryos. Also, hatchlings resulting from eggs incubated at these temperatures are generally prone to have congenital deformities. Excessive moisture or a very high relative humidity does not seem to adversely affect the eggs. Relative humidity below 60% on the other hand, may lead to dehydration of the eggs, causing the death of the embryo.

CARE OF HATCHLINGS

Acharjyo and Misra (1976) report that out of 30 hatchlings from the 1974 batch of 54 eggs at the Nandankanan Zoological Park, 24 died within the first 3½ months; 17 due to accidental cannibalism, 6 due to starvation and 1 while trying to escape. These then are the chief problems in rearing hatchlings. At MSPT we have all but eliminated these problems through the following simple measures:

1. Hatchlings are not housed together in large numbers but rather in small groups of 3 or 4.
2. Accidental cannibalism which is extremely common among juveniles is avoided by feeding each snake separately.
3. Cages are escape proof. Hatchlings are prone to damage their snouts by rubbing them against the mesh in their cage. This is avoided simply by eliminating the use of wire mesh.
4. Juveniles refusing food over long periods and which have as a consequence become very weak, are force fed on a special diet. Chicken or rats are skinned, and after bones and guts are removed, the rest is finely ground in a meat grinder and fed to the snake through a tube attached to a hand grease gun. Force feeding is done only as a last resort as it involves a certain amount of trauma for the snake. Normally, one or two such feedings are sufficient as the snakes start feeding on their own once they have regained their strength. A better alternative to force feeding is "assisted feeding" in which a dead mouse of appropriate size is manually placed in between a snake's jaws. This stimulus often encourages the snake to swallow in the normal way.

When rodents are unavailable our juvenile pythons are fed one day old chicken (1-2 per snake). However, we do not recommend this diet as it is neither nutritious nor well balanced.

Growth rate. Growth greatly depends upon the type of food offered and frequency of feeding. It is therefore, difficult to say what is optimum. Acharjyo and Misra (1976) give a table of growth figures for captive raised hatchling pythons up to the age of one year. Since their figures closely correspond with our own for healthy python hatchlings raised at MSPT,

TABLE 3

FEEDING HATCHLINGS

Days	Food offered	Quantity	Frequency of feeding
1-30:	Adult *Mus booduga* (field mice)	4-8 per snake	Once a week
30-60:	Subadult *Rattus rattus* or *Tatera indica* (40-50 g. size)	1-2 per snake	Once a week
60 days and above adult	*R. rattus or T. indica* (50-60 g. size)	1-2 per snake	Once a week

they could be considered optimum growth rates. At birth hatchlings measure an average of 70 cm (total length) and weigh an average of 140 g (sample size 15). By the age of 12 months their length has doubled and the weight increase is approximately ten fold. 3 captive raised male pythons at MSPT measured an average of 1.77 m (range 1.66-1.94 m) at the age of 28 months. A female of the same age measured 2.15 m.

SUMMARY

The following recommendatons can be made regarding the maintenance and captive breeding of Indian pythons:

1. The breeding unit should consist of interconnected indoor and outdoor enclosures.
2. Sexes should be kept separate prior to the mating season.
3. Several males should be used for each breeding female whenever available.
4. Males should be removed from the breeding enclosure after mating.
5. Males and females should come from entirely different stocks to prevent interbreeding.
6. Temperature and humidity in breeding enclosure should be manipulated to provide ideal conditions for the females to brood their eggs.
7. Eggs removed for artificial incubation should be separated when possible.
8. Optimum temperature for one egg is 32°C ± 1.
9. Optimum humidity is in the range of 80-100%.
10. Gravid females or eggs should not be handled or moved about unnecessarily.

Ross (1980), after a worldwide survey of python breeders on behalf of the Institute for Herpetological Research, Stanford, California, lists nine sound suggestions for breeders, a few of which are reproduced below:

1. Removal of spoiled or dead eggs from incubators appears to be unnecessary..... (as there is) little risk to incubating eggs from eggs that have died. Once growth of contaminents is observed, it is likely that the egg has died.
2. It is beneficial to open incubating python eggs once our initial egg has been slit. After slitting eggs, the young should be left to emerge on their own, and should not be removed from the egg.

3. Eggs should not be opened to see if they are fertile. This gives no useful information inasmuch as the egg opened, if fertile, may actually be the only fertile egg, and if infertile, may be the only infertile egg.
4. Potentially gravid pythons (or any animals) should never be X-rayed unless the animal is ill and an X-ray is needed for diagnosis. He further states that 4 cases were reported in which X-rays were used under such circumstances, and the resulting eggs either failed to hatch, or when hatched, produced young with severe congenital deformities.[1]

[1]Reproductive Biology and Diseases of Captive Reptiles. SSAR Publ. 1980. Eds. James B. Murphy and Joseph T. Collins.

LITERATURE CITED

ACHARJYO, L.N. & MISRA, R. (1976): Aspects of reproduction and growth of the Indian Python, *Python m. molurus* in captivity, *Brit. Jour. of Herp.* **5:** 562-65.

BROWN, W.S. & PARKER, WILLIAM S. (1976): A ventral scale clipping system for permanently marking snakes, *Jour. of Herp.* **10:** 247-249.

DATTARI, S. (1982): Captive propagation of endangered snakes as a conservation tool. Proc. of the IUCN/SSC Snake Specialist Group meeting.

HUFF, THOMAS A. (1980):* Captive propagation of the subfamily *Boinae* with emphasis on the genus *Epicrates.*

JONES, J.P. (1978): Photoperiod and reptile reproduction. *Herp. Review* **9,** No. 3, September.

ROSS, R. (1980):* The breeding of pythons (Subfamily Pythoninae) in captivity.

SMITH, M.S. (1953): The Fauna of British India, Reptilia and Amphibia, Vol. III Serpentes. Francis & Taylor, London.

Mahseer an endangered species of Game Fish, needs artificial propagation for its conservation

(*With a plate*)

C.V. KULKARNI

Mahseers are well-known riverine fish of India which grow to large sizes, the longest being 3 m, and the heaviest about 54.5 kg (Thomas). They are renowned all over the world as excellent sportfish (angling) and innumerable foreign anglers visit India to lure these denizens of our riverine stretches. Being large and bright scaled they are magnificent members of our fish fauna. They comprise six different species, namely *Tor putitora, T. tor, T. mosal, T. progeneius, T. khudree* and *T. mussullah,* spread over the different waters of the Indian subcontinent though at one time they were all included under one species *Barbus tor* (Ham.). As this piscine group was considered as carnivorous and slow growing, it was not accepted as a cultivable species in inland pisciculture; but recent studies by Desai (1970) indicated that *T. tor* was not a piscivorous fish and observation on *T. khudree* by Kulkarni (1980) showed that it was only mildly piscivorous and being omnivorous it played a very useful role in the reservoir fisheries. It is also relished as good food. Despite these qualities very little attention was paid to this fish and its fishery has been seriously declining. The National Commission on Agriculture (1976) in its report on 'Fisheries' stated "it has been reported that there has been a general decline in the Mahseer fishery due to indiscriminate fishing of brood fish and juveniles and the adverse effects of river valley projects"; and recommended "detailed ecological and biological investigations". Fortunately biological investigations had already commenced in 1970 in the lakes of Tata Hydro-Electric Company at Lonavla (Dist. Pune) on the peninsular species, *T. khudree* and provided some significant information (Kulkarni 1971). These studies indicated the dire need for conservation of this species.

THE PRESENT STATUS OF THE SPECIES

As the mahseers were considerably reduced in their numbers, they rarely figured in the commercial catches in the rivers of Indo-Gangetic plains. In the rivers of sub-Himalayan ranges of Jammu, Himachal Pradesh and Uttar Pradesh, the fishery consisted largely of individuals of *T. putitora,* either ascending hill stream for breeding or the spent ones returning to perennial pools in the plains (Sahgal 1972). As exact numerical statements of commercial landings of this fish are wanting, one has to depend on whatever reports are available from anglers and Directors of Fisheries of different states. These communications invariably indicate considerable reduction in the fishery, especially in riverine areas. Details of landings at Govind Sagar recorded by Raizada (1981) show a distressing fall in the catches of mahseers from 63% to 10% of the total catch and in the mahseers alone, the decline was 33%, despite much increased efforts in later years when fishing was intensified. In some of the lakes of Rajasthan and in the Chambal river between the Gandhi Sagar reservoir and Rana Pratap reservoir, mahseers do occur, but their fishery status cannot be determined in the

Above: Deccan Mahseer (*Tor khudree*) from Lonavla
Below: Mahseer (*Tor khudree*) male being stripped and eggs being fertilised
(*Photos*: Author)

absence of catch data. In the Kumaon hill area and especially in the Nainital lakes, both *T. putitora* and *T. tor* are found but their numbers have considerably attenuated. Same is the case about Ramganga river near Corbett Park. One ardent angler (M.L. Mehta) gave a vivid pen-picture in *The Times of India* (6.6.1976) of the wanton destruction of these fish in the rivers near Dehra Dun (U.P.). The well-known critic and commentator Melville de Mellow also corroborated this situation in an article in *The Times of India, Sunday Review,* dated 19.7.1981. In Madhya Pradesh especially in the Narmada river near Hoshangabad and in the Tapi near Bahranpur, *T. tor* figured predominantly in the commercial catches about 15 years ago (Karamchandani *et al.* 1967) but the landings are reported to have dwindled drastically in recent years. In Maharashtra, *T. khudree* and *T. mussullah* (photo 1) have been practically a rarity in the rivers Bhima, Krishna, Koyna, etc. except at a few temple sanctuaries and in the reservoirs such as Walwhan, Shirota, Mulshi, etc. A few occur in the Godavari river near Nasik but only in the monsoon. In the south also, the situation is not any brighter as regards occurrence of these fish in the Kaveri and its tributaries (Kabini etc) which were at one time the home of large specimens. However, a silver lining to the dark cloud was a report in *The Deccan Herald,* Bangalore dated 4.4.1978, that a catch of 12 mahseers including a largest one of 42 kg was landed by a British team of three Transworld Anglers. But even this bounty was amassed after intensive efforts by these three expert anglers over a period of about 10 weeks with their modern gadgets, and this hardly does any credit to the mahseer resources of the rivers of Karnataka. According to recent observations, the Bhadra river forming the Bhadra reservoir also has a small population of mahseers, but they show up only during the early part of the monsoon when they leave the reservoir to migrate upstream for spawning.

Causes of Depletion and Present Approach to Conservation

The aforesaid drastic reduction in the catches of mahseer is beyond any doubt when compared with the reports of earlier anglers. One of the main reasons for this decline is the thoughtless destruction of this fish by illegal means such as the use of explosives wherein a large number of big and small, i.e. both wanted and unwanted fish are killed on account of underwater explosions. General fishing intensity has also increased considerably as fishermen can now-a-days approach distant streams easily on account of the present improved transport system. Secondly, when the brood fish migrate for spawning, they travel through shallow streams; at this time greedy fisherfolk and others kill these fish ruthlessly with the help of spears, arrows or swords. Another serious handicap the fish suffers from, is the change in the habitat or the ecological condition of the riverine systems by erection of several new multipurpose dams across streams, large and small, all over the country. Such dams are beneficial to the country for irrigation, power, potable water and in several other ways. A number of large impoundments which would not have otherwise come into existence are created by these dams. This expansion of water bodies is advantageous to fish and fisheries in general, but migratory fish such as mahseer which migrate to clear upstream waters for breeding, can no longer ascend the streams unmolested, as human interference has penetrated into most of the previously secluded waters. Since the aforesaid developmental activities are essential for the general well-being and prosperity of the local population as a whole, a compromise has to be struck, as is done in the case of the famous Salmon fisheries in Europe and America. Fish passes and ladders are provided for this purpose to enable gravid and migratory Salmon to cross the dams and reach their ancestral spawning grounds. In addition to this, hatcheries are also established where gravid Salmon are caught, stripped, eggs artificially fertilised and fingerlings (juveniles) raised to be released back into the natural streams to propagate the species (Photo 2). In the case of mahseer, though it can adapt itself to lacustrine (reservoir) conditions and breed in the adjoining streams on a small scale, additional efforts, as in the Salmon, are essential, for continued propagation of the species in full strength.

In the case of sport fish like the mahseer where quantitative data of catches in regular sequence are not available, it is dangerous to wait for conclusive proof of depletion. We may then unknowingly reach a point of no return when it would be too late to mend matters. It is necessary, therefore, to analyse the situation objectively from the information available and to chalk out a strategy for the conservation and continued propagation of the species, which appears to be threatened in the present circumstances. As a result of recommendations of the Agricultural Commission, investigations on the ecology and biology of the Kumaon mahseer have recently commenced (Pathani 1982) but effective action to protect the fish is the imperative need of the day.

Fish ladders. Although mahseer is a migratory fish ascending small streams for breeding, it is not yet clear whether the conventional fish ladders in the shape of ascending flight of small tanks will be helpful in climbing and crossing dams during their migration. This is because it has not yet been ascertained whether the heavy gravid mahseer will jump from tank to tank of the traditional fish ladders, like the Salmon. It is felt that mahseer may negotiate fish passes or fish-ways, but this too has to be thoroughly investigated, otherwise they will become varitable traps for capture of these fish by the unscrupulous people as it had reportedly happened in the case of some of the old dams in the Punjab.

Another factor to contend with while providing fish ladders is that these efforts even if successful will be nullified by the unscrupulous attitude of the local fishermen and other people frequenting the streams during spawning season as mentioned earlier. The menace is constantly increasing and the situation worsening with the ever increasing human population and its decreasing life standards and food availability. This makes the second method, namely the artificial propagation as the only method to ensure conservation and continued propagation of the species.

CONSTRAINTS IN NATURAL BREEDING

Before considering the artificial propagation of mahseer, natural constraints in the early life cycle of the fish have to be understood. The fish requires rigorous specialised conditions for successful post-natal development. Recent observations on the early development and growth of hatchlings of *T. khudree* at Lonavla indicate that it has very low fecundity, hardly 1000-15000 per kg body weight, as compared to 1,33,000 and 2,60,000 for Catla and Rohu. Secondly the hatching period is 80 hours in water temperature of 22 to 26°C (Kulkarni *et al.* 1978), against only 18 hours for Catla, Rohu, etc. This hatching period is likely to be longer in colder streams of the sub-Himalayas, which are inhabited by the other species of mahseer, namely *T. putitora* and the Katli mahseer, *Acrossocheilas hexagonolepes*. Further, the semi-quiescent stage after hatching which is only three days in other carps is extended to as long as six days in *T. khudree*. During this period the hatchlings do not swim freely but remain at the bottom mostly huddled up in large numbers in the corners and crevices with their heads tucked away from light, and their tails vibrating. In this condition they are subject to severe depredation by animals of all sorts. Thus, this semi-quiescent stage is the most critical stage in the life history of mahseer and since it is prolonged, the mortality is also very high. *T. putitora* and *T. tor* are also likely to have similar long quiescent stage making them equally vulnerable to infantile mortality. In the past, the number of streams unfrequented by man was large and a greater number of mahseers had an opportunity to spawn unmolested and hence the long critical semi-quiescent stage in their life history did not matter very much. Moreover, with the increasing number of blocking of streams to create more reservoirs for developmental activities, the traditional spawning grounds are lost to the fish. Besides this, many streams are affected by harmful industrial pollution which kills the fish fauna and especially the tiny delicate hatchlings and fry in enormous numbers. All these handicaps combined together are affecting adversely the fish fauna which, in general and mahseer in particular suffer grievously.

ROLE OF FISH SANCTUARIES

Mahseer being a large sized fish capable of getting accustomed to taking artificial feeds many people adore them, along with other fish, at temple sanctuaries established by tradition. Here the mahseers are protected from the depredation of illegal poachers and others. Several such sanctuaries exist in different parts of the country, the most outstanding being at Haredwar and Rishikesh temples on the banks of the Ganga river after its confluence with the Alakananda. In Madhya Pradesh too, there are sanctuaries on the Narmada at Kapileswar, several places such as Mangalnath, Sahasradhara, etc. In Maharashtra, long stretches of river Indrayani at Alandi and Dehu and at Pandharpur on Bhima river all tributaries of Krishna are forbidden to fishing of any sort. In Karnataka, sanctuaries exist at Shringeri (Bhadra river), Ramanathapuram and Chipalgudda on the Kaveri and Shishima on the Sharavati. These fish sanctuaries like those of wildlife, serve useful purpose in protecting the mahseer but they being in the open courses of the rivers, movements of the fish are not restricted when the rivers are in spate. The gravid fish by their very instinct leave the sanctuaries and migrate to shallow streams for spawning. At this time they are exposed to the usual onslaughts by the illegal operators and are also affected by the natural constraints or vicissitudes of their early life cycle mentioned earlier. Thus, though the sanctuaries protect the fish in fair season, during the flooded condition or the post-flood period which coincides with their breeding season, they are not protected and hence the survival of young ones suffers resulting in very low recruitment to new generation.

The fisheries department of Karnataka has recently been alive to the problem of conservation of their famous mahseer resources and have started stocking their waters, though sporadically, with mahseer fry obtained from the aforesaid fish farm at Lonavla. The Department has also commenced another experiment of leasing out some sections of their rivers to angling associations which prevent illegal fishing by explosives etc. As a result of this step better catches by angling etc. are reported. The off-take by angling being very small, the fish are comparatively protected but they suffer from the same problems as the fish from the sanctuaries.

Action Plan (Recommendations)

As stated earlier, the fish sanctuaries afford only a limited protection and taking into consideration the increasing interference by the human population which is unavoidable in the developing economy of our country, supplementary methods of conservation and rehabilitation of mahseer have to be thought of. Improvement of habitat is also linked up with construction of dams which too are essential for the prosperity of the country. Effective prevention of pollution is uncertain. Under these circumstances, the only other method of conservation of the species is artificial propagation for stocking perennial waters and observation of conservation rules, such as prevention of killing of brood fish, juveniles, etc.

These efforts have to be three-pronged: (1) stricter enforcement of fishery rules to prevent illegal methods of fishing such as use of explosives, etc.; (2) by preventing killing of brood fish and the juveniles; (3) by replenishment of stock by artificial propagation of the fish. Incidentally the fish farm at Lonavla has followed this practice by raising 2-3 lakhs of mahseer fry every year for restocking Tata lakes and also for supplying state governments in the country.

In the case of new reservoirs the following steps are necessary to conserve the species:

1. A fish farm should be established in close proximity of every new dam as a part of the reservoir project.

2. A few tanks of the farm should be reserved for mahseers.

3. The fish should be bred either by collecting spawners from the reservoirs and stripping them for artificial fertilisation of eggs or by induced breeding with the help of *pituitary* hormones.

4. Raising of hatchlings to fingerling stage.

5. Release of fingerlings into the reservoir and also down-stream waters as a rehabilitation measure.

Location of spawning grounds and collection of spawners involve special efforts but these can be achieved by experience and insight into the problem. Similarly, if the fish has to be bred by induced breeding method (hypophysation) mahseer fingerlings will have first to be grown in the fish farm and then used for breeding. In this case, however the fecundity is much lower than usual. The female fish takes three years to ripen while the male ripens earlier. More proteinous feed than what is given to other carps is required for the mahseer.

The aforesaid rehabilitation has to be undertaken as an obligation arising out of the change in the ecosystem on account of construction of the dam concerned and has to be undertaken by the authorities involved as a compensatory measure. No total ban on fishing for mahseer is proposed but if the aforesaid steps are taken and the matter kept under observation, the fish can be conserved for the benefit of future generations.

India's Freshwater Turtle resource with recommendations for Management

EDWARD O. MOLL
Department of Zoology, Eastern Illinois University, Charleston Illinois 61920, USA

ABSTRACT

The status of India's freshwater turtles as a protein resource is examined respective to usage, threats and present protective measures.

Of 22 freshwater species inhabiting India, ten are commonly used as food with soft-shells (Trionychidae) being most popular. Peak consumption of turtle meat occurs in West Bengal where the demand is sufficiently great to support an extensive marketing channel involving much of the Ganges and Mahanadi river systems. Base line data are few but indicate many chelonian populations are undergoing serious declines. Over-exploitation and habitat alterations appear to be the chief causative factors.

To stem declines and allow rehabilitation of depleted populations the following actions are recommended: 1) Revise lists of endangered species on the Indian Wildlife (Protection) Act 1972 and the Convention on International Trade in Endangered Species by removing common species and adding truly threatened ones. 2) Train wildlife officers to identify endangered reptiles. 3) Prohibit exploitation of chelonians during nesting seasons. 4) Establish sanctuaries, hatcheries and/or protected nesting sites on major river systems. 5) Encourage captive breeding programmes for conservation and commercial purposes. 6) Provide educational programmes for the public.

Freshwater turtles have long served as an important protein resource in tropical and subtropical Asia. However, most countries of the region have made little attempt to control or manage the resource. Malaysia has been an exception—there protective laws, licensed egg collecting and hatcheries help to prevent over exploitation (Siow and Moll 1981; Moll 1976).

The importance of Indian turtles as food and the need for conserving and managing their populations was expressed over thirty years ago by M.N. Acharji (1950). To date little attempt has been made to follow up these recommendations. One of the major obstacles to doing so is the dearth of recent information on the status and even the distribution of the important Indian species. No extensive field studies of freshwater turtles have been conducted since before World War II. Smith (1931) is still the best major reference to the chelonian fauna of India.

When the IUCN/SSC[1] Freshwater Chelonian Specialist Group (FCSG) met along with CITES[2] in New Delhi during February 1981 to plan conservation action for the Indian species, they found a confusing situation. Eight species of the families Emydidae and Trionychidae from India and/or Bangladesh were listed as endangered on Appendix I of CITES. However, only four of these species were listed as endangered on Schedule I of the Indian Wildlife (Protection) Act, 1972 (IWL(P)A) and no freshwater turtle had been so categorized by the Zoological Survey of India (1981).

[1]Special Survival Commission (SSC) International Union for the Conservation of Nature and Natural Resources (IUCN)

[2]Convention on International Trade in Endangered Species of Wild flora and Fauna.

Inasmuch as conservation and management action could not be planned until populations actually threatened with extinction could be identified, the FCSG listed a status survey of Indian freshwater turtles as "highest priority" in their 1981 global action plan.

Two such surveys have now been completed: a two-month survey in 1981 and 1982 of turtle markets and habitats chiefly within West Bengal (Vijaya and Manna 1982, *unpublished*) and a nine month survey (Sept. 1982-June 1982) by the author and two assistants, J. Vijaya and S. Bhaskar, of turtle markets and river systems in Andhra Pradesh, Bihar, Kerala, Madhya Pradesh, Orissa and Uttar Pradesh. Based on findings of these surveys, this paper presents an overview of the usage of turtles in India, the status of the exploited species, and recommendations for protection and management.

THE RESOURCE

Description and Ecology

The freshwater turtle[1] fauna of India comprises some 22 species belonging to two families—the pond turtles, Emydidae (16) and the soft-shells, Trionychidae (6). Both are widespread groups showing maximum diversification in the Oriental Region. This section briefly examines the characteristics of the group which are directly and indirectly important to man and to planning of their management in India.

At least potentially this assemblage is an important protein resource for the region. Many of the species are large, prolific and locally abundant. In terms of biomass, turtles may be the dominant vertebrates in aquatic habitats (Bury 1979). Single species standing crop biomass estimates are among the highest reported for vertebrates and, based on preliminary studies, the annual production per unit area may only be exceeded by certain fishes (Iverson 1982). Species possessing such characteristics can, if properly managed, withstand considerable long term exploitation.

Another positive characteristic of the group in regard to exploitation is that majority feed chiefly at the primary consumer (herbivore) level as adults. Strict herbivory (or carnivory) is rare among turtles—rather most are opportunistic with aquatic plants being a dietary staple. Even among the soft-shells, a group so admirably adapted for carnivory, diets of certain species (e.g. *Trionyx gangeticus, Lissemys punctata*) may contain considerable amounts of vegetation (Minton 1966). The nature of the diet is advantageous in that there is little competition with man for food. By harvesting turtles, man can convert a relatively unused resource (aquatic plants) into a usable one (turtle protein). To be sure some turtles do compete with man by eating fish. However, in a natural (unconfined) habitat, most species have neither the speed nor manouverability to regularly catch healthy fish and thus are unlikely to be a major limiting factor of their populations. At the same time, they may benefit fishermen by helping to maintain open water by controlling production of waterweeds.

Another indirect benefit to man concerns the role turtles play in cleansing aquatic habitats. Certain species (e.g. *Tryionyx gangeticus, Lissemys punctata*) are excellent scavengers. They are often abundant in the vicinity of aquatic burial sites and burning ghats. With their jaws and forelimbs, they speed the decomposition process by opening the integument and mascerating the flesh of bodies allowing smaller scavengers, bacteria, etc. to enter and assist the

[1]The term, freshwater turtles, is here used in a broad sense for any member of the Emydidae or Trionychidae even though a few may inhabit brackish water or be terrestrial.

recycling. In this respect they can be regarded as an aquatic equivalent of vultures. In fact *Lyssemys* will also congregate in large numbers around large dead vertebrates on land some distance removed from their aquatic habitat (Krishnan 1981).

Generally the aquatic turtles of India can be divided into two somewhat overlapping habitat groups—those inhabiting rivers and streams and those occupying the more lentic habitats such as lakes, ponds, swamps, and marshes. Members of the former group tend to be highly aquatic (seldom leaving the water except to bask or nest), powerful swimmers that may reach a very large size. This group include both soft-shells (*Trionyx, Chitra* and *Pelochelys*) and the emydids (*Batagur* and *Kachuga*). Lentic species typically are the smaller, often semi-aquatic forms such as *Cuora, Cyclemys, Geoclemys, Melanochelys,* and *Morenia*. However, *Hardella* which also falls in this group attains an impressively large size (to 500 mm shell length). These categories are far from absolute. Large *Triyonix* also inhabits, reservoirs and, on occasion, surprisingly small ponds. Highly generalized species such as the flap-shell *Lissemys punctata* are common in both lentic and lotic habitats.

Reproductive cycles of the Indian species are poorly known but from data collected during the surveys, it appears that the peak nesting seasons for trionychids and emydids are largely mutually exclusive. The major nesting season for trionychids appears to be August-November whereas most emydids nest from November-April.

Usage

In Asia freshwater turtles are little exploited for jewellery, tourist souvenirs or leather. They are heavily utilized for food and to some extent as medicine. This holds generally true for India; however, the extent of usage varies with the section of the country and with the religion of the peoples involved.

Due to religion-related restrictions, Moslems do not usually eat turtle meat but eggs are acceptable fare. Hindus are sometimes strict vegetarians but the majority accept meat including that of turtles. Nevertheless some species are considered unclean and are avoided (footnote in Annandale and Shastri 1914). Certain tribal groups regularly eat turtles. Chaudhuri (1912) reported that on the Ganges near Rajmahal, turtles are caught and eaten by the Santals, Binds, Banpars, Teors and Gondris but are shunned by the Malas and Myfarases. The Irulas in Tamil Nadu enjoy *Lissemys* but seldom eat *Melanochelys*. The Kadans of Kerala eat the rare *Heosemys silvatica*.

Turtle meat attains the zenith of its popularity in northern India especially among the Bengalis of West Bengal. The major marketing centre is located in Calcutta (Howrah). Other large wholesale markets in the state are located near Malda, Murshidabad, Raghunathgarj and Siliguri. Over the rest of India the meat is less highly regarded, being eaten chiefly by tribals, fishermen and by the poor as a cheap source of protein[1]. Nevertheless due to the burgeoning demand in West Bengal, the turtling industry thrives throughout much of the Ganges and Mahanadi river drainages involving a complex marketing channel with trappers, local jobbers, second level wholesalers (i.e. in marketing centres such as Howrah) and retailers.

It is difficult to obtain reliable data on the volume of this industry as many of the key species are protected by the IWL(P)A. A few dealers and wholesalers have been willing to discuss their trade. However, as the figures they

[1]We were told by vendors in the Hyderabad markets that turtles sold for 5 Rs/kg are purchased by lower income groups.

provided generally came from recollection rather than written records, their accuracy is suspect. The information presented below comes form the soruces I consider the most reliable.

As an example of the volume being traded in a single area, I quote one supplier of West Bengal markets located in Uttar Pradesh who receives turtles from the Chambal, Jumna, Betwa and Ganges rivers. He estimated his monthly trade averages "5000 to 7500 *Lissemys punctata,* 350 to 500 *Chitra indica,* and 200 to 300 hard-shelled turtles (chiefly *Kachuga dhongoka* and *Hardella*)". The above species can be legally traded with a permit in Uttar Pradesh despite the fact that *Lissemys* was listed as Schedule I on the IWL(P)A. No information was provided for *Trionyx gangeticus* which could not be legally traded[1].

The largest wholesale turtle market in India is at Howrah just across the Hooghli river from Calcutta. Most turtles arrive here by rail packed in large wicker baskets. A survey of these markets made for the Freshwater Chelonian Specialist Group in late 1981 and early 1982 estimated that 50,000 to 75,000 Indian flapshells (*Lissemys punctata*), 7000 to 8000 large trionychids (chiefly *Trionyx gangeticus, T. hurum* and *Chitra indica*) and at least 1000 to 1500 emydids reached Howrah annually (Vijaya and Manna 1982, *unpublished*)[2]. There seemed to be a large number of mortalities in each shipment but observations were insufficient to estimate numbers.

[1]The figures provided for *Chitra* probably include *T. gangeticus* as well.

[2]The emydids were probably underestimated in this survey, for when we revisited these markets in May 1983, some 300 to 400 large hard-shells were being auctioned off in one day.

We visited the Siliguri area in May of 1983. Trains bring turtles here from Bihar, Uttar Pradesh, Assam and Orissa. Most shipments arrive at New Jalpaiguri where they are divided and distributed to jobbers in smaller towns such as Belekoba and Mainaguri. Vendors attend daily auctions in these towns and then sell their acquisitions at daily or weekly markets ("hats") held in the local villages. We found from 1 to 4 (mode 2) stalls selling turtles in the eight "hats" that we visited at this time. Turtle meat sold at 10 to 14 Rs/kg retails depending on the species and place. Again the illegal nature of the trade made it impossible to obtain reliable information on its volume. However, a railway official at Belekoba told us that during the peak season (December-March) some 400 to 600 baskets (weighing *c.* 1 quintal = 100 kg each) arrived monthly and that, even during May, they were still receiving 150 to 200 baskets monthly.

Considering the difficulty in obtaining information, the economic importance of the resource is difficult to assess. The lowest wholesale prices at Howrah market in May, were 10 Rs/kg for soft-shells and 5 Rs/kg for hardshells. Using these figures with the aforementioned annual estimates of turtles coming into Howrah and estimating weight (8 kg for an average large soft-shell, 0.75 kg for the average flap-shell and 8 kg for an average emydid), we conservatively estimated that the annual rupee income from turtles at Howrah alone at between 12 and 13 lakhs.

Soft-shelled turtles are in greatest demand. This may be due partially to taste but more importantly, soft-shells are easier to butcher and a greater percentage of the body weight is edible than in emydids[3]. In 35 sites (markets or

[3]The massive shell of a large emydid may comprise some 20 percent of the body weight compared to 15 percent for a trionychid.

villages) where we recorded turtles being sold or eaten, soft-shells were represented at 32 and were the most abundant type at 26. Emydids (or hard-shells) were present at 17 but were the most abundant type in only 9 (Table 1). The two most widely exploited species were the Indian flap-shell, *Lissemys punctata,* and the Indian soft-shell, *Trionyx gangeticus* both listed on Schedule I of the IWL(P)A having a frequency of occurrence of 0.63 and 0.49 respectively. These same two species were also utilized in the greatest numbers at more sites than any other species—9 sites each. The most widely utilized emydids were the coronated turtle, *Hardella thurjii,* and the striped-roof turtle, *Kachuga dhongoka,* having a frequency of occurrence of 0.26 and 0.20 respectively. *Kachuga dhongoka* was found to be used in the greatest numbers at four sites—more than any other emydid.

In addition to their use as food, turtles are widely used in India for various home cures or medicines. In most cases a powder is made from trionychid shells and is usually mixed with coconut oil, milk or some other medium. Externally the preparation is used for piles, inflamed eyes, and to heal sores and burns. It is taken internally to cure a variety of other ailments such as stomach problems, colds and menorrhagia.

A few other miscellaneous uses were observed. In some areas it is common to put turtles in wells to clean out algae and insects, etc. We observed this in Tamil Nadu, Andhra Pradesh and Madhya Pradesh. Flap-shells were most commonly used for this purpose. In Madhya Pradesh, villagers near the Chambal river hung pieces of *Lissemys* shell on their cows and buffaloes to keep them producing good quantities of milk. In Bihar we even saw a stringed musical instrument called a "Sarangi" that used a *Lissemys* shell as a sounding drum. Fishermen in several riverine villages were observed using trionychid shells a scoops to throw water from their boats and as receptacles for carrying various items (e.g. mud, sand etc.).

Threats to the Resource

The most serious threats to this resource are undoubtedly over-exploitation and habitat alteration. Certainly the great demand for turtle meat in West Bengal has created a drain on turtle populations throughout the Ganges and associated river systems. However, there are few baseline data for comparison, making it difficult to ascertain just how serious this drain has been. A few indications have been derived from the literature and from talking with long-time fishermen and market vendors in the study areas.

As West Bengal is the main centre of turtle consumption in India, it might be expected that problems with over-exploitation would be most obvious here. Biswas and Biswas (*unpublished manuscript*) state that in recent years the turtle catch from West Bengal has dwindled to the point that it is no longer profitable to fish for them. The FCSG Survey (Vijaya and Manna 1982, *unpublished*) made similar observations. It concluded that a few turtles were now being caught in West Bengal and these are usually sold at local markets. Catches within West Bengal are highest at Murshidabad on the Ganges which still sends 2-3 baskets of turtles per month in peak months to the Sealdah markets in Calcutta. As sources within the state have become depleted, West Bengal has had to reach further afield to obtain supplies of turtles. Thus today the supply network extends to Orissa, Bihar, Madhya Pradesh, Uttar Pradesh and to a lesser extent Bangladesh, Assam, Andhra Pradesh, Rajasthan and Gujarat. The number of jobbers dealing in turtles in these areas is unknown. However, Vijaya (1982) has reported that at least 20 agents send turtles to West Bengal from the Rapti river (Uttar Pradesh) alone.

Baseline data for individual species are largely lacking but a few statements in the scientific literature indicate declines in populations of specific species.

Batagur baska was reported by Blyth in Günther (1864) to abound in the mouth of the Hooghly from where large numbers were being shipped to Calcutta markets. Similarly Theobald (1868) related that in Calcutta, *Batagur baska* was commonly being used as a substitute for sea turtles in the making of turtle soup. Today *Batagur* is no longer seen in the Calcutta markets nor has it recently been reported at the mouth of the Hooghly. In our survey of West Bengal (April 1983), J. Vijaya visited the Sunderbans near Bangladesh and determined that a few *Batagur* were still extant in India. She discovered that several were being raised by local people in small ponds probably for food. No direct information was obtained on the status of wild populations but people of the area claimed that some nesting still occurred in the vicinity

Acharji (1955) reported on a survey of chelonians made by the Zoological Survey of India on the Ganges below Rajmahal, Bihar in 1954. Based on their collections and inquiries made from turtle hunters in the area, he listed the local species and categorized them as to abundance. Four species listed as common to very common were *Kachuga kachuga, K. dhongoka, Hardella thurjii* and *Trionyx gangeticus*. In March of 1983 we briefly surveyed this area and interviewed fishermen. We found *Kachuga dhongoka* was still common. *Trionyx gangeticus* was present but no longer common. We found no evidence of recent catches of either *Hardella* or *Kachuga kachuga*. Both were regarded as rare by local fishermen.

A scattering of evidence from other sources

TABLE 1

THE MOST IMPORTANT FOOD SPECIES BASED ON OCCURRENCE AND RELATIVE ABUNDANCE OF SPECIMENS IN 35 MARKETS AND VILLAGES. N IS THE NUMBER OF SITES WHERE EACH SPECIES WAS FOUND, FO THE FREQUENCY OF OCCURRENCE AND MN THE NUMBER OF SITES WHERE THAT SPECIES WAS MOST NUMEROUS. *TRIONYX* SP. LUMPS THE THREE SPECIES OF *TRIONYX* WHICH OCCUPY SOMEWHAT EXCLUSIVE RANGES. ALL OTHERS ARE INDIVIDUAL SPECIES.

Species	*N(35)*	*FO(N/35)*	*MN*
Trionyx sp.	23	.66	13
Lissemys punctata	22	.63	9
Trionyx gangeticus	17	.49	9
Chitra indica	11	.31	3
Trionyx hurum	9	.26	2
Hardella thurjii	9	.26	2
Kachuga dhongoka	7	.20	4
Kachuga tentoria	7	.20	3
Kachuga smithii	3	.09	1
Kachuga kachuga	3	.09	1
Trionyx leithii	2	.06	2

further points to a serious decline in populations of *Hardella* and *Kachuga kachuga.* Market vendors at Howrah and Siliguri told us that shipments of these species have been declining for some time. *Hardella,* though still being received, was coming in smaller numbers each year whereas any *K. kachuga* in a shipment was rare. Dr. Falconer (*in* Günther 1864) stated that *K. kachuga* was common at "Saharumpoor" (presumably Serampore on the Hooghly river near Calcutta). All species of turtles now appear to be rare near Calcutta (Biswas and Biswas, *unpublished manuscript*). Our survey further supports these findings. *Hardella* or their shells were encountered in several markets and villages in the Ganges drainage (FO .26 — Table 1) but always in small numbers. *Kachuga kachuga* was generally much rarer (FO .09) but moderate populations were found in two protected areas, the National Chambal river Gharial Sanctuary and in a stretch of the Jumna river flowing past a number of Jain Hindoo Temples in the town of Bateswar, Uttar Pradesh.

Habitat alteration is perhaps even more important than over-exploitation in the decline of India's freshwater resources. However, as these factors act indirectly on turtle populations, it is far more difficult to determine their importance.

India has been very active in water develpment projects and it is likely that the large numbers of dams and barrages built have affected various species. For example, dams affect riverine species by replacing their lotic habitats with lentic ones. Damming of small tributaries lowers the productivity of the main river. Obstructions can also prevent the movements of migratory species (e.g. *Batagur*) to their nesting sites thus preventing reproduction. Biswas and Biswas (*unpublished manuscript*) attributed much of the decline of turtle populations on the Bhagirathi and Hooghli rivers to the effects of the Farrakka barrage. The creation of large reservoirs has seemingly favoured certain species however. *Trinoyx gangeticus* and *T. leithii* seem to do very well in such habitats.

There are other potentially damaging practices. Cultivation of river banks is a common practice along many rivers that can destroy or alter nesting sites. Continued clearing of vegetation along watersheds leads to siltation, turbidity, decreased productivity and increased flooding. Use of organochlorine pesticides and polychlorinated biphenyls has been widespread in India (Kalra and Chawla 1981); contamination of aquatic habitats with these substances can directly and indirectly deplete turtle populations (see Hall 1980 for review).

These and other forms of alterations need to be studied in regard to their effects on the aquatic wildlife of India.

To summarize there is some good suggestive evidence that the turtle resources of India have been undergoing a serious decline for some time. Table 2 summarizes our findings concerning the present status of the Indian species encountered in our surveys. Though partially based on subjective judgments and secondhand accounts, I feel confident that this assessment is reasonably accurate. Certainly it utilizes the most complete and current information presently available for Indian chelonians. The conclusion drawn from these observations is that for freshwater turtles to remain a viable protein resource in India, greater protection and management are urgently needed.

PROTECTING AND MANAGING THE RESOURCE

Evaluation and improvement of existing protection

Until 1972 wildlife protection and management has been chiefly the prerogative of each

TABLE 2

DISTRIBUTION, RELATIVE ABUNDANCE AND STATUS OF TURTLES IN 20 LOCALITIES* SURVEYED SEPTEMBER 1982 - JUNE 1983. LETTERS A, B, C, D INDICATE THAT A SPECIES WAS RESPECTIVELY RARE, UNCOMMON, COMMON, OR ABUNDANT AT A PARTICULAR SITE. ROMAN NUMERAL I INDICATES A WIDESPREAD SPECIES THAT IS RELATIVELY COMMON OVER THE MAJORITY OF THE RANGE; II A SPECIES WHICH IS RELATIVELY COMMON OVER A RESTRICTED RANGE; III A WIDESPREAD BUT UNCOMMON SPECIES OVER THE MAJORITY OF THE RANGE; IV AN UNCOMMON SPECIES WITH A RESTRICTED RANGE.

Species	1	2	3	4	5	6	7	8	9	10	11	12	13	14	15	16	17	18	19	20	Status in India
TRIONYCHIDAE																					
Lissemys punctata	—	C	C	—	—	C	C	C	C	—	C	C	C	C	B	—	—	—	C	C	I
Chitra indica	—	A	—	—	—	A	B	—	D	—	—	—	B	—	—	—	—	—	—	—	III
Pelochelys bibronii	—	—	—	—	—	—	—	—	—	B	—	—	—	—	—	—	—	—	—	—	III
Trionyx gangeticus	—	—	—	—	—	C	C	C	C	—	B	—	B	—	C	C	C	—	—	—	I
Trionyx hurum	—	—	—	—	—	—	—	—	—	—	—	—	C	C	—	A	B	—	—	—	I
Trionyx leithii	—	C	—	—	—	—	—	—	—	—	—	—	—	—	—	—	—	—	—	B	I
EMIDIDAE																					
Batagur baska	—	—	—	—	—	—	—	—	—	—	—	—	—	—	—	—	—	B	—	—	IV
Geoclemys hamiltonii	—	—	—	—	—	—	—	—	—	—	—	—	A	—	—	—	—	—	—	—	III
Heosemys silvatica	C	—	—	—	—	—	—	—	—	—	—	—	—	—	—	—	—	—	—	—	II
Hardella thurjii	—	—	—	B	B	—	—	—	—	—	—	—	B	—	—	B	B	—	—	—	III
Kachuga dhongoka	—	—	—	—	—	C	—	C	—	—	D	—	B	—	—	D	B	—	—	—	I
Kachuga kachuga	—	—	—	—	—	B	—	B	—	—	—	—	A	—	—	—	A	—	—	—	III
Kachuga smithii	—	—	—	—	B	—	—	—	—	—	C	—	C	—	—	—	—	—	—	—	I
Kachuga tecta	—	—	—	C	B	—	—	—	—	—	—	—	C	—	B	—	—	—	—	—	I
Kachuga tentoria	—	C	—	C	B	D	C	D	D	—	B	—	C	—	—	—	—	—	—	—	I
Melanochelys trijuga	C	—	C	—	—	—	—	—	—	—	—	—	C	—	—	—	—	—	C	C	I
M. tricarinata	—	—	—	—	—	—	—	—	—	—	—	—	B	—	—	—	—	—	—	—	IV
Morenia petersii	—	—	—	—	—	—	—	—	—	—	—	—	C	—	—	—	—	—	—	—	II

Table 2 cont.

* LOCALITIES SURVEYED

1. Vicinity of Anaipandam, Chalakudy District, Kerala
2. Godaveri river, Manthani to Coast, Andhra Pradesh
3. Vicinity of Hyderabad, Andhra Pradesh
4. Gomti river and vicinity near Lucknow, Uttar Pradesh
5. Ghagra river, Katerniaghat Gharial Sanctuary, vicinity of Girija Barrage, Bhariach District, Uttar Pradesh
6. Chambal river, Morena and Bhind Districts, Madhya Pradesh
7. Kuarr and Sank rivers, vicinity of Morena, Madhya Pradesh
8. Jumna river, Bah to Etawah, Uttar Pradesh
9. Mahanadi river, Tikerpara to Cuttack, Orissa
10. Subarnarekha river, Udaipur Village 3 mi NE Chandaeswar, Orissa
11. Ganges river, Kahalgaon to Rajmahal, Bihar
12. Saranda Forest, Singhbhum District, Bihar
13. Gandak river and vicinity, Gandak Dam to Bettiah, West Champaran District, Bihar
14. Burhi Gandak river, Muzaffarpur, Bihar
15. Narmada river, Maheshwar to Hosangabad, Madhya Pradesh
16. Howrah Markets, West Bengal
17. Markets in Jalpaiguri District, West Bengal
18. Sunderbans, 24 Parganas District, West Bengal
19. Vicinity of Madras, Tamil Nadu
20. Moyar, Bhavani and Amaravati Tributaries of the Cauvery river, Periyar, Nilgiris and Coimbatore Districts, Tamil Nadu.

state, being administrated through the Forest Department. The roll of the central government was chiefly advisory. This situation has been altered by passing the Indian Wildlife (Protection) Act 1972 and through inclusion of wildlife protection on the Concurrent List of the Union, in the Constitution of India. Now the central government has some administrative control over the states in wildlife conservation matters (Saharia 1982).

The IWL(P)A provides the only protection for freshwater turtles in most states today. The initial document listed no freshwater turtles in need of protection but a later revision (Table 3) included four species (3 trionychids and 1 emydid) on Schedule I (rare and endangered species) and placed all tortoises, the remaining soft-sheels and an emydid on Schedule IV (small game species). According to provisions of this act the Schedule I species are completely protected and a permit is required to capture any species on Schedule IV.

At the international level, the Convention on International Trade of Endangered Species of Wild Flora and Fauna (CITES) provides the chief means of controlling trade between countries. Seven Indian species are on Appendix I indicating that they cannot be traded (Table 3).

Certain problems presently exist which limit the effectiveness of these protective measures. First not all of the species listed on Appendix I and/or Schedule I are rare or endangered. In fact some of the more common widespread species in India (e.g. *Lissemys punctata, Trionyx gangeticus, Kachuga tecta*) are on both lists while a number of other truly rare species (e.g. *Batagur baska, Kachuga kachuga, Pelochelys bibroni*) are on only one or neither. If these lists are to perform their intended function, revisions are necessary.

Table 3 summarizes my recommended revisions for these lists based on findings of our surveys. For the IWL(P)A, I recommended adding five rare species to Schedule I and removing or down-listing four common ones. Further, the more important commercial species should be placed on Schedule IV (small game) allowing for better monitoring of the trade. As permits are required to exploit small game, the number of permits issued for each species can provide an indication of volume of trade. Also, herein lies a mechanism through which exploiters can be charged the costs of managing the resource—i.e. by levying permit fees for this purpose.

My recommendations for the CITES appendices would reduce the Indian species on Ap-

TABLE 3

SUGGESTED REVISIONS IN LISTINGS OF TURTLES ON THE SCHEDULES OF THE INDIAN WILDLIFE (PROTECTION) ACT 1972 AND ON THE APPENDICES OF THE CONVENTION ON INTERNATIONAL TRADE IN ENDANGERED SPECIES

	Present		Revised		
Species	IWL(P)A *Schedule*	CITES *Appendix*	IWL(P)A *Schedule*	CITES *Appendix*	*Explanation**
Batagur baska	—	I	I	I	1
Geoclemys hamiltonii	—	I	I	I	1
Hardella thurjii	—	—	IV	—	1
Heosemys silvatica	—	—	I	—	2
Kachuga tecta	I	I	—	—	3,4
Kachuga kachuga	—	—	I	—	1
Kachuga dhongoka	—	—	IV	—	5
Melanochelys tricarinata	IV	I	I	I	6
Chitra indica	IV	—	IV	—	3,4
Pelochelys bibronii	IV	—	I	—	6,4
Trionyx gangeticus	I	I	IV	II	3,5
Trionyx hurum	I	I	IV	II	3,5
Trionyx leithii	IV	—	IV	—	3,4
Lissemys punctata	I	I	IV	—	3,5

* 1. Serious declines in population numbers or small population numbers indicated
2. Limited range with threats to habitats
3. Survey indicates moderate to large populations
4. More extensive range than previously known
5. Heavy trade in this species needs monitoring
6. Insufficient data available on species

pendix I from 7 to 3 by down-listing 2 and removing 2 others. No new species have been added—the philosophy being that for species occurring largely or wholly in India, the protection offered by the IWL(P)A is sufficient.

A second problem with the existing protective measures has been lax enforcement. The fact that 3 out of 4 most common market species seen on our surveys were on Schedule I underscores this fact. An important contributing factor to the lax enforcement has been that most forest departments lack personnel trained to distinguish the protected from unprotected chelonians. Wildlife officers usually are trained only in the identification of game mammals and birds, not reptiles. To rectify this problem, I recommend that a section of the curricula at the government training schools for wildlife officers be devoted to reptile identification and conservation techniques.

Management and Rehabilitation

The IWL(P)A provides an important foundation for safeguarding India's chelonian resources. However, it should be considered a beginning rather than the final solution to present problems. If further steps are not taken, continued habitat alteration and heavy exploitation will lead to the inclusion of additional species on Schedule I. The following measures for protection and management are recommended to augment the IWL(P)A . Chief objectives of these actions are to permit some exploitation while protecting the resource base and promoting growth of the populations to former levels. To achieve these objectives the government must first set aside favourable habitat and then enhance recruitment and growth of depleted populations. Recommendations for specific actions follow.

The sanctuary or source area concept. This technique completely protects an area containing a nucleus of breeding individuals. Ideally the nuclear or source population increases in size until population pressure forces dispersal to unprotected areas where the turtles can be exploited. So long as the breeding nucleus is protected the population will not be exterminated.

Certain sanctuaries, already extant in India, demonstrate the effectiveness of such areas in turtle conservation. As part of India's successful crocodile rehabilitation programme, crocodile sanctuaries have been established on several river systems. Due to prohibition of hunting and fishing in these areas, turtle populations have usually increased along with the crocodilians. An excellent example is the National Chambal River Sanctuary which was the second richest area in terms of turtle diversity and abundance (6 species, 4 of which were quite common) that we encountered in our surveys.

Religious sanctuaries in which turtles are fed and protected are also scattered throughout India. In some cases turtles are kept in tanks (ponds) associated with a temple. Here they are fed by local people and pilgrims in the belief that merit is gained by such action. Typically such tanks contain a population of one of the large species of *Trionyx* (Annandale and Shastri 1914). We saw an example of a turtle tank at a Hindoo temple near the mouth of the Godaveri river at Kotipalle, Andhra Pradesh. Here numbers of *Trionyx leithii* were seen eating puffed rice and hibiscus flowers provided by local villagers. We visited another temple tank at Puri, Orissa but this site no longer maintains the population of *Trionyx gangeticus* described by Annandale and Shastri (1914).

In other cases, turtles in a stretch of river near a temple will be given protection and food. At Bateshwar, Uttar Pradesh along a temple-lined stretch of the Jumna river, I observed large numbers of the otherwise rare *Kachuga kachuga* along with *K. dhongoka, K. tentoria, Lissemys punctata* and *Trionyx gangeticus* being fed dough balls from the steps of one temple. This site was also used for aquatic burials which may further explain the abundance and diversity of turtles present.

Sanctuaries such as the above are already functioning as source areas supplying turtles to nonprotected regions. However, additional ones are needed on rivers where few or none exist. Multiple purpose sanctuaries should be considered. For example they might be done in cooperation with the Fisheries Department as fish benefit in the same manner as turtles and crocodiles. The areas chosen should include both favourable nesting sites and feeding habitats. The larger the better, but areas of even a kilometre in length would be beneficial.

Hatcheries and protected nesting areas. As the mortality rates of early ontogenetic stages in the life history far exceed those of older animals, any actions taken to limit egg or hatchling predation can greatly increase recruitment. Hatcheries and protected areas are among the most common techniques used to maintain and rehabilitate populations in turtle conservation programmes. Detailed hatchery techniques are described by Pritchard *et al.* (1982). Briefly a hatchery functions by removing eggs from nests and replanting them either in a protected area of beach or in a container until incubation is complete. I recently worked with the Madhya Pradesh Forest Department to initiate a pilot hatchery for *Kachuga kachuga* and *K. dhongoka* at the National Chambal River Sanctuary headquarters near Morena, Madhya Pradesh.

Hatcheries do have certain drawbacks: They require space, fencing and personnel for several weeks. Moving of eggs from one site to another can reduce viability. Recent finds have also shown that in certain species incubation temperatures can affect the sex ratio of the hatchlings (Morreale *et al.* 1982). It is possible to produce all males unless temperatures are controlled.

A simpler and usually cheaper method is to hire one to several personnel to patrol the nesting beaches during peak periods. Nests can be protected from many predators by putting wire cages over them for a couple of weeks after which time the characteristics that allow a predator to locate the nest will have largely disappeared. Another simple technique which has been successful in protecting sea turtle nests is to replant the eggs a few yards away from the nest (Stancyk 1981). Again this seems to eliminate many of the cues that a predator utilizes to find a nest.

Captive breeding programmes. Although every attempt should be made to maintain species in their natural environment, it may be necessary in some cases to initiate captive breeding programmes to restock dwindling populations. Such programmes can also provide valuable information on the reproductive biology of the species.

The Madras Crocodile Bank with funding from the Wildlife Institute is currently constructing facilities for a threatened species breeding programme and already has begun feasibility studies for certain species. Breeding stock is available for *Heosemys silvatica, Hardella thurjii* and *Kachuga dhongoka.* Pairs of *Batagur baska, Kachuga kachuga* and commercially important trionychids will be sought during the coming year. Such pilot projects should be encouraged to work out the techniques and conditions needed for breeding these animals in captivity.

Another type of captive breeding programme deserving study is that for commercial purposes. In China, Japan and Thailand, soft-shell turtles are being raised in ponds for markets. In particular, the feasibility of such projects should be investigated in West Bengal. It seems likely that turtles could be provided to the West Bengal markets more cheaply and efficiently than the present system in which they are shipped long distances by rail during which time many die. Such programmes utilizing non-endangered species in West Bengal could reduce the demand for wild-caught out-of-state turtles. However, a similar issue concerning farming of sea turtles has been the subject of much controversy in recent years. Arguments for and against are summarized by Ehrenfeld (1981), Reichart (1981), and Dodd (1981). However, as the programmes suggested herein would be utilizing non-endangered species, many of the objections discussed by the above authors should not apply.

Other studies are needed to determine how turtles can be raised along with to achieve maximum productivity in small private ponds. Many of these ponds exist in W. Bengal but according to Biswas and Biswas (*unpublished manuscript*) present fishery practices dictate that all turtles be removed from these ponds prior to stocking of fish. Nevertheless it is likely that vegetarian species of turtles could coexist with the fish without competing thus increasing the overall productivity of the ponds. Again such private supplies of turtles could lessen the drain on wild populations.

For commercial purposes either the Indian flap-shell, *Lissemys punctata,* or one of its larger relatives (e.g. *Trionyx gangeticus, T. leithii*) show the greatest potential. These are highly adaptable, omnivorous species that do well in ponds. They are already the most popular market species. However, being omnivorous these species could lower the fish productivity in private ponds (*Lissemys* being smaller would probably have the least deleterious effect). For fish ponds an herbivorous emydid such as *Hardella thurjii* or *Kachuga tentoria* might be a more suitable choice to coexist with fish. Experimental studies on the subject are greatly needed.

Closed season. This general protective measure would benefit all of the commercially valuable species. As stated previously, the nesting season is the most vulnerable to capture at this time and if they are not allowed to reproduce the population will continue to decline. Conversely prohibiting the collection of turtles during their nesting season should lead to greater recruitment and population growth.

With Indian turtles a simple, effective and easily enforcible system could be established having only two closed seasons corresponding with the peak nesting seasons of hard-shells (December-April) and soft-shells (August-November). The simplicity of enforcing two closed seasons is a big selling point. Spot checks of the major West Bengal markets could be made periodically. Wildlife officers would not have to identify different species but only make the simple distinction between a hard-shell and soft-shell turtle. Only hard-shells should be present in markets from August through November and only soft-shells from December through April.

Education. The long term success of any conservation programme requires public support. Cooperation is more likely when the public understands the needs for the programme (IUCN 1980). A turtle fisherman is far more likely to respect the law (a closed season, a sanctuary area) if he understands that these practices are designed to benefit him by increasing the numbers of turtles. It is recommended that wildlife departments designate public relations personnel to disseminate educational information to the public concerning game laws and conservation programmes. Mass media should be utilized along with on-site visits to villages in key areas and the provision of environmental education in the schools.

ACKNOWLEDGEMENTS

Many persons and institutions have contributed to this project and while all names cannot be mentioned, hopefully I can collectively thank all concerned.

The Forest Departments of Kerala, Andhra Pradesh, Uttar Pradesh, Bihar, Orissa, West Bengal and Madhya Pradesh have been very helpful, providing transportation into difficult to reach areas, allowing us to use their resthouse facilities and for allowing various personnel to accompany and assist us.

My thanks to Mr. J.C. Daniel and the Bombay Natural History Society for serving respectively as my advisor and host institution during my stay in India; to Romulus and Zai Whitaker and the Madras Snake Park personnel who have provided so much, including housing, office space, and secretarial help; to Dennis Johnson, Robert Stella and V.V. Nanda of the United States. Embassy Science who have advised and assisted in getting the project going; to the Zoological Survey of India and World Wildlife Fund-India of the Eastern Region for their hospitality while I was in Calcutta. Mr S. Biswas of the Zoological Survey of India provided many useful suggestions and allowed me to read unpublished work.

My special appreciation to Shri Samar Singh, Joint Secretary for Wildlife and his staff (particularly Shri Kishore Rao and Shri P. Kannan) for their help in getting this project started, for writing numerous letters of introduction to state forest departments and in general for their support and encouragement.

I was very ably assisted throughout the project by Ms J. Vijaya and Mr Satish Bhaskar and much of the success of the work can be attributed to their efforts.

Funding for the 2 months survey (1981-82) was provided by a World Wildlife Fund Grant. My participation in the second survey was supported chiefly by an Indo-American Fellowship. For this I thank the Indo-American subcommission on Education and Culture along with the Council on International Exchange of Scholars and the American Institute of Indian Studies that administered the award. Supplementary funds were provided by a grant of the New York Zoological Society administered through the Office of International Affairs of the United States Fish and Wildlife Service. Eastern Illinois University provided me with a one year sabbatical leave to conduct the survey.

LITERATURE CITED

ACHARJI, M.N. (1950): Edible chelonians and their products. *J. Bombay nat. Hist. Soc.* **49**: 529-532.

__________ (1955): A collection of chelonians and snakes from Chota Nagpur, Bihar. *Rec. Indian Mus.* **53**: 383-392.

ANNANDALE, N. & SHASTRI, H. (1914): Relics of the worship of Mud-turtles (Trionychidae) in India and Burma. *Proc. Asiatic Soc., Bengal* **10**: 131-135.

BISWAS, S. & BISWAS, B.: Conservation problems with Indian freshwater turtles. Unpublished manuscript.

BURY, R.B. (1979): Population ecology of freshwater turtles. pp. 571-602. In Harless M. and Morlock H. (eds.) Turtles: Perspectives and research. Wiley Interscience, New York.

CHAUDHURI, B.L. (1912): Aquatic tortoises of the middle Ganges and Brahmaputra *Rec. Indian Mus.* **7**: 212-214.

DODD, C.K. (1981): Does sea turtle aquacultre benefit conservaton? pp. 473-480. In K.A. Bjorndal (ed.). Biology and conservation of sea turtles. Smithsonian Instit. Press. Washington D.C.

EHRENFELD, D.(1981): Options and limitations in the conservation of sea turtles. pp. 457-463. In K.A. Bjorndal (ed.). Biology and conservation of sea turtles. Smithsonian Instit. Press. Washington D.C.

GÜNTHER, A.C.L.G. (1864): The reptiles of British India. London.

HALL, R.J. (1980): Effects of environmental contaminants on reptiles: A review. *U.S. Fish Wild. Serv. Spec. Sc. Rep.-Wild.* No. 228. 12 pp.

IUCN (1980): World conservation strategy. International Union for conservation of nature and natural resources.

IVERSON, J.B. (1982): Biomass in turtle populations: A neglected subject. *Oecologia (Berl)* **55**: 69-76.

KALRA, R.L. & CHAWLA, R.P. (1981): Impact of pesticidal pollution in the environment. *J. Bombay nat. Hist. Soc.* **78**(1): 1-15.

KRISHNAN, M. (1981): Moving cobble-stones. *The Sunday Statesman* **30**: 8.

MINTON, S.A. (1966): A contribution to the herpetology of West Pakistan. *Bull. Amer. Mus. Nat. Hist.* **134**(2): 27-184.

MOLL, E.O. (1976): West Malaysian turtles: Utilization and conservation. *Herp. Rev.* **7**(4): 163-166.

MORREALE, S.J., RUIZ, G.J., SPOTILA, J.R. & STANDORA, E.A. (1982): Temperature-dependent sex determination: Current practices threaten conservation of sea turtles. *Science* **216**: 1245-1247.

PRITCHARD, P. *et al.* (1982): Sea turtle manual of research and conservation techniques. Western Atlantic Turtle Symposium, Costa Rica.

REICHART, H.A. (1981): Farming and ranching as a strategy for sea turtle Conservation. pp. 465-471. In K.A. Bjorndal (ed.). Biology and conservation of sea turtles. Smithsonian Instit. Press. Washington D.C.

SAHARIA, V.B. (1982): Wildlife in India. Natraj Publishers, Dehra Dun.

SIOW, K.T. & MOLL, E.O. (1981): Status and conservation of estuarine and sea turtles in West Malaysian waters. pp. 339-347. In K.A. Bjorndal (ed.). Biology and conservation of sea turtles. Smithsonian Instit. Press, Washington D.C.

SMITH, M.A. (1931): The fauna of British India, including Ceylon and Burma. Reptilia and Amphibia. Vol. 1. London.

STANCYK, S.E. (1981): Non-human predators of sea turtles and their control. pp. 139-152. In K.A. Bjorndal (ed.). Biology and conservation of sea turtles. Smithsonian

Instit. Press, Washington, D.C.

THEOBALD, W. (1868): Catalogue of the reptiles of British Burma, embracing the provinces of Pegu, Martaban and Tenasserium; with descriptions of new or little known species. *J. Linn. Soc. Zool.* 1868: 4-67.

VIJAYA, J. (1982): Freshwater turtles. *Hamadryad* 7(1): 11-13.

______ & MANNA, P. (1982): A preliminary status survey of freshwater turtles in West Bengal, India. Unpublished report to World Wildlife Fund-U.S.

ZOOLOGICAL SURVEY OF INDIA (1981): Rare and endangered animals of India. Government of India, Calcutta.

Trends in Wildlife Trade from India to the United States[1]

(*With a text-figure*)

LYNN GRAY-SCHOFIELD & LINDA MCMAHAN

ABSTRACT

India, once one of the largest exporters of wildlife and wildlife products to the United States, has taken many measures to protect its species from possible excessive trade, including the implementation of protective legislation and conservation programmes. In this report I analyze wildlife trade statistics to the U.S. from India and discuss how legislation has reduced trade in most wildlife categories.

An analysis of wildlife trade trends shows that exports to the U.S. from India have fallen dramatically over past decades. U.S. imports of rhesus monkeys (*Macaca mulatta*), after reaching a peak of 200,000 in the late 1950's, declined until 1978 when India banned primate exports. In the early 1970's, India was the second largest exporters of live mammals to the U.S. with primates composing the majority of exports.

The number of wild birds imported into the U.S. from India dropped from an average of over 200,000 per year in the early 1970's to an annual average of only a few thousand in the early 1980's.

India has traditionally maintained a large trade in reptile skins. Conscious of the possible deleterious effects of this trade on native reptile populations, Indian officials imposed bans on reptile skin exports. Despite these bans, however, it appears that trade, particularly in snakeskins, still flourishes. The U.S. continues to import annually hundred thousand Ratsnake (*Ptyas mucosus*) skins originating in India.

In 1981 and 1982, India exported several other wildlife items to the U.S., including several million shells, nearly one million mammal bone and skin products (from water buffaloes, *Bubalus bubalis* and dromedary camels, (*Camelus dromedarius*), and thousands of manufactured African elephant ivory products.

Wildlife trade from India to the United States has undergone many changes over past decades, including changes in the types and numbers of species traded. Live primates once traded extensively for research purposes are no longer exported. The number of birds exported for the pet trade has decreased, but the percent composition of psittacines has increased. Products and skins from Indian reptiles, traditionally heavily traded, continue to be imported by the U.S. in large numbers despite legislative protection in India.

Indian legislation has been an important factor in the overall decline in wildlife trade. Some laws and regulations have been enforced effectively, thereby protecting the species concerned. However, others appear to be violated, resulting in a continuation of trade at levels possibly detrimental to wild populations. India ratified the Convention on International Trade in Endangered Species of Wild Fauna and Flora (CITES) in July 1976, thereby agreeing to regulate trade in some species that were not covered under domestic legislation and were not subject to prior export control.

The data presented in this report were derived from several U.S. sources for import

[1]TRAFFIC (U.S.A.) Report 1983

statistics. These include U.S. Department of Commerce statistics, U.S. CITES Annual Reports, and U.S. Fish and Wildlife Service 3-177 declaration data supplied to TRAFFIC (U.S.A.) under a Freedom of Information Act request. I also used India's 1981 CITES Annual Report to supplement U.S. import data.

Primate Trade

In the early 1970's, India was the second largest exporter of live mammals to the United States. Between 1970 and 1972, the U.S. imported 66,178 mammals from India, almost all of which were rhesus monkeys (*Macaca mulatta*) (Clapp 1974; Clapp & Paradiso 1973, Paradiso & Fisher 1972). In 1955, the U.S. and India entered into an agreement permitting rhesus monkey exports from India to the U.S. for use in the development and testing of the polio vaccine and in other biomedical research. U.S. imports of rhesus monkeys from India averaged 120,000 animals annually between 1956 and 1960 (Conway 1966), and as a result, populations of the monkeys began to decline drastically. In the province of Uttar Pradesh (northern India), intensive trapping for export had caused a pronounced change in the age structure of rhesus populations. The populations, once thought to be between 10-20 million, was estimated at only one million in 1961 (Southwick *et al.* 1975).

In an attempt to regulate the trade, India established several export quotas: the first at 50,000 rhesus monkeys per year, then 30,000 per year in 1973, and finally 20,000 per year in 1974. Between 1964 and 1978, the U.S. imported 332,000 primates from India, most of which were probably rhesus monkeys (Mack & Eudey, *in press*). Conscious of their seriously depleted monkey populations and also of U.S. research violations of the initial 1955 agreement, Indian officials banned all exports of rhesus monkeys effective April 1978. Since that date, primates have not been imported into the United States from India (see Figure).

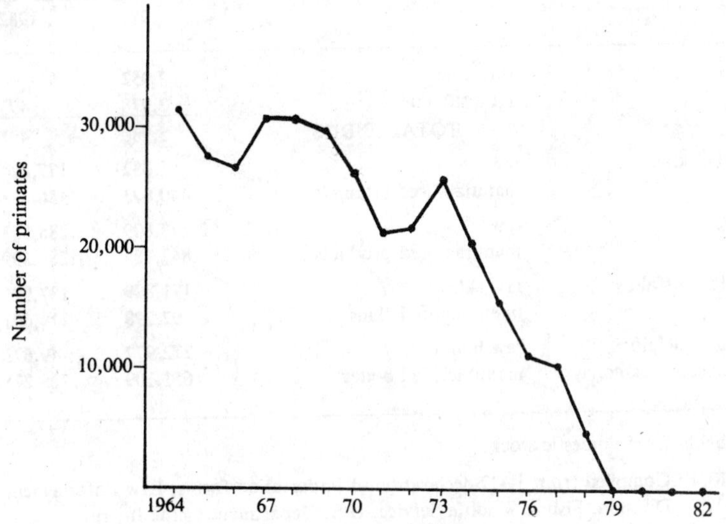

Figure. Primates imported into the United States from India.
SOURCE: U.S. Imports for consumption, compiled by Bureau of the Census, U.S. Department of Commerce.

Despite the unavailability of rhesus monkeys from India, research programmes in the U.S. continue. Captive-breeding programmes in the U.S. have produced over 20,000 rhesus monkeys between 1978 and 1981 (Mack 1982). In addition, researchers have begun substituting long-tailed macaques (*Macaca fascicularis*) for rhesus monkeys in many studies (Mack & Eudey, *in press*).

Live Bird Trade

Between 1970 and 1976, India exported nearly 13 million birds worldwide, an average of 1.85 million annually (Inskipp 1981a). Over 60 countries imported these birds, with the U.S. being fifth-largest importer after Japan, Italy, France, and Belgium. The U.S. imported more live birds from India between 1970 and 1972 than from any other single nation, averaging over 210,000 birds annually and representing more than one quarter of all live birds imported by the U.S. during that period (Clapp 1975; Clapp & Banks 1973a and b).

Since 1972, U.S. imports of live birds originating in India have decreased greatly. Annual U.S. imports averaged 3,212 birds in 1981 and 1982 (Table 1). The decline is due in part to the temporary U.S. ban on all bird imports in August 1972 and to U.S. quarantine restrictions implemeted to help eliminate outbreaks of exotic Newcastle disease (Inskipp 1981a). The U.S. resumed importing live birds in 1974 but imports from India have yet to reach the levels attained in the early 1970's. It also appears that U.S. imports of birds from India have decreased due to the availability of less expensive birds from other countries, such as small seedeaters from Senegal (ibid.).

TABLE 1

U.S. WILDLIFE IMPORTS ORIGINATING IN INDIA

Wildlife category		Quantity 1981	Quantity 1982
Birds	psittacines	2,952	4
	non-psittacines	2,978	493
	TOTAL BIRDS	5,930	497
Reptile skins	raw	451,032	177,024
	manufactured products	440,673	456,438
Shells	raw	2,247,809	3,288,533
	manufactured products	847,784	1,284,399
*Water buffalo	raw skins	171,899	137,996
	manufactured skins	97,299	214,601
*Water buffalo &	raw bones	272,977	49,673
*Dromedary camel	manufactured bones	651,109	728,278

*Probably from domestic stock.

SOURCE: Compiled from 3-177 declaration of importation forms, Law Enforcement Division, Fish & Wildlife Service, U.S. Department of the Interior.

The export of birds from India is controlled by the Exports (Control) Order (made under the Imports and Exports [Control] Act, 1947). The Order consists of two parts and is revised each year. The Indian government does not generally allow exports of species listed on Part A. Species listed on Part B may be exported if certain conditions are met. The number of species added to both lists has increased annually, although changes to the lists in 1979 decreased the number of birds on Part B by half.

In the early 1970's, species of the family Estrildidae composed almost 90 percent of India's bird exports to the United States. Red avadavat or munia (*Amandava amandava*), black-headed (or chestnut) mannikin (*Lonchura malacca*), spotted (or nutmeg) mannikin (*L. punctulata*), and Indian silverbill (*Euodice malabarica*) were among the most frequently traded species (ibid.). Today the number of these species found in trade are greatly reduced.

The percentage of psittacines out of the total number of birds imported by the U.S. from India form an annual of 3 percent between 1970 and 1972 to an average of 46 percent for 1981 and 1982 combined. However, due to lack of data for the intermediate years, it is difficult to determine if the percent increase has been a continuous one. Psittacines imported from India totalled 1,986 in 1970, 13,200 in 1971, and 3,665 in 1972 (Clapp 1970, 1971, 1972), with ringnecked parakeets (*Psittacula krameri*) and blossom-headed parakeets (*P. cyanocephala*) being the most commonly traded species. In 1981 and 1982, the U.S. imported 2,956 psittacines out of a total of 6,427 birds (Table 1). More than half of the psittacines originated in India and were re-exported to the U.S. through Belgium. The vast majority of birds were ringnecked parakeets, one of the three psittacine species not covered by the general parrot listing under CITES.

Reptile Skin Trade

Historically, reptile skins and products from India have been an important trade (Inskipp 1981b). The Indian snakeskin trade peaked in the 1950's, with an estimated 12 million skins exported from India has declined considerably since that time, the number still in trade appears high when one considers that India has enacted a total ban on the export of reptile skins (Export [Control] Order 1979). By 1973, India had banned the export of the Indian python (*Python molurus molurus*) and all poisonous snakes and had placed quotas on all other reptiles (Inskipp 1981b). In 1976, exports of raw snakeskin were banned in India and in 1979, all commercial exports of other skins were prohibited.

Despite this legislation, large quantities of reptile skins originating in India continue to enter the U.S. each year. Indian snakeskin compose the vast majority of these reptile items, with oriental rat snake (*Ptyas mucosus*), called "whipsnake" in trade,* being the most commonly traded species.

Some of the Indian reptile skins currently in trade may be from stockpiles. At the time of the ban, these stockpiles were declared to the government and dealers were allowed to continue trade within the country with only these legally acquired skins (ibid.). There may also have been stockpiles in several European countries (ibid.). The large quantity of snakeskins still in trade, however, possibly indicates the illegal smuggling of these skins out of the country. In 1979 for example, 150,000 snakeskins were seized by Indian Customs authorities at the Calcutta airport, with part of the shipment destined for West Germany (CITES Secretariat, *pers. comm.*). The three main

*In fact the Rat snake skin is called the "whips" in the trade; not as Rat snake — Editors

species involved in this seizure were whipsnake, Asiatic cobra (*Naja naja*), and Indian python.

In 1981 and 1982, 628,056 semi-tanned reptile skins originating in India arrived in the U.S., most of which were re-exported through West Germany and the United Kingdom (Table 1). Of these skins, 4,663 came from CITES-listed reptile species. Ratsnake skins composed the vast majority of the non-CITES listed imports. Only 1,705 snakeskins were directly exported from India to the United States for the two years.

In addition, the U.S. imported 897,111 manufactured Indian reptile products in 1981 and 1982; Italy and Spain were the primary re-exporting countries of manufactured Indian reptile leather. Less than three percent of the manufactured items imported involved CITES-listed species (totalling 23,941 manufactured products). According to the U.S. 1981 CITES Annual Report, the U.S. imported over 16,000 manufactured products from India made from Pacific monitor skins (*Varanus indicus*). Water monitors (*V. salvator*), reticulated pythons (*Python reticulatus*), and Burmese pythons (*P. molurus bivittatus*) were the other CITES-listed reptile species most often found in trade, and declared as originating in India. However, Pacific monitor lizards and Burmese pythons do not occur in India, water monitor lizards are found on Andaman Islands, and reticulated pythons are native to the Nicobar Islands only (Groombridge 1981).

Shell Trade

India exports millions of shells to the United States each year, the vast majority (over 95 percent) of which are directly exported from India. Imports for 1981 and 1982 totalled 5,536,342 raw shells and 2,132,183 manufactured products such as jewelry pieces,. lamp shades and plant hangers (Table 1). Among the most commonly imported shells were cowries (*Cypraea* spp., particularly *C. tigris*), turbans (*Turbo* spp.) and window-pane oysters (*Placuna placenta*).

Mammal Products Trade

In 1981 and 1982, hundreds of thousands of mammal skins and manufactured products were in trade from India to the United States. The vast majority of these imports were products made from water buffalo (*Bubalus bubalis*) skins and bones. The U.S. imported 309,895 raw skins and 311,900 manufactured skins from India in 1981 and 1982 (Table 1).

In addition to the water buffalo skin trade, the U.S. imported large quantities of bones from water buffaloes and dromedary camels (*Camelus dromedarius*) to carve into beads, necklaces, and bracelets. Over 322,000 raw bones and nearly 1.4 million manufactured bone products made from these two mammals were imported in 1981 and 1982. Almost all U.S. imports of water buffalo and dromedary camel products came directly from India.

Although it is likely that most of the water buffalo and camel products in trade came from domestic stock, the information is included since these imports compose a significant part of current U.S. trade in animal products from India.

Elephant Ivory Trade

Historically, India had been one of the principal carving centres for elephant ivory worldwide. Asian elephants have traditionally supplied only a small proportion of India's demand for ivory, possibly as little as three to five percent (Parker 1979). Therefore, the vast majority of India's ivory has originated from African elephants.

In 1975, The Asian elephant was listed on CITES Appendix I; this action prohibited any legal commercial trade in its products. However, African elephants, listed on CITES

Appendix II in 1977, still could be traded legally, provided certain requirements were met.

It has been only recently that India's role as a major ivory market has decreased (ibid.). There are several reasons for this decline; probably the most important occurred in 1978 when the Indian government levied a 120 percent import duty on the value of raw ivory. This, coupled with sharp price rises and regulations imposed by CITES in the 1970's, caused the Indian ivory trade to drop.

Parker (1979), in his voluminous report on the ivory trade states that 85 to 90 percent of all Indian ivory work is destined for export or the tourist trade. According to India's 1981 CITES Annual Report, the U.S. was the third largest consumer of Indian ivory, importing 13 percent of India's total ivory exports in 1981. The U.S. 1981 CITES Annual Report shows that only Hong Kong and Japan re-exported more ivory to the U.S. than did India. In 1981 and 1982 combined, the U.S. imported 128,240 items and 56,061 kg of worked ivory products from India (Table 2).

TABLE 2

MANUFACTURED ELEPHANT IVORY PRODUCTS RE-EXPORTED FROM INDIA TO THE U.S.

	1981		1982	
Declared country of origin	Quantity	Declared US$ Value	Quantity[1]	Declared US$ Value
Commercial imports				
Africa	2	539	—	—
Botswana	2,000	ND	1,648	13,522
			12 kg	3,451
Kenya	41,936	211,585	318	9,605
South Africa	—	—	71	1,081
Tanzania	37,776	190,738	28,818	207,144
			& 56,022 kg	132,219
Thailand*	—	—	741	5,462
Zimbabwe	—	—	8,622	49,689
			27 kg	7,624
Unknown	1	100	6,154	92,102
Subtotal	81,715	402,962	46,372 & 56,061 kg	521,899
Non-commercial imports				
Africa	5	615	1	52
India*	31	1,234	5	315
Kenya	2	770	3	950
Tanzania	1	407	32	ND
Unknown	65	2,523	8	346
Subtotal	104	5,549	49	1,663

[1]Number of items, unless otherwise specified.

*This ivory may have been from Asian elephants (antique or pre-Convention ivory) or the reported information may have been miscoded.

SOURCE: Compiled from 3-177 declaration of importation forms, Law Enforcement Division, Fish & Wildlife Service, U.S. Department of the Interior.

Conclusion

India was once one of the largest exporters of live wildlife and wildlife products to the United States and other consuming nations. As a result of laws and regulations passed over the last two decades, trade in many wildlife categories has declined dramatically. Although legislation and enforcement have appeared to control possibly excessive trade in Indian rhesus monkeys, birds, and Asian elephant ivory, it is unclear whether these measures have also been effective for trade in reptile products, particularly snakeskins.

References

CLAPP, R. (1974): Mammals imported into the United States in 1972. Fish and Wildlife Service, U.S. Department of the Interior. Special Scientific Report, No. 181.

_________(1975): Birds imported into the United States in 1972. Fish and Wildlife Service, U.S. Department of the Interior. Ibid., No. 193.

_______ & PARADISO, J. (1973): Mammals imported into the United States in 1971. Fish and Wildlife Service, U.S. Department of the Interior. Ibid., No. 171.

_________ & BANKS, R.C. (1973a): Birds imported into the United States in 1971. Fish and Wildlife Service, U.S. Department of the Interior. Ibid., No. 170.

_______ (1973b): Birds imported into the United States in 1970. Fish and Wildlife Service, U.S. Department of the Interior. Ibid., No. 164.

CONWAY, W.G. (1966): The availability and longterm supply of primates for medical research: a report on the conference held in New York *in* International Zoo yearbook **6**: 284-288.

GROOMBRIDGE, B. (1981): World checklist of endangered amphibians and reptiles. Nature Conservancy Council.

INSKIPP, T. (1981a): The Indian bird trade *in* The Bird Business, by Greta Nilsson pp. 35-48.

_________ (1981b): Indian trade in reptile skins. IUCN Conservation Monitoring Centre, Cambridge.

_______ & WELLS, S. (1979): International trade in wildlife. Earthscan/Fauna Preservation Society publication.

MACK, D. (1982): Trends in primate imports into the United States, 1981. ILAR News **25**, No. 4, pp. 10-13.

_________ & EUDEY, A. (*in press*): Primate trade in the United States *in* The International Primate Trade. (D. Mack and R. Mittermeier, eds.), World Wildlife Fund-U.S. publication.

Ministry of Agriculture, Government of India. 1982. Convention on international trade in endangered species of wild fauna and flora anuual report—1981.

PARADISO, J.L. & FISHER, R.D. (1972): Mammals imported into the United States in 1970. Fish and Wildlife Service, U.S. Department of the Interior. Special Scientific Report, No. 161.

PARKER, I.S.C. (1979): The ivory trade. Typescript report to the U.S. Fish and Wildlife Service.

SOUTHWICK, C.H., SIDDIQI, M.R. & SIDDIQI, M.F. (1975): Primate populations and biomedical research *in* primate utilization and conservation. (G. Bermant and D.G. Lindburg, eds.), Wiley, New York.

U.S. FISH AND WILDLIFE SERVICE (1983): Convention on international trade in endangered species of wild fauna and flora annual report for 1981.

Some aspects of the Wildlife/Pet Trade in India

SHARAD R. SANE, M. Sc.[1]

INTRODUCTION

"JEEVO JEEVASYA JEEVANAM" has been the way of life from the time life started on earth and will continue in the same fashion till life continues on earth. This confirms Darwin's theory of the survival of the better adapted. As civilization is progressing the only difference has been that earlier it was the might or the actual strength, while today it is economic position, i.e. the money value of the person or the nation. So when you take these basic facts into consideration the trade in wildlife, dead or alive has to continue till the human race continues to remain on this planet.

The trade in wildlife/pets has been going on for centuries. That some species like horses, rabbits, cattle, goats, sheep, canary, budgerigar, domestic fowl are descendants of the wild forms is a well known fact. Apart from these the Indian large green parakeet *P. eupatria* is known as the Alexandrine parakeet named after Alexander the Great who had these tame and talking birds.

Collection for the pet trade can really never cause a stress on wild populations, but collection of the species meant for food like frogs, pheasants, partridges, quails etc. can cause a substantial drain on wild populations as well as other species involved in products of wildlife. It is also not economical for any country to import live animals for food or for their products like fur, coats etc. as the air freight involved in importing live animals for this purpose does not make it a commercially viable proposition. For example, the weight of the frog leg in proportion to the entire body of the frog is about 33%. The frogs have to be fed and have to be shipped by air only, so the air freight alone costs about Rs. 4/- per frog while a kilo of frog legs fetches between Rs. 35/- and Rs. 40/-. Same is the case with any other product like crocodile skins, snake skins, or even as a matter of fact the napes of Grey Junglefowl.

To the best of my knowledge there has not been even one species of wildlife which has been extinct or even threatened to an endangered level by the pet trade. In fact the pet trade has saved several species from possibilities of extinction like the Splendid Grass Parakeets, Turquosine Grass Parakeets etc. where the captive populations are far more than those in the wild. It should be also noted that the captive breeding programme was boosted by a wild animals dealer who is still considered an authority.

Even hunting as sport does not cause a significant stress on the population, as is caused by trapping or hunting of the species used as food or as products.

Whatever one may say, the human stomach has to be filled prior to conservation of any species of wildlife. The second fact is that as the agricultural areas grow the forested areas become less. Apart from this the government as well as the conservationist have to take into consideration whether they want to protect wildlife and have population explosions of species which are or could be termed as agricultrual pests like munias, parakeets, bulbuls, rats, fruit bats, striped squirrels etc. by putting unwarranted restrictions on their collections or should allow as many species to live in the restricted forest and agricultural areas.

[1]Proprietor, SACHETAN, L 4/5, Sitaram Building, Palton Road, Bombay-400 001

Major markets in India

The British settled at Calcutta and with their interests in tea gardens in the eastern region, the trade in wildlife pets first started there. Avicultural literature shows that exports used to take place from Calcutta even in the late 19th century. Today Calcutta has more than 50% share of the pet trade. The hobby of keeping pets is best developed at Calcutta, in comparison to other major cities and towns. Apart from being a seaport, to the best of my knowledge, Calcutta was the first well developed commercial airport in comparison to Bombay.

Patna has a peculiar status and these dealers act as middlemen in the pet industry. The wildlife from the Eastern region, Nepal terai region and parts of Uttar Pradesh, Orissa and of course Bihar are gathered by these dealers and supplied to trade all over the country; and through these dealers one could buy wildlife like clouded leopards, tigers, panthers, black bear, lesser pandas, falcons, king and other hornbills, pheasants and of course commoner stuff like redbreasted parakeets, slatyheaded parakeets, hill mynas and so on. Patna being nearer to Calcutta has a distinct advantage.

Bareilly and Lucknow played a major part as middleman dealers, Bareilly specialised in the Himalayan softbills like tits, redstarts, thrushes etc., while Lucknow dealt in different parakeets and other low altitude birds like common and other mynas, bulbuls etc.

Though Bombay has been a seaport and airport for a long time the trade has not developed as the journey involved to bring the livestock to Bombay from the middlemen/dealers from Patna, Lucknow, Bareilly, Kanpur, Varanasi, etc. is more time consuming and difficult in comparison to Caluctta. Though Bombay has been the major city of revenue the hobby of pet keeping is hardly developed here. But Bombay has very peculiar trade of *Bhootadaya* which involves releasing of birds in large numbers for attaining *Poonya*.

The airport at Delhi was developed comparatively recently to those of Calcutta and Bombay. Hence exports never used to take place from Delhi in the olden days. But now, as the Delhi airport is well connected with the international and internal network, the export is picking up and the exporters from Varanasi/Banaras and Meerut use Delhi as their port of export, mainly in species from Western Himalayas and the Ganga plains.

Madras, though it used to supply the trade with some birds like quails, painted and grey partridges, grey junglefowl, munias like red, tri-coloured, spotted and silverbill and though on the air map, has never had significant exports.

Bangalore/Mysore and Hyderabad were mainly the supply lines for munias like spotted, silverbills, red and tri-coloured, some quails, partridges and spurfowl. Supply of mouse deer, slender loris and star tortoises, painted bush quails used to be the speciality of Bangalore/Mysore and Madras dealers.

Alwaye in Kerala State was the main source of the lesser hill mynas, bluewinged parakeets and lorikeets. There are also several other places like Kanpur, Rampur, Sahranpur, Bhagalpur, Jalpaiguri and so on where middlemen collect the wildlife for supply to the export trade centres.

Until early nineteen sixties every year several species of pheasants like Satyr's Tragopan, Impayans, Kalij Koklass, Cheer and sometimes Blood Pheasants along with other game birds like chukor, hill partridge, snow pigeons were brought generally to Lucknow by Lepchas, Bhutias and other tribal people who carried them on their shoulders in baskets and traded. This continued till the borders with Tibet and Nepal were sealed off. The birds that were not absorbed in the pet trade were sold for meat which is even today done surreptitiously.

Since I knew that several birds like the Fairy Blue birds, Imperial pigeons, ruby throated, greyheaded and yellowbrowed bulbuls etc. which were never kept in captivity before, were found along with Lesser Hill mynas and I was interested in collecting them. I visited my supplier in Kerala whose family trade had been supplying Lesser Hill Mynas as well as other forest produce. I was amazed to find that all these birds though trapped along with mynas were eaten, while only mynas were brought alive.

Even after the enforcement of the Wildlife Act 1972, the situation still remains the same, i.e. the tribals collect birds and try to sell them either alive or dead as these and other forest produce are the main—if not only—means of their livelihood. If one visits the local village markets especially in Bihar, Uttar Pradesh, West Bengal, Maharashtra, Manipur, Arunachal Pradesh etc. one can confirm this according to seasons. Now the venues of sales in major cities have changed and keep on changing as old venues are discovered by the forest department.

The general outlook towards animals—wild or domesticated—in the developing countries is altogether different to that in the developed countries. The tribal and village people will give baby birds, turtles, tortoise etc. to their children as toys without any consideration, and do not feel any sense of cruelty. The wildlife is collected by the tribals and other economically backward classes of society. They try to collect forest products to meet their day-to-day needs and when they get more than their immediate requirement on a particular day, being naturally lazy do not go for collction but enjoy or rest. Primarily the tribals used to hunt or collect wildlife, dead or alive, as their own food. Today they prefer to sell them because the returns they get from these sale proceeds are much more than the meat they can get from these animals. The flesh obtained by killing 100 munias or similar sized birds will hardly be 300 gm in comparison to Rs. 20/- to Rs. 100/- he can get by their sale. This in turn helps him to maintain his family in better condition than by eating the flesh of 100 munias.

In the old State of Bombay, a Wild Animals and Birds Protection Act was enacted sometime in 1951 or 1952 and no trapping permits for trade were given and from that time till today, i.e. from 1973 onwards under the Wildlife Protection Act, 1972. Even then there has been no change in the situation as the tribals used to collect munias and other birds which were taken out of the State and resold to the dealers in Bombay/Maharashtra.

Hence the assumption by the government or conservationist that, prohibiting trade in a particular species or a numbr of species will help those species in increasing their numbers in the wild is wrong. In fact these undue restrictions will only lead to the tribals killing the animals more in number for eating instead of selling them. Nagas will eat any wild animal and I have seen in South India tribals eating jungle cats and civets.

Apart from these species regularly involved in the trade I used to specialise in other species which are considered a problem or difficult to keep birds in the avicultural field like jacanas, lapwings, plovers, curlews, bee-eaters, swallow shrikes, cuckoo shrikes, penduline tits or other birds which were never exported before, like the southern treepies, greyheaded bulbuls, Nilgiri wood pigeons, Jerdon's imperial pigeons and so on in very small quantities, say a maximum of 25 of a species a year and these small quantities exported could really never cause any drain on the wild population.

I also used to export frogs, toads, newts, turtles, terrapins, tortoises, smaller species of lizards like different geckos or house lizards, calotes, mabuyas or skinks, chameleons and non-venomous snakes.

At the same time, the efforts made by the hobbyist to keep them alive and try to breed from them led to quite an amount of knowledge which in turn could be very helpful in the captive breeding programme of similar endangered species from other, or even, our country. So science has been deprived of this knowledge by the unwarranted restriction on their collection as well as export.

Impact of Agriculture and Horticulture on Wildlife

The parakeets are nest hole builders and so also are several other birds like barbets, woodpeckers, mynas, magpie robins, owlets. As the agricultural areas increase there is an abundance of food, i.e. grain and fruits, for parakeets in comparison to other, mainly insectivorous birds. With the abudance of food for parakeets there has been a disproportionate growth in their population and with the tree line reduced there is a severe competition for the nest hole sites. The parakeets being more powerful than most of the other nest hole breeders, there is an automatic depletion in their numbers, as these are being deprived of nesting sites.

The other example is of the munias, buntings and other seed eating passerines. These birds mainly eat grain and seeds once they reach adult stages, while only up to the fledgeling stage they do require insect or live food. The crops and orchards are continuously sprayed with insecticides and pesticides, with the effect that a large number of insects and other live food required by the other species like thrushes, warblers, babblers, etc. is reduced considerably, with the result that these species are dwindling in numbers while seed-eating species like munias and other finches have population explosion, apart from this they do rampant destruction of crops. Hence it is necessary to remove all the restriction for trade as used to be before 1977, including trapping, export, etc. except for singular species like green munias, bluewinged parakeet, while Intermediate parakeets should be transferred to schedule I of the Wildlife Act, 1972.

In this present structure when the ecological balance is upset due to man's activity, allowing exploitation for the pet trade is one way to conserve more species with the minimum of destruction.

Economics of Wildlife/Pet Trade

There is a lot of difference between the live wildlife trade and other perishable commodities like vegetables, meat etc. One has to take this basic fact into consideration. Each munia requires about 10 g and the parakeets like Roseringed, Blossomheaded, Redbreasted etc. require 30 g of seeds every day which means that to feed 100 munias it costs Rs. 2/- per day while for 100 parakeets it costs around Rs. 15/- per day, apart from the dealer's normal establishment expenses like rent, electricity, water, salaries, etc. Secondly the livestock has to be attended to 24 hours a day to avoid any mishaps resulting in mortality. Hence, though apparently it looks that the profit margin is very high, it is not so.

In the book THE BIRD BUSINESS — A STUDY OF THE COMMERCIAL CAGE BIRD TRADE, by Greta Nilson with Foreword by S. Dillon Ripley, the 2nd chapter is on the Indian Bird Trade by Tim Inskipp. Table 5 in this chapter is reproduced below:

PRICE CHAIN FOR BIRDS TRANSPORTED FROM INDIA (£ STERLING)

	TRAPPER	MIDDLEMAN	EXPORTER	IMPORTER	RETAILER
Spotted Mannikin (*Lonchura punctulata*)	0.01	0.02	0.05		3.00
Ringnecked Parakeet (*Psittacula krameri*)	0.06		0.30		16.00
Whiterumped Shama (*Copsychus malabaricus*)	0.60		3.00		38.00
Purple Gallinule (*Porphyrio porphyrio*)	0.85		4.40		50.00

This is probably to educate the general public, conservationist and governmental agencies to point out the fantastic profit margin a pet dealer has. If this was the fact then every pet dealer/exporter would be a *Lakhopati*.

The cost structure of the Indian exporter, if the shipment moved out normally, i.e. in a week's time, is as follows:

	100 Spotted Munia	100 Roseringed Parakeet	Whiterumped Shama per bird
Trapper	18.00	108.00	10.80
Middleman	36.00		
Feeding cost for a week	15.00	105.00	9.00
Packing cost	12.00	180.00	10.00
Average mortality	(5%) 3.60	(5%) 5.40	(25%) 2.70
Mortality replacement	3.60	5.40	2.70
Total cost	70.20	403.80	35.20
Export price F.O.B.	90.00	540.00	54.00

If by a chance the shipment is delayed by a week to 10 days the costs cut at par and any further delay beyond that will result in a loss. On an average there is a delay of one shipment in every ten.

The U.K. importer who is a wholeseller has to keep the birds in quarantine for a minimum period of 35 days and also to pay an air-freight of over Rs. 300/- for a cage containing 100 munias. Apart from the cost of feeding and maintenance it costs between £ Stg. 125/- and 250/- depending upon size and location of the quarantine station. These costs include veterinary inspections, post-mortem examination etc. and about another 5% mortality on an average. The figures between the wholeseller and retailer are not given, probably to protect interests of the importer in the U.K.

In the case of soft-billed passerines like Shamas, these are individually packed which used to cost Rs. 10/- per bird and the feeding is very specialised. Food like live insects or ant eggs may cost between Rs. 20/- & 60/- per kg, while the basic insectile mixture which soft-bills require around Rs. 20/- per kg, against Rs. 2/-to Rs. 5/- per kg for the seed-eating birds, and the average mortality is around 25%.

FLOOR PRICE — A MUST

Keeping pets is a luxury in comparison to the daily necessities like food, shelter and clothing. One observes that, as the price of these daily necessities goes up, that sale of these daily necessity commodities in terms of quantities go down according to the parchasing power of the person. The same rule applies more truly to the acquiring of pets. No sensible citizen likes to destroy the national wealth until such time his daily necessities are met.

One can also observe that even today after the introduction of quota system and other measures taken by the government, Indian Wildlife is the cheapest wildlife available to the pet trade. Under these circumstances the only way to conserve wildlife as well as to benefit the economically backward tribal and minority communities will be to open out once again the export pet trade as in 1973/74 with a floor price and at the same time form co-operative societies like the one of the Irula tribes which is under formation due to the efforts of Mr. Romulus Whitaker. This will enable one to obtain a better price for the wildlife, in this case mainly snakes to the Irula tribal who has been earning his living for generations by collection of snakes.

From the compilation by the British Pet Trade Association, one can easily find out that the cheapest wildlife available is from India. It can be easily observed that the variation in the range of prices from the Indian exporters is unimaginable and could be seen from the table below for the years 1979 or 1980.

NAME	MAXIMUM PRICE PER BIRD IN RUPEES	LOWEST PRICE PER BIRD IN RUPEES
Alexandrine Parakeet	67.50	24.00 or U.S. $ 3.00
Roseringed Parakeet	10.50	4.00 U.S. $ 1.00 a pair
Blossomheaded Parakeet	25.00	5.00 U.S. $ 1.25 a pair
Redbreasted Parakeet	45.00	24.00 U.S. $ 3.00 each

The introduction of a floor price at a relatively higher price than the existing prices today will automatically reduce the number of animals exported. At the same time the destruction caused by the tribals and other economically backward people of the society by killing wildlife in numbers just to feed their families to keep going will also be reduced markedly. To cite an example, the spotted munia which used to be exported at Rs. 90/- to Rs. 100/- per 100 birds can easily get a price of Rs. 400/- to Rs. 500/- per 100 birds with the result that it becomes expensive to the importer, thus resulting in automatic reduction in the numbers exported; at the same time our country gets more foreign exchange. If this supply is channelled through co-operative societies the collector will get a better price. This will further reduce the competition between the Indian exporters. As the costs of imported birds rise in the importing countries, the choice of the importer is not to buy cheap stuff, but to buy better livestock which has been kept well and packed well, since the cost of air freight involved acts as a deterrent. Thus opening out of the trade will help the legitimate trade, at the same time acting as a check against smuggling.

Export Policy and Quota System

Our parliament promulgated the Wildlife Protection Act, 1972 in 1973. It was for the first time under the Export trade notice 71/73 dt. 30/4/1973 and 96/73 dt. 13/7/73, Bombay that a registration with Jt. C.C.I. & E was required. This registration was given only to those persons who were in the trade and also had obtained licence to deal in captive animals, trophies etc. issued under the Wildlife Protection Act, 1972. This was the first major change but did not affect the export, except for a few months until such time the licences under Wildlife Protection Act, 1972 were issued.

The export policy for Wildlife—part thereof or produced therefrom till 1978-79—used to be, part A for lists of species of Wildlife normally banned for export. Part B, a list of species of wildlife allowed for export with the legal procurement certificate, was divided into (a) Animals, (b) Reptiles, (c) Birds (ii) Peacock tail feathers, (iii) Others. The export of other species of Wild Animals, Birds, Reptiles and Insects etc. not mentioned elsewhere in these Annexures will also be regulated through four major ports of Bombay, Calcutta, Madras and airport of Delhi. Export will be allowed only by registered exporters of wildlife and wildlife products without any consideration of production of certificate of legal procurement.

The addition and omission of some species from part A to part B and *vice versa* did not make any significant difference to the export trade.

The export policy changed radically for the year 1979-80 for the first time by reverse listing, i.e. list of species allowed for export and introduction of quota system. It was said among the pet/wildlife exporters that this sudden change was at the special recommendation of Dr Salim Ali. So, before I met Dr Salim Ali with others from the trade I myself wanted to compile statistics of the exports made during the years 1977 and 1978. All the exporters did not respond but a large number did. The figures calculated are as per the statements given by the exporters plus a little addition for the exporters who did not respond. The figures given below are best exports, for these particular varieties, either during 1977 or 1978 (Appendix I).

So the statistics collected by me show that out of birds and mammals involved in the export trade 10,63,950 birds are parakeets and seed eating passerines, i.e. approximatley 97%, which are agricultural pests or crop raiders. The remaining species, though insignificant in numbers, are also important from the trade point of view. I was given to understand that the export of these species has been banned which used to be exported in such small numbers because the concerned advisors thought it was insignificant and at the same time they forget that each drop added constitutes to the formation of the ocean.

Their argument about the birds which were being exported in large numbers was that it would cause a population drain. Though the trade exported about 9,38,300 munias, it was reliably learnt that a quota of 50,000 munias per year for all the ports was allocated.

It is understood that the present system of allocating quotas on first-come first-served basis was to accommodate or encourage newcomers in this export field. When the quotas allocated are so low that existing exporters find it extremely difficult to continue with the export trade the question of encouraging or accommodating the newcomers does not arise. I have myself not been able to effect a single shipment during policy years 1981/82, 1982/83 and till today. I have been in the export trade from 1960.

In the export policy announced for 1979-80, 21 items of live wildlife were allowed on quota. Hence I personally met, on behalf of the pet trade Dr Salim Ali, requesting him to request the government to give relaxation in the existing export policy. Which he did by requesting that 47 items should be allowed for export, some of them without any quota restrictions. But instead of getting any relaxation government further restricted the items (see statement in Appendix II).

In the meantime, as far as my information goes a study group under the chairmanship of Dr Salim Ali was formed and a report submitted to the government some time in December 1980 wherein the study group had requested the government for further drastic relaxation for export of wildlife for pet trade. Instead of giving any further relaxation, government further reduced the item of wildlife exported alive to only 3 in animals, which include rats and mice, and 8 in live birds which include crows, sparrows and pigeons (Blue Rock and its domesticated varieties).

The study group must have recommended to the government drastic relaxation for export. Dr Salim Ali explained on T.V. national programme in August 1983 and, as I understand it, while he encourages *Realistic* conservation, he does not want us to indulge in *Sentimental* conservation.

Import and Export Policy April 1983-March 1984 on pages 8 and 9 No. 4 Wildlife states the following: (a) Live Animals, (b) Animal Products on page 9, (c) Live birds state item 5; Munias (Spotted, Red, Blackheaded, Whiteheaded and Whitethroated). I fail to understand since when the Malaysian Whiteheaded Munia — *Lonchura maja* became a bird of Indian origin and if so, where in India it is found in the wild.

Item (8) Pigeons (Blue Rock and its domesticated varieties). How do the domesticated varieties of Blue Rock Pigeon form Indian Wildlife? If the authorities feel that the domesticated forms also are Wildlife and there should be a legal procurement certificate, then why other domesticated species like mules, camel, buffaloes, sheep and goats and poultry should not be covered with the Legal Procurement Certificate of the Wildlife department.

The present quota system for export, where the quotas are not made known officially to the exporter apart from the restriction of 20% of the quota allotment per day per exporter, is an absolutely unreasonable one. To cite an example, suppose there is a quota of 125 White-eyes for a port, which means an exporter can get maximum licence for 25 White-eyes. The price for White-eyes used to be Rs. 6/- per bird. One cannot expect to go through all the paper work for a shipment of Rs. 150/-. Since the quota is not known and one is not sure of his exports there is still further unhealthy competition for grabbing whatever an exporter can, resulting ultimately in loss of foreign exchange for the country. As against this if individual quota is given to each exporter then he can plan his business better, and can command a better price.

For the same White-eyes an exporter can get

as much as Rs. 20/- or Rs. 25/- per bird. He can then look after his birds in a better manner.

As per the customs regulation in Bombay, an advance payment/Inward Remittance Certificate or an L/C must be produced at the time of getting the Shipping Bills approved for any perishable cargo like live pets. The Jt. C.C.I. must have a firm contract with terms and conditions. So how can one ask for advance without knowing whether he is going to get a licence for export or not? If one does not get the licence for the required number of birds the shipment becomes uneconomical to the buyer as the shipment may not even cover his quarantine expenses. In Bombay one has to have a prior approval from the Reserve Bank of India to address the shipment directly to the buyer; a fact which I came to know only after 10 years of exports. I think all these restrictions are not either compulsory or adhered to at the other ports of export.

If the above recommendation is not acceptable to the conservationist at whose advice government acts by banning exports the former should at least recommend to the government that individual quotas to the existing exports should be given for a complete year, year after year so that he can at least obtain the best price for the quota that is allocated to him. If the exporter does not utilize his quota completely then it is better from the conservation point of view, as so many numbers of animals have not been collected from the wild.

PRE-SHIPMENT EXAMINATIONS

Some years back I had an occasion to handle some shipments en route to Europe from Delhi. The flight was diverted to Bombay, after taking off from Delhi. Since there was an indefinite delay for the taking off, my services were requested for feeding, watering and removing dead birds. The cages were sealed and I could do the entire operation without breaking the seals. I really do not know the purpose of these seals. These seals were supposed to be of the Wildlife Department.

It is said in the trade that at Delhi and Calcutta the empty packing cages are sealed by the staff of the Asstt. Director, Wildlife and the contents are examined separately during the office hours. The birds are then released in the cages according to the time of the flight and then taken for customs examination. It is also said that the quantity, and sometimes the species of birds differ from those mentioned in the export licence. Since I do not have documentary evidence I cannot prove it. However, I do have documentary evidence stating that Roseringed Parakeet exported from Delhi and certificate "The Parrots (Parakeets) have been stayed in quarantine for at least 6 months". The price charged was U.S. $ 1.00 per pair. I do not think even if someone gets the birds free of cost he can feed them for 6 months for U.S. $ 1.00 per pair and also does not charge any packing. It was surprising for me to note that none of the inspecting authorities at both the ends took notice of this impossible situation.

As against this, the system of examination at Bombay is totally different. According to the customs regulations the perishable cargo is to be brought for customs examination minimum 4 hours and maximum 6 hours in advance before the scheduled departure of the flight. Both customs and Wildlife department examinations are carried out simultaneously. Of course this means either the staff from the Asstt. Director, Wildlife has to come at odd hours or the shipper has to drop the idea of utilizing the flights which depart around midnight till early morning, say 09.00 hrs. The live pets in general sleep during the night that means if they are packed in the evening and brought to the airport by 20.00 hrs. for customs and Wildlife examinations it does not cause noticeable stress to the birds or mammals as they are then asleep. Hence for those flights which depart after midnight and before 09.00 a.m. the joint examination should be done before 20.00 hrs. The shipments remain with the customs; hence sealing is not necessary.

It is also surprising to note that the Dy. Director, Wildlife, Northern Region, i.e. Delhi and Eastern Region, namely Calcutta can now issue certificate under the "CITES" recommendations but at the same time the same power is not assigned to Dy. Director, Wildlife, Western Region, i.e. Bombay, and if my information is correct, to Dy. Director, Southern Region, i.e. Madras. I do not understand this step-motherly treatment, and we have to apply to Delhi for "CITES" certificates which may take weeks, thus making shipments uneconomical.

Another important consideration is that actually there should be some officer on duty for 24 hours, on the same system as the Plant Quarantine office, so that the Wildlife that is going out of the country as personal baggage also could be checked.

Smuggling

The smuggling of wildlife generally involves species which demand high prices with hobbyist and at the same time are easily available and generally are not controlled by special restrictions in the country of origin.

When I visited the Perth University campus, I could see twenty eight parakeets sitting on telephone wires. They were offered for sale in the local pet shops for 10 Australian dollars each.

Two years later when I visited a dealer in Belgium, he had these 28 parakeets for sale at 500/- U.S. dollars each. Australia has a total ban on export on any kind of wildlife, at the same time they poison water holes and kill their wildlife by the ton-load. Being an affluent country, they can afford this. Apparently these twenty eight parakeets had been smuggled out.

I am also giving two extracts as published in the Parrot Society Magazines, U.K. (Appendix III).

In the paper "Present Distribution and Status of Pheasant in Himachal Pradesh, Western Himalayas" by Gaston *et al,* in *WPA* journal VI, 1980-81 it is stated "For the Western Tragopan, however which is thought to be endangered with extinction (IUCN 1978) we have refrained on the advice of the World Wildlife Fund—India from specifying particular localities in case we might aid people interested in trapping the birds illegally".

Even if the exact localities of the Western Tragopan were published there would not be any danger to the birds from the trade as going to these places and collecting the birds in summer is the only possibility, but the chances of their survival by bringing them down to the port of export and the enormous costs involved in collecting the birds prohibit the dealers in making an attempt, even assuming that they might get the fantastic value of 2000 to 3000 U.S. dollars per pair. Collecting these Tragopans in winter is also not possible because of the altitude and the difficult terrain in which they are found though they could be acclimatised to withstand the temperatures at the port of export. The same remains true for other commoner species like Blood Pheasant, Snow Cocks, Snow Partridges, Grandalas, certain species of Grosbeak, etc. which are basically high altitude birds and do not descend between 4000 and 6000 ft even during winter months. At the same time I would not be surprised if a wealthy hobbyist makes an attempt for collecting a pair or two where financial aspect does not play any part, at the same time there is joy or pleasure of possession, a natural instinct of a human being.

While in the case of other birds like the shahin, Peregrine and other falcons, birds of prey the presence of the illegal trade is possible because, during the winter months they can be collected in the normal bird collecting areas and hence no special financial economic restraints are involved.

The rigidity in the export policy by the reverse listing of the species allowed for export with insignificant quotas and that to be allocated on first-come first-served basis, at the same time a large number of species being open for trade within the country, will definitely attract people involved in the smuggling trade as the demand for these common species increased with high profit margins like those with the Australian birds.

Our Hill myna could be one of the most prone species for this trade. So let us study the case of Hill Myna including the race *peninsularis,* in the trade known as the *Morbhanj* variety of Myna. It is estimated that between 15000 and 20000 Greater Hill Mynas were collected for the trade, out of which about 3000 to 5000 were collected as adults or semi-adults, the rest as young fledgelings, in the trade known as *Baby Mynas.* Only between 3000 and 4000 were of the race *peninsularis.*

It was reported in BNHS/Avicultural Magazine that in the Garo Hills an artificial nest is provided by the Garo tribals for these Hill Mynas to breed. Each family has a number of nests which it guards and removes the fledgelings. The very fact that these Hill Mynas accept these nests proves that this process must have been taking place for generations. Bertram (*Avi. Mag.* Vol. 75 No. 5, 1968) states "The advantages to the Garo are obvious, he has good source of revenue, collected with little difficulty since the nests are reasonably accessible (to a Garo)"

According to my estimate the number of birds collected varies from year to year; approximate figures are: 2500 Lower Shillong/Kamrukh where Forest Dept. used to charge a royalty of Rs. 3.50 per bird; 6000 at Garo Hills, 2000 in Naga Hills and Mizoram, 8000 Nepal/W. Bengal/Bangladesh (Sylhet). Out of this approximately 60% were smuggled into India through Nepal and Bangladesh, and about 4500 (only adults) from upper Assam/Manipur Road around village outskirts.

Bertram (*Avi. Mag.* Vol. 75 No. 7, 1969 page 245) states "In North India, Greater Hill Mynas (i.e. the race *intermedia*) are occasionally captured when adult by some of the hill peoples. Sticks coated with bird lime are attached to trees just coming into fruit and the winter flocks of Hill Mynas land on these and become entangled. All the birds so caught used to be eaten—curried Hill Mynas is apparently a Naga delicacy. Recently, however, the bird dealers in India have discovered that they can buy cheaply these wild-caught adult *intermedia.*"

He also states on the same page, "In South India Hill Myna of the race *indica* are captured in large numbers with *neta* bird lime, when large flocks, gather to feed on local concentration of fruit or nectar. Around 25,000 were collected every year"

If I remember correctly, some years back the Orissa Forest Dept. used to buy these Hill Mynas from the tribals between Rs. 15/- and Rs. 22/- per bird and sell them to the dealers by auction where they used to get a price between Rs. 39/- and Rs. 42/- per bird. Since the export of Hill Mynas has been banned, I do not know if this practice still continues.

With the ban on export of Hill Mynas, there should have been a population explosion, but how can one expect this as the collection of these mynas is still continued by the tribals and even today the birds which are not sold are curried and enjoyed by the tribals, which puts the tribals to more hardship. Still quite a good number of mynas appear in different markets at the ports of export. What happens to these? Where do they go? How is it that Hill mynas are still advertised in the market abroad? Has the export ban helped in any way in the conservation of this species? The answer is No. Only one has to wait and watch for the Mafia to enter into this venture.

HANDICAPS

It will be observed that most persons from the forest departments as well as from other agencies enforcing Wildlife Protection Act, 1972 cannot even identify the popular species of wildlife, a fact which I have experienced on several occasions.

Before the appointment of the Asstt. Director, Wildlife in Bombay, forest dept. etc. used to seek my help for on-the-spot identification of live birds etc. In one case my help was not requested and the concerned officer, instead of seizing all the animals belonging to the Schedules of Wildlife Act, 1972 seized some scheduled animals at the same time some expensive exotic birds. When I came to know about this I requested the concerned officer that seizing birds like Cockatoos etc. was not proper and if something went wrong with these birds, he could be sailing in troubled waters.

Could one imagine the consequences of this advice? The officer concerned sent his junior officer for a raid on me (I was brought back from my office to my residence in their jeep). Of course neither this officer nor his assisting staff could identify any of the birds from my collection but when he saw an African Grey Parrot he remarked what a beautiful falcon that was. I now really feel that instead of explaining to him that it was a parrot I should have allowed him to seize the bird and prosecute me for keeping that falcon.

Apart from this I have seen a licence issued under the Wildlife Protection Act, 1972 to deal in Zebra Finches and Love birds, the birds of foreign origin, and another to deal in Indian birds as foreign birds like 'Mina' (Myna), Madna (Redbreasted parakeet). I just fail to understand how animals of foreign origin, highly domesticated, come under the purview of the Wildlife Act, 1972.

Scientists or naturalists have not recorded the Malabar Bluewinged Parakeet, *Psitacula columboides,* from the northern or northeastern states but the forest departments of some northern states have issued legal procurement certificate for this species. As far as I know there have been no permits issued for trapping of wildlife in the Southern, Western and South Central States like Gujarat, Maharashtra, Kerala, Andhra Pradesh, Karnataka and Goa. In Tamilnadu it is said some trapping permits were issued for quails, partridges and munia only. To the the best of knowledge there are no records of breeding this species in captivity in commercial quantities. I am also given to understand that to legalise the species in the zoos in the northern or northeastern regions, mainly managed by the forest departments by issuing trapping or *special purpose* permits for species which are not supposed to occur in their areas. Otherwise how can zoos acquire schedule I or part II of schedule II animals for thier exhibition?

Governmental, semi-governmental, or private agencies undertake surveys of different areas. Unless these surveys last continuously for 2 to 3 years, in that specified area, a more or less true picture cannot be had. It has been also observed that there is a cycle of occurrence for each species.

The only other way is to take the trade into confidence and acquire along with the survey the information from the trade which is equally important. To cite an example is the recent so-called "re-discovery" of the Indian Cane Turtles after 79 years, which I used to get collected from 1964 to 1977 every year for export. Or Rothchild's Parakeet supposed to have never been in existence and described from the skins exported from India in 1895 and 1924; I have till today myself obtained 2 of these birds; one is living while the other died and skin is with the B.N.H.S. The trade was also responsible for the so-called re-discovery of the Finn's Baya which is common in their natural habitat in the Himalayan grasslands. It should also be noted that identifications, including those working especially with the Zoological Survey of India, are wrong, e.g. *Puntius narayani* as *Puntius nigrofasciatus* or *Botia striata* as *Botia dayi*.

In 1977 when the amendments to schedule of the Wildlife Act, 1972 came in for the first time I had, in a personal communication, pointed out that expert advisors to the government have omitted the species of turtles and tortoise which should have protection, while some very common species should be free for the trade as before, but no action was taken on this, being a recommendation from a dealer. Now Dr Edward Moll, world authority on Chelonians and the head of IUCN/SSC Freshwater Chelonian group has recommended that *Kachuga tectum, Lysemys punctata, Tryonix gangeticum* and *hurrum* should be transferred to schedules IV of the Wildlife Act, 1972 so that these species should be open for the trade.

Another instance to show these conservation minded people or organizations have a prejudiced mind about the trade is described in World Pheasant Association Journal No. VI.

1980-81, Gaston *et al.* in their paper "Present Distribution and Status of Pheasants in Himachal Pradesh, Western Himalayas" have several wrong statements like Cheer-*Catreas wallichis,* 4 Nadar (Bandal), 11 Sara, 12 Siul Valley "not protected". When the species is listed in Schedule I of the Wildlife Protection Act, 1972, how can one say "not protected", and it clearly shows the ignorance about the provisions in the Wildlife Protection Act, 1972.

Further amendments to Wildlife Protection Act, 1972 came in force from 2/10/1980, covering a list which runs to several pages, of butterflies, moths, beetles, etc. I wonder if the students and teachers from the departments of Zoology at undergraduate or post-graduate level, including those specializing in entomology are aware of these amendments and the punishment they are liable to, by infringement of Wildlife Act, 1972, when they go out for their normal field collections. Are the concerned authorities going to take the action recommended under the provision of the Wildlife Act?

"Even after knowing these facts the attitude of the government officials and most of the conservationists as trained or taught by the British, though we are in the 36th year of Independence is so biased that they do not want to believe or listen to the trade, and this attitude is doing more harm to the conservation of wildlife also."

Cruelty and Sentimental Aspects

People talk of the imagined cruelty that is supposed to be taking place in pet/wildlife trade or the way the imported animals are used by the importing countries. They do not visualize the benefits human life has derived by experimenting on these animals and which they are themselves enjoying, like modern drugs, cosmetics etc. Unless these animals are used the only alternative will be to use human beings as guinea pigs. How could one have studied different principles of Genetics?

These same people who talk of cruelty cannot insist upon the I.S.I. to improve upon their standards which are so cruel. I had personally pointed this out in 1977 that even a dealer himself will not pack the birds as tightly as recommended in the I.S.I. standard for small and medium sized birds. In fact so tightly that one will have to convert these birds into minced meat to accommodate them. In this connection I.A.T.A. Live Animal Board has been more cooperative and after the visit of I.A.T.A. Live Animal Board members to India, had recommended to Air India to form a mini I.A.T.A. Live Animal Board for Indian subcontinent to advise about the livestock packing recommendations, which even today has not been formed. Some of the "CITES" packing recommendations are also cruel and unrealistic but fortunately have not been enforced. I have seen a paper published by 'experts' on packaging of livestock who have just discussed this with me for a short time, got information as to how I pack, and by photographing my packings.

The so-called conservation minded people agree that a particular species of animal could be on the vermin list but are against recommending to the government to allow free export alive or of their derivatives. Our country is not rich like Australia that we can afford to waste such an amount of our national wealth by just killing and wasting the vermin and other agricultural pests.

Let us study the case of export of live frogs. As explained earlier, the export of live frogs by air is not economical in comparison to import of frozen frog legs. This assorted live frogs export was only for the pet trade. The figure of live frogs and toads exported had never reached 1000 animals a year. The price used to be a minimum of Rs. 3/- to maximum Rs. 15/- per animal, depending upon the species. I was developing this trade as we have plenty of colourful small-sized frogs like *Rana malabarica, Rhacophorus,* etc. and hardly at any time *Rana tigerina* or *hexadactyla.* Today technically the export of live frogs is allowed after the clearance from Marine Products Export Development Authority. First of all, one cannot understand how live frogs could be included as "Marine Product" when there is nothing marine about them; not even one species of Indian frog or toad is marine. Anyway, apart from this, M.P.F.D.A. wants a signed contract to give a clearance. How can one obtain a signed contract without knowing what one can export and if the export is not allowed then who is to bear a loss for not fulfilling the contract? I was the only regular exporter of this item.

As against this, M.P.E.D.A. in their statistics of 1981 show that 43,67,889 kg of frozen froglegs were exported which means at least 8,73,57,780 number of *Rana tigerina* & *hexadactyla* were slaughtered during the year. The governmental and other conservation minded agencies do not feel concerned over this slaughter but feel that export of a few thousand live assorted frogs and toads will cause a substantial drain on the wild population.

Different species of *Varanus,* popularly known as the Monitor lizards and *Chamaeleon* spp. are included in the schedules of the Wildlife Protection Act, 1972. Geckos are considered a bad omen and are immediately killed or chased out of the house. A number of species of *Calotes, Mabuya, Riopa, Samophilus* etc. are very common and export of a few thousand of these lizards every year cannot cause any significant drain on the population. These used to be exported at between Rs. 5/- and Rs. 50/-per animal. I was the only regular exporter for these smaller species of lizards from India, now totally banned for export.

The conservationists say that snakes should be protected as they control the rat and other rodent populations; at the same time they ignore the fact that every snake seen in village areas is killed or at least an attempt is made to do so. Secondly the number of species of snakes that eat rats is very small. The breeding capacity of these snakes in comparision to rats and mice is extremely low. In olden days when forest areas were more or practically same as the agricultural areas, snakes might have been effective in controlling the rat population. As far as I remember the first ban came on export of live venomous snakes said to be at the recommedation of Haffkine Institute as they were not getting sufficient snakes for milking. How could they get the snakes when they were paying only a price of Rs. 3/- per foot — length of venomous snake and the skins were being sold for around Rs. 7/- to Rs. 10/- per piece. The risk of handling, mortality and non-acceptance of live snakes by railways did not make it worthwhile to supply these venomous snakes to the Haffkine Institute. Even this ban did not have any effect on bettering the snake supplies to the Institute, so a total ban on export of live snakes of all species came into force. The species involved in snake-skin trade are mainly the larger snakes like python, rat snakes, cobras, Russel's vipers. The very fact that several lakhs of skins are confiscated from the clandestine trade and yet the snake population has not dwindled to any great extent and still is the main source of income to the tribals mainly from northeastern region and southern region shows the inefficiency of the ban. The effort made by Romulus Whitaker in the formation of the Irula Tribals' Co-operative Society is much more appreciable as this will help in regulating the collection of snakes and providing a better price for their collection, which today are purchased by the underground trade for a very low price. At the same time the smaller snake species like the sand boas, tree snakes, cat snakes, rough-tailed snakes, racers, watersnakes etc. should be opened for pet trade.

A book ALL HEAVEN IN A RAGE — A STUDY INTO THE IMPORTATION OF BIRDS INTO THE UNITED KINGDOM, by T.P. Inskipp was published first by the Royal Society for the Protection of Birds in U.K. In the foreword by its Director it is mentioned "Many of the catchers and exporters regard the colourful birds as most valuable; indeed we know that they do not always bother to send off the dull coloured females and immatures which are therefore torn from the lime stick and left to die" Does the Director as well as the other members of R.S.P.B. know the basic fact that all the wild birds are collected by the tribals in India as food and that it is because they get better return in kind or money which helps them in bettering their living condition? Do the members of R.S.P.B. know that persons who want to keep the pet birds for singing or taming, generally want only male birds which are colourful, and at the same time make a lot of noise and the dull coloured females and immatures are used by the pet trade as painted finches? Spray painting with the edible colours does not do any harm to these birds or may do the same amount of harm when the pets are bathed with sprays, shampoos etc. specially advertised for this purpose in the pet trade. The painted finches moult into perfectly normal birds and there is no excessive mortality in comparison to the normal birds. The finches are painted with colours as per the orders from the buyers including those in Britain. The Indian exporter has not been cheating the buyer in anyway. R.S.P.B. also had another publication *"Airborne Birds"* but even after all these sentimental efforts, the British government has not promulgated a TOTAL ban on imports of wild birds. Whatever restrictions have been enforced in the U.K. as well as U.S.A. have been with the main intention of preventing diseases like Newcastle etc. which harm mainly the poultry and other table bird production.

As mentioned in my paper earlier, random sampling and taking random photographs as an assignment can never emphasize, and can never give a true picture. It is necessary for responsible organizations like R.S.P.B. or Animal Welfare Institutes or even as a matter of fact any conservation minded organization to have a detailed picture including general economic condition of the people living in that country than just making emotional charges on anybody or even the trade if they really feel the urge for conservation of wildlife.

STATUS OF ZOOS AND CAPTIVE BREEDING PROJECTS

Since the hobby of pet keeping is not well developed in India or, in fact, in any of the developing countries, the standard and concepts of zoo keeping are also relatively primitive.

Secondly the specialization seen in the people involved in zoo keeping in affluent countries is also not seen in most of the Indian zoos. This is because of the fact that the staffing pattern and the credentials required for the zoo staff are entirely different in comparison to those in the European or American zoos. In these zoos the personnel involved may change jobs but they will still be working in a zoo. So the experience and the knowledge they have is much while in case of most of the Indian zoos this is not the case. The zoo director today may become a conservator of forest tomorrow or may be transferred to some other job which has nothing to do with zoo-keeping. This means the experience he has gained is wasted and therefore one cannot specialize in the field. The policy of the colonial rulers was to have "Jacks of all trades" but at the same time they did not want anybody other than themselves to be the master. We still continue the same policy. Hence we have hardly any experts in this field who have knowledge like Dr Lang, (Director, Basel Zoo), Dr Schroder (Director, Berlin Aquarium), Dr Gizmik (Director, Frankfurt Zoo), or Dr Veselvosky of Prague Zoo who had spent in the zoo keeping field 25 years or even more. With this sort of experience, it is easy for them to specify what is rare or common and the economics of maintenance. The experience also reduces the rate of mortality as well as increases the number of births in the zoo, while here we have to have a replacement of dead zoo animals very often and also breeding is poor.

The same more or less applies to the captive breeding especially with birds. As explained earlier the hobby of bird keeping is not at all well developed. Hence there are only a very few hobbyists in India.

Now the organizations involved basically in promoting these captive breeding projects do not want these hobbyists to play any role as, inspite of his limited experience, the hobbyist can challenge these "expert's" advice, like "However, hatching from the start in Bombay may be successful, provided you keep the chicks cool with use of fans and may be water sprinkled on the floor etc., particularly after the first 4-5 days".

While it is a well known fact that most of the pheasants including the Cheer Pheasants, especially chicks cannot tolerate dampness or high humidity, the "experts" still insist on sending eggs for hatching during the rainy season, or they do not encourage exchange of experience with others of their projects in the country.

At the same time they will advise sending a local person for some months training in their country. How can one gain experience in a few months when the trainee has never kept birds in captivity?

If the zoos and the captive breeding projects become successful in raising these captive birds and have them available to the hobbyist, the pressure on the collections from the wild will be automatically reduced and after some time they could be again had for pet trade like the Splendid Grass Parakeet or Turquoisine Grass Parakeet.

RECOMMENDATIONS

1. All the restrictions on trapping and export of seed-eating passerine birds (like munias, bayas, buntings, finches and parakeets should be totally removed as before, i.e. when the Wildlife Protection Act, 1972 came into force for the first time in 1973.
2. Considering the fact that even today, after all the restrictions imposed, the prices of Indian Wildlife exported for the pet trade are the cheapest in the world, floor price for each species should be fixed. This will help in the reduction of numbers exported.
3. Trade representation should be there at all levels including State Wildlife Boards as well as I.B.W.L.
4. Most of the amendments to schedules of the Wildlife Act, 1972 should be scrapped except for some species.
5. If a particular species is banned for export, then the trade in that species should also be banned within the country. This will have a definite effect on curbing smuggling.
6. There should be some Wildlife personnel all the 24 hours on duty like that of plant quarantine, to restrict mainly smuggling of wildlife as personal baggage by air.
7. The export policy for pet trade as well as the change in the schedules of the Wildlife Protection Act should be made at the recommendations of eminent and realistic conservationists/scientists and not at the recommendations of emotional conservationists.
8. The present quota of issuing licences on first-come first-served basis should be totally abolished, but individual quotas should be given to each exporter.
9. If individual quota is acceptable to the government, then a charge of 1 or 2% cess should be collected by the office of the Director, Wildlife. This money should be entirely used for training of personnel to identify Wildlife and its products.

APPENDIX I

BIRDS

Munia assorted	—	938300
Parakeet assorted	—	97600
Bunting assorted, mainly Redheaded & Blackheaded	—	20546
Rose Finches	—	3164
Green and Gold Finches	—	700
Weavers	—	3640
Bulbul assorted, mainly Redvented, Redwhiskered, White-cheeked and Black-headed Yellow	—	2798
Mynas and Starlings, other than Hill Mynas	—	5381
Hill Mynas	—	4500
Thrushes assorted	—	978
Chloropsis	—	5594
Mesia	—	290
Yuhina (including Small Babblers like Redbilled and Quacker Babblers)	—	594
Flycatchers assorted	—	501
White-eyes	—	4806
Sibia	—	275
Siva	—	464
Robins, mainly Pecking Robins	—	1676
Barbets assorted	—	392
Pittas	—	371
Sunbirds	—	507
Tits	—	168
Nuthatch	—	39

Chats	—	27
Flowerpeckers	—	44
Tree Pies	—	32
Jays	—	18
Drongos	—	12
Pelicans	—	50
Storks	—	62
Magpie Robin	—	384
Magpies	—	308
Cranes, mainly Demoiselle	—	191
Storks	—	71
Redstarts	—	97
Babblers	—	277
Flowerpeckers	—	44
Purple Moorhen	—	52

MAMMALS

Striped Palm Squirrels	—	1970
Fruit Bats	—	390
Himalayan Black Bear cubs	—	31

APPENDIX – II

	1979-80	DR SALIM ALI'S RECOMMENDATION	1980-81	REMARKS
1) Barbets	On quota	No remarks	Banned for export	Further restriction
2) Bayas	On quota, all species	Total relaxation for 4 common species except Finn's Baya	On quota except Finn's Baya.	Further restriction
3) Bulbuls	On quota, all species	Total relaxation for 4 common species, remaining species on quota	Only 4 common species on quota, rest banned	Further restriction
4) Buntings	On quota	On quota	On quota	No change
5) Chloropsis	On quota	On quota	Banned for export	Further restriction
6) Finches (Fringillidae)	On quota, all species	Common Rose Finch & H. Green Finch on quota	Rose Finch & H. Green Finch on quota	Further restriction
7) Mynas other than Hill Myna	On quota, all species	Total relaxation	Only common, Bank & Blackheaded Myna on quota	Further restriction
8) Parakeets	On quota, all species	a) Rose Ringed Parakeet Total relaxation b) Other species except *intermedia* and *derbyana* on quota	On quota except Blue-winged, Slatyheaded & Rothchild's Parakeet	Further restriction
9) Peckin Robins	On quota	On quota	On quota	No change
10) Pittas	On quota	On quota	On quota	No change
11) Rosy Pastors	On quota	Total relaxation	Banned for export	Further restriction
12) Robins	On quota, all species	On quota Indian Magpie Robin & Shama	On quota only Indian Robin	Further restriction
13) Rubythroats	On quota	On quota	On quota	Same
14) Sibia	On quota	On quota	On quota	Same
15) Sivas	On quota	On quota	On quota	Same
16) Sparrows	On quota	Spanish & House total relaxation Yellowthroated on quota	On quota—2 separate items shown	Same

	1979-80	Dr Salim Ali's recommendation	1980-81	Remarks
17) Starling	On quota	Total relaxation	Banned for export	Further restriction
18) Sunbirds including Spiderhunters	On quota	On quota	Banned for export	Further restriction
19) Thrushes	All species on quota	On quota	*Turdus, Myophonus, Zoothera & Monticola* allowed on quota, rest banned for export like *Garrulax*	Further restriction
20) White-eyes	On quota	On quota	On quota	Same
21) Woodpeckers	On quota	No remarks	Banned for export	Further restriction
22) Babblers		On quota	On quota	Relaxation
23) Bee-eaters		On quota	On quota	Relaxation
24) Bluethroats		On quota	On quota	Relaxation
25) Doves		On quota	On quota	Relaxation
26) Magpies		On quota	On quota	Relaxation
27) Munia		Total relaxation except Green Munia	On quota except Red & Green Munia	Relaxation
28) Treepies		On quota	On quota except Southern Treepie	Relaxation
29) Silver-eared Mesia		On quota	On quota	Same
30) Yuhinas		On quota	On quota	Relaxation
31) Crows		Total relaxation	Total Ban	Same
32) Tits		On quota	Ban for export	Same
33) Flowerpeckers		On quota	Ban for export	Same
34) Flycatchers		On quota	Ban for export	Same
35) Kingfishers		On quota	Ban for export	Same
36) Pigeon—Green, Wood, Imperial		On quota	Ban for export	Same
37) Redstarts		On quota	Ban for export	Same
38) Pigeon—Blue Rock		Total relaxation	Ban for export	Same
Other Live Animals				
39) Striped Palm Squirrels	On quota	Total relaxation for Three & Five-striped Palm Squirrels on quota	On quota	On quota
40) Live Snakes		Total relaxation except Python, Egg eating & Venomous Snakes	Ban for export	Same
41) Live Lizards		On quota except ***Varanus*** **sp.**	Ban for export	Same

	1979-80	DR SALIM ALI'S RECOMMENDATION	1980-81	REMARKS
42) *Testudo elegans*		On quota		
43) *Lissemys punctata*		On quota	Ban for export	Same
44) *Kachuga tectum*		On quota	Ban for exprot	Same
45) Live Frogs & Toads	Only by recommendation from Marine Products Development Authority	Total relaxation	Only by recommendation from Marine Products Development Authority	Same
46) Fruit Bats	Ban for export	Total relaxation	Ban for export	Same
47) Rats, Field Rats, Gerbiles, Mice	Ban for export	Total relaxation	Ban for export	Same

APPENDIX III

A FLY-BY-NIGHT PLOT IN AUSTRALIA

The panel truck meandered through the muggy tropical forests of Australia's remote Cape York peninsula all day long, then headed for a dirt airstrip as night fell. The driver and his cohort were to meet a plane to transport their cargo—worth $2.5 million—to the United States. But they never made their flight. Police surrounded the truck, arrested the two would-be smugglers and seized the contraband—$51 birds.

It was the first successful Australian raid on a burgeoning racket: bird smuggling. In recent months, the demand in the U.S. for protected red and grey galahs and sulfur-crested cockatoos, has spawned highly profitable clandestine industry. The sulfur-crested cockatoo; a bird featured on the American television programme "Baretta" is a particularly hot item. The birds can be purchased for as little as $1.25 in Australia and resold for as much as $3,500 in the United States. This year alone, the estimated turnover for smuggled Austalian wildlife is $30 million, and birds are not the only endangered species. Koala bears and kangaroos are frequently smuggled out of the country and Darwin police arrested one man for trying to take out five pythons—including one he tucked into his underwear.

Casualty rate: At a press conference after the Cape York bird bust, the Commonwealth Police contended that the Mafia in the United States was behind the smuggling. With its boost from organised crime, bird smuggling has increased dramatically in the last three years. Smugglers now roam the Australian outback full-time, trapping birds in "mist nets" strung between trees, with nylon nooses and even with sticky substances that glue birds to tree branches or to the ground. Birds that do not die from shock or starvation are packed into crates and flown out of Australia from isolated airstrips, or are drugged and stuffed into false-bottomed suitcases and smuggled through major airports. "The casualty rate is often extremely high" said one official, "but with the prices the birds are getting, you could lose half and still be doing well".

State government differ on how to combat the smuggling. A special twenty-man squad has been formed to patrol the outback areas of Queensland, while officials in Victoria have imposed strict fines of up to $ 5,000 for anyone possessing species protected under the Fauna Conservation Act. The state of South Australia recently urged the federal government to lift some export bans altogether, a suggestion that has met with some public support. "They should really legalize the export of the unendangered birds" said Sydney bird dealer Bob Green. "They should set up quarantine stations and cut out the attraction of smuggling." Until that happens, however, a bird on the black market is still worth thousands in the bush.

Australian 'Newsweek/October 1, 1979'

****

COCKATOO CAPER:

MAFIA GETS THE BIRD

SYDNEY: Four men are to appear in court today following the smashing of a multi-million pound bird smuggling ring. Squads of Sydney police arrested the men over the weekend in dawn raids. Last night police revealed that U.S. Mafia boss 'Big Vinnie' Teresa was behind the smuggling racket.

A spokesman said: "Extradition is impossible as Mr Teresa is a portected witness in America on another matter."

The four men, including a Customs official, have been charged with illegally exporting 816 galahs and 335 sulphur-crested cockatoos worth £ 1 million. They were found packed into cantainers marked 'computer parts'. The drug Valium had been used to quieten them. Police claim that Teresa set up a multi-million pound organisation to smuggle the birds from Australia for sale in America. A spokesman said: "Millions of pounds-worth of birds have been smuggled out since 1978."

The birds which can be bought from gangs of hunters for 60p each will fetch up to £ 1,800 in America.

(Extract from 'Daily Express' — 17.9.'79)

****

Threatened Endemic Plants from Maharashtra

S.M. ALMEIDA[1] AND M.R. ALMEIDA[2]

According to estimates of the recent surveys there are about 15,000 species of vascular plants found in India (Jain 1976). There are nearly 1275 species of monocotyledons and around 5000 of dicotyledons endemic to this country. Recent studies have shown that about 1500-2000 species (i.e. 10-15% of the flora) fall in one or the other category of threatened plants. Chatterjee (1962) estimated flowering plants of peninsular India as about 2545 species (about 2045 dicots. and about 500 monocots. Subramanyan & Nayar (1974) reported about 90 endemic species from the Western Ghats. Henry *et al.* (1979) listed 264 species of rare flowering plants in South India of which 54 were reported by Hooker (1872-1897). According to these authors many of these 54 species are not represented in the Madras Herbarium (MH), today. Recently Mehrotra and Jain (1982 *pers. comm.*) have attempted a survey of Monocotyledon and have found that out of 15,000 vascular plants reported from India, about 3500 are monocotyledons. Out of these 1260 (about 36%) are endemic to India and 427 of these (about 12%) could be classified as rare or threatened.

Since the publication of CATALOGUE OF PLANTS GROWING IN BOMBAY AND ITS VICINITY, by Graham (1839), various authors have described some 587 new species and about 50 new varieties from Maharashtra. Out of these, 442 species and 30 varieties had been reported till the time of publication of the FLORA OF PRESIDENCY OF BOMBAY, by Cooke (1902-1905) and 145 species and 20 intraspecific taxa have been added thereafter.

Blatter Herbarium which houses 200,000 specimens mainly from Western India, still lacks a number of species which are described from that region, particularly from Maharashtra. The present study was undertaken to reinvestigate and to search for such missing species from Maharashtra.

Cooke (1902-1905) mentioned 76 taxa apparently endemic to Bombay Presidency (excluding areas now in Sind, Gujarat and North Kanara). According to the recent data compiled by us as well as by Kartikeyan, this number should now be revised to 182 taxa. More and more endemic species from Maharashtra are being discovered in contiguous areas in nearby states making their distribution wider than presumed earlier.

There are about 40 families found in Maharashtra, out of which Poaceae (Graminae) 49, Fabaceae (= Leguminosae) 20, Asclepiadaceae 19, Acanthaceae 10, and Liliaceae 10 show the major number of endemic species.

Our study from the fields as well as from Herbarium materials now reports that there are 18 endemic species with a wide range of distribution in Maharashtra and grow quite abundantly. Sixty two species have been found to be rare in their habitats and eight are known

[1] *Blatter Herbarium, St Xavier's College, Bombay* 400 001

[2] *Alchemie Research Centre, Thane-Belapur Road, Thane* 400 601

only from types or rarely from a second collection. About 78 endemic species have no representative collection in Blatter Herbarium (BLAT). We have been so far successful in adding 18 missing species to the collection of Blatter Herbarium thereby reducing the margin of missing endemic species to 78. However, out of these 78 species about 66 species are represented in Poona Herbarium (BSI) at least by a single representative specimen. There are about 184 species which are distributed widely in other states in India as well as in some neighbouring countries and about 280 species have been so far relegated to the synonymy.

The Endemic species from Maharashtra, which we feel are threatened, can be classified in three groups and these are discussed in the following pages. Appendices covering endemic plants (A) With wide distribution, (B) Rare in their habitats, (C) Known from type collections only or rarely a second collection, (D) Not represented in Blatter Herbarium and in the herbarium of Botanical Survey of India, Western Circle (BSI), and (E) Recently collected and added to Blatter Herbarium (BLAT) have been given at the end of the text.

1. Plants of rare natural occurrence

Frerea indica Dalz. (Asclepiadaceae)

This species which was originally described by Dalzell from Hewra, near Junnar, in Poona district, so far has been only known from these areas. Its occurrence has been reported on sloping rocks, inaccessible to plant collectors. Even in the original description, Dalzell mentions to have found this plant growing on bare rocks. It has beautiful flowers and it is worth introducing in gardens. Although Raghavan and Singh (1983) reported it to be extinct at Junnar we have collected a fresh plant on the way to Junnar Fort on 15th August, 1982.

ii) **Seshagiria sahyadrica** Ansari *et* Hemadri (Asclepiadaceae)

This is also a rare endemic species so far known to occur in Satara district and from its type locality in Poona district. We have been able to locate a few plants of this species from Amboli Hills, in Sindhudurg district. This climber produces a large number of purple flowers and deserves a place in gardens.

iii) **Balanophora elkinsii** Blatter (Balanophoraceae)

This species is so far known from its type locality from Mahabaleshwar, in Satara district. It is parasitic on the roots of *Carissa carandas*.

iv) **Acroblastus ambavanense** Reddi (Balanophoraceae)

This rare parasite is known only from its type locality Ambavane, in Maharashtra.

v) **Begonia prixophylla** Blatter & McCann (Begoniaceae)

A rare Begonia only known from its type locality, Mahabaleshwar in Satara district. Its distribution in Mahabaleshwar is restricted to a single spot which is a very steep rocky slope inaccessible to botanical collectors. It has beautiful pink flowers and deserves a place in gardens. Unfortunately, our attempts to introduce this species in cultivation from small seedlings collected from Mahabaleshwar were fruitless, because the plant does not last very long in Bombay climate.

vi) **Thalictrum dalzelli** Hook. f. and **T. obovatum** Blatter (Ranunculaceae)

Both these species have been described from Mahabaleshwar in Satara district, and are very poorly represented in herbaria in Maharashtra.

vii) **Abutilon ranadei** Woodrow *ex* Stapf (Malvaceae)

The type of this species comes from Amba Ghat, along the Kolhapur-Ratnagiri road in Kolhapur district. Both at Blatter Herbarium (BLAT) and the herbarium of Botanical Survey of India, Western Circle (BSI), there are no recent collections of this species other than the types.

viii) **Maytenus puberula** (Laws.) Loes. (= *Gymnosporia puberula* Laws., *G. konkanensis* Talbot) (Celastraceae)

Subsequent to its original collection by Lawson and later by Talbot from Bassein, in Thana district, the only collection of this species deposited in Blatter Herbarium is that of Bhide from Pratapgarh Fort near Mahabaleshwar, in Satara district. We have recently been able to collect a few specimens of this species from Amboli Hills, Sindhudurg district. In sterile condition the plant looks very similar to *Turraea villosa* Benn. (Meliaceae) but it can be easily distinguished in fruiting samples.

ix) **Salacia brunoniana** Wt. & Arn. (Celastraceae)

Very little information is available about this species. Raghavan and Singh have reported that it is represented by a single and incomplete specimen at Kew Herbarium (KEW). Recently we have been able to collect this species from Amboli Ghat, along Amboli-Ramghat road, and found it to be identical with a specimen of *S. brunoniana* available at Poona (BSI). It resembles *S. macrosperma* Wt. in its habit and foliage, but has very small (0.5 cm across) orange-yellow ripe fruits as compared to the large fruits (over 2.5 cm across) of *S. macrosperma* Wt.

x) **Euphorbia katrajensis** Gage (Euphorbiaceae)

A rare species known only from its type locality at Katraj Ghat in Poona district. In Blatter Herbarium, it is represented by a single specimen from Katraj collected by Vartak (VDV-5477).

2. PLANTS THREATENED DUE TO DESTRUCTION OF THEIR NATURAL HABITATS

Plants in this group generally grow quite in abundance, but the vast areas where they occur are being utilised for developing residential and cultivable lands and hence these have become threatened.

i) ORDER **Strobilanthinae** (Acanthaceae): The entire genus *Strobilanthes* (*sensu lato*) has become endangered due to acquiring of more and more forest areas. Most of the species in this group are known to produce massive flowers periodically once in three to twenty one years. All these species are reputed for good quality nectar and during the time of their flowering season are useful for generating honey. Endangered species in this group are **Nilgirianthus reticulatus** Bremek., **N. lupulinus** Bremek. **N. ciliatus** Bremek., **N. wareensis** Bremek., **N. asper** Bremek., **Pleocaulis ritchiei** Bremek., and **Mackenzia integrifolia** Bremek.

ii) Due to over-felling of forest trees, epiphytic orchids and other epiphytes are gradually vanishing from Maharashtra. **Sarcochilus viridiflora** T. Cooke, **Dendrobium chlorops** Lindl. and **Hoya pendula** Wt. are on the verge of extinction from their habitats.

iii) Climbers like **Ventilago bombaiensis** Dalz., **Cissus woodrowii** (Stapf) Santapau, and **Rourea praineana** Talbot depend on forest trees for support and are gradually becoming rarer due to indiscriminate felling of forest trees.

iv) **Impatiens dalzellii** Hook. f. **Indigofera dalzellii** T. Cooke, **Senecio hewrensis** (Dalz.) Hook. f., **Blumea malcolmii** Hook. f. and **Vicoa cernua** Dalzell have become endangered because of overgrazing of grasslands where they grow.

3. PLANTS THREATENED DUE TO OVER COLLECTIONS

i) Medicinal plants used in various systems of traditional medicines are the targets of large scale exploitation. **Nothopodytes nimmoniana** (Graham) Maberley. Recently it has been discovered to contain some anti-cancer principles Mappicin and camptothecin, and therefore is being collected on a large scale for the extraction of drugs. Seeds of **Iphigenia stellata** Blatter and **Iphigenia pallida** Baker have been found to contain colchicine, a chemical which is used in agriculture to induce polyploidy of chromosomes in plants. Large quantities of bulbs and seeds of these species have started vanishing from their natural habitats. **Swertia deccusata** Nimmo is used as an antidysenteric drug and plants of this species are on the verge of extinction from their natural habitat at Mahabaleshwar. Fruits of **Capparis moonii** Wt. are used as potent antitubercular agents as well as in the treatment of septic wounds. Continuous collection on large scale will ultimately leave no seeds for future natural propagation.

ii) Tubers and bulbs of the following species are used for edible purposes by the locals reducing their populations year by year. **Ceropegia evansii** McCann, **C. media** (Huber) Ansari, **C. macannii** Ansari, **C. mahabalei** Hemadri & Ansari, **C. noorjahaniae** Ansari, **Ceropegia panchganiensis** Blatter & McCann, **C. rollae** Hemadri, **C. sahyadrica** Ansari, **C. santapaui** Wadhwa & Ansari are endemic species with relatively rare distribution. **Ceropegias** are known for their fascinating floral structures and in some countries they are considered as plants of highly commercial value by horticulturists.

iii) Some attractive ground orchids, like **Habenaria longecorniculata** Gaertn., **H. panchganiensis** Blatter & McCann, **Habenaria grandifloriformis** Blatter & McCann and all the **Ceropegia** species mentioned above are dug out from the ground by enthusiastic plant collectors without any concern of the destruction from their natural habitats.

Because of the various reasons mentioned above, many of our endemic species from Maharashtra have become endangered and if immediate steps are not taken, soon they will be permanently lost from their habitats.

The best way of conservation of these species could be only by creating Biosphere reserves for these plants near their natural habitats.

ACKNOWLEDGEMENTS

The authors are grateful, to Prof. P.V. Bole, for suggesting the study and supervision of the work, the Rev. Fr John Corriea-Afonso, S.J., Principal of St Xavier's College and B.D. Sharma, Deputy Director, Botanical Survey of India for facilities in consulting the herbaria, to Mr. G.M. Chopra, General Manager, Research, Alchemie Research Centre, for encouragement in preparation of this article.

Species mentioned in this paper, whichever available, are deposited in Blatter Herbarium, (BLAT). All the figures mentioned in the text are approximate.

APPENDICES

A. PLANTS WITH WIDE DISTRIBUTION

(*Localities in brackets*)

1. *Flemingia tuberosa* Dalz. (Jogeshwari, Borivli, Malad, Goregaon, Dapoli).

2. *Indigofera dalzelli* T. Cooke (Panchgani, Mahabaleshwar, Amboli).

3. *Smithia purpurea* Hook.f. (Lonavla, Khandala, Poona, Igatpuri, Mahabaleshwar, Bhimashankar).

4. *Phaseolus khandalensis* Santapau syn. *Phaseolus grandis* Dalz. (Khandala, Igatpuri, Purandhar, Bhandardhara, Sinhagad).

5. *Oldenlandia maheshwarii* Santapau & Merchant (Khandala, Mahabaleshwar, Panchgani, Igatpuri, Savantwadi).

6. *Senecio gibsoni* Hook.f. (Purandhar, Amboli hills, Poona, Tungar hills).

7. *Ipomoea salsettensis* Santapau & Patel (Mumbra, Borivli, Bhandup, Vehar Lake, Trombay, Goregaon).

8. *Crotalaria leptostachya* Benth. (Purandhar, Goregaon, Ghodbunder, Powai, Borivli, Matheran, Poona, Khandala, Salsette, Dangs, Vehar Lake, Malad, Katraj, Mumbra).

9. *Alysicarpus belgaumensis* Wight (Mahabaleshwar, Amboli, Khandala).

10. *Clitoria biflora* Dalz. (Khandala, Salsette, Kalyan, Borivli, Goregaon).

11. *Peucedanum grande* (Dalz. & Gibs) C.B. Clarke syn. *Pastinaca grandis* Dalz. & Gibs. (Khandala, Junnar, Mahabaleshwar, Panchgani).

12. *Heracleum concanense* Dalz. (Khandala, Matheran, Mahabaleshwar, Savantwadi).

13. *Senecio grahami* Hook.f. (Thana, Mahabaleshwar, Khandala, Amboli).

14. *Ipomoea clarkei* Hook.f. (Khandala, Poona, Igatpuri, Junnar).

15. *Nilgirianthus reticulatus* (Stapf.) Bremek. (Khandala, Mahabaleshwar).

16. *Euphorbia coccinea* Roth. (Poona, Alibag, Ahmednagar).

17. *Ischaemum diplopogon* Hook.f. (Khandala, Mahabaleshwar, Borivli, Poona, Igatpuri, Sakharpathar).

18. *Ischaemum tumidum* Stafp. ex Bor. (Borivli, Mumbra, Malad).

B. PLANTS WHICH ARE RARE IN THEIR HABITATS

1. *Impatiens dalzellii* Hook.f. & Thoms. (Panchgani, Purandhar, Mahabaleshwar).

2. *Crotalaria decasperma* Naik (Purandhar).

3. *Canavalia stocksii* Dalz. (Mahabaleshwar).

4. *Senecio hewrensis* (Dalz.) Hook.f. (Purandhar, Junnar).

5. *Ceropegia evansii* McCann (Khandala).

6. *Ceropegia lawii* Hook.f. (Khandala, Mahabaleshwar, Sinhagad, Torna).

7. *Ceropegia media* (Heber) Ansari (Khandala, Mahabaleshwar, Purandhar, Sinhagad, Bhimashankar, Matheran).

8. *Ceropegia huberi* Ansari (Ambaghat, Ratnagiri).

9. *Ceropegia polyantha* Blatt. & McCann (*Ceropegia vinçaefolia* Hook.) (Mahabaleshwar, Mumbra).

10. *Ceropegia mahabalei* Hemadri & Ansari (Talegaon, Poona District).

11. *Ceropegia rollae* Hemadri (Khilla, Poona district).

12. *Ceropegia sahyadrica* Ansari & Kulkarni (Ambavane, Sakharpathar).

13. *Ceropegia santapaui* Wadhwa & Ansari (Mahabaleshwar).

14. *Frerea indica* Dalz. (Junnar, Purandhar).

15. *Gymnema khandalensis* Santapau (Khandala).

16. *Marsdenia lanceolata* T. Cooke (Lohagaon).

17. *Oianthus deccanensis* Talbot (Pashan, Tungar).

18. *Seshagiria sahyadrica* Hemadri & Ansari (Poona, Amboli).

19. *Canscora khandalensis* Santapau (Khandala).

20. *Argyreia boseana* Santapau & Patel (Mahabaleshwar, Savantwadi).

21. *Operculina tansaensis* Santapau & Patel (Tansa lake).

22. *Bonnayodes limnophiloides* Blatter & Hall. (Lonavala, Khandala).

23. *Lepidagathis lutea* Dalz. (Dapoli, Diva).

24. *Achyranthes coynei* Santapau (Khandala, Matheran, Tungar, Amboli).

25. *Balanophora elkinsii* Blatter (Mahabaleshwar).

26. *Euphorbia katrajensis* Gage (Katraj).

27. *Euphorbia khandalensis* Blatter & Hall. (Khandala, Matheran).

28. *Euphorbia panchganiensis* Blatter & McCann (Mahabaleshwar, Panchgani, Purandhar, Savantwadi).

29. *Zingiber cernuum* Dalz. (Savantwadi)

30. *Pancratium sanctae-mariae* Blatter & Hall, (Khandala).

31. *Chlorophytum borivilianum* Santapau & Fernandez (Borivli, Matheran).

32. *Chlorophytum glaucoides* Blatter (Mahabaleshwar, Purandhar, Khandala).

33. *Dipcadi maharashtrensis* Deb & Dasgupta (Panchgani).

34. *Dipcadi saxorum* Blatter (Borivli).

35. *Dipcadi ursulae* Blatter (Trombay, Panchgani, Junnar, Khamgaon).

36. *Scilla viridis* Blatter & Hallb. (Khandala).

37. *Urgenia polyantha* Blatter & McCann (Panchgani).

38. *Iphigenia stellata* Blatter (Panchgani).

39. *Erinocarpus nimmonii* Graham (Khandala, Savantwadi).

40. *Gymnosporia puberula* Laws. (Amboli).

41. *Smithia pycnantha* Benth. & Hook. (Khandala).

42. *Desmodium rotundifolium* Baker (Mahabaleshwar, Purandhar).

43. *Galactea malvanensis* (Dalz. & Gibs.) S.M. Almeida (comb. nov.) syn. *Leucodyctyon malvanensis* Dalz. & Gibs. (Malvan). (Malvensis by misprint).

44. *Canavalia stocksii* Dalz. (Mahabaleshwar).

45. *Bauhinia foveolatus* Dalz. syn. *B. lawii* Benth. (Khandala, Matheran, Thana).

46. *Ammania floribunda* C.B. Clarke (Mahabaleshwar).

47. *Begonia concanensis* DC. (Khandala, Lonavala, Amboli).

48. *Pimpinella tomentosa* Dalz. (Mahabaleshwar, Purandhar).

49. *Centranthera hookeri* C.B. Clarke (Poona, Purandhar, Concan).

50. *Cyathocline lutea* Lour. (Khandala, Concan).

51. *Nanothamnus sericeus* Thoms. (Igatpuri, Khandala, Concan).

52. *Pogonachne racemosa* Bor (Khandala).

53. *Manisuris santapaui* Jain & Hemadri (Ratnagiri).

54. *Manisuris ratnagirica* Kulk. & Hemadri (Amboli hills).

55. *Ischaemum bolei* Almeida (Savantwadi).

56. *Ischaemum bombaiensis* Bor (Khandala, Mira Road).

57. *Christisonia lawii* Wight (Khandala, Tungar).

58. *Christisonia calcarata* Wight (Khandala, Matheran).

59. *Dichoriste dalzellii* Kuntze (Purandhar, Vazirgad, Poona).

60. *Dysophylla salicifolia* Dalz. (Mahabaleshwar, Concan).

61. *Dysophylla gracilis* Dalz. (Mahabaleshwar).

62. *Nilgirianthus scrobiculatus* (Dalz.) Bremek. syn. *Strobilathes scrobiculatus* Dalz. (Mahabaleshwar).

C. PLANTS WHICH ARE KNOWN FROM TYPE COLLECTIONS ONLY OR RARELY A SECOND COLLECTION

1. *Cleome asperrima* Blatter (Dhulia, Western Khandesh).
2. *Abutilon ranadei* Woodrow (Ambaghat).
3. *Smithia agharkarii* Hemadri (Mahabaleshwar, Khandala).
4. *Begonia prixophylla* Blatter & McCann (Mahabaleshwar).
5. *Heracleum pinda* Dalz. & Gibs. (Harischandragad Fort).
6. *Barleria gibsonioides* Blatter (Panchgani).
7. *Dicliptera ghatica* Santapau (Khandala).
8. *Panicum obscurans* Woodrow (Jeur).

D. PLANTS NOT REPRESENTED IN BLATTER HERBARIUM: (Plants with asterisks are not represented in Poona (BSI) Herbarium also):

*1. *Salacia talbotii* Gamble
2. *Vitis araneosa* Lour.
3. *Dolichos bracteatus* Baker
4. *Indigofera duthiei* Drum. ex Naik
5. *Indigofera monosperma* Blatter
*6. *Moghania gracilis* Mukherjee
7. *Smithia oligantha* Blatter
*8. *Tephrosia collina* Sharma
9. *Kalanchoe bhidei* T. Cooke
*10. *Cucumella ritchiei* (Chakr.) Jeffrey.
11. *Pimpinella katrajensis* Rao & Hemadri
12. *Blumea venkataramanii* Rao & Hemadri
13. *Gnaphalium luteum* Lour. ex Wight
14. *Aegiceras parviflora* Talb.
15. *Ceropegia noorjahaniae* Ansari
16. *Ceropegia stocksii* Hook.f.
17. *Ceropegia vincaefolia* Hook.f.
18. *Ceropegia odorata* Hook.f.
*19. *Canscora stricta* Sedgw.
*20. *Nicotiana glauca* Graham
*21. *Lindernia quinqueloba* Blatter
*22. *Utricularia scadens* Benj.
*23. *Barleria gibsonioides* Blatter
*24. *Synnema anomalum* (Blatter) Sant.
*25. *Lepidagathis bandraensis* Blatter
*26. *Neesiella longipedunculata* Sreemadh.
27. *Dysophylla stocksii* Hook.f.
28. *Leucus deodikarii* Billore & Hemadri
*29. *Piper talbotti* C.B. Clarke
30. *Acroblastus ambavanense* Reddy
*31. *Blyxa echinospermoides* Blatter
*32. *Crinum eleonarae* Blatt. & McCann.
*33. *Pancratium donaldi* Blatter
34. *Iphigenia stellata* Blatter
35. *Chlorophytum bharuchae* Ansari *et. al.*
36. *Urginia polyphylla* Hook.f.
*37. *Curcuma purpurea* Blatter
38. *Eriolaena stocksii* Hook.f.
39. *Impatiens stocksii* Hook.f.
40. *Indigofera wightii* Graham
41. *Atylosia glandulosa* Dalz.
42. *Eugenia stocksii* Duthie
43. *Senecio lawii* Clarke
44. *Habenaria spencei* Blatter & McCann
45. *Ceropegia mahabalei* Hemadri & Ansari
*46. *Cryptocorine cognotoides* Blatter & McCann
*47. *Typhonium incurvatum* Blatter & McCann
48. *Eriocaulon sedgwickii* Fyson
49. *Cyperus decumbens* Govindarajalu
50. *Cyperus pentabracteatus* Govindarajalu & Hemadri
51. *Fimbristylis ligulata* Govindarajalu

52. *Fimbristylis unispicularis* Govindarajalu & Hemadri
53. *Mariscus blatteri* McCann
54. *Arthraxon junnarensis* Jain et Hemadri
55. *Arthraxon raizadae* Jain, Hemadri & Deshpande
56. *Bothriochloa jainii* Deshpande & Hemadri
57. *Isachne bicolor* Naik & Patunkar
58. *Isachne borii* Hemadri
59. *Ischaemum hugelii* Hack
60. *Ischaemum inerme* Stapf. ex Bor
61. *Ischaemum zeylanicolum* Bor
62. *Oropetium villosulum* Stapf. ex Bor
*63. *Pseudanthistiria intermedia* Birari & D'Cruz
64. *Tripogon polyanthos* Naik & Patunkar
65. *Ipomoea annua* Dalz
66. *Argyreia lawii* C.B. Clarke
67. *Nilgirianthus lupulinus* (Nees) Bremek
68. *Nilgirianthus ciliatus* (Nees) Bremek
69. *Dysophylla stocksii* Hook. f.
*70. *Boerhavia fruticosa* Dalz
71. *Loranthus gibbosus* Talbot
72. *Phyllanthus scabrifolius* Hook.f.
73. *Jatropha nana* Dalz
74. *Croton gibsonianus* Nimmo
*75. *Sarcochilus maculatus* Benth
*76. *Aerides radicosum* A. Rich
77. *Habenaria lawii* Wight
78. *Habenaria caranjensis* Dalz

E. PLANTS RECENTLY COLLECTED AND ADDED TO BLATTER HERBARIUM

1. *Maytenus puberula* (Laws.) Loes. (Savantwadi).
2. *Salacia brunoniana* Wight & Arn. (Amboli hills, Savantwadi).
3. *Allophyllus concanensis* Radlk. (Amboli hills, Savantwadi).
4. *Rourea praineana* Talbot (Amboli hills, Savantwadi).
5. *Heracleum aquilegifolium* C.B. Clarke (Uran, Raigad District).
6. *Torenia bicolor* Dalz. (Savantwadi).
7. *Nilgirianthus wareensis* (Dalz.) Bremek. (Tilari).
8. *Myristica beddomei* King (Amboli).
9. *Antidesma menasu* Miq. (Amboli).
10. *Agrostistachys indica* Dalz. (Amboli).
11. *Bulbophyllym neilgherrensis* Wight (Savantwadi).
12. *Porpax jerdoniana* Reichb. (Amboli).
13. *Sarcochilus viridiflorus* T. Cooke (Amboli).
14. *Rungia crenata* T. Anders. (Savantwadi).
15. *Ventilago bombaiensis* Dalz. (Amboli Ghat).
16. *Schizachyrium paranjpyeanum* (Bhide) Raizada & Jain (Chaukul).
17. *Merremia rhynchoriza* Hook. f. (Amboli).
18. *Argyreia involucrata* C.B. Clarke (Bhedsi).

BIBLIOGRAPHY

CHATTERJEE, D. (1940): Studies on the Endemic Flora of India and Burma, *J. Asiat. Soc. Bengal (New series)* **5**:19-67.

________________ (1962): Floristic Patterns of Indian Vegetation. *Proc. Summer School of Botany, Darjeeling,* 1960: 32-42, New Delhi.

COOKE, T. (1902-1905): Flora of Presidency of Bombay vol. 1-3.

GAMBLE, J.S. (1915-1936): Flora of Presidency of Madras, vols, 1-3.

GRAHAM, J. (1839): Catalogue of plants growing in Bombay and its vicinity.

HENRY, A.N. *et al.* (1979): Rare and threatened flowering Plants of South India. *J. Bombay. nat. Hist. Soc.* **75**:684-697.

HOOKER, J.D. *et al.* (1872-97): Flora of British India vol. 1-7.

JAIN, S.K. (1976): Rare and endangered plants — the problem and its solution. *Ind. Sci. Ann.* **2**:20-23.

KARTIKEYAN, S. *et al.* (1981): A catalogue of species added to Cooke's Flora of the Presidency of Bombay, during 1908-1978. *Rec. Bot. Surv. India* **21**:(2):153-206.

RAGHAVAN, R.S. & SINGH, N.P. (1983): Endemic and threatened Plants of Western India. *Plant conservation Bull.* **3**.1983.

SUBRAMANYAN, K. & NAYAR, M.P. (1974): Vegetation and phytogeography of the Western Ghats, Ecology and Biogeography in India 178-196. The Hague.

Regeneration of tree cover after aerial seeding in the sand dune ecosystem of arid region

(With four text-figures)

K.A. SHANKARNARAYAN[1]

Sandy soils are a characteristic feature of the arid region. Being single grained and structureless and poor in organic matter, the sandy soils are highly prone to wind erosion (Gupta 1981). These limitations are further accentuated by adverse climatic conditions, namely low and erratic rainfall, high wind velocity and low humidity which make plant production very difficult (Singh 1981). The problem becomes more complex because of the increasing human and animal pressure on the land and the gradual but inexorable attenuation of vegetal cover leading to the exposure of soil mantle causing accelerated wind erosion. In areas like left bank of Rajasthan canal in Bikaner, the process of wind erosion has not only led to the loss of top soil but also caused siltation of the costly irrigation canals like Rajasthan canal. Some rapid methods are, therefore of urgent and paramount need to afforest such areas for stabilisation of soil and prevention of wind-erosion.

New Zealand was afflicted with serious problem of soil erosion from hills which was depriving the country of much needed pasture lands. The Agriculture Department undertook an experiment in 1947 by using two primitive, second world war aircraft for spreading fertilizer and seeds on the hill slopes. The experiment proved a great success on the barren hills and where the fertilizer and seeds fell became luscious green. This venture not only solved the soil erosion problems but provided rich and large quantities of forage for increased animal production. By 1949 aerial seeding had become an established industry and today over 150 aircrafts are used in the aerial seeding programme (Sahni 1983).

Realising the success achieved by a small country like New Zealand, the Planning Commission, which was seized of the problem on the left bank of Rajasthan Canal, felt that India can also use the same aerial technology for reclaiming the difficult, inaccessible deserts or hill areas. Luckily the Agricultural Aviation Division of the Ministry of Agriculture, Government of India, pari-passu with the development of Agro-Aviation technology has the potent tool in the form of specialised agriculture aircraft which has the capacity to do this job speedily and effectively.

Against this background, the Planning Commission suggested CAZRI to undertake a pilot project to study the feasibility of aerial seeding in desert ecosystem with proven tree species and grasses, adapted to the arid region (Kaul 1970). The present paper is the outcome of this endeavour.

MATERIALS AND METHODS

Site. Two sites, namely Sardarpura (300 ha area) and Motigarh (400 ha area) on left bank of Rajasthan canal located 45 and 60 km north of Bikaner on the Chattargarh road were selected and fenced. While Sardarpura constituted single block, Motigarh area consisted of three sub-blocks A, B and C.

The following land treatments, namely time of sowing, seed rate, species choice, use of

[1]*Director, Central Arid Zone Research Institute, Jodhpur.*

repellents etc. were adopted in the technical programme in order to ensure success of aerial seeding which would help and evaluate the efficacy of treatments.

I. **Land treatment and strata**

1. Mulched dune
2. Unmulched dune
3. Ploughed interdune
4. Unploughed interdune
5. Windward slope
6. Leeward slope

II. **Time of sowing**

1. Pre-monsoon sowing in the end of June. This was carried out in Motigarh site (plots A, B and C).
2. Monsoon sowing in July after a soaking shower of rain. This was carried out in Sardarpura site.

III. **Species choice**

In a feasibility study of aerial seeding method, for quick revegetation, it need not be emphasised that only well-adapted and proven species should be considered for choice of species in order to ensure success of the programme. Accordingly, the following species, which have already identified as promising for arid region by research efforts at CAZRI for conventional afforestation and revegetation techniques, have been chosen for trial in the current feasibility studies.

1) *Acacia tortilis,* 2) *Colophospermum mopane,* 3) *Dichrostachys nutans,* 4) *Prosopis cineraria,* 5) *Zizyphus rotundifolia,* 6) *Citrullus colocynthis* and *Lasiurus sindicus*.

IV. **Seed rate.** It was determined at 14 kg/ha as follows:

Acacia tortilis	3 kg
Prosopis cineraria	2 kg
Colophospermum mopane	1 kg
Zizyphus rotundifolia	2 kg
Dichrostachys nutans	1 kg
Citrullus colocynthis	1 kg
Lasiurus sindicus	4 kg
	14 kg

The seeds of tree species were given a treatment of scarification with 50% sulphuric acid to increase seed coat permeability. Only seed of *Lasiurus sindicus* grass was pelleted using a mixture of dung, sand and clay in the ratio of 1:1:2. Bird and insect repellents such as Aldrin 400 ml/q of seed and Thiram at 2.5 g/kg of seed were applied to the seeds.

V. **Construction of air strip.** The air strip 30 m × 600 m was constructed about 4 to 5 km from the Motigarh plot for take-off and landing. The flight traverse, number of sorties, payload and height of aircraft flight were predetermined in relation to wind direction and terrain characteristics. In all 30 sorties were made with an average payload of 475 kg/sortie for aerial seeding of entire 700 hectare area in about 11 hours period.

VI. **Estimation of seedling population.** Estimates of the seedling germinated and established were accomplished by random location of quadrats along five transect lines at Sardarpura and eleven transect lines (5 + 3 + 3 in A, B, C plots) in Motigarh plot (Mueller-Dombois Ellenberg 1974). Since the density of seedling population was high in Sardarpura (monsoon sowing) the quadrat size (1 × 1 m) was considered adequate whereas in Motigarh (representing pre-monsoon sowing) the population was sparse and hence 10 × 10 m quadrats were employed for estimation of the seedling population. The data on presence-absence and density of seedling were analysed to get the estimate of Mean and Variance in each of the six strata sampled as given in Table 1.

Results and Discussion

The results obtained in Sardarpura and Motigarh are discussed separately below.

Sardarpura. Table 1 shows that seedling density was maximum in ploughed interdunes, followed by unploughed interdune and windward slope. There was none in leeward slope. Species-wise, *Acacia tortilis* recorded the maximum number of seedling (44,800/ha) in ploughed interdune, 3500/ha in unploughed interdune and 2700/ha in windward slope. This was followed by *Citrullus colocynthis, Prosopis cineraria, Colophospermum mopane, Lasiurus sindicus, Zizyphus rotundifolia* and *Dichrostachys nutans,* in that order. It is significant to mention that while *Lasiurus sindicus* was altogether absent in both unploughed interdunes and windward slopes, *Zizyphus rotundifolia* and *Dichrostachys nutans* did not germinate and establish in the windward side.

The large number of seedlings in the ploughed interdunes is mainly due to better seed bed conditions with adequate soil moisture compared with hard crust soil obtainable in unploughed dunes where the number of seedlings was very low.

An idea of the distribution of seedlings in the various strata can be judged by the frequency diagram (Fig. 1) which shows that *Acacia tortilis* has 70% frequency in ploughed interdune and the least 20% in the windward slope.

The next best distribution appears to be that of *Citrullus colocynthis* which was about 20% frequency, while the remaining five species have a frequency of less than 10% indicating

TABLE 1

MEAN, VARIANCE AND RANGE OF SEEDLING DENSITY IN SARDARPURA

Names of species	Strata					
	Ploughed interdune		Unploughed interdune		Windward slope	
	Mean	Variance	Mean	Variance	Mean	Variance
Acacia tortilis	1.48 (14,800)	0.022	0.35 (3500)	0.004	0.27 (2700)	0.001
Citrullus colocynthis	0.45 (4500)	0.68	0.02 (200)	—	0.06 (600)	0.001
Colophospermum mopane	0.07 (700)	0.001	0.02 (200)	—	0	
Dichrostachys nutans	0.02 (200)	—	0.01 (100)	—	0	—
Prosopis cineraria	0.08 (800)	0.001	0.01 (100)	—	0.02 (200)	—
Zizyphus rotundifolia	0.04 (400)	0.001	0.05 (500)	—	—	—
Lasiurus sindicus	0.06 (600)	-	0	—	0	—

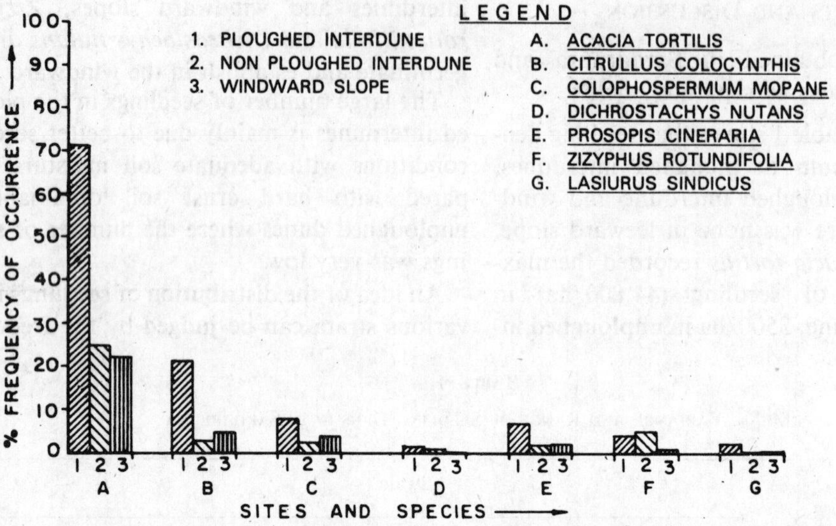

Fig.1: FREQUENCY DIAGRAM OF DIFFERENT SPECIES AT SARDARPURA

very poor distribution.

Motigarh. Tables 2 to 4 present the data on mean variance and density of seedlings in plots A, B, C at Motigarh.

In plot 'A', (Table 2) *Acacia tortilis* recorded the highest seedlings number in Mulched crest 82/ha followed by ploughed interdune, leeward slope. The next best performance is shown by *Lasiurus sindicus* which recorded highest number of seedlings in mulched crest followed by leeward slope and ploughed interdune. While *Zizyphus rotundifolia* was altogether absent in any of the strata, *Colophospermum* and *Prosopis cineraria* were absent in leeward slope, unmulched crest and unploughed interdune although mulched crest and ploughed interdune seemed to favour marginal establishment.

In plot B of Motigarh also (Table 3) *Acacia tortilis* showed a consistent trend in the germination in all the strata except unmulched crest where it has failed to establish. Among the strata, leeward slope recorded the highest number of seedlings of *Acacia tortilis* followed by ploughed interdune, mulched crest and windward slope in that order. *Lasiurus sindicus* seemed to have a distinct affinity for mulched crest where it had the highest number of seedlings (396) compared with all others. The high adaptability of *Lasiurus* becomes further demonstrated when it is the only species recorded in unmulched crest with a fairly high density (118/ha). *Citrullus colocynthis* shows leeward slope and mulched crest as its preferred habitat with a density of 100/ha and 52/ha respectively. Its performance in ploughed dune and windward slope is poor and it is totally unable to survive in unmulched crest and unploughed interdune. Both *Dichrostachys nutans* and *Zizyphus rotundifloia* failed to establish in any of the six strata.

In plot C Motigarh (Table 4), the mulched crest had the highest density with 466/ha of *Lasiurus sindicus* followed by *Acacia tortilis* (61/ha) and *Citrullus colocynthis* (34/ha). The ploughed interdune proved very favourable stratum for all plants under trial except *Dichrostachys nutans* which failed to establish in any strata. *Acacia tortilis* was dominant with

TABLE 2

MEAN, VARIANCE AND DENSITY OF SEEDLINGS AT MOTIGARH PLOT A

Name of species	Strata											
	Windward slope		Leeward slope		Mulched crest		Unmulched crest		Ploughed interdune		Unploughed interdune	
	Mean	Varia-nce	Mean	Varia-nce	Mean	Varia-nce	Mean	Varia-nce	Mean	Varia-nce	Mean	Varia-nce
Acacia tortilis	0.21 (21)	0.002	0.42 (42)	0.025	0.82 (82)	0.043	0	—	0.59 (59)	0.427	0.05 (5)	—
Cirtullus colocynthis	0.11 (11)	0.001	0.26 (26)	0.01	0.36 (36)	0.019	0	—	0	—	0	—
Colophospermum mopane	0.12 (12)	0.001	0	—	0.11 (11)	0.002	0	—	0.05 (5)	—	0	—
Dichrostachys nutans	0	—	0	—	0	—	0	—	0	—	0	—
Prosopis cineraria	0.01 (1)	—	0	—	0.05 (5)	—	0	—	0.08 (8)	—	0	—
Zizyphus rotundifolia	0	—	0	—	0	—	0	—	0	—	0	—
Lasiurus sindicus	0.08 (8)	—	0.32 (32)	—	0.82 (82)	0.076	0	—	0.14 (14)	—	0	—

TABLE 3

MEAN, VARIANCE AND SEEDLING DENSITY IN PLOT B MOTIGARH

Name of species	Strata											
	Windward slope		Leeward slope		Mulched crest		Unmulched crest		Ploughed interdune		Unploughed interdune	
	Mean	Varia-nce	Mean	Varia-nce	Mean	Varia-nce	Mean	Varia-nce	Mean	Varia nce	Mean	Varia-nce
Acacia tortilis	0.77 (77)	0.019	3.18 (318)	3.106	1.0 (100)	0.124	0	—	1.08 (108)	0.096 (33)	0.33	—
Citrullus colocynthis	0.14 (14)	—	1.0 (100)	0.182	0.52 (52)	0.039	0	—	0.23 (23)	—	0	—
Colophospermum mopane	0.07 (7)	0.004	0.18 (18)	—	0.17 (17)	—			0	—	0	—
Dichrostachys nutans	0	—	0	—	0	—	0	—	0	—	0	—
Prosopis cineraria	0.02 (2)	—	0.27 (27)	—	0.04 (4)	—	0	—	0	—	0	—
Zizyphus rotundifolia	0	—	0	—	0	—	0	—	0	—	0	—
Lasiurus sindicus	0.10 (10)	0.002	0.36 (36)	—	3.96 (396)	2.322	1.18 (118)	—	0.38 (38)	—	0	—

TABLE 4

MEAN, VARIANCE AND SEEDLING DENSITY IN PLOT C MOTIGARH

Name of species	Strata											
	Windward slope		Leeward slope		Mulched crest		Unmulched crest		Ploughed interdune		Unploughed interdune	
	Mean	Varia-nce	Mean	Varia-nce	Mean	Varia-nce	Mean	Varia-nce	Mean	Varia nce	Mean	Varia-nce
Acacia tortilis	0.57 (57)	0.013	0	—	0.61 (61)	0.031	0	—	1.9 (190)	1.019	0	—
Citrullus colocynthis	0.19 (19)	0.002	0.23 (23)	—	0.34 (34)	0.033	0	—	0.47 (47)	0.066	0	—
Colophospermum mopane	0.03 (3)	0.001	0	—	0	—	0	—	0.03 (3)	—	0	—
Dichrostachys nutans	0	—	0	—	0	—	0	—	0	—	0	—
Prosopis cineraria	0	—	0	—	0	—	0	—	0.13 (13)	—	0	—
Zizyphus rotundifolia	0	—	0	—	0	—	0	—	0.02 (2)	—	0	—
Lasiurus sindicus	0.12 (12)	0.004	0.09 (9)	—	4.66 (466)	3.34	0	—	0.08 (8)	—	0	—

190/ha followed by *Citrullus* (47/ha), *Prosopis cineraria* (13/ha), *Lasiurus* (8/ha), *Colophospermum* (3/ha) and *Zizyphus* (2) in that order.

The unploughed interdune in view of its hard crust surface did not enable any of the species to survive. Further *Prosopis cineraria* and *Zizyphus rotundifolia* did not also find the strata of windward or leeward slope mulched or crest suitable for establishment.

Frequency diagram (Fig. 2) shows that all the species in the trial had less than 50% frequency in plot A of Motigarh. This implies that more than 50% of the quadrats were recorded as blanks which goes to confirm that the germination has been poor in plot 'A'. Here again it is only the mulched crest which gave highest frequency of 42% as recorded by *Acacia tortilis* and about 35% in *Lasiurus sindicus*. Interestingly ploughed interdune was next best with 35% frequency by *Acacia tortilis* the latter also recording about 30% frequency in leeward slope.

In plot B the picture is different with ploughed interdune giving frequency of 55% in *Acacia tortilis*. The next best frequency was of *Lasiurus* with 55% frequency in mulched crest and 45% in unmulched crest which indicates its high adaptablity on the dunes. The third position in terms of frequency goes to *Citrullus colocynthis* which also showed better establishment in mulched crest and leeward slope. The remaining species showed very poor frequency distribution.

In general the frequency distribution in plot C (Fig. 3) was low compared with plot B or A. It is only in this plot that *Lasiurus sindicus* annexed the highest frequency percent (about 50%) in the mulched crest followed by *Acacia tortilis* (34%). Others were extremely poor.

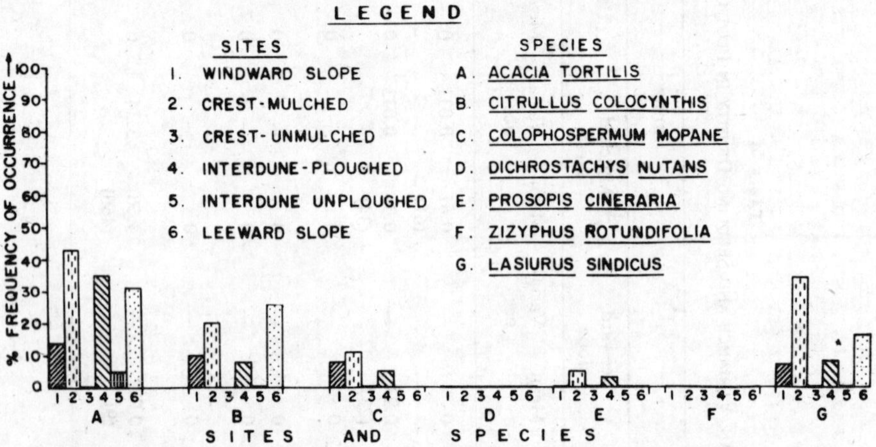

Fig. 2 : FREQUENCY DIAGRAM OF DIFFERENT SPECIES AT MOTIGARH PLOT A

Comparative Performance of Pre-monsoon and Monsoon Aerial Seedlings

The results of the overall comparative performance of aerial seeding in pre-monsoon as represented by Motigarh site vis-a-vis monsoon period as represented by Sardarpura site are presented in Tables 5 and 6 which are self-explanatory.

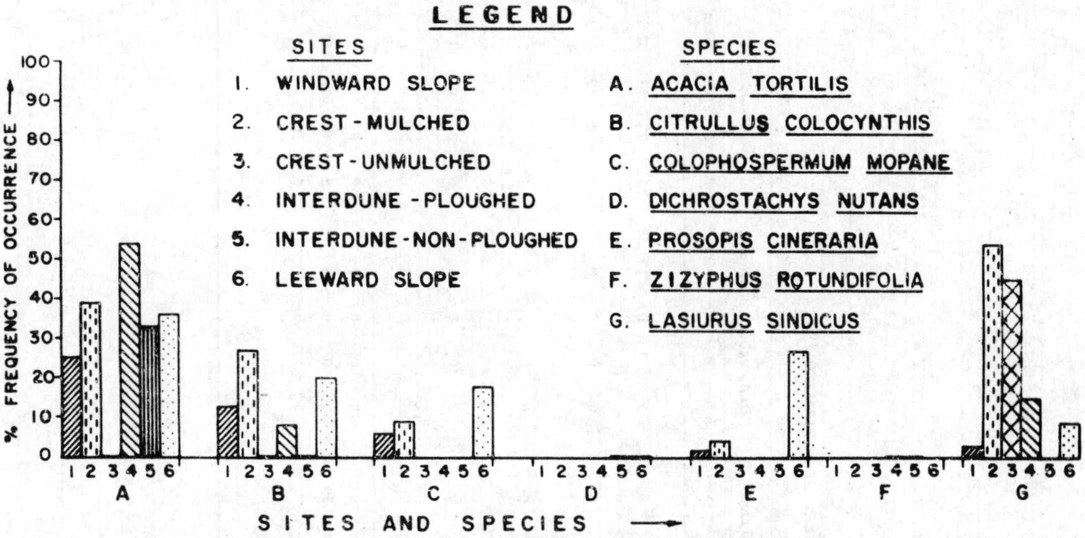

Fig. 3 : FREQUENCY DIAGRAM OF DIFFERENT SPECIES AT MOTIGARH PLOT B

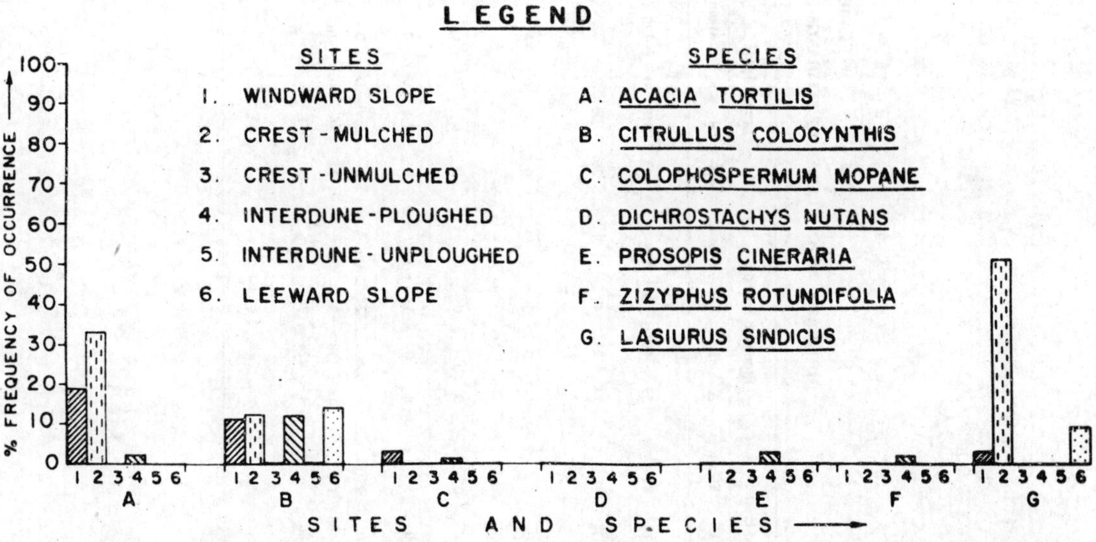

Fig. 4 : FREQUENCY DIAGRAM OF DIFFERENT SPECIES AT MOTIGARH PLOT C

TABLE 5

MOTIGARH: MEAN NUMBER OF SEEDLINGS/HA AS ON LAST WEEK OF SEPTEMBER 1982

Name of species	Mulched crest				Ploughed interdune				Leeward side				Unmulched crest				Unploughed interdune				Windward slope			
	A	B	C	Mean	A	B	C	Mean	A	B	C	Mean	A	B	C	Mean	A	B	C	Mean	A	B	C	Mean
Acacia tortilis	82	100	61	81	59	108	190	119	42	318	0	120	0	0	0	0	5	33	0	13	21	77	57	52
Citrullus colocynthis	36	52	34	41	24	23	47	31	26	100	0	42	0	0	0	0	0	0	0	0	11	14	19	15
Colophos-permum mopane	11	17	0	9	5	0	3	3	0	18	0	6	0	0	0	0	0	0	0	0	12	7	3	7
Dichros-tachys nutans	0	0	0	0	0	0	0	0	0	0	0	0	0	0	0	0	0	0	0	0	0	0	0	0
Prosopis cineraria	5	4	0	3	8	0	13	7	0	27	0	0	0	0	0	0	0	0	0	0	0	2	0	1
Z. rotundi-folia	0	0	0	0	0	0	2	0.6	0	0	0	0	0	0	0	0	0	0	0	0	0	0	0	0
L. sindicus	82	396	466	315	14	38	8	20	32	36	9	26	0	118	0	39	0	0	0	0	8	10	12	10
Mean	31	81	80		37	24	38		33	71	1		0	17	0		0.7	5	0		8	16	13	
Overall mean		64				33				35				6				2				12		

It will be observed that excepting the mulched crest, *Acacia tortilis* recorded the highest number of seedlings in all the strata. In the mulched strata, however, *Lasiurus sindicus* was predominant (315/ha). The next best performance was shown by *Citrullus colocynthis* followed by *Colophospermum mopane*. The performance of *Prosopis cineraria* was poor and *Dichrostachys nutans* and *Zizyphus rotundifolia* have altogether failed to establish.

Zizyphus rotundifolia (300/ha) and *Lasiurus sindicus* (200/ha) and *Dichrostachys nutans* (100/ha).

CONCLUSIONS

Monsoon sowing has obviously given a higher germination, seedling density and better distribution compared with the pre-monsoon sowing. Here again *Acacia tortilis* has given the highest germination and seedling density

TABLE 6

SARDARPURA: MEAN NUMBER OF SEEDLINGS/HA AS ON LAST WEEK OF SEPTEMBER 1982.

Name of species	Ploughed interdune	Unploughed interdune	Windward slope	Mean
Acacia tortilis	14800	3500	2700	7000
Citrullus colocynthis	4500	1200	600	2766
Colophospermum mopane	700	200	300	400
Dichrostachys nutans	200	100	0	100
Prosopis cineraria	800	100	200	366
Zizyphus rotundifolia	400	500	0	300
Lasiurus sindicus	600	0	0	200
Mean	3143	800	543	

Frequency data reveal that *Acacia tortilis* and *Lasiurus sindicus* have about 50% occurrence. Others have a frequency of less than 30% which give an indication of the measure of blanks.

In Sardarpura representing monsoon sowing (Table 6), the density of seedling was phenomenally high recording a mean of 3143 seedlings/ha on ploughed interdune, 800 in unploughed interdune and 543 in windward slope.

Of these, *Acacia tortilis* again recorded the highest density in all the three strata (Mean 7000/ha) followed by *Citrullus colocynthis* (2766/ha), *Colophospermum mopane* (400/ha), *Prosopis cineraria* (366/ha), thereby emerging itself as not only the king-pin in arid silviculture but also in aerial seeding technology. This has been followed by *Citrullus colocynthis, Colophospermum mopane, Prosopis cineraria, Zizyphus rotundifolia, Lasiurus sindicus* and *Dichrostachys nutans* in that order. Further the monsoon sowing has not only ensured better germination and seedling establishment of plants but has also ensured the germination and establishment of all the species tried in the seed mixture including *Dichrostachys nutans* and *Zizyphus rotundifolia* which had totally failed to germinate and establish in the pre-monsoon sowing treatment. The process of seed germination and seedling establishment has been profoundly influenced in mulched crest and soil worked interdune.

The feasibility and potential of aerial seeding for quick revegetation of desert areas, therefore, become established by foregoing studies. The expenditure and effort on aerial seeding would be wasted if we do not keep animals away from entering the treated area. For pasture lands, controlled grazing would have to be ensured and for afforestation, animals need to be kept out till trees attain a safe height.

Above all, soil conservation cum silvipasture programme hold the key to reclaim the vast desert lands into lush green productive pastures and forests which while providing sustenance to both human and animal population prevent wind erosion and silting up of the costly irrigation canals.

ACKNOWLEDGEMENTS

The facilities provided by Rajasthan State Forest Department are gratefully acknowledged.

REFERENCES

GUPTA, J.P. (1981): Management of sandy soils for higher productivity. *Proceedings of the Summer Institute on Agroforestry in arid and semi-arid zones*, Vol. 3, pp. 78-91.

KAUL, R.N. (1970): Afforestation in Arid Zones. Dr W. Junk N.V. Publishers. The Hague, pp. 1-435.

MUELLER-DOMBOIS, DIEFER & ELLENBERG HEINZ, (1974): Aims and Methods of Vegetation Ecology, John Wiley and Sons, USA. pp. 1-547.

SAHNI, S. (Air Vice-Marshal, Retd.) (1983): Aerial seeding. *Indian Express*, p. 6.

SINGH, H.P. (1981): Soil physical constraints in relation to increasing the arid zone productivity with particular reference to Agroforestry. *Proceedings of the Summer Institute on Agroforestry in arid and semi-arid zones*, pp. 44-48.

Dry-zone afforestation and its impact on Blackbuck population

K. ULLAS KARANTH[1] AND MEWA SINGH[2]

ABSTRACT

A field study was carried out in Ranebennur Blackbuck Sanctuary area and supplementary observations were made in Onkara-Naganapura State Forest in Karnataka. In these dry-zone areas, afforestation work, primarily with eucalyptus, using mechanised techniques, has been carried out by the State Forest Department. Initially, these areas contained remnant populations of blackbuck and other plains' fauna. Though the plantations were sylviculturally very successful, some conservationists anticipated that the changed ecological conditions on account of these plantations may make the area unsuitable for the above fauna. The present study, however, revealed that with the increased area under these plantations, the blackbuck populations seem to have increased parallely. This paper discusses the role played by these plantations in meeting the ecological requirements of blackbuck in these particular study areas, keeping in view the biotic factors prevailing there.

INTRODUCTION

The plains' fauna of penninsular India has suffered a drastic decline in populations in the last few decades. This decline has been rather marked in the case of Blackbuck (*Antelope cervicapra*), whose formerly widespread range in the Deccan Plateau has shrunk to a few miniscule pockets at present (Krishnan 1972).

Apart from poaching, the other major reason for the decline of blackbuck has been the widespread habitat loss. Its scrub forest habitats have, on one hand, physically shrunked due to expansion of agriculture, and on the other hand, deteriorated due to biotic factors such as grazing, tree cutting, fires etc.

In response to the problems of soil erosion and fuelwood shortage caused by loss of scrub forest, the Forest Department have taken up revegetation of degraded scrub forests in dry zones using mechanised techniques and fast growing exotic plants, particularly *Eucalyptus* species. Rannebennur Blackbuck Sanctuary in Karnataka State is an example of such efforts.

Rannebennur has blackbuck and other endangered fauna like Wolf (*Canis lupus*) and Great Indian Bustard (*Choriotis nigriceps*). The intensive mechanised dry-zone afforestation works carried out by the Forest Department were thought to be turning the habitat unsuitable for this fauna by some naturalists (Krishnan 1975; Neginhal 1977). The Forest Department, however, felt that this was not true (Shyamsunder 1980 — *Deccan Herald Newspaper*).

The present paper describes a study of the impact of dry-zone afforestation on blackbuck populations in the Ranebennur Sanctuary.

STUDY AREA

Ranebennur Sanctuary is located at longitude 75.41°E and latitude 14.33°N. The 123 sq. km area is on the Deccan Plateau at an average altitude of 610 metres. It is ribbed with a chain of low hillocks about 150 metres higher than

[1]499, J.T. Extension, Mysore 570 009

[2]Department of Psychology, University of Mysore, Mysore 570 006

the plains. The soil structure is described as "Gneisses, schists and granite of archean era and Deccan trap rocks of tertiary era" (Jagadishchandra 1974). The soil is generally poor and is in degraded condition. The temperature ranges between 20-38° C, and the average rainfall is between 424 mm and 740 mm. There are some seasonal streams within the Sanctuary, but in the dry season, water is available only in some of the farmlands and in the River Tungabhadra nearby.

The original forest of Ranebennur area was of the Southern Tropical Thorn Forest (Champion's Classification 6A/C1) type. The tree cover of a stunted nature (3 m-6 m) consisted chiefly of *Acacia arabica, A. latronum, A. leucophloea, Hardwickia binata, Albizzia amara* etc. The ground cover had species like *Dodonaea viscosa, Cassia auriculata, Carissa carandas* and *Lantana camara* etc., and grasses of several species.

This native thorn forest has, however, almost disappeared now, and the afforestation works have established *Eucalyptus* hybrid (*E. tereticornis* and *E. camaldulensis*) as the redominant tree species. Some of the other species used in afforestation have been *Santalum album, Albizzia lebbek, Cassia* sp., *Acacia* sp., *Prosopis juliflora, Leucaena* sp. etc. There is fairly good grass growth within the eucalyptus plantations as well as in the few blank patches inside the Sanctuary. The surrounding areas are used for seasonal monsoon cultivation of millets, sorghum, groundnut and cotton, and appear to be badly eroded.

The Sanctuary has over 80 species of birds. The major mammals are listed in Table 1.

TABLE 1

THE STATUS OF SOME WILD MAMMALS IN RANEBENNUR BLACKBUCK SANCTUARY AND ITS SURROUNDINGS

Sl. No.	Common name	Scientific name	Status*
1.	Common langur°	*Presbytis entellus*	3
2.	Common mongoose	*Herpestes edwardsi*	3
3.	Wolf	*Canis lupus*	3
4.	Jackal	*Canis aureus*	3
5.	Indian fox	*Vulpes bengalensis*	4
6.	Striped hyena	*Hyaena hyaena*	1
7.	Common otter@	*Lutra lutra*	1
8.	Porcupine	*Hystrix indica*	2
9.	Blacknaped hare	*Lepus nigricollis*	3
10.	Blackbuck	*Antelope cervicapra*	4
11.	Wild pig	*Sus scrofa*	2
12.	Pangolin	*Manis crassicaudata*	2

*4 - Very common; 3 - Frequent; 2 - Present; 1 - Rare

° Along the highway on roadside trees

@ Near Tungabhadra river

Eucalyptus plantations provide an open natured cover suitable for Blackbuck

Eucalyptus Hybrid appears to be only species which can withstand the adverse biotic pressures at Ranebennur

OBSERVATIONS

1. Biotic factors affecting the Sanctuary

Semi-nomadic pastoral castes living in the 50 surrounding villages have grazing rights in the Sanctuary for the livestock owned by them (approximately 42,000 sheep, 16,000 goats and 8,000 cattle). The pastoralists migrate away from the Sanctuary in December taking away about 90 percent of the sheep and goats. They return in June with the onset of monsoons. Therefore, the full pressure of grazing on the Sanctuary is exerted between June and November, which ecologically is the period when the vegetation has to regenerate and establish itself. The grazing pressure has been assessed using the data and assumptions mentioned in Table 2. From this it can be seen that during the peak period the domestic livestock overgraze the Sanctuary by an index of 6 times when considered from the point of view of optimum pasture use. This is also supported by the fact that the domestic livestock population in this area has been almost stable during the last 20 years. It is also reported that the shepherds burn the Sanctuary area illegally to encourage the early regeneration of grass. Of all the species used in afforestation work, only *Eucalyptus* hybrid appears to withstand the grazing pressure. On the whole, the grazing seems to be a major socio-economic activity whose total prevention seems to be impossible.

Approximately 110,000 people live in the vicinity of the Sanctuary. For most of them the domestic fuel is firewood. In view of the ex-

TABLE 2

GRAZING PRESSURE BY DOMESTIC LIVESTOCK ON RANEBENNUR SANCTUARY*

Name of the Block	Area Hectares	No. of sheep and goat		No. of cattle × 5	Total sheep equivalent population		Grazing pressure index: sheep equivalent per hectare	
		June-Dec.	Dec.-May		June-Dec.	Dec.-May	June-Dec.	Dec.-May
Hunashi Katti	4257	12750	1275	10200	22950	11475	4.04	2.02
Hullatti	3662	30375	3037	24300	54675	27337	11.20	5.60
Alalgeri	4414	15000	1500	7500	22500	9000	3.82	1.53
Total Sanctuary	12333	58125	5812	42000	100125	47812	6.09	2.91

*1. We have assumed that about 75 per cent of the fodder requirements of domestic livestock are obtained from the Sanctuary.

2. During June-December period, all the domestic livestock are presumed to be present in the Sanctuary and during December-May period, about 90 per cent of the sheep and goat are taken away to their summer pastures in Malnad region.

3. For purpose of calculating grazing pressure, the 'sheep equivalent' figures are obtained using the equation—1 sheep = 1 goat = 1/5 cow or buffalo (cattle) (personal communication: Dr. Srinivas, Veterinary Doctor, Mysore Zoo).

4. According to the officials (T.R. Chandrasekhar) of Sheep Development Corporation at Ranebennur, the optimum grazing pressure is one sheep equivalent per hectare.

treme paucity of firewood resources in the surroundings, bulk of this firewood requirement appears to be removed from the Santuary. Quite a few of the landless poor people of the area, particularly Lambani tribals, are forced to eke out an existence by illegally removing and selling firewood from the Sanctuary. Since eucalyptus is identified easily and seized by the Forest Department staff during transport, the tribals cut chiefly the miscellaneous indigenous species particularly *Acacia*. Further, the regeneration from coppices in the case of these native tree species is practically non-existant. Being a good coppicer, *Eucalyptus* hybrid is the only species which withstands this large scale cutting. This is a socio-economic factor total elimination of which is not possible. Some local castes like Areyavaru occasionally are reported to net blackbuck during moon-lit nights. Poachers from some urban areas might occasionally raid the Sanctuary. However, we believe that poaching is not a major adverse factor. The herds of sheep that graze in the Sanctuary are usually accompanied by dogs which guard them against wolves. A large number of dogs enter the Sanctuary everyday and it is likely that they may kill new-born blackbuck and other smaller mammals.

2. Afforestation works

The original scrub forests of Ranebennur were already in a degraded condition in 1924 due to the influence of biotic factors like overgrazing, cutting and fires. Between 1925 and 1955, these degraded forests were extracted by the Forest Department in an attempt to rehabilitate them by "vigorous coppice and seedling growth" (Kanitkar 1924). However, these attempts failed due to the biotic factors, and as a result by 1958 the entire reserved forest area was totally denuded of all tree cover and reduced to barren hillocks with sparse grass growth. An example of such degraded habitat can still be seen in the nearby Kakola area.

Afforestation works were taken up as a soil conservation measure from 1958 onwards. Every year during monsoon, native tree species and *Eucalyptus* hybrid were planted in trench mounds laid 9.15 metres apart. For the first two years, such afforested patches were closed to grazing. It was, however, observed that once the areas were opened to grazing, the native species were rapidly eliminated. This can still be observed by the gaps in the trench mounds. Only *Eucalyptus* hybrid survived in a stunted condition.

In 1972, to improve the growth rate of these plantations, mechanised afforestation replaced the earlier trench mound system, and greater emphasis was given to *Eucalyptus* hybrid in the choice of tree species. The planting was done in furrows, 1.25 to 1.50 metres apart, ripped across the contour using specially equipped bulldozers. Approximately 640 hectares were planted up every year and by 1979, most of the unplanted area as well as the older trench mound plantations were covered by the mechanised plantations. These plantations were stopped in 1979 in response to criticisms that they might adversely affect the blackbuck habitat.

3. Blackbuck populations

Though the Deccan thorn forest of the type that existed in Ranebennur is essentially a good habitat for blackbuck, Kanitkar (1924) does not record anything regarding their status. However, a few remnant populations must have existed even then. In 1958 when the afforestation works were taken up, blackbuck appeared to have been extremely rare according to local sources.

Consequent to the protection afforded to the afforested patches and the decline in poaching due to the presence of Forest Department staff involved in afforestation activities, stray groups of blackbuck were reported to be seen colonising these areas. The blackbuck population increased gradually and was estimated at 600 during 1970 and 1000 during 1974 (Neginhal 1977). A census conducted in November 1979 by means of visual counting put the population at 2794 animals (Table 3). Our own impressionistic estimate in March 1981 was about 2500 animals. Since some seasonal migrations are likely due to water scarcity, the 1979 figures appear reasonable. According to the local sources also, the blackbuck population increase has been rapid, particularly since mid 1970s.

TABLE 3

1979 BLACKBUCK CENSUS FIGURES IN RANEBENNUR

Name of Block	Adult male	Adult female	Young	Total
Hunashi Katti	177	440	166	783
Hullatti	403	801	340	1544
Alalgeri	125	254	88	467
Total	705	1495	594	2794

Date of census : 11-11-1979 to 13-11-1979

Method of census : Total visual counting by enumerators moving on foot, by dividing the area into smaller units.

Source : Assistant Conservator of Forest (Wildlife), Dharwad.

Early in the morning, blackbuck herds are found grazing in the cultivated lands adjoining the plantations. Around 9.00 a.m. they retreat into the interior of the plantations when the shepherds reach the Sanctuary. During the day, they are found inside the plantations and emerge out in the evenings when the sheep herds retreat. At night, they seem to be straying away from the plantations to feed on crop stubble. During the monsoon, when the surrounding areas containing crops are guarded, they are reported to stay inside the plantations for longer hours feeding on the grass and come out at night to raid the crops. When alarmed in the open areas, they rush headlong into the plantations, with ease. There are no blackbuck except in the vicinity of the afforested patches.

DISCUSSION

Some naturalists (Krishnan 1975; Neginhal 1977) had advocated the total removal of the *Eucalyptus* hybrid from Ranebennur Sanctuary for the following reasons:

1. The *tall, dense forest* habitat created as a result of mechanised afforestation would be ecologically unsuitable for blackbuck which is an animal adapted to the open plains habitat.
2. Shunning this unsuitable habitat, blackbuck would move away from the Sanctuary and their place will be taken by forest-dwelling species like spotted deer (*Axis axis*) due to ecological succession.

Our observations reveal the following facts:

The eucalyptus plantations established since 1972 have been forests of a very open nature containing good grass growth. Under the extremely harsh edaphic and biotic conditions prevailing in Ranebennur, these plantations have not grown into tall, dense forests.

Estimated blackbuck population growth rates appear to be of the order of 14 per cent between 1970 and 1974, and 22 percent between 1974 and 1979. This increase in population has taken place inspite of the predation by domestic dogs and in severe competition with the livestock, during the years when the Sanctuary was being covered by mechanised afforestation. This high growth rate can only be attributed to two reasons, i.e. optimum ecological conditions for reproduction and for immigration of remnant herds from surrounding areas. This seems to be corroborated by the fairly high (21 per cent) percentages of young animals in the population. This clearly shows that the mechanised plantations of eucalyptus, under the conditions prevailing in Ranebennur, have not turned the habitat unsuitable for blackbuck. On the other hand, quick establishment of tree cover appears to have fulfilled a basic ecological need, i.e. cover for survival.

Blackbuck, even in its open habitats, need a fair amount of cover which is a key ecological factor affording protection against predation and persecution by humans. Elsewhere in its open habitat, patches of natural scrub and woodland provide this cover. In Ranebennur, the long narrow strip of eucalyptus plantations with good forage and an open natured cover has met this need. Supplementing this, similar response to eucalyptus plantations on the part of blackbuck is being observed in other dry-zone areas like Onkara and Naganapura State Forests in Mysore District. Adaptation of blackbuck to moist-deciduous forests in Madhya Pradesh and Orissa (Schaller 1967) and their preference to denser vegetation in Rajasthan desert (Sharma 1981) have also been reported.

Establishment of this ecologically crucial cover in the form of native tree species, though highly desirable, is impracticable under the adverse biotic conditions caused by overgrazing, cutting and fires in areas like Ranebennur. Further these biotic factors are results of deeper socio-economic causes and their immediate elimination appears unlikely and in any case beyond the purview of wildlife management. In view of this, wherever such adverse biotic factors are severe on the Deccan plains, establishing this cover by mechanised afforestation using hardy exotic like *Eucalyptus* hybrid may be desirable from the point of view of Blackbuck conservation.

ACKNOWLEDGEMENTS

The authors are indebted to the World Wildlife Fund-India which supported this study, and the Krnataka Forest Department for its whole-hearted cooperation.

REFERENCES

JAGADISCHNDRA, B.K. (1974): Working plans for the forests of Dharwad and Gadag divisions. 1976-77 to 1996-97. Karnataka Forest Department.

KANITKAR, R.K. (1924): Working plan report for the scrub forests of Dharwad and Kod Ranges. Karnataka Forest Department.

KRISHNAN, M. (1972): An ecological survey of mammals of India. *J. Bombay nat. Hist. Soc.* **69**: 469-501.

——— (1975): Report on the Ranebennur Sanctuary sent to the Director, Wildlife Preservation, Bangalore.

NEGINHAL, S.G. (1977): Ecological impact of afforestation at Ranebennur Blackbuck Sanctuary. *J. Bombay nat. Hist. Soc.* **75** (Supplement)

SCHALLER, G.B. (1967): THE DEER AND THE TIGER. The Chicago Universty Press.

SHARMA, I.K. (1981): Survival of the Blackbuck. Newsletter No. 37. World Wildlife Fund-India.

Utilisation of Organic Waste for Fish Cultivation

DHIRENDRA KUMAR[1], B. VENKATESH[2], AND P.V. DEHADRAI[3]

ABSTRACT

Results of utility of organic waste as feed in monoculture experiments of *C. batrachus* and *H. fossilis* at low and high stocking densities are discussed in the present communication. The experiment at low stocking density resulted high productivity of organic waste items like carcass meat meal, damaged rice and wheat bran (unfit for human and cattle consumption), gobar gas slurry and poultry dropping, in semi-intensive culture of air-breathing fishes.

INTRODUCTION

Utilisation of organic waste in a profitable manner has been a burning problem in small towns and villages throughout the country. Efforts are being made in different directions; however, one such method is its use in fish culture.

Semi-intensive culture technology of magur (*Clarias batrachus*) and singhi (*Heteropneustes fossilis*), two air breathing catfishes of India, is feed oriented and has some constraints in the widespread adaptability in rural areas. However, utilisation of nitrogen bearing organic waste as feed will help in utilizing the natural waste and also in bringing down the cost of expensive input component in the culture operations. Incorporation of organic waste, such as biogas slurry, poultry dropping, cowdung, damaged wheat/rice bran (unfit for human and cattle consumption) and carcass meat meal, in the feed will project the possibilities of integration of the technology with rural based industry.

With a view to finding a suitable and cheap alternative to fish and also testing the utility of aforesaid cheap organic waste items as feed in fish cultivation, three mono-culture experiments of air-breathing fishes were conducted during January to June 1980. The results of experiments are embodied in the present communication.

MATERIAL AND METHODS

Three air-breathing fish culture experiments were conducted in shallow ponds each of 0.04 ha in water area at Rahra Fish Farm of Central Inland Fisheries Research Institute (ICAR). Stocking and production details of all the three experiments are given in Table 1. *Clarias batrachus* were stocked in two different ponds at high and low stocking densities. After fifth week of culture, in the pond with low stocking density, 25 fingerlings of silver carps (*Hypophthalmichthys molitrix*) of av. size 13 g/103 mm were released to control algal bloom of *Cosmarium* and *Closterium* which had appeared during the period. *Heteropneustes fossilis* were stocked in a pond at high stocking density. Water replenishment was not done in any pond during culture period. The physico-chemical conditions of water of experimental ponds are given in Table 2.

Organic waste items used as supplementary feed for *C. batrachus* were carcass meat meal,

Present Address:

1. Officer-in-charge, Air-breathing Fish Culture Unit, Central Fisheries (ICAR) Mithapur Fish Farm, Patna (Bihar)
2. Development Officer (Technical), National Bank for Agriculture and Rural Development, 101, Janpath, Station Square, Bhubneshwar, Orissa.
3. Fisheries Development Commissioner, Govt. of India, Krishi Bhavan, New Delhi.

TABLE 1

EXPERIMENT—WISE STOCKING AND PRODUCTION DETAILS

Species cultured and experiments	Pond No. and its area (ha)	STOCKING DENSITY Stocking density /ha	No. stocked & date of stocking	Av. length (mm)	Av. wt. (g)	PRODUCTION DETAILS Number recovered	Recovery (%)	Av. wt. attained (g)	Production /ha
C. batrachus (Mono-culture at low stocking rate)	I (0.04)	45,000 + 625 silver carp	1,800 (1.2.80) + 25 Silver carp* (17.3.80)	109.0	11.0	1,386	77.0	51.0	2,034 kg in 4 and half months (87 % magur)
C. batrachus (Mono-culture at high stocking rate)	II (0.04)	1,05,000	4,200 (10.1.80)	113.0	15.0	1,793	42.7	25.0	1,129 kg in 5 months
H. fossilis (Mono-culture at high stocking rate)	III (0.04)	1,59,000	6,371 (14.1.80)	82.0	5.9	3,013	47.3	25.0	1,898 kg in 5 months

* Silver carp (*Hypophthalmichthys molitrix*) of av. size of 13 g/103 mm were released in the pond for control of algal bloom.

TABLE 2

PHYSICO-CHEMICAL CONDITIONS OF WATER OF THREE EXPERIMENTAL PONDS

Month of observation	Experiment pond No.	Water temperature °C	pH	Free carbon-dioxide (ppm)	Dissolved oxygen (ppm)	Free ammonia (ppm)	Total alkanity (ppm)	Phosphate (ppm)	Transperency (cm)
February '80	II	24.5	8.5	10.0	8.4	0.63	250	0.01	23.0
		24.5							
	III	24.5	8.6	5.0	4.2	0.47	248	0.38	23.5
March '80	I	25.0	7.5	3.0	3.1	0.23	200	0.10	17.5
	II	25.5	8.0	6.7	4.6	0.49	244	0.10	18.5
	III	26.5	8.0	13.5	3.4	0.22	260	0.25	18.0
April '80	I	29.0	7.5	4.0	6.0	0.12	265	0.16	15.5
	II	29.0	7.5	13.0	2.0	0.50	385	0.24	17.0
	III	29.0	7.5	3.0	7.5	0.30	270	0.17	13.0
May '80	I	30.0	7.3	14.0	6.0	Trace	290	Trace	16.0
	II	30.0	7.4	8.0	8.0	0.56	320	Trace	16.5
	III	30.0	7.3	13.0	9.2	0.20	330	Trace	17.5

Pond No. I : Mono-culture experiment of magur at low stocking rate.
Pond No. II : Mono-culture experiment of magur at high stocking rate.
Pond No. III: Mono-culture experiment of singhi at high stocking rate.

damaged rice and wheat bran having a total protein content of 44 percent, 6.48 percent and 20 percent respectively. Carcass meat meal was procured from the Khadhi and Village Industries Commission, Kalyani, (W.B.) at a rate of Rs.150/- per quintal and damaged rice and wheat bran were procured from Food Corporation of India Godown where these were declared unfit for human and cattle consumption. Feeding rates varied from 5 to 10 percent of the body weight of the stocked fish and the ratio of carcass meat meal: rotten rice/wheat bran was varied depending on the season. For *H. fossilis*, supplementary feed inrgredients were gobar gas slurry/poultry droppings and damaged rice/wheat bran in the ratio of 2:3. The av. total nitrogen content of gobar gas slurry and poultry dropping was 2.5 percent and 1.8 percent respectively. The feeding rate varied from 5 to 7 percent of the body weight of the stocked fish.

RESULTS

Best result was obtained in mono-culture of *C. batrachus* at the low stocking density. As can be seen from Table 1, in this experiment, a total production of 2034 kg/ha/4½ months of magur (87 percent) was obtained with a survival rate of 77 percent. Algal bloom of *Cosmarium* and *Closterium* observed during the fifth week of culture was successfully controlled by introduction of silver carp fingerlings in the pond. 80 percent survival of silver carp was recovered which had attained an av. weight of 530 g. in 90 days.

In another mono-culture experiment of *C. batrachus* at high stocking density, the production could be obtained to 1129 kg/ha/5 months with a poor survival rate of 42.7 percent only. As can be seen from Table 1, the poor growth and low production was due to heavy mortality caused by periodic outburst of disease, characterised by symptoms like loss of barbles, frayed fins and degenerated tail. Also heavy predation by water snakes was noticed which not only killed the fishes but also left them injured making them vulnerable for bacterial infection. The disease could be checked by feeding the fish with terramycin tablets at the rate of 100 mg/kg of feed for the first three days, 50 mg/kg for next two days and 25 mg/kg of feed for another two days. During culture period, there was periodical appearance of algal bloom of *Closterium, Cosmarium* and *Microcystis* which caused wide fluctuation in the dissolved oxygen level. The algal bloom could be controlled partially by shading half of the pond with water hycinth. These varied problems had bearing on poor growth and survival and as such the efficiency of the supplementary feed could not be evaluated.

Mono-culture experiment of *H. fossilis* at high stocking density, yielded production of 1898 kg/ha/5 months. As given in Table 1, the poor retrieval and growth was due to excessive growth of *Spirogyra* which formed thick mat on the bottom of the pond after about a month of rearing. It was manually removed and water level was increased to prevent subsequent growth of algae on the pond bottom.

Monthly quantitative and qualitative analysis of plankton of experimental ponds revealed that their volume in 50 litres of water varied from 0.4 ml to 2.1 ml, 0.8 to 2.9 ml and 0.35 ml to 2.5 ml in ponds I, II and III (Table 2) respectively. The type of phyto and zooplanktons in each pond were *Cosmarium, Closterium, Nitzschia, Pediastrum, Euglena, Navicula, Cyclop, Ceriodaphnia, Keratella, Brachionus* and *Polyarthra* in pond I; *Microcystis, Closterium, Cosmarium, Nitzschia, Pediastrum, Euglena, Spirogyra, Cyclop, Keratella, Brachionus, Polyarthra* and *Filinia* in pond II; and *Spirogyra, Closterium, Euglena, Nitzschia, Pediastrum, Keratella, Brachionus, Polyarthra* and *Cyclop* in pond III.

Discussion

The best utility of organic waste ingredients used as supplementary feed in these experiments, was in mono-culture experiment of magur at low stocking density or semi-intensive culture with moderate feeding. According to Dehadrai in semi-intensive culture, production of 5 tones/ha/year is possible. Based on this, a production of 2034 kg/ha/4½ months from a shallow pond that too without replenishment of water under semi-intensive condition is quite encouraging. Silver carp attained an av. weight of 530 g in 90 days in shallow pond which indicates that its introduction was well suited for biological control of algal bloom in such type of culture system. The high stocking densities which were adopted in other two experiments on mono-culture of *C. batrachus* and *H. fossilis* seem to be undesirable for semi-intensive culture without water replenishment. In these experiments, many hazards were encountered during the course of experiment which resulted in heavy mortality, poor growth of fish and low production. As such the efficiency of the supplementary feed could not be evaluated.

The result of these experiments clearly reflects that used organic waste items can be utilised as supplementary feed of *C. batrachus* and *H. fossilis* for high yielding operation but the stocking density should be kept between 20,000/ha and 45,000/ha for high survival, high growth and low key management with less risk. However, high stocking density more than 50,000/ha can be recommended for culture of these species in shallow ponds where water replenishment is easily possible without incurring heavy expenditure on it.

ACKNOWLEDGEMENTS

The authors are grateful to Dr. A. V. Natarajan, Director, Central Inland Fisheries Research Institute, Barrackpore for taking interest in the study. They convey their sincere thanks to the staff of Rahra Fish Farm of CIFRI for extending all possible help in conducting the experiments.

REFERENCES

GHOSH, A., RAO, L.H. & SAHA, S.K. (1976): Culture possibilities of Air-breathing catfish, *Clarias batrachus* in domestic waste waters. *J. Inland Fish. Soc., India,* **8**: 151-152.

JHINGRAN, V.G. (1969): Potential of Inland Fisheries, *Indian Farming,* **19**(9): 22-25.

THAKUR, N.K. (1978): On the food of the air-breathing catfish, *Clarias batrachus* (Linn.) occurring in wild waters. *Int. Revue ges. Hydrobiol.* **63**(3): 421-431.

Orchid Sanctuary Sessa, Arunachal Pradesh — An effort towards habitat conservation

SADANAND N. HEGDE

INTRODUCTION

Although orchids are known as plants of ornamentation, conservation of species belonging to this group in their natural habitat had long remained of little interest to the people world over. However, with the activities of IUCN, MAB, WWF, etc, the gravity of situation in respect of endangered status of this unique group, was brought into focus and the entire family Orchidaceae has now been treated as protected and brought under the convention on the International Trade in Endangered species of Wild Fauna and Flora (CITIES 1973).

In our country, there has been a growing concern over the last two decades about the depleting orchid species from their natural habitats. As early as 1936, in Assam two species of orchids, namely *Renanthera imshootiana* and *Vanda coerulea* were considered endangered and a fine of Re 1/- used to be imposed by the Government for unauthorised collection of these orchids (in ASSAM MANNUAL — for Unclassed State Forests of Nagaland Govt. Notification No. 459-R, of 12.2.1936). Subsequently, in 1960s, Government of India opened three National Orchidaria under Botanical Survey of India each situated at Yercaud in Tamil Nadu, Indian Botanic Garden, Howrah and Shillong, Meghalaya respectively, for preserving the rare orchids in different geographical regions. Yet, the situation did not improve. Subramanyam and Sreemadhavan (1970) reviewing the Indian situation on endangered plant species and their habitats report several orchids under 'threat'. With further survey in the North-East India, there were alarming reports of depleting and diminishing orchid species and their habitats (Jain and Sastry 1980, Hegde 1980a, 1981a, b, c). Further, studying the various causes responsible for the threatened status of the species, the author (Hegde 1980b, 1981c) outlined certain measures for conserving the depleting and diminishing orchid flora in Arunachal Pradesh. As a follow-up programme, an Orchid Sanctuary was established at Sessa during 1979 under State Plan, for ensuring *in situ* conservation of orchids which forms the subject matter of the present paper.

Orchid Research and Development Centre, Tipi: Bhalukpong 790 114, Arunachal Pradesh

What is an Orchid Sanctuary?

Orchid Sanctuary, in a broad sense in this paper, is referred to 'Wild Life Sanctuary' (Cf. IUNC report 1979) as orchids are an integral part of an ecosystem. However, the term 'Orchid Sanctuary' indicates/emphasizes the purpose of the particular area so declared as meant for *in situ* conservation of a number of *Orchid* species in their natural habitat. The area is managed to provide optimum conditions to several orchid species in their own ecosystem. Primary purpose is the protection of germplasm of orchids in nature permitting study and education.

Based on this concept, orchid sanctuary, Sessa has been created during 1979 under the Wildlife Act issued vide Govt. order No. For. 32/IND-I/82/17706 — 45 of 19.7.82 and being developed at present.

Orchid Sanctuary, Sessa

Orchid Sanctuary, Sessa, is situated in West Kameng District of Arunachal Pradesh, about 24 km away from Orchid Research and Development Centre, Tipi and falls on Tezpur — Bomdila main road. It is located between Doimarah Forest Reserve on the south and Tenga Forest Reserve on the north, lying between the parallels of Lat. 27°6′-27°7′N and meridian of Longi. 92°31′-92°32′E (Cf. ground plan).

Physiography. The Sanctuary stretches over an area of 85 hect. surrounded by high mountains on the north and west, the perennial Sessa nala on the south and Tezpur—Bomdila Highway on the east. The place is situated at an elevation of 1100 m MSL rising up to 1800 m on the north and the west.

Climate. The area receives heavy to moderate rainfall throughout the year excepting a brief period during winter. As a result, the Sanctuary remains characteristically cool and humid in most part of the year. It enjoys a temperature ranging from 3°C minimum in winter to 25°C maximum in summer. The top ridges of the Sanctuary also experience brief snowing for a day or two during peak winter.

General Vegetation. The most attractive part of the Sanctuary is dense evergreen vegetation with mixed elements of tropical and subtropical flora at the lower ridges and culminating in temperate elements on the top ridges, with *Quercus, Rhododendron, Pinus* sp., etc. The flora here are *Schima wallichii, Terminalia myriocarpa, Phoebe acuminata, Magnolia* sp., *Castanopsis indica,* etc.

The Forest here is subtropical wet evergreen type with multitiered tree canopy formation and with undergrowth. Every tree is heavily moss-covered which is congenial to the epiphytic orchids. Similarly the ground orchids thrive well in different habitat conditions.

The very fact that the saprophytic orchids like *Epipogium* and *Galeola* occur naturally in the Sanctuary speaks of the virginity and primitivity of the forest type here.

Soil. The soil type is either rigolith or woody peat. Organic content is found to be very high. The pH of the soil varies from 5.39 to 6.90.

Orchid Flora. That the Sanctuary provides diverse ecological conditions conducive to various orchid species, there are as many as 130 species in 53 genera found to occur and is about 35% of the total estimated number of species of Arunachal Pradesh (Cf. list of orchids at the end). Out of the 130 species occurring in the Sanctuary, 5 are saprophytes, 23 terrestrials and 102 epiphytes. Dominant genera among them are those of *Dendrobium* with 12 species, *Bulbophyllum, Coelogyne* and *Eria* with 11 each and *Liparis* with 8 species respectively. It is further worthy to note that four new species (+) and one new record to India have been recorded from this area alone. Endangered species like *Galeola lindleyana, Dendrobium densiflorum, Coelogyne barbata, Cymbidium longifolium,* etc. find natural occurrence here.

Maintenance and Management

As pointed out earlier, the purpose of an Orchid Sanctuary is to ensure *in situ* conservation of orchids in their habitat. Accordingly, the species known to have their natural occurrence in that area should be provided perpetual environment of their own, not withstanding the process of ecological succession or evolution. For an effective maintenance and management, therefore, one should have the adequate knowledge of orchid ecology. Accordingly, the saprophytic, terrestrial and epiphytic orchids are to be maintained.

Saprophytes. The basic requirement of

saprophytic orchids is decaying wood with rich humus having the soil pH nearer 6.8 and 6.9. Cool and humid atmosphere with partial sunlight are the other necessities. Normally, they appear with the onset of monsoon. It is interesting to note that the *Epipogium* species occur in decayed wood matter under partial shade condition. On the other hand, *Galeola lindleyana* grows in lot of decaying wood amongst banana groves or damp forest floor preferably nearer perennial springs. Once the decaying wood completely mixes up with the soil resulting in the variation in pH, these orchid species give way to other plant species to take over in succession. It has been observed that with the advancement of ferns in the area, the saprophytes lose battle. In such a situation, ferns are to be weeded out to the extent of keeping up equilibrium. This is of considerable importance in maintaining the saprophytic orchids in the Sanctuary.

Terrestrials. On the ground strata, as many as 23 species of terrestrial orchids are found to occur within the Sanctuary. However, no single species is found in abundance, excepting *Anthogonium gracile* which is found in large patches on sunny rocky slopes. The genera *Anoectochilus, Goodyera, Chrysoglossum, Liparis, Malaxis* etc, are well distributed in the ground strata near the stream sides in the sanctuary. The species like *Phaius mishmensis, Phaius flavus, Hetaeria rubens* etc. are found in the thickets under dense shade in woody peat or regolith soil having pH ranging from 5.39 to 6.57. On the other hand, *Goodyera procera, Spathoglottis pubescens* var. *parviflora, Habenaria* sp., *Pleione praecox* and *Satyrium nepalense* are found on open grassy land at the top ridges.

Periodical weeding around their habitat reducing the pressure of competition for space, light and nutrition, is required for their happy growth in the Sanctuary. However, under no circumstances the associate plants that provide shade and congenial habitat should be disturbed.

Epiphytes. The large majority of species found in the Sanctuary are epiphytes. The tall trees of *Schima wallichii, Terminalia myriocarpa,* etc. are found to harbour a number of epiphytic species at different heights. The species of *Aerides, Bulbophyllum, Cleisostoma, Coelogyne, Dendrobium, Eria, Bulbophyllum, Pholidota, Thunia, Vanda,* etc. are the common sights. The rare and endangered species like *Dendrobium densiflorum, Cymbidium longifolium, Arachnis cathcartii, A. clarkei* are also found to occur here. The latter two species are generally seen pendulously hanging down the main trunks of large trees. The rocky cliffs covered with moss are also congenial habitats for *Coelogyne, Pleione, Neogyne,* etc.

It has been observed that the epiphytic species often compete between themselves and also with other epiphytic forms like aroids, ferns, etc. within the same habitat environment. For instance, *a single large tree, bears as many as 30-60 species of orchids along with other epiphytic forms, which compete for space, light and nutrition and one or the other becomes the loser.* Therefore, it is essential to study the ecology of orchids and provide the necessary space and environment to every orchid species within the sanctuary. To this extent, human interference is necessary in an Orchid Sanctuary to conserve every germ-plasm and to maintain the equilibrium in the ecosystem by checking competition without damaging the original environment.

Based on this principle, Orchid Sanctuary, Sessa has been maintained and managed. There are sections of orchid species of major orchid genera as shown below (Cf. ground plan also) where their habitat environment is created and maintained for their proliferation.

Major Orchid Sections in the Sanctuary

1. Anthogonium Section
2. Oberonia ,,
3. Coelogyne ,,
4. Cymbidium ,,
5. Phaius ,,
6. Calanthe ,,
7. Galeola ,,
8. Epipogium ,,
9. Chrysoglossum ,,
10. Liparis ,,
11. Eria ,,
12. Bulbophyllum ,,
13. Pholidota ,,
14. Otochilus ,,
15. Goodyera ,,
16. Dendrobium ,,
17. Thunia ,,
18. Vandaceous ,,
19. Anoectochilus ,,
20. Acanthephippium ,,

Man-power requirment: Effective maintenance and management of an Orchid Sanctuary much depends upon the man-power used. As experienced over the last three years, a skilled and trained personnel with two assisting field officals is a minimum requirement for maintaining a Sanctuary of this kind. Of course, they need to be given adequate labourers. Four daily labourers are minimum requirement for maintaining an area of about 5 ha consisting of various orchid sectiôns. Other areas can be maintained once a year in appropriate season depending upon the necessity. It is necessary therefore, to set up an adequate operating fund to meet these recurring expenditures of day-to-day maintenance including the salaries of staff. There is need to emphasize adequate housing facilities also to the staff.

Importance of Orchid Sanctuary: Realising the physical feature that harbours diverse habitat conditions for a large number of orchid species within a reasonably manageable area, the Orchid Sanctuary has been created. It is indeed a positive pioneering step towards habitat conservation of cool-loving orchids of this region. The Sanctuary ensures protection of orchid species on the one hand and promotes an interest among the public for conservation, education and research in various aspects of Orchidology — especially in orchid ecology, taxonomy, and as a source of germ-plasm for plant improvement and breeding.

Further, it is suggested to have chains of such Orchid Sanctuaries in different geographical regions to ensure conservation of this specialized group of plants.

ORCHID FLORA OF THE ORCHID SANCTUARY, SESSA

Saprophytes

1. *Epipogium roseum* (Don) Lindl.
2. *E. sessanum* Hegde *et* Rao +
3. *E. tuberosum* Duthie
4. *Galeola javanica* (Bl.) Benth & Hk.f.
5. *G. lindleyana* (Rchb.f.) Rchb.f.

Terrestrials

6. *Acanthephippium striatum* Lindl.
7. *Anoectochilus lanceolatus* (Benth.) K. & P.
8. *A. roxburghii* var. *regalis* (Bl.) Pradhan
9. *Anthogonium gracile* Wall. *ex* Lindl.
10. *Calanthe biloba* Lindl.
11. *C. herbacea* Lindl.
12. *C. masuca* (D. Don) Lindl.
13. *Chrysoglossum erraticum* Hk.f.
14. *Cremastra appendiculata* (D.Don) Makino
15. *Goodyera procera* Hk.f.
16. *Habenaria clavigera* (Lindl.) Dandy
17. *H. polytricha* (Hk.f.) Pradhan
18. *Herpysma longicaulis* Lindl.
19. *Hetaeria rubens* Benth *ex* Hk.f.
20. *Malaxis acuminata* D.Don.
21. *M. josephiana* (Rchb.f.) Rchb.f.
22. *Phaius flavus* (Bl.) Lindl.

23. *P. mishmensis* (Lindl.) Rchb.f.
24. *P. tankervilliae* (Ait.) Bl.
25. *Spathoglottis pubescens* var. *parviflora* Lindl.
26. *Tainia latifolia* Lindl. Benth *ex* Hk.f.
27. *Tainia wrayana* (Hk.f.) J.J.Sm.
28. *Zeuxine goodyeroides* Lindl.

Epiphytes

29. *Acrochanena punctata* Lindl.
30. *Aerides multiflorum* Roxb.
31. *A. odoratum* Lour.
32. *Agrostophyllum callosum* Rchb.f.
33. *Arachnis cathcartii* J.J.Sm.
34. *A. clarkei* (Rchb.f.) J.J.Sm.
35. *Biermannia jainiana* Hedge *et* Rao +
36. *Bulbophyllum cauliflorum* Hk.f.
37. *B. clarkeanum* K. & P.
38. *B. gamblei* Hk.f.
39. *B. guttulatum* Wall *ex.* Hk.f.
40. *B. obrienianum* Rolf.
41. *B. odoratissimum* Lindl.
42. *B. penicillium* Par. & Rchb.f.
43. *B. piluliferum* K. & P.
44. *B. protractum* Hk.f.
45. *B. reptans* Lindl.
46. *B. scabratum* Rchb.f.
47. *Ceratostylis himalaica* Hk.f.
48. *Cleisostoma discolor* Lindl.
49. *C. racemiferum* (Lindl.) Garay
50. *C. sagittiforme* Garay.
51. *C. subulatum* Bl.
52. *C. tricallosa* Hegde *et* Rao. +
53. *Coelogyne barbata* Griff.
54. *C. elata* Lindl.
55. *C. fimbriata* Lindl.
56. *C. flavida* Wall *ex* Lindl.
57. *C. fuscescens* Lindl.
58. *C. griffithii* Hk.f.
59. *C. nitida* (Wall. *ex* Don) Lindl.
60. *C. prolifera* Lindl.
61. *C. punctulata* Lindl.
62. *C. rigida* Par. & Rchb.f.
63. *Cryptochilus sanguinea* Wall.
64. *Cymbidium devonianum* Paxt.
65. *C. elegans* Lindl.
66. *C. iridioides* D.Don.
67. *C. longifolium* D.Don.
68. *C. mastersii* Grill.
69. *Dendrobium aphyllum* (Roxb.) Fischer.
70. *D. bicameratum* Lindl.
71. *D. chrysanthum* Lindl. *ex* Wall.
72. *D. chrysotoxum* Lindl.
73. *D. desnsiflorum* Lindl.
74. *D. devonianum* Paxt.
75. *D. eriaeflorum* Griff.
76. *D. falconeri* Hk.f.
77. *D. fimbriatum* var. *oculatum* Hk.f.
78. *D. hookerianum* Lindl.
79. *D. longicornu* Lindl. *ex* Wall.
80. *D. nobile* Lindl.
81. *D. wardianum* Warner.
82. *Ephemerantha macraei* (Lindl.) Hunt & Summerh.
83. *Epigeneium amplum* (Lindl.) Summerh.
84. *Gastrochilus acutifolium* (Lindl.) O.K.
85. *Gastrochilus dasypogon* (Sm.) O.K.
86. *G. inconspicuum* (Hk.f.) Seienf.
87. *G. intermedius* (Griff. *ex* Lindl.) O.K.
88. *Eria acervata* Lindl.
89. *E. amica* Rchb.f.
90. *E. carinata* Gibs.
91. *E. clausa* K. & P.
92. *E. connata* Joseph, Hegde *et* Rao +
93. *E. hindei* Summerh.
94. *E. paniculata* Lindl.
95. *E. pannea* Lindl.
96. *E. pubescens* Wt.
97. *E. spicata* (Don.) Hand-Mazz.
98. *E. stricta* Lindl.
99. *Kingidium taenialis* (Lindl.) Hunt.
100. *Liparis bituberculata* (Hk.f.) Lindl.
101. *L. bootanensis* Griff.
102. *L. coespitosa* K. & P.
103. *L. cordifolia* Hk.f.
104. *L. delicatula* Hk.f.
105. *L. mannii* Rchb.f.
106. *L. plantaginea* Lindl.
107. *L. viridiflora* (Bl.) Lindl.
108. *Micropera mannii* (Hk.f.) Tang & Wang.
109. *Neogyne gardnerana* (Lindl.) Rchb.f. *ex.* Pfitz.
110. *Oberonia acaulis* Griff.
111. *O. falconeri* Hk.f.
112. *Ornithochilus fuscus* Wall *ex* Lindl.
113. *Otochilus albus* Lindl.
114. *O. fuscus* Lindl.
115. *Phalaenopsis parishii* var. *lobbii* Rchb.f.
116. *Pholidota articulata* Lindl.
117. *P. imbricata* Lindl.
118. *P. rubra* Lindl.
119. *Phreatia elegans* Lindl.
120. *Pleione praecox* (Sm.) Don.

121. *Podochilus khasianus* Hk.f.
122. *Pteroceras suaveolens* (Roxb.) Holtt.
123. *Smitinandia micrantha* (Lindl.) Holtt.
124. *Sunipia andersoni* (K. & P.) Hunt.
125. *S. racemosa* (J.J. Sm.) Tang & Wang
126. *Thelasis longifolia* Hk.f.
127. *Thunia alba* (Lindl.) Rchb.f.
128. *Uncifera acuminata* Lindl.
129. *Vanda alpina* Lindl.
130. *V. cristata* Wall. *ex* Lindl.

* New record.

ACKNOWLEDGEMENTS

Grateful thanks are due to Shri R.N. Kaul, IFS, Chief Conservator of Forests, Arunachal Pradesh, Itanagar and Shri J.K. Mehta, IFS, Conservator of Forests, Western Circle, Banderdewa for their encouraging interest and facilities to carry out the present investigation.

REFERENCES

ANON. (1976): Convention on International Trade in Endangered Species of Wild Fauna and Flora. Govt. of India Press, New Delhi.

HEGDE, S.N. (1980a): Preliminary observations and list of orchids of Arunachl Pradesh. *Arunachal Forest News* **3(3)**: 1-11.

HEGDE, S.N. (1980b): Orchids of Arunachal Pradesh—their conservation and commercialization strategies. *Proc. National Symposium on Orchids, Bangalore.*

__________ (1981a): Cultivation and conservation of lost orchids. *Indian Horticulture.* **25(4)**: 7-9.

__________ (1981b): Three Saporphyptic orchids from Arunachal Pradesh. *Am. Orchid Soc. Bull.* **50(10)**: 1220-1222.

__________ (1981c): Field Observations on the depleting orchids of Arunachal Pradesh. Seminar on depleting plant resources in North-East India, Shillong.

__________ & RAO, A. NAGESHWARA (1982): *Epipogium sessanum* Hegde *et* Rao—A new species of orchid from Arunachal Pradesh, India. *J. Econ. Tax. Bot.* 3: 597-601.

__________ (1983): Further contributions to the Orchid Flora of Arunachal Pradesh India, ibid. **4(2)**: 383-392.

__________ (1983): *Cleisostoma tricallosum* Hegde *et* Rao —A new orchid from Arunachal Pradesh, India. *Orchid Review.* **91:(1074)**.

IUCN (1979): The Biosphere Reserve and its Relationship to other protected area.

JAIN, S.K. & SASTRY, A.R.K. (1980): Threatened plants of India. Govt. of India.

SUBRAMNYAM, K. & SREEMANDHAVAN, C.P. (1970): Endangered plant species and their habitats. A review of the Indian situation. IUCN Publications N.S. No. **18**: 108-114.

Environmental impact of hydro electric projects

B. VIJAYARAGHAVAN[1]

Beauty resides in the hills and the rivers, so it does in the laughter of the poor and the broken. This epitomises the conflict between the conservation of the environment and the development of the economy. There can be no standard formula for the resolution of this conflict applicable for all climes, for all times. In the developing countries where starvation and absence of even the basic needs for a bare existence are the lot of large numbers of the human race, a clamour about environmental degradation as a consequence of economic development may appear not only irrelevant but even cruel. Therefore, one has to be extremely cautious and balanced in any discussion on the environmental impact of development projects in developing countries.

Recognition of the environmental consequences of the energy industry is a comparatively recent phenomenon the world over. In the developing countries especially, there can be no economic development without massive investments in the power sector. Till recent times, decisions on power projects were being taken exclusively on the basis of technical feasibility and economic viability. 'Social desirability' (an insufficiently expressive term in the context) has rarely, if ever, been a relevant consideration.

The energy industry everywhere faces a dilemma. While the non-renewable sources of power, such as fossil fuel, oil and nuclear fuel, are of limited availability and likely to get exhausted over a period of time, the renewable sources, such as solar, wind, ocean thermal and tidal, are not yet capable of exploitation on a commercial scale and the technology for their exploitation is undeveloped. The only exception in regard to renewable sources of power is water. Water has always been a primary source of power generation and there are many reasons for this. Firstly, it is a renewable resource. Secondly, the technology is simple and well-developed and is the earliest known power generation technology. Thirdly, compared to thermal and nuclear stations, in hydro electric stations the operation costs are negligible. Fourthly, unlike thermal or nuclear stations, hydel stations are capable of easy regulation and can function effectively as peaking stations. This last mentioned consideration is of special importance in Indian states like Tamil Nadu where the agricultural load is substantial and this comes on to the grid about the same time every day for a limited duration. Then again, where the fossil/nuclear share of power generation in the total grid capacity is high, as is progressively happening in many states of India, hydro electric stations can have a special significance. While thermal and nuclear stations will have to be operated as base load stations at fairly constant levels and should not be called upon to reduce generation below specific levels to suit the dips in the grid demand, hydro stations can come to the rescue of the grid by stepping up or stepping down generation with facility to match the requirements of the grid from time to time.

In India, the utilisation of the hydro electric potential increased from 582 MW in 1951, when the first Five Year Plan was initiated, to 13,165 MW in 1983. At present, hydro power plants account for 41% of electricity generation in India. The total economically exploitable

[1]*Chairman, Tamil Nadu Electicity Board, India.*

hydro electric potential in India is estimated as the equivalent of 396.4 TWH of annual energy generation. The schemes now in operation account for only 11% of this potential, and the schemes under execution account for another 7%. The balance of about 82% is yet to be exploited. In the years to come, the pressures for development of this balance potential of hydro power will mount. Therefore, there is every need for the conservationists to be vigilant so that such further development of hydro power will not inflict any excessive or irreversible damage to the environment.

The consequences of hydro electric projects on the environment are by now fairly well known. These can be briefly summed up as follows:

The immediate and obvious effect is the submersion of considerable forest areas by the reservoir and destruction of forests in the surrounding areas also for the construction of the power house and other ancillary structures and for the infra-structural requirements. While such submersion and destruction of forests is generally harmful, particular care is required where forests having special features such as rain forests are involved. The quiddity of rain forests has been the subject matter of much discussion. Notwithstanding this, very little information is forthcoming on the floristic or faunistic diversity of rain forersts. Our knowledge of the utilisation potential and the evolutionary significance of many of the genetic resources that are cradled in the rain forests is inadequate and, therefore, when rain forests as in the Western Ghats of India are destroyed for the execution of hydro-electric projects we are losing irreplaceable biotic wealth without even knowing what exactly we are losing. It is not the direct destruction or submersion of forests alone by such projects that matters. Nor even the destruction of forests for the readily identifiable and unavoidable ancillary activites and infra-structural requirements. What is equally bad is that the project has a catalistic effect in accelerating the destruction of forests in the surrounding areas also. This is particularly attributable to two factors. Firstly, the labour camps that come to be set up in these areas during the construction phase. And, secondly, the easy accessiblity provided by extensions of roads which are an inevitable part of projects activities. The execution of hydro-electric projects is extremely labour intensive and huge armies of labourers take up encampment in these areas. To make matters worse, such projects have a very prolonged gestation period and the labour camps continue for long periods in the heart of the forest. In most cases, even after the projects are commissioned it becomes impossible to remove these labour camps and they become a permanent feature of the area. During the long construction period, the labourers and their families would have entrenched themeselves by resorting to illicit cultivation and also illicit felling of trees. Even a casual study of the many of our hydro-electric projects would show that there has been a marked spurt in cultivation activities in the forest areas as a result of such projects and such cultivation often involve heavy destruction of forests. Large bodies of men unconnected with project activities also flow in search of a living, who further contribute to the despoilation of the forests. In the POST FACTO ENVIRONMENTAL IMPACT STUDY OF THE IDUKKI PROJECT, IN KERALA published by the Department of Environment, Government of India, (1983) it has been pointed out that while during 1910-15 the area of the Periyar-Thodupuzha basins in the back drop of the Idukki dam was mostly covered by forest which occupied nearly 95% of the total area, the forest cover had by

1968-78 been reduced to less than 50%. The report also points out that "the population distribution and density in the study area had increased considerably from the period 1961-71 to 1971-81". Similarly, there had been a tremendous increase in the establishment of small scale industries in these areas. Thus, the indirect and long-term effects of hydro-electric projects on forests are as damaging as the direct and immediate effects.

The opening up of rain forests and other special types of forests by hydro-electric projects also encourage various forms of so-called forest development which ultimately results in the original forest losing its special characteristics. Extensive plantation of eucalyptus, teak, cardamom etc., in the Western Ghat has inflicted serious damage to the ecosystem. The diversified and highly complex forest types are destroyed and replaced by relatively simple mono-culture with no floristic diversity. This has an effect also on the fauna and has led to the decline of the native fauna. Krishnan says that "the spread of exotics into the natural forests is directly related to their opening up by human activities and has in some areas resulted in serious ecological imbalance. Practically all exotics specially cultivated departmentally such as casuarina, cashew, rubber, and *Prosopis juliflora* serve to deprive the wild animals of territory in long-held homes".

Cutting up of virgin forest areas leads to invasion by noxious exotic species such as *Lantana, Eupatorium* and *Mikana*. These inhibit the natural regeneration of the forest.

In the wake of the increased human activity in forests which takes the form of tree felling, forest fires, artificial regeneration, indiscriminate grazing etc. secondary forests emerge in the place of the old humid tropical evergreen forests. Studies by Jasbir Singh of the Botanical Survey of India in Idukki (Kerala, India) confirm that the tropical wet evergreen forests get converted into semi-evergreen forests due to human intervention in project areas. "From the comparative studies of phytosociology, litter production and and soil characteristics of the different successional communities at Idukki, it is clear that the evergreen forests have undergone tremendous environmental degradations. This fact shows that the evergreen species have a narrow ecological amplitude as they are restricted to valleys, hollows and depressions...... The woody species which occupy the openings of the evergreen forests are of semi-deciduous to deciduous stock and have a wide ecological range to survive the adverse edaphic conditions".

The adverse impact of human habitations and human intervention facilitated by extensive roads, faster modes of conveyance etc. may be direct or indirect. The direct impact takes the form of reduction of animal habitat, destruction through poaching, reduction in grazing for herbivores because of competition by domestic cattle etc., loss of feeding grounds and safe waters etc. There are also indirect and less pronounced impacts on faunal habits. It has been noticed that elephants in such disturbed territories become aggressive. Diurnal animals such as gaur and sambar become nocturnal upsetting their nutrition and making them vulnerable to predators. Gregarious associations of animals also get broken up. In his ECOLOGICAL SURVEY OF THE LARGER MAMMALS OF PENINSULAR INDIA, Krishnan observes: "The most obvious reaction of wild animals to sustained distrubance by humanity ...... is to convert them into shy fugitive creatures of the night and to cause them a greater degree of nervous tension than is normal in their lives. Animals which are normally abroad by day like gaur, sambar and pig retreat into cover with dawn and stay in hiding till near sun set: the difference between the behaviour of gaur in the Mudumalai and Bandipur sanctuaries and in the Kanha National Park is significant''.

Changes in the faunal composition take place in respect of birds also. It is noticed that with increasing human activity in project areas birds of the forest edge ecotone displace the true forest birds.

The damming of the river upsets the natural rhythm between the dry-weather flow and the flood discharges. The dynamic equilibrium which the river has attained during the ages is upset all of a sudden. Such changes in the hydraulic and hydrological regime can have far reaching implications on aquatic life, both in the reservoir and in the down stream stretches. The conversion of a fast flowing river system into a static environment also affects the inter-relationship among the various organisms. The segmentation of the fluvial system by the dam has long-term consequences on the geomorphology of the drainage basin and sediment distribution of the river system. Such segmentation also affects the floristic features. Krishnan has referred to the ecological changes induced by the artificial formation of the reservoir and water-spread of the Periyar hydro-electric project by the pent-up waters banking against the hill slopes which by their very steepness could have had no source of water originally except during the rains. ''No study of these changes has been made but it is apparent that at least certain waterside plants such as *Ochlandra* spp. and some sedges could not have been found in such profusion on the hill slopes and terraces abutting the water before the formation of the lakes''.

Dams and other structures have an adverse effect on fish populations. Such effect may be either obstructional or ecological. Dams, weirs and anicuts act as physical barriers to migration of fish, tending to prevent access of the fish to their customary breeding, rearing and feeding grounds. The restriction or prevention of migration may lead to reduction of fish stocks, thus leading to extermination. Changes in water velocity, water chemistry, trubidity, temperature etc., as a result of impoundments also have a disturbing effect on fish life. The sudden steep decline in the *Hilsa* fishery in the inshore areas of the Bay of Bengal and the Hoogly estuary coinciding with the construction of the Maithon dam in 1957 has attracted much attention. Sometimes, the dam can have an effect even on the marine fishery far removed from the dam itself. The trapping of silt in the Aswan Dam in Egypt is reported to have resulted in the collapse of a substantial sardine fishery. It is surmised that since the floods stopped, the aquatic food chain in the eastern Mediterranean has been broken along a stretch of continental shelf 12 miles wide and 600 miles long. The lack of the Nile sediment has reduced the plankton and organic carbon — all these having a cumulative adverse impact on the sardine fishery.

Eutrophication is a known phenomenon in stagnant waters. Unlike in fast flowing rivers there is less of re-charging with oxygen in stagnant waters. Added to this the nutrients washed into the reservoir by surface run-off and the warmer waters of a static reservoir favour the blooming of algae to levels exceeding the carrying capacity of the reservoir leading to depletion of the limited oxygen and destruction of aquatic life.

The dams also have an indirect impact on the tropical estuarine ecosystem. The delicately balanced interactions amongst the various biotic and abiotic factors in the shallow and fertile water area of the estuaries are seriously affected by the obstruction of the flow by dams.

Since the tropical estuaries are valuable nursery grounds for many marine and freshwater fisheries, dams can have a very adverse impact on the fisheries.

Many reservoirs are susceptible to the accumulation of non-biodegradable toxic matter. The catchment areas of rivers are extensively cultivated. As already stated, the activities surrounding dam construction may result in the acceleration of such agricultural activities in the catchment area. With the increasing use of pesticides and chemical fertilisers, the toxic matter is washed into the reservoirs by surface run-off and left to accumulate there slowly. This can inflict severe damage to aquatic life, since the accumulation of dissolved, suspended or sedimented toxic matter in the water body is almost irreversible. The only way to tackle this problem is by enforcing strict rules governing agricultural practices in the catchment areas of rivers draining into reservoirs.

It is, however, not as if that dams are an unmitigated disaster as far as fish life is concerned. The reservoirs in many cases have provided excellent environment for the multiplication of fish life. Notwithstanding the decline in the population of individual species in the river system as a result of the dam construction, there has been a total quantitative increase in fish population in a submerged river. Vast quantities of fish food develop in the reservoirs in the expanded aquatic environment. Some species of fish native to fast flowing river systems adapt well and even thrive in static lacustrine environment. Examples are provided by the Indian Carps such as *Catla catla, Labeo rohita* and *Cirrhinus mrigala*. The substantial development of the inland fisheries in India over the last few decades would not have been possible without the help of man-made reservoirs.

An excellent example of other kinds of beneficial effects of reservoirs is provided by the Periyar Dam executed in 1897. This diverts the waters of a west flowing river in South India into an east flowing river, the Vaigai, through a long subterranean channel. Originally constructed as an irrigation project, this has subsequently been developed into a power generation project also. The impoundment has insulated many land areas which have provided sanctuary for wild animals. Similarly, some of the reservoirs also attract significant numbers of water birds.

The aerobic and anaerobic decomposition of submerged vegetation is particularly pronounced when the forest areas likely to be submerged are not properly cleared of vegetation before the waters are impounded. This results in the production of methane, hydrogen and hydrogen sulphide. The hydrogen sulphide when it gets converted into sulphuric acid has a deleterious effect not only on the aquatic life but also on the mechanical structures of the dam, the concrete structures and the power house equipments. In Kodayar Power House I (Tamil Nadu, India), the turbine runner failed in December 1971. It was noticed that a radial crack had developed in the runner disc even though it had been in service for only a limited period. It was suspected that one of the causes could have been change in the crystalline structure of the metal due to hydrogen sulphide.

The reservoir provides breeding sites for vectors such as snails and mosquitoes. The margins of reservoirs and the hollows and indentation of the shore line, especially when vegetation such as *Eichhornia, Salvinia* and *Pistia* are present, provided abundant scope for the breeding of the vectors. Similarly, the irrigation system carries water-borne diseases to hitherto uncontaminated areas. The incidence of malaria, filariasis, encephalitis, schistosomiasis, onchocerciasis etc. had been aggravated by reservoirs and irrigation systems in various countries. However, it must be mentioned that, as far as India is concerned, unlike countries in Africa, natural impoundments and stagnant waters abound and, therefore, the adverse role of man-made lakes and irrigation systems in the spread of diseases can be only of comparatively marginal proportions.

Documented studies of many dams confirm that large impoundments of water lead to an increase in seismic activity. The overload of water reactivates faults that are endemic in the geological strata which over the eras have remained stable. The Koyna earthquake of December 10, 1967, in Maharashtra which claimed 200 lives and rendered thousands injured and homeless provides a classic example of such reservoir-induced seismicity. This region had long been a non-seismic one but had experienced a series of tremors after the impounding of water in Koyna dam reservoir in 1962. In addition to the tectonic setting, the quantum and duration of water loading and the rapidity with which the reservoir is loaded have also a bearing on the extent of seismicity of a particular area.

Extensive quarrying done in many projects during construction needs to be kept under check since the blasting operations loosen the slopes and make them susceptible to land slides.

The displacement of tribal settlements arising from the occupation of forest areas by projects is another significant impact. The displaced tribals may take to poaching, illicit tree-cutting, etc. which will further promote the degradation of the environment. It is not always easy also to provide satisfactory resettlement of such displaced tribal population. Sometimes, the resettlement itself may inflict further damages to the environment. Madhav Gadgil (1981) has pointed out that the clearance of the forest in Ramanagar (Karnataka, India) for the settlement of the refugees from the Kali Hydro Electric Project and failure to effect any soil conservation measures have resulted in grave damage to the land and it has been rendered a "desert unfit for cultivation". Particularly disastrous is the re-settlement of such diplaced population in catchment areas since the increased agricultural activities in such areas loosen the soil and promote soil erosion. Observations have also been made of the "cultural shock" inflicted on tribal populations by certain resettlement programmes. The tribal folks are forced to surrender their cultural ego, become subject to the domination of other communities and are forced to imbibe the social and cultural values of the resident population.

Not much attention seems to have been given in the past to the adverse effect of hydroelectric penstocks, trolley lines and flume channels which act as effective barriers to the movement of the larger mammals: A study to be mentioned here is the one made by E.R.C. Davidar in his "Investgation of Elephant migration paths in the Nilgri hills". The corridor concept applied to wildlife management is the provision of a free and as far as possible unimpeded way for the passage of wild animals between two wildlife zones. Movement of wildlife over a wide area is necessary for a variety of reasons and "a corridor might make the difference between survival and extinction particularly in the case of large animals such as elephant and gaur in certain areas. A corridor's more important function is to prevent wildlife from getting isolated in small pockets, like islands in an ocean, without a line of retreat in times of need". Davidar points out that penstock pipes and trolley lines leading to power houses invariably dismember elephant country into two parts as they occupy the entire hill slope. The International Workshop on the Management of Elephants (December 1982) organised by the IUCN also took note of hydro-electric penstocks becoming effective barriers to movement of the less agile, larger mammals and recommended that "Designs of crossing points be included in the hydro-electric projects as an essential component and effort be made to provide such corridors on existing penstocks, channels and other barriers". Such obstructions by penstocks in elephant country have been noticed in Singara, Moyar and Sholayar (Tamil Nadu, India) and it is now proposed to provide suitable ramps across the penstocks to facilitate the crossing by the larger mammals.

The increase in cultivation in catchment areas which is an inevitable sequel to the increased human activity in project areas leads to marked soil erosion resulting in quick sedimentation of reservoirs. The extensive and unscientific cultivation of the hill slopes with potato and other vegetable crops in the catchment areas of the river systems in the Nilgiris district (Tamil Nadu, India) has resulted in the heavy silting up of the Kundapallam forebay reservoir, the Pegambahalla forebay reservoir and the Pillur reservoir. The storage capacity has been drastically reduced. The intake trash racks and the scourvent trash racks have got choked up. The heavy choking of the intake trash rack has resulted in the drawal of power draft up to the minimum draw down level not becoming possible and thus the flexibility of operation has been affected. The choking of the trash rack has made it difficult to flush the silt through the scourvent. Where the sedimentation has a high content of sand, it can also seriously damage the runners of the machines in the power houses because of the abrasive effect of sand passing through. Severe damages were noticed in the Pelton wheel buckets of machines in Kundah Power House 3 (Tamil Nadu, India) in 1967 because of accumulation of sand in the Niralapallam tunnel from the eroded stream bed of the upper reaches of Niralapallam accentuated by the diversion of the flow from Katteri catchment into Niralapallam basin. The damage happened within a year of the diversion but, subsequently everything stabilised. In the Periyar Power House (Tamil Nadu, India) the damage has been of bigger proportions and more persistent. The damage to the turbine parts was noticed in the early 1960s on account of sand and the damage was severe in April 1979. The source of sand was identified as Anaivaikkal which joins the leading channel about 300 metres above the entry to the tunnel. During 1980-82, check dams were constructed and the Anaivaikkal stream diverted away from the leading channel. The effect of this modification is under observation.

Impoundments and irrigation systems lead to a rise in sub-soil water level which can cause water logging. This has been noticed in the Ukai-Kakrapar project (Gujarat, India), Chambal canal system (Madhya Pradesh, India) and the Cauvery Delta (Tamil Nadu, India).

The rise in the sub-soil water also increases salinity of the soil as observed in areas like Ukai-Kakrapar project (Gujarat, India).

The elevation of the sub-soil water level also brings in its wake higher contents of calcium and trace metal leading to the aggravation of the incidence of fluorosis in areas where it is already endemic. Similarly, Genuvalgum, another crippling disease, has been found to occur in the villages in Coimbatore district (Tamil Nadu, India) within a radius of 30 km from the Parambikulam Aliyar Project and this again is attributed partly to this project.

Obstruction by the dam increases the erosion downstream. This is because of the increased aggressiveness of flow of the silt-free waters in residual rivers which scours the river beds and banks much faster than a normal river.

The limited flow down stream as a result of the dam affects the self purification capacity of the river system and increases the pollution load. Dhanpat Rai reports (Bhageerath July 1983) that the "Upper Ganga Canal diverts so much water at Haridwar that the meagre flow remaining in the main stream cannot absorb the pollution load of the tanneries at Kanpur".

So far we have referred mostly to the impact of hydro-electric projects on the biogeophysical environment. Equally important is the impact on the socio-economic environment which covers changes such as those in employment, transportation, recreation, changes in the aesthetic value of landscape etc. If biogeophysical impacts are difficult to quantify even more difficult is the quantification of socio-economic impacts. This should not result in socio-economic impacts being ignored or slurred over in a scientific impact assessment.

There are three paramount considerations to be borne in mind while evolving a sound and durable system of environmental impact assessment. Firstly, the formulation of a widely acceptable methodolgy; secondly, the right timing of environmental impact assessment; and, thirdly, the need for cohesion among the environmentalists in presenting their case.

Inspite of all the noise being made about conservation of the environment, it is a fact that we have not been able to evolve generally acceptable norms for such assessments. The environment is highly variable in time and space. The available environmental data are often widely scattered, incomplete and incompatible. The shortcomings in the evolution of a methodolgy in this field call for early rectification. The diversity of disciplines involved in such assessments deserves special attention. In the absence of a generally acceptable methodology there is every possibility of mutually contradictory assessments being made and the uncertainty is bound to be exploited by sectarian interests. Many of the so-called environmental impact studies are superficial accounts without valid data collected over a period of time and are designed only to justify preconceived notions or reinforce postures already assumed. S.S. Rachagon (1983) refers to the controversy over the Tembelling dam in Malaysia where vested interests took advantage of the confusion over the uncertain data available though ultimately the project came to be abandoned and ecologists scored a victory. Similarly, nearer home, a profusion of 'instant literature' has appeared in recent years on the Silent Valley (Kerala, India), either supporting or opposing the proposed hydel project. This controversy exemplifies many shortcomings on either side which are a general feature of most such debates. While some ecologists tend to disguise lack of scientific data with poetry, some power engineers and administrators are apt to exploit the slogan that, of all forms of pollution, the pollution of poverty is the worst. Ultimately, this is likely to degenerate into a hand-to-hand fight between 'econuts' and 'hydronuts'. Therefore, systematisation of the methodology is a prime requirement and emotive overtones should be kept well under control.

Detailed researching of the particular ecosystem is necessary and generalisation of extrapolation from findings elsewhere will not do. No two river systems are alike, especially if in different ecological zones. In fact, ecology itself is an infant science and many of the theories in ecology are themselves to be put to severe test. For instance, it is sometimes said that stability in an ecosystem is a function of diversity and that complex saturated ecosystems where the habitats and micro-habitats are fully filled by many species are least likely to suffer any permanent damage if a few habitats are altered or if a few species are eliminated. This is a theory which can, in unscrupulous hands, be exploited with disastrous consequences. Ecologists will do well to assess the soundness of theories such as this and arrive at some generally acceptable conclusions.

The environmental impact assessment should also make full use of modern techniques such as satellite aerial remote sensing techniques, aerial multispectral scanning and thermal scanning.

As important as methodology is the timing of the environmental impact assessment. It needs to be emphasised that the environmental impact assessment should be made well before the project proposal is formulated. At the very least, the assessment should be paralleled with project investigation. Most of the proposed hydro electric projects will be in ecosystems not researched or inadequately researched. If impact assessment is delayed commitments may come to be made on behalf of the power sector from which it will be difficult to retract later on. Such delay may also contribute to attitudes on either side getting hardened and a dispassionate appraisal rendered difficult. an example of such a situation is the controversy over the Silent Valley Project (Kerala, India) where the ecologists woke up very late but, fortunately, not too late. It must also be noted that a delayed environmental impact assessment will inflict a damage on the economy if, ultimately, the project is found to be feasible and not ecologically objectionable since the approval and execution of the project will get delayed with consequent loss of power and cost escalations if the impact assessment report is not available well in time.

The third aspect I referred to in this context is the need for cohesion among the environmentalists. While the benefits conferred by development projects are identifiable, quantifiable and enjoyed by a compact group, the consequential damage to the environment is, to a large extent, imperceptible, dispersed in time and space and suffered by anonymous populations. Similarly, while the case for the project is forcibly put forth by well-organised lobbies of politicians, administrators and engineers with command over money, men and the media, the ecologists who protest are mostly 'lone wolves', feeble, scattered and disunited. There is, therefore, little wonder that the ecologists' lamentation becomes a cry in the wilderness. If the ecologists want themselves to be heard they should come together and organise themselves into cohesive groups.

It is not sufficient to confine the environmental impact assessment to the period prior to the project sanction alone. Where the project is sanctioned and is executed, the impact assessment should continue concurrently during the execution of the project and during the post-execution phase. It will be necessary to have a satisfactory system for the correlation and comparison of data collected during these periods with data relating to the pre-execution phase so that correctives wherever necessary can be applied promptly. The environmental impact assessment should become the responsibility of a separate department of environment under the State and Central Governments, independent of the organisation or department incharge of the formulation and execution of projects.

Surveillance of dam safety should be a regular and permanent feature of all project maintenance activities. This does not appear to have received much attention in our country so far notwithstanding the failure of a few dams inflicting tremendous loss in life and property. Even though instances of total failure have been few they should make us alive to the need for evolving a regular machinery for exercising continuous surveillance over the safety of the dams. The external and internal forces bearing on the dam, the effect of ageing, the effects of the environment on the dam and the arrangements for operation, maintenance, repair etc., should all be continuously monitored. Hazard rating procedures have to be evolved and so also formulation of early warning systems. This work should form a part of the job of the Electricity Boards or Irrigation Departments which are in charge of the dams.

Another essential point to be remembered is that environmental safeguards should be built into the project plan itself and not treated as something alien to the project. The expenditure necessary for ensuring such safeguards should be treated as part of the project cost. Such environmental safeguards will include afforestation of catchment areas, grading of borrow areas to harmonize with the natural grounds, benching of quarries so that they could be planted with vegetation, sloping of spoil from tunnel excavations to blend with the surroundings, provision of corridors and crossing points for the larger mammals etc. and landscape architecture in general. The necessary expertise for such works should be employed by the Electricity Boards/Irrigation Departments as part of their organisation.

Demands are often made for identification of reserves where unique biotic features exist. There has to be a total ban on all developmental activities in such areas. A certain amount of dogmatism in such reservation policy is inevitable and even essential. Once such areas have been chosen with care, there should be a ban even on consideration of proposals for locating projects there. Such absolute reservations exist in other spheres of developmental activities. For example, it is now well recognised that for protecting the integrity of urban zones rigid rules have to be enforced in regard to town planning, lay outs, provision of open spaces, ban on growth of slums etc. If compromises are made in these regards as piece-meal concessions to the needs of a growing population, within a very brief period, our urban settlements will be converted to gigantic slums. This awareness has necessitated a rigid and dogmatic policy in regard to urban planning. A similar dogmatism and rigidity in the conservation of biosphere reserves is unavoidable.

One very important consideration that should engage the attention of all Govermental agencies is the need to educate administrators and engineers on environmental conservation. This is no doubt a part of the need for environmental education and training programmes in general, starting from the school stage itself. But the problem is more pressing and urgent in respect of administrators and engineers who are in charge of formulation and execution of projects in forest areas. Once this awareness is created among administrators and engineers the present conflict between them and the environmentalists will disappear to a great extent and there will be a more balanced and enlightened approach to conservation issues.

In the management of hydro electric projects one essential point to be remembered is that after the construction phase is over, only the minimum staff required for the maintenance of the project is allowed to remain at the project site. The long gestation period of the project and the large army of workers required for such projects are conducive to the growth of permanent settlements in forest areas unless very strict measures are enforced to prevent this. Experience shows that even where damage has been done to the environment during the construction phase, once nature is left to itself after the construction, there is a certain amount of récupération possible. In the course of the study report on Idukki project by the Department of Environment, Government of India, it has been pointed out that Sabarigiri (Kerala, India) once disturbed greatly during the construction period has recovered considerably over the years, the forest is once again lush and wildlife which once left the area in fright has all come back and that all this has happened because the Sabarigiri site was abandoned after construction except for very few maintenance staff and the single access road was left to deteriorate.

It is essential that there should be full legislative support for all environmental conservation. Various steps have already been in India in this regard with the enactment of the Wildlife Protection Act 1972, Water (Prevention and Control of Pollution) Act 1974, Water Pollution Cess Act 1978 and the Air (Prevention and Control of Pollution) Act 1981. But there are areas left uncovered by legislation also. For example, there is an urgent need to regulate and control forestry and agricultural practices in the catchment areas. Unrestricted cultivation with crops like potato, vegetables etc., as has been going on in the Nilgiris (India), loosen up the soil resulting in heavy erosion and siltation of reservoirs. Similarly, the unrestricted use of fertilisers and pesticides in the catchment areas results in toxic matter getting washed into the reservoirs inflicting damage on the aquatic life. All these should be strictly controlled through legislative measures.

There is need for effective nodal agencies in the government both at the Central clearance of projects and monitoring of environmental clearance of projects and monitoring of environmental impact assessment. In recent times, such departments have been constituted in the Government of India and in certain States like Tamil Nadu.

The history of civilisation has been the history of man taming nature. No progress would have been possible if efforts had not been made to interfere with forces of nature and nature had been left in its primitive glory. In respect of water resources, projects to harness the hydro potential have brought in tremendous benefits to mankind in the form of hydro power irrigation, flood control, drinking water schemes, fishery development, facilities for recreation etc. Economic growth is a continuous exercise of making one trade-off after another. But, a time comes when we are in danger of making the wrong trade-off and exchanging long-term advantages for short term gains. In fact, most of the disagreements between economists and ecologists hinge largely on their different perspectives of time. In general, 5 to 10 years is considered to be a sufficiently long period by economists but this is a short period for ecologists. The basic questions then to be answered are what a proper time-frame should be to assess the relative advantages of economic development and environmental conservation, and what is the true cost of a kilowatt of energy. For answering such questions a segmented or sectarian approach by either ecologists or economists will not serve the purpose and we have to go in for total measurement techniques which encompass much more than growth in GNP or rise in per capita income. In other words, such questions can be answered only jointly by economists and ecologists and not separately as two different mutually opposed camps.

Select References

INTERNATIONAL WATER POWER AND DAM CONSTRUCTION. October 1980 and July 1983.

BHAGIRATH – The irrigation and Power Quarterly, July 1983. Published by the Central Water Commission, New Delhi.

The state of India's Environment (1982): Published by the Centre for Science and Environment, New Delhi.

Post facto Environmental Impact Study of the Idukki

Project in Kerala (1983). Compiled by C.L. Trisal and N.L. Ramanathan, Department of Environment, Government of India.

Scope Report on Environmental Impact Assessment — *Principles and Procedures* — Edited by R.E. Munn (1975). Scientific Committee on the Problems of the Environment of the International Council of Scientific Unions.

Major Dams — A Second Look (1981): Edited by L.T. Sharma and Ravi Sharma — Environment Cell, Gandhi Peace Foundation, New Delhi.

V.R. PANTULU (1975): Environmental Aspects of River Development in Tropical Asia with particular reference to the Mekong Basin (Proceedings of the Second World Congress on Water Resources — Vol. V — Technology and Ecology).

M. KRISHNAN: An Ecological Survey of the Larger Mammals of Peninsular India.

E.R.C. DAVIDAR: Investigation of Elephant Migration paths in the Nilgiri Hills.

The impact of the loss of forest on the birds of the Eastern Ghats of Andhra Pradesh

(*With 4 text-figures*)

Trevor D. Price[1]

Introduction

The Eastern Ghats of the Vishakapatnam District in Andhra Pradesh are rapidly losing their remaining forest cover. Of the three plateaux making up the area — Araku, Paderu, and Chintapalle, only the Chintapalle plateau still has substantial forest and this is being reduced to fragments on steep hillsides and the ghatface itself. Denudation is largely due to the pressures of an expanding agricultural population and clearfelling of natural forests for replacement with teak and other economic species of timber, and to a lesser extent to other private and public enterprise (roads, electric power schemes, forest contractors, coffee plantations etc.).

The loss of forest habitat is affecting the abundance and distribution of organisms. It will probably cause some populations in the area to disappear, and some may already have disappeared. However, the fauna and flora of the region have been little studied. Whistler & Kinnear (1932-39) named seven endemic subspecies of birds from the area. As it is a mountain block, separate from other mountainous regions, the area may well contain endemic species in other less vagile groups.

I studied the birds at one locality in the Eastern Ghats for a total of 13 months between 1976 and 1978 (Price 1978, 1979, 1981), and visited the area briefly in November, 1983. My study was not designed to investigate problems associated with forest destruction. Indeed, it was only the partial loss of one of my study sites to agriculture which impressed on me the extent of habitat loss. Nevertheless, observations such as mine on species occurrences in an area are obviously needed for conservation planning. Therefore in this paper I use the data I obtained to draw some tentative conclusions about the impact of development on the bird life in the area. To do this I studied as to which populations are particularly forest dependent, and therefore likely to be threatened by continued forest destruction.

To assess changes in the bird fauna it would be ideal to census birds from each habitat in widely separated areas (cf. Terborgh 1977) and to follow temporal changes in species diversity associated with habitat modification (e.g. Willis 1974, Leck 1979, Karr 1982*a*, 1982*b*). Without such data I can only present quantitative results on patterns of species diversity in the two habitats I studied, mature forest and an adjacent area of regenerating scrub, and indicate how species composition differs between these two habitats. I use these results, scanty published data, and personal observations elsewhere on the plateau to assess potential changes in species diversity in the face of a continuing trend of habitat modification. Finally I consider what steps can be taken to lessen the impact on birds, and the arguments for a reserve in the area.

Methods

The study was based at the village of Lamasinghi on the edge of the Chintapalle plateau, at an altitude of 2,300 ft. It lasted from

[1]Division of Biological Sciences, The University of Michigan, Ann Arbor, Mi. 48109-1048 U.S.A.

August 1976 to July 1977, and for three weeks in January and February 1978. Methods are reported in detail in Price (1979). Throughout this paper quantitative results are restricted to the following groups of birds: pigeons and doves, parrots, trogons, bee-eaters, hoopoes, barbets, woodpeckers, and all passerines. Scientific names for resident species are given in Table 1. Birds were trapped in mist nets in the area of regenerating secondary growth ('disturbed habitat') next to the forest, and below the mature forest. Nets were placed in similar positions in these two sites each week. Trapping effort was between 1.5 and 2.5 times more intense in the disturbed habitat than in the forest: more nets were placed there for a longer period of time (Price 1979). Captured birds were colour ringed and released. Casual observations of birds elsewhere in the Ghats were made during 10 weekend expeditions.

TABLE 1

A CLASSIFICATION OF RESIDENT SPECIES BY HABITAT AT LAMMASINGHI, TOGETHER WITH NUMBERS CAPTURED IN THE FORSET AND SECONDARY GROWTH.

		Numbers Trapped: Secondary Growth	Forest
Group 1. Forest species.			
*Emerald dove	*Chalcophaps indica*	12	1
*Malabar trogon	*Harpactes fasciatus*	0	3
Lesser yellownaped woodpecker	*Picus chlorolophus*	3	0
Bronzed drongo	*Dicrurus aeneus*	2	0
+ Hill myna	*Gracula religiosa*	0	0
Blackheaded yellow bulbul	*Pycnonotus melanicterus*	2	7
*Greyheaded flycatcher	*Culicicapa ceylonensis*	2	6
Whitebrowed fantail flycatcher	*Rhipidura aureola*	0	1
Blacknaped blue flycatcher	*Monarcha azurea*	10	10
*Shama	*Copsychus malabaricus*	30	16
Thickbilled flowerpecker	*Dicaeum agile*	4	1
Group 2. Forest + edge species			
+ Blossomheaded parakeet	*Psittacula cyanocephala*	3	0
+ Indian lorikeet	*Loriculus vernalis*	1	0
Baybanded cuckoo	*Cacomantis sonnerati*	4	0
Bluebearded bee-eater	*Nyctyornis athertoni*	3	1
Large green barbet	*Megalaima zeylanica*	18	5
Coppersmith	*Megalaima haemacephala*	11	0
Speckled piculet	*Picumnus innominatus*	20	3
Fulvousbreasted pied woodpecker	*Picoides macei*	3	1
Pigmy woodpecker	*Picoides nanus*	3	0
+ Blackheaded oriole	*Oriolus xanthornus*	0	0
Grey drongo	*Dicrurus leucophaeus*	5	0
+ Jungle crow	*Corvus macrorhynchos*	0	0

		Numbers Trapped: Secondary Growth	Forest
Large woodshrike	*Tephrodornis gularis*	7	3
Scarlet minivet	*Pericrocotus flammeus*	6	0
Small minivet	*Pericrocotus cinnamomeus*	0	1
Goldfronted chloropsis	*Chloropsis aurifrons*	2	0
Slatyheaded scimitar babbler	*Pomatorhinus schistriceps*	8	0
Spotted babbler	*Pellorneum ruficeps*	23	14
Redfronted babbler	*Stachyris rufifrons*	19	5
Yellowbreasted babbler	*Macronous gularis*	21	7
Quaker babbler	*Alcippe poiocephala*	36	21
*Brook's flycatcher	*Muscicapa poliogenys*	20	14
Whitethroated ground thrush	*Zoothera citrina*	24	8
Blackbird	*Turdus merula*	16	1
Chestnut-bellied nuthatch	*Sitta castanea*	5	5
Velvet-fronted nuthatch	*Sitta frontalis*	9	6
Tickell's flowerpecker	*Dicaeum erythrorhynchos*	32	10
Purplerumped sunbird	*Nectarinia zeylonica*	21	3
Purple sunbird	*Nectarinia asiatica*	16	2
Little spiderhunter	*Archnothera longirostris*	1	0
Group 3. Edge + forest species			
*Spotted dove	*Streptopelia chinensis*	15	0
Himalayan tree pie	*Dendrocitta formosae*	1	0
Pied flycatcher shrike	*Hemipus picatus*	20	2
Common woodshrike	*Tephrodornis pondicerianus*	4	2
Common iora	*Aegithina tiphia*	40	0
Redwhiskered bulbul	*Pycnonotus jocosus*	196	15
Redvented bulbul	*Pycnonotus cafer*	143	4
Rufousbellied babbler	*Dumetia hyperythra*	38	2
White-throated fantail flycatcher	*Rhipidura albicollis*	4	0
*Tailor bird	*Orthotomus sutorius*	85	15
Magpie robin	*Copsychus saularis*	25	2
Blackspotted yellow tit	*Parus xanthogenys*	50	6
White-eye	*Zosterops palpebrosa*	182	31
Group 4. Scrub species			
+ Crow pheasant	*Centropus sinensis*	0	0
+ Yellowfronted pied woodpecker	*Picoides mahrattensis*	0	0
Striated swallow	*Hirundo daurica*	9	0
Rufousbacked shrike	*Lanius schach*	14	0
+ Ashy swallow-shrike	*Artamus fuscus*	0	0
+ Whitebellied drongo	*Dicrurus caerulescens*	0	0
+ Pied myna	*Sturnus contra*	0	0

		Numbers Trapped: Secondary Growth	Forest
Jungle myna	*Acridotheres fuscus*	1	0
Blackheaded cuckoo shrike	*Coracina melanoptera*	11	0
Whitebrowed bulbul	*Pycnonotus luteolus*	8	1
Jungle babbler	*Turdoides striatus*	1	0
Yellow-eyed babbler	*Chrysomma sinense*	28	0
Ashy grey wren warbler	*Prinia hodgsonii*	12	0
Ashy wren warbler	*Prinia socialis*	25	0
Jungle wren warbler	*Prinia sylvatica*	7	1
Pied bush chat	*Saxicola caprata*	11	0
+Green munia	*Estrilda formosa*	0	0
Whitebacked munia	*Lonchura striata*	39	1
Jerdon's munia	*Lonchura kelaarti*	37	2
Spotted munia	*Lonchura punctulata*	6	0

+. — Species not included in the trapping data (figures 1-3).
*. — Species largely confined to the understory when found in the forest.

RESULTS

Habitats near Lammasinghi

The area, at least from an altitude of 3,000 feet to sea level is primevally dry deciduous, moist deciduous and semi-evergreen forest (Champion & Seth 1968); the forest types changing as one passes from dryer to wetter areas, and from higher to lower altitudes. True semi-evergreen forest, which must have once covered much of the coastal plain, is now present only in small fragments, mainly along the edge of the Ghats (e.g. at Merripakala).

On the Chintapalle plateau there are now some widely cultivated areas as well as substantial areas of more or less permanent scrub maintained by the pressures of heavy grazing. Teak monocultures at all stages of growth are becoming more widespread and better managed, in that the understory is kept clear. There are also some pine plantations. Coffee plantations are being developed. In these plantations a proprotion of the mature trees are felled, and the undergrowth replaced with the coffee plants.

My study at Lammasinghi was carried out in mainly moist deciduous forest and in secondary growth regenerating from clearance 5-20 years previously which is adjacent to this forest. There are a few evergreen trees in the forest and also deciduous trees which often have extensive overlap between old leaf fall and new leaf gain. The understory, which contains evergreen plants, is sparse and regularly burns towards the end of the dry season. The secondary growth contains a substantial number of fruiting and flowering trees (e.g. *Ficus* spp., *Mangifera indica, Bombax* and *Erythrina*), and trees that have been selectively retained along a road, and many fruiting bushes (e.g. *Lantana*). A full description of the locality and climate is given in Price (1979).

Species at Lammasinghi

Abundance of species. Among residents in the area 1643 individuals of 64 species were captured in mist nets during the study (Table 1). Cumulative species and individual abudnance curves for the 1976-1977 study period are presented in figure 1. The species curve for the partly the abundance of a few species (notably bulbuls) in the edge habitat. However, rare species typically account for 70% of all species in humid tropical forests (Karr 1971, Lovejoy 1974, Pearson 1977, Wong 1984).

Comparison of two habitats. Although trapping effort in the disturbed habitat was between

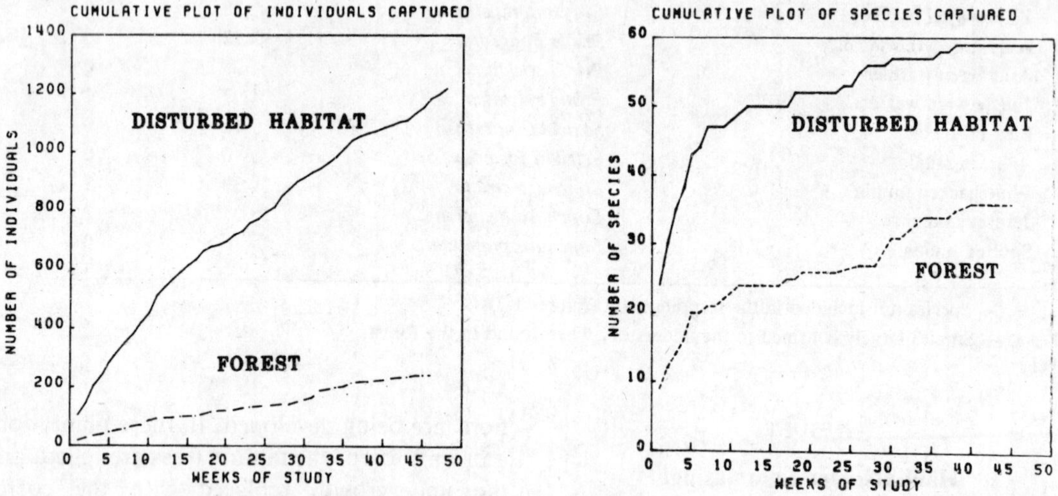

Fig. 1. — *A*: Cumulative numbers of species captured in the secondary growth and forest. *B*: Cumulative number of individuals. For the period 1976-1977 only.

disturbed habitat appears to be close to an asymptote, that for the forest less so. This indicates, for the disturbed habitat at least, that the resident species have been rather thoroughly sampled (MacArthur & MacArthur 1974). There is a lognormal distribution of species' relative abundance (figure 2) whether observational or trapping data are used, although individual species' abundances do differ according to the method of estimation (Price 1979). The abundance of 42 (66%) of the species form less than 2% of the total number of individuals in the catch, which is the criterion for rarity suggested by Karr (1971). Such a large number of rare species partly reflects stragglers from open scrubland, and 1.5 and 2.5 times as intensive in the zone below the forest canopy, almost six times as many individuals were captured in this habitat (figures 1 and 3). A greater habitat complexity and productivity at net level, and the presence of fruiting bushes (e.g. *Lantana*), probably contribute to the greater abundance. However among those species restricted to the understory in the forest only the Tailor bird and the doves show a marked increase in the secondary growth areas (table 1).

Species abundance curves for the two areas are shown in figure 3. 38 species were trapped in the forest, whereas 59 were trapped in the secondary growth area. Figure 3 indicates that part of this difference may be due to incomplete

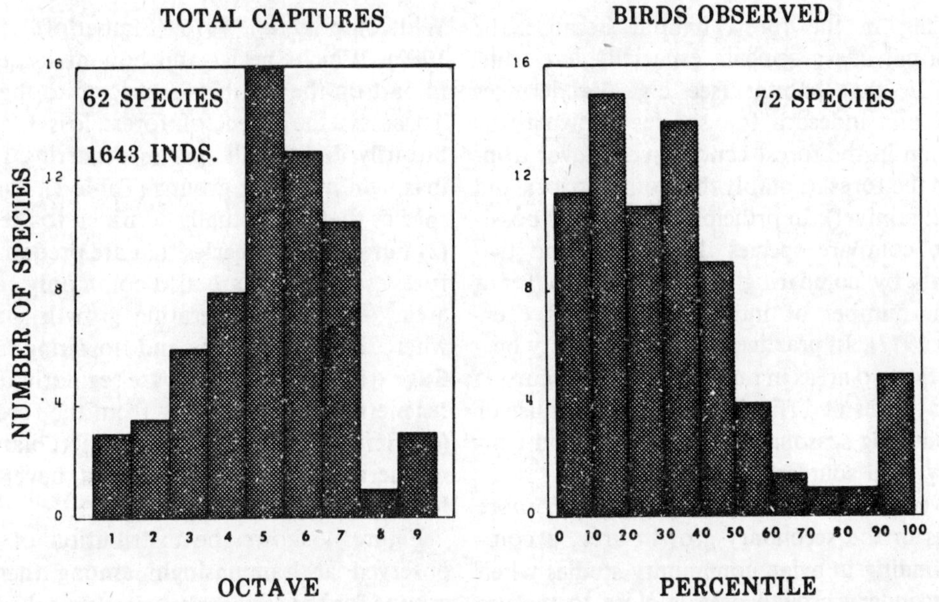

Fig. 2. — Species abundance curves. *A*: Abundance curves based on trapping. Species are grouped into octaves, such that the first octave contains all species for which zero to one individual were trapped, the second octave one to two individuals, the third two to four individuals, and so on (see Vandermeer 1981). Thus the abscissa is on a logarithmic scale. *B*: Abundance curves based on days of observation, as a proportion of the total days spent at Lammasinghi. Species are grouped into ten-percentiles, thus the scale on the abscissa is arithmetic. Based on data in Price (1979).

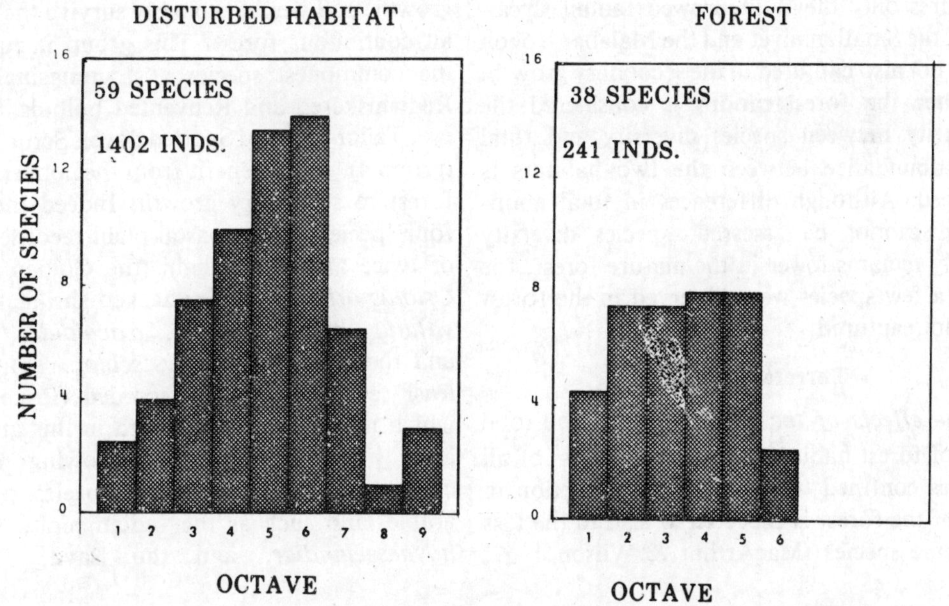

Fig. 3. — Species abundance curves based on trapping in (*a*) the secondaory growth area and (*b*) the forest. From data in Table 1.

sampling in the forest habitat because the lognormal curve appears especially left truncated in that habitat (see e.g. Vandermeer 1981), and indeed a few species known to be common in the forest canopy were never trapped in the forest (notably the Common iora and Scarlet minivet). In principle it should be possible to compare species diversity in the two habitats by comparing species diversity for a similar number of individuals trapped (Terborgh 1977). In practice the large disparity between the two areas in numbers caught (figure 1) makes the result difficult to interpret because of confounding seasonal effects, flocking on temporary food sources, etc.

Nevertheless it is clear that there are more species in the secondary growth area, a common finding in avian community studies when the secondary growth area is close to mature forest (e.g. MacArthur 1964, Schemske & Brokaw 1981). The secondary growth area has some specialist species, and others typical of the more open areas of scrub, as well as sampling nearly all the species from the forest. Of forest captures only the Whitebrowed fantail flycatcher, the Small minivet and the Malabar trogon were not also captured in the secondary growth.

When the forest canopy is considered the disparity between species diversity and total bird abundance between the two habitats is reduced. Although differences in total abundance cannot be assessed, species diversity clearly remains lower in the mature forest, for only a few species were observed in the forest but not captured.

Threatened species

The effects of the loss of forest. The total loss of forest habitat will lead to the loss of all species confined to this habitat. Reduction in size of the forest is expected to lead to the loss of some species (MacArthur & Wilson 1967, Whitcomb *et al.* 1976, Simberloff & Abele 1982). Which species and how many, depends in part on the numbers restricted to the forest. To assess the effect of forest loss I have arbitrarily divided all species occurring at Lammasinghi into four groups (Table 1): (1) **Forest species** that are virtually confined to the forest; (2) **Forest + edge species** that are predominantly forest species but are also commonly found in areas of thick regenerating growth, and also where there are fruiting and flowering trees; (3) **Edge + forest species** that are regularly found in regenerating growth away from the forest; and (4) **Scrub species** found in scrubland and regenerating growth but almost never in the forest.

Figure 4 shows the distribution of species observed at Lammasinghi among these four groups for the resident species (see table 1), for the winter visitors (including passage migrants) and for the summer visitors (see table 1 of Price 1979).

Edge + forest species (group 3) are likely to be able to exploit isolated trees and secondary growth, and would probably survive the loss of all continuous forest. This group includes all the commonest species at Lammasinghi (the Redwhiskered and Redvented bulbuls, White-eye, Tailor bird and Spotted dove). Scrub species (group 4) would benefit from the conversion of forest to secondary growth. Indeed there are four species of the coastal plain recorded once or twice at Lammasinghi (the Golden oriole, *Oriolus oriolus,* the Baybacked shrike, *Lanius vittatus,* the Indian robin, *Saxicoloides fulicata* and the Koel, *Eudynamys scolopacea*) and at least seven others not recorded (Price 1979) which have not been included in this analysis, and which may appear following further clearance. Finally there are species of pure arable land such as the Indian pipit, *Anthus novaeseelandiae,* and the Baya, *Ploceus phillipinus,* which have also not been included in the analysis. Of course none of the species in this group can be considered threatened.

Forest species (group 1) are particularly susceptible to forest loss, and forest + edge species (group 2) may also disappear. Thus between 11 and 41 of the resident species observed at Lammasinghi are dependent on forest, bet-

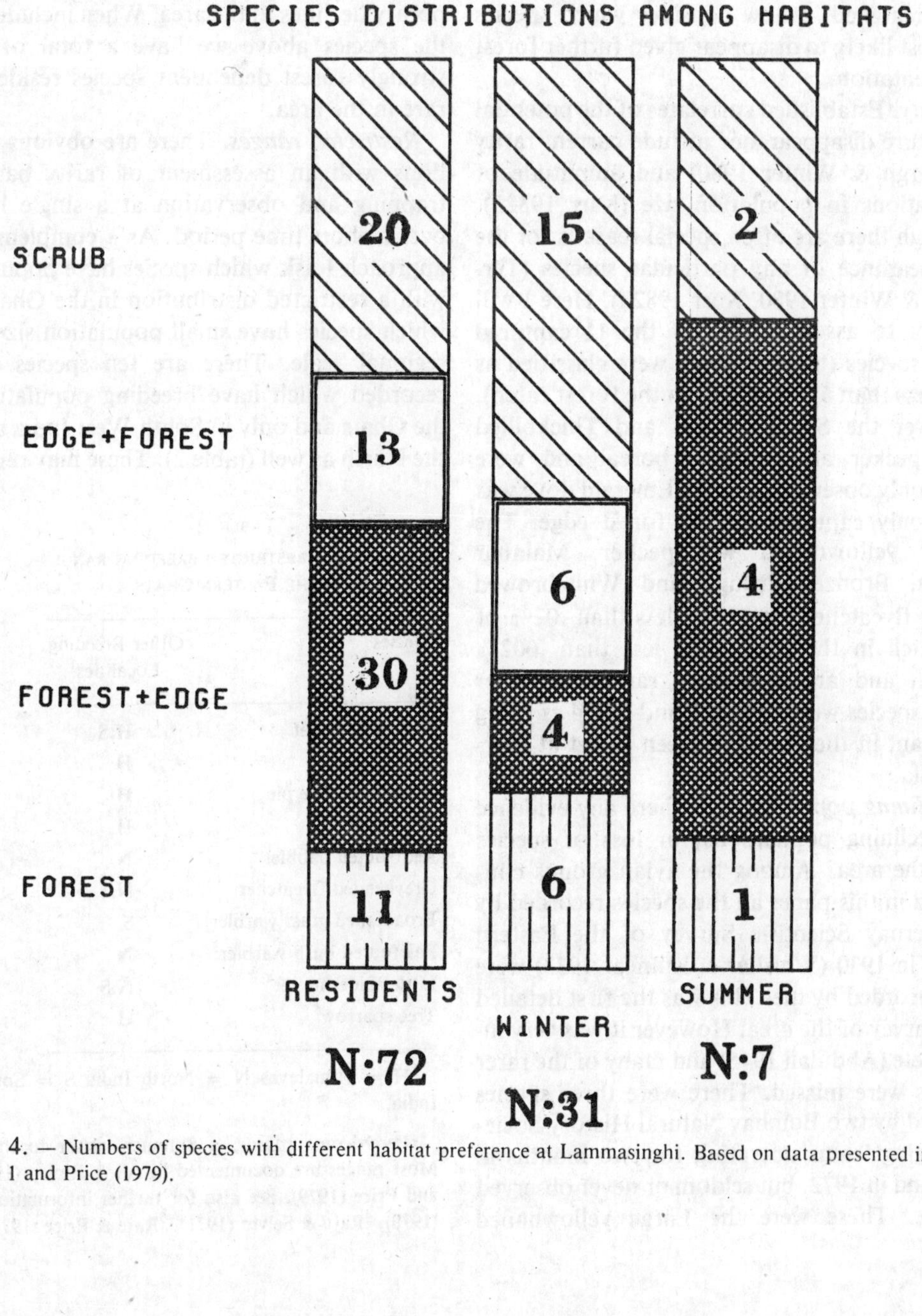

Fig. 4. — Numbers of species with different habitat preference at Lammasinghi. Based on data presented in table 1 and Price (1979).

ween 6 and 10 of the Winter visitors and between 1 and 5 of the Summer visitors (figure 4). Up to 50% of the species currently occurring at Lammasinghi are dependent on the forest. To a varying extent all species dependent on forest are threatened. I now consider which species are most likely to disappear given further forest fragmentation.

Rarity. Established correlates of the potential for future disappearance include current rarity (Terborgh & Winter 1980) and amplitude of fluctuations in population size (Karr 1982*b*), although there are often special reasons for the disappearance of any particular species (Terborgh & Winter 1980, Karr 1982*a*). Here I will attempt to assess rarity. Of the 11 captured forest species (table 1) seven were classified as rare (less than 5 individuals in the forest catch). However the Small minivet and Thickbilled flowerpecker are mainly arboreal and were commonly observed, and the Emerald dove was commonly captured on the forest edge. The Lesser yellownaped woodpecker, Malabar trogon, Bronzed drongo and Whitebrowed fantail flycatcher comprised less than .02% of the catch in the forest and less than .002% overall, and are considered rare. The other forest species were common and noted as being abundant in the semi-evergreen forest at Merripakala.

Declining populations. Is there any evidence for declining populations, or loss of species from the area? Among the avian groups considered in this paper all the species recorded by the Vernay Scientific Survey of the Eastern Ghats in 1930 (Whistler & Kinnear 1933) were also recorded by me. This was the first detailed bird survey of the area. However it was very incomplete (Abdulali 1945) and many of the rarer species were missed. There were three species trapped by two Bombay Natural History Society ringing teams operating for two months in 1971 and in 1972, but seldom or never observed by me. These were the Large yellownaped woodpecker, *Picus flavinucha* (not trapped by me), Jerdon's chloropsis, *(Chloropsis cochinchinensis* (not trapped or observed) and the Little spiderhunter (one trapped). It is not possible to say if these represent permanent or temporary declines in the area. When included with the species above we have a total of seven strongly forest dependent species resident but rare in the area.

Restricted ranges. There are obvious limitations with an assessment of rarity based on trapping and observation at a single locality over a short time period. As a complementary approach I ask which species have populations with a restricted distribution in the Ghats, i.e. which species have small population sizes on a regional scale. There are ten species so far recorded which have breeding populations in the Ghats and only in South West India and/or the North as well (table 2). These may represent

TABLE 2

SPECIES WITH RESTRICTED BREEDING RANGES IN THE EASTERN GHATS.

Species	Other Breeding Localities[1]
Speckled piculet	H,S
Grey drongo	H
Himalayan tree pie	H
Rosy minivet[2]	H
Redfronted babbler	N
Greyheaded flycatcher	N,S
Broadtailed grass warbler[3]	S
Palefooted bush warbler[3]	N
Little spiderhunter[4]	N,S
Tree sparrow[5]	H

[1]H = Himalayas N = North India S = South West India.

[2]*Percrocotus roseus,* a Summer visitor to the Ghats. Most ranges are documented in Ali & Ripley (1969-1974) and Price (1979). See also for further information. [3]Price (1978), [4]Raju & Selvin (1971), [5]Raju & Price (1973).

relicts of formerly more extensive populations (Price 1979). Most of these species are common in the Ghats; seven are forest or forest + edge species. Two — the Pale-footed bush warbler, *Cettia pallidipes,* and the Broadtailed grass warbler, *Schoenicola platyura,* do not occur at Lammasinghi, being found on the wetter agricultural land. Only two species are apparently rare in the area: the Tree sparrow, *Passer montanus,* and the Broadtailed grass warbler, known only from a sight record of a single breeding pair (Price 1978). The Tree sparrow may now be extinct in the Ghats, for I was unable to locate it in November, 1983, in either of the two villages where it had been previously recorded (Price 1979).

Causes of population decline

Loss of habitat may be the ultimate cause of population decline, but the proximate cause must relate to a decreasing reproductive rate and/or increasing mortality. Considerations of factors affecting mortality can indicate why some species are becoming rare and how their population size could be increased.

Food limitation. My studies at Lammasinghi showed that the late dry season (February-April) was a time of critical food shortage for many species, and may have been the main factor in limiting their population sizes. Winter feeding strategies are reported in Price (1979). I note from that paper that (1) Insectivorous foliage gleaners concentrate on those trees retaining leaf; (2) The occasional fruiting tree is very important for several species and (3) Once the Cotton flower tree (*Bombax malabarica*) flowers (from early March onwards) it is a very important food source (as is Eucalyptus which is being planted in localised areas). I recorded 17 species feeding on *Bombax* flowers, with representatives from all four groups in Table 1. All have been noted as feeding at this tree species by Ali (1932). Thus the selective retention of a) evergreen trees, b) fruiting trees and c) flowering trees in cut over areas would greatly enhance the overwinter survival of many species, and should therefore be encouraged. In fact mangoes and fig trees are often selectively retained by villagers, and these form the main evergreen trees in the area. *Ficus benghalensis* is an important dry season fruiting tree. Thus cutting over need not have as great an effect as it might, but in many areas there is now clear felling.

Other causes of mortality. The absence of the Peafowl (*Pavo cristatus*) from Lammasinghi is certainly attributable to shooting, the species is reasonably common around Merripakala where the bow and arrow is still the most lethal weapon.

One for one replacements by congeneric species commonly occur in association with a habitat change (e.g. Ward 1968), and this may be due to direct interspecific competition. House sparrows and Tree sparrows bred side by side in thatched roofs at Lammasinghi but the larger House sparrow was dominant over the tree sparrow when feeding (*personal observations*), and probably also when competing for nest sites. It seems likely that the presence of House sparrows is the main reason for the probable disappearance of the Tree sparrow in the Ghats.

Plantations

Teak. Mature teak plantations are no substitute for forest. The tree has a prolonged leafless period, during which arboreal species must virtually disappear. In contrast I observed over 20 species in natural forest in the late dry season feeding at trees which retained some leaf and/or were in fruit, and there were many others at the *Bombax* trees. The presence of a natural understory in some plantations improves the area for the ten or so species which regularly exploit this habitat, but the overall conclusion must be that teak is poor for birds.

Coffee. Coffee, which is usually grown beneath a selectively logged forest, and is evergreen is not expected to be as detrimental to birds, particularly if attention is paid to the selectivity of the logging (see above), and pesticides are not extravagantly applied. Wong (1984) examined the effect of selective logging in Malaysia on understory birds. She showed that after 25 years of regeneration most of the species in nearby virgin forest were also present in the logged forest, but population sizes were lower. A well tended coffee plantation would probably prevent complete recovery of all species.

DISCUSSION

As forest cover is lost, bird species are likely to disappear from the area, but only a few are rare enough to expect their imminent disappearance, and of these rare species most are widespread over a large area of India (Ali & Ripley 1968-1974). Among known rare species with restricted ranges the Tree sparrow may be extinct and the Broadtailed grass warbler may be very rare. The status of these species can hardly be blamed on forest disappearance. However it should be noted first, that some avian groups, for example the birds of prey and the owls, have not been studied in the Ghats, or considered in this paper. Species in these groups may be especially prone to extinction (Terborgh & Winter 1980). Second, some rare breeding species have probably still to be discovered in the Ghats. For example, I observed a pair of Brown flycatchers, *Musciciapa. latirostris,* displaying throughout April 1977, but I was unable to prove breeding (Price 1979).

At present it is undoubtedly the loss of habitat *per se* that is the single most serious impact of human development in the Eastern Ghats. Moist semi-evergreen forest is now rare. I do not wish to dwell on general problems associated with such forest destruction (see for example Whitmore 1980, Anon 1980, Myers 1980). The reader is also referred to studies from Malaysia (Johns 1983, Wong 1984) and the neotropics (Willis 1974, Leck 1979, Karr 1982*a,b,*) which have specifically investigated the effect of habitat destruction on birds.

From the point of view of conservation in the Eastern Ghats it is unfortunate that there are no special endemic species for which a clear case for a reserve could be made, for there are several outstanding areas of habitat which are at present only semi-protected, for example at Merripakala and Sapparlla. I visited Merripakala in December, 1983. Large areas of forest had been cleared since my previous visit in February, 1978. Nevertheless the area still contains abundant wildlife; for example, I observed or heard ten species of large mammals.

It would be desirable to have observations on other groups of animals and plants besides birds (Terborgh & Winter 1983, Lovejoy 1982). Birds do have a special advantage over other groups which makes them especially worth studying in that they are more widely appreciated by the general public, and people may be more concerned over potential extinctions. It is to be hoped that documentation of changes in bird species diversity may to some extent mirror changes in species diversity of other groups. More research in the area would clearly be very useful. The importance of further research is illustrated by the results of a recent ornithological expedition to the Eastern Ghats (B. Behler and K.S.R. Krishna Raju, *personal communication*). At a site 30 miles from Lammasinghi they found the Little Spiderhunter to be common. In earlier drafts of this paper I had stated that this species appeared to be particularly threatened, based on my results from Lammasinghi.

Research and well patrolled reserves may be wishful thinking, so I would like to conclude by reiterating that abundance and diversity of many species in secondary growth and plantations could be enhanced by the retention of adjacent true forest, and in particular selective retention of preferred trees. In the Eastern Ghats this includes evergreens and those trees that fruit and flower in the late dry season.

SUMMARY

I use the results from a year long mist netting and observational study at Lammasinghi in the Eastern Ghats to assess the affects on birds of continued forest clearance for agriculture and plantations. Analysis is restricted to those species which can be easily sampled by the mist netting technique. Population sizes of forest dwelling resident and migrant species are being reduced. However most of the resident forest species are either widely distributed or locally common, and do not appear to be threatened at present. Species diversity in cleared areas, particularly those close to forests, could be enhanced by the selective retention of favoured trees. To some extent this is practised by villagers, and such a policy should be encouraged, and if possible expanded to include forest plantations. Since the area is undergoing accelerated deforestation, there is a case for a well-patrolled reserve in the area.

ACKNOWLEDGEMENTS

I thank K.S.R. Krishna Raju, J.C. Daniel and S. Dillon Ripley for encouragement during and after the study, and B. Behler, A. Diamond, K.S.R. Krishna Raju, P. Grant, W. Newmark and M. Wong for commenting on the manuscript. The research was funded by the Leverhulme Trust Fund, with some additional support from the British Ornithologists' Union and the Smithsonian Institution. I thank the Smithsonian Institution for the financial support enabling me to attend this conference.

REFERENCES

ABDULALI, H. (1945): Birds of the Vizagapatnam District. *J. Bombay nat. Hist. Soc.* **45**: 333-347.

ALI, S. (1932): Flower birds and Bird Flowers of India. Ibid. **35**: 573-605.

________, & RIPLEY, S.D. (1968-1974): Handbook of the birds of India and Pakistan. Ten volumes. Oxford University Press. Anon. 1980. Research priorities in tropical biology. National Academy of Sciences. Washington, D.C.

CHAMPION, H.G. & SETH, S.K. (1968): A revised survey of the forest types of India. Delhi, Manager of Publications.

JOHNS, A. (1983): Wildlife can live with logging. *New Scientist* **99**: 206-209.

KARR, J.R. (1971): Structure of avian communities in selected Panama and Illinois habitats. *Ecol. Monogr.* 41: 207-233.

________ (1982*a*): Avian extinction on Barro Colorado island, Panama: a reassessment. *Amer. Nat.* **119**: 220-239.

________ (1982*b*): Population variability and extinction in the avifauna of a tropical land bridge island. *Ecology* **63**: 1975-1978.

LECK, C.F. (1979): Avian extinctions in an isolated tropical wet-forest preserve, Ecuador. *Auk* **96**: 343-352.

LOVEJOY, T.E. (1974): Bird diversity and abundance in Amazon forest communities. *Living Bird* **13**: 127-191.

________ (1982): Designing refugia for tomorrow. *In* Proc. Fifth Int. Symp. Assoc. for Tropical Biology. Columbia University Press.

MACARTHUR, R.H. (1964): Environmental factors affecting bird species diversity. *Amer. Nat.* **98**: 387-397.

________ & MACARTHUR, A.T. (1974): On the use of mist nets for population studies of birds. *Proc. Nat. Acad. Sci. U.S.A.* **71**: 3230-3233.

________ & WILSON, E.O. (1967): The theory of island biogeography. Princeton University Press, Princeton, N. J.

MYERS, N. (1980): Conversion of tropical moist forests. National Academy of Sciences. Washington, DC.

PEARSON, D. (1977): A pantropical comparison of bird community structure on six lowland rain forest sites. *Condor* **79**: 232-244.

PRICE, T.D. (1978): Some observations on the warblers of the upland perennial wetlands in the Eastern Ghats. *J. Bombay nat. Hist. Soc.* **75**: 488-490.

________ (1979): The seasonality and occurrence of

birds in the Eastern Ghats of Andhra Pradesh. Ibid **76**: 379-422.

PRICE, T.D. (1981): The ecology of the Greenish warbler *Phylloscopus trochiloides* in its Winter quarters. *Ibis* **123**: 131-144.

RAJU, K., KRISHNA, S.R. & PRICE, T.D. (1973): Tree sparrow, *Passer montanus* (L.) in the Eastern Ghats. *J. Bombay nat. Hist. Soc.* **70**: 557.

__________ & SELVIN, J.P. (1971): Little spiderhunter, *Arachnothera longirostris* (Latham) in the Eastern Ghats. ibid. **68**: 454.

SCHEMSKE, D.W. & BROKAW, N. (1981): Treefalls and the distribution of understory birds in a tropical forest. *Ecology* **62**: 938-945.

SIMBERLOFF, D.S. & ABELE, L.G. (1982): Refugia design and island biogeographic theory: effects of fragmentation. *Amer. Nat.* **120**: 41-50.

TERBORGH, J. (1977): Bird species diversity on an Andean elevational gradient. *Ecology* **58**: 1007-1019.

__________ & WINTER, B. (1980): Some causes of extinction. Pages 119-133 *in* M.E. Soulé and B.A. Wilcox, eds. Conservation Biology: an evolutionary-ecological perspective. Sinauer, Sunderland, Mass.

__________ (1983): A method for siting parks and reserves with special reference to Columbia and Ecuador. *Biol. Conserv.* **27**: 45-58.

VANDERMEER, J. (1981): Elementary mathematical ecology. Wiley and Sons, New York.

WARD, P. (1968): Origin of the avifauna of urban and suburban Singapore. *Ibis* **110**: 239-253.

WHISTLER, H. & KINNEAR, N.B. (1932-1939): The Vernay scientific survey of the Eastern Ghats. In 16 parts. *J. Bombay nat. Hist Soc.* **39**: 447-463.

WHITCOMBE, R.F., LYNCH, J.F., OPLER, P.A. & ROBBINS, C.S. (1976): Island biogeography and conservation: strategy and limitations, a reply. *Science* **193**: 1030-1032.

WHITMORE, T.C. (1980). The conservation of tropical rain forest. Pages 303-318 *in* M.E. Soulé and B.A. Wilcox, eds. Conservation Biology: an evolutionary-ecological perspective. Sinauer, Sunderland, Mass.

WILLIS, E.O. (1974): Populations and local extinctions of birds on Barro Colorado Island, Panama. *Ecol. Monogr.* **44**: 153-169.

WONG, M. (1984): Understory birds as indicators of regeneration in a patch of selectively logged West Malaysian rain forest. *In* A.W. Diamond & T.E. Lovejoy (eds.) I.C.B.P. Technical Pub. (*In press*).

Agastyamalai proposal for a Biosphere Reserve in the Western Ghats

RAUF ALI[1]

SUMMARY

The feasibility of the forests centred around Agastyamalai peak (8°36'N, 77°15'E) being converted into a major biosphere reserve is examined. Problems and research potential are briefly outlined. It is concluded that in terms of uniqueness, number of endemics, endangered species, representativeness of floral and faunal types, and ease of protection, Agastyamalai is an ideal choice for a biosphere reserve, with a potential area of 2000 km^2.

INTRODUCTION

The peak, Agastyamalai, is today of great religious significance. Rising to an altitude of 1869 metres (at 8°36'N, 77°15'E) it is the tallest peak in the southern portion of the Western Ghats. On its slopes, and in the adjoining areas in Tirunelveli and Kanyakumari districts of Tamil Nadu, and Quilon and Trivandrum districts of Kerala, lie some of the most diverse, and also the most unknown ecosystems in peninsular India.

The area is bounded by 8°15'-9°N and 77°-77°33'E, roughly lying diagonally across the rectangle described. It is roughly elliptic in shape being roughly 100 km long along one axis, and 40 km long along the other. The altitude in the area changes from sea level to 1869 metres and contains several different habitat types covering the entire spectrum, from scrub jungle to wet evergreen forest (which incidentally is the only non-dipterocarp rainforest in the Western Ghats) with rainfall also varying from 500 mm in the dry plains of Tirunelveli District to over 4000 mm on the crestline of the Western Ghats. Special habitat types such as euphorbiaceous scrub as a consequence of shifting cultivation, and fire subclimaxes are also represented. A very large number of mammal and bird species have been recorded from here, and will be listed in the appropriate place.

[1]Dept. of Biology, Faculty of Science, Mahidol University, Rama VI Rd., Bangkok 10400, Thailand

ADMINISTRATIVE AND GEOGRAPHIC BOUNDARIES

A compact area was identified, beginning south of the Shencottah gap (9° N) and extending to where the Western Ghats end at Aramboly just 20 km north of Cape Camorin.

Detailed information could not be gathered on all the areas within the proposed Biosphere reserve. Area descriptions of each of the Reserved Forests and sanctuaries listed is given below. Exact area calculations have not been made separately for each area, but the total area is 3100 km^2, of which over 300 km^2 is rainforest.

PULIYARAM RF COURTALAM RESERVE FOREST (approx. 70 km^2)

This is mainly a moist-deciduous forest in its lower reaches and wet-evergreen higher up, rising abruptly to 1500 metres on the state boundary. A very large portion of Puliyaram RF has been converted to teak plantations. There are few small cardamom and coffee estates within Courtalam RF, mainly on land leased from the forest department. Sambar deer have been sighted in the RF area, as well as liontailed macaques. Elephant droppings have also been seen in the area.

Courtalam has a major tourist centre, based on its waterfalls, under which visitors come to bathe. The importance of preserving the catchment that services these falls, as well as ensuring that the water supply is clean, is extremely important. It is proposed that the 500 m contour be taken as the boundary of the core area, with special emphasis on studying the impact of the cardamom plantations on the ecosystem. Any decision about the continuation of cardamom leases, would obviously follow a review of the extent to which such leases affect biological diversity as a whole, in the area.

MUNDANTHURAI WILDLIFE SANCTUARY (568 km^2)

This was formed by merging the Papanasam RF and the Singampatti ex-Zamin Forest. By itself, this area is probably the most diverse in terms of habitats in the entire biosphere reserve.

To the north of the sanctuary, in the Sivasailam area, a small population of the highly endangered Grizzled Giant Squirrel (*Ratufa macroura*) has been recorded. In the last few years, this population seems to have become extinct (Johnson, *pers. comm.*).

The upper reaches of the sanctuary, together with the adjoining areas of Kalakad sanctuary, contain the largest single population of the lion-tailed macaque now known. An initial estimate of 90-210 (Green and Minkowski 1977) is almost certainly an underestimate, in the light of further research done there. In the interior, the population is fairly inaccessible to humans, and is relatively secure.

The most disturbed part of the sanctuary is the Mundanthurai plateau, bounded approximately by the Thambraparni and Servalar rivers, an area of approximately 60 km^2. There are three existing hydel and irrigation projects—the Upper Thambraparni, the Papanasam Lower Dam, and the Manimuthar. A fourth is under construction: the Servalar project.

A consequence of these hydel projects is the presence of human settlements at the dam sites. There is considerable grazing pressure, and pressure for firewood, in the absence of any initiative by the Electricity Board. Enforcement has not been successful. The construction of the hydel projects have caused the forest type below them to deteriorate from moist to dry deciduous. The reason for this is not entirely clear, but a preliminary investigation appears to indicate that a change in soil hydrology is the most likely explanation.

There have also been efforts to resettle the local tribal population—Kanis—on the plateau. However, their needs have not been adequately considered. A few pockets exist which still contain tribal settlements in their original condition, but the practice of shifting cultivation has now been banned. A few pockets of cardamom cultivaton also exist, with the leases to expire within the next 5 years.

There are two major enclaves within the sanctuary—one is the Kattalamalai estate, on the fringes of the rain forest, and the other is Sandpit farm. Both constitute fairly major disturbances to the movements of the larger animals.

Johnson (1978) has clarified the different vegetation types within the sanctuary as follows: 1. Thorn scrub; 2. Deciduous forest; 3. Mixed deciduous forest; 4. Moist deciduous forest; 5. Semi evergreen; 6. Tropical wet evergreen; 7. Euphorbiaceous scrub.

These represent a rainfall gradient. The euphorbiaceous scrub is a consequence of the shifting cultivation. Many rare and endangered plant species occur in this area. These are documented under Kalakad sanctuary.

Further to the south, a large tea estate run by

the Bombay Burmah Trading Corporation extends from about 750 to 1350 m. and occupies roughly 35 km^2. However, BBTC has in general been extremely effective in preserving animal populations around the estate, in spite of the disturbance caused by fellings and expansion. Recently the Company agreed to preserve a belt of forest to provide a corridor between two patches of evergreen forest. The corridor was meant mainly to ensure that the population of liontailed macaques was not fragmented, but serves as a mechanism for ensuring geneflow for other rainforest species as well. Another corridor between the BBTC Manimuthar estate and Hope Lake (Upper Thambraparni dam) also connects the rainforest patches, and these are ideally suited for monitoring species dispersal patterns.

In summary, the Mundanthurai plateau provides a perfect natural laboratory to study most man-nature interactions, and work out methods of ensuring that man and nature can live in harmony. The area's ease of access makes scientific study here extremely feasible.

This area contains over 30 mammal species and over 130 bird species. These include 5 primate species which are abundant: the common langur, the Nilgiri langur, the bonnet macaque, the liontailed macaque and the slender loris. Since the langurs only have a small area of partial sympatry, a situation similar to that of the macaques and these areas of partial sympatry correspond to shifts in vegetation type, the sensitivity of primates to changes in plant diversity is indicated here. Other mammals of the area are the elephant, spotted deer, sambar, mouse deer, wild pig, common mongoose, ruddy mongoose, gaur and the otter. Tigers are rare whereas both leopard and dhole are frequently seen on the Mundanthurai plateau.

KALAKAD WILDLIFE SANCTUARY (223 km^2)

This is one of the newest and still the most inaccessible of sanctuaries in peninsular India. Apart from 5 enclosures: Kuliraati estate (31 ha), the Vanaramalai mutt tea and cardamom estates (59.7 ha), which are currently on lease, Narakadu estate (14.9 ha), Agailandampillai (12 ha) and 16 blocks leased to cardamom growers at Sengaltheri (98.36 ha), there is no human habitation inside the sanctuary.

Vegetation zones in this portion are as varied as in Mundanthurai sanctuary. Ramanathan (1978) recognises 6 basic forest types.

1. 1A/C4. Tropical West Coast evergreen.

This includes the practically pure stands of *Podocarpus* in patches near the Sengaltheri Rest House, in the heart of Kalakad sanctuary. Almost 200 km^2 of this rainforest patch and that of adjoining portions of Mundanthurai and Virapuli is virgin—making it a natural laboratory of unique biological significance.

2. 2A/C3 Tirunelveli Semi-evergeen

3. 3B/C2 Southern mixed deciduous

4. 5/A Dry Teak

5. 5A/C3 Southern Dry mixed deciduous

Within this type a variety of stunted teak occurs naturally. This does not grow higher than 7 metres.

6. 8/E1 Ochlandra reed brakes

These are extensive patches of reeds, consisting of *Ochlandra travancorica, O. rheedii* and *O. brandisii,* which occur within the wet evergreen forest.

Apart from these primary vegetation types, several seral stages exist. In the vicinty of Sengaltheri there are large patches of fire subclimax—savannah with a very low tree density. The main grass is *Cymbopogon* sp., and the tree species found within this are *Syzygium cumini, Buchannia lanzan, Careya arborea, Terminalia chebula* and *Semecarpus anacardium*. Adjoining these patches rich secondary succession exists, where the trees mentioned above form the top canopy. Currently, this successional growth is all in the sapling stage. The hill tops represent yet another climax type, with stunted vegetation and very diverse grassland. A third type is *Phoenix* scrub, patchily distributed all over the sanctuary.

A variety of gaur different from those seen elsewhere has been seen often here. These pale to chestnut in the middle of the body. Their rump and hind quarters are buff. In the lower regions of the sanctuary, a brown morph of the Nilgiri Langur is occasionally seen and it has been speculated that this aberrant coat colouring may actually be of greater survival advantage in the light-coloured foliage at lower elevations (Oates, *pers. comm.*).

Kalakad, with the adjoining rainforest areas contains the largest single known population of liontailed macaques, as mentioned earlier. There are also an estimated 15,000 Nilgiri langurs in the area (Oates 1979). Bonnet macaques live in the dry evergreen forest here, and their social structure is dramatically different from the lowland populations in the same area (R. Ali, 1981).

At the southern part of the sanctuary, the crestline of Thiruvannamalai forms the boundary with Mahendragiri RF. There is a population of about 40 Nilgiri Tahr here. The access to the peak involves going through some excellent patches of moist-deciduous forest.

MAHENDRAGIRI AND ASHAMBU RFs.

These, with smaller adjoining Reserved Forests, such as Poigaimalai, Tadakamalai and Velimalai lie in Kanyakumari district. These have very recently been declared reserved forests, and the rights of settlers in the area have not been settled yet, with over 100 cases of encroachment pending in the High Court, and some in the Supreme Court. Due to these problems, large parts of these areas may have to be excluded from the Biosphere Reserve—or alternatively treated as a special manipulation zone with intensive monitoring of human impacts.

The forest is evergreen on the upper stretches, largely interspersed with scrub vegetation. *Macaca radiata diluta* was described with the type specimen from Boothapandi, which is an enclave within the reserve forest.

POIGAIMALAI RF

This lies on the southern edge of Ashambu RF, and good vegetation still exists in patches. Southwest of this is Velimalai RF, which has been islanded. Given adequate protection this area would be an ideal site for biogeographic studies on rates of colonization by different plant and animal taxa.

VIRAPULI RF (*c.* 150 km^2)

Virapuli adjoins Mundanthurai sanctuary on the BBTC tea estate to the north east, and Kalakad sanctuary to the north. The RF has a high-altitude section within which the Kodayar dam has been built. While severely disturbed near the dam site, the upper reaches still contain about 40 km^2 of dense wet evergreen forest, and extensive reed brakes. The ground here tends to be swampy over an extensive area, which was not found in other parts of the proposed biosphere reserve. Liontailed macaques are found in this area, with several relatively inaccessible valleys still being relatively undisturbed.

The Muthukuzhi plateau, towards the southeast of the reserve forest, contains extensive grassland—sholla ecosystems, with fragmented forest patches ideally suited for studies on biological diversity. The lower reaches of the Virapuli RF have been largely fragmented by rubber plantations. Lower Kodayar Lake (Pechiparai) makes a natural boundary for the Biosphere Reserve in this area.

KALAMALAI RF

North of Pechiparai Lake, Kalamalai RF still contains some very good patches of moist-deciduous forest. The disturbance is much heavier on the Kerala side, and a number of encroachments exist on this side.

NEYYAR SANCTUARY

The area around Neyyar Dam is very heavily disturbed, though several animal species, such as elephant, are seen here. The slopes of Agastyamalai, on the Kerala side, are lush and undisturbed, again consisting of wet evergreen forest.

YERUR AND KOLATHUPUZHA RFS.

These start from Ponmudi and extend north to Tenmalai. There is very variable vegetation in this area, changing from moist-deciduous to wet evergreen. The inner valleys are still undisturbed, whereas the forest on the western side has been heavily disturbed, largely due to selection felling with 265 ha currently being selectionfelled about 2 km north of the KIP boundary. Ponmudi would be the boundary of the Biosphere reserve at this end.

Elephants were seen in this area. Primates densities are much lower than expected, and a little protection would certainly see a major comeback of the Nilgiri langur in this area, given the tremendously high populations on the eastern slopes.

The Northern boundary of Kolathupuzha RF, specially along the Kolathupuzha-Arayankavu road, has been very heavily encroached. Continuity with the northern parts of the RF, north of this road, is tenuous at best, and this area is suited for ecological restoration, to provide the links with forests further north.

ENDANGERED PLANTS

Pure stands of *Bentinckia codapanna* have been seen at Upper Kodayar, and almost pure stands of *Podocarpus latifolia* near Sengaltheri. Other threatened plants in the area include *Apama barberi, Dioscorea wightii, Gluta travancorica* (endemic), *Entada pursaetha, Gnetum ula, Piper barberi* and *Pterospermum obtusifolium* (Ramanathan, 1978).

PROBLEMS AND THREATS IN THE REGION

River Valley Projects. These, as appears to be the case in all other important forest reserves, are the major threat to the environment. The consequences of hydel projects have been well documented elsewhere, and are beyond the scope of this report. A listing of the dams being built or proposed, and a statement of their immediate impact is given.

i) *Servalar Hydel Project*: This is under construction. A detailed discussion of the current problems being experienced there is given separately (Appendix 1). In the long run, with all the waters from the Upper Thambraparni being diverted through a tunnel to Servalar, the river course of the Thambraparni will dry up. This will result in the destruction of the finest existing riverine forest on the Mundanthurai Plateau and lead to far-reaching consequence as far as animal distribution patterns within the whole area are concerned.

ii) *Injikuli Hydel Project*: Proposed on the Thambraparni above the Upper Dam, this will open up areas which are currently inaccessible, and lead to the destruction of large patches of evergreen forest under investigation at the moment.

iii) *The Upper Manimuthar Hydel Project*: This is an ambitious scheme to construct and link three dams, and will effectively destroy the heartland of the virgin rainforest existing in these hills. It will also effectively destory the corridor between the rainforests on the Kalakad side with those on the Papanasam side. Following representations by conservation organizations such as Bombay Natural History Society and World Wildlife Fund, an enlightened decision to shelve the project has been taken, pending more research. This research has unfortunately not been forthcoming. In any case, this area is ecologically as sensitive and deserving of protection as Silent Valley; for instance, there are at least 23 endangered plant species in the area (Daniel, *pers. comm.*) and efforts should continue to ensure that the project is finally abandoned.

iv) *Pachayar Dam*, a dam on the Pachayar river, in Kalakad sanctuary. This will destory the lowland vegetation near Kalakad, and again open up access to areas which are difficult to reach right now.

v) *Kodamadi Dam*, is a small dam below Tiruvannamalai. Some scrub and dry deciduous forest will be submerged. A detailed environmental assessment, at least, is necessay.

It must be noted that most patches of water that are impounded here develop blooms of *Microcystis* spp. algae. This algae releases toxic substances which are toxic to fish, animals and potentially to humans as well. There has been *no* research conducted on this aspect in this country.

vi) *The Kallada Irrigation Project* under construction in the Kolathupuzha RF, is another prime example of ecologically thoughtless planning, with the observed damage far more than necessary.

Roads. A proposed highway from Tirunelveli to Trivandrum goes through Mundanthurai, across the Agastyamalai slopes to Trivandrum. The new route will be approximately 135 km long (estimated from map distances) as opposed to the current 160 km—a saving in distance that is offset by steep ghat sections over almost 40 km.

This road will open up one of the most inaccessible areas of the sanctuary—the Agastyamalai slopes, and protection problems are likely to increase tremendously—apart from the habitat disturbance that is bound to occur.

Encroachments. There are over 100 encroachments in the Ashambu and Mahendragiri areas. Most of these are pending court settlement at the moment. There are possibly more in the Kerala area, near Kolathupuzha and Tenmalai but accurate figures are not available.

Private Enclaves. A farm on the Mundanthurai plateau owned by influential local figures provides a perfect example of the harm that enclaves within sanctuaries do. A bridge was constructed to provide access to this farm in the guise of benefitting pilgrims to the Sorimuthaianar temple, and has destroyed one of the most scenic areas along the Thambraparni. There are now proposals for tourist development in this area, sponsored by the Banatheertham Improvement Trust.

Another private enclave at Kuliraati in Kalakad creates a major disturbance in the middle of the evergreen forest, with the understorey recently having been removed and converted to citrus trees. The evidence of soil erosion can be seen in the streams in the area, and there are moves to log the timber standing on this 73 acre enclave—moves that are currently being resisted by the forest department.

Rubber Plantations. There has been talk of expanding the Government Rubber Plantations at Nagercoil. This replaces rainforest with ecologically valueless rubber—a species in which only a few insectivorous bird species are found, compared to the rich bird diversity in adjoining natural forest.

RESEARCH DONE AND FUTURE OPPORTUNITIES

The first systematic mammal research work done in this area was a study on liontailed macaques between 1973 and 1975. Ecological results from this study are given in Green and Minkowski (1975). This was followed by a study of Nilgiri Langurs (e.g. Oates, 1979; *pers. comm.*). This was subsequently followed by a study on the bonnet macaque (R. Ali, 1981). During this period, between 1973 and 1978, monitoring of two groups of liontailed macaques was done, and is at present being continued by the Tamilnadu Forest Department. These data have however not been collated yet. Recently the Zoological Survey of India has also initiated some studies on the common langur in this area.

Botanically, the area is very poorly known. Apart from surveys done by Bourdillon in the last century, the only recent work is that of A.N. Henry of the Botanical Survey of India. A rough idea of the floral diversity of even lowland dry deciduous forest can be given by the fact that a plant enumeration of a 15 ha patch near Mundanthurai gave over 250 species of trees, shrubs and climbers over 3 metres in height (R. Ali, 1981).

The scope for future research is limitless. A major population study of the different primates in the region and the effects of various disturbances on their distribution could well be done here, and this fits very neatly with the goals of the Biosphere Reserve programme. A similar study on predator-prey interactions would also be valuable.

Since there are many habitat islands of various types, biogeographic studies on colonization rates and extinction rates could also be carried out here with ease. The long term ecological effects of the conversion of different forest types into plantations is another research possibility. These would supplement routine monitoring operations.

IMMEDIATE RECOMMENDATIONS

Before the Biosphere Reserve is established a timelag of two to three years is bound to occur. To cover this timelag, the following steps are recommended for immediate implementation.

1. Upgrading all the Reserved Forests and sanctuaries in the area to National Parks. Provisional boundaries to be contained, without regard to zonation, which can be done by the concerned DFOs.

2. Shelving all projects proposed within the Biosphere Reserve area pending a detailed review of their environmental impact, and the preparation of an interim management plan.

3. Posting of extra protective staff to 'sensitive areas such as the Mundanthurai Plateau, Mahendragiri and Tenmalai.

4. Beginning of acquisition proceedings for acquiring land holdings in ecologically sensitive areas, or where it is felt that they are likely to cause adverse consequence. The question of renewal of leases within the area can be taken up during the preparation of the final management plan after monitoring to see what type of adverse consequences ensue from the operation of such leases, and the extent to which they can be mitigated.

ACKNOWLEDGEMENTS

The field work on which this study is based was funded through the Salim Ali Nature Conservation Fund. I was a research associate in the School of Biological Sciences, Madurai Kamaraj University during this period, and thank Professor S. Krishnaswamy for permitting me to carry out the survey. Mr G. Narayanaraj helped with the field work.

I would like to thank the Chief Conservator of Forests, Tamil Nadu, for permission to do the work. Without Mr J.M. Johnson's help and encouragement, the preparation of this report would not have been possible. The list of forest officers who assisted is too lengthy to put down here, but I would like to acknowledge my indebtedness to them.

Last but not least — to my colleagues at the Indian Institute of Science, especially Dr Niranjan Joshi and Dr S. Narendra Prasad — whose presence provided the environment for preparing this report.

REFERENCES

ALI, R. (1981): The ecology and social behaviour of the Agastyamalai Bonnet Macaque. Ph.D. Thesis, University of Bristol.

GREEN, S. & MINKOWSKI, K. (1977): The Liontailed Macaque and its South Indian Rain Forest habitat. In 'Primate Conservation' (G.H. Bourne and Prince Rainier, eds.). Academic Press, N.Y.

JOHNSON, J.M. (1978): Management plan for the Mundanthurai Wildlife Sanctuary. Government of Tamil Nadu, Forest Department.

OATES, J.F. (1979): Comments on the geographical distribution and status of the South Indian Black Leaf Monkey (*Presbytis johnii*). *Mammalia* **43**: 485-493.

RAMANATHAN, S. (1978): Management plan for the Kalakad Wildlife Sanctuary, Government of Tamil Nadu, Forest Department.

Appendix

SERVALAR HYDEL PROJECT

Construction was resumed on the Servalar Hydel Project in 1978, after being suspended for over two years because of lack of funds. During this period, Forest Department efforts to get the project shelved were unsuccesful, largely because support was not forthcoming from any other organization.

The Servalar is a tributary of the Thambraparni. The idea is to divert the water from the Upper Thambraparni Dam, which is about 5 km upstream from the confluence of the Servalar and Thambraparni, through an underground tunnel into the Servalar Dam. There will be about 20 Mw of electricity generated.

Though comparatively small in area, the Servalar Project will submerge more than a 5 sq. km length of prime riverine deciduous forest. Also, the riverine forest on the Thambraparni is expected to dry up because of the stoppage of water along the original river course. It is obvious that these two factors together are going to affect the movement of animals on the Mundanthurai plateau very adversely.

There are currently 4,000 people working at the project site. They have brought in 500 cattle with them, despite it being illegal to graze cattle within the reserve forest area. The 1976 plantations in the area have been a failure due to these cattle, and soils within a radius of over 2 km from the project site have been churned up due to excessive grazing and cattle use. Signs of extensive erosion can already be seen.

These 4,000 people get all their firewood from the forest. The protective staff for Servalar consists of 5 foresters, 11 guards and 4 watchers. Due to inadequate staff strength and the extreme hostility of the project staff to the forest department, enforcement is not possible, and no cases were booked in 1980-81. (It may be noted that in August 1980 a group of Electiricity Board employees led by a senior engineer attacked Forest Department staff at Papanasam. No action was taken against this individual, leading to a total demoralization of the Forest staff.)

There is also a large domestic dog population, with one local estimate placing the number of dogs around 200. These are not properly fed, and currently obtain most of their food by pack-hunting in the forest.

There is considerable distillation of arrack in the area, which is also causing major damage to the forest. There are at least 7 distillation units, with the major ones being at Thailathoda and Netaluvodai. The police are aware of these but have refused to take any action. Dynamite fishing is also prevalent. Dead fish have been seen floating on the river on several occasions. The use of dynamite in the area has also resulted in the movement upwards in the hills of both elephant and wild boar, where they are causing considerable damage to cardamom plantations. This phenomenon is very recent.

A good example of faulty planning is the location of the workers' camp. This could have been within the submergible area to minimise environmental damage.

Vehicular movement is now permitted at night, and this has resulted in major changes in the behaviour of the animal populations, especially the nocturnal ones. The populations of Blacknaped Hare, Nilgiri Langur, and Sambar Deer have declined noticeably.

Areas such as this would need special protective measures in the proposed Biosphere reserve.

LIQUID FUEL TESTING FACILITY

The Indian Space Research Organization (ISRO) began the construction of a liquid fuel testing facility in the Mahendragiri Reserved Forest, about 3 km southwest of Panagudi town and 20 km north of Nagercoil, in April 1982. By January 1983 only the approach roads had been built.

There will be one test approximately every six weeks over a period of three years. Each test involves burning 33 tonnes of a highly carcinogenic amine, UDMH (unsymmetrical di-methyl hydrazine). High levels of noise and air pollution are expected, and contamination of the water table cannot be ruled out, according to reliable sources.

An area of 1 km radius around the test site has already been clearfelled. This was good dry deciduous forest, one of the best patches existing in the proposed Biosphere reserve area. A 3 km zone around the test site constitutes the safety zone, and this is expected to receive high levels of chemical pollutants. This zone includes excellent patches of moist deciouous and wet evergreen forest.

A proper ecological survey of the area was not carried out, and we have been unable to find a single trained ecologist who has visited the site, in spite of ISRO's contention that an environmental impact assessment was done. At least three endangered species are known to occur within the safety zone: the liontailed macaque, the Nilgiri Tahr, and an endemic snake, *Uropeltis myhendrae.*

Objections raised by the forest department were overruled, with the answers being given in reply being farcical. An example: 'There would be a problem of water pollution'. Reply: 'There would be a problem of pollution wherever we go.' ISRO in spite of having done an impact assessment, has yet to produce a species inventory for the affected area, and actually claims that there are no animals in the area. The calculations made by them of noise levels at various sites reveal that the formulas used were straight out of a high school textbook, and no possible effect of the terrain on noise levels was considered. There has also been no study of the effect of the pollution on the animal populations in the area.

The Dept. of Environment has refused to get involved in the issue. Representations to them have merely brought forth the response that an official committee has cleared the project.

The chief factor in selecting this site appears to be its proximity to the Vikram Sarabhai Space Centre in Trivandrum. An assumption made in the selection of the site was that selecting a site in hilly terrain would save on the cost of a gantry. The value of the forest already clearfelled probably exceeds this. It may still be possible to persuade the Government to shift the site.

Eco-Development as a solution for India's environmental problems

(*With one plate*)

M.A. RASHID I.F.S. (Retd)
Ex-Chief Conservator of Forests, Wildlife, Gujarat State

SUMMARY

As a rapidly developing country, India today is beset with a host of environmental problems. It is, also, an unfortunate fact that our spectacular progress in the field of science and technology has become synonymous with a steady pollution and degradation of our natural environment due to indiscriminate and injudicious use of our limited natural resources, thereby creating serious ecological imbalances which can ultimately jeopardise our very survival on this planet. In a desparate attempt to satisfy the ever-increasing demands for goods and services of our burgeoning population, which now doubles almost every 25 years, we persistently indulge in the suicidal folly of indiscriminately cutting down our natural forests and denuding our vulnerable hill slopes in the interest of agriculture, irrigation, power generation, mining, urbanisation and procuring of raw materials to feed our mushrooming industries, without giving a second thought to the disastrous repercussions such large scale deforestation has on the climate, on the fertile top soil and the hydrological cycle which together constitute the very life blood of our agriculture, and on the tribals and the wildlife whose home and habitat the forests represent. The ravages of disforestation are further compounded by the subsequent scourges of forest fires and over-grazing, recurring floods and droughts, the continuing pollution of our rivers and sea coasts through the discharge of industrial effluents and raw sewage from towns and cities, through the increasing use of pesticides and insecticides by the agricultural sector which takes its own insidious toll of the insect and bird life in the countryside, and last, though by no means the least, through poisoning of the very air we breathe by the carcinogenous fumes ceaselessly belching forth from factory chimneys and automobile exhausts which have transformed our major cities into veritable gas chambers. What a heavy price, indeed, to pay for the ephemeral trappings of the so-called civilization of this ultra-modern atomic age!

Are we then ultimately destined to become the victims of our own technological advancement? Is there no escape from the impending self-engineered doom we are precipitately heading for? Our only hope of deliverance lies in a realisation, even at this belated stage, of the basic fact that this planet earth and its bounties belong to all living creatures inhabiting it and not to man alone. Man must understand and respect nature's law of equilibrium and learn to live in perfect harmony with his natural environment and with other living creatures who share the earth with him, without disturbing nature's delicate balance. In fact, by virtue of his superior intellect and the power of reasoning that nature has endowed him with, Man must adopt a mode of life and abide by a code of conduct which will ensure not only a good quality of life for himself but a mutually beneficial relationship with other living creatures as well. His new motto should be "Development without Destruction". In other words, his salvation lies in "ECO-DEVELOPMENT".

The author particularly emphasises the vital role which big industrial houses dependent on natural raw material resources or causing serious pollution hazards affecting the local community can play in this context by providing the finances essential for the implementation of eco-development projects. They can thus make at least some amends for the environmental degradation which has resulted from their industrial exploitation of the areas in which they operate. In this way, they would not only be doing a social service to the community but would also themselves be benefited by such involvement since expenditure on such projects, which are a form of rural

Above: A roadside plantation under Gujarat Social Forestry Programme
Below: Canal bank plantation under Gujarat Social Forestry Programme
(*Photos*: Gujarat Forest Department)

development activity, would render them eligible for income tax relief. A modest beginning in this direction has already been made in Gujarat and Maharashtra by the enlightened house of Tatas which has always played a pioneering role in industrial innovations. If other business houses follow suit, this could usher in a healthy trend which would bring about a revolution in the field of nature conservation in this country.

A. THE GENESIS OF INDIA'S ENVIRONMENTAL PROBLEMS

In the world community, India has always been the cynosure of all eyes on account of its wealth and variety of natural resources. These attracted hordes of foreign invaders to her shores down the ages, some of whom even annexed and ruled over her territories for long periods.

In the wake of the attainment of Independence from foreign domination in the forties followed an era of rapid industrialisation and development in the fields of science and technology leading to injudicious use of natural resources and general degradation of the environment, mainly through large scale deforestation and pollution of the soil, water and atmosphere. The rapid disappearance of the protective mantle of natural vegetation triggered off a violent chain reaction giving rise to serious ecological imbalances by disrupting nature's delicate life support systems so essential to our very survival.

B. SOLUTION TO THE PROBLEM

Today, as we stand at the crossroads of human history, it is essential that we pause and take careful stock of the grave crisis in the form of all round environmental degradation which we have brought upon ourselves through selfish exploitation of our natural resources and thoughtless application of science and technology, thereby jeopardising the very survival not only of ourselves but of all living creatures which share this earth with us. The economics of a prosperous welfare society which we are trying to build up must necessarily undergo a fundamental reorientation so as to bring them in conformity with the basic concepts of nature conservation if we hope to live at peace with ourselves and in harmony with our environment. "Development without Destruction" must become the new strategy for our future planning. In other words, the solution of our environmental problems lies in "ECO-DEVELOPMENT".

What precisely do we mean by "Eco-development"? Although this term has been vaguely bandied about of late, no attempt appears to have been made to define it, and may therefore mean different things to different people. To avoid any confusion or ambiguity, I propose to define it as under:

"Eco-development" of any region may be defined as its integrated development in conformity with the recognized concept and principles of environmental conservation with the object of ensuring that

(i) A proper balance between the components of all natural ecosystems is maintained so that existing life forms are not needlessly endangered.

(ii) The natural flora and fauna of the area is preserved and restored where it has been depleted.

(iii) Damage from all forms of pollution and from any other factors capable of causing environmental degradation is eliminated or at least minimised.

(iv) All land is put to optimum use so that it produces the most and deteriorates the least.

(v) There is a general improvement in the quality of life for the people residing in the area.

In the light of its above concept and definition, an eco-development project could possibly involve activities of the following nature:

(a) *Forest Conservation and Development Activities.*

(i) Control of cattle grazing through effective closure by fencing, appointment of watchmen, penning of cattle with the cooperation of local people, etc.

(ii) Carrying out soil and moisture conservation works, such as contour trenching (gradonis), check damming, gully plugging, construction of ring bunds, soil mulching, making shallow saucer-shaped pits (in arid areas), etc.

(iii) Establishment of nurseries near sources of perennial water supply for raising adequate planting stock of the desired species (preferably indigenous).

(iv) Large scale afforestation/revegetation of barren/degraded areas, adopting specialised sowing/planting techniques, such as aerial seeding where large or inaccessible areas are to be covered within a limited time schedule or where adequate local labour is not available when required. The problem is so gigantic that the conventional afforestation techniques involving manual labour adopted by the Forest Departments with their limited staff would appear to be hopelessly inadequate. Afforestation through aerial seeding on an experimental scale has already been undertaken in Arunachal Pradesh, Madhya Pradesh, Rajasthan and Maharashtra in recent years.

(v) Creation of shelterbelts and windbreaks along roadsides, canal banks, railway tracks, individual field boundaries, etc.

(vi) Afforestation along coastal strips, and desert border and on shifting sand dunes, catchment areas of rivers, lakes and reservoirs, mangrove afforestation in tidal swamps, reboisement of areas after quarrying and mining, etc.

vii) Raising urban forests for public recreation.

viii) Setting up of arboreta and botanical gardens.

(b) *Wildlife Conservation Activities.*

(i) Establishment of Sanctuaries, National Parks and Biosphere reserves.

(ii) Breeding and propagation of endangered species.

(iii) Establishment of breeding farms for game animals and birds as a commercial activity by Government and private agencies. These could also be utilised for restocking depleted areas. Local tribals should be involved in this activity.

(iv) Establishment of zoological parks.

(v) Improving food, water and shelter facilities for wildlife, providing nest boxes for birds, salt licks, etc.

(c) *Rural Development Activities*

(i) *Community Forestry*

Creation of village woodlots so as to make villagers self-sufficient in meeting their requirements of small timber, bamboos, fuel and fodder, thereby relieving the tremendous pressure on Government forests which suffer heavy damage on this account.

Strip planting along roadsides, canal banks and railway tracks.

Helping farmers to raise trees on their field boundaries to act as windbreaks.

Encouraging agriculturists to take to commercial tree farming, particularly on marginal lands.

Establishment of 'kissan' and school nurseries. Pasture improvement in village commons (*gaochars*). Promotion of fuel-saving devices in villages, namely smokeless *'chulas'* and improved crematoria, for meeting the acute shortage of fuelwood in rural areas.

Gujarat State has already given a pioneering lead to the rest of the country in the field of community forestry by launching a gigantic programme of the above activities at a cost of Rs. 64 crores with financial assistance from the World Bank. The results achieved have been spectacular and worthy of emulation by other States.

(2) *Miscellaneous Activities*

(i) Anti-pollution measures.

(ii) Protective and bioaesthetic tree planting.

(iii) Animal husbandry — improvement of cattle breeds through castration of scrub cattle and artificial insemination, stoppage of free forest grazing and encouragement of stall feeding.

(iv) Dairy cooperatives.

(v) Poultry farming.

(vi) Apiculture.

(vii) Sericulture (where climatic factors are favourable).

(viii) Pisciculture — fish, prawn and oyster culture.

(ix) Alternative sources of energy — biogas, solar energy, windmills (where strong winds prevail).

(x) Subsidized cottage industries based on various forest, wildlife and marine products (e.g. bamboo matches, toys, baskets and mats, katha, oil seeds, fans and dyestuffs, aromatic oils, lac, *bidi* leaves, *agarbattis,* medicinal plants and products, peacock feathers, fillets and protein tablets from trash fish, fish *'kheema'*, tooth and talcum powders, shell grit and cleansing powder from sea shells, cultured pearls, edible sea algae, etc.). This list is illustrative and not exhaustive.

(xi) Encouraging the development of tribal art, culture and handicrafts.

(d) *Conservation Education Programme*

6. Our efforts to save the natural environment stand little chance of success in the absence of a general public awareness of the gravity of the problem and the creation of an enlightened public opinion in favour of nature conservation. The launching of an intensive nature education programme for the benefit of the public in general and of the younger generation in particular is, therefore, the need of the hour. The State Wildlife Departments as well as conservation organisations like the World Wildlife Fund and Bombay Natural History Society have a key role to play in organising such programmes. The Gujarat Wildlife Department has already taken a lead in this direction by organising a series of subsidized nature education camps for thousands of school children over the past few years at selected places like Hingolgadh near Rajkot (Nature Education Sanctuary), Pirotan Island in the Gulf of Kutch (Marine National Park). Gir National Park (last abode of the Asiatic Lion), Gandhinagar (under the auspices of the Gujarat Ecological Education & Research Foundation) and at Dabka and Jambughoda around Baroda, in collaboration with the local branches of WWF. While the Department bears the cost of providing boarding and lodging facilities at these outdoor camps, WWF contributes camping equipment and volunteers who act as guides for conducting the camps. These camps have evoked an enthusiastic response from the children who have been coming forward to participate in them in increasing numbers from year to year.

(C) INVOLVEMENT OF INDUSTRIAL HOUSES

The preparation and implementation of eco-development projects calls for substantial investment of money. Looking to the magnitude of the problem, this would be a heavy drain on the financial resources of the State Governments which would not be in a position to shoulder this heavy burden all by themselves. It would, however, be in the fitness of things if all industrial houses were to come forward to share this responsibility by funding such projects in the talukas where they operate. After all, there is no denying the fact that industries take a heavy toll of the natural environment either through exploitation of the natural resources which constitute their raw material or by creating pollution hazards which adversely affect the surrounding population. By contributing their mite to the cause of eco-development, they would be making at least some amends for the environmental damage resulting from their operations and also discharging their moral obligation to society by helping to improve the general quality of life in their area of operation.

A modest beginning in this direction has already been made in Gujarat and Maharashtra by the enlightened house of Tatas which has always been a pioneer in the field of industrial reforms and innovations. For example, Tata Chemicals located it Mithapur in Jamnagar district of Gujarat have done a commendable job in successfully raising a belt of *Casuarina* trees along the coastal sand dunes for checking wind-blown sand and by undertaking bio-aesthetic tree planting to beautify the Mithapur township which is mostly made up of their own employees. They have even set up a separate Society for Rural Development for undertaking such works in addition to other welfare activities such as constructing link roads, setting up primary schools, supply of drinking water, etc. They have also developed some of their low concentration saltpans into a refuge for water-birds. In Maharashtra, Tata Electric Companies have provided funds for a pilot project involving reafforestation of the denuded catchments of their water reservoirs by aerial seeding.

Hopefully, the pioneering lead given by Tatas will, in due course, be emulated by other progressive industrial houses. Such active involvement of industrial houses in eco-development process would provide a vital breakthrough in the field of environmental conservation in a rapidly developing country such as ours.

I am quite confident that this august body of eminent conservationists, who have gathered here on the auspicious occasion of the Centenary of the Bombay Natural History Society, will deliberate at length on this new facet of the country's development process and lend their whole-hearted support to the innovative concept of eco-development which I have outlined above. This is positively our only hope of averting the ecological disaster which our present mode and trend of technological development otherwise have in store for us.

I close my presentation with a fervent prayer to the Almighty to bestow on all of us the wisdom and good sense to give a fairer deal to our bounteous and magnanimous Mother Earth than we have given her hitherto and to desist from the suicidal folly of killing the very goose that lays the golden egg. Let us not forget that Mother Earth produces enough to meet everyone's reasonable needs but not to satisfy everyone's greed!

Non-Government Organisations and Conservation

E. R. C. DAVIDAR

Prior to independence, the Indian subcontinent was divided into princely states and British India. The administration in the states set-up left little scope for non-governmental activity particularly in the field of Conservation of Nature and Natural Resources as the emphasis was on hunting and game was the rulers' prerogative for sport and entertainment. As far as British India was concerned true to British tradition and culture non-governmental organisations were encouraged and they flourished. In the natural history field there were two types of organisations. One was science-oriented, devoted to the setting up of museums, organising natural history expeditions and collections and the like — the general objective being the acquisition and dissemination of knowledge. The foremost among these was the Bombay Natural History Society. The other type of societies were the shikar, hunt and tent clubs. Shikar clubs went by the name of Game Associations. This paper proposes to deal with this type of non-governmental organisation.

A need has to be felt for any organisation to come into being, a motivating factor in fact, particularly if organisations that call for sacrifices on the part of their members are to be set up. When game was abundant no such need was felt for regulating their pursuit. It was the decline in the status of animals and birds that were the object of pursuit that led to the formation of game associations. The areas where these associations were set up were the ones which saw concentrated sporting activity such as hill stations, cantonment areas and plantation districts.

To give an example of the butchery that went on in the eighteen hundreds the following extracts are taken from the October 1829 issue of the *Oriental Sporting Magazine.*

"Neilgherry sport" — List of game killed by a gentleman in the Neilgherries within six months:

"Thirty three and a half couple of Woodcock; 30 head of Black Deer, Commonly known as Elk, one of which was measured and proved 14 hands 2″ (4ft 10″); 1 Jungle Sheep; 3 Wild dogs; 7 Bears; 7 Hogs; 1 Royal Tiger, length 9′ 7″; 1 Cheeta; 100 brace and upwards of Jungle Fowl and Spurfowl; 20 Brace and more of Hares, some weighing as much as an English hare; quail, often 8 or 10 brace a day; snipe often 4 or 5 brace a day; Imperial Pigeon about 20 brace". Besides the damage these hunters caused, the practice of employing local shikaries to procure game was also prevalent.

The firearms used for hunting during that period were primitive and placed the hunter at a disadvantage. The scales started tilting against game once the quality of sporting weapons began to improve. For almost one hundred years from the 1730s single barrel, smooth bore guns using flint locks and firing black powder propelled balls were used for big game. These were slow and inaccurate. Percussion locks replaced flint locks. The late 1860s saw the advent of the breech loader and the centre fire cartridge. By 1880s the black powder express rifle had arrived. Low bullet weight, larger powder charge gave the bullet higher velocity, lower trajectory, greater accuracy and longer range. The bore size was reduced and fire arms became lighter and faster to operate. These improved weapons proved very efficient.

The sportsmen among the hunters began to realise that the slaughter must stop if hunting was to be preserved. And game associations were born.

It fell to the lot of the Nilgiri Game Association with which I was closely associated in various capacities for nearly 30 years to be the pioneer in the field. On third October 1877 twenty five resident sportsmen of the Nilgiri hills met and decided to form a Game Association. The first step they took was to recommend close seasons to give game rest and a chance to breed and prohibition of shooting females and young of game animals. The voluntary ban the members placed on themselves to abide by their recommendations probably gained for the Association respect and eventually recognition. The Government of the Presidency of Madras did not take long to place the recommendations on the statute. The Nilgiri Fish and Game Preservation Act of 1879, was the first piece of legislation in the country for preserving wildlife.

Although the N.G.A., which later became the Nilgiri Wildlife Association was a non-Governmental organisation, it was a happy blend of governmental and non-governmental functionaries. And the membership was composed of game licence holders.

The District Collector as the authority under the Nilgiri Game Rules let the Association act for him in the matter of issue of licences, framing of bye laws and generally administer the Nilgiri Game Preservation Act. Once a vested interest in wildlife was created it was a simple step thereafter for the hunter to become a conservationist. Instead of an exploiter he became a husbandman.

Close seasons and protection given to females, immature males and the young yielded rich dividends. In the case of some species total protection had to be given. In the slaughter that preceded the formation of the Association the animal that suffered most was the Nilgiri thar (*Hemitragus hylocrius*), which was and continues to be called the 'ibex'. In his SPORT IN THE NILGIRIS AND THE WYNAAD, Fletcher writes "Owing to incessant persecution the numbers were thinned at such a rapid rate that at one time ibex stood in imminent danger of extermination". Phythian-Adams, who managed the affairs of the N. G. A. for many years estimated that there were less than a dozen heads of tahr all told when the Association was formed. The protection given to this species through the strict observance of the ban rehabilitated the species so completely that by 1908 'saddle backs' were thrown open to hunting.

Hunters elsewhere, particularly resident planters who had a vested interest in keeping game hunting going to bring a little pleasure and excitement into their lives began to realise that like the plantation crops they raised game was also a crop to be harvested if it was to last. Game associations sponsored by planters were formed. One of the first (and even to this day, the foremost) among these was the High Range Game Preservation Association, sponsored and supported by the Kannan Devan Hill Produce Co. Ltd, now a member of the Tata group. When the Association took control the Nilgiri tahr on the High Range plateau which includes Eravikulam and Rajamallay was gravely endangered and was on the verge of extinction due to the depredations of Muduvan poaching gangs. The present stock of about 600 tahr was built from almost scratch.

Peermade adjoining Periyar had its association. The Anamalai Hills had the Konalar fishing association in the wildliferich Grass hills. Most planting districts, whether in the south or northeast of India had their own, game preservation associations.

The transformation of the hunter from a blood thirsty butcher to a trophy hunter inbibed with a spirit of sportsmanship was the greatest contribution that game associations made to the cause of conservation of wildlife. Many of the wildlife sanctuaries and national parks in the country today are living monuments to these associations and bear witness to their effectiveness.

In the changed environment of Independent India, the weaker organisations collapsed and some remain only on paper. But the more vigorous ones such as the Nilgiri and High Range Associations continue to function, and function effectively through broad basing their membership and activities. Among its new projects, the Nilgiri Association has been helping the authorities by sending out anti-poaching patrols into remote tahr country and has set up an intelligence service to prevent ivory poaching. The High Range Association continues to protect tahr on the Rajamallay plateau. These bodies also act in an advisory capacity and are represented on wildlife boards at the Centre as well as in the States. They have programmes to involve the youth in conservation efforts. It has proved to be a case of 'where there is a will there is a way'.

A different breed of organisations have come into being in the past twenty years or so. Wildlife conservation has crossed national frontiers and has become a subject of international concern. Discounting the self interest group societies that mushroomed following popular interest in conservation the rest are doing valuable work in spreading the message of conservation, funding research projects, etc. All these efforts hardly scratch the surface.

For its part the Government of India has enacted the Wildlife (Protection) Act of 1972, gathering within its purview all the wild animal and plant life wherever found within the Indian Union, deeming all wildlife to be state property. But the executive arm charged with the enforcement of the legislation is puny and its reach is short. Sanctuaries, National parks and reserved forests occupy just a fraction of the land and littoral mass of the country. The rest is a vast no man's land where the Wildlife Act's writ does not run. It would be unwise to write off the wildlife wealth in this tract. The pace at which wild animal and plant life is disappearing from this region is cause for concern. The nineteen eighties are no different from the eighteen eighties in this respect. The need of the hour is conservation-oriented non-governmental organisations based in rural India. No doubt the initiative must come from the people themselves. It is heartening to find that there are already movements such as the 'chipko' in the field.

The sportsmen who formed game associations in the late nineteen hundreds had a vested interest in preserving game for their hunting pleasure. Similarly, the people of rural India have a vested interest in protecting their environment. But this proposition is a little difficult to comprehend as it is a long term objective. It is here that the enlightend and experienced urban organisations have a duty to perform. The advantages of conservation should be explained to the rural people in terms that they can understand. Once the motivating factor is found then it will not be a difficult task to involve rural communities in conservation efforts. Without such involvement conservation of nature will remain a mere concept.

Concepts for a Civilization based on Conservation

R. ASHOK KUMAR

ABSTRACT

Civilization today is synonymous with soil destruction. But all previous civilizations which neglected their soils and exhausted them met with the same fate — ruin. Nature's rough and ready justice is evident everywhere — floods, droughts, landslides, erosion, impoverishment, squalor, disease, wars and spiritual decline; and man, unable to understand himself, exploits and destroys all life and everything. The paper urges the conservation of natural resources in the village and in the city through specific organised actions of an immediate nature:

1. Like the existing network for handling agricultural outputs and conventional inputs (artificial fertilisers, water, energy), either use existing organisation or modify it to give equal importance to soil quality — physical, chemical biological — by strictly recycling human and animal excreta in the form of organic manure via sewerless systems in the villages and other small towns. With villages being where the majority live, and villages being nicely decentralised this should be feasible — the biolatrine. In cities sewage and garbage must be converted to organic fertiliser and transported, weighing money against soil quality.

2. Give as much importance to trees, pastures and other plants and animals as given to industries. Money should be in everything. A stone is as vital as gold.

3. Strengthen existing transport systems based on utilising natural resources—the cycle, the cyclerickshaw, the bullock cart, the horse, the horse-driven carriage, the boat, the inland river system.

4. Strengthen existing cottage crafts like those using renewable energy and materials, like mechanical advantaged human animal power.

5. Organisation of 150 million Solar Cookers in two years in such a way that the solar cookers are self financing.

6. Adoption of box type solar cookers in establishments and homes by attractive advertising via information campaigns using roadside demonstration along with spiritual commentaries.

7. Spreading use of pond type solar collectors.

8. Extensive use of daylight in the performance of work in all human activity areas.

9. Work culture may be modified to include physical work for all human beings. A healthy mind in a healthy body achieved by full development of the human being, rather than only desk work or only physical work.

10. Stop maldevelopment like large dams so that people do not become refugees in their own homeland.

11. Emphasise the development of self-sufficient communites with the city also participating in organic farming of vegetable and fruit gardens.

12. Form local nature study groups and inculcate conservation ethic while meeting basic needs by providing means to these for the community.

13. Develop the faculty of understanding human nature and the spirit through Gandhi's interpretations of the Bhagavadgita.

14. Basic education through non-formal means — earning while learning.

15. Introduction of "research now, pay later" schemes in living on true income.

16. Ensure that all people in a community are spiritually involved in conservation while earning a living in the process of building a self sustaining economy.

What are the signals for a change in the way of living away from the present?

In India the signals are:

Regarding the soil: In 1980-81, when 130 million tonnes of food grains were produced, 18 million tonnes of plant nutrients were taken out of the soil, but only 11 million tonnes were added back. Further, another 8 million plus of nutrients are being lost annually through water erosion. If we consider the amount of nutrients in Indian human excreta alone (faeces and urine), they amount annually to some 21 million tonnes which to an extent make up for the nutrients lost above. This signals a change from the present: *Do not waste these nutrients.*

In the form of organic manure obtained from efficiently designed biolatrines of the community type, or individual type, using plug flow designs where productivity is maximized for biogas and distilled water is recovered using solar stills, the soil can be renewed.

On account of the shortage of cooking energy, crop residues and cowdung are being used as fuel, thus the micronutrients in these as well as NPK are lost to the soil. It has been estimated that the application of a tonne of cowdung as manure enhances grain yield by 50 kg per hectare (FAO 1978), so much so that with the application of cowdung now used as fuel, annual foodgrain production can be increased enabling the return of uneconomical agricultural land to the planting of trees.

Considering that 70% of the Indian population, 502 million lives in villages, biolatrines using sewerless systems of biogas and organic manure production are practical. In other words the present village civilization should be strengthened by organising the people to produce energy (biogas) and organic fertiliser in a biogas digester attached to the biolatrine. Kitchen and other garbage can be used to mix with the excreta and hence the village household get energy income, fertiliser income and with a solar still get pure water from the fertiliser slurry. In this way some 230 million tonnes of human wastes will be reused, annually.

The 100 million tonnes of human wastes and an equal amount of garbage produced in cities should be converted in economical biogas plants and the cooking energy produced piped to individual communities. For this purpose the city should be converted into suitable zones. At present a lot of water is mixed with human excreta in raw sewage. A redesign of this costly system into a sewerless system with biolatrines, a biogas digester of the anaerobic type and means to collect the fertiliser with separate handling of bathroom waste water is indicated. This would lead to redesign of cities on the model of small self-sufficient communities. Organic gardening here would enable cheap production of vegetables and fruits. Regarding organic farming it is worth quoting some individual examples, as its importance to conservation cannot be sufficiently underscored:

WENDELL BERRY. Wendell Berry who personally does organic farming in America addressed Purdue University Agricultural School on the dangers of high technology farming. After his talk he was asked on organic farming. "Mr Berry, what you say about farming on a human scale sounds attractive. But who's going to decide who is going to starve when we cut down today's enormous productivity to start farming your way?"

Answer. "A few powerful people will always decide who'll starve in scarcity and who will not." He went on to make some points of his own. "I have seen figures", he said, "which suggest intensive organic farming is less productive but not much less productive, than industrial chemical farming. Often today organic farming, is the only way to revitalize and conventional farming has run out." "The question should be" 'he added, "do we want to feed an enormous amount of people as we do now a little while longer until our fossil fuels run out and our top soil runs into the sea, or do we want to feed as many people as we can forever on farms which can renew their own fertility" (Ananthu 1983).

Trees. The elimination of trees to meet various commercial needs and fuelwood for cities has resulted in loss of top soil by erosion, and degradation of soil. Soil protection by trees is so fundamental that we can say that a permanent civilization is impossible without proper tree cover of sufficient diversity in a total ecologically balanced community. Thus while 'only God can make a tree', soil erosion "has made a knowledge of the underlying principles of human ecology—the art of living together with animals, insects and plants—one of the most urgent needs of mankind." The following example dramatically brings out the power of the tree:

'In the deepest woods
Lies the heart of our country
A people without forests
Is a dying race. That is why
When a tree perishes we grow
Another on its grave.'

—A verse found on a forest cabin wall in Juriens.

"For a long time people were not able to grasp the essential fact that ecology means balance. Nor could they see that forest ecology was the controlling factor in watersheds, in holding the delicate line between supply and flood. The aerated texture of forest soil will easily hold 14 times as much water as soil in an open field. The experience of two towns in Utah, Farmington and Centerville, both on the Great Salt Lake at the foot of the Wasatch Mountains is an illustration.

"Drenching rains had all but buried Farmington in mud and rocks that came sliding down from the mountains. Highways, farms, orchards and houses were buried in feet of mud. Each summer the sudden heavy storms of the area repeated the disasters. No one seemed to know why. The rain did not appear to be heavier than in other years. Even more baffling, it was not happening in nearby Centerville, which was receiving the same amount of rains.

"Investigation finally made it clear that the mountains behind Farmington had been stripped of tree cover by over-grazing and by fire. At Centerville the cattle had been kept out of the mountain forests and the fires had been controlled. Run off measurements showed one stream in Farmington carrying 160 times the water of a similar stream whose watershed had not been cropped bare. Once the problem was understood, a replanting programme was undertaken in Farmington; cattle were barred from mountain slopes, and fire control instituted. Since 1936 there have been no floods in Farmington." (Mines 1971).

The signals regarding the trees are very strong in India for a change in the way of our life styles. Centre for Science and Environment (1982): "Every six months more top soil gets washed away than has been used to build all the brick houses across the country."

"In the highly grazed Shivalik hills six centimetres of top soil representing nearly 2400 years of local ecological history often disappears with one monsoon." "Already 175 million hectares of land — 66% of the total area needing proper management are already degraded." "Of the 143 million hectares of agricultural land, 87 million hectares have been degraded by erosion, salinity and waterlogging." Further: "25 million hectares have been endangered by floods and recent canal irrigation schemes... The land area prone to floods has increased from 20 million hectares to about 40 million hectares in the last ten years."

Now consider the power of the tree to draw water. In dry climates plants growing in the fields may consume hundreds of tonnes of water for each tonne of vegetative growth. Plants transmit more than 90% of the water they extract from the soil to the atmosphere. The pressure between the soil and the atmosphere across the tree amounts to hundreds of bars and in an arid climate exceeds 1000 bars. Plants transpire more than their own weight of water in India daily. At a density of 45 kg/m^2 biomass dry weight, vegetation represents electric power equivalent of 3 kw/m^2 They however do more. They produce goods and perform services as well — all automatically. This signal points then unmistakably to a culture of tree plantation and treating it as a friend of all of us. The individual must have a stake in the tree he has planted; thus the community would be made to take interest in the tree.

A massive tree plantation programme of types of trees useful to the local population should be selected, and the people (spiritually) involved in the programme.

SOLAR COOKERS. Soil renewal can be made easier by slowing down the requirement for fuelwood for industrial purposes and for cooking — in urban as well as in rural areas by deploying the solar cooker for cooking purposes wherever there is sunlit space. The government and private organisations can use the cooker to generate finances for deployment of biomanure production in biogas plants and in biolatrines equipped with a digester.

The generation of financial resources can be easy. The first cooker is bought and used daily to cook a hundred eggs. The eggs are sold and a daily profit of Rs. 30/- made. Thus in a month enough money will have been recovered to buy one more solar cooker. With two cookers in the second month selling food cooked with the solar cooker, enough money would be generated for the purchase of two more cookers at the end of the second month. At the end of the third month, there would be enough to buy 4 more cookers. Thus in this way with proper organization, 150 million cookers would be deployed in around two years. A dedicated programme like this would save 1200 million trees during the time the cookers are in service. Fuelwood and gas would also be saved. At biomass density (dry basis) of 45 kg/m^2 and each tree of 10 m^2 projected crown area, 1200 million trees represent 36 million MW of electrical power — natural renewable electricity!

POND TYPE SOLAR COLLECTORS. Hot Water up to 90°C can be supplied by such collectors boosted with aluminised polyester mirrors. For a typical canteen with hot water requirements of 500 litres per day, cement concrete pond type collectors costing about 11,000 rupees would save about 5000 kg of gas of 10000 kcal/kg heating value per dry season. Also if the application displaces the use of firewood, it would aid in conservation.

REFUGEES IN THEIR OWN HOMELAND. A new concept of civilization has to take into account strong maldevelopment signals emanating from the destruction of habitat, involving the uprooting of thousands of families from their homeland. Examples are huge dams which submerge large areas of rich agricultural land and displaced persons are provided with non irrigated hilly land for every piece of rich land submerged. Attempts may not even be made to provide the refugees with alternative non-agricultural occupations such a large development would create. Another aspect is ill planned attempts to resettle refugees on forested land by cutting down the forests and exposing the top soil to be eroded by making it lie fallow without any soil conservation measures. Such development is causing large scale movement of tribals.

The large movement of people living in the rural areas to urban areas has caused the concentration of some 24% of India's population to be squeezed into towns and cities covering just 1.3% of the country's land area. Overcrowding has led to curtailment severely of clean water availability. Of 1027 towns lacking drinking water supply systems, 902 are towns with population below 20,000. This congestion has led to leaving garbage and defecating in the open.

Suffice it to say that the refugee problem

within India's borders is closely interlinked with deforestation and encroachment of mechanisation and is serious enough to require a rethinking of India's road to civilization. These aspects are brought out in sickening details of people — farmers tribals, nomads and fisherfolk as well as of plants, animals and soil in 'The State of India's Environment 1982', an annual review issued by the Centre for Science and Environment, New Delhi.

Such signals point to the following norm which must be adopted. "Voluntary protection of plant, human and animal power against the competition of machinery as the price of social insurance" (Pyarelal 1959).

CONCLUSION. There are enough signals in India that point out that civilization is being destroyed because soil is being destroyed. Even human beings are wasted because they are in plenty instead of converting wastage into an advantage. The new civilization should conserve while enjoying the tremendous amount of material and spiritual energy. The Bhagavadgita can show the way. Why, the message of the Father of the Nation is clear: Swadeshi — regional self sufficiency — Conservation.

REFERENCES

ANANTHU, T.S. (1983): Events and Comments in *Gandhi Marg*. 52, July 1983, pp. 241-246.

CARTER, V. & DALE, T. (1974): Topsoil and Civilization. University of Oklahoma. Oklahoma.

CENTRE FOR SCIENCE AND ENVIRONMENT (1982): State of India's Environment, 1982. New Delhi.

DASMANN, R.F. (1975): The Conservation Alternative. Wiley. New York.

DORE (1982): Energy Conservation in the Japanese Industry. Energy Paper No. 3. Policy Studies. Royal Institute of International Affairs. UK.

FAO (1978): Forestry for Rural Communities. FAO, Rome, p. 14.

MAHATMA GANDHI (1926): The Bhagavadgita. *Navjivan*. Ahmedabad.

MINES, S. (1971): Last days of Mankind — Ecological Survival or Extinction. Simon and Shuster. New York.

PYARELAL (1959): Towards New Horizons. *Navjivan*. Ahmedabad.

Abstracts of papers read but not submitted for publication

Wildlife and Conservation problems in Ashambu hills

The Ashambu hills form the southern limit of the great irregular chain of Western Ghats south of Ariankavu Pass. Vegetation of these hills varies from thorny scrub jungle to evergreen forests. Biologically this area is interesting and important because: a) this area has certain endangered plants, herpetofauna, birds and mammals and, b) some of the wildlife seen here are represented in the Himalayas either by the same species or by a closely allied species.

This tract has a wide varitey of mammal life including the endangered Nilgiri tahr, liontailed monkey and the elephant. Tiger is also said to occur. So far extensive research has been done on bonnet macaque, Nilgiri langur and liontailed monkey. More research involving trapping, marking and radio telemetry is needed particularly to know more about the ecology and behaviour of such mammals as the slender loris, mouse deer and the carnivores.

Major conservation problems in this area are proposals to build more hydel projects, existing plantations, firewood extraction, smuggling of valuable timber, cattle, forest fires, poaching and arrack distillation.

The best way to conserve and manage this area is to declare Kalakadu-Mundanthurai sanctuaries and adjoining wildlife areas as one wildlife unit, improve protection and plant multi-purpose social forests in areas outside the forest partly atleast to meet the unemployment problem and firewood and timber demands of the villagers. Knowledge acquired in Auroville could be used in the afforestation programme here.

A.J.T. JOHNSINGH,
Project Scientist,
Bombay Natural History Society,
Hornbill House, Bombay.

Ecological diversity of the vegetation in the desert environment

Vegetation of the Indian Desert is continuously exposed to a full impact of extreme and drastic environmental conditions. Indian Desert which lies between 24° & 30° North latitude to 69° to 78° East longitude, occupying the eastern extremity of the north tropical desert belt, covering an area of 3,36,000 square kilometres, is one of the most arid parts of the world. Climatic aridity prevails throughout the region, low rainfall, dry atmosphere and extremes of temperatures. Apart from its scantiness, the rainfall is characterised by its variability both in space and in time. This variation in rainfall together with the topographical variability, induces a appreciable diversity of vegetation in the desert zone.

Like all deserts, the Indian desert is also distinguished by its sparse vegetation and the plant cover is structurally open. The vegetation mostly consists of a permanent frame work of perennials, the interspaces of which are occupied by ephemerals after rains. Phenology of plants is also largely related to environmental conditions.

Life forms which predominantly consist of Therophytes and Nanophanerophytes, also reflect a major feature of climate.

Pressure on food, fodder and fuel has been greatest in the desert environment. Coupled with the paucity of water it has led to the overexploitation of the already sparse vegetation cover which in turn causes erosion leading to the loss of soil and soil fertility.

Plant communities of the Indian desert demonstrate a great variability. The three principal landforms, the predominating sand covered Thar, the plains including the central dune free country and the hills, demonstrate a marked variability in their vegetal covers. The character of the plant communities change when one goes from one landform to the other. Saline areas are dominated by many halophytic species. The successional phenomenon operative within a group of communities in various habitats are closely related to the modifications in the physical properties of the soils and topographic features and consequently to the water resources of each community.

M.M. BHANDARI,
Professor of Botany,
University of Jodhpur,
Jodhpur, India.

Stochastic extinction and reserve size A focal species report

Populations of endangered species are almost by definition small and, as such, vulnerable to extinction as a result of stochastic fluctuations in abundance. We examine the effectiveness with which one large reserve (OLR) or two small reserves of the same total area (TSR) protect endangered populations from such demographic stochasticity. To do this, we model the random walk of the abundance of a local population whose numbers fluctuate according to a stochastic analog of logistic growth. The model is Markovian but it is more general than pure birth and death processes because immigration is allowed.

Reserve recommendations follow. When the endangered or focal species receives extra-reserve immigrants (such as when conspecific populations exist elsewhere), the difference between OLR and TSR is negligible. More importantly, the focal species switches from being nearly always absent to nearly always present over a narrow range of reserve sizes. Hence, when the conservation goal to maintain local populations which receive outside immigrants, reserves should be larger than this critical size.

When the focal species cannot receive immigrants from outside the system of reserves, the population must eventually random walk to extinction. The time to extinction can be very long, however, and is longer for OLR than for TSR. This result is robust even when migration between TSR is allowed. Hence, when the conservation goal is to protect the last populations of endangered species from demographic stochasticity, reserves should be as large as possible.

S. JOSEPH WRIGHT,
Department of Zoology,
University of Iowa
Iowa City, Iowa 52242
USA.

Tropical Bees and ecological diversity: New paradigms and prospects

All highly social bees are native to the tropics, and their ecological roles are only beginning to be clarified. Perennial colonies of such species are eclogically far more varied than solitray bees and forage throughout the year. Their activity as pollinators, pollen and spore predators, nectar and pollen robbers, and competitors with pollinating insects, birds and bats creates strong selective pressures which influence the diversity of tropical biota. Tropical plants have responded with an array of adaptations to combat predation by social bees or to enhance pollination by social species. Protection of flowers, mixing of needless with pollen, production of extrafloral nectar which attracts aggressive ants, and regulation of nectar quality are among plant adaptations likely caused by persistent interaction with social bees.

Plant species visited by a single colony of social bees may number in the hundreds during one year. Although pollen collected by bees rapidly loses power of germination, recent advances in pollination biology suggest that pollen trapped from bee colonies may be used to preserve the gene pool of tropical plants. In addition, study of pollen harvested by bees provides a powerful tool for documenting flowering phenology in tropical forest.

DAVID W. ROUBIK,
Smithsonian Tropical Research Institute,
APDO 2072,
Balboa, Panama.

A multitude of fiddlers; and yet threatened?

The film talk focuses on the behavioural and ecological variety encountered in the ninety-odd species of fiddler crabs (genus *Uca*) and emphasizes the apparent multitude of individuals in certain habitats. In spite of some notorious fiddler predators (birds, mammals, fishes, other crabs), *Uca* has so far withstood these pressures. Due to anthropogenic influences, however, there has already been a marked reduction of this multitude in certain places, and one each of such places is referred to: one in Europe, one in Africa (*U. tangeri*), one in America (*U. panamensis, U. terpsichores*), and two in India (*U. annulipes, U. urvillei*).

RUDOLF ALTEVOGT,
Munster University,
Federal Republic of Germany.

Deer, plant phenology, and succession in South Asian monsoonal lowland forests

The monsoonal lowland forests of South Asia are notably rich in number of deer species. In the Royal Karnali-Bardia Wildlife Reserve, Nepal, 5 cervids occurred sympatrically: barking deer (*Muntiacus muntjak*); hog deer (*Axis porcinus*); chital (*Axis axis*); swamp deer (*Cervus duvauceli*); and sambar (*Cervus unicolor*). Deer responded dramatically to seasonal changes in plant phenology and to changes in plant succession. Biotic and abiotic factors, such as fire and the monsoon rains, triggered major changes in plant phenology which directly influenced deer forage abundance and quality. Cervid biomass estimates indicated that grasslands and successional forests supported more deer than did mature sal (*Shorea robusta*) forests. Mangement efforts to enhance deer habitat in continuous sal forest are discussed. The role of disturbance in maintaining high levels of forage abundance in deer habitat is stressed.

ERIC DINERSTEIN,
Wildlife Science Group,
College of Forest Resources AR-10,
University of Washington,
Seattle, Wa. 98195.

Case history of the Cooperative Conservation Programme: The Nepal Tiger Ecology Project

The Nepal Tiger Ecology Project was launched in 1973 to generate biological information for rational long term management of tiger populations and habitats. The objective of this paper is to describe the system of management that was employed and analyze its strengths, weaknesses, and cost effectiveness. The project was carried out in Chitawan National Park in collaboration with the Department of National Parks and Wildlife Conservation, HMG Nepal, (and) under the auspices of the Smithsonian Institution and the World Wildlife Fund (U.S. Appeal).

The field team operated from a base camp in Sauraha village using 4 elephants and up to 2 vehicles for field excursions into the Park and adjacent area. Temporary camps were made for extended stays in remote areas. Research project design was the responsibility of principal investigators (PI's) and their academic committee or advisor. The field team at any one time consisted of the 2 PI's (Nepali and American), 2 research assistants (undergraduate or baccalaureate students), and 28 support personnel locally hired on the basis of jungle experience and trained in wildlife research techniques.

To date the project has resulted in the completion of 4 doctoral dissertations on tiger and ungulate ecology, publication of over two dozen reports, and recommendations for a park extension which was implemented by HMG. The project also facilitated the establishment of an international trust for conservation in Nepal.

C. WEMMER, R. SIMONS AND H.R. MISHRA,
National Zoological Park,
Smithsonian Institution,
Washington, D.C. 20560.
GPO Box 38.
Kathmandu, Nepal.

The need to conserve Spotted-billed Pelican nesting habitat in India

The Spotted-billed Pelican *Pelecanus philippensis* has become very rare, and is among the most endangered of the world's birds. The primary cause for the reduction in numbers is probably cutting of the trees in which they once nested in India, Burma, and Sri Lanka. Fewer than 500 pairs are known to have nested in recent years in India in 3 colonies and fewer than 1000 in Sri Lanka in 23 small colonies. The current status of the Spotted-billed Pelican in Burma is not known. In India, large trees used by the Pelicans for nesting in two of the three colonies have been recently cut and nesting has not been obeserved there for the past 2 years. Necessary conservation measures involve steps to ensure that trees in the remaining nesting area are not cut. The cost of such conservation measures would not be great, but would be of crucial benefit to this severely endangered species.

G. GENE MONTGOMERY[1] AND
RALPH W. SCHREIBER[2],
[1]Smithsonian Tropical Research Institute,
Balboa, Panama.
[2]Natural History Museum,
900 Exposition Blvd., Los Angeles,
California 900 007.

The Grey Pelican at Nelapattu

The Grey Pelican were studied for 3 consecutive seasons at Nelapattu. The data highlights importance of ecological factors in the habitat and survival requirements as revealed in study of feeding and breeding habits.

Some of the factors necessary for survival of the Grey Pelican are: 1. Nesting space. 2. Nesting material. 3. Proximity of water as insulating medium and 4. fishing grounds. 5. Protection from human activity including pollution. The importance of food for survival and successful breeding is well documented. One of the factors in mortality is overcrowding due to shortage of nesting space. The other factors in mortality are predation and human interference, as approach of human beings creates a commotion in the colony and inadvertant dislocation of eggs and young leading to their falling out of nests. Of the climatic causes, temperature is a major factor at the height of summer resulting in many deaths. At the commencement of the season, if sufficient water does not accumulate in the tank the birds may over fly and not tenant the trees. The success of Nelapattu as a sanctuary is attributed to favourable ecological conditions. Conservation measure may augment favourable components to assure continued survival here or elsewhere where it is sought to conserve pelicanries.

V. NAGULU AND J.V. RAMANA RAO,
Department of Zoology,
Osmania Univesity,
Hyderabad-7.

Habitat management for the Conservation of the Great Indian Bustard *Choriotis nigriceps*

The ecology of the Great Indian Bustard *Choriotis nigriceps* (Vigors) was studied at Nanaj (Solapur, Maharashtra) and Karera (Shivpuri, Madhya Pradesh). Micro-habitat utilization by the bustard in both the places was similar. It was found that the density and height of the vegetation is very important. The bustard prefers open flat or slightly undulating grassland with scattered trees and bushes. The height of the vegetation must not be above their eye-level. They avoid thick stands of grasses and bushes of more than a metre high and also, thickly wooded scrub. All the nests were found in open low vegetation areas from where the incubating bird can see all around. Micro-habitat preference for night roost, day rest and display was studied. It was found that habitat management in the bustard sanctuaries is essential. There are chances that some of the sanctuaries if over-protected without active management will become unsuitable for the bustard. Habitat management plan is suggested.

ASAD RAFI RAHMANI,
Project Scientist,
Endangered Species Project (Bustard),
Bombay Natural History Society.

Rehabilitation of Saltwater Crocodile, *Crocodylus porosus* Schneider in Orissa, India—a case history

This paper deals with the rehabilitation of Saltwater Crocodile, *Crocodylus porosus* Schneider into the Bhitarkanika Wildlife Sanctuary of Orissa as part of the Conservation Programme of the Species using the 'grow and release' technique. Uptil now, 200 young crocodiles of more than 1.2 m length were released in four phases into the wild to recover the most depleted populations in the nature. Movement and dispersal of these crocodiles are regularly being monitored and their adaptability have been observed. A few released crocodiles created a problem—so-called 'man and crocodile conflict' which has been overcome to a greater extent by capture and release of those crocodiles elsewhere as well as selection of suitable release sites away from human habitation.

SUDHAKAR KAR,
Research Officer,
Crocodile Project,
Dangmal, Via. Rajkanika,
Dist. Cuttack, Orissa, India.

Butterfly farming and Conservation in Papua New Guinea, with controlled utilization of insect resources as a new village industry

Papua New Guinea is one of the few places in the world where the Commercial Dealing in Insects, as Entomological Specimens, has gone beyond mere collecting to include the Farming (or more correctly, Ranching) of Insects on a large scale as a Village Industry. It involves hundreds of villagers in widely scattered and often remote areas, who, through a Government backed organisation, encourage habitat enrichment to reduce the need for taking wild butterflies by producing a steady flow of high quality specimens for export through the Government's insect marketing agency. The programme provides a means for numerous individuals to have a cash economy in surroundings where there is little chance of making a living or obtaining employment, but where the insect resources have a great potential. With careful guidance the conservation of the insect resources has emerged as a paramount byproduct of this programme and no longer do a handful of Expatriate Dealers take away huge profits at the expense of the Country and its People. Instead a solid and growing contribution has been added to the rural economy. No more are large numbers of Butterflies (many of them very rare and consequently very valuable), indiscriminately collected without any thought of population survival, instead, a substantial amount of the export volume is farmed. The principle of combining Conservation with Development, as enshrined in the World Conservation Strategy, is particularly relevent and the system pioneered in Papua New Guinea, unique in the World, could be used for many developing Countries in South East Asia.

ANGUS F. HUTTON

The trade in Wild Falcons in Egypt

Large numbers of falcons are captured in Egypt every year and exported to other countries for use in falconry. The demand for these falcons is so high that a captive wild peregrine can be sold for as high as $10,000. Migratory peregrine (*Falco peregrinus*) and saker (*Falco cherrug*) falcons and the resident barbary falcon (*Falco peregrinoides*) are the birds of choice. Peregrine and saker falcons are captured during their fall passage and to a lesser extent during their spring passage, while barbary falcons are caught throughout the year. Only female falcons are used for falconry because of their large size and more aggressive nature. Many lanner falcons (*Falco biarmicus*) as well as the males of other falcons are also caught and used in the process of capturing other falcons using special lures.

It is difficult to determine the real number of falcons caught annually in Egypt since the people involved in the capture and export of these birds are usually very reluctant to give any information on their business. An estimate of the number of falcons caught in Egypt, based on observations made during numerous visits to families and individuals involved in the trapping and exporting of falcons during the past four years was made. At least 80 peregrine and barbary falcons, 10 to 15 sakers and 100 lanners are caught and exported from Egypt. In addition, since the method of capture is not very selective, hundreds of other raptors with no value for falconry are caught. These birds are usually destroyed after their capture.

Falcon trapping is also known to take place in most other Middle East countries. Most of these falcons end up in Saudi Arabia and Arab Gulf states and to a lesser extent in Europe, particularly West Germany. It is estimated that 3,000-5,000 falcons are kept captive by falconers in these countries.

Although Egypt is a co-signer of a number of international treaties controlling trade in wildlife, the government has not yet interfered with the trade in wild falcons in Egypt.

Already threatened by the use of pesticides, destruction of habitat and other forms of human interference, the capture and removal of significant numbers of these falcons from the wild population may form another major threat to their existence. A significant drop in the population of wild barbary and lanner falcons in Egypt coincides with the increased demand for falcons that occurred in the last few years. The impact of the capture of the migratory peregrine and saker falcons on their wild populations in Europe is difficult to make. However, judging by the small number of these falcons in their breeding ranges, the number of falcons caught every year may exceed what these populations could withstand, at least in some parts of their European range.

MOSTAFA ABBAS SALEH,
Associate Professor of Zoology,
Department of Zoology,
Faculty of Science,
Al Azhar University,
Cairo, Egypt.

Implications of mutualistic seed-dispersal for Tropical Reserve Management

Many tropical trees bear fruits adapted for consumption by animals, and many tropical animals depend on fruits for food at least part of the year. The purpose of this paper is to discuss the potential importance of (1) uneven (canonical) species abundance distributions, (2) the imperative of local seed dispersal for plant recruitment, and (3) seasonability of fruit production in influencing the stability of small tropical reserves. A review of recent literature shows that some mutualistic seed-dispersal systems are "pivotal" for forest communities. Although most trees bear fruits when fruit is readily available in the forests, others (e.g. *Casearia corymbosa* in Costa Rican rainforest and *Virola sebifera* in Panamanian rainforest) bear fruits during annual periods of fruit scarcity in the forest, and consequently maintain fruit-eating animals that are critical for the dispersal and ultimate recruitment of many tree species at other times of the year. The question of species abundance presents peculiar problems when some "pivotal" plants, such as *Casearia corymbosa* in eastern Costa Rica, are rare and confined to special habitats. This paper outlines ecological relationships which would accelerate species loss from habitat islands over and above "random" loss predicted from biogeographic theory, and suggests management methods that can reduce such loss.

Human needs for living space, agricultural land, and firewood in tropical regions have created imperatives for government and private agencies which are concerned with selecting and maintaining habitat remanants. Refuges may be designed to maintain particular "focal" endangered species, or to protect entire communities. Either kind of reserve is likely to become a habitat island, and will consequently lose species through random extinctions (MacArthur & Wilson 1987). The process will be especially rapid in small reserves harbouring small populations of animals and plants (Willson & Wills 1975). The most mathematically tractable predictions from biogeographic theory assume no interactions between species (Wright & Hubbell 1983). Such theory is directly applicable to animals with generalized feeding habits, to plants that do not require animals for pollination or dispersal, and to plants that are pollinated and dispersed by a wide variety of animals. But in tropical forests "all species are not equal;" critically important interactions occur. Futuyma (1973) asserts that such forests are particularly vulnerable to human perturbation because obligate mutualisms between plants and animals produce ecological links among them. Local extinction of a common fruit-eating animal might, for instance, reduce recruitment of fruiting trees dependent upon it for reproduction, and consequently increase the changes of local extinction of those trees and other animals that eat their fruits (Howe 1976). The general consequence could be a widening circle of extinctions, precipitated by the disappearance of one "pivotal" species (Howe 1977; see Futuyma 1973). This paper develops the biological assumptions behind such a prediction, reviews relevant evidence from neotropical forests, and makes qualitative recommendations for selection and maintenance of tropical reserves.

Henry F. Howe,
Smithsonian Tropical Research Inst.
Apartado 2072,
Balboa, Republica de Panama.

Desertic Trees and their influences on companion vegetation

The need for introducing more of useful and adapted trees in dry regions has been recognised. Since trees, under all situations of land use, exist always with a ground cover of vegetation, their influence on the companion vegetation assumes reckonable importance. In this regard variabilities of rainfall interception by different trees and consequent differences in soil moisture enrichment have a special significance in the arid regions. With a few exceptions, most adapted trees under desertic environment display rapid transpiration as a measure against high heat load and they also maintain a high DPD in the foliage. Under low water regime total water use is normally reduced by the reduction of leaf area and not by the reduction of transpiration rate except under severe drought stress. It has been estimated that a *Prosopis cineraria* community of 50 trees/ha lose annually about 222 mm of water. This large water need of trees is met from deep and extensive root system. Study on rooting behaviour of trees, has indicated that some roots extend just below the surface, while others go deep down. Surface roots in all possibility compete for moisture with the shallow rooted annual companion vegetation. Therefore, trees with only a deep root system may be more desirable. Water balance studies have revealed that under desertic condition limitation of soil moisture is the principal cause of reduction of growth and water use of the ground cover. Again, there are evidences that soil microbial population differs significantly under different tree species and thus fertility buildup, though slow under arid conditions, markedly differs under different trees. It seems that systematic and scientific lopping schedule for trees is necessary to avoid adverse shade effects which limit the growth of the companion vegetation. Furthermore, germination and growth inhibitors, found in the leaf litter of some desertic trees, often pose a serious problem for regeneration and growth of the ground cover. Such species are to be, therefore, avoided in agro-forestry or silvipastoral programme. In the light of these, research thrust is necessary for careful scientific evaluation of diverse merits and impacts of different tree components for deriving durable benefits from afforestation projects in arid regions.

A.N. Lahiri,
Division of Soil-Water-Plant Relationship,
Central Arid Zone Research Institute,
Jodhpur 342 003.

Environmental consequences of hydro-electric projects in Bastar District, Central India

Our country is progressing in the development of water resources by the construction of multipurpose hydro-electric projects on all major and minor river systems to meet the ever increasing demand for electrical energy for domestic and industrial consumption and also to bring land under irrigation to maximise food production. Dam construction brings about environmental changes, causing both beneficial and detrimental effects. In India 42 dams were built before year 1900, 1033 built between 1901 and 1979 and 479 under construction or being completed presently. Over 700 major new dams are under consideration by Central and State Governments, central water power commission, National Hydro-Power Corporation, State Irrigation Departments and State Electricity Boards.

Several rivers in Bastar district, M.P. and in adjoining forested areas (as also in the Himalayan region) which are inaccessible due to heavily forested, hilly and difficult terrain are under the Dam Engineers' immediate and special attention to harvest hitherto untapped enormous renewable energy available in these rivers.

The present study is about the Bhopalpattanam and Bodhghat dam projects on Indravati river in Bastar District, Madhya Pradesh.

The Bhopalpattanam and Bhodghat dams are a series of dams (over 15) being planned and constructed across Indravati and Godavari River systems in Bastar district and adjoining areas. The Bhodghat dam project was commenced in 1976 and is estimated to be completed in 1991. It is a purely hydro-electric project dam with an estimated cost of over 400 crores (1981 estimate), whereas the Bhopalpattanam dam project is yet to commence.

This paper touches on various effects of the man-made lakes in this undisturbed heavily forested region, on the wildlife, forest, fisheries, resettlement of tribals and other related considerations.

The paper indicates the various types of investigations that might be taken up so as to fully understand the problems in all its aspects.

H.K. DIVEKAR,
B/22, Balasunder Society,
M.G. Road, Naupada,
Thane 400 602.

The development of Birdlife in Auroville

Auroville was founded on February 28, 1968, in the South Arcot District of Tamil Nadu. The area in which Auroville chose to locate itself was typical of much of the district and indeed of much of the developing world: deforested, eroded, populated by village agriculturists who found it more and more difficult to make a living out of their windswept fields which were becoming desert.

As might be expected, the bird population of such a degenerating ecology was thin, consisting mainly species which thrive in open arid spaces such as palm swifts, drongos, nightjars, larks, blue jays, yellow wattled lapwings and kites, and those which live around human settlements or in the few scattered groves such as house crows, hawk cuckoos, screech owls, babblers and also the great horned owl which lives in the canyons. During the growing season visits were made by flocks of rose ringed parakeets which were attracted by the grains in the fields.

As Auroville grew, the bird population began to increase gradually, centering around the mini-oases (a well with trees and gardens) of the first Auroville settlements. In 1972, for example, the first redvented bulbul was seen. In that year also Auroville began a comprehensive, wide-scale programme of reafforestation and erosion control which today, after a decade of development, has begun to change the face of the whole environment where hundreds of acres have been planted in trees with some 80 wells scattered amidst more than 40 settlements. On the palteau the area is becoming more and more hospitable to bird life and the population is expanding year by year. Some of the species present in Auroville today include sunbirds, flycatchers, cuckoos and flower-peckers. In some areas with an abundance of water the pied kingfisher and the whitebreasted waterhen can be found.

As Auroville continues to develop, the bird population is certain to grow; and steps are being taken to ensure that Auroville will continue to be a sanctuary for birds.

PIETER CENTERFIELD,
Auroville,
Pondicherry, India,
605 101.

INDEX

Abutilon indica, 90
ranadei, 546, 550
Acacia, 88, 192, 243, 401, 446, 566, 568
Acacia-Anogeissus, 182
Acacia-Anogeissus latifolia, 107, 187, 189
Acacia arabica, 566
Acacia-Capparis, 107, 182, 187, 189
Acacia-Capparis decidua, 107
Acacia catechu, 96, 106, 182, 192
Acacia catechu-Anogeissus pendula, 182, 187, 189
Acacia latronum, 566
leucophloea, 566
nilotica, 192, 405
pinnata, 90
planifrons, 106
senegal, 96, 106, 182, 192
Acacia senegal-Anogeissus pendula, 182, 186, 187, 189
Acacia tortilis, 554-560, 562, 563
Acanthaster, 272
planci, 271, 272
Acanthephippium striatum, 579
Acanthus sp., 456
Achyranthes coynei, 549
Acridotheres fuscus, 597
Acridotheres tristis melanosternus, 265
Acroplastus ambayanense, 545, 550
Acrochanena punctata, 580
Acropora, 272, 273
aspera, 272
cervicornis, 29
corymbosa, 272
palifera, 272
palmata, 29
teres, 272
Acrossocheilas hexagonolepes, 499
Adina, 190
Aegiceras parviflora, 550
Aegithina tiphia, 596
Aegle marmelos, 432
Aerides, 578
multiflorum, 580
odoratum, 580
radicosum, 551
Aerne scandeuse, 90
Aerva lanata, 269
Aeypodius, 350, 353
arfakianus, 350
bruijni, 350
Agrostistachys indica, 551
Agrostophyllum callosum, 580
Ahaetulla, 229
dispar, 229
perroteti, 229
Ailurus, 193
fulgens, 235
Albizia amara, 99, 106, 186, 192
lebbek, 432, 566
Albizia amara-Acacia, 182, 186, 189
Alcedo meninting phillipsi, 264
Alcippe poiocephala, 596
Alectoris chukor, 288
Alectura, 345, 350
lathami, 350, 352
Allophyllus concanensis, 551
Alona guttata, 279
Amandava amandava, 519
Ammania floribunda, 549
Amphiesma, 229
beddomei, 229
monticola, 229
Anacardium, 145
excelsum, 145
occidentale, 145
Anas andamanensis, 237
Andropogon lividus, 389
sorghum, 404
Anguinicephalus deraniyagalei, 255
hickanala, 255
Anoectochilus, 573
lanceolatus, 579
roxburghii var. *regalis*, 579
Anogeissus latifolia, 96, 106, 107, 182, 191, 192, 213
pendula, 96, 99, 106, 107, 182, 187
Anogeissus latifolia-Chloroxylon-Albizia amara, 106, 182, 187, 189
Anogeissus pendula-Anogeissus latifolia, 182, 187, 189
Anogeissus-Terminalia-Tectona, 181, 185, 189
Ansonia, 227
ornata, 227
rubigena, 227
Anthogonium gracile, 578, 579
Anthracoceros coronatus, 264
Anthus novaeseelandiae, 598
Antidesma menasu, 551
Antilope cervicapra, 236, 286, 407-409, 565, 566
Apama barberi, 611
Aphanizomenon flosaque, 279
Apodytes, 101
Apogon spp., 371
Arachis hypogea, 404

Arachnis cathcartii, 578, 580
clarkei, 578, 580
Archamia spp., 271, 273
Archnothera longirostris, 596
Ardea alba, 429
Ardeola grayii, 429
Ardisia solanacea, 101
Argostemma vappi, 124
Argyreia boseana, 549
involucrata, 551
lawii, 551
Artamus fuscus, 596
Artemisia, 416
Arthraxon Junnarensis, 551
raizadae, 551
Artocarpus altilis, 269
heterophyllus, 222
Arundinella fuscata, 389
Arundo, 416
Asparagus sp., 89
Astromuricea stellifera, 7
Astropecten polycanthus, 7
Attergatis inermis, 7
Atylosia gladulosa, 550
Adviceda jerdoni, 265
Avicennia alba, 8
officinalis, 8
sp., 8
Axis axis, 2, 76, 255, 263, 417, 631
porcinus, 264, 411, 418
Azadiracta indica, 269, 432

Balanitis roxburghii, 90
Balanophora elkinsii, 545, 549
Balanus complentata, 7
sp., 7
Bambusa sp., 73
Bandicota benghalensis, 488
indica, 489
Barbus bimaculatus, 255
cummingi, 255
srilankensis, 255
titteya, 255
tor, 496
Barleria gibsonioides, 550
pratens, 89
Barringtonia sp., 269
Batagur, 296, 503, 506, 507
baska, 295, 296, 311, 313, 506, 508, 510, 512
Bauhinia foveolatus, 549
racemosa, 89
Begonia concanensis, 549
Begonia prixophylla, 545, 550
Beilschmiedia, 101
Belontia signata, 255
Bentinckia codapanna, 611
Berberis tinctoria, 100
Bhesa, 101
Biermannia jainiana, 580
Blumea malcolmii, 547
venkataramanii, 550
Blyxa echinospermoides, 550
Boerhavia diffusa, 269
fruticosa, 551
Boiga dightoni, 229
Boleophthalmus, 438
Bombax, 16, 597, 603
malabarica, 603
Bonnayodes limnophiloides, 549
Bos gaurus, 65, 75, 392
grunniens, 235
Boselaphus tragocamelus, 408
Bothriochloa jainii, 551
Brachionus, 574
angularis, 279
Botia dayi, 535
striata, 535
Brachyophidium rhodogaster, 230
Bridelia-Syzygium-Ficus-Terminalia, 98, 100
Bridelia-Syzygium-Terminalia-Ficus, 181, 185, 189
Bubalus bubalis, 264, 418, 516, 520
Bubulcus ibis, 429
Buchanania lanzan, 610
latifolia, 96
Budorcos taxicolor, 235
Bufo, 227
atukoralei, 255
beddomii, 227
hololius, 227
parietalis, 227
silentvalleyensis, 227
Bulbophyllum, 577, 578
cauliflorum, 580
clarkeanum, 580
gamblei, 580
guttulatum, 580
neilgherrensis, 551
obrienianum, 580
odoratissimum, 580
penicillium, 580
piluliferum, 580
protractum, 580
reptans, 580

Bulbophyllum scabratum, 580
Bungarus ceylonicus, 255
Butea, 446

Cacomantis sonnerati, 595
Caesio, 271, 273
Cairina scutulata, 237, 313
Cajanus indicus, 404
Calanthe biloba, 579
  herbacea, 579
  masuca, 579
Calatodactylus, 255
Calceolaria mexicana, 100
Callicarpa, 416
Calligonum, 193
  polygonoides, 96, 107
Calliophis, 230
  beddomei, 230
  bibroni, 230
  nigrescens, 230
Callosciurus, 213, 216
  erythraeus, 213
  notatus, 213
  prevostii, 213
  pygerythrus, 213
Calophyilum, 146, 221, 223
  inophyllum, 269
Calotes, 229, 536
  ceylonensis, 255
  ellioti, 229
  grandisquamis, 229
  liocephalus, 255
  nemoricola, 229
  rouxi, 229
Calycogonium squamulosum, 125, 129
Calycopteris floribunda, 341
Camelus dromedarius, 516, 520
Canavalia stocksii, 548, 549
Canis aureus, 65, 263, 566
  lupus, 565, 566
    pallipes, 236
Canscora khandalensis, 549
  stricta, 550
Capparis, 193
  decidua, 96, 192
  moonii, 547
Capra, *193*
  falconeri, 235
Capricornis sumatraensis, 313
Caprolagus hispidus, 235, 313
Carax, 413
Caretta, 366-369, 371-373
Caretta caretta, 292, 294, 364, 366
Careya arborea, 610
Carissa carandas, 566
Carmona microphylla, 106
Caryca papaya, 269
Casearia, 147
  corymbosa, 636
Cassia, 401, 566
  auriculata, 566
  fistula, 341
  punnila, 89
  tora, 90
Castanopsis indica, 577
Casuarina equisetifolia, 269
Catla catla, 586
Catreus wallichii, 237, 286
Cedrela, 130
Cedrus deodara, 253
Celastrus paniculatus, 89
Celosia argentia, 90
Centranthera hookeri, 549
Centropus chlororhynchus, 264
  sinensis, 596
Ceraspis carinatus, 265
Ceratophora, 265
Ceratostylis himalaica, 580
Ceriodphnia, 574
Ceriops taqal, 8
Ceropegia, 547
  evansii, 547, 548
  huberi, 548
  lawii, 548
  macannii, 547
  mahabalei, 547, 548, 550
  media, 547, 548
  noorjahaniae, 547, 550
  odorata, 550
  panchganensis, 547
  polyantha, 548
  rollae, 547, 548
  sahyadrica, 547, 548
  santapaui, 547, 549
  stocksii, 550
  vincaefolia, 548, 550
Cervus duvauceli, 418, 631
  eldi eldi, 411
  elephas hanglu, 234
  unicolor, 65, 75, 255, 264, 418, 613
Cettia pallidipes, 603
Chalcides pentadactylus, 229
Chalcophaps indica, 595

Chamaeleon, 536
zeylanicus, 295, 298
Channa orientalis, 255
Charybdis spp., 7
Chelonia, 366-373, 378
mydas, 288, 292, 294, 364, 366, 370
Chenopodium album, 146
Chitra, 503
indica, 293, 504, 566-568, 510
Chlorophytum bharuchae, 550
borivillanum, 549
glaucoides, 549
Choriotis nigriceps, 237, 565, 633
Chloropsis aurifrons, 596
cochinchinensis, 602
Christisonia calcarata, 549
lawii, 549
Chromis caeruleus, 271, 273, 274, 275
Chrysipelea taprobanica, 256
Chrysoglossum, 578
erraticum, 579
Chrysopogon zelanica, 389
Chrysomma sinense, 597
Chukrassia tabularis, 96
Chydorus sphaericus, 279
Cinnamomum, 101
wightii, 122
Cirrhinus mricala, 586
Cissus quadrangularis, 106
woodrowii, 546
Citrullus, 560
colocynthis, 554-560, 562, 563
Clarius batrachus, 571-574
Cliesostoma discolor, 580
racemiferum, 580
sagittiforme, 580
subulatum, 580
tricallosa, 580
Cliestanthus, 103
collinus, 103
Cleome asperrima, 550
Clerodendron, 269
viscosum, 341
Clerodendrum, 516
Clitoria biflora, 548
Closterium, 571, 573, 574
Clusia, 130
Clypeaster humilis, 7
Cnemaspis, 225, 229
beddomei, 229
goaensis, 229
Cnemaspis indica, 229
littoralis, 229
ornata, 229
podihuna, 255
sisparensis, 229
wynadensis, 229
Cocos nucifera, 432
Coelogyne, 577, 578
barbata, 577, 580
elata, 580
fimbriata, 580
flavida, 580
fuscescens, 580
griffithii, 580
nitida, 580
prolifera, 580
punctulata, 580
rigida, 580
Colebrokea, 416
Colophospermum, 556, 560
mopane, 554, 555, 557-559, 562, 563
Copsychus malabaricus, 527, 595
indicus, 340
malabaricus, 340
saularis, 596
Coracina melanoptera, 597
Corchorus oletorieus, 89
triama, 89
Cordia gharaf, 432
Corvus macrorhynchos, 265, 596
splendens, 265
Cosmarium, 571, 573, 574
Cremastra appendiculata, 579
Crinum eleonarae, 550
Crocodylus paulustris, 76, 255, 265, 294, 297, 464
porosus, 265, 294, 297, 312, 313, 464, 634
Crotalaria burhia, 408
decasperma, 548
leptostchya, 548
Croton gibsonianus, 551
Cryptochilus sanguinea, 580
Cryptocorine cognotoides, 550
Ctenopharyngodon idella, 203
Cucumella ritchiei, 550
Culicicapa ceylonensis, 595
Cullenia-Mesua-Palaquium, 181, 185, 189, 190
Cuon alpinus, 65, 75, 313, 392
Cuora, 503
Curcuma purpurea, 550
Cyathea arborea, 129
Cyathocline lutea, 549

Cyclemys, 503
Cyclop, 574
Cymbidium devonianum, 580
  elegans, 580
  iridioides, 580
  longifolium 577, 578, 580
  matersii, 580
Cymbopogon sp., 609
Cynodon dactylon, 408
Cypraea, 580
  tigris, 520
Cyperpus, 403, 456, 460, 461
  decumbens, 550
  pentabracteatus, 550
Cyprinus carpio, 202
Cyrtodactylus albofasciatus, 229

Dacrydium, 123
  comosum, 123
Dalbergia latifolia, 96, 341
  paniculata, 90
Daseyllus aruanus, 273
Dasia haliana, 255
  subcaerulea, 229
Dendrelaphis grandoculis, 230
Dendrobium, 577, 578
  aphyllum, 580
  bicameratum, 580
  chlorops, 546
  chrysanthum, 580
  chrysotoxum, 580
  densiflorum, 577, 578, 580
  devonianum, 580
  eriaeflorum, 580
  falconeri, 580
  fimbriatum var., *oculatum*, 580
  hookerianus, 580
  longicornu, 580
  nobile, 580
  wardianum, 580
Dendrocitta formosae, 596
Dendrocopus maharattensis, 265
Dendrophthoe falcata, 213
Dendronephthya brevirama, 7
  dendrophyta, 7
Dermochelys, 366-370, 372
  coriacea, 294, 366
Desmodium rotundifolium, 549
Dibamus, 298
Dicaeum agile, 595
  erythrorhynchos, 596
Dichoriste dalzellii, 550
Dichrostachys nutans, 554-559, 562, 563
Dicliptera ghatica, 550
Dicrurus aeneus, 595
  caerulescens, 596
  leucophaeus, 595
Didymocarpus sp., 124
Didymopanax, 145
  pittieri, 130, 145
Dillenia pentagyna, 102
Dillenia-Terminalia paniculata, 181, 185
Dioscorea wightii, 611
Diosphyros, 88, 113
  ferrea, 106
  montana, 401
Dipcadi maharashtrensis, 549
  saxorum, 549
  ursulae, 549
Diplerygonatus leucogrammicus, 271, 273
Diploastrea heliopora, 272
Diploria strigosa, 29
Dipterocarpus, 223
  indicus, 221
Dipterocarpus indicus-Vateria indica, 113
Dipterocarpus-Mesua-Palaquium, 98, 181, 185, 189, 190
Discora hispida, 90
Dadonaea viscosa, 566
Dolichos bracteatus, 550
Dravidogecko anamallensis, 229
Drosera peltata, 394
Dryanobalanops aromatica, 147
Drypetes roxburghii, 432
  sepiaria, 106
Dugong dugon, 237, 264
Dumetia hyperythra, 596
Dussia, 130
Dysophylla gracilis, 550
  salicifolia, 550
  stocksii, 550, 551

Egretta, 430
  garzetta, 430
  gularis, 429
Eichhornia, 586
Eichornea, 196
Elachistodon westermanii, 290, 294
Elaeocarpus ganitrus, 101
Elephas maximus, 75, 263, 266, 313, 392, 518
    maximus, 254, 484
Elettaria cardamomum, 221
Emblica officinalis, 89
Entada pursaetha, 611
Ephemerantha macraei, 580

Epigeneium amolum, 580
Epipogium, 577, 578
roseum, 579
sessanum, 579
tuberosum, 579
Eptesicus fuscus, 424
Equus hemionus khur, 237
Eretmochelys, 336-372, 378
coriacea, 292
imbricata, 294, 364, 366
Eria, 577, 578
amica, 580
carinata, 580
clausa, 580
connata, 580
hindei, 580
paniculata, 580
pannea, 580
pubescens, 580
spicata, 580
stricta, 580
Erinocarpus nimmonii, 549
Eriocaulon sedgwickii, 550
Eriolaena stocksii, 550
Eriphia laeyimenus, 7
Erythrina, 597
variegata, 269
Erythroxylon monogynum, 106
Eryx conicus, 295
johnii, 295
Estrilda formosa, 597
Eucalyptus, 73, 102, 192, 196, 565-569
camadulensis, 566
tecticornis, 566
Eudynamis scolopacea, 598
Eugenia boringuensis, 124
stoksii, 550
Euglena, 574
Eulalia phaeothrix, 389
Eulipoa, 348-351
wallacei, 349, 350, 352, 354
Euodice malabarica, 519
Euonymus, 101
Eupatorium, 209, 584
Eupatorium (= *Chromalaena*), 196
glandulosum, 389
odoratum, 341
Euphorbia, 183
antiquorum, 166
cauducifolia, 192
coccinea, 548
Euphorbia katranjensis, 546, 549
khandalensis, 549
panchganiensis, 549
Euphodotis bengalensis, 237, 313, 452
Eurya japonica, 100
Eurystomus orientalis, 264
Eurythoe complanata, 7
Exilisciurus, 215
Evodia lunu-ankenda, 101, 122

Fagus sp., 146
Falco biarmicus, 635
cherrug, 635
peregrinoides, 635
peregrinus, 635
peregrinator, 265
Faramea occidentalis, 147
Favia spp., 7
Felis bengalensis, 65, 313
caracal, 235
chaus, 65, 74, 313, 411
lynx isabellina, 235
manul, 235
marmorata, 236
rubiginosa, 236
temmincki, 235, 313
viverrina, 263, 313
Ficus, 269, 597
amplissima, 432, 435, 438
benghalensis, 90, 432, 603
hispida, 341
racemosa, 432
religiosa, 430, 432
Filinia, 574
opliensis, 279
Fimbristylis ligulata, 550
unispicularis, 551
Flacourtia indica, 89
Flemingia tuberosa, 548
Fluggea macrocarpa, 90
Fragilaria corotonesis, 279
Francolinus francolinus, 287
pictus watsoni, 264
pondicerianus, 265
Frerea indica, 545, 549,
Freycinet sp., 348
Fulica atra, 265
Funambulus, 215, 216
palmarum, 65

Galactea malyanensis, 549
Galeola, 577
javanica, 579

Galeola lindleyana, 577-579
Galloperdix bicalcarata, 256
Gallus lafayetti, 256, 264
Gambusia, 203
affinis, 202
Garcinia, 113
Garra lamta, 255
Garrulax, 541
Gastrochilus acutifolium, 580
dasypogon, 580
inconspicuum, 580
intermedius, 580
Gaultheria, 100, 101
fragrantissima, 160
Gavialis gangeticus, 294, 296, 297, 312, 313, 464
Gazella bennetti, 236
Geckoella yakhuna, 255
Gegeneophis, 228
carnosus, 228
ramaswamii, 228
Geochelone elegans, 293, 295
elongata, 295
emys, 313
travancorica, 22, 231, 236, 293, 295
Geoclemys, 503
hamiltonii, 508, 510
Glochidion heyneanum, 101
velutinum, 101
Gluta travancorica, 611
Gmelina arborea, 96
asiatica, 106
Gnaphalium luteum, 550
Gnetum ula, 611
Goniastrea retiformis, 272
Goodyera, 578
Gracula religiosa, 595
indica, 533
intermedia, 533
peninsularis, 533
Grewia hirsuta, 90
tilaefolia, 213
Gutteria dumetorum, 146, 168
Gymnema khandalensis, 249
Gymnodactylus frenatus, 255
Gymnogyps californianus, 360
Gymnosporia konkanensis, 546
puberula, 546, 549
Gyps, 360
africanus, 361
bengalensis, 361, 362
coprothers, 361
Gyps fulvus, 361
fulvescence, 361
himalayensis, 361
indicus, 362
ruppellii, 361

Habenaria, 578
caranjensis, 551
clavigera, 579
grandifloriformis, 547
lawii, 551
longicorniculata, 547
panchganiensis, 547
polytricha, 579
spencei, 550
Haplocerus ceylonensis, 265
Hardella, 503-507
thurjii, 505, 506, 508, 510-513
Hardwickia, 99, 103, 182
binata, 103, 191, 566
Hardwickia binata-Albizia amara, 182
Hardwickia binata-Anogeissus latifolia, 186, 189
Harpactes fasciatus, 595
Hasseltia floribunda, 145
Helicteres isora, 88, 89
Heliopora, 272
Hemidactylus depressus, 255
flaviviridis, 310
Hemidesmus indica, 89
Hemipus picatus, 596
Hemitragus hylocrius, 70, 75, 177, 224, 235, 387, 622
jayakari, 387
jemlahicus, 177, 387
Heosemys, 225
silvatica, 222, 225, 231, 236, 293, 295, 503, 508, 510, 512
Heracleum aquilegifolium, 551
concanense, 548
pinda, 550
Herpestis edwardsi, 65, 566
smithi, 74
Herpysma longicaulis, 579
Hetaeria rubens, 578, 579
Heteropneustes fossilis, 571-574
Heteropogon, 196
Hexarthra mira, 279
Hibiscus spp., 89
Hipposideros bicolor, 425
speoris, 425
Hirundo daurica, 596
Hopea, 221
Hoya pendula, 546
Hugonia mystax, 106

Humboldtia brunonis, 113
Hyaena hyaena, 65, 566
Hydnocarpus laurifolia, 341, 342
Hylobates hoolock, 235
Hyosciurus, 245
Hypophthalmichthys molitrix, 571, 572
Hystrix indica, 65, 75, 566

Ichthyophis, 223, 228, 255
    beddomei, 228
    bombayensis, 228
    malabarensis, 228
    peninsularis, 228
    subterrestris, 228
    tricolor, 228
Ikedella misakiensis, 7
Ikedosoma pirotanensis, 7
Ilex, 101, 168
    myrtillus, 145
Impatiens dalzellii, 547, 548
    stocksii, 550
    spp., 89
Indigofera dalzellii, 547, 548
    duthieri, 550
    monosperma, 550
    wightii, 550
Indotyphlus battersbyi, 228
Inga dulce, 401
Iphigenia pallida, 547
    stellata, 547, 549, 550
Ipomoea, 89
    annua, 551
    clarkei, 548
    salsettensis, 548
Irena puella, 264
Isachne bicolor, 551
    borii, 551
Ischaemum bolei, 549
    bombaiensis, 549
    diplopogon, 548
    hugelii, 551
    indicum, 389
    inerme, 551
    tumidum, 548
    zeylanicolum, 551

Jatropha nana, 551
Juncella juncea, 7

Kachuga, 503
    dhongoka, 296, 504-506, 508, 510-512
    kachuga, 296, 506-512
    smithii, 506, 508
    sylhetensis, 311
Kachuga tecta, 294, 508-510
    tectum, 535, 542
    tentoria, 506, 508, 511, 513
Kalanchoe bhidei, 550
Kaloula, 311
    pulchra, 311
Keratella, 574
    tropica, 279
Kingidium taenialis, 580

Labeo fisheri, 255
    rohita, 586
Lagerstroemia, 96, 190
    lanceolata, 96, 102, 341
Lamprometra palmata, 7
Lanius schach, 596
    vittatus, 598
Lantana, 209, 416, 446, 584, 597, 598
    camara, 341, 566
Lasianthus, 101
    venulosa, 122
Lasiosiphon, 101
Lasiurus, 408, 556, 560
    sindicus, 409, 554-560, 562, 563
Leersia hexandra, 412, 414
Leipoa, 348, 350
    ocellata, 350, 352
Leo pardus, 313
    tigris, 313
Lepidogathis bandraensis, 550
    lutea, 549
Lepidochelys, 366, 367, 369, 370-373
    olivacea, 292, 294, 313, 364, 366
    cristata, 90
Lepidozygus, 273
    tapeinosoma, 271, 273
Leptospermum, 123
    flavescens, 123
Lepus nigricollis, 65, 566
        singhala, 266
Leucaena sp., 566
Leucodyctyon malvanensis, 549
Leucus deodikarii, 550
Limonia acidissima, 432
Lindernia quinqueloba, 550
Linociera, 101
Liparis, 577, 578
    bituberculata, 580
    bootanensis, 580
    coespitosa, 580
    cordifolia, 580

Liparis delicatula, 580
mannii, 580
plantaginea, 580
viridiflora, 580
Lissemys, 296, 503, 505, 513
punctata, 293, 294, 502-506, 509-511, 513, 535, 542
Litsaea sebifera, 101
zeylanica, 101
Livistonia routundifolia, 358
Lobophyllia, 272
Lonchura kelaarti, 597
maja, 527
malacca, 519
punctulata, 519, 527, 597
striata, 597
Lophogorgia lutkeni, 7
Lophotriorchis kienerii, 265
Loranthus gibbosus, 551
Loriculus beryllinus, 256
vernalis, 595
Luchea seemannii, 168
Lumnitzera, 146
Lutra, 75
lutra, 566
perspicillata, 65
Lynx rufus, 420
Lytocarpus sp., 7
Mabuya, 536
carinata, 269
Macaca arctoides, 313
mulatta, 313, 516
radiata, 73
silenus, 70, 73, 224, 235
sinica, 255, 256, 263
Macrocephalon, 348, 350
maleo, 350, 352, 356
Macronous gularis, 596
Macrophiothrix sp., 7
Magnolia, 96, 577
Mahonia, 100, 101
Makenzia integrifolia, 546
Malaxis, 578
acuminata, 579
josephiana, 579
Mangifera indica, 145, 432, 597
Manilkara-Chloroxylon, 182, 187, 189
Manis crassicaudata, 65, 75, 313, 566
Manisuris ratnagirica, 549
santapaui, 549
Mappia, 101
Mariscus blatteri, 551
Marsdenia lanceolata, 549
Martes gwatkinsi, 392
Mayteanus emarginatus, 408
Maytenus puberula, 546, 551
Megaderma lyra, 425
Megalaima fuscocapillum, 256
haemacephala, 595
zeylanica, 595
Megapodius, 342, 349, 354
freycinet, 237, 349, 352, 357
laperonse, 349, 350
pritchardii, 349, 350
Melanobatrachus indicus, 224, 227
Melanochelys, 293, 503
tricarinata, 295, 508, 510
trijuga, 265, 298, 508
Melanophidium, 230
bilineatum, 230
punctatum, 230
wynaudense, 230
Melia ?, 213
Melicone, 101
Meliosma siplicifolia, 101
Melursus ursinus, 65, 67, 75, 255, 263, 313
Memecylon, 124
umbellatum, 106
Memecylon-Syzgium-Actinodaphne, 98, 181, 185, 189
Merremia rhynchoriza, 551
Mesua, 223
ferrea, 221
Michelia champaca, 101
Micrixalus, 227
fuscus, 227
herrei, 227
Microxalus nudis, 227
opistorhodes, 227
saxicola, 227
silvaticus, 227
thampii, 227
Microcystis aeruginosa, 279
Microsystis, 574
Micropara mannii, 580
Microtropis, 101
Mikana, 584
Millingtonia hortensis, 432
Mimusops elengi, 432
Moghania gracilis, 550
Monarcha azurea, 595
Montastrea annularis, 29
Monticola, 541
Montipora, 273

Morenia, 503
Morenia petersii, 508
Morinda sp., 269
Moringa oleifera, 432
Moschus moschiferus, 235
Muntiacus muntjak, 65, 67, 76, 264, 418, 631
Mus rattus, 269
rufescens, 269
Muscicapa latirostris, 604
poliogenys, 596
Mycteria leucocephala, 429
Myophonus, 541
Myotis grisescens, 424
velifer, 424
Myristica, 113, 124
beddomei, 551

Naja naja, 291, 520
kaouthia, 291
Nannobatrachus, 225, 227
anamallaiensis, 227
beddomii, 227
kempholeyensis, 227
Nanothamnus sericeus, 549
Narenga porphyrochroma, 413, 414
Navicula, 574
Nectarinia asiatica, 596
zeylonica, 596
Neesiella longipedunculata, 550
Neofelis nebulosa, 236
Neogyne, 578
gardnerana, 580
Nepenthes, 123, 124
Neptunus pelagicus, 7
Neris versicolor, 7
Nicotiana glauca, 550
Nilgirianthus asper, 546
ciliatus, 546, 551
lupulinus, 546, 551
reticulatus, 546, 548
scrobiculatus, 550
wareensis, 546, 551
Nitzschia, 574
Nothofagus, 169
Nothopegia, 113
Nothopodytes nimmoniana, 547
Nyctibatrachus, 225, 227
humayuni, 227
major, 227
pygmaeus, 227
sanctipalustris, 227
sylvaticus, 227
Nycticebus coucang, 313
Nycticorax nycticorax, 429
Nyctyornis athertoni, 595
Nysicarpus belgaumensis, 548

Oberonia acaulis, 580
falconeri, 580
Ochlandra, 73, 585
brandisii, 609
rheedii, 609
travancorica, 609
Ocotea, 124
spathulata, 124, 147, 168
Oegenia dahlberzioides, 213
Oianthus deccanensis, 549
Oldenlandia, 456, 460
maheshwarii, 548
Oligodon, 225, 230
affinis, 230
brevicauda, 230
travancoricus, 230
venustus, 230
Olmedia aspera, 146
Operculina tansaensis, 549
Ophiophagus hannah, 291, 312
Ophiops beddomei, 229
Ophiothrix sp., 7
Oreortyx pictus, 288
Oriolus oriolus, 598
xanthornus, 595
Ornithochilus fuscus, 580
Orthotomus sutorius, 595
Oryctes rhinoceros, 269
Otis tarda, 446
Otochilus albus, 580
fuscus, 580
Otocryptis, 225
weigmanni, 255
Ovis, 193
ammon hodgsoni, 235
poli, 235
vignei, 235

Pagarus sp., 7
Pancratius donaldi, 550
sanctae-mariae, 549
Pandanus, 123, 269
odaratissimus, 269
Panicum obscurans, 550
Panthera leo persica, 81
pardus, 65, 74, 263, 392, 415
tigris, 65, 70, 74, 392, 416
uncia, 235

Panthera pardus fusca, 254
Pantholops hodgsoni, 235
Panulirus homarus, 7
polyphagus, 7
Parus xanthogenys, 596
Paradoxurus ceylonensis, 256
hermaphroditus, 64, 74
Parthenium, 196, 209
Paspalum scrobiculaetum, 404
Passer montanus, 603
Pastinaca grandis, 548
Pateria sp., 7
Pavo cristatus, 264, 603
muticus, 313
Pavonia, 130
Pediastrum, 574
Pedostibes tuberculosa, 225, 227
Pelecanus philippensis, 264, 632
Pellorneum ruficeps, 596
Pelochelys, 503
bibroni, 508-510
Peltophorum pterocarpus, 432
Pemphia acidula, 269
Pennisetum typhoideum, 404
Pentaphylax euryoides, 123
Pericrocotus cinnamomeus, 596
flammeus, 596
roseus, 602
Persea americana, 146
Persea-Holigarna-Diosphyros, 98, 181, 185, 189
Petaurista petaurista, 65, 255, 263
Petinomys fuscocapillus, 255, 263
Peucedanum grande, 548
Phaenicophaeus pyrrohocephalus, 256
Phaius flavus, 578, 579
mishmensis, 578, 580
tankervilliae, 580
Phalacrocorax niger, 434
Phalaenopsis parishii var. *lobbii*, 580
Phaseolus aconitifolius, 404
aureus, 404
grandis, 548
khandalensis, 548
minima, 89
Phasianus colchicus, 288
Phelsuma andamanense, 298
Philautus, 228
beddomii, 228
bombayensis, 228
charius, 228
elegans, 228
Philautus glandulosus, 228
kottigeharensis, 288
longicrus, 228
melanesis, 228
montanus, 228
narainensis, 228
pulcherrimus, 228
swamianus, 228
travancoricus, 228
Phoebe acuminata, 577
lanceolata, 101
Phoenix, 501, 610
sylvestris, 405
Pholidota, 578
articulata, 580
imbricata, 580
rubra, 580
Photinia notoniana, 101
Phragmitis, 416
karka, 412, 414
Phreatia elegans, 580
Phyllanthus, 416
niruri, 269
scabrifolius, 551
Picoides macei, 595
maharattensis, 596
nanus, 595
Picumnus innominatus, 595
Picus chlorolophus, 595
flavinucha, 595
Pimephales promelas, 203
Pimpinella katrajensis, 550
tomentosa, 549
Pinus, 577
excelsa, 246
roxburghii, 101, 183, 187, 189, 193, 245
Piper barberi, 611
nigrum, 221
talbotti, 550
Pipistrellus, 425
Pistia, 586
Pithecelobium, 124
dulce, 532
Pittosporum floribundum, 101
Placuna placenta, 520
Platalea leucorodia, 409
Platanista gangetica, 313
indi, 285, 286
Platyplectrurus, 230
madurensis, 230
trilineatus, 230

Platypodium elegans, 168
Plectrurus, 230
aureus, 230
canaricus, 230
guentheri, 230
perroteti, 230
Plegadis falcinellus, 264
falcinellus falcinellus, 255
Pleione, 578
praecox, 578, 580
Pleocaulis ritchiei, 546
Ploceus phillipinus, 598
Plumeria rubra, 145
Podocarpus, 130
latifolia, 611
Podochilus khasianus, 581
Poeoiloneuron indicum-Dipterocarpus indicus, 113
Pogonachne racemosa, 549
Pogostemom, 416
Polyarthra, 574
vulgaris, 279
Polypedetes cruciger, 255
Polyplectron bicalcaratum, 313
Pomatorhinus schisticeps, 596
Pongamia pinnata, 90
Porites, 7, 272
Porpax jerdoniana, 551
Porphyrio porphyrio, 527
Portulalia oleracea, 90
Presbytis entellus, 65, 73, 255, 263, 313, 516
geei. 235
johni, 73
phayri, 313
pileatus, 313
senex, 255, 256
vetulus, 263
Prinia hodgsoni, 597
socialis, 597
sylvatica, 597
Procapra picticaudata, 235
Prosopis, 193
Prosopis-Capparis-Ziziphus-Salvadora-Calligonum, 183, 187
cineraria, 96, 432, 554-560, 562, 563, 637
Prosopis cineraria-Capparis-Zizyphus-Salvadora oleoides, 107
juliflora, 433, 456, 460, 566, 584
Protosciurus, 215, 216
Prunus amygdalia, 269
Pseudois nayaur, 235
Pseudotyphlops philippinus, 235
Psittacula calthropae, 256
columboides, 534
cyanocephala, 519, 595
derbyana, 537
eupatria, 523
krameri, 265, 519, 527
intermedia, 537
Psychotria, 101, 122, 146
acuminata, 145
bisulcata, 122
elongata, 122
furcata, 145
Pterocarpus marsupium, 96
santalinus, 103, 191
Pteroceras suaveolens, 581
Pteroides sp., 7
Pterolobium hexapetalum, 106
Pteropus giganteus, 440
Pterospermum obtusifolium, 611
suberifolium, 106
Ptyas mucosus, 291, 312, 516, 519
Puntius narayani, 335
nigrofasciatus, 535
Pycnonotus cafer, 596
jocosus, 596
luteolus, 597
melanicterus, 595
Pygeum, 101
Python molurus, 236, 290, 291, 312, 313
bivittatus, 520
molurus, 294, 488, 519
reticulatus, 290, 294, 312, 520

Quercus, 96, 577
dilata, 246
incana, 101, 246

Ramanella triangularis, 227
Rana, 227
aurantica, 228
beddomii, 228
bhagmandlensis, 228
curtipes, 228
diplostica, 228
dobsoni, 228
hexadactyla, 289, 311, 536
(Hylarana) gracilis, 255
leithii, 228
leptodactyla, 228
malabarica, 536
murthii, 228
phrynoderma, 228
rufescens, 228

Rana sauriceps, 228
semipalmata, 228
tigerina, 289, 311, 536
verrucosa, 228
Randia dumetorum, 90
Ratufa, 212-217
affinis, 212-214
bicolor, 212-214
gigantea, 212
indica, 65, 75, 212-214, 216, 217
centralis, 212
dealbata, 212
Rtufa macroura, 212, 213, 226, 255, 263, 608
dandolena, 212
Renanthera imshootiana, 576
Rhabdops olivaceus, 230
Rhacophorus, 228, 536
calcadensis, 228
malabaricus, 228
noblei, 228
parkeri, 228
Rheedia spp., 147
Rhinoceros unicornis, 417
Rhinophis, 230
fergusonianus, 230
oxyrhynchus, 255
sanguineus, 230
travancoricus, 230
Rhinopoma, 425
hardwickei, 424-426
Rhipidura albicollis, 596
aureola, 595
Rhizophora, 146
mucronata, 8
Rhododendron, 100, 101, 145, 577
arboreum, 122
Rhodoyrtus tomentosa, 122
Rhyticeros narcondami, 237
Ricinus communis, 269
Riopa, 536
goaensis, 229
Ristella, 229
beddomei, 229
guentheri, 229
rurki, 229
travancorica, 229
Rivea spp., 90
Rostratula benghalensis, 456, 461
Rourea praineana, 546, 551
Rubrisciurus, 215
Rungia crenata, 551
Sabella sp., 7
Saccharum, 403, 416
munja, 413, 414
procenus, 413
procerum, 414
Salacia brunoniana, 456, 551
macrosperma, 546
talbotii, 550
Salea, 225, 229
anamallayana, 229
horsfieldii, 229
Salmaca bicolor, 7
Salmo gairdneri, 202
Salvadora, 193
Salvinia, 586
Samòphilus, 536
Santalúm album, 566
Sapindus emarginatus, 341
laurifolius, 432
Sarcochilus viridiflora, 546
viridiflorus, 551
Sarkidiornis melanotos, 255, 264, 313
Sarotherodon mosambicus, 275
Satyrium nepalense, 578
Saxicola caprata, 597
Saxicoloides fulicata, 598
Schefflera venulosa, 101
Schizachyrium paranjpyeanum, 551
Schoenicola platyura, 603
Scincella, 229
beddomei, 229
bilineatum, 229
laterimaculatum, 229
palnicum, 229
travancoricum, 229
Scilla viridis, 549
Sciurotamis, 215
Sciurus, 215
Screbera sweiferriorrides, 90
scylla serrata, 7
Sehima nervosum, 389
wallichii, 577, 578
Selenarctos thibetanus, 313
Semecarpus anacardium, 610
Senecio gibsoni, 548
grahami, 548
hewrensis, 547, 548
lawii, 550
Sequoia sempervirens, 113
Sesamum indicum, 404
Sashagiria sahyadrica, 545, 548

Setaria, 413
italica, 404
Shorea, 221
Shorea-Buchanania-Cleistanthus, 103, 181, 186, 189
Shorea-Buchanania-Terminalia, 103, 182, 186, 189
Shorea-Cleistanthus-Croton, 181, 186, 189
Shorea-Cleistanthus collinus-Croton oblongifolius, 103
Shorea-Dillenia-Pterospermum, 182, 186, 189
Shorea-Dillenia-Pterospermum heyneanum-Cycas circinalis, 103
Shorea robusta, 96, 102, 243, 416, 632
Shorea-Syzygium operculatum-Toona, 182, 186, 189
Shorea-Syzygium operculatum-Toona ciliata-Symolocos spicata, 103
Shorea-Terminalia-Adina, 103, 182, 186, 189
Siderestrea spp., 7
Sideroxylon, 101
Simocephalus vetulus, 279
Sitta castanea, 596
frontalis, 596
Smithia agharkarii, 550
oligantha, 550
purpurea, 548
pycnantha, 549
Smitinandia micrantha, 581
Sonerila, 124
Sorocea affinis, 146
Soymida fabrifuga, 90
Sphenomorphus fallax, 256
Spathoglottis pubescens var. *parviflora*, 578, 580
Spirogyra, 574
Spizaetus nipalensis, 265
Spratelloides delicatulus, 271, 274, 275
japonicus, 271, 273
Stachyris rufifrons, 596
Sterculia foetida, 432
Streptopelia chinensis, 596
ceylonensis, 265
Strobilanthes, 546
kunthianus, 389
scrobiculatus, 550
Strychnos nux-vomica, 341
Sturnus contra, 596
senex, 264
Sunipia andersoni, 581
racemosa, 581
Sus salvanius, 235
scrofa, 65, 67, 76, 266, 408, 411, 417, 566
Swertia deccusata, 547
Sympolocos spicata, 101
Synnema anomalum, 550
Sypheotides indica, 237
Syzygium, 123
arnottianum, 122
calophyllifolia, 122, 123
cumini, 432, 610
Tabebuia, 124
rigida, 124
Tadarida aegyptiaca, 425
Tainia latifolia, 580
wrayana, 580
Talegalla, 348, 350, 353
cuvieri, 350
fuscirostris, 350
fuscirostris, 350
occidentalis, 350
jobiensis, 350
jobiensis, 350
longicauda, 350
Tamarindus indica, 432, 435
Taphozous kachenensis, 425
melanopogon, 425
Tapirus indicus, 3
Tectona, 190, 446
grandis, 96, 213, 242, 341
Tectona-Lagerstroemia-Dillenia-T. paniculata, 189
Tectona-Lagerstroemia lanceolata, 185
Tectona-Lagerstroemia lanceolata-Dillenia pentagyna-Terminalia paniculata, 101
Tectona-Lagerstroemia paniculata, 181
Tectona-Terminalia, 181, 185, 188, 189
Tectona-Terminalia-Adina-Anogeissus, 101, 181, 189
Tephrodornis gularis, 596
pondicerianus, 596
Tephrosia collina, 550
Teretrurus sanguineus, 230
Terminalia, 96, 190
Terminalia-Anogeissus-Cleistanthus, 181, 185, 189
Terminalia-Anogeissus latifolia, 103, 181, 186, 189
Terminalia-Anogeissus latifolia-Cleistanthus, 103
bellerica, 401
chebula, 610
crenulata, 90
myriocarpa, 577, 578
paniculata, 102, 341
tomentosa, 213, 401
Testudo elegans, 265, 542
Tetracerus quadricornis, 408
Tetramelas, 96
Thalamita prymna, 7
Thalictrum dalzellii, 545
obovatum, 545

Thespesia populnea, 269
Thelasis longifolia, 581
Thevetia ahouvai, 146
Threskiornis aethiopica, 429
Thunia, 578
    alba, 581
Tilapia, 203
Tinospora cordifolia, 89
Toona ciliata, 96
Toona-Garuga, 103, 182, 186, 189
Tor khudree, 496-499
    mosal, 496
    mussullah, 496, 497
    progeneius, 496
    putitora, 496-499
    tor, 497, 499
Tragulus meminna, 65, 67, 76, 264
Tragopan blythi, 237
    molesworthi, 237
    melanocephalus, 237, 287
Trewia, 416
Tridax procumbens, 90, 405
Trimeresurus, 231
Trimeresurus huttoni, 231
    macrolepis, 231
    malabaricus, 231
    trigonocephalus, 256
Trionyx, 503, 506, 511
    gangeticum, 535
    gangeticus, 293, 294, 502, 504-511, 513
    hurum, 293, 294, 504, 506, 508, 510, 535
    leithii, 506-508, 510, 511, 513
    nigricana, 295, 310, 312, 313
Tripogon ananthaswamianus, 389
    bromoides, 389
Triumfetta rotundifolia, 89
Tubicolor, 7
Turbo spp., 520
Turdoides striatus, 597
Turdus, 541
    merula, 596
Turraca villosa, 546
Tylotriton, 289
Typhlops, 230
    beddomei, 230
    thurstoni, 230
    tindalli, 230
Typloscincus, 298

Uca, 7, 631
    annulipes, 631
    panamensis, 631
Uca tangeri, 631
    terpisichores, 631
    urvillei, 631
Uncifera acuminata, 581
Unonopsis pittieri, 147
Uperodon, 311
    globulosum, 311
Uraeotyphlus, 225, 228
    malabaricus, 228
    menoni, 228
    narayani, 228
    oxyurus, 228
Urgenia polyantha, 549
Urginia polyphylla, 550
Uromastix, 298
    hardwickii, 295, 298
Uropeltis, 223, 230
    arcticeps, 230
    beddomii, 230
    broughami, 230
    ceylonicus, 230
    dindigalensis, 230
    ellioti, 231
    liura, 231
    macrolepis, 231
    macrorhynchus, 231
    maculatus, 231
    myhendrae, 231
    nitidus, 231
    ocellatus, 231
    petersi, 231
    phillipsi, 231
    pulneyensis, 231
    rubrolineatus, 231
    rubromaculatus, 231
    smithi, 231
    woodmasoni, 231
Uricularia scandens, 550

Vaccinium, 101
Valeria, 221
Vanda, 578
    alpina, 581
    coerulea, 576
    cristata, 581
Varanus, 76, 356, 536, 537
    bengalensis, 222, 244, 255, 265, 294, 298
    bomodoensis, 356
    flavescens, 294
    griseus, 294
    indicus, 520
    salvator, 244, 255, 294, 298, 312, 313, 520

Vateria, 221
Ventilago bombaiensis, 546, 551
Vicoa cernua, 547
Vigna catjung, 404
Vinca rosea, 269
Virgularia rumphii, 7
Virola, 147
    sebifera, 636
    surinamensis, 168
Vitis, 89
    araneosa, 550
Viveria megaspila, 235
    zibetha, 411
Viverricula indica, 65, 74
Vulpes bengalensis, 566
Vultur gryphus, 360

Weinmannia, 130, 155

Xeromphis, 401
Xylia, 342
    xylocarpa, 341, 342
Xylophis, 225, 230
    perroteti, 230
    stenorhynchus, 230

Zeuxine goodyeroides, 580
Zinziber cernuum, 549
Zizania latifolia, 412-414
Ziziphus nummularia, 96, 192, 408
Zizyphus, 446, 560
    muritiana, 432
    oenoplia, 89
    rotundifolia, 554-560, 562, 563
Zoothera, 541
    citrina, 596
    spiloptera, 256
Zosterops palpebrosa, 596
Zuelania guidonia, 147, 168